# THE SUCCESS
# BIBLE

# THE SUCCESS BIBLE

### THE WORLD'S GREATEST INSPIRATIONAL CLASSICS ABRIDGED AND INTRODUCED BY MITCH HOROWITZ

*Sun Tzu • Henry David Thoreau*

*Ralph Waldo Emerson • Napoleon Hill*

*Florence Scovel Shinn • James Allen*

*Niccolò Machiavelli • Khalil Gibran*

*Dale Carnegie • Wallace D. Wattles*

*Norman Vincent Peale and more*

INCLUDES: *101 RULES OF EFFECTIVE LIVING*

Published 2025 by Gildan Media LLC
aka G&D Media
www.GandDmedia.com

THE SUCCESS BIBLE. Copyright © 2025 Mitch Horowitz. All rights reserved.

No part of this book may be used, reproduced or transmitted in any manner whatsoever, by any means (electronic, photocopying, recording, or otherwise), without the prior written permission of the author, except in the case of brief quotations embodied in critical articles and reviews. No liability is assumed with respect to the use of the information contained within. Although every precaution has been taken, the author and publisher assume no liability for errors or omissions. Neither is any liability assumed for damages resulting from the use of the information contained herein.

Front cover design by David Rheinhardt of Pyrographx

Interior design by Meghan Day Healey of Story Horse, LLC

Library of Congress Cataloging-in-Publication Data is available upon request

ISBN: 978-1-7225-0733-6

10   9   8   7   6   5   4   3   2   1

# Contents

Preface: 101 Rules of Effective Living   by Mitch Horowitz . . . . . . . . . . . 7

The Art of War (c. 500 BC)   Sun Tzu . . . . . . . . . . . . . . . . . . . . 13

The Prince (1532)   Niccolò Machiavelli . . . . . . . . . . . . . . . . . . . . 39

Self-Reliance (1841)   Ralph Waldo Emerson . . . . . . . . . . . . . . . . . . 71

Walden (1854)   Henry David Thoreau . . . . . . . . . . . . . . . . . . . 87

Power and Wealth (1860)   Ralph Waldo Emerson . . . . . . . . . . . . . . . . . 119

The Gospel of Wealth (1889)   Andrew Carnegie . . . . . . . . . . . . . . . . . . 143

Acres of Diamonds (1890)   Russell H. Conwell . . . . . . . . . . . . . . . . . . 179

In Tune with the Infinite (1897)   Ralph Waldo Emerson . . . . . . . . . . . . 193

A Message to Garcia (1899)   Elbert Hubbard . . . . . . . . . . . . . . . . . . 235

The Magic Story (1900)   Frederick van Rensselaer Dey . . . . . . . . . . . . 249

As a Man Thinketh (1903)   James Allen . . . . . . . . . . . . . . . . . . 269

The Kybalion (1908)   Three Initiates . . . . . . . . . . . . . . . . . . . . 289

The Science of Getting Rich (1910)   Wallace D. Wattles . . . . . . . . . . . . 329

The Science of Being Great (1911)   Wallace D. Wattles . . . . . . . . . . . . 345

The Power of Concentration (1916)   Theron Q. Dumont . . . . . . . . . . . . 361

The Master Mind (1918)   Theron Q. Dumont . . . . . . . . . . . . . . . . . 401

The Prophet (1923)   Khalil Gibran . . . . . . . . . . . . . . . . . . . . . 439

The Game of Life And How to Play It (1925)   Florence Scovel Shinn . . . 465

Public Speaking to Win! (1926)   Dale Carnegie . . . . . . . . . . . . . . . . 481

## Contents

Richest Man in Babylon (1926)    George S. Clason . . . . . . . . . . . . . . . . 499

The Secret of the Ages (1926)    Robert Collier . . . . . . . . . . . . . . . . . . . 535

The Law of Success (1928)    Napoleon Hill. . . . . . . . . . . . . . . . . . . . . . 551

The Magic Ladder to Success (1930)    Napoleon Hill . . . . . . . . . . . . . . 569

Think and Grow Rich (1937)    Napoleon Hill . . . . . . . . . . . . . . . . . . . . 599

Alcoholics Anonymous (1939) . . . . . . . . . . . . . . . . . . . . . . . . . . . . . . 619

The Power of Faith (1940)    Norman Vincent Peale . . . . . . . . . . . . . . . 649

The Secret Door to Success (1940)    Florence Scovel Shinn . . . . . . . . . 681

Your Faith Is Your Fortune (1941)    Neville . . . . . . . . . . . . . . . . . . . . . 701

The Master Key to Riches (1945)    Napoleon Hill . . . . . . . . . . . . . . . . 715

The Magic of Believing (1948)    Claude M. Bristol. . . . . . . . . . . . . . . . 747

Think Your Way to Wealth (1948)    Napoleon Hill. . . . . . . . . . . . . . . . 767

Atom-Smashing Power of Mind (1949)    Charles Fillmore . . . . . . . . . . 809

How to Attract Good Luck (1952)    A.H.Z. Carr. . . . . . . . . . . . . . . . . . 837

The Power of Awareness (1952)    Neville . . . . . . . . . . . . . . . . . . . . . . 855

Magic of Faith (1954)    Joseph Murphy . . . . . . . . . . . . . . . . . . . . . . . 873

How to Attract Money (1955)    Joseph Murphy. . . . . . . . . . . . . . . . . . 911

The Power of Your Subconscious Mind (1963)    Joseph Murphy . . . . . . 949

The Million Dollar Secret Hidden in Your Mind (1963)    Anthony Norvell. . . 965

About the Authors. . . . . . . . . . . . . . . . . . . . . . . . . . . . . . . . . . . . . . . 991

## Preface
# 101 Rules of Effective Living
### *by Mitch Horowitz*

In more than thirty years as a writer, editor, and publisher, I have, to my best reckoning, introduced, abridged, issued or reissued, and read nearly every major work of inspirational literature produced or translated into English.

Based on experience, the "rules" of effective living—at least those I consider befitting an ethical and accountable person—are reducible to these:

1. Do your work—do it on time and fully, if not early and overabundantly.
2. Deal plainly.
3. Acknowledge failure.
4. There exists uncanny congruity between thought and experience.
5. Pay people on time.
6. Be willing to clean toilets and wash floors.
7. Do not over-talk.
8. Speak only of what you know well.
9. Apologize.
10. Judge quality not category.
11. Research every important question independently.
12. Expect corruption.
13. "Beware the devastation of conflict; war must never be pursued lightly." (Sun Tzu)
14. The loftier the language, the lower the behavior.
15. Take due credit. You'll get blame when you don't deserve it.
16. Don't complain.
17. Thank people sincerely.
18. Argue with a fool, make a fool your colleague.

19. Measure twice.
20. Get away from cruel people—at all costs.
21. People lie.
22. Great execution matters far more than great ideas.
23. Never humor or accommodate bullies.
24. Humiliate no one.
25. People see only those traits they possess.
26. Focus on one area of expertise and know it comprehensively.
27. Relationships define your life and happiness.
28. Never underestimate money or sex.
29. Far better to find your group than to win people over.
30. "The art of war is the art of deception." (Sun Tzu)
31. In terms of investments, virtually nothing, over time, outpaces an index fund.
32. Brilliant people are wrong all the time
33. When you feel a sense of unease, honor it without question.
34. The only real emergency is a medical emergency.
35. Give no second chances to anyone who shows disrespect.
36. "In the long run, we find what we expect. We shall be fortunate then if we expect great things." (Thoreau)
37. Honor every religion.
38. Look people in the eye, recognize them, acknowledge them.
39. Tip well.
40. Eschew rhetorical questions.
41. Use sarcasm rarely, unless you're George Carlin.
42. Don't be an asshole.
43. Learn to fight.
44. Reduce food intake by twenty percent.
45. Better to be nobly alone than settle for low company.
46. Write nothing you wouldn't want read aloud in public.
47. You don't know someone until witnessing him in crisis.
48. If you see someone mistreat another, he will mistreat you.
49. No one cares about your political opinions; they care only whether you agree with theirs.
50. Anger solves nothing.
51. "Who is evil? He who borrows and does not repay." (*Ethics of the Fathers, Talmud*)

# Preface

52. Unflinching perseverance is your single best chance of deliverance. Consider this lawful.
53. Act decisively.
54. Keep your hallowed wishes private.
55. Be willing to pay qualified people for sound information or services.
56. Beware those who keep pets that bite (including people).
57. Respect workers.
58. "If we must choose between them, it is far safer to be feared than loved." (Machiavelli)
59. There is no such thing as common sense.
60. Emotions are far stronger than intellect.
61. "To work intelligently is education." (Elbert Hubbard)
62. Cynics know nothing.
63. Recheck your work—especially beginnings, endings, and the "easy parts."
64. Practice constantly.
65. "To feel brave, act as if we were brave." (William James)
66. Nothing does more to squander goodwill than being a smartass.
67. Concentration produces power.
68. "The past controls the future but the present controls the past." (G.I. Gurdjieff)
69. Know your preferences, even if you cannot act on them.
70. "The way bread smells depends on how hungry a man is." (Arab proverb)
71. Morality judges another; ethics judges self.
72. A positive mental attitude means evaluating circumstances based on their capacity for self-development.
73. "A chief feature of false life is that it cannot stand alone, but frantically demands allies to support its false positions." (Vernon Howard)
74. War or natural disaster abrogates nearly all of these rules; in such case health and survival are the laws.
75. Eschew gossip, talebearing, and trash talk—especially for entertainment.
76. Know who you are talking to.
77. Do your absolute best to carry your own load before bothering another.
78. "Opposition is true Friendship" (Blake)—but only if it is worthy opposition.

79. Curiosity cannot be taught.
80. "Any reasonable order in an emergency is better than no order." (Major C.A. Bach)
81. "Be wise as serpents and harmless as doves." (Christ)
82. We rarely work hard enough; cease only when you feel bodily fatigue.
83. Boredom invites trouble.
84. It is better and nobler to give away than lend money.
85. Never give up hope that your tormenter will disappear or die. It happens constantly.
86. Extra-physicality or spirituality is as real as the words you are now reading.
87. There is no dishonor in electing to give in. Each conflict must end.
88. "He who proceeds violently across the earth will meet with a weary end. Know this and you know all my teachings." (Lao Tzu)
89. Arrogance is stupidity.
90. Never pick on people or make jokes at their expense; they have more problems than you know.
91. "What is fear of need but need itself?" (Khalil Gibran)
92. The only things you can really give another are money or time.
93. "Persistence amounting to madness should be avoided." (I Ching)
94. Accept paradox.
95. "Chance favors the prepared mind." (Pasteur)
96. Prepare for the day when your best friend betrays you.
97. Keep your word.
98. No one is as confident as someone who knows the least.
99. Show respect.
100. Those who bill by the hour work not for you but for the hour.
101. "The power of instruction is seldom of much efficacy, except in those happy dispositions where it is almost superfluous." (Edward Gibbon)

In reading the abridged works that makeup this collection, you will undoubtedly find different ideas or new wrinkles and applications among those I have attempted to distill. I can promise you that I have made every effort to excise these great books, ancient and modern, to their true essentials, omitting nothing based on taste or fickleness.

I write the following without sentiment: if you are reading this anthology the great likelihood is that you stand to benefit from it, as those who learn the lessons of successful living are those who already (or innately) know them but turn to literature, as I do, for reminder and support. In some cases, those of us who seek to lead an ethical and positive life are taken advantage of by others. This book helps in those instances, too, without sacrificing honor or selfhood.

Laws or rules that counsel deception are neither: they are breakage of the laws you find here. Seen from a certain perspective, the person who breaks his word violates no law—but violates the spirit of every law.

I have no idea whether nice guys finish first, last, or not at all. But I do know that honor is what builds powerful (not forceful) individuals and sound communities and companies, without which nothing can thrive. I believe this book places the motivated querent on the path to both.

---

**Mitch Horowitz** is a PEN Award-winning historian whose books include *Occult America, The Miracle Club, Daydream Believer, Uncertain Places, Modern Occultism,* and *Practical Magick*. He plays himself in AMC-Shudder's V/H/S/BEYOND, a 2025 Critics' Choice Award nominee for Best Movie made for Television. His work is censored in China.

# The Art of War
(c. 500 BC)

## by Sun Tzu

*History's Greatest Work on Strategy—
Now in a Special Condensation*

## Contents

Introduction   *The Unlikeliest Classic* by Mitch Horowitz   14
Chapter I   Laying Plans   16
Chapter II   Waging War   18
Chapter III   Attack by Stratagem   19
Chapter IV   Tactical Dispositions   21
Chapter V   Energy   22
Chapter VI   Weak Points and Strong   24
Chapter VII   Maneuvering   27
Chapter VIII   Variation in Tactics   29
Chapter IX   The Army on the March   30
Chapter X   Dangers and Opportunities   33
Chapter XI   The Use of Spies   38

## Introduction
# The Unlikeliest Classic

Since its first creditable English translation in 1910, the ancient Chinese martial text *The Art of War* has enthralled Western readers. First gaining the attention of military officers, sinologists, martial artists, and strategy aficionados, *The Art of War* is today read by business executives, athletes, artists, and seekers from across the self-help spectrum. This is a surprising destiny for a work on ancient warfare estimated to be written around 500 BC by Zhou dynasty general Sun Tzu, an honorific title meaning "Master Sun." Very little is known about the author other than a historical consensus that such a figure actually existed as a commander in the dynastic emperor's army.

What, then, accounts for the enduring popularity of a text that might have been conscripted to obscurity in the West?

Like the best writing from the Taoist tradition, *The Art of War* is exquisitely simple, practical, and clear. Its insights into life and its inevitable conflicts are so organic and sound—Taoism is based on aligning with the natural order of things—that many people who have never been on a battlefield are immediately drawn into wanting to apply Sun Tzu's maxims to daily life.

Indeed, this gentle condensation is intended to highlight those aphorisms and lessons that have the broadest general applicability. I have no doubt that as you experience this volume you will immediately discover ideas that you want to note and use. This is because Sun Tzu's genius as a writer is to return us to natural principles—things that we may have once understood intuitively but lost in superfluous and speculative analysis, another of life's inevitabilities.

I have based this abridgment on the aforementioned and invaluable 1910 English translation by British sinologist Lionel Giles. Giles' translation has stood up with remarkable relevance over the past century. Rather than laden his words with the flourish of late-Victorian prose, Giles honored the starkness and sparseness of the original work. I have occasionally altered an obscure or antiquated term, but, overall, the economy and elegance of Giles' translation is an art form in itself, and deserves to be honored as such.

Why then a condensation at all? In some instances, Sun Tzu, a working military commander, necessarily touched upon battlefield intricacies—such as the fine points of terrain or attacking the enemy with fire—that prove less immediately applicable to modern life than his observations on the movements and motives of men. In a few spots I also add a clarifying note to bring out Sun Tzu's broader points.

I ask the reader to take special note of Sun Tzu's frequent references to adhering to the natural landscape. It is a classically Taoist approach to blend with the curvature and qualities of one's surroundings—to find your place in the organic order of things. Within the Vedic tradition this is sometimes called dharma. Transcendentalist philosopher Ralph Waldo Emerson also notes the need to cycle yourself with the patterns of nature. As the great Hermetic dictum put it: "As above, so below."

Another key to Sun Tzu's popularity is the manner in which he unlocks the universality of true principles. What applies in warfare, if authentic, must apply to other areas of life. Human nature is consistent. So are the ebb and flow of events, on both macro and intimate levels. Be on the watch for this principle throughout the text.

Another central aspect of Sun Tzu's thought—again in harmony with Taoism—is that the greatest warrior prevails without ever fighting. If a fighter has observed conditions, deciphered the enemy, and diligently prepared and marshaled his forces, the ideal is to overwhelm his foe without shooting a single arrow. "Supreme excellence," Sun Tzu writes, "consists in breaking the enemy's resistance without fighting."

If an attack does prove necessary, it should be launched with irresistible force, like a seismic shifting of the earth. After your enemy's defeat, quickly return to normalcy. "In war then," the master writes, "let your object be victory, not lengthy campaigns." Sun Tzu warns against protracted operations. "There is no instance of a country having benefited from prolonged warfare," he writes.

Rather than seek glory, Sun Tzu counsels that the excellent commander practices subtlety, inscrutability, watchfulness, and flexibility. The good fighter, he writes, should be like water: dwelling unnoticed at his enemy's lowest depths and then striking with overwhelming power at his weakest points, the way a torrent of water rushes downhill. This constitutes ideal preparation and formation for attack: practice patience, carefully study the enemy, know his limits and strengths and your own, never be lured or tricked into battle—and then strike with ferocity. And never fight unless victory is assured.

If I had to put *The Art of War* into a nutshell, I would use this one of the master's maxims: "Let your plans be dark and impenetrable as night, and when you move, fall like a thunderbolt."

In a sense, *The Art of War* is about unlearning the complexities of life and returning to the simple and true. This voice from millennia ago can teach us how to strip away obfuscation. May its wisdom bring you your highest effectiveness.

—Mitch Horowitz

## Chapter I

# Laying Plans

Sun Tzu said: The art of war is of vital importance to the State.

It is a matter of life and death, a road either to safety or to ruin. Hence, it is a subject of inquiry that can on no account be neglected.

The art of war, then, is governed by five constant factors, to be taken into account in one's deliberations when seeking to determine the conditions obtaining in the field.

These are:

(1) The Moral Law;

(2) Heaven;

(3) Earth;

(4) The Commander;

(5) Method and Discipline.

The Moral Law causes the people to be in complete accord with their ruler, so that they will follow him regardless of their lives, undismayed by any danger.

Heaven signifies night and day, cold and heat, times and seasons.

Earth comprises distances, great and small; danger and security; open ground and narrow passes; the chances of life and death.

The Commander stands for the virtues of wisdom, sincerity, benevolence, courage, and strictness.

By method and discipline are to be understood the marshaling of the army in its proper subdivisions, the graduations of rank among the officers, the maintenance of roads by which supplies may reach the army, and the control of military expenditure.

These five heads should be familiar to every general: he who knows them will be victorious; he who knows them not will fail.

Therefore, in your deliberations, when seeking to determine the military conditions, let them be made the basis of a comparison, in this way:

(1) Which of the two sovereigns is imbued with the Moral Law?
(2) Which of the two generals has most ability?
(3) With whom lie the advantages derived from Heaven and Earth?
(4) On which side is discipline most rigorously enforced?
(5) Which army is stronger?
(6) On which side are officers and men more highly trained?
(7) In which army is there the greater constancy both in reward and punishment?

By means of these seven considerations I can forecast victory or defeat.

The general that hearkens to my counsel and acts upon it, will conquer: let such a one be retained in command! The general that hearkens not to my counsel nor acts upon it, will suffer defeat—let such a one be dismissed!

While heeding the profit of my counsel, avail yourself also of any helpful circumstances over and beyond the ordinary rules.

According as circumstances are favorable, one should modify one's plans.

All warfare is based on deception.

Hence, when able to attack, we must seem unable; when using our forces, we must seem inactive; when we are near, we must make the enemy believe we are far away; when far away, we must make him believe we are near.

Hold out baits to entice the enemy. Feign disorder, and crush him.

If he is secure at all points, be prepared for him. If he is in superior strength, evade him.

If your opponent is bad-tempered, seek to irritate him. Pretend to be weak, that he may grow arrogant.

If he is at ease, give him no rest. If his forces are united, separate them.

Attack him where he is unprepared, appear where you are not expected.

These military devices, leading to victory, must not be divulged beforehand.

Now the general who wins a battle makes many calculations in his temple ere the battle is fought. The general who loses a battle makes but few calculations beforehand. Thus do many calculations lead to victory, and few calculations to defeat: how much more no calculation at all! It is by attention to this point that I can foresee who is likely to win or lose.

## Chapter II

# Waging War

When you engage in actual fighting, if victory is long in coming, then men's weapons will grow dull and their ardor will be dampened. If you lay siege to a town, you will exhaust your strength.

Again, if the campaign is protracted, the resources of the State will not be equal to the strain.

Now, when your weapons are dulled, your ardor dampened, your strength exhausted and your treasure spent, other chieftains will spring up to take advantage of your extremity. Then no man, however wise, will be able to avert the consequences that must ensue.

Thus, though we have heard of stupid haste in war, cleverness has never been seen associated with long delays.

There is no instance of a country having benefited from prolonged warfare.

It is only one who is thoroughly acquainted with the evils of war that can thoroughly understand the profitable way of carrying it on.

The skillful soldier does not levy a second tax, neither are his supply-wagons loaded more than twice.

Bring war material with you from home, but forage on the enemy. Thus the army will have food enough for its needs.

Poverty of the State treasury causes an army to be maintained by contributions from a distance. Contributing to maintain an army at a distance causes the people to be impoverished.

On the other hand, the proximity of an army causes prices to go up; and high prices cause the people's substance to be drained away.

When their substance is drained away, the peasantry will be afflicted by heavy exactions.

With this loss of substance and exhaustion of strength, the homes of the people will be stripped bare, and three-tenths of their income will be dissipated; while government expenses for broken chariots, worn-out horses, breast-plates and helmets, bows and arrows, spears and shields, protective mantles, draught-oxen and heavy wagons, will amount to four-tenths of its total revenue.

Hence a wise general makes a point of foraging on the enemy. One cart-load of the enemy's provisions is equivalent to twenty of one's own, and likewise a single parcel from his stores is equivalent to twenty from one's own stores.

Now in order to kill the enemy, our men must be roused to anger; that there may be advantage from defeating the enemy, they must have their rewards.

Therefore in chariot fighting, when ten or more chariots have been taken, those should be rewarded who took the first. Our own flags should be substituted for those of the enemy, and the chariots mingled and used in conjunction with ours. The captured soldiers should be kindly treated and kept.

This is called, using the conquered foe to augment one's own strength.

In war, then, let your great object be victory, not lengthy campaigns.

Thus it may be known that the leader of armies is the arbiter of the people's fate, the man on whom it depends whether the nation shall be in peace or in peril.

## Chapter III
# Attack by Stratagem

Sun Tzu said: In the practical art of war, the best thing of all is to take the enemy's country whole and intact; to shatter and destroy it is not so good. So, too, it is better to recapture an army entire than to destroy it, to capture a regiment, a detachment or a company entire than to destroy them.

Hence to fight and conquer in all your battles is not supreme excellence; supreme excellence consists in breaking the enemy's resistance without fighting.

Thus the highest form of generalship is to block the enemy's plans; the next best is to prevent the junction of the enemy's forces; the next in order is to attack the enemy's army in the field; and the worst policy of all is to besiege walled cities.

The rule is, not to besiege walled cities if it can possibly be avoided. The preparation of mantlets, movable shelters, and various implements of war, will take up three whole months; and the piling up of mounds over against the walls will take three months more.

The general, unable to control his irritation, will launch his men to the assault like swarming ants, with the result that one-third of his men are slain, while the town still remains untaken. Such are the disastrous effects of a siege.

Therefore the skillful leader subdues the enemy's troops without any fighting; he captures their cities without laying siege to them; he overthrows their kingdom without lengthy operations in the field.

With his forces intact he will dispute the mastery of the Empire, and thus, without losing a man, his triumph will be complete. This is the method of attacking by stratagem.

It is the rule in war, if our forces are ten to the enemy's one, to surround him; if five to one, to attack him; if twice as numerous, to divide our army into two.

If equally matched, we can offer battle; if slightly inferior in numbers, we can avoid the enemy; if quite unequal in every way, we can flee from him.

Hence, though an obstinate fight may be made by a small force, in the end it must be captured by the larger force.

Now the general is the bulwark of the State; if the bulwark is complete at all points, the State will be strong; if the bulwark is defective, the State will be weak.

There are three ways in which a ruler can bring misfortune upon his army:

(1) By commanding the army to advance or to retreat, being ignorant of the fact that it cannot obey. This is called hobbling the army.

(2) By attempting to govern an army in the same way as he administers a kingdom, being ignorant of the conditions which obtain in an army. This causes restlessness in the soldiers' minds.

(3) By employing the officers of his army without discrimination, through ignorance of the military principle of adaptation to circumstances. This shakes the confidence of the soldiers.

But when the army is restless and distrustful, trouble is sure to come from the other feudal princes. This is simply bringing anarchy into the army, and flinging victory away.

Thus we may know that there are five essentials for victory:

(1) He will win who knows when to fight and when not to fight.

(2) He will win who knows how to handle both superior and inferior forces.

(3) He will win whose army is animated by the same spirit throughout all its ranks.

(4) He will win who, prepared himself, waits to take the enemy unprepared.

(5) He will win who has military capacity and is not interfered with by the sovereign.

Hence the saying: If you know the enemy and know yourself, you need not fear the result of a hundred battles. If you know yourself but not the enemy, for every victory gained you will also suffer a defeat. If you know neither the enemy nor yourself, you will succumb in every battle.

## Chapter IV
# Tactical Dispositions

Sun Tzu said: The good fighters of old first put themselves beyond the possibility of defeat, and then waited for an opportunity of defeating the enemy.

To secure ourselves against defeat lies in our own hands, but the opportunity of defeating the enemy is provided by the enemy himself.

Thus the good fighter is able to secure himself against defeat, but cannot make certain of defeating the enemy.

Hence the saying: One may know how to conquer without being able to do it.*

Security against defeat implies defensive tactics; ability to defeat the enemy means taking the offensive.

Standing on the defensive indicates insufficient strength; attacking, a superabundance of strength.

The general who is skilled in defense hides in the most secret recesses of the earth; he who is skilled in attack flashes forth from the topmost heights of heaven. Thus on the one hand we have ability to protect ourselves; on the other, a victory that is complete.

To see victory only when it is within the ken of the common herd is not the acme of excellence.

Neither is it the acme of excellence if you fight and conquer and the whole Empire says, "Well done!"

To lift an autumn hair is no sign of great strength; to see the sun and moon is no sign of sharp sight; to hear the noise of thunder is no sign of a quick ear.

What the ancients called a clever fighter is one who not only wins, but excels in winning with ease.

---

\* This is natural law: where two parties are involved the outcome depends on both.—MH

Hence his victories bring him neither reputation for wisdom nor credit for courage.

He wins his battles by making no mistakes. Making no mistakes is what establishes the certainty of victory, for it means conquering an enemy that is already defeated.

Hence the skillful fighter puts himself into a position which makes defeat impossible, and does not miss the moment for defeating the enemy.

Thus it is that in war the victorious strategist only seeks battle after the victory has been won, whereas he who is destined to defeat first fights and afterwards looks for victory.

The consummate leader cultivates the moral law, and strictly adheres to method and discipline; thus it is in his power to control success.*

In respect of military method, we have, firstly, Measurement; secondly, Estimation of quantity; thirdly, Calculation; fourthly, Balancing of chances; fifthly, Victory.

Measurement owes its existence to Earth; Estimation of quantity to Measurement; Calculation to Estimation of quantity; Balancing of chances to Calculation; and Victory to Balancing of chances.

A victorious army opposed to a routed one, is as a pound's weight placed in the scale against a single grain.

The onrush of a conquering force is like the bursting of pent-up waters into a chasm a thousand fathoms deep.

## Chapter V

# Energy

Sun Tzu said: The control of a large force is the same principle as the control of a few men: it is merely a question of dividing up their numbers.

Fighting with a large army under your command is in no way different from fighting with a small one: it is merely a question of instituting signs and signals.

To ensure that your whole army may withstand the brunt of the enemy's attack and remain unshaken—this is effected by maneuvers direct and indirect.

---

* It is useful here to note that Sun Tzu adheres not to inspiration, which can come and go, but to "method and discipline," where are permanent.—MH

That the impact of your army may be like a grindstone dashed against an egg—this is effected by the science of weak points and strong.

In all fighting, the direct method may be used for joining battle, but indirect methods will be needed in order to secure victory.

Indirect tactics, efficiently applied, are inexhaustible as Heaven and Earth, unending as the flow of rivers and streams; like the sun and moon, they end but to begin anew; like the four seasons, they pass away to return once more.*

There are not more than five musical notes, yet the combinations of these five give rise to more melodies than can ever be heard.

There are not more than five primary colors (blue, yellow, red, white, and black), yet in combination they produce more hues than can ever been seen.

There are not more than five cardinal tastes (sour, acrid, salt, sweet, bitter), yet combinations of them yield more flavors than can ever be tasted.

In battle, there are not more than two methods of attack—the direct and the indirect; yet these two in combination give rise to an endless series of maneuvers.

The direct and the indirect lead on to each other in turn. It is like moving in a circle—you never come to an end. Who can exhaust the possibilities of their combination?

The onset of troops is like the rush of a torrent, which will even roll stones along in its course.

The quality of decision is like the well-timed swoop of a falcon, which enables it to strike and destroy its victim.

Therefore the good fighter will be terrible in his onset, and prompt in his decision.

Energy may be likened to the bending of a crossbow; decision, to the releasing of a trigger.

Amid the turmoil and tumult of battle, there may be seeming disorder and yet no real disorder at all; amid confusion and chaos, your array may be without head or tail, yet it will be proof against defeat.

Simulated disorder postulates perfect discipline, simulated fear postulates courage; simulated weakness postulates strength.

Hiding order beneath the cloak of disorder is simply a question of subdivision; concealing courage under a show of timidity presupposes a fund of

---

* This precept should be read and contemplated carefully with the one immediately preceding it.—MH

latent energy; masking strength with weakness is to be effected by tactical dispositions.

Thus one who is skillful at keeping the enemy on the move maintains deceitful appearances, according to which the enemy will act. He sacrifices something, that the enemy may snatch at it.

By holding out baits, he keeps him on the march; then with a body of picked men he lies in wait for him.

The clever combatant looks to the effect of combined energy, and does not require too much from individuals. Hence his ability to pick out the right men and utilize combined energy.*

When he utilizes combined energy, his fighting men become as it were like unto rolling logs or stones. For it is the nature of a log or stone to remain motionless on level ground, and to move when on a slope; if four-cornered, to come to a standstill, but if round-shaped, to go rolling down.

Thus the energy developed by good fighting men is as the momentum of a round stone rolled down a mountain thousands of feet in height.

## Chapter VI

# Weak Points and Strong

Sun Tzu said: Whoever is first in the field and awaits the coming of the enemy, will be fresh for the fight; whoever is second in the field and has to hasten to battle will arrive exhausted.**

Therefore the clever combatant imposes his will on the enemy, but does not allow the enemy's will to be imposed on him.

By holding out advantages to him, he can cause the enemy to approach of his own accord; or, by inflicting damage, he can make it impossible for the enemy to draw near.

If the enemy is taking his ease, he can harass him; if well supplied with food, he can starve him out; if quietly encamped, he can force him to move.

Appear at points that the enemy must hasten to defend; march swiftly to places where you are not expected.

---

\* Sun Tzu is saying that you must not over-rely on any one person or factor.—MH
\*\* This is one of Sun Tzu's most practical lessons: always arrive first.—MH

An army may march great distances without distress, if it marches through country where the enemy is not.

You can be sure of succeeding in your attacks if you only attack places that are undefended. You can ensure the safety of your defense if you only hold positions that cannot be attacked.

Hence that general is skillful in attack whose opponent does not know what to defend; and he is skillful in defense whose opponent does not know what to attack.

O divine art of subtlety and secrecy! Through you we learn to be invisible, through you inaudible; and hence we can hold the enemy's fate in our hands.

You may advance and be absolutely irresistible, if you make for the enemy's weak points; you may retire and be safe from pursuit if your movements are more rapid than those of the enemy.

If we wish to fight, the enemy can be forced to an engagement even though he be sheltered behind a high rampart and a deep ditch. All we need do is attack some other place that he will be obliged to relieve.

If we do not wish to fight, we can prevent the enemy from engaging us even though the lines of our encampment be merely traced out on the ground. All we need do is to throw something odd and unaccountable in his way.

By discovering the enemy's dispositions and remaining invisible ourselves, we can keep our forces concentrated, while the enemy's must be divided.

We can form a single united body, while the enemy must split up into fractions. Hence there will be a whole pitted against separate parts of a whole, which means that we shall be many to the enemy's few.

And if we are able thus to attack an inferior force with a superior one, our opponents will be in dire straits.

The spot where we intend to fight must not be made known; for then the enemy will have to prepare against a possible attack at several different points; and his forces being thus distributed in many directions, the numbers we shall have to face at any given point will be proportionately few.

For should the enemy strengthen his approach, he will weaken his rear; should he strengthen his rear, he will weaken his approach; should he strengthen his left, he will weaken his right; should he strengthen his right, he will weaken his left. If he sends reinforcements everywhere, he will everywhere be weak.

Numerical weakness comes from having to prepare against possible attacks; numerical strength, from compelling our adversary to make these preparations against us.

Knowing the place and the time of the coming battle, we may concentrate from the greatest distances in order to fight.

Though the enemy be stronger in numbers, we may prevent him from fighting. Scheme so as to discover his plans and the likelihood of their success.

Rouse him, and learn the principle of his activity or inactivity. Force him to reveal himself, so as to find out his vulnerable spots.

Carefully compare the opposing army with your own, so that you may know where strength is superabundant and where it is deficient.

In making tactical dispositions, the highest pitch you can attain is to conceal them; conceal your dispositions, and you will be safe from the prying of the subtlest spies, from the machinations of the wisest brains.

How victory may be produced for them out of the enemy's own tactics—that is what the multitude cannot comprehend.

All men can see the tactics whereby I conquer, but what none can see is the strategy out of which victory is evolved.

Do not repeat the tactics that have gained you one victory, but let your methods be regulated by the infinite variety of circumstances.

Military tactics are like unto water; for water in its natural course runs away from high places and hastens downwards.

So in war, the way is to avoid what is strong and to strike at what is weak.

Water shapes its course according to the nature of the ground over which it flows; the soldier works out his victory in relation to the foe that he is facing.*

Therefore, just as water retains no constant shape, so in warfare there are no constant conditions.

He who can modify his tactics in relation to his opponent and thereby succeed in winning, may be called a heaven-born captain.

The five elements (water, fire, wood, metal, earth) are not always equally predominant; the four seasons make way for each other in turn. There are short days and long; the moon has its periods of waning and waxing.

---

* Sun Tzu is counseling flexibility, morphing, and response to changed circumstances. Do not be rigid.—MH

## Chapter VII
# Maneuvering

Sun Tzu said: In war, the general receives his commands from the sovereign. Having collected an army and concentrated his forces, he must blend and harmonize the different elements thereof before pitching his camp.

After that, comes tactical maneuvering, than which there is nothing more difficult. The difficulty of tactical maneuvering consists in turning the devious into the direct, and misfortune into gain.

Thus, to take a long and circuitous route, after enticing the enemy out of the way, and though starting after him, to contrive to reach the goal before him, shows knowledge of the artifice of DEVIATION.

Maneuvering with an army is advantageous; with an undisciplined multitude, most dangerous.

If you set a fully equipped army to march in order to snatch an advantage, the chances are that you will be too late. On the other hand, to detach a flying column for the purpose involves the sacrifice of its baggage and stores.

Thus, if you order your men to roll up their buff-coats, and make forced marches without halting day or night, covering double the usual distance at a stretch in order to wrest an advantage, the leaders of all your three divisions will fall into the hands of the enemy.

The stronger men will be in front, the jaded ones will fall behind, and on this plan only one-tenth of your army will reach its destination.

If you march long distances to outmaneuver the enemy, you will lose the leader of your first division, and only half your force will reach the goal. Even you modify the long distance, two-thirds of your army will arrive.

Hence it follows that an army without its baggage-train is lost; without provisions it is lost; without bases of supply it is lost.

We cannot enter into alliances until we are acquainted with the designs of our neighbors.

We are not fit to lead an army on the march unless we are familiar with the face of the country—its mountains and forests, its pitfalls and precipices, its marshes and swamps.

We shall be unable to turn natural advantage to account unless we make use of local guides.

In war, practice concealment, and you will succeed.

Whether to concentrate or to divide your troops, must be decided by circumstances.

Let your rapidity be that of the wind, your compactness that of the forest.

In raiding and plundering be like fire, as immovability is like a mountain.

Let your plans be dark and impenetrable as night, and when you move, fall like a thunderbolt.

When you plunder a countryside, let the spoils be divided amongst your men; when you capture new territory, cut it up into allotments for the benefit of the soldiery.

Ponder and deliberate before you make a move.

He will conquer who has learnt the artifice of deviation. Such is the art of maneuvering.

The Book of Army Management says: On the field of battle, the spoken word does not carry far enough: hence the institution of gongs and drums. Nor can ordinary objects be seen clearly enough: hence the institution of banners and flags.

Gongs and drums, banners and flags, are means whereby the ears and eyes of the army may be focused on one particular point.

The army thus forming a single united body, it is impossible either for the brave to advance alone, or for the cowardly to retreat alone. This is the art of handling large masses of men.

In night-fighting, then, make much use of signal-fires and drums, and in fighting by day, of flags and banners, as a means of influencing the ears and eyes of your army.

A whole army may be robbed of its spirit; a commander-in-chief may be robbed of his presence of mind.

Now a soldier's spirit is keenest in the morning; by noonday it has begun to flag; and in the evening, his mind is bent only on returning to camp.

A clever general, therefore, avoids an army when its spirit is keen, but attacks it when it is sluggish and inclined to return. This is the art of studying moods.

Disciplined and calm, to await the appearance of disorder and hubbub amongst the enemy—this is the art of retaining self-possession.

To be near the goal while the enemy is still far from it, to wait at ease while the enemy is toiling and struggling, to be well-fed while the enemy is famished—this is the art of husbanding one's strength.

To refrain from intercepting an enemy whose banners are in perfect order, to refrain from attacking an army drawn up in calm and confident array—this is the art of studying circumstances.

It is a military axiom not to advance uphill against the enemy, nor to oppose him when he comes downhill.

Do not pursue an enemy who simulates flight; do not attack soldiers whose temper is keen.

Do not swallow bait offered by the enemy. Do not interfere with an army that is returning home.

When you surround an army, leave an outlet free. Do not press a desperate foe too hard.*

Such is the art of warfare.

## Chapter VIII

# Variation in Tactics

Sun Tzu said: In war, the general receives his commands from the sovereign, collects his army, and concentrates his forces

When in difficult country, do not encamp. In country where high roads intersect, join hands with your allies. Do not linger in dangerously isolated positions. In hemmed-in situations, you must resort to stratagem. In desperate position, you must fight.

There are roads that must not be followed, armies that must be not attacked, towns that must be besieged, positions that must not be contested, commands of the sovereign that must not be obeyed.

The general who thoroughly understands the advantages that accompany variation of tactics knows how to handle his troops.

The general who does not understand these may be well acquainted with the configuration of the country, yet he will not be able to turn his knowledge to practical account.

So, the student of war who is unversed in the art of war of varying his plans, even though he is acquainted with the Five Advantages, will fail to make the best use of his men.**

---

\* By pressing a desperate foe, and leaving him no way out, you ensure he will fight to the death.—MH
\*\* For the "Five Advantages," see Sun Tzu's note on the "five essentials for victory" in chapter III.—MH

Hence in the wise leader's plans, considerations of advantage and of disadvantage will be blended together.

If our expectation of advantage is tempered in this way, we may succeed in accomplishing the essential part of our schemes.

If, on the other hand, in the midst of difficulties we are always ready to seize an advantage, we may extricate ourselves from misfortune.

Reduce the hostile chiefs by inflicting damage on them; and make trouble for them, and keep them constantly engaged; hold out specious allurements, and make them rush to any given point.

The art of war teaches us to rely not on the likelihood of the enemy's not coming, but on our own readiness to receive him; not on the chance of his not attacking, but rather on the fact that we have made our position unassailable.

There are five dangerous faults which may affect a general:

(1) Recklessness, which leads to destruction;

(2) cowardice, which leads to capture;

(3) a hasty temper, which can be provoked by insults;

(4) a delicacy of honor which is sensitive to shame;

(5) over-solicitude for his men, which exposes him to worry and trouble.

These are the five besetting sins of a general, ruinous to the conduct of war.

When an army is overthrown and its leader slain, the cause will surely be found among these five dangerous faults. Let them be a subject of meditation.

## Chapter IX

# The Army on the March

Sun Tzu said: We come now to the question of encamping the army, and observing signs of the enemy. Pass quickly over mountains, and keep in the neighborhood of valleys.

Camp in high places, facing the sun. Do not climb heights in order to fight.

After crossing a river, you should get far away from it.

When an invading force crosses a river in its onward march, do not advance to meet it in midstream. It will be best to let half the army get across, and then deliver your attack.

If you are anxious to fight, you should not go to meet the invader near a river that he has to cross.*

Moor your craft higher up than the enemy, and facing the sun. Do not move upstream to meet the enemy.

In crossing saltmarshes, your sole concern should be to get over them quickly, without any delay.

If forced to fight in a saltmarsh, you should have water and grass near you, and get your back to a clump of trees.

In dry, level country, take up an easily accessible position with rising ground to your right and on your rear, so that the danger may be in front, and safety lie behind.

All armies prefer high ground to low and sunny places to dark.

If you are careful of your men, and camp on hard ground, the army will be free from disease of every kind, and this will spell victory.

When you come to a hill or a bank, occupy the sunny side, with the slope on your right rear. Thus you will at once act for the benefit of your soldiers and utilize the natural advantages of the ground.

When, in consequence of heavy rains up-country, a river you wish to ford is swollen and flecked with foam, you must wait until it subsides.

Country in which there are precipitous cliffs with torrents running between, deep natural hollows, confined places, tangled thickets, quagmires and crevasses, should be left with all possible speed and not approached.

While we keep away from such places, we should get the enemy to approach them; while we face them, we should let the enemy have them on his rear.

If in the neighborhood of your camp there should be any hilly country, ponds surrounded by aquatic grass, hollow basins filled with reeds, or woods with thick undergrowth, they must be carefully routed out and searched; for these are places where men in ambush or insidious spies are likely to be lurking.

When the enemy is close at hand and remains quiet, he is relying on the natural strength of his position.

When he keeps aloof and tries to provoke a battle, he is anxious for the other side to advance.

If his place of encampment is easy of access, he is tendering a bait.

---

* In these passages, Sun Tzu is staying that you must exhaust your enemy by enticing him to cross a river.—MH

Movement amongst the trees of a forest shows that the enemy is advancing. The appearance of a number of screens in the midst of thick grass means that the enemy wants to make us suspicious.

The rising of birds in their flight is the sign of an ambush. Startled beasts indicate that a sudden attack is coming.

Humble words and increased preparations are signs that the enemy is about to advance. Violent language and driving forward as if to the attack are signs that he will retreat.

When the light chariots come out first and take up a position on the wings, it is a sign that the enemy is forming for battle.

Peace proposals unaccompanied by a sworn covenant indicate a plot.

When there is much running about and the soldiers fall into rank, it means that the critical moment has come.

When some are seen advancing and some retreating, it is a lure.

When the soldiers stand leaning on their spears, they are faint from want of food.

If those who are sent to draw water begin by drinking themselves, the army is suffering from thirst.

If the enemy sees an advantage to be gained and makes no effort to secure it, the soldiers are exhausted.

If birds gather on any spot, it is unoccupied. Clamor by night betokens nervousness.

If there is disturbance in the camp, the general's authority is weak. If the banners and flags are shifted about, sedition is afoot. If the officers are angry, it means that the men are weary.

When an army feeds its horses with grain and kills its cattle for food, and when the men do not hang their cooking-pots over the camp-fires, showing that they will not return to their tents, you may know that they are determined to fight to the death.*

The sight of men whispering together in small knots or speaking in subdued tones points to disaffection amongst the rank and file.

Too frequent rewards signify that the enemy is at the end of his resources; too many punishments betray a condition of dire distress.

To begin by bluster, but afterwards to take fright at the enemy's numbers, shows a supreme lack of intelligence.

---

* Men eat grain; horses eat grass. Hence, the slaying of cattle means a preparation for the end.—MH

When envoys are sent with compliments in their mouths, it is a sign that the enemy wishes for a truce.

If the enemy's troops march up angrily and remain facing ours for a long time without either joining battle or taking themselves off again, the situation is one that demands great vigilance and circumspection.

If our troops are no more in number than the enemy that is amply sufficient; it only means that no direct attack can be made. What we can do is simply to concentrate all our available strength, keep a close watch on the enemy, and obtain reinforcements.

He who exercises no forethought but makes light of his opponents is sure to be captured by them.

If soldiers are punished before they have grown attached to you, they will not prove submissive; and, unless submissive, then will be practically useless. If, when the soldiers have become attached to you, punishments are not enforced, they will still be useless.

Therefore soldiers must be treated in the first instance with humanity, but kept under control by means of iron discipline. This is a certain road to victory.

If in training soldiers commands are habitually enforced, the army will be well disciplined; if not, its discipline will be bad.

If a general shows confidence in his men but always insists on his orders being obeyed, the gain will be mutual.

## Chapter X

# Dangers and Opportunities

Now an army is exposed to six varying calamities, not arising from natural causes, but from faults for which the general is responsible. These are: (1) flight; (2) insubordination; (3) collapse; (4) ruin; (5) disorganization; (6) rout.

Other conditions being equal, if one force is hurled against another ten times its size, the result will be the flight of the former.

When the common soldiers are too strong and their officers too weak, the result is insubordination. When the officers are too strong and the common soldiers too weak, the result is collapse.

When the higher officers are angry and insubordinate, and on meeting the enemy give battle on their own account from a feeling of resentment, before the commander-in-chief can tell whether or not he is in a position to fight, the result is ruin.

When the general is weak and without authority; when his orders are not clear and distinct; when there are no fixed duties assigned to officers and men, and the ranks are formed in a slovenly haphazard manner, the result is utter disorganization.

When a general, unable to estimate the enemy's strength, allows an inferior force to engage a larger one, or hurls a weak detachment against a powerful one, and neglects to place picked soldiers in the front rank, the result must be rout.

These are six ways of courting defeat, which must be carefully noted by the general who has attained a responsible post.

The natural formation of the country is the soldier's best ally; but a power of estimating the adversary, of controlling the forces of victory, and of shrewdly calculating difficulties, dangers, and distances, constitutes the test of a great general.

He who knows these things, and in fighting puts his knowledge into practice, will win his battles. He who knows them not, nor practices them, will surely be defeated.

If fighting is sure to result in victory, then you must fight, even though the ruler forbid it; if fighting will not result in victory, then you must not fight, even at the ruler's bidding.

The general who advances without coveting fame and retreats without fearing disgrace, whose only thought is to protect his country and do good service for his sovereign, is the jewel of the kingdom.

Regard your soldiers as your children, and they will follow you into the deepest valleys; look upon them as your own beloved sons, and they will stand by you even unto death.

If, however, you are indulgent, but unable to make your authority felt; kind-hearted, but unable to enforce your commands; and incapable, moreover, of quelling disorder: then your soldiers must be likened to spoilt children; they are useless for any practical purpose.

If we know that our own men are in a condition to attack, but are unaware that the enemy is not open to attack, we have gone only halfway towards victory.

If we know that the enemy is open to attack, but are unaware that our own men are not in a condition to attack, we have gone only halfway towards victory.

If we know that the enemy is open to attack, and also know that our men are in a condition to attack, but are unaware that the nature of the ground makes fighting impracticable, we have still gone only halfway towards victory.

Hence the experienced soldier, once in motion, is never bewildered; once he has broken camp, he is never at a loss.

Hence the saying: If you know the enemy and know yourself, your victory will not stand in doubt; if you know Heaven and know Earth, you may make your victory complete.

If asked how to cope with a great army of the enemy in orderly array and on the point of marching to the attack, I should say: "Begin by seizing something which your opponent holds dear; then he will be amenable to your will."

Rapidity is the essence of war: take advantage of the enemy's unreadiness, make your way by unexpected routes, and attack unguarded spots.

The following are the principles to be observed by an invading force: The further you penetrate into a country, the greater will be the solidarity of your troops, and thus the defenders will not prevail against you.

Make forays in fertile country in order to supply your army with food.

Carefully study the wellbeing of your men, and do not overtax them. Concentrate your energy and hoard your strength. Keep your army continually on the move, and devise unfathomable plans.

Throw your soldiers into positions whence there is no escape, and they will prefer death to flight. If they will face death, there is nothing they may not achieve. Officers and men alike will put forth their uttermost strength.

Soldiers when in desperate straits lose the sense of fear. If there is no place of refuge, they will stand firm. If they are in hostile country, they will show a stubborn front. If there is no help for it, they will fight hard.

Thus, without waiting to be marshaled, the soldiers will be constantly on the alert; without waiting to be asked, they will do your will; without restrictions, they will be faithful; without giving orders, they can be trusted.

Prohibit the taking of omens, and do away with superstitious doubts. Then, until death itself comes, no calamity need be feared.

If our soldiers are not overburdened with money, it is not because they have a distaste for riches; if their lives are not unduly long, it is not because they are disinclined to longevity.

On the day they are ordered out to battle, your soldiers may weep. But let them once be brought to bay, and they will display great courage.

The principle on which to manage an army is to set up one standard of courage which all must reach.

How to make the best of both strong and weak—that is a question involving the proper use of ground.

Thus the skillful general conducts his army just as though he were leading a single man, in all places, by the hand.

It is the business of a general to be quiet and thus ensure secrecy; upright and just, and thus maintain order.

He must be able to mystify his officers and men by false reports and appearances, and thus keep them in total ignorance.

By altering his arrangements and changing his plans, he keeps the enemy without definite knowledge. By shifting his camp and taking circuitous routes, he prevents the enemy from anticipating his purpose.

At the critical moment, the leader of an army acts like one who has climbed up a height and then kicks away the ladder behind him. He carries his men deep into hostile territory before he shows his hand.

He burns his boats and breaks his cooking-pots; like a shepherd driving a flock of sheep, he drives his men this way and that, and nothing knows whither he is going.*

To muster his army and bring it into danger—this may be termed the business of the general.

It is the soldier's disposition to offer an obstinate resistance when surrounded, to fight hard when he cannot help himself, and to obey promptly when he has fallen into danger.

We cannot enter into alliance with neighboring princes until we are acquainted with their designs. We are not fit to lead an army on the march unless we are familiar with the face of the country—its mountains and forests, its pitfalls and precipices, its marshes and swamps. We shall be unable to turn natural advantages to account unless we make use of local guides.

To be ignorant of any one of the following four or five principles does not befit a warlike prince.

When a warlike prince attacks a powerful state, his generalship shows itself in preventing the concentration of the enemy's forces. He overawes his opponents, and their allies are prevented from joining against him.

---

* The reference to burning boats and breaking cooking pots is akin to the Western expression to "burn the fleet"—in other words, to eliminate any way out and thus to guarantee victory or demise. This also makes a show of determination to troops and foes.—MH

Hence he does not strive to ally himself with all and sundry, nor does he foster the power of other states. He carries out his own secret designs, keeping his antagonists in awe. Thus he is able to capture their cities and overthrow their kingdoms.

Bestow rewards without regard to rule, issue orders without regard to previous arrangements; and you will be able to handle a whole army as though you had to do with but a single man.

Confront your soldiers with the deed itself; never let them know your design. When the outlook is bright, bring it before their eyes; but tell them nothing when the situation is gloomy.*

Place your army in deadly peril, and it will survive; plunge it into desperate straits, and it will come off in safety.

For it is precisely when a force has fallen into harm's way that is capable of striking a blow for victory.

Success in warfare is gained by carefully accommodating ourselves to the enemy's purpose.

By persistently hanging on the enemy's flank, we shall succeed in the long run in killing the commander-in-chief.

This is called ability to accomplish a thing by sheer cunning.

If the enemy leaves a door open, you must rush in.

Forestall your opponent by seizing what he holds dear, and subtly contrive to time his arrival on the ground.

Walk in the path defined by rule, and accommodate yourself to the enemy until you can fight a decisive battle.

At first, then, exhibit the coyness of a maiden, until the enemy gives you an opening; afterwards emulate the rapidity of a running hare, and it will be too late for the enemy to oppose you.

Unhappy is the fate of one who tries to win his battles and succeed in his attacks without cultivating the spirit of enterprise; for the result is waste of time and general stagnation.

Hence the saying: The enlightened ruler lays his plans well ahead; the good general cultivates his resources.

Move not unless you see an advantage; use not your troops unless there is something to be gained; fight not unless the position is critical.

---

* In the first part of this principle, Sun Tzu is saying to focus troops on the goal not on the means to the goal.—MH

No ruler should put troops into the field merely to gratify his own spleen; no general should fight a battle simply out of irritation.

If it is to your advantage, make a forward move; if not, stay where you are.

Anger may in time change to gladness; vexation may be succeeded by content.

But a kingdom that has once been destroyed can never come again into being; nor can the dead ever be brought back to life.

Hence the enlightened ruler is heedful, and the good general full of caution. This is the way to keep a country at peace and an army intact.

## Chapter XI
# The Use of Spies

Hostile armies may face each other for years, striving for the victory that is decided in a single day. This being so, to remain in ignorance of the enemy's condition simply because one grudges the outlay of a hundred ounces of silver in honors and payments is the height of inhumanity.

One who acts thus is no leader of men, no present help to his sovereign, no master of victory.

Thus, what enables the wise sovereign and the good general to strike and conquer, and achieve things beyond the reach of ordinary men, is foreknowledge.

Now this foreknowledge cannot be elicited from spirits; it cannot be obtained inductively from experience, nor by any deductive calculation.

Knowledge of the enemy's dispositions can only be obtained from other men.

Spies cannot be usefully employed without a certain intuitive sagacity.

They cannot be properly managed without benevolence and straightforwardness.

Without subtle ingenuity of mind, one cannot make certain of the truth of their reports.

Be subtle! be subtle! and use your spies for every kind of business.

Whether the object be to crush an army, to storm a city, or to assassinate an individual, it is always necessary to begin by finding out the names of the attendants, the aides-de-camp, and doorkeepers and sentries of the general in command. Our spies must be commissioned to ascertain these.

The enemy's spies who have come to spy on us must be sought out, tempted with bribes, led away, and comfortably housed. Thus they will become converted spies and available for our service.

# The Prince
(1532)

# by Niccolò Machiavelli

*History's Greatest Guide to
Attaining and Keeping Power*

## Contents

Introduction  *A Different Side of The Prince* by Mitch Horowitz  40
To the Reader  42
Chapter I  On Acquiring a New Kingdom  42
Chapter II  Against Occupation  44
Chapter III  The Example of Alexander the Great  44
Chapter IV  How to Control Formerly Independent Territories  45
Chapter V  When a Prince Conquers by Merit  46
Chapter VI  When a Prince Conquers with Help of Others or by Luck  48
Chapter VII  When a Prince Conquers by Crime  49
Chapter VIII  When a Prince Rules by Popular Consent  50
Chapter IX  How the Strength of Princedoms Should Be Measured  53
Chapter X  Of Soldiers and Mercenaries  54
Chapter XI  The Prince and Military Affairs  55
Chapter XII  Better to Be Loved or Feared?  57
Chapter XIII  Truth and Deception  59
Chapter XIV  How to Avert Conspiracies  60
Chapter XV  How a Prince Should Defend Himself  62
Chapter XVI  How a Prince Should Preserve His Reputation  64
Chapter XVII  A Prince's Court  65
Chapter XVIII  Flatterers Should Be Shunned  66
Chapter XIX  The Role of Fortune  67
Chapter XX  Aphorisms from The Prince  69

## Introduction
# A Different Side of *The Prince*

It does not come naturally to me to introduce and abridge Niccolò Machiavelli's 1532 classic *The Prince*. The Renaissance-era guide to gaining and holding power has been known for centuries as a blueprint to ruthlessness, deception, and even brutality. I have inveighed against current books, like *The 48 Laws of Power*, that endorse amoral or unethical methods of personal advancement.

"But that's the real world," argue the defenders of such books. Not my world. And not the one I encourage others to dwell in.

How, then, do I justify this condensed and reader-friendly new edition of *The Prince*, a book considered the urtext of guides to ruthless attainment? The fact is—as you will discover in this careful abridgement—the writer and diplomat Machiavelli imbued his work with a greater sense of purpose and ethics than is commonly understood. Although Machiavelli unquestionably endorses absolutist and, at times, bloody ways of dealing with adversaries, he repeatedly notes that these are efforts of a last or near-last resort, when peaceable means of governance prove either unpromising or unworkable. He justifies resorting to deception or faithlessness only as a defense against the depravity of men, who shift alliances like the winds. This logic by no means approaches the morality of Christ's principle to be "wise as serpents and harmless as doves," but it belies the general notion that Machiavelli was a one-dimensional schemer.

Moreover, the author also emphasizes rewarding merit; leaving the public to its own devices and personal pursuits as much as possible (which is the essential ingredient to developing culture and economy); trusting subjects enough to allow them to bear arms—and even to arm them yourself if confident in their loyalty (which the good leader should be); surrounding oneself with wise counselors (the true measure of an able ruler); avoiding and not exploiting civic divisions; and striving to ensure the public's general satisfaction.

One of the most striking parts of the book for me is when Machiavelli expounds on the best kind of intellect for an adviser or minister. In chapter XVII he writes:

> There are three scales of intelligence, one which understands by itself, a second which understands what it is shown by others, and a third, which

understands neither by itself nor by the showing of others, the first of which is most excellent, the second good, but the third worthless.

This has always been my favorite passage of Machiavelli's. To add a further dimension to his observation, here is an alternate translation (and I challenge you to consider what place you have earned on its scale):

> There exist three kinds of intellects: that belonging to the one who can do the thing itself, that belonging to the one who can judge the thing, and that belonging to the one who can neither do nor judge. The first is excellent, the second is good, and the third is worthless.

Some contemporary critics suggest that *The Prince* is actually a satire of monarchy: that under the guise of a guide to ruthless conduct Machiavelli sends up the actions of absolute rulers and covertly calls for more republican forms of government. I think this assessment probably stretches matters. But it would be equally wrong, as noted, to conclude that Machiavelli was a narrow-eyed courtier bent on keeping others down. On balance, Machiavelli was a pragmatic tutor interested in promoting the unity, stability, and integrity of nation states, chiefly his own Italy, in a Europe that lacked cohesive civics and reliable international treaties. His harsher ideas were then considered acceptable quivers in the bow of statecraft; you will also see his efforts to leaven them with keen observations about the vicissitudes of human nature, fate, and virtue.

In actuality, I believe that businesspeople, leaders, and entrepreneurs who read *The Prince* today will discover subtleties that are missing from current power-at-any-cost guides. I advise experiencing *The Prince* through the filter of your own ethical standards and inner truths; sifting among its practical lessons; taking in its tough observations about human weaknesses; and using it as a guide to the realities —and foibles—of how we live.

Let me say a brief word about my method of abridgment. First, I have used the 1910 translation of Renaissance scholar N.H. Thomson, which originally appeared as part of the Harvard Classics line. My aim in condensing Thomson's translation is to provide the full range of Machiavelli's lessons and observations, but without most of his historical portraiture (which is well worth reading in the original, if you are engaged by what you encounter here). I have taken Machiavelli's most relatable and practical passages and ordered them into individual segments, each with a new and clarifying title. I have striven to eliminate repetition. I have occasionally substituted modern terms for antiquated ones. Finally, I have included a closing section of Machiavelli's most poignant aphorisms.

—Mitch Horowitz

## To the Reader

I have found among my possessions none that I prize and esteem more than a knowledge of the actions of great men, acquired in the course of long experience in modern affairs and a continual study of antiquity. This knowledge has been most carefully and patiently pondered over and sifted by me, and now reduced into this little book. I can offer no better gift than the means of mastering, in a very brief time, all that in the course of so many years, and at the cost of so many hardships and dangers, I have learned, and know.

—Niccolò Machiavelli

## Chapter I
# On Acquiring a New Kingdom

The Prince cannot avoid giving offense to new subjects, either in respect of the troops he quarters on them, or of some other of the numberless vexations attendant on a new acquisition. And in this way you may find that you have enemies in all those whom you have injured in seizing the Princedom, yet cannot keep the friendship of those who helped you to gain it; since you can neither reward them as they expect, nor yet, being under obligations to them, use violent remedies against them. For however strong you may be in respect of your army, it is essential that in entering a new Province you should have the good will of its inhabitants.

Hence it happened that Louis XII of France speedily gained possession of Milan, and as speedily lost it. For the very people who had opened the gates to the French King, when they found themselves deceived in their expectations and hopes of future benefits, could not put up with the insolence of their new ruler.

True it is that when a State rebels and is again got under, it will not afterwards be lost so easily. For the Prince, using the rebellion as a pretext, will not hesitate to secure himself by punishing the guilty, bringing the suspected to trial, and otherwise strengthening his position in the points where it was weak.

I say, then, that those States which upon their acquisition are joined onto the ancient dominions of the Prince who acquires them are either of the same religion and language as the people of these dominions, or they are not. When they are, there is great ease in retaining them, especially when they have not been accustomed to live in freedom. To hold them securely it is enough to have rooted out the line of the reigning Prince; because if in other respects the old condition of things be continued, and there be no discordance in their customs, men live peaceably with one another. Even if there be some slight difference in their languages, provided that customs are similar, they can easily get on together. He, therefore, who acquires such a State, if he mean to keep it, must see to two things: first, that the blood of the ancient line of Princes be destroyed; second, that no change be made in respect of laws or taxes; for in this way the newly acquired State speedily becomes incorporated.

But when States are acquired in a country differing in language, usages, and laws, difficulties multiply, and great good fortune, as well as actions, are needed to overcome them. One of the best and most efficacious methods for dealing with such a State is for the Prince who acquires it to go and dwell there in person, since this will tend to make his tenure more secure and lasting. For when you are on the spot, disorders are detected in their beginnings and remedies can be readily applied; but when you are at a distance, they are not heard of until they have gathered strength and the case is past cure. Moreover, the Province in which you take up your abode is not pillaged by your officers; the people are pleased to have a ready recourse to their Prince; and have all the more reason if they are well disposed, to love, if disaffected, to fear him. A foreign enemy desiring to attack that State would be cautious how he did so. In short, where the Prince resides in person, it will be extremely difficult to oust him.

Another excellent expedient is to send colonies into one or two places, so that these may become, as it were, the keys of the Province; for you must either do this, or else keep up a numerous force of men-at-arms and foot soldiers. A Prince need not spend much on colonies. He can send them out and support them at little or no charge to himself, and the only persons to whom he gives offence are those whom he deprives of their fields and houses to bestow them on the new inhabitants. Those who are thus injured form but a small part of the community, and remaining scattered and poor can never become dangerous. All others being left unmolested, are in consequence easily quieted, and at the same time are afraid to make a false move, lest they share the fate of those who have been deprived of their possessions. In few words, these colonies cost less than soldiers, are more faithful, and give less offense, while those who are offended, being, as I have said, poor and dispersed, cannot hurt. And let it here be noted that men are either to be kindly treated, or utterly crushed, since they can revenge lighter injuries, but not graver. Wherefore the injury we do to a man should be of a sort to leave no fear of reprisals.

## Chapter II
# Against Occupation

If instead of colonies you send troops, the cost is vastly greater, and the whole revenues of the country are spent in guarding it; so that the gain becomes a loss, and much deeper offense is given; since in shifting the quarters of your soldiers from place to place the whole country suffers hardship, which as all feel, all are made enemies; and enemies who remaining, although vanquished, in their own homes, have power to hurt. In every way, therefore, this mode of defense is as disadvantageous as that by colonizing is useful.

In dealing with the countries of which they took possession the Romans diligently followed the methods I have described. They planted colonies, conciliated weaker powers without adding to their strength, humbled the great, and never suffered a formidable stranger to acquire influence.

## Chapter III
# The Example of Alexander the Great

Alexander the Great having achieved the conquest of Asia in a few years and, dying before he had well entered on possession, it might have been expected, given the difficulty of preserving newly acquired States, that on his death the whole country would rise in revolt.

Nevertheless, his successors were able to keep their hold, and found in doing so no other difficulty than arose from their own ambition and mutual jealousies.

If anyone think this strange and ask the cause, I answer that all the Princedoms of which we have record have been governed in one of two ways: 1) either by a sole Prince, all others being his servants permitted by his grace and favor to assist in governing the kingdom as his ministers; or 2) by a Prince with his Barons who hold their rank, not by the favor of a superior Lord, but by antiquity of bloodline, and who have States and subjects of their own who recognize them as their rulers and entertain for them a natural affection.

States governed by a sole Prince and by his servants—as with Alexander—vest in him a more complete authority; because throughout the land none but he is recognized as sovereign, and if obedience be yielded to any others, it is yielded as to his ministers and officers for whom personally no special love is felt.*

## Chapter IV
# How to Control Formerly Independent Territories

When a newly acquired State has been accustomed to live under its own laws and in freedom, there are three methods whereby it may be held. The first is to destroy it; the second, to go and reside there in person; the third, to suffer it to live on under its own laws, subjecting it to a tribute and entrusting its government to a few of the inhabitants who will keep the rest your friends. Such a Government, since it is the creature of the new Prince, will see that it cannot stand without his protection and support, and must therefore do all it can to maintain him; and a city accustomed to live in freedom, if it is to be preserved at all, is more easily controlled through its own citizens than in any other way.

We have examples of all these methods in the histories of the Spartans and the Romans. The Spartans held Athens and Thebes by creating oligarchies in these cities, yet lost them in the end. The Romans, to retain Capua, Carthage, and Numantia, destroyed them and never lost them. On the other hand, when they thought to hold Greece as the Spartans had held it, leaving it its freedom

---

* Machiavelli is saying that civic and military authority surpasses bloodline.—MH

and allowing it to be governed by its own laws, they failed, and had to destroy many cities of that Province before they could secure it. For, in truth, there is no sure way of holding other than by destroying, and whoever becomes master of a City accustomed to live in freedom and does not destroy it, may reckon on being destroyed by it. For if it should rebel, it can always screen itself under the name of liberty and its ancient laws, which no length of time, nor any benefits conferred will ever cause it to forget; and do what you will, and take what care you may, unless the inhabitants be scattered and dispersed, this name, and the old order of things, will never cease to be remembered, but will at once be turned against you whenever misfortune overtakes you.

If, however, the newly acquired City or Province has been accustomed to live under a Prince, and his line is extinguished, it will be impossible for the citizens, used, on the one hand, to obey, and deprived, on the other, of their old ruler, to agree to choose a leader from among themselves; and as they know not how to live as freemen, and are therefore slow to take up arms, a stranger may readily gain them over and attach them to his cause. But in Republics there is a stronger vitality, a fiercer hatred, a keener thirst for revenge. The memory of their former freedom will not let them rest; so that the safest course is either to destroy them, or to go and live in them.

## Chapter V
# When a Prince Conquers by Merit

Since men for the most part follow in the footsteps and imitate the actions of others, and yet are unable to adhere exactly to those paths which others have taken, or attain to the virtues of those whom they would resemble, the wise man should always follow the roads that have been trodden by the great, and imitate those who have most excelled, so that if he cannot reach their perfection, he may at least acquire something of its savor. Acting in this like the skillful archer, who seeing that the object he would hit is distant, and knowing the range of his bow, takes aim much above the destined mark; not designing that his arrow should strike so high, but that flying high it may strike the point intended.

I say, then, that in entirely new Princedoms where the Prince himself is new, the difficulty of maintaining possession varies with the greater or less ability of him who acquires possession. And, because the mere fact of a private person rising to be a Prince presupposes either merit or good fortune, it will be seen that the presence of one or other of these two conditions lessens, to some extent, many difficulties. And yet, he who is less beholden to Fortune has often in the end the better success; and it may be for the advantage of a Prince that, from his having no other territories, he is obliged to reside in person in the State which he has acquired.

Looking first to those who have become Princes by their merit and not by their good fortune, I say that the most excellent among them are Moses, Cyrus, Romulus, Theseus, and the like. And though perhaps I ought not to name Moses, he being merely an instrument for carrying out the Divine commands, he is still to be admired for those qualities which made him worthy to converse with God. But if we consider Cyrus and the others who have acquired or founded kingdoms, they will all be seen to be admirable. And if their actions and the particular institutions of which they were the authors be studied, they will be found not to differ from those of Moses, instructed though he was by so great a teacher. Moreover, on examining their lives and actions, we shall see that they were debtors to Fortune for nothing beyond the opportunity which enabled them to shape things as they pleased, without which the force of their spirit would have been spent in vain; as on the other hand, opportunity would have offered itself in vain had the capacity for turning it to account been wanting. It was necessary, therefore, that Moses should find the children of Israel in bondage in Egypt, and oppressed by the Egyptians, in order that they might be disposed to follow him, and so escape from their servitude. It was fortunate for Romulus that he found no home in Alba, but was exposed at the time of his birth, to the end that he might become king and founder of the City of Rome. It was necessary that Cyrus should find the Persians discontented with the rule of the Medes, and the Medes enervated and effeminate from a prolonged peace. Nor could Theseus have displayed his great qualities had he not found the Athenians disunited and dispersed. But while it was their opportunities that made these men fortunate, it was their own merit that enabled them to recognize these opportunities and turn them to account, to the glory and prosperity of their country.

They who come to the Princedom, as these did, by virtuous paths, acquire with difficulty, but keep with ease. The difficulties which they have in acquiring arise mainly from the new laws and institutions that they are forced to introduce in founding and securing their government. And let it be noted that there is no more delicate matter to take in hand, nor more dangerous to conduct, nor more doubtful in its success, than to set up as a leader in the introduction of changes. For he who innovates will have for his enemies all those who are well off under the existing order of things, and only lukewarm supporters in those who might be better off under the new. This lukewarm temper arises partly from the fear of adversaries who have the laws on their side, and partly from the incredulity of mankind, who will never admit the merit of anything new, until they have seen it proved by the event. The result, however, is that whenever the enemies of change make an attack, they do so with all the zeal of partisans, while the others defend themselves so feebly as to endanger both themselves and their cause.

It should be borne in mind that the temper of the multitude is fickle, and that while it is easy to persuade them of a thing, it is hard to fix them in that persuasion. Wherefore, matters should be so ordered that when men no longer believe of their own accord, they may be compelled to believe by force. Moses, Cyrus, Theseus, and Romulus could never have made their ordinances be observed for any length of time had they been unarmed, as was the case, in our own days, with the Friar Girolamo Savonarola, whose new institutions came to nothing so soon as the multitude began to waver in their faith; since he had not the means to keep those who had been believers steadfast in their belief, or to make unbelievers believe.

Such persons, therefore, have great difficulty in carrying out their designs; but all their difficulties are on the road, and may be overcome by courage. Having conquered these, and coming to be held in reverence, and having destroyed all who were jealous of their influence, they remain powerful, safe, honored, and prosperous.

## Chapter VI

# When a Prince Conquers with Help of Others or by Luck

They who from private life become Princes by mere good fortune, do so with little trouble, but have much trouble to maintain themselves. They meet with no hindrance on their way, being carried as it were on wings to their destination, but all their difficulties overtake them when they alight. Of this class are those on whom States are conferred either in return for money, or through the favor of him who confers them.

Such Princes are wholly dependent on the favor and fortunes of those who have made them great; of supports none could be less stable or secure; and they lack both the knowledge and the power that would enable them to maintain their position. They lack the knowledge because, unless they have great parts and force of character, it is not to be expected that having always lived in a private station they should have learned how to command. They lack the power since they cannot look for support from attached and faithful troops. Moreover, States suddenly acquired, like all else that is produced and grows up rapidly, can never have such root or hold as that the first storm which strikes them shall not overthrow them; unless, indeed that they who suddenly become Princes have a capacity for learning quickly how to defend what Fortune has placed in their lap, and can lay those foundations after they rise which by others are laid before.

He who does not lay his foundations at first, may, if he be of great ability, succeed in laying them afterwards, though with inconvenience to the builder and risk to the building.

A certain type of man will judge it necessary, on entering a new Princedom, to rid himself of enemies, to conciliate friends, to prevail by force or fraud, to make himself feared yet not hated by his subjects, respected and obeyed by his soldiers, to crush those who can or ought to injure him, to introduce changes in the old order of things, to be at once severe and affable, magnanimous and liberal, to do away with a mutinous army and create a new one, to maintain relations with Kings and Princes on such a footing that they must see it for their interest to aid him, and dangerous to offend.

## Chapter VII

# When a Prince Conquers by Crime

A man may also rise from privacy to be a Prince in one of two ways, neither of which can be ascribed wholly either to merit or to fortune. The ways I speak of are, first, when the ascent to power is made by paths of wickedness and crime; and, second, when a private person becomes ruler of his country by the favor of his fellow-citizens.

Whoever examines the first man's actions and achievements will discover little or nothing in them which can be ascribed to Fortune, seeing that it was not through the favor of any but by the regular steps of the military service, gained at the cost of a thousand hardships and hazards, he reached the princedom, which he afterwards maintained by so many daring and dangerous enterprises. Still, to slaughter fellow-citizens, to betray friends, to be devoid of honor, pity, and religion, cannot be counted as merits, for these are means which may lead to power, but which confer no glory.

On seizing a state, the usurper should make haste to inflict what injuries he must, at a stroke, that he may not have to renew them daily, but be enabled by their discontinuance to reassure men's minds and afterwards win them over by benefits. Whosoever, either through timidity or from following bad counsels adopts a contrary course must keep the sword always drawn, and can put no trust in his subjects, who suffering from continued and constantly renewed severities, will never yield him their confidence. Injuries, therefore, should be inflicted all at once that their ill savor being less lasting may the less offend; whereas, benefits should be conferred little by little that so they may be more fully relished.

But, above all things, a Prince should so live with his subjects that no vicissitude of good or evil fortune shall oblige him to alter his behavior; because, if a need to change should come through adversity, it is then too late to resort to severity; while any leniency that you may use will be thrown away, for it will be seen to be compulsory and gain you no thanks.

## Chapter VIII
# When a Prince Rules by Popular Consent

I come now to the second case, namely, of the leading citizen who, not by crimes or violence, but by the favor of his fellow-citizens is made Prince of his country. This may be called a Civil Princedom, and its attainment depends not wholly on merit, nor wholly on good fortune, but rather on what may be termed a fortunate astuteness. I say then that the road to this Princedom lies either through the favor of the people or of the nobles. For in every city are to be found these two opposed humors having their origin in this: that the people desire not to be domineered over or oppressed by the nobles, while the nobles desire to oppress and domineer over the people. And from these two contrary appetites there arises in cities one of three results: a Princedom, or Liberty, or License. A Princedom is created either by the people or by the nobles, according as one or other of these factions has occasion for it. For when the nobles perceive that they cannot withstand the people, they set to work to magnify the reputation of one of their number, and make him their Prince, to the end that under his shadow they may be enabled to indulge their desires. The people, on the other hand, when they see that they cannot make head against the nobles, invest a single citizen with all their influence and make him Prince, that they may have the shelter of his authority.

He who is made Prince by the favor of the nobles, has greater difficulty to maintain himself than he who comes to the Princedom by aid of the people, since he finds many about him who think themselves as good as he, and whom, on that account, he cannot guide or govern as he would. But he who reaches the Princedom by the popular support, finds himself alone, with none, or but a very few about him who are not ready to obey. Moreover, the demands of the nobles cannot be satisfied with credit to the Prince, nor without injury to others, while those of the people well may, the aim of the people being more honorable than that of the nobles, the latter seeking to oppress, the former not to be oppressed. Add to this, that a Prince can never secure himself against a disaffected people, their number being too great, while he may against a disaffected nobility, since their number is small. The worst that a Prince need fear from a disaffected people is that they may desert him, whereas when the nobles are his enemies he has to fear not only that they may desert him but also that they may turn against him; because, as they have greater craft and foresight, they always choose their time to suit their safety, and seek favor with the side they think will win. Again, a Prince must always live with the same people but need not always live with the same nobles, being able to make and unmake these from day to day, and give and take away their authority at his pleasure.

But to make this part of the matter clearer, I say that as regards the nobles there is this first distinction to be made. They either so govern their conduct as to bind themselves wholly to your fortunes, or they do not. Those who so bind themselves, and who are not grasping, should be loved and honored. As to those who do not so bind themselves, there is this further distinction. For the most part they are held back by pusillanimity and a natural defect of courage, in which case you should make use of them, and of those among them more especially who are prudent, for they will do you honor in prosperity, and in adversity give you no cause for fear. But where they abstain from attaching themselves to you of set purpose and for ambitious ends, it is a sign that they are thinking more of themselves than of you, and against such men a Prince should be on his guard, and treat them as though they were declared enemies, for in his adversity they will always help to ruin him.

He who becomes a Prince through the favor of the people should always keep on good terms with them; which it is easy for him to do, since all they ask is not to be oppressed. But he who against the will of the people is made a Prince by the favor of the nobles, must, above all things, seek to conciliate the people, which he readily may by taking them under his protection. For since men who are well treated by one whom they expected to treat them ill feel the more beholden to their benefactor, the people will at once become better disposed to such a Prince when he protects them than if he owed his Princedom to them.

There are many ways in which a Prince may gain the goodwill of the people, but, because these vary with circumstances, no certain rule can be laid down respecting them, and I shall, therefore, say no more about them. But this is the sum of the matter, that it is essential for a Prince to be on a friendly footing with his people since otherwise he will have no resource in adversity.

And what I affirm let no one controvert by citing the old saw that 'he who builds on the people builds on mire,' for that may be true of a private citizen who presumes on his favor with the people, and counts on being rescued by them when overpowered by his enemies or by the magistrates. In such cases a man may often find himself deceived. But when he who builds on the people is a Prince capable of command, of a spirit not to be cast down by ill-fortune, who, while he animates the whole community by his courage and bearing, neglects no prudent precaution, he will not find himself betrayed by the people, but will be seen to have laid his foundations well.

The most critical juncture for Princedoms of this kind, is at the moment when they are about to pass from the popular to the absolute form of government: and as these Princes exercise their authority either directly or through the agency of the magistrates, in the latter case their position is weaker and more hazardous, since they are wholly in the power of those citizens to whom the magistracies are entrusted, who can, and especially in difficult times with the greatest ease, deprive them of their authority, either by opposing or by not obeying them. And in times of peril it is too late for a Prince to assume to himself an absolute authority, for the citizens and subjects who are accustomed to take their orders from the magistrates will not when dangers threaten take them from the Prince, so that at such seasons there will always be very few in whom he can trust. Such Princes, therefore, must not build on what they see in tranquil times when the citizens feel the need of the State. For then everyone is ready to run, to promise, and, danger of death being remote, even to die for the State. But in troubled times, when the State has need of its citizens, few of them are to be found. And the risk of the experiment is the greater in that it can only be made once. Wherefore, a wise Prince should devise means whereby his subjects may at all times, whether favorable or adverse, feel the need of the State and of him, and then they will always be faithful to him.

## Chapter IX
# How the Strength of Princedoms Should Be Measured

In examining the character of these Princedoms, another circumstance has to be considered, namely, whether the Prince is strong enough, if occasion demands, to stand alone, or whether he needs continual help from others. To make the matter clearer, I pronounce those to be able to stand alone who, with the men and money at their disposal, can get together an army fit to take the field against any assailant; and, conversely, I judge those to be in constant need of help who cannot take the field against their enemies, but are obliged to retire behind their walls, and to defend themselves there. As to the latter there is nothing to be said, except to exhort such Princes to strengthen and fortify the towns in which they dwell, and take no heed of the country outside. For whoever has thoroughly fortified his town, and put himself on such a footing with his subjects as I have already indicated and shall further speak of, will always be attacked with much caution; for men are always averse to enterprises that are attended with difficulty, and it is impossible not to foresee difficulties in attacking a Prince whose town is strongly fortified and who is not hated by his subjects.

A Prince, therefore, who has a strong city, and who does not make himself hated, cannot be attacked, or should he be so, his assailant will come badly off, since human affairs are so variable that it is almost impossible for anyone to keep an army posted for a whole year without interruption of some sort. Should it be objected that if the citizens have possessions outside the town and see them burned they will lose patience, and that self-interest, together with the hardships of a protracted siege, will cause them to forget their loyalty, I answer that a capable and courageous Prince will always overcome these difficulties by holding out hopes to his subjects that the evil will not be of long continuance; by exciting their fears of the enemy's cruelty; and by dexterously silencing those who seem to him too forward in their complaints. Moreover, it is to be expected that the enemy will burn and lay waste the country immediately on their arrival, at a time when men's minds are still heated and resolute for defense. And for this very reason the Prince has less to fear because after a few days, when the first ardor has abated, the injury is already done and suffered and cannot be undone; and the people will now, all the more readily, make common cause with their Prince from his seeming to be under obligations to them, their houses having been burned and their lands wasted in his defense. For it is the nature of men to incur obligation as much by the benefits they render as by those they receive.

If the whole matter be well considered, it ought not to be difficult for a prudent Prince, both at the outset and afterwards, to maintain the spirits of his subjects during a siege; provided always that provisions and other means of defense do not run short.

## Chapter X
# Of Soldiers and Mercenaries

The arms with which a Prince defends his State are either his own subjects, or they are mercenaries, or they are auxiliaries, or they are partly one and partly another. Mercenaries and auxiliaries are at once useless and dangerous, and he who holds his State by means of mercenary troops can never be solidly or securely seated. For such troops are disunited, ambitious, insubordinate, treacherous, insolent among friends, cowardly before foes, and without fear of God or faith with man. Whenever they are attacked defeat follows; so that in peace you are plundered by them, in war by your enemies. And this is because they have no tie or motive to keep them in the field beyond their paltry pay, in return for which it would be too much to expect them to give their lives. They are ready enough, therefore, to be your soldiers while you are at peace, but when war is declared they make off and disappear. I ought to have little difficulty in getting this believed, for the present ruin of Italy is due to no other cause than her having for many years trusted to mercenaries, who though heretofore they may have helped the fortunes of some one man, and made a show of strength when matched with one another, have always revealed themselves in their true colors so soon as foreign enemies appeared.

The second sort of unprofitable arms are auxiliaries, by whom I mean troops brought to help and protect you by a potentate whom you summon to your aid; as when in recent times, Pope Julius II, observing the pitiful behavior of his mercenaries at the enterprise of Ferrara, betook himself to auxiliaries, and arranged with Ferdinand of Spain to be supplied with horse and foot soldiers.*

Auxiliaries may be excellent and useful soldiers for themselves, but are always hurtful to him who calls them in; for if they are defeated, he is undone; if victorious, he becomes their prisoner. Ancient histories abound with instances of this.

Let him, therefore, who would deprive himself of every chance of success, have recourse to auxiliaries, these being far more dangerous than mercenary arms, bringing ruin with them ready made. For they are united, and wholly under the control of their own officers; whereas, before mercenaries, even after gaining a victory, can do you hurt, longer time and better opportunities are needed; because, as they are made up of separate companies, raised and paid by you, he whom you place in command cannot at once acquire such authority over them as will be injurious to you. In short, with mercenaries your greatest danger is from their inertness and cowardice, with auxiliaries from their valor. Wise Princes, therefore, have always eschewed these arms, and trusted rather to their own, and have preferred defeat with the latter to victory with the former, counting that as no true victory which is gained by foreign aid.

## Chapter XI

# The Prince and Military Affairs

A Prince, therefore, should have no care or thought other than for war, and for the regulations and training it requires, and should apply himself exclusively to this as his peculiar province; for war is the sole art looked for in one who rules, and is of such efficacy that it not merely maintains those who are born Princes, but often enables men to rise to that eminence from a pri-

---

* Julius was later forced to make territorial concessions to Ferdinand. —MH

vate station; while, on the other hand, we often see that when Princes devote themselves rather to pleasure than to arms, they lose their dominions. And as neglect of this art is the prime cause of such calamities, to be proficient in it is the surest way to acquire power.

Between an armed and an unarmed man no proportion holds, and it is contrary to reason to expect that the armed man should voluntarily submit to him who is unarmed, or that the unarmed man should stand secure among armed retainers. For with contempt on one side and distrust on the other it is impossible that men should work well together. Wherefore, as has already been said, a Prince who is ignorant of military affairs, besides other disadvantages, can neither be respected by his soldiers, nor can he trust them. A Prince, therefore, ought never to allow his attention to be diverted from warlike pursuits, and should occupy himself with them even more in peace than in war. This he can do in two ways, by practice or by study.

As to the practice, he ought, besides keeping his soldiers well trained and disciplined, to be constantly engaged in the chase, that he may inure his body to hardships and fatigue, and gain at the same time a knowledge of places, by observing how the mountains slope, the valleys open, and the plains spread; acquainting himself with the characters of rivers and marshes, and giving the greatest attention to this subject. Such knowledge is useful to him in two ways; for first, he learns thereby to know his own country, and to understand better how it may be defended; and next, from his familiar acquaintance with its localities, he readily comprehends the character of other districts when obliged to observe them for the first time. For the hills, valleys, plains, rivers, and marshes of Tuscany, for example, have a certain resemblance to those elsewhere; so that from a knowledge of the natural features of that province, similar knowledge in respect of other provinces may readily be gained. The Prince who is wanting in this kind of knowledge, is wanting in the first qualification of a good captain for by it he is taught how to surprise an enemy, how to choose an encampment, how to lead his army on a march, how to array it for battle, and how to post it to the best advantage for a siege.

Among the commendations that Philopoemen, Prince of the Achaeans, has received from historians is this: that in times of peace he was always thinking of methods of warfare, so that when walking in the country with his friends he would often stop and talk with them on the subject. "If the enemy," he would say, "were posted on that hill, and we found ourselves here with our army, which of us would have the better position? How could we most safely and in the best order advance to meet them? If we had to retreat, what direction should we take? If they retired, how should we pursue?" In this way he put to his friends, as he went along, all the contingencies that can befall an army. He listened to their opinions, stated his own, and supported them with reasons; and from his being constantly occupied with such meditations, it resulted, that when in actual command no complication could ever present itself with which he was not prepared to deal.

As to the mental training of which we have spoken, a Prince should read histories, and in these should note the actions of great men, observe how they conducted themselves in their wars, and examine the causes of their victories and defeats. And above all, he should, as many great men of past ages have done, assume for his models those persons who before his time have been renowned and celebrated, whose deeds and achievements he should constantly keep in mind.

A wise Prince, therefore, should pursue such methods as these, never resting idle in times of peace but strenuously seeking to turn them to account, so that he may derive strength from them in the hour of danger, and find himself ready should Fortune turn against him.

## Chapter XII
# Better to Be Loved or Feared?

I say that every Prince should desire to be accounted merciful and not cruel. Nevertheless, he should be on his guard against the abuse of this quality of mercy.

A Prince should disregard the reproach of being thought cruel where it enables him to keep his subjects united and obedient. For he who quells disorder by a very few signal examples will in the end be more merciful than he who from too great leniency permits things to take their course and so to result in pillage and bloodshed; for these hurt the whole State, whereas the severities of the Prince injure individuals only. And for a new Prince, of all others, it is impossible to escape a name for cruelty, since new States are full of dangers.

Nevertheless, the new Prince should not be too ready of belief, nor too easily set in motion; nor should he himself be the first to raise alarms; but should so temper prudence with kindliness that too great confidence in others shall not throw him off his guard nor groundless distrust render him insupportable.

And here comes in the question whether it is better to be loved rather than feared, or feared rather than loved. It might perhaps be answered that we should wish to be both; but since love and fear can hardly exist together, if we must choose between them, it is far safer to be feared than loved. For of men it may generally be affirmed that they are thankless, fickle, false, studious to avoid danger, greedy of gain, devoted to you while you are able to confer benefits upon them, and ready, as I said before, while danger is distant, to shed their blood, and sacrifice their property, their lives, and their children for you; but in the hour of need they turn against you. The Prince, therefore, who without otherwise securing himself builds wholly on their professions is undone. For the friendships which we buy with a price, and do not gain by greatness and nobility of character, though they be fairly earned are not made good, but fail us when we have occasion to use them.

Moreover, men are less careful how they offend him who makes himself loved than him who makes himself feared. For love is held by the tie of obligation, which, because men are a sorry breed, is broken on every whisper of private interest; but fear is bound by the apprehension of punishment which never relaxes its grasp.

Nevertheless a Prince should inspire fear in such a fashion that if he do not win love he may escape hate. For a man may very well be feared and yet not hated, and this will be the case so long as he does not meddle with the property or with the women of his citizens and subjects. And if constrained to put any to death, he should do so only when there is manifest cause or reasonable justification. But, above all, he must abstain from seizing the property of others. For men will sooner forget the death of their father than the loss of their estate. Moreover, pretexts for confiscation are difficult to find, and he who has once begun to live by pillaging always finds reasons for taking what is not his; whereas reasons for shedding blood are fewer and sooner exhausted.

Among other things remarkable in Hannibal, this has been noted: that having a very great army, made up of men of many different nations and brought to fight in a foreign country, no dissension ever arose among the soldiers themselves, nor any mutiny against their leader, either in his good or in his evil fortunes. This we can only ascribe to the transcendent cruelty, which, joined with numberless great qualities, rendered him at once venerable and terrible in the eyes of his soldiers, for without this reputation for cruelty these other virtues would not have produced the like results.

## Chapter XIII
# Truth and Deception

Everyone understands how praiseworthy it is in a Prince to maintain trust, and to live uprightly and not craftily. Nevertheless, we see from what has taken place in our own days that Princes who have set little store by their word, but have known how to overreach men by their cunning, have accomplished great things, and in the end got the better of those who trusted to honest dealing.

Be it known, then, that there are two ways of contending, one in accordance with the laws, the other by force; the first of which is proper to men, the second to beasts. But since the first method is often ineffectual, it becomes necessary to resort to the second. A Prince should, therefore, understand how to use well both the man and the beast. And this lesson has been covertly taught by the ancient writers who relate how Achilles and many others of these old Princes were given over to be brought up and trained by Chiron the Centaur; the only meaning of their having for an instructor one who was half man and half beast is that it is necessary for a Prince to know how to use both natures, and that the one without the other has no stability.

But since a Prince should know how to use the beast's nature wisely, he ought of beasts to choose both the lion and the fox; for the lion cannot guard himself from the traps nor the fox from wolves. He must therefore be a fox to discern traps and a lion to drive off wolves.

To rely wholly on the lion is unwise; and for this reason a prudent Prince neither can nor ought to keep his word when to keep it is hurtful to him, and the causes which led him to pledge it are removed. If all men were good this would not be good advice, but since they are dishonest and do not keep faith with you, you in return need not keep faith with them; and no prince was ever at a loss for plausible reasons to cloak a breach of faith. Of this numberless recent instances could be given, and it might be shown how many solemn treaties and engagements have been rendered inoperative and idle through want of faith in Princes, and that he who was best known to play the fox has had the best success.

It is necessary, indeed, to put a good color on this nature, and to be skillful in simulating and dissembling. But men are so simple, and governed so absolutely by their present needs, that he who wishes to deceive will never fail in finding willing dupes.

And you are to understand that a Prince, and most of all a new Prince, cannot observe all those rules of conduct in respect whereof men are accounted good, being often forced, in order to preserve his Princedom, to act in opposition to good faith, charity, humanity, and religion. He must therefore keep his mind ready to shift as the winds and tides of Fortune turn, and, as I have already said, he ought not to quit good courses if he can help it, but should know how to follow evil courses if he must.

A Prince should therefore be very careful that nothing ever escapes his lips that does not make him seem the embodiment of mercy, good faith, integrity, humanity, and religion. And there is no virtue which it is more necessary for him to seem to possess than this last; because men in general judge rather by the eye than by the hand, for everyone can see but few can touch. Everyone sees what you seem, but few know what you are, and these few dare not oppose themselves to the opinion of the many who have the majesty of the State to back them up.

Moreover, in the actions of all men, and most of all of Princes, where there is no tribunal to which we can appeal we look to results. Wherefore if a Prince succeeds in establishing and maintaining his authority the means will always be judged honorable and be approved by everyone. For the vulgar are always taken by appearances and by results, and the world is made up of the vulgar, the few only finding room when the many have no longer ground to stand on.

A certain Prince of our own days, whose name it is as well not to mention, is always preaching peace and good faith, although the mortal enemy of both; and both, had he practiced them as he preaches them, would, oftener than once, have lost him his kingdom and authority.

## Chapter XIV

# How to Avert Conspiracies

A Prince should consider how he may avoid such courses as would make him hated or despised; and that whenever he succeeds in keeping clear of these, he has performed his part, and runs no risk though he incur other infamies.

A Prince, as I have said before, sooner becomes hated by being rapacious and by interfering with the property and with the women of his subjects than in any other way. From these, therefore, he should abstain. For so long as neither their property nor their honor are touched the mass of mankind live contentedly, and the Prince has only to cope with the ambition of a few, which can in many ways and easily be kept within bounds.

A Prince is despised when he is seen to be fickle, frivolous, effeminate, pusillanimous, or irresolute, against which defects he ought therefore most carefully to guard, striving so to bear himself that greatness, courage, wisdom, and strength may appear in all his actions. In his private dealings with his subjects his decisions should be irrevocable, and his reputation such that no one would dream of overreaching or cajoling him.

The Prince who inspires such an opinion of himself is greatly esteemed, and against one who is greatly esteemed conspiracy is difficult; nor, when he is known to be an excellent Prince and held in reverence by his subjects, will it be easy to attack him. For a Prince is exposed to two dangers: from within in respect of his subjects, and from without in respect of foreign powers. Against the latter he will defend himself with good arms and good allies, and if he have good arms he will always have good allies; and when things are settled abroad, they will always be settled at home, unless disturbed by conspiracies; and even should there be hostility from without, if he has taken those measures, and has lived in the way I have recommended, and if he never abandons hope, he will withstand every attack.

As regards his own subjects, when affairs are quiet abroad, he has to fear they may engage in secret plots; against which a Prince best secures himself when he escapes being hated or despised, and keeps on good terms with his people; and this, as I have already shown, is essential. Not to be hated or despised by the body of his subjects is one of the surest safeguards that a Prince can have against conspiracy. For he who conspires always reckons on pleasing the people by putting the Prince to death; but when he sees that instead of pleasing he will offend them, he cannot summon courage to carry out his design. For the difficulties that attend conspirators are infinite, and we know from experience that while there have been many conspiracies, few of them have succeeded.

He who conspires cannot do so alone, nor can he assume as his companions any save those whom he believes to be discontented; but so soon as you impart your design to a discontented man, you supply him with the means of removing his discontent, since by betraying you he can procure for himself every advantage; so that seeing on the one hand certain gain and on the other a doubtful and dangerous risk, he must either be a rare friend to you or the mortal enemy of his Prince, if he keep your secret.

To put the matter shortly, I say that on the side of the conspirator there are distrust, jealousy, and dread of punishment to deter him; while on the side of the Prince there are the laws, the majesty of the throne, the protection of friends and of the government to defend him, to which if the general goodwill of the people be added, it is hardly possible that any should be rash enough to conspire. For while in ordinary cases, the conspirator has ground for fear only before the execution of his villainy, in this case he has also cause to fear after the crime has been perpetrated since he has the people for his enemy and is thus cut off from every hope of shelter.

In brief, a Prince has little to fear from conspiracies when his subjects are well disposed towards him; but when they are hostile and hold him in detestation he has then reason to fear everything and everyone. And well ordered States and wise Princes have provided with extreme care that the nobility shall not be driven to desperation, and that the commons shall be kept satisfied and contented; for this is one of the most important matters that a Prince must look to.

## Chapter XV
# How a Prince Should Defend Himself

To govern more securely some Princes have disarmed their subjects, others have kept the towns subject to them divided by factions; some have fostered hostility against themselves, others have sought to gain over those who at the beginning of their reign were looked on with suspicion; some have built fortresses, others have dismantled and destroyed them; and though no definite judgment can be pronounced respecting any of these methods, without regard to the special circumstances of the State to which it is proposed to apply them, I shall nevertheless speak of them in as comprehensive a way as the subject will admit.

It has never chanced that any new Prince has disarmed his subjects. On the contrary, when he has found them unarmed he has always armed them. For the arms thus provided become yours, those whom you suspected grow faithful, while those who were faithful at the first continue so, and from your subjects become your partisans. And though all your subjects cannot be armed yet if those of them whom you arm be treated with marked favor you can deal more securely with the rest. For the difference which those whom you supply with arms perceive in their treatment will bind them to you, while the others will excuse you recognizing that those who incur greater risk and responsibility merit greater rewards. But by disarming, you at once give offense, since you show your subjects that you distrust them, either as doubting their courage or as doubting their fidelity, each of which imputations begets hatred against you. Moreover, as you cannot maintain yourself without arms you must have recourse to mercenary troops. What these are I have already shown, but even if they were good, they could never avail to defend you at once against powerful enemies abroad and against subjects whom you distrust. Wherefore, as I have said already, new Princes in new Princedoms have always provided for their being armed; and of instances of this History is full.

But when a Prince acquires a new State, which thus becomes joined on like a limb to his old possessions, he must disarm its inhabitants, except such of them as have taken part with him while he was acquiring it; and even these, as time and occasion serve, he should seek to render soft and effeminate; and he must so manage matters that all the arms of the new State shall be in the hands of his own soldiers who have served under him in his ancient dominions.

I do not believe that divisions purposely caused can ever lead to good; on the contrary, when an enemy approaches, divided cities are lost at once, for the weaker faction will always side with the invader, and the other will not be able to stand alone.

Moreover methods like these argue weakness in a Prince, for under a strong government divisions would never be permitted, since they are profitable only in time of peace as an expedient whereby subjects may be more easily managed; but when war breaks out their insufficiency is demonstrated.

It has been customary for Princes, with a view to hold their dominions more securely, to build fortresses which might serve as a curb and restraint on such as have designs against them, and as a safe refuge against a first onset. I approve this custom, because it has been followed from the earliest times.

Fortresses are useful or not according to circumstances, and if in one way they benefit, in another they injure you. We may state the case thus: the Prince who is more afraid of his subjects than of strangers ought to build fortresses, while he who is more afraid of strangers than of his subjects should leave them alone.

All considerations taken into account, I shall applaud him who builds fortresses and him who does not; but I shall blame him who, trusting in them, reckons it a light thing to be held in hatred by his people.

## Chapter XVI
# How a Prince Should Preserve His Reputation

Nothing makes a Prince so well thought of as to undertake great enterprises and give striking proofs of his capacity.

It greatly profits a Prince in conducting the internal government of his State to follow striking methods. The remarkable actions of anyone in civil life, whether for good or for evil, afford him notability; and to choose such ways of rewarding and punishing cannot fail to be much spoken of. But above all, he should strive by all his actions to inspire a sense of his greatness and goodness.

A Prince is likewise esteemed who is a stanch friend and a thorough foe, that is to say, who without reserve openly declares for one against another, this being always a more advantageous course than to stand neutral. For supposing two of your powerful neighbors come to blows, it must either be that you have, or have not, reason to fear the one who comes off victorious. In either case it will always be well for you to declare yourself, and join in frankly with one side or other. For should you fail to do so you are certain, in the former of the cases put, to become the prey of the victor to the satisfaction and delight of the vanquished, and no reason or circumstance that you may plead will avail to shield or shelter you; for the victor dislikes doubtful friends, and such as will not help him at a pinch; and the vanquished will have nothing to say to you, since you would not share his fortunes sword in hand.

A Prince should be careful never to join with one stronger than himself in attacking others, unless he is driven to it by necessity. For if he whom you join prevails, you are at his mercy; and Princes, so far as in them lies, should avoid placing themselves at the mercy of others.

A Prince should show himself a patron of merit, and should honor those who excel in every art. He ought accordingly to encourage his subjects by enabling them to pursue their callings, whether mercantile, agricultural, or any other, in security, so that this man shall not be deterred from beautifying his possessions from the apprehension that they may be taken from him, or that other refrain from opening a trade through fear of taxes; and he should provide rewards for those who desire so to employ themselves, and for all who are disposed in any way to add to the greatness of his City or State.

He ought, moreover, at suitable seasons of the year to entertain the people with festivals and shows. And because all cities are divided into guilds and companies, he should show attention to these societies, and sometimes take part in their meetings, offering an example of courtesy and munificence, but always maintaining the dignity of his station, which must under no circumstances be compromised.

## Chapter XVII

# A Prince's Court

The choice of Ministers is a matter of no small moment to a Prince. Whether they shall be good or not depends on his prudence, so that the readiest conjecture we can form of the character and sagacity of a Prince is from seeing what sort of men he has about him. When they are at once capable and faithful, we may always account him wise, since he has known to recognize their merit and to retain their fidelity. But if they be otherwise, we must pronounce unfavorably of him, since he has committed a first fault in making this selection.

There are three scales of intelligence, one which understands by itself, a second which understands what it is shown by others, and a third which understands neither by itself nor by the showing of others, the first of which is most excellent, the second good, but the third worthless.

As to how a Prince is to know his Minister, this unerring rule may be laid down. When you see a Minister thinking more of himself than of you, and in all his actions seeking his own ends, that man can never be a good Minister or one that you can trust. For he who has the charge of the State committed to him, ought not to think of himself, but only of his Prince, and should never bring to the notice of the latter what does not directly concern him. On the other hand, to keep his Minister good, the Prince should be considerate of him, dignifying him, enriching him, binding him to himself by benefits, and sharing with him the honors as well as the burdens of the State, so that the abundant honors and wealth bestowed upon him may divert him from seeking them at other hands; while the great responsibilities wherewith he is charged may lead him to dread change, knowing that he cannot stand alone without his master's support. When Prince and Minister are upon this footing they can mutually trust one another; but when the contrary is the case, it will always fare ill with one or other of them.

## Chapter XVIII
# Flatterers Should Be Shunned

One error into which Princes, unless very prudent or very fortunate in their choice of friends, are apt to fall, is of so great importance that I must not pass it over. I mean in respect of flatterers. These abound in Courts, because men take such pleasure in their own concerns, and so deceive themselves with regard to them, that they can hardly escape this plague; while even in the effort to escape it there is risk of their incurring contempt.

For there is no way to guard against flattery but by letting it be seen that you take no offense in hearing the truth: but when everyone is free to tell you the truth respect falls short. Wherefore a prudent Prince should follow a middle course, by choosing certain discreet men from among his subjects, and allowing them alone free leave to speak their minds on any matter on which he asks their opinion, and on none other. But he ought to ask their opinion on everything, and after hearing what they have to say, should reflect and judge for himself. And with these counselors collectively, and with each of them separately, his bearing should be such, that each and all of them may know that the more freely they declare their thoughts the better they will be liked. Besides these, the Prince should hearken to no others, but should follow the course determined on, and afterwards adhere firmly to his resolves. Whoever acts otherwise is either undone by flatterers, or from continually vacillating as opinions vary, comes to be held in light esteem.

A Prince ought always to take counsel, but at such times and reasons only as he himself pleases, and not when it pleases others; nay, he should discourage every one from obtruding advice on matters on which it is not sought. But he should be free in asking advice, and afterwards as regards the matters on which he has asked it, a patient hearer of the truth, and even displeased should he perceive that any one, from whatever motive, keeps it back.

But those who think that every Prince who has a name for prudence owes it to the wise counselors he has around him, and not to any merit of his own, are certainly mistaken; since it is an unerring rule and of universal application that a Prince who is not wise himself cannot be well advised by others, unless by chance he surrender himself to be wholly governed by some one adviser who happens to be supremely prudent; in which case he may, indeed, be well advised; but not for long, since such an adviser will soon deprive him of his Government. If he listen to a multitude of advisers, the Prince who is not wise will never have consistent counsels, nor will he know of himself how to reconcile them. Each of his counselors will study his own advantage, and the Prince will be unable to detect or correct them. Nor could it well be otherwise, for men will always grow rogues on your hands unless they find themselves under a necessity to be honest.

Hence it follows that good counsels, whenever they come, have their origin in the prudence of the Prince, and not the prudence of the Prince in wise counsels.

## Chapter XIX
# The Role of Fortune

I am not ignorant that many have been and are of the opinion that human affairs are so governed by Fortune and by God that men cannot alter them by any prudence of theirs, and indeed have no remedy against them, and for this reason have come to think that it is not worthwhile to labour much about anything, but that they must leave everything to be determined by chance.

Often when I turn the matter over, I am in part inclined to agree with this opinion, which has had readier acceptance in our own times from the great changes in things which we have seen and everyday see happen contrary to all human expectation. Nevertheless, that our freewill be not wholly set aside, I think it may be the case that Fortune is the mistress of one half our actions, and yet leaves the control of the other half, or a little less, to ourselves. And I would liken her to one of those wild torrents which, when angry, overflow the plains, sweep away trees and houses, and carry off soil from one bank to throw it down upon the other. Everyone flees before them, and yields to their fury without the least power to resist. And yet, though this be their nature, it does not follow that in seasons of fair weather men cannot, by constructing dams and barriers, take such precautions as will cause them when again in flood to pass off by some artificial channel, or at least prevent their course from being so uncontrolled and destructive. And so it is with Fortune, who displays her might where there is no organized strength to resist her, and directs her onset where she knows that there is neither barrier nor embankment to confine her.

I note that one day we see a Prince prospering and the next day overthrown, without detecting any change in his nature or character. This, I believe, comes chiefly from a cause already dwelt upon, namely, that a Prince who rests wholly on Fortune is ruined when she changes. Moreover, I believe that he will prosper most whose mode of acting best adapts itself to the character of the times; and conversely that he will be unprosperous with whose mode of acting the times do not accord. For we see that men in these matters which lead to the end that each has before him, namely, glory and wealth, proceed by different ways, one with caution, another with impetuosity, one with violence, another with subtlety, one with patience, another with its contrary; and that by one or other of these different courses each may succeed.

Again, of two who act cautiously, you shall find that one attains his end, the other not, and that two of different temperament, the one cautious, the other impetuous, are equally successful. All which happens from no other cause than that the character of the times accords or does not accord with their methods of acting. And hence it comes, as I have already said, that two operating differently arrive at the same result, and two operating similarly, the one succeeds and the other not. On this likewise depend the vicissitudes of Fortune. For if to one who conducts himself with caution and patience, time and circumstances are propitious, so that his method of acting is good, he goes on prospering; but if these change he is ruined, because he does not change his method of acting.

For no man is found so prudent as to know how to adapt himself to these changes, both because he cannot deviate from the course to which nature inclines him, and because, having always prospered while adhering to one path, he cannot be persuaded that it would be well for him to forsake it. And so when occasion requires the cautious man to act impetuously, he cannot do so and is undone: whereas, had he changed his nature with time and circumstances, his fortune would have been unchanged.

To be brief, I say that since Fortune changes and men stand fixed in their old ways, they are prosperous so long as there is congruity between them, and the reverse when there is not. Of this, however, I am well persuaded, that it is better to be impetuous than cautious. For Fortune to be kept under must be beaten and roughly handled; and we see that she suffers herself to be more readily mastered by those who so treat her than by those who are more timid in their approaches. And always she favors the young, because they are less scrupulous and fiercer, and command her with greater audacity.

## Chapter XX
# Aphorisms from *The Prince*

"One change always leaves a dovetail into which another will fit."

"Men are either to be kindly treated or utterly crushed since they can revenge lighter injuries but not graver.

"The wise man should always follow the roads that have been trodden by the great, and imitate those who have most excelled."

"Take aim much above the destined mark."

"He who is less beholden to Fortune has often in the end the better success."

"Those who come to the Princedom by virtuous paths acquire with difficulty but keep with ease."

"It should be borne in mind that the temper of the multitude is fickle, and that while it is easy to persuade them of a thing, it is hard to fix them in that persuasion."

"He who does not lay his foundations at first, may, if he be of great ability, succeed in laying them afterwards, though with inconvenience to the builder and risk to the building."

"A Prince can never secure himself against a disaffected people, their number being too great, while he may against a disaffected nobility, since their number is small."

"Men are always averse to enterprises that are attended with difficulty."

"Mercenaries and auxiliaries are at once useless and dangerous, and he who holds his State by means of mercenary troops can never be solidly or securely seated."

"A Prince ought never to allow his attention to be diverted from warlike pursuits, and should occupy himself with them even more in peace than in war."

"Many Republics and Princedoms have been imagined that were never seen or known to exist in reality."

"If we must choose between them, it is far safer to be feared than loved."

"If a man have good arms he will always have good allies."

"I do not believe that divisions purposely caused can ever lead to good."

"A Prince should show himself a patron of merit."

"The readiest conjecture we can form of the character and sagacity of a Prince is from seeing what sort of men he has about him."

"A Prince who is not wise himself cannot be well advised by others."

"A Prince who rests wholly on Fortune is ruined when she changes."

"It is better to be impetuous than cautious. Fortune suffers herself to be more readily mastered by those who so treat her than by those who are timid in their approaches."

# Self-Reliance
(1841)

## by Ralph Waldo Emerson

*The Masterwork of Esoteric Wisdom for Living with Power and Purpose*

### Contents

Introduction  *Heretical or Helpful? The Challenge of Abridging "Self-Reliance"* by Mitch Horowitz   72

Self-Reliance   74

## Introduction
# Heretical or Helpful?
## *The Challenge of Abridging "Self-Reliance"*

How can you possibly abridge a classic statement of the search for good living like "Self-Reliance?" Why would you even want to?

Those questions hung over me as I attempted to create a digest-sized portion of Ralph Waldo Emerson's epic work.

Is it an act of secular sacrilege, or frivolity, to shorten the best-known essay of America's greatest philosopher? Well, if it is sacrilege, I take succor in Emerson's own words from this essay:

> On my saying, "What have I do to with the sacredness of traditions, if I live wholly from within?" my friend suggested,—"But these impulses may be from below, not from above." I replied, "They do not seem to me to be such; but if I am the Devil's child, I will live then from the Devil." No law can be sacred to me but that of my nature.

In actuality, I provide this Condensed Classics edition of "Self-Reliance" for three reasons:

1. I have no idea whether Emerson would have approved, but he was very keen—and shrewd—about seeing that his works reached a broad general readership. After delivering a public lecture, the philosopher would quickly and adroitly issue it in pamphlet form, ensuring that the approval or calumny that greeted his public address—and he was served by both responses—would lift the work's notability and publication.
2. Emerson was not shy about revisions. He revised and edited some of his best-known essays until his death in 1882. He was not priggish about editorial changes, provided those changes served a good and noble end, about which I will say more.
3. I harbor the conviction that some readers and listeners will be introduced to the insights of this splendorous work in no other form than that which

is containable within a lunch hour or morning commute. I harbor equal conviction that some among that number—and you will know yourselves by the end of this short volume—will be so moved by the ideas found in it that you will become lifelong readers of Emerson's original.

Indeed, an abridgment doesn't detract from the original; it advertises a work to new readers, and shines its rays into the lives of those who otherwise might not experience it at all.

Speaking of advertising, I am reminded of a wonderful essay that the legendary ad man David Ogilvy once wrote in defense of *Reader's Digest*. Ogilvy noted:

> Some highbrows may look down their noses at The Digest, charging it with superficiality and over-simplification. There is a modicum of justice in this charge; you can learn more about the Congo if you read about it in Foreign Affairs Quarterly, and you can learn more about Abraham Lincoln in Carl Sandburg's books about him. But have you time?

I claim the same mantle of practicality for this work.

Finally, how does one abridge "Self-Reliance?" How do you select among the master's well-chosen and lapidary words? Well, that part was easy. I have read and reread "Self-Reliance" more times than I can keep track of over the past twenty years. Again and again, I have underlined, highlighted, and bracketed passages that speak to my heart. By the very logic of Emerson's essay, those portions that repeatedly speak to my heart, speak to all hearts.

It is those penetrating words that I have preserved here. May they deliver you to your highest insights, as they illuminate what you already know within, and are waiting to rediscover.

When this rediscovery occurs, may you join the fraternity of people for whom Emerson's masterwork is a lifetime companion.

—Mitch Horowitz

# Self-Reliance

I read the other day some verses written by an eminent painter which were original and not conventional. The soul always hears an admonition in such lines, let the subject be what it may. The sentiment they instil is of more value than any thought they may contain. To believe your own thought, to believe that what is true for you in your private heart is true for all men,—that is genius.

In every work of genius we recognize our own rejected thoughts: they come back to us with a certain alienated majesty.

There is a time in every man's education when he arrives at the conviction that envy is ignorance; that imitation is suicide; that he must take himself for better, for worse, as his portion; that though the wide universe is full of good, no kernel of nourishing corn can come to him but through his toil bestowed on that plot of ground which is given to him to till.

We but half express ourselves, and are ashamed of that divine idea which each of us represents. It may be safely trusted as proportionate and of good issues, so it be faithfully imparted, but God will not have his work made manifest by cowards. A man is relieved and gay when he has put his heart into his work and done his best.

Trust thyself: every heart vibrates to that iron string. Accept the place the divine providence has found for you, the society of your contemporaries, the connection of events. Great men have always done so, and confided themselves childlike to the genius of their age.

Infancy conforms to nobody: all conform to it, so that one babe commonly makes four or five out of the adults who prattle and play to it. So God has armed youth and puberty and manhood no less with its own piquancy and charm, and made it enviable and gracious and its claims not to be put by, if it will stand by itself.

The nonchalance of boys who are sure of a dinner, and would disdain as much as a lord to do or say aught to conciliate one, is the healthy attitude of human nature. A boy cumbers himself never about consequences, about interests: he gives an independent, genuine verdict. You must court him: he does not court you.

Society everywhere is in conspiracy against the manhood of every one of its members. Society is a joint-stock company, in which the members agree, for the better securing of his bread to each shareholder, to surrender the liberty and culture of the eater. The virtue in most request is conformity. Self-reliance is its aversion. It loves not realities and creators, but names and customs.

Whoso would be a man must be a nonconformist. He who would gather immortal palms must not be hindered by the name of goodness, but must explore if it be goodness. Nothing is at last sacred but the integrity of your own mind. Absolve you to yourself, and you shall have the suffrage of the world. I remember an answer which when quite young I was prompted to make to a valued adviser, who was wont to importune me with the dear old doctrines of the church. On my saying, "What have I to do with the sacredness of traditions, if I live wholly from within?" my friend suggested,—"But these impulses may be from below, not from above." I replied, "They do not seem to me to be such; but if I am the Devil's child, I will live then from the Devil." No law can be sacred to me but that of my nature. Good and bad are but names very readily transferable to that or this; the only right is what is after my constitution, the only wrong what is against it. A man is to carry himself in the presence of all opposition, as if every thing were titular and ephemeral but he. I am ashamed to think how easily we capitulate to badges and names, to large societies and dead institutions. Every decent and well-spoken individual affects and sways me more than is right. I ought to go upright and vital, and speak the rude truth in all ways.

Your goodness must have some edge to it,—else it is none. The doctrine of hatred must be preached as the counteraction of the doctrine of love when that pules and whines. I shun father and mother and wife and brother, when my genius calls me. I would write on the lintels of the door-post, *Whim*. I hope it is somewhat better than whim at last, but we cannot spend the day in explanation.

There is a class of persons to whom by all spiritual affinity I am bought and sold; for them I will go to prison, if need be.

My life is for itself and not for a spectacle. I much prefer that it should be of a lower strain, so it be genuine and equal, than that it should be glittering and unsteady.

Few and mean as my gifts may be, I actually am, and do not need for my own assurance or the assurance of my fellows any secondary testimony.

What I must do is all that concerns me, not what the people think. This rule, equally arduous in actual and in intellectual life, may serve for the whole distinction between greatness and meanness. It is the harder, because you will always find those who think they know what is your duty better than you know it. It is easy in the world to live after the world's opinion; it is easy in solitude to live after our own; but the great man is he who in the midst of the crowd keeps with perfect sweetness the independence of solitude.

The objection to conforming to usages that have become dead to you is that it scatters your force. It loses your time and blurs the impression of your character.

But do your work, and I shall know you. Do your work, and you shall reinforce yourself. A man must consider what a blindman's-buff is this game of conformity. If I know your sect, I anticipate your argument.

It is easy enough for a firm man who knows the world to brook the rage of the cultivated classes. Their rage is decorous and prudent, for they are timid as being very vulnerable themselves. But when to their feminine rage the indignation of the people is added, when the ignorant and the poor are aroused, when the unintelligent brute force that lies at the bottom of society is made to growl and mow, it needs the habit of magnanimity and religion to treat it godlike as a trifle of no concernment.

The other terror that scares us from self-trust is our consistency; a reverence for our past act or word, because the eyes of others have no other data for computing our orbit than our past acts, and we are loath to disappoint them.

But why should you keep your head over your shoulder? Why drag about this corpse of your memory, lest you contradict somewhat you have stated in this or that public place? Suppose you should contradict yourself; what then? It seems to be a rule of wisdom never to rely on your memory alone, scarcely even in acts of pure memory, but to bring the past for judgment into the thousand-eyed present, and live ever in a new day. In your metaphysics you have denied personality to the Deity: yet when the devout motions of the soul come, yield to them heart and life, though they should clothe God with shape and color. Leave your theory, as Joseph his coat in the hand of the harlot, and flee.

A foolish consistency is the hobgoblin of little minds, adored by little statesmen and philosophers and divines. With consistency a great soul has simply nothing to do. He may as well concern himself with his shadow on the wall. Speak what you think now in hard words, and to-morrow speak what to-morrow thinks in hard words again, though it contradict every thing you said to-day.—'Ah, so you shall be sure to be misunderstood.'—Is it so bad, then, to be misunderstood? Pythagoras was misunderstood, and Socrates, and Jesus, and Luther, and Copernicus, and Galileo, and Newton, and every pure and wise spirit that ever took flesh. To be great is to be misunderstood.

I suppose no man can violate his nature. All the sallies of his will are rounded in by the law of his being, as the inequalities of Andes and Himmaleh are insignificant in the curve of the sphere. Nor does it matter how you gauge and try him. A character is like an acrostic or Alexandrian stanza;—read it forward, backward, or across, it still spells the same thing. In this pleasing, contrite wood-life which God allows me, let me record day by day my honest thought without prospect or retrospect, and, I cannot doubt, it will be found symmetrical, though I mean it not, and see it not. My book should smell of pines and resound with the hum of insects. The swallow over my window should interweave that thread or straw he carries in his bill into my web also. We pass for what we are. Character teaches above our wills. Men imagine that they communicate their virtue or vice only by overt actions, and do not see that virtue or vice emit a breath every moment.

There will be an agreement in whatever variety of actions, so they be each honest and natural in their hour. For of one will, the actions will be harmonious, however unlike they seem. These varieties are lost sight of at a little distance, at a little height of thought. One tendency unites them all. The voyage of the best ship is a zigzag line of a hundred tacks. See the line from a sufficient distance, and it straightens itself to the average tendency. Your genuine action will explain itself, and will explain your other genuine actions. Your conformity explains nothing. Act singly, and what you have already done singly will justify you now. Greatness appeals to the future. If I can be firm enough to-day to do right, and scorn eyes, I must have done so much right before as to defend me now. Be it how it will, do right now. Always scorn appearances, and you always may. The force of character is cumulative.

Honor is venerable to us because it is no ephemeris. It is always ancient virtue. We worship it to-day because it is not of to-day. We love it and pay it homage, because it is not a trap for our love and homage, but is self-dependent, self-derived, and therefore of an old immaculate pedigree, even if shown in a young person.

I hope in these days we have heard the last of conformity and consistency. Let the words be gazetted and ridiculous henceforward. Instead of the gong for dinner, let us hear a whistle from the Spartan fife. Let us never bow and apologize more. A great man is coming to eat at my house. I do not wish to please him; I wish that he should wish to please me. I will stand here for humanity, and though I would make it kind, I would make it true. Let us affront and reprimand the smooth mediocrity and squalid contentment of the times, and hurl in the face of custom, and trade, and office, the fact which is the upshot of all history, that there is a great responsible Thinker and Actor working wherever a man works; that a true man belongs to no other time or place, but is the centre of things. Where he is, there is nature. The man must be so much, that he must make all circumstances indifferent. Every true man is a cause, a country, and an age; requires infinite spaces and numbers and time fully to accomplish his design;—and posterity seem to follow his steps as a train of clients. A man Caesar is born, and for ages after we have a Roman Empire. Christ is born, and millions of minds so grow and cleave to his genius, that he is confounded with virtue and the possible of man. An institution is the lengthened shadow of one man.

Our reading is mendicant and sycophantic. In history, our imagination plays us false. Kingdom and lordship, power and estate, are a gaudier vocabulary than private John and Edward in a small house and common day's work; but the things of life are the same to both; the sum total of both is the same. Why all this deference to Alfred, and Scanderbeg, and Gustavus? Suppose they were virtuous; did they wear out virtue? As great a stake depends on your private act to-day, as followed their public and renowned steps. When private men shall act with original views, the lustre will be transferred from the actions of kings to those of gentlemen.

The magnetism which all original action exerts is explained when we inquire the reason of self-trust. Who is the Trustee? What is the aboriginal Self, on which a universal reliance may be grounded? What is the nature and power of that science-baffling star, without parallax, without calculable elements, which shoots a ray of beauty even into trivial and impure actions, if the least mark of independence appear? For the sense of being which in calm hours rises, we know not how, in the soul, is not diverse from things, from space, from light, from time, from man, but one with them, and proceeds obviously from the same source whence their life and being also proceed. We first share the life by which things exist, and afterwards see them as appearances in nature, and forget that we have shared their cause. Here is the fountain of action and of thought. Here are the lungs of that inspiration which giveth man wisdom, and which cannot be denied without impiety and atheism. We lie in the lap of immense intelligence, which makes us receivers of its truth and organs of its activity. When we discern justice, when we discern truth, we do nothing of ourselves, but allow a passage to its beams. Every man discriminates between the voluntary acts of his mind, and his involuntary perceptions, and knows that to his involuntary perceptions a perfect faith is due. He may err in the expression of them, but he knows that these things are so, like day and night, not to be disputed. For my perception of it is as much a fact as the sun.

The relations of the soul to the divine spirit are so pure, that it is profane to seek to interpose helps. It must be that when God speaketh he should communicate, not one thing, but all things; should fill the world with his voice; should scatter forth light, nature, time, souls, from the centre of the present thought; and new date and new create the whole. Whenever a mind is simple, and receives a divine wisdom, old things pass away,—means, teachers, texts, temples fall; it lives now, and absorbs past and future into the present hour. All things are made sacred by relation to it,—one as much as another. All things are dissolved to their centre by their cause, and, in the universal miracle, petty and particular miracles disappear. If, therefore, a man claims to know and speak of God, and carries you backward to the phraseology of some old mouldered nation in another country, in another world, believe him not. Is the acorn better than the oak which is its fulness and completion? Is the parent better than the child into whom he has cast his ripened being? Whence, then, this worship of the past? The centuries are conspirators against the sanity and authority of the soul. Time and space are but physiological colors which the eye makes, but the soul is light; where it is, is day; where it was, is night; and history is an impertinence and an injury, if it be any thing more than a cheerful apologue or parable of my being and becoming.

Man is timid and apologetic; he is no longer upright; he dares not say 'I think,' 'I am,' but quotes some saint or sage. He is ashamed before the blade of grass or the blowing rose. These roses under my window make no reference to former roses or to better ones; they are for what they are; they exist with God to-day. There is no time to them. There is simply the rose; it is perfect in every moment of its existence. Before a leaf-bud has burst, its whole life acts; in the full-blown flower there is no more; in the leafless root there is no less. Its nature is satisfied, and it satisfies nature, in all moments alike. But man postpones or remembers; he does not live in the present, but with reverted eye laments the past, or, heedless of the riches that surround him, stands on tiptoe to foresee the future. He cannot be happy and strong until he too lives with nature in the present, above time.

If we live truly, we shall see truly. It is as easy for the strong man to be strong, as it is for the weak to be weak. When we have new perception, we shall gladly disburden the memory of its hoarded treasures as old rubbish. When a man lives with God, his voice shall be as sweet as the murmur of the brook and the rustle of the corn.

And now at last the highest truth on this subject remains unsaid; probably cannot be said; for all that we say is the far-off remembering of the intuition. That thought, by what I can now nearest approach to say it, is this. When good is near you, when you have life in yourself, it is not by any known or accustomed way; you shall not discern the foot-prints of any other; you shall not see the face of man; you shall not hear any name;—the way, the thought, the good, shall be wholly strange and new. It shall exclude example and experience. You take the way from man, not to man. All persons that ever existed are its forgotten ministers. Fear and hope are alike beneath it. There is somewhat low even in hope. In the hour of vision, there is nothing that can be called gratitude, nor properly joy. The soul raised over passion beholds identity and eternal causation, perceives the self-existence of Truth and Right, and calms itself with knowing that all things go well.

Life only avails, not the having lived. Power ceases in the instant of repose; it resides in the moment of transition from a past to a new state, in the shooting of the gulf, in the darting to an aim. This one fact the world hates, that the soul becomes; for that for ever degrades the past, turns all riches to poverty, all reputation to a shame, confounds the saint with the rogue, shoves Jesus and Judas equally aside. Why, then, do we prate of self-reliance? Inasmuch as the soul is present, there will be power not confident but agent. To talk of reliance is a poor external way of speaking. Speak rather of that which relies, because it works and is. Who has more obedience than I masters me, though he should not raise his finger. Round him I must revolve by the gravitation of spirits.

All things real are so by so much virtue as they contain. Commerce, husbandry, hunting, whaling, war, eloquence, personal weight, are somewhat, and engage my respect as examples of its presence and impure action. I see the same law working in nature for conservation and growth. Power is in nature the essential measure of right. Nature suffers nothing to remain in her kingdoms which cannot help itself. The genesis and maturation of a planet, its poise and orbit, the bended tree recovering itself from the strong wind, the vital resources of every animal and vegetable, are demonstrations of the self-sufficing, and therefore self-relying soul.

Thus all concentrates: let us not rove; let us sit at home with the cause. Let us stun and astonish the intruding rabble of men and books and institutions, by a simple declaration of the divine fact. Bid the invaders take the shoes from off their feet, for God is here within. Let our simplicity judge them, and our docility to our own law demonstrate the poverty of nature and fortune beside our native riches.

But now we are a mob. Man does not stand in awe of man, nor is his genius admonished to stay at home, to put itself in communication with the internal ocean, but it goes abroad to beg a cup of water of the urns of other men. We must go alone. I like the silent church before the service begins, better than any preaching. How far off, how cool, how chaste the persons look, begirt each one with a precinct or sanctuary! So let us always sit. Why should we assume the faults of our friend, or wife, or father, or child, because they sit around our hearth, or are said to have the same blood? All men have my blood, and I have all men's. Not for that will I adopt their petulance or folly, even to the extent of being ashamed of it. But your isolation must not be mechanical, but spiritual, that is, must be elevation. At times the whole world seems to be in conspiracy to importune you with emphatic trifles.—'Come Friend, client, child, sickness, fear, want, charity, all knock at once at thy closet door, and say, out unto us.' But keep thy state; come not into their confusion. The power men possess to annoy me, I give them by a weak curiosity. No man can come near me but through my act.

Check this lying hospitality and lying affection. Live no longer to the expectation of these deceived and deceiving people with whom we converse. Say to them, 'O father, O mother, O wife, O brother, O friend, I have lived with you after appearances hitherto. Henceforward I am the truth's. Be it known unto you that henceforward I obey no law less than the eternal law. I will have no covenants but proximities. I shall endeavour to nourish my parents, to support my family, to be the chaste husband of one wife,—but these relations I must fill after a new and unprecedented way. I appeal from your customs. I must be myself. I cannot break myself any longer for you, or you. If you can love me for what I am, we shall be the happier. If you cannot, I will still seek to deserve that you should. I will not hide my tastes or aversions. I will so trust that what is deep is holy, that I will do strongly before the sun and moon whatever inly rejoices me, and the heart appoints. If you are noble, I will love you; if you are not, I will not hurt you and myself by hypocritical attentions. If you are true, but not in the same truth with me, cleave to your companions; I will seek my own. I do this not selfishly, but humbly and truly. It is alike your interest, and mine, and all men's, however long we have dwelt in lies, to live in truth. Does this sound harsh to-day? You will soon love what is dictated by your nature as well as mine, and, if we follow the truth, it will bring us out safe at last.'—But so you may give these friends pain. Yes, but I cannot sell my liberty and my power, to save their sensibility. Besides, all persons have their moments of reason, when they look out into the region of absolute truth; then will they justify me, and do the same thing.

And truly it demands something godlike in him who has cast off the common motives of humanity, and has ventured to trust himself for a taskmaster. High be his heart, faithful his will, clear his sight, that he may in good earnest be doctrine, society, law, to himself, that a simple purpose may be to him as strong as iron necessity is to others!

Our housekeeping is mendicant, our arts, our occupations, our marriages, our religion, we have not chosen, but society has chosen for us. We are parlour soldiers. We shun the rugged battle of fate, where strength is born.

Let a Stoic open the resources of man, and tell men they are not leaning willows, but can and must detach themselves; that with the exercise of self-trust, new powers shall appear; that a man is the word made flesh, born to shed healing to the nations, that he should be ashamed of our compassion, and that the moment he acts from himself, tossing the laws, the books, idolatries, and customs out of the window, we pity him no more, but thank and revere him,—and that teacher shall restore the life of man to splendor, and make his name dear to all history.

It is easy to see that a greater self-reliance must work a revolution in all the offices and relations of men; in their religion; in their education; in their pursuits; their modes of living; their association; in their property; in their speculative views.

1. In what prayers do men allow themselves! That which they call a holy office is not so much as brave and manly. Prayer looks abroad and asks for some foreign addition to come through some foreign virtue, and loses itself in endless mazes of natural and supernatural, and mediatorial and miraculous. Prayer that craves a particular commodity,—any thing less than all good,—is vicious. Prayer is the contemplation of the facts of life from the highest point of view. It is the soliloquy of a beholding and jubilant soul. It is the spirit of God pronouncing his works good. But prayer as a means to effect a private end is meanness and theft. It supposes dualism and not unity in nature and consciousness. As soon as the man is

at one with God, he will not beg. He will then see prayer in all action. The prayer of the farmer kneeling in his field to weed it, the prayer of the rower kneeling with the stroke of his oar, are true prayers heard throughout nature, though for cheap ends.

Another sort of false prayers are our regrets. Discontent is the want of self-reliance: it is infirmity of will. Regret calamities, if you can thereby help the sufferer; if not, attend your own work, and already the evil begins to be repaired. Our sympathy is just as base. We come to them who weep foolishly, and sit down and cry for company, instead of imparting to them truth and health in rough electric shocks, putting them once more in communication with their own reason. The secret of fortune is joy in our hands. Welcome evermore to gods and men is the self-helping man. For him all doors are flung wide: him all tongues greet, all honors crown, all eyes follow with desire. Our love goes out to him and embraces him, because he did not need it. "To the persevering mortal," said Zoroaster, "the blessed Immortals are swift."

2. It is for want of self-culture that the superstition of Travelling, whose idols are Italy, England, Egypt, retains its fascination for all educated Americans. They who made England, Italy, or Greece venerable in the imagination did so by sticking fast where they were, like an axis of the earth. In manly hours, we feel that duty is our place. The soul is no traveller; the wise man stays at home, and when his necessities, his duties, on any occasion call him from his house, or into foreign lands, he is at home still, and shall make men sensible by the expression of his countenance, that he goes the missionary of wisdom and virtue, and visits cities and men like a sovereign, and not like an interloper or a valet.

I have no churlish objection to the circumnavigation of the globe, for the purposes of art, of study, and benevolence, so that the man is first domesticated, or does not go abroad with the hope of finding somewhat greater than he knows. He who travels to be amused, or to get somewhat which he does not carry, travels away from himself, and grows old even in youth among old things. In Thebes, in Palmyra, his will and mind have become old and dilapidated as they. He carries ruins to ruins.

Travelling is a fool's paradise. Our first journeys discover to us the indifference of places. At home I dream that at Naples, at Rome, I can be intoxicated with beauty, and lose my sadness. I pack my trunk, embrace my friends, embark on the sea, and at last wake up in Naples, and there beside me is the stern fact, the sad self, unrelenting, identical, that I fled from. I seek the Vatican, and the palaces. I affect to be intoxicated with sights and suggestions, but I am not intoxicated. My giant goes with me wherever I go.

3. But the rage of travelling is a symptom of a deeper unsoundness affecting the whole intellectual action. The intellect is vagabond, and our system of education fosters restlessness. Our minds travel when our bodies are forced to stay at home. We imitate; and what is imitation but the travelling of the mind? Our houses are built with foreign taste; our shelves are garnished with foreign ornaments; our opinions, our tastes, our faculties, lean, and follow the Past and the Distant. The soul created the arts wherever they have flourished. It was in his own mind that the artist sought his model. It was an application of his own thought to the thing to be done and the conditions to be observed.

Insist on yourself; never imitate. Your own gift you can present every moment with the cumulative force of a whole life's cultivation; but of the adopted talent of another, you have only an extemporaneous, half possession. That which each can do best, none but his Maker can teach him. No man yet knows what it is, nor can, till that person has exhibited it. Where is the master who could have taught Shakspeare? Do that which is assigned you, and you cannot hope too much or dare too much. Abide in the simple and noble regions of thy life, obey thy heart, and thou shalt reproduce the Foreworld again.

4. As our Religion, our Education, our Art look abroad, so does our spirit of society. All men plume themselves on the improvement of society, and no man improves.

Society never advances. It recedes as fast on one side as it gains on the other. It undergoes continual changes; it is barbarous, it is civilized, it is christianized, it is rich, it is scientific; but this change is not amelioration. For every thing that is given, something is taken. Society acquires new arts, and loses old instincts.

The civilized man has built a coach, but has lost the use of his feet. He is supported on crutches, but lacks so much support of muscle. He has a fine Geneva watch, but he fails of the skill to tell the hour by the sun. His note-books impair his memory; his libraries overload his wit; the insurance-office increases the number of accidents; and it may be a question whether machinery does not encumber; whether we have not lost by refinement some energy, by a Christianity entrenched in establishments and forms, some vigor of wild virtue. For every Stoic was a Stoic; but in Christendom where is the Christian?

The harm of the improved machinery may compensate its good. Galileo, with an opera-glass, discovered a more splendid series of celestial phenomena than any one since. Columbus found the New World in an undecked boat. We reckoned the improvements of the art of war among the triumphs of science, and yet Napoleon conquered Europe by the bivouac, which consisted of falling back on naked valor, and disencumbering it of all aids. The Emperor held it impossible to make a perfect army, says Las Casas, "without abolishing our arms, magazines, commissaries, and carriages, until, in imitation of the Roman custom, the soldier should receive his supply of corn, grind it in his hand-mill, and bake his bread himself."

And so the reliance on Property, including the reliance on governments which protect it, is the want of self-reliance. Men have looked away from themselves and at things so long, that they have come to esteem the religious, learned, and civil institutions as guards of property, and they deprecate assaults on these, because they feel them to be assaults on property. They measure their esteem of each other by what each has, and not by what each is. But a cultivated man becomes ashamed of his property, out of new respect for his nature. Especially he hates what he has, if he see that it is accidental,—came to him by inheritance, or gift, or crime; then he feels that it is not having; it does not belong to him, has no root in him, and merely lies there, because no revolution or no robber takes it away. But that which a man is, does always by necessity acquire, and what the man acquires is living property, which does not wait the beck of rulers, or mobs, or revolutions, or fire, or storm, or bankruptcies, but perpetually renews itself wherever the man breathes. "Thy lot or portion of life," said the Caliph Ali, "is seeking after thee; therefore be at rest from seeking after it." Our dependence on these foreign goods leads us to our slavish respect for numbers.

Not so, O friends! will the God design to enter and inhabit you, but by a method precisely the reverse. It is only as a man puts off all foreign support, and stands alone, that I see him to be strong and to prevail. He is weaker by every recruit to his banner. Is not a man better than a town? Ask nothing of men, and in the endless mutation, thou only firm column must presently appear the upholder of all that surrounds thee. He who knows that power is inborn, that he is weak because he has looked for good out of him and elsewhere, and so perceiving, throws himself unhesitatingly on his thought, instantly rights himself, stands in the erect position, commands his limbs, works miracles; just as a man who stands on his feet is stronger than a man who stands on his head.

So use all that is called Fortune. Most men gamble with her, and gain all, and lose all, as her wheel rolls. But do thou leave as unlawful these winnings, and deal with Cause and Effect, the chancellors of God. In the Will work and acquire, and thou hast chained the wheel of Chance, and shalt sit hereafter out of fear from her rotations. A political victory, a rise of rents, the recovery of your sick, or the return of your absent friend, or some other favorable event, raises your spirits, and you think good days are preparing for you. Do not believe it. Nothing can bring you peace but yourself. Nothing can bring you peace but the triumph of principles.

# Walden
(1854)

## by Henry David Thoreau

*The Landmark Classic of Simple Living—
Now in a Special Abridgment*

## Contents

Introduction  *Why Read Walden?* by Mitch Horowitz  88
I. Economy  90
II. Where I Lived, and What I Live For  97
III. Reading  100
IV. Sounds  101
V. Solitude  102
VI. Visitors  104
VII. The Bean-Field  106
VIII. The Village  106
IX. The Ponds  108
X. Baker Farm  109
XI. Higher Laws  110
XII. House-Warming  112
XIII. Former Inhabitants; and Winter Vistors  113
XIV. Spring  114
Conclusion  115

## Introduction
# Why Read *Walden*?

As I lay down these words to a new introduction to *Walden*, I am sitting under the gaze of the Great Sphinx at Giza—and I am deeply struck by something. As incredible a monument as the Sphinx is, and as deeply affected as I am by its antiquity and mystery, I had a more emotional response about twenty years ago when I visited the all-but-barren spot where Thoreau built his tiny cabin on the shores of Walden Pond in Concord, Massachusetts.

I will never forget my first visit. It was a snowy day near Christmas and I arrived at the spot to find that the only original remains were of Thoreau's hearthstone. I knelt down in the snow and cleared away the mounting flurries from the stone. I kissed it—and began to cry. I was so deeply struck that this was the place to which one man came to experience life in its fullness. I later wrote that what was there was a kind of Sphinx of air. When writing that I forgot that Thoreau himself had written: " If you have built castles in the air, your work need not be lost."

A woman who had been walking in the woods nearby later approached me and said that she saw me kneeling in the snow and wondered what, if anything, was wrong? No, I smiled, I had just dropped my car keys. How can you explain an emotional reaction at such a moment? It's not part of casual talk.

In the years since, a few literary critics have questioned Thoreau's sincerity and have accused him of pursuing hype by living two years on the shores of the Concord town pond in what they considered make-believe hermitage. I believe that that kind of hero-toppling is overblown and, at times, shallow. You can still find in Thoreau's book observations that could not arise from any but the person who yearns to peer into life at its core.

Here is one of them: "The best works of art are the expression of man's struggle to free himself."

For all of Thoreau's personal enterprise, why should anyone still read his 1854 memoir, a classic that can seem overly familiar or event a remnant of grade-school assignments?

Because *Walden* created a culture of rebellion and independent thought that reflects the best of American life, especially at the current moment when coarseness, unlearned opinion, and groupthink threaten to overrun us.

The philosophy called Transcendentalism, as shaped by Thoreau, Ralph Waldo Emerson, and their collaborators, reflected America's sharpest break with the religious dogma and intellectual conformities of the Old World. Transcendentalism embraced inner experiment, personal experience, and the individual search for meaning.

The New England Transcendentalists rejected the idea of rewards in the afterlife as the aim of religious practice. Instead, they believed in living out your highest potential in the present, deriving power and purpose from a palpably felt relationship to the Higher. The Transcendentalists also embraced mystical ideas from the East to which they gave a practical and can-do tone, familiarizing Americans with concepts of meditation, karma, and nonattachment. Thoreau and Emerson further drew upon esoteric ideas from Hermeticism—the Greek-Egyptian philosophy that flourished in the decades following Christ—to suggest the creative and causative powers of the human mind, and how to apply them in the here and now.

Thanks in part to Thoreau, the idea of the individual spiritual search now seems like a national birthright. In polls, most Americans agree that spiritual truth can be found outside of allegiance to any one faith or tradition. "Unaffiliated" is the fastest-growing category of religious identity. In recovery groups, twelve-step programs, and other nontraditional forms of spiritual search, we are encouraged to seek our own conception of a Higher Power. Even those Americans who affiliate with the traditional faiths are taught to believe that their own paths to the Divine are many—that the gates of prayer and forgiveness are always open; that the house of God, the seat of the ineffable, exists all around us. A spark of divinity, many believe, exists within. Such concepts were foreign, if not heretical, in the hierarchical religiosity of the Old World.

Consider, for example, the physical structure of the fourteenth-century Pope's Palace in Avignon, France. In the enormous church that dominates the palace's ground floor, the front pews were, naturally, reserved for aristocracy. A few rows back, space was reserved for those who served the powerful, such as merchants and teachers. And the remainder of the enormous cathedral was designated for everybody else. Here was a structure built in the name of a man who taught, "Blessed are the poor in spirit," resembling nothing so much as an emperor's court.

Thoreau and Transcendentalism upended that. Today one can visit Walden Pond, as I did, and walk to the spot where Thoreau built his tiny cabin. As noted, nothing remains of the physical structure, aside from the hearthstone. There is just open air where the cabin stood. But that empty space is, in a sense, Transcendentalism's greatest monument, and perhaps America's, as well. One can stand in this space and *feel* that this is a place in which one individual lived, determined to learn what it means to be a real human being, to look inside life and discover what really penetrates the human psyche. It is an invisible monument to the quest to know oneself. It is America's sphinx. And that is Transcendentalism.

Read *Walden* not because it is old and venerated—that is the last thing Thoreau would want. Read it because it summons you to all that is new within yourself. To ask, to seek, and to experiment—these are the most radical acts a person can undertake. These are the Thoreau's tools.

This condensed edition of *Walden* brings you some of the most valuable ideas in the book. I hope that you will return to it several times, and read the original itself. Ask yourself: What in Thoreau's memoir calls to you? Your response will point the way toward your most authentic direction in life.

—Mitch Horowitz

## I. Economy

When I wrote the following pages, or rather the bulk of them, I lived alone, in the woods, a mile from any neighbor, in a house which I had built myself, on the shore of Walden Pond, in Concord, Massachusetts, and earned my living by the labor of my hands only. I lived there two years and two months.

Some have asked what I got to eat; if I did not feel lonesome; if I was not afraid; and the like.

I should not talk so much about myself if there were anybody else whom I knew as well. Unfortunately, I am confined to this theme by the narrowness of my experience. Moreover, I, on my side, require of every writer, first or last, a simple and sincere account of his own life, and not merely what he has heard of other men's lives.

I see young men, my townsmen, whose misfortune it is to have inherited farms, houses, barns, cattle, and farming tools; for these are more easily acquired than got rid of. Better if they had been born in the open pasture and suckled by a wolf, that they might have seen with clearer eyes what field they were called to labor in.

Men labor under a mistake. The better part of the man is soon plowed into the soil for compost. By a seeming fate, commonly called necessity, they are employed, as it says in an old book, laying up treasures which moth and rust will corrupt and thieves break through and steal.

Most men, even in this comparatively free country, through mere ignorance and mistake, are so occupied with the factitious cares and superfluously coarse labors of life that its finer fruits cannot be plucked by them. Their fingers, from excessive toil, are too clumsy and tremble too much for that. He has no time to be anything but a machine. How can he remember well his ignorance—which his growth requires—who has so often to use his knowledge?

The masses of men lead lives of quiet desperation.

When we consider what, to use the words of the catechism, is the chief end of man, and what are the true necessaries and means of life, it appears as if men had deliberately chosen the common mode of living because they preferred it to any other. Yet they honestly think there is no choice left.

One farmer says to me, "You cannot live on vegetable food solely, for it furnishes nothing to make bones with;" and so he religiously devotes a part of his day to supplying his system with the raw material of bones; walking all the while he talks behind his oxen, which, with vegetable-made bones, jerk him and his lumbering plough along in spite of every obstacle. Some things are really necessaries of life in some circles, the most helpless and diseased, which in others are luxuries merely, and in others still are entirely unknown.

We might try our lives by a thousand simple tests.

The greater part of what my neighbors call good I believe in my soul to be bad, and if I repent of anything, it is very likely to be my good behavior. What demon possessed me that I behaved so well? You may say the wisest thing you can, old man,—you who have lived seventy years, not without honor of a kind,—I hear an irresistible voice which invites me away from all that. One generation abandons the enterprises of another like stranded vessels.

I think that we may safely trust a good deal more than we do. We may waive just so much care of ourselves as we honestly bestow elsewhere. Nature is as well adapted to our weakness as to our strength. The incessant anxiety and strain of some is a well nigh incurable form of disease. We are made to exaggerate the importance of what work we do; and yet how much is not done by us! or, what if we had been taken sick?

Let us consider for a moment what most of the trouble and anxiety which I have referred to is about, and how much it is necessary that we be troubled, or, at least, careful. It would be some advantage to live a primitive and frontier life, though in the midst of an outward civilization, if only to learn what are the gross necessaries of life and what methods have been taken to obtain them.

The improvements of ages have had but little influence on the essential laws of man's existence; as our skeletons, probably, are not to be distinguished from those of our ancestors.

The necessaries of life for man in this climate may, accurately enough, be distributed under the several heads of Food, Shelter, Clothing, and Fuel; for not till we have secured these are we prepared to entertain the true problems of life with freedom and a prospect of success.

Most of the luxuries, and many of the so called comforts of life, are not only not indispensable, but positive hindrances to the elevation of mankind. With respect to luxuries and comforts, the wisest have ever lived a more simple and meagre life. None can be an impartial or wise observer of human life but from the vantage ground of what we should call voluntary poverty.

There are nowadays professors of philosophy, but not philosophers. To be a philosopher is not merely to have subtle thoughts, nor even to found a school, but so to love wisdom as to live according to its dictates, a life of simplicity, independence, magnanimity, and trust. It is to solve some of the problems of life, not only theoretically, but practically. The success of great scholars and thinkers is commonly a courtier-like success, not kingly, not manly. They make shift to live merely by conformity, practically as their fathers did, and are in no sense the progenitors of a nobler race of men.

A man who has at length found something to do will not need to get a new suit to do it in; for him the old will do, that has lain dusty in the garret for an indeterminate period. Old shoes will serve a hero longer than they have served his valet,—if a hero ever has a valet,—bare feet are older than shoes, and he can make them do. Only they who go to soirées and legislative halls must have new coats, coats to change as often as the man changes in them. But if my jacket and trousers, my hat and shoes, are fit to worship God in, they will do; will they not?

When the farmer has got his house, he may not be the richer but the poorer for it, and it be the house that has got him.

Most men appear never to have considered what a house is, and are actually though needlessly poor all their lives because they think that they must have such a one as their neighbors have. It is possible to invent a house still more convenient and luxurious than we have, which yet all would admit that man could not afford to pay for. Shall we always study to obtain more of these things, and not sometimes to be content with less? Shall the respectable citizen thus gravely teach, by precept and example, the necessity of the young man's providing a certain number of superfluous glow-shoes, and umbrellas, and empty guest chambers for empty guests, before he dies? Why should not our furniture be as simple as the Arab's or the Indian's? When I think of the benefactors of the race, whom we have apotheosized as messengers from heaven, bearers of divine gifts to man, I do not see in my mind any retinue at their heels, any car-load of fashionable furniture.

The best works of art are the expression of man's struggle to free himself.

When I consider how our houses are built and paid for, or not paid for, and their internal economy managed and sustained, I wonder that the floor does not give way under the visitor while he is admiring the gewgaws upon the mantel-piece, and let him through into the cellar, to some solid and honest though earthy foundation. I cannot but perceive that this so called rich and refined life is a thing jumped at, and I do not get on in the enjoyment of the fine arts which adorn it. The first question which I am tempted to put to the proprietor of such great impropriety is, Who bolsters you? Are you one of the ninety-seven who fail, or of the three who succeed? Answer me these questions, and then perhaps I may look at your bawbles and find them ornamental. The cart before the horse is neither beautiful nor useful. Before we can adorn our houses with beautiful objects the walls must be stripped, and our lives must be stripped, and beautiful housekeeping and beautiful living be laid for a foundation: now, a taste for the beautiful is most cultivated out of doors, where there is no house and no housekeeper.

Near the end of March, 1845, I borrowed an axe and went down to the woods by Walden Pond, nearest to where I intended to build my house, and began to cut down some tall, arrowy white pines, still in their youth, for timber. It is difficult to begin without borrowing, but perhaps it is the most generous course thus to permit your fellow-men to have an interest in your enterprise. The owner of the axe, as he released his hold on it, said that it was the apple of his eye; but I returned it sharper than I received it. It was a pleasant hillside where I worked, covered with pine woods, through which I looked out on the pond.

My days in the woods were not very long ones; yet I usually carried my dinner of bread and butter, and read the newspaper in which it was wrapped, at noon, sitting amid the green pine boughs which I had cut off, and to my bread was imparted some of their fragrance, for my hands were covered with a thick coat of pitch. Before I had done I was more the friend than the foe of the pine tree, though I had cut down some of them, having become better acquainted with it. Sometimes a rambler in the wood was attracted by the sound of my axe, and we chatted pleasantly over the chips which I had made.

By the middle of April, for I made no haste in my work, but rather made the most of it, my house was framed and ready for the raising. The roof was the soundest part, though a good deal warped and made brittle by the sun. There was a stove, a bed, and a space to sit, an infant in the house where it was born, a silk parasol, gilt-framed looking-glass, and a patent new coffee-mill bailed to an oak sapling, all told.

I dug my cellar in the side of a hill sloping to the south, where a woodchuck had formerly dug his burrow, down through sumach and blackberry roots, and the lowest stain of vegetation, six feet square by seven deep, to a fine sand where potatoes would not freeze in any winter. The sides were left shelving, and not stoned.

In those days, when my hands were much employed, I read but little, but the least scraps of paper which lay on the ground, my holder, or tablecloth, afforded me as much entertainment, in fact answered the same purpose as the Iliad.

Before I finished my house, wishing to earn ten or twelve dollars by some honest and agreeable method, in order to meet my unusual expenses, I planted about two acres and a half of light and sandy soil near it chiefly with beans, but also a small part with potatoes, corn, peas, and turnips. The whole lot contains eleven acres, mostly growing up to pines and hickories, and was sold the preceding season for eight dollars and eight cents an acre. I put no manure whatever on this land, not being the owner, but merely a squatter, and not expecting to cultivate so much again, and I did not quite hoe it all once. I got out several cords of stumps in ploughing, which supplied me with fuel for a long time, and left small circles of virgin mould, easily distinguishable through the summer by the greater luxuriance of the beans there. The dead and for the most part unmerchantable wood behind my house, and the driftwood from the pond, have supplied the remainder of my fuel. I was obliged to hire a team and a man for the ploughing, though I held the plough myself.

I was more independent than any farmer in Concord, for I was not anchored to a house or farm, but could follow the bent of my genius, which is a very crooked one, every moment. Beside being better off than they already, if my house had been burned or my crops had failed, I should have been nearly as well off as before.

I am wont to think that men are not so much the keepers of herds as herds are the keepers of men, the former are so much the freer. Men and oxen exchange work; but if we consider necessary work only, the oxen will be seen to have greatly the advantage, their farm is so much the larger. Man does some of his part of the exchange work in his six weeks of haying, and it is no boy's play. Certainly no nation that lived simply in all respects, that is, no nation of philosophers, would commit so great a blunder as to use the labor of animals. True, there never was and is not likely soon to be a nation of philosophers, nor am I certain it is desirable that there should be. However, *I* should never have broken a horse or bull and taken him to board for any work he might do for me, for fear I should become a horse-man or a herds-man merely.

I learned from my two years' experience that it would cost incredibly little trouble to obtain one's necessary food, even in this latitude; that a man may use as simple a diet as the animals, and yet retain health and strength. I have made a satisfactory dinner, satisfactory on several accounts, simply off a dish of purslane which I gathered in my cornfield, boiled and salted.

Bread I at first made of pure Indian meal and salt, genuine hoe-cakes, which I baked before my fire out of doors on a shingle or the end of a stick of timber sawed off in building my house; but it was wont to get smoked and to have a piny flavor. I tried flour also; but have at last found a mixture of rye and Indian meal most convenient and agreeable. In cold weather it was no little amusement to bake several small loaves of this in succession, tending and turning them as carefully as an Egyptian his hatching eggs. They were a real cereal fruit which I ripened, and they had to my senses a fragrance like that of other noble fruits, which I kept in as long as possible by wrapping them in cloths. I made a study of the ancient and indispensable art of bread-making, consulting such authorities as offered, going back to the primitive days and first invention of the unleavened kind, when from the wildness of nuts and meats men first reached the mildness and refinement of this diet, and travelling gradually down in my studies through that accidental souring of the dough which, it is supposed, taught the leavening process, and through the various fermentations thereafter, till I came to "good, sweet, wholesome bread," the staff of life.

There is a certain class of unbelievers who sometimes ask me such questions as, if I think that I can live on vegetable food alone; and to strike at the root of the matter at once,—for the root is faith,—I am accustomed to answer such, that I can live on board nails. If they cannot understand that, they cannot understand much that I have to say. For my part, I am glad to hear of experiments of this kind being tried; as that a young man tried for a fortnight to live on hard, raw corn on the ear, using his teeth for all mortar. The squirrel tribe tried the same and succeeded. The human race is interested in these experiments, though a few old women who are incapacitated for them, or who own their thirds in mills, may be alarmed.

My furniture, part of which I made myself, and the rest cost me nothing of which I have not rendered an account, consisted of a bed, a table, a desk, three chairs, a looking-glass three inches in diameter, a pair of tongs and andirons, a kettle, a skillet, and a frying-pan, a dipper, a wash-bowl, two knives and forks, three plates, one cup, one spoon, a jug for oil, a jug for molasses, and a japanned lamp.

I would observe, by the way, that it costs me nothing for curtains, for I have no gazers to shut out but the sun and moon, and I am willing that they should look in. The moon will not sour milk nor taint meat of mine, nor will the sun injure my furniture or fade my carpet, and if he is sometimes too warm a friend, I find it still better economy to retreat behind some curtain which nature has provided, than to add a single item to the details of housekeeping. A lady once offered me a mat, but as I had no room to spare within the house, nor time to spare within or without to shake it, I declined it, preferring to wipe my feet on the sod before my door. It is best to avoid the beginnings of evil.

For more than five years I maintained myself thus solely by the labor of my hands, and I found, that by working about six weeks in a year, I could meet all the expenses of living. The whole of my winters, as well as most of my summers, I had free and clear for study.

As I preferred some things to others, and especially valued my freedom, as I could fare hard and yet succeed well, I did not wish to spend my time in earning rich carpets or other fine furniture, or delicate cookery, or a house in the Grecian or the Gothic style just yet.

In short, I am convinced, both by faith and experience, that to maintain one's self on this earth is not a hardship but a pastime, if we will live simply and wisely.

One young man of my acquaintance, who has inherited some acres, told me that he thought he should live as I did, *if he had the means*. I would not have any one adopt *my* mode of living on any account; for, beside that before he has fairly learned it I may have found out another for myself, I desire that there may be as many different persons in the world as possible; but I would have each one be very careful to find out and pursue *his own* way, and not his father's or his mother's or his neighbor's instead. The youth may build or plant or sail, only let him not be hindered from doing that which he tells me he would like to do.

Probably I should not consciously and deliberately forsake my particular calling to do the good which society demands of me, to save the universe from annihilation; and I believe that a like but infinitely greater steadfastness elsewhere is all that now preserves it. But I would not stand between any man and his genius; and to him who does this work, which I decline, with his whole heart and soul and life, I would say, Persevere, even if the world call it doing evil, as it is most likely they will.

## II. Where I Lived, and What I Lived For

When first I took up my abode in the woods, that is, began to spend my nights as well as days there, which, by accident, was on Independence Day, or the Fourth of July, 1845, my house was not finished for winter, but was merely a defence against the rain, without plastering or chimney, the walls being of rough, weather-stained boards, with wide chinks, which made it cool at night. The upright white hewn studs and freshly planed door and window casings gave it a clean and airy look, especially in the morning, when its timbers were saturated with dew, so that I fancied that by noon some sweet gum would exude from them. To my imagination it retained throughout the day more or less of this auroral character, reminding me of a certain house on a mountain which I had visited the year before. This was an airy and unplastered cabin, fit to entertain a travelling god, and where a goddess might trail her garments. The winds which passed over my dwelling were such as sweep over the ridges of mountains, bearing the broken strains, or celestial parts only, of terrestrial music. The morning wind forever blows, the poem of creation is uninterrupted; but few are the ears that hear it. Olympus is but the outside of the earth every where.

I was seated by the shore of a small pond, about a mile and a half south of the village of Concord and somewhat higher than it, in the midst of an extensive wood between that town and Lincoln, and about two miles south of that our only field known to fame, Concord Battle Ground; but I was so low in the woods that the opposite shore, half a mile off, like the rest, covered with wood, was my most distant horizon. For the first week, whenever I looked out on the pond it impressed me like a tarn high up on the side of a mountain, its bottom far above the surface of other lakes, and, as the sun arose, I saw it throwing off its nightly clothing of mist, and here and there, by degrees, its soft ripples or its smooth reflecting surface was revealed, while the mists, like ghosts, were stealthily withdrawing in every direction into the woods, as at the breaking up of some nocturnal conventicle. The very dew seemed to hang upon the trees later into the day than usual, as on the sides of mountains.

This small lake was of most value as a neighbor in the intervals of a gentle rain storm in August, when, both air and water being perfectly still, but the sky overcast, mid-afternoon had all the serenity of evening, and the wood-thrush sang around, and was heard from shore to shore. A lake like this is never smoother than at such a time; and the clear portion of the air above it being shallow and darkened by clouds, the water, full of light and reflections, becomes a lower heaven itself so much the more important. From a hill top near by, where the wood had been recently cut off, there was a pleasing vista southward across the pond, through a wide indentation in the hills which form the shore there, where their opposite sides sloping toward each other suggested a stream flowing out in that direction through a wooded valley, but stream there was none. That way I looked between and over the near green hills to some distant and higher ones in the horizon, tinged with blue. Indeed, by standing on tiptoe I could catch a glimpse of some of the peaks of the still bluer and more distant mountain ranges in the north-west, those true-blue coins from heaven's own mint, and also of some portion of the village. But in other directions, even from this point, I could not see over or beyond the woods which surrounded me. It is well to have some water in your neighborhood, to give buoyancy to and float the earth. One value even of the smallest well is, that when you look into it you see that earth is not continent but insular. This is as important as that it keeps butter cool. When I looked across the pond from this peak toward the Sudbury meadows, which in time of flood I distinguished elevated perhaps by a mirage in their seething valley, like a coin in a basin, all the earth beyond the pond appeared like a thin crust insulated and floated even by this small sheet of interverting water, and I was reminded that this on which I dwelt was but dry land.

Though the view from my door was still more contracted, I did not feel crowded or confined in the least. There was pasture enough for my imagination. The low shrub-oak plateau to which the opposite shore arose, stretched away toward the prairies of the West and the steppes of Tartary, affording ample room for all the roving families of men. "There are none happy in the world but beings who enjoy freely a vast horizon,"—said Damodara, when his herds required new and larger pastures.

Every morning was a cheerful invitation to make my life of equal simplicity, and I may say innocence, with Nature herself. I have been as sincere a worshipper of Aurora as the Greeks. I got up early and bathed in the pond; that was a religious exercise, and one of the best things which I did. They say that characters were engraven on the bathing tub of king Tching-thang to this effect: "Renew thyself completely each day; do it again, and again, and forever again." I can understand that. Morning brings back the heroic ages. There was something cosmical about it; a standing advertisement, till forbidden, of the everlasting vigor and fertility of the world. The Vedas said, "All intelligences awake with the morning." Morning is when I am awake and there is a dawn in time. Moral reform is the effort to throw off sleep.

I went to the woods because I wished to live deliberately, to front only the essential facts of life, and see if I could not learn what it had to teach, and not, when I came to die, discover that I had not lived. I did not wish to live what was not life, living is so dear; nor did I wish to practise resignation, unless it was quite necessary. I wanted to live deep and suck out all the marrow of life, to live so sturdily and Spartan-like as to put to rout all that was not life, to cut a broad swath and shave close, to drive life into a corner, and reduce it to its lowest terms, and, if it proved to be mean, why then to get the whole and genuine meanness of it, and publish its meanness to the world; or if it were sublime, to know it by experience, and be able to give a true account of it in my next excursion. For most men, it appears to me, are in a strange uncertainty about it, whether it is of the devil or of God, and have *somewhat hastily* concluded that it is the chief end of man here to "glorify God and enjoy him forever."

Why should we live with such hurry and waste of life? We are determined to be starved before we are hungry. Men say that a stitch in time saves nine, and so they take a thousand stitches to-day to save nine to-morrow.

Let us spend one day as deliberately as Nature, and not be thrown off the track by every nutshell and mosquito's wing that falls on the rails. Let us rise early and fast, or break fast, gently and without perturbation; let company come and let company go, let the bells ring and the children cry,—determined to make a day of it. Why should we knock under and go with the stream?

## III. Reading

The heroic books, even if printed in the character of our mother tongue, will always be in a language dead to degenerate times; and we must laboriously seek the meaning of each word and line, conjecturing a larger sense than common use permits out of what wisdom and valor and generosity we have. The modern cheap and fertile press, with all its translations, has done little to bring us nearer to the heroic writers of antiquity. They seem as solitary, and the letter in which they are printed as rare and curious, as ever. It is worth the expense of youthful days and costly hours, if you learn only some words of an ancient language, which are raised out of the trivialness of the street, to be perpetual suggestions and provocations. It is not in vain that the farmer remembers and repeats the few Latin words which he has heard. Men sometimes speak as if the study of the classics would at length make way for more modern and practical studies; but the adventurous student will always study classics, in whatever language they may be written and however ancient they may be. For what are the classics but the noblest recorded thoughts of man? They are the only oracles which are not decayed, and there are such answers to the most modern inquiry in them as Delphi and Dodona never gave. We might as well omit to study Nature because she is old. To read well, that is, to read true books in a true spirit, is a noble exercise, and one that will task the reader more than any exercise which the customs of the day esteem.

No wonder that Alexander carried the Iliad with him on his expeditions in a precious casket. A written word is the choicest of relics. It is something at once more intimate with us and more universal than any other work of art. It is the work of art nearest to life itself. It may be translated into every language, and not only be read but actually breathed from all human lips;—not be represented on canvas or in marble only, but be carved out of the breath of life itself. The symbol of an ancient man's thought becomes a modern man's speech.

## IV. Sounds

I did not read books the first summer; I hoed beans. Nay, I often did better than this. There were times when I could not afford to sacrifice the bloom of the present moment to any work, whether of the head or hands. I love a broad margin to my life. Sometimes, in a summer morning, having taken my accustomed bath, I sat in my sunny doorway from sunrise till noon, rapt in a revery, amidst the pines and hickories and sumachs, in undisturbed solitude and stillness, while the birds sing around or flitted noiseless through the house, until by the sun falling in at my west window, or the noise of some traveller's wagon on the distant highway, I was reminded of the lapse of time.

The Fitchburg Railroad touches the pond about a hundred rods south of where I dwell. I usually go to the village along its causeway, and am, as it were, related to society by this link. The men on the freight trains, who go over the whole length of the road, bow to me as to an old acquaintance, they pass me so often, and apparently they take me for an employee; and so I am. I too would fain be a track-repairer somewhere in the orbit of the earth.

I watch the passage of the morning cars with the same feeling that I do the rising of the sun, which is hardly more regular. Their train of clouds stretching far behind and rising higher and higher, going to heaven while the cars are going to Boston, conceals the sun for a minute and casts my distant field into the shade, a celestial train beside which the petty train of cars which hugs the earth is but the barb of the spear.

What recommends commerce to me is its enterprise and bravery. It does not clasp its hands and pray to Jupiter. I see these men every day go about their business with more or less courage and content, doing more even than they suspect, and perchance better employed than they could have consciously devised. I am less affected by their heroism who stood up for half an hour in the front line at Buena Vista, than by the steady and cheerful valor of the men who inhabit the snow-plough for their winter quarters; who have not merely the three-o'-clock in the morning courage, which Bonaparte thought was the rarest, but whose courage does not go to rest so early, who go to sleep only when the storm sleeps or the sinews of their iron steed are frozen.

Commerce is unexpectedly confident and serene, alert, adventurous, and unwearied. It is very natural in its methods withal, far more so than many fantastic enterprises and sentimental experiments, and hence its singular success. I am refreshed and expanded when the freight train rattles past me, and I smell the stores which go dispensing their odors all the way from Long Wharf to Lake Champlain, reminding me of foreign parts, of coral reefs, and Indian oceans, and tropical climes, and the extent of the globe. I feel more like a citizen of the world at the sight of the palm-leaf which will cover so many flaxen New England heads the next summer, the Manilla hemp and cocoa-nut husks, the old junk, gunny bags, scrap iron, and rusty nails.

Now that the cars are gone by and all the restless world with them, and the fishes in the pond no longer feel their rumbling, I am more alone than ever. For the rest of the long afternoon, perhaps, my meditations are interrupted only by the faint rattle of a carriage or team along the distant highway.

## V. Solitude

This is a delicious evening, when the whole body is one sense, and imbibes delight through every pore. I go and come with a strange liberty in Nature, a part of herself. As I walk along the stony shore of the pond in my shirt sleeves, though it is cool as well as cloudy and windy, and I see nothing special to attract me, all the elements are unusually congenial to me. The bullfrogs trump to usher in the night, and the note of the whippoorwill is borne on the rippling wind from over the water. Sympathy with the fluttering alder and poplar leaves almost takes away my breath; yet, like the lake, my serenity is rippled but not ruffled. These small waves raised by the evening wind are as remote from storm as the smooth reflecting surface. Though it is now dark, the wind still blows and roars in the wood, the waves still dash, and some creatures lull the rest with their notes. The repose is never complete. The wildest animals do not repose, but seek their prey now; the fox, and skunk, and rabbit, now roam the fields and woods without fear. They are Nature's watchmen,—links which connect the days of animated life.

When I return to my house I find that visitors have been there and left their cards, either a bunch of flowers, or a wreath of evergreen, or a name in pencil on a yellow walnut leaf or a chip. They who come rarely to the woods take some little piece of the forest into their hands to play with by the way, which they leave, either intentionally or accidentally. One has peeled a willow wand, woven it into a ring, and dropped it on my table. I could always tell if visitors had called in my absence, either by the bended twigs or grass, or the print of their shoes, and generally of what sex or age or quality they were by some slight trace left, as a flower dropped, or a bunch of grass plucked and thrown away, even as far off as the railroad, half a mile distant, or by the lingering odor of a cigar or pipe. Nay, I was frequently notified of the passage of a traveller along the highway sixty rods off by the scent of his pipe.

Yet I experienced sometimes that the most sweet and tender, the most innocent and encouraging society may be found in any natural object, even for the poor misanthrope and most melancholy man. There can be no very black melancholy to him who lives in the midst of Nature and has his senses still. There was never yet such a storm but it was Æolian music to a healthy and innocent ear. Nothing can rightly compel a simple and brave man to a vulgar sadness. While I enjoy the friendship of the seasons I trust that nothing can make life a burden to me. The gentle rain which waters my beans and keeps me in the house to-day is not drear and melancholy, but good for me too. Though it prevents my hoeing them, it is of far more worth than my hoeing. If it should continue so long as to cause the seeds to rot in the ground and destroy the potatoes in the low lands, it would still be good for the grass on the uplands, and, being good for the grass, it would be good for me. Sometimes, when I compare myself with other men, it seems as if I were more favored by the gods than they, beyond any deserts that I am conscious of; as if I had a warrant and surety at their hands which my fellows have not, and were especially guided and guarded. I do not flatter myself, but if it be possible they flatter me. I have never felt lonesome, or in the least oppressed by a sense of solitude, but once, and that was a few weeks after I came to the woods, when, for an hour, I doubted if the near neighborhood of man was not essential to a serene and healthy life. To be alone was something unpleasant. But I was at the same time conscious of a slight insanity in my mood, and seemed to foresee my recovery. In the midst of a gentle rain while these thoughts prevailed, I was suddenly sensible of such sweet and beneficent society in Nature, in the very pattering of the drops, and in every sound and sight around my house, an infinite and unaccountable friendliness all at once like an atmosphere sustaining me, as made the fancied advantages of human neighborhood insignificant, and I have never thought of them since.

Some of my pleasantest hours were during the long rain storms in the spring or fall, which confined me to the house for the afternoon as well as the forenoon, soothed by their ceaseless roar and pelting; when an early twilight ushered in a long evening in which many thoughts had time to take root and unfold themselves. In those driving north-east rains which tried the village houses so, when the maids stood ready with mop and pail in front entries to keep the deluge out, I sat behind my door in my little house, which was all entry, and thoroughly enjoyed its protection. In one heavy thunder shower the lightning struck a large pitch-pine across the pond, making a very conspicuous and perfectly regular spiral groove from top to bottom, an inch or more deep, and four or five inches wide, as you would groove a walking-stick. I passed it again the other day, and was struck with awe on looking up and beholding that mark, now more distinct than ever, where a terrific and resistless bolt came down out of the harmless sky eight years ago. Men frequently say to me, "I should think you would feel lonesome down there, and want to be nearer to folks, rainy and snowy days and nights especially." I am tempted to reply to such,—This whole earth which we inhabit is but a point in space. How far apart, think you, dwell the two most distant inhabitants of yonder star, the breadth of whose disk cannot be appreciated by our instruments? Why should I feel lonely? is not our planet in the Milky Way? This which you put seems to me not to be the most important question. What sort of space is that which separates a man from his fellows and makes him solitary? I have found that no exertion of the legs can bring two minds much nearer to one another.

I find it wholesome to be alone the greater part of the time. To be in company, even with the best, is soon wearisome and dissipating. I love to be alone. I never found the companion that was so companionable as solitude. We are for the most part more lonely when we go abroad among men than when we stay in our chambers. A man thinking or working is always alone, let him be where he will. Solitude is not measured by the miles of space that intervene between a man and his fellows.

Society is commonly too cheap. We meet at very short intervals, not having had time to acquire any new value for each other.

# VI. Visitors

I think that I love society as much as most, and am ready enough to fasten myself like a bloodsucker for the time to any full-blooded man that comes in my way. I am naturally no hermit, but might possibly sit out the sturdiest frequenter of the bar-room, if my business called me thither.

I had three chairs in my house; one for solitude, two for friendship, three for society. When visitors came in larger and unexpected numbers there was but the third chair for them all, but they generally economized the room by standing up. It is surprising how many great men and women a small house will contain. I have had twenty-five or thirty souls, with their bodies, at once under my roof, and yet we often parted without being aware that we had come very near to one another. Many of our houses, both public and private, with their almost innumerable apartments, their huge halls and their cellars for the storage of wines and other munitions of peace, appear to me extravagantly large for their inhabitants. They are so vast and magnificent that the latter seem to be only vermin which infest them.

Many a traveller came out of his way to see me and the inside of my house, and, as an excuse for calling, asked for a glass of water. I told them that I drank at the pond, and pointed thither, offering to lend them a dipper. Far off as I lived, I was not exempted from the annual visitation which occurs, methinks, about the first of April, when every body is on the move; and I had my share of good luck, though there were some curious specimens among my visitors. Half-witted men from the almshouse and elsewhere came to see me; but I endeavored to make them exercise all the wit they had, and make their confessions to me; in such cases making wit the theme of our conversation; and so was compensated. Indeed, I found some of them to be wiser than the so called overseers of the poor and selectmen of the town, and thought it was time that the tables were turned. With respect to wit, I learned that there was not much difference between the half and the whole. One day, in particular, an inoffensive, simple-minded pauper, whom with others I had often seen used as fencing stuff, standing or sitting on a bushel in the fields to keep cattle and himself from straying, visited me, and expressed a wish to live as I did. He told me, with the utmost simplicity and truth, quite superior, or rather inferior, to any thing that is called humility, that he was "deficient in intellect." These were his words. The Lord had made him so, yet he supposed the Lord cared as much for him as for another. "I have always been so," said he, "from my childhood; I never had much mind; I was not like other children; I am weak in the head. It was the Lord's will, I suppose." And there he was to prove the truth of his words. He was a metaphysical puzzle to me. I have rarely met a fellow-man on such promising ground,—it was so simple and sincere and so true all that he said. And, true enough, in proportion as he appeared to humble himself was he exalted. I did not know at first but it was the result of a wise policy. It seemed that from such a basis of truth and frankness as the poor weak-headed pauper had laid, our intercourse might go forward to something better than the intercourse of sages.

Objects of charity are not guests. Men who did not know when their visit had terminated, though I went about my business again, answering them from greater and greater remoteness.

## VII. The Bean-Field

Meanwhile my beans, the length of whose rows, added together, was seven miles already planted, were impatient to be hoed, for the earliest had grown considerably before the latest were in the ground; indeed they were not easily to be put off. What was the meaning of this so steady and self-respecting, this small Herculean labor, I knew not. I came to love my rows, my beans, though so many more than I wanted. They attached me to the earth.

Early in the morning I worked barefooted, dabbling like a plastic artist in the dewy and crumbling sand, but later in the day the sun blistered my feet. There the sun lighted me to hoe beans, pacing slowly backward and forward over that yellow gravelly upland, between the long green rows, fifteen rods, the one end terminating in a shrub oak copse where I could rest in the shade, the other in a blackberry field where the green berries deepened their tints by the time I had made another bout. Removing the weeds, putting fresh soil about the bean stems, and encouraging this weed which I had sown, making the yellow soil express its summer thought in bean leaves and blossoms rather than in wormwood and piper and millet grass, making the earth say beans instead of grass,—this was my daily work.

## VIII. The Village

Every day or two I strolled to the village to hear some of the gossip which is incessantly going on there, circulating either from mouth to mouth, or from newspaper to newspaper, and which, taken in homœopathic doses, was really as refreshing in its way as the rustle of leaves and the peeping of frogs. As I walked in the woods to see the birds and squirrels, so I walked in the village to see the men and boys; instead of the wind among the pines I heard the carts rattle. In one direction from my house there was a colony of muskrats in the river meadows; under the grove of elms and buttonwoods in the other horizon was a village of busy men, as curious to me as if they had been prairie dogs, each sitting at the mouth of its burrow, or running over to a neighbor's to gossip. I went there frequently to observe their habits. The village appeared to me a great news room; and on one side, to support it, as once at Redding & Company's on State Street, they kept nuts and raisins, or salt and meal and other groceries. Some have such a vast appetite for the former commodity, that is, the news, and such sound digestive organs, that they can sit forever in public avenues without stirring, and let it simmer and whisper through them like the Etesian winds, or as if inhaling ether, it only producing numbness and insensibility to pain,—otherwise it would often be painful to hear,—without affecting the consciousness.

It was very pleasant, when I stayed late in town, to launch myself into the night, especially if it was dark and tempestuous, and set sail from some bright village parlor or lecture room, with a bag of rye or Indian meal upon my shoulder, for my snug harbor in the woods, having made all tight without and withdrawn under hatches with a merry crew of thoughts, leaving only my outer man at the helm, or even tying up the helm when it was plain sailing. I had many a genial thought by the cabin fire "as I sailed." I was never cast away nor distressed in any weather, though I encountered some severe storms. It is darker in the woods, even in common nights, than most suppose.

One afternoon, near the end of the first summer, when I went to the village to get a shoe from the cobbler's, I was seized and put into jail, because, as I have elsewhere related, I did not pay a tax to, or recognize the authority of, the state which buys and sells men, women, and children, like cattle at the door of its senate-house. I had gone down to the woods for other purposes. But, wherever a man goes, men will pursue and paw him with their dirty institutions, and, if they can, constrain him to belong to their desperate oddfellow society. It is true, I might have resisted forcibly with more or less effect, might have run "amok" against society; but I preferred that society should run "amok" against me, it being the desperate party. However, I was released the next day, obtained my mended shoe, and returned to the woods in season to get my dinner of huckleberries on Fair-Haven Hill. I was never molested by any person but those who represented the state. I had no lock nor bolt but for the desk which held my papers, not even a nail to put over my latch or windows. I never fastened my door night or day, though I was to be absent several days; not even when the next fall I spent a fortnight in the woods of Maine. And yet my house was more respected than if it had been surrounded by a file of soldiers. The tired rambler could rest and warm himself by my fire, the literary amuse himself with the few books on my table, or the curious, by opening my closet door, see what was left of my dinner, and what prospect

I had of a supper. Yet, though many people of every class came this way to the pond, I suffered no serious inconvenience from these sources, and I never missed anything but one small book, a volume of Homer, which perhaps was improperly gilded, and this I trust a soldier of our camp has found by this time. I am convinced, that if all men were to live as simply as I then did, thieving and robbery would be unknown. These take place only in communities where some have got more than is sufficient while others have not enough.

## IX. The Ponds

Sometimes, after staying in a village parlor till the family had all retired, I have returned to the woods, and, partly with a view to the next day's dinner, spent the hours of midnight fishing from a boat by moonlight, serenaded by owls and foxes, and hearing, from time to time, the creaking note of some unknown bird close at hand.

The scenery of Walden is on a humble scale, and, though very beautiful, does not approach to grandeur, nor can it much concern one who has not long frequented it or lived by its shore; yet this pond is so remarkable for its depth and purity as to merit a particular description. It is a clear and deep green well, half a mile long and a mile and three quarters in circumference, and contains about sixty-one and a half acres; a perennial spring in the midst of pine and oak woods, without any visible inlet or outlet except by the clouds and evaporation. The surrounding hills rise abruptly from the water to the height of forty to eighty feet, though on the south-east and east they attain to about one hundred and one hundred and fifty feet respectively, within a quarter and a third of a mile. They are exclusively woodland. All our Concord waters have two colors at least; one when viewed at a distance, and another, more proper, close at hand.

The water is so transparent that the bottom can easily be discerned at the depth of twenty-five or thirty feet. Paddling over it, you may see, many feet beneath the surface the schools of perch and shiners, perhaps only an inch long, yet the former easily distinguished by their transverse bars, and you think that they must be ascetic fish that find a subsistence there. Once, in the winter, many years ago, when I had been cutting holes through the ice in order to catch pickerel, as I stepped ashore I tossed my axe back on to the ice, but, as if some evil genius had directed it, it slid four or five rods directly into one of the holes, where the water was twenty-five feet deep. Out of curiosity,

I lay down on the ice and looked through the hole, until I saw the axe a little on one side, standing on its head, with its helve erect and gently swaying to and fro with the pulse of the pond; and there it might have stood erect and swaying till in the course of time the handle rotted off, if I had not disturbed it. Making another hole directly over it with an ice chisel which I had, and cutting down the longest birch which I could find in the neighborhood with my knife, I made a slip-noose, which I attached to its end, and, letting it down carefully, passed it over the knob of the handle, and drew it by a line along the birch, and so pulled the axe out again.

# X. Baker Farm

I set out one afternoon to go a-fishing to Fair-Haven, through the woods, to eke out my scanty fare of vegetables. My way led through Pleasant Meadow, an adjunct of the Baker Farm.

I thought of living there before I went to Walden. I "hooked" the apples, leaped the brook, and scared the musquash and the trout. It was one of those afternoons which seem indefinitely long before one, in which many events may happen, a large portion of our natural life, though it was already half spent when I started. By the way there came up a shower, which compelled me to stand half an hour under a pine, piling boughs over my head, and wearing my handkerchief for a shed; and when at length I had made one cast over the pickerel-weed, standing up to my middle in water, I found myself suddenly in the shadow of a cloud, and the thunder began to rumble with such emphasis that I could do no more than listen to it. The gods must be proud, thought I, with such forked flashes to rout a poor unarmed fisherman. So I made haste for shelter to the nearest hut, which stood half a mile from any road, but so much the nearer to the pond, and had long been uninhabited.

My Good Genius seemed to say,—Go fish and hunt far and wide day by day,—farther and wider,—and rest thee by many brooks and hearth-sides without misgiving. Remember thy Creator in the days of thy youth. Rise free from care before the dawn, and seek adventures. Let the noon find thee by other lakes, and the night overtake thee everywhere at home. There are no larger fields than these, no worthier games than may here be played. Grow wild according to thy nature, like these sedges and brakes, which will never become English hay. Let the thunder rumble; what if it threaten ruin to farmers' crops? that is not its errand to thee. Take shelter under the cloud, while they flee to carts and sheds. Let not to get a living be thy trade, but thy sport. Enjoy the land, but own it not. Through want of enterprise and faith men are where they are, buying and selling, and spending their lives like serfs.

# XI. Higher Laws

As I came home through the woods with my string of fish, trailing my pole, it being now quite dark, I caught a glimpse of a woodchuck stealing across my path, and felt a strange thrill of savage delight, and was strongly tempted to seize and devour him raw; not that I was hungry then, except for that wildness which he represented. Once or twice, however, while I lived at the pond, I found myself ranging the woods, like a half-starved hound, with a strange abandonment, seeking some kind of venison which I might devour, and no morsel could have been too savage for me. The wildest scenes had become unaccountably familiar. I found in myself, and still find, an instinct toward a higher, or, as it is named, spiritual life, as do most men, and another toward a primitive rank and savage one, and I reverence them both. I love the wild not less than the good. The wildness and adventure that are in fishing still recommended it to me. I like sometimes to take rank hold on life and spend my day more as the animals do. Perhaps I have owed to this employment and to hunting, when quite young, my closest acquaintance with Nature. They early introduce us to and detain us in scenery with which otherwise, at that age, we should have little acquaintance. Fishermen, hunters, woodchoppers, and others, spending their lives in the fields and woods, in a peculiar sense a part of Nature themselves, are often in a more favorable mood for observing her, in the intervals of their pursuits, than philosophers or poets even, who approach her with expectation. She is not afraid to exhibit herself to them. The traveler on the prairie is naturally a hunter, on the head waters of the Missouri and Columbia a trapper, and at the Falls of St. Mary a fisherman. He who is only a traveler learns things at second-hand and by the halves, and is poor authority. We are most interested when science reports what those men already know practically or instinctively, for that alone is a true humanity, or account of human experience.

I have found repeatedly, of late years, that I cannot fish without falling a little in self-respect. I have tried it again and again. I have skill at it, and, like many of my fellows, a certain instinct for it, which revives from time to time, but always when I have done I feel that it would have been better if I had not fished. I think that I do not mistake. It is a faint intimation, yet so are the first streaks of morning. There is unquestionably this instinct in me which belongs to the lower orders of creation; yet with every year I am less a fisherman, though without more humanity or even wisdom; at present I am no fisherman at all. But I see that if I were to live in a wilderness I should again be tempted to become a fisher and hunter in earnest. Beside, there is something essentially unclean about this diet and all flesh, and I began to see where housework commences, and whence the endeavor, which costs so much, to wear a tidy and respectable appearance each day, to keep the house sweet and free from all ill odors and sights. Having been my own butcher and scullion and cook, as well as the gentleman for whom the dishes were served up, I can speak from an unusually complete experience. The practical objection to animal food in my case was its uncleanness; and, besides, when I had caught and cleaned and cooked and eaten my fish, they seemed not to have fed me essentially. It was insignificant and unnecessary, and cost more than it came to. A little bread or a few potatoes would have done as well, with less trouble and filth. Like many of my contemporaries, I had rarely for many years used animal food, or tea, or coffee, &c.; not so much because of any ill effects which I had traced to them, as because they were not agreeable to my imagination. The repugnance to animal food is not the effect of experience, but is an instinct. It appeared more beautiful to live low and fare hard in many respects; and though I never did so, I went far enough to please my imagination. I believe that every man who has ever been earnest to preserve his higher or poetic faculties in the best condition has been particularly inclined to abstain from animal food, and from much food of any kind.

It is hard to provide and cook so simple and clean a diet as will not offend the imagination; but this, I think, is to be fed when we feed the body; they should both sit down at the same table. Yet perhaps this may be done. The fruits eaten temperately need not make us ashamed of our appetites, nor interrupt the worthiest pursuits. But put an extra condiment into your dish, and it will poison you. It is not worth the while to live by rich cookery. Most men would feel shame if caught preparing with their own hands precisely such a dinner, whether of animal or vegetable food, as is every day prepared for them by others. Yet till this is otherwise we are not civilized, and, if gentlemen and ladies, are not true men and women. This certainly suggests what change is to be made. It may be vain to ask why the imagination will not be reconciled to flesh and fat. I am satisfied that it is not. Is it not a reproach that man is a carnivorous animal? True, he can and does live, in a great measure, by preying on other animals; but this is a miserable way,—as any one who will go to snaring rabbits, or slaughtering lambs, may learn,—and he will be regarded as a benefactor of his race who shall teach man to confine himself to a more innocent and wholesome diet. Whatever my own practice may be, I have no doubt that it is a part of the destiny of the human race, in its gradual improvement, to leave off eating animals, as surely as the savage tribes have left off eating each other when they came in contact with the more civilized.

## XII. House-Warming

When I came to build my chimney I studied masonry. My bricks being second-hand ones required to be cleaned with a trowel, so that I learned more than usual of the qualities of bricks and trowels. The mortar on them was fifty years old, and was said to be still growing harder; but this is one of those sayings which men love to repeat whether they are true or not. Such sayings themselves grow harder and adhere more firmly with age, and it would take many blows with a trowel to clean an old wiseacre of them. Many of the villages of Mesopotamia are built of second-hand bricks of a very good quality, obtained from the ruins of Babylon, and the cement on them is older and probably harder still. However that may be, I was struck by the peculiar toughness of the steel which bore so many violent blows without being worn out. As my bricks had been in a chimney before, though I did not read the name of Nebuchadnezzar on them, I picked out as many fire-place bricks as I could find, to save work and waste, and I filled the spaces between the bricks about the fire-place with stones from the pond shore, and also made my mortar with the white sand from the same place. I lingered most about the fire-place, as the most vital part of the house.

The north wind had already begun to cool the pond, though it took many weeks of steady blowing to accomplish it, it is so deep. When I began to have a fire at evening, before I plastered my house, the chimney carried smoke particularly well, because of the numerous chinks between the boards. Yet I passed some cheerful evenings in that cool and airy apartment, surrounded by the rough brown boards full of knots, and rafters with the bark on high overhead. My house never pleased my eye so much after it was plastered, though I was obliged to confess that it was more comfortable.

The pond had in the mean while skimmed over in the shadiest and shallowest coves, some days or even weeks before the general freezing. The first ice is especially interesting and perfect, being hard, dark, and transparent, and affords the best opportunity that ever offers for examining the bottom where it is shallow; for you can lie at your length on ice only an inch thick, like a skater insect on the surface of the water, and study the bottom at your leisure, only two or three inches distant, like a picture behind a glass.

At length the winter set in in good earnest, just as I had finished plastering, and the wind began to howl around the house as if it had not had permission to do so till then. Night after night the geese came lumbering in in the dark with a clangor and a whistling of wings, even after the ground was covered with snow, some to alight in Walden, and some flying low over the woods toward Fair Haven, bound for Mexico. Several times, when returning from the village at ten or eleven o'clock at night, I heard the tread of a flock of geese, or else ducks, on the dry leaves in the woods by a pond-hole behind my dwelling, where they had come up to feed, and the faint honk or quack of their leader as they hurried off. In 1845 Walden froze entirely over for the first time on the night of the 22d of December.

# XIII. Former Inhabitants; and Winter Visitors

weathered some merry snow storms, and spent some cheerful winter evenings by my fire-side, while the snow whirled wildly without, and even the hooting of the owl was hushed. For many weeks I met no one in my walks but those who came occasionally to cut wood and sled it to the village. The elements, however, abetted me in making a path through the deepest snow in the woods, for when I had once gone through the wind blew the oak leaves into my tracks, where they lodged, and by absorbing the rays of the sun melted the snow, and so not only made a dry bed for my feet, but in the night their dark line was my guide. For human society I was obliged to conjure up the former occupants of these woods. Within the memory of many of my townsmen the road near which my house stands resounded with the laugh and gossip of inhabitants, and the woods which border it were notched and dotted here and there with their little gardens and dwellings, though it was then much more shut in by the forest than now.

At this season I seldom had a visitor. When the snow lay deepest no wanderer ventured near my house for a week or fortnight at a time, but there I lived as snug as a meadow mouse, or as cattle and poultry which are said to have survived for a long time buried in drifts, even without food; or like that early settler's family in the town of Sutton, in this state, whose cottage was completely covered by the great snow of 1717 when he was absent, and an Indian found it only by the hole which the chimney's breath made in the drift, and so relieved the family. But no friendly Indian concerned himself about me; nor needed he, for the master of the house was at home.

## XIV. Spring

One attraction in coming to the woods to live was that I should have leisure and opportunity to see the spring come in. The ice in the pond at length begins to be honey-combed, and I can set my heel in it as I walk. Fogs and rains and warmer suns are gradually melting the snow; the days have grown sensibly longer; and I see how I shall get through the winter without adding to my wood-pile, for large fires are no longer necessary. I am on the alert for the first signs of spring, to hear the chance note of some arriving bird, or the striped squirrel's chirp, for his stores must be now nearly exhausted, or see the woodchuck venture out of his winter quarters. On the 13th of March, after I had heard the bluebird, song-sparrow, and red-wing, the ice was still nearly a foot thick.

Every incident connected with the breaking up of the rivers and ponds and the settling of the weather is particularly interesting to us who live in a climate of so great extremes. When the warmer days come, they who dwell near the river hear the ice crack at night with a startling whoop as loud as artillery, as if its icy fetters were rent from end to end, and within a few days see it rapidly going out.

At the approach of spring the red-squirrels got under my house, two at a time, directly under my feet as I sat reading or writing, and kept up the queerest chuckling and chirruping and vocal pirouetting and gurgling sounds that ever were heard; and when I stamped they only chirruped the louder, as if past all fear and respect in their mad pranks, defying humanity to stop them. No you don't—chickaree—chickaree. They were wholly deaf to my arguments, or failed to perceive their force, and fell into a strain of invective that was irresistible.

The first sparrow of spring! The year beginning with younger hope than ever! The faint silvery warblings heard over the partially bare and moist fields from the blue-bird, the song-sparrow, and the red-wing, as if the last flakes of winter tinkled as they fell!

The change from storm and winter to serene and mild weather, from dark and sluggish hours to bright and elastic ones, is a memorable crisis which all things proclaim. It is seemingly instantaneous at last. Suddenly an influx of light filled my house, though the evening was at hand, and the clouds of winter still overhung it, and the eaves were dripping with sleety rain. I looked out the window, and lo! where yesterday was cold gray ice there lay the transparent pond already calm and full of hope as in a summer evening.

A single gentle rain makes the grass many shades greener. So our prospects brighten on the influx of better thoughts. We should be blessed if we lived in the present always, and took advantage of every accident that befell us, like the grass which confesses the influence of the slightest dew that falls on it; and did not spend our time in atoning for the neglect of past opportunities, which we call doing our duty. We loiter in winter while it is already spring. In a pleasant spring morning all men's sins are forgiven. Such a day is a truce to vice. While such a sun holds out to burn, the vilest sinner may return. Through our own recovered innocence we discern the innocence of our neighbors.

On the 29th of April, as I was fishing from the bank of the river near the Nine-Acre-Corner bridge, standing on the quaking grass and willow roots, where the muskrats lurk, I heard a singular rattling sound, somewhat like that of the sticks which boys play with their fingers, when, looking up, I observed a very slight and graceful hawk, like a night-hawk, alternately soaring like a ripple and tumbling a rod or two over and over, showing the underside of its wings, which gleamed like a satin ribbon in the sun, or like the pearly inside of a shell.

Early in May, the oaks, hickories, maples, and other trees, just putting out amidst the pine woods around the pond, imparted a brightness like sunshine to the landscape, especially in cloudy days, as if the sun were breaking through mists and shining faintly on the hill-sides here and there.

Thus was my first year's life in the woods completed; and the second year was similar to it. I finally left Walden September 6th, 1847.

# Conclusion

I left the woods for as good a reason as I went there. Perhaps it seemed to me that I had several more lives to live, and could not spare any more time for that one. It is remarkable how easily and insensibly we fall into a particular route, and make a beaten track for ourselves. I had not lived there a week before my feet wore a path from my door to the pond-side; and though it is five or six years since I trod it, it is still quite distinct. It is true, I fear that others may have fallen into it, and so helped to keep it open. The surface of the earth is soft and impressible by the feet of men; and so with the paths which the mind travels. How worn and dusty, then, must be the highways of the world, how deep the ruts of tradition and conformity!

I learned this, at least, by my experiment; that if one advances confidently in the direction of his dreams, and endeavors to live the life which he has imagined, he will meet with a success unexpected in common hours. He will put some things behind, will pass an invisible boundary; new, universal, and more liberal laws will begin to establish themselves around and within him; or the old laws be expanded, and interpreted in his favor in a more liberal sense, and he will live with the license of a higher order of beings. In proportion as he simplifies his life, the laws of the universe will appear less complex, and solitude will not be solitude, nor poverty poverty, nor weakness weakness. If you have built castles in the air, your work need not be lost; that is where they should be. Now put the foundations under them.

It is a ridiculous demand which England and America make, that you shall speak so that they can understand you.

Why level downward to our dullest perception always, and praise that as common sense? The commonest sense is the sense of men asleep, which they express by snoring. Sometimes we are inclined to class those who are once-and-a-half-witted with the half-witted, because we appreciate only a third part of their wit. Some would find fault with the morning-red, if they ever got up early enough.

If a man does not keep pace with his companions, perhaps it is because he hears a different drummer. Let him step to the music which he hears, however measured or far away. It is not important that he should mature as soon as an apple-tree or an oak. Shall he turn his spring into summer?

However mean your life is, meet it and live it; do not shun it and call it hard names. It is not so bad as you are. It looks poorest when you are richest. The fault-finder will find faults even in paradise. Love your life, poor as it is. You may perhaps have some pleasant, thrilling, glorious hours, even in a poor-house. The setting sun is reflected from the windows of the alms-house as brightly as from the rich man's abode; the snow melts before its door as early in the spring. I do not see but a quiet mind may live as contentedly there, and have as cheering thoughts, as in a palace. Do not trouble yourself much to get new things, whether clothes or friends. Turn the old; return to them. Things do not change; we change. Sell your clothes and keep your thoughts. God will see that you do not want society.

There is an incessant influx of novelty into the world, and yet we tolerate incredible dulness. I need only suggest what kind of sermons are still listened to in the most enlightened countries. There are such words as joy and sorrow, but they are only the burden of a psalm, sung with a nasal twang, while we believe in the ordinary and mean. We think that we can change our clothes only. It is said that the British Empire is very large and respectable, and that the United States are a first-rate power. We do not believe that a tide rises and falls behind every man which can float the British Empire like a chip, if he should ever harbor it in his mind. The government of the world I live in was not framed, like that of Britain, in after-dinner conversations over the wine.

The life in us is like the water in the river. It may rise this year higher than man has ever known it, and flood the parched uplands; even this may be the eventful year, which will drown out all our muskrats.

Who knows what beautiful and winged life, whose egg has been buried for ages under many concentric layers of woodenness in the dead dry life of society, deposited at first in the alburnum of the green and living tree, which has been gradually converted into the semblance of its well-seasoned tomb,— heard perchance gnawing out now for years by the astonished family of man, as they sat round the festive board,—may unexpectedly come forth from amidst society's most trivial and handselled furniture, to enjoy its perfect summer life at last!

I do not say that John or Jonathan will realize all this; but such is the character of that morrow which mere lapse of time can never make to dawn. The light which puts out our eyes is darkness to us. Only that day dawns to which we are awake. There is more day to dawn. The sun is but a morning star.

# Power and Wealth
(1860)

# by Ralph Waldo Emerson

*The Immortal Classics on Will & Money—
Now in Special Condensations*

### Contents

Introduction  *Genius and Practicality* by Mitch Horowitz   120
I. Power   122
II. Wealth   131

## Introduction
# Genius and Practicality

Part of Ralph Waldo Emerson's greatness as a writer is that he never shied away from practicality. This was true of his philosophical descendant William James, as well. It can be argued that Emerson's most practical works—which include his essays *Power* and *Wealth*—were not among his greatest. Critic Irving Howe wrote that in such works the philosopher "merely tugs the complexities . . . into the shallows of the explicit."

There is truth in this charge. And yet this judgment fails to take account of Emerson's bravery. Emerson felt obligated to be direct—to provide his readers with plans of action. If this approach reduced philosophical heights, it also banished authorial cowardice. Emerson would not dodge the question of *how* to practice the kinds of self-driven living that his philosophical essays endorsed.

Hence, it is in his essays *Power* and *Wealth*, which Emerson published in *The Conduct of Life* in 1860, that the Transcendentalist prescribed exactly how and under what conditions a person can successfully assert his will in outer life.

In *Power*, Emerson names four essential elements to exercising personal power. The first—and that which sustains all the others—is to be "in sympathy with the course of things." Displaying his innate instinct for Taoism and other Eastern philosophies, Emerson believed that an individual could read the *nature of things* and seek to merge with it, like a twig carried downstream. "The mind that is parallel with the laws of nature," he writes, "will be in the current of events, and strong with their strength."

The second element of power is *health*. Emerson means this on different levels. He is speaking broadly of the vitality of body and spirit; the state of physicality and personal morale that sustains risks, seeks adventure, and completes plans. But he also speaks of routine bodily health, without which the individual's energies are sapped.

The third element is *concentration*. One of nature's laws is that concentration of energies brings impact. The concentration of a striking blow delivers the greatest force. Too often we deplete our energies by dispersing or spreading thin our aims and efforts. In *Power*, an imaginary oracle says: "Enlarge not thy destiny, endeavor not to do more than is given thee in charge." Like light focused in a laser, concentration into a single beam brings the greatest power.

The fourth and final element of power is *drilling*. By this Emerson means repeating a practice over and over until you can perform it with excellence. The martial artist repeats his movements and routines to the point where they enter his physical memory and are available to him under all conditions. Likewise, we must drill—or practice or rehearse—to the point where we have mastered our chosen task.

In the essay *Wealth*, Emerson declares, chin out, that the individual is "born to be rich." And by riches, the philosopher is not employing a coy metaphor. He means cold, hard cash. But he also identifies accumulation of capital as befitting only that person who uses it to productive ends. Emerson writes,

> Every man is a consumer, and ought to be a producer. He fails to make his place good in the world, unless he not only pays his debt, but also adds something to the common wealth. Nor can he do justice to his genius, without making some larger demand on the world than a bare subsistence. He is by constitution expensive, and needs to be rich.

Only those purchases that expand your power and abilities, he writes, leave you any richer. Indeed, wealth that fails to accompany expansion is wealth thrown away. "Nor is the man enriched," Emerson writes, "in repeating the old experiments of animal sensation." Rather, you are enriched when you increase your ability to earn, to do, and to grow. Wealth, properly understood, is power. That is why these essays are conjoined.

So, how do you earn wealth? Emerson outlines roughly three steps: 1) First filling some nonnegotiable, subsistence-level need in your own life: this what drove the primeval farmers, hunter-gathers, and villagers. 2) Next, applying one's particular talents to nature, and expansively filling the needs of others. If you do not know or understand your talents, you must start there before anything is possible. Your particular talent is a source of excellence. And, finally, 3) using your wealth for the purposes of productiveness: paying down debts, making compound investments, and procuring the tools and talents of your trade. Building and expanding is the only sound way to riches. And such things also reflect your code and fiber as a progressing being.

By entering the mechanics of practicality, did Emerson sacrifice some of his transcendental splendor? Some thought so; I see it differently. If Emerson had avoided such an approach he would have been guilty of failing to take his philosophy onto the road. Complexity does not excuse inaction. And here I am reminded of an observation by the flawed and brilliant poet Ezra Pound, to whom I cede the last word: "But to have done instead of not doing/ This is not vanity."

—Mitch Horowitz

# I. Power

Who shall set a limit to the influence of a human being? There are men, who, by their sympathetic attractions, carry nations with them, and lead the activity of the human race. And if there be such a tie, that, wherever the mind of man goes, nature will accompany him, perhaps there are men whose magnetisms are of that force to draw material and elemental powers, and, where they appear, immense instrumentalities organize around them. Life is a search after power; and this is an element with which the world is so saturated,—there is no chink or crevice in which it is not lodged,—that no honest seeking goes unrewarded. A man should prize events and possessions as the ore in which this fine mineral is found; and he can well afford to let events and possessions, and the breath of the body go, if their value has been added to him in the shape of power. If he have secured the elixir, he can spare the wide gardens from which it was distilled. A cultivated man, wise to know and bold to perform, is the end to which nature works, and the education of the will is the flowering and result of all this geology and astronomy.

All successful men have agreed in one thing,—they were *causationists*. They believed that things went not by luck, but by law; that there was not a weak or a cracked link in the chain that joins the first and last of things. A belief in causality, or strict connection between every trifle and the principle of being, and, in consequence, belief in compensation, or, that nothing is got for nothing,—characterizes all valuable minds, and must control every effort that is made by an industrious one. The most valiant men are the best believers in the tension of the laws. "All the great captains," said Bonaparte, "have performed vast achievements by conforming with the rules of the art,—by adjusting efforts to obstacles."

The key to the age may be this, or that, or the other, as the young orators describe; —the key to all ages is—Imbecility; imbecility in the vast majority of men, at all times, and, even in heroes, in all but certain eminent moments; victims of gravity, custom, and fear. This gives force to the strong,—that the multitude have no habit of self-reliance or original action.

We must reckon success a constitutional trait. Courage,—the old physicians taught, (and their meaning holds, if their physiology is a little mythical,)—courage, or the degree of life, is as the degree of circulation of the blood in the arteries. Where the arteries hold their blood, is courage and adventure possible. Where they pour it unrestrained into the veins, the spirit is low and feeble. For performance of great mark, it needs extraordinary health. If Eric is in robust health, and has slept well, and is at the top of his condition, and thirty years old, at his departure from Greenland, he will steer west, and his ships will reach Newfoundland. But take out Eric, and put in a stronger and bolder man,—Biorn, or Thorfin,—and the ships will, with just as much ease, sail six hundred, one thousand, fifteen hundred miles further, and reach Labrador and New England. There is no chance in results. With adults, as with children, one class enter cordially into the game, and whirl with the whirling world; the others have cold hands, and remain bystanders; or are only dragged in by the humor and vivacity of those who can carry a dead weight. The first wealth is health. Sickness is poor-spirited, and cannot serve any one: it must husband its resources to live. But health or fulness answers its own ends, and has to spare, runs over, and inundates the neighborhoods and creeks of other men's necessities.

All power is of one kind, a sharing of the nature of the world. The mind that is parallel with the laws of nature will be in the current of events, and strong with their strength. One man is made of the same stuff of which events are made; is in sympathy with the course of things; can predict it. Whatever befalls, befalls him first; so that he is equal to whatever shall happen. A man who knows men, can talk well on politics, trade, law, war, religion. For, everywhere, men are led in the same manners.

The advantage of a strong pulse is not to be supplied by any labor, art, or concert. It is like the climate, which easily rears a crop, which no glass, or irrigation, or tillage, or manures, can elsewhere rival. It is like the opportunity of a city like New York, or Constantinople, which needs no diplomacy to force capital or genius or labor to it. They come of themselves, as the waters flow to it.

This affirmative force is in one, and is not in another, as one horse has the spring in him, and another in the whip. "On the neck of the young man," said Hafiz, "sparkles no gem so gracious as enterprise." Import into any stationary district, as into an old Dutch population in New York or Pennsylvania, or among the planters of Virginia, a colony of hardy Yankees, with seething brains, heads full of steam-hammer, pulley, crank, and toothed wheel,—and everything begins to shine with values. In every company, there is not only the active and passive sex, but, in both men and women, a deeper and more important *sex of mind*, namely, the inventive or creative class of both men and women, and the uninventive or accepting class. Each plus man represents his set, and, if he have the accidental advantage of personal ascendency,—which implies neither more nor less of talent, but merely the temperamental or taming eye of a soldier or a schoolmaster, (which one has, and one has not, as one has a black moustache and one a blond,) then quite easily and without envy or resistance, all his coadjutors and feeders will admit his right to absorb them.

There is always room for a man of force, and he makes room for many. Society is a troop of thinkers, and the best heads among them take the best places. A feeble man can see the farms that are fenced and tilled, the houses that are built. The strong man sees the possible houses and farms. His eye makes estates, as fast as the sun breeds clouds.

When a new boy comes into school, when a man travels, and encounters strangers every day, or, when into any old club a new comer is domesticated, that happens which befalls, when a strange ox is driven into a pen or pasture where cattle are kept; there is at once a trial of strength between the best pair of horns and the new comer, and it is settled thenceforth which is the leader. So now, there is a measuring of strength, very courteous, but decisive, and an acquiescence thenceforward when these two meet. Each reads his fate in the other's eyes. The weaker party finds, that none of his information or wit quite fits the occasion. He thought he knew this or that: he finds that he omitted to learn the end of it. Nothing that he knows will quite hit the mark, whilst all the rival's arrows are good, and well thrown. But if he knew all the facts in the encyclopaedia, it would not help him: for this is an affair of presence of mind, of attitude, of aplomb: the opponent has the sun and wind, and, in every cast, the choice of weapon and mark; and, when he himself is matched with some other antagonist, his own shafts fly well and hit. 'Tis a question of stomach and constitution. The second man is as good as the first,—perhaps better; but has not stoutness or stomach, as the first has, and so his wit seems over-fine or under-fine.

Health is good,—power, life, that resists disease, poison, and all enemies, and is conservative, as well as creative. Vivacity, leadership, must be had, and we are not allowed to be nice in choosing. And we have a certain instinct, that where is great amount of life, though gross and peccant, it has its own checks and purifications, and will be found at last in harmony with moral laws.

We prosper with such vigor, that, like thrifty trees, which grow in spite of ice, lice, mice, and borers, so we do not suffer from the profligate swarms. The huge animals nourish huge parasites, and the rancor of the disease attests the strength of the constitution.

All kinds of power usually emerge at the same time; good energy, and bad; power of mind, with physical health; the ecstasies of devotion, with the exasperations of debauchery. The same elements are always present, only sometimes these conspicuous, and sometimes those; what was yesterday foreground, being to-day background,—what was surface, playing now a not less effective part as basis. The longer the drought lasts, the more is the atmosphere surcharged with water. The faster the ball falls to the sun, the force to fly off is by so much augmented. And, in morals, wild liberty breeds iron conscience; natures with great impulses have great resources, and return from far. In politics, the sons of democrats will be whigs; whilst red republicanism, in the father, is a spasm of nature to engender an intolerable tyrant in the next age. On the other hand, conservatism, ever more timorous and narrow, disgusts the children, and drives them for a mouthful of fresh air into radicalism.

Those who have most of this coarse energy,—the 'bruisers,' who have run the gauntlet of caucus and tavern through the county or the state, have their own vices, but they have the good nature of strength and courage. Fierce and unscrupulous, they are usually frank and direct, and above falsehood. Our politics fall into bad hands, and churchmen and men of refinement, it seems agreed, are not fit persons to send to Congress. Politics is a deleterious profession, like some poisonous handicrafts. Men in power have no opinions, but may be had cheap for any opinion, for any purpose,—and if it be only a question between the most civil and the most forcible, I lean to the last.

In trade, also, this energy usually carries a trace of ferocity. Philanthropic and religious bodies do not commonly make their executive officers out of saints. The communities hitherto founded by Socialists,—the Jesuits, the Port-Royalists, the American communities at New Harmony, at Brook Farm, at Zoar, are only possible, by installing Judas as steward. The rest of the offices may be filled by good burgesses. The pious and charitable proprietor has a foreman not quite so pious and charitable. The most amiable of country gentlemen has a certain pleasure in the teeth of the bull-dog which guards his orchard. Of the Shaker society, it was formerly a sort of proverb in the country, that they always sent the devil to market. And in representations of the Deity, painting, poetry, and popular religion have ever drawn the wrath from Hell. It is an esoteric doctrine of society, that a little wickedness is good to make muscle; as if conscience were not good for hands and legs, as if poor decayed formalists of law and order cannot run like wild goats, wolves, and conies; that, as there is a use in medicine for poisons, so the world cannot move without rogues; that public spirit and the ready hand are as well found among the malignants. 'Tis not very rare, the coincidence of sharp private and political practice, with public spirit, and good neighborhood.

Whilst thus the energy for originating and executing work, deforms itself by excess, and so our axe chops off our own fingers,—this evil is not without remedy. All the elements whose aid man calls in, will sometimes become his masters, especially those of most subtle force. Shall he, then, renounce steam, fire, and electricity, or, shall he learn to deal with them? The rule for this whole class of agencies is,—all plus is good; only put it in the right place.

Men of this surcharge of arterial blood cannot live on nuts, herb-tea, and elegies; cannot read novels, and play whist; cannot satisfy all their wants at the Thursday Lecture, or the Boston Athenaeum. They pine for adventure, and must go to Pike's Peak; had rather die by the hatchet of a Pawnee, than sit all day and every day at a counting-room desk. They are made for war, for the sea, for mining, hunting, and clearing; for hair-breadth adventures, huge risks, and the joy of eventful living. Some men cannot endure an hour of calm at sea.

The excess of virility has the same importance in general history, as in private and industrial life. Strong race or strong individual rests at last on natural forces, which are best in the savage, who, like the beasts around him, is still in reception of the milk from the teats of Nature. Cut off the connection between any of our works, and this aboriginal source, and the work is shallow. The people lean on this, and the mob is not quite so bad an argument as we sometimes say, for it has this good side. "March without the people," said a French deputy from the tribune, "and you march into night: their instincts are a finger-pointing of Providence, always turned toward real benefit."

The best anecdotes of this force are to be had from savage life, in explorers, soldiers, and buccaneers. But who cares for fallings-out of assassins, and fights of bears, or grindings of icebergs? Physical force has no value, where there is nothing else. Snow in snow-banks, fire in volcanoes and solfataras is cheap. The luxury of ice is in tropical countries, and midsummer days. The luxury of fire is, to have a little on our hearth: and of electricity, not volleys of the charged cloud, but the manageable stream on the battery-wires.

In history, the great moment is, when the savage is just ceasing to be a savage, with all his hairy Pelasgic strength directed on his sense of beauty;—and you have Pericles and Phidias,—not yet passed over into the Corinthian civility. Everything good in nature and the world is in that moment of transition, when the swarthy juices still flow plentifully from nature, but their astringency or acridity is got out by ethics and humanity.

The triumphs of peace have been in some proximity to war. Whilst the hand was still familiar with the sword-hilt, whilst the habits of the camp were still visible in the port and complexion of the gentleman, his intellectual power culminated: the compression and tension of these stern conditions is a training for the finest and softest arts, and can rarely be compensated in tranquil times, except by some analogous vigor drawn from occupations as hardy as war.

We say that success is constitutional; depends on a *plus* condition of mind and body, on power of work, on courage; that it is of main efficacy in carrying on the world, and, though rarely found in the right state for an article of commerce, but oftener in the supersaturate or excess, which makes it dangerous and destructive, yet it cannot be spared, and must be had in that form, and absorbents provided to take off its edge.

The affirmative class monopolize the homage of mankind. They originate and execute all the great feats. What a force was coiled up in the skull of Napoleon! Of the sixty thousand men making his army at Eylau, it seems some thirty thousand were thieves and burglars. The men whom, in peaceful communities, we hold if we can, with iron at their legs, in prisons, under the muskets of sentinels, this man dealt with, hand to hand, dragged them to their duty, and won his victories by their bayonets.

This aboriginal might gives a surprising pleasure when it appears under conditions of supreme refinement, as in the proficients in high art. When Michel Angelo was forced to paint the Sistine Chapel in fresco, of which art he knew nothing, he went down into the Pope's gardens behind the Vatican, and with a shovel dug out ochres, red and yellow, mixed them with glue and water with his own hands, and having, after many trials, at last suited himself, climbed his ladders, and painted away, week after week, month after month, the sibyls and prophets. He surpassed his successors in rough vigor, as much as in purity of intellect and refinement. He was not crushed by his one picture left unfinished at last. Michel was wont to draw his figures first in skeleton, then to clothe them with flesh, and lastly to drape them. "Ah!" said a brave painter to me, thinking on these things, "if a man has failed, you will find he has dreamed instead of working. There is no way to success in our art, but to take off your coat, grind paint, and work like a digger on the railroad, all day and every day."

Success goes thus invariably with a certain *plus* or positive power: an ounce of power must balance an ounce of weight. And, though a man cannot return into his mother's womb, and be born with new amounts of vivacity, yet there are two economies, which are the best *succedanea* which the case admits. The first is, the stopping off decisively our miscellaneous activity, and concentrating our force on one or a few points; as the gardener, by severe pruning, forces the sap of the tree into one or two vigorous limbs, instead of suffering it to spindle into a sheaf of twigs.

"Enlarge not thy destiny," said the oracle: "endeavor not to do more than is given thee in charge." The one prudence in life is concentration; the one evil is dissipation: and it makes no difference whether our dissipations are coarse or fine; property and its cares, friends, and a social habit, or politics, or music, or feasting. Everything is good which takes away one plaything and delusion more, and drives us home to add one stroke of faithful work. Friends, books, pictures, lower duties, talents, flatteries, hopes,—all are distractions which cause oscillations in our giddy balloon, and make a good poise and a straight course impossible. You must elect your work; you shall take what your brain can, and drop all the rest. Only so, can that amount of vital force accumulate, which can make the step from knowing to doing. No matter how much faculty of idle seeing a man has, the step from knowing to doing is rarely taken. 'Tis a step out of a chalk circle of imbecility into fruitfulness. Many an artist lacking this, lacks all: he sees the masculine Angelo or Cellini with despair. He, too, is up to Nature and the First Cause in his thought. But the spasm to collect and swing his whole being into one act, he has not. The poet Campbell said, that "a man accustomed to work was equal to any achievement he resolved on, and, that, for himself, necessity not inspiration was the prompter of his muse."

Concentration is the secret of strength in politics, in war, in trade, in short, in all management of human affairs. One of the high anecdotes of the world is the reply of Newton to the inquiry, "how he had been able to achieve his discoveries?"—"By always intending my mind." Or if you will have a text from politics, take this from Plutarch: "There was, in the whole city, but one street in which Pericles was ever seen, the street which led to the market-place and the council house. He declined all invitations to banquets, and all gay assemblies and company. During the whole period of his administration, he never dined at the table of a friend." Or if we seek an example from trade,—"I hope," said a good man to Rothschild, "your children are not too fond of money and business: I am sure you would not wish that."—"I am sure I should wish that: I wish them to give mind, soul, heart, and body to business,—that is the way to be happy. It requires a great deal of boldness and a great deal of caution, to make a great fortune, and when you have got it, it requires ten times as much wit to keep it. If I were to listen to all the projects proposed to me, I should ruin myself very soon. Stick to one business, young man. Stick to your brewery, and you will be the great brewer of London. Be brewer, and banker, and merchant, and manufacturer, and you will soon be in the Gazette."

Many men are knowing, many are apprehensive and tenacious, but they do not rush to a decision. But in our flowing affairs a decision must be made,—the best, if you can; but any is better than none. There are twenty ways of going to a point, and one is the shortest; but set out at once on one. A man who has that presence of mind which can bring to him on the instant all he knows, is worth for action a dozen men who know as much, but can only bring it to light slowly. The good Speaker in the House is not the man who knows the theory of parliamentary tactics, but the man who decides off-hand. The good judge is not he who does hair-splitting justice to every allegation, but who, aiming at substantial justice, rules something intelligible for the guidance of suitors. The good lawyer is not the man who has an eye to every side and angle of contingency, and qualifies all his qualifications, but who throws himself on your part so heartily, that he can get you out of a scrape. Dr. Johnson said, in one of his flowing sentences, "Miserable beyond all names of wretchedness is that unhappy pair, who are doomed to reduce beforehand to the principles of abstract reason all the details of each domestic day. There are cases where little can be said, and much must be done."

The second substitute for temperament is drill, the power of use and routine. The hack is a better roadster than the Arab barb. In chemistry, the galvanic stream, slow, but continuous, is equal in power to the electric spark, and is, in our arts, a better agent. So in human action, against the spasm of energy, we offset the continuity of drill. We spread the same amount of force over much time, instead of condensing it into a moment. 'Tis the same ounce of gold here in a ball, and there in a leaf. At West Point, Col. Buford, the chief engineer, pounded with a hammer on the trunnions of a cannon, until he broke them off. He fired a piece of ordnance some hundred times in swift succession, until it burst. Now which stroke broke the trunnion? Every stroke. Which blast burst the piece? Every blast. The worst provincial company of actors would go through a play better than the best amateur company. The worst regular troops will beat the best volunteers. Practice is nine tenths. A course of mobs is good practice for orators. All the great speakers were bad speakers at first. Stumping it through England for seven years, made Cobden a consummate debater. Stumping it through New England for twice seven, trained Wendell Phillips. The way to learn German, is, to read the same dozen pages over and over a hundred times, till you know every word and particle in them, and can pronounce and repeat them by heart. No genius can recite a ballad at first reading, so well as mediocrity can at the fifteenth or twentieth reading. A humorous friend of mine thinks, that the reason why Nature is so perfect in her art, and gets up such inconceivably fine sunsets, is, that she has learned how, at last, by dint of doing the same thing so very often. Cannot one converse better on a topic on which he has experience, than on one which is new? Hence the use of drill, and the worthlessness of amateurs to cope with practitioners. Six hours every day at the piano, only to give facility of touch; six hours a day at painting, only to give command of the odious materials, oil, ochres, and brushes. The masters say, that they know a master in music, only by seeing the pose of the hands on the keys;—so difficult and vital an act is the command of the instrument. To have learned the use of the tools, by thousands of manipulations; to have learned the arts of reckoning, by endless adding and dividing, is the power of the mechanic and the clerk.

I remarked in England, in confirmation of a frequent experience at home, that, in literary circles, the men of trust and consideration, bookmakers, editors, university deans and professors, bishops, too, were by no means men of the largest literary talent, but usually of a low and ordinary intellectuality, with a sort of mercantile activity and working talent. Indifferent hacks and mediocrities tower, by pushing their forces to a lucrative point, or by working power, over multitudes of superior men.

I have not forgotten that there are sublime considerations which limit the value of talent and superficial success. We can easily overpraise the vulgar hero. There are sources on which we have not drawn. I know what I abstain from. But this force or spirit, being the means relied on by Nature for bringing the work of the day about,—as far as we attach importance to household life, and the prizes of the world, we must respect that. And I hold, that an economy may be applied to it; it is as much a subject of exact law and arithmetic as fluids and gases are; it may be husbanded, or wasted; every man is efficient only as he is a container or vessel of this force, and never was any signal act or achievement in history, but by this expenditure. This is not gold, but the gold-maker; not the fame, but the exploit.

If these forces and this husbandry are within reach of our will, and the laws of them can be read, we infer that all success, and all conceivable benefit for man, is also, first or last, within his reach, and has its own sublime economies by which it may be attained. The world is mathematical, and has no casualty, in all its vast and flowing curve. Success has no more eccentricity, than the gingham and muslin we weave in our mills. I know no more affecting lesson to our busy, plotting New England brains, than to go into one of the factories with which we have lined all the watercourses in the States. A man hardly knows how much he is a machine, until he begins to make telegraph, loom, press, and locomotive, in his own image. But in these, he is forced to leave out his follies and hindrances, so that when we go to the mill, the machine is more moral than we. Let a man dare go to a loom, and see if he be equal to it. Let machine confront machine, and see how they come out. The world-mill is more complex than the calico-mill, and the architect stooped less. In the gingham-mill, a broken thread or a shred spoils the web through a piece of a hundred yards, and is traced back to the girl that wove it, and lessens her wages. The stockholder, on being shown this, rubs his hands with delight. Are you so cunning, Mr. Profitloss, and do you expect to swindle your master and employer, in the web you weave? A day is a more magnificent cloth than any muslin, the mechanism that makes it is infinitely cunninger, and you shall not conceal the sleezy, fraudulent, rotten hours you have slipped into the piece, nor fear that any honest thread, or straighter steel, or more inflexible shaft, will not testify in the web.

# II. Wealth

As soon as a stranger is introduced into any company, one of the first questions which all wish to have answered, is, How does that man get his living? And with reason. He is no whole man until he knows how to earn a blameless livelihood. Society is barbarous, until every industrious man can get his living without dishonest customs.

Every man is a consumer, and ought to be a producer. He fails to make his place good in the world, unless he not only pays his debt, but also adds something to the common wealth. Nor can he do justice to his genius, without making some larger demand on the world than a bare subsistence. He is by constitution expensive, and needs to be rich.

Wealth has its source in applications of the mind to nature, from the rudest strokes of spade and axe, up to the last secrets of art. Intimate ties subsist between thought and all production; because a better order is equivalent to vast amounts of brute labor. The forces and the resistances are Nature's, but the mind acts in bringing things from where they abound to where they are wanted; in wise combining; in directing the practice of the useful arts, and in the creation of finer values, by fine art, by eloquence, by song, or the reproductions of memory. Wealth is in applications of mind to nature; and the art of getting rich consists not in industry, much less in saving, but in a better order, in timeliness, in being at the right spot. One man has stronger arms, or longer legs; another sees by the course of streams, and growth of markets, where land will be wanted, makes a clearing to the river, goes to sleep, wakes up rich. Steam is no stronger now, than it was a hundred years ago; but is put to better use. A clever fellow was acquainted with the expansive force of steam; he also saw the wealth of wheat and grass rotting in Michigan. Then he cunningly screws on the steam-pipe to the wheat-crop. Puff now, O Steam! The steam puffs and expands as before, but this time it is dragging all Michigan at its back to hungry New York and hungry England. Coal lay in ledges under the ground since the Flood, until a laborer with pick and windlass brings it to the surface. We may well call it black diamonds. Every basket is power and civilization. For coal is a portable climate. It carries the heat of the tropics to Labrador and the polar circle: and it is the means of transporting itself whithersoever it is wanted. Watt and Stephenson whispered in the ear of mankind their secret, that *a half-ounce of coal will draw two tons a mile*, and coal carries coal, by rail and by boat, to make Canada as warm as Calcutta, and with its comfort brings its industrial power.

When the farmer's peaches are taken from under the tree, and carried into town, they have a new look, and a hundredfold value over the fruit which grew on the same bough, and lies fulsomely on the ground. The craft of the merchant is this bringing a thing from where it abounds, to where it is costly.

Wealth begins in a tight roof that keeps the rain and wind out; in a good pump that yields you plenty of sweet water; in two suits of clothes, so to change your dress when you are wet; in dry sticks to burn; in a good double-wick lamp; and three meals; in a horse, or a locomotive, to cross the land; in a boat to cross the sea; in tools to work with; in books to read; and so, in giving, on all sides, by tools and auxiliaries, the greatest possible extension to our powers, as if it added feet, and hands, and eyes, and blood, length to the day, and knowledge, and good-will.

Wealth begins with these articles of necessity. And here we must recite the iron law which Nature thunders in these northern climates. First, she requires that each man should feed himself. If, happily, his fathers have left him no inheritance, he must go to work, and by making his wants less, or his gains more, he must draw himself out of that state of pain and insult in which she forces the beggar to lie. She gives him no rest until this is done: she starves, taunts, and torments him, takes away warmth, laughter, sleep, friends, and daylight, until he has fought his way to his own loaf. Then, less peremptorily, but still with sting enough, she urges him to the acquisition of such things as belong to him. Every warehouse and shop-window, every fruit-tree, every thought of every hour, opens a new want to him, which it concerns his power and dignity to gratify. It is of no use to argue the wants down: the philosophers have laid the greatness of man in making his wants few; but will a man content himself with a hut and a handful of dried pease? He is born to be rich. He is thoroughly related; and is tempted out by his appetites and fancies to the conquest of this and that piece of nature, until he finds his well-being in the use of his planet, and of more planets than his own. Wealth requires, besides the crust of bread and the roof,—the freedom of the city, the freedom of the earth, travelling, machinery, the benefits of science, music, and fine arts, the best culture, and the best company. He is the rich man who can avail himself of all men's faculties. He is the richest man who knows how to draw a benefit from the labors of the greatest number of men, of men in distant countries, and in past times. The same correspondence that is between thirst in the stomach, and water in the spring, exists between the whole of man and the whole of nature. The elements offer their service to him. The sea, washing the equator and the poles, offers its perilous aid, and the power and empire that follow it,—day by day to his craft and audacity. "Beware of me," it says, "but if you can hold me, I am the key to all the lands." Fire offers, on its side, an equal power. Fire, steam, lightning, gravity, ledges of rock, mines of iron, lead, quicksilver, tin, and gold; forests of all woods; fruits of all climates; animals of all habits; the powers of tillage; the fabrics of his chemic laboratory; the webs of his loom; the masculine draught of his locomotive, the talismans of the machine-shop; all grand and subtile things, minerals, gases, ethers, passions, war, trade, government, are his natural playmates, and, according to the excellence of the machinery in each human being, is his attraction for the instruments he is to employ. The world is his tool-chest, and he is successful, or his education is carried on just so far, as is the marriage of his faculties with nature, or, the degree in which he takes up things into himself.

The strong race is strong on these terms. The Saxons are the merchants of the world; now, for a thousand years, the leading race, and by nothing more than their quality of personal independence, and, in its special modification, pecuniary independence. No reliance for bread and games on the government, no clanship, no patriarchal style of living by the revenues of a chief, no marrying-on,—no system of clientship suits them; but every man must pay his scot. The English are prosperous and peaceable, with their habit of considering that every man must take care of himself, and has himself to thank, if he do not maintain and improve his position in society.

The subject of economy mixes itself with morals, inasmuch as it is a peremptory point of virtue that a man's independence be secured. Poverty demoralizes. A man in debt is so far a slave; and Wall-street thinks it easy for a millionaire to be a man of his word, a man of honor, but, that, in failing circumstances, no man can be relied on to keep his integrity. And when one observes in the hotels and palaces of our Atlantic capitals, the habit of expense, the riot of the senses, the absence of bonds, clanship, fellow-feeling of any kind, he feels, that, when a man or a woman is driven to the wall, the chances of integrity are frightfully diminished, as if virtue were coming to be a luxury which few could afford, or, as Burke said, "at a market almost too high for humanity." He may fix his inventory of necessities and of enjoyments on what scale he pleases, but if he wishes the power and privilege of thought, the chalking out his own career, and having society on his own terms, he must bring his wants within his proper power to satisfy.

The manly part is to do with might and main what you can do. The world is full of fops who never did anything, and who have persuaded beauties and men of genius to wear their fop livery, and these will deliver the fop opinion, that it is not respectable to be seen earning a living; that it is much more respectable to spend without earning; and this doctrine of the snake will come also from the elect sons of light; for wise men are not wise at all hours, and will speak five times from their taste or their humor, to once from their reason. The brave workman, who might betray his feeling of it in his manners, if he do not succumb in his practice, must replace the grace or elegance forfeited, by the merit of the work done. No matter whether he make shoes, or statues, or laws. It is the privilege of any human work which is well done to invest the doer with a certain haughtiness. He can well afford not to conciliate, whose faithful work will answer for him. The mechanic at his bench carries a quiet heart and assured manners, and deals on even terms with men of any condition. The artist has made his picture so true, that it disconcerts criticism. The statue is so beautiful, that it contracts no stain from the market, but makes the market a silent gallery for itself. The case of the young lawyer was pitiful to disgust,—a paltry matter of buttons or tweezer-cases; but the determined youth saw in it an aperture to insert his dangerous wedges, made the insignificance of the thing forgotten, and gave fame by his sense and energy to the name and affairs of the Tittleton snuffbox factory.

Society in large towns is babyish, and wealth is made a toy. The life of pleasure is so ostentatious, that a shallow observer must believe that this is the agreed best use of wealth, and, whatever is pretended, it ends in cosseting. But, if this were the main use of surplus capital, it would bring us to barricades, burned towns, and tomahawks, presently. Men of sense esteem wealth to be the assimilation of nature to themselves, the converting of the sap and juices of the planet to the incarnation and nutriment of their design. Power is what they want,—not candy;—power to execute their design, power to give legs and feet, form and actuality to their thought, which, to a clear-sighted man, appears the end for which the Universe exists, and all its resources might be well applied. Columbus thinks that the sphere is a problem for practical navigation, as well as for closet geometry, and looks on all kings and peoples as cowardly landsmen, until they dare fit him out. Few men on the planet have more truly belonged to it. But he was forced to leave much of his map blank. His successors inherited his map, and inherited his fury to complete it.

So the men of the mine, telegraph, mill, map, and survey,—the monomaniacs, who talk up their project in marts, and offices, and entreat men to subscribe:—how did our factories get built? how did North America get netted with iron rails, except by the importunity of these orators, who dragged all the prudent men in? Is party the madness of many for the gain of a few? This speculative genius is the madness of few for the gain of the world. The projectors are sacrificed, but the public is the gainer. Each of these idealists, working after his thought, would make it tyrannical, if he could. He is met and antagonized by other speculators, as hot as he. The equilibrium is preserved by these counteractions, as one tree keeps down another in the forest, that it may not absorb all the sap in the ground. And the supply in nature of railroad presidents, copper-miners, grand-junctioners, smoke-burners, fire-annihilators, &c., is limited by the same law which keeps the proportion in the supply of carbon, of alum, and of hydrogen.

To be rich is to have a ticket of admission to the master-works and chief men of each race. It is to have the sea, by voyaging; to visit the mountains, Niagara, the Nile, the desert, Rome, Paris, Constantinople; to see galleries, libraries, arsenals, manufactories. The reader of Humboldt's "Cosmos" follows the marches of a man whose eyes, ears, and mind are armed by all the science, arts, and implements which mankind have anywhere accumulated, and who is using these to add to the stock. So is it with Denon, Beckford, Belzoni, Wilkinson, Layard, Kane, Lepsius, and Livingston. "The rich man," says Saadi, "is everywhere expected and at home." The rich take up something more of the world into man's life. They include the country as well as the town, the ocean-side, the White Hills, the Far West, and the old European homesteads of man, in their notion of available material. The world is his, who has money to go over it. He arrives at the sea-shore, and a sumptuous ship has floored and carpeted for him the stormy Atlantic, and made it a luxurious hotel, amid the horrors of tempests. The Persians say, "'Tis the same to him who wears a shoe, as if the whole earth were covered with leather."

Kings are said to have long arms, but every man should have long arms, and should pluck his living, his instruments, his power, and his knowing, from the sun, moon, and stars. Is not then the demand to be rich legitimate? Yet, I have never seen a rich man. I have never seen a man as rich as all men ought to be, or, with an adequate command of nature. The pulpit and the press have many commonplaces denouncing the thirst for wealth; but if men should take these moralists at their word, and leave off aiming to be rich, the moralists would rush to rekindle at all hazards this love of power in the people, lest civilization should be undone. Men are urged by their ideas to acquire the command over nature. Ages derive a culture from the wealth of Roman Caesars, Leo Tenths, magnificent Kings of France, Grand Dukes of Tuscany, Dukes of Devonshire, Townleys, Vernons, and Peels, in England; or whatever great proprietors. It is the interest of all men, that there should be Vaticans and Louvres full of noble works of art; British Museums, and French Gardens of Plants, Philadelphia Academies of Natural History, Bodleian, Ambrosian, Royal, Congressional Libraries. It is the interest of all that there should be Exploring Expeditions; Captain Cooks to voyage round the world, Rosses, Franklins, Richardsons, and Kanes, to find the magnetic and the geographic poles. We are all richer for the measurement of a degree of latitude on the earth's surface. Our navigation is safer for the chart. How intimately our knowledge of the system of the Universe rests on that!—and a true economy in a state or an individual will forget its frugality in behalf of claims like these.

Whilst it is each man's interest, that, not only ease and convenience of living, but also wealth or surplus product should exist somewhere, it need not be in his hands. Often it is very undesirable to him. Goethe said well, "nobody should be rich but those who understand it." Some men are born to own, and can animate all their possessions. Others cannot: their owning is not graceful; seems to be a compromise of their character: they seem to steal their own dividends. They should own who can administer; not they who hoard and conceal; not they who, the greater proprietors they are, are only the greater beggars, but they whose work carves out work for more, opens a path for all. For he is the rich man in whom the people are rich, and he is the poor man in whom the people are poor: and how to give all access to the masterpieces of art and nature, is the problem of civilization. The socialism of our day has done good service in setting men on thinking how certain civilizing benefits, now only enjoyed by the opulent, can be enjoyed by all. For example, the providing to each man the means and apparatus of science, and of the arts. There are many articles good for occasional use, which few men are able to own. Every man wishes to see the ring of Saturn, the satellites and belts of Jupiter and Mars; the mountains and craters in the moon: yet how few can buy a telescope! and of those, scarcely one would like the trouble of keeping it in order, and exhibiting it. So of electrical and chemical apparatus, and many the like things. Every man may have occasion to consult books which he does not care to possess, such as cyclopaedias, dictionaries, tables, charts, maps, and public documents: pictures also of birds, beasts, fishes, shells, trees, flowers, whose names he desires to know.

There is a refining influence from the arts of Design on a prepared mind, which is as positive as that of music, and not to be supplied from any other source. But pictures, engravings, statues, and casts, beside their first cost, entail expenses, as of galleries and keepers for the exhibition; and the use which any man can make of them is rare, and their value, too, is much enhanced by the numbers of men who can share their enjoyment. In the Greek cities, it was reckoned profane, that any person should pretend a property in a work of art, which belonged to all who could behold it. I think sometimes,—could I only have music on my own terms;—could I live in a great city, and know where I could go whenever I wished the ablution and inundation of musical waves,—that were a bath and a medicine.

If properties of this kind were owned by states, towns, and lyceums, they would draw the bonds of neighborhood closer. A town would exist to an intellectual purpose. In Europe, where the feudal forms secure the permanence of wealth in certain families, those families buy and preserve these things, and lay them open to the public. But in America, where democratic institutions divide every estate into small portions, after a few years, the public should step into the place of these proprietors, and provide this culture and inspiration for the citizen.

Man was born to be rich, or, inevitably grows rich by the use of his faculties; by the union of thought with nature. Property is an intellectual production. The game requires coolness, right reasoning, promptness, and patience in the players. Cultivated labor drives out brute labor. An infinite number of shrewd men, in infinite years, have arrived at certain best and shortest ways of doing, and this accumulated skill in arts, cultures, harvestings, curings, manufactures, navigations, exchanges, constitutes the worth of our world to-day.

Commerce is a game of skill, which every man cannot play, which few men can play well. The right merchant is one who has the just average of faculties we call common sense; a man of a strong affinity for facts, who makes up his decision on what he has seen. He is thoroughly persuaded of the truths of arithmetic. There is always a reason, in the man, for his good or bad fortune, and so, in making money. Men talk as if there were some magic about this, and believe in magic, in all parts of life. He knows, that all goes on the old road, pound for pound, cent for cent,—for every effect a perfect cause,—and that good luck is another name for tenacity of purpose. He insures himself in every transaction, and likes small and sure gains. Probity and closeness to the facts are the basis, but the masters of the art add a certain long arithmetic. The problem is, to combine many and remote operations, with the accuracy and adherence to the facts, which is easy in near and small transactions; so to arrive at gigantic results, without any compromise of safety. Napoleon was fond of telling the story of the Marseilles banker, who said to his visitor, surprised at the contrast between the splendor of the banker's chateau and hospitality, and the meanness of the counting-room in which he had seen him,—"Young man, you are too young to understand how masses are formed,—the true and only power,—whether composed of money, water, or men, it is all alike,—a mass is an immense centre of motion, but it must be begun, it must be kept up:"—and he might have added, that the way in which it must be begun and kept up, is, by obedience to the law of particles.

Success consists in close appliance to the laws of the world, and, since those laws are intellectual and moral, an intellectual and moral obedience. Political Economy is as good a book wherein to read the life of man, and the ascendency of laws over all private and hostile influences, as any Bible which has come down to us.

Money is representative, and follows the nature and fortunes of the owner. The coin is a delicate meter of civil, social, and moral changes. The farmer is covetous of his dollar, and with reason. It is no waif to him. He knows how many strokes of labor it represents. His bones ache with the day's work that earned it. He knows how much land it represents;—how much rain, frost, and sunshine. He knows that, in the dollar, he gives you so much discretion and patience so much hoeing, and threshing. Try to lift his dollar; you must lift all that weight. In the city, where money follows the skit of a pen, or a lucky rise in exchange, it comes to be looked on as light. I wish the farmer held it dearer, and would spend it only for real bread; force for force.

The farmer's dollar is heavy, and the clerk's is light and nimble; leaps out of his pocket; jumps on to cards and faro-tables: but still more curious is its susceptibility to metaphysical changes. It is the finest barometer of social storms, and announces revolutions.

The value of a dollar is social, as it is created by society. Every man who removes into this city, with any purchasable talent or skill in him, gives to every man's labor in the city, a new worth. If a talent is anywhere born into the world, the community of nations is enriched; and, much more, with a new degree of probity. The expense of crime, one of the principal charges of every nation, is so far stopped. In Europe, crime is observed to increase or abate with the price of bread.

Wealth brings with it its own checks and balances. The basis of political economy is non-interference. The only safe rule is found in the self-adjusting meter of demand and supply. Do not legislate. Meddle, and you snap the sinews with your sumptuary laws. Give no bounties: make equal laws: secure life and property, and you need not give alms. Open the doors of opportunity to talent and virtue, and they will do themselves justice, and property will not be in bad hands. In a free and just commonwealth, property rushes from the idle and imbecile, to the industrious, brave, and persevering.

Our nature and genius force us to respect ends, whilst we use means. We must use the means, and yet, in our most accurate using, somehow screen and cloak them, as we can only give them any beauty, by a reflection of the glory of the end. That is the good head, which serves the end, and commands the means. The rabble are corrupted by their means: the means are too strong for them, and they desert their end.

1. The first of these measures is that each man's expense must proceed from his character. As long as your genius buys, the investment is safe, though you spend like a monarch. Nature arms each man with some faculty which enables him to do easily some feat impossible to any other, and thus makes him necessary to society. This native determination guides his labor and his spending. He wants an equipment of means and tools proper to his talent. Do your work, respecting the excellence of the work, and not its acceptableness. Nothing is beneath you, if it is in the direction of your life: nothing is great or desirable, if it is off from that. I think we are entitled here to draw a straight line, and say, that society can never prosper, but must always be bankrupt, until every man does that which he was created to do.

Spend for your expense, and retrench the expense which is not yours. Allston, the painter, was wont to say, that he built a plain house, and filled it with plain furniture, because he would hold out no bribe to any to visit him, who had not similar tastes to his own. We are sympathetic, and, like children, want everything we see. But it is a large stride to independence,—when a man, in the discovery of his proper talent, has sunk the necessity for false expenses.

2. Spend after your genius, and by system. Nature goes by rule, not by sallies and saltations. There must be system in the economies. Saving and unexpensiveness will not keep the most pathetic family from ruin, nor will bigger incomes make free spending safe. The secret of success lies never in the amount of money, but in the relation of income to outgo; as if, after expense has been fixed at a certain point, then new and steady rills of income, though never so small, being added, wealth begins.

3. The rule is not to dictate, nor to insist on carrying out each of your schemes by ignorant wilfulness, but to learn practically the secret spoken from all nature, that things themselves refuse to be mismanaged, and will show to the watchful their own law. Nobody need stir hand or foot. The custom of the country will do it all. I know not how to build or to plant; neither how to buy wood, nor what to do with the house-lot, the field, or the wood-lot, when bought. Never fear: it is all settled how it shall be, long beforehand, in the custom of the country, whether to sand, or whether to clay it, when to plough, and how to dress, whether to grass, or to corn; and you cannot help or hinder it. Nature has her own best mode of doing each thing, and she has somewhere told it plainly, if we will keep our eyes and ears open.

4. Another point of economy is to look for seed of the same kind as you sow: and not to hope to buy one kind with another kind. Friendship buys friendship; justice, justice; military merit, military success. Good husbandry finds wife, children, and household. The good merchant large gains, ships, stocks, and money. The good poet fame, and literary credit; but not either, the other. Yet there is commonly a confusion of expectations on these points. Hotspur lives for the moment; praises himself for it; and despises Furlong, that he does not. Hotspur, of course, is poor; and Furlong a good provider. The odd circumstance is, that Hotspur thinks it a superiority in himself, this improvidence, which ought to be rewarded with Furlong's lands.

5. Now these things are so in Nature. All things ascend, and the royal rule of economy is, that it should ascend also, or, whatever we do must always have a higher aim. Thus it is a maxim, that money is another kind of blood. So there is no maxim of the merchant, e.g., "Best use of money is to pay debts;" "Every business by itself;" "Best time is present time;" "The right investment is in tools of your trade;" or the like, which does not admit of an extended sense. The counting-room maxims liberally expounded are laws of the Universe. The merchant's economy is a coarse symbol of the soul's economy. It is, to spend for power, and not for pleasure. It is to invest income; that is to say, to take up particulars into generals; days into integral eras,—literary, emotive, practical, of its life, and still to ascend in its investment. The merchant has but one rule, absorb and invest: he is to be capitalist: the scraps and filings must be gathered back into the crucible; the gas and smoke must be burned, and earnings must

not go to increase expense, but to capital again. Well, the man must be capitalist. Will he spend his income, or will he invest? His body and every organ is under the same law. His body is a jar, in which the liquor of life is stored. Will he spend for pleasure? The way to ruin is short and facile. Will he not spend, but hoard for power? It passes through the sacred fermentations, by that law of Nature whereby everything climbs to higher platforms, and bodily vigor becomes mental and moral vigor. The bread he eats is first strength and animal spirits: it becomes, in higher laboratories, imagery and thought; and in still higher results, courage and endurance. This is the right compound interest; this is capital doubled, quadrupled, centupled; man raised to his highest power.

The true thrift is always to spend on the higher plane; to invest and invest, with keener avarice, that he may spend in spiritual creation, and not in augmenting animal existence. Nor is the man enriched, in repeating the old experiments of animal sensation, nor unless through new powers and ascending pleasures, he knows himself by the actual experience of higher good, to be already on the way to the highest.

# The Gospel of Wealth
(1889)

## by Andrew Carnegie

*The Definitive Edition of the
Wealth-Building Classic*

### Contents

Introduction  *The Gospel of Carnegie* by Mitch Horowitz   144
The Gospel of Wealth   146

## Introduction
# The Gospel of Carnegie

Success author Napoleon Hill described his first encounter with steel magnate Andrew Carnegie—"the richest man that the richest nation on earth ever produced"—in terms that brought to mind Moses receiving the tablets on Mount Sinai. Hill said that he interviewed the industrialist in 1908 and received marching orders to codify a philosophy of success, which formed the basis for his 1928 book *The Law of Success* and the wealth-building classic that followed nine years later, *Think and Grow Rich*.

Whatever impression Hill left on Carnegie, the industrialist made no mention of the younger man in his writings. Nor did Hill begin making references to the fateful meeting until nearly a decade after Carnegie's death in 1919. Critics question whether the encounter ever took place. I am agnostic on the point. Hill was working that year for *Bob Taylor's Magazine*, an inspirational and general-interest monthly that featured up-by-the-bootstraps stories of millionaires—a staple of the day's popular literature—and the job could have facilitated contact between journalist and subject. In any case, Carnegie's memoirs do paint the image of a man who enjoyed discussing the metaphysics of success. In his autobiography, published posthumously in 1920, Carnegie recalled that as an adolescent he "became deeply interested in the mysterious doctrines of Swedenborg." A Spiritualist aunt encouraged the young Carnegie to develop his psychical talents, or "ability to expound 'spiritual sense.'"

Carnegie was eager to be taken seriously as an author and he reveled in probing whether there exist natural laws of money and accumulation. In June 1889, Carnegie published his essay "Wealth" for the *North American Review*, which might have been forgotten if not for its near-immediate republication by England's evening newspaper *The Pall Mall Gazette* under the more alluring title by which it became internationally famous and is reprinted here: "The Gospel of Wealth."

Taking a leaf from the neo-Darwinian views of philosopher Herbert Spencer, Carnegie described a "law of competition," which he believed brought a rough, necessary order to the world:

> While the law may be sometimes hard to the individual, it is best for the race, because it ensures the survival of the fittest in every department. We accept and welcome, therefore, as conditions to which we must accom-

modate ourselves, great inequality of environment, the concentration of business, industrial and commercial, in the hands of a few, and the law of competition between these, as being not only beneficial but essential for the future progress of the race.

Although contemporaneous success authors such as Ralph Waldo Trine and Wallace D. Wattles extolled creativity above competition, Carnegie welcomed "laws of accumulation" as a necessary means of separating life's winners from losers. At his steel mills, the magnate sometimes backed his belief through ruthless and, by way of surrogates and business partners, brutal labor practices. Seven of his workers were killed by Pinkerton guards during the Homestead Strike of 1892.

Yet Carnegie's essay had a surprising wrinkle. He emphasized that great wealth—which he attributed chiefly to raw materials, real estate, utilities, and inventions (the manufacturer disdained financial speculation)—was the product of the community. And should ultimately be returned to it. Wealth, Carnegie argued, is amassed as a passive result of an industrialist or investor benefiting from mass shifts in demography, migration, and public needs. The world's reputedly richest man wrote that wealth should be restored to the community rather than passed down through family inheritance. In a sentiment that would win him few admirers among radicals and reformers, Carnegie counseled that millionaires should electively dispense their money in acts of philanthropy during their lifetimes. He called that the legitimate culmination of success. In essence, Carnegie argued that monopolistic capitalism should be leavened by voluntary largesse or noblesse oblige. But the millionaire's sense of volunteerism had its limits. If the rich didn't find a way to disperse their fortunes through philanthropy, Carnegie called for a nearly 100 percent estate tax to settle the matter for them.

"The Gospel of Wealth" proved so popular that Carnegie issued two sequels in the *North American Review*—the first in December 1889 called "The Best Fields for Philanthropy" and the second seventeen years later in December 1906 called "The Gospel of Wealth II."

In this Condensed Classics edition I have combined all three "Gospel" essays for a panoramic view of Carnegie's wealth philosophy. I have excised, shortened, or clarified a few policy references or news-related tangents reflective of his immediate era, and also eliminated some superfluous prefatory material so that these three works can be read as one whole. I have modernized spellings and added a few clarifying footnotes. Although Carnegie wrote a handful of related pieces in response to his critics, these interwoven essays provide a more or less complete perspective on his views of how wealth is generated—and how it should be dispensed.

Whether one agrees with Carnegie on every point—and I do not—it is worth noting that he followed through on his statements with wide-ranging acts of structured philanthropy. In so doing, the industrialist helped presage the nonprofit field as it exists today. His business advice is for each individual to assess, but of one point he leaves no doubt: great fortunes accrue due not primarily to the ability of their holders but to ancillary events and circumstances that emerge from public need and growth.

—Mitch Horowitz

# The Gospel of Wealth

The problem of our age is the proper administration of wealth, so that the ties of brotherhood may still bind together the rich and poor in harmonious relationship. The conditions of human life have not only been changed, but revolutionized, within the past few hundred years. In former days there was little difference between the dwelling, dress, food, and environment of the chief and those of his retainers. The Indians are today where civilized man then was. When visiting the Sioux, I was led to the wigwam of the chief. It was just like the others in external appearance, and even within the difference was trifling between it and those of the poorest of his braves. The contrast between the palace of the millionaire and the cottage of the laborer with us today measures the change which has come with civilization.

This change, however, is not to be deplored, but welcomed as highly beneficial. It is well, nay, essential for the progress of the race, that the houses of some should be homes for all that is highest and best in literature and the arts, and for all the refinements of civilization, rather than that none should be so. Much better this great irregularity than universal squalor. Without wealth there can be no Mæcenas.* The "good old times" were not good old

---

* Carnegie refers here to the wealthy Roman statesman who was a patron to the arts.

times. Neither master nor servant was as well situated then as today. A relapse to old conditions would be disastrous to both—not the least so to him who serves—and would sweep away civilization with it. But whether the change be for good or ill, it is upon us, beyond our power to alter, and therefore to be accepted and made the best of. It is a waste of time to criticize the inevitable.

It is easy to see how the change has come. One illustration will serve for almost every phase of the cause. In the manufacture of products we have the whole story. It applies to all combinations of human industry, as stimulated and enlarged by the inventions of this scientific age. Formerly articles were manufactured at the domestic hearth or in small shops which formed part of the household. The master and his apprentices worked side by side, the latter living with the master, and therefore subject to the same conditions. When these apprentices rose to be masters, there was little or no change in their mode of life, and they, in turn, educated in the same routine succeeding apprentices. There was, substantially, social equality, and even political equality, for those engaged in industrial pursuits had then little or no political voice in the State.

But the inevitable result of such a mode of manufacture was crude articles at high prices. Today the world obtains commodities of excellent quality at prices which even the generation preceding this would have deemed incredible. In the commercial world similar causes have produced similar results, and the race is benefited thereby. The poor enjoy what the rich could not before afford. What were the luxuries have become the necessaries of life. The laborer has now more comforts than the landlord had a few generations ago. The farmer has more luxuries than the landlord had, and is more richly clad and better housed. The landlord has books and pictures rarer, and appointments more artistic, than the King could then obtain.

The price we pay for this salutary change is, no doubt, great. We assemble thousands of operatives in the factory, in the mine, and in the counting-house, of whom the employer can know little or nothing, and to whom the employer is little better than a myth. All intercourse between them is at an end. Rigid Castes are formed, and, as usual, mutual ignorance breeds mutual distrust. Each Caste is without sympathy for the other, and ready to credit anything disparaging in regard to it. Under the law of competition, the employer of thousands is forced into the strictest economies, among which the rates paid to labor figure prominently, and often there is friction between the employer and the employed, between capital and labor, between rich and poor. Human society loses homogeneity.

The price which society pays for the law of competition, like the price it pays for cheap comforts and luxuries, is also great; but the advantages of this law are also greater still, for it is to this law that we owe our wonderful material development, which brings improved conditions in its train. But, whether the law be benign or not, we must say of it, as we say of the change in the conditions of men to which we have referred: It is here; we cannot evade it; no substitutes for it have been found; and while the law may be sometimes hard for the individual, it is best for the race, because it ensures the survival of the fittest in every department. We accept and welcome therefore, as conditions to which we must accommodate ourselves, great inequality of environment, the concentration of business, industrial and commercial, in the hands of a few, and the law of competition between these, as being not only beneficial, but essential for the future progress of the race. Having accepted these, it follows that there must be great scope for the exercise of special ability in the merchant and in the manufacturer who has to conduct affairs upon a great scale. That this talent for organization and management is rare among men is proved by the fact that it invariably secures for its possessor enormous rewards, no matter where or under what laws or conditions. The experienced in affairs always rate the MAN whose services can be obtained as a partner as not only the first consideration, but such as to render the question of his capital scarcely worth considering, for such men soon create capital; while, without the special talent required, capital soon takes wings. Such men become interested in firms or corporations using millions; and estimating only simple interest to be made upon the capital invested, it is inevitable that their income must exceed their expenditures, and that they must accumulate wealth. Nor is there any middle ground which such men can occupy, because the great manufacturing or commercial concern which does not earn at least interest upon its capital soon becomes bankrupt. It must either go forward or fall behind: to stand still is impossible. It is a condition essential for its successful operation that it should be thus far profitable, and even that, in addition to interest on capital, it should make profit. It is a law, as certain as any of the others named, that men possessed of this peculiar talent for affair, under the free play of economic forces, must, of necessity, soon be in receipt of more revenue than can be judiciously expended upon themselves; and this law is as beneficial for the race as the others.

Objections to the foundations upon which society is based are not in order, because the condition of the race is better with these than it has been with any others which have been tried. Of the effect of any new substitutes proposed we cannot be sure. The Socialist or Anarchist who seeks to overturn present conditions is to be regarded as attacking the foundation upon which civilization itself rests, for civilization took its start from the day that the capable, industrious workman said to his incompetent and lazy fellow, "If thou dost not sow, thou shalt not reap," and thus ended primitive Communism by separating the drones from the bees. One who studies this subject will soon be brought face to face with the conclusion that upon the sacredness of property civilization itself depends—the right of the laborer to his hundred dollars in the savings bank, and equally the legal right of the millionaire to his millions. To these who propose to substitute Communism for this intense Individualism the answer, therefore, is: The race has tried that. All progress from that barbarous day to the present time has resulted from its displacement. Not evil, but good, has come to the race from the accumulation of wealth by those who have the ability and energy that produce it. But even if we admit for a moment that it might be better for the race to discard its present foundation, Individualism—that it is a nobler ideal that man should labor, not for himself alone, but in and for a brotherhood of his fellows, and share with them all in common, realizing Swedenborg's idea of Heaven, where, as he says, the angels derive their happiness, not from laboring for self, but for each other—even admit all this, and a sufficient answer is, This is not evolution, but revolution. It necessitates the changing of human nature itself a work of aeons, even if it were good to change it, which we cannot know. It is not practicable in our day or in our age. Even if desirable theoretically, it belongs to another and long-succeeding sociological stratum. Our duty is with what is practicable now; with the next step possible in our day and generation. It is criminal to waste our energies in endeavoring to uproot, when all we can profitably or possibly accomplish is to bend the universal tree of humanity a little in the direction most favorable to the production of good fruit under existing circumstances. We might as well urge the destruction of the highest existing type of man because he failed to reach our ideal as favor the destruction of Individualism, Private Property, the Law of Accumulation of Wealth, and the Law of Competition; for these are the highest results of human experience, the soil in which society so far has produced the best fruit. Unequally or unjustly, perhaps, as these laws sometimes operate, and imperfect as they appear to the Idealist, they are, nevertheless, like the highest type of man, the best and most valuable of all that humanity has yet accomplished.

We start, then, with a condition of affairs under which the best interests of the race are promoted, but which inevitably gives wealth to the few. Thus far, accepting conditions as they exist, the situation can be surveyed and pronounced good. The question then arises—and, if the foregoing be correct, it is the only question with which we have to deal—What is the proper mode of administering wealth after the laws upon which civilization is founded have thrown it into the hands of the few? And it is of this great question that I believe I offer the true solution. It will be understood that *fortunes* are here spoken of, not moderate sums saved by many years of effort, the returns on which are required for the comfortable maintenance and education of families. This is not *wealth,* but only *competence* which it should be the aim of all to acquire.

There are but three modes in which surplus wealth can be disposed of. It can be left to the families of the decedents; or it can be bequeathed for public purposes; or, finally, it can be administered during their lives by its possessors. Under the first and second modes most of the wealth of the world that has reached the few has hitherto been applied. Let us in turn consider each of these modes. The first is the most injudicious. In monarchical countries, the estates and the greatest portion of the wealth are left to the first son, that the vanity of the parent may be gratified by the thought that his name and title are to descend to succeeding generations unimpaired. The condition of this class in Europe today teaches the futility of such hopes or ambitions. The successors have become impoverished through their follies or from the fall in the value of land. Even in Great Britain the strict law of entail has been found inadequate to maintain the status of an hereditary class. Its soil is rapidly passing into the hands of the stranger. Under republican institutions the division of property among the children is much fairer, but the question which forces itself upon thoughtful men in all lands is: Why should men leave great fortunes to their children? If this is done from affection, is it not misguided affection? Observation teaches that, generally speaking, it is not well for the children that they should be so burdened. Neither is it well for the state. Beyond providing for the wife and daughters moderate sources of income, and very moderate allowances indeed, if any, for the sons, men may well hesitate, for it is no longer questionable that great sums bequeathed oftener work more for the injury than for the good of the recipients. Wise men will soon conclude that, for the best interests of the members of their families and of the state, such bequests are an improper use of their means.

It is not suggested that men who have failed to educate their sons to earn a livelihood shall cast them adrift in poverty. If any man has seen fit to rear his sons with a view to their living idle lives, or, what is highly commendable, has instilled in them the sentiment that they are in a position to labor for public ends without reference to pecuniary considerations, then, of course, the duty of the parent is to see that such are provided for *in moderation*. There are instances of millionaires' sons unspoiled by wealth, who, being rich, still perform great services in the community. Such are the very salt of the earth, as valuable as, unfortunately, they are rare; still it is not the exception, but the rule, that men must regard, and, looking at the usual result of enormous sums conferred upon legatees, the thoughtful man must shortly say, "I would as soon leave to my son a curse as the almighty dollar," and admit to himself that it is not the welfare of the children, but family pride, which inspires these enormous legacies.

As to the second mode, that of leaving wealth at death for public uses, it may be said that this is only a means for the disposal of wealth, provided a man is content to wait until he is dead before it becomes of much good in the world. Knowledge of the results of legacies bequeathed is not calculated to inspire the brightest hopes of much posthumous good being accomplished. The cases are not few in which the real object sought by the testator is not attained, nor are they few in which his real wishes are thwarted. In many cases the bequests are so used as to become only monuments of his folly. It is well to remember that it requires the exercise of not less ability than that which acquired the wealth to use it so as to be really beneficial to the community. Besides this, it may fairly be said that no man is to be extolled for doing what he cannot help doing, nor is he to be thanked by the community to which he only leaves wealth at death. Men who leave vast sums in this way may fairly be thought men who would not have left it at all, had they been able to take it with them. The memories of such cannot be held in grateful remembrance, for there is no grace in their gifts. It is not to be wondered at that such bequests seem so generally to lack the blessing.

The growing disposition to tax more and more heavily large estates left at death is a cheering indication of the growth of a salutary change in public opinion. The State of Pennsylvania now takes—subject to some exceptions—one-tenth of the property left by its citizens. The budget presented in the British Parliament the other day proposes to increase the death-duties; and, most significant of all, the new tax is to be a graduated one. Of all forms of taxation, this seems the wisest. Men who continue hoarding great sums all their lives, the proper use of which for public ends would work good to the community, should be made to feel that the community, in the form of the state, cannot thus be deprived of its proper share. By taxing estates heavily at death the state marks its condemnation of the selfish millionaire's unworthy life.

It is desirable that nations should go much further in this direction. Indeed, it is difficult to set bounds to the share of a rich man's estate which should go at his death to the public through the agency of the state, and by all means such taxes should be graduated, beginning at nothing upon moderate sums to dependents, and increasing rapidly as the amounts swell, until of the millionaire's hoard, as of Shylock's, at least—The other half Comes to the privy coffer of the state.

This policy would work powerfully to induce the rich man to attend to the administration of wealth during his life, which is the end that society should always have in view, as being that by far most fruitful for the people. Nor need it be feared that this policy would sap the root of enterprise and render men less anxious to accumulate, for to the class whose ambition it is to leave great fortunes and be talked about after their death, it will attract even more attention, and, indeed, be a somewhat nobler ambition to have enormous sums paid over to the state from their fortunes.

There remains, then, only one mode of using great fortunes; but in this we have the true antidote for the temporary unequal distribution of wealth, the reconciliation of the rich and the poor—a reign of harmony—another ideal, differing, indeed, from that of the Communist in requiring only the further evolution of existing conditions, not the total overthrow of our civilization. It is founded upon the present most intense individualism, and the race is projected to put it in practice by degree whenever it pleases. Under its sway we shall have an ideal state, in which the surplus wealth of the few will become, in the best sense the property of the many, because administered for the common good, and this wealth, passing through the hands of the few, can be made a much more potent force for the elevation of our race than if it had been distributed in small sums to the people themselves. Even the poorest can be made to see this, and to agree that great sums gathered by some of their fellow-citizens and spent for public purposes, from which the masses reap the principal benefit, are more valuable to them than if scattered among them through the course of many years in trifling amounts.

If we consider what results flow from the Cooper Institute, for instance, to the best portion of the race in New York not possessed of means, and compare these with those which would have arisen for the good of the masses from an equal sum distributed by Mr. Cooper in his lifetime in the form of wages, which is the highest form of distribution, being for work done and not for charity, we can form some estimate of the possibilities for the improvement of the race which lie embedded in the present law of the accumulation of wealth. Much of this sum if distributed in small quantities among the people, would have been wasted in the indulgence of appetite, some of it in excess, and it may be doubted whether even the part put to the best use, that of adding to the comforts of the home, would have yielded results for the race, as a race, at all comparable to those which are flowing and are to flow from the Cooper Institute from generation to generation. Let the advocate of violent or radical change ponder well this thought.

We might even go so far as to take another instance, that of Mr. Tilden's bequest of five millions of dollars for a free library in the city of New York, but in referring to this one cannot help saying involuntarily, how much better if Mr. Tilden had devoted the last years of his own life to the proper administration of this immense sum; in which case neither legal contest nor any other cause of delay could have interfered with his aims.\* But let us assume that Mr. Tilden's millions finally become the means of giving to this city a noble public library, where the treasures of the world contained in books will be open to all forever, without money and without price. Considering the good of that part of the race which congregates in and around Manhattan Island, would its permanent benefit have been better promoted had these millions been allowed to circulate in small sums through the hands of the masses? Even the most strenuous advocate of Communism must entertain a doubt upon this subject. Most of those who think will probably entertain no doubt whatever.

Poor and restricted are our opportunities in this life; narrow our horizon; our best work most imperfect; but rich men should be thankful for one inestimable boon. They have it in their power during their lives to busy themselves in organizing benefactions from which the masses of their fellows will derive lasting advantage, and thus dignify their own lives. The highest life is probably to be reached, not by such imitation of the life of Christ as Count Tolstoi gives us, but, while animated by Christ's spirit, by recognizing the changed conditions of this age, and adopting modes of expressing this spirit suitable

---

\* Carnegie refers here to the bequest of wealthy American statesman Samuel J. Tilden, which was subject to numerous legal challenges by his family after Tilden's death in 1886.

to the changed conditions under which we live; still laboring for the good of our fellows, which was the essence of his life and teaching, but laboring in a different manner.

This, then, is held to be the duty of the man of Wealth: First, to set an example of modest, unostentatious living, shunning display or extravagance; to provide moderately for the legitimate wants of those dependent upon him; and after doing so to consider all surplus revenues which come to him simply as trust funds, which he is called upon to administer, and strictly bound as a matter of duty to administer in the manner which, in his judgment, is best calculated to produce the most beneficial results for the community—the man of wealth thus becoming the mere agent and trustee for his poorer brethren, bringing to their service his superior wisdom, experience and ability to administer, doing for them better than they would or could do for themselves.

We are met here with the difficulty of determining what are moderate sums to leave to members of the family; what is modest, unostentatious living; what is the test of extravagance. There must be different standards for different conditions. The answer is that it is as impossible to name exact amounts or actions as it is to define good manners, good taste, or the rules of propriety; but, nevertheless, these are verities, well known although undefinable. Public sentiment is quick to know and to feel what offends these. So in the case of wealth. The rule in regard to good taste in the dress of men or women applies here. Whatever makes one conspicuous offends the canon. If any family be chiefly known for display, for extravagance in home, table, equipage, for enormous sums ostentatiously spent in any form upon itself, if these be its chief distinctions, we have no difficulty in estimating its nature or culture. So likewise in regard to the use or abuse of its surplus wealth, or to generous, freehanded cooperation in good public uses, or to unabated efforts to accumulate and hoard to the last, whether they administer or bequeath. The verdict rests with the best and most enlightened public sentiment. The community will surely judge and its judgments will not often be wrong.

The best uses to which surplus wealth can be put have already been indicated. These who would administer wisely must, indeed, be wise, for one of the serious obstacles to the improvement of our race is indiscriminate charity. It were better for mankind that the millions of the rich were thrown into the sea than so spent as to encourage the slothful, the drunken, the unworthy. Of every thousand dollars spent in so-called charity today, it is probable that $950 is unwisely spent; so spent, indeed as to produce the very evils which it proposes to mitigate or cure. A well-known writer of philosophic books admitted the other day that he had given a quarter of a dollar to a man who approached him as he was coming to visit the house of his friend. He knew nothing of the habits of this beggar; knew not the use that would be made of this money, although he had every reason to suspect that it would be spent improperly. This man professed to be a disciple of Herbert Spencer; yet the quarter-dollar given that night will probably work more injury than all the money which its thoughtless donor will ever be able to give in true charity will do good. He only gratified his own feelings, saved himself from annoyance—and this was probably one of the most selfish and very worst actions of his life, for in all respects he is most worthy.

In bestowing charity, the main consideration should be to help those who will help themselves; to provide part of the means by which those who desire to improve may do so; to give those who desire to use the aids by which they may rise; to assist, but rarely or never to do all. Neither the individual nor the race is improved by almsgiving. Those worthy of assistance, except in rare cases, seldom require assistance. The really valuable men of the race never do, except in cases of accident or sudden change. Everyone has, of course, cases of individuals brought to his own knowledge where temporary assistance can do genuine good, and these he will not overlook. But the amount which can be wisely given by the individual for individuals is necessarily limited by his lack of knowledge of the circumstances connected with each. He is the only true reformer who is as careful and as anxious not to aid the unworthy as he is to aid the worthy, and, perhaps, even more so, for in almsgiving more injury is probably done by rewarding vice than by relieving virtue.

The rich man is thus almost restricted to following the examples of Peter Cooper, Enoch Pratt of Baltimore, Mr. Pratt of Brooklyn, Senator Stanford, and others, who know that the best means of benefiting the community is to place within its reach the ladders upon which the aspiring can rise—parks, and means of recreation, by which men are helped in body and mind; works of art, certain to give pleasure and improve the public taste, and public institutions of various kinds, which will improve the general condition of the people—in this manner returning their surplus wealth to the mass of their fellows in the forms best calculated to do them lasting good.

Thus is the problem of Rich and Poor to be solved. The laws of accumulation will be left free; the laws of distribution free. Individualism will continue, but the millionaire will be but a trustee for the poor; entrusted for a season with a great part of the increased wealth of the community, but administering it for the community far better than it could or would have done for itself. The best minds will thus have reached a stage in the development of the race in which it is clearly seen that there is no mode of disposing of surplus wealth creditable to thoughtful and earnest men into whose hands it flows save by using it year by year for the general good. This day already dawns. Man may die without incurring the pity of their fellows, still sharers in great business enterprises from which their capital cannot be or has not been withdrawn, and is left chiefly at death for public uses, yet the man who dies leaving behind many millions of available wealth, which was his to administer during life, will pass away "unwept, unhonored, and unsung," no matter to what uses he leaves the dross which he cannot take with him. Of such as these the public verdict will then be: "The man who dies thus rich dies disgraced."

Such, in my opinion, is the true Gospel concerning Wealth, obedience to which is destined someday to solve the problem of the Rich and the Poor, and to bring "Peace on earth, among men Good-Will."

Some argue that the gospel of wealth is not lived up to by the acts. To this the reply seems obvious: the gospel of Christianity is also killed by the acts. The same objection that is urged against the gospel of wealth lies against the commandment "Thou shalt not steal." It is no argument against a gospel that it is not lived up to; indeed, it is an argument in its favor, for a gospel must be higher than the prevailing standard. It is no argument against a law that it is broken: in that disobedience lies the reason for making and maintaining the law; the law which is never to be broken is never required.

Let us turn attention to some of the best methods of performing this duty of administering surplus wealth for the good of the people. The first requisite for a really good use of wealth by the millionaire who has accepted the gospel which proclaims him only a trustee of the surplus that comes to him is to take care that the purpose for which he spends it shall not have a degrading, pauperizing tendency upon its recipients, and that his trust should be so administered as to stimulate the best and most aspiring poor of the community to further efforts for their own improvement. It is not the irreclaimably destitute, shiftless, and worthless that it is truly beneficial or truly benevolent to attempt to reach and improve. For these there exists the refuge provided by the city or the state, where they can be sheltered, fed, clothed, and kept in comfortable existence, and—most important of all—where they can be isolated from the well-doing and industrious poor, who are liable to be demoralized by contact with these unfortunates. One man or woman who succeeds in living comfortably by begging is more dangerous to society, and a greater obstacle to the progress of humanity, than a score of wordy Socialists. The individual administrator of surplus wealth has as his charge the industrious and ambitious; not those who need everything done for them, but those who, being most anxious and able to help themselves, deserve and will be benefited by help from others and the extension of their opportunities at the hands of the philanthropic rich.

It is ever to be remembered that one of the chief obstacles which the philanthropist meets in his efforts to do real and permanent good in this world is the practice of indiscriminate giving; and the duty of the millionaire is to resolve to cease giving to objects that are not proved clearly to his satisfaction to be deserving. He must remember Mr. Rice's belief, that nine hundred and fifty out of every thousand dollars bestowed today upon so-called charity had better be thrown into the sea. As far as my experience of the wealthy extends, it is unnecessary to urge them to give of their superabundance in charity so-called. Greater good for the race is to be achieved by inducing them to cease impulsive and injurious giving. As a rule, the sins of millionaires in this respect are not those of omission, but of commission, because they will not take time to think, and chiefly because it is much easier to give than to refuse. Those who have surplus wealth give millions every year which produce more evil than good, and which really retard the progress of the people, because most of the forms in vogue today for benefiting mankind only tend to spread among the poor a spirit of dependence upon alms, when what is essential for progress is that they should be inspired to depend upon their own exertions. The miser millionaire who hoards his wealth does less injury to society than the careless millionaire who squanders his unwisely, even if he does so under cover of the mantle of sacred charity. The man who gives to the individual beggar commits a grave offense, but there are many societies and institutions soliciting alms which it is nonetheless injurious to the community to aid. These are as corrupting as individual beggars. Plutarch's "Morals" contains this lesson: "A beggar asking an alms of a Lacedaemonian, he said: 'Well, should I give thee anything, thou wilt be the greater beggar, for he that first gave thee money made thee idle, and is the cause of this base and dishonorable way of living'." As I know them, there are few millionaires, very few indeed, who are clear of this sin of having made beggars.

Bearing in mind these considerations, let us endeavor to present some of the best uses to which a millionaire can devote the surplus of which he should regard himself as only the trustee.

*First*—Standing apart by itself there is the founding of a university by men enormously rich, such men as must necessarily be few in any country. Perhaps the greatest sum ever given by an individual for any purpose is the gift of Senator Stanford, who undertakes to establish upon the Pacific coast, where he amassed his enormous fortune, a complete university, which is said to involve the expenditure of ten millions of dollars, and upon which he may be expected to bestow twenty millions of his surplus. He is to be envied. A thousand years hence some orator, speaking his praise upon the then-crowded shores of the Pacific, may repeat Griffith's eulogy of Wolsey, "In bestowing he was most princely: ever witness for him this great seat of learning." Here is a noble use of wealth.

We have many such institutions, Hopkins, Cornell, Packer, and others, but most of these have only been bequeathed, and it is impossible to extol any man greatly for simply leaving what he cannot take with him. Cooper, and Pratt, and Stanford, and others of this class deserve credit and the admiration of their fellows as much for the time and the attention given during their lives, as for their expenditure, upon their respective monuments.

We cannot have the Pacific coast in mind without recalling another important work of a different character which has recently been established there, the Lick Observatory. If any millionaire be interested in the ennobling study of astronomy—and there should be and would be such if they but gave the subject the slightest attention—here is an example which could well be followed, for the progress made in astronomical instruments and appliances is so great and continuous that every few years a new telescope might be judiciously given to one of the observatories upon this continent, the last being always the largest and the best, and certain to carry further and further the knowledge of the universe and of our relation to it here upon the earth. As one among many of the good deeds of the late Mr. Thaw, of Pittsburg, his constant support of the observatory there may be mentioned. This observatory enabled Professor Langley to make his wonderful discoveries. The professor is now at the head of the Smithsonian Institution, a worthy successor to Professor Henry. Connected with him was Mr. Braeshier, of Pittsburg, whose instruments are in most of the principal observatories of the world. He was a common millwright, but Mr. Thaw recognized his genius and was his main support through trying days. This common workman has been made a professor by one of the foremost scientific bodies of the world. In applying part of his surplus in aiding these two now famous men, the millionaire Thaw did a noble work. Their joint labors have brought great, and are destined to bring still greater, credit upon their country in every scientific center throughout the world.

It is reserved for very few to found universities, and, indeed, the use for many, or perhaps any, new universities does not exist. More good is henceforth to be accomplished by adding to and extending those in existence. But in this department a wide field remains for the millionaire as distinguished from the Croesus among millionaires.* The gifts to Yale University have been many, but there is plenty of room for others. The School of Fine Arts, founded by Mr. Street, the Sheffield Scientific School, endowed by Mr. Sheffield, and Professor Loomis's fund for the observatory, are fine examples. Mrs. O.J. Osborne's building for reading and recitation is to be regarded with especial pleasure as being the wise gift of a woman. Harvard University has not been forgotten; the Peabody Museum, and the halls of Wells, Matthews, and Thayer may be cited. Seber Hall is worthy of special mention, as showing what a genius like Richardson could do with the small sum of a hundred thousand dollars. The Vanderbilt University at Nashville, Tennessee, may be mentioned as a true product of the gospel of wealth. It was established by members of the Vanderbilt family during their lives—mark this vital feature—during their lives; for nothing counts for much that is left by a man at his death. Such funds are torn from him, not given by him. If any millionaire is at a loss to know how to accomplish great and indisputable good with his surplus, here is a field which can never be fully occupied, for the wants of our universities increase with the development of the country.

*Second*—The result of my own study of the question, What is the best gift which can be given to a community? is that a free library occupies the first place, provided the community will accept and maintain it as a public institution, as much a part of the city property as its public schools, and, indeed, an adjunct to these. It is, no doubt, possible that my own personal experience may have led me to value a free library beyond all other forms of beneficence. When I was a boy in Pittsburg, Colonel Anderson, of Allegheny—a name I

---

* Carnegie refers to the ancient Greek ruler who conquered parts of Persia and was legendary for his wealth.

can never speak without feelings of devotional gratitude—opened his little library of four hundred books to boys. Every Saturday afternoon he was in attendance himself at his house to exchange books. No one but he who has felt it can know the intense longing with which the arrival of Saturday was awaited, that a new book might be had. My brother and Mr. Phipps, who have been my principal business partners through life, shared with me Colonel Anderson's precious generosity, and it was when reveling in these treasures that I resolved, if ever wealth came to me, that it should be used to establish free libraries, that other poor boys might receive opportunities similar to those for which we were indebted to that noble man.

Great Britain has been foremost in appreciating the value of free libraries for its people. Parliament passed an act permitting towns and cities to establish and maintain these as municipal institutions, and whenever the people of any town or city voted to accept the provisions of the act, the authorities were authorized to tax the community to the extent of one penny in the pound valuation. Most of the towns already have free libraries under this act. Many of these are the gifts of rich men, whose funds have been used for the building, and in some cases for the books also, the communities being required to maintain and to develop the libraries; and to this feature I attribute most of their usefulness. An endowed institution is liable to become the prey of a clique. The public ceases to take interest in it, or, rather, never acquires interest in it. The rule has been violated which requires the recipients to help themselves. Everything has been done for the community instead of its being only helped to help itself.

Many free libraries have been established in our country, but none that I know of with such wisdom as the Pratt Library, of Baltimore. Mr. Pratt presented to the city of Baltimore one million dollars, requiring it to pay 5 percent, per annum, amounting to fifty thousand dollars per year, which is to be devoted to the maintenance and development of the library and its branches. During last year 430,217 books were distributed; 37,196 people of Baltimore are registered upon the books as readers; and it is safe to say that the 37,000 frequenters of the Pratt Library are of more value to Baltimore, to the State, and to the country than all the inert, lazy, and hopelessly-poor in the whole nation. And it may further be safely said that, by placing within the reach of 37,000 aspiring people books which they were anxious to obtain, Mr. Pratt has done more for the genuine progress of the people than has been done by all the contributions of all the millionaires and rich people to help those who cannot help themselves. The one wise administrator of his surplus has poured his fertilizing stream upon soil that was ready to receive it and return a hundred-fold. The many squanderers have not only poured their streams into sieves which never can be filled—they have done worse; they have poured them into stagnant sewers that breed the diseases which afflict the body politic. And this is not all. The million dollars of which Mr. Pratt has made so grand a use are something, but there is something greater still. When the fifth branch library was opened in Baltimore, the speaker said:

> Whatever may have been done in these four years, it was his pleasure to acknowledge that much, very much, was due to the earnest interest, the wise councils, and the practical suggestions of Mr. Pratt. He never seemed to feel that the mere donation of great wealth for the benefit of his fellow-citizens was all that would be asked of him, but he wisely labored to make its application as comprehensive and effective as possible. Thus he constantly lightened burdens that were, at times, very heavy, brought good cheer and bright sunshine when clouds flitted across the sky, and made every officer and employee feel that good work was appreciated, and loyal devotion to duty would receive hearty commendation.

This is the finest picture I have ever seen of any of the millionaire class. As here depicted, Mr. Pratt is the ideal disciple of the "Gospel of Wealth." We need have no fear that the mass of toilers will fail to recognize in such as he their best leaders and their most invaluable allies; for the problem of poverty and wealth, of employer and employed, will be practically solved whenever the time of the few is given, and their wealth is administered during their lives, for the best good of that portion of the community which has not been burdened by the responsibilities which attend the possession of wealth. We shall have no antagonism between classes when that day comes, for the high and the low, the rich and the poor, shall then indeed be brothers.

No millionaire will go far wrong in his search for one of the best forms for the use of his surplus who chooses to establish a free library in any community that is willing to maintain and develop it. John Bright's words should ring in his ear: "It is impossible for any man to bestow a greater benefit upon a young man than to give him access to books in a free library." Closely allied to the library, and, where possible, attached to it, there should be rooms for an art gallery and museum, and a hall for such lectures and instruction as are provided in the Cooper Union. The traveler upon the Continent is surprised to find that every town of importance has its art gallery and museum; these may be large or small, but in any case each has a receptacle for the treasures of the locality, which is constantly receiving valuable gifts and bequests. The free library and art gallery of Birmingham are remarkable among these, and every now and then a rich man adds to their value by presenting books, fine pictures, or other works of art. All that our cities require to begin with is a proper fireproof building. Their citizens who travel will send to it rare and costly things from every quarter of the globe they visit, while those who remain at home will give or bequeath to it of their treasures. In this way these collections will grow until our cities will ultimately be able to boast of permanent exhibitions from which their own citizens will derive incalculable benefit, and which they will be proud to show to visitors. In the Metropolitan Museum of Art in this city we have made an excellent beginning. Here is another avenue for the proper use of surplus wealth.

*Third*—We have another most important department in which great sums can be worthily used—the founding or extension of hospitals, medical colleges, laboratories, and other institutions connected with the alleviation of human suffering, and especially with the prevention rather than the cure of human ills. There is no danger of pauperizing a community in giving for such purposes, because such institutions relieve temporary ailments or shelter only those who are hopeless invalids. What better gift than a hospital can be given to a community that is without one?—the gift being conditioned upon its proper maintenance by the community in its corporate capacity. If hospital accommodation already exists, no better method for using surplus wealth can be found than in making additions to it. The late Mr. Vanderbilt's gift of half a million of dollars to the medical department of Columbia College for a chemical laboratory was one of the wisest possible uses of wealth. It strikes at the prevention of disease by penetrating into its causes. Several others have established such laboratories, but the need for them is still great.

If there be a millionaire in the land who is at a loss what to do with the surplus that has been committed to him as trustee, let him investigate the good that is flowing from these chemical laboratories. No medical college is complete without its laboratory. As with universities, so with medical colleges; it is not new institutions that are required, but additional means for the more thorough equipment of those that exist. The forms that benefactions to these may wisely take are numerous, but probably none is more useful than that adopted by Mr. Osborne when he built a school for training female nurses at Bellevue College. If from all gifts there flows one-half of the good that comes from this wise use of a millionaire's surplus, the most exacting may well be satisfied. Only those who have passed through a lingering and dangerous illness can rate at their true value the care, skill, and attendance of trained female nurses. Their employment as nurses has enlarged the sphere and influence of woman. It is not to be wondered at that a Senator of the United States and a physician distinguished in this country for having received the highest distinctions abroad should find their wives from this class.

*Fourth*—In the very front rank of benefactions public parks should be placed, always provided that the community undertakes to maintain, beautify, and preserve inviolate the parks given to it. No more useful or more beautiful monument can be left by any man than a park for the city in which he was born or in which he has long lived, nor can the community pay a more graceful tribute to the citizen who presents it than to give his name to the gift. If a park be already provided, there is still room for many judicious gifts in connection with it. Mr. Phipps, of Allegheny, has given conservatories to the park there, which are visited by many every day of the week and crowded by thousands of working people every Sunday, for, with rare wisdom, he has stipulated as a condition of the gift that the conservatories shall be open on Sundays. The result of his experiment has been so gratifying that he is justified in adding to them from his surplus, as he is doing largely this year. To any lover of flowers among the wealthy I commend a study of what is possible for them to do in the line of Mr. Phipps's example; and may they please note that Mr. Phipps is a wise as well as a liberal giver, for he requires the city to maintain these conservatories, and thus secures for them forever the public ownership, the public interest, and the public criticism of their management. Had he undertaken to manage and maintain them, it is probable that popular interest in the gift would never have been awakened.

The parks and pleasure-grounds of small towns throughout Europe are not less surprising than their libraries, museums, and art galleries. We saw nothing more pleasing during our recent travels than the hillside of Bergen, in Norway. It has been converted into one of the most picturesque of pleasure-grounds; fountains, cascades, waterfalls, delightful arbors, fine terraces, and statues adorn what was before a barren mountainside. Here is a field worthy of study by the millionaire who would confer a lasting benefit upon his fellows. Another beautiful instance of the right use of wealth in the direction of making cities more and more attractive we found in Dresden. The owner of the leading paper there bequeathed its revenues forever to the city, to be used in beautifying it. An art committee decides from time to time what new artistic feature is to be introduced or what hideous feature is to be changed, and as the revenues accrue they are expended in this direction. Thus through the gift of this patriotic newspaper proprietor his native city of Dresden is fast becoming one of the most artistic places of residence in the whole world.

A work having been completed, it devolves upon the city to maintain it forever. May I be excused if I commend to our millionaire newspaper proprietors the example of their colleague in the capital of Saxony?

Scarcely a city of any magnitude in the older countries is without many structures and features of great beauty. Much has been spent upon ornament, decoration, and architectural effect: we are still far behind in these things upon this side of the Atlantic. Our Republic is great in some things—in material development unrivalled; but let us always remember that in art and in the finer touches we have scarcely yet taken a place. Had the exquisite memorial arch recently erected temporarily in New York been shown in Dresden, the art committee there would probably have been enabled, from the revenue of the newspaper given by its owner for just such purposes, to order its permanent erection to adorn the city forever.

While the bestowal of a park upon a community as one of the best uses for surplus wealth will be universally approved, in embracing such additions to it as conservatories, or in advocating the building of memorial arches and works of adornment, it is probable that many will think we go too far, and consider these somewhat fanciful. The material good to flow from them may not be so directly visible; but let not any practical mind, intent only upon material good, depreciate the value of wealth given for these or for kindred aesthetic purposes as being useless as far as the mass of the people and their needs are concerned. As with libraries and museums, so with these more distinctively artistic works; these perform their great use when they reach the best of the masses of the people. It is worth more to reach and touch the sentiment for beauty in the naturally bright minds of this class than that those incapable of being so touched should be pandered to. For what the improver of the race must endeavor to do is to reach those who have the divine spark ever so feebly developed, that it may be strengthened and grow. For my part, I think Mr. Phipps put his money to better use in giving the workingmen of Allegheny conservatories filled with beautiful flowers, orchids, and aquatic plants, which they, with their wives and children, can enjoy in their spare hours, and on which they can feed the love for the beautiful, than if he had given his surplus money to furnish them with bread, for those in health who cannot earn their bread are scarcely worth considering by the individual giver; the care of such being the duty of the state. The man who erects in a city a truly artistic arch, statue, or fountain makes a wise use of his surplus. "Man does not live by bread alone."

*Fifth*—We have another good use for surplus wealth, in providing for our cities halls suitable for meetings of all kinds, especially for concerts of elevating music. Our cities are rarely provided with halls for these purposes, being in this respect also very far behind European cities. The Springer Hall, of Cincinnati, that valuable addition to the city, was largely the gift of Mr. Springer, who was not content to bequeath funds from his estate at death, but who gave during his life, and, in addition, gave—what was equally important—his time and business ability to ensure the successful results which have been achieved. The gift of a hall to any city lacking one is an excellent use for surplus wealth for the good of a community. The reason why the people have only one instructive and elevating, or even amusing, entertainment when a dozen would be highly beneficial, is that the rent of a hall, even when a suitable hall exists (which is rare), is so great as to prevent managers from running the risk of financial failure. If every city in our land owned a hall which could be given or rented for a small sum for such gatherings as a committee or the mayor of the city judged advantageous, the people could be furnished with proper lectures, amusements, and concerts at an exceedingly small cost. The town halls of European cities, many of which have organs, are of inestimable value to the people, when utilized as they are in the manner suggested. Let no one underrate the influence of entertainments of an elevating or even of an amusing character, for these do much to make the lives of the people happier and their natures better. If any millionaire born in a small village, which has now become a great city, is prompted in the day of his success to do something for his birthplace with part of his surplus, his grateful remembrance cannot take a form more useful than that of a public hall with an organ, provided the city agrees to maintain and use it.

*Sixth*—In another respect we are still much behind Europe. A form of beneficence which is not uncommon there is providing swimming baths for the people. The donors of these have been wise enough to require the city benefited to maintain them at its own expense, and as proof of the contention that everything should never be done for anyone or for any community, but that the recipients should invariably be called upon to do part, it is significant that it is found essential for the popular success of these healthful establishments to exact a nominal charge for their use. In many cities, however, the school children are admitted free at fixed hours upon certain days, different hours being fixed for the boys and the girls to use the great swimming baths, hours or days being also fixed for the use of these baths by ladies. In inland cities the young of both sexes are thus taught to swim. Swimming clubs are organized, and matches are frequent, at which medals and prizes are given. The reports published by the various swimming baths throughout Great Britain are filled with instances of lives saved because those who fortunately escaped shipwreck had been taught to swim in the baths, and not a few instances are given in which the pupils of certain bathing establishments have saved the lives of others. If any disciple of the "Gospel of Wealth "gives his favorite city large swimming and private baths (provided the municipality undertakes their management as a city affair), he will never be called to account for an improper use of the funds entrusted to him.

*Seventh*—Churches as fields for the use of surplus wealth have purposely been reserved until the last, because, these being sectarian, every man will be governed by his own attachments; therefore gifts to churches, it may be said, are not, in one sense, gifts to the community at large, but to special classes. Nevertheless, every millionaire may know of a district where the little cheap, uncomfortable, and altogether unworthy wooden structure stands at the crossroads, to which the whole neighborhood gathers on Sunday, and which is the center of social life and source of neighborly feeling. The administrator of wealth has made a good use of part of his surplus if he replaces that building with a permanent structure of brick, stone, or granite, up the sides of which the honeysuckle and columbine may climb, and from whose tower the sweet-tolling bell may sound. The millionaire should not figure how cheaply this structure can be built, but how perfect it can be made. If he has the money, it should be made a gem, for the educating influence of a pure and noble specimen of architecture, built, as the pyramids were built, to stand for ages, is not to be measured by dollars. Every farmer's home, heart, and mind in the district will be influenced by the beauty and grandeur of the church. But having given the building, the donor should stop there; the support of the church should be upon its own people; there is not much genuine religion in the congregation or much good to flow from the church which is not supported at home.

Many other avenues for the wise expenditure of surplus wealth might be indicated. I enumerate but a few—a very few—of the many fields which are open, and only those in which great or considerable sums can be judiciously used. It is not the privilege, however, of millionaires alone to work for or aid measures which are certain to benefit the community. Every one who has but a small surplus above his moderate wants may share this privilege with his richer brothers, and those without surplus can give at least part of their time, which is usually as important as funds, and often more so. Someday, perhaps, with your permission, I will endeavor to point out some fields and modes in which these may perform well their part as trustees of wealth or leisure, according to the measure of their respective fortunes.

It is not expected, neither is it desirable, that there should be a general concurrence as to the best possible use of surplus wealth. For different men and different localities there are different uses. What commends itself most highly to the judgment of the administrator is the best use for him, for his heart should be in the work. It is as important in administering wealth as it is in any other branch of a man's work that he should be enthusiastically devoted to it and feel that in the field selected his work lies. Besides this, there is room and need for all kinds of wise benefactions for the common weal. The man who builds a university, library, or laboratory performs no more useful work than he who elects to devote himself and his surplus means to the adornment of a park, the gathering together of a collection of pictures for the public, or the building of a memorial arch. These are all true laborers in the vineyard. The only point required by the "Gospel of Wealth" is that the surplus which accrues from time to time in the hands of a man should be administered by him in his own lifetime for that purpose which is seen by him, as trustee, to be best for the good of the people. To leave at death what he cannot take away, and place upon others the burden of the work which it was his own duty to perform, is to do nothing worthy. This requires no sacrifice, nor any sense of duty to his fellows.

Time was when the words concerning the rich man entering heaven were regarded as a hard saying. Today, when all questions are probed to the bottom and the standards of faith receive the most liberal interpretations, the startling verse has been relegated to the rear, to await the next kindly revision as one of those things which cannot be quite understood, but which meanwhile—it is carefully to be observed—are not to be understood literally. But is it so very improbable that the next stage of thought is not to restore the doctrine in all its pristine purity and force, as being in perfect harmony with sound ideas upon the subject of wealth and poverty, the rich and the poor, and the contrasts everywhere seen and deplored? In Christ's day, it is evident, reformers were against the wealthy. It is nonetheless evident that we are fast recurring to that position today; and there will be nothing to surprise the student of sociological development if society should soon approve the text which has caused so much anxiety: "It is easier for a camel to enter the eye of a needle than for a rich man to enter the Kingdom of Heaven." Even if the needle were the small casement at the gates, the words betoken serious difficulty for the rich. It will be but a step for the theologian to take from the doctrine that he who dies rich dies disgraced to that which brings upon the man punishment or deprivation hereafter.

The "Gospel of Wealth" but echoes Christ's words. It calls upon the millionaire to sell all that he hath and give it in the highest and best form to the poor, by administering his estate himself for the good of his fellows, before he is called upon to lie down and rest upon the bosom of Mother Earth. So doing, he will approach his end no longer the ignoble hoarder of useless millions, poor, very poor indeed, in money, but rich, very rich, twenty times a millionaire still, in the affection, gratitude, and admiration of his fellow-men, and—sweeter far—soothed and sustained by the still small voice within, which, whispering, tells him that, because he has lived, perhaps one small part of the great world has been bettered just a little. This much is sure: against such riches as these no bar will be found at the Gates of Paradise.

The problem of wealth will not down. It is obviously so unequally distributed that the attention of civilized man must be attracted to it from time to time. He will ultimately enact the laws needed to produce a more equal distribution. It is again foremost in the public mind today.

We have evidence of this in President Teddy Roosevelt's recent speech of April 14th, 1906, in which he gives direct and forcible expression to public sentiment. We quote:

> It is important to this people to grapple with the problems connected with the amassing of enormous fortunes, and the use of those fortunes, both corporate and individual, in business. We should discriminate in the sharpest way between fortunes well won and fortunes ill won; between those gained as an incident to performing great services to the community as a whole, and those

gained in evil fashion by keeping just within the limits of mere law-honesty. Of course, no amount of charity in spending such fortunes in any way compensates for misconduct in making them. As a matter of personal conviction, and without pretending to discuss the details or formulate the system, I feel that we shall ultimately have to consider the adoption of some such scheme as that of a progressive tax on all fortunes beyond a certain amount, either given in life or devised or bequeathed upon death to any individual—a tax so framed as to put it out of the power of the owner of one of these enormous fortunes to hand on more than a certain amount to any one individual; the tax, of course, to be imposed by the national and not the State government. Such taxation should, of course, be aimed merely at the inheritance or transmission in their entirety of those fortunes swollen beyond all healthy limits.

It is seventeen years since *The North American Review* published "The Gospel of Wealth," written by this writer, which strongly urged graduated taxation of estates at death of possessors as the easiest and best mode of ensuring for the community a just share of great fortunes. He is in full accord with the President's views, as quoted, upon this vital question. Continued study has only confirmed him in his conviction of their justice, their beneficent effect upon society, and their necessity in the not-distant future. Much has been written of a contrary character. Graduated taxation has been denounced as unjust and Socialistic, fatal to Individualism and sure to sap the springs of enterprise. If the writer thought it favorable to Socialism or Communism, or in the least degree opposed to Individualism, he would be the last to favor it, for of nothing is he more fully convinced than that in Individualism lies the secret of the steady progress of civilization. Except we build upon the foundation of "As ye sow so shall ye reap," we labor in vain to establish a higher, or even to maintain the present, civilization. Virtue must bring reward, vice punishment, work wages, sloth misery. Energy and skill must win a prize denied to indolence and ignorance. He who sows the wind must reap the whirlwind.

The rights of private property emerged slowly from ages when property was held mostly in common; as civilization advanced men became less communistic and more individualistic. Public sentiment at last sustained private property because it was found favorable, and discarded Communism because it was found unfavorable, to progress; but there is nothing sacred about individual ownership except as man has established it as the system under which progress can be made. There is no cause to fear, therefore, that man is ever to turn round and creep backward toward the barbarism from which he has finally emerged. The law of evolution forbids, for his march is upward. Should he go too far in assessing wealth, he will inevitably reverse his action and adopt that policy which is best for the general good.

First, as to the justice of taxing large fortunes left at death upon a graduated scale for the benefit of the community. Graduated taxes are no new feature. Britain long since adopted them.

They are advocated by no less an authority than Adam Smith, who says, "The subjects of every state ought to contribute to the support of government as nearly as possible in proportion to their respective abilities."

Let us go to the root of the matter and inquire how these fortunes are created, from whence and how they arise.

Imagine an honest hardworking farmer who finds himself able to give to each of his two sons a farm. They have married admirable young women of the neighborhood, of good kith and kin, friends from youth—no mistake about their virtues. The sons find farms, one in the center of Manhattan Island, the other beyond the Harlem. They cast lots for the farms as the fairest method, thus letting the fates decide. Neither has a preference. The Harlem farm falls to the elder, the Manhattan to the younger. Mark now the problem of wealth, how it develops.

A few hundred dollars buy the farms, and the loving brothers set out for themselves. They are respected by all; loved by their intimates. To the extent of their means, they are liberal contributors to all good causes, and especially to the relief of neighbors who through exceptional troubles need friendly aid and counsel. They are equally industrious, cultivate their farms equally well and in every respect are equally good citizens of the state. Their children grow up and are educated together.

The growth of New York City northwards soon makes the children of the younger millionaires, while those of the elder remain simple farmers in comfortable circumstances, but still of the class who, fortunate in this beyond their cousins, have to perform some service to their fellows and thus earn a livelihood.

Now, who or what made this difference in wealth? Not labor, not skill. No, nor superior ability, sagacity, nor enterprise, nor greater public service. The Community created the millionaire's wealth. While he slept, it grew as fast as when he was awake. It would have arisen exactly as it did had he been on the Harlem and his brother on the Manhattan farm.

The younger farmer, now a great property-holder, dies and his children in due time pass away, each leaving millions, since the farm has become part of a great city, and immense buildings upon it produce annual rents of hundreds of thousands of dollars.

When these children die, who have neither toiled nor spun, what canon of justice would be violated were the nation to step in and say that, since the aggregation of their fellow men called "the community" created the decedent's wealth, it is entitled to a large portion of it as they pass away. The community has refrained from exacting any part during their lives. The heirs have been allowed to enjoy it all, because although in their case the wealth was a purely communal growth, yet in other cases wealth often comes largely from individual effort and ability, and hence it is better for the community to allow such ability to remain in charge of fortune-making, because most likely to succeed, and in so doing develop our country's resources.

It would be unwise to interfere with the working bees; better allow them to continue gathering honey during their lives. When they die, the nation should have a large portion of the honey remaining in the hives; it is immaterial at what date collection is made, so that it comes to the National Treasury at last.

In a prosperous country, increasing rapidly in population, like our own, by far the greatest amount of wealth created in any department comes from enhanced values of real property.

The census shows that from 1890 to 1900 the value of real estate increased by nearly $13 billion.

The obvious creator of this wealth is not the individual but the community, as we see in the case of the two brother farmers. Property may pass through many proprietors, each paying more for it than his predecessor; but whether each succeeding owner sells to his successor at a profit depends almost solely upon whether the surrounding population increases. Let population remain stationary and so do values of property. Let it decline, and values fall even more rapidly. In other words, increased population—the community—creates the wealth in each successive generation. Decrease of population reduces it, and this law holds in the whole of that vast and greatest field of wealth, real estate. In no other field is the making of wealth so greatly dependent upon the community, so little upon the owner, who may wholly neglect it without injury. Therefore no other form of wealth should contribute to the nation so generously.

Let us now trace the acquisition of wealth by the active businessman who has some personal part, and often not a small one, in creating it.

Imagine four brothers, sons of another hardworking farmer. The first settles in New York City, the second in Pittsburgh, the third in Chicago and the fourth in Montana. The first sees that railroads in every direction are essential to the coming Metropolis and devotes himself to this field, obtains large interests therein; and, as the population of the country increases and that of New York City bounds ahead into the millions, these lines of transport laden with traffic justify increasing bonded debt. Having the figures under his eye, he sees that the shares of these railways are sure to become dividend-paying, that even already there are surplus earnings beyond the bonded interest, which, if not needed for pressing extensions, could be paid in dividends and make the stock par. He strains his credit, borrows great sums, buys the shares when prices are low, and, floating upon a tidal wave of swelling prosperity, caused by the increased traffic of rapidly increasing communities, he soon becomes a multimillionaire and at his death his children are all left millionaires. In the consolidation of the various short lines into one great whole there was margin for a stupendous increase of capital; and in other collateral fields there lay numerous opportunities for profitable exploitation, all, however, dependent upon an expanding population for increased values. Now, while the founder of the family must be credited with remarkable ability and with having done the state some service in his day and generation, it cannot be denied that the chief creator of his wealth was the increasing communities along the railroads, which gave the traffic that lifted these lines into dividend-payers upon a capital far beyond the actual cost of the property.

In the work and its profits the nation was an essential partner, and equally entitled with the individual to share in the dividends.

The second son is so fortunate as to settle in Pittsburgh when it has just been discovered that some of the coalfields of which it is the center produced a coking-coal admirably adapted for iron-ore smelting. Another vein easily mined proved a splendid steam-coal. Small iron mills soon sprang up. Everything indicated that here was indeed the future iron city, where steel could be produced more cheaply than in any other location in the world. Naturally, his attention was turned in this direction. He wooed the genius of the place. This was not anything extraordinarily clever. It was in the air. He is entitled to credit for having abiding faith in the future of his country and of steel, and for risking with his young companions not only all he had, which was little or nothing, but all they could induce timid bankers to lend from time to time. He and his partners built mills and furnaces, and finally owned a large concern making millions yearly. This son and his partners looked ahead. They visited other lands and noted conditions, and finally concluded that a large supply of raw materials was the key to permanent prosperity. Accordingly, they bought or leased many mines of iron ore, many thousands of acres of coal and of limestone and also of natural-gas territory, and at last had for many long years a full supply of all the minerals required to produce iron and steel. This was wise policy, but it did not require genius, only intelligent study and good judgment, to see that. They did not produce these minerals; they saw them lying around open for sale at prices that are now deemed only nominal. Much of the wealth of the concern came from these minerals which were once the public property of the community, and were easily secured by this fortunate son and his partners upon trifling royalties.

Their venture was made profitable by the demand for their products, iron and steel, from the expanding population engaged in settling a new continent. Without new populous communities far and near, no milliondom was possible for them. The increasing population was always the important factor in their success. Why should the Nation be denied participation in the results when the gatherers cease to gather and a division has to be made?

The third son was attracted to Chicago, and quite naturally became an employee in a meatpacking concern, in which he soon made himself indispensable. A small interest in the business was finally won by him, and he rose in due time to millionairedom, just as the population of the country swelled. If Chicago today, and our country generally, had only the population of early days, there could have been no great fortune for the third son. Here, as before, it was the magnitude of the business, based solely upon the wants of the population, that swelled the yearly profits and produced prodigious fortunes.

The fourth son, attracted by the stories of Hecla and Calumet, and other rich mines which "far surpass the wealth of Ormus or of Ind" settled in Montana and was lucky after some years of rude experience. His ventures gave him the coveted millionairedom. The amount of copper and silver required by the teeming population of the country and of other lands kept prices high, and hence his enormous profits mined from land for which only a trifle was paid to the General Government not so long ago. He did not create his wealth; he only dug it out of the mine as the demands of the people gave value to the previously worthless stones. Here especially we cannot but feel that the people who created the value should share the dividends when these must pass into other hands.

The fifth son had a melancholy career. He settled in New York City while young and unfortunately began his labors in a stockbroker's office, where he soon became absorbed in the fluctuations of the Exchange, while his fond mother proudly announced to all she met that he "was in business." From this the step was easy to taking chances with his small earnings.

His gambling ventures proved successful. It was an era of rising values, and he soon acquired wealth without increasing values, for speculation is the parasite of business feeding upon values, creating none. A few years and the feverish life of the gamester told upon him. He was led into a scheme to corner a certain stock, and, as was to have been expected, he found that men who will conspire to entrap others will not hesitate to deceive their partners upon occasion if sure it will pay and be safe from exposure. He ended his life by his own hand. His end serves to keep his brothers resolute in the resolve never to gamble. The speculator seldom leaves a millionaire's fortune, unless he breaks down or passes away when his ventures are momentarily successful. In such a case, his ill-gotten gold should be levied upon by the state at the highest rate of all, even beyond that imposed upon real estate values. Wealth is often, we may say generally, accumulated in such manner as benefits the nation in the process; here the means employed demoralizes the getter as well as the people, and lowers the standard of ethics. It is taken without returning any valid consideration.

There is one class of millionaires whose wealth in very much greater degree than others may be credited to themselves. Graham Bell of the telephone, Edison of numerous inventions, Westinghouse of the airbrake, and others, who originated or first applied processes hitherto unused, and were sufficiently alive to their pecuniary interests to hold large shares in the companies formed to develop and introduce them to the public. Their wealth had its origin in their own inventive brains. All honor to the inventor! He stands upon a higher platform than the others.

It may be said that in greater or less degree our leading manufacturers, railroad-builders, department-store projectors, meatpackers, and other specialists in one line or other had to adopt new methods; and, with few, if any, exceptions, there can be traced in their careers some special form of ability upon which their success depended, thus distinguishing them from the mass of competitors. No doubt this is correct, yet the inventions or processes used were the work of others, so that all they did was to introduce new methods of management or to recognize and utilize opportunities. This the inventor class have also done if they have become millionaires, but in addition they have invented the new processes. So that these deserve to reap beyond the other class, yet only in degree, because both classes alike depend upon increasing population—the masses, who require, or consume, the article produced, so that even the inventor's wealth is in great part dependent upon the community which uses his productions.

It is difficult to understand why, at the death of its possessor, great wealth, gathered or created in any of these or in other forms, should not be shared by the community which has been the most potent cause or partner of all in its creation. We have seen that enormous fortunes are dependent upon the community; without great and increasing population, there could be no great wealth. Where wealth accrues honorably, the people are always silent partners.

It is not denied that the great administrator, whether as railroad-builder, steamship-owner, manufacturer, merchant, banker, is an exceptional man, or that millions honestly made in any useful occupation give evidence of ability, foresight, and assiduity above the common and prove the man who has made them a valuable member of society. In no wise, therefore, should such men be unduly hampered or restricted as long as they are spared. After all, they can absorb comparatively little; and, generally speaking, the money-making man, in contrast to his heirs, who generally become members of the smart or fast set, is abstemious, retiring and little of a spendthrift. The millionaire himself is probably the least expensive bee in the industrial hive, taking into account the amount of honey he gathers and what he consumes.

An Income Tax is sometimes proposed as one of the best possible modes of correcting the uneven distribution of wealth, but of all taxes this is the most pernicious. It demoralizes a nation. Mr. Gladstone, one of the greatest financial ministers, advocated its abolition in Britain, alleging that it made a "Nation of Liars." During the Civil War, we had such a tax and paid it loyally, but public sentiment demanded its repeal and it was the first tax remitted when war ceased—justly so because it penalized the honest citizen. Its imposition would be strenuously opposed unless it were graduated and the exemption line placed high, so that the tax should be restricted to the few enormous fortunes. The Supreme Court has declared such a tax to be unconstitutional. No great gain would result to the state from it compared to what would accrue from the easier plan of exacting heavy taxes at death. The date of collection matters little, so that the payment is certain at last. Such proportions can be exacted as are deemed proper from time to time, until it is generally agreed that great wealth at last pays its fair share to the people of the Nation, who were so highly instrumental in creating it or from whom it was gathered.

The collection of an Income Tax would require a large trained body of permanent officials to collect from indignant, discontented people, naturally resenting intrusive inquiries regarding their private affairs. The honest would always pay, the dishonest would usually escape. Much better that Corporations should be required to pay a dividend tax to the Nation which would be really a tax upon Incomes. It is by doing so that Britain realizes such enormous sums from its Income Tax. Were she to attempt to collect these direct from each individual, it would be found much less productive. So should we find if we made the attempt. There is no reason for so doing. Every dividend-paying Corporation can be made the rigid collector of Income Tax for the Government.

It is clearly at the rich man's death that the community should exact a large share of estate, a graduated share, increasing in proportion to its extent. It should be paid over to the Government and applied to the service of the people, the silent but contributive partner from whom it has been so largely derived. The graduated death duties exacted by Britain might guide us in the beginning. The maximum assessment upon estates to the lineal successors is eight percent, upon the valuation, but to distant legatees it is very much higher. Smaller estates pay less in proportion.

Such contributions from the owners of enormous fortunes at death would do much to reconcile dissatisfied but fair-minded people to the alarmingly unequal distribution of wealth arising from the new industrial conditions of our day and the era of unprecedented prosperity our country has enjoyed for years.

The millionaire himself should rejoice at the thought of being a useful laborer in the national vineyard and in knowing that his contribution to the general fund at death will lessen the drain upon the scanty resources of his less successful fellows. Wealth left at death seldom does better service than this.

The people see how equivocally in many cases, how unfairly in others, fortunes have been made. Especially have the numerous failures of prominent men in official position to perform their duties properly deeply impressed them, and produced a strong feeling of antagonism to wealth and millionaires as a class. The appeal to them in the June number of this *Review* should not pass unheeded. As wealth comes mainly from the community, it should be administered as a sacred trust, by the temporary recipient, for the public good. Property in one sense is a mere creature of the law. Whether the holder be permitted to bequeath it to his successors and to what extent and how, are simply questions of policy for the people through the Government to determine. France has long restricted it. Our States generally designate the widow's share. There is here no question of right or wrong, but simply one of policy—what is best in all respects for the Nation.

Fortunes have recently been more easily made with us than ever, both in number and amount, with the inevitable result that sudden wealth is bound to produce in a new land, which, not so long ago, was much freer from immense fortunes than the older lands of Europe. Millionaires are a recent growth in the Republic. Multimillionaires were unheard of before our day.

Some sixty-odd years ago, Britain, then in the beginning of the speculative period of railroad construction and manufacturing supremacy, had a somewhat similar experience. Greater fortunes were made than ever before; but the makers, imbued with the aristocratic ambition to become great landowners and county magnates, were soon absorbed into that class. They regarded wealth only as a means to an end—entrance to the aristocratic and fashionable circle. This refuge new millionaires lack under our democratic system, hence the vulgar, extravagant and offensive character of the follies to which they are driven, that evoke so much adverse criticism from people of education, good sense, and quiet respectable living, with whom mere dollars count for little. Funds collected by the Government from the estates of the millionaires at death would never be likely otherwise to be put to so good a use as the payment of Government expenditures, relieving the people in part from the burden of taxation.

We are yet as a nation in the heyday of youth. In time we shall tone down and live simpler lives and create different standards. Wealth will be dethroned as higher tastes prevail, its pursuit become less absorbing and less esteemed, and, above all, the mere man of wealth himself will come to realize that in the estimation of those of wisest judgment he has no place with the educated, professional man. He occupies a distinctly lower plane intellectually, and in the coming day Brain is to stand above Dollars, Conduct above both. The making of money as an aim will then be rated as an ignoble ambition. No man has ever secured recognition, much less fame, from mere wealth. It confers no distinction among the good or the great.

Meanwhile, as the masses become more intelligent, they may be expected to criticize and denounce the growth of fortunes which fail to contribute largely to the public good, and finally to insist that they shall be made to do so. The first step to this end should be heavy graduated death taxes upon wealth, in pursuance of Adam Smith's dictum already quoted.

Indications of alarm are sometimes seen regarding present conditions. Fears are expressed that a war of classes may arise. On the contrary, there are none but healthful signs in the awakening intelligence and deep interest of the masses in this problem. Its final solution upon right lines cannot but place the body politic in a much better position than before.

The American people can be trusted to deal with improper methods of business and excessive wealth accumulations wisely and well, to the advantage of the Nation, as they have met and solved other pressing problems, some of which for a time were thought by many likely to cause serious trouble, whereas the commotion only indicated that another step nearer the light was about to be taken. So will it be with this new problem of regulating, as needed, both corporations and individuals, that there may be fairer acquisition and fairer distribution of wealth.

# Acres of Diamonds
(1890)

# by Russell H. Conwell

*The Classic Work on Finding Your Fortune Where You Least Expect It*

## Contents

Introduction  *Serve and Grow Rich* by Mitch Horowitz   180
Acres of Diamonds   181

## Introduction
# Serve and Grow Rich

Author Russell H. Conwell belonged to a generation of late nineteenth-century motivational writers who regarded good character as the indispensible ingredient to success. Without character, the minister and educator said, you could attain no success worthy of the name.

Conwell began giving his famous lecture *Acres of Diamonds* in the 1870s, and was said to have delivered it more than 6,152 times around the nation before his death in 1925. He maintained a grueling speaking schedule not only to encourage young people in the ways of ethical achievement, but also to use his speaking fees to found a college dedicated to placing education in reach of working-class students. That school today is Temple University in Philadelphia.

*Acres of Diamonds* remains as sturdy a guide to life as when Conwell first received inspiration for the lecture (and its title) while travelling as a journalist through Persia and Northern Africa in 1869. The ex-Civil War officer spent many hours (not always happily) listening to folk stories that his Arab guides insisted on reciting for travellers. One of the guides told him an intriguing morality tale about a wealthy Persian farmer who had squandered his money and life searching the world for diamonds—dying a pauper before diamonds were finally discovered, on the very farm that he had abandoned to embark on his quest.

The lesson that Conwell took from this story forms the heart of *Acres of Diamonds*: Success can be found right where you stand—provided you possess the simplicity and soundness of character to see it. While *Acres of Diamonds* holds many lessons for today's success-hungry reader, it differs in tone from later generations of motivational literature. Conwell insisted that good character and good business are innately joined: one could not exist without the other. The chief aim of the good businessman, he taught, is to figure out what the people around you need, and devote yourself to filling those needs. This can also make you very wealthy.

Conwell did not believe that it was the job of the capitalist to fleece his customers and workers, but rather to profit from them on the same scale as they profited from him. "I should sell each bill of goods," Conwell wrote, "so that the person to whom I sell shall make as much as I make."

Conwell's book made a surprising return to the news in 2015 when high-tech entrepreneur Dan Price responded to the national rise in income inequality by announcing a minimum salary of $70,000 for workers at his Seattle credit-card processing firm. Price's move generated headlines and controversy. "If there was a 19th-century thinker Mr. Price drew inspiration from," wrote *The New York Times*, "it would be not Karl Marx, but Russell Conwell, the Baptist minister and Temple University founder, whose famed 'Acres of Diamonds' speech fused Christianity and capitalism."

The *Times* was right. Conwell saw the good Christian and the good businessman as one and the same, though he noted that his ideas were for motivated people of all backgrounds.

In this condensed edition of *Acres of Diamonds*, be on the lookout for four principles, which form the foundation of Conwell's success philosophy:
1. Greatness is achieved where you are.
2. Success, including wealth, comes from *filling a human need*.
3. The truly great are *simple*—in speech, methods, ideas, and inventions.
4. Money is power, greatness, and good—but only in the hands someone who will *use it well*.

Although Conwell's examples often focused on entrepreneurship, his principles can be used in any job or pursuit. Conwell's ideal of success—as radical today as it was in the Victorian age—boils down to this: If you sincerely care enough about people to understand and provide for their needs, you will receive material rewards, which, in turn, can be used to uplift others. This is the circle of sound business, good ethics, and meaningful existence.

—Mitch Horowitz

# Acres of Diamonds

The title of this lecture originated in 1869. My travelling party and I had hired a guide from Baghdad to take us down the Tigris River to the Arabian Gulf. Our guide resembled the barbers found in America. That is, he resembled the barbers in certain mental characteristics. He thought it was not only his duty to guide us down the river, but also to entertain us with stories: curious and weird, ancient and modern, strange and familiar. Many of them I have forgotten, and I am glad that I have. But there is one that has stayed with me always.

At a certain point in our journey, the guide had grown irritable over my lack of appreciation for his tales. As he led my camel by the halter he introduced a new story by saying: "This is a tale that I reserve for my *particular friends*." He immediately had my close attention.

He then told me that there once lived near the shore of the River Indus, toward which we were travelling, an ancient Persian by the name of Ali Hafed. He said that Ali Hafed owned a large farm, with orchards, grain fields, and gardens; that he loaned money at interest; had a beautiful wife and lovely children; and was a wealthy and contented man.

One day there visited this old Persian farmer one of those ancient Buddhist priests, one of the wise men of the East, who sat down by Ali Hafed's fireside and told the farmer how this world was created in fascinating—and not unscientific—detail. The priest concluded by telling the farmer that a diamond was the last and the highest of God's mineral creations. The old priest told Ali Hafed that if the farmer had a diamond the size of his thumb, he could purchase a dozen farms like his.

"And," said the priest, "if you had a handful of diamonds, you could purchase the county, and if you had a mine of diamonds you could purchase kingdoms."

Ali Hafed heard all about diamonds that night—and went to bed a poor man in his mind. He wanted a whole mine of diamonds. Early in the morning he sought out the priest.

"Will you tell me where I can find diamonds?" Ali Hafed asked.

"Diamonds?" the priest said. "What do you want of diamonds?"

"I want to be immensely rich," said Ali Hafed.

"Well," said the priest, "if you want diamonds, all you have to do is go find them, and then you will have them."

"But I don't know where to go," said Ali Hafed.

"If you will find a river that runs over white sands between high mountains, in those white sands you will always find diamonds," replied the priest.

"But," asked Ali Hafed, do you believe there is such a place?"

"Plenty of them," said the priest. "You just have to go where they are."

So, Ali Hafed sold his farm, left his family in charge of a neighbor, and away he went in search of diamonds.

He began at the mountain range at the source of the Nile River. Afterward he went to the Holy Land, and then into Europe. At last, when his money was all gone and he was in rags and starving, he stood on the shores at Barcelona in Spain, and he cast himself into the incoming tide, sank beneath its foaming crest, never to rise in this life again.

When the old Arab guide told me this story he stopped to rearrange some of our belongings and I had an opportunity to muse over what he had said. I asked myself: "Why did this old guide reserve this story for his *particular friends?*" But when he began again I discovered that this was the first story that I had ever heard where the hero died in the first chapter—for the guide began a second chapter just as though there had been no break.

The guide went on to say that the man who had purchased Ali Hafed's farm led his camel out into the garden to drink, and as the animal put his nose into the shallow waters of the garden brook, Ali Hafed's successor noticed a curious flash of light from the white sands of the stream. Reaching in he pulled out a black stone containing a strange eye of light. He took it into the house as a curiosity, placed it on the mantel, and forgot about it.

Not long after that same old priest came to visit Ali Hafed's successor. The moment he stepped in the room he noticed the flash of light. The priest rushed to the mantel and said: "Here is a diamond! Here is a diamond! Has Ali Hafed returned?"

"Oh no, Ali Hafed has not returned and we have not heard from him," the new owner said. "And that is not a diamond; it is nothing but a stone we found out in our garden."

"But I know a diamond when I see one," said the priest, "and *that* is a diamond."

Together they rushed out into the garden. They stirred up the white sands, and came upon other more beautiful, more valuable gems than the first.

In this way, said the guide—and, friends, it is historically true—was discovered the diamond mines of Golconda, the most valuable diamond mines in the ancient world.

Well, when the guide had finished the second chapter to his story he took off his cap and swung it in the air to call attention to the moral. He said to me: "Had Ali Hafed remained at home, and dug in his own cellar, or underneath his own wheat field, instead of wretchedness, starvation, poverty, and death in a strange land, he would have had *acres of diamonds.*"

When the guide added his moral I saw why he reserved the story for his *particular friends*. I didn't tell him that I could see it. He had a way of going around a thing, like a lawyer, and saying indirectly what he didn't dare say directly: That in his personal opinion there was a certain young man travelling down the Tigris River who might be better off at home in America.

I told him that his tale reminded me of one. I told him that a man in Northern California owned a ranch in 1847. The rancher heard they had discovered gold in Southern California, though they had not. He sold his ranch to Colonel John Sutter, who put a mill on the little stream below the house. One day the next year, his little girl gathered some of the sand in her hands at the raceway, and brought it into the house. While she was sifting it through her fingers, a visitor noticed the first shining scales of real gold that were ever discovered in California. Acres and acres of gold.

But before we judge the unfortunate California rancher, or poor Ali Hafed, keep in mind that you and I have done the same as they. Ah, now you will say: "Oh no, I never had any acres of diamonds or gold mines." But I say to you that you *did* have gold mines and acres of diamonds—and you have them right now.

Now, let me speak with the greatest care lest my eccentricity of manner should mislead my listeners, and make you think that I am here to entertain more than to help. I want to hold your attention with sufficient interest to leave my lesson with you.

You have had an opportunity to become rich; and to some of you it has been a hardship to purchase a ticket to this lecture. You have no right to be poor. It is all wrong. You have no right to be poor. It is your duty to be rich.

You ought to make money. Money is power, and you ought to be reasonably ambitious to have it. You ought to because you can do more good with it than you could without it. Money printed your Bible, money builds your churches, money sends your missionaries, money pays your preachers, and you would not have many of them, either, if you did not pay them.

Think of how much good you could do if you had money now. Again, money is power—and it ought to be in the hands of good men. It would be in the hands of good men if we comply with Scripture, in which God promises prosperity to the righteous man. That means more than being goody-goody—it means the all-around righteous man. You should be a righteous man, and if you were, you would be rich.

"Oh," you will say, "Mr. Conwell, can you, as a Christian teacher, tell the young people to spend their lives making money? Don't you think there are some things in this world that are better than money?"

Of course I do, but I am talking about money now. Of course there are some things higher than money. Oh, yes, I know by the grave that has left me standing alone that there are some things in this world that are higher and sweeter and purer than money. I also know that there is not one of those things that is not greatly enhanced by the use of money. Love is the grandest thing on God's earth, but fortunate the lover who has plenty of money. I say again, money is power, money is force, money will do good, as well as harm. In the hands of good men and women it could accomplish, and has accomplished, good.

I need to guard myself right here. Because one of my theological students came to me once to charge me with heresy inasmuch as I had said that money was power.

He said: "Mr. Conwell, I feel it my duty to tell you that Scripture says that money 'is the root of all evil.'"

I said: "I would like you to find that passage for me. I have never seen it."

He triumphantly brought a Bible, and with all the bigoted pride of a narrow sectarian, who founds his creed on some misinterpretation of Scripture, threw it down before me and said: "There it is!" And he read: "The *love* of money is the root of all evil."

Indeed it is. The *love* of money is the root of all evil. The love of money—rather than the love of the good it secures—*is* a dangerous evil in the community. The desire to grab hold of money, and to hold onto it, "hugging the dollar until the eagle squeals," is the root of all evil. But it is a grand ambition for men to desire money that they may use it for the benefit of their fellow men.

I say to you, then, that you ought to be rich.

"Well," you say, "I would like to be rich, but I have never had an opportunity. I have never had any diamonds about me!"

My friends you did have an opportunity. And let us see where your mistake was.

What business have you been in?

"Oh," some man or woman will say, "I keep a store on one of these side streets, and I am so far from the great commercial center that I cannot make any money."

"How long have you kept that store?"

"Twenty years."

"Twenty years and not turning a handsome profit now? There is something wrong with you. Nothing wrong with the side street. It is with you."

"Oh now," you will say, "anybody knows that you must be in the center of trade if you are going to make money."

The man of common sense will not admit that that is necessarily true at all. If you are keeping that store and you are not making money, it would have been better for the community if they had kicked you out of that store nineteen years ago.

No man has a right to go into business and not make money. It is a crime to go into business and lose money, because it is a curse to the rest of the community. No man has a moral right to transact business unless he makes something out of it. He has also no right to transact business unless the man he deals with has an opportunity to make something. Unless he lives and lets live, he is not an honest man in business. There are no exceptions to this great rule.

You ought to have been rich. You have no right to keep a store for twenty years and still be poor. You will say to me: "Now, Mr. Conwell, I know the mercantile business better than you do."

My friend, let us consider this a minute.

When I was young my father kept a country store in western Massachusetts, and once in while he left me in charge of that store. Fortunately for him it was not often. When I had it in my charge a man came in the door and asked: "Do you keep jackknives?"

"No, we don't keep jackknives." Then I went off and whistled a tune, and what did I care for that man?

Then another man would come in the same door and say, "Do you keep jackknives?"

"No, we don't keep jackknives." Then I went off and whistled another tune, and what did I care for that man?

Then another man would come in that same door and say, "Do you keep jackknives?"

"No, we don't keep jackknives. Do you suppose we are keeping this store just for the purpose of supplying the whole neighborhood with jackknives?"

Do you carry on your business like that? Do you ask what was the problem with it? The problem was that I had not learned that the foundational principles of business success and the foundational principles of Christianity are both the same. It is the whole of every man's life to be doing for his fellow men. And he who can do the most to help his fellow men is entitled to the greatest reward himself. Not only so says God's holy book, but so says every man's business common sense.

If I had been carrying on my father's store on a Christian plan, or on a plan that leads to success, I would have had a jackknife for the third man when he called for it. Then I would have actually done him a kindness, and I would have received a reward myself, which it would have been my duty to take.

There are some overly pious Christians who think that if you take any profit on anything you sell that you are an unrighteous man. On the contrary, you would be a criminal to sell goods for less than they cost. You have no right to do that. You cannot trust a man with your money who cannot take care of his own. You cannot trust a man in your family who is not true to his own wife. You cannot trust a man in the world who does not begin with his own heart, his own character, his own life.

It would have been my duty to have furnished a jackknife to the third man, or the second, and to have sold it to him and actually profited myself. I have no more right to sell goods without making a profit on them than I have to overcharge dishonestly beyond what they are worth. I should sell each bill of goods so that the person to whom I sell shall make as much as I make.

To live and let live is the principle of the gospel, and the principle of everyday common sense. Oh young man, hear me: live as you go along. Do not wait until you have reached my years before you begin to enjoy anything in life. The man who has gone through life dividing fairly with his fellow men, making and demanding his own rights and his own profits, and given to every other man his rights and profits, lives every day, and not only that, but he is on the royal road to wealth.

But you say: "I don't carry on my business like you did back in Massachusetts." But if you have not made any money, you are carrying on your business like that, and I can tell you what you will say to me tomorrow morning when I go into your store.

I come to you and ask: "Do you know Mr. A?"

"Oh yes. He lives up in the next block. He shops here at my little store."

"Well, where is he originally from?"

"I don't know."

"Does he own his own house?"
"I don't know."
"What business is he in?"
"I don't know."
"Do his children go to school?"
"I don't know."
"What party does he vote?"
"I don't know."
"What church does he go to?"
"I don't know, and I don't care."

Do you answer me like that tomorrow morning in your store? Then you are carrying on your business just as I carried on my father's business back in Massachusetts.

You don't know where Mr. A came from and you *don't care*. You don't care whether he has a happy home. You don't know what church he attends, and you don't care! If you had cared, you would have been a rich man right now.

You never thought it was part of your duty to help him make money. So you cannot succeed! You are acting against every law of business and every rule of political economy, and failure is guaranteed and deserved. What right have you to be in business taking no interest in your fellow men, and not endeavoring to supply them with what they need? You cannot succeed.

I know of a merchant in Boston who made millions of dollars and who began his enterprises out in the suburbs where there were not a dozen houses on the street; although there were other stores scattered about. He became such a necessity to the neighborhood that when he wished to move into the city, the community came to him with a great petition, signed by all the people, begging him not to close that store. He had always looked after the community's interests. He had always carefully studied what they wanted and advised them rightly. He was a necessity; and they must make him wealthy; for in proportion as you are of use to fellow men, in that proportion can they afford to pay you.

You are poor because you are not wanted. You should have made yourself a necessity to the world, and the world would have paid you your own price.

Young man, remember: if you are going to invest your life or talent or money, you must look around and see what people need and then invest yourself, or your money, in that which they need most. Then will your fortune be made, for they must take care of you. It is a difficult lesson to learn.

Why does one merchant surpass another? Why does one manufacturer outsell another? It is simply because that one has found out what people want, and does not waste his time or money on things they do not need. That is the whole of it. A great merchant once said: "I am not going to buy things people do not want. I will take an interest in people and study their needs."

"But," you will say, "I cannot do that here." Yes you can. It is being done in smaller places now, and you can do it as well as another.

The farmer will be more successful when he gives more attention to what people want and not so much to what will grow, though he needs them both. But now the whole time of most of our farmers is taken up with the finding out of "what will grow."

Who are the great inventors? Always the men who are the simplest and plainest. The great inventor has the simple mind, and invents the simplest machine. Did you ever think how simple the first telephones and the telegraph were? The simplest mind is always the greatest. Did you ever see a great man? Great in every noble and true sense? If so, you could walk right up to him and say, "How are you, Jim?" Just think of the great men you have met and you find this is true.

When I was an officer in the Civil War one my soldiers had been sentenced to death for desertion. I went up to the White House—sent there for the first time in my life—to see the President and petition for the boy's life.

I went into the waiting room and sat down with a lot of others on the benches, and the secretary asked one after another to tell him what they wanted. After the secretary had been through the line, he went in, and then came back to the door and motioned for me. I went up to that anteroom, and the secretary said: "That is the president's door right over there. Just rap on it and go right in."

I was never so taken aback in all my life, never. The secretary himself made it worse for me, because he had told me how to go in and then went out another door to the left and shut that. There I was, in the hallway by myself before the President of the United States of America's door. I had been on fields of battle, where the shells did sometimes shriek and the bullets did sometimes hit me, but I always wanted to run. I have no sympathy with the old man who says, "I would just as soon march up to the cannon's mouth as eat my dinner." I have no faith in a man who doesn't know enough to be afraid when he is being shot at. I never was so afraid when the shells came around us at Antietam as I was when I went into that room that day; but I finally mustered the courage—I don't know how I ever did—and at arm's length tapped on the door. The man inside did not help me at all, but yelled out: "Come in and sit down!"

Well, I went in and sat down on the edge of a chair, and wished I were in Europe. The man at the table did not look up. He was one of the world's greatest men, and was great by one single rule. Oh, that I could say this one thing to all the young people of our nation, and that they would remember it. I would give a lifetime for the effect it would have on our community and on our civilization. Abraham Lincoln's principle for greatness can be adopted by nearly all. This was his rule: Whatever he had to do at all, he put his whole mind into it and held it all there until he was done. That makes men great almost anywhere. He stuck to those papers at that table and did not look up at me, and I sat there trembling.

Finally, when he had put the string around his papers, he pushed them over to one side and looked over to me, and a smile came over his worn face. He said: "I am a very busy man and have only a few minutes to spare. Now tell me in the fewest words what it is you want."

I began to tell him, and mentioned the case, and he said: "I have heard all about it and you do not need to say any more. Mr. Stanton"—his secretary of war—"was talking to me only a few days ago about that. You can go back to the hotel and rest assured that the president never did sign an order to shoot a boy under twenty years of age, and never will. You can say that to his mother anyhow."

Then he said to me, "How is it going in the field?" I said, "We sometimes get discouraged." And he said: "It is all right. We are going to win out now. We are getting very near the light. No man ought to wish to be president of the United States, and I will be glad when I get through; then my son Tad and I are going out to Springfield, Illinois. I have a bought a farm out there and I don't care if I again earn only twenty-five cents a day. Tad has a mule team, and we are going to plant onions."

Then he asked, "Were you brought up on a farm?" I said, "Yes; in the Berkshire Hills of Massachusetts." He then threw his leg over the corner of the big chair and said, "I have heard many a time, ever since I was young, that up there in those hills you have to sharpen the noses of the sheep in order to get down to the grass between the rocks." He was so familiar, so everyday, so farmer-like, that I felt right at home with him at once.

He then took hold of another roll of paper, and looked up at me and said: "Good morning." I took the hint then and got up and went out. After I had gotten out I could not realize I had seen the President of the United States at all.

Did you ever see a man who struts around altogether too large to notice an ordinary working mechanic? Do you think he is great? He is nothing but a puffed-up balloon, held down by his big feet. There is no greatness there. There may be greatness in self-respect but there is no greatness in feeling above one's fellow men. The simple men are the greatest always.

Once I went up to New Hampshire to lecture and when I returned I said I would never lecture in New Hampshire again. I told a relative of mine, who was a professor at Harvard: "I was cold all the time I was there and I shivered so much that my teeth shook."

"Why did you shiver?" he asked.

"Because it was cold."

"No, that is not the reason you shivered."

Then I said: "I shivered because I had not bedclothes enough."

"No, that is not the reason."

"Well," I said, "Professor, you are a scientific man. I am not. I would like to have an expert, scientific opinion of why I shivered."

He arose in his facetious way and said to me: "Young man you shivered because you did not know any better! Did you have in your pocket a two-cent newspaper?"

"Oh, yes, I had a *Herald* and a *Journal*."

"That is it. You had them in your pocket, and if you had spread one newspaper over your sheet when you want to bed, you would've been as a warm as the richest man in America under all his silk coverlids. But you shivered because you didn't know enough to put a two-cent newspaper on your bed, and you had it in your pocket."

It is the power to appreciate the little things that brings success. The greatest inventors are those who see what the people need, and then invent something to fill that need. If you know what people need, you have gotten more knowledge of a fortune than any amount of capital can give you. Indeed, the moment a young man or woman gets more money than he or she has grown to by practical experience, that moment he has gotten a curse. I tell you this great secret: Your wealth is too near to you. You are looking right over it.

And note, too, that greatness does not consist in holding high office or in rank, even in times of war. The office does not make the man. Every great general is credited with many victories he never knew anything about, simply because they were won by his subordinates. But it is unfair to give the credit to a general who did not know anything about it. I tell you if the lightening of heaven had struck out of existence every man who wore shoulder straps in our wars, there would have arisen out of the ranks of our private soldiers just as great men to lead the nation to victory.

Greatness really consists in doing great deeds with little means—in the accomplishment of vast purposes from the private ranks of life—in benefiting one's own neighborhood, in blessing one's own city, the community in which he dwells. There, and there only, is the great test of human goodness and human ability. He who waits for a high office before he does great and noble deeds must fail altogether.

I have learned the lesson from being around men who hold high office that you and I should call no man great simply because he holds an office. Greatness! It is something more than office, more than fame, more than genius! It is the great-heartedness that encloses those in need, reaches down to those below, and lifts them up. May this thought come to every one of the young men and women who hear me speak and abide through future years.

I close with the words of Philip James Bailey. He was not one of our greatest writers, but, after all, in this he was one of our best:

We live in deeds, not years; in thoughts, not breaths;
In feelings, not in figures on a dial.
We should count time by heart-throbs. He most lives
Who thinks most . . .

Oh, friends, if you forget everything else I say, don't forget these two lines; for if you think *two* thoughts where I think *one*, you live twice as much as I do in the same length of time:

. . . He most lives
Who thinks most, feels the noblest, acts the best.

# In Tune With the Infinite
(1897)

# by Ralph Waldo Trine

*The Timeless Classic on the Power of Your Eternal Mind*

## Contents

Introduction   *Bringing the Infinite to Earth* by Mitch Horowitz   194
Author's Preface   197
Chapter One   Fullness of Peace, Power, and Plenty   197
Chapter Two   The Supreme Fact of the Universe   198
Chapter Three   The Supreme Fact of Human Life   200
Chapter Four   Fullness of Life—Bodily Health and Vigor   204
Chapter Five   Wisdom and Interior Illumination   206
Chapter Six   The Realization of Perfect Peace   211
Chapter Seven   Coming Into Fullness of Power   214
Chapter Eight   Plenty of All Things—The Law of Prosperity   219
Chapter Nine   How Men Have Become Prophets, Seers, Sages, and Saviors   224
Chapter Ten   The Basic Principle of All Religions—The Universal Religion   225
Chapter Eleven   Entering Now Into the Realization of the Highest Riches   228
Chapter Twelve   "The Way"   230

## Introduction
# Bringing the Infinite to Earth

In one of my favorite scenes from *The Wizard of Oz* Dorothy is running away from home and happens upon the wagon of a Professor Marvel who sympathetically invites her inside to his fortunetelling parlor. Seating Dorothy before a crystal ball, Professor Marvel tells the wide-eyed girl:

> That's right. Here—sit right down here. That's it. Ha ha! This—this is the same genuine, magic, authentic crystal used by the Priests of Isis and Osiris in the days of the Pharaohs of Egypt—in which Cleopatra first saw the approach of Julius Caesar and Marc Antony, and—and so on—and so on. Now, you—you'd better close your eyes, my child, for a moment—in order to be better in tune with the infinite.

*In tune with the infinite.* The title of Ralph Waldo Trine's 1897 book retained posterity as a catchphrase for numinous realities in the 1939 movie, more than a generation after its publication. (Neither the scene nor phrase appears in Theosophist L. Frank Baum's original novel from 1900.) The reference testifies to the enormity of the book's cultural reach and recognition in the first half of the twentieth century. In many respects, *In Tune With the Infinite* was the nation's first mass bestseller of therapeutic spirituality, laying the template for future works such as *Alcoholics Anonymous* in 1939 and Norman Vincent Peale's *The Power of Positive Thinking* in 1952, both of which use Trine's phraseology, if not always with attribution.

Although the *Oz* screenwriters were poking gentle fun at the author, the movie also presented the perfect framing of Trine's metaphysics, which echoed and augmented the popular spiritual vision of the nation itself: belief in the innocence of the individual, the capacity to break through to other realms, and the transcendent promise of self-improvement.

Indeed, many of Trine's phrases and themes entered the lexicon of American spirituality. The term "Higher Power"—central to Alcoholics Anonymous and the 12-step movement—probably came from *In Tune With the Infinite*, where Trine repeatedly used the phrase with particular reference to alcohol: "In the degree that we come into the realization of the higher powers of the mind and spirit... there also falls away the desire for the heavier, grosser, less valuable kinds of food and drink, such as the flesh of animals, alcoholic drinks..." Trine helped popularize the term "Law of Attraction," which until his book was a little-known phrase from deep within the folds of metaphysical culture (and was only just coming into coinage for the concept of like thoughts attracting like circumstances). Many writers, including Neville Goddard, adopted Trine's term "enter the silence" to signal communion with the infinite. William James mentioned Trine as among the New Thought figures who moved him to conclude that "it really looks as if a good start might be made in the direction of changing our American mental habit into something more indifferent and strong." (By *indifferent* James meant serviceable and utilitarian.) Henry Ford called the book a major factor in his success and pressed copies on friends and visitors to his office. Even televangelist Oral Roberts echoed Trine, encouraging readers to reflect: "I am in tune with God."

---

The man who started it all was born in Northern Illinois in 1866, the same year as the death of mental-healing pioneer Phineas Quimby. Ralph Waldo Trine, named for Transcendentalist philosopher Ralph Waldo Emerson, studied history and political science at Johns Hopkins University and later won a $100 prize for an essay on "The Effects of Humane Education on the Prevention of Crime." Little is known about Trine personally, including the mystical influences that led to his signature work soon after he turned 31. What is evident is that beneath the placid, almost priestly exterior that appears in his photographs burned a desire to unite mysticism and social reform. A 1902 profile in the New Thought magazine *Mind* said that Trine believed in the cooperative ethos of socialism and that he planned to write a book "from the viewpoint of a socialist who is such because of his New Thought philosophy."

It is not clear that Trine ever wrote such a book, but something very close appeared under his byline in 1910: *Land of Living Men*. While *In Tune With the Infinite* employed a gentle, folksy tone emphasizing gratitude and generosity, *Land of Living Men* revealed different colors. The New Thought pioneer called for "a great people's movement to bring back to the people the immense belongings that have been taken away from them." Trine advocated busting up monopolies, striking for higher wages, and placing essential utilities and industries into public hands. This was one book that Henry Ford didn't give away to friends. In fact, *Land of Living Men* seemed to make little impact at all on Trine's followers. By 1928, Trine was an honored guest in Ford's office, where he engaged in an almost fawning interview with the automaker. Their conversation was turned into a popular book, *The Power That Wins*, which ranged from Ford's love for avocados to his belief in reincarnation. Whatever Trine's innermost commitments, he would never again be seen—nor succeed as—a political Jeremiah.

The power of *In Tune With the Infinite* rests on two counts. The first is that Trine created perhaps not the earliest but the most effective and widely accessible iteration of the New Thought gospel that thoughts are causative. Trine's popularization remained unmatched until Norman Vincent Peale published *The Power of Positive Thinking* more than fifty years later. But Trine's book was something that Peale's was not—and this forms the second basis of its achievement. Although Trine's reference points are chiefly Christian, *In Tune With the Infinite* is one of the first widely popular works of *religious universalism*.

Peale's book was explicitly Christian; the Dutch Reform minister reimagined New Thought in language that was reassuringly familiar to the churchgoing public. (Although even in this regard Peale snuck in some radically mystical concepts and references.) Trine, by contrast, incorporated principles, if not always language, from broad-spanning religious traditions. In some respects, *In Tune With the Infinite* is as much a popularization of New Thought as it is of Hermetic philosophy. Hermeticism is a late-ancient Greek-Egyptian mystical school that taught that the individual is an extension of a higher mind, or *Nous*, and possesses the same creative potentials. You'll see this on display in chapter three, "The Supreme Fact of Human Life," where Trine talks about the nature of the "God-man." In chapter four, "Fullness of Life—Bodily Health and Vigor," Trine remakes the core Hermetic dictum "As above, so below" into "As within, so without; cause, effect." The Hermetic outlook is likewise present when Trine talks about a "divine inflow" into the individual. This also echoes eighteenth-century mystic Emanuel Swedenborg's concept of a "Divine influx."

Trine, for all his folksy language, was a radical thinker. And *In Tune With the Infinite*, a book that ultimately sold more than two million copies when the nation itself was far less populous than today, brought everyday Americans ideas that were jarring, fresh, anti-mainstream, and transcendent. That such themes of spiritual possibility sound so familiar to us today is testament to the author's legacy.

—Mitch Horowitz

## Author's Preface

There is a golden thread that runs through every religion in the world. There is a golden thread that runs through the lives and the teachings of all the prophets, seers, sages, and saviors in the world's history, through the lives of all men and women of truly great and lasting power. All that they have ever done or attained to has been done in full accordance with law. What one has done, all may do.

This same golden thread must enter into the lives of all who today, in this busy work-a-day world of ours, would exchange impotence for power, weakness and suffering for abounding health and strength, pain and unrest for perfect peace, poverty of whatever nature for fullness and plenty.

Each is building his own world. We both build from within and we attract from without. Thought is the force with which we build, for thoughts are forces. Like builds like and like attracts like. In the degree that thought is spiritualized does it become more subtle and powerful in its workings. This spiritualizing is in accordance with law and is within the power of all.

Everything is first worked out in the unseen before it is manifested in the seen, in the ideal before it is realized in the real, in the spiritual before it shows forth in the material. The realm of the unseen is the realm of cause. The realm of the seen is the realm of effect. The nature of effect is always determined and conditioned by the nature of its cause.

There is a divine sequence running throughout the universe. Within and above and below the human will incessantly works the Divine will. To come into harmony with it and thereby with all the higher laws and forces, to come then into league and to work in conjunction with them, in order that they can work in league and in conjunction with us, is to come into the chain of this wonderful sequence. This is the secret of all success.

## Chapter One

# Fullness of Peace, Power and Plenty

The optimist is right. The pessimist is right. The one differs from the other as the light from the dark. Yet both are right. Each is right from his own particular point of view, and this point of view is the determining factor in the life of each. It determines as to whether it is a life of power or of impotence, of peace or of pain, of success or of failure.

The optimist has the power of seeing things in their entirety and in their right relations. The pessimist looks from a limited and a one-sided point of view. The one has his understanding illumined by wisdom, the understanding of the other is darkened by ignorance. Each is building his world from within, and the result of the building is determined by the point of view of each. The optimist, by his superior wisdom and insight, is making his own heaven, and in the degree that he makes his own heaven is he helping to make one for all the world beside. The pessimist, by virtue of his limitations, is making his own hell, and in the degree that he makes his own hell is he helping to make one for all mankind.

You and I have the predominating characteristics of an optimist or the predominating characteristics of a pessimist. We then are making, hour by hour, our own heaven or our own hell; and in the degree that we are making the one or the other for ourselves are we helping make it for all the world beside.

## Chapter Two
# The Supreme Fact of the Universe

The great central fact of the universe is that Spirit of Infinite Life and Power is behind all, animates all, manifests itself in and through all; that self-existent principle of life is that from which all has come, and not only from which all has come, but from which all is continually coming. If there is an individual life, there must of necessity be an infinite source of life from which it comes. If there is a quality or a force of love, there must of necessity be an infinite source of love whence it comes. If there is wisdom, there must be the all-wise source behind it from which it springs. The same is true in regard to peace, the same in regard to power, the same in regard to what we call material things.

There is, then, this Spirit of Infinite Life and Power behind all, which is the source of all. This Infinite Power is creating, working, ruling through the agency of great immutable laws and forces that run through all the universe, that surround us on every side. Every act of our every-day lives is governed by these same great laws and forces. Every flower that blooms by the wayside, springs up, grows, blooms, fades, according to certain great immutable laws. Every snowflake that plays between earth and heaven, forms, falls, melts, according to certain great unchangeable laws.

In a sense there is nothing in all the great universe but law. If this is true there must of necessity be a force behind it all that is the maker of these laws and a force greater than the laws that are made. This Spirit of Infinite Life and Power that is behind all is what I call God. I care not what term you may use, be it Kindly Light, Providence, the Over Soul, Omnipotence, or whatever term may be most convenient. I care not what the term may be as long as we are agreed in regard to the great central fact itself.

God, then, is this Infinite Spirit which fills all the universe with Himself alone, so that all is from Him and in Him, and there is nothing that is outside. Indeed and in truth, then, in Him we live and move and have our being. He is the life of our life, our very life itself. We have received, we are continually receiving our life from Him. We are partakers of the life of God; and though we differ from Him in that we are individualized spirits, while He is the Infinite Spirit including us as well as all else beside, yet *in essence the life of God and the life of man are identically the same, and so are one*. They differ not in essence, in quality; they differ in degree.

There have been and are highly illumined souls who believe that we receive our life from God after the manner of a divine inflow. And again, there have been and are those who believe that our life is one with the life of God, and so that God and man are one. Which is right? Both are right; both right when rightly understood.

In regard to the first: if God is the Infinite Spirit of Life behind all, whence all comes, then clearly our life as individualized spirits is continually coming from this Infinite Source by means of this divine inflow. In the second place, if our lives as individualized spirits are directly from, are parts of this Infinite Spirit of Life, then the degree of the Infinite Spirit that is manifested in the life of each must be identical in quality with that Source, the same as a drop of water taken from the ocean is, in nature, in characteristics, identical with that ocean, its source. And how could it be otherwise? The liability to misunderstanding in this latter case, however, is this: in that although the life of God and the life of man in essence are identically the same, the life of God so far transcends the life of individual man that it includes all else beside. In other words, so far as the quality of life is concerned, in essence they are the same; so far as the degree of life is concerned, they are vastly different.

There is a reservoir in a valley which receives its supply from an inexhaustible reservoir on the mountain side. It is then true that the reservoir in the valley receives its supply by virtue of the inflow of the water from the larger reservoir on the mountain side. It is also true that the water in this smaller reservoir is in nature, in quality, in characteristics identically the same as that in the larger reservoir which is its source. The difference, however, is this: the reservoir on the mountain side, in the *amount* of its water, so far transcends the reservoir in the valley that it can supply an innumerable number of like reservoirs and still be unexhausted.

If this is true, does it not then follow that in the degree that man opens himself to this divine inflow does he approach to God? If so, it then necessarily follows that in the degree that he makes this approach does he take on the God-powers. And if the God-powers are without limit, does it not then follow that the only limitations man has are the limitations he sets to himself, by virtue of not knowing himself?

## Chapter Three
# The Supreme Fact of Human Life

From the great central fact of the universe in regard to which we have agreed, namely, this Spirit of Infinite Life that is behind all and from which all comes, we are led to inquire as to what is the great central fact in human life. From what has gone before, the question almost answers itself.

*The great central fact in human life, in your life and in mine, is the coming into a conscious, vital realization of our oneness with this Infinite Life, and the opening of ourselves fully to this divine inflow.* This is the great central fact in human life, for in this all else is included, all else follows in its train. In just the degree that we come into a conscious realization of our oneness with the Infinite Life, and open ourselves to this divine inflow, do we actualize in ourselves the qualities and powers of the Infinite Life.

And what does this mean? It means simply this: that we are recognizing our true identity, that we are bringing our lives into harmony with the same great laws and forces, and so opening ourselves to the same great inspirations, as have all the prophets, seers, sages, and saviors in the world's history, all men of truly great and mighty power. For in the degree that we come into this realization and connect ourselves with this Infinite Source, do we make it possible for the higher powers to play, to work, to manifest through us.

We can keep closed to this divine inflow, to these higher forces and powers, through ignorance, as most of us do, and thus hinder or even prevent their manifesting through us. Or we can intentionally close ourselves to their operations and thus deprive ourselves of the powers to which, by the very nature of our being, we are rightful heirs. On the other hand, we can come into so vital a realization of the oneness of our real selves with this Infinite Life, and can open ourselves so fully to the incoming of this divine inflow, and so to the operation of these higher forces, inspirations, and powers, that we can indeed and in truth become what we may well term, God-men.

And what is a God-man? One in whom the powers of God are manifesting, though yet a man. No one can set limitations to a man or a woman of this type; for the only limitations he or she can have are those set by the self. Ignorance is the most potent factor in setting limitations to the majority of mankind; and so the great majority of people continue to live their little, dwarfed, and stunted lives simply by virtue of the fact that they do not realize the larger life to which they are heirs. They have never as yet come into a knowledge of the real identity of their true selves.

Mankind has not yet realized that the real self is one with the life of God. Through its ignorance it has never yet opened itself to the divine inflow, and so has never made itself a channel through which the infinite powers and forces can manifest. When we know ourselves merely as men, we live accordingly, and have merely the powers of men. When we come into the realization of the fact that we are God-men, then again we live accordingly, and have the powers of God-men. *In the degree that we open ourselves to this divine inflow are we changed from mere men into God-men.*

Before we proceed farther let us consider very briefly the nature of thought. Thought is not, as is many times supposed, a mere indefinite abstraction, or something of a like nature. It is, on the contrary, a vital, living force, the most vital, subtle, and irresistible force there is in the universe.

Everything in the material universe about us, everything the universe has ever known, had its origin first in thought. From this it took its form. Every castle, every statue, every painting, every piece of mechanism, everything had its birth, its origin, first in the mind of the one who formed it before it received its material expression or embodiment. The very universe in which we live is the result of the thought energies of God, the Infinite Spirit that is back of all. And if it is true, as we have found, that we in our true selves are in essence the same, and in this sense are one with the life of this Infinite Spirit, do we not then see that in the degree that we come into a vital realization of this stupendous fact, *we, through the operation of our interior, spiritual, thought forces, have in like sense creative power?*

Everything exists in the unseen before it is manifested or realized in the seen, and in this sense it is true that the unseen things are the real, while the things that are seen are the unreal. The unseen things are *cause*; the seen things are *effect*. The unseen things are the eternal; the seen things are the changing, the transient.

Much is said in regard to "building castles in the air," and one who is given to this building is not always looked upon with favor. But castles in the air are always necessary before we can have castles on the ground, before we can have castles in which to live. The trouble with the one who gives himself to building castles in the air is not that he builds them in the air, but that he does not go farther and actualize in life, in character, in material form, the castles he thus builds. He does a part of the work, a very necessary part; but another equally necessary part remains still undone.

There is in connection with the thought forces what we may term, the drawing power of mind, and the great law operating here is one with that great law of the universe, that like attracts like. We are continually attracting to us from both the seen and the unseen side of life, forces and conditions most akin to those of our own thoughts.

This law is continually operating whether we are conscious of it or not. We are all living, so to speak, in a vast ocean of thought, and the very atmosphere around us is continually filled with the thought forces that are being continually sent or that are continually going out in the form of thought waves. We are all affected, more or less, by these thought forces, either consciously or unconsciously; and in the degree that we are more or less sensitively organized, or in the degree that we are negative and so are open to outside influences, rather than positive, thus determining what influences shall enter into our realm of thought, and hence into our lives.

There are those among us who are much more sensitively organized than others. As an organism their bodies are more finely, more sensitively constructed. These, generally speaking, are people who are always more or less affected by the mentalities of those with whom they come in contact, or in whose company they are.

Some think it unfortunate for one to be sensitively organized. By no means. It is a good thing, for one may thus be more open and receptive to the higher impulses of the soul within, and to all higher forces and influences from without. It may, however, be unfortunate and extremely inconvenient to be so organized unless one recognize and gain the power of closing himself, of making himself positive to all detrimental or undesirable influences. This power everyone, however sensitively organized he may be, can acquire.

This he can acquire through the mind's action. And, moreover, there is no habit of more value to anyone, be he sensitively or less sensitively organized, than that of occasionally taking and holding himself continually in the attitude of mind—I close myself, I make myself positive to all things below, and open and receptive to all higher influences, to all things above. By taking this attitude of mind consciously now and then, it soon becomes a habit, and if one is deeply in earnest in regard to it, it puts into operation silent but subtle and powerful influences in effecting the desired results. In this way all lower and undesirable influences from both the seen and the unseen side of life are closed out, while all higher influences are invited, and in the degree that they are invited will they enter.

Says one who knows full well whereof he speaks: "The law of attraction works universally on every plane of *action*, and we attract whatever we desire or expect. If we desire one thing and expect another, we become like houses divided against themselves, which are quickly brought to desolation. Determine resolutely to expect only what you desire, then you will attract only what you wish for.... Carry any kind of thought you please about with you, and so long as you retain it, no matter how you roam over land or sea, you will unceasingly attract to yourself, knowingly or inadvertently, exactly and only what corresponds to your own dominant quality of thought. Thoughts are our private property, and we can regulate them to suit our taste entirely by steadily recognizing our ability so to do."

We have just spoken of the drawing power of mind. Faith is nothing more nor less than the operation of the *thought forces* in the form of an earnest desire, coupled with expectation as to its fulfillment. And in the degree that faith, the earnest desire thus sent out, is continually held to and watered by firm expectation, in just that degree does it either draw to itself, or does it change from the unseen into the visible, from the spiritual into the material, that for which it is sent.

Let the element of doubt or fear enter in, and what would otherwise be a tremendous force will be so neutralized that it will fail of its realization.

Continually held to and continually watered by firm expectation, it becomes a force, a drawing power, that is irresistible and absolute, and the results will be absolute in direct proportion as it is absolute.

## Chapter Four
# Fullness of Life—Bodily Health and Vigor

God is the Spirit of Infinite Life. If we are partakers of this life, and have the power of opening ourselves fully to its divine inflow, it means more, so far as even the physical life is concerned, than we may at first think. For very clearly, the life of this Infinite Spirit, from its very nature, can admit of no disease; and if this is true, no disease can exist in the body where it freely enters, through which it freely flows.

Let us recognize at the outset that, so far as the physical life is concerned, *all life is from within out*. There is an immutable law which says: "As within, so without; cause, effect." In other words, the thought forces, the various mental states and the emotions, all have in time their effects upon the physical body.

Someone says: "I hear a great deal said today in regard to the effects of the mind upon the body, but I don't know as I place very much confidence in this." Don't you? Someone brings you sudden news. You grow pale, you tremble, or perhaps you fall into a faint. It is, however, through the channel of your mind that the news is imparted to you. A friend says something to you, perhaps at the table, something that seems very unkind. You are hurt by it, as we say. You have been enjoying your dinner, but from this moment your appetite is gone. But what was said entered into and affected you through the channel of your mind.

Again, a sudden emergency arises. You stand trembling and weak with fear. Why are you powerless to move? Why do you tremble? And yet you believe that the mind has but little influence upon the body. You are for a moment dominated by a fit of anger. For a few hours afterwards you complain of a violent headache. And still you do not seem to realize that the thoughts and emotions have an effect upon the body.

Fear and worry have the effect of closing up the channels of the body, so that the life forces flow in a slow and sluggish manner. Hope and tranquility open the channels of the body, so that the life forces go bounding through it in such a way that disease can rarely get a foothold.

I am aware of the fact that in connection with the matter we are now considering there has been a great deal of foolishness during the past few years. Many absurd and foolish things have been claimed and done; but this says nothing against, and it has absolutely nothing to do with, the great underlying laws themselves. The same has been true of the early days of practically every system of ethics or philosophy or religion the world has ever known. But as time has passed, these foolish, absurd things have fallen away, and the great eternal principles have stood out ever more and more clearly defined.

I know *personally* of many cases where an entire and permanent cure has been effected, in some within a remarkably short period of time, through the operation of these forces. Some of them are cases that had been entirely given up by the regular practice, *materia medica*. We have numerous accounts of such cases in all times and in connection with all religions. And why should not the power of effecting such cures exist among us today? The *power does exist*, and it will be actualized in just the degree that we recognize the same great laws that were recognized in times past.

The whole of human life is cause and effect; there is no such thing in it as chance, nor is there even in all the wide universe. Are we not satisfied with whatever comes into our lives? The thing to do, then, is not to spend time in railing against the imaginary something we create and call fate, but to look to the within, and change the causes at work there, in order that things of a different nature may come, for there will come exactly what we cause to come. This is true not only of the physical body, but of all phases and conditions of life.

The time will come when the work of the physician will not be to treat and attempt to heal the body, but to heal the mind, which in turn will heal the body. In other words, the true physician will be a teacher; his work will be to keep people well, instead of attempting to make them well after sickness and disease comes on; and still beyond this there will come a time when each will be his own physician. In the degree that we live in harmony with the higher laws of our being, and so, in the degree that we become better acquainted with the powers of the mind and spirit, will we give less attention to the body,—no less *care*, but less *attention*.

The bodies of thousands today would be much better cared for if their owners gave them less thought and attention. As a rule, those who think least of their bodies enjoy the best health. Many are kept in continual ill health by the abnormal thought and attention they give them.

Give the body the nourishment, the exercise, the fresh air, the sunlight it requires, keep it clean, and then think of it as little as possible. In your thoughts and in your conversation never dwell upon the negative side. Don't talk of sickness and disease. By talking of these you do yourself harm and you do harm to those who listen to you. Talk of those things that will make people the better for listening to you. Thus you will infect them with health and strength and not with weakness and disease.

To dwell upon the negative side is always destructive. This is true of the body the same as it is true of all other things.

The whole matter may then be summed up in the one sentence, "God is well and so are you." You must awaken to the knowledge of your *real being*. When this awakening comes, you will have, and you will see that you have, the power to determine what conditions are externalized in your body. You must recognize, you must realize yourself as one with Infinite Spirit. God's will is then your will; your will is God's will, and "with God all things are possible."

## Chapter Five
# Wisdom and Interior Illumination

If you would find the highest, the fullest, and the richest life that not only this world but that any world can know, then do away with the sense of the separateness of your life from the life of God. Hold to the thought of your oneness. In the degree that you do this you will find yourself realizing it more and more, and as this life of realization is lived, you will find that no good thing will be withheld, for all things are included in this. Then it will be yours, without fears or forebodings, simply to do today what your hands find to do, and so be ready for tomorrow, *when it comes*, knowing that tomorrow will bring tomorrow's supplies for the mental, the spiritual, and the physical life. Remember, however, that tomorrow's supplies are not needed until tomorrow comes.

If one is willing to trust himself *fully* to the Law, the Law will never fail him. It is the half-hearted trusting to it that brings uncertain, and so, unsatisfactory results. Nothing is firmer and surer than Deity. It will never fail the one who throws himself wholly upon it. The secret of life then, is to live continually in this realization, whatever one may be doing, wherever one may be, by day and by night, both waking and sleeping. It can be lived in while we are sleeping no less than when we are awake. And here shall we consider a few facts in connection with sleep, in connection with receiving instruction and illumination while asleep?

During the process of sleep it is merely the physical body that is at rest and in quiet; the soul life with all its activities goes right on. Sleep is nature's provision for the recuperation of the body, for the rebuilding and hence the replacing of the waste that is continually going on during the waking hours. It is nature's great restorer. If sufficient sleep is not allowed the body, so that the rebuilding may equalize the wasting process, the body is gradually depleted and weakened, and any ailment or malady, when it is in this condition, is able to find a more ready entrance. It is for this reason that those who are subject to it will take a cold, as we term it, more readily when the body is tired or exhausted through loss of sleep than at most any other time. The body is in that condition where outside influences can have a more ready effect upon it, than when it is in its normal condition. And when they do have an effect they always go to the weaker portions first.

Our bodies are given us to serve far higher purposes than we ordinarily use them for. Especially is this true in the numerous cases where the body is master of its owner. In the degree that we come into the realization of the higher powers of the mind and spirit, in that degree does the body, through their influence upon it, become less gross and heavy, finer in its texture and form. And then, because the mind finds a kingdom of enjoyment in itself, and in all the higher things it becomes related to, *excesses* in eating and drinking, as well as all others, naturally and of their own accord fall away. There also falls away the desire for the heavier, grosser, less valuable kinds of food and drink, such as the flesh of animals, alcoholic drinks, and all things of the class that stimulate the body and the passions rather than build the body and the brain into a strong, clean, well-nourished, enduring, and fibrous condition. In the degree that the body thus becomes less gross and heavy, finer in its texture and form, is there less waste, and what there is is more easily replaced, so that it keeps in a more regular and even condition. When this is true, less sleep is actually required. And even the amount that is taken does more for a body of this finer type than it can do for one of the other nature.

As the body in this way grows finer, in other words, as the process of its evolution is thus accelerated, it in turn helps the mind and the soul in the realization of ever higher perceptions, and thus body helps mind the same as mind builds body. It was undoubtedly this fact that Browning had in mind when he said:

> Let us cry "All good things
> Are ours, nor soul helps flesh, more now,
> Than flesh helps soul."

Sleep, then, is for the resting and the rebuilding of the body. The soul needs no rest, and while the body is at rest in sleep the soul life is active the same as when the body is in activity.

There are some, having a deep insight into the soul's activities, who say that we travel when we sleep. Some are able to recall and bring over into the conscious, waking life the scenes visited, the information gained, and the events that have transpired. Most people are not able to do this and so much that might otherwise be gained is lost. They say, however, that it is in our power, in proportion as we understand the laws, to go where we will, and to bring over into the conscious, waking life all the experiences thus gained. Be this, however, as it may, it certainly is true that while sleeping we have the power, in a perfectly normal and natural way, to get much of value by way of light, instruction, and growth that the majority of people now miss.

If the soul life, that which relates us to Infinite Spirit, is always active, even while the body is at rest, why may not the mind so direct conditions as one falls asleep, that while the body is at rest, it may continually receive illumination from the soul and bring what it thus receives over into the conscious, waking life? This, indeed, can be done, and is done by some to great advantage; and many times the highest inspirations from the soul come in this way, as would seem most natural, since at this time all communications from the outer, material world no longer enter. I know those who do much work during sleep, the same as they get much light along desired lines. By charging the mind on going to sleep as to a particular time for waking, it is possible, as many of us know, to wake on the very minute. Not infrequently we have examples of difficult problems, problems that defied solution during waking hours, being solved during sleep.

A friend, a well-known journalist, had an extended newspaper article clearly and completely worked out for her in this way. She frequently calls this agency to her aid. She was notified by the managing editor one evening to have the article ready in the morning—an article requiring more than ordinary care, and one in which quite a knowledge of facts was required. It was a matter in connection with which she knew scarcely anything, and all her efforts at finding information regarding it seemed to be of no avail.

She set to work, but it seemed as if even her own powers defied her. Failure seemed imminent. Almost in desperation she decided to retire, and putting the matter into her mind in such a way that she would be able to receive the greatest amount of aid while asleep, she fell asleep and slept soundly until morning. When she awoke her work of the previous evening was the first thing that came into her mind. She lay quietly for a few minutes, and as she lay there, the article, completely written, seemed to stand before her mind. She ran through it, arose, and without dressing took her pen and transcribed it onto paper, literally acting simply as her own amanuensis.

The mind acting intently along a particular line will continue so to act until some other object of thought carries it along another line. And since in sleep only the body is in quiet while the mind and soul are active, then the mind on being given a certain direction when one drops off to sleep, will take up the line along which it is directed, and can be made, in time, to bring over into consciousness the results of its activities. Some will be able very soon to get results of this kind; for some it will take longer. Quiet and continued effort will increase the faculty.

Then by virtue of the law of the drawing power of mind, since the mind is always active, we are drawing to us even while sleeping, influences from the realms kindred to those in which we in our thoughts are living before we fall asleep. In this way we can put ourselves into relation with whatever kinds of influence we choose and accordingly gain much during the process of sleep. In many ways the interior faculties are more open and receptive while we are in sleep than while we are awake. Hence the necessity of exercising even greater care as to the nature of the thoughts that occupy the mind as we enter into sleep, for there can come to us only what we by our own order of thought attract. We have it entirely in our own hands.

And for the same reason—this greater degree of receptivity during this period—we are able by understanding and using the law, to gain much of value more readily in this way than when the physical senses are fully open to the material world about us. Many will find a practice somewhat after the following nature of value: When light or information is desired along any particular line, light or information you feel it is right and wise for you to have, as, for example, light in regard to an uncertain course of action, then as you retire, first bring your mind into the attitude of peace and goodwill for all. You in this way bring yourself into an harmonious condition, and in turn attract to yourself these same peaceful conditions from without.

Then resting in this sense of peace, quietly and calmly send out your earnest desire for the needed light or information; cast out of your mind all fears or forebodings lest it come not, for "in quietness and in confidence shall be your strength." Take the expectant attitude of mind, firmly believing and expecting that when you awake the desired results will be with you. Then on awaking, before any thoughts or activities from the outside world come in to absorb the attention, remain for a little while receptive to the intuitions or the impressions that come. When they come, when they manifest themselves clearly, then act upon them without delay. In the degree that you do this, in that degree will the power of doing it ever more effectively grow.

Or, if for unselfish purposes you desire to grow and develop any of your faculties, or to increase the health and strength of your body, take a corresponding attitude of mind, the form of which will readily suggest itself in accordance with your particular needs or desires. In this way you will open yourself to, you will connect yourself with, and you will set into operation within yourself, the particular order of forces that will make for these results. Don't be afraid to voice your desires. In this way you set into operation vibratory forces which go out and which make their impress felt somewhere, and which, arousing into activity or uniting with other forces, set about to actualize your desires. No good thing shall be withheld from him who lives in harmony with the higher laws and forces. There are no desires that shall not be satisfied to the one who knows and who wisely uses the powers with which he or she is endowed.

Your sleep will be more quiet and peaceful and refreshing, and so your power increased mentally, physically, and spiritually, simply by sending out as you fall asleep, thoughts of love and goodwill, thoughts of peace and harmony for all. In this way you are connecting yourself with all the forces in the universe that make for peace and harmony.

Visions and inspirations of the highest order will come in the degree that we make for them the right conditions.

When one awakes from sleep and so returns to conscious life, he is in a peculiarly receptive and impressionable state. All relations with the material world have for a time been shut off, the mind is in a freer and more natural state, resembling somewhat a sensitive plate, where impressions can readily leave their traces. This is why many times the highest and truest impressions come to one in the early morning hours, before the activities of the day and their attendant distractions have exerted an influence. This is one reason why many people can do their best work in the early hours of the day.

But this fact is also a most valuable one in connection with the molding of everyday life. The mind is at this time as a clean sheet of paper. We can most valuably use this quiet, receptive, impressionable period by wisely directing the activities of the mind along the highest and most desirable paths, and thus, so to speak, set the pace for the day.

Each morning is a fresh beginning. We are, as it were, just beginning life. We have it *entirely* in our own hands. And when the morning with its fresh beginning comes, all yesterdays should be yesterdays, with which we have nothing to do. Sufficient is it to know that the way we lived our yesterday has determined for us our today. And, again, when the morning with its fresh beginning comes, all tomorrows should be tomorrows, with which we have nothing to do. Sufficient to know that the way we live our today determines our tomorrow.

## Chapter Six
# The Realization of Perfect Peace

To recognize the fact that we are spirit, and to live in this thought, is to be spiritually minded, and so to be in harmony and peace. Oh, the thousands of men and women all about us weary with care, troubled and ill at ease, running hither and thither to find peace, weary in body, soul, and mind; going to other countries, travelling the world over, coming back, and still not finding it. Of course they have not found it and they never will find it in this way, because they are looking for it where it is not. They are looking for it without when they should look within. Peace is to be found only within, and unless one find it there he will never find it at all.

The moment we fear anything we open the door for the entrance of the actualization of the very thing we fear. An animal will never harm a person who is absolutely fearless in regard to it. The instant he fears he opens himself to danger; and some animals, the dog for example, can instantly detect the element of fear, and this gives them the courage to do harm. In the degree that we come into a full realization of our oneness with this Infinite Power do we become calm and quiet, undisturbed by the little occurrences that before so vex and annoy us. We are no longer disappointed in people, for we always read them aright. We have the power of penetrating into their very souls and seeing the underlying motives that are at work there.

A gentleman approached a friend the other day, and with great show of cordiality grasped him by the hand and said, "Why, Mr. _____, I am so glad to see you." Quick as a flash my friend read him, and looking him steadily in the eye, replied, "No, you are mistaken, you are not glad to see me; but you are very much disconcerted, so much so that you are now blushing in evidence of it." The gentleman replied, "Well, you know in this day and age of conventionality and form we have to put on the show and sometimes make believe what we do not really feel." My friend once more looked him in the face and said, "Again you are mistaken. Let me give you one little word of advice: You will always fare better and will think far more of yourself, always to recognize and to tell the truth rather than to give yourself to any semblance of it."

As soon as we are able to read people aright we will then cease to be disappointed in them, we will cease to place them on pedestals, for this can never be done without some attendant disappointment. The fall will necessarily come, sooner or later, and moreover, we are thus many times unfair to our friends. When we come into harmony with this Spirit of Peace, evil reports and apparent bad treatment, either at the hands of friends or of enemies, will no longer disturb us. When we are conscious of the fact that in our life and our work we are true to that eternal principle of right, of truth, of justice that runs through all the universe, that unites and governs all, that always eventually prevails, then nothing of this kind can come nigh us, and come what may we will always be tranquil and undisturbed.

The things that we open ourselves to always come to us. People in the olden times expected to see angels and they saw them; but there is no more reason why they should have seen them than that we should see them now; no more reason why they should come and dwell with them than that they should come and dwell with us, for the great laws governing all things are the same today as they were then. If angels come not to minister unto us it is because we do not invite them, it is because we keep the door closed through which they otherwise might enter.

In the degree that we are filled with this Spirit of Peace by thus opening ourselves to its inflow does it pour through us, so that we carry it with us wherever we go. In the degree that we thus open ourselves do we become magnets to attract peace from all sources; and in the degree that we attract and embody it in ourselves are we able to give it forth to others. We can in this way become such perfect embodiments of peace that wherever we go we are continually shedding benedictions.

Within each one lies the cause of whatever comes to him. Each has it in his own hands to determine what comes. Everything in the visible, material world has its origin in the unseen, the spiritual, the thought world. This is the world of cause, the former is the world of effect. The nature of the effect is always in accordance with the nature of the cause. What one lives in his invisible, thought world, he is continually actualizing in his visible, material world. If he would have any conditions different in the latter he must make the necessary change in the former. A clear realization of this great fact would bring success to thousands of men and women who all about us are now in the depths of despair. It would bring health, abounding health and strength to thousands now diseased and suffering. It would bring peace and joy to thousands now unhappy and ill at ease.

And oh, the thousands all about us who are continually living in the slavery of fear. The spirits within that should be strong and powerful are rendered weak and impotent. Their energies are crippled, their efforts are paralyzed. "Fear is everywhere—fear of want, fear of starvation, fear of public opinion, fear of private opinion, fear that what we own today may not be ours tomorrow, fear of sickness, fear of death. Fear has become with millions a fixed habit. The thought is everywhere. The thought is thrown upon us from every direction.... To live in continual dread, continual cringing, continual fear of anything, be it loss of love, loss of money, loss of position or situation, is to take the readiest means to lose what we fear we shall."

By fear nothing is to be gained, but on the contrary, everything is to be lost. "I know this is true," says one, "but I am given to fear; it's natural to me and I can't help it." Can't help it! In saying this you indicate one great reason of your fear by showing that you do not even know yourself as yet. You must know yourself in order to know your powers, and not until you know them can you use them wisely and fully. Don't say you can't help it. If you think you can't, the chances are that you can't. If you think you can, and act in accordance with this thought, then not only are the chances that you can, but if you act fully in accordance with it, that you can and that you will is an absolute certainty. It was Virgil who in describing the crew which in his mind would win the race, said of them—They can because they think they can. In other words, this very attitude of mind on their part will infuse a spiritual power into their bodies that will give them the strength and endurance which will enable them to win.

Then take the thought that you *can*; take it merely as a seed-thought, if need be, plant it in your consciousness, tend it, cultivate it, and it will gradually reach out and gather strength from all quarters. It will focus and make positive and active the spiritual force within you that is now scattered and of little avail. It will draw to itself force from without. It will draw to your aid the influence of other minds of its own nature, minds that are fearless, strong, courageous. You will thus draw to yourself and connect yourself with this order of thought. If earnest and faithful, the time will soon come when all fear will loose its hold; and instead of being an embodiment of weakness and a creature of circumstances, you will find yourself a tower of strength and a master of circumstances.

Materialism leads naturally to pessimism. And how could it do otherwise? A knowledge of the Spiritual Power working in and through us as well as in and through all things, a power that works for righteousness, leads to optimism. Pessimism leads to weakness.

Optimism leads to power. The one who is centered in Deity is the one who not only outrides every storm, but who through the faith, and so, the conscious power that is in him, faces storm with the same calmness and serenity that he faces fair weather; for he knows well beforehand what the outcome will be.

## Chapter Seven
# Coming Into Fullness of Power

This is the Spirit of Infinite Power, and in the degree that we open ourselves to it does power become manifest in us. With God all things are possible—that is, in conjunction with God all things are possible. The true secret of power lies in keeping one's connection with the God who worketh all things; and in the degree that we keep this connection are we able literally to rise above every conceivable limitation.

Why, then, waste time in running hither and thither to acquire power? Why waste time with this practice or that practice? Why not go directly to the mountain top itself, instead of wandering through the byways, in the valleys, and on the mountain sides? That man has absolute dominion, as taught in all the scriptures of the world, is true not of physical man, but of *spiritual man*. There are many animals, for example, larger and stronger, over which from a physical standpoint he would not have dominion, but he can gain supremacy over even these by calling into activity the higher mental, psychic, and spiritual forces with which he is endowed.

Whatever can't be done in the physical can be done in the spiritual. And in direct proportion as a man recognizes himself as spirit, and lives accordingly, is he able to transcend in power the man who recognizes himself merely as material. All the sacred literature of the world is teeming with examples of what we call miracles. They are not confined to any particular times or places. There is no age of miracles in distinction from any other period that may be an age of miracles. Whatever has been done in the world's history can be done again through the operation of the same laws and forces. These miracles were performed not by those who were more than men, but by those who through the recognition of their oneness with God became God-men, so that the higher forces and powers worked through them.

For what, let us ask, is a miracle? Is it something supernatural? Supernatural only in the sense of being above the natural, or rather above that which is natural to man in his ordinary state. A miracle is nothing more nor less than this. One who has come into a knowledge of his true identity, of his oneness with the all-pervading Wisdom and Power, thus makes it possible for laws higher than the ordinary mind knows of to be revealed to him. These laws he makes use of; the people see the results, and by virtue of their own limitations, call them miracles and speak of the person who performs these apparently supernatural works as a supernatural being. But they as supernatural beings could themselves perform these supernatural works if they would open themselves to the recognition of the same laws, and consequently to the realization of the same possibilities and powers.

And let us also remember that the supernatural of yesterday becomes, as in the process of evolution we advance from the lower to the higher, from the more material to the more spiritual, the common and the natural of today, and what seems to be the supernatural of today becomes in the same way the natural of tomorrow, and so on through the ages. Yes, it is the God-man who does the things that appear supernatural, the man who by virtue of his realization of the higher powers transcends the majority and so stands out among them. But any power that is possible to one human soul is possible to another. The same laws operate in every life. We can be men and women of power or we can be men and women of impotence. The moment one vitally grasps the fact that he can rise he will rise, and he can have absolutely no limitations other than the limitations he sets to himself. Cream always rises to the top. It rises simply because *it is the nature of cream to rise.*

We hear much said of "environment." We need to realize that environment should never be allowed to make the man, but that man should always, *and always can*, condition the environment. When we realize this we will find that many times it is not necessary to take ourselves out of any particular environment, because we may yet have a work to do there; but by the very force we carry with us we can so affect and change matters that we will have an entirely new set of conditions in an old environment.

The same is true in regard to "hereditary" traits and influences. We sometimes hear the question asked, "Can they be overcome?" Only the one who doesn't yet know himself can ask a question such as this. If we entertain and live in the belief that they cannot be overcome, then the chances are that they will always remain. The moment, however, that we come into a realization of our true selves, and so of the tremendous powers and forces within—the powers and forces of the mind and spirit—hereditary traits and influences that are harmful in nature will begin to lessen, and will disappear with a rapidity directly in proportion to the completeness of this realization.

Again there are many who are living far below their possibilities because they are continually handing over their individualities to others. Do you want to be a power in the world? Then be yourself. Don't class yourself, don't allow yourself to be classed among the second-hand, among the *they-say* people. Be true to the highest within your own soul, and then allow yourself to be governed by no customs or conventionalities or arbitrary man-made rules that are not founded upon *principle*. Those things that are founded upon principle will be observed by the right-minded, the right-hearted man or woman, in any case.

Don't surrender your individuality, which is your greatest agent of power, to the customs and conventionalities that have gotten their life from the great mass of those who haven't enough force to preserve their individualities—those who in other words have given them over as ingredients to the "mush of concession" which one of our greatest writers has said characterizes our modern society. If you do surrender your individuality in this way, you simply aid in increasing the undesirable conditions; in payment for this you become a slave, and the chances are that in time you will be unable to hold even the respect of those whom you in this way try to please.

If you preserve your individuality then you become a master, and if wise and discreet, your influence and power will be an aid in bringing about a higher, a better, and a more healthy set of conditions in the world. All people, moreover, will think more of you, will honor you more highly for doing this than if you show your weakness by contributing yourself to the same "mush of concession" that so many of them are contributing themselves to. With all classes of people you will then have an influence. "A great style of hero draws equally all classes, all extremes of society to him, till we say the very dogs believe in him."

To be one's self is the only worthy, and by all means the only satisfactory, thing to be. "May it not be good policy," says one, "to be governed sometimes by one's surroundings?" What is good policy? To be yourself, first, last, and always.

The men and the women who are truly awake to the real powers within are the men and women who seem to be doing so little, yet who in reality are doing so much. They seem to be doing so little because they are working with higher agencies, and yet are doing so much because of this very fact. They do their work on the higher plane. They keep so completely their connection with the Infinite Power that *It* does the work for them and they are relieved of the responsibility. They are the care-less people. They are care-less because it is the Infinite Power that is working through them, and with this Infinite Power they are simply cooperating.

*The secret of the highest power is simply the uniting of the outer agencies of expression with the Power that works from within.*

I had rather be an amanuensis of the Infinite God, as it is my privilege literally to be, than a slave to the formulated rules of any rhetorician, or to the opinions of any critic. Oh, the people, the people over and over! Let me give something to them that will lighten the everyday struggles of our common life, something that will add a little sweetness here, a little hope there, something that will make more thoughtful, kind, and gentle this thoughtless, animal-natured man, something that will awaken into activity the dormant powers of this timid, shrinking little woman, powers that when awakened will be irresistible in their influence and that will surprise even herself. Let me give something that will lead each one to the knowledge of the divinity of every human soul, something that will lead each one to the conscious realization of *his own divinity*, with all its attendant riches, and glories, and powers—let me succeed in doing this, and I can then well afford to be careless as to whether the critics praise or whether they blame. If it is blame, then under these circumstances it is as the cracking of a few dead sticks on the ground below, compared to the matchless music that the soft spring gale is breathing through the great pine forest.

If when born into the world you came into a family of the English-speaking race, then in all probability you are a Christian. To be a Christian is to be a follower of the *teachings* of Jesus, the Christ; to live in harmony with the same laws he lived in harmony with: in brief, *to live his life*. The great central fact of his teaching was this conscious union of man with the Father. It was the complete realization of this oneness with the Father on his part that made Jesus the Christ. It was through this that he attained to the power he attained to, that he spake as never man spake.

He never claimed for himself anything that he did not claim equally for all mankind. "The mighty works performed by Jesus were not exceptional, they were the natural and necessary concomitants of his state; he declared them to be in accordance with unvarying order; he spoke of them as no unique performances, but as the outcome of a state to which all might attain if they chose. As a teacher and demonstrator of truth, according to his own confession, he did nothing for the purpose of proving his solitary divinity.... The life and triumph of Jesus formed an epoch in the history of the race. His coming and victory marked a new era in human affairs; he introduced a new because a more complete ideal to the earth, and when his three most intimate companions saw in some measure what the new life really signified, they fell to the earth, speechless with awe and admiration."

By coming into this complete realization of his oneness with the Father, by mastering, absolutely mastering every circumstance that crossed his path through life, even to the death of the body, and by pointing out to us the great laws which are the same for us as they were for him, he has given us an ideal of life, an ideal for us to attain to *here and now*, that we could not have without him. *One has conquered first; all may conquer afterward.* By completely realizing it first for himself, and then by pointing out to others this great law of the at-one-ment with the Father, he has become probably the world's greatest savior.

Don't mistake his mere person for his life and his teachings, an error that has been made in connection with most all great teachers by their disciples over and over again. And if you have been among the number who have been preaching a dead Christ, then for humanity's sake, for Christ's sake, for

God's sake, and I speak most reverently, don't steal the people's time any longer, don't waste your own time more, in giving them stones in place of bread, dead form for the spirit of living truth. In his own words, "let the dead bury their dead." Come out from among them. Teach as did Jesus, *the living Christ*. Teach as did Jesus, *the Christ within*. Find this in all its transcendent beauty and power—find it as Jesus found it, then you also will be one who will speak with authority. Then you will be able to lead large numbers of others to its finding. This is the pearl of great price.

## Chapter Eight
# Plenty of All Things—The Law of Prosperity

This is the Spirit of Infinite Plenty, the Power that has brought, that is continually bringing, all things into expression in material form. He who lives in the realization of his oneness with this Infinite Power becomes a magnet to attract to himself a continual supply of whatsoever things he desires.

If one hold himself in the thought of poverty, he will be poor, and the chances are that he will remain in poverty. If he hold himself, whatever present conditions may be, continually in the thought of prosperity, he sets into operation forces that will sooner or later bring him into prosperous conditions. The law of attraction works unceasingly throughout the universe, and the one great and never-changing fact in connection with it is, as we have found, that like attracts like. If we are one with this Infinite Power, this source of all things, then in the degree that we live in the realization of this oneness, in that degree do we actualize in ourselves a power that will bring to us an abundance of all things that it is desirable for us to have. In this way we come into possession of a power whereby we can actualize at all times those conditions that we desire.

As all truth exists *now*, and awaits simply our perception of it, so all things necessary for present needs exist *now*, and await simply the power in us to appropriate them. God holds all things in His hands. His constant word is, My child, acknowledge me in all your ways, and in the degree that you do this, in the degree that you live this, then what is mine is yours. Jehovah-jireh—the Lord will provide. "He giveth to all men liberally and upbraideth not." He giveth liberally to all men who put themselves in the right attitude to receive from Him. He forces no good things upon any one.

The old and somewhat prevalent idea of godliness and poverty has absolutely no basis for its existence, and the sooner we get away from it the better. It had its birth in the same way that the idea of asceticism came into existence, when the idea prevailed that there was necessarily a warfare between the flesh and the spirit. It had its origin therefore in the minds of those who had a distorted, a one-sided view of life. True godliness is in a sense the same as true wisdom. The one who is truly wise, and who uses the forces and powers with which he is endowed, to him the great universe always opens her treasure house. The supply is always equal to the demand—equal to the demand when the demand is rightly, wisely made. When one comes into the realization of these higher laws, then the fear of want ceases to tyrannize over him.

Are you out of a job? Let the fear that you will not get another take hold of and *dominate* you, and the chances are that it may be a long time before you will get another, or the one that you do get may be a very poor one indeed. Whatever the circumstances, you must realize that you have within you forces and powers that you can set into operation that will triumph over any and all apparent or temporary losses. Set these forces into operation and you will then be placing a magnet that will draw to you a situation that may be far better than the one you have lost, and the time may soon come when you will be even thankful that you lost the old one.

Recognize, working in and through you, the same Infinite Power that creates and governs all things in the universe, the same Infinite Power that governs the endless systems of worlds in space. Send out your thought—thought is a force, and it has occult power of unknown proportions when rightly used and wisely directed—send out your thought that the right situation or the right work will come to you at the right time, in the right way, and that you will recognize it when it comes. Hold to this thought, never allow it to weaken, hold to it, and continually water it with firm expectation. You in this way put your advertisement into a psychical, a spiritual newspaper, a paper that has not a limited circulation, but one that will make its way not only to the utmost bounds of the earth, but of the very universe itself. It is an advertisement, moreover, which if rightly placed on your part, will be far more effective than any advertisement you could possibly put into any printed sheet, no matter what claims are made in regard to its being "the great advertising medium." In the degree that you come into this realization and live in harmony with the higher laws and forces, in that degree will you be able to do this effectively.

If you wish to look through the "want" columns of the newspapers, then do it not in the ordinary way. Put the higher forces into operation and thus place it on a higher basis. As you take up the paper, take this attitude of mind: If there is here an advertisement that it will be well for me to reply to, the moment I come to it I will recognize it. Affirm this, believe it, expect it. If you do this in full faith you will somehow feel the intuition the moment you come to the right one, and this intuition will be nothing more nor less than your own soul speaking to you. When it speaks then act at once.

If you get the job and it does not prove to be exactly what you want, if you feel that you are capable of filling a better one, then the moment you enter upon it take the attitude of mind that this situation is the steppingstone that will lead you to one that will be still better. Hold this thought steadily, affirm it, believe it, expect it, and all the time be faithful, *absolutely faithful* to the situation in which you are at present placed. If you are *not* faithful to it then the chances are that it will not be the steppingstone to something better, but to something poorer. If you are faithful to it, the time may soon come when you will be glad and thankful, when you will rejoice, that you lost your old position.

This is the law of prosperity: When apparent adversity comes, be not cast down by it, but make the best of it, and always look forward for better things, for conditions more prosperous. To hold yourself in this attitude of mind is to set into operation subtle, silent, and irresistible forces that sooner or later will actualize in material form that which is today merely an idea. But ideas have occult power, and ideas, when rightly planted and rightly tended, are the seeds that actualize material conditions.

Never give a moment to complain, but utilize the time that would otherwise be spent in this way in looking forward and actualizing the conditions you desire. Suggest prosperity to yourself. See yourself in a prosperous condition. Affirm that you will before long be in a prosperous condition. Affirm it calmly and quietly, but strongly and confidently. Believe it, believe it absolutely. Expect it—keep it continually watered with expectation. You thus make yourself a magnet to attract the things that you desire. Don't be afraid to suggest, to affirm these things, for by so doing you put forth an ideal which will begin to clothe itself in material form. In this way you are utilizing agents among the most subtle and powerful in the universe. If you are particularly desirous for anything that you feel it is good and right for you to have, something that will broaden your life or that will increase your usefulness to others, simply hold the thought that at the right time, in the right way, and through the right instrumentality, there will come to you or there will open up for you the way whereby you can attain what you desire.

I know of a young lady who a short time ago wanted some money very badly. She wanted it for a good purpose; she saw no reason why she shouldn't have it. She is one who has come into an understanding of the power of the interior forces. She took and held herself in the attitude of mind we have just pointed out. In the morning she entered into the silence for a few moments. In this way she brought herself into a more complete harmony with the higher powers. Before the day closed a gentleman called, a member of a family with which she was acquainted. He asked her if she would do for the family some work that they wanted done. She was a little surprised that they should ask her to do this particular kind of work, but she said to herself, "Here is a call. I will respond and see what it will lead to." She undertook the work. *She did it well.* When she had completed it there was put into her hands an amount of money far beyond what she had expected. She felt that it was an amount too large for the work she had done. She protested. They replied, "No; you have done us a service that transcends in value the amount we offer to pay you." The sum thus received was more than sufficient for the work she wished to accomplish.

This is but one of many instances in connection with the wise and effective use of the higher powers. It also carries a lesson,—Don't fold your hands and expect to see things drop into your lap, but set into operation the higher forces and then take hold of the first thing that offers itself. Do what your hands find to do, *and do it well.* If this work is not thoroughly satisfactory to you, then affirm, believe, and expect that it is the agency that will lead you to something better. "The basis for attracting the best of all the world can give to you is to first surround, own, and live in these things in mind, or what is falsely called imagination. All so-called imaginings are realities and forces of unseen element. Live in mind in a palace and gradually palatial surroundings will gravitate to you. But so living is *not* pining, or longing, or complainingly wishing. It is when you are 'down in the world,' calmly and persistently seeing yourself as up. It is when you are now compelled to eat from a tin plate, regarding that tin plate as only the certain step to one of silver. It is not envying and growling at other people who have silver plate. That growling is just so much capital stock taken from the bank account of mental force."

A friend who knows the power of the interior forces, and whose life is guided in every detail by them, has given a suggestion in this form: When you are in the arms of the bear, even though he is hugging you, look him in the face and laugh, but all the time keep your eye on the bull. If you allow all of your attention to be given to the work of the bear, the bull may get entirely out of your sight. In other words, if you yield to adversity the chances are that it will master you, but if you recognize in yourself the power of mastery over conditions then adversity will yield to you, and will be changed into prosperity. If when it comes you calmly and quietly recognize it, and use the time that might otherwise be spent in regrets, and fears, and forebodings, in setting into operation the powerful forces within you, it will soon take its leave.

Faith, absolute dogmatic faith, is the only law of true success. When we recognize the fact that a man carries his success or his failure with him, and that it does not depend upon outside conditions, we will come into the possession of powers that will quickly change outside conditions into agencies that make for success. When we come into this higher realization and bring our lives into complete harmony with the higher laws, we will then be able so to focus and direct the awakened interior forces, that they will go out and return laden with that for which they are sent. We will then be great enough to attract success, and it will not always be apparently just a little ways ahead. We can then establish in ourselves a center so strong that instead of running hither and thither for this or that, we can stay at home and draw to us the conditions we desire. If we firmly establish and hold to this center, things will seem continually to come our way.

The one who has come into the realization of the higher life no longer has a desire for the accumulation of enormous wealth, any more than he has a desire for any other *excess*. In the degree that he comes into the recognition of the fact that he is wealthy within, external wealth becomes less important in his estimation. When he comes into the realization of the fact that there is a source within from which he can put forth a power to call to him and actualize in his hands at any time a sufficient supply for all his needs, he no longer burdens himself with vast material accumulations that require his constant care and attention, and thus take his time and his thought from the real things of life. In other words, he first finds the *kingdom*, and he realizes that when he has found this, all other things follow in full measure.

It is as hard for a rich man to enter into the kingdom of heaven, said the Master—he who having nothing had everything—as it is for a camel to pass through the eye of a needle. In other words, if a man give all his time to the accumulation, the hoarding of outward material possessions far beyond what he can possibly ever use, what time has he for the finding of that wonderful kingdom, which when found, brings all else with it. Which is better, to have millions of dollars, and to have the burden of taking care of it all—for the one always involves the other—or to come into the knowledge of such laws and forces that every need will be supplied in good time, to know that no good thing shall be withheld, to know that we have it in our power to make the supply always equal to the demand?

Wealth beyond a certain amount cannot be used, and when it cannot be used it then becomes a hindrance rather than an aid, a curse rather than a blessing. There is no wiser use that those who have great accumulations can make of them than wisely to put them into life, into character, *day by day while they live*. In this way their lives will be continually enriched and increased. The time will come when it will be regarded as a disgrace for a man to die and leave vast accumulations behind him.

## Chapter Nine
# How Men Have Become Prophets, Seers, Sages, and Saviors

All the prophets, seers, sages, and saviors in the world's history became what they became, and consequently had the powers they had, through an entirely natural process. They all recognized and came into the conscious realization of their oneness with the Infinite Life. God is no respecter of persons. He doesn't create prophets, seers, sages, and saviors as such. He creates men. But here and there one recognizes his true identity, recognizes the oneness of his life with the Source whence it came. He lives in the realization of this oneness, and in turn becomes a prophet, seer, sage, or savior. Neither is God a respecter of races or of nations. He has no chosen people; but here and there a race or nation becomes a respecter of God and hence lives the life of a chosen people.

There has been no age or place of miracles in distinction from any other age or place. What we term miracles have abounded in all places and at all times where conditions have been made for them. They are being performed today just as much as they ever have been when the laws governing them are respected. Mighty men, we are told they were, mighty men who walked with God; and in the words "who walked with God" lies the secret of the words "mighty men." Cause, effect.

The Lord never prospers any man, but the man prospers because he acknowledges the Lord, and lives in accordance with the higher laws. Solomon was given the opportunity of choosing whatever he desired; his better judgment prevailed and he chose wisdom. But when he chose wisdom he found that it included all else beside. We are told that God hardened Pharaoh's heart. I don't believe it. God never hardens any one's heart. Pharaoh hardened his own heart and God was blamed for it. But when Pharaoh hardened his heart and disobeyed the voice of God, the plagues came. Again, cause, effect. Had he, on the contrary, listened—in other words, had he opened himself to and obeyed the voice of God, the plagues would not have come.

We can be our own best friends or we can be our own worst enemies. In the degree that we become friends to the highest and best within us, we become friends to all; and in the degree that we become enemies to the highest and best within us, do we become enemies to all. In the degree that we open ourselves to the higher powers and let them manifest through us, then by the very inspirations we carry with us do we become in a sense the saviors of our fellow-men, and in this way we all are, or may become, the saviors one of another. In this way you may become, indeed, one of the world's redeemers.

## Chapter Ten
# The Basic Principle of all Religions— The Universal Religion

The great truth we are considering is the fundamental principle running through all religions. We find it in everyone. In regard to it all agree. It is, moreover, a great truth in regard to which all people can agree, whether they belong to the same or to different religions. People always quarrel about the trifles, about their personal views of minor insignificant points. They always come together in the presence of great fundamental truths, the threads of which run through all. The quarrels are in connection with the lower self, the agreements are in connection with the higher self.

A place may have its factions that quarrel and fight among themselves, but let a great calamity come upon the land, flood, famine, pestilence, and these little personal differences are entirely forgotten and all work shoulder to shoulder in the one great cause. The changing, the evolving self gives rise to quarrels; the permanent, the soul-self unites all in the highest efforts of love and service.

Patriotism is a beautiful thing; it is well for me to love my country, but why should I love my own country more than I love all others? If I love my own and hate others, I then show my limitations, and my patriotism will stand the test not even for my own. If I love my own country and in the same way love all other countries, then I show the largeness of my nature, and a patriotism of this kind is noble and always to be relied upon.

The view of God in regard to which we are agreed, that He is the Infinite Spirit of Life and Power that is back of all, that is working in and through all, that is the life of all, is a matter in regard to which all men, all religions can agree. With this view there can be no infidels or atheists. There are atheists and infidels in connection with many views that are held concerning God, and thank God there are. Even devout and earnest people among us attribute things to God that no respectable men or women would permit to be attributed to themselves. This view is satisfying to those who cannot see how God can be angry with his children, jealous, vindictive. A display of these qualities always lessens our respect for men and women, and still we attribute them to God.

The earnest, sincere heretic is one of the greatest friends true religion can have. Heretics are among God's greatest servants. They are among the true servants of mankind. Christ was one of the greatest heretics the world has ever known. He allowed himself to be bound by no established or orthodox teachings or beliefs. Christ is preëminently a type of the universal. John the Baptist is a type of the personal. John dressed in a particular way, ate a particular kind of food, belonged to a particular order, lived and taught in a particular locality, and he himself recognized the fact that he must decrease while Christ must increase. Christ, on the other hand, gave himself absolutely no limitations. He allowed himself to be bound by nothing. He was absolutely universal and as a consequence taught not for his own particular day, but for all time.

This mighty truth which we have agreed upon as the great central fact of human life is the golden thread that runs through all religions. When we make it the paramount fact in our lives we will find that minor differences, narrow prejudices, and all these laughable absurdities will so fall away by virtue of their very insignificance, that a Jew can worship equally as well in a Catholic cathedral, a Catholic in a Jewish synagogue, a Buddhist in a Christian church, a Christian in a Buddhist temple. Or all can worship equally well about their own hearthstones, or out on the hillside, or while pursuing the avocations of everyday life. For true worship, only God and the human soul are necessary. It does not depend upon times, or seasons, or occasions.

Anywhere and at any time God and man in the bush may meet.

This is the great fundamental principle of the universal religion upon which all can agree. This is the great fact that is permanent. There are many things in regard to which all cannot agree. These are the things that are personal, nonessential, and so as time passes they gradually fall away. One who doesn't grasp this great truth, a Christian, for example, asks "But was not Christ inspired?" Yes, but he was not the only one inspired. Another who is a Buddhist asks, "Was not Buddha inspired?" Yes, but he was not the only one inspired. A Christian asks, "But is not our Christian Bible inspired?" Yes, but there are other inspired scriptures. A Brahmin or a Buddhist asks, "Are not the Vedas inspired?" Yes, but there are other inspired sacred books. Your error is not in believing that your particular scriptures are inspired, but your error is—and you show your absurdly laughable limitations by it—your inability to see that other scriptures are also inspired.

The sacred books, the inspired writings, all come from the same source—God, God speaking through the souls of those who open themselves that He may thus speak. Some may be more inspired than others. It depends entirely on the relative degree that this one or that one opens himself to the Divine voice. Says one of the inspired writers in the Hebrew scriptures, Wisdom is the breath of the power of God, and *in all ages* entering into holy souls she maketh them friends of God and prophets.

The great fundamental principles of all religions are the same. They differ only in their minor details according to the various degrees of unfoldment of different people. I am sometimes asked, "To what religion do you belong?" What religion? Why, bless you, there is only one religion—the religion of the living God. There are, of course, the various creeds of the same religion arising from the various interpretations of different people, but they are all of minor importance. The more unfolded the soul the less important do these minor differences become. There are also, of course, the various so-called religions. There is in reality, however, but one religion.

## Chapter Eleven
# Entering Now Into the Realization of the Highest Riches

I hear the question, What can be said in a concrete way in regard to the method of coming into this realization? The facts underlying it are, indeed, most beautiful and true, but how can we actualize in ourselves the realization that carries with it such wonderful results?

The method is not difficult if we do not of ourselves make it difficult. The principal word to be used is the word—Open. Simply to open your mind and heart to this divine inflow which is waiting only for the opening of the gate, that it may enter. It is like opening the gate of the trough which conducts the water from the reservoir above into the field below. The water, by virtue of its very nature, will rush in and irrigate the field if the gate is but opened. As to the realization of our oneness with this Infinite Life and Power, after seeing, as I think we have clearly seen by this time, the relations it bears to us and we to it, the chief thing to be said is simply—Realize your oneness with it. The open mind and heart whereby one is brought into the receptive attitude is the first thing necessary. Then the earnest, sincere desire.

It may be an aid at first to take yourself for a few moments each day into the quiet, into the silence, where you will not be agitated by the disturbances that enter in through the avenues of the physical senses. There in the quiet alone with God, put yourself into the receptive attitude. Calmly, quietly, and expectantly desire that this realization break in upon and take possession of your soul. As it breaks in upon and takes possession of the soul, it will manifest itself to your mind, and from this you will feel its manifestations in every part of your body. Then in the degree that you open yourself to it you will feel a quiet, peaceful, illuminating power that will harmonize body, soul, and mind, and that will then harmonize these with all the world. You are now on the mountain top, and the voice of God is speaking to you. *Then, as you descend, carry this realization with you.* Live in it, waking, working, thinking, walking, sleeping. In this way, although you may not be continually on the mountain top, you will nevertheless be continually living in the realization of all the beauty, and inspiration, and power you have felt there.

Moreover, the time will come when in the busy office or on the noisy street you can enter into the silence by simply drawing the mantle of your own thoughts about you and realizing that there and everywhere the Spirit of Infinite Life, Love, Wisdom, Peace, Power, and Plenty is guiding, keeping, protecting, leading you. This is the spirit of continual prayer. This it is to pray without ceasing. This it is to know and to walk with God. *This it is to find the Christ within.* This is the new birth, the second birth. First that which is natural, then that which is spiritual. It is thus that the old man Adam is put off and the new man Christ is put on. This it is to be saved unto life eternal, whatever one's form of belief or faith may be; for it is life eternal to know God. "The Sweet By and By" will be a song of the past. We will create a new song—"The Beautiful Eternal Now."

This is the realization that you and I can come into this very day, this very hour, this very minute, if we desire and if we will it. And if now we merely set our faces in the right direction, it is then but a matter of time until we come into the full splendors of this complete realization. To set one's face in the direction of the mountain and then simply to journey on, whether rapidly or more slowly, will bring him to it. But unless one set his face in the right direction and make the start, he will not reach it. It was Goethe who said:

*Are you in earnest? Seize this very minute:*
*What you can do, or dream you can, begin it;*
*Boldness has genius, power, and magic in it.*
*Only engage and then the mind grows heated;*
*Begin and then the work will be completed.*\*

Said the young man, Gautama Siddhârtha, I have awakened to the truth and I am resolved to accomplish my purpose—Verily I shall become a Buddha. It was this that brought him into the life of the Enlightened One, and so into the realization of Nirvana right here in this life. That this same realization and life is within the possibilities of all here and now was his teaching. It was this that has made him the Light Bearer to millions of people.

Said the young man, Jesus, Know ye not that I must be about my Father's business? Making this the one great purpose of his life he came into the full and complete realization—I and the Father are one. He thus came into the full realization of the Kingdom of Heaven right here in this life. That all could come into this same realization and life here and now was his teaching. It was this that has made him the Light Bearer to millions of people.

---

\* Trine is quoting a very loose 1835 translation of Goethe's *Faust* by Irish poet John Anster.—MH

And so far as practical things are concerned, we may hunt the wide universe through and we shall find that there is no injunction more practical than, Seek ye first the kingdom of God and His righteousness and all other things shall be added unto you. And in the light of what has gone before, I think there is no one who is open to truth and honest with himself who will fail to grasp the underlying reason and see the great laws upon which it is based.

As one comes into and lives continually in the full, conscious realization of his oneness with the Infinite Life and Power, then all else follows. This it is that brings the realization of such splendors, and beauties, and joys as a life that is thus related with the Infinite Power alone can know. This it is to come into the realization of heaven's richest treasures while walking the earth. This it is to bring heaven down to earth, or rather to bring earth up to heaven. This it is to exchange weakness and impotence for strength; sorrows and sighings for joy; fears and forebodings for faith; longings for realizations. This it is to come into fullness of peace, power, and plenty. This it is to be in tune with the Infinite.

## Chapter Twelve
# "The Way"

Life is not so complex if we do not so persistently make it so. We accept the results or the effects; but we concern ourselves all too little with the realm of cause. The springs of life are all from within. Invariably it is true—as is the inner so always and inevitably will be the outer.

There is a Divine current that will bear us with peace and safety on its bosom if we are sufficiently alert and determined to find it and go with it. The natural, normal life is by a law divine under the guidance of the Spirit.

There is a mystic force that transcends the powers of the intellect and likewise of the body. There are certain faculties that we have that are not a part of the active, thinking mind; they transcend any possible activities of the active, thinking mind. Through them we have intuitions, impulses, leadings, that instead of being merely the occasional, *should be the normal and habitual.*

They would be if we understood better the laws that pertain to them and observed them; for here, as in connection with everything in the universe and everything in human life, all is governed by law—the Elemental law of cause and effect. Supreme Intelligence, Creative Power, works only through law. There is an inner spirit or guide that rules and regulates the life when the life is brought into that state or condition whereby it can make itself known, and in turn dominate the life.

Jesus, Master of the laws of life, and supreme revealer of them to men, had a full and practical knowledge of it. He not only abundantly demonstrated it in His own life; but He made clear the way whereby it may become the common possession of other lives. Do not worry about your life, was the Master's clear-cut and repeated command. He not only gave the injunction or command, but He demonstrated the method whereby the fears and forebodings and uncertainties of life can be displaced by a force or a power that will bring them to an end.

It was embodied in His other injunction or command that He gave utterance to so repeatedly: "Seek ye first the Kingdom of God and His righteousness and all these things shall be added to you." And by all these things, He meant, all of the common needs and necessities of the daily life.

The finding of the Kingdom of God is the recognition of the indwelling Divine Life as the source, and therefore as the Essence, of our own lives. It is the bringing of men's minds and therefore acts into harmony with the Divine will and purpose. It is the saving of men from their lower conceptions and selves, and a lifting them up to a realization of their higher selves, which, as He taught, is eternally one with God, the Father; and which, when realized, lifts a man's thoughts, acts, purposes, and conduct—his entire life—up to that pattern or standard.

It was not merely a poetic fancy, but the recognition of a fundamental law, as well-known laws of modern psychology, mental and spiritual science, are now clearly demonstrating, that induced the Master to say: "And thine ears shall hear a word behind thee, saying, This is the way, walk ye in it, when ye turn to the righthand and when ye turn to the left." And again: "The Lord in the midst of thee is mighty." And still again: "He that dwelleth in the secret place of the Most High shall abide under the shadow of the Almighty."

How often do the meager accounts of the Master's life tell us of His going up to the mountain to pray—*for communion with the Father*. And then we find Him invariably down among men, always where the need for help and for human service was the greatest.

This habit of taking a little time daily alone, in the quiet, in communion with one's Source that the illumination and guidance of the Holy

Spirit may become alive and active in the life, and going then about one's daily work ever open to and conscious of this Divine guidance, trusting and resting in it, strengthened and sustained always by this Divine power, will bring definiteness and direction, will bring hope and courage, will bring peace and power to everyone who will heed the Master's injunction and will follow His example. These it has brought to great numbers to whom before, life was an enigma, and this because the life had been lived entirely from the outside.

The higher forces and powers of the inner life, those of the mind and spirit, always potential within, become of actual value only as they are recognized, realized, and used.

The Master's *Way of the Spirit*, the finding of the Kingdom within, leads into no blind alley. It leads out and triumphantly out onto the great plain of clear vision, of un-self-centered activity, of heroic endeavor and accomplishment.

If we would spend a fraction of the time that we spend in needless anxiety in definite constructive thought, in "silent demand," visualizing the conditions that we would have, with faith in their fulfillment, we would soon know that the Master's illustration of the carefree bird is fact and not fancy. It is, He said, what life should be.

The little time spent in the quiet each day, alone with one's God, that we may make and keep our connection with the Infinite Source, "our source and our life," will be a boon to any life. It will prove, if we are faithful, to be the most priceless possession that we have.

While it is impossible for one to make a formula which another should follow, the following may perchance contain some little suggestions—each must follow his or her own leading and, therefore, method.

> My Father in Heaven, Infinite Spirit of life and love and wisdom and power, in whom I live and move and have my being, whence cometh my help, manifest Thyself in me.
>
> Help me to open myself to the highest wisdom and insight and love and power, that I may serve Thee and my fellow-man, and all my fellow-creatures faithfully, and that I may have the Divine guidance and care, and that all my needs be supplied.
>
> Oh *Christ within*, enfold and lead me and reign supreme, that the One Life that is my life I may realize and manifest ever more fully.

I am strong in the Infinite Spirit of life and love and wisdom and power. I have and shall have the Divine guidance and care; for it is the Father that worketh in me—My Father works and I work.

---

The following little motto—a resolve for today—may contain a little aid for the following of the *Way*.

### *I AM RESOLVED*

*I believe that my Master intended that I take His teachings in the simple, frank, and open manner in which He gave them, out on the hillside, by the calm blue waters of the Galilean sea, and out under the stars of heaven.*

*I believe that He knew what He meant, and that He meant what He said, when He gave the substance of all religion and the duty of man as love to God, and love and service for His fellow-men.*

*I am therefore resolved at this, the beginning of another day, this fresh beginning of life, to go forth eager and happy and unafraid, in that I can come into the same filial relations of love and guidance and care with my Father in Heaven that my Master realized and lived, and going before revealed to me.*

*I shall listen intently to know, and shall run with eager feet to do my Father's will, calm and quiet within, knowing that I shall have the Divine guidance and care, and that no harm therefore shall befall me; for I am now living in God's life and there I shall live forever.*

*I am resolved in all human contact to meet petulance with patience, questionings with kindness, hatred with love, eager always to do the kindly deed that brings the joy of service—and that alone makes human life truly human.*

*I shall seek no advantage for myself to the detriment or the harm of my neighbor, knowing that it is only through the law of mutuality that I can fully enjoy what I gain—or can even be a man.*

*I am resolved therefore so to live this day that, when the twilight comes and the night falls, I shall be not only another day's journey nearer home; but I shall have lived a man's part and done a man's work in the world and shall indeed deserve my Father's love and care.*

# A Message to Garcia
## and Treasured Wisdom
### (1899)

## by Elbert Hubbard

*Discover the Simple, Life-Changing Secret of this Motivational Classic— Now in a Definitive Edition*

*"We work to become, not to acquire."*
—ELBERT HUBBARD

## Contents

Introduction   *The Message That Shook the World* by Mitch Horowitz   236
A Message to Garcia   239
Uncommon Commonsense Passages by Elbert Hubbard   243

## Introduction

# The Message That Shook the World

This "literary trifle," as author Elbert Hubbard described *A Message to Garcia,* may be the most important piece of practical philosophy that you ever encounter.

I call Hubbard's writing "uncommon commonsense." This is because his work conveys truths that we should know, and perhaps innately know, but have forgotten amid the calls of modern commerce to turn everything into short-term profit and to expect that every experience deliver entertainment and pleasure.

Hubbard intended his short essay as a guiding light to illuminate, very simply, what separates the few exceptional people from the mass of mediocrity. His core truth is: "the hero is the man who does his work"—thoroughly, energetically, and intelligently. The workplace hero does not make needless demands on others or require superfluous guidance and assistance; he does not deliver a job half-done or done only according to pro forma standards; but he *does his work* so that no one will have to fix it, embellish it, worry about it, or do it again.

Do not mistake this as a formula for worker-bee conformity. It is the opposite. Hubbard's credo, if you take it seriously and *act* on it, will show you what you're really capable of—and help you become a useful, constructive, and generative person.

Hubbard derived the title *A Message to Garcia* and his lesson from the experience of Lieutenant Andrew S. Rowan, an intelligence officer in US Army during the Spanish-American War. At the outset of the conflict in 1898, Rowan was ordered to deliver a vital US military message to General Calixto Garcia, the leader of a rebellion against Spanish rule of Cuba. All that was known of Garcia's whereabouts was that he was hunkered down at a jungle base in eastern Cuba. With little strategic briefing or material help from the US Army, Rowan succeeded in landing on the island, locating the rebel general, and delivering his "Message to Garcia," thus solidifying the US alliance with Cuban partisans, and leading to Spain's defeat in the war.

Hubbard wasn't making a political judgment about the war. He grew deeply critical of the intermingling of war and commerce in the years that immediately followed, as will be seen. Rather, Hubbard's focus was the character of Lieutenant Rowan: the young officer displayed independence of thought, resourcefulness, and tremendous determination, all of it applied with careful judgment and good sense. Those traits, Hubbard reasoned, are in alarmingly short supply in the lives of most men and women, who quickly vacillate from excitement to boredom, and often approach their work with apathy.

Hubbard first published his essay as a kind of space-filler in the March 1899 issue of his cultural magazine *The Philistine*. He said that he wrote it in just one hour after dinner one night. It was so minor a piece to him that he originally ran it with no headline. But the brief statement quickly gained national attention. Employers, managers, college presidents, and generals ordered copies and reprinted it, first by the thousands and eventually the millions. The essay became so popular that for many years the term "carry a message to Garcia" was slang for attempting a challenging task. *A Message to Garcia* got translated around the world and read by foreign armies and workforces. Parents gave copies to children who were starting college or entering working life. Enterprising clerks, with eyes on the corner office, gobbled up copies.

*A Message to Garcia* remained a mainstay of American success literature for close to fifty years. While the work's popularity is now nowhere near what it once was, it remains possible in the twenty-first century to find an employer here and there who still gives copies to new hires. It would be a help to the human situation if *all* employers handed it out today. Although the essay's message is chiefly about work and duty, its principles of personal enterprise and dedication are an excellent formula for peace at home: When you do things for people, rather than demand things from them (which can take subtle forms in the home environment), it demonstrates that you truly care about them. Every marriage therapist should hand out *A Message to Garcia*. Parents and children should receive it from family counselors. Prisoners working toward early release would benefit from it. So would law enforcement. Students who follow it would excel.

In short, there is almost no one today who wouldn't benefit from reading and following *A Message to Garcia*. Why is the pamphlet no longer widely read? Some readers may be put off by its unfamiliar historical references to the Spanish-American War. But these are easily illuminated, as I've attempted above.

There is one more reason why Garcia has fallen from its peak—and it involves a fair, but incomplete, criticism of the work. Hubbard's critics disparaged his essay for promoting servility and loyalty to unjust causes or employers. Some social writers saw Hubbard as a kind of false prophet to the workingman; someone who reinforced existing power structures and promulgated a message of complacency and know-thy-place toadyism. Hubbard reinforced this judgment by boasting that generals and industrialists had distributed his pamphlet by the millions. The pamphlet was given to Russian soldiers in the Tsar's army, and to every member of the early twentieth-century Japanese military. Both forces were known to commit acts of brutality and even atrocities. Hubbard's philosophy in *A Message to Garcia* can be taken amorally. But this is untrue of the man himself.

Although he had a flamboyant and somewhat media-catered personality, and although he betrayed instances of cloyingness toward industry titans, Hubbard's body of writing, as a social-reform journalist and an aphorist, loudly called for economic justice, legal protections for workers, and the criminalization of war profiteering. Hubbard helped expose child-labor abuses in Southern cotton mills—a social blight that chiefly profited mill owners in the North. His reportage led to some of America's first anti child-labor laws. He advocated for women's rights and suffrage. He experimented with voluntary communism and communal living. He thought it should be illegal to profit from the sale of military weaponry. He vociferously and vocally opposed World War One. This last commitment cost him his life. Hubbard and his second wife, Alice, a student of New Thought and a women's rights activist, were killed along with nearly 1,200 other civilians when a German U-boat torpedoed the British passenger liner the Lusitania in May 1915 off the Irish coast. The Hubbards were on a self-described peace mission to Europe to protest the war to the German Kaiser. Hubbard had hoped to gain a personal interview with the Kaiser (a reasonable possibility given Hubbard's fame at the time) and inveigh against the conflict.

"Big business has been to blame in this thing," Hubbard wrote of the war before his journey, "... let it not escape this truth—that no longer shall individuals be allowed to thrive by selling murder machines to the mob."

Seen in perspective, *A Message to Garcia* is an incomplete rendering of Hubbard's philosophy. Hubbard would have strengthened the work if he had infused it with a sense of his own moral purpose and discrimination. That said, Garcia is a *necessary* philosophy. Not just for ambitious employees, or for managers who are trying to overcome workplace apathy; but for artists, scholars, and those who work for social justice. People who see themselves as standing outside of traditional commerce often neglect the principles that Hubbard said make an individual effective and powerful. His methods—namely, throwing yourself into a task with absolute dedication, independence, and accountability—are as necessary for the artist and activist as for the executive and field commander. Artists who blow deadlines, activists who forget their pamphlets on the way to a rally, or union organizers who dither, hesitate, or put off needed tasks, benefit no one.

To fill some of the moral blanks Hubbard left in his great work, this edition of *A Message to Garcia* includes selections from some of his most stirring statements of moral philosophy. These passages flesh out Hubbard's full point of view. But be warned: Hubbard will frustrate any reader looking for surface consistency. At varying turns Hubbard celebrates capitalism, socialism, and anarchism. This isn't because he was fickle or erratic. Rather, it is because Hubbard had the capacity to see and embrace the highest good in philosophies that others might view as incompatible. In Hubbard's experience as a manufacturer, publisher, muckraker, and founder of a successful arts-and-crafts community, he proved his ability to combine tenets of all these outlooks. This was one of the marks of his greatness.

Although it is a short and brisk piece of writing, *A Message to Garcia* will take on new shades of meaning and provide new truths each time you examine it. Return to Hubbard's words again and again. Recommend them to those you love. It is one of the greatest gifts you could ever give or receive.

—Mitch Horowitz

# A Message To Garcia

In all this Cuban business there is one man stands out on the horizon of my memory like Mars at perihelion.

When war broke out between Spain and the United States, it was very necessary to communicate quickly with the leader of the Insurgents. Garcia was somewhere in the mountain fastnesses of Cuba—no one knew where. No mail or telegraph message could reach him. The President must secure his co-operation, and quickly.

What to do!

Some one said to the President, "There is a fellow by the name of Rowan will find Garcia for you, if anybody can."

Rowan was sent for and was given a letter to be delivered to Garcia. How the "fellow by the name of Rowan" took the letter, sealed it up in an oilskin pouch, strapped it over his heart, in four days landed by night off the coast of Cuba from an open boat, disappeared into the jungle, and in three weeks came out on the other side of the Island, having traversed a hostile country on foot, and delivered his letter to Garcia—are things I have no special desire now to tell in detail. The point that I wish to make is this: McKinley gave Rowan a letter to be delivered to Garcia; Rowan took the letter and did not ask, "Where is he at?"

By the Eternal! there is a man whose form should be cast in deathless bronze and the statue placed in every college of the land. It is not book-learning young men need, nor instruction about this and that, but a stiffening of the vertebrae which will cause them to be loyal to a trust, to act promptly, concentrate their energies: do the thing—"Carry a message to Garcia."

General Garcia is dead now, but there are other Garcias. No man who has endeavored to carry out an enterprise where many hands were needed, but has been well-nigh appalled at times by the imbecility of the average man—the inability or unwillingness to concentrate on a thing and do it.

Slipshod assistance, foolish inattention, dowdy indifference, and half-hearted work seem the rule; and no man succeeds, unless by hook or crook or threat he forces or bribes other men to assist him; or mayhap, God in His goodness performs a miracle, and sends him an Angel of Light for an assistant.

You, reader, put this matter to a test: You are sitting now in your office—six clerks are within call. Summon any one and make this request: "Please look in the encyclopedia and make a brief memorandum for me concerning the life of Correggio."

Will the clerk quietly say, "Yes, sir," and go do the task?

On your life he will not. He will look at you out of a fishy eye and ask one or more of the following questions:

Who was he?

Which encyclopedia?

Where is the encyclopedia?

Was I hired for that?

Don't you mean Bismarck?
What's the matter with Charlie doing it?
Is he dead?
Is there any hurry?
Sha'n't I bring you the book and let you look it up yourself?
What do you want to know for?

And I will lay you ten to one that after you have answered the questions, and explained how to find the information, and why you want it, the clerk will go off and get one of the other clerks to help him try to find Garcia—and then come back and tell you there is no such man. Of course I may lose my bet, but according to the Law of Average I will not. Now, if you are wise, you will not bother to explain to your "assistant" that Correggio is indexed under the C's, not in the K's, but you will smile very sweetly and say, "Never mind," and go look it up yourself. And this incapacity for independent action, this moral stupidity, this infirmity of the will, this unwillingness to cheerfully catch hold and lift—these are the things that put pure Socialism so far into the future. If men will not act for themselves, what will they do when the benefit of their effort is for all?

A first mate with knotted club seems necessary; and the dread of getting "the bounce" Saturday night holds many a worker to his place. Advertise for a stenographer, and nine out of ten who apply can neither spell nor punctuate—and do not think it necessary to.

Can such a one write a letter to Garcia?

"You see that bookkeeper," said a foreman to me in a large factory.

"Yes; what about him?"

"Well, he's a fine accountant, but if I'd send him up-town on an errand, he might accomplish the errand all right, and on the other hand, might stop at four saloons on the way, and when he got to Main Street would forget what he had been sent for."

Can such a man be entrusted to carry a message to Garcia?

We have recently been hearing much maudlin sympathy expressed for the "downtrodden denizens of the sweat-shop" and the "homeless wanderer searching for honest employment," and with it all often go many hard words for the men in power.

Nothing is said about the employer who grows old before his time in a vain attempt to get frowsy ne'er-do-wells to do intelligent work; and his long, patient striving with "help" that does nothing but loaf when his back is turned. In every store and factory there is a constant weeding-out process going on. The employer is continually sending away "help" that have shown their incapacity to further the interests of the business, and others are being taken on. No matter how good times are, this sorting continues: only if times are hard and work is scarce, the sorting is done finer—but out and forever out the incompetent and unworthy go. It is the survival of the fittest. Self-interest prompts every employer to keep the best—those who can carry a message to Garcia.

I know one man of really brilliant parts who has not the ability to manage a business of his own, and yet who is absolutely worthless to any one else, because he carries with him constantly the insane suspicion that his employer is oppressing, or intending to oppress, him. He can not give orders; and he will not receive them. Should a message be given him to take to Garcia, his answer would probably be, "Take it yourself!"

Tonight this man walks the streets looking for work, the wind whistling through his threadbare coat. No one who knows him dare employ him, for he is a regular firebrand of discontent. He is impervious to reason, and the only thing that can impress him is the toe of a thick-soled Number Nine boot.

Of course I know that one so morally deformed is no less to be pitied than a physical cripple; but in our pitying let us drop a tear, too, for the men who are striving to carry on a great enterprise, whose working hours are not limited by the whistle, and whose hair is fast turning white through the struggle to hold in line dowdy indifference, slipshod imbecility, and the heartless ingratitude which, but for their enterprise, would be both hungry and homeless.

Have I put the matter too strongly? Possibly I have; but when all the world has gone a-slumming I wish to speak a word of sympathy for the man who succeeds—the man who, against great odds, has directed the efforts of others, and having succeeded, finds there's nothing in it: nothing but bare board and clothes. I have carried a dinner-pail and worked for day's wages, and I have also been an employer of labor, and I know there is something to be said on both sides. There is no excellence, per se, in poverty; rags are no recommendation; and all employers are not rapacious and high-handed, any more than all poor men are virtuous. My heart goes out to the man who does his work when the "boss" is away, as well as when he is at home. And the man who, when given a letter for Garcia, quietly takes the missive, without asking any idiotic questions, and with no lurking intention of chucking it into the nearest sewer, or of doing aught else but deliver it, never gets "laid off," nor has to go on a strike for higher wages. Civilization is one long, anxious search for just such individuals. Anything such a man asks shall be granted. His kind is so rare that no employer can afford to let him go. He is wanted in every city, town and village—in every office, shop, store and factory. The world cries out for such: he is needed and needed badly—the man who can "Carry a Message to Garcia."

# Uncommon Commonsense:
## *Passages by Elbert Hubbard*

### LIFE LIES IN THE QUEST

We need the colleges, but not for segregation, nor for noisy yells and sophomoric pride in smug futility of Greek-letter societies, with their senseless, soulless mummery.

Why not a workshop instead?

The university of the future will supply certain conditions of growth and these will be free to all who care to work for them, and all who care to work for them will be free to do so.

If a man will not work, neither shall he eat.

If a man will not work, neither shall he be educated.

In future, our children shall go to school—not be sent nor sentenced. Nothing is of any value to you except what you work for. Things given you and thrust upon you are forever alien to you—separate and apart, and will be molted very shortly.

That which is worth having is worth working for.

Education is not an acquisition, it is an achievement. Like liberty you must earn it, or you'll wander forever in the desert, a slave in spirit still.

—1904

### HORSE SENSE

If you work for a man, in Heaven's name work for him. If he pays wages that supply you your bread and butter, work for him, speak well of him, think well of him, and stand by him, and stand by the institution he represents. I think if I worked for a man, I would work for him. I would not work for him a part of his time, but all of his time. I would give an undivided service or none. If put to the pinch, an ounce of loyalty is worth a pound of cleverness. If you must vilify, condemn, and eternally disparage, why, resign your position, and when you are outside, damn to your heart's content. But, I pray you, so long as you are a part of an institution, do not condemn it. Not that you will injure the institution—not that—but when you disparage the concern of which you are a part, you disparage yourself. And don't forget—"I forgot" won't do in business.   —Circa 1899

## Jesus Was an Anarchist

An Anarchist is one who minds his own business. An Anarchist does not believe in sending warships across wide oceans to kill brown men, and lay waste rice fields, and burn the homes of people fighting for liberty. An Anarchist does not drive women with babes at their breasts and other women with babes unborn, children and old men into the jungle to be devoured by beasts or fever or fear, or die of hunger, homeless, unhoused and undone.

... I believe that brutality tends to defeat itself. Prize fighters die young, gourmands get the gout, hate hurts worse the man who nurses it, and all selfishness robs the mind of its divine insight, and cheats the soul that would know. Mind alone is eternal! He, watching over Israel, slumbers not nor sleeps. My faith is great: out of the transient darkness of the present the shadows will flee away, and Day will yet dawn.

... I am an Anarchist.

No man who believes in force and violence is an Anarchist. The true Anarchist decries all influences save those of love and reason. Ideas are his only arms.

Being an Anarchist I am also a Socialist. Socialism is the antithesis of Anarchy. One is the North Pole of Truth, the other the South. The Socialist believes in working for the good of all, while Anarchy is pure Individualism. I believe in every man working for the good of self; and in working for the good of self, he works for the good of all. To think, to see, to feel, to know; to deal justly; to bear all patiently; to act quietly; to speak cheerfully; to moderate one's voice—these things will bring you the highest good. They will bring you the love of the best, and the esteem of that Sacred Few, whose good opinion alone is worth cultivating. And further than this, it is the best way you can serve Society—live your life. The wise way to benefit humanity is to attend to your own affairs, and thus give other people an opportunity to look after theirs.

If there is any better way to teach virtue than by practicing it, I do not know it. Would you make men better—set them an example.   —1901

## An Educated Person

1. Man's education is never complete, and life and education should go hand in hand to the end.
2. By separating education from practical life society has inculcated the vicious belief that education is one thing and life another.
3. Five hours of intelligently directed work a day will supply ample board, lodging, and clothing to the adolescent student, male or female.
4. Five hours of manual labor will not only support the student, but it will add to his intellectual vigor and conduce to his better physical, mental and, spiritual development.
5. This work should be directly in the line of education, and part of the school curriculum.
6. No effort of life need be inutile, but all effort should be useful in order to satisfy the consciousness.
7. Somebody must do the work of the world. There is a certain amount of work to do, and the reason some people have to labor from daylight until dark is because others never work at all.
8. To do a certain amount of manual labor every day, should be accounted a privilege to every normal man and woman.
9. No person should be overworked.
10. All should do some work.
11. To work intelligently is education.
12. To abstain from useful work in order to get an education, is to get an education of the wrong kind, that is to say, a false education.
13. From fourteen years up, every normal individual can be self-supporting, and to be so is a God-given privilege, conductive to the best mental, moral, and spiritual development.
14. The plan of examinations, in order to ascertain how much the pupil knows, does not reveal how much the pupil knows, causes much misery, is conducive to hypocrisy, and is like pulling up the plant to examine its roots. It further indicates that we have small faith in our methods.
15. People who have too much leisure consume more than they should, and do not produce enough.
16. To go to school for four years, or six, is no proof of excellence; any more than to fail in an examination is proof of incompetence.

17. The giving of degrees and diplomas to people who have done no useful things is puerile and absurd, since degrees so secured are no proof of competence, and tend to inflate the holder with the idea that he is some great one when, probably, he isn't.
18. All degrees should be honorary, and be given for meritorious service to society—that is, for doing something useful for somebody.
19. The walls of the old-time college are crumbing, and the University of the future will have around it no twelve-foot-high iron fence.

The chief error of the colleges lies in the fact that they have separated the world of culture from the world of work.

They have fostered the fallacy that one set of men should do the labor, and another set should have the education—that one should be ornamental and the other useful.

Then, to bolster their position, they have manufactured specious arguments trying to show that the professionals who supply truth and art to the poor people who have neither, are better than the folks who toil to feed and clothe the folks who make the arguments.

The fact is that the opportunities for education should be within the reach of every individual, not for the lucky few. Nature is opposed to monopolies and so she nips the selfish ambitions of your exclusively educated person and says, "Go to! get your education and be damned!"

And he often is.

Hence we get a condition approaching that which existed in the Fifteenth Century, when nobody was educated because the schools graduated only the top-heavy. —1904

## I Believe

I believe in myself.

I believe in the goods I sell.

I believe in my colleagues and helpers.

I believe in the efficacy of printer's ink.

I believe in producers, creators, manufacturers, distributors, and in all the workers of the world who have a job and hold it down.

I believe that truth is an asset.

I believe that the first requisite in success is not to achieve a dollar but to confer a benefit, and that the reward will come automatically and usually as a matter of course.

I believe that the greatest word in the English language is "Sufficiency."

I believe that when I make a sale I must make a friend.

I believe that when I part with you I must do it in such a way that when you see me again you will be glad—and so will I.

I believe in the hands that work, in the brains that think, and in the hearts that love. —1912, adapted form Elbert Hubbard's *Credo*

# The Magic Story
(1900)

## by Frederick van Rensselaer Dey

*"If you have skill, apply it; the world must profit by it, and, therefore, you."*

## Contents

Introduction  *Discovering Your Story Within* The Magic Story by Mitch Horowitz   250

Preface   253

Part One   253

Part Two   In the Old Scrap Book   260

## Introduction
# Discovering Your Story Within *The Magic Story*

If you're like me, you often walk around feeling like there are "two of you"—dual selves fighting for dominance.

And you are right: There are, in a sense, two personas struggling within us all, like Jacob and Esau.

We experience this when we feel ourselves divided between ordinary life and peak possibility. People often harbor the feeling that they *could* become a writer, or *could* get straight A's, or *could* excel at work, or *could* find a positive relationship . . . if only they were able to freely throw themselves upon the energies of their higher, better, more formidable doppelgänger, waiting to be released. This possibility is real, but it is rarely, or only fleetingly, exercised.

Many modern fiction writers and psychologists, not to mention their ancient and folkloric forebears, have posited the existence of this "other self." Psychologist Carl Jung famously called it the shadow, which he identified as a fount of unacknowledged desires and proclivities; if acknowledged and integrated into your day-to-day consciousness, these shadow traits could lead to the growth of untapped powers, confidence, and abilities. For fantasy writer Robert Louis Stevenson, the other self was the malevolent "Mr. Hyde," a feral counterpart to the refined and approachable persona of Dr. Jekyll. For Edgar Allan Poe, the other side was represented by "William Wilson," the title of Poe's 1839 short story in which his protagonist, the debauched Wilson, grows up alongside an uncanny double who shares his name, appearance, and birthdate, and who eventually turns out to be the maleficent hero's alienated conscience.

Many fiction writers, like Stephen King in his 1989 novel, *The Dark Half*, see the other self as a figure of repressed violence and evil. But that reflects only one sliver of the split-self riddle of human nature. More important for our purposes, your counter-self can be a figure of relative fearlessness, effectiveness, and ability. Author Napoleon Hill highlighted these possibilities in his 1937 self-help classic, *Think and Grow Rich*. (A book that you do yourself a disservice by not reading if you permit yourself to be put off by its seemingly gauche title.) Hill wrote:

> O. Henry discovered the genius which slept within his brain, after he had met with great misfortune, and was confined to a prison cell in Columbus,

Ohio. Being FORCED, through misfortune, to become acquainted with his "other self," and to use his IMAGINATION, he discovered himself to be a great author instead of a miserable criminal and outcast. Strange and varied are the ways of life, and stranger still are the ways of Infinite Intelligence, through which men are sometimes forced to undergo all sorts of punishments before discovering their own brains, and their own capacity to create useful ideas through imagination.

One of the oddest inspirational works ever written, *The Magic Story*, reprinted here from one of its earliest extant editions, featured this theme of a positive double, which author Frederick van Rensselaer Dey (1861–1922) called your "plus-entity." In Dey's brief and oddly compelling instructional tale from 1900, he depicts the life of a down-and-out 17th-century craftsman who discovers that a haunting Presence, or other self, is hovering around his periphery. Dey's hero finds that his counter-self is a real part of him, one that is "calm, steadfast, and self-reliant." As soon as he comes to identify, literally, with his plus-entity, his life is happily transformed. "Make a daily and nightly companion of your plus-entity," the hero counsels.

As it happens, the author Dey's life was less than happy: After a middling and prolific career writing pulp crime fiction, including the popular Nick Carter detective tales, the wearied writer shot himself to death in 1922. He left behind a stoic suicide note, asking only that his older brother be taken care of. Dey's widow, Haryot Holt Dey, was herself a notable writer and suffragist who lived until 1950. To use the terms of Dey's own allegory, the author succumbed to his "minus-entity."

How can you get in touch with your stronger plus-entity?

### Dress the Part

Never neglect the power of simple things. The manner in which you dress and comport yourself has tremendous impact on your psyche. Most people instinctively sense this without fully acting on it. (This is one reason why the process of transitioning can feel enormously liberating to a transgender person.) Become a thespian, trying out, perhaps subtly at first, different styles of dress, makeup, accessories, and body art. In one of my favorite episodes of *The Simpsons*, a teacher tells young Lisa, "Being tough comes from the inside. First step—change your outside." It's a joke, of course, but like most jokes, it conceals a core truth.

## Feed Your Other Self

Allow yourself to become immersed in music, movies, and media that feed your sense of power and self-agency. As an example, consider the elegant but deadly robot named David in the 2012 science fiction movie *Prometheus*; take note of how David studiously models his persona after the cinematic *Lawrence of Arabia*. Although brief, these scenes are no passing trifle; they are mini-models of the kinds of self-making that we all engage in, sometimes without awareness.

## Talk Like It

Consider the manner in which you speak. I once knew a crime reporter at a newspaper in upstate New York who had a slight build and appearance—but he spoke in a commanding, self-confident bass voice. It earned him the respect of the police and his newsroom colleagues. Whether natural or affected (I could never tell), his voice altered his entire persona.

## Find a Manifesto

You may question the value of reading *The Magic Story* given its author's tragic end. Do not be deterred. Read it tonight. Make its lessons your own. Dey possessed a keen instinct for human nature, including its shadowy and occultic paths to power. If this book doesn't speak to you (although I suspect it will), select another from the works I've mentioned, or find ones of your own.

## Stand for Something

The chief cause of mediocrity is purposelessness. We are never more aroused, sensitive, and capable than when we are striving for something. What are you striving for? A watch-the-clock job and entertainment won't bring out more than your most average traits. Above all, you must find a chief aim in life. You should never be embarrassed by your aim. Your aim can be public or intimate. It requires no one's approval—it must be uniquely your own. The only tragedy is not having one.

*　*　*

Since earliest childhood, you have probably felt, as I have, that you are two selves. Be guided by the principle of *The Magic Story*: select the self that builds you. It represents a more powerful choice than may at first appear.

—Mitch Horowitz

# Preface

This wonderful little story, written by Frederick van Rensselaer Dey, first appeared in the December, 1900, and January, 1901, issues of *Success Magazine*. It created an immediate sensation, and urgent requests were made for its reprint in book form. A small edition of a little silver-gray book was published to meet these requests, and this, the First Edition, has virtually disappeared from sight. The fact that the publishers of *Success Magazine* are in almost daily receipt of requests for additional copies is sufficient evidence of the value placed by the holders of the original edition upon the copies in their possession, and of their desire to bring it to the attention of their friends; and the demand has now become so insistent as to lead to the production of this, the Second Edition.

Mr. Dey has woven into this story, in a remarkably effective way, some of the fundamental principles of the "New Thought Movement" which is sweeping over this country, and it is safe to say that the application of these principles, as outlined in the "Magic Story," will accomplish almost, if not quite, all that is herein claimed for them towards the upbuilding and development of a manly, self-reliant, *success-compelling* spirit.

—The Publishers

# PART ONE

I was sitting alone in the *café*, and had just reached for the sugar preparatory to putting it into my coffee. Outside, the weather was hideous. Snow and sleet came swirling down, and the wind howled frightfully. Every time the outer door opened, a draft of unwelcome air penetrated the uttermost corners of the room. Still, I was comfortable. The snow and sleet and wind conveyed nothing to me except an abstract thanksgiving that I was where it could not affect me. While I dreamed and sipped my coffee, the door opened and closed, and admitted—Sturtevant.

Sturtevant was an undeniable failure, but, withal, an artist of more than ordinary talent. He had, however, fallen into the rut traveled by ne'er-do-wells, and was out at the elbows as well as insolvent.

As I raised my eyes to Sturtevant's, I was conscious of mild surprise at the change in his appearance. Yet he was not dressed differently. He wore the same threadbare coat in which he always appeared, and the old brown hat was the same. And yet there was something new and strange in his appearance. As he swished his hat around to relieve it of the burden of snow deposited by the howling nor'wester, there was something new in the gesticulation. I could not remember when I had invited Sturtevant to dine with me, but involuntarily I beckoned to him. He nodded, and presently seated himself opposite to me. I asked him what he would have, and he, after scanning the bill of fare carelessly, ordered from it leisurely, and invited me to join him in coffee for two. I watched him in stupid wonder, but, as I had invited the obligation, I was prepared to pay for it, although I knew I hadn't sufficient cash to settle the bill. Meanwhile, I noted the brightness of his usual lackluster eyes, and the healthful, hopeful glow upon his cheek, with increasing amazement.

"Have you lost a rich uncle?" I asked.

"No," he replied, calmly, "but I have found my mascot."

"Brindle bull, or terrier?" I inquired.

"Currier," said Sturtevant, at length, pausing with his coffee cup half way to his lips, "I see that I have surprised you. It is not strange, for I am a surprise to myself. I am a new man, a different man,—and the alteration has taken place in the last few hours. You have seen me come into this place broke' many a time, when you have turned away, so that I would think you did not see me. I knew why you did that. It was not because you did not want to pay for a dinner, but because you did not have the money to do it. Is that your check? Let me have it. Thank you. I haven't any money with me to-night, but I,—well, this is my treat."

He called the waiter to him, and, with an inimitable flourish, signed his name on the backs of the two checks, and waved him away. After that he was silent a moment while he looked into my eyes, smiling at the astonishment which I in vain strove to conceal.

"Do you know an artist who possesses more talent than I?" he asked, presently. "No. Do you happen to know anything in the line of my profession that I could not accomplish, if I applied myself to it? No. You have been a reporter on the dailies for—how many?—seven or eight years. Do you remember when I ever had any credit until to-night? No. Was I refused just now? You have seen for yourself. To-morrow my new career begins. Within a month I shall have a bank account. Why? Because I have discovered the secret of success."

"Yes," he continued, when I did not reply, "my fortune is made. I have been reading a strange story, and, since reading it, I feel that my fortune is assured. It will make your fortune, too. All you have to do is to read it. You have no idea what it will do for you. Nothing is impossible after you know that story. It makes everything as plain as A, B, C. The very instant you grasp its true meaning, success is certain. This morning I was a hopeless, aimless bit of garbage in the metropolitan ash can; to-night I wouldn't change places with a millionaire. That sounds foolish, but it is true. The millionaire has spent his enthusiasm; mine is all at hand."

"You amaze me," I said, wondering if he had been drinking absinthe. "Won't you tell me the story? I should like to hear it."

"Certainly. I mean to tell it to the whole world. It is really remarkable that it should have been written and should remain in print so long, with never a soul to appreciate it until now. This morning I was starving. I hadn't any credit, nor a place to get a meal. I was seriously meditating suicide. I had gone to three of the papers for which I had done work, and had been handed back all that I had submitted. I had to choose quickly between death by suicide and death slowly by starvation. Then I found the story and read it. You can hardly imagine the transformation. Why, my dear boy, everything changed at once—and there you are."

"But what is the story, Sturtevant?"

"Wait; let me finish. I took those same old drawings to other editors, and every one of them was accepted at once."

"Can the story do for others what it has done for you? For example, would it be of assistance to me?" I asked.

"Help you? why not? Listen and I will tell it to you, although, really, you should read it. Still, I will tell it as best I can. It is like this: you see—," The waiter interrupted us at that moment. He informed Sturtevant that he was wanted at the telephone, and, with a word of apology, the artist left the table. Five minutes later I saw him rush out into the sleet and wind and disappear. Within the recollection of the frequenters of that *café*, Sturtevant had never before been called out by telephone. That, of itself, was substantial proof of a change in his circumstances.

One night, on the street, I encountered Avery, a former college chum, then a reporter on one of the evening papers. It was about a month after my memorable interview with Sturtevant, which, by that time, was almost forgotten.

"Hello, old chap," he said; "how's the world using you? Still on space?"

"Yes," I replied, bitterly, "with prospects of being on the town, shortly. But you look as if things were coming your way. Tell me all about it."

"Things have been coming my way, for a fact, and it is all remarkable, when all is said. You know Sturtevant, don't you? It's all due to him. I was plumb down on my luck—thinking of the morgue and all that—looking for you, in fact, with the idea that you would lend me enough to pay my room rent, when I met Sturtevant. He told me a story, and, really, old man, it is the most remarkable story you ever heard; it made a new man of me. Within twenty-four hours I was on my feet, and I've hardly known a care or a trouble since."

Avery's statement, uttered calmly, and with the air of one who had merely pronounced an axiom, recalled to my mind the conversation with Sturtevant in the *café* that stormy night, nearly a month before.

"It must be a remarkable story," I said, incredulously. "Sturtevant mentioned it to me once. I have not seen him since. Where is he now?"

"He has been making war sketches in Cuba, at two hundred a week; he's just returned. It is a fact that everybody that has heard that story has done well since. There are Cosgrove and Phillips—friends of mine—you don't know them. One's a real estate agent; the other a broker's clerk. Sturtevant told them the story, and they have experienced the same result that I have; and they are not the only ones, either."

"Do you know the story?" I asked. "Will you try its effect on me?"

"Certainly; with the greatest pleasure in the world. I would like to have it printed in big black type, and posted on the elevated stations throughout New York. It certainly would do a lot of good, and it's as simple as A, B, C; like living on a farm. Excuse me a minute, will you? I see Danforth over there. Back in a minute, old chap."

He nodded and smiled,—and was gone. I saw him join the man whom he had designated as Danforth. My attention was distracted for a moment, and, when I looked again, both had disappeared.

If the truth be told, I was hungry. My pocket at that moment contained exactly five cents; just enough to pay my fare up-town, but insufficient also to stand the expense of filling my stomach. There was a "night owl" wagon in the neighborhood, where I had frequently "stood up" the purveyor of midnight dainties, and to him I applied. He was leaving the wagon as I was on the point of entering it, and I accosted him.

"I'm broke again," I said, with extreme cordiality. "You'll have to trust me once more. Some ham and eggs, I think, will do for the present."

He coughed, hesitated a moment, and then re-entered the wagon with me.

"Mr. Currier is good for anything he orders," he said to the man in charge; "one of my old customers. This is Mr. Bryan, Mr. Currier. He will take good care of you, and 'stand for' you, just the same as I would. The fact is, I have sold out. I've just turned over the outfit to Bryan. By the way, isn't Mr. Sturtevant a friend of yours?"

I nodded. I couldn't have spoken if I had tried.

"Well," continued the ex-night-owl man, "he came here one night, about a month ago, and told me the most wonderful story I ever heard. I've just bought a place in Eighth Avenue, where I am going to run a regular restaurant—near Twenty-third Street. Come and see me." He was out of the wagon, and the sliding door had been banged shut before I could stop him; so I ate my ham and eggs in silence, and resolved that I would hear that story before I slept. In fact, I began to regard it with superstition. If it had made so many fortunes, surely it should be capable of making mine.

The certainty that the wonderful story—I began to regard it as magic—was in the air, possessed me. As I started to walk homeward, fingering the solitary nickel in my pocket and contemplating the certainty of riding down town in the morning, I experienced the sensation of something stealthily pursuing me, as if Fate were treading along behind me, yet never overtaking, and I was conscious that I was possessed with or by the story. When I reached Union Square, I examined my address book for the home of Sturtevant. It was not recorded there. Then I remembered the *café* in University Place, and, although the hour was late, it occurred to me that he might be there.

He was! In a far corner of the room, surrounded by a group of acquaintances, I saw him. He discovered me at the same instant, and motioned to me to join them at the table. There was no chance for the story, however. There were half a dozen around the table, and I was the farthest removed from Sturtevant. But I kept my eyes upon him, and bided my time, determined that, when he rose to depart, I would go with him. A silence, suggestive of respectful awe, had fallen upon the party when I took my seat. Every one seemed to be thinking, and the attention of all was fixed upon Sturtevant. The cause was apparent. He had been telling the story. I had entered the *café* just too late to hear it. On my right, when I took my seat, was a doctor; on my left a lawyer.

Facing me on the other side was a novelist with whom I had some acquaintance. The others were artists and newspaper men.

"It's too bad, Mr. Currier," remarked the doctor; "you should have come a little sooner. Sturtevant has been telling us a story; it is quite wonderful, really. I say, Sturtevant, won't you tell that story again, for the benefit of Mr. Currier?"

"Why, yes. I believe that Currier has, somehow, failed to hear the magic story, although, as a matter of fact, I think he was the first one to whom I mentioned it at all. It was here, in this *café*, too,—at this very table. Do you remember what a wild night that was, Currier? Wasn't I called to the telephone, or something like that? To be sure! I remember, now; interrupted just at the point when I was beginning the story. After that, I told it to three or four fellows, and it 'braced them up,' as it had me. It seems incredible that a mere story can have such a tonic effect upon the success of so many persons who are engaged in such widely different occupations, but that is what it has done. It is a kind of never failing remedy, like a cough mixture that is warranted to cure everything, from a cold in the head to galloping consumption. There was Parsons, for example. He is a broker, you know, and had been on the wrong side of the market for a month. He had utterly lost his grip, and was on the verge of failure. I happened to meet him at the time he was feeling the bluest, and, before we parted, something brought me around to the subject of the story, and I related it to him. It had the same effect upon him that it had on me, and has had upon everybody who has heard it, as far as I know. I think you will all agree with me, that it is not the story itself that performs the surgical operation on the minds of those who are familiar with it; it is the way it is told—in print, I mean. The author has, somehow, produced a psychological effect which is indescribable. The reader is hypnotized. He receives a mental and moral tonic. Perhaps, doctor, you can give some scientific explanation of the influence exerted by the story. It is a sort of elixir manufactured out of words, eh?"

From that the company entered upon a general discussion of theories. Now and then slight references were made to the story itself, and they were just sufficient to tantalize me—the only one present who had not heard it.

At length, I left my chair, and, passing around the table, seized Sturtevant by one arm, and succeeded in drawing him away from the party.

"If you have any consideration for an old friend who is rapidly being driven mad by the existence of that confounded story, which Fate seems determined that I shall never hear, you will relate it to me now," I said, savagely.

Sturtevant stared at me in mild surprise.

"All right," he said. "The others will excuse me for a few moments, I think. Sit down here, and you shall have it. I found it pasted in an old scrapbook I purchased in Ann Street, for three cents; and there isn't a thing about it by which one can get any idea in what publication it originally appeared, or who wrote it. When I discovered it, I began casually to read it, and in a moment I was interested. Before I left it, I had read it through many times, so that I could repeat it almost word for word. It affected me strangely—as if I had come in contact with some strong personality. There seems to be in the story a personal element that applies to every one who reads it. Well, after I had read it several times, I began to think it over. I couldn't stay in the house, so I seized my coat and hat and went out. I must have walked several miles, buoyantly, without realizing that I was the same man who, only a short time before, had been in the depths of despondency. That was the day I met you here—you remember."

We were interrupted at that instant by a uniformed messenger, who handed Sturtevant a telegram. It was from his chief, and demanded his instant attendance at the office. The messenger had already been delayed an hour, and there was no help for it; he must go at once.

"Too bad!" said Sturtevant, rising and extending his hand. "Tell you what I'll do, old chap. I'm not likely to be gone any more than an hour or two. You take my key and wait for me in my room. In the *escritoire* near the window you will find an old scrapbook, bound in rawhide. It was manufactured, I have no doubt, by the author of the magic story. Wait for me in my room until I return."

With that he went out, and I lost no time in taking advantage of the permission he had given me.

I found the book without difficulty. It was a quaint, home-made affair, covered, as Sturtevant had said, with rawhide, and bound with leather thongs. The pages formed an odd combination of yellow paper, vellum and home-made parchment. I found the story, curiously printed on the last-named material. It was quaint and strange. Evidently, the printer had "set" it under the supervision of the writer. The phraseology was an unusual combination of seventeenth and eighteenth century mannerisms, and the interpolation of italics and capitals could have originated in no other brain than that of its author.

In reproducing the following story, the peculiarities of type, spelling, etc., are eliminated, but in other respects it remains unchanged.

*Nothing worth while is attainable without effort. By the same token, a thoughtful reading of "The Magic Story" and a correct interpretation of its "lessons" are essential to a full appreciation of its inspirational value.*

*The author has woven into this story in a remarkably effective way the basic principles of a successful life, and it is safe to say that persistent application of these principles will accomplish almost, if not quite, all that is claimed for them in the development of a self-reliant, success-compelling spirit.*

*Enthusiastic readers of this unusual book, appreciating its inspiring force, give it generous publicity, and as a result its sphere of influence is being constantly enlarged.*

# PART TWO
## *In the Old Scrap Book*

INASMUCH as I have evolved from my experience the one great secret of success for all worldly undertakings, I deem it wise, now that the number of my days is nearly counted, to give to the generations that are to follow me the benefit of whatsoever knowledge I possess. I do not apologize for the manner of my expression, nor for lack of literary merit, the latter being, I wot, its own apology. Tools much heavier than the pen have been my portion, and, moreover, the weight of years has somewhat palsied hand and brain; nevertheless, the fact I can tell, and that I deem the meat within the nut. What mattereth it, in what manner the shell be broken, so that the meat be obtained and rendered useful? I doubt not that I shall use, in the telling, expressions that have clung to my memory since childhood; for, when men attain the number of my years, happenings of youth are like to be clearer to their perceptions than are events of recent date; nor doth it matter much how a thought is expressed, if it be wholesome and helpful, and findeth the understanding.

Much have I wearied my brain anent the question, how best to describe this recipe for success that I have discovered, and it seemeth advisable to give it as it came to me; that is, if I relate somewhat of the story of my life, the directions for agglomerating the substances, and supplying the seasoning for the accomplishment of the dish, will plainly be perceived. Happen they may;

and that men may be born generations after I am dust, who will live to bless me for the words I write.

My father, then, was a seafaring man who, early in life, forsook his vocation, and settled on a plantation in the colony of Virginia, where, some years thereafter, I was born, which event took place in the year 1642; and that was over a hundred years ago. Better for my father had it been had he hearkened to the wise advice of my mother, that he remain in the calling of his education; but he would not have it so, and the good vessel he captained was bartered for the land I spoke of. Here beginneth the first lesson to be acquired:

*Man should not be blinded to whatsoever merit exists in the opportunity which he hath in hand, remembering that a thousand promises for the future should weigh as naught against the possession of a single piece of silver.*

When I had achieved ten years, my mother's soul took flight, and two years thereafter my worthy father followed her. I, being their only begotten, was left alone; howbeit, there were friends who, for a time, cared for me; that is to say, they offered me a home beneath their roof,—a thing which I took advantage of for the space of five months. From my father's estate there came to me naught; but, in the wisdom that came with increasing years, I convinced myself that his friend, under whose roof I lingered for some time, had defrauded him, and therefore me.

Of the time from the age of twelve and a half until I was three and twenty, I will make no recital here, since that time hath naught to do with this tale; but some time after, having in my possession the sum of sixteen guineas, ten, which I had saved from the fruits of my labor, I took ship to Boston town, where I began work first as a cooper, and thereafter as a ship's carpenter, although always after the craft was docked; for the sea was not amongst my desires.

Fortune will sometimes smile upon an intended victim because of pure perversity of temper. Such was one of my experiences. I prospered, and, at seven and twenty, owned the yard wherein, less than four years earlier, I had worked for hire. Fortune, howbeit, is a jade who must be coerced; she will not be coddled. Here beginneth the second lesson to be acquired:

*Fortune is ever elusive, and can only be retained by force. Deal with her tenderly and she will forsake you for a stronger man. [In that, methinks, she is not unlike other women of my knowledge.]*

About this time, Disaster (which is one of the heralds of broken spirits and lost resolve), paid me a visit. Fire ravaged my yards, leaving nothing in its blackened paths but debts, which I had not the coin wherewith to defray. I labored with my acquaintances, seeking assistance for a new start, but the fire that had burned my competence seemed also to have consumed their sympathies. So it happened, within a short time, that not only had I lost all, but I was hopelessly indebted to others; and for that they cast me into prison. It is possible that I might have rallied from my losses but for this last indignity, which broke down my spirits so that I became utterly despondent. Upward of a year was I detained within the gaol; and, when I did come forth, it was not the same hopeful, happy man, content with his lot, and with confidence in the world and its people, who had entered there.

Life has many pathways, and of them by far the greater number lead downward. Some are precipitous, others are less abrupt; but ultimately, no matter at what inclination the angle may be fixed, they arrive at the same destination—failure. And here beginneth the third lesson:

*Failure exists only in the grave. Man, being alive, hath not yet failed; always he may turn about and ascend by the same path he descended by; and there may be one that is less abrupt (albeit longer of achievement), and more adaptable to his condition.*

When I came forth from prison, I was penniless. In all the world I possessed naught beyond the poor garments which covered me, and a walking stick which the turnkey had permitted me to retain, since it was worthless. Being a skilled workman, howbeit, I speedily found employment at good wages; but, having eaten of the fruit of worldly advantage, dissatisfaction possessed me. I became morose and sullen; whereat, to cheer my spirits, and for the sake of forgetting the losses I had sustained, I passed my evenings at the tavern. Not that I drank overmuch of liquor, except on occasion (for I have ever been somewhat abstemious), but that I could laugh, and sing, and parry wit and badinage with my ne'er-do-well companions; and here might be included the fourth lesson:

*Seek comrades among the industrious, for those who are idle will sap your energies from you.*

It was my pleasure at that time to relate, upon slight provocation, the tale of my disasters, and to rail against the men whom I deemed to have wronged me, because they had seen fit not to come to my aid. Moreover, I found childish delight in filching from my employer, each day, a few moments of the time for which he paid me. Such a thing is less honest than downright theft.

This habit continued and grew upon me until the day dawned which found me not only without employment, but also without character, which meant that I could not hope to find work with any other employer in Boston town.

It was then that I regarded myself a failure. I can liken my condition at that time for naught more similar than that of a man who, descending the steep side of a mountain, loses his foothold. The farther he slides, the faster he goes. I have also heard this condition described by the word Ishmaelite, which I understand to be a man whose hand is against everybody, and who thinks that the hands of every other man are against him; and here beginneth the fifth lesson:

*The Ishmaelite and the leper are the same, since both are abominations in the sight of man—albeit they differ much, in that the former may be restored to perfect health. The former is entirely the result of imagination; the latter has poison in his blood.*

I will not discourse at length upon the gradual degeneration of my energies. It is not meet ever to dwell much upon misfortunes (which saying is also worthy of remembrance). It is enough if I add that the day came when I possessed naught wherewith to purchase food and raiment, and I found myself like unto a pauper, save at infrequent times when I could earn a few pence, or, mayhap, a shilling. Steady employment I could not secure, so I became emaciated in body, and naught but a skeleton in spirit.

My condition, then, was deplorable; not so much for the body, be it said, as for the mental part of me, which was sick unto death. In my imagination I deemed myself ostracised by the whole world, for I had sunk very low indeed; and here beginneth the sixth and final lesson to be acquired (which cannot be told in one sentence, nor in one paragraph, but must needs be adapted from the remainder of this tale).

Well do I remember my awakening, for it came in the night, when, in truth, I did awake from sleep. My bed was a pile of shavings in the rear of the cooper shop where once I had worked for hire; my roof was the pyramid of casks, underneath which I had established myself. The night was cold, and I was chilled, albeit, paradoxically, I had been dreaming of light and warmth and of the repletion of good things. You will say, when I relate the effect the vision had on me, that my mind was affected. So be it, for it is the hope that the minds of others might be likewise influenced which disposes me to undertake the labor of this writing. It was the dream which converted me to the belief—nay, to the knowledge—that I was possessed of two identities; and it was my own better self that afforded me the assistance for which I had pleaded in vain from my acquaintances. I have heard this condition described by the word "double." Nevertheless, that word does not comprehend my meaning. A double can be naught more than a double, neither half being possessed of individuality. But I will not philosophize, since philosophy is naught but a suit of garments for the decoration of a dummy figure.

Moreover, it was not the dream itself which affected me; it was the impression made by it, and the influence that it exerted over me, which accomplished my enfranchisement. In a word, then, I encouraged my other identity. After toiling through a tempest of snow and wind, I peered into a window and saw that other being. He was rosy with health; before him, on the hearth, blazed a fire of logs; there was conscious power and force in his demeanor; he was physically and mentally muscular. I rapped timidly upon the door, and he bade me enter. There was a not unkindly smile of derision in his eyes as he motioned me to a chair by the fire; but he uttered no word of welcome; and, when I had warmed myself, I went forth again into the tempest, burdened with the shame which the contrast between us had forced upon me. It was then that I awoke; and here cometh the strange part of my tale, for, when I did awake, I was not alone. There was a Presence with me; intangible to others, I discovered later, but real to me.

The Presence was in my likeness, yet was it strikingly unlike. The brow, not more lofty than my own, yet seemed more round and full; the eyes, clear, direct, and filled with purpose, glowed with enthusiasm and resolution; the lips, chin—ay, the whole contour of face and figure was dominant and determined.

He was calm, steadfast, and self-reliant; I was cowering, filled with nervous trembling, and fearsome of intangible shadows. When the Presence turned away, I followed, and throughout the day I never lost sight of it, save when it disappeared for a time beyond some doorway where I dared not enter; at such places, I awaited its return with trepidation and awe, for I could not help wondering at the temerity of the Presence (so like myself, and yet so unlike), in daring to enter where my own feet feared to tread.

It seemed also, as if purposely I was led to the place and to the men where and before whom I most dreaded to appear; to offices where once I had transacted business; to men with whom I had financial dealings. Throughout the day I pursued the Presence, and at evening saw it disappear beyond the portals of a hostelry famous for its cheer and good living. I sought the pyramid of casks and shavings.

Not again in my dreams that night did I encounter the Better Self (for that is what I have named it), albeit, when, perchance, I awakened from slumber, it was near to me, ever wearing that calm smile of kindly derision which could not be mistaken for pity, nor for condolence in any form. The contempt of it stung me sorely.

The second day was not unlike the first, being a repetition of its forerunner, and I was again doomed to wait outside during the visits which the Presence paid to places where I fain would have gone had I possessed the requisite courage. It is fear which deporteth a man's soul from his body and rendereth it a thing to be despised. Many a time I essayed to address it, but enunciation rattled in my throat, unintelligible; and the day closed like its predecessor.

This happened many days, one following another, until I ceased to count them; albeit, I discovered that constant association with the Presence was producing an effect upon me; and one night, when I awoke among the casks and discerned that he was present, I made bold to speak, albeit with marked timidity.

"Who are you?" I ventured to ask; and I was startled into an upright posture by the sound of my own voice; and the question seemed to give pleasure to my companion, so that I fancied there was less of derision in his smile when he responded.

"I am that I am," was the reply. "I am he who you have been; I am he who you may be again; wherefore do you hesitate? I am he who you were, and whom you have cast out for other company. I am the man made in the image of God, who once possessed your body. Once we dwelt within it together, not in harmony, for that can never be, nor yet in unity, for that is impossible, but as tenants in common who rarely fought for full possession. Then you were a puny thing, but you became selfish and exacting until I could no longer abide with you, wherefore I stepped out. There is a plus-entity and a minus-entity in every human body that is born into the world. Whichever one of these is favored by the flesh becomes dominant; then is the other inclined to abandon its habitation, temporarily or for all time. I am the plus-entity of yourself; you are the minus-entity. I own all things; you possess naught. That body which we both inhabited is mine, but it is unclean, and I will not dwell within it. Cleanse it, and I will take possession.

"Why do you pursue me?" I next asked the Presence.

"You have pursued me, not I you. You can exist without me for a time, but your path leads downward, and the end is death. Now that you approach the end, you debate if it be not politic that you should cleanse your house and invite me to enter. Step aside, then, from the brain and the will; cleanse them of your presence; only on that condition will I ever occupy them again."

"The brain hath lost its power," I faltered. "The will is a weak thing, now; can you repair them?"

"Listen!" said the Presence, and he towered over me while I cowered abjectly at his feet. "To the plus-entity of a man, all things are possible. The world belongs to him—is his estate. He fears naught, dreads naught, stops at naught; he asks no privileges, but demands them; he *dominates*, and cannot cringe; his requests are orders; opposition flees at his approach; he levels mountains, fills in vales, and travels on an even plane where stumbling is unknown."

Thereafter, I slept again, and, when I awoke, I seemed to be in a different world. The sun was shining and I was conscious that birds twittered above my head. My body, yesterday trembling and uncertain, had become vigorous and filled with energy. I gazed upon the pyramid of casks in amazement that I had so long made use of it for an abiding place, and I was wonderingly conscious that I had passed my last night beneath its shelter.

The events of the night recurred to me, and I looked about me for the Presence. It was not visible. But anon I discovered, cowering in a far corner of my resting place, a puny, abject, shuddering figure, distorted of visage, deformed of shape, disheveled and unkempt of appearance. It tottered as it walked, for it approached me piteously; but I laughed aloud, mercilessly. Perchance I knew then that it was the minus-entity, and that the plus-entity was within me; albeit I did not then realize it. Moreover, I was in haste to get away; I had no time for philosophy. There was much for me to do—much; strange it was that I had not thought of that yesterday. But yesterday was gone—to-day was with me—it had just begun.

As had once been my daily habit, I turned my steps in the direction of the tavern where formerly I had partaken of my meals. I nodded cheerily as I entered, and smiled in recognition of returned salutations. Men who had ignored me for months bowed graciously when I passed them on the thoroughfare. I went to the washroom, and from there to the breakfast table; afterwards, when I passed the taproom, I paused a moment and said to the landlord:

"I will occupy the same room that I formerly used, if, perchance, you have it at disposal. If not, another will do as well, until I can obtain it."

Then I went out and hurried with all haste to the cooperage. There was a huge wain in the yard, and men were loading it with casks for shipment. I asked no questions, but, seizing barrels, began hurling them to the men who worked atop of the load. When this was finished, I entered the shop. There was a vacant bench; I recognized its disuse by the litter on its top. It was the same at which I had once worked. Stripping off my coat, I soon cleared it of *impedimenta*. In a moment more I was seated, with my foot on the vice-lever, shaving staves.

It was an hour later when the master workman entered the room, and he paused in surprise at sight of me; already there was a goodly pile of neatly shaven staves beside me, for in those days I was an excellent workman; there was none better, but, alas! now, age hath deprived me of my skill. I replied to his unasked question with the brief but comprehensive sentence: "I have returned to work, sir." He nodded his head and passed on, viewing the work of other men, albeit anon he glanced askance in my direction.

Here endeth the sixth and last lesson to be acquired, although there is more to be said, since from that moment I was a successful man, and ere long possessed another shipyard, and had acquired a full competence of worldly goods.

I pray you who read, heed well the following admonitions, since upon them depend the word "success" and all that it implies:

*Whatsoever you desire of good is yours. You have but to stretch forth your hand and take it.*

Learn that the consciousness of dominant power within you is the possession of all things attainable.

*Have no fear* of any sort or shape, for fear is an adjunct of the minus-entity.

If you have skill, apply it; the world must profit by it, and, therefore, you.

Make a daily and nightly companion of your plus-entity; if you heed its advice, you cannot go wrong.

Remember, philosophy is an argument; the world, which is your property, is an accumulation of facts.

Go, therefore, and do that which is within you to do; take no heed of gestures which would beckon you aside; *ask of no man permission to perform.*

The minus-entity requests favors; the plus-entity grants them. Fortune waits upon every footstep you take; seize her, bind her, hold her, for she is yours; she belongs to you.

Start out now, with these admonitions in your mind. Stretch out your hand, and grasp the plus, which, maybe, you have never made use of, save in grave emergencies. Life is an emergency most grave.

Your plus-entity is beside you now; cleanse your brain, and strengthen your will. It will take possession. It waits upon you.

*Start to-night; start now upon this new journey.*

Be always on your guard. Whichever entity controls you, the other hovers at your side; beware lest the evil enter, even for a moment.

My task is done. I have written the recipe for "success." If followed, it cannot fail. Wherein I may not be entirely comprehended, the plus-entity of whosoever reads will supply the deficiency; and upon that Better Self of mine, I place the burden of imparting to generations that are to come, the secret of this all-pervading good—*the secret of being what you have it within you to be.*

[THE END]

# As a Man Thinketh
(1903)

## by James Allen

*The Extraordinary Classic on Remaking Your Life Through Your Thoughts*

## Contents

Introduction   *Why James Allen Still Matters* by Mitch Horowitz   270

Foreword   274

Chapter One   Thought and Character   274

Chapter Two   Effect of Thought on Circumstances   276

Chapter Three   Thought and Purpose   281

Chapter Four   The Thought-Factor in Achievement   283

Chapter Five   Visions and Ideals   285

Chapter Six   Serenity   287

## Introduction
# Why James Allen Still Matters

James Allen's literary career was short, ranging roughly from the publication of his first book in 1901 to his death in 1912. Yet these few years of output resulted in nearly twenty books, including one of the most widely read inspirational works of our time: *As a Man Thinketh*.

Allen's book became read in households where few or no other positive-mind books were found. His methods of mental creativity and ethical self-seeking set the template for much of the metaphysical culture in America in the twentieth century. In a sense, the key to understanding Allen's work appears in the details of his own life. The writer's journey from "poverty to power," to use his phrase, was Allen's greatest creation.

\* \* \*

James Allen was born in 1864 in Leicester, an industrial town in central England. His father, William, was a successful knitting manufacturer who cultivated James's taste in books and philosophy. A downturn in the textile trade drove William out of business, and in 1879 he traveled to New York City to look for new work. His plan was to get settled and pay for the rest of the family to join him. But the unthinkable occurred. On the brink of the Christmas season, just after James had turned 15, word came back to the Allen household that the family patriarch was dead. William had been found robbed and murdered two days after reaching New York. His battered body, with pockets emptied, lay in a city hospital.

James's mother, Martha, a woman who could not read or write, found herself in charge of James and his two younger brothers, with no means of support. "Young Jim" would have to leave school and find work as a factory knitter. The teenager had been his father's favorite. An avid reader, James had spent hours questioning him about life, death, religion, politics, and Shakespeare. "My boy," William told him, "I'll make a scholar of you." Those hopes were gone.

James took up employment locally as a framework knitter, a job that occupied his energies for the next nine years. He sometimes worked fifteen-hour days. But even amid the strains of factory life, he retained the refined, studious bearing that his father had cultivated. When his workmates went out drinking, or caught up on sleep, Allen studied and read two to three hours a day. Coworkers called him "the Saint" and "the Parson."

Allen read through his father's collected works of Shakespeare, as well as books of ethics and religion. He grew determined to discover the "central purpose" of life. At age twenty-four, he found the book that finally seemed to reveal it to him: *The Light of Asia* by Edwin Arnold. The epic poem introduced Allen, along with a generation of Victorians, to the ideas of Buddhism. Under its influence, Allen came to believe that the true aim of all religion is self-development and inner refinement.

Shortly after discovering *The Light of Asia*, Allen experienced a turning point in his outer life, as well. Around 1889 he found new employment in London as a private secretary and stationer—markedly friendlier vocations to the bookish man than factory work. In London he also met his wife and intellectual partner, Lily.

By the mid-1890s, Allen had deepened his inquiry into spiritual philosophies, immersing himself in the works of John Milton, Ralph Waldo Emerson, Walt Whitman, and early translations of the *Bhagavad Gita, Tao Te Ching*, and the sayings of Buddha.

He marveled over the commonalities in the world's religions. "The man who says, 'My religion is true, and my neighbor's is false,' has not yet discovered the truth in his own religion," he wrote, "for when a man has done that, he will see the Truth in all religions."

Allen also grew interested in the ideas of America's New Thought culture through the work of Ralph Waldo Trine, Orison Swett Marden, and, later, Christian D. Larson. His reading of New Thought, or positive-mind, literature sharpened his spiritual outlook—in particular his idea that our thoughts are causative and determine our destiny.

By 1898, Allen found an outlet for his intellectual interests. He began writing for the *Herald of the Golden Age*. In addition to metaphysical topics, the journal was an early voice for vegetarianism and humane treatment of animals, ideas that Allen had discovered in Buddhism. In 1901, he published his first book of practical philosophy, *From Poverty to Power*. The work extolled the creative agencies of the mind, placing equal emphasis on Christian ethics and New Thought metaphysics. The following year, Allen launched his own mystical magazine, the *Light of Reason*, and soon came another book, *All These Things Added*.

It was a period of tremendous productivity, capped in 1903 by Allen's third and most influential work—the short, immensely powerful meditation, *As a Man Thinketh*, which you are about to experience. The title is loosely adapted from a caution against hypocrisy in Proverbs 23:7: "As he thinketh in his heart, so is he." In Allen's eyes, that brief statement captured his core philosophy—that a man's thought, if not the cause of his circumstances, is the cause of *himself,* and shapes the tenor of his life.

The phrase "as a man thinketh" became the informal motto of the New Thought movement, adopted and repeated by motivational writers throughout the century. Allen's book is marked by memorable, aphoristic lessons, which have withstood the passage of time. *As a Man Thinketh* defines achievement in deeply personal terms: "You will become as small as your controlling desire; as great as your dominant aspiration."

Toward the end of *As a Man Thinketh*, Allen writes in a manner that amounts to autobiography:

> Here is a youth hard pressed by poverty and labor; confined long hours in an unhealthy workshop; unschooled, and lacking all the arts of refinement. But he dreams of better things: he thinks of intelligence, of refinement, of grace and beauty. He conceives of, mentally builds up, an ideal condition of life; vision of a wider liberty and a larger scope takes possession of him; unrest urges him to action, and he utilizes all his spare time and means, small though they are, to the development of his latent powers and resources. Very soon so altered has his mind become that the workshop can no longer hold him.

As a personal rule, Allen always used his life experiences as the backbone of his teaching. "He never wrote *theories*," Lily noted in 1913, "or for the sake of writing; but he wrote when he had a message, and it became a message *only when he had lived it out in his own life*, and knew that it was good."

The impact of *As a Man Thinketh* was not fully felt during Allen's lifetime, but the book brought him enough of an audience (and sufficient pay) so that he was able to quit secretarial work and commit himself to writing and editing fulltime. On its publication, Allen, Lily, and their daughter, Nora, moved to the southern English costal town of Ilfracombe, where he spent the remainder of his life. He wrote books at a remarkable pace, often more than one a year, producing nineteen works. Allen's days assumed a meticulous routine of meditating, writing, walking in nature, and gardening. He work habits never flagged. "Thoroughness is genius," he wrote in 1904.

For all of his creative output, Allen struggled with fragile health. Lily wrote of her husband faltering from an illness in late 1911. On January 24, 1912, Allen died at home in Ilfracombe at age 47, probably of tuberculosis.

In an obituary of January 27, the *Ilfracombe Chronicle* noted: "Mr. Allen's books . . . are perhaps better known abroad, especially in America, than in England." Indeed, the twentieth century's leading American writers of motivational thought—from Napoleon Hill to Norman Vincent Peale—read and noted the influence of *As a Man Thinketh*. Dale Carnegie said the book had "a lasting and profound effect on my life." The cofounder of Alcoholics Anonymous, Bob Smith, called it a favorite. The black-nationalist pioneer Marcus Garvey embraced the book's do-for-self ethic and adapted the slogan "As Man Thinks So Is He" on the cover of his newspaper, *Blackman*. In years ahead, the book's influence showed up in myriad places: An adolescent Michael Jackson told a friend that it was his "favorite book in the world;" NFL Hall of Famer Curtis Martin credited *As a Man Thinketh* with helping him overcome pain and injury; businessman and Oprah Winfrey partner Stedman Graham said Allen's work helped him attain "real freedom."

Yet the full impact of *As a Man Thinketh* can best be seen in the successive generations of everyday readers who embraced its aphoristic lessons in directing one's thoughts to higher aims, and to understanding success as the outer manifestation of inner development.

"Men do not attract that which they *want*," Allen told readers, "but that which they *are*." In that sense, Allen attracted a vast following of people who mirrored the ordinary circumstances from which he arose—and whose hopes for a better, nobler existence were reflected back to them in the example of his life.

This gentle abridgement of *As a Man Thinketh* is intended to make the work and its message available to you in a single sitting. I have based it upon the earliest American edition of *As a Man Thinketh*, published in Chicago in 1905, and it contains the full nature of Allen's message. My one significant excision has been his short chapter on health, in which I think the author drew too complete and hasty a confluence, at least in my mind as an observer and lover of New Thought, between thoughts and disease. With this excision, I believe the book functions better as a moral philosophy, and it is possible that in hindsight, the author, himself a publisher and editor, would have agreed.

What you are about to experience is a philosophy of spiritual and mental governance of character and circumstance, which may prove as life-altering to you as it has to countless devotees of this powerful meditation for more than a century.

—Mitch Horowitz

---

*Mind is the Master power that moulds and makes, And Man is Mind, and evermore he takes The tool of Thought, and, shaping what he wills, Brings forth a thousand joys, a thousand ills:—He thinks in secret, and it comes to pass: Environment is but his looking-glass.*

---

## Foreword

This little volume (the result of meditation and experience) is not intended as an exhaustive treatise on the much-written-upon subject of the power of thought. It is suggestive rather than explanatory, its object being to stimulate men and women to the discovery and perception of the truth that—

---

### "They themselves are makers of themselves"

---

by virtue of the thoughts which they choose and encourage; that mind is the master-weaver, both of the inner garment of character and the outer garment of circumstance, and that, as they may have hitherto woven in ignorance and pain they may now weave in enlightenment and happiness.

—James Allen

## Chapter One
# Thought and Character

The aphorism, "As a man thinketh in his heart so is he," not only embraces the whole of a man's being, but is so comprehensive as to reach out to every condition and circumstance of his life. A man is literally *what he thinks,* his character being the complete sum of all his thoughts.

As the plant springs from, and could not be without the seed, so every act of a man springs from the hidden seeds of thought, and could not have appeared without them. This applies equally to those acts called "spontaneous" and "unpremeditated," as to those that are deliberately executed.

Act is the blossom of thought, and joy and suffering are its fruits; thus does a man garner in the sweet and bitter fruitage of his own husbandry.

Man is a growth by law, and not a creation by artifice, and cause and effect is as absolute and undeviating in the hidden realm of thought as in the world of visible and material things. A noble and Godlike character is not a thing of favor or chance, but is the natural result of continued effort in right thinking, the effect of long-cherished association with Godlike thoughts. An ignoble and bestial character, by the same process, is the result of the continued harboring of groveling thoughts.

Man is made or unmade by himself; in the armory of thought he forges the weapons by which he destroys himself; he also fashions the tools with which he builds for himself heavenly mansions of joy and strength and peace. By the right choice and true application of thought, man ascends to the Divine Perfection; by the abuse and wrong application of thought, he descends below the level of the beast. Between these two extremes are all the grades of character, and man is their maker and master.

Of all the beautiful truths pertaining to the soul which have been restored and brought to light in this age, none is more gladdening or fruitful of divine promise and confidence than this—that man is the master of thought, the moulder of character, and the maker and shaper of condition, environment, and destiny.

As a being of Power, Intelligence, and Love, and the lord of his own thoughts, man holds the key to every situation, and contains within himself that transforming and regenerative agency by which he may make himself what he wills.

Man is always the master, even in his weaker and most abandoned state; but in his weakness and degradation he is the foolish master who misgoverns his "household." When he begins to reflect upon his condition, and to search diligently for the Law upon which his being is established, he then becomes the wise master, directing his energies with intelligence, and fashioning his thoughts to fruitful issues. Such is the *conscious* master, and man can only thus become by discovering *within himself* the laws of thought; which discovery is totally a matter of application, self analysis, and experience.

Only by much searching and mining, are gold and diamonds obtained, and man can find every truth connected with his being, if he will dig deep into the mine of his soul; and that he is the maker of his character, the moulder of his life, and the builder of his destiny, he may unerringly prove, if he will watch, control, and alter his thoughts, tracing their effects upon himself, upon others, and upon his life and circumstances, linking cause and effect by patient practice and investigation, and utilizing his every experience, even to the most trivial, everyday occurrence, as a means of obtaining that knowledge of himself which is Understanding, Wisdom, Power. In this direction, as in no other, is the law absolute that "He that seeketh findeth; and to him that knocketh it shall be opened;" for only by patience, practice, and ceaseless importunity can a man enter the Door of the Temple of Knowledge.

## Chapter Two
# Effect of Thought on Circumstances

A man's mind may be likened to a garden, which may be intelligently cultivated or allowed to run wild; but whether cultivated or neglected, it must, and will, *bring forth*. If no useful seeds are *put* into it, then an abundance of useless weed-seeds will *fall* therein, and will continue to produce their kind.

Just as a gardener cultivates his plot, keeping it free from weeds, and growing the flowers and fruits which he requires, so may a man tend the garden of his mind, weeding out all the wrong, useless, and impure thoughts, and cultivating toward perfection the flowers and fruits of right, useful, and pure thoughts. By pursuing this process, a man sooner or later discovers that he is the master-gardener of his soul, the director of his life. He also reveals, within himself, the laws of thought, and understands, with ever-increasing accuracy, how the thought-forces and mind elements operate in the shaping of his character, circumstances, and destiny.

Thought and character are one, and as character can only manifest and discover itself through environment and circumstance, the outer conditions of a person's life will always be found to be harmoniously related to his inner state. This does not mean that a man's circumstances at any given time are an indication of his *entire* character, but that those circumstances are so intimately connected with some vital thought-element within himself that, for the time being, they are indispensable to his development.

Every man is where he is by the law of his being; the thoughts which he has built into his character have brought him there, and in the arrangement of his life there is no element of chance, but all is the result of a law which cannot err. This is just as true of those who feel "out of harmony" with their surroundings as of those who are contented with them.

As a progressive and evolving being, man is where he is that he may learn that he may grow; and as he learns the spiritual lesson that any circumstance contains for him, it passes away and gives place to other circumstances.

Man is buffeted by circumstances so long as he believes himself to be the creature of outside conditions, but when he realizes that he is a creative power, and that he may command the hidden soil and seeds of his being out of which circumstances grow, he then becomes the rightful master of himself.

The soul attracts that which it secretly harbors; that which it loves, and also that which it fears; it reaches the height of its cherished aspirations; it falls to the level of its unchastened desires—and circumstances are the means by which the soul receives its own.

Every thought-seed sown or allowed to fall into the mind, and to take root there, produces its own, blossoming sooner or later into act, and bearing its own fruitage of opportunity and circumstance. Good thoughts bear good fruit, bad thoughts bad fruit.

The outer world of circumstance shapes itself to the inner world of thought, and both pleasant and unpleasant external conditions are factors, which make for the ultimate good of the individual. As the reaper of his own harvest, man learns both by suffering and bliss.

Following the inmost desires, aspirations, thoughts, by which he allows himself to be dominated, a man at last arrives at their fruition and fulfillment in the outer conditions of his life. The laws of growth and adjustment everywhere obtain.

Circumstance does not make the man; it reveals him to himself. No such conditions can exist as descending into vice and its attendant sufferings apart from vicious inclinations, or ascending into virtue and its pure happiness without the continued cultivation of virtuous aspirations; and man, therefore, as the lord and master of thought, is the maker of himself, the shaper and author of environment. Even at birth the soul comes to its own, and through every step of its earthly pilgrimage it attracts those combinations of conditions which reveal itself, which are the reflections of its own purity and impurity, its strength and weakness.

Men do not attract that which they *want*, but that which they *are*. Their whims, fancies, and ambitions are thwarted at every step, but their inmost thoughts and desires are fed with their own food, be it foul or clean. The "divinity that shapes our ends" is in ourselves; it is our very self. Man is manacled only by himself: thought and action are the jailers of Fate—they imprison, being base; they are also the angels of Freedom—they liberate, being noble. Not what he wishes and prays for does a man get, but what he justly earns. His wishes and prayers are only gratified and answered when they harmonize with his thoughts and actions.

In the light of this truth, what, then, is the meaning of "fighting against circumstances?" It means that a man is continually revolting against an *effect* without, while all the time he is nourishing and preserving its *cause* in his heart. That cause may take the form of a conscious vice or an unconscious weakness; but whatever it is, it stubbornly retards the efforts of its possessor, and thus calls aloud for remedy.

Men are anxious to improve their circumstances, but are unwilling to improve themselves; they therefore remain bound. The man who does not shrink from self-crucifixion can never fail to accomplish the object upon which his heart is set. This is as true of earthly as of heavenly things. Even the man whose sole object is to acquire wealth must be prepared to make great personal sacrifices before he can accomplish his object; and how much more so he who would realize a strong and well-poised life?

Here is a man who is wretchedly poor. He is extremely anxious that his surroundings and home comforts should be improved, yet all the time he shirks his work, and considers he is justified in trying to deceive his employer on the ground of the insufficiency of his wages. Such a man does not understand the simplest rudiments of those principles which are the basis of true prosperity, and is not only totally unfitted to rise out of his wretchedness, but is actually attracting to himself a still deeper wretchedness by dwelling in, and acting out, indolent, deceptive, and unmanly thoughts.

Here is a rich man who is the victim of a painful and persistent disease as the result of gluttony. He is willing to give large sums of money to get rid of it, but he will not sacrifice his gluttonous desires. He wants to gratify his taste for rich and unnatural viands and have his health as well. Such a man is totally unfit to have health, because he has not yet learned the first principles of a healthy life.

Here is an employer of labor who adopts crooked measures to avoid paying the regulation wage, and, in the hope of making larger profits, reduces the wages of his work-people. Such a man is altogether unfitted for prosperity, and when he finds himself bankrupt, both as regards reputation and riches, he blames circumstances, not knowing that he is the sole author of his condition.

I have introduced these three cases merely as illustrative of the truth that man is the causer (though nearly always unconsciously) of his circumstances, and that, whilst aiming at a good end, he is continually frustrating its accomplishment by encouraging thoughts and desires which cannot possibly harmonize with that end. Such cases could be multiplied and varied almost indefinitely, but this is not necessary, as the reader can, if he so resolves, trace the action of the laws of thought in his own mind and life, and until this is done, mere external facts cannot serve as a ground of reasoning.

Circumstances, however, are so complicated, thought is so deeply rooted, and the conditions of happiness vary so vastly with individuals, that a man's entire soul-condition (although it may be known to himself) cannot be judged by another from the external aspect of his life alone. A man may be honest in certain directions, yet suffer privations; a man may be dishonest in certain directions, yet acquire wealth; but the conclusion usually formed that the one man fails *because of his particular honesty,* and that the other prospers *because of his particular dishonesty,* is the result of a superficial judgment, which assumes that the dishonest man is almost totally corrupt, and the honest man almost entirely virtuous. In the light of a deeper knowledge and wider experience, such judgment is found to be erroneous. The dishonest man may have some admirable virtues, which the other does not possess; and the honest man obnoxious vices which are absent in the other. The honest man reaps the good results of his honest thoughts and acts; he also brings upon himself the sufferings which his vices produce. The dishonest man likewise garners his own suffering and happiness.

Good thoughts and actions can never produce bad results; bad thoughts and actions can never produce good results. This is but saying that nothing can come from corn but corn, nothing from nettles but nettles. Men understand this law in the natural world, and work with it; but few understand it in the mental and moral world (though its operation there is just as simple and undeviating), and they, therefore, do not cooperate with it.

Suffering is *always* the effect of wrong thought in some direction. It is an indication that the individual is out of harmony with himself, with the Law of his being. The sole and supreme use of suffering is to purify, to burn out all that is useless and impure. Suffering ceases for him who is pure. There could be no object in burning gold after the dross had been removed, and a perfectly pure and enlightened being could not suffer.

The circumstances that a man encounters with suffering are the result of his own mental inharmony. The circumstances that a man encounters with blessedness are the result of his own mental harmony. Blessedness, not material possessions, is the measure of right thought; wretchedness, not lack of material possessions, is the measure of wrong thought. A man may be cursed and rich; he may be blessed and poor. Blessedness and riches are only joined together when the riches are rightly and wisely used; and the poor man only descends into wretchedness when he regards his lot as a burden unjustly imposed.

Indigence and indulgence are the two extremes of wretchedness. They are both equally unnatural and the result of mental disorder. A man is not rightly conditioned until he is a happy, healthy, and prosperous being; and happiness, health, and prosperity are the result of a harmonious adjustment of the inner with the outer, of the man with his surroundings.

A man only begins to be a man when he ceases to whine and revile, and commences to search for the hidden justice that regulates his life. And as he adapts his mind to that regulating factor, he ceases to accuse others as the cause of his condition, and builds himself up in strong and noble thoughts; ceases to kick against circumstances, but begins to *use* them as aids to his more rapid progress, and as a means of discovering the hidden powers and possibilities within himself.

Law, not confusion, is the dominating principle in the universe; justice, not injustice, is the soul and substance of life; and righteousness, not corruption, is the moulding and moving force in the spiritual government of the world. This being so, man has but to right himself to find that the universe is right; and during the process of putting himself right he will find that as he alters his thoughts towards things and other people, things and other people will alter towards him.

Let a man radically alter his thoughts, and he will be astonished at the rapid transformation it will effect in the material conditions of his life. Men imagine that thought can be kept secret, but it cannot; it rapidly crystallizes into habit, and habit solidifies into circumstance. A particular train of thought persisted in, be it good or bad, cannot fail to produce its results on the character and circumstances. A man cannot *directly* choose his circumstances, but he can choose his thoughts, and so indirectly, yet surely, shape his circumstances.

Nature helps every man to the gratification of the thoughts which he most encourages, and opportunities are presented which will most speedily bring to the surface both the good and evil thoughts.

Let a man cease from his sinful thoughts, and all the world will soften towards him, and be ready to help him; let him put away his weakly and sickly thoughts, and lo! opportunities will spring up on every hand to aid his strong resolves; let him encourage good thoughts, and no hard fate shall bind him down to wretchedness and shame. The world is your kaleidoscope, and the varying combinations of colors, which at every succeeding moment it presents to you, are the exquisitely adjusted pictures of your ever-moving thoughts.

## Chapter Three
# Thought and Purpose

Until thought is linked with purpose there is no intelligent accomplishment. With the majority the bark of thought is allowed to "drift" upon the ocean of life. Aimlessness is a vice, and such drifting must not continue for him who would steer clear of catastrophe and destruction.

They who have no central purpose in their life fall an easy prey to petty worries, fears, troubles, and self-pityings, all of which are indications of weakness, which lead, just as surely as deliberately planned sins (though by a different route) to failure, unhappiness, and loss, for weakness cannot persist in a power-evolving universe.

A man should conceive of a legitimate purpose in his heart, and set out to accomplish it. He should make this purpose the centralizing point of his thoughts. It may take the form of a spiritual ideal, or it may be a worldly object, according to his nature at the time being; but whichever it is, he should steadily focus his thought-forces upon the object which he has set before him. He should make this purpose his supreme duty, and should devote himself to its attainment, not allowing his thoughts to wander away into ephemeral fancies, longings, and imaginings. This is the royal road to self-control and true concentration of thought. Even if he fails again and again to accomplish his purpose (as he necessarily must until weakness is overcome), the *strength of character gained* will be the measure of his *true* success, and this will form a new starting-point for future power and triumph.

Those who are not prepared for the apprehension of a *great* purpose should fix the thoughts upon the faultless performance of their duty, no matter how insignificant their task may appear. Only in this way can the thoughts be gathered and focused, and resolution and energy be developed, which being done, there is nothing which may not be accomplished.

The weakest soul, knowing its own weakness, and believing this truth—*that strength can only be developed by effort and practice,* will, thus believing, at once begin to exert itself, and, adding effort to effort, patience to patience, and strength to strength, will never cease to develop, and will at last grow divinely strong.

As the physically weak man can make himself strong by careful and patient training, so the man of weak thoughts can make them strong by exercising himself in right thinking.

To put away aimlessness and weakness, and to begin to think with purpose, is to enter the ranks of those strong ones who only recognize failure as one of the pathways to attainment; who make all conditions serve them, and who think strongly, attempt fearlessly, and accomplish masterfully.

Having conceived of his purpose, a man should mentally mark out a *straight* pathway to its achievement, looking neither to the right nor the left. Doubts and fears should be rigorously excluded; they are disintegrating elements, which break up the straight line of effort, rendering it crooked, ineffectual, useless. Thoughts of doubt and fear never accomplished anything, and never can. They always lead to failure. Purpose, energy, power to do, and all strong thoughts cease when doubt and fear creep in.

The will to do springs from the knowledge that we *can* do. Doubt and fear are the great enemies of knowledge, and he who encourages them, who does not slay them, thwarts himself at every step.

He who has conquered doubt and fear has conquered failure. His every thought is allied with power, and all difficulties are bravely met and wisely overcome. His purposes are seasonably planted, and they bloom and bring forth fruit, which does not fall prematurely to the ground.

Thought allied fearlessly to purpose becomes creative force: he who *knows* this is ready to become something higher and stronger than a mere bundle of wavering thoughts and fluctuating sensations; he who *does* this has become the conscious and intelligent wielder of his mental powers.

## Chapter Four
# The Thought-Factor in Achievement

All that a man achieves and all that he fails to achieve is the direct result of his own thoughts. In a justly ordered universe, where loss of equipoise would mean total destruction, individual responsibility must be absolute. A man's weakness and strength, purity and impurity, are his own, and not another man's; they are brought about by himself, and not by another; and they can only be altered by himself, never by another. His condition is also his own, and not another man's. His suffering and his happiness are evolved from within. As he thinks, so he is; as he continues to think, so he remains.

A strong man cannot help a weaker unless that weaker is *willing* to be helped, and even then the weak man must become strong of himself; he must, by his own efforts, develop the strength which he admires in another. None but himself can alter his condition.

It has been usual for men to think and to say, "Many men are slaves because one is an oppressor; let us hate the oppressor." Now, however, there is amongst an increasing few a tendency to reverse this judgment, and to say, "One man is an oppressor because many are slaves; let us despise the slaves." The truth is that oppressor and slave are cooperators in ignorance, and, while seeming to afflict each other, are in reality afflicting themselves. A perfect Knowledge perceives the action of law in the weakness of the oppressed and the misapplied power of the oppressor; a perfect Love, seeing the suffering, which both states entail, condemns neither; a perfect Compassion embraces both oppressor and oppressed.

He who has conquered weakness, and has put away all selfish thoughts, belongs neither to oppressor nor oppressed. He is free.

A man can only rise, conquer, and achieve by lifting up his thoughts. He can only remain weak, and abject, and miserable by refusing to lift up his thoughts.

Before a man can achieve anything, even in worldly things, he must lift his thoughts above slavish animal indulgence. He may not, in order to succeed, give up *all* animality and selfishness, by any means; but a portion of it must, at least, be sacrificed. A man whose first thought is bestial indulgence could neither think clearly nor plan methodically; he could not find and develop his latent resources, and would fail in any undertaking. Not having commenced to manfully control his thoughts, he is not in a position to control affairs and to adopt serious responsibilities. He is not fit to act independently and stand alone. But he is limited only by the thoughts which he chooses.

There can be no progress, no achievement without sacrifice, and a man's worldly success will be in the measure that he sacrifices his confused animal thoughts, and fixes his mind on the development of his plans, and the strengthening of his resolution and self-reliance. And the higher he lifts his thoughts, the more manly, upright, and righteous he becomes, the greater will be his success, the more blessed and enduring will be his achievements.

The universe does not favor the greedy, the dishonest, the vicious, although on the mere surface it may sometimes appear to do so; it helps the honest, the magnanimous, the virtuous. All the great Teachers of the ages have declared this in varying forms, and to prove and know it a man has but to persist in making himself more and more virtuous by lifting up his thoughts.

Intellectual achievements are the result of thought consecrated to the search for knowledge, or for the beautiful and true in life and nature. Such achievements may be sometimes connected with vanity and ambition, but they are not the outcome of those characteristics; they are the natural outgrowth of long and arduous effort, and of pure and unselfish thoughts.

Spiritual achievements are the consummation of holy aspirations. He who lives constantly in the conception of noble and lofty thoughts, who dwells upon all that is pure and unselfish, will, as surely as the sun reaches its zenith and the moon its full, become wise and noble in character, and rise into a position of influence and blessedness.

Achievement, of whatever kind, is the crown of effort, the diadem of thought. By the aid of self-control, resolution, purity, righteousness, and well-directed thought a man ascends; by the aid of animality, indolence, impurity, corruption, and confusion of thought a man descends.

A man may rise to high success in the world, and even to lofty altitudes in the spiritual realm, and again descend into weakness and wretchedness by allowing arrogant, selfish, and corrupt thoughts to take possession of him.

Victories attained by right thought can only be maintained by watchfulness. Many give way when success is assured, and rapidly fall back into failure.

All achievements, whether in the business, intellectual, or spiritual world, are the result of definitely directed thought, are governed by the same law and are of the same method; the only difference lies in *the object of attainment*.

He who would accomplish little must sacrifice little; he who would achieve much must sacrifice much; he who would attain highly must sacrifice greatly.

## Chapter Five
# Visions and Ideals

The dreamers are the saviors of the world. As the visible world is sustained by the invisible, so men, through all their trials and sins and sordid vocations, are nourished by the beautiful visions of their solitary dreamers. Humanity cannot forget its dreamers; it cannot let their ideals fade and die; it lives in them; it knows them as the *realities* which it shall one day see and know.

Composer, sculptor, painter, poet, prophet, sage, these are the makers of the after-world, the architects of heaven. The world is beautiful because they have lived; without them, laboring humanity would perish.

He who cherishes a beautiful vision, a lofty ideal in his heart, will one day realize it. Cherish your visions; cherish your ideals; cherish the music that stirs in your heart, the beauty that forms in your mind, the loveliness that drapes your purest thoughts, for out of them will grow all delightful conditions, all heavenly environment; of these, if you but remain true to them, your world will at last be built.

To desire is to obtain; to aspire is to achieve. Shall man's basest desires receive the fullest measure of gratification, and his purest aspirations starve for lack of sustenance? Such is not the Law: such a condition of things can never obtain: "Ask and receive."

Dream lofty dreams, and as you dream, so shall you become. Your Vision is the promise of what you shall one day be; your Ideal is the prophecy of what you shall at last unveil.

The greatest achievement was at first and for a time a dream. The oak sleeps in the acorn; the bird waits in the egg; and in the highest vision of the soul a waking angel stirs. Dreams are the seedlings of realities.

Your circumstances may be uncongenial, but they shall not long remain so if you but perceive an Ideal and strive to reach it. You cannot travel *within* and stand still *without*. Here is a youth hard pressed by poverty and labor; confined long hours in an unhealthy workshop; unschooled, and lacking all the arts of refinement. But he dreams of better things; he thinks of intelligence, of refinement, of grace and beauty. He conceives of, mentally builds up, an ideal condition of life; the vision of a wider liberty and a larger scope takes possession of him; unrest urges him to action, and he utilizes all his spare time and means, small though they are, to the development of his latent powers and resources. Very soon so altered has his mind become that the workshop can no longer hold him. It has become so out of harmony with his mentality that it falls out of his life as a garment is cast aside, and, with the growth of opportunities which fit the scope of his expanding powers, he passes out of it forever.

And you, too, will realize the Vision (not the idle wish) of your heart, be it base or beautiful, or a mixture of both, for you will always gravitate toward that which you, secretly, most love. Into your hands will be placed the exact results of your own thoughts; you will receive that which you earn; no more, no less. Whatever your present environment may be, you will fall, remain, or rise with your thoughts, your Vision, your Ideal. You will become as small as your controlling desire; as great as your dominant aspiration.

The thoughtless, the ignorant, and the indolent, seeing only the apparent effects of things and not the things themselves, talk of luck, of fortune, and chance. Seeing a man grow rich, they say, "How lucky he is!" Observing another become intellectual, they exclaim, "How highly favored he is!" And noting the saintly character and wide influence of another, they remark, "How chance aids him at every turn!" They do not see the trials and failures and struggles which these men have voluntarily encountered in order to gain their experience; have no knowledge of the sacrifices they have made, of the undaunted efforts they have put forth, of the faith they have exercised, that they might overcome the apparently insurmountable, and realize the Vision of their heart. They do not know the darkness and the heartaches; they only see the light and joy, and call it "luck." They do not see the long and arduous journey, but only behold the pleasant goal, and call it "good fortune," do not understand the process, but only perceive the result, and call it "chance."

In all human affairs there are *efforts,* and there are *results,* and the strength of the effort is the measure of the result. Chance is not. "Gifts," powers, material, intellectual, and spiritual possessions are the fruits of effort; they are thoughts completed, objects accomplished, visions realized.

The Vision that you glorify in your mind, the Ideal that you enthrone in your heart—this you will build your life by, this you will become.

## Chapter Six
# Serenity

Calmness of mind is one of the beautiful jewels of wisdom. It is the result of long and patient effort in self-control. Its presence is an indication of ripened experience, and of a more than ordinary knowledge of the laws and operations of thought.

A man becomes calm in the measure that he understands himself as a thought-evolved being, for such knowledge necessitates the understanding of others as the result of thought, and as he develops a right understanding, and sees more and more clearly the internal relations of things by the action of cause and effect, he ceases to fuss and fume and worry and grieve, and remains poised, steadfast, serene.

The calm man, having learned how to govern himself, knows how to adapt himself to others; and they, in turn, reverence his spiritual strength, and feel that they can learn of him and rely upon him. The more tranquil a man becomes, the greater is his success, his influence, his power for good. Even the ordinary trader will find his business prosperity increase as he develops a greater self-control and equanimity, for people will always prefer to deal with a man whose demeanor is strongly equable.

The strong, calm man is always loved and revered. He is like a shade-giving tree in a thirsty land, or a sheltering rock in a storm. "Who does not love a tranquil heart, a sweet-tempered, balanced life? It does not matter whether it rains or shines, or what changes come to those possessing these blessings, for they are always sweet, serene, and calm. That exquisite poise of character, which we call serenity, is the last lesson of culture; it is the flowering of life, the fruitage of the soul. It is precious as wisdom, more to be desired than gold—yea, than even fine gold. How insignificant mere money seeking looks in comparison with a serene life—a life that dwells in the ocean of Truth, beneath the waves, beyond the reach of tempests, in the Eternal Calm!

"How many people we know who sour their lives, who ruin all that is sweet and beautiful by explosive tempers, who destroy their poise of character, and make bad blood! It is a question whether the great majority of people do not ruin their lives and mar their happiness by lack of self-control. How few people we meet in life who are well balanced, who have that exquisite poise which is characteristic of the finished character!"

Yes, humanity surges with uncontrolled passion, is tumultuous with ungoverned grief, is blown about by anxiety and doubt. Only the wise man, only he whose thoughts are controlled and purified, makes the winds and the storms of the soul obey him.

Tempest-tossed souls, wherever ye may be, under whatsoever conditions ye may live, know this—in the ocean of life the isles of Blessedness are smiling, and the sunny shore of your ideal awaits your coming. Keep your hand firmly upon the helm of thought. In the bark of your soul reclines the commanding Master; He does but sleep: wake Him. Self-control is strength; Right Thought is mastery; Calmness is power. Say unto your heart, "Peace, be still!"

# The Kybalion
(1908)

# by Three Initiates

*The Masterwork of Esoteric Wisdom
For Living with Power and Purpose*

*To Hermes Trismegistus
known by the ancient Egyptians as "The Great Great" and
"Master of Masters" this little volume of Hermetic teachings
is reverently dedicated*

## Contents

Introduction  *Why The Kybalion Matters* by Mitch Horowitz  290
Foreword  292
Chapter One  The Hermetic Philosophy  293
Chapter Two  The Seven Hermetic Principles  295
Chapter Three  Mental Transmutation  301
Chapter Four  The Mental Universe  302
Chapter Five  The Divine Paradox  304
Chapter Six  The Planes of Correspondence  307
Chapter Seven  Vibration  308
Chapter Eight  Polarity  310
Chapter Nine  Rhythm  313
Chapter Ten  Causation  316
Chapter Eleven  Gender  319
Chapter Twelve  Hermetic Axioms  324

## Introduction

# Why *The Kybalion* Matters

The short book called *The Kybalion*, published in 1908, is probably the most popular and, in my estimation, most important occult work of the twentieth century.

The book is rivaled in significance only by a much longer and very different work, Manly P. Hall's magisterial encyclopedia arcana, *The Secret Teachings of All Ages*, which appeared twenty years later. The landscape of mythical and esoteric philosophies that the scholar Hall curated, illustrated, and documented in his volume are, in a sense, distilled into their practical philosophical essentials in the precise guidebook *The Kybalion*, written under the pseudonymous byline of Three Initiates.

As I've written elsewhere, and will not cover in any great detail here, Three Initiates was one of several pseudonyms used by Chicago publisher, lawyer, and New Thought philosopher, William Walker Atkinson, whom historical and documentary sources have identified as the book's sole author. Atkinson was also its publisher at his Yogi Publication Society, a longtime and widely loved occult press. But unveiling the mystery of the book's authorship in no way detracts from its scope and achievement.

The greatness of *The Kybalion* is that Atkinson successfully captures—and makes relevant for modern seekers—elements of the late-ancient Greek-Egyptian philosophy called Hermeticism. Hermeticism grew out of the intellectual ferment of the city of Alexandria in the decades immediately following Christ. In the closing generations of Egyptian antiquity, a diffuse collection of Greek writers—who were part of the Hellenic ruling class that presided over the fading empire—encountered the priesthoods, temple orders, and initiatory religions of Egypt's dissipating spiritual culture. Using Greek literary form, these scribes produced a variety of dialogues attributed to the man-god Hermes Trismegistus—the honorific title of "thrice-greatest Hermes," which the Greeks bestowed upon the Egyptian god of intellect Thoth, whom they venerated above their own Hermes.

These unsigned tracts became broadly known as the Hermetica. When rediscovered and translated by Renaissance scholars, the Hermetic texts, covering philosophic, magical, alchemical, and occult ideas, formed an essential part of the Renaissance outlook, and shaped elements of scientific and rational thought associated with the Age of Enlightenment—an era that would soon relegate Hermeticism to the fringes of history, treating it as little more than a curio of late-Greek mystical thought.

But the Hermetica represents far more than that, a fact Atkinson understood and placed on display in *The Kybalion*. History, especially religious history, is an admixture of crosscurrents, frictions, and influences. The value of the Hermetica is that it preserves a sample of Egyptian thought, enfolded within Greek literary style and intermingled with Neo-Platonic and Hellenic philosophy. This is of immense importance, since our insight into Ancient Egyptian thought, which was often passed on through oral tradition or encoded in hieroglyphs and myths, is limited. Indeed, until very recently, we possessed few serviceable translations of the Hermetic literature, which was neglected after the Renaissance.

In *The Kybalion*, Atkinson expertly and artfully, using the few Victorian-era translations available to him, summarized the metaphysical psychology of the Hermetica, and combined it with his own insights into New Thought, or what William James termed "the religion of healthy mindedness." The occult revival of the late-nineteenth century and the New Thought flowering of Atkinson's own era, provided the writer-publisher a perfect moment to reinterpret Hermetic ideas for a popular audience.

Hermeticism is not exactly the religious ancestor to New Thought. The paucity of translations and the rural surroundings of most of America's New Thought pioneers placed these ideas off their path. Early New Thoughters were largely independent investigators and reached their insights about the mind's causative abilities chiefly through self-experiment. But aspects of Hermeticism do represent a distant historical parallel to New Thought, especially Hermeticism's core idea that a Great Mind of Creation brought all things into being, and that this same creative mental faculty dwells in all men, beings the Higher Mind created not only in its own image but to function in its own likeness.

". . . your mind is god the father; they are not divided from one another for their union is life," says the Hermetica. This statement would be at home in any New Thought book.

Atkinson brilliantly surmises the possibilities—and limits—of the mind's power for earthbound men and women. If it were somehow possible for contemporary metaphysical seekers to reach back in time and have an exchange with the ancient Hermeticists, something like *The Kybalion* is probably as good an estimation as we can venture of what would appear.

I have reread *The Kybalion* many times, and encourage all who encounter these words to do so. But I have created this shortened version for several reasons: Brief as the original book is, its opening chapters present a detailed casebook in the nature of mental causation and the immaterial basis of reality—ideas that are perhaps more readily accepted today than in Atkinson's generation, and some readers may find his lawyerly style of argumentation a barrier to entry. That barrier has been somewhat eased in this abridgement, but without sacrificing any of his ideas. I have also shortened some of Atkinson's more speculative investigations—and I think he would have agreed that they were such—into the figurative nature of various corresponding planes of reality. I have also reduced the verbiage of certain arguments, in which he restated, as any good lawyer would, certain key premises.

The result, I hope, is an abridgment that retains the overall mission and, above all, the practicality of Atkinson's original. This digest-sized edition is not a substitute for the original, but it is an excellent entry point for the newcomer and, perhaps most importantly, a way for longtime readers and lovers of the book to re-experience or remind themselves of key points.

Most importantly, it falls to you, the reader and listener, to enact and experience these ideas in your life. "For otherwise," the book counsels, "the Hermetic Teachings will be as 'words, words, words' to you."

—Mitch Horowitz

## Foreword

We take great pleasure in presenting to the attention of students and investigators of the Secret Doctrines this little work based upon the world-old Hermetic Teachings.

The purpose of this work is not the enunciation of any special philosophy or doctrine, but rather is to give to the students a statement of the Truth that will serve to reconcile the many bits of occult knowledge that they may have acquired, but which are apparently opposed to each other and which often serve to discourage the beginner in the study. Our intent is not to erect a new Temple of Knowledge, but rather to place in the hands of the student a Master-Key with which he may open the many inner doors in the Temple of Mystery through the main portals he has already entered.

There is no portion of the occult teachings possessed by the world which have been so closely guarded as the fragments of the Hermetic Teachings, which have come down to us over the tens of centuries that have elapsed since the lifetime of its great founder, Hermes Trismegistus, the "scribe of the gods," who dwelt in old Egypt in the days when the present race of men was in its infancy. Contemporary with Abraham, and, if the legends be true, an instructor of that venerable sage, Hermes was, and is, the Great Central Sun of Occultism, whose rays have served to illumine the countless teachings which have been promulgated since his time. All the fundamental and basic teachings embedded in the esoteric teachings of every race may be traced back to Hermes.

The original truths taught by him have been kept intact in their original purity by a few men in each age who followed the Hermetic custom and reserved their truth for the few who were ready to comprehend and master it. From lip to ear, the truth has been handed down among the few. There have always been Initiates in each generation, in the various lands of the earth, who kept alive the sacred flame of the Hermetic Teachings. These men have never sought popular approval, nor numbers of followers. They are indifferent to these things, for they know how few there are in each generation who are ready for the truth, or who would recognize it if it were presented to them. They reserve the "strong meat for men," while others furnish the "milk for babes."

In this little work, we have endeavored to give you an idea of the fundamental teachings of *The Kybalion*, striving to give you the working Principles, leaving you to apply them yourselves, rather than attempting to work out the teaching in detail. If you are a true student, you will be able to work out and apply these Principles—if not, then you must develop yourself into one, for otherwise the Hermetic Teachings will be as "words, words, words" to you.

—Three Initiates

## Chapter One
# The Hermetic Philosophy

*"The lips of wisdom are closed, except to the ears of Understanding."*
—THE KYBALION

From old Egypt have come the fundamental esoteric and occult teachings, which have so strongly influenced the philosophies of all races, nations, and peoples, for several thousand years. Egypt, the home of the Pyramids and the Sphinx, was the birthplace of the Hidden Wisdom and Mystic Teachings. From her Secret Doctrine all nations have borrowed. India, Persia, Chaldea, Medea, China, Japan, Assyria, ancient Greece and Rome, and other ancient countries partook liberally at the feast of knowledge which the Hierophants and Masters of the Land of Isis so freely provided for those who came prepared to partake of the great store of Mystic and Occult Lore which the masterminds of that ancient land had gathered together.

Among these great Masters of Ancient Egypt there once dwelt one whom Masters hailed as "The Master of Masters." This man, if "man" indeed he was, dwelt in Egypt in the earliest days. He was known as Hermes Trismegistus. He was the father of the Occult Wisdom; the founder of Astrology; the discoverer of Alchemy. The details of his life are lost to history, owing to the lapse of the years, though several of the ancient countries disputed with each other in their claims to the honor of having furnished his birthplace—and this thousands of years ago. The date of his sojourn in Egypt, in his last incarnation on this planet, is not now known, but it has been fixed at the early days of the oldest dynasties of Egypt—long before the days of Moses.

The Egyptians deified Hermes, and made him one of their gods, under the name of Thoth. Years after, the people of Ancient Greece also made him one of their many gods—calling him "Hermes, the god of Wisdom." The Egyptians revered his memory for many centuries, calling him "the Scribe of the Gods," and bestowing upon him, distinctively, his ancient title, "Trismegistus," which means "the thrice-great."

In the early days, there was a compilation of certain Basic Hermetic Doctrines, passed on from teacher to student, which was known as "THE KYBALION," the exact significance and meaning of the term having been lost for several centuries. This teaching, however, is known to many to whom it has descended, from mouth to ear, on and on throughout the centuries. Its precepts have never been written down, or printed, so far as we know. It was merely a collection of maxims, axioms, and precepts, which were nonunderstandable to outsiders, but which were readily understood by students, after the axioms, maxims, and precepts had been explained and exemplified by the Hermetic Initiates to their Neophytes. These teachings really constituted the basic principles of "The Art of Hermetic Alchemy," which, contrary to the general belief, dealt in the mastery of Mental Forces, rather than Material Elements—the Transmutation of one kind of Mental Vibrations into others, instead of the changing of one kind of metal into another. The legends of the "Philosopher's Stone," which would turn base metal into Gold, was an allegory relating to Hermetic Philosophy, readily understood by all students of true Hermeticism.

In this little book, of which this is the First Lesson, we invite our students to examine into the Hermetic Teachings, as set forth in THE KYBALION, and as explained by ourselves, humble students of the Teachings, who, while bearing the title of Initiates, are still students at the feet of HERMES, the Master.

The original maxims, axioms, and precepts of THE KYBALION are printed herein, in quotation marks. Our own work is printed in the regular way, in the body of the work. We trust that the many students to whom we now offer this little work will derive as much benefit from the study of its pages as have the many who have gone on before.

In the words of THE KYBALION:

> *"Where fall the footsteps of the Master, the ears of those ready for his Teaching open wide."* —THE KYBALION

> *"When the ears of the student are ready to hear, then cometh the lips to fill them with Wisdom."* —THE KYBALION

So that according to the Teachings, the passage of this book to those ready for the instruction will attract the attention of such as are prepared to receive the Teaching. And, likewise, when the pupil is ready to receive the truth, then will this little book come to him or her. Such is The Law. The Hermetic Principle of Cause and Effect, in its aspect of the Law of Attraction, will bring lips and ear together—pupil and book in company.

## Chapter Two
# The Seven Hermetic Principles

> *"The Principles of Truth are Seven; he who knows these, understandingly, possesses the Magic Key before whose touch all the Doors of the Temple fly open."*
> —THE KYBALION

The Seven Hermetic Principles, upon which the entire Hermetic Philosophy is based, are as follows:

I. THE PRINCIPLE OF MENTALISM
II. THE PRINCIPLE OF CORRESPONDENCE
III. THE PRINCIPLE OF VIBRATION
IV. THE PRINCIPLE OF POLARITY
V. THE PRINCIPLE OF RHYTHM
VI. THE PRINCIPLE OF CAUSE AND EFFECT
VII. THE PRINCIPLE OF GENDER

These Seven Principles will be discussed and explained as we proceed with these lessons. A short explanation of each, however, may be given at this point.

## I. The Principle of Mentalism

*"THE ALL IS MIND; The Universe is Mental."* —The Kybalion

This Principle embodies the truth that "All is Mind." It explains that THE ALL (which is the Substantial Reality underlying all the outward manifestations and appearances which we know under the terms of "The Material Universe;" the "Phenomena of Life;" "Matter;" "Energy;" and, in short, all that is apparent to our material senses) is SPIRIT, which in itself is UNKNOWABLE and UNDEFINABLE, but which may be considered and thought of as A UNIVERSAL, INFINITE, LIVING MIND. It also explains that all the phenomenal world or universe is simply a Mental Creation of THE ALL, subject to the Laws of Created Things, and that the universe, as a whole, and in its parts or units, has its existence in the Mind of THE ALL, in which Mind we "live and move and have our being." This Principle explains the true nature of "Energy," "Power," and "Matter," and why and how all these are subordinate to the Mastery of Mind. One of the old Hermetic Masters wrote, long ages ago: "He who grasps the truth of the Mental Nature of the Universe is well advanced on The Path to Mastery."

## II. The Principle of Correspondence

*"As above, so below; as below, so above."* —The Kybalion

This Principle embodies the truth that there is always a Correspondence between the laws and phenomena of the various planes of Being and Life. The old Hermetic axiom ran in these words: "As above, so below; as below, so above." And the grasping of this Principle gives one the means of solving many a dark paradox and hidden secret of Nature. There are planes beyond our knowing, but when we apply the Principle of Correspondence to them we are able to understand much that would otherwise be unknowable to us. This Principle is of universal application and manifestation on the various planes of the material, mental, and spiritual universe—it is a Universal Law.

## III. The Principle of Vibration

*"Nothing rests; everything moves; everything vibrates."* —THE KYBALION

This Principle embodies the truth that "everything is in motion;" "everything vibrates;" "nothing is at rest;" facts which Modern Science endorses, and which each new scientific discovery tends to verify. From THE ALL, which is Pure Spirit, down to the grossest form of Matter, all is in vibration—the higher the vibration, the higher the position in the scale. The vibration of Spirit is at such an infinite rate of intensity and rapidity that it is practically at rest—just as a rapidly moving wheel seems to be motionless. At the other end of the scale, there are gross forms of matter whose vibrations are so low as to seem at rest. Between these poles are millions upon millions of varying degrees of vibration. From corpuscle and electron, atom and molecule, to worlds and universes, everything is in vibratory motion. An understanding of this Principle, with the appropriate formulas, enables Hermetic students to control their own mental vibrations as well as those of others. The Masters also apply this Principle to the conquering of Natural phenomena, in various ways. "He who understands the Principle of Vibration, has grasped the scepter of power," says one of the old writers.

## IV. The Principle of Polarity

*"Everything is Dual; everything has poles; everything has its pair of opposites; like and unlike are the same; opposites are identical in nature, but different in degree; extremes meet; all truths are but half-truths; all paradoxes may be reconciled."*
—THE KYBALION

This Principle embodies the truth that "everything is dual;" "everything has two poles;" "everything has its pair of opposites," all of which were old Hermetic axioms. It explains the old paradoxes, that have perplexed so many, which have been stated as follows: "Thesis and antithesis are identical in nature, but different in degree;" "opposites are the same, differing only in degree;" "the pairs of opposites may be reconciled;" "extremes meet;" "everything is and isn't, at the same time;" "all truths are but half-truths;" etc. It explains that in everything there are two poles, or opposite aspects, and that "opposites" are really only the two extremes of the same thing, with many varying degrees between them. To illustrate: Heat and Cold, although "opposites," are really the same thing, the differences consisting merely of degrees. Look at your thermometer and see if you can discover where "heat" terminates and "cold" begins! There is no such thing as "absolute heat" or "absolute cold"—the two terms simply indicate varying degrees of the same thing, and that "same thing" that manifests as "heat" and "cold" is merely a form, variety, and rate of Vibration. The same Principle manifests in the case of "Light and Darkness," which are the same thing, the difference consisting of varying degrees between the two poles of the phenomena. What is the difference between "Large and Small?" Between "Hard and Soft?" Between "Black and White?" Between "Sharp and Dull?" Between "Noise and Quiet?" Between "High and Low?" Between "Positive and Negative?" The Principle of Polarity explains these paradoxes, and no other Principle can supersede it. The same Principle operates on the Mental Plane. Let us take a radical and extreme example—that of "Love and Hate," two mental states apparently totally different. And yet there are degrees of Hate and degrees of Love, and a middle point in which we use the terms "Like or Dislike," which shade into each other so gradually that sometimes we are at a loss to know whether we "like" or "dislike" or "neither." All are simply degrees of the same thing, as you will see if you will but think a moment. And, more than this (and considered of more importance by the Hermetists), it is possible to change the vibrations of Hate to the vibrations of Love, in one's own mind, and in the minds of others. Many of you, who read these lines, have had personal experiences of the involuntary rapid transition from Love to Hate, and the reverse, in your own case and that of others. And you will therefore realize the possibility of this being accomplished by the use of the Will, by means of the Hermetic formulas. "Good and Evil" are but the poles of the same thing, and the Hermetist understands the art of transmuting Evil into Good, by means of an application of the Principle of Polarity. In short, the "Art of Polarization" becomes a phase of "Mental Alchemy" known and practiced by the ancient and modern Hermetic Masters. An understanding of the Principle will enable one to change his own Polarity, as well as that of others, if he will devote the time and study necessary to master the art.

## V. The Principle of Rhythm

*"Everything flows, out and in; everything has its tides; all things rise and fall; the pendulum-swing manifests in everything; the measure of the swing to the right is the measure of the swing to the left; rhythm compensates."*
—The Kybalion

This Principle embodies the truth that in everything there is manifested a measured motion, to and fro; a flow and inflow; a swing backward and forward; a pendulum-like movement; a tide-like ebb and flow; a high-tide and low-tide; between the two poles which exist in accordance with the Principle of Polarity described a moment ago. There is always an action and a reaction; an advance and a retreat; a rising and a sinking. The Hermetists have grasped this Principle, finding its universal application, and have also discovered certain means to overcome its effects in themselves by the use of the appropriate formulas and methods. They apply the Mental Law of Neutralization. They cannot annul the Principle, or cause it to cease its operation, but they have learned how to escape its effects upon themselves to a certain degree depending upon the Mastery of the Principle. They have learned how to USE it, instead of being USED BY it. The Master of Hermetics polarizes himself at the point at which he desires to rest, and then neutralizes the Rhythmic swing of the pendulum which would tend to carry him to the other pole. All individuals who have attained any degree of Self-Mastery do this to a certain degree, more or less unconsciously, but the Master does this consciously, and by the use of his Will, and attains a degree of Poise and Mental Firmness almost impossible of belief on the part of the masses who are swung backward and forward like a pendulum.

## VI. The Principle of Cause and Effect

*"Every Cause has its Effect; every Effect has its Cause; everything happens according to Law; Chance is but a name for Law not recognized; there are many planes of causation, but nothing escapes the Law."* —The Kybalion

This Principle embodies the fact that there is a Cause for every Effect; an Effect from every Cause. It explains that: "Everything Happens according to Law;" that nothing ever "merely happens;" that there is no such thing as Chance; that while there are various planes of Cause and Effect, the higher dominating the lower planes, still nothing ever entirely escapes the Law. The masses of people are carried along, obedient to environment; the wills and desires of others stronger than themselves; heredity; suggestion; and other outward causes moving them about like pawns on the Chessboard of Life. But the Masters, rising to the plane above, dominate their moods, characters, qualities, and powers, as well as the environment surrounding them, and become Movers instead of pawns. They help to PLAY THE GAME OF LIFE, instead of being played and moved about by other wills and environment. They USE the Principle instead of being its tools. The Masters obey the Causation of the higher planes, but they help to RULE on their own plane. In this statement there is condensed a wealth of Hermetic knowledge—let him read who can.

## VII. The Principle of Gender

*"Gender is in everything; everything has its Masculine and Feminine Principles; Gender manifests on all planes."* —THE KYBALION

This Principle embodies the truth that there is GENDER manifested in everything—the Masculine and Feminine Principles ever at work. This is true not only of the Physical Plane, but of the Mental and even the Spiritual Planes. On the Physical Plane, the Principle manifests as SEX, on the higher planes it takes higher forms, but the Principle is ever the same. No creation, physical, mental or spiritual, is possible without this Principle. An understanding of its laws will throw light on many a subject that has perplexed the minds of men. Everything, and every person, contains the two Elements or Principles, or this great Principle, within it, him or her. Every Male thing has the Female Element also; every Female contains also the Male Principle. If you would understand the philosophy of Mental and Spiritual Creation, Generation, and Re-generation, you must understand and study this Hermetic Principle. It contains the solution of many mysteries of Life.

## Chapter Three
# Mental Transmutation

*"Mind (as well as metals and elements) may be transmuted, from state to state; degree to degree; condition to condition; pole to pole; vibration to vibration. True Hermetic Transmutation is a Mental Art."* —THE KYBALION

"Mental Transmutation" means the art of changing and transforming mental states, forms, and conditions, into others. So you may see that Mental Transmutation is the "Art of Mental Chemistry," if you like the term—a form of practical Mystic Psychology.

But this means far more than appears on the surface. Transmutation, Alchemy, or Chemistry, on the Mental Plane is important enough in its effects, to be sure, and if the art stopped there it would still be one of the most important branches of study known to man. But this is only the beginning. Let us see why!

The first of the Seven Hermetic Principles is the Principle of Mentalism, the axiom of which is "THE ALL is Mind; the Universe is Mental," which means that the Underlying Reality of the Universe is Mind; and the Universe itself is Mental— that is, "existing in the Mind of THE ALL." We shall consider this Principle in succeeding lessons, but let us see the effect of the principle if it be assumed to be true.

If the Universal is Mental in its nature, then Mental Transmutation must be the art of CHANGING THE CONDITIONS OF THE UNIVERSE, along the lines of Matter, Force, and Mind. So you see, therefore, that Mental Transmutation is really the "Magic" of which the ancient writers had so much to say in their mystical works, and about which they gave so few practical instructions. If All be Mental, then the art which enables one to transmute mental conditions must render the Master the controller of material conditions as well as those ordinarily called "mental."

None but advanced Mental Alchemists have been able to attain the degree of power necessary to control the grosser physical conditions, such as the control of the elements of Nature.

But students and Hermetists of lesser degree than Masters—the Initiates and Teachers—are able to freely work along the Mental Plane, in Mental Transmutation. In fact all that we call "psychic phenomena;" "mental influence;" "mental science;" "new-thought phenomena;" etc., operates along the same general lines, for there is but one principle involved, no matter by what name the phenomena be called.

The student and practitioner of Mental Transmutation works among the Mental Plane, transmuting mental conditions, states, etc., into others. Not only may the mental states, etc., of one's self be changed or transmuted by Hermetic Methods; but also the states of others may be, and are, constantly transmuted in the same way, usually unconsciously.

We shall now proceed to a consideration of the first of the Hermetic Seven Principles—the Principle of Mentalism, in which is explained the truth that "THE ALL is Mind; the Universe is Mental," in the words of The Kybalion. We ask the close attention, and careful study of this great Principle, on the part of our students, for it is really the Basic Principle of the whole Hermetic Philosophy.

## Chapter Four
# The Mental Universe

*"The Universe is Mental—held in the Mind of THE ALL."* —The Kybalion

THE ALL is SPIRIT! But what is Spirit? This question cannot be answered, for the reason that its definition is practically that of THE ALL, which cannot be explained or defined. Spirit is simply a name that men give to the highest conception of Infinite Living Mind—it means "the Real Essence"—it means Living Mind, as much superior to Life and Mind as we know them, as the latter are superior to mechanical Energy and Matter. Spirit transcends our understanding, and we use the term merely that we may think or speak of THE ALL. For the purposes of thought and understanding, we are justified in thinking of Spirit as Infinite Living Mind, at the same time acknowledging that we cannot fully understand it.

Let us now proceed to a consideration of the nature of the Universe, as a whole and in its parts. What is the Universe? We have seen that there can be nothing outside of THE ALL. Then is the Universe THE ALL? No, this cannot be, because the Universe seems to be made up of MANY, and is constantly changing, and in other ways it does not measure up to the ideas that we are compelled to accept regarding THE ALL, as stated in our last lesson. Then if the Universe be not THE ALL, then it must be Nothing—such is the inevitable conclusion of the mind at first thought. But this will not satisfy the question, for we are sensible of the existence of the Universe. Then if the Universe is neither THE ALL, nor Nothing, what can it be? Let us examine this question.

If the Universe exists at all, or seems to exist, it must proceed in some way from THE ALL—it must be a creation of THE ALL. But as something can never come from nothing, from what could THE ALL have created it? Some philosophers have answered this question by saying that THE ALL created the Universe from ITSELF—that is, from the being and substance of THE ALL. But this will not do, for THE ALL cannot be subtracted from, nor divided, as we have seen, and then again if this be so, would not each particle in the Universe be aware of its being THE ALL—THE ALL could not lose its knowledge of itself, nor actually BECOME an atom, or blind force, or lowly living thing.

But, what indeed is the Universe, if it be not THE ALL, yet not created by THE ALL having separated itself into fragments? What else can it be—of what else can it be made? This is the great question. Let us examine it carefully. We find that the "Principle of Correspondence" comes to our aid here. The old Hermetic axiom, "As above so below," may be pressed into service at this point. Let us endeavor to get a glimpse of the workings on higher planes by examining those on our own. The Principle of Correspondence must apply to this as well as to other problems.

On his own plane of being, how does Man create? He CREATES MENTALLY! And in so doing he uses no outside materials, nor does he reproduce himself, and yet his Spirit pervades the Mental Creation.

Following the Principle of Correspondence, we are justified in considering that THE ALL creates the Universe MENTALLY, in a manner akin to the process whereby Man creates Mental Images. THE ALL can create in no other way except mentally, without either using material (and there is none to use), or else reproducing itself (which is also impossible). There is no escape from this conclusion of the Reason, which agrees with the highest teachings of the Illumined. Just as you, student, may create a Universe of your own in your mentality, so does THE ALL create Universes in its own Mentality. But your Universe is the mental creation of a Finite Mind, whereas that of THE ALL is the creation of an Infinite. The two are similar in kind, but infinitely different in degree. We shall examine more closely into the process of creation and manifestation, as we proceed. But this is the point to fix in your minds at this stage: THE UNIVERSE, AND ALL IT CONTAINS, IS A MENTAL CREATION OF THE ALL. Verily, indeed, ALL IS MIND!

## Chapter Five
# The Divine Paradox

*"The half-wise, recognizing the comparative unreality of the Universe, imagine that they may defy its Laws—such are vain and presumptuous fools, and they are broken against the rocks and torn asunder by the elements by reason of their folly. The truly wise, knowing the nature of the Universe, use Law against laws; the higher against the lower; and by the Art of Alchemy transmute that which is undesirable into that which is worthy, and thus triumph. Mastery consists not in abnormal dreams, visions, and fantastic imaginings or living, but in using the higher forces against the lower—escaping the pains of the lower planes by vibrating on the higher. Transmutation, not presumptuous denial, is the weapon of the Master."*
—The Kybalion

This is the Paradox of the Universe, resulting from the Principle of Polarity which manifests when THE ALL begins to Create—hearken to it for it points the difference between half-wisdom and wisdom. While to THE INFINITE ALL, the Universe, its Laws, its Powers, its Life, its Phenomena, are as things witnessed in the state of Meditation or Dream; yet to all that is Finite, the Universe must be treated as Real, and life and action and thought, must be based thereupon, accordingly, although with an ever understanding of the Higher Truth. Each according to its own Plane and Laws. If Man, owing to half-wisdom, acts and lives and thinks of the Universe as merely a dream (akin to his own finite dreams) then indeed does it so become for him, and like a sleep-walker he stumbles ever around and around in a circle, making no progress, and being forced into an awakening at last by his falling bruised and bleeding over the Natural Laws which he ignored. Keep your mind ever on the Star, but let your eyes watch over your footsteps, lest you fall into the mire by reason of your upward gaze. Remember the Divine Paradox that while the Universe IS NOT, still IT IS. Remember ever the Two Poles of Truth—the Absolute and the Relative. Beware of Half-Truths.

What Hermetists know as "the Law of Paradox" is an aspect of the Principle of Polarity. The Hermetic writings are filled with references to the appearance of the Paradox in the consideration of the problems of Life and Being. The Teachers are constantly warning their students against the error of omitting the "other side" of any question. And their warnings are particularly directed to the problems of the Absolute and the Relative, which perplex all students of philosophy, and which cause so many to think and act contrary to what is generally known as "common sense." And we caution all students to be sure to grasp the Divine Paradox of the Absolute and Relative, lest they become entangled in the mire of the Half-Truth. With this in view this particular lesson has been written. Read it carefully!

The first thought that comes to the thinking man after he realizes the truth that the Universe is a Mental Creation of THE ALL, is that the Universe and all that it contains is a mere illusion; an unreality; against which idea his instincts revolt. But this, like all other great truths, must be considered both from the Absolute and the Relative points of view. From the Absolute viewpoint, of course, the Universe is in the nature of an illusion, a dream, a phantasmagoria, as compared to THE ALL in itself. We recognize this even in our ordinary view, for we speak of the world as "a fleeting show" that comes and goes, is born and dies—for the element of impermanence and change, finiteness and unsubstantiality, must ever be connected with the idea of a created Universe when it is contrasted with the idea of THE ALL.

Anything that has a beginning and an ending must be, in a sense, unreal and untrue, and the Universe comes under that rule, in all schools of thought. From the Absolute point of view, there is nothing Real except THE ALL.

But the Absolute point of view shows merely one side of the picture—the other side is the Relative one. Absolute Truth has been defined as, "Things as the mind of God knows them," while Relative Truth is, "Things as the highest reason of Man understands them." And so while to THE ALL the Universe must be unreal and illusionary, a mere dream or result of meditation—nevertheless, to the finite minds forming a part of that Universe, and viewing it through mortal faculties, the Universe is very real indeed, and must be so considered. In recognizing the Absolute view, we must not make the mistake of ignoring or denying the facts and phenomena of the Universe as they present themselves to our mortal faculties—we are not THE ALL, remember.

To take familiar illustrations, we all recognize that Matter "exists" to our senses—we will fare badly if we do not. And yet, even our finite minds understand the scientific dictum that there is no such thing as Matter from a scientific point of view—that which we call Matter is held to be merely an aggregation of atoms, which atoms themselves are merely a grouping of units of force, vibrating and in constant circular motion. We kick a stone and we feel the impact—it seems to be real, notwithstanding that we know it to be merely what we have stated above. But remember that our foot, which feels the impact by means of our brains, is likewise Matter, so constituted of electrons, and for that matter so are our brains. And, at the best, if it were not by reason of our Mind, we would not know the foot or stone at all.

Oh, friends, to mortals this Universe of Mentality is very real indeed—it is the only one we can ever know, though we rise from plane to plane, higher and higher in it. To know it otherwise, by actual experience, we must be THE ALL itself. It is true that the higher we rise in the scale—the nearer to "the mind of the Father" we reach—the more apparent becomes the illusory nature of finite things, but not until THE ALL finally withdraws us into itself does the vision actually vanish.

So, we need not dwell upon the feature of illusion. Rather let us, recognizing the real nature of the Universe, seek to understand its mental laws, and endeavor to use them to the best effect in our upward progress through life, as we travel from plane to plane of being. The Laws of the Universe are nonetheless "Iron Laws" because of the mental nature. All, except THE ALL, are bound by them. What is IN THE INFINITE MIND OF THE ALL is REAL in a degree second only to that Reality itself which is vested in the nature of THE ALL.

The Hermetic Principle of Mentalism, while explaining the true nature of the Universe upon the principle that all is Mental, does not change the scientific conceptions of the Universe, Life, or Evolution. So, the student of Hermetics need not lay aside any of his cherished scientific views regarding the Universe. All he is asked to do is to grasp the underlying principle of, "THE ALL is Mind; the Universe is Mental—held in the Mind of THE ALL." He will find that the other six of the Seven Principles will "fit into" his scientific knowledge, and will serve to bring out obscure points and to throw light in dark corners.

The purpose of this lesson is to impress upon the minds of our students the fact that, to all intents and purposes, the Universe and its laws, and its phenomena, are just as REAL, so far as Man is concerned, as they would be under the hypotheses of Materialism or Energism. Under any hypothesis the Universe in its outer aspect is changing, everflowing, and transitory— and therefore devoid of substantiality and reality. But (note the other pole of the truth) under any of the same hypotheses, we are compelled to ACT AND LIVE as if the fleeting things were real and substantial. With this difference, always, between the various hypotheses—that under the old views Mental Power was ignored as a Natural Force, while under Mentalism it becomes the Greatest Natural Force. And this one difference revolutionizes Life, to those who understand the Principle and its resulting laws and practice.

## Chapter Six
# The Planes of Correspondence

*"As above, so below; as below, so above."* —THE KYBALION

The great Second Hermetic Principle embodies the truth that there is a harmony, agreement, and correspondence between the several planes of Manifestation, Life, and Being. This truth is a truth because all that is included in the Universe emanates from the same source, and the same laws, principles, and characteristics apply to each unit, or combination of units of activity, as each manifests its own phenomena upon its own plane.

For the purpose of convenience of thought and study, the Hermetic Philosophy considers that the Universe may be divided into three great classes of phenomena, known as the Three Great Planes, namely:

I. The Great Physical Plane
II. The Great Mental Plane
III. The Great Spiritual Plane

These divisions are more or less artificial and arbitrary, for the truth is that all of the three divisions are but ascending degrees of the great scale of Life, the lowest point of which is undifferentiated Matter, and the highest point that of Spirit. And, moreover, the different Planes shade into each other, so that no hard and fast division may be made between the higher phenomena of the Physical and the lower of the Mental.

You will kindly remember, however, that the Three Great Planes are not actual divisions of the phenomena of the Universe, but merely arbitrary terms used by the Hermetists in order to aid in the thought and study of the various degrees and forms of universal activity and life. The atom of matter, the unit of force, the mind of man, and the being of the archangel are all but degrees in one scale, and all fundamentally the same, the difference between solely a matter of degree, and rate of vibration—all are creations of THE ALL, and have their existence solely within the Infinite Mind of THE ALL.

We would again remind you that according to the Principle of Correspondence, which embodies the truth, "As Above so Below; as Below, so Above," all of the Seven Hermetic Principles are in full operation on all of the many planes, Physical, Mental and Spiritual. The Principle of Mental Substance, of course, applies to all the planes, for all are held in the Mind of THE ALL. The Principle of Correspondence manifests in all, for there is a correspondence, harmony, and agreement between the several planes. The Principle of Vibration manifests on all planes, in fact the very differences that go to make the "planes" arise from Vibration, as we have explained. The Principle of Polarity manifests on each plane, the extremes of the Poles being apparently opposite and contradictory. The Principle of Rhythm manifests on each Plane, the movement of the phenomena having its ebb and flow, rise and flow, incoming and outgoing. The Principle of Cause and Effect manifests on each Plane, every Effect having its Cause and every Cause having its effect. The Principle of Gender manifests on each Plane, the Creative Energy being always manifest, and operating along the lines of its Masculine and Feminine Aspects.

"As Above so Below; as Below, so Above." This centuries old Hermetic axiom embodies one of the great Principles of Universal Phenomena. As we proceed with our consideration of the remaining Principles, we will see even more clearly the truth of the universal nature of this great Principle of Correspondence.

## Chapter Seven

# Vibration

*"Nothing rests; everything moves; everything vibrates."* —THE KYBALION

The great Third Hermetic Principle—the Principle of Vibration—embodies the truth that Motion is manifest in everything in the Universe—that nothing is at rest—that everything moves, vibrates, and circles.

The Hermetic Teachings are that not only is everything in constant movement and vibration, but that the "differences" between the various manifestations of the universal power are due entirely to the varying rate and mode of vibrations. Not only this, but that even THE ALL, in itself, manifests a constant vibration of such an infinite degree of intensity and rapid motion that it may be practically considered as at rest, the teachers directing the attention of the students to the fact that even on the physical plane a rapidly moving object (such as a revolving wheel) seems to be at rest. The Teachings are to the effect that Spirit is at one end of the Pole of Vibration, the other Pole being certain extremely gross forms of Matter. Between these two poles are millions upon millions of different rates and modes of vibration.

Scientists have offered the illustration of a rapidly moving wheel, top, or cylinder, to show the effects of increasing rates of vibration. The illustration supposes a wheel, top, or revolving cylinder, running at a low rate of speed— we will call this revolving thing "the object" in following out the illustration. Let us suppose the object moving slowly. It may be seen readily, but no sound of its movement reaches the ear. The speed is gradually increased. In a few moments its movement becomes so rapid that a deep growl or low note may be heard. Then as the rate is increased the note rises one in the musical scale. Then, the motion being still further increased, the next highest note is distinguished. Then, one after another, all the notes of the musical scale appear, rising higher and higher as the motion is increased. Finally, when the motions have reached a certain rate the final note perceptible to human ears is reached and the shrill, piercing shriek dies away, and silence follows. No sound is heard from the revolving object, the rate of motion being so high that the human ear cannot register the vibrations. Then comes the perception of rising degrees of Heat.

When the object reaches a certain rate of vibration its molecules disintegrate, and resolve themselves into the original elements or atoms. Then the atoms, following the Principle of Vibration, are separated into the countless corpuscles of which they are composed. And, finally, even the corpuscles disappear and the object may be said to be composed of The Ethereal Substance. Science does not dare to follow the illustration further, but the Hermetists teach that if the vibrations be continually increased the object would mount up the successive states of manifestation and would in turn manifest the various mental stages, and then on Spiritward, until it would finally reenter THE ALL, which is Absolute Spirit.

The Hermetic Teachings go much further than do those of modern science. They teach that all manifestation of thought, emotion, reason, will or desire, or any mental state or condition, are accompanied by vibrations, a portion of which are thrown off, and which tend to affect the minds of other persons by "induction." This is the principle which produces the phenomena of "telepathy;" mental influence, and other forms of the action and power of mind over mind. Every thought, emotion or mental state has its corresponding rate and mode of vibration. And by an effort of the will of the person, or of other persons, these mental states may be reproduced, just as a musical tone may be reproduced by causing an instrument to vibrate at a certain rate—just as color may be reproduced in the same way. By a knowledge of the Principle of Vibration, as applied to Mental Phenomena, one may polarize his mind at any degree he wishes, thus gaining a perfect control over his mental states, moods, etc. In the same way he may affect the minds of others, producing the desired mental states in them. In short, he may be able to produce on the Mental Plane that which science produces on the Physical Plane—namely, "Vibrations at Will."

A little reflection on what we have said will show the student that the Principle of Vibration underlies the wonderful phenomena of the power manifested by the Masters and Adepts, who are able to apparently set aside the Laws of Nature, but who, in reality, are simply using one law against another; one principle against others; and who accomplish their results by changing the vibrations of material objects, or forms of energy, and thus perform what are commonly called "miracles."

As one of the old Hermetic writers has truly said: "He who understands the Principle of Vibration, has grasped the scepter of Power."

## Chapter Eight
# Polarity

*"Everything is dual; everything has poles; everything has its pair of opposites; like and unlike are the same; opposites are identical in nature, but different in degree; extremes meet; all truths are but half-truths; all paradoxes may be reconciled."* —The Kybalion

The great Fourth Hermetic Principle—the Principle of Polarity—embodies the truth that all manifested things have "two sides;" "two aspects;" "two poles;" a "pair of opposites," with manifold degrees between the two extremes. The old paradoxes, which have ever perplexed the mind of men, are explained by an understanding of this Principle. Man has always recognized something akin to this Principle.

The Hermetic Teachings are to the effect that the difference between things seemingly diametrically opposed to each other is merely a matter of degree. It teaches that "the pairs of opposites may be reconciled," and that "thesis and anti-thesis are identical in nature, but different in degree," and that the "universal reconciliation of opposites" is affected by a recognition of this Principle of Polarity. The teachers claim that illustrations of this Principle may be had on every hand, and from an examination into the real nature of anything. They begin by showing that Spirit and Matter are but the two poles of the same thing, the intermediate planes being merely degrees of vibration. They show that THE ALL and The Many are the same, the difference being merely a matter of degree of Mental Manifestation.

Light and Darkness are poles of the same thing, with many degrees between them. The musical scale is the same—starting with "C" you move upward until you reach another "C," and so on, the differences between the two ends of the board being the same, with many degrees between the two extremes.

Good and Bad are not absolute—we call one end of the scale Good and the other Bad, or one end Good and the other Evil, according to the use of the terms. A thing is "less good" than the thing higher in the scale; but that "less good" thing, in turn, is "more good" than the thing next below it—and so on, the "more or less" being regulated by the position on the scale.

And so it is on the Mental Plane. "Love and Hate" are generally regarded as being things diametrically opposed to each other; entirely different; unreconcilable. But we apply the Principle of Polarity; we find that there is no such thing as Absolute Love or Absolute Hate, as distinguished from each other. The two are merely terms applied to the two poles of the same thing. The Pairs of Opposites exist everywhere. Where you find one thing you find its opposite—the two poles.

And it is this fact that enables the Hermetist to transmute one mental state into another, along the lines of Polarization. Things belonging to different classes cannot be transmuted into each other, but things of the same class may be changed, that is, may have their polarity changed. Thus Love never becomes East or West, or Red or Violet—but it may and often does turn into Hate—and likewise Hate may be transformed into Love, by changing its polarity. Courage may be transmuted into Fear, and the reverse. Hard things may be rendered Soft. Dull things become Sharp. Hot things become Cold. And so on, the transmutation always being between things of the same kind of different degrees. Take the case of a Fearful man. By raising his mental vibrations along the line of Fear-Courage, he can be filled with the highest degree of Courage and Fearlessness. And, likewise, the Slothful man may change himself into an Active, Energetic individual, simply by polarizing along the lines of the desired quality.

The student who is familiar with the processes by which the various schools of Mental Science, etc., produce changes in the mental states of those following their teachings, may not readily understand the principle underlying many of these changes. When, however, the Principle of Polarity is once grasped, and it is seen that the mental changes are occasioned by a change of polarity—a sliding along the same scale—the matter is more readily understood. The change is not in the nature of a transmutation of one thing into another thing entirely different—but is merely a change of degree in the same things, a vastly important difference.

The student will readily recognize that in the mental states, as well as in the phenomena of the Physical Plane, the two poles may be classified as Positive and Negative, respectively. Thus Love is Positive to Hate; Courage to Fear; Activity to Non-Activity, etc. And it will also be noticed that even to those unfamiliar with the Principle of Vibration, the Positive pole seems to be of a higher degree than the Negative, and readily dominates it. The tendency of Nature is in the direction of the dominant activity of the Positive pole.

In addition to the changing of the poles of one's own mental states by the operation of the art of Polarization, the phenomena of Mental Influence, in its manifold phases, shows us that the principle may be extended so as to embrace the phenomena of the influence of one mind over that of another. When it is understood that Mental Induction is possible, that is that mental states may be produced by "induction" from others, then we can readily see how a certain rate of vibration, or polarization of a certain mental state, may be communicated to another person, and his polarity in that class of mental states thus changed. It is along this principle that the results of many of the "mental treatments" are obtained. For instance, a person is "blue," melancholy and full of fear. A mental scientist bringing his own mind up to the desired vibration by his trained will, and thus obtaining the desired polarization in his own case, then produces a similar mental state in the other by induction, the result being that the vibrations are raised and the person polarizes toward the Positive end of the scale instead toward the Negative, and his Fear and other negative emotions are transmuted to Courage and similar positive mental states. A little study will show you that these mental changes are nearly all along the line of Polarization, the change being one of degree rather than of kind.

A knowledge of the existence of this great Hermetic Principle will enable the student to better understand his own mental states, and those of other people. He will see that these states are all matters of degree, and seeing thus, he will be able to raise or lower the vibration at will—to change his mental poles, and thus be Master of his mental states, instead of being their servant and slave. And by his knowledge he will be able to aid his fellows intelligently, and by the appropriate methods change the polarity when the same is desirable. We advise all students to familiarize themselves with this Principle of Polarity, for a correct understanding of the same will throw light on many difficult subjects.

## Chapter Nine

# Rhythm

*"Everything flows out and in; everything has its tides; all things rise and fall; the pendulum-swing manifests in everything; the measure of the swing to the right, is the measure of the swing to the left; rhythm compensates."*
—THE KYBALION

The great Fifth Hermetic Principle—the Principle of Rhythm—embodies the truth that in everything there is manifested a measured motion; a to-and-from movement; a flow and inflow; a swing forward and backward; a pendulum-like movement; a tide-like ebb and flow; a high-tide and a low-tide; between the two-poles manifest on the physical, mental or spiritual planes. The Principle of Rhythm is closely connected with the Principle of Polarity described in the preceding chapter. Rhythm manifests between the two poles established by the Principle of Polarity. This does not mean, however, that the pendulum of Rhythm swings to the extreme poles, for this rarely happens; in fact, it is difficult to establish the extreme polar opposites in the majority of cases. But the swing is ever "toward" first one pole and then the other.

There is always an action and reaction; an advance and a retreat; a rising and a sinking; manifested in all of the airs and phenomena of the Universe.

Suns, worlds, men, animals, plants, minerals, forces, energy, mind and matter, yes, even Spirit, manifests this Principle. The Principle manifests in the creation and destruction of worlds; in the rise and fall of nations; in the life history of all things; and, finally, in the mental states of Man.

The Principle of Rhythm is well understood by modern science, and is considered a universal law as applied to material things. But the Hermetists carry the principle much further, and know that its manifestations and influence extend to the mental activities of Man, and that it accounts for the bewildering succession of moods, feelings, and other annoying and perplexing changes that we notice in ourselves. But the Hermetists by studying the operations of this Principle have learned to escape some of its activities by Transmutation.

The Hermetic Masters long since discovered that while the Principle of Rhythm was invariable, and ever in evidence in mental phenomena, still there were two planes of its manifestation so far as mental phenomena are concerned. They discovered that there were two general planes of Consciousness, the Lower and the Higher, the understanding of which enabled them to rise to the higher plane and thus escape the swing of the Rhythmic pendulum which manifested on the lower plane. In other words, the swing of the pendulum occurred on the Unconscious Plane, and the Consciousness was not affected. This they call the Law of Neutralization. Its operations consist in the raising of the Ego above the vibrations of the Unconscious Plane of mental activity, so that the negative-swing of the pendulum is not manifested in consciousness, and therefore they are not affected. It is akin to rising above a thing and letting it pass beneath you. The Hermetic Master, or advanced student, polarizes himself at the desired pole, and by a process akin to "refusing" to participate in the backward swing, or, if you prefer, a "denial" of its influence over him, he stands firm in his polarized position, and allows the mental pendulum to swing back along the unconscious plane. All individuals who have attained any degree of self-mastery, accomplish this, more or less unknowingly, and by refusing to allow their moods and negative mental states to affect them, they apply the Law of Neutralization. The Master, however, carries this to a much higher degree of proficiency, and by the use of his Will he attains a degree of Poise and Mental Firmness almost impossible of belief on the part of those who allow themselves to be swung backward and forward by the mental pendulum of moods and feelings.

The importance of this will be appreciated by any thinking person who realizes what creatures of moods, feelings, and emotion the majority of people are, and how little mastery of themselves they manifest. If you will stop and consider a moment, you will realize how much these swings of Rhythm have affected you in your life—how a period of Enthusiasm has been invariably followed by an opposite feeling and mood of Depression. Likewise, your moods and periods of Courage have been succeeded by equal moods of Fear. And so it has ever been with the majority of persons—tides of feeling have ever risen and fallen with them, but they have never suspected the cause or reason of the mental phenomena. An understanding of the workings of this Principle will give one the key to the Mastery of these rhythmic swings of feeling, and will enable him to know himself better, and to avoid being carried away by these in flows and out flows. The Will is superior to the conscious manifestation of this Principle, although the Principle itself can never be destroyed. We may escape its effects, but the Principle operates, nevertheless. The pendulum ever swings, although we may escape being carried along with it.

There are other features of the operation of this Principle of Rhythm of which we wish to speak at this point. There comes into its operations that which is known as the Law of Compensation. One of the definitions or meanings of the word "Compensate" is "to counterbalance," which is the sense in which the Hermetists use the term. It is this Law of Compensation to which The Kybalion refers when it says: "The measure of the swing to the right is the measure of the swing to the left; rhythm compensates."

The Law of Compensation is that the swing in one direction determines the swing in the opposite direction, or to the opposite pole—the one balances, or counterbalances, the other. The pendulum, with a short swing in one direction, has but a short swing in the other; while the long swing to the right invariably means the long swing to the left. An object hurled upward to a certain height has an equal distance to traverse on its return. The force with which a projectile is sent upward a mile is reproduced when the projectile returns to the earth on its return journey. This Law is constant on the Physical Plane.

But the Hermetists carry it still further. They teach that a man's mental states are subject to the same Law. The man who enjoys keenly, is subject to keen suffering; while he who feels but little pain is capable of feeling but little joy.

There are temperaments which permit of but low degrees of enjoyment, and equally low degrees of suffering; while there are others which permit the most intense enjoyment, but also the most intense suffering. The rule is that the capacity for pain and pleasure, in each individual, are balanced. The Law of Compensation is in full operation here.

But the Hermetists go still further in this matter. They teach that before one is able to enjoy a certain degree of pleasure, he must have swung as far, proportionately, toward the other pole of feeling. They hold, however, that the Negative is precedent to the Positive in this matter, that is to say that in experiencing a certain degree of pleasure it does not follow that he will have to "pay up for it" with a corresponding degree of pain; on the contrary, the pleasure is the Rhythmic swing, according to the Law of Compensation, for a degree of pain previously experienced either in the present life, or in a previous incarnation. This throws a new light on the Problem of Pain.

The Hermetists claim that the Master or advanced student is able, to a great degree, to escape the swing toward Pain, by the process of Neutralization before mentioned. By rising on to the higher plane of the Ego, much of the experience that comes to those dwelling on the lower plane is avoided and escaped.

The Law of Compensation plays an important part in the lives of men and women. It will be noticed that one generally "pays the price" of anything he possesses or lacks. If he has one thing, he lacks another—the balance is struck. The things that one gains are always paid for by the things that one loses. And so it is through life. The Law of Compensation is ever in operation, striving to balance and counter-balance, and always succeeding in time, even though several lives may be required for the return swing of the Pendulum of Rhythm.

## Chapter Ten
# Causation

*"Every Cause has its Effect; every Effect has its Cause; everything happens according to Law; Chance is but a name for Law not recognized; there are many planes of causation, but nothing escapes the Law."* —THE KYBALION

The great Sixth Hermetic Principle—the Principle of Cause and Effect—embodies the truth that Law pervades the Universe; that nothing happens by Chance; that Chance is merely a term indicating cause existing but not recognized or perceived; that phenomena is continuous, without break or exception.

A little consideration will show you that there can be no such agent as "Chance," in the sense of something outside of Law—something outside of

Cause and Effect. How could there be a something acting in the phenomenal universe, independent of the laws, order, and continuity of the latter? Such a something would be entirely independent of the orderly trend of the universe, and therefore superior to it. We can imagine nothing outside of THE ALL being outside of the Law, and that only because THE ALL is the LAW in itself. There is no room in the universe for a something outside of and independent of Law. The existence of such a Something would render all Natural Laws ineffective, and would plunge the universe into chaotic disorder and lawlessness.

What we call "Chance" is merely an expression relating to obscure causes; causes that we cannot perceive; causes that we cannot understand. The word Chance is derived from a word meaning "to fall" (as the falling of dice), the idea being that the fall of the dice (and many other happenings) are merely a "happening" unrelated to any cause. And this is the sense in which the term is generally employed. But when the matter is closely examined, it is seen that there is no chance whatsoever about the fall of the dice. Each time a die falls, and displays a certain number, it obeys a law as infallible as that which governs the revolution of the planets around the sun. Back of the fall of the die are causes, or chains of causes, running back further than the mind can follow. The position of the die in the box; the amount of muscular energy expended in the throw; the condition of the table, etc., all are causes, the effect of which may be seen. But back of these seen causes are chains of unseen preceding causes, all of which had a bearing upon the number of the die which fell uppermost.

If a die be cast a great number of times, it will be found that the numbers shown will be about equal, that is, there will be an equal number of one-spot, two-spot, etc., coming upper-most. Toss a penny in the air, and it may come down either "heads" or "tails;" but make a sufficient number of tosses, and the heads and tails will about even up. This is the operation of the law of average. But both the average and the single toss come under the Law of Cause and Effect, and if we were able to examine into the preceding causes, it would be clearly seen that it was simply impossible for the die to fall other than it did, under the same circumstances and at the same time. Given the same causes, the same results will follow. There is always a "cause" and a "because" to every event. Nothing ever "happens" without a cause, or rather a chain of causes.

There is a continuity between all events precedent, consequent, and subsequent. There is a relation existing between everything that has gone before, and everything that follows. Stop to think a moment. If a certain man had not met a certain maid, away back in the dim period of the Stone Age—you who are now reading these lines would not now be here. And if, perhaps, the same couple had failed to meet, we who now write these lines would not now be here. And the very act of writing, on our part, and the act of reading, on yours, will affect not only the respective lives of yourself and ourselves, but will also have a direct, or indirect, affect upon many other people now living and who will live in the ages to come. Every thought we think, every act we perform, has its direct and indirect results, which fit into the great chain of Cause and Effect.

We do not wish to enter into a consideration of Free-Will, or Determinism, in this work, for various reasons. Among the many reasons, is the principal one that neither side of the controversy is entirely right—in fact, both sides are partially right, according to the Hermetic Teachings. The Principle of Polarity shows that both are but Half-Truths—the opposing poles of Truth. The Teachings are that a man may be both Free and yet bound by Necessity, depending upon the meaning of the terms, and the height of Truth from which the matter is examined. The ancient writers express the matter thus: "The further the creation is from the Centre, the more it is bound; the nearer the Centre it reaches, the nearer Free is it."

The majority of people are more or less the slaves of heredity, environment, etc., and manifest very little Freedom. They are swayed by the opinions, customs and thoughts of the outside world, and also by their emotions, feelings, moods, etc. The majority of people are carried along like a falling stone, obedient to environment, outside influences and internal moods, desires, etc., not to speak of the desires and wills of others stronger than themselves, carrying them along without resistance on their part, or the exercise of the Will. Moved like the pawns on the checkerboard of life, they play their parts and are laid aside after the game is over. But the Masters, knowing the rules of the game, rise above the plane of material life, and placing themselves in touch with the higher powers of their nature, dominate their own moods, characters, qualities, and polarity, as well as the environment surrounding them, and thus become Movers in the game, instead of Pawns—Causes instead of Effects. The Masters do not escape the Causation of the higher planes, but fall in with the higher laws, and thus master circumstances on the lower plane. They thus form a conscious part of the Law, instead of being mere blind instruments. While they Serve on the Higher Planes, they Rule on the Material Plane.

The Hermetic Teachings are that Man may use Law to overcome laws, and that the higher will always prevail against the lower, until at last he has reached the stage in which he seeks refuge in the LAW itself. Are you able to grasp the inner meaning of this?

## Chapter Eleven

# Gender

*"Gender is in everything; everything has its Masculine and Feminine Principles; Gender manifests on all planes."* —THE KYBALION

The great Seventh Hermetic Principle—the Principle of Gender—embodies the truth that there is Gender manifested in everything—that the Masculine and Feminine principles are ever present and active in all phases of phenomena, on each and every plane of life. At this point we think it well to call your attention to the fact that Gender, in its Hermetic sense, and Sex in the ordinarily accepted use of the term, are not the same.

The word "Gender" is derived from the Latin root meaning "to beget; to procreate; to generate; to create; to produce." A moment's consideration will show you that the word has a much broader and more general meaning than the term "Sex," the latter referring to the physical distinctions between male and female living things. Sex is merely a manifestation of Gender on a certain plane of the Great Physical Plane—the plane of organic life. The office of Gender is solely that of creating, producing, generating, etc., and its manifestations are visible on every plane of phenomena.

It is not necessary to take up your time with the well known phenomena of the "attraction and repulsion" of the atoms; chemical affinity; the "loves and hates" of the atomic particles; the attraction or cohesion between the molecules of matter. These facts are too well known to need extended comment from us. But, have you ever considered that all of these things are manifestations of the Gender Principle? And more than this, can you not see the reasonableness of the Hermetic Teachings which assert that the very Law of Gravitation—that strange attraction by reason of which all particles and bodies of matter in the universe tend toward each other—is but another manifestation of the Principle of Gender, which operates in the direction of attracting the Masculine to the Feminine energies, and vice versa?

Let us now pass on to a consideration of the operation of the Principle on the Mental Plane.

The idea of Mental Gender may be explained in a few words to students who are familiar with modern psychological theories. The Masculine Principle of Mind corresponds to the so-called Conscious Mind; Objective Mind; Voluntary Mind; Active Mind, etc. And the Feminine Principle of Mind corresponds to the so-called Sub-conscious Mind; Subjective Mind; Involuntary Mind; Passive Mind, etc. Of course the Hermetic Teachings do not agree with the many modern theories regarding the nature of the two phases of mind, nor do they admit many of the facts claimed for the two respective aspects.

The Hermetic Teachers impart their instruction regarding this subject by bidding their students examine the report of their consciousness regarding their Self. The students are bidden to turn their attention inward upon the Self dwelling within each. Each student is led to see that his consciousness gives him first a report of the existence of his Self—the report is "I Am." This at first seems to be the final words from the consciousness, but a little further examination discloses that this "I Am" may be separated or split into two distinct parts, or aspects, which while working in unison and in conjunction, yet, nevertheless, may be separated in consciousness.

While at first there seems to be only an "I" existing, a more careful and closer examination reveals the fact that there exists an "I" and a "Me." These mental twins differ in their characteristics and nature, and an examination of their nature and the phenomena arising from them will throw much light upon many of the problems of mental influence.

Let us begin with a consideration of the "Me," which is usually mistaken for the "I" by the student, until he presses the inquiry a little further back into the recesses of consciousness. A man thinks of his Self (in its aspect of "Me") as being composed of certain feelings, tastes, likes, dislikes, habits, peculiar ties, characteristics, etc., all of which go to make up his personality, or the "Self" known to himself and others. He knows that these emotions and feelings change; are born and die away; are subject to the Principle of Rhythm, and the Principle of Polarity, which take him from one extreme of feeling to another. He also thinks of the "Me" as being certain knowledge gathered together in his mind, and thus forming a part of himself. This is the "Me" of a man.

But we have proceeded too hastily. The "Me" of many men may be said to consist largely of their consciousness of the body and their physical appetites, etc. Their consciousness being largely bound up with their bodily nature, they practically "live there." Some men even go so far as to regard their personal apparel as a part of their "Me," and actually seem to consider it a part of themselves. They cannot conceive of a Self independent of the body. Their mind seems to them to be practically "a something belonging to" their body—which in many cases it is indeed.

But as man rises in the scale of consciousness he is able to disentangle his "Me" from his idea of body, and is able to think of his body as "belonging to" the mental part of him. But even then he is very apt to identify the "Me" entirely with the mental states, feelings, etc., which he feels to exist within him. He is very apt to consider these internal states as identical with himself, instead of their being simply "things" produced by some part of his mentality, and existing within him—of him, and in him, but still not "himself." He sees that he may change these internal states of feelings by an effort of will, and that he may produce a feeling or state of an exactly opposite nature, in the same way, and yet the same "Me" exists. And so after a while he is able to set aside these various mental states, emotions, feelings, habits, qualities, characteristics, and other personal mental belongings—he is able to set them aside in the "not-me" collection of curiosities and encumbrances, as well as valuable possessions. This requires much mental concentration and power of mental analysis on the part of the student. But still the task is possible for the advanced student, and even those not so far advanced are able to see, in the imagination, how the process may be performed.

After this laying-aside process has been performed, the student will find himself in conscious possession of a "Self" which may be considered in its "I" and "Me" dual aspects. The "Me" will be felt to be a Something mental in which thoughts, ideas, emotions, feelings, and other mental states may be produced. It may be considered as the "mental womb," as the ancients styled it—capable of generating mental offspring. It reports to the consciousness as a "Me" with latent powers of creation and generation of mental progeny of all sorts and kinds. Its powers of creative energy are felt to be enormous. But still it seems to be conscious that it must receive some form of energy from either its "I" companion, or else from some other "I," ere it is able to bring into being its mental creations. This consciousness brings with it a realization of an enormous capacity for mental work and creative ability.

But the student soon finds that this is not all that he finds within his inner consciousness. He finds that there exists a mental Something which is able to Will that the "Me" act along certain creative lines, and which is also able to stand aside and witness the mental creation. This part of himself he is taught to call his "I." He is able to rest in its consciousness at will. He finds there not a consciousness of an ability to generate and actively create, in the sense of the gradual process attendant upon mental operations, but rather a sense and consciousness of an ability to project an energy from the "I" to the "Me"—a process of "willing" that the mental creation begin and proceed. He also finds that the "I" is able to stand aside and witness the operations of the "Me's" mental creation and generation. There is this dual aspect in the mind of every person. The "I" represents the Masculine Principle of Mental Gender—the "Me" represents the Female Principle. The "I" represents the Aspect of Being; the "Me" the Aspect of Becoming.

The tendency of the Feminine Principle is always in the direction of receiving impressions, while the tendency of the Masculine Principle is always in the direction of giving out, or expressing. The Feminine Principle has a much more varied field of operation than has the Masculine Principle. The Feminine Principle conducts the work of generating new thoughts, concepts, ideas, including the work of the imagination. The Masculine Principle contents itself with the work of the "Will," in its varied phases. And yet without the active aid of the Will of the Masculine Principle, the Feminine Principle is apt to rest content with generating mental images which are the result of impressions received from outside, instead of producing original mental creations.

Persons who can give continued attention and thought to a subject actively employ both of the Mental Principles—the Feminine in the work of active mental generation, and the Masculine Will in stimulating and energizing the creative portion of the mind. The majority of persons really employ the Masculine Principle but little, and are content to live according to the thoughts and ideas instilled into the "Me" from the "I" of other minds.

The Masculine Principle in the average person is too lazy to act—the display of Will-Power is too slight—and the consequence is that such persons are ruled almost entirely by the minds and wills of other persons. How few original thoughts or original actions are performed by the average person? Are not the majority of persons mere shadows and echoes of others having stronger wills or minds than themselves? The trouble is that the average person dwells almost altogether in his "Me" consciousness, and does not realize that he has such a thing as an "I." He is polarized in his Feminine Principle of Mind, and the Masculine Principle, in which is lodged the Will, is allowed to remain inactive and not employed.

The strong men and women of the world invariably manifest the Masculine Principle of Will, and their strength depends materially upon this fact. Instead of living upon the impressions made upon their minds by others, they dominate their own minds by their Will, obtaining the kind of mental images desired, and moreover dominate the minds of others likewise, in the same manner. Look at the strong people, how they manage to implant their seed-thoughts in the minds of the masses of the people, thus causing the latter to think thoughts in accordance with the desires and wills of the strong individuals. This is why the masses of people are such sheep-like creatures, never originating an idea of their own, nor using their own powers of mental activity.

The manifestation of Mental Gender may be noticed all around us in everyday life. The magnetic persons are those who are able to use the Masculine Principle in the way of impressing their ideas upon others. The actor who makes people weep or cry as he wills, is employing this principle. And so is the successful orator, statesman, preacher, writer or other people who are before the public attention. In this principle lies the secret of personal magnetism, personal influence, fascination, etc., as well as the phenomena generally grouped under the name of Hypnotism.

The student who has familiarized himself with the phenomena generally spoken of as "psychic" will have discovered the important part played in the said phenomena by that force which science has styled "Suggestion," by which term is meant the process or method whereby an idea is transferred to or "impressed upon" the mind of another, causing the second mind to act in accordance. A correct understanding of Suggestion is necessary in order to intelligently comprehend the varied psychical phenomena which Suggestion underlies. But, still more is a knowledge of Vibration and Mental Gender necessary for the student of Suggestion. For the whole principle of Suggestion depends upon the principle of Mental Gender and Vibration.

If you will think of the matter in the light of the Hermetic Teachings, you will be able to see that the energizing of the Feminine Principle by the Vibratory Energy of the Masculine Principle is in accordance to the universal laws of nature. The Hermetic Teachings show that the very creation of the Universe follows the same law, and that in all creative manifestations, upon the planes of the spiritual, the mental, and the physical, there is always in operation this principle of Gender—this manifestation of the Masculine and the Feminine Principles. "As above, so below; as below, so above." And more than this, when the principle of Mental Gender is once grasped and understood, the varied phenomena of psychology at once becomes capable of intelligent classification and study. The principle "works out" in practice, because it is based upon the immutable universal laws of life.

With the aid of The Kybalion one may go through any occult library anew, the old Light from Egypt illuminating many dark pages and obscure subjects. That is the purpose of this book. We do not come expounding a new philosophy, but rather furnishing the outlines of a great world-old teaching, which will make clear the teachings of others—which will serve as a Great Reconciler of differing theories, and opposing doctrines.

## Chapter Twelve
# Hermetic Axioms

"The possession of Knowledge, unless accompanied by a manifestation and expression in Action, is like the hoarding of precious metals—a vain and foolish thing. Knowledge, like Wealth, is intended for Use. The Law of Use is Universal, and he who violates it suffers by reason of his conflict with natural forces." —THE KYBALION.

The Hermetic Teachings, while always having been kept securely locked up in the minds of the fortunate possessors thereof, for reasons that we have already stated, were never intended to be merely stored away and secreted. The Law of Use is dwelt upon in the Teachings, as you may see by reference to the above quotation from The Kybalion, which states it forcibly. Beware of Mental Miserliness, and express into Action that which you have learned. Study the Axioms and Aphorisms, but practice them also.

We give below some of the more important Hermetic Axioms from The Kybalion, with a few comments added to each. Make these your own, and practice and use them, for they are not really your own until you have Used them.

"To change your mood or mental state—change your vibration."—The Kybalion

One may change his mental vibrations by an effort of Will, in the direction of deliberately fixing the Attention upon a more desirable state. Will directs the Attention, and Attention changes the Vibration. Cultivate the Art of Attention, by means of the Will, and you have solved the secret of the Mastery of Moods and Mental States.

"To destroy an undesirable rate of mental vibration, put into operation the Principle of Polarity and concentrate upon the opposite pole to that which you desire to suppress. Kill out the undesirable by changing its polarity."—The Kybalion

This is one of the most important of the Hermetic Formulas. We have shown you that a mental state and its opposite were merely the two poles of one thing, and that by Mental Transmutation the polarity might be reversed. This principle is known to modern psychologists, who apply it to the breaking up of undesirable habits by bidding their students concentrate upon the opposite quality. If you are possessed of Fear, do not waste time trying to "kill out" Fear, but instead cultivate the quality of Courage, and the Fear will disappear. Some writers have expressed this idea most forcibly by using the illustration of the dark room. You do not have to shovel out or sweep out the Darkness, but by merely opening the shutters and letting in the Light the Darkness has disappeared. To kill out a Negative quality, concentrate upon the Positive Pole of that same quality, and the vibrations will gradually change from Negative to Positive, until finally you will become polarized on the Positive pole instead of the Negative. The reverse is also true, as many have found out to their sorrow, when they have allowed themselves to vibrate too constantly on the Negative pole of things. By changing your polarity you may master your moods, change your mental states, remake your disposition, and build up character. Much of the Mental Mastery of the advanced Hermetics is due to this application of Polarity, which is one of the important aspects of Mental Transmutation. Remember the Hermetic Axiom (quoted previously), which says:

"Mind (as well as metals and elements) may be transmuted from state to state; degree to degree; condition to condition; pole to pole; vibration to vibration."—The Kybalion

The mastery of Polarization is the mastery of the fundamental principles of Mental Transmutation or Mental Alchemy, for unless one acquires the art of changing his own polarity, he will be unable to affect his environment. An understanding of this principle will enable one to change his own Polarity, as well as that of others, if he will but devote the time, care, study, and practice necessary to master the art. The principle is true, but the results obtained depend upon the persistent patience and practice of the student.

"Rhythm may be neutralized by an application of the Art of Polarization."—The Kybalion

As we have explained in previous chapters, the Hermetists hold that the Principle of Rhythm manifests on the Mental Plane as well as on the Physical Plane, and that the bewildering succession of moods, feelings, emotions, and other mental states, are due to the backward and forward swing of the mental pendulum, which carries us from one extreme of feeling to the other. The Hermetists also teach that the Law of Neutralization enables one, to a great extent, to overcome the operation of Rhythm in consciousness. As we have explained, there is a Higher Plane of Consciousness, as well as the ordinary Lower Plane, and the Master by rising mentally to the Higher Plane causes the swing of the mental pendulum to manifest on the Lower Plane, and he, dwelling on his Higher Plane, escapes the consciousness of the swing backward. This is effected by polarizing on the Higher Self, and thus raising the mental vibrations of the Ego above those of the ordinary plane of consciousness. It is akin to rising above a thing, and allowing it to pass beneath you. The advanced Hermetist polarizes himself at the Positive Pole of his Being—the "I Am" pole rather than the pole of personality, and by "refusing" and "denying" the operation of Rhythm, raises himself above its plane of consciousness, and standing firm in his Statement of Being he allows the pendulum to swing back on the Lower Plane without changing his Polarity. This is accomplished by all individuals who have attained any degree of self-mastery, whether they understand the law or not. Such persons simply "refuse" to allow themselves to be swung back by the pendulum of mood and emotion, and by steadfastly affirming the superiority, they remain polarized on the Positive pole. The Master, of course, attains a far greater degree of proficiency, because he understands the law which he is overcoming by a higher law, and by the use of his Will he attains a degree of Poise and Mental Steadfastness almost impossible of belief on the part of those who allow themselves to be swung backward and forward by the mental pendulum of moods and feelings.

Remember, always, however, that you do not really destroy the Principle of Rhythm, for that is indestructible. You simply overcome one law by counter-balancing it with another, and thus maintain an equilibrium.

"Nothing escapes the Principle of Cause and Effect, but there are many Planes of Causation, and one may use the laws of the higher to overcome the laws of the lower."—The Kybalion

By an understanding of the practice of Polarization, the Hermetists rise to a higher plane of Causation and thus counter-balance the laws of the lower planes of Causation. By rising above the plane of ordinary Causes they become themselves, in a degree, Causes instead of being merely Caused. By being able to master their own moods and feelings, and by being able to neutralize Rhythm, as we have already explained, they are able to escape a great part of the operations of Cause and Effect on the ordinary plane. The masses of people are carried along, obedient to their environment; the wills and desires of others stronger than themselves; the effects of inherited tendencies; the suggestions of those about them; and other outward causes; which tend to move them about on the chessboard of life like mere pawns. By rising above these influencing causes, the advanced Hermetists seek a higher plane of mental action, and by dominating their moods, emotions, impulses, and feelings, they create for themselves new characters, qualities, and powers, by which they overcome their ordinary environment. Such people help to play the game of life understandingly, instead of being moved about this way and that way by stronger influences and powers and wills. As The Kybalion says:

"The wise ones serve on the higher, but rule on the lower. They obey the laws coming from above them, but on their own plane, and those below them, they rule and give orders. And, yet, in so doing, they form a part of the Principle, instead of opposing it. The wise man falls in with the Law, and by understanding its movements he operates it instead of being its blind slave. Just as does the skilled swimmer turn this way and that way, going and coming as he will, instead of being as the log which is carried here and there—so is the wise man as compared to the ordinary man—and yet both swimmer and log, wise man and fool, are subject to Law. He who understands this is well on the road to Mastery."

In conclusion let us again call your attention to the Hermetic Axiom: "True Hermetic Transmutation is a Mental Art."—The Kybalion

In the above axiom, the Hermetists teach that the great work of influencing one's environment is accomplished by Mental Power. The Universe being wholly mental, it follows that it may be ruled only by Mentality. Back of and under the teachings of the various cults and schools, remains ever constant the principle of the Mental Substance of the Universe. If the Universe be Mental in its substantial nature, then it follows that Mental Transmutation must change the conditions and phenomena of the Universe. If the Universe is Mental, then Mind must be the highest power affecting its phenomena. If this be understood then all the so-called "miracles" and "wonder-workings" are seen plainly for what they are.

*"THE ALL is MIND; The Universe is Mental."* —The Kybalion

# The Science of Getting Rich
(1910)

## by Wallace D. Wattles

*The Legendary Mental Program to Wealth and Mastery*

### Contents

Introduction   *The Ethic of Success* by Mitch Horowitz   330
Chapter One   For Those Who Want Money   331
Chapter Two   The Right to Be Rich   332
Chapter Three   There is a Science of Getting Rich   333
Chapter Four   Is Opportunity Monopolized?   333
Chapter Five   The First Principle in the Science of Getting Rich   335
Chapter Six   Increasing Life   336
Chapter Seven   How Riches Come to You   338
Chapter Eight   Gratitude   339
Chapter Nine   Thinking in a Certain Way   340
Chapter Ten   How to Use the Will   341
Chapter Eleven   Further Use of the Will   342
Chapter Twelve   Acting In the Certain Way   343

## Introduction
# The Ethic of Success

Some people have deeply contradictory feelings about the idea of "getting rich." They believe that getting rich sounds gauche, unspiritual, or selfish. This book by American social reformer and New Thought pioneer Wallace D. Wattles will put those mixed feelings to rest.

Wattles, a fighter for progressive causes as well as a pioneering mind theorist, believed that the true aim of enrichment was not the mere accumulation of personal resources, but the establishment of a better world: a world of shared abundance and possibility for all people.

His guidebook *The Science of Getting Rich* was obscure until about ten years ago. In 2007, word spread that *The Science of Getting Rich* was a source behind the mega-selling book and movie *The Secret*. The book began to hit bestseller lists, nearly than a century after the author's death in 1911. I published an edition myself that reached number-one on the *Businessweek* bestseller list.

But what many of Wattles's new generation of readers missed was his dedication to the ethic of collective advancement and creativity above animal competition; his belief that competition itself was an outmoded idea, soon to be supplanted but the creative capacities found within the mind. And that once unlocked, these higher capacities would grant working men and women the keys to a life of prosperity for themselves and for all around them.

Was his vision really so utopian? We live in an age of remarkable advances in placebo studies, extending even to "placebo surgery" and mentally based weight-loss; new findings in the field called neuroplasticity, which show that the brain's neural pathways are literally "rewired" by habits of thought; extraordinary questions posed by quantum physics experiments, which suggest causality between thought and object; and ongoing and serious experiments in ESP, which repeatedly demonstrate some kind of nonphysical conveyance of data in laboratory settings.

Wattles's vision, now more than a century old, was simply to ask whether these remarkable abilities, which were only hinted at in the science labs of his day, could be applied and experimented with on the material scale of daily life.

Wattles did not live long enough to see the influence of his book. He died of tuberculosis less than a year after it appeared. But his calm certainty and profoundly confident yet gentle tone suggest that he understood the portent of what he was writing.

Like every great thinker, Wattles left us not with a doctrine, but rather with articles of experimentation. The finest thing you can do to honor the memory of this good man—and to advance your own place in life—is to heed his advice: Go and experiment. Go and try. And if you experience results, as I think you will, do what he did: Tell the people.

—Mitch Horowitz

## Chapter One
# For Those Who Want Money

This book is a practical manual, not a treatise upon theories. It is intended for men and women whose most pressing need is money; who wish to get rich first, and philosophize afterward. It is for those who have, so far, found neither the time, the means, nor the opportunity to go deeply into the study of metaphysics, but who want results and who are willing to take the conclusions of science as a basis for action, without going into all the processes by which those conclusions were reached.

It is expected that the reader will take the fundamental statements of this book upon faith; and, taking the statements upon faith, that he will prove their truth by acting upon them without fear or hesitation.

Every man or woman who does this will certainly get rich; for the science herein is an exact science, and failure is impossible. For the benefit, however, of those who wish to investigate philosophical theories and secure a logical basis for faith, I will here cite certain authorities.

The monistic theory of the universe—the theory that One is All, and that All is One; that one Substance manifests itself as the seeming many elements of the material world—is of Hindu origin, and has been gradually winning its way into the thought of the western world for two hundred years. It is the foundation of all the Oriental philosophies, and of those of Descartes, Spinoza, Leibnitz, Schopenhauer, Hegel, and Emerson.

In writing this book I have sacrificed all other considerations to plainness and simplicity of style, so that all might understand. The plan of action laid down herein was deduced from the conclusions of philosophy; it has been thoroughly tested, and bears the supreme test of practical experiment:

*it works*. If you wish to know how the conclusions were arrived at, read the writings of the authors mentioned above; and if you wish to reap the fruits of their philosophies in actual practice, read this book, and do exactly as it tells you to do.

## Chapter Two
# The Right to be Rich

The object of life is development; and everything that lives has an inalienable right to all the development that it is capable of attaining.

Man's right to life means his right to have the free and unrestricted use of all things necessary to his fullest mental, spiritual, and physical unfoldment; or, in other words, his right to be rich.

In this book, I do not speak of riches in a figurative way; to be really rich does not mean to be satisfied or contented with a little. No man ought to be satisfied with a little if he is capable of using and enjoying more. The purpose of Nature is the advancement and unfoldment of life; and every man should have all that can contribute to the power, elegance, beauty, and richness of life. To be content with less is sinful.

The desire for riches is really the desire for a richer, fuller, and more abundant life.

There are three motives for which we live: the body, the mind, and the soul. No one of these is better or holier than the other; all are alike desirable, and no one of the three—body, mind, or soul—can live fully if either of the others is cut short of full life and expression.

*Real* life means the complete expression of all that man can give forth through body, mind, and soul.

Wherever there is unexpressed possibility, or function not performed, there is unsatisfied desire. Desire is possibility seeking expression, or function seeking performance.

It is perfectly right that you should desire to be rich; if you are a normal man or woman you cannot help doing so. It is perfectly right that you should give your best attention to the Science of Getting Rich, for it is the noblest and most necessary of all studies. If you neglect this study, you are derelict in your duty to yourself, to God and humanity; for you can render to God and humanity no greater service than to make the most of yourself.

## Chapter Three
# There Is a Science of Getting Rich

There is a Science of Getting Rich, and it is an exact science, like algebra or arithmetic. There are certain laws that govern the process of acquiring riches.

The ownership of money and property comes as a result of doing things in a *certain way*; those who do things in this Certain Way, whether on purpose or accidentally, get rich; while those who do not do things in this Certain Way, no matter how hard they work or how able they are, remain poor.

The ability to do things in this certain way is not due solely to birth or talent, for many people who have great talent remain poor, while others who have little talent get rich.

Studying the people who have gotten rich, we find that they are an average lot in all respects, having no greater talents and abilities than other men. It is evident that they do not get rich because they possess talents and abilities that other men have not, but because they happen to do things in a Certain Way.

Some degree of ability to think and understand is, of course, essential; but insofar as natural ability is concerned, any man or woman who has sense enough to read and understand these words can get rich.

It is true that you will do best in a business that you like, and that is congenial to you; and if you have certain talents that are well developed, you will do best in a business that calls for those talents.

Also, you will do best in a business that is suited to your locality; an ice-cream parlor would do better in a warm climate than in Greenland, and a salmon fishery will succeed better in the Northwest than in Florida, where there are no salmon.

But, aside from these general limitations, getting rich is not dependent upon your engaging in some particular business, but upon your learning to do things in a Certain Way that causes success. It is this to which we now turn.

## Chapter Four
# Is Opportunity Monopolized?

It is quite true that if you are a workman in the employ of the steel trust you have very little chance of becoming the owner of the plant for which you work; but it is also true that if you will commence to act in a Certain Way, you can soon leave the employ of the steel trust for new opportunity.

At different periods the tide of opportunity sets in different directions, according to the needs of the whole, and the particular stage of social evolution that has been reached.

There is abundance of opportunity for the man who will go with the tide, instead of trying to swim against it.

The workers are not being "kept down" by their masters. As a class, they are where they are because they do not do things in a Certain Way. If the workers of America chose to do so, they could follow the example of their brothers in Belgium and other countries, and establish great department stores and co-operative industries; they could elect men of their own class to office, and pass laws favoring the development of such co-operative industries; and in a few years they could take peaceable possession of the industrial field.

The working class may become the master class whenever they will begin to do things in a Certain Way; the law of wealth is the same for them as it is for all others. This they must learn; and they will remain where they are as long as they continue to do as they do. The individual worker, however, is not held down by the ignorance or the mental slothfulness of his class; he can follow the tide of opportunity to riches.

The visible supply is practically inexhaustible; and the invisible supply really IS inexhaustible.

*Everything you see on earth is made from one original substance, out of which all things proceed.*

New forms are constantly being made, and older ones are dissolving; but all are shapes assumed by One Thing.

There is no limit to the supply of Formless Stuff, or Original Substance. The universe is made out of it; but it was not all used in making the universe. The spaces in, through, and between the forms of the visible universe are permeated and filled with the Original Substance; with the formless Stuff; with the raw material of all things. Ten thousand times as much as has been made might still be made, and even then we should not have exhausted the supply of universal raw material.

Nature is an inexhaustible storehouse of riches; the supply will never run short. Original Substance is alive with creative energy, and is constantly producing more forms. When the supply of building material is exhausted, more will be produced; when the soil is exhausted so that foodstuffs and materials for clothing will no longer grow upon it, it will be renewed or more soil will be made. When all the gold and silver has been dug from the earth, if man is still in such a stage of social development that he needs gold and silver, more will produced from the Formless. The Formless Stuff responds to the needs of man; it will not let him be without any good thing.

The Formless Stuff is intelligent; it is stuff that thinks. It is alive, and is always impelled toward more life.

It is the natural and inherent impulse of life to seek to live more; it is the nature of intelligence to enlarge itself, and of consciousness to seek to extend its boundaries and find fuller expression. The universe of forms has been made by Formless Living Substance, throwing itself into form in order to express itself more fully.

The universe is a great Living Presence, always moving inherently toward more life and fuller functioning.

Nature is formed for the advancement of life; its impelling motive is the increase of life. For this cause, everything that can possibly minister to life is bountifully provided; there can be no lack unless God is to contradict himself and nullify his own works.

I shall demonstrate shortly that the resources of the Formless Supply are at the command of the man or woman who will act and think in a Certain Way.

## Chapter Five
# The First Principle in the Science of Getting Rich

Thought is the only power that can produce tangible riches from the Formless Substance. The stuff from which all things are made is a substance that thinks, and a thought of form in this substance produces the form.

Original Substance moves according to its thoughts; every form and process you see in nature is the visible expression of a thought in Original Substance. As the Formless Stuff thinks of a form, it takes that form; as it thinks of a motion, it makes that motion. That is the way all things were created. We live in a thought world, which is part of a thought universe. The thought of a moving universe extended throughout Formless Substance, and the Thinking Stuff moving according to that thought, took the form of systems of planets, and maintains that form. Thinking Substance takes the form of its thought, and moves according to the thought.

Every thought of form held in thinking Substance, causes the creation of the form but always, or at least generally, along lines of growth and action already established.

*No thought of form can be impressed upon Original Substance without causing the creation of the form.*

Man is a thinking center, and can originate thought. All the forms that man fashions with his hands must first exist in his thought; he cannot shape a thing until he has thought that thing.

Yet so far man has confined his efforts wholly to the work of his hands; he has applied manual labor to the world of forms, seeking to change or modify what already exists. He has never thought of trying to cause the creation of new forms by impressing his thoughts upon Formless Substance.

As our first step, we must lay down three fundamental propositions:

*1) There is a thinking stuff from which all things are made, and which, in its original state, permeates, penetrates, and fills the interspaces of the universe.*

*2) A thought, in this substance, produces the thing that is imaged by the thought.*

*3) Man can form things in his thought, and, by impressing his thought upon formless substance, can cause the thing he thinks about to be created.*

Read these creed statements over and over again; fix every word upon your memory, and meditate upon them until you firmly believe what they say.

There is no labor from which most people shrink as they do from that of sustained and consecutive thought; it is the hardest work in the world. This is especially true when truth is contrary to appearances. Every appearance in the visible world tends to produce a corresponding form in the mind that observes it; and this can be prevented only by holding the thought of the TRUTH.

Do not ask why these things are true, nor speculate as to how they can be true; simply take them on trust.

The science of getting rich begins with the absolute acceptance of this faith.

## Chapter Six
# Increasing Life

The desire for riches is simply the capacity for larger life seeking fulfillment; every desire is the effort of an unexpressed possibility to come into action. It is power seeking to manifest that causes desire. That which makes you want more money is the same as that which makes the plant grow: it is Life, seeking fuller expression.

The One Living Substance must be subject to this inherent law of all life; it is permeated with the desire to live more; that is why it is under the necessity of creating things.

It is the desire of God that you should get rich. He wants you to get rich because He can express himself better through you if you have plenty of things to use in giving Him expression. He can live more in you if you have unlimited command of the means of life.

The universe desires you to have everything you want to have.

Nature is friendly to your plans.

Everything is naturally for you.

Make up your mind that this is true.

It is essential, however that *your purpose should harmonize with the purpose that is in All.*

You must want real life, not mere pleasure of sensual gratification. Life is the performance of function; and the individual really lives only when he performs every function, physical, mental, and spiritual, of which he is capable, without excess in any.

Remember, however, that the desire of Substance is for all, and its movements must be for more life to all; it cannot be made to work for less life to any, because it is equally in all, seeking riches and life.

Intelligent Substance will make things for you, but it will not take things away from some one else and give them to you.

You are to become a creator, not a competitor; you are going to get what you want, but in such a way that when you get it every other man will have more than he has now.

I am aware that there are men who get a vast amount of money by proceeding in direct opposition to the statements above, and may add a word of explanation here. Men of the plutocratic type, who become very rich, do so sometimes purely by their extraordinary ability on the plane of competition; and sometimes they unconsciously relate themselves to Substance in its great purposes and movements for the general racial upbuilding through industrial evolution. Rockefeller, Carnegie, Morgan, et al., have been the unconscious agents of the Supreme in the necessary work of systematizing and organizing productive industry; and in the end, their work will contribute immensely toward increased life for all. Their day is nearly over; they have organized production, and *will soon be succeeded by the agents of the multitude, who will organize the machinery of distribution.*

The multi-millionaires are like the monster reptiles of the prehistoric eras; they play a necessary part in the evolutionary process, but the same Power that produced them will dispose of them. And it is well to bear in mind that they have never been really rich; a record of the private lives of most of this class will show that they have really been the most abject and wretched of the poor.

Riches secured on the competitive plane are never satisfactory and permanent; they are yours today, and another's tomorrow. Remember, if you are to become rich in a scientific and certain way, you must rise entirely out of the competitive thought.

Let us consider once more:

*There is a thinking stuff from which all things are made, and which, in its original state, permeates, penetrates, and fills the interspaces of the universe.*

*A thought, in this substance, produces the thing that is imaged by the thought.*

*Man can form things in his thought, and, by impressing his thought upon formless substance, can cause the thing he thinks about to be created.*

The supply is limitless.

## Chapter Seven
# How Riches Come to You

When I say that you do not have to drive sharp bargains, I do not mean that you do not have to drive any bargains at all, or that you are above the necessity for having any dealings with your fellow men. I mean that you will not need to deal with them unfairly; you do not have to get something for nothing, *but can give to every man more than you take from him.*

You cannot give every man more in cash market value than you take from him, but you can give him more in use value than the cash value of the thing you take from him. The paper, ink, and other material in this book may not be worth the money you pay for it; but if the ideas suggested by it bring you thousands of dollars, you have not been wronged by those who sold it to you; they have given you a great use value for a small cash value.

Give every man more in use value than you take from him in cash value; then you are adding to the life of the world by every business transaction.

If you have people working for you, you must take from them more in cash value than you pay them in wages; but you can so organize your business that it will be filled with the principle of advancement, and so that each employee who wishes to do so may advance a little every day.

You can make your business do for your employees what this book is doing for you. You can so conduct your business that it will be a sort of ladder, by which every employee who will take the trouble may climb to riches himself; and given the opportunity, if he will not do so it is not your fault.

## Chapter Eight
# Gratitude

The whole process of mental adjustment and atonement can be summed up in one word: gratitude.

First, you believe that there is one Intelligent Substance, from which all things proceed; second, you believe that this Substance gives you everything you desire; and third, you relate yourself to it by a feeling of deep and profound gratitude.

Many people who order their lives rightly in all other ways are kept in poverty by their lack of gratitude. Having received one gift from God, they cut the wires that connect them with Him by failing to make acknowledgment.

It is easy to understand that the nearer we live to the source of wealth, the more wealth we shall receive; and it is easy also to understand that the soul that is always grateful lives in closer touch with God than the one that never looks to Him in thankful acknowledgment.

The more gratefully we fix our minds on the Supreme when good things come to us, the more good things we will receive, and the more rapidly they will come; and the reason simply is that the mental attitude of gratitude draws the mind into closer touch with the source from which the blessings come.

There is a Law of Gratitude, and it is absolutely necessary that you should observe the law, if you are to get the results you seek.

The Law of Gratitude is the natural principle that action and reaction are always equal, and in opposite directions.

The grateful outreaching of your mind in thankful praise to the Supreme *is a liberation or expenditure of force; it cannot fail to reach that to which it addressed, and the reaction is an instantaneous movement towards you.*

"Draw nigh unto God, and He will draw nigh unto you." That is a statement of psychological truth.

## Chapter Nine
# Thinking in a Certain Way

It is not enough that you should have a general desire for wealth "to do good." Everybody has that desire.

It is not enough that you should have a wish to travel, see things, live more, etc. Everybody has those desires, too. If you were going to relay a radio message to a friend, you would not send the letters of the alphabet in their order, and let him construct the message for himself; nor would you take words at random from the dictionary. You would send a coherent sentence; one that meant something.

When you try to impress your wants upon Substance it must be done by a coherent statement; you must know what you want, and be definite. You can never get rich, or start the creative power into action, by sending out unformed longings and vague desires.

You must have a clear mental picture continually in mind, and you must keep your face toward it all the time.

It is not necessary to take exercises in concentration, nor to set apart special times for prayer and affirmation. These things are well enough, but all you need is to know what you want, and to want it badly enough so that it will stay in your thoughts.

Spend as much of your leisure time as you can in contemplating your picture, but no one needs to take exercises to concentrate his mind on a thing that he really wants; it is the things you do not really care about that require effort to focus upon.

The more clear and definite you make your picture then, and the more you dwell upon it, bringing out all its delightful details, the stronger your desire will be; and the stronger your desire, the easier it will be to hold your mind fixed upon the picture of what you want.

Something more is necessary, however, than merely to see the picture clearly.

Behind your clear vision must be the purpose to realize it; to bring it out in tangible expression.

And behind this purpose must be an invincible and unwavering FAITH that the thing is already yours; that it is "at hand" and you have only to take possession of it.

Live in the new house, mentally, until it takes form around you physically. In the mental realm, enter at once into full enjoyment of the things you want.

"Whatsoever things ye ask for when ye pray, believe that ye receive them, and ye shall have them," said Jesus.

You do not need to pray repeatedly for things you want; it is not necessary to tell God about it every day.

"Use not vain repetitions as the heathen do," Jesus told his pupils, "for your Father knoweth that ye have need of these things before ye ask Him."

Your part is to intelligently formulate your desires for the things which make for a larger life, and to get these desires arranged into a coherent whole; and then to impress this Whole Desire upon the Formless Substance, which has the power and the will to bring you what you want.

You do not make this impression by repeating strings of words; you make it by holding the vision with unshakable PURPOSE to attain it, and with steadfast FAITH that you do attain it.

The answer to prayer is not according to your faith while you are talking, but according to your faith while you are working.

## Chapter Ten
# How to Use the Will

To set about getting rich in a scientific way, do not try to apply your will power to anything outside of yourself.

You have no right to, anyway.

It is wrong to apply your will to other men and women in order to get them to do what you wish done.

It is as flagrantly wrong to coerce people by mental power as it is to coerce them by physical power. If compelling people by physical force to do things for you reduces them to slavery, compelling them by mental means accomplishes the same thing.

You have no right to use your will power upon another person, even "for his own good;" for you do not know what is for his good.

To get rich, you need only to use your will power upon yourself.

When you know what to think and do, then you must use your will to compel yourself to think and do the right things. That is the legitimate use of the will in getting what you want—to use it in holding yourself to the right course. Use your will to keep yourself thinking and acting in the Certain Way.

Do not try to project your will, or your thoughts, or your mind out into space, to "act" on things or people.

Keep your mind at home; it can accomplish more there than elsewhere.

Use your mind to form a mental image of what you want, and to hold that vision with faith and purpose; and use your will to keep your mind working in the Right Way.

The more steady and continuous your faith and purpose, the more rapidly you will get rich, because you will make only POSITIVE impressions upon Substance; and you will not neutralize or offset them by negative impressions.

The picture of your desires, held with faith and purpose, is taken up by the Formless. As this impression spreads, all things are set moving toward its realization; every living thing, every inanimate thing, and the things yet uncreated, are stirred toward bringing into being that which you want. All force begins to be exerted in that direction; all things begin to move toward you. The minds of people, everywhere, are influenced toward doing the things necessary to the fulfilling of your desires; and they work for you, unconsciously.

Since belief is all-important, it behooves you to guard your thoughts; and as your beliefs will be shaped to a very great extent by the things you observe and think about, it is important that you should command your attention.

## Chapter Eleven
# Further Use of the Will

You cannot retain a true and clear vision of wealth if you are constantly turning your attention to opposing pictures, whether they are external or imaginary.

Do not tell of your past troubles of a financial nature; if you have had them, do not think of them at all. Do not tell of the poverty of your parents, or the hardships of your early life; to do any of these things is to mentally class yourself with the poor for the time being, and it will certainly check the movement of things in your direction.

"Let the dead bury their dead," as Jesus said.

Put poverty and all things that pertain to poverty completely behind you.

You have accepted a certain theory of the universe as being correct, and are resting all your hopes of happiness on its being correct; and what can you gain by giving heed to conflicting theories?

You can aim at nothing so great or noble, I repeat, as to become rich; and you must fix your attention upon your mental picture of riches, to the exclusion of all that may tend to dim or obscure the vision.

You must learn to see the underlying TRUTH in all things; you must see beneath all seemingly wrong conditions the Great One Life ever moving forward toward fuller expression and more complete happiness.

The very best thing you can do for the whole world is to make the most of yourself.

## Chapter Twelve
# Acting in the Certain Way

This is the crucial point in the Science of Getting Rich—right here, where thought and personal action must be combined. Many people, consciously or unconsciously, set the creative forces in action by the strength and persistence of their desires, yet they remain poor because they do not provide for the reception of the thing they want when it comes.

By thought, the thing you want is brought to you; by action you receive it.

Whatever your action is to be, it is evident that you must act NOW. You cannot act in the past, and it is essential to the clearness of your mental vision that you dismiss the past from your mind. You cannot act in the future, for the future is not here yet. And you cannot tell how you will want to act in any future contingency until that contingency has arrived.

Because you are not in the right business, or the right environment now, do not think that you must postpone action until you get into the right business or environment. And do not spend time in the present taking thought as to the best course in possible future emergencies; have faith in your ability to meet any emergency when it arrives.

Put your whole mind into present action.

Do not bother as to whether yesterday's work was well done or ill done; do to-day's work well.

Do not try to do tomorrow's work now; there will be plenty of time to do that when you get to it.

Do not try, by occult or mystical means, to act on people or things that are out of your reach.

Do not wait for a change of environment, before you act; get a change of environment by action.

You can so act upon the environment in which you are now, as to cause yourself to be transferred to a better environment.

Hold with faith and purpose the vision of yourself in the better environment, but act upon your present environment with all your heart, and with all your strength, and with all your mind.

You can advance only by being larger than your present place; and no man is larger than his present place who leaves undone any of the work pertaining to that place.

Doing what you want to do is life; and there is no real satisfaction in living if we are compelled to be forever doing something that we do not like to do. And it is certain that you can do what you want because the *desire* to do it is proof that you have within you the power that *can* do it.

Desire is a manifestation of power.

The desire to play music is the power that can play music seeking expression and development.

If there are past mistakes whose consequences have placed you in an undesirable business or environment, you may be obliged for some time to do that which you do not like to do; but you can make the doing of it pleasant by knowing that it is making it possible for you to come to the doing of what you want to do.

Remember always that definiteness of purpose, the ability of your thoughts to impress themselves upon the great Original Substance of the universe, the sincere impulse toward creative function, the desire to build—not to best—your neighbor, and the dedication to doing all you can wherever you are, place at your back an awesome power of Truth, to which nothing can be denied.

Build the world that you dream of for yourself and others; bring prosperity and beauty into creation; improve yourself—and you improve the world. That is the noblest goal to which any man or woman can aspire.

# The Science of Being Great
(1911)

## by Wallace D. Wattles

*The Secret to Living Your Greatest Life Now
From the Author of* The Science of Getting Rich

## Contents

Introduction  *"You Can Become What You Want to Be"* by Mitch Horowitz  346
Chapter One   Any Person May Become Great   347
Chapter Two   The Source of Power   348
Chapter Three   The Mind of God   349
Chapter Four   Consecration   350
Chapter Five   Identification   351
Chapter Six   Idealization   352
Chapter Seven   Realization   353
Chapter Eight   Hurry and Habit   355
Chapter Nine   Thought   356
Chapter Ten   Action at Home   357
Chapter Eleven   Jesus's Idea of Greatness   358
Chapter Twelve   Serving God   359

## Introduction

# "You Can Become What You Want to Be"

The title of this preface is the final line of author Wallace D. Wattles's opening chapter, and the heart of this book. But it is more than an author's credo. It is, in a sense, an encapsulation of American metaphysical ideals—the outlook of a still-young nation when Wattles wrote *The Science of Being Great* in 1911, and an outlook still held today.

In the era in which Wattles lived, America was suffused with the influence of a new metaphysics—Christian Science, New Thought, mental healing, and other spiritual philosophies taught modern people to believe that what we think and feel concretizes in the experience of our lives; that thoughts are causative. This spiritual vision harmonized with the sense of limitless possibility that many Americans felt in the early twentieth century, when the nation's growth and expansion seemed endless.

This book, which appeared the year that Wattles died, was, in my view, his greatest work. It captured everything that he saw around him, and put a sharper focus on the ideas that he explored in his widely read book *The Science of Getting Rich*, which preceded this one in 1910.

Wattles was far more than a cheerleader for personal and national growth. He was also a fiery social reformer who was forced out of his Methodist pulpit in northern Indiana after refusing to accept collection-basket offerings from parishioners who ran sweatshops. He believed in a voluntary, democratic socialism, and he foresaw a new world where cooperation would replace animal competition. He ran for office twice on the ticket of Eugene V. Debs's Socialist Party. He advocated for the rights of striking workers and suffragists. Yet his reputation was sealed, and he received posthumous fame in our own time, for a book dedicated to personal money-getting, *The Science of Getting Rich*.

None of this was contradictory. Wattles believed, without any sense of personal conflict, that the potential of the individual must be expressed both socially and materially. "Man is formed for growth," he wrote, "and he is under the necessity of growing. It is essential to his happiness that he should continually advance. Life without progress is unendurable."

Although Wattles had no way of knowing that his life would be lost to tuberculosis at age fifty, shortly after finishing this book, *The Science of Being Great* formed a culminating manifesto and testament to all that he believed. In its pages, abridged to their essential points in this Condensed Classics edition, you will discover Wattles's complete philosophy of life: namely, that each of us is run through by a Divine influx, which can raise us to extraordinary heights of personal excellence, acts of creativity, and skills marked by virtuosity. But to fully place ourselves within this eternal, creative current we must first be in alignment with Gospel ethics, and possess a sense of duty to God and our fellow beings.

Self-refinement, he wrote, is the key to transforming ourselves into vehicles for the Higher Principle of life, or God, which yearns for expression through us, and can deliver us to greatness.

Everything that this good and thoughtful man believed necessary for a powerful life can be found in this short and compelling book. May it deliver you to your greatest heights of achievement—and your deepest sense of responsibility.

—Mitch Horowitz

## Chapter One
# Any Person May Become Great

There is a Principle of Power in every person. By the intelligent use and direction of this principle, man can develop his own mental faculties. Man has an inherent power by which he may grow in whatsoever direction he pleases.

The possibility is in the Original Substance from which man is made. Genius is Omniscience flowing into man. Genius is more than talent. Talent may merely be one faculty developed out of proportion to other faculties, but genius is the union of man and God in the acts of the soul. Great men are always greater than their deeds. They are in connection with a reserve power that is without limit.

The purpose of life for man is growth, just as the purpose of life for trees and plants is growth. Trees and plants grow automatically and along fixed lines; man can grow as he will. Trees and plants can only develop certain possibilities and characteristics; man can develop any power that is or has been shown by any person, anywhere. Nothing that is possible in spirit is impossible in flesh and blood. Nothing that man can think is impossible in action. Nothing that man can imagine is impossible of realization.

Man is formed for growth, and he is under the necessity of growing. It is essential to his happiness that he should continuously advance.

Life without progress becomes unendurable. The greater and more harmonious and well-rounded his growth, the happier man will be.

Every man comes into the world with a predisposition to grow along certain lines, and growth is easier for him along those lines than in any other way.

The Principle of Power gives us just what we ask of it; if we only undertake little things, it only gives us power for little things; but if we try to do great things in a great way it gives us all the power there is.

No greater good can come to any man or woman than to become self-active. All the experiences of life are designed by Providence to force men and women into self-activity; to compel them to cease being creatures of circumstances and master their environment.

Nothing was ever in any man that is not in you; no man ever had more spiritual or mental power than you can attain, or did greater things than you can accomplish. You can become what you want to be.

## Chapter Two
# The Source of Power

Wisdom is the power to perceive the best ends to aim at and the best means for reaching those ends. It is the power to perceive the right thing to do. The man who is wise enough to know the right thing to do, who is good enough to wish to do only the right thing, and who is able and strong enough to do the right thing is a truly great man.

Wisdom is dependent upon knowledge. Man's knowledge is comparatively limited and so his wisdom is small, unless he can connect his mind with a knowledge greater than his own and draw from it, by inspiration, the wisdom that his own limitations deny him. This he can do; this is what the really great men and women have done.

I proceed to give an illustration: Abraham Lincoln had limited education; but he had the power to perceive truth. When Lincoln became president he was surrounded by a multitude of so-called able advisers, hardly any two of whom were agreed. At times they were all opposed to his policies; at times the whole North was opposed to what he proposed to do. But he saw the truth when others were misled by appearances; his judgment was seldom or never wrong. He was at once the ablest statesman and the best solider of the period. Where did he, a comparatively unlearned man, get this wisdom?

Knowledge of truth is not often reached by the processes of reason. It was due to spiritual insight. He perceived truth. But where did he perceive it and whence did the perception come? We see something similar in Washington, whose faith and courage, due to his perception of truth, held the colonies together during the long and often apparently hopeless struggle of the Revolution.

We discover back of Washington and Lincoln something greater than either Washington or Lincoln. We see the same thing in all great men and women. They perceive truth; but truth cannot be perceived until it exists; and there can be no truth until there is a mind to perceive it. Truth does not exist apart from mind. Washington and Lincoln were in touch and communication with a mind that knew all knowledge and contained all truth. So of all who manifest wisdom.

*Wisdom is obtained by reading the mind of God.*

## Chapter Three
# The Mind of God

There is a Cosmic Intelligence that is in all things and through all things. This is the one real substance. From it all things proceed. It is Intelligent Substance or Mind Stuff. It is God.

Where there is thought there must be a substance which thinks. But thought is not in the brain substance, for brain substance, without life, is quite unintelligent and dead. Thought is the life-principle that animates the brain, in the spirit-substance, which is the real man. The brain does not think, the man thinks and expresses his thought through the brain.

There is a spirit substance that thinks. Just as the spirit substance of man permeates his body, and thinks and knows in the body, so the Original Spirit Substance, God, permeates all nature and thinks and knows in nature. The All-Mind has been in touch with all things from the beginning, and it contains all knowledge. The truths men perceive by inspiration are thoughts held in the mind.

Man is thinking substance, a portion of the Cosmic Substance; but man is limited, while the Cosmic Intelligence from which he sprang, which Jesus calls the Father, is unlimited. All intelligence, power, and force come from the Father. Jesus recognized this and stated it very plainly. Over and over again, he ascribed all his wisdom and power to his unity with the Father, and to his perceiving the thoughts of God. "My father and I are one." This was the foundation of his knowledge and power.

## Chapter Four
# Consecration

No one will deny the statement that if you are to be great, the greatness must be a manifestation of something within; nor can you question that this something must be the very greatest and highest that is within. It is not the mind, or the intellect, or the reason. You cannot be great if you go no farther back for principle than to your reasoning power. Reason knows neither principle nor morality. Your reason is like a lawyer in that it will argue for either side. The intellect of a thief will plan robbery or murder as readily as the intellect of a saint will plan a great philanthropy.

Intellect helps us to see the best means and manner of doing the right thing, but intellect never shows us the right thing. Intellect and reason serve the selfish man for his selfish ends as readily as they serve the unselfish man for his unselfish ends. Use intellect and reason without regard to principle, and you may become known as a very able person, but you will never become known as a person whose life shows the power of real greatness.

There is too much training of the intellect and reasoning powers and too little training in obedience to the soul. This is the only thing that can be wrong with your personal attitude—when it fails to be one of obedience to the Principle of Power.

By going back to your own center you can always find the pure idea of right for every relationship. To be great and to have power it is only necessary to conform your life to the pure idea as you find it in the GREAT WITHIN. Every compromise on this point is made at the expense of a loss of power. This you *must* remember.

There are many ideas in your mind that you have outgrown, and which, from force of habit, you still permit to dictate the actions of your life. Cease all this; abandon everything you have outgrown. There are many ignoble customs, social and other, which you still follow, although you know they tend to dwarf and belittle you and keep you acting in a small way. Rise above all this. I do not say that you should absolutely disregard conventionalities, or the commonly accepted standards of right and wrong. You cannot do this; but you can deliver your soul from most of the narrow restrictions which bind the majority of your fellow men. Do not give your time and strength to the support of obsolete institutions, religious or otherwise; do not be bound by creed in which you do not believe. Be free.

You have perhaps formed some sensual habits of mind or body; abandon them. You still indulge in distrustful fears that things will go wrong, or that people will betray you, or mistreat you; get above all of them. You still act selfishly in many ways and on many occasions; cease to do so. Abandon all these, and in place of them put the best actions you can form a conception of in your mind. If you desire to advance, and you are not doing so, remember that it can be only because your thought is better than your practice. You must do as well as you think.

Let your attitude in business, in politics, in neighborhood affairs, and in your own home be the expression of the best thoughts you can think. Let your manner toward all men and women, great and small, and especially to your own family circle, always be the most kindly, gracious, and courteous you can picture in your imagination.

Say: "I surrender my body to be ruled by my mind; I surrender my mind to be governed by my soul; and I surrender my soul to the guidance of God."

## Chapter Five
# Identification

Having recognized God as the advancing presence in nature, society, and your fellow men, and harmonized yourself with all these, and having consecrated yourself to that within you which impels toward the greatest and the highest, the next step is to become aware of and recognize fully the fact that the Principle of Power within you is God Himself. You must consciously identify yourself with the Highest. This is not some false or untrue position to be assumed; it is a fact to be recognized. You are already one with God; you want to become consciously aware of it.

There is one substance, the source of all things, and this substance has within itself the power that creates all things; all power is inherent in it. There cannot be one kind of intelligence in God and another kind of intelligence in man. Man is of one stuff with God, and so all the talents, powers, and possibilities that are in God are in man; not in a few exceptional men but in every man.

The Principle of Power in man is man himself, and man himself is God. But while man is original substance, and has within him all the power and possibilities, his consciousness is limited. He does not know all there is to know, and so he is liable to error and mistake. To save himself from these he must unite his mind to That outside him which does know all; he must become consciously one with God. There is a Mind surrounding him on every side, closer than breathing, nearer than hands and feet, and in this mind is the memory of all that has ever happened, from the greatest convulsions of nature in prehistoric days to the fall of a sparrow in the present time; and all that is in existence now as well. Held in this Mind is the great purpose that is behind all nature, and so it knows what is going to be.

Man is surrounded by a Mind that knows all there is to know, past, present, and to come. Everything that men have said or done or written is present there. Man is of one identical stuff with this Mind; he proceeded from it; and he can so identify himself with it that he may know what it knows.

You must affirm, "There is only one and that one is everywhere. I surrender myself to conscious unity with the highest. Not I, but the Father. I will to be one with the Supreme and to lead the divine life. I am one with infinite consciousness; there is but one mind, and I am that mind. I that speak unto you am he."

## Chapter Six

# Idealization

A thought held in thinking substance is a real thing; a form, and has actual existence, although it is not visible to you. You internally take the form in which you think of yourself; and you surround yourself with the invisible forms of those things with which you associate in your thoughts.

If you desire a thing, picture it clearly and hold the picture steadily in mind until it becomes a definite thought-form; and if your practices are not such as to separate you from God, the thing you want will come to you in material form. It must do so in obedience to the law by which the universe was created.

Make a thought-form of yourself as strong and hearty and perfectly well; impress this thought-form on creative intelligence, and if your practices are not in violation of the laws by which the physical body is built, your thought-form will become manifest in your flesh. This also is certain; it comes by obedience to law.

Fix upon your ideal of what you wish to make of yourself; consider well and be sure that you make the right choice; that is, the one that will be the most satisfactory to you in a general way. Do not pay too much attention to the advice or suggestions of those around you: do not believe that any one can know, better than yourself, what is right for you. Listen to what others have to say, but always form your own conclusions. DO NOT LET OTHER PEOPLE DECIDE WHAT YOU ARE TO BE. BE WHAT YOU FEEL THAT YOU WANT TO BE.

Do not be misled by a false notion of obligation or duty. You can owe no possible obligation or duty to others that should prevent you from making the most of yourself.

Be true to yourself, and you cannot then be false to any man. When you have fully decided what thing you want to be, form the highest conception of that thing that you are capable of imagining, and make that conception a thought-form. Hold that thought-form as a fact, as the real truth about yourself, and believe in it.

## Chapter Seven

# Realization

If you were to stop with the close of the last chapter, you would never become great; you would be indeed a mere dreamer of dreams, a castle-builder. Too many do stop there; they do not understand the necessity for present action in realizing the vision and bringing the thought-form into manifestation. Two things are necessary; firstly, the making of the thought-form and secondly, the actual appropriation to yourself of all that goes into, and around, the thought-form.

We have discussed the first, now we will proceed to give directions for the second. When you have made your thought-form, you are already, in your interior, what you want to be; next you must become externally what you want to be. You are already great within, but you are not yet doing the great things without. You cannot begin, on the instant, to do the great things; you cannot be before the world the great actor, or lawyer, or musician, or personality you know yourself to be; no one will entrust great things to you as yet for you have not made yourself known. But you can always begin to do small things in a great way.

Here lies the whole secret. You can begin to be great today in your own home, in your store or office, on the street, everywhere; you can begin to make yourself known as great, and you can do this by doing everything you do in a great way. You must put the whole power of your great soul into every act, however small and commonplace, and so reveal to your family, your friends, and neighbors what you really are. Do not brag or boast of yourself; do not go about telling people what a great personage you are, simply live in a great way. In your domestic circle be so just, so generous, so courteous, and kindly that your family, your wife, husband, children, brothers, and sisters shall know that you are a great and noble soul. In all your relations with men be great, just, generous, courteous, and kindly. The great are never otherwise. This is your attitude.

Next, and most important, you must have absolute faith in your own perceptions of truth. Never act in haste or hurry; be deliberate in everything; wait until you feel that you know the true way. And when you do feel that you know the true way, be guided by your own faith though the entire world shall disagree with you. If you do not believe what God tells you in little things, you will never draw upon his wisdom and knowledge in larger things. When you feel deeply that a certain act is the right act, do it and have perfect faith that the consequences will be good.

Rely upon your perception of truth in all the facts and circumstances of life. If you deeply feel that a certain man will be in a certain place on a certain day, go there with perfect faith to meet him; he will be there, no matter how unlikely it may seem. If you feel sure that certain people are making certain combinations, or doing certain things, act in the faith that they are doing those things. If you feel sure of the truth of any circumstance or happening, near or distant, past, present, or to come, trust in your perception. You may make occasional mistakes at first because of your imperfect understanding of the within; but you will soon be guided almost invariably right. Soon your family and friends will begin to defer, more and more, to your judgment and to be guided by you. Soon your neighbors and townsmen will be coming to you for counsel and advice; soon you will be recognized as one who is great in small things, and you will be called upon more and more to take charge of larger things.

## Chapter Eight
# Hurry and Habit

No doubt you have many problems, domestic, social, physical, and financial, which seem to you to be pressing for instant solution. You have debts that must be paid, or other obligations that must be met; you are unhappily or inharmoniously placed, and feel that something must be done at once. Do not get into a hurry and act from superficial impulses. You can trust God for the solution of all your personal riddles. There is no hurry. There is only God, and all is well with the world.

There is an invincible power in you, and the same power is in the things you want. It is bringing them to you and bringing you to them. This is a thought that you must grasp, and hold continuously—that the same intelligence that is in you is in the things you desire. They are impelled toward you as strongly and decidedly as your desire impels you toward them. The tendency, therefore, of a steadily held thought must be to bring the things you desire to you and to group them around you. So long as you hold your thought and your faith right, all must go well. *Nothing can be wrong but your own personal attitude, and that will not be wrong if you trust and are not afraid.* Hurry is a manifestation of fear; he who fears not has plenty of time. If you act with perfect faith in your own perceptions of truth, you will never be too late or too early

Next, as to habit, it is probable that your greatest difficulty will be to overcome your old habitual ways of thought, and to form new habits. The world is ruled by habit. Kings, tyrants, masters, and plutocrats hold their positions solely because the people have come to habitually accept them. Things are as they are only because people have formed the habit of accepting them as they are. When the people change their habitual thought about governmental, social, and industrial institutions, they will change the institutions. Habit rules us all.

You have formed, perhaps, the habit of thinking of yourself as a common person, as one of a limited ability, or as being more or less of a failure. Whatever you habitually think yourself to be, that you are. You must form, now, a greater and better habit; you must form a conception of yourself as a being of limitless power, and habitually think that you are that being. It is the habitual, not the periodical thought that decides your destiny. It will avail you nothing to sit apart for a few moments several times a day to affirm that you are great, if during all the balance of the day, while you are about your regular vocation, you think of yourself as not great. No amount of praying or affirmation will make you great if you still habitually regard yourself as being small. The use of prayer and affirmation is to change your habit of thought.

Any act, mental or physical, often repeated, becomes a habit. The purpose of mental exercises is to repeat certain thoughts over and over until the thinking of those thoughts becomes constant and habitual. The thoughts we continually repeat become convictions. What you must do is to repeat the new thought of yourself until it is the only way in which you think of yourself. Habitual thought, and not environment or circumstance, has made you what you are. Every person has some central idea or thought-form of himself, and by this idea he classifies and arranges all his facts and external relationships. You are classifying your facts either according to the idea that you are a great and strong personality, or according to the idea that you are limited, common, or weak. If the latter is the case you must change your central idea. Get a new mental picture of yourself. Do not try to become great by repeating mere strings of words or superficial formulas; but repeat over and over the THOUGHT of your own power and ability until you classify external facts, and decide your place everywhere by this idea.

## Chapter Nine

# Thought

Greatness is only attained by the constant thinking of great thoughts. No man can become great in outward personality until he is great internally; and no man can be great internally until he THINKS. No amount of education, reading, or study can make you great without thought; but thought can make you great with very little study. There are altogether too many people who are trying to make something of themselves by reading books without thinking; all such will fail. You are not mentally developed by what you read, but by what you think about what you read.

Thinking is the hardest and most exhausting of all labor; and hence many people shrink from it. God has so formed us that we are continuously impelled to thought; we must either think or engage in some activity to escape thought. The headlong, continuous chase for pleasure in which most people spend all their leisure time is only an effort to escape thought. If they are alone, or if they have nothing amusing to take their attention, as a novel to read or a show to see, they must think; and to escape from thinking they resort to novels, shows, and all the endless devices of the purveyors of amusement. Most people spend the greater part of their leisure time running away from thought, hence they are where they are.

Read about great things and think about great questions and issues. Thinking, not mere knowledge or information, makes personality. Thinking is growth; you cannot think without growing. Every thought engenders another thought. There can be no real greatness without original thought.

Action is the second form of thought, and personality is the materialization of thought. Environment is the result of thought; things group themselves or arrange themselves around you according to your thought. There is, as Emerson says, some central idea or conception of yourself by which all the facts of your life are arranged and classified. Change this central idea and you change the arrangement or classification of all the facts and circumstances of your life.

## Chapter Ten
# Action at Home

Do not merely think that you are going to become great; think *that you are great now*. Do not think that you will begin to act in a great way at some future time; begin now.

If you are not in an environment where there is scope for your best powers and talents you can move in due time; but meanwhile you can be great where you are.

Never mind how the people around you, including those of your own household, may treat you. That has nothing at all to do with your being great; that is, it cannot hinder you from being great. People may neglect you and be unthankful and unkind in their attitude toward you; does that prevent you from being great in your manner and attitude toward them? "Your Father," said Jesus, "is kind to the unthankful and the evil." Would God be great if he should go away and sulk because people were unthankful and did not appreciate him? Treat the unthankful and the evil in a great and perfectly kind way, just as God does.

Then assume the same mental attitude with your neighbors, friends, and those you meet in business, you will soon find that people are beginning to depend on you. Your advice will be sought, and a constantly increasing number of people will look to you for strength and inspiration, and rely upon your judgment. Here, as in the home, you must avoid meddling with other people's affairs. Help all who come to you, but do not go about officiously endeavoring to set other people right. Mind your own business. It is no part of your mission in life to correct people's morals, habits, or practices. Lead a great life, doing all things with a great spirit and in a great way; give to him that asketh of you as freely as you have received, but do not force your help or your opinions upon any man.

Form your mental vision of yourself with care. Make the thought-form of yourself as you wish to be, and hold this with the faith that it is being realized, and with the purpose to realize it completely. Do every common act as a god should do it; speak every word as a god should speak it; meet men and women of both low and high estate as a god meets other divine beings. Begin thus and continue thus, and your unfoldment in ability and power will be great and rapid.

## Chapter Eleven
# Jesus's Idea of Greatness

In the twenty-third chapter of Matthew, Jesus makes a very plain distinction between true and false greatness; and also points out the one great danger to all who wish to become great. Speaking to the multitude and to his disciples he bids them beware of adopting the principle of the Pharisees. He points out that while the Pharisees are just and righteous men, honorable judges, true lawgivers and upright in their dealings with men, they "love the uppermost seats at feasts and greetings in the marketplace, and to be called Master, Master"; and in comparison with this principle, he says: "He that will be great among you let him serve."

The average person's idea of a great man, rather than of one who serves, is of one who succeeds in getting himself served. He gets himself in a position to command men; to exercise power over them, making them obey his will. The exercise of dominion over other people, to most persons, is a great thing. Nothing seems to be sweeter to the selfish soul than this. You will always find every selfish and undeveloped person trying to domineer over others, to exercise control over other men. Savage men were no sooner placed upon the earth than they began to enslave one another. For ages the struggle in war, diplomacy, politics, and government has been aimed at the securing of control over other men. Kings and princes have drenched the soil of the earth in blood and tears in the effort to extend their dominions and their power to rule more people. The struggle of the business world today is the same as that on the battlefields of Europe a century ago so far as the ruling principle is concerned.

I want you to contrast these two ideas of greatness sharply in your minds. "He that will be great among you let him serve." I speak not of servility, but service. Lincoln was a great man because he knew how to be a great servant. Napoleon, able, cold, selfish, seeking the high places, was a brilliant man. Lincoln was great; Napoleon was not.

The very moment you begin to advance and are recognized as one who is doing things in a great way you will find yourself in danger. The temptation to patronize, advise, or take upon yourself the direction of other people's affairs is sometimes almost irresistible. Avoid, however, the opposite danger of falling into servility, or of completely throwing yourself away in the service of others.

Thousands of people imitating Jesus, as they suppose, have belittled themselves and given up all else to go about doing good; practicing an altruism that is really as morbid and as far from great as the rankest selfishness. The finer instincts that respond to the cry of trouble or distress are not by any means all of you; they are not necessarily the best part of you. There are other things you must do besides helping the unfortunate, although it is true that a large part of the life and activities of every great person must be given to helping other people. As you begin to advance they will come to you. Do not turn them away. But do not make the fatal error of supposing that the life of complete self-abnegation is the way of greatness.

## Chapter Twelve

# Serving God

I have brought you thus far with a view to finally settling the question of duty. This is one that puzzles and perplexes very many people who are earnest and sincere. When they start to make something of themselves and to practice the science of being great, they find themselves necessarily compelled to rearrange many of their relationships. There are friends who perhaps must be alienated, there are relatives who misunderstand and who feel that they are in some way being slighted; the really great man is often considered selfish by a large circle of people who are connected with him and who feel that he might bestow upon them more benefits than he does. The question at the outset is: Is it my duty to make the most of myself regardless of everything else?

The answer lies in service to God. The only service you can render God is to give expression to what he is trying to give the world, through you. The only service you can render God is to make the very most of yourself in order that God may live in you to the utmost of your possibilities. The Spirit of God is over, about, around, and in all of us, seeking to do great things with us, so soon as we will train our hands and feet, our minds, brains, and bodies to do His service.

Your first duty to God, to yourself, and to the world is to make yourself as great a personality, in every way, as you possibly can. And that, it seems to me, disposes of the question of duty.

The world needs demonstration more than it needs teaching. For this mass of people, our duty is to become as great in personality as possible in order that they may see and desire to do likewise. It is our duty to make ourselves great for their sakes; so that we may help prepare the world that the next generation shall have better conditions for thought.

One last point. I frequently hear from people who wish to make something of themselves and to move out into the world, but who are hampered by home ties, having others more or less dependent upon them, whom they fear would suffer if left alone. In general I advise such people to move out fearlessly, and to make the most of themselves. If there is a loss at home it will be only temporary and apparent, for in a little while, if you follow the leading of Spirit, you will be able to take better care of your dependents than you have ever done before.

# The Power of Concentration

(1916)

## by Theron Q. Dumont

*The Classic to Harnessing Your Mental Power
From the Immortal Author of* The Kybalion

## Contents

Introduction   *The Voice of a Pioneer* by Mitch Horowitz   362
Foreword   363
Lesson I   Concentration Finds the Way   364
Lesson II   The Self-Mastery Power of Concentration   365
Lesson III   How to Gain What You Want Through Concentration   369
Lesson IV   The Silent Force that Produces Results   371
Lesson V   How Concentrated Thought Links All Humanity   372
Lesson VI   The Training of the Will to Do   374
Lesson VII   The Concentrated Mental Demand   376
Lesson VIII   Concentrating Gives Mental Poise   377
Lesson IX   Concentration Can Overcome Bad Habits   380
Lesson X   Business Results Gained Through Concentration   382
Lesson XI   Concentrate on Your Courage   384
Lesson XII   Concentrate on Wealth   387
Lesson XIII   You Can Concentrate, But Will You?   389
Lesson XIV   The Art of Concentration with Practical Exercises   390
Lesson XV   Concentrate So You Will Not Forget   393
Lesson XVI   How Concentration Can Fulfill Your Desire   394
Lesson XVII   Ideals Develop by Concentration   395
Lesson XVIII   Concentration Reviewed   397

## Introduction
# The Voice of a Pioneer

If you're an avid reader of metaphysical books, as I am, you might find the voice in this valuable little volume, published in 1916, somewhat familiar.

It belongs to the remarkably energetic New Thought philosopher and publisher William Walker Atkinson, who wrote under several pseudonyms and produced nearly one hundred New Thought books in the three decades leading up to his death in 1932. The most popular of these works was *The Kybalion*, which Atkinson wrote under the name "Three Initiates" in 1908, eight years before this similarly enduring volume.

In *The Power of Concentration,* Atkinson used the name French name of Theron Q. Dumont, which was often his chosen byline to explore matters of psychology, willpower, suggestion, and self-hypnosis, all of which were closely associated with French thinkers in the early twentieth century. This was particularly the case with hypnosis, which was introduced in its earliest form in Paris in the late 1770s by occult healer Franz Anton Mesmer. Although the arrival of the France Revolution, and the ensuing years of social upheaval, interrupted the progress of hypnotic theory in France, the nation once more popularized the therapeutic uses of the craft in the late-nineteenth century through the so-called Nancy School of hypnotism, which promoted practices of suggestion and hypnotherapy. The Nancy movement produced the immensely popular French healer Emile Coué, who became famous in Europe and America in the 1910s and 20s for his self-help mantra, "Day by day, in every way, I am getting better and better."

This was the tradition to which Atkinson sought to attach himself with his persona Theron Q. Dumont. Under the name Dumont, he wrote several works on the power of personal magnetism, the uses of will and suggestion, and the self-shaping forces of the mind, of which *The Power of Concentration* is probably the most compelling, persuasive, and enduring.

As is often the case with Atkinson's works, the book is a feast of practicality and idealism. It is at once inspiring and hard-knuckled—there is no toleration for dreamy visualizations unmoored from outer action. Rather, *The Power of Concentration* shows how to harness your thoughts and habits to heighten your personal performance. Nearly every page contains injunctions to act, do, and strive.

The book's advice, reduced to its essentials in this condensation, remains potent and fresh more than a century after its publication. Atkinson's language often prefigures terms and concepts heard today in the fields of neuroplasticity and cognitive behavioral therapy. Yet his book contains an infectious dynamism and scale of purpose rarely found in either of those fields. The book captures both the epic hopes and the applicability of the early days of New Thought. Its techniques have never been eclipsed or surpassed.

—Mitch Horowitz

## Foreword

We all know that in order to accomplish a certain thing we must concentrate. It is of the utmost value to learn how to concentrate. To make a success of anything, you must be able to concentrate your entire thought upon the idea.

Do not become discouraged if you are unable to hold your thought on the subject very long at first. Very few can. It seems a peculiar fact that it is easier to concentrate on something that is *not* good for us than on something that is beneficial. This tendency is overcome when we learn to concentrate consciously.

Did you ever stop to think what an important part your thoughts play in your life? This book shows their far-reaching and all-abiding effects.

Man is a wonderful creature, but requires training and development to be useful. A great work can be accomplished by every man if he can be awakened to do his very best. But the greatest man would accomplish little if he lacked concentration and effort. Dwarfs can do the work of giants when they are transformed by the almost-magical power of great mental concentration. But giants will only do the work of dwarfs when they lack this power.

We accomplish more by concentration than by fitness; the man that is apparently best suited for a place does not always fill it best. It is the man who concentrates on every possibility that makes an art of both his work, and his life.

This course will stimulate and inspire you to achieve success; it will bring you into perfect harmony with the laws of success. It will give you a firmer hold on your duties and responsibilities.

The methods of thought-concentration given in this work, if put into practice, will open up interior avenues that will connect you with the everlasting laws of Being and their exhaustless foundation of unchangeable truth.

## Lesson I
# Concentration Finds the Way

Everyone has two natures. One wants to advance and the other wants to pull back. The one that we cultivate and concentrate on decides what we are at the end. Both natures are vying for control. The will alone decides the issue. A man by one supreme effort of the will may change his whole career, and almost accomplish miracles. You may be that man. You can be if you Will to be, for Will can find a way, or make one.

It is a matter of choice whether we allow our diviner self to control us, or whether we get controlled by the brute within. No man has to do anything he does not want to do. He is therefore the director of his life, if he wills to be. What we do is the result of our training. We are like putty, and can be completely controlled by our willpower.

Many people read good books, but say they do not get much out of them. They do not realize that all any book or lesson can do is to awaken them to their possibilities. One of the most beneficial practices I know of is looking for the good in everyone and everything, for there is good in all things. We encourage a person by seeing his good qualities, and we also help ourselves by looking for them. We gain their good wishes, a most valuable asset. We get back what we give out. The time comes when most all of us need encouragement; need buoying up. So, form the habit of encouraging others, and you will find it a wonderful tonic for both others and yourself, for you will get back encouraging and uplifting thoughts.

The first of each month, a person should sit down and examine the progress he has made. If he has not come up to expectations he should discover the reason, and by extra exertion measure up to what is demanded.

I know that every man who is willing to pay the price can be a success. The price is not in money, but in effort. The first essential quality for success is the desire to do—*to be something*. The next thing is to learn how to do it; the next to carry it into execution. The man best able to accomplish anything is the one with a broad mind; a man may acquire knowledge that is foreign to a particular case, but is, nevertheless, of some value in all cases. So, the man who wants to be successful must be liberal; he must acquire all the knowledge he can; he must be well posted not only in one branch of his business but in every part of it. Such a man achieves success.

The secret of success is to try always to improve yourself no matter where you are or what your position. Learn all you can. Don't see how little you can do, but how much you can do. Such a man will always be in demand.

The man with grit and will may be poor today and wealthy in a few years; willpower is a better asset than money. Will will carry you over chasms of failure, if you but give it the chance.

Everyone *really wants* to do something, but few will put forward the effort to make the necessary sacrifice to secure it. There is only one way to accomplish anything, and that is to go ahead and do it. A man may accomplish almost anything today, if he just sets his heart on it and lets nothing interfere with his progress. Obstacles are quickly overcome by the man that sets out to accomplish his heart's desire. The "bigger" the man, the smaller the obstacle appears. The "smaller" the man the greater the obstacle appears. Always look at the advantage you gain by overcoming obstacles, and it will give you the needed courage for their conquest.

## Lesson II
# The Self-Mastery Power of Concentration

Man from a psychological standpoint of development is not what he should be. He does not possess the self-mastery, the self-directing power of concentration that is his right.

He has not trained himself to promote his self-mastery. Every balanced mind possesses faculties whose chief duties are to engineer, direct, and concentrate the operations of the mind, both in a mental and physical sense. Man must learn to control not only his mind but also his bodily movements.

When the self-regulating faculties are not developed the impulses, appetites, emotions, and passions have full swing, and the mind becomes impulsive, restless, emotional, and irregular. This makes mental concentration poor.

When the self-guiding faculties are weak, the person always lacks the power of mental concentration. Therefore, you cannot concentrate until you develop those very powers that *qualify* you to concentrate. If you cannot concentrate, one of the following is the cause:

1. Deficiency of the motor centers.
2. An impulsive and emotional mind.
3. An untrained mind.

The last fault can soon be removed by systematic practice. It is easiest to correct.

The impulsive and emotional state of mind can best be corrected by restraining anger, passion and excitement, hatred, strong impulses, intense emotions, fretfulness, etc. It is impossible to concentrate when you are in any of these excited states. You can help naturally decrease these by avoiding food and drinks as have nerve weakening or stimulating influences, or a tendency to stir up the passions, impulses, and emotions. It is also a good practice to watch and associate with people who are steady, calm, controlled, and conservative.

Many have the idea that when they get into a negative state they are concentrating, but this is not so. Their power of concentration becomes weaker, and they find it difficult to concentrate on anything. The mind that cannot center itself on a special subject or thought, is weak; as is the mind that cannot draw itself from a subject or thought. But the person who can center his mind on any problem, no matter what it is, and remove any unharmonious impressions, has strength of mind. Concentration, first, last, and all the time, means strength of mind.

A concentrated mind pays attention to thoughts, words, acts, and plans. The person who allows his mind to roam at will, will never accomplish a great deal in the world. He wastes his energies. You concentrate the moment you say, "I want to, I can, I will."

Concentration of the mind can only be developed by watching yourself closely. All kinds of development commence with close attention. You should regulate your every thought and feeling. When you commence to watch yourself, your own acts, and also the acts of other people, you use the faculties of autonomy, and, as you continue to do so, you improve your faculties, until in time you can engineer your every thought, wish, and plan. Only the trained mind can focalize. To hold a thought before it until all the faculties have had time to consider that thought is concentration.

The person who cannot direct his thoughts, wishes, plans, resolutions, and studies cannot possibly succeed to the fullest extent. The person who is impulsive one moment and calm the next has not the proper control over himself. He is not a master of his mind, nor of his thoughts, feelings, and wishes. Such a person cannot be a success. When he becomes irritated, he irritates others and spoils all chances of any concerned doing their best. But the person who can direct his energies and hold them at work in a concentrated manner controls his every work and act, and thereby gains power to control others. He can make his every move serve a useful end, and every thought a noble purpose.

He is consciously attentive and holds his mind to one thing at a time. He shuts out everything else. When you are talking to anyone give him your sole and undivided attention. Do not let your attention wander or be diverted. Give no heed to anything else, but make your will and intellect act in unison.

Start out in the morning and see how self-poised you can remain all day. At times, take an inventory of your actions during the day and see if you have kept your determination. If not, see that you do tomorrow. The more self-poised you are the better your concentration. Never be in too much of a hurry; and, remember, the more you improve your concentration, the greater are your possibilities. Concentration means success, because you are better able to govern yourself and centralize your mind; you become more in earnest in what you do, and this almost invariably improves your chances for success.

When you are talking to a person have your own plans in mind. Concentrate your strength upon the purpose you are talking about. Watch his every move, but keep your own plans before you. Unless you do, you will waste your energy and not accomplish as much as you should.

I want you to watch the next person you see who has the reputation of being a strong character, a man of force. Watch and see what a perfect control he has over his body. Then I want you to watch just an ordinary person. Notice how he moves his eyes, arms, fingers; notice the useless expenditure of energy. These movements lessen the person's power in vital and nerve directions. Center your mind on one purpose, one plan, one transaction.

There is nothing that uses up nerve force so quickly as excitement. This is why an irritable person is never magnetic; he is never admired or loved; he does not develop those finer qualities that a real gentleman possesses. Anger, sarcasm, and excitement weaken a person in this direction. The person that allows himself to get excited will become nervous in time, because he uses up his nerve forces and his vital energies. The person that cannot control himself and keep from becoming excited cannot concentrate.

But those whose actions are slower and directed by their intelligence develop concentration. Sometimes dogmatic, willful, excitable persons can concentrate, but it is spasmodic, erratic concentration instead of controlled and uniform concentration. Their energy works by spells; sometimes they have plenty, other times very little; it is easily excited; easily wasted. The best way to understand it is to compare it with the discharge of a gun. If the gun goes off when you want it to, it accomplishes the purpose, but if it goes off before you are ready, you not only waste ammunition, but are also likely to do some damage. That is just what most people do. They allow their energy to explode, thus not only wasting it, but also endangering others. They waste their power, their magnetism, and so injure their chance of success.

The brain is the storehouse of the energy. Most all persons have all the dynamic energy they need if they would concentrate it. They have the machine, but they must also have the engineer, or they will not go very far. The engineer is the self-regulating, directing power. The good engineer controls his every act. By what you do you either advance or degenerate. This is a good idea to keep always in mind. When you are uncertain whether you should do something, just think whether by doing it you will grow or deteriorate, and act accordingly.

I am a firm believer in "work when you work, play when you play." When you give yourself up to pleasure you can develop concentration by thinking of nothing else but pleasure; when your mind dwells on love, think of nothing but this and you will find you can develop a more intense love than you ever had before. When you concentrate your mind on the "you" or real self, and its wonderful possibilities, you develop concentration and a higher opinion of yourself. By doing this systematically, you develop power, because you cannot be systematic without concentrating on what you are doing. When you walk out into the country and inhale the fresh air, studying vegetation, trees, etc., you are concentrating. Whenever you fix your mind on a certain thought and hold your mind on it at successive intervals, you develop concentration.

If you hold your mind on some chosen object, you centralize your attention, just like the lens of the camera centralizes on a certain landscape. Therefore, always hold your mind on what you are doing, no matter what it is.

Practice inhaling long, deep breaths, not simply for the improvement of health, although that is no small matter, but also for the purpose of developing more power, more love, more life. All work assists in development.

If you want to get more out of life you must think more of love. Unless you have real affection for something, you have no sentiment, no sweetness, no magnetism. So arouse your love affections by your will, and enter into a fuller life.

The next time you feel yourself becoming irritable, use your will and be patient. This is a very good exercise in self-control. It will help you to keep patient if you will breathe slowly and deeply. If you find you are commencing to speak fast, just control yourself and speak slowly and clearly. Keep from either raising or lowering your voice, and concentrate on the fact that you are determined to keep your poise, and you will improve your power of concentration.

If you feel yourself getting irritable, nervous or weak, stand squarely on your feet with your chest up and inhale deeply, and you will see that your irritability will disappear and a silent calm will pass over you.

If you are in the habit of associating with nervous, irritable people, quit it until you grow strong in the power of concentration, because irritable, angry, fretful, dogmatic, and disagreeable people will weaken what powers of resistance you have.

When your eye is steady, your mind is steady. One of the best ways to study a person is to watch his physical movements, for, when we study his actions, we are studying his mind. Because actions are the expressions of the mind. As the mind is, so is the action. When you learn to control the body, you are gaining control over the mind.

## Lesson III
# How to Gain What You Want Through Concentration

The ignorant person may say, "How can you get anything by merely wanting it?" I say that through concentration you can get anything you want. Every desire can be gratified. But whether it is, will depend upon you concentrating to have that desire fulfilled. Merely wishing for something will not bring it. Wishing you had something shows a weakness, and not a belief that you will really get it. So never merely wish, as we are not living in a "fairy age." You use up just as much brain force in "vain imaginings" as you do when you think of something worthwhile.

Be careful of your desires, make a mental picture of what you want and set your will to this until it materializes. Never allow yourself to drift without helm or rudder. Know what you want to do, and strive with all your might to do it, and you will succeed.

Feel that you can accomplish anything you undertake. Many undertake to do things, but feel when they start they are going to fail, and usually they do. I will give an illustration. A man goes to a store for an article. The clerk says, "I am sorry, we do not have it." But the man that is determined to get that thing inquires if he doesn't know where he can get it. Again receiving an unsatisfactory answer the determined buyer consults the manager, and finally finds where the article can be bought.

That is the whole secret of concentrating on getting what you want. And, remember, your soul is a center of all-power, and you can accomplish what you will to. "I'll find a way or make one!" is the spirit that wins. I know a man who is now head of a large bank. He started there as a messenger boy. His father had a button made for him with a "P" on it and put it on his coat. He said, "Son, that 'P' is a reminder that some day you are to be the president of your bank. I want you to keep this thought in your mind. Every day do something that will put you nearer your goal." Each night after supper he would say, "Son, what did you do today?" In this way the thought was always kept in mind. He concentrated on becoming president of that bank, and he did. His father told him never to tell anyone what that "P" stood for. His associates made a good deal of fun of it. And they tried to find out what it stood for, but they never did until he was made president, and then he told the secret.

Don't waste your mental powers in wishes. Don't dissipate your energies by trying to satisfy every whim. Concentrate on doing something really worthwhile. The man that sticks to something is not the man that fails.

> "Power to him who power exerts."
> —EMERSON

This great universe is interwoven with myriad forces. You make your own place, and whether it is important depends upon you. Through the Indestructible and Unconquerable Law you can, in time, accomplish all right things, and therefore do not be afraid to undertake whatever you really desire to accomplish and are willing to pay for in effort. *Anything that is right is possible.* That which is necessary will inevitably take place. If something is right, it is your duty to do it, though the whole world thinks it to be wrong.

"God and one are always a majority," or in plain words, that omnipotent interior law which is God, and the organism that represents you, is able to conquer the whole world if your cause is absolutely just. Don't say, "I wish I were great." You can do anything that is proper, and that you want to. Just say: You can. You will. You must. *Realize this* and the rest is easy.

## Lesson IV
# The Silent Force That Produces Results

Through concentrated thought power you can make yourself whatever you please. By thought you can greatly increase your efficiency and strength. You are surrounded by all kinds of thoughts, some good, others bad, and you are sure to absorb some of the latter if you do not build up a positive mental attitude.

If you will study the needless moods of anxiety, worry, despondency, discouragement, and others that are the result of uncontrolled thoughts, you will realize how important the control of your thoughts are. Your thoughts make you what you are.

When I walk along the street and study the different people's faces I can tell how they spent their lives. It all shows in their faces, just like a mirror reflects their physical countenances. In looking in those faces I cannot help thinking how most of the people you see have wasted their lives.

Understanding the power of thought will awaken possibilities within you that you never dreamed of. Never forget that your thoughts are making your environment and your friends, and as your thoughts change these will also. The desire to do right carries with it a great power. I want you to thoroughly realize the importance of your thoughts, and how to make them valuable, to understand that your thoughts come to you over invisible wires and influence you.

In order to speak wisely you must secure at least a partial concentration of the faculties and forces upon the subject at hand. Speech interferes with the focusing powers of the mind, as it withdraws the attention to the external and therefore is hardly to be compared with that deep silence of the subconscious mind, where deep thoughts, and the silent forces of high potency, are evolved. It is necessary to be silent before you can speak wisely. The person who is really alert, well poised, and able to speak wisely under trying circumstances, is the person who has practiced in the silence. Most people do not know what the silence is and think it is easy to go into the silence, but this is not so. In the real silence, we become attached to that interior law and the forces become silent, because they are in a state of high potency. Hold the thought: In-silence-I-will-allow-my-higher-self-to-have-complete-control. I-will-be-true-to-my-higher-self. I-will-live-true-to-my-conception-of-what-is-right. I-realize-that-it-is-in-my-self-interest-to-live-up-to-my-best. I-demand-wisdom-so-that-I-may-act-wisely-for-myself-and-others.

In the next chapter, I tell you of the mysterious law that links all humanity together by the powers of cooperative thought, and chooses for us companionship and friends.

## Lesson V
# How Concentrated Thought Links All Humanity

Success is the result of how you think. I will show you how to think to be successful.

The power to rule and attract success is within yourself. The barriers that shut these off from you are subject to your control. You have unlimited power to think, and this is the link that connects you with your omniscient source.

Success is the result of certain moods of mind or ways of thinking. These moods can be controlled by you, and produced at will.

Concentrated thought will accomplish seemingly impossible results and make you realize your fondest ambitions. At the same time that you break down barriers of limitation new ambitions will be awakened. If you will just realize that through deep concentration you become linked with thoughts of omnipotence, you will kill out entirely your belief in your limitations, and at the same time will drive away all fear and other negative and destructive thought forces, which constantly work against you.

It is just as easy to surround your life with what you want as it is with what you don't. It is a question to be decided by your will. There are no walls to prevent you from getting what you want, *providing you want what is right*. If you choose something that is not right, you are in opposition to the omnipotent plans of the universe, and deserve to fail. *But, if you base your desires on justice and good will, you avail yourself of the helpful powers of universal currents, and instead of having a handicap to work against, can depend upon ultimate success, though the outward appearances may not at first be bright.*

Never stop to think of temporary appearances, but maintain an unfaltering belief in your ultimate success. Make your plans carefully, and see that they are not contrary to the tides of universal justice. The main thing for you to remember is to keep at bay the destructive and opposing forces of fear, anger, and their satellites.

There is no power so great as the belief which comes from the knowledge that your thought is in harmony with the divine laws of thought, and the sincere conviction that your cause is right.

All just causes succeed in time, though temporarily they may fail. So if you should face the time when everything seems against you, quiet your fears, drive away all destructive thoughts, and uphold the dignity of your moral and spiritual life.

The following method may assist you in gaining better thought control. If you are unable to control your fears, just say to your faulty determination, "Do not falter or be afraid, for I am not really alone. I am surrounded by invisible forces that will assist me to remove the unfavorable appearances." Soon you will have more courage. The only difference between the fearless man and the fearful one is in his will, his hope. So if you lack success, believe in it, hope for it, claim it. You can use the same method to brace up your thoughts of desire, aspiration, imagination, expectation, ambition, understanding, trust, and assurance.

If you get anxious, angry, discouraged, undecided or worried, it is because you are not receiving the cooperation of the higher powers of your mind. By your Will you can so organize the powers of the mind that your moods change only as you want them to instead of as circumstances affect you. If you allow the mind to wander while you are doing small things, it will be likely to get into mischief and make it hard to concentrate on the important act when it comes.

The will does not act with clearness, decision and promptness *unless it is trained to do so.* Comparatively few people really know what they are doing every minute of the day. This is because they do not observe with sufficient orderliness and accuracy. It is not difficult to know what you are doing all the time, if you will just practice concentration, and with a reposeful deliberation train yourself to think clearly, promptly, and decisively.

If you allow yourself to worry or hurry in what you are doing, it will not be clearly photographed upon the sensitized plate of the subjective mind, and therefore you will not be really conscious of your actions. So practice accuracy and concentration of thought, and also absolute truthfulness, and you will soon be able to concentrate.

## Lesson VI
# The Training of the Will to Do

The Will To Do is the greatest power in the world that is concerned with human accomplishment, and no one can predetermine its limits.

The Will To Do is a force that is strictly practical, yet it is difficult to explain just what it is. It can be compared to electricity because we know it only through its cause and effects. Every time you accomplish any definite act, consciously or unconsciously, you use the principle of the Will. You can Will to do anything, whether right or wrong, and therefore how you use your will makes a big difference in your life.

Every person possesses some "Will To Do." It is the inner energy that controls all conscious acts. *Genius is but a will to do little things with infinite pains. Little things done well open the door of opportunity for bigger things.*

Study yourself carefully. Find out your greatest weakness and then use your willpower to overcome it. In this way eradicate your faults, one by one, until you have built up a strong character and personality.

**Rules for Improvement.** A desire arises. Now think whether this would be good for you. If it is not, use your Willpower to kill out the desire; but, on the other hand, if it is a righteous desire, summon all your Willpower to your aid, crush all obstacles that confront you, and secure possession of the coveted Good.

**Slowness in Making Decisions.** This is a weakness of Willpower. You know you should do something, but you delay doing it through lack of decision. It is easier not to do a certain thing, but conscience says to do it. The vast majority of people are failures because of the lack of deciding to do a thing when it should be done. Those that are successful have been quick to grasp opportunities by making a quick decision. This power of will can be used to bring culture, wealth, and health.

**Some Special Pointers.** For the next week try to make quicker decisions in your little daily affairs. Set the hour you wish to get up and arise exactly at the fixed time. Anything that you should accomplish, do on or ahead of time. You want, of course, to give due deliberation to weighty matters, but by making quick decisions on little things you will acquire the ability to make quick decisions in bigger things.

**You Are as Good as Anyone.** You have willpower, and if you use it, you will get your share of the luxuries of life. So use it to claim your own. Don't depend on anyone else to help you. We have to fight our own battles. All the world loves a fighter, while the coward is despised by all. Every person's problems are different, so I can only say "analyze your opportunities and conditions and study your natural abilities." Don't make an indefinite plan, but a definite one, and then don't give up until your object has been accomplished. Put these suggestions into practice with true earnestness, and you will soon note astonishing results, and your whole life will be completely changed. An excellent motto for one of pure motives is: *Through my willpower I dare do what I want to.* You will find this affirmation has a very strengthening effect.

**The Spirit of Perseverance.** The spirit of "sticktoitiveness" is the one that wins. Many go just so far and then give up, whereas, if they had persevered a little longer, they would have won out. Many have much initiative, but instead of concentrating it into one channel they diffuse it through several, thereby dissipating it to such an extent that its effect is lost.

**Lack of Perseverance** is nothing but the lack of the Will To Do. It takes the same energy to say, "I will continue," as to say, "I give up." Just the moment you say the latter you shut off your dynamo, and your determination is gone. Every time you allow your determination to be broken you weaken it. Don't forget this. Just the instant you notice your determination beginning to weaken, concentrate on it and by sheer Will Power make it continue on the "job."

Never try to make a decision when you are not in a calm state of mind. If in a "quick temper," you are likely to say things you regret. In anger, you follow impulse rather than reason. No one can expect to achieve success if he makes decisions when not in full control of his mental forces. Therefore make it a fixed rule to make decisions only when at your best.

**Special Instructions to Develop the Will To Do.** This is a form of mental energy, but requires the proper mental attitude to make it manifest. We hear of people having wonderful willpower, which really is wrong. It should be said that they *use* their willpower, while with many it is a latent force. I want you to realize that no one has a monopoly on willpower. What we speak of as willpower is but the gathering together of mental energy, the concentration of power at one point. So never think of someone as having a stronger will than you. Each person will be supplied with just that amount of willpower that he demands.

## Lesson VII
# The Concentrated Mental Demand

The Mental Demand is the potent force in achievement. The attitude of the mind affects the expression of the face, determines action, changes our physical condition, and regulates our lives.

The mental demand must be directed by every power of the mind, and every possible element should be used to make the demand materialize. You can so intently desire a thing that you can exclude all distracting thoughts. When you practice this singleness of concentration until you attain the end sought, you have developed a Will capable of accomplishing whatever you wish.

The men looked upon as the world's successes have not always been men of great physical power, nor at the start did they seem very well adapted to the conditions around them. In the beginning, they were not considered men of superior genius, but they won their success by their resolution to achieve results by permitting no setback to dishearten them; no difficulties to daunt them. Nothing could turn them or influence them against their determination. They never lost sight of their goal. In all of us there is this silent force of wonderful power. If developed, it can overcome conditions that would seem insurmountable. It is constantly urging us on to greater achievement. The more we become acquainted with it the better strategists we become, the more courage we develop, and the greater the desire within us for self-expression along many lines.

No one will ever be a failure if he becomes conscious of this silent force within that controls his destiny. But without the consciousness of this inner force, you will not have a clear vision, and external conditions will not yield to the power of your mind. It is the mental resolve that makes achievement possible. Once this has been formed it should never be allowed to cease to press its claim until its object is attained.

Perseverance is the first element of success. In order to persevere you must be ceaseless in your application. It requires you to concentrate your thoughts upon your undertaking, and bring every energy to bear upon keeping them focused upon it until you have accomplished your aim. To quit short of this is to weaken all future efforts.

The Mental Demand seems an unreal power because it is intangible; but it is the mightiest power in the world. It is a power that is free for you to use. No one can use it for you. Every time you make a Mental Demand you strengthen the brain centers by drawing to you external forces.

Few realize the power of a Mental Demand. It is possible to make your demand so strong that you can impart what you have to say to another without speaking to him. Have you ever, after planning to discuss a certain matter with a friend, had the experience of having him broach the subject before you had a chance to speak of it? These things are neither coincidences nor accidents, but are the results of mental demand launched by strong concentration. The person that never wants anything gets little. To demand resolutely is the first step toward getting what you want.

Once the Mental Demand is made, however, never let it falter. If you do, the current that connects you with your desire is broken. Take all the necessary time to build a firm foundation, so that there need not be even an element of doubt to creep in. Just the moment you entertain "doubt" you lose some of the demand force, and force once lost is hard to regain. So whenever you make a mental demand hold steadfastly to it until your need is supplied.

And every man of AVERAGE ability, the ordinary man that you see about you, can be really successful, independent, free of worry, HIS OWN MASTER, if he can manage to do just two things: First, remain forever dissatisfied with what he IS doing and with what he HAS accomplished. Second, develop in his mind a belief that the word "impossible" was not intended for him. Build up in his mind the confidence that enables the mind to use its power.

Lesson VIII

# Concentration Gives Mental Poise

You will find that the man that concentrates is well poised, whereas the man that allows his mind to wander is easily upset. When in this state wisdom does not pass from the subconscious storehouse into the consciousness. There must be mental quiet before the two forms of consciousness can work in harmony. When you are able to concentrate, you have peace of mind.

If you are in the habit of losing your poise, form the habit of reading literature that has a quieting power. Just the second you feel your poise slipping, say, "Peace," and then hold this thought in mind and you will never lose your self-control. Think of yourself as a child of the infinite, possessing infinite possibilities. Write on a piece of paper, "I have the power to do and to be whatever I wish to do and be." Keep this mentally before you, and you will find the thought will be of great help to you.

**The Mistake of Concentrating on Your Business While Away.** In order to be successful today, you must concentrate, but don't become a slave to concentration, and carry your business cares home. Just as sure as you do, you will be burning the life forces at both ends, and the fire will go out much sooner than intended.

Many men become so absorbed in their business that when they go to church they do not hear the preacher because their minds are on their business. If they go to the theater they do not enjoy it because their business is on their minds. When they go to bed they think about business instead of sleep. This is the wrong kind of concentration and is dangerous. It is involuntary. It is a big mistake to let a thought rule you, instead of ruling it. He who does not rule himself is not a success. If you cannot control your concentration, your health will suffer.

Never become so absorbed with anything that you cannot lay it aside and take up another. This is self-control. Concentration is paying attention to a chosen thought.

**Self-Study Valuable.** Everyone has some habits that can be overcome by concentration. We will say for instance, you are in the habit of complaining, or finding fault with yourself or others; or, imagining that you do not possess the ability of others; or feeling that you are not as good as someone else; or that you cannot rely on yourself; or harboring any similar thoughts. These should be cast aside, and instead thoughts of strength should be put in their place. Just remember that every time you think of yourself as being weak, in some way you are making yourself so. Our mental conditions make us what we are. Just watch yourself and see how much time you waste in worrying, fretting, and complaining. The more of it you do, the worse off you are.

Just the minute you are aware of thinking a negative thought immediately change to a positive one. If you start to think of failure, change to thinking of success. You have the germ of success within you. Care for it the same as the setting hen broods over the eggs, and you can make it a reality.

You can make those that you come in contact with feel as you do, because you radiate vibrations of the way you feel, and your vibrations are felt by others. When you concentrate on a certain thing you turn all the rays of your vibrations on this. Thought is the directing power of all Life's vibrations. If a person should enter a room with a lot of people and feel as if he were a person of no consequence, no one would know he was there unless they saw him; and even if they did, they would not remember seeing him, because they were not attracted towards him. But let him enter the room feeling that he was magnetic and concentrating on this thought, others would feel his vibration. So remember, the way you feel you can make others feel.

If you will study all of the great characters of history you will find that they were enthusiastic. First, they were enthusiastic themselves, and then they could arouse others' enthusiasm. It is latent in everyone. It is a wonderful force when once aroused. This is the keynote of success.

"Think, speak, and act just as you wish to be, And you will be that which you wish to be."

You are just what you think you are, and not what you may appear to be. You may fool others, but not yourself. You may control your life and actions just as you can control your hands. If you want to raise your hand, you must first think of raising it. If you want to control your life, you must first control your thinking. Easy to do, is it not? Yes it is, if you will but concentrate on what you think about.

How can we secure concentration? To this question, the first and last answer must be: by interest and strong motive. The stronger the motive, the greater the concentration.

**Successful Lives Are the Concentrated Lives.** Train yourself so that you will be able to centralize your thought, develop your brainpower, and increase your mental energy, or you can be a slacker, a drifter, a quitter, or a sleeper. It all depends on how you concentrate, or centralize your thoughts. Your thinking then becomes a fixed power and you do not waste time thinking about something that would not be good for you. You pick out the thoughts that will be the means of bringing you what you desire, and they become a material reality. Whatever we create in the thought world will some day materialize. That is the law. Never forget this.

**Why People Often Do Not Get What They Concentrate On.** Because they sit down in hopeless despair and expect it to come to them. But if they will just reach out for it with their biggest effort they will find it is within their reach. No one limits us but ourselves.

Through our concentration we can attract what we want, because we became en rapport with the Universal forces, from which we can get what we want.

A man starts to think on a certain subject. He has all kinds of thoughts come to him, but by concentration he shuts out all these but the one he has chosen. Concentration is just a case of willing to do a certain thing, and doing it.

If you want to accomplish anything, first put yourself in a concentrating, reposeful, receptive, acquiring frame of mind. In tackling unfamiliar work make haste slowly and deliberately, and then you will secure that interior activity, which is never possible when you are in a hurry or under a strain. When you "think hard," or try to hurry results too quickly, you generally shut off the interior flow of thoughts and ideas. You have often no doubt tried hard to think of something but could not, but just as soon as you stopped trying to think of it, it came to you.

## Lesson IX
# Concentration Can Overcome Bad Habits

Habits make or break us to a far greater extent than we like to admit. Habit is both a powerful enemy and wonderful ally of concentration. You must learn to overcome habits that are injurious to concentration, and to cultivate those that increase it.

Most people are controlled by their habits, and are buffeted around by them like waves of the ocean tossing a piece of wood. They do things in a certain way because of the power of habit. They seldom ever think of concentrating on why they do them this or that way, or study to see if they could do them in a better way.

The first thing I want you to realize is that all habits are governed consciously or unconsciously by the will. Most of us are forming new habits all the time. Very often, if you repeat something several times in the same way, you will have formed the habit of doing it that way. But the oftener you repeat it the stronger that habit grows, and the more deeply it becomes embedded in your nature. After a habit has been in force for a long time, it becomes almost a part of you, and is therefore hard to overcome. But you can still break any habit by strong concentration on its opposite.

You will find the following maxims worth remembering.

**First Maxim:** "We must make our nervous system our ally instead of our enemy."

**Second Maxim:** "In the acquisition of a new habit as in the leaving off of an old one, we must take care to launch ourselves with as strong and decided an initiative as possible."

Surround yourself with every aid you can. Don't play with fire by forming bad habits. Make a new beginning today. Study why you have been doing certain things. If they are not for your good, shun them henceforth. Don't give in to a single temptation, for every time you do, you strengthen the chain of bad habits. Every time you keep a resolution you break the chain that enslaves you.

**Third Maxim:** "Never allow an exception to occur till the new habit is securely rooted in your life."

**Fourth Maxim:** "Seize the very first possible opportunity to act on every resolution you make, and on every emotional prompting you may experience in the direction of the habits you aspire to gain."

Keep every resolution you make, for you not only profit by the resolution, but it furnishes you with an exercise that causes the brain cells and physiological correlatives to form the habit of adjusting themselves to carry out resolutions. A tendency to act becomes effectively engrained in us in proportion to the uninterrupted frequency with which the actions actually occur, and the brain "grows" to their use.

**Fifth Maxim:** "Keep the faculty of effort alive in you by a little gratuitous exercise every day."

The more we exercise the will, the better we can control our habits. Every few days, do something for no other reason than its difficulty, so that when the hour of dire need draws near, it may find you not unnerved or untrained to stand the test. Asceticism of this sort is like the insurance that a man pays on his house and goods. So with the man who has daily insured himself to habits of concentrated attention, energetic volition, and self-denial in unnecessary things.

Habits have often been called a labor-saving invention, because when they are formed they require less of both mental and material strength. The more deeply the habit becomes ingrained, the more automatic it becomes. Therefore habit is an economizing tendency of our nature, for if it were not for habit we should have to be more watchful. We walk across a crowded street; the habit of stopping and looking prevents us from being hurt. Habits mean less risk, less fatigue, and greater accuracy.

In order to overcome undesirable habits, two things are necessary. You must have trained your will to do what you want it to do, and the stronger the will the easier it will be to break a habit. Then you must make a resolution to do just the opposite of what the habit is. I will bring this chapter to a close by giving Doctor Oppenheim's instructions for overcoming a habit:

"If you want to abolish a habit, and its accumulated circumstances as well, you must grapple with the matter as earnestly as you would with a physical enemy. You must go into the encounter with all tenacity of determination, with all fierceness of resolve—and yea, even with a passion for success that may be called vindictive. No human enemy can be as insidious, so persevering, as unrelenting as an unfavorable habit. It never sleeps, it needs no rest.

"It is like a parasite that grows with the growth of the supporting body, and, like a parasite, it can best be killed by violent separation and crushing."

It is not in the easy, contented moments of our life that we make our greatest progress, for then it requires no special effort to keep in tune. But it is when we are in the midst of trials and misfortunes, when we think we are sinking, being overwhelmed, then it is important for us to realize that we are linked to a great Power, and if we live as we should, there is nothing that can occur in life that could permanently injure us, nothing can happen that should disturb us. Always remember you have within you unlimited power, ready to manifest itself in the form which fills our need at the moment.

### Lesson X
# Business Results Through Concentration

Business success depends on well-concentrated efforts. You must use every mental force you can master. The more these are used, the more they increase. Therefore the more you accomplish today the more force you will have at your disposal to solve your problems tomorrow. Then when you have resolved what you want to do, you will be drawn towards it. There is a law that opens the way to the fulfillment of your desires. Of course, back of your desire you must put forward the necessary effort to carry out your purpose; you must use your power to put your desires into force. Once they are created, and you keep up your determination to have them fulfilled, you both consciously and unconsciously work toward their materialization. Set your heart on your purpose, concentrate your thought upon it, direct your efforts with all your intelligence, and in due time you will realize your ambition.

Feel yourself a success, believe you are a success, and thus put yourself in the attitude that demands recognition and the thought current draws to you what you need to make you a success. Don't be afraid of big undertakings. Go at them with grit, and pursue methods that you think will accomplish your purpose. You may not at first meet with entire success, but aim so high that if you fall a little short you will still have accomplished much.

What others have done you can do. You may even do what others have been unable to do. Always keep a strong desire to succeed in your mind. Be in love with your aim and work, and make it, as far as possible, square with the rule of the greatest good to the greatest number, and your life cannot be a failure.

The successful business attitude must be cultivated to make the most out of your life: the attitude of expecting great things from both yourself and others. This alone will often cause men to make good; to measure up to the best that is in them.

It is not the spasmodic spurts that count on a long journey, but the steady efforts. Spurts fatigue, and make it hard for you to continue.

When once you reach a conclusion abide by it. Let there be no doubt, or wavering. If you are uncertain about every decision you make, you will be subject to harassing doubts and fears, which will render your judgment of little value. The man that decides according to what he thinks right, and who learns from every mistake, acquires a well-balanced mind that gets the best results. He gains the confidence of others. He is known as the man who knows what he wants, and not as one that is as changeable as the weather. Reliable firms want to do business with men of known qualities, with men of firmness, judgment, and reliability.

So, if you wish to start in business for yourself, your greatest asset, with the single exception of a sound physique, is that of a good reputation.

A successful business is not hard to build if we can concentrate all our mental forces upon it. We hear people say that business is trying on the nerves, but it is the unsettling elements of fret, worry, and suspense that are nerve exhausting, and not the business. Executing one's plans may cause fatigue, but enjoyment comes with rest. If there has not been any unnatural strain, the recuperative powers replace what energy has been lost.

By attending to each day's work properly, you develop the capacity to do a greater work tomorrow. It is this gradual development that makes possible the carrying out of big plans.

Even brilliant men's conceptions of the possibilities of their mental forces are so limited and below their real worth that they are far more likely to belittle their possibilities than they are to exaggerate them. You don't want to think that an aim is impossible because it has never been realized in the past. Everyday someone is doing something that was never done before.

The natural leader always draws to himself, by the law of mental attraction, all the ideas in his chosen subject that have ever been conceived by others. This is of the greatest importance and help. If you are properly trained you benefit much by others' thoughts, and, providing you generate from within yourself something of value, they will benefit from yours. "We are heirs of all the ages," but we must know how to use our inheritance.

The confident, pushing, hopeful, determined man influences all with whom he associates, and inspires the same qualities in them. There is no reason why your work or business should burn you out. When it does, something is wrong. You are attracting forces and influence that you should not, because you are not in harmony with what you are doing. There is nothing so tiring as trying to do work for which we are unfitted both by temperament and training.

Each one should be engaged in a business that he loves; he should be furthering movements with which he is in sympathy. Only then will he do his best, and take intense pleasure in his business. In this way, while constantly growing and developing his powers, he is at the same time rendering through his work genuine and devoted service to humanity.

## Lesson XI
# Concentrate On Your Courage

Courage is the backbone of man. The man with courage has persistence. He states what he believes, and puts it into execution.

Lack of courage creates financial, as well as mental and moral difficulties. When a new problem comes, instead of looking upon it as something to be achieved, the man or woman without courage looks for reasons why it cannot be done, and failure is naturally the almost inevitable result. This is a subject well worth your study. Look upon everything within your power as a possibility, and you will accomplish a great deal more, because by considering a thing as impossible you immediately draw to yourself all the elements that contribute to failure. Lack of courage destroys your confidence in yourself.

The man without courage unconsciously draws to himself all that is contemptible, weakening, demoralizing, and destructive. We must first have the courage to *strongly desire something*. A desire to be fulfilled must be backed by the strength of all our mental forces. Such a desire has enough commanding force to change all unfavorable conditions.

What is courage? It is the *Will To Do*. It takes no more energy to be courageous than to be cowardly. It is a matter of the right training, in the right way. Courage concentrates the mental forces on the task at hand. It then directs them thoughtfully, steadily, deliberately, while attracting all the forces of success toward the desired end.

As we are creatures of habits, we should avoid people who lack courage. They are easy to discover because of their habits of fear in attacking new problems. The man with courage is never afraid.

Start out today with the idea that there is no reason why you should not be courageous. If any fear-thoughts come to you, cast them off as you would the deadly viper. Form the habit of never thinking of anything unfavorable to yourself or anyone else. In dealing with difficulties, new or old, hold ever the thought: "I am courageous." Whenever a doubt crosses the threshold of your mind, banish it. Remember, you as master of your mind control its every thought, and here is a good one to often affirm: "I have courage because I desire it; because I need it; because I use it; and because I refuse to become such a weakling as cowardice produces."

There is no justification for the loss of courage. The evils by which you will almost certainly be overwhelmed without it are far greater than those which courage will help you to meet and overcome. Right, then, must be the moralist who says that the only thing to fear is fear.

Never let another's opinion affect you; he cannot tell what you are able to do; he does not know what you can do with your forces. The truth is, you do not know yourself until you put yourself to the test. Therefore, how can someone else know? Never let anyone else put a valuation on you.

Almost all wonderful achievements have been accomplished after it had been "thoroughly" demonstrated that they were impossibilities. Once we understand the law, all things are possible. If they were impossibilities, we could not conceive them.

Just the moment you allow someone to influence you against what you think is right, you lose that confidence that inspires courage and carries with it all the forces that courage creates. Just the moment you begin to swerve in your plan you begin to carry out another's thought, and not your own. You become the directed and not the director. You forsake the courage and resolution of your own mind, and you therefore lack the very forces that you need to sustain and carry out your work. Instead of being self-reliant you become timid, and this invites failure. When you permit yourself to be influenced from your plan by another, you are unable to judge as you should, because you have allowed another's influence to deprive you of your courage and determination without absorbing any of his in return, so you are in much the same predicament as you would be in if you turned over all your worldly possessions to another without getting value received.

Concentrate on just the opposite of fear, want, poverty, sickness, etc. Never doubt your own ability. You have plenty, *if you will just use it*. A great many men are failures because they doubt their own capacity. Instead of building up strong mental forces, which would be of the greatest use to them, their fear thoughts tear them down. Fear paralyzes energy. It keeps us from attracting the forces that make success. Fear is the worst enemy we have.

Few people really know that they can accomplish much. They desire the full extent of their powers, but alas, it is only occasionally that you find a man who is aware of the great possibilities within him. When you believe with all your mind and heart and soul that you can do something, you thereby develop the courage to steadily and confidently live up to that belief. You have now gone a long way towards accomplishing it. Strong courage eliminates the injurious and opposing forces by summoning their masters, the yet-stronger forces that will serve you.

Courage is yours for the asking. All you have to do is to believe in it, claim it, and use it. One man of courage can fire with his spirit a whole army of men, whether military or industrial, because courage, like cowardice, is contagious.

## Lesson XII
# Concentrate on Wealth

It was never intended that man should be poor. When wealth is obtained under the proper conditions, it broadens the life. Everything has its value. Everything has a good use and a bad use. The forces of mind, like wealth, can be directed either for good or evil. A little rest will re-create forces. Too much rest degenerates into laziness, and brainless, dreamy longings.

So, the first step toward acquiring wealth is to surround yourself with helpful influences; to claim for yourself an environment of culture, place yourself in it, and be molded by its influences.

Wealth is usually the fruit of achievement. It is not, however, altogether the result of being industrious. Thousands of persons work hard who never grow wealthy. Others with much less effort acquire wealth. Seeing possibilities is another step toward acquiring wealth. A man may be as industrious as he can possibly be, but if he does not use his mental forces he will be a laborer, to be directed by the man who uses to good advantage his mental forces.

No one can become wealthy in an ordinary lifetime by mere savings from earnings. Many scrimp and economize all their lives; but by so doing waste all their vitality and energy. For example, I know a man who used to walk to work. It took him an hour to go and an hour to return. He could have taken a car and gone in twenty minutes. He saved ten cents a day, but wasted an hour and a half. It was not a very profitable investment, unless the time spent in physical exercise yielded him large returns in the way of health.

The same amount of time spent in concentrated effort to overcome his unfavorable business environment might have firmly planted his feet in the path of prosperity.

One of the big mistakes made by many people is that they associate with those who fail to call out or develop the best that is in them. When the social side of life is developed too exclusively, and recreation or entertainment becomes the leading motive of a person's life, he acquires habits of extravagance instead of economy; habits of wasting his resources, physical, mental, moral, and spiritual, instead of conserving them.

The other day I attended a lecture on Prosperity. I knew the lecturer had been practically broke for ten years. I wanted to hear what he had to say. He spoke very well. He no doubt benefited some of his hearers, but he had not profited by his own teachings. I introduced myself and asked him if he believed in his maxims. He said he did. I asked him if they had made him prosperous. He said not exactly. I asked him why. He answered that he thought he was fated not to experience prosperity.

In half an hour, I showed that man why poverty had always been his companion. He had dressed poorly. He held his lectures in poor surroundings. By his actions and beliefs he attracted poverty. He did not realize that his thoughts and his surroundings exercised an unfavorable influence. I said: "Thoughts are moving forces; great powers. Thoughts of wealth attract wealth. Therefore, if you desire wealth you must attract the forces that will help you to secure it. Your thoughts attract a similar kind of thoughts. If you hold thoughts of poverty you attract poverty. If you make up your mind you are going to be wealthy, you will instill this thought into all your mental forces, and you will at the same time use every external condition to help you."

Business success depends on foresight, good judgment, grit, firm resolution, and settled purpose. But never forget that thought is as real a force as electricity. Let your thoughts be such that you will send out as good as you receive; if you do not, you are not enriching others, and therefore deserve not to be enriched.

Again I repeat that the first as well as the last step in acquiring wealth is to surround yourself with good influences—good thought, good health, good home and business environment, and successful business associates. Cultivate, by every legitimate means, the acquaintance of men of big caliber. Bring your thought vibrations in regard to business into harmony with theirs. This will make your society not only agreeable, but sought after, and, when you have formed intimate friendships with clean, reputable men of wealth, entrust to them, for investment, your surplus earnings, however small, until you have developed the initiative and business acumen to successfully manage your own investments. By this time you will, through such associations, have found your place in life which, if you have rightly concentrated upon and used your opportunities, will not be among men of small parts.

There is somewhere in every brain the energy that will get you out of that rut and put you far up on the mountain of success, if you can only use the energy. And hope, self-confidence, and the determination to do something supply the spark that makes the energy work.

## Lesson XIII
# You Can Concentrate, But Will You?

All have the ability to concentrate, but will you? You can, but whether you will or not depends on you. It is one thing to be able to do something, another to do it. There is far more ability not used than is used. Why do not more men of ability make something of themselves? There are comparatively few successful men, but many ambitious ones. Why do not more get along? Cases may differ, but the fault is usually their own. They have had chances, perhaps better ones than some others that have made good.

What would you like to do that you are not doing? If you think you should be "getting on" better, why don't you? Study yourself carefully. Learn your shortcomings. Sometimes only a mere trifle keeps one from branching out and becoming a success. Discover why you have not been making good—the cause of your failure. Have you been expecting someone to lead you, or to make a way for you? If you have, concentrate on a new line of thought.

There are two things absolutely necessary for success—energy and the will to succeed. Nothing can take the place of either of these.

When we see those with handicaps amounting to something great in the world, the able-bodied man should feel ashamed of himself if he does not make good. There is nothing that can resist the force of perseverance. The way ahead for all of us is not clear sailing, but all hard passages can be bridged.

Many men will not begin an undertaking unless they feel sure they will succeed in it. What a mistake! This would be right, if we were sure of what we could and could not do. But who knows? *There may be an obstruction there now that might not be there next week. There may not be an obstruction there now that will be there next week.* The trouble with most people is that just as soon as they see their way blocked they lose courage. They forget that usually there is a way around the difficulty. It's up to you to find it. If you tackle something with little effort, when the conditions call for a big effort, you will, of course, not win. Tackle everything with a feeling that you will use all the power within you to make it a success. This is the kind of concentrated effort that succeeds.

Most people are beaten before they start. They think they are going to encounter obstacles, and they look for them instead of for means to overcome them. The result is that they increase their obstacles instead of diminishing them. Have you ever undertaken something that you thought would be hard, but afterwards found it easy? That is the way a great many times. Things that look difficult in advance turn out to be easy of conquest when once encountered. So start out on your journey with the idea that the road is going to be clear for you, and that if it is not you will clear the way.

The one great keynote of success is to do whatever you have decided on. Don't be turned from your path, but resolve that you are going to accomplish what you set out to do. Don't be frightened at a few rebuffs, for they cannot stop the man that is determined—the man that knows in his heart that success is only bought by tremendous resolution, by concentrated and wholehearted effort.

It is not so much skill that wins victories, as it is activity and great determination. There is no such thing as failure for the man who does his best. No matter what you may be working at, don't let this make you lose courage. *The tides are continually changing, and tomorrow or some other day they will turn to your advantage if you are a willing and ambitious worker.* There is nothing that develops you and increases your courage like work. If it were not for work how monotonous life would become!

So I say to the man who wants to advance: "Don't look upon your present position as your permanent one. Keep your eyes open, and add those qualities to your makeup that will assist you when your opportunity comes. Be ever alert and on the watch for opportunities. Remember, we attract what we set our minds on. If we look for opportunities, we find them."

## Lesson XIV
# The Art of Concentration with Practical Exercises

Select some thought, and see how long you can hold your mind on it. It is well to have a clock at first and keep track of the time. If you decide to think about health, you can get a great deal of good from your thinking besides developing concentration. Think of health as being the greatest blessing in the world. Don't let any other thought drift in. The moment one starts to obtrude, make it get out.

Make it a daily habit of concentrating on this thought for, say, ten minutes. Practice until you can hold it to the exclusion of everything else. You will find it of the greatest value to centralize your thoughts on health. Regardless of your present condition, see yourself as you would like to be, and be blind to everything else. You will find it hard at first to forget your ailments, if you have any, but after a short while you can shut out these negative thoughts and see yourself as you want to be. Each time you concentrate, you form a more perfect image of health, and, as you come into its realization, you become healthy, strong, and wholesome.

I want to impress upon your mind that the habit of forming mental images is of the greatest value. It has always been used by successful men of all ages, but few realize its full importance.

Do you know that you are continually acting according to the images you form? If you allow yourself to mold negative images, you unconsciously build a negative disposition. You will think of poverty, weakness, disease, fear, etc., just as surely as you think of these will your objective life express itself in a like way. Just what we think, we will manifest in the external world.

In deep concentration you become linked with the great creative spirit of the universe, and the creative energy then flows through you, vitalizing your creations into form. In deep concentration your mind becomes attuned with the infinite and registers the cosmic intelligence and receives its messages. You become so full of the cosmic energy that you are flooded with divine power. This is a most desired state. It is then we realize the advantages of being connected with the supra-consciousness. The supra-consciousness registers the higher cosmic vibrations. It is often referred to as the wireless station, the message recorded coming from the universal mind.

Watch yourself during the day and see that your muscles do not become tense or strained. See how easy and relaxed you can keep yourself. See how poised you can be at all times. Cultivate a self-poised manner, instead of a nervous, strained appearance. This mental feeling will improve your carriage and demeanor. Stop all useless gestures and movements of the body. These mean that you have not proper control over your body. After you have acquired this control, notice how "ill-at-ease" people are that have not gained this control.

Get rid of any habit you have of twitching or jerking any part of your body. You will find that you make many involuntary movements. You can quickly stop any of these by merely centering your attention on the thought: "I will not."

No matter what you may be doing, imagine that it is your chief object in life. Imagine you are not interested in anything else in the world but what you are doing. Do not let your attention get away from the work you are at. Your attention will no doubt be rebellious, but control it, and do not let it control you. When once you conquer the rebellious attention, you have achieved a greater victory than you can realize at the time.

By concentration you can control your temper. If you are one of those that flare up at the slightest "provocation" and never try to control yourself, just think this over a minute. Does it do you any good? Do you gain anything by it? Doesn't it put you out of poise for some time? Don't you know that this grows on you, and will eventually make you despised by all that have any dealings with you?

Many of you that read this may think you are not guilty of either of these faults, but if you will carefully watch yourself, you will probably find that you are, and, if so, you will be greatly helped by repeating this affirmation each morning:

"I am going to try today not to make a useless gesture or to worry over trifles, or become nervous or irritable. I intend to be calm, and, no difference what may be the circumstances, I will control myself. Henceforth, I resolve to be free from all signs that show lack of self-control."

Now, a word on needless talking. It seems natural to want to tell others what you know; but, by learning to control these desires, you can wonderfully strengthen your powers of concentration. Remember, you have all you can do to attend to your own business. Do not waste your time in thinking of others, or in gossiping about them.

If, from your own observation, you learn something about another person that is detrimental, keep it to yourself. Your opinion may afterwards turn out to be wrong anyway; but whether right or wrong, you have strengthened your will by controlling your desire to communicate your views.

If you hear good news, resist the desire to tell it to the first person you meet and you will be benefited thereby. It will require the concentration of all your powers of resistance to prohibit the desire to tell. After you feel that you have complete control over your desires, you can then tell your news. But you must be able to suppress the desire to communicate the news until you are fully ready to tell it. Persons that do not possess this power of control over desires are apt to tell things that they should not, thereby often involving both themselves and others in needless trouble.

If you are in the habit of getting excited when you hear unpleasant news, just control yourself and receive it without any exclamation of surprise. Say to yourself, "Nothing is going to cause me to lose my self-control." You will find from experience that this self-control will be worth much to you in business. You will be looked upon as a cool-headed businessman, and this in time becomes a valuable asset. Of course, circumstances alter cases. At times it is necessary to become enthused. But be ever on the lookout for opportunities for the practice of self-control. "He that ruleth his spirit is greater than he that ruleth a city."

## Lesson XV
# Concentrate So You Will Not Forget

We remember only that which makes a deep impression; hence we must first deepen our impressions by associating in our minds certain ideas that are related to them.

Let's say a wife gives her husband a letter to mail. He does not think about it, but automatically puts it in his pocket and forgets all about it. When the letter was given to him had he said to himself, "I will mail this letter. The box is at the next corner and when I pass it I must drop this letter," it would have enabled him to recall the letter the instant he reached the mailbox.

The same rule holds good in regard to more important things. For example, if you are instructed to drop in and see Mr. Smith while out to lunch today, you will not forget it, if, at the moment the instruction is given, you say to yourself something similar to this: "When I get to the corner of Blank Street, on my way to lunch, I shall turn to the right and call on Mr. Smith." In this way the impression is made, the connection established, and the sight of the associated object recalls the errand.

The important thing to do is to deepen the impression at the very moment it enters your mind. This is made possible not only by concentrating the mind upon the idea itself, but by surrounding it with all possible association of ideas, so that each one will reinforce the others.

The mind is governed by laws of association, such as the law that ideas that enter the mind at the same time emerge at the same time, one assisting in recalling the others. You can train yourself to remember in this way by the concentration of the attention on your purpose, in accordance with the laws of association.

## Lesson XVI
# How Concentration Can Fulfill Your Desire

It is a spiritual law that the desire to do necessarily implies the ability to do."

All natural desires can be realized. It would be wrong for the Infinite to create wants that could not be supplied. Man's very soul is in his power to think, and it, therefore, is the essence of all created things. Every instinct of man leads to thought, and in every thought there is great possibility because true thought development, when allied to those mysterious powers which perhaps transcend it, has been the cause of all the world's true progress.

Silent, concentrated thought is more potent than spoken words, for speech distracts from the focusing power of the mind by drawing more and more attention to the without.

Man must learn more and more to depend on himself; to seek more for the Infinite within. It is from this source alone that he gains the power to solve his practical difficulties. No one should give up when there is always the resources of Infinity. The cause of failure is that men search in the wrong direction for success, because they are not conscious of their real powers, which when used are capable of guiding them.

The Infinite within is foreign to those who go through life without developing their spiritual powers. But the Infinite helps only he who helps himself. There is no such thing as a Special "Providence." Man will not receive help from the Infinite except to the extent that he believes and hopes and prays for help from this great source.

Remember that the first step in concentration is to form a Mental Image of what you wish to accomplish. This image becomes a thought-seed that attracts thoughts of a similar nature. Around this thought, when it is once planted in the imagination or creative region of the mind, you group or build associated thoughts, which continue to grow as long as your desire is keen enough to compel close concentration.

Form the habit of thinking of something you wish to accomplish for five minutes each day. Shut every other thought out of consciousness. Be confident that you will succeed; make up your mind that all obstacles will be overcome, and that you can rise above any environment.

A great aid in the development of concentration is to write out your thoughts on that which lies nearest your heart and to continue, little by little, to add to it until you have as nearly as possible exhausted the subject. You will find that each day as you focus your forces on this thought at the center of the stream of consciousness, new plans, ideas, and methods will flash into your mind.

We can attract those things that will help us. Very often we seem to receive help in a miraculous way. It may be slow in coming, but once the silent unseen forces are put into operation, they will bring results so long as we do our part. By forming a strong mental image of your desire, you plant the thought-seed that begins working in your interest and, in time, that desire, if in harmony with your higher nature, will materialize.

It may seem that it would be unnecessary to caution you to concentrate only upon achievement that will be good for you, and work no harm to another, but there are many who forget others and their rights, in their anxiety to achieve success. All good things are possible for you to have, but only as you bring your forces into harmony with that law that requires that we mete out justice to fellow travelers as we journey along life's road. So first think over the thing wanted and if it would be good for you to have. Say: "I want to do this; I am going to work to secure it. The way will be open for me."

If you fully grasp mentally the thought of success and hold it in mind each day, you gradually make a pattern or mold, which in time will materialize. But by all means keep free from doubt and fear, the destructive forces. Never allow these to become associated with your thoughts.

At last you will create the desired conditions, and receive help in many unlooked-for ways that will lift you out of the undesired environment. Life will then seem very different to you, for you will have found happiness through awakening within yourself the power to become the master of circumstances, instead of their slave.

Remember the mystical words of Jesus, the Master: "Whatsoever thing ye desire when ye pray, pray as if ye had already received and ye shall have."

## Lesson XVII
# Ideals Developed by Concentration

We often hear people spoken of as idealists. The fact is we are all idealists to a certain extent, and upon the ideals we picture depend our ultimate success. You must have the mental image if you are to produce the material thing. Everything is first created in the mind. When you control your thoughts, you become a creator. You receive divine ideas and shape them to your individual needs. All things of this world are to you just what you think they are. Your happiness and success depend upon your ideals.

**Concentrate Upon Your Ideals and They Will Become Material Actualities.** Through concentration we work out our ideals in physical life. Your future depends upon the ideals you are forming now. Your past ideals are determining your present. Therefore, if you want a bright future, you must begin to prepare for it today.

We say that a man is as changeable as the weather. What is meant is his ideals change. Every time you change your ideal you think differently. You become like a rudderless boat on an ocean. Therefore realize the importance of holding to your ideal until it becomes a reality.

You get up in the morning determined that nothing will make you lose your temper. This is your ideal of a person of real strength and poise. Something takes place that upsets you completely, and you lose your temper. For the time being you forget your ideal. If you had just thought a second of what a well-poised person implies you would not have become angry. *You lose your poise when you forget your ideal.* Each time we allow our ideals to be shattered we also weaken our willpower. Holding to your ideals develops willpower. Never forget this.

Why do so many fail? Because they don't hold to their ideal until it becomes a mental habit. When they concentrate on it to the exclusion of all other things, it becomes a reality. "I am that which I think myself to be."

You must give some hours to concentrated, consistent, persistent thought. You must study yourself and your weaknesses.

No man gets over a fence by wishing himself on the other side. He must climb.

No man gets out of the rut of dull, tiresome, monotonous life by merely wishing himself out of the rut. He must climb.

If you are standing still, or going backward, there is something wrong. You are the person to find out what is wrong.

Don't think that you are neglected, or not understood, or not appreciated. Such thoughts are the thoughts of failure.

You know that the only thing in the world that you have got to count upon is yourself.

## Lesson XVIII
# Concentration Reviewed

In this closing chapter, I want to impress you to concentrate on what you do, instead of performing most of your work unconsciously or automatically, until you have formed habits that give you the mastery of your work, and your life powers and forces.

Very often the hardest part of work is thinking about it. When you get right into it, it does not seem so disagreeable. This is the experience of many when they first commence to learn how to concentrate. So never think it a difficult task, but undertake it with the "I Will Spirit," and you will find that its acquirement will be as easy as its application will be useful.

Read the life of any great man, and you will generally find that the dominant quality that made him successful was the ability to concentrate. Study those who have been failures, and you will often find that lack of concentration was the cause.

Never say, "I can't concentrate today." You can do it just the minute you say, "I will." You *can* keep your thoughts from straying, just the same as you can control your arms. Once you realize this fact, you can train the will to concentrate on anything you wish. If it wanders, it is your fault. You are not using your will. But don't blame it on your will, and say it is weak. The will is the same whether you act as if it were weak or as if it were strong. When you act as if your will is strong you say, "I can." When you act as if it were weak you say, "I can't." It requires the same amount of effort.

Some men get in the habit of thinking, "I can't," and they fail. Others think, "I can," and succeed. So remember, it is for you to decide whether you will join the army of "I can't" or "I can."

The big mistake with so many is that they don't realize that when they say, "I can't," they really say, "I won't try." You cannot tell what you can do until you try. "Can't" means you will not try.

Before going to bed tonight, repeat: "I am going to choose my own thoughts, and to hold them as long as I choose. I am going to shut out all thoughts that weaken or interfere, that make me timid. My Will is as strong as anyone else's." While going to work the next morning, repeat this Keep this up for a month, and you will find you will have a better opinion of yourself. These are the factors that make you a success. Hold fast to them always.

Concentration is nothing but willing to do a certain thing. All foreign thoughts can be kept out by willing that they stay out. You cannot realize your possibilities until you commence to direct your mind.

You have at times been in a position that required courage, and you were surprised at the amount you showed. Now, when once you arouse yourself, you have this courage all the time and it is not necessary to have a special occasion reveal it. My object in so strongly impressing this on your mind is to make you aware that the same courage, the same determination that you show at certain exceptionable times, you have at your command at all times. It is a part of your vast resources. Use it often and well, in working out the highest destiny of which you are capable.

Father Time keeps going on and on. Every day he rolls around means one less day for you on this planet. Most of us only try to master the external conditions of this world. We think our success and happiness depend on us doing so. These are, of course, important, and I don't want you to think they are not; but I want you to realize that when death comes, only those inherent and acquired qualities and conditions within the mentality—your character, conduct, and soul growth—will go with you. If these are what they should be, you need not be afraid of not being successful and happy, for with these qualities you can mold external materials and conditions.

Now start from this minute to act according to the advice of the higher self in everything you do. If you do, its ever-harmonious forces will necessarily ensure a successful fulfillment of all your life purposes. Whenever you feel tempted to disobey your higher promptings, hold the thought: "My-higher-self-ensures-to-me-the-happiness-of-doing-that-which-best-answers-my-true-relations-to-all-others."

You possess latent talents, which when developed and used are of assistance to you and others. But if you do not properly use them, you shirk your duty, and you will be the loser and suffer from the consequences. Others will also be worse off if you do not fulfill your obligations.

Hold the thought: "I-will-live-for-my-best. I-seek-wisdom, self-knowledge, happiness-and-power-to-help-others. I-act-from-the-higher-self, therefore-only-the-best-can-come-to-me."

The more we become conscious of the presence of the higher self, the more we should try to become a true representative of the human soul in all its wholeness and holiness, instead of wasting our time dwelling on some trifling external quality or defect. We should try to secure a true conception of what we really are so as not to over value the external furnishings. You will then not surrender your dignity or self-respect when others ignorantly make a display of material things to show off. Only the person who realizes that he is a permanent Being knows what the true self is

# The Master Mind

(1918)

# by Theron Q. Dumont

*The Unparalleled Classic on Wielding Your Mental Powers From the Author of The Kybalion*

## Contents

Introduction   *The Enduring Genius of The Master Mind* by Mitch Horowitz   402
Chapter One   The Master Mind   404
Chapter Two   The Mind Master   407
Chapter Three   The Slave Will and the Master Will   411
Chapter Four   Positive and Negative Mentality   413
Chapter Five   Attention   415
Chapter Six   The Mastery of Perception   417
Chapter Seven   The Mastery of Emotion   419
Chapter Eight   The Mastery of Desire   420
Chapter Nine   The Mastery of Thought   426
Chapter Ten   Subconscious Mentality   428
Chapter Eleven   The Mastery of Will   499

## Introduction
# The Enduring Genius of *The Master Mind*

This is a distinctly different kind of book to come from the author who used the pseudonymous byline "Theron Q. Dumont." The man behind this penetrating, practical work of psychology was William Walker Atkinson, a prolific writer and publisher of New Thought and metaphysical literature in the early-twentieth century. Atkinson's most successful and influential work was the 1908 occult classic, *The Kybalion*, which he also wrote pseudonymously under the mysterious byline "Three Initiates."

Yet this work, *The Master Mind*, published ten years later, is notable for its absence of any mystical content. For a man who intensively studied the spiritual ideas of New Thought—or what William James called "the religion of healthy-mindedness"—this book represented a sharp departure. *The Master Mind* is probably Atkinson's most straightforward work of psychology. In fact, the book's great value is that it may be the best popularization ever of the psychological and self-development ideas of William James. James, like Atkinson, believed in the ability of the individual to harness and direct the practical faculties of his mind. A person's failure to use his mental forces, James reasoned, regulated him to a random and automatized existence, in which covert motives and desires shoved and shuffled him around.

The chief aim of this book is to teach you to become aware of and command your mental and emotional faculties. The book's techniques are drawn from the work of James and other practical psychologists of the era, whose ideas have proven remarkably resilient and, in many ways, remain as radical today as they were in the early part of the last century. The continued urgency of these methods is due not only to their truthfulness, but also to their persistent neglect. People typically acknowledge but fail to attempt most techniques of inner development. Hence, much of the material in *The Master Mind* awaits rediscovery and full use by the intrepid reader.

Another philosophical correspondence, if not influence, found in this book is between Atkinson's ideas and those of early-twentieth century spiritual teacher G.I. Gurdjieff. The Russian mystic and philosopher, more than any other figure of the last century, described man's state of automatism and his alienation from the forces, interior and exterior, that rule his life. Atkinson's analysis of the individual as an ineptly steered chariot in chapter four corresponds remarkably well with Gurdjieff's metaphor of an unruly horse-and-carriage representing man's disordered state. Atkinson also shares, to some degree, Gurdjeff's identification of a lost but central "I" within the individual.

Although Atkinson's death in 1932 made him contemporaneous to Gurdjieff, it is not clear to me that he ever actually encountered the teacher's ideas—I have come across no such reference in his work. But some of Atkinson's coinciding insights demonstrate just how insightful the writer-publisher was to evince points of commonality with the vitally important esoteric philosopher Gurdjieff.

Some observers have made the mistake—and I was once among them—of underestimating Atkinson as a thinker due to his frequent use of dramatic-sounding bylines and covert identities. Today, however, Atkinson is rightly becoming recognized not only for the breadth of his output, but also for the sturdiness of his ideas. I believe that within a generation Atkinson will be recognized as one of the two or three brightest and most literate voices to emerge from the New Thought tradition. Another is the mystic Neville Goddard, whose work emerged in the generation following Atkinson's.

In this condensed book, I have endeavored to preserve Atkinson's shrewdest insights into human nature, and his most practical and doable exercises for mental and emotional self-development. All of these exercises are canny and realistic. There is no excuse for not doing them. The long-term payoff, Atkinson promised, is honing your command over the instrumentalities of your thought, emotions, and willpower—which will result in the development of a Master Mind, and a true sense of selfhood. It is an epic promise, and one worthy of striving toward.

Finally, in this abridgment, I have identified the philosophers and psychologists that Atkinson quotes, who he sometimes referenced only generally and not by name in his original edition. I have also omitted quotation marks and attributions from passages where Atkinson quotes his own writing as published under a different byline.

This new edition of *The Master Mind* gives you a sense of the hope and excitement that early-twentieth century readers found in the theories of "healthy-mindedness." I think you will come to share my conviction that the book's immensely practical ideas await new discovery and use today.

—Mitch Horowitz

## Chapter One
# The Master Mind

In this book there will be nothing said concerning metaphysical theories or philosophical hypotheses; instead, there will be a very strict adherence to the principles of psychology. There will be nothing said of "spirit" or "soul;" but very much said of "mind." There will be no speculation concerning the question of "what is the soul?" or "what becomes of the soul after death?" These subjects, while highly important and interesting, belong to a different class of investigation, and are outside of the present inquiry. We shall not even enter into a discussion of the subject of "what is the mind?" Instead, we shall confine our thought to the subject of "how does the mind work?"

Many philosophers and metaphysicians have sought to tell us "just what" the mind is; but they usually leave us as much in doubt as before. As the old Persian poet has said, we "come out the door in which we went." We know much about **how the mind works**, but little or nothing about **what the mind really is**. So far as practical purposes are concerned, it makes very little difference to us just what the mind **is**, providing we know just how it **works**, and how it may be controlled and managed.

We shall operate according to the principle of pragmatism, as described by William James: "Pragmatism is the attitude of looking away from first things, principles, categories, supposed necessities; and of looking forward toward last things, fruits, consequences, facts."

What is the difference between a Master Mind and any other form of Mind? Simply that the Master Mind is consciously, deliberately, and voluntarily built up, cultivated, developed, and used; whereas the ordinary mind is usually unconsciously built up, cultivated, and developed, without voluntary effort on its own part, but solely by the force and power of impressions from the outside world, and is usually employed and used with little or no conscious direction by its own will.

In short, the ordinary mind is a mere creature of circumstances, driven by the winds of outside forces, and lacking the guidance of the hand on the wheel, and without the compass of knowledge; while the Master Mind proceeds in the true course mapped out by Intelligence, and determined by will—with sails set so as to catch the best breeze from the outside world, and steered by the master-hand at the wheel, under the direction of the compass of intelligence. The ordinary mind is like a dumb, driven animal; while the Master Mind is like the strong-willed, intelligent, masterful Man.

We can deliberately and voluntarily select and choose the particular wind which is to force our mental boat forward or, changing the figure, to choose and select the particular stream of thought and feeling which is to be allowed to flow through our mind.

There are three general conditions of human mentality: (1) Mental Slavery, in which the mind is the slave and servant of outside forces and influences; (2) Partial Freedom, in which the mind is largely controlled by outside influences, while at the same time a limited amount of voluntary control and direction has been acquired; and (3) Mental Mastery, in which the mental faculties, and emotional organism, have been brought under the control of the will and judgment, and the individual is a master of, and not a slave to, environment and circumstances. The great masses of people are in the first class; a comparatively small number have passed into the second; while a still smaller number have passed into the third class, and have become the Master Minds of their time and place.

We moderns are unaccustomed to the mastery over our inner thoughts and feelings. That a man should fall prey to any thought that happens to take possession of his mind is commonly assumed as unavoidable. It may be a matter of regret that he should be kept awake all night from anxiety, and that he should have the power of determining whether he be kept awake seems an extravagant demand. The image of an impending calamity is no doubt odious, but its very odiousness (we say) makes it haunt the mind all the more pertinaciously, and it is useless to expel it. Yet this is an absurd position for man, the heir of all the ages, to be lag-ridden by the flimsy creatures of his own brain. If a pebble in our boot torments us, we expel it. We take off the boot and shake it out. And once the matter is fairly understood, it is just as easy to expel an intruding and obnoxious thought. It *should* be as easy to expel an obnoxious thought from the mind as to shake a stone out of your shoe; and until a man can do that, it is nonsense to talk about his ascendancy over nature. He is a mere slave, and a prey to the bat-winged phantoms that flit through the corridors of his own brain.

It is one of the prominent doctrines of some of the Eastern schools of practical psychology that the power of expelling thoughts, or if need be, killing them dead on the spot, **must** be attained. Naturally the art requires practice; but, like other arts, when once acquired there is no mystery or difficulty about it. It is *worth practice*. It may be fairly said that life only begins when this art has been acquired. For obviously when, instead of being ruled by individual thoughts, the whole flock of them in their immense multitude, variety, and capacity is ours to direct, dispatch, and employ where we will, life becomes so vast and grand, compared to what it was before, that its former condition may well appear almost ante-natal. If you can kill a thought dead, for the time being, you can do anything else with it that you please. And therefore is this power so valuable. It not only frees a man from mental torment (which is at least nine-tenths the torment of life), but it also gives him a concentrated power of handling mental work absolutely unknown to him before.

Another facet of the Master Mind is that while at work your thought is absolutely concentrated upon and in it, undistracted by anything whatever irrelevant to the matter in hand. Then when the work is finished, if there is no more occasion for the use of the machine, it stops equally, absolutely, and entirely—with no **worrying**—and the man retires into that region of his consciousness where his true self dwells. The power of the thought-machine is enormously increased by this faculty of letting it alone on the one hand, and of using it singly and with concentration on the other.

The subjection of thought is closely related to the subjection of desire, and consequently has especially moral as well as especially intellectual relation to the question in hand. Nine-tenths of the scattered or sporadic thought with which the mind occupies itself, when not concentrated on any definite work, is what may be called *self-thought*—thought which dwells on and exaggerates the sense of self. This is hardly realized in its full degree until the effort is made to suppress it; and one of the most excellent results of such an effort is that with the stilling of all the phantoms which hover around the lower self, one's relations to others, to one's friends, to the world at large, and one's perceptions of all that is concerned in these relations, come out into a purity and distinctness unknown before. Obviously, when the mind is full of little desires and fears, which concern the local self, and is clouded over by the thought images, which such desires and fears evoke, it is impossible that it should see and understand the greater facts beyond, and its own relation to them. But with the subsiding of the former, the great vision begins to dawn; and a man never feels less alone than when he has ceased to think whether he is alone.

The Master Mind creates a world for itself, in which it dwells supreme, and to which it attracts and draws what is conducive to its welfare and happiness, its success and achievement.

You are invited to become a Master Mind. Will you accept the invitation? If so, you will carefully study the principles herein explained, and apply the methods described.

## Chapter Two

# The Mind Master

The idea of "mastery" carries with it the notion of dominion, power, or supremacy exercised by some person or thing, which is regarded as the "master." The spirit and essence of the term "master" is that of governor, ruler, director, leader, manager, or controller.

Some psychologists would have us believe that the intellectual faculties are the governing powers of the mind. But it will take but little thought to inform us that in many cases the intellectual powers are not the masterful forces in the mental activities of the individual; in many cases the feelings, desires, and emotional factors of the person run away with his reason, and not only cause him to do things that his reason tells him he should not, but also so influence his reason that his "reasons" are usually merely excuses for his actions performed in response to feelings and emotions.

Other psychologists would have us believe that the desires, feelings, and emotions of the individual are his mental masters; and in many cases it would appear that this is true, for many persons allow their feelings, emotions, and passions to govern them almost entirely, all else being subordinated to these. But when we begin to examine closely into the matter we find that in the case of certain individuals there is a greater or lesser subordination of the feelings and emotions to the dictates of reason; and in the case of persons of excellent self-control, the reason would appear to be higher in authority than the feelings. In the case of recognized Mental Masters, it is even found that the very feelings, passions, and emotions are so obedient to higher mental authority that in many cases they may actually be transformed and transmuted into other forms of feeling and emotion in response to the orders or commands of the central authority.

The thoughtful investigator usually discovers that the Mind Master is not found in the respective realms of the first two of the three great divisions of the mental kingdom, i.e., in the division of Thought, or that of Feeling, respectively. The investigator then turns to the third great division of the mental kingdom, i.e., that of Will, in his search for the sovereign power. And at first, it would appear that here, in the region of the Will, he had found the object of his search; and that the Will must be acclaimed the master. But when the matter is gone into a little deeper, the investigator discovers that not in Will itself, but in a *Something* lying at the very center of Will, is found the Mind Master.

While it is seen that the Will is higher in power and authority than either Thought or Feeling, it is also seen by the careful investigator that, in most cases, the Will is controlled and brought into activity by the Feelings; and that in other cases, it is started into action by the result of Thought, or intellectual effort. This being so, the Will cannot be considered as being always the Mind Master. And, discovering this, the investigator at first begins to feel discouraged, and to imagine that he is but travelling around a circle; in fact, many thinkers would have us believe that the mental processes work around in a circle, and that like a ring the process has no point of beginning or ending. But those who have persisted in the search have been rewarded by a higher discovery. They have found that while many persons are impelled to will by reason of their feelings and emotions, and others by reason of their thoughts, there is a third class of individuals—a smaller class to be sure—who seem to be masters of the will-activity, and who, standing in the position of a judge and sovereign power, first carefully weigh the merits of both feelings and thoughts, and then decide to exercise the willpower in a certain determined direction. This last class of individuals may be said to really *will to will* by the exercise of some higher authority within them. These are the real Master Minds. Let us seek to discover the secret of their power.

## The Central Authority

There is in the mental realm of every individual a certain *Something* that occupies the position of Central Authority, Power, and Control over the entire mental kingdom of that person. In many case—in **most** cases, we regret to say—this *Something* seems to be asleep, and the kingdom is allowed to run itself, "higgledy-piggledy," automatically and like a piece of senseless machinery, or else under the control of outside mentalities and personalities. In other cases—in **many** cases, in fact—this Central Authority has partially awakened, and consequently exerts at least a measure of its authority over its kingdom, but at the same time fails to realize its full powers, or to exert its full authority; it acts like a man only half-awakened from his sleep, and still in a state of partial doze.

Rising in the scale, we find cases of still greater degree of "awakening," until finally we discover the third great class of individuals—a very small class!—in whom the Central Authority has become almost or quite fully awake; and in whom this Mind Master has taken active control of his kingdom, and has begun to assert his authority and power over it.

You, the person now reading these words—YOU, yourself—are now asked to make this search of your mental kingdom, this search that has for its aim the discovery of the *Something Within* yourself that is the Mind Master, and which, when fully aroused into conscious power and activity, makes you a Master Mind.

All "voluntary attention" is performed by the exercise of this power of the will, exerted by this *Something Within* that we call "I," and which proves itself to be the Master of Thoughts.

The individual who has trained his mind to obey his will, is able to direct his thought processes just as he directs his feet, hands, or body, or just as he guides and manages his team of horses or his car. This being so, we cannot consider our Thought processes or faculties as the Mind Master; but must look for the Master in something still higher in authority.

There seems to be but one other region of the mind in which to search for our Mind Master, or Central Authority. You naturally say here, "He means The Will." But is it merely the Will? Stop a moment and consider. If the Will, in itself, is the Mind Master, why is it that the Will, in the case of so many persons, allows itself to be controlled and called into action by ordinary feelings, desires, emotions, or passions, or on the other hand is called into action by the most trifling, passing thought or idea? In such cases it appears that the Will is really the obedient, "easy" servant, rather than the Master.

That the machinery of the Will is the mechanism of control and action, is undoubted; but what is it that controls and directs the Will in the cases of individuals of strong Willpower? In such cases it would seem that not only must the Will be strong, but there must be some stronger *Something* that is able to control, direct, and apply the power of the Will. In moments in which you have exerted your Willpower, did you identify yourself with your Will, or did you feel that your Will was an instrument of power "belonging to" you, and being operated by you? Were you not at such moments aware of feeling an overwhelming consciousness of the existence of your **self**, or "I," at the center of your mental being? And of feeling that, at least for the time, this "I" was the Master of all the rest of your mental equipment? We think that you will agree to this statement, if you will carefully live over again the experiences of such moments, and in imagination and memory reenact the experience.

All mental analysis brings the individual to the realization that at the very center of his mental being there dwells a *Something*—and he always calls this "I"— which is the **permanent** element of his being. While his sensations, feelings, emotions, tastes, thoughts, beliefs, ideas, and even ideals have changed from time to time, he knows to a certainty that this "I" has been permanent, and that it is the same old "I" that has always been present throughout his life, from his earliest days. He knows that although his emotional nature, and general mental-physical character may have undergone an almost total transformation, this "I" has never really changed at all, but has ever remained "the same I."

Moreover, while the individual may change his sensations, feelings, tastes, passions, emotions, and whole general character in some cases, he is never able to change in the slightest degree this *Something Within* that he calls "I." He can never run away from this "I," nor can he ever move it from its position. He can never lift his "I" by means of his mental bootstraps; nor can his personal shadow run away from this "I" of his individuality. He may set apart for consideration each and every one of his mental experiences, sensations, thoughts, feelings, ideas, and all the rest; but he can never set off from himself this "I" for such inspection. He can know this "I" only as his self, that *Something Within* at the very center of his consciousness.

We are conscious of something closer to the center than anything else. Sensations originate outside and inside of the body. Emotions originate inside of the body. But this *Something* is deeper than either, and both are objective to it. We cannot classify it with anything else. We cannot describe it in terms of any other form of consciousness. Other forms of consciousness are objective in their relation to it, but it is never objective to them. There is nothing in our consciousness deeper. It underlies and overlies and permeates all other forms, and, moreover,—what is of immeasurably greater importance—it can, if need be, create them.

Just what this "I" is, we cannot tell. This riddle has never been solved by the reason of man. So subtle is its essence that it is almost impossible to think of it as a something apart from its mental states. All that can be said of it is that *it is*. Its only report of itself is "I Am."

This *Something Within*—this "I"—is that entity in philosophy and metaphysics that has been called "The Ego;" but such name does nothing in the way of defining it. You need not speculate over just what the Ego is, for you will never learn this. All that you can know is that it IS.

Your task is not to try to learn what the Ego is, for as has been said, you will never know this. Your task is to strive to awaken it into active consciousness, so that it may realize its power, and begin to employ it. You can awaken it by the proper mental attitude—by the conscious realization of its presence and power. And you can gradually cause it to realize its power, and to use it, by means of exercises calling into play that power. This is what Willpower really means. Your Will is strong already—it does not need strengthening; what is needed is that you urge your Ego into realizing that it can use your Willpower. You must learn to gradually awaken the half-asleep Giant, and set it to work in its own natural field of endeavor.

He who will carefully consider the above statements, and will make them a part of his mental armament, will have grasped the secret of the Master Mind.

Chapter Three

# The Slave Will and The Master Will

The masses of people are really little more than automatons. Their wills are called into activity by every passing desire, their passions and desires are uncontrolled, and their thought-processes are the result of suggestions made by others, which they accept and then fondly imagine they have thought for themselves.

The wills of such persons are Slave Wills, subject to the influence, control, and direction of others. The will-processes of such persons are almost entirely what are known as "reflex" activities, requiring the employment of but little powers of judgment, and little or no exercise of voluntary control.

Some may object that we are making too strong a statement when we say that the mental activity of the great masses of people are practically akin to reflex actions. People "think" about what they do before doing it, these objectors say. Of course "people think;" or, rather, they "think that they think;" but in reality the process of their "thinking" is almost reflex, that is to say it is automatic and mechanical, rather than deliberate. Their thought is usually based upon some suggested premise—some so-called fact accepted through suggestion and without verification or real consideration. Their accepted "facts" are usually found to agree with their likes, feelings, or prejudices, rather than based upon careful investigation. Their so-called "reasons" are but excuses or explanations evolved to justify their decision or action, both of these really based upon desires, wishes, likes, or prejudices.

Practically all our voluntary acts of will result from the power of **desire**. But this does not imply, by any means, that **all** desires result in action. The rule is this: **The greater the degree of the willpower of the individual, the greater is his degree of control over his desires**. And, as we have seen that the degree of willpower is the degree of the "wakefulness" of the Ego, it follows that **the greater the wakefulness of the Ego, the greater the degree of its control over the desires found within its mental realm.**

Every human being is, from the cradle to the grave, subject to external restraint. If a man declares that he is free to go without food, air, and sleep, and tries to act accordingly, consequences will soon deprive him of that liberty. The circle of freedom is much smaller than is sometimes thought; the fish is never free to become an eagle. Human freedom may be likened to a vessel sailing—freedom consists in being able to choose between two or more alternative courses of action.

The average man will indignantly deny that his freedom of will-action is in any way affected or restricted by outside or inside influences. He says triumphantly: "**I can act as I wish**," thinking that he has answered the argument against free will. But here is the point: he can act **only** as he **wishes**; and if his **wishes** are controlled or determined in any way, then so are his actions controlled and determined. And as his "wishes" are but forms of his **desires**, then unless he controls his desires he does not control his wishes, but is controlled by them. And as the average man has not acquired a strong control of his desires, he is lacking to that extent in his freedom of will-action. And right here is the main distinction between the Slave Will and the Master Will.

The Slave Will obeys the orders of its desires, feelings, and other "wishes," the latter coming from Lord-knows-where into his mental field. Such a man is not free, in the true sense of the word. He is a slave to his wishes, feelings, desires, passions—and he has no control over the thoughts and ideas that feed these desires, and that often actually **create** them. The Master Will not only refuses to be controlled by the intruding desires, if these are deemed against his best interests, but he actually controls them—by controlling the ideas and thoughts that serve to feed and nourish these desires, and in many cases, have also created them.

Our world is very much what we choose to pay attention to.

Ideas detained in consciousness tend to fan the flame of feeling; these ideas may be dismissed and others summoned to repress the flame of feeling. **In the higher type of action, the will can go out only in the direction of an idea. Every idea that becomes an object of desire is a motive.** It is true that the will tends to go out in the direction of the greatest motive, that is, toward the object that seems the most desirable; but the will, through voluntary attention, puts energy into a motive idea and thus makes it strong. It is impossible to center the attention long on an idea without developing positive or negative interest, attraction or repulsion. **Thus does the will develop motives.** We may state it as a law that **the will determines which motives shall become the strongest, by determining which ideas shall occupy the field of consciousness.**

If one idea is kept before the mind, a desire and a strong motive may gather around that idea. If another idea is called in, the power of the first idea will decline. Voluntary attention makes the motive. The motive does not make the attention. Hence, the motive is a product of the will. If I withdraw my attention from a motive idea, it loses vigor. The only way to develop and maintain a free will is to direct the attention and thought by means of the awakened Ego—the Master Mind and Mind Master.

## Chapter Four
# Positive and Negative Mentality

There is always a "two-sidedness" in individuals. Every individual finds within a constant struggle between these two opposing elements—the positive and the negative. Upon the outcome of this battle depends largely the advancement, success, welfare, and progress of the individual. Goethe has said: "In my breast, alas, two souls dwell, all there is unrest. Each with the other strives for mastery, each from the other struggles to be free." The ordinary individual seems content to remain a passive spectator of this struggle; but the individual of the awakened Ego takes part in the struggle, and by throwing the weight of his freewill into the balance, he brings down the scales on the positive side.

When the individual is forced to consider any feeling, emotion, idea, action, advice, suggestion, or teaching, he should always submit it to the

Touchstone of Positivity, by asking himself: **"Will this make me stronger, more powerful, more capable, more efficient, better?"** It becomes the duty of every individual wishing to progress on the Path of Life, and desiring to become proficient and capable in his expression and manifestation of mentality and character, to cultivate the positive qualities of the mind, and to restrain and inhibit the negative ones. In the consideration of this matter you should always remember that every positive quality has its negative opposite. This is an invariable rule, and one that you may test for yourself. And arising from it is this important rule of the new psychology: "To develop a positive quality, you should restrain or inhibit its opposing negative: To restrain or inhibit a negative quality, you should develop and encourage its opposing positive."

Man should be more than a mere creature of chance, environment, and outside influences. He should be ruled from within—be self-ruled—instead of being merely a weak instrument of desire, emotion, and feeling, influenced by suggestions and impressions from every passing person or thing. Man should be directed and guided by the strong instrument of his will, held firmly to its task by the Ego.

The fundamental idea of the new psychology is embodied in the symbol of the charioteer driving his fiery steeds under full control and with taut rein. The chariot represents the being of the man; the charioteer, the Ego; the reins, the will; the steeds, the mental states of feeling, emotion, desire, imagination, and the rest. Unless the reins be strong, they will not be sufficient to control the horses. Unless the charioteer be trained and vigilant, the horses will run away with the chariot and dash to pieces the driver in the general wreck. But controlled and mastered, the fiery steeds will lead forward to attainment and accomplishment, and at the same time will travel the road in safety.

There comes a time in the life of each one of us when the following question must be answered, and your course chosen. It may be that this time has come to you in the reading of these lines. Are you ready to answer it, and to make the decision? Remember the question. It is this: "Mastery or Servitude—Which?"

A man grows to resemble his ideals. And a man's ideals are the outgrowth of his feelings and emotions. The ideal held by the man arouses interest in all things connected with it. Interest is the strong motive of attention; and attention is the beginning of all the activities of the will. So the man's ideals serve to set into activity the chain of mental cause and effect that results in storing away in his mind the strong impressions that have so much to do with the building up of character. A man tends to grow to resemble the things he likes, and in which he is interested.

So true is this that a writer has suggested that we say, "As a man loveth, so is he." But here again the Master Mind asserts its power, and says: "I love that which I want to love—I am free here as in all else in my realm."

Modern psychology teaches us that the two following principles are operative in the character of each individual: (1) That feelings manifest themselves in will-action, unless inhibited or controlled; and (2) that the will-action follows the lines of the strongest interest.

We constantly act, often unconsciously, in accordance with our strongest desires, feelings, likes or dislikes, prejudices, etc. The Master Mind recognizes this and places in that storehouse only what he chooses to go into it, and what he chooses to come out of it as the incentive to action—being always governed in his choice by the Rule of Positivity heretofore announced: **"Will this make me stronger, more powerful, more capable, more efficient, better?"**

To many people the suggestion that they have the **power** to select the objects of their interest may seem absurd. They are accustomed to regard interest, feelings, desires, emotions, and even passions, as things beyond their control, so that they make no attempt to exercise a voluntary control over them. It is true that these mental states do not spring from pure intellectual effort—they spring from the depths of the subconscious mentality, unbidden, in most cases. But the facts of the new psychology show us plainly that the Ego may assume control of these involuntary mental states, and either encourage and develop them, or else restrain or inhibit them entirely. Just as the will may assume control of certain muscles of the body, so may the Ego assume control of the entire mental kingdom, and mold, build, change, and improve each and every department of its mental workshop. Interest results from attention, and may be controlled by the will. **And the will is the chief instrument of the Ego.**

Chapter Five

# Attention

Considering how frequently we employ the term "Attention," and its importance in our mental processes and their resulting action, it is strange how little thought we have given to the question: "What is Attention?"

Philosopher William Hamilton has said: "Attention is consciousness, and something more. It is consciousness voluntarily applied to some determinate object. **It is consciousness concentrated.**"

Attention is not an enlargement or increase in consciousness, but rather a narrowing, condensing, or limiting of consciousness. The act of Attention may be said to consist of three phases: (1) The earnest **fixing** of the mind upon some particular object; (2) the persistent **holding** of the mind upon that object; and (3) the determined **shutting-out** of the mind (for the time being) the perception of any other objects struggling for conscious recognition and attention.

To paraphrase one authority: The most important intellectual habit that I know of is attending exclusively to the matter in hand. It is commonly said that genius cannot be infused by education, yet this is the power of **concentrated Attention.**

And another: The force wherewith anything strikes the mind is generally in proportion to the degree of Attention bestowed upon it. The more completely the mental energy can be brought into one focus, and all distracting objects excluded, by the act of Attention, the more powerful will be the volitional effort.

There are two phases of Attention: (1) **reflex**, and (2) **voluntary** attention. **Reflex Attention** is drawn from us by a nervous response to some stimulus. **Voluntary Attention** is given by us to some object of our own selection, and is accompanied by a peculiar sense of effort. Many persons scarcely get beyond the reflex stage. Any chance stimulus will take their attention away.

In voluntary Attention, we make a deliberate selection of the object to which we wish our mind to attend. Again, in involuntary Attention there is no sense of effort; while in voluntary Attention there is always a peculiar sense of effort, sometimes to a very marked degree.

The first step toward the development of the will lies in the exercise of Attention. There is a sense of conscious effort in voluntary Attention. This suffices to mark it off from the involuntary type. If we take two ideas of the same intensity, and center the attention upon one, we shall notice how much it grows in power. If we, at the start, want several things in about an equal degree, whether a bicycle, a typewriter, or an encyclopedia, we shall end by wanting the one most on which our attention has been most strongly centered. Attention is the most important element in will. In order to act in the direction of one idea in preference to another, we must dismiss the one and voluntarily attend to the other. The motor force thus developed in connection with the dominant idea lies at the foundation of every higher act of will.

Psychologist Rueben Post Halleck has written: "When it is said that Attention will not take hold on an uninteresting object, we must not forget that anyone not shallow and fickle can soon discover something interesting in most objects. Here cultivated minds show their especial superiority, for the Attention that they are able to give generally finds a pearl in the most uninteresting looking oyster. When an object necessarily loses interest from one point of view, such minds discover in it new attributes. The essence of genius is to present an old thing in new ways, whether it be some force in nature or some aspect in humanity."

## Chapter Six
# The Mastery of Perception

Psychologist William Walter Smith has given us perhaps the most comprehensive, and at the same time the most condensed, statement of the Laws of Attention, which I paraphrase:

(1) Attention will not attach itself to uninteresting things. (2) It will soon decline in vigor (a) if the stimulus is unvarying, or (b) if some new attribute is not discovered in the object. (3) Attention cannot remain constant in the same direction for a long period, because (a) the nervous apparatus of the senses soon tire under the strain of continuous attention toward any one object, and consequently respond with less vigor, (b) the same is true of brain cells. To prove the truth of this one has only to focus the eye continuously on one object, or to keep the attention fixed on the same phase of a subject. (4) When one kind of attention is exhausted, we may rest ourselves in two ways: (a) by giving ourselves up to the play of reflex (involuntary) attention, or (b) by directing our voluntary attention into a new channel. The amount of fatigue must determine which is better. (5) Attention too continuously centered upon the same unvarying sensation, or upon any unchanging object, has been proved by experiment to tend to induce either the hypnotic state or a comatose condition.

The first of the above laws states the difficulty of attaching the Attention to uninteresting things. But there is a remedy for this as follows: (a) in the application of the equally true principle that interest may be developed in a previously uninteresting thing by studying and analyzing it. Everything has its interesting side, and examination will bring this into view. (b) By viewing a thing from varying viewpoints, and from different angles of physical and mental vision, new facts are discovered regarding it, and these discoveries awaken interest and renewed Attention.

The same remedy applies in the case of the second law. For by changing the point of view, and by discovering new qualities, properties, and attributes in a thing, the stimulus is varied, and renewed interest is obtained.

The third law explains why the Attention cannot long remain focused in the same direction. A remedy for this will be found in the well-known psychological rule to study a thing by piecemeal. That is to say, instead of considering attentively the entire subject, or object, one should break it (mentally) into as many small sections as possible, and then proceed to study it by sections. This will vary the stimulus.

The fourth law informs us that we may obtain rest for the tired Attention by (a) relaxing the voluntary Attention, and opening our consciousness to the impressions of involuntary, or reflex Attention—paying attention to the sights and sounds reaching us from outside, as for instance by closing our book and looking out of the window at the passing persons and things; or (b) by directing our voluntary Attention into a new channel, as by closing our book and picking up and reading another book along entirely different lines; or changing from an abstract subject to a concrete proposition, or vice versa. This expresses an important psychological principle, i.e., that the best way to rest and relax the Attention is to change the direction of its effort and activity. Change of occupation gives the best kind of rest to physical or mental muscles.

The fifth law merely serves to emphasize the effect of the unnatural concentration of Attention; and the fact that a varying stimulus is necessary for continued consciousness. It serves to point us to the middle of the road, avoiding the extreme of undue concentration on a single object on the one hand, and the other extreme of bestowing no voluntary Attention at all.

The average person is able to arouse and maintain Attention only when interest already attaches to the object to be considered. But the Master Mind rides over this obstacle by first awakening interest in the thing by means of a careful examination under concentrated voluntary Attention, and thereafter allowing the Attention to flow freely along the channels of interest thus made. Here we have an instance of the will first creating a channel, and then travelling over its course.

## Chapter Seven
# The Mastery of Emotion

Feeling and Emotion are the great incentives to action, and the great motive-power of mental and physical manifestations. Even Intellect, that supposed monarch of the mental world, really is "under the thumb" of that "power behind the throne," which we know as Feeling and Emotion. Not only do we act according to our feelings, but in most cases we also think according to them. Instead of reasoning coldly and without prejudice, we really generally reason along the lines of our strong feelings. Instead of finding real "reasons" for our actions, we usually seek merely for "excuses" to justify our actions in accordance with our feelings.

There are few people able to detach themselves, even in a small degree, from their feelings, so as to decide questions by pure reason or intellectual effort. Moreover, there are few whose wills are guided by pure reason; their feelings supply the motive for the majority of the acts of will. The intellect, even when used, is generally employed to carry out the dictates of Feeling and Desire. Much of our reasoning is performed in order to justify our feelings, or to find proofs for the position dictated by our desires, feelings, sympathies, prejudices, or sentiments. It has been said that "men seek not reasons, but excuses, for their actions."

Our judgments are affected by our feelings. It is much easier to approve of the actions of some person whom we like, or whose views accord with our own, than of an individual whose personality and views are distasteful to us. It is very difficult to prevent prejudice, for or against anything, from influencing our judgments. It is also true that "we find that for which we look" in things and people, and that which we expect and look for is often dependent upon our feelings. If we dislike a person or thing, we usually perceive no end of undesirable qualities in him or it; while if we are favorably inclined we easily find many admirable qualities in the same person or thing. A little change in our feeling often results in the formation of an entirely new set of judgments regarding a person or thing.

The true Master Mind impresses its dominion upon the Feelings and Emotions, and then **sets them to work** in the right direction. In fact, it is by means of the powers of Feeling and Emotion that the Master Mind accomplishes much of its work. This should be borne in mind by the reader who wishes to develop the Master Mind.

Particularly in its phase of Desire does the Master Mind make use of Feeling and Emotion. Desire may be said to be *concentrated Feeling*. Before we can have ambition or aspiration, there must be desire. Before we can manifest courage or energy, there must be desire. Desire for something must underlie all life-action—desire conscious or subconscious. Abstract thought is a cold, bare thing, lacking vitality and warmth—desire is filled with life, throbbing, longing, wanting, craving, insisting, and ever pressing forward into action. Desire, indeed, is the motive power of all action. We may call desire by the favorite terms of ambition, aspiration, longing for attainment, etc., but **desire is ever the basic principle of all longing, all wishing, all wanting.**

There have been many attempts to define Desire. Perhaps the best and clearest in its analysis of the essential qualities of Desire is that of Reuben Post Halleck, who has furnished the following definition: **"Desire has for its object something that will bring pleasure or get rid of pain, immediate or remote, for the individual or for someone else in whom he is interested. Aversion, or a striving away from something, is merely the negative aspect of desire."**

**Most men act from motives of securing what will bring them the greatest amount of pleasure, or the least amount of pain, immediate or remote, for themselves or for others.** In short, men ever strive for **Pleasure** and away from **Pain**.

## Chapter Eight
# The Mastery of Desire

The Mastery of Desire does not mean (as some suppose) the "killing out" of all Desire. In fact, as careful students of the subject well know, it would be impossible to kill out all Desire, for the very act of "killing out" would be actually, itself, a response to a desire—a desire not to desire, as it were. Mastery of Desire really means the control, management, and direction of Desire by the Ego.

In beginning the study of the Mastery of Desire, however, we must, of course, begin with the subject of the handling, direction, culture, and control of the Feelings and Emotions, for these are the stuff of which Desire is made. The Ego must learn how to manufacture certain grades and kinds of Feeling and Emotion into Desire, and at the same time to discard and throw into the scrap pile other kinds of Feelings and Emotions, which would make only the wrong kind of Desire.

How to Restrain Feelings, Emotions, or Desires

The general rules for the restraint of any class of feelings, emotions, and the desires arising therefrom, are:

I. Refrain as far as possible from the physical expression of the feeling, or emotion, or the desire arising therefrom, which are deemed objectionable.
II. Refuse to permit the formation of the habit of expressing in action the feeling, or emotion, or the desire arising therefrom, which are deemed objectionable.
III. Refuse to dwell upon the idea or mental picture of the object or subject exciting the feeling, or emotion, or the desire arising therefrom, which are deemed objectionable.
IV. Cultivate the class of feelings or emotions, or the desires arising therefrom, which are opposed to those deemed objectionable.

Let us now consider each one of these rules in further detail:

### I. Refrain from the Physical Expression.

A strong feeling or emotion, and the desire arising therefrom, tends toward expression in physical action of some kind. In fact, the feeling is said not to have been fully manifested unless this outward expression is had in at least some degree. This being so, it is seen that if one refrains from the physical expression, he has done something to prevent the full manifestation of the feeling.

So closely are the two—feelings and their physical expression—connected, that some psychologists have actually held that the physical expression precedes and practically causes the mental state of feeling. Some men in important positions make it a rule to maintain an even, low tone of voice when they are threatened with a rush of angry feeling—they have found that such a plan enables them to keep their temper, even under the most trying circumstances. And, in passing, it may be said that such a course will often result in the other person in the quarrel also lowering his voice, and abating his angry feeling.

There is a mutual action and reaction between emotional mental states and the physical expression thereof; each in a measure being the cause of the other, and each at the same time being the effect of the other.

Halleck has noted: "Actors have frequently testified to the fact that emotion will arise if they go through the appropriate muscular movements. In talking to actors on the stage, if they clinch the fists and frown, they often find themselves becoming really angry; if they start with counterfeit laughter, they find themselves growing cheerful ... If we wish to conquer undesirable emotional tendencies in ourselves, we must assiduously, and in the first instance cold-bloodedly, go through the outward movements of those contrary dispositions which we wish to cultivate. Soothe the brow, brighten the eye, contract the dorsal rather than the ventral aspect of the frame, and speak in a major key, and your heart must be frigid indeed if it does not gradually thaw."

The essence, then, of the above is: **Refrain so far as is possible from indulging in the physical expression of a feeling, emotion, or desire that you wish to conquer, control, and repress.**

## II. Refuse to Form the Habit of Expression in Action.

Habits build a mental path over which the Will thereafter travels. Or, to use another figure of speech, Habit cuts a channel, through which the Will afterward flows. When you express a feeling, emotion, or desire in action you begin to form a habit; when you express it the second time the habit takes on force; and so on, each repetition widening the mental path, or deepening the mental channel over which it is easy for subsequent action to travel. The oftener the feeling, emotion, or desire travels this path of action, the stronger it becomes.

The essence of the above is: **Don't get into the habit of expressing in action a feeling, emotion, or desire which you wish to conquer, control, and repress.**

## III. Refuse to Dwell upon the Idea or Mental Picture.

This rule is based upon the accepted fact of psychology that Feeling, Emotion, and Desire are fed, nourished, and strengthened by the representative idea, or mental image of the object or subject which has originally inspired them, or which is associated with that object or subject. Feelings are often caused by an idea, resulting from the process of thought or recalled in memory. Likewise they are deepened and strengthened by the recalling into consciousness of such ideas. In the same way, they are fed and nourished by ideas connected with the original object or subject by the ties of association.

The remembrance of an insult, an act of unkindness, a wrong done, may cause acute feeling. There may be no immediately preceding change in the sense organ when an idea flashes into the mind, but the feeling may be just as pronounced as if it were. A **representative idea** is a revived sensation, or a complex of revived sensations. Some ideas cause a joyful, others a sorrowful mental state; accordingly, feelings differ qualitatively according to the idea. Our feelings also differ quantitatively as the idea has a more or less pleasurable or painful element.

To sum up: Inasmuch as it is a psychological fact that ideas not only cause feelings, emotions, and desires, but also tend to revive, deepen, strengthen, and nourish them, it follows that if one wishes to inhibit, repress, or weaken any disadvantageous feeling, emotion, or desire, he should studiously and insistently refrain from allowing his attention to dwell upon the ideas tending to arouse or stimulate such feelings, emotions, or desires. He should refuse to feed the feeling, emotion, or desire with the nourishing food of associated ideas. Instead, he should set to starve out the objectionable feeling, emotion, or desire by refusing it the mental food needed for its growth.

## IV. Cultivate the Opposite.

It is a law of psychology that one set of feelings, emotions, or desires may be weakened, repressed, and controlled by a careful and determined cultivation of the opposite set of feelings, emotions, or desires. Every mental state in the emotional field has its opposite. The two states are antagonistic, and each tends to annihilate the other. The two cannot coexist. One cannot feel happy and miserable at the same time and place. Consequently, there is always a struggle between opposing mental states.

By the *Cultivation of the Opposites*, the person takes advantage of the fight already under way between the two opposing emotional armies, and instead of fighting the battle all alone by a frontal attack, he forms an alliance with the friendly army, and throws the weight of his own will in its favor—he brings up a powerful reserve force, with men, equipment, ammunition, and supplies, and thus gives to the friendly army an enormously increased advantage. One has but to consider the matter in this light in order to see that this is **the best, easiest, and quickest way** to conquer the objectionable mental army.

The above statement is based upon the acknowledged psychological fact expressed in the axiom that: **"To develop a positive quality, it is important to restrain or inhibit its opposing negative; to restrain or inhibit a negative quality, develop and encourage its opposing positive."** In this axiom is condensed a whole philosophy of character-building and self-improvement.

It is equally important to cultivate positive or desired emotions. Here are the general rules for the Cultivation, Development, and Strengthening of *Desirable* Feelings, Emotions, and Desires:

I. Frequently express, mentally and physically, the feeling, emotion, or desire that you wish to cultivate, develop, and strengthen.

II. Form the habit of expressing in action the feeling, emotion, or desire that you wish to cultivate, develop, or strengthen.

III. Keep before you as much as possible the idea or mental image associated with the feeling, emotion, or desire which you wish to cultivate, develop or strengthen.

IV. Restrain the classes of feelings, emotions, and desires opposed to those you wish to cultivate, develop, or strengthen.

Let us now consider each one of these rules in further detail.

## I. Frequently Express the Positive Feelings, Emotions, and Desires.

As we have seen, a feeling, emotion, or desire is developed by the physical expression thereof, and also by the frequent repetition of the same in consciousness. The expression of the outward physical manifestations of the inner state tends not only to add fuel to the fire of the latter, but also nourishes and strengthens it. Likewise, the frequent bringing into the field of consciousness of the feeling, emotion, or desire tends to deepen the impression, and to cause the mental state to take deep roots in the mental being of the individual.

Exercise and practice develops the emotional muscles, just as they do the physical muscles. Repetition is a potent factor in forming and strengthening mental impressions, and in the cultivation of the mental habits. Consequently, lose no opportunity for exercising and using the feeling, emotion, or desire that you wish to cultivate and develop. If you wish to be courageous, bring up often the idea of courage, and endeavor to feel its thrill through you; and at the same time, deliberately assume the physical attitude of courage. Think of yourself as the courageous individual, and try to walk, carry yourself, and in general act like that individual. Form the correct mental picture, and then endeavor to **act it out.**

Get control of your physical channels of expression, and master the physical expression connected with the mental state you are trying to develop. For instance, if you are trying to develop your will along the lines of Self-Reliance,

Confidence, Fearlessness, etc., the first thing for you to do is to get a perfect control of the muscles by which the physical manifestations or expressions of those feelings are shown. Get control of the muscles of your shoulders, that you may throw them back manfully. Look out for the stooping attitude of lack of confidence. Then get control of the muscles by which you hold up your head, with eyes front, gazing the world fearlessly in the face. Get control of your vocal organs, by which you may speak in the resonant, vibrant tones that compel attention and inspire respect.

You must learn to occasionally actually perform some act requiring physical or moral courage. You must exercise your mental state and will by actual use. Grow by expression and action. Do the deeds, and you will acquire the power to do still greater.

The essence, then, of the above is: **Express frequently, mentally and physically, in "acting out" and actual doing, the feeling, emotion, and desire which you wish to cultivate and develop.**

## II. Acquire the Habit of Expression.

By acquiring the Habit of Expression of the feeling, emotion, or desire which you may wish to cultivate and develop, you make a mental path or channel over which the will will naturally and easily travel. Habit renders the expression second nature. Habit is formed by exercise and repetition. Every time you express a mental state, the easier it becomes to express it again, for you have started the formation of a habit. Habit is a form of mental impression, and the oftener you sink the die of action into the soft wax of the mind, the deeper will be the impression. Habit increases ease of performance. When a habit is built, it constitutes the line of least resistance, and you will find it easy to move in that direction, and hard to move in the opposite.

Here you must fight with all your might, but, the first battle once won, the after-fights are less severe, and finally degenerate into mere skirmishes.

The essence, of the above is: **Establish firmly the habit of expressing in action the feeling, emotion, or desire that you wish to cultivate.**

## III. Visualize the Associated Subject or Object.

It is an established principle of psychology that the mental picture of the object or subject of a feeling, emotion, or desire, when held before the mind, tends to add force, power, and vitality to the emotional state representing it. And the stronger, deeper, clearer, and more frequently repeated such a mental picture is, the stronger, deeper, and more does the emotional mental state associated with it become. Feelings, emotions, and desires are fed by **ideas**—and the strongest kinds of ideas are those taking form in clear mental pictures of the imagination or memory.

The essence, of the above is: **Feed your mind with the ideas and mental pictures of the object or subject of the feeling, emotion, or desire you wish to develop.**

IV. RESTRAIN AND SUPPRESS THE OPPOSITES.
As we have seen, the development of an opposite set of feelings, emotions, or desires tends to restrain, suppress, and eventually destroy any particular set of these mental states. Contrariwise, it follows that if we will studiously and determinedly restrain and suppress (by the methods already given) the feelings, emotions, and desires opposed to those we wish to cultivate, then will the favored ones be given the best possible opportunity to nourish, grow, develop, and wax strong. Regard the opposing set as **weeds**, which if allowed to grow will choke and weaken, or possibly even kill, your favorite valuable plants. And you know what you should do in such a case, of course: determinedly **weed out** the harmful growths—pluck them by the roots and cast them out of your mental garden the moment they appear.

By refusing to permit the growth of the objectionable emotional weeds of the "opposites" in your mental garden, you greatly promote the growth of the valuable plants. Remember, there is not room in the mental garden for both of the two opposing sets of emotional qualities to thrive. It is up to you to determine which ones shall be the victors— which ones shall be the fittest to survive. The fittest in such cases is not always the **best**—rather is the one that you strengthen, stimulate, and feed. Will you bear a crop of sturdy, strong and vigorous plants and fruits, which are conducive to your wellbeing, strength, efficiency, and ultimate happiness? It is up to you to **decide**—and then to **act**.

## Chapter Nine
# The Mastery of Thought

Speaking in the figurative sense, it may be said that the Kingdom of Mind over which the Ego—or Master Mind—rules (or may rule if it will assert its right and power to rule) is composed of three grand divisions, or states: (1)

Feeling; (2) Thought; and (3) Will. The activities of the mind consist of Feeling, Thinking, and Willing. All mental states or processes will be found to come under one or the other of the said classes. And yet, the mental activities are so complex that each of these three respective classes are usually found manifesting in connection with one or more of the others.

We seldom find a Thought without also finding a blending of Feelings, and usually a manifestation of Will, as well. Likewise, we seldom find a Feeling without a Thought connected or associated with it, and usually a manifestation of the presence of Will in connection with it. And, finally, we seldom find a manifestation of Will without the presence of Feeling, and of the Thought associated with the Feeling. But, nevertheless, there is a clear distinction among these three great classes of mental states or processes.

To begin with, let us ask, "What is thought?"

Halleck states: "To think is to compare things with each other, to notice wherein they agree and differ, and to classify them according to these agreements and differences. It enables us to put into a few classes the billions of things that strike our perceptive faculties; to the things with like qualities into a bundle by themselves, and to infer that what is true of one of these things will be true of the others, without actual experience in each individual case; and to introduce law and order into what at first seemed a mass of chaotic materials."

Man has one resource denied to the animals—**the power of progressive thought.** He has harnessed the forces of Nature, proceeding from the grosser to the finer—from steam to electricity—and still has a far more wonderful field to explore.

Many people believe they are "thinking" when they are but exercising their faculty of memory, and even that in merely an idle and passive manner. They are simply allowing the stream of memory to flow through their field of consciousness, while the Ego stands on the banks and idly watches the passing waters of memory flow by. They call this "thinking," while in reality there is no process of Thought under way.

Henry Hazlitt writes: "When I use the word 'thinking,' I mean thinking with a purpose, with an end in view, thinking to solve a problem. I mean the kind of thinking that is forced on us when we are deciding on a course to pursue, on a life work you take up perhaps: the kind of thinking that was forced upon us in our younger days when we had to find a solution to a problem in mathematics... I do not mean 'thinking' in snatches, or holding petty opinions on this subject and on that. I mean thought on significant questions which lie outside the bounds of your narrow personal welfare."

The same writer has said: "**If a man were to know everything, he could not think.** Nothing would ever puzzle him, his purposes would never be thwarted, he would never experience perplexity or doubt, he would have no problems . . . If our lives and the lives of our ancestors had always run smoothly, if our every desire were immediately satisfied, if we never met an obstacle in anything we tried to do, thinking would never have appeared on this planet. But adversity forced us to it."

Real thinking is a process directly under the control, direction, and management of the Master Mind. The importance of this fact can be correctly estimated only when one realizes the all-important part played by Thought in the life and welfare of the individual. We are the result of what we have thought. The Master Mind thinks what it wills to think, not what others will it to think, or what Chance determines it shall think. Thus is the Master Mind the Master of Itself.

## Chapter Ten
# Subconscious Mentality

A large share of the mental processes of the individual play out on some fields or on planes of mentality under or above the ordinary plane of consciousness.

The so-called subconscious or unconscious planes of mind **are not unconscious**, but are really conscious in various degrees of consciousness peculiar to themselves. The term "subconscious" is used simply to indicate that the processes and activities of these particular planes of mind are outside of the field of the ordinary consciousness. When I speak of the passing of impressions, ideas, or records in and out of consciousness, I am not trying to convey the idea of passing these mental images from one mind to another, but rather of passing them in and out of the narrow field of the ordinary consciousness, just as the tiny living creatures in a drop of stagnant water under a microscope pass in and out of the field of vision of the apparatus; or as the stars pass in and out of the field of a stationery telescope as the earth revolves.

Mental events imperceptible to consciousness are far more numerous than the others, and we perceive only the highest points of the world that makes up our being—the lighted-up peaks of a continent whose lower levels remain in the shade. Examine closely, and without bias, the ordinary mental operations of daily life, and you will discover that consciousness has not one-tenth the functions we commonly ascribe to it. In every conscious state there are conscious, subconscious, and infra-conscious energies, each one indispensable.

It must not be supposed that the mind is at any time conscious of all its materials and powers. At any moment we are not conscious of a thousandth part of what we know. It is well that such is the case; for when we are studying a subject, or an object, we should not want all we know to rush into our minds at once. If this occurred, our mental confusion would be indescribable. Between the perception and the recall, the treasures of memory are, metaphorically speaking, away from the eye of consciousness. How these facts are preserved, before they are summoned by memory, consciousness can never tell us. An event may not be thought of for fifty years, and then it may suddenly appear in consciousness.

### The Processes of Imagination

Imagination, the second class of the processes of the Subconscious Mentality, very closely resembles its brother, the Memory, but there is an important distinction between the two, as follows: Memory reproduces only the original impressions placed within its realm, while Imagination reproduces the recorded impressions of Memory, not in their original condition, but in new groupings, arrangements, and forms.

Memory is the storehouse of impressions, but Imagination is the artist working with these stored up impressions, and making new and wonderful things with them. Imagination takes these stored-away impressions, and **creates** new forms of things from them, but always uses the materials it finds in the Memory storehouse—it makes new combinations, new arrangements, new forms, **but it never makes new materials.**

Imagination is subject to misuse, as well—in fact, the word is frequently employed to indicate the misuse of it, in the form of idle daydreams and vain fanciful flights of the imagination. This misuse arises from the **involuntary** exercise of the Imagination—allowing this subconscious faculty to indulge in purposeless and useless activity. This is like mere daydreaming, and is a habit that often obtains quite a hold over a person if too freely indulged in. It is a mild form of mental intoxication, and the effects are undesirable, for they often manifest in a weakening of the will, and rendering infirm the voluntary purposive faculties of the mind.

The most harmful effects of the idle exercise of the imagination is that it usurps the place rightfully belonging to **action**. It is so much easier and more pleasant to dream of accomplishment than to attempt to make them come true in actual life The habitual daydreamer gradually loses the desire to participate in the activities of life, and slowly sinks into a passive existence.

The best modern psychology recognizes this danger of the misuse of the Imagination, and lays great stress upon the necessity of transmuting the energies of the Imagination into the images of things connected with the life work of the individual, character-building, self-mastery, and general creative work along the lines of the Constructive Imagination. Creative and constructive imagination furnishes the pattern, design, or mold of future action or material manifestation. Properly used, the imagination is the architect of deeds, actions, and accomplishments.

In this constructive and creative work of the Imagination we have but another example of what has been so positively insisted upon: **the principle of the Ego using its instruments of expression, instead of allowing them to use the Ego.** It is the **positive** use of the faculties, instead of the **negative**.

Here follow a few carefully selected rules for the cultivation of the right habits of using the Imagination.

**The Supply of Material.** Before the Imagination can build, construct, and create, it must be supplied with the proper materials. The materials with which the Imagination works are to be had only in the subconscious storehouse of Memory. Therefore, the Memory must be supplied with a stock of information concerning the particular subject or object. The impressions stored away should be clear, distinct, and strong.

**Develop by Exercise.** The Imagination should be developed, cultivated, and strengthened by voluntary and directed exercise and use. Acquire the habit of mapping out the work you have to do in advance, and allowing the creative Imagination to fill in the details of the map after you have made the general outlines. Turn your attention upon the tasks before you, and you will discover, providing you have the strong desire for improvement, that the Imagination will set to work suggesting improvements.

**Avoid Idle Daydreaming.** Avoid the habit of idle daydreaming, for this only dissipates and wastes the energies of the Imagination. Instead, strive to acquire the habit of the purposeful, voluntary use of the Imagination.

**Hold to the Central Idea.** In the work of Constructive Imagination, always hold firmly to the central idea and purpose of your thought. Build up, tear down, alter, and change the details as much as you see fit, but always with the idea of improving and creating—never allow yourself to be sidetracked. Allow the central idea and its purpose to be the framework upon which you build.

**Discard Useless Material.** Acquire the habit of discarding all ideas and mental images that are not conducive to your creative work. Hold your mind one-pointed while engaged in your imaginative work. Subject all your ideas and mental images to the test: "Is this conducive to the task in view? Does this tend to efficiency?"

**See the Result as You Desire It to Be.** Always hold before your mental eye the picture of yourself accomplishing the thing you have set out to do, and picture the result taking on proper form and power.

Describing a scene from his novel *Dr. Jekyll and Mr. Hyde*, author Robert Louis Stevenson offered this portrait of his subconscious and imaginative faculties: "My Brownies! God bless them! who do one-half of my work for me when I am fast asleep, and in all human likelihood do the rest for me as well when I am wide awake and foolishly suppose that I do it for myself. I had long been wanting to write a book on man's double being. For two days I went about racking my brains for a plot of any sort, and on the second night I dreamt the scene in *Dr. Jekyll and Mr. Hyde* at the window; and a scene, afterward split in two, in which Hyde, pursued, took the powder and underwent the change in the presence of his pursuer."

Many pages could be filled with similar testimony to the reality of the processes of Subconscious Thought, to which has been given the names "automatic thinking," "unconscious rumination," or even the picturesque term "the helpful Brownies" of Stevenson.

In the Inner Consciousness of each of us there are forces that act much the same as would countless tiny mental brownies or helpers who are eager to assist us in our mental work, if we will have confidence and trust in them. This is a psychological truth expressed in the terms of the old fairytales. The process of summoning these Inner Consciousness helpers is similar to that we constantly employ to recall some forgotten fact or name. We find that we cannot recollect a desired fact, date, or name, and instead of racking our brains with an increased effort, we (if we have learned the secret) pass on the matter to the Inner Consciousness with a silent command, "Recollect this name for me," and then continue with our ordinary work. After a few minutes—or it may be hours—all of a sudden, pop! will appear the missing name or fact—flashed from the planes of the Inner Consciousness by the help of the kindly workers or "brownies" of those planes. The experience is so common that we have ceased to marvel at it, and yet it is a wonderful manifestation of the Inner Consciousness workings of the mind.

Furthermore, if you will look carefully into a subject you wish to master, and will pass along the results of your observations to these Subconscious Brownies, you will find that they will work the raw materials of thought into shape for you in a comparatively short time. They will arrange, analyze, systematize, collate, and arrange in consecutive order the various details of information that you have passed on to them, and will add articles of similar information that they will find stored away in the various recesses of your memory. In this way, they will group together scattered bits of knowledge that you have forgotten.

There are many ways of setting the brownies to work. Perhaps the best way for the average person is for one to get a very clear idea of what one really wants to know—a clear idea or mental image of the question you wish answered. Then after rolling it around in your mind—mentally chewing it, as it were—giving it a high degree of voluntary attention, you can pass it on to your Subconscious Mentality with the mental command: **"Attend to this for me—work out the answer!"** or some similar order. This command may be given silently, or else spoken aloud—either will do. Speak to the Subconscious Mentality—or its little workers—just as you would speak to people in your employ, kindly but firmly. Talk to the little workers, and command them to do your work. And then forget all about the matter—throw it off your conscious mind, and attend to other tasks. In due time will come your answer—flashed into your consciousness—perhaps not until the very minute that you must decide upon the matter, or need the information. You may give your brownies orders to report at such and such a time—just as you do when you tell them to awaken you at a certain time in the morning, or just as they remind you of the hour of your appointment, if you have them well trained.

The above instruction, though conveyed in a fanciful style, really contains the essence and substance of the most approved methods of making use of the faculties of the subconscious mentality. The reader should carefully study this method, and begin to practice it as he wishes to make use of this wonderful power of the mind. He will find that after a little practice his mental powers will be enormously increased, and his general efficiency added to.

## Chapter Eleven
# The Mastery of Will

The modern conception of the Will is that of **mental states concerned with action**, the other phases being regarded as subordinate to this.

The Will may be said to present three general phases: (1) The phase in which Desire is being transformed into Will; (2) the phase in which there is the process of Deliberation concerning the respective values of several desires, or several courses of action represented by their respective ideas or mental images; this phase of Deliberation begins with conflicting motives, and ends with a Decision or Choice; (3) the phase of action resulting from the Decision or Choice. The following somewhat fuller statement of each of these phases will aid the reader in perceiving the special characteristics of each.

1. DESIRE-WILL.
All activities of the Will are preceded by Desire. One may Desire without actually setting the Will into operation, but one can scarcely be thought of as Willing without having first experienced the Desire to Will (it being, of course, understood that such Desire may have manifested subconsciously rather than in the conscious field). It is almost impossible to conceive of one willing to do a thing other than from the motive of Desire, either in the form of "wanting to" on the one hand, or of fear on the other hand. Will is always the active expression of some form of Desire.

2. DELIBERATIVE WILL.
In this second phase of Will activity, there is **a balancing and weighing of desires, or at least a weighing and balancing of several courses of action, in order to determine their values as a channel of expression of the strongest desires.**

Sometimes there is a dominant desire that presses aside all other desires, and asserts its strength and power; in such a case, the deliberation is simply that of determining the best possible channel of expression. But, as a rule, there is first a conflict of desires, which results either in the victory of **the strongest desire present at that moment,** or else **an average struck between several strong desires then present.**

### 3. Action-Will.

Some persons can never seem to understand that **resolving** to do a thing is not the same as doing it. Such are utterly worthless in this world of action. They **talk**; they **feel**; they do anything **but act.** They appear to derive almost as much comfort from resolving to answer a letter, which should have been answered two months earlier, as they would from actually writing the reply. There may be desire, deliberation, and decision; but if these do not result in action, the process of will is practically incomplete.

### Training the Will

Just as the Master Mind may train the faculties of Thought, Feeling, and Emotion, so may it train, control, direct, and master the faculties of the Will. And this last is perhaps the most important of all the various forms of mastery manifested by the Ego, or Master Mind, because the Will is the instrument the Ego uses to control the other mental faculties—and control of the Will is control of the entire situation.

The following Rules of Will Development provide a simple, practical system of training and cultivating the Will.

### 1. Finding the Center of Power.

This rule consists of bidding the student to find the center of his mental being—the place where dwells the Ego, the Master of Mind, the "I." This involves not only assenting to the presence of the Ego on the part of the intellect, but also of the conscious **feeling** of the presence, reality and power of the "I" in the center of the mental field, where it masters, directs, controls, and manages the feelings, emotions, thought processes, objects of attention and desire, and, finally, of the **activities of the will.**

The Ego must learn to turn its attention inward upon itself, and to be conscious of its own presence and existence. It must inwardly cognize itself as the "I"—an actual living entity or being. To do this fully, the Ego must for the moment separate itself from the various instruments and faculties belonging to it—it must see and feel itself simply as the pure Ego—the "I AM!" Each time you control or direct the mind, say to yourself "**I, the Ego, the Master Mind, am doing this**"—and you will be made conscious of a dawning realization of the Ego, which is Yourself—your **Real Self**.

## 2. Exert Your Will Power.

Exert Your Will Power by practicing the control over the several mental and emotional faculties: **Will** to think; **Will** to **feel**; **Will** to **act**. For instance, you may feel a desire to do, or not do a certain thing—here is your chance to prove your Willpower. Deliberately determine that you **shall and will** desire and feel the exact opposite of your present desire, and then proceed to manifest in action that idea and determination. You will find that the original desire or feeling will struggle and rebel—it will fight hard for life and power—but you must oppose it to the deadly cold steel of your will, as directed by the Master Mind. Persevere, and yield not an inch—assert your mastery of your mental domain. Ask no quarter, and give none; and as sure as tomorrow's sun will rise, so surely will your will triumph. For the Will is positive to other mental states, when it is properly applied and persistently exerted.

## 3. Consider Your Actions.

Cultivate the faculty of careful deliberation and intelligent determination. In short, look before you leap. Test your feelings, emotions, impulses, and desires by the light of intellect. Test every desire and impulse by the Touchstone of Positivity: "Will this make me stronger, better, and more efficient?" Do not prolong your deliberation too long, however—learn to decide carefully but at the same time quickly and without dawdling. **Then,** when you have determined upon your course of action—have decided **what** to do, and **how** to do it, as well as understanding **why** you should do it—proceed to **actually do it with all your might**. Follow the old maxim: "Be sure you're right, then go ahead!"

## 4. Cultivate the Attention.

Carefully cultivate the Attention until you can focus it upon any object or subject with concentrated force and insistent direction. The Attention determines the path of the will—either toward or away from the object of the Attention. Attention is the eye of the Ego, or Master Mind, the driver of the mental chariot.

### 5. Acquire the Habit of Mastery.

Carefully cultivate and acquire the habit of controlling your mental faculties, feelings, desires, and thoughts, as well as your actions, by the power of your awakened will. When you have acquired this habit, half the battle is over. Then will the wild horses of the mind have learned the lesson of control, and will interpose a constantly decreasing degree of resistance, and a constantly increasing obedience.

### 6. Occasionally Perform Disagreeable Tasks.

You will find that it is of great benefit to occasionally drive your mental steeds in directions contrary to that which they wish to travel. This course is advisable, not because the agreeable way is necessarily wrong, but simply because such exercise of control trains them and accustoms them to the direction of the Master Mind.

One writer mentions the case of a man who was found reading a particularly dry work on political economy. His friend expressed surprise at his choice of a book, and the man replied: **"I am doing this because I dislike it!"** He was training his mental horses. One of the best and simplest methods of putting this rule into practice is that of heeding the popular adage: "DO IT NOW!" Procrastination is a particularly balky horse, and one that requires careful and persistent attention.

## The "James Formulas"

No presentation of the best modern thought concerning the Cultivation of Willpower would be complete without mentioning the celebrated formulas of the great American psychologist William James. Professor James based these formulas upon those of philosopher Alexander Bain, elaborating the latter and adding some equally good advice to them. Here is a condensed statement of the "James Formulas."

1. "In the acquisition of a new habit, or the leaving off of an old one, launch yourself with as strong and decided an initiative as possible. This will give your new beginning such a momentum that the temptation to break down will not occur as soon as it otherwise might; and every day during

which a breakdown is postponed adds to the chances of it not occurring at all."
2. "Never suffer an exception to occur till the new habit is securely rooted in your life. Every lapse is like the letting fall of a ball of string which one is carefully winding up—a single slip undoes more than a great many turns will wind again." "It is necessary, above all things, in such a situation, never to lose a battle. Every gain on the wrong side undoes the effect of many conquests on the right. The essential precaution is so to regulate the two opposing powers that the one may have a series of uninterrupted successes, until repetition has fortified it to such a degree as to enable it to cope with the opposition, under any circumstances."
3. "Seize the very first possible opportunity to act on every resolution you make, and on every emotional prompting you may experience in the direction of the habits you wish to gain. It is not the moment of their forming, but in the moment of their producing motor effects, that resolves, and aspirations communicate their new 'set' to the brain. The actual presence of the practical opportunity alone furnishes the fulcrum upon which the lever can rest, by which the moral will may multiply its strength and raise itself aloft. He who has no solid ground to press against will never get beyond the stage of empty gesture making."
4. "Keep the faculty alive in you by a little gratuitous exercise every day. That is, be systematically ascetic or heroic in little, unnecessary points; do every day something for no other reason than that you would rather not do it, so that when the hour of dire need draws nigh, it may find you not unnerved and untrained to stand the test. The man who has daily inured himself to habits of concentrated attention, energetic volition, and self-denial in unnecessary things will stand like a tower when everything rocks around him, and when his softer mortals are winnowed like chaff in the blast."

In closing, the student who is striving to develop his Willpower will do well to hold before his mental vision the Inspiring Ideal of the Goal toward which he is struggling and striving.

Benjamin Disraeli wrote: "I have brought myself by long meditation to the conviction that a human being with a settled purpose must accomplish it, and that nothing can resist a will which will stake even existence upon its fulfillment."

Decide which you wish to be: Master Mind or Slave Mind. You have the choice—make it! I have led you to the spring from which bubbles the Waters of Mastery—but I cannot force you to drink. In the words of an old writer: "Man must be either the Anvil or the Hammer—let each make his choice, and then complain not."

# The Prophet
(1923)

## by Khalil Gibran

*The Unparalleled Classic on Life's Meaning—
Now in a Special Condensation*

### Contents

Introduction   *A Guide to Powerful Living* by Mitch Horowitz   440

The Prophet   442

## Introduction
# A Guide to Powerful Living

Poet Khalil Gibran's *The Prophet* is probably the most widespread and influential work of modern inspirational literature. Its impact is difficult to overstate, touching the lives of readers from politicians and radicals to movie stars and pop singers. *The Prophet* impacted the revolution in alternative spirituality that was travelling the globe when the book first appeared in 1923. It impacted the Beat culture of the 1950s, with its calls for a boundary-free search for truth. Its spirit of love and rebelliousness influenced the Woodstock generation. And today it remains a standard work for people who consider themselves spiritual but not religious—yet it also finds a place on the bookshelves of traditional seekers since none of its principles run counter to mainline religion.

Gibran's brilliance in writing *The Prophet*—in which an unnamed figure delivers a series of aphorisms to a group of villagers—is that he distilled the highest and most universal principles of all faiths, East and West, ancient and modern. That his book resonates so deeply with readers of diffuse backgrounds testifies to the truth, sensed instinctively by so many people and enunciated within the book's pages, that, issues of doctrine and dogma aside, there really *does* exist a common core of ethics and values at the heart of the world's enduring faiths. This core is distilled in *The Prophet*.

In terms of meaning and influence, I group *The Prophet* with works like the *Tao Te Ching* and the *Meditations* of Marcus Aurelius. All of these expressions have attained posterity because they return us to what was being sought from religions before religions themselves were formed.

In essence, *The Prophet* is a guide to ethical living. The purpose of my condensation is not to replace the original, which no book can do, but rather to distill the poet's most poignant and applicable ideals. That you can experience the book in a single sitting makes me hope you will become a lifelong reader of it, and also venture into the original text.

Gibran's verse has so fully permeated our culture that you may be surprised to encounter passages that remind you of some of our best-known expressions. Take for example Gibran's maxim: "And what is fear of need but need itself?" Ten years after he wrote those words, Franklin Roosevelt in 1933 announced in his first inaugural speech: "The only thing we have to fear is fear itself."

Writer Joseph Wakim detected a similar parallel in the widely repeated lines from John F. Kennedy's 1961 inaugural address: "Ask not what your country can do for you. Ask what you can do for your country." Writing in 2011 in the *Sydney Morning Herald*, Wakim noted that the Lebanese-American poet Gibran "never intended these words to be addressed by a president to his people." Rather:

> He was writing an open letter, in Arabic, to Lebanese parliamentarians in 1925, during the fall of the Ottoman Empire. His letter was titled 'The New Frontier,' which gives a completely different meaning and context. 'Are you a politician asking what your country can do for you or a zealous one asking what you can do for your country?' he wrote.

What's more, JFK had used the phrase "New Frontier" as the signature of his convention acceptance speech several months earlier and, as Wakim notes, made it a keynote of his administration, saying: "We stand today on the edge of a new frontier—the frontier of the 1960s, the frontier of unknown opportunities and perils, the frontier of unfilled hopes and unfilled threats." Few Americans would have connected the president's soaring words with the work of an Arab-American poet who had died nearly three decades earlier.

Part of the power of Gibran's work is that every reader seems to find within it exactly what he or she most needs. This has been my personal experience. For about ten years I was a vegetarian for ethical reasons. Shortly before writing these words, I had, as a personal decision, returned to eating meat. I felt conflicted. Then I encountered these lines by Gibran, which seemed to offer a way out of my conflict:

> But since you must kill to eat, and rob the newly born of its mother's milk to quench your thirst, let it then be an act of worship...
> When you kill a beast say to him in your heart,
> "By the same power that slays you, I too am slain; and I too shall be consumed..."

This outlook is not for everyone but it gave me an open door.

Likewise, we can find wisdom in Gibran's work for the run-amuck tone and content of much of today's social media: "And in much of your talking, thinking is half murdered."

Another facet of today's social media is the widespread pirating of intellectual property and the feckless conviction that all songs, art, movies, books, and imagery should be free. Gibran issued a call to always compensate artists and those who create:

> And suffer not the barren-handed to take part in your transactions, who would sell their words for your labour.
> To such men you should say,
> "Come with us to the field, or go with our brothers to the sea and cast your net;
> For the land and the sea shall be bountiful to you even as to us."

Above all, Gibran believed that the contemplative life and the search for meaning are not bound to any ideology or doctrine—nor do they reject any. On this count he wrote: "Your daily life is your temple and your religion."

That one line could sum up his entire philosophy. May this short volume bring you phrases and ideas that enable you to find your own personal philosophy within its folds.

—Mitch Horowitz

## The Prophet

The prophet walked among the people. One woman said, Speak to us of Love. The prophet spoke thus:
When love beckons to you, follow him,
Though his ways are hard and steep.
And when his wings enfold you yield to him,
Though the sword hidden among his pinions may wound you.
And when he speaks to you believe in him,
Though his voice may shatter your dreams as the north wind lays waste the garden.

For even as love crowns you so shall he crucify you. Even as he is for your growth so is he for your pruning.
Even as he ascends to your height and caresses your tenderest branches that quiver in the sun,

So shall he descend to your roots and shake them in their clinging to the earth.
Like sheaves of corn he gathers you unto himself.
He threshes you to make you naked.
He sifts you to free you from your husks.
He grinds you to whiteness.
He kneads you until you are pliant;
And then he assigns you to his sacred fire, that you may become sacred bread for God's sacred feast.

All these things shall love do unto you that you may know the secrets of your heart, and in that knowledge become a fragment of Life's heart.

But if in your fear you would seek only love's peace and love's pleasure,
Then it is better for you that you cover your nakedness and pass out of love's threshing-floor,
Into the seasonless world where you shall laugh, but not all of your laughter, and weep, but not all of your tears.

Love gives naught but itself and takes naught but from itself.
Love possesses not nor would it be possessed;
For love is sufficient unto love.

Love has no other desire but to fulfill itself.

To know the pain of too much tenderness.
To be wounded by your own understanding of love;
And to bleed willingly and joyfully.

༄༅

Love one another, but make not a bond of love:
Let it rather be a moving sea between the shores of your souls.

Sing and dance together and be joyous, but let each one of you be alone,
Even as the strings of a lute are alone though they quiver with the same music.

Give your hearts, but not into each other's keeping.
For only the hand of Life can contain your hearts.

And stand together yet not too near together:
For the pillars of the temple stand apart,
And the oak tree and the cypress grow not in each other's shadow.

---

And a woman who held a babe against her bosom said, Speak to us of Children.
And he said:
Your children are not your children.
They are the sons and daughters of Life's longing for itself.
They come through you but not from you,
And though they are with you yet they belong not to you.

You may give them your love but not your thoughts,
For they have their own thoughts.
You may house their bodies but not their souls,
For their souls dwell in the house of to-morrow, which you cannot visit, not even in your dreams.
You may strive to be like them, but seek not to make them like you.
For life goes not backward nor tarries with yesterday.

You are the bows from which your children as living arrows are sent forth.
The archer sees the mark upon the path of the infinite, and He bends you with His might that His arrows may go swift and far.
Let your bending in the Archer's hand be for gladness;
For even as He loves the arrow that flies, so He loves also the bow that is stable.

---

Then said a rich man, Speak to us of Giving.
And he answered:
You give but little when you give of your possessions.
It is when you give of yourself that you truly give.
For what are your possessions but things you keep and guard for fear you may need them tomorrow?
And tomorrow, what shall to-morrow bring to the over-prudent dog burying bones in the trackless sand as he follows the pilgrims to the holy city?

And what is fear of need but need itself?

Is not dread of thirst when your well is full, the thirst that is unquenchable?

There are those who give little of the much which they have—and they give it for recognition and their hidden desire makes their gifts unwholesome.

And there are those who have little and give it all.

These are the believers in life and the bounty of life, and their coffer is never empty.

There are those who give with joy, and that joy is their reward.

And there are those who give with pain, and that pain is their baptism.

And there are those who give and know not pain in giving, nor do they seek joy, nor give with mindfulness of virtue;

They give as in yonder valley the myrtle breathes its fragrance into space.

Through the hands of such as these God speaks, and from behind their eyes He smiles upon the earth.

It is well to give when asked, but it is better to give unasked, through understanding;

And to the open-handed the search for one who shall receive is joy greater than giving.

And is there aught you would withhold?

All you have shall some day be given;

Therefore give now, that the season of giving may be yours and not your inheritors'.

You often say, "I would give, but only to the deserving."

The trees in your orchard say not so, nor the flocks in your pasture.

They give that they may live, for to withhold is to perish.

Surely he who is worthy to receive his days and his nights is worthy of all else from you.

And he who has deserved to drink from the ocean of life deserves to fill his cup from your little stream.

And what desert greater shall there be, than that which lies in the courage and the confidence, nay the charity, of receiving?

And who are you that men should rend their bosom and unveil their pride, that you may see their worth naked and their pride unabashed?

See first that you yourself deserve to be a giver, and an instrument of giving.
For in truth it is life that gives unto life-while you, who deem yourself a giver, are but a witness.

And you receivers—and you are all receivers—assume no weight of gratitude, lest you lay a yoke upon yourself and upon him who gives.
Rather rise together with the giver on his gifts as on wings;
For to be overmindful of your debt is to doubt his generosity who has the free-hearted earth for mother, and God for father.

---

Then an old man, a keeper of an inn, said, Speak to us of Eating and Drinking.
And he said:
Would that you could live on the fragrance of the earth, and like an air plant be sustained by the light.
But since you must kill to eat, and rob the newly born of its mother's milk to quench your thirst, let it then be an act of worship.
And let your board stand an altar on which the pure and the innocent of forest and plain are sacrificed for that which is purer and still more innocent in man.

When you kill a beast say to him in your heart,
"By the same power that slays you, I too am slain; and I too shall be consumed.
For the law that delivered you into my hand shall deliver me into a mightier hand.
Your blood and my blood is naught but the sap that feeds the tree of heaven."

And when you crush an apple with your teeth, say to it in your heart,
"Your seeds shall live in my body,
And the buds of your to-morrow shall blossom in my heart,
And your fragrance shall be my breath,
And together we shall rejoice through all the seasons."

And in the autumn, when you gather the grapes of your vineyards for the winepress, say in your heart,
"I too am a vineyard, and my fruit shall be gathered for the winepress,
And like new wine I shall be kept in eternal vessels."

And in winter, when you draw the wine, let there be in your heart a song for each cup;

And let there be in the song a remembrance for the autumn days, and for the vineyard, and for the winepress.

***

Then a ploughman said, Speak to us of Work.

And he answered, saying:

You work that you may keep pace with the earth and the soul of the earth.

For to be idle is to become a stranger unto the seasons, and to step out of life's procession that marches in majesty and proud submission towards the infinite.

When you work you are a flute through whose heart the whispering of the hours turns to music.

Which of you would be a reed, dumb and silent, when all else sings together in unison?

Always you have been told that work is a curse and labour a misfortune.

But I say to you that when you work you fulfill a part of earth's furthest dream, assigned to you when that dream was born,

And in keeping yourself with labour you are in truth loving life,

And to love life through labour is to be intimate with life's inmost secret.

You have been told also that life is darkness, and in your weariness you echo what was said by the weary.

And I say that life is indeed darkness save when there is urge,

And all urge is blind save when there is knowledge,

And all knowledge is vain save when there is work,

And all work is empty save when there is love;

And when you work with love you bind your self to yourself, and to one another, and to God.

***

And a merchant said, Speak to us of Buying and Selling.

And he answered and said:

To you the earth yields her fruit, and you shall not want if you but know how to fill your hands.

It is in exchanging the gifts of the earth that you shall find abundance and be satisfied.

Yet unless the exchange be in love and kindly justice it will but lead some to greed and others to hunger.

When in the market-place you toilers of the sea and fields and vineyards meet the weavers and the potters and the gatherers of spices,—

Invoke then the master spirit of the earth, to come into your midst and sanctify the scales and the reckoning that weighs value against value.

And suffer not the barren-handed to take part in your transactions, who would sell their words for your labour.

To such men you should say,

"Come with us to the field, or go with our brothers to the sea and cast your net;

For the land and the sea shall be bountiful to you even as to us."

And if there come the singers and the dancers and the flute players,—buy of their gifts also.

For they too are gatherers of fruit and frankincense, and that which they bring, though fashioned of dreams, is raiment and food for your soul.

And before you leave the market-place, see that no one has gone his way with empty hands.

For the master spirit of the earth shall not sleep peacefully upon the wind till the needs of the least of you are satisfied.

※

Then one of the judges of the city stood forth and said, Speak to us of Crime and Punishment.

And he answered, saying:

It is when your spirit goes wandering upon the wind,

That you, alone and unguarded, commit a wrong unto others and therefore unto yourself.

And for that wrong committed must you knock and wait a while unheeded at the gate of the blessed.

Like the ocean is your god-self;
It remains for ever undefiled.
And like the ether it lifts but the winged.
Even like the sun is your god-self;
It knows not the ways of the mole nor seeks it the holes of the serpent.
But your god-self dwells not alone in your being.
Much in you is still man, and much in you is not yet man,
But a shapeless pigmy that walks asleep in the mist searching for its own awakening.
And of the man in you would I now speak.
   For it is he and not your god-self nor the pigmy in the mist that knows crime and the punishment of crime.

   Oftentimes have I heard you speak of one who commits a wrong as though he were not one of you, but a stranger unto you and an intruder upon your world.
   But I say that even as the holy and the righteous cannot rise beyond the highest which is in each one of you,
   So the wicked and the weak cannot fall lower than the lowest which is in you also.
   And as a single leaf turns not yellow but with the silent knowledge of the whole tree,
   So the wrong-doer cannot do wrong without the hidden will of you all.
   Like a procession you walk together towards your god-self.
   You are the way and the wayfarers.
   And when one of you falls down he falls for those behind him, a caution against the stumbling stone.
   Ay, and he falls for those ahead of him, who, though faster and surer of foot, yet removed not the stumbling stone.

   And this also, though the word lie heavy upon your hearts:
   The murdered is not unaccountable for his own murder,
   And the robbed is not blameless in being robbed.
   The righteous is not innocent of the deeds of the wicked,
   And the white-handed is not clean in the doings of the felon.
   Yea, the guilty is oftentimes the victim of the injured,

And still more often the condemned is the burden bearer for the guiltless and unblamed.

You cannot separate the just from the unjust and the good from the wicked;

For they stand together before the face of the sun even as the black thread and the white are woven together.

And when the black thread breaks, the weaver shall look into the whole cloth, and he shall examine the loom also.

If any of you would bring to judgment the unfaithful wife,

Let him also weigh the heart of her husband in scales, and measure his soul with measurements.

And let him who would lash the offender look unto the spirit of the offended.

And if any of you would punish in the name of righteousness and lay the axe unto the evil tree, let him see to its roots;

And verily he will find the roots of the good and the bad, the fruitful and the fruitless, all entwined together in the silent heart of the earth.

And you judges who would be just.

What judgment pronounce you upon him who though honest in the flesh yet is a thief in spirit?

What penalty lay you upon him who slays in the flesh yet is himself slain in the spirit?

And how prosecute you him who in action is a deceiver and an oppressor,

Yet who also is aggrieved and outraged?

And how shall you punish those whose remorse is already greater than their misdeeds?

Is not remorse the justice which is administered by that very law which you would fain serve?

Yet you cannot lay remorse upon the innocent nor lift it from the heart of the guilty.

Unbidden shall it call in the night, that men may wake and gaze upon themselves.

And you who would understand justice, how shall you unless you look upon all deeds in the fullness of light?

Only then shall you know that the erect and the fallen are but one man standing in twilight between the night of his pigmy-self and the day of his god self,

And that the corner-stone of the temple is not higher than the lowest stone in its foundation.

⁕

Then a lawyer said, But what of our Laws, master?
And he answered:
You delight in laying down laws,
Yet you delight more in breaking them.
Like children playing by the ocean who build sand-towers with constancy and then destroy them with laughter.
But while you build your sand-towers the ocean brings more sand to the shore,
And when you destroy them the ocean laughs with you.
Verily the ocean laughs always with the innocent.

But what of those to whom life is not an ocean, and man-made laws are not sand-towers,
But to whom life is a rock, and the law a chisel with which they would carve it in their own likeness?
What of the cripple who hates dancers?
What of the ox who loves his yoke and deems the elk and deer of the forest stray and vagrant things?
What of the old serpent who cannot shed his skin, and calls all others naked and shameless?
And of him who comes early to the wedding feast, and when over-fed and tired goes his way saying that all feasts are violation and all feasters lawbreakers?

What shall I say of these save that they too stand in the sunlight, but with their backs to the sun?
They see only their shadows, and their shadows are their laws.
And what is the sun to them but a caster of shadows?
And what is it to acknowledge the laws but to stoop down and trace their shadows upon the earth?
But you who walk facing the sun, what images drawn on the earth can hold you?
You who travel with the wind, what weather vane shall direct your course?

What man's law shall bind you if you break your yoke but upon no man's prison door?

What laws shall you fear if you dance but stumble against no man's iron chains?

And who is he that shall bring you to judgment if you tear off your garment yet leave it in no man's path?

⊸⧖⊷

And the priestess spoke and said: Speak to us of Reason and Passion.

And he answered, saying:

Your soul is oftentimes a battlefield, upon which your reason and your judgment wage war against your passion and your appetite.

Would that I could be the peacemaker in your soul, that I might turn the discord and the rivalry of your elements into oneness and melody.

But how shall I, unless you yourselves be also the peacemakers, nay, the lovers of all your elements?

Your reason and your passion are the rudder and the sails of your seafaring soul.

If either your sails or your rudder be broken, you can but toss and drift, or else be held at a standstill in mid-seas.

For reason, ruling alone, is a force confining; and passion, unattended, is a flame that burns to its own destruction.

Therefore let your soul exalt your reason to the height of passion, that it may sing;

And let it direct your passion with reason, that your passion may live through its own daily resurrection, and like the phoenix rise above its own ashes.

I would have you consider your judgment and your appetite even as you would two loved guests in your house.

Surely you would not honour one guest above the other; for he who is more mindful of one loses the love and the faith of both.

Among the hills, when you sit in the cool shade of the white poplars, sharing the peace and serenity of distant fields and meadows—then let your heart say in silence, "God rests in reason."

And when the storm comes, and the mighty wind shakes the forest, and thunder and lightning proclaim the majesty of the sky,—then let your heart say in awe, "God moves in passion."

And since you are a breath in God's sphere, and a leaf in God's forest, you too should rest in reason and move in passion.

---

And a woman spoke, saying, Tell us of Pain.

And he said:

Your pain is the breaking of the shell that encloses your understanding.

Even as the stone of the fruit must break, that its heart may stand in the sun, so must you know pain.

And could you keep your heart in wonder at the daily miracles of your life, your pain would not seem less wondrous than your joy;

And you would accept the seasons of your heart, even as you have always accepted the seasons that pass over your fields.

And you would watch with serenity through the winters of your grief.

Much of your pain is self-chosen.

It is the bitter potion by which the physician within you heals your sick self.

Therefore trust the physician, and drink his remedy in silence and tranquillity:

For his hand, though heavy and hard, is guided by the tender hand of the Unseen,

And the cup he brings, though it burn your lips, has been fashioned of the clay which the Potter has moistened with His own sacred tears.

---

AND a man said, Speak to us of Self-Knowledge.

And he answered, saying:

Your hearts know in silence the secrets of the days and the nights.

But your ears thirst for the sound of your heart's knowledge.

You would know in words that which you have always known in thought.

You would touch with your fingers the naked body of your dreams.

And it is well you should.

The hidden well-spring of your soul must needs rise and run murmuring to the sea;

And the treasure of your infinite depths would be revealed to your eyes.

But let there be no scales to weigh your unknown treasure;

And seek not the depths of your knowledge with staff or sounding line.

For self is a sea boundless and measureless.

Say not, "I have found the truth," but rather, "I have found a truth."

Say not, "I have found the path of the soul." Say rather, "I have met the soul walking upon my path."

For the soul walks upon all paths.

The soul walks not upon a line, neither does it grow like a reed.

The soul unfolds itself, like a lotus of countless petals.

---

Then said a teacher, Speak to us of Teaching.

And he said:

No man can reveal to you aught but that which already lies half asleep in the dawning of your knowledge.

The teacher who walks in the shadow of the temple, among his followers, gives not of his wisdom but rather of his faith and his lovingness.

If he is indeed wise he does not bid you enter the house of his wisdom, but rather leads you to the threshold of your own mind.

The astronomer may speak to you of his understanding of space, but he cannot give you his understanding.

The musician may sing to you of the rhythm which is in all space, but he cannot give you the ear which arrests the rhythm, nor the voice that echoes it.

And he who is versed in the science of numbers can tell of the regions of weight and measure, but he cannot conduct you thither.

For the vision of one man lends not its wings to another man.

And even as each one of you stands alone in God's knowledge, so must each one of you be alone in his knowledge of God and in his understanding of the earth.

---

And a youth said, Speak to us of Friendship.

And he answered, saying:

Your friend is your needs answered.
He is your field which you sow with love and reap with thanksgiving.
And he is your board and your fireside.
For you come to him with your hunger, and you seek him for peace.

When your friend speaks his mind you fear not the "nay" in your own mind, nor do you withhold the "ay."
And when he is silent your heart ceases not to listen to his heart;
For without words, in friendship, all thoughts, all desires, all expectations are born and shared, with joy that is unclaimed.
When you part from your friend, you grieve not;
For that which you love most in him may be clearer in his absence, as the mountain to the climber is clearer from the plain.
And let there be no purpose in friendship save the deepening of the spirit.
For love that seeks aught but the disclosure of its own mystery is not love but a net cast forth: and only the unprofitable is caught.

And let your best be for your friend.
If he must know the ebb of your tide, let him know its flood also.
For what is your friend that you should seek him with hours to kill?
Seek him always with hours to live.
For it is his to fill your need, but not your emptiness.
And in the sweetness of friendship let there be laughter, and sharing of pleasures.
For in the dew of little things the heart finds its morning and is refreshed.

And then a scholar said, Speak of Talking.
And he answered, saying:
You talk when you cease to be at peace with your thoughts;
And when you can no longer dwell in the solitude of your heart you live in your lips, and sound is a diversion and a pastime.
And in much of your talking, thinking is half murdered.
For thought is a bird of space, that in a cage of words may indeed unfold its wings but cannot fly.

There are those among you who seek the talkative through fear of being alone.

The silence of aloneness reveals to their eyes their naked selves and they would escape.

And there are those who talk, and without knowledge or forethought reveal a truth which they themselves do not understand.

And there are those who have the truth within them, but they tell it not in words.

In the bosom of such as these the spirit dwells in rhythmic silence.

When you meet your friend on the roadside or in the market-place, let the spirit in you move your lips and direct your tongue.

Let the voice within your voice speak to the ear of his ear;

For his soul will keep the truth of your heart as the taste of the wine is remembered.

When the colour is forgotten and the vessel is no more.

༺༻

And one of the elders of the city said, Speak to us of Good and Evil.
And he answered:
Of the good in you I can speak, but not of the evil.
For what is evil but good tortured by its own hunger and thirst?
Verily when good is hungry it seeks food even in dark caves, and when it thirsts it drinks even of dead waters.

You are good when you are one with yourself.
Yet when you are not one with yourself you are not evil.
For a divided house is not a den of thieves; it is only a divided house.
And a ship without rudder may wander aimlessly among perilous isles yet sink not to the bottom.

You are good when you strive to give of yourself.
Yet you are not evil when you seek gain for yourself.
For when you strive for gain you are but a root that clings to the earth and sucks at her breast.
Surely the fruit cannot say to the root, "Be like me, ripe and full and ever giving of your abundance."

For to the fruit giving is a need, as receiving is a need to the root.

You are good when you are fully awake in your speech.
Yet you are not evil when you sleep while your tongue staggers without purpose.
And even stumbling speech may strengthen a weak tongue.

You are good when you walk to your goal firmly and with bold steps.
Yet you are not evil when you go thither limping.
Even those who limp go not backward.
But you who are strong and swift, see that you do not limp before the lame, deeming it kindness.

You are good in countless ways, and you are not evil when you are not good,
You are only loitering and sluggard.
Pity that the stags cannot teach swiftness to the turtles.

In your longing for your giant self lies your goodness: and that longing is in all of you.
But in some of you that longing is a torrent rushing with might to the sea, carrying the secrets of the hillsides and the songs of the forest.
And in others it is a flat stream that loses itself in angles and bends and lingers before it reaches the shore.
But let not him who longs much say to him who longs little, "Wherefore are you slow and halting?"
For the truly good ask not the naked, "Where is your garment?" nor the houseless, "What has befallen your house?"

Then a priestess said, "Speak to us of Prayer."
And he answered, saying:
You pray in your distress and in your need; would that you might pray also in the fullness of your joy and in your days of abundance.

For what is prayer but the expansion of your self into the living ether?
And if it is for your comfort to pour your darkness into space, it is also for your delight to pour forth the dawning of your heart.

And if you cannot but weep when your soul summons you to prayer, she should spur you again and yet again, though weeping, until you shall come laughing.

When you pray you rise to meet in the air those who are praying at that very hour, and whom save in prayer you may not meet.

Therefore let your visit to that temple invisible be for naught but ecstasy and sweet communion.

For if you should enter the temple for no other purpose than asking you shall not receive:

And if you should enter into it to humble yourself you shall not be lifted:

Or even if you should enter into it to beg for the good of others you shall not be heard.

It is enough that you enter the temple invisible.

I cannot teach you how to pray in words.

God listens not to your words save when He Himself utters them through your lips.

And I cannot teach you the prayer of the seas and the forests and the mountains.

But you who are born of the mountains and the forests and the seas can find their prayer in your heart,

And if you but listen in the stillness of the night you shall hear them saying in silence:

"Our God, who art our winged self, it is thy will in us that willeth.

It is thy desire in us that desireth.

It is thy urge in us that would turn our nights, which are thine, into days, which are thine also.

We cannot ask thee for aught, for thou knowest our needs before they are born in us:

Thou art our need; and in giving us more of thyself thou givest us all."

Then a hermit came forth and said, Speak to us of Pleasure.

And he answered, saying:

Pleasure is a freedom-song,

But it is not freedom.

It is the blossoming of your desires,
But it is not their fruit.
It is a depth calling unto a height,
But it is not the deep nor the high.
It is the caged taking wing,
But it is not space encompassed.
Ay, in very truth, pleasure is a freedom-song.
And I fain would have you sing it with fullness of heart; yet I would not have you lose your hearts in the singing.

Some of your youth seek pleasure as if it were all, and they are judged and rebuked.
I would not judge nor rebuke them. I would have them seek.
For they shall find pleasure, but not her alone;
Seven are her sisters, and the least of them is more beautiful than pleasure.
Have you not heard of the man who was digging in the earth for roots and found a treasure?

And some of your elders remember pleasures with regret like wrongs committed in drunkenness.
But regret is the beclouding of the mind and not its chastisement.
They should remember their pleasures with gratitude, as they would the harvest of a summer.
Yet if it comforts them to regret, let them be comforted.

And there are among you those who are neither young to seek nor old to remember;
And in their fear of seeking and remembering they shun all pleasures, lest they neglect the spirit or offend against it.
But even in their foregoing is their pleasure.
And thus they too find a treasure though they dig for roots with quivering hands.
But tell me, who is he that can offend the spirit?
Shall the nightingale offend the stillness of the night, or the firefly the stars?
And shall your flame or your smoke burden the wind?
Think you the spirit is a still pool which you can trouble with a staff?

Oftentimes in denying yourself pleasure you do but store the desire in the recesses of your being.

Who knows but that which seems omitted to day, waits for to-morrow?

Even your body knows its heritage and its rightful need and will not be deceived.

And your body is the harp of your soul,

And it is yours to bring forth sweet music from it or confused sounds.

And now you ask in your heart, "How shall we distinguish that which is good in pleasure from that which is not good?"

Go to your fields and your gardens, and you shall learn that it is the pleasure of the bee to gather honey of the flower,

But it is also the pleasure of the flower to yield its honey to the bee.

For to the bee a flower is a fountain of life,

And to the flower a bee is a messenger of love,

And to both, bee and flower, the giving and the receiving of pleasure is a need and an ecstasy.

And an old priest said, "Speak to us of Religion."

And he said:

Have I spoken this day of aught else?

Is not religion all deeds and all reflection,

And that which is neither deed nor reflection, but a wonder and a surprise ever springing in the soul, even while the hands hew the stone or tend the loom?

Who can separate his faith from his actions, or his belief from his occupations?

Who can spread his hours before him, saying,"This for God and this for myself;

This for my soul and this other for my body?"

All your hours are wings that beat through space from self to self.

He who wears his morality but as his best garment were better naked.

The wind and the sun will tear no holes in his skin.

And he who defines his conduct by ethics imprisons his song-bird in a cage.

The freest song comes not through bars and wires.

And he to whom worshipping is a window, to open but also to shut, has not yet visited the house of his soul whose windows are from dawn to dawn.

Your daily life is your temple and your religion.
Whenever you enter into it take with you your all.
Take the slough and the forge and the mallet and the lute,
The things you have fashioned in necessity or for delight.
For in reverie you cannot rise above your achievements nor fall lower than your failures.
And take with you all men:
For in adoration you cannot fly higher than their hopes nor humble yourself lower than their despair.

And if you would know God, be not therefore a solver of riddles.
Rather look about you and you shall see Him playing with your children.
And look into space; you shall see Him walking in the cloud, outstretching His arms in the lightning and descending in rain.
You shall see Him smiling in flowers, then rising and waving His hands in trees.

―――

Than another spoke, saying, "We would ask now of Death."
And he said:
You would know the secret of death.
But how shall you find it unless you seek it in the heart of life?
The owl whose night-bound eyes are blind unto the day cannot unveil the mystery of light.
If you would indeed behold the spirit of death, open your heart wide unto the body of life.
For life and death are one, even as the river and the sea are one.

In the depth of your hopes and desires lies your silent knowledge of the beyond;
And like seeds dreaming beneath the snow your heart dreams of spring.
Trust the dreams, for in them is hidden the gate to eternity.
Your fear of death is but the trembling of the shepherd when he stands before the king whose hand is to be laid upon him in honour.

Is the shepherd not joyful beneath his trembling, that he shall wear the mark of the king?

Yet is he not more mindful of his trembling?

For what is it to die but to stand naked in the wind and to melt into the sun?

And what is it to cease breathing but to free the breath from its restless tides, that it may rise and expand and seek God unencumbered?

Only when you drink from the river of silence shall you indeed sing.

And when you have reached the mountain top, then you shall begin to climb.

And when the earth shall claim your limbs, then shall you truly dance.

---

And then the prophet declared, you called unto me, not in words and said,

"Stranger, stranger, lover of unreachable heights, why dwell you among the summits where eagles build their nests?

Why seek you the unattainable?

What storms would you trap in your net,

And what vaporous birds do you hunt in the sky?

Come and be one of us.

Descend and appease your hunger with our bread and quench your thirst with our wine."

In the solitude of their souls they said these things;

But were their solitude deeper they would have known that I sought but the secret of your joy and your pain,

And I hunted only your larger selves that walk the sky.

But the hunter was also the hunted;

For many of my arrows left my bow only to seek my own breast.

And the flier was also the creeper;

For when my wings were spread in the sun their shadow upon the earth was a turtle.

And I the believer was also the doubter;

For often have I put my finger in my own wound that I might have the greater belief in you and the greater knowledge of you.

And it is with this belief and this knowledge that I say,
You are not enclosed within your bodies, nor confined to houses or fields.
That which is you dwells above the mountain and roves with the wind.
It is not a thing that crawls into the sun for warmth or digs holes into darkness for safety,
But a thing free, a spirit that envelops the earth and moves in the ether.

If these be vague words, then seek not to clear them.
Vague and nebulous is the beginning of all things, but not their end,
And I fain would have you remember me as a beginning.
Life, and all that lives, is conceived in the mist and not in the crystal.
And who knows but a crystal is mist in decay?

This would I have you remember in remembering me:
That which seems most feeble and bewildered in you is the strongest and most determined.
Is it not your breath that has erected and hardened the structure of your bones?
And is it not a dream which none of you remember having dreamt, that built your city and fashioned all there is in it?
Could you but see the tides of that breath you would cease to see all else,
And if you could hear the whispering of the dream you would hear no other sound.

But you do not see, nor do you hear, and it is well.
The veil that clouds your eyes shall be lifted by the hands that wove it,
And the clay that fills your ears shall be pierced by those fingers that kneaded it.
And you shall see.
And you shall hear.
Yet you shall not deplore having known blindness, nor regret having been deaf.

For in that day you shall know the hidden purposes in all things,
And you shall bless darkness as you would bless light.

After saying these things he looked about him, and he saw the pilot of his ship standing by the helm and gazing now at the full sails and now at the distance.

And he said:

Patient, over patient, is the captain of my ship.

The wind blows, and restless are the sails;

Even the rudder begs direction;

Yet quietly my captain awaits my silence.

And these my mariners, who have heard the choir of the greater sea, they too have heard me patiently.

Now they shall wait no longer.

I am ready.

The stream has reached the sea, and once more the great mother holds her son against her breast.

Fare you well.

This day has ended.

It is closing upon us even as the waterlily upon its own to-morrow.

What was given us here we shall keep,

And if it suffices not, then again must we come together and together stretch our hands unto the giver.

Forget not that I shall come back to you.

A little while, and my longing shall gather dust and foam for another body.

A little while, a moment of rest upon the wind, and another woman shall bear me.

"A little while, a moment of rest upon the wind, and another woman shall bear me."

# The Game of Life and How to Play It
(1925)

## by Florence Scovel Shinn

*The Timeless Classic on Successful Living*

## Contents

Introduction  *Philosopher of Everyday Life* by Mitch Horowitz  466
Chapter One  The Game  467
Chapter Two  The Law of Prosperity  469
Chapter Three  The Power of the Word  470
Chapter Four  The Law of Nonresistance  471
Chapter Five  The Law of Karma  472
Chapter Six  Casting the Burden (Impressing the Subconscious)  473
Chapter Seven  Love  475
Chapter Eight  Intuition or Guidance  476
Chapter Nine  Perfect Self-Expression or the Divine Design  477
Chapter Ten  Denials and Affirmations  478

## Introduction
# Philosopher of Everyday Life

Ask any fan of motivational or New Thought literature to name his or her favorite books, and chances are the list will include Florence Scovel Shinn's *The Game of Life and How to Play It*.

Shinn's book has been beloved among self-help readers since it first appeared in 1925. Yet it almost didn't appear at all. Shinn, a respected illustrator of children's literature, could not get New York publishers interested in her metaphysical philosophy. Finding no takers, the artist published the book herself.

Shinn's outlook is simple and decisive. Within you, she writes, exist three minds: the *conscious mind*, which you use to navigate daily life; the *subconscious mind*, which acts on suggestions, good or bad, from your conscious mind; and the *superconscious mind*, a spark of divine power within you. Your superconscious, she writes, possesses infinite awareness and the creative ability to remake your world. Shinn provides methods to get in tune with this higher mind, and thus "win" at the game of life.

What accounts for Shinn's longstanding popularity? Her ideas were not unique to her time. Contemporaneous metaphysical writers, such as William Walker Atkinson and Wallace D. Wattles, held similar views. Yet listening to Shinn always feels like hearing from a trusted friend—someone who understands our daily struggles and who doesn't talk above us; but who also isn't afraid to deliver tough advice and won't tolerate excuses. She insists that we get out there and test her methods on the field of life.

Shinn was a lasting influence on many leaders in the positive-thinking movement, including Emmett Fox, Norman Vincent Peale, and Louise Hay. It is notable that each of these figures is from a different generation: Fox, a popular New Thought minister, was a contemporary of Shinn's; Peale, a Methodist minister, rose to worldwide fame in the 1950s as the author of *The Power of Positive Thinking*; and Hay is widely known today as a pioneering New Age publisher and writer. Martin Luther King's eldest daughter, Yolanda, told me shortly before her death in 2007 that Shinn's writing had influenced her. This gives some sense of Shinn's range of impact.

While Shinn called life a "game," her own life was not easy—nor did she seek ease. Born Florence Scovel in Camden, New Jersey in 1871, she took a rare path as a female artist, attending the Pennsylvania Academy of Fine Arts. There she met her future husband, realist painter Everett Shinn. Married in 1898, they moved to New York's Greenwich Village, where they became part of the Ashcan School of American artists, a cohort known for depicting street scenes, tenements, and the immigrant experience. The couple divorced in 1912. While pursuing her own career as an illustrator, Shinn became a student of metaphysics, leading her to write *The Game of Life* and several other books. She also became a popular spiritual lecturer and counselor. She died in Manhattan in 1940.

One of the defining elements of Shinn's work is its bravery. Shinn neither sought, nor received, mainstream approval. Instead, she embodied a core ideal of American metaphysics: that the common person, the everyday man or woman, is as capable of receiving higher truths as the Biblical prophets of antiquity. Nearly a century after her first book, Shinn has proven the endurance of her message.

—Mitch Horowitz

## Chapter One
# The Game

Most people consider life a battle, but it is not a battle, it is a game.

It is a game, however, that cannot be played successfully without knowledge of spiritual law, and the Old and New Testaments give the rules of the game with wonderful clarity. Jesus Christ taught that life is a great game of *Giving* and *Receiving*.

"Whatsoever a man soweth that shall he also reap." This means that whatever a person sends out in word or deed, will return to him; what he gives, he will receive—hate for hate; love for love; criticism for criticism.

We are also taught that the imaging faculty of the mind plays a leading part in the game of life. "Keep thy heart (or imagination) with all diligence, for out of it are the issues of life." (Proverbs 4:23) This means that what you image in your mind, sooner or later, externalizes in your life.

To successfully play the game of life you must train the imaging faculty. A person with an imaging faculty disciplined to image only good brings into his life "every righteous desire of his heart"—health, wealth, love, friends, perfect self-expression, and high ideals.

To train the imagination successfully, you must understand the workings of your mind. It has three departments: the *subconscious, conscious,* and *superconscious*. The subconscious is simply power without direction. It is like steam or electricity, and it does what it is directed to do. Whatever you feel deeply or image clearly is impressed upon your subconscious, and carried out in minutest detail.

The conscious mind has been called mortal or carnal mind. It is your ordinary human mind, and it sees life as it *appears to be*. It sees death, disaster, sickness, poverty, and limitation of every kind, which it impresses on your subconscious.

The *superconscious* mind is the God Mind within us all, and is the realm of perfect ideas. In it is the "perfect pattern" spoken of by Plato, *The Divine Design*—for there is a *Divine Design* for each one of us.

*There is a place that you are to fill and no one else can fill, something you are to do, that no one else can do.*

A perfect picture of this divine plan exists in your *superconscious mind*. It usually flashes across your conscious mind as an unattainable ideal—"something too good to be true." In reality, this is your true destiny (or destination) coming to you from Infinite Intelligence, which is *within you*.

Many people are ignorant of their true destinies. They strive for things and situations that do not belong to them, and would bring only failure and dissatisfaction if attained.

For example, a woman asked me to "speak the word" that she would marry a certain man. (She called him A.B.) I replied that this would be a violation of spiritual law, but that I would speak the word for the *right man*, the "divine selection."

I added, "If A.B. is the right man you can't lose him; and if he isn't, you will receive his equivalent." She saw A.B. frequently but made no headway in their friendship. One evening she said, "You know, for the last week A.B. hasn't seemed so wonderful to me." I replied, "Maybe he is not the divine selection—another man may be the right one."

Soon after, she did meet another man, who fell in love with her at once and who told her she was his ideal. In fact, he said all the things that she had always wished A.B. would say to her.

This illustration shows the law of substitution. A right idea was substituted for a wrong one and, hence, no loss or sacrifice was entailed. Jesus said, "Seek ye first the Kingdom of God and his righteousness; and all these things shall be added unto you," and he said the Kingdom is *within man*.

The Kingdom is the realm of *right ideas*, or the divine pattern, revealed to us by our superconscious mind, or Christ within. In the following chapters we will learn more about the awesome possibilities of this power within us.

Chapter Two

# The Law of Prosperity

One of the greatest messages given to humanity through Scripture is that God is man's supply, and that man can release, *through his spoken word*, all that is his by divine right. He must, however, have *perfect faith in his spoken word*.

Isaiah said, "My word shall not return unto me void, but shall accomplish that where unto it is sent." Words and thoughts are a tremendous vibratory force, ever molding man's body and affairs.

But remember, if one asks for success and prepares for failure, he will get the situation he has prepared for. A man once asked me to speak the word that a certain debt would be wiped out. I found that he spent his time planning what he would say to his debtor when he did not pay his bill, thereby neutralizing my words. He should have seen himself paying the debt.

We see a wonderful depiction of this in the Bible, relating to three kings in the desert, who were without water for their men and horses. They consulted the prophet Elisha, who gave them this astonishing message: "Thus saith the Lord—Ye shall not see wind, neither shall ye see rain, yet make this valley full of ditches."

You must prepare for the thing you have asked for *when there isn't the slightest sign of it.*

Your adverse thoughts, doubt, and fear surge from the subconscious. They are the "army of the aliens," which must be put to flight. Having made a statement of high spiritual truth, you have challenged the old beliefs in your subconscious, and "error is exposed" to be put out. In fact, a big demonstration is usually preceded by tormenting thoughts. This explains why it is often "darkest before the dawn."

At these times of challenge, you must make your affirmations of truth repeatedly, and rejoice and give thanks that you have already received. "Before ye call I shall answer." This means that "every good and perfect gift" is already yours, awaiting your recognition.

The children of Israel were told that they could have all the land they could see. This is true for each of us. You have only the land within your own mental vision. Every great work, every big accomplishment, has been brought into manifestation through holding to the vision, and often just before the big achievement, comes apparent failure and discouragement.

When the children of Israel reached the "Promised Land" they were afraid to enter, for they said it was filled with giants who made they feel like grasshoppers. This is almost everyone's experience. The one who knows spiritual law, however, is undisturbed by appearance, and rejoices while he is "yet in captivity." He holds to his vision, and gives thanks that the end is accomplished.

## Chapter Three
# The Power of the Word

A person who knows *the power of the word* becomes very careful of his conversation. He has only to watch the reaction of his words to know that they do "not return void." Through his spoken word man is continually making laws for himself.

I have a friend who often says on the phone, "Do come to see me and have a fine old-fashioned chat." This "old-fashioned chat" means an hour of about five hundred to a thousand destructive words, the principal topics being loss, lack, failure, and sickness.

I reply: "No, thank you, I've had enough old-fashioned chats in my life; they are too expensive. But I will be glad to have a new-fashioned chat, and talk about what we want, not what we don't want."

There is an old saying that man only dares use his words for three purposes: to "heal, bless, or prosper." What you say of others will be said of you, and what you wish for another, you are wishing for yourself.

Your only true enemies are within. The enlightened person, therefore, endeavors to perfect himself on his neighbor. His work is to send out goodwill and blessings to every being. And the marvelous thing is, if you bless a man he has no power to harm you. *Goodwill produces a great aura of protection about the one who sends it, and "No weapon that is formed against him shall prosper." In other words, love and goodwill destroy the enemies within one's self—therefore, one has no enemies on the external.*

There is peace on earth for him who sends goodwill to man.

## Chapter Four
# The Law of Nonresistance

Nothing on earth can resist an absolutely nonresistant person.

The Chinese say that water is the most powerful element because it is perfectly nonresistant. It can wear away a rock, and sweep all that is before it.

Jesus said, "Resist not evil," for He knew, in reality, there is no evil, therefore nothing to resist. Evil has come of man's "vain imagination," or a belief in two powers: good and evil.

There is an old legend that Adam and Eve ate of "Maya the Tree of Illusion," and saw two powers instead of one power, God. *Therefore, evil is a false law that man has made for himself.*

Man's soul is his subconscious mind, and whatever he feels deeply, good or bad, is outpictured by that faithful servant. His body and affairs reflect what he has been picturing. The sick man has pictured his sickness, the poor man, poverty, the rich man, wealth. Children are sensitive and receptive to the thoughts of others about them, and often outpicture the fears of their parents.

A metaphysician once said, "If you do not run your subconscious mind yourself, someone else will run it for you." The man who is centered and established in right thinking, the man who sends out only goodwill, and who is without fear, cannot be *touched or influenced by the negative thoughts of others.*

Some of us are kept in bondage by thoughts of the past. Living in the past is a failure and a violation of spiritual law. The past keeps you blocked. You must bless it and forget it; you should likewise bless the future, knowing that it has in store for you endless joys; but you must live *fully in the now.*

Make this affirmation immediately upon waking: *Thy will be done this day! Today is a day of completion; I give thanks for this perfect day, miracle shall follow miracle, and wonders shall never cease.*

Make this a daily habit—and you *will* see wonders and miracles enter your life.

## Chapter Five
# The Law of Karma

The Game of Life is a game of boomerangs. Man's thoughts, deeds, and words return to him, sooner or later, with astounding accuracy.

This is the Law of Karma, which is another way of saying, "Whatsoever a man soweth, that also shall he reap."

The more you know about the Game of Life, the more you are responsible for. Someone with knowledge of Spiritual Law who does not practice it, suffers greatly in consequence. In the Bible, if we read the word Lord as law it will make many passages much clearer. "The fear of the Lord (law) is the beginning of wisdom."

Always remember that *your desires are a tremendous force; they must be directed in the right channels or chaos ensues.*

In demonstrating, the first and most important step is to *ask aright*. Man should always demand only that which is his by *divine right*. We are admonished: "My will be done not thine." And man always gets just what he desires when he *relinquishes personal will*, thereby enabling Infinite Intelligence to work through him. "Stand ye still and see the salvation of the Lord (law)."

A woman came to me in great distress. Her daughter had determined to take a very hazardous trip, and the mother was filled with fear. She had used every argument, had pointed out the dangers, and forbidden her to go. But the daughter became only more rebellious and determined. I told the mother, "You are forcing your personal will upon your daughter, which you have no right to do. Your fear of the trip is only attracting it, for we attract what we fear."

I added, "Let go, and take your mental hands off. *Put it in God's hands, and use this statement*: 'I put this situation in the hands of Infinite Love and Wisdom; if this trip is the Divine plan, I bless it and no longer resist; but if it is not divinely planned, I give thanks that it is now dissolved and dissipated.'"

A day or so later, her daughter told her, "Mother I have given up the trip," and the situation returned to its "native nothingness."

Sometimes our most difficult challenge is that of "standing still." But when we can do that, and turn life over to the Divine Will, events have their perfect outcome.

## Chapter Six

# Casting the Burden
# (Impressing the Subconscious)

When you understand the workings of your mind, your great desire is to find an easy and quick way to impress the subconscious with good; for simply an intellectual knowledge of Truth will not bring results.

I have found that the easiest way is in "casting the burden."

In the fifty-fifth Psalm we are told to "cast thy burden upon the Lord." Many passages in the Bible state that the *battle is God's* not man's, and that man is always to *"stand still"* and *see the Salvation of the Lord.*

That is what Jesus meant when he said, "My yoke is easy and my burden is light." He further said: "Come to me all ye that labor and are heavy laden, and I will give you rest."

This indicates that the superconscious mind (or Christ within) is the department that fights man's battle and relieves him of burdens. We see, therefore, that man violates the law if he carries a burden. And a burden is an adverse thought or condition, and this thought or condition has its root in the subconscious.

It seems almost impossible to make any headway directing the subconscious from the conscious, or reasoning, mind, as the reasoning mind (the intellect) is limited in its conceptions and filled with doubts and fears.

How scientific it then is to cast the burden upon the superconscious mind (or Christ within) where it is "made light," or dissolved into its "native nothingness."

A woman in urgent need of money "made light" upon the Christ within, the superconscious, with this statement: "I cast this burden of lack on the Christ within and I go free to have plenty." The belief in lack was her burden, and as she cast it upon the superconscious, with its belief in plenty, an avalanche of supply resulted.

I knew a woman whose burden was resentment. For years, resentment held her in a state of torment and imprisoned her soul (the subconscious mind). She said: "I cast this resentment on the Christ within and I go free to be loving, harmonious, and happy." The Almighty superconscious flooded the subconscious, and her whole life was changed.

When you "cast the burden," your statement should be made over and over and over, sometimes for hours at a time, silently or audibly, with quietness but determination.

I have noticed in "casting the burden" that after a little while one seems to see clearly. It is impossible to have clear vision while in the throes of the carnal mind. In steadily repeating the affirmation, "I cast this burden on the Christ within and go free," the vision clears, and with it comes a feeling of relief and, sooner or later, *the manifestation of good.*

A student once asked me to explain the "darkness before the dawn." As noted earlier, often before a big demonstration "everything seems to go wrong," and deep depression clouds the consciousness. This means that out of the subconscious are rising doubts and fears of the ages. These old derelicts of the subconscious rise to the surface *to be put out.* It is just then that a man should clap his symbols, like Jehoshaphat, and give thanks that he is saved, even though he seems surrounded by the enemy.

The student continued, "How long must one remain in the dark?" I replied, "Until one *can see in the dark*," and *"Casting the burden enables one to see in the dark."*

In order to impress the subconscious, active faith is essential. Jesus showed active faith when "He commanded the multitude to sit down on the ground," before He gave thanks for the loaves and fishes.

Active faith is the bridge over which man passes to the Promised Land. I will give another example showing how necessary this step is.

A woman I knew had, through misunderstanding, been separated from her husband, whom she loved deeply. He refused all offers of reconciliation. Coming into knowledge of Spiritual Law, she denied the appearance of separation. She made this statement: "There is no separation in Divine Mind, therefore, I cannot be separated from the love and companionship which are mine by divine right."

She showed active faith by arranging a place for him at the table every day, thereby impressing the subconscious with a picture of his return. More than a year passed, but she never wavered, and *one day he walked in.*

The student must remember not to despise the "day of small things." Invariably, before a demonstration come "signs of land." Before Columbus reached America, he saw birds and twigs, which showed him land was near. So it is with a demonstration; but often the student mistakes it for the demonstration itself, and is disappointed.

For example, a woman had "spoken the word" for a set of dishes. Not long afterwards a friend gave her a dish that was old and cracked. She came to me and said, "Well, I asked for a set of dishes, and all I got was a cracked plate."

I replied, "The plate was only 'signs of land.' It shows your dishes are coming—look upon it as birds and twigs." And not long afterward the dishes came.

## Chapter Seven
# Love

A woman came to me in deep distress. The man she loved had left her for another women, and said he had never intended to marry her. She was torn with jealousy and resentment, and said she hoped he would suffer as he had made her suffer. She added, "How could he leave me when I loved him so much?"

I replied, "You are not loving that man, you are hating him," and added, "*You can never receive what you have never given. Give a perfect love and you will receive a perfect love.* Perfect yourself on this man. Give him *unselfish* love, demanding nothing in return; do not criticize or condemn, and *bless him wherever he is.*"

I continued, "When you *send out real love*, real love will return to you. Either from this man or his equivalent, for if this man is not the divine selection you will not want him. As you are one with God, you are one with the love that is yours by divine right."

I told her of a brotherhood in India who never said, "Good morning" to each other. They used the words: *"I salute the Divinity in you."* They saluted the divinity in every man, for they *saw only God in every living thing.*

I said, "Salute the divinity in this man, and say, 'I see your divine self only. I see you as God sees you: perfect, made in His image and likeness.'"

She did so—and gradually she grew more poised and began losing her resentment. One morning I received a letter saying, "We are married."

There is an old proverb, "No man is your enemy, no man is your friend, every man is your teacher." This woman's lover was teaching her selfless love.

Suffering is not necessary for man's development; it is the result of violation of spiritual law, but few seem able to rouse themselves from their "soul sleep" without it. When people are happy, they usually become selfish, and automatically the Law of Karma is set in action. Man often suffers loss through lack of appreciation.

No one can attract money, for example, if he despises it. Many people are kept in poverty by saying "money means nothing to me." This is why so many artists are poor. Their contempt for money separates them from it. I remember hearing one artist say of another, "He's no good as an artist; he has money in the bank." This attitude of mind separates man from his supply; you must be in harmony with a thing in order to attract it.

Follow the path of love, and all things are added. For *God is love*—and *God is supply.*

## Chapter Eight
# Intuition or Guidance

No accomplishment is too great for the man who knows the power of his word, and who follows his intuitive leads. By the word he sets in action unseen forces, and can rebuild his body or remold his affairs.

It is, therefore, of utmost importance that the student choose the *right words,* and carefully select the affirmation he wishes to catapult into the invisible. He knows that God is his supply, that there is a supply for every demand, and that his spoken word releases this supply. "Ask and ye shall receive."

But it falls to man to make the first move. "Draw nigh to God and He will draw nigh to you."

I am often asked just how to make a demonstration. I reply, "Speak the word and then do nothing until you get a definite lead." Demand the lead, saying, "Infinite Spirit, reveal to me the way, let me know if there is anything for me to do."

The answer will come through intuition (or hunch); a chance remark from someone, or a passage in a book, etc. Intuition is a spiritual faculty and does not explain but simply *points the way.* The answers coming from intuition are sometimes startling in their exactness.

For example, a woman desired a large sum of money. She spoke the words: "Infinite Spirit, open the way for my immediate supply, let all that is mine by divine right now reach me, in great avalanches of abundance." Then she added: "Give me a definite lead, let me know if there is anything for me to do."

The thought came quickly, "Give a certain friend" (who had helped her spiritually) "a hundred dollars." She told her friend, who said, "Wait and get another lead before giving it." So she waited, and that day met a woman who said to her, "I gave someone a dollar today; it was just as much for me as it would be for you to give someone a hundred." This was an unmistakable lead, so she knew she was right in giving the hundred dollars. It was a gift that proved a great investment, for shortly after, a large sum of money came to her in a remarkable way.

Giving opens the way for receiving. In order to create activity in finances, one should give. Tithing, or giving one-tenth of one's income, is an old Jewish custom, and is sure to bring increase. The tenth-part goes forth and returns blessed and multiplied. But the gift or tithe must be given with love and cheerfulness, for "God loveth a cheerful giver." Bills should be paid cheerfully; all money should be sent forth happily and with a blessing.

This attitude of mind makes you a master of money. It obeys you, and your spoken word opens vast reservoirs of wealth.

## Chapter Nine
# Perfect Self-Expression or the Divine Design

There is for each of us perfect self-expression. *There is a place for you to fill that no one else can fill; something you are to do that no one else can do; it is your destiny.*

Your personal achievement is held as a perfect idea in Divine Mind awaiting your recognition. As the imaging faculty is the creative faculty, it is necessary for you to see the idea before it can manifest.

So, your highest demand is for the *Divine Design of your life.*

You may not have the faintest conception of what it is. There is, possibly, some marvelous talent hidden deep within you.

Your demand should be: *"Infinite Spirit, open the way for the Divine Design of my life to manifest; let the genius within me now be released; let me see clearly the perfect plan."*

Your plan includes health, wealth, love, and perfect self-expression. This is the *square of life*, which brings perfect happiness. When you have made this demand, you may find great changes occurring in your life, for nearly everyone has wandered far from the Divine Design.

Many a genius has struggled for years with the problem of supply, when his spoken word, and faith, would have quickly released the necessary funds. After class one day a man came to me and handed me a cent. He said: "I have just seven cents in the world, and I'm going to give you one; for I have faith in the power of your spoken word. I want you to speak the word for my perfect self-expression and prosperity."

I "spoke the word," and did not see him again until a year later. He came in one day, successful and happy, with a roll of bills in his pocket. He said, "Immediately after you spoke the word, I had a position offered me in a distant city, and am now demonstrating health, happiness, and supply."

Demand definite leads for yourself, and the way will be made easy and successful.

One should not visualize or force a mental picture. When you demand the Divine Design to come into your conscious mind, you will receive flashes of inspiration and begin to see yourself making some great accomplishment. This is the picture, or idea, you must hold without wavering.

The thing you seek is seeking you—*the telephone was seeking Alexander Graham Bell.*

Now, one sure way of blocking your Divine Plan is *anger.* Anger blurs the visions, poisons the blood, is the root of many diseases, and causes wrong decision. It has been called one of the worst "sins" as its reaction is so harmful. The student learns that in metaphysics sin has a much broader meaning than in the old teaching. "Whatsoever is not of faith is of sin."

Fear and worry are deadly sins. They are inverted faith, and through distorted mental pictures, bring to pass the thing one fears. Your work is to drive out these enemies (from the subconscious mind).

You can vanquish fear only by walking up to the thing you are afraid of. When Jehoshaphat and his army prepared to meet the enemy singing, "Praise the Lord, for his mercy endureth forever" they found their enemies had destroyed each other—and there was nothing to fight.

## Chapter Ten

# Denials and Affirmations

All the good that is to be made manifest in your life is already an accomplished fact in the Divine Mind, and is released through your recognition, or spoken word. So you must be careful to decree that only the Divine Idea be made manifest; for often we decree through our "idle words," bringing failure and misfortune.

Again, it is of the utmost importance to word your demands correctly.

If you a desire home, friend, position, or any other good thing, make the demand for the "divine selection." For example, say: "Infinite Spirit, open the way for my right home, my right friend, my right position. I give thanks *that it now manifests under grace in a perfect way."*

As you grow in financial consciousness, you should demand that the enormous sums of money, which are yours by divine right, reach you under grace in perfect ways.

It is impossible for you to release more than you think is possible, for you are bound by the limited expectancies of the subconscious. You must enlarge your expectancies in order to receive in a larger way.

The French illustrate this in a legend. A poor man was walking along a road when he met a traveler, who stopped him and said: "My good friend, I see you are poor. Take this gold nugget, sell it, and you will be rich all your days."

The man was overjoyed at his good fortune, and took the nugget home. He immediately found work and became so prosperous that he did not sell the nugget. Years passed, and he became very rich. One day he met a poor man on the road. He stopped him and said: "My good friend, I will give you this gold nugget, which, if you sell it, will make you rich for life." The mendicant took the nugget, had it valued, and found it was only brass. So, we see, the first man became rich through feeling rich, thinking the nugget was gold.

Feeling that a thing is so establishes it in the subconscious. It would not be necessary to make an affirmation more than once if one had perfect faith. One should not plead or supplicate, but give thanks repeatedly that he has received.

The Lord's Prayer is in the form of command and demand: "Give us this day our daily bread, and forgive us our debts as we forgive our debtors," and ends in praise: "For thine is the Kingdom and the Power and the Glory, forever. Amen."

Prayer is command and demand, praises and thanksgiving. The student's work is in making himself believe "with God all things are possible."

Demonstrations often come at the eleventh hour because one then lets go, stops reasoning, and Infinite Intelligence has a chance to work.

I am often asked the difference between *visualizing* and *visioning*. Visualizing is a mental process governed by the reasoning or conscious mind; visioning is a spiritual process governed by intuition, or the superconscious mind. The student should train his mind to receive these flashes of inspiration, and work out the "divine pictures" through definite leads.

When you can say, "I desire only that which God desires for me," your false desires fade from the consciousness, and a new set of blueprints is given to you by the Master Architect, the God within. God's plan transcends the limitation of your reasoning mind, and is always the square of life, containing health, wealth, love, and perfect self-expression.

Turn always to the Christ within. This is your own higher self, made in God's image. This is the self that has never failed, never known sickness or sorrow, was never born, and has never died. It is "the resurrection and the life" within us all.

As you now experience these words, may you be freed from the thing that has held you in bondage, stood between you and your birthright; may you "know the Truth that makes you free"—free to fulfill your destiny, to bring into manifestation the *Divine Design of your life*.

*"Be ye transformed by the renewing of your mind."*

# Public Speaking to Win!
## (1926)

## by Dale Carnegie

*The Original Formula to Speaking with Power*

## Contents

Introduction  *The Power of What You Say* by Mitch Horowitz  482
Chapter One  Developing Courage and Self-Confidence  483
Chapter Two  Self-Confidence Through Preparation  484
Chapter Three  Keeping Your Audience Awake  486
Chapter Four  The Secret of Good Delivery  488
Chapter Five  Platform Presence and Personality  488
Chapter Six  How to Open a Talk  490
Chapter Seven  How to Close a Talk  491
Chapter Eight  How to Make Your Meaning Clear  492
Chapter Nine  How to Interest Your Audience  493
Chapter Ten  Improving Your Language  494
Chapter Eleven  How to Get Action  495

## Introduction
# The Power of What You Say

Nearly everything worth accomplishing in life comes down to communication. Your ability to sway others, win support, gain resources, succeed in your work, and correct injustice rests on your power of persuasion.

Even in our social-media age, the spoken word remains paramount. Candidates are elected because of what they say and how. Court trials hang on spoken testimony. Job interviews are face-to-face encounters. The same holds true for pitches to clients, donors, investors, customers, and financial backers. If you are seeking a career as a teacher, military officer, actor, broadcaster, or leader in any almost any field, your speaking ability is vital to your success.

Strikingly little has changed in human relations since Dale Carnegie wrote this guide to speaking in 1926, a decade before he gained international fame as the author of *How to Win Friends and Influence People*. When Carnegie produced this book he was making his living as the teacher of a popular seminar on public speaking. Carnegie had begun teaching his methods in 1912 at a YMCA in New York City. Requests for his course came in from around the country. By the mid-1930s, *Ripley's Believe-It-Or-Not* anointed Carnegie the king of public speaking with a cartoon reporting that he had personally critiqued 150,000 speeches.

Whether this is exaggerated, Carnegie's guidebook remains probably the best ever on how to speak with conviction and power. The book shows how to capture people's attention and win their confidence, whether you are speaking at a local club, a national sales conference, or in front of a class. But, as you will discover, this book delivers far more than instructions on how to give a good talk. Its greater value is that it teaches how to communicate effectively in virtually every sphere of life, on any occasion, and on behalf of any aim or purpose.

If you are a salesman, the book will help you will sell more. If you are a writer or editor, you will learn to better connect with readers. If you are an activist, you will find new ways to rally people to your cause.

What is the secret of Carnegie's formula? It comes down to three principles.

First, have an airtight knowledge of your subject—*know more than you need*.

Second, when speaking, use plain language, personal examples, and tell stories of people.

Third, and finally, appeal to your listeners' sense of self-interest: We all crave safety, success, health, and prosperity. We also have a yearning for justice and fairness. Speak on these points, and you will likely bring people to your side.

Unless you are one of a very few naturally gifted speakers, implementing these simple guidelines requires persistence, inspiration, and strategy. You will find all of that—and more—in this book.

Carnegie's methods will bring you increased power. Use it for good ends.

—Mitch Horowitz

## Chapter One
# Developing Courage and Self-Confidence

Thousands of businessmen have taken my public-speaking courses. The vast majority have told me the same thing: "When I am called upon to stand up and speak, I become so self-conscious, so frightened, that I can't think clearly, can't concentrate, and can't remember what I wanted to say. I want to gain self-confidence, poise, and the ability to think on my feet."

Gaining self-confidence and courage, and the ability to think calmly and clearly while talking to a group, is not nearly as difficult as most imagine. It is not a gift bestowed by Providence. It is like the ability to play golf. Anyone can develop his own latent capacity, if he has sufficient desire to do so.

Rather than being frightened to speak publicly, you ought to think and speak *better* in front of a group. Their presence ought to lift and stir you. Many speakers will tell you that an audience is a stimulus, an inspiration that drives their brains to function more clearly, more keenly. At such times, thoughts, facts, and ideas that they did not know they possessed come to them. This will probably be your experience if you practice and persevere.

In order to get the most from this book, and to get it quickly, four things are essential:

### First
Start with a persistent desire. This is of far greater importance than you may realize. If I could look into your heart and mind right now, and ascertain the depth of your desires, I could foretell with near-certainty the swiftness of your

progress. If your desire is pale and flabby, your achievements will be the same. But if you go after this subject with persistence, nothing will defeat you. Therefore, arouse your enthusiasm for this study. Think of what additional self-confidence and speaking ability will mean to you. Think of what it may mean in profits. Think of what it may mean socially—of the friends it will bring, of the increase of your personal influence, of the leadership it will give you.

## Second

Know thoroughly what you intend to talk about. Unless a speaker has thought out and planned what he is going to say, he can't feel very comfortable when facing his auditors. An unprepared speaker *ought* to be self-conscious—and ought to be ashamed of his negligence.

## Third

Act confident. "To feel brave," advises philosopher William James, "act as if we *were* brave, use all our will to that end, and a courage-fit will very likely replace the fit of fear." To develop courage when facing an audience, act as if you already have it. Unless you are prepared, of course, all the acting in the world will amount to little.

## Fourth

Practice! Practice! Practice! This is the most vital point of all. The first way, the last way, the never-failing way to overcome fear and develop self-confidence in speaking is—to speak. The whole matter finally simmers down to one essential: *practice*.

## Chapter Two
# Self-Confidence Through Preparation

It has been my professional duty, as well as my pleasure, to listen to and criticize approximately six thousand speeches a year. Most were made by ordinary businesspeople. If that experience has engraved one thing on my mind it is this: the urgent necessity of preparing a talk before one starts to make it, and of having something clear and definite to say.

Aren't you unconsciously drawn to a speaker who you feel has a real message, which he zealously desires to communicate? That is half the secret of speaking. When a speaker is in that kind of mental and emotional state he will discover a significant fact: his talk almost makes itself. A well-prepared speech is already nine-tenths delivered. The one fatal mistake is neglecting to prepare. "Perfect love," wrote the apostle John, "casteth out fear." So does perfect preparation.

What is preparation? Reading a book? That is one kind, but not the best. Reading may help; but if one attempts to lift a lot of "canned" thoughts out of a book and give them out as his own, the whole performance will be lacking.

Does preparation mean pulling together some faultless phrases, written down or memorized? No. Does it mean assembling a few casual thoughts that really convey very little to you personally? Not at all.

It means assembling *your* thoughts, *your* ideas, *your* convictions, *your* urges. You have them everyday of your life. They swarm through your dreams. Your whole existence has been filled with feelings and experiences. These things are lying deep in your subconscious as thick as pebbles on the seashore. Preparation means thinking, brooding, recalling, selecting the ones that speak to you most, polishing them, working them into a pattern, a mosaic of your own. That doesn't sound so difficult, does it? It isn't. It just requires a little concentration and thinking to a purpose.

What topics should you speak on? Anything that truly interests you. Ask yourself all possible questions concerning your topic. For example, if you are to speak on divorce, ask yourself what causes divorce, what are the effects economically, socially, domestically? Should we have uniform divorce laws? Should divorce be more difficult? Easier?

When preparing a speech, assemble a hundred thoughts, and discard ninety. Collect more material than there is any possibility of using. Get it for that additional confidence it will give you, for that sureness of touch. Get it for the effect it will have on your mind and heart and whole manner of speaking. That is a basic factor of preparation—yet most speakers constantly ignore it.

You must practice your speaking. If you stand up and think clearly and keep going for two or three minutes, that is a perfect way to practice delivering a talk. Try this a few times. What you can do first on a small scale you can do later on a large scale.

When making your practice talk, do not attempt to tell us everything in three minutes. It can't be done. Take one, and only one, phase of your topic: expand and enlarge that. For example, you can tell us how you came to be in your particular business or profession. Was it due to accident or choice? Relate your early struggles, your defeats, your hopes, and your triumphs. Give us a human-interest narrative, a real-life picture based on first-hand experience. The truthful, inside story of almost anyone's life—if told modestly and without egotism—is sure-fire speech material.

Many wonder if they should use notes while speaking. As a listener, don't notes destroy about fifty percent of your interest in a talk? Notes prevent, or at least render difficult, a very precious intimacy that ought to exist between the speaker and the audience. They create an air of artificiality. They restrain an audience from feeling that a speaker has confidence, spontaneity, and power.

Make notes during your preparation—elaborate ones, profuse ones. You may wish to refer to them when you are practicing your talk alone. You may possibly feel more comfortable if you have them stored away in your pocket when facing an audience. But they should be emergency tools, used only in case of a total wreck.

If you *must* use notes while speaking, make them extremely brief and write them in large letters on an ample sheet of paper. Then arrive early where you are speaking and discretely place your notes on the lectern, or conceal them behind books on a table. Glance at them if you must, but be brief.

In a few limited instances it may be wise to use notes. Some people during their first few talks are so nervous that they are unable to remember what they wanted to say. In such cases, it is fine to hold a few very condensed notes in your hands.

Get comfortable with your talk. After you have thought it out and arranged it, practice it silently as you walk along the street. Also get off somewhere by yourself and go over it from beginning to end, using gestures, letting yourself go. Imagine that you are addressing a real audience. The more of this you do, the more comfortable you will feel when the time comes to deliver your talk.

## Chapter Three
# Keeping Your Audience Awake

What is the secret of success? "Nothing great," said Ralph Waldo Emerson, "was ever achieved without enthusiasm." This quality is the most effective, most important factor in advertising, selling goods, and getting things done.

I once put considerable reliance on the *rules* of public speaking. But with the passing of years I have come to put more and more faith in the *spirit* of speaking.

Remember always that every time we speak we determine the attitude of our listeners. If we are lackadaisical, they will be lackadaisical. If we are reserved, they will be reserved. If we are only mildly concerned, they will be only mildly concerned. But if we are deadly in earnest about what we say, and if we say it with feeling and spontaneity and force and conviction, they cannot keep from catching our spirit to a degree.

So, to feel earnest and enthusiastic, stand up and *act* in earnest and *be* enthusiastic. Stop leaning against the table. Stand tall. Stand still. Don't rock back and forth. Don't bob up and down. Don't shift your weight from one foot to the other and back again. In short, don't make a lot of nervous movements. They proclaim your lack of ease and self-possession. Control yourself physically. It conveys a sense of poise and power. Fill your lungs with oxygen. Look straight at your audience. Look at them as if you have something urgent to say. Look at them with the confidence and courage of a teacher, for you *are* a teacher, and they are there to hear you and to be taught.

Use emphatic gestures. Never mind, just now, whether they are beautiful or graceful. Think only of making them forceful and spontaneous. Make them now, not for the sense they will convey to others, but for what they will do for *you*. And they will do wonders. Even if you are speaking to a radio audience, *gesture, gesture*. Your gestures won't, of course, be visible to the hearers, but the result of your gestures will be audible to them. They will give increased aliveness and energy to your tone.

I have made a special study of Abraham Lincoln as a public speaker. He is perhaps the most loved man America has ever produced; and unquestionably he delivered some of America's greatest speeches. Although he was a genius in some ways, I am inclined to believe that his power with audiences was due, in large measure, to his sympathy and honesty and goodness. He loved people. "His heart," said his wife, "is as large as his arms are long." He was Christlike.

The finest thing in speaking is neither physical nor mental. It is spiritual. Jesus loved men and their hearts burned within them as He talked with them by the way. If you want a splendid text on public speaking, read your New Testament.

## Chapter Four
# The Secret of Good Delivery

We are often told to be natural, to be ourselves. But the same society that gives this advice often bleeds naturalness out of us by imposing all kinds of preconceptions of just what "naturalness" ought to be.

The problem of teaching or training people in delivery is not one of superimposing additional characteristics; it is largely one of removing impediments, of freeing people, of getting them to speak, albeit with a different vocabulary and judgment, as they did when they were four years old.

As you practice, if you find yourself talking in a stilted manner, pause and say sharply to yourself mentally: "What is wrong? Wake up. Be human." In the end, even the matter of delivery comes back to a point that has already been emphasized: namely, *put your heart in your talks*.

Here are four things that all of us do unconsciously and naturally in conversation. You should do them when speaking in public.

1. Stress the important words in a sentence and subordinate the unimportant ones. When you speak conversationally you naturally give emphasis to keywords, such as *ambition*, *affliction*, and *skyscraper*. But not to unimportant words, such as *the*, *and*, or *but*.
2. Allow the pitch of your voice to flow up and down the scale from high to low and back again—as the pitch of a little child does when speaking.
3. Vary your rate of speaking, running rapidly over the unimportant words, spending more time on the ones you wish to make stand out.
4. And, finally, pause before and after your important ideas.

This is exactly how you speak to your friends, coworkers, or spouse—and it is how you should address an audience.

## Chapter Five
# Platform Presence and Personality

*Personality*—with the exception of *preparation* and *ideas*—is probably the most important factor in public speaking. But personality is a vague and elusive thing. It is the whole combination of the man: the physical, the spiritual, the mental; his traits, his predilections, his tendencies, his temperament, his cast of mind, his vigor, his experience, his training, his life.

If you wish to make the most of your individuality, go before your audience well rested. A tired person is not magnetic or attractive. When you have to make an important talk, beware of your hunger. Eat as sparingly as a saint. Do nothing to dull your senses or energy.

To maintain high spirits in the room, make sure that your audience—whether it is large or small—is grouped closely together. No audience will be easily moved when it is scattered. Nothing so dampens enthusiasm as wide, open spaces and empty chairs between the listeners.

If you are going to talk to a small group, choose a small room. Better to pack the aisles of a small place than to have people dispersed through the lonely, deadening spaces of a large hall. If your hearers are scattered, ask them to move down front and be seated near you. Insist on this before you start speaking.

Unless the audience is a fairly large one, and there is a real reason, a necessity, for you to stand on a platform, do not do so. Get down on the same level with your listeners. Stand near them. Break up all formality. Get an intimate contact. Make the thing conversational.

Take a deep breath. Look over your audience for a moment. If there is a noise or disturbance, pause until it quiets down. Hold your chest high. But why wait until you get before an audience to do this? Do it daily in private life. Then you will do it unconsciously in public.

And what shall you do with your hands? Forget them. If they fall naturally to your sides, that is ideal. And this returns us to the much-abused question of gesture. A man's gestures, like his toothbrush, should be very personal things. As all of us are different, our gestures will be individual if only we act natural. No two people should be drilled to gesture in precisely the same fashion.

I can't give you rules for gesturing—and neither can anyone else. For everything depends on the temperament of the speaker, upon his preparation, his enthusiasm, his personality, the subject, the audience, the occasion. Above all, be truthful; be comfortable; be yourself.

## Chapter Six
# How to Open a Talk

For some unfortunate reason, the novice often feels that he ought to be funny as a speaker. So he is inclined to open with a humorous story, especially if the occasion is an after-dinner affair. The chances are his stories don't "click." In the immortal language of Hamlet, they prove "weary, stale, flat, and unprofitable."

In the difficult realm of speechmaking, what is more difficult, more rare, than the ability to make an audience laugh? Remember, it is seldom the story that is funny. It is *the way it is told* that makes it a success. Ninety-nine people out of a hundred will fail woefully with the identical stories that made Mark Twain famous.

The second egregious blunder that the beginner is likely to make in his opening is this: He apologizes. "I am no speaker... I am not prepared to talk... I have nothing to say..." Don't! Don't! Why insult your audience by suggesting that you did not think them worth preparing for, that just any old thing you happened to have on the fire would be good enough to serve them? We don't want to hear your apologies. We are there to be informed and interested—to be *interested,* remember that.

Arouse your audience's curiosity with your first sentence—and you have their attention. An article in *The Saturday Evening Post* entitled "With the Gangsters," began: "Are gangsters really organized? As a rule they are. How?" With ten words the writer announced his subject, told you something about it, and aroused your curiosity.

Everyone who aspires to speak in public ought to study the techniques that magazine writers use to immediately hook the reader's interest. You can learn far more from them about how to open a speech than you can by studying collections of speeches.

## Chapter Seven
# How to Close a Talk

If you want to know how to end a speech, you can do no better than study the close of Lincoln's Second Inaugural:

> *With malice toward none, with charity for all, with firmness in the right as God gives us to see the right, let us strive on to finish the work we are in, to bind up the nation's wounds, to care for him who shall have borne the battle and for his widow and his orphan, to do all which may achieve and cherish a just and lasting peace among ourselves and with all nations.*

You have just encountered what is, in my opinion, the most beautiful speech ending ever delivered. But you are not going to deliver immortal pronouncements as president in Washington or prime minister in Ottawa. Your problem, perhaps, will be how to close a simple talk before a group of businessmen. How shall you set about it? Here are some suggestions.

### First

Even in a short talk of three to five minutes, a speaker is very apt to cover so much ground that at the close his listeners are a little hazy about all his main points. Some anonymous Irish politician is reported to have given this famous recipe for making a speech: "First, tell them what you are going to tell them; then, tell them; then, tell them what you told them." It is often highly advisable to "tell them what you told them." Briefly, of course, speedily—a mere outline, a summary.

### Second

Try closing with a poetical quotation. If you can get a proper verse of poetry for your closing, it is almost ideal. It will give the desired flavor. It will give dignity. It will give individuality. It will give beauty. A choice Biblical quotation often has a profound effect.

### Third

Build to a climax. The climax is a popular way of ending. It is often difficult to manage and is not an ending for all speakers or all subjects. But, when well done, it is excellent. It works up to a crest, a peak, getting stronger sentence by sentence. It often means ending with a tribute to someone or something, or an appeal for action—a topic we will cover in a future chapter.

## Chapter Eight
# How to Make Your Meaning Clear

Napoleon's most emphatic instruction to his secretaries was: "Be clear! Be clear!"

When the disciples asked Christ why He taught the public by parables, He answered: "Because they seeing, see not; and hearing, hear not; neither do they understand."

And when you talk about a subject strange to your hearers, can you hope that they will understand you any more readily than people understood the Master?

Hardly. So what can we do about it? What did he do? He solved it in the most simple and natural manner imaginable: described the things people did not know by likening them to things they did know. The kingdom of Heaven... what would it be like?

"The kingdom of Heaven is like unto leaven... The kingdom of Heaven is like unto a merchant seeking goodly pearls... The kingdom of Heaven is like unto a net that was cast into the sea."

That was lucid; they could understand that. The housewives in the audience were using leaven every week; the fishermen were casting their nets into the sea daily; the merchants were dealing in pearls.

I once heard a lecturer on Alaska who failed, in many places, to be either clear or interesting because he neglected to talk in terms of what his audience knew. He told us, for example, that Alaska had a gross area of 590,804 miles.

Half-a-million square miles—what does that mean to the average person? Precious little. He is not used to thinking in square miles. They conjure up no mental picture. He does not have any idea whether half-a-million square miles are approximately the size of Maine or Texas. Suppose the speaker had said that the coastline of Alaska and its islands is longer than the distance around the globe, and that its area more than equals the combined areas of Vermont, New Hampshire, Maine, Massachusetts, Rhode Island, Connecticut, New York, New Jersey, Pennsylvania, Delaware, Maryland, West Virginia, North

Carolina, South Carolina, Georgia, Florida, Mississippi, and Tennessee. Would that not give everyone a fairly clear conception of the area of Alaska?

If you belong to a profession that does technical work—if you are a lawyer, physician, engineer, or are in a highly specialized line of businesses—be doubly careful when you talk to outsiders to express yourself in *plain terms*, and to fill in necessary details.

Put your ideas into language plain enough for any boy to understand.

## Chapter Nine
# How to Interest Your Audience

What would you say are the three most interesting subjects in the world? They are: *sex, property,* and *religion*. By the first we can create life, by the second we maintain it, and by the third we hope to continue it in the world to come.

But it is *our* sex, *our* property, and *our* religion that interests us. Our interests swarm around our own egos.

When a British newspaper baron was asked what interests people, he answered with one word: "themselves." Do you want to know what kind of person you are? Ah, now we are on an interesting topic. We are talking about *you*.

Remember that people spend most of their time, when they are not concerned with the problems of business, thinking about and justifying and glorifying themselves. The average man will be more wrought up over a dull razor than over a revolution in South America. His own toothache will distress him more than an earthquake in Asia destroying half-a-million lives. He would rather listen to you say some nice thing about him than hear you discuss the ten greatest men in history.

A successful magazine editor once told me the secret of capturing people's attention: "People are selfish," he said. "They are interested chiefly in themselves. They are not very much concerned about whether the government should own the railroads; but they do want to know how to get ahead, how to draw more salary, how to keep healthy, how to take care of their teeth, how to take baths, how to keep cool in the summer, how to get a job, how to handle employees, how to buy homes, how to remember, how to avoid grammatical errors, and so one. People are always interested in human stories, so I have some rich man tell how he made a million in real estate. I get prominent bankers and presidents of various corporations to tell their stories of how they battled their way up to power and wealth."

This editor has attracted millions of readers by appealing to their selfish interests.

But interest is also *contagious*. Your hearers are almost sure to catch it if you have a bad case of it yourself. A short time ago I heard a speaker warn his audience that if the present methods of catching rockfish in Chesapeake Bay were continued the species would become extinct. And in a very few years! He *felt* his subject. It was important. He was in real earnest about it. When he finished all of us probably would have been willing to sign a petition to protect the rockfish by law.

Always remember, your audience will feel interested in your topic to the degree that you are sincerely interested in it yourself.

## Chapter Ten
# Improving Your Language

The world judges us by four things: by what we do, by how we look, by what we say, and by how we say it.

Many people blunder through life with no conscious effort to enrich their stock of words, to master their shades of meaning, and to speak with precision. Many people habitually use the overworked and exhausted phrases of the office and street. Small wonder that their way of speaking lacks distinction and individuality.

But how are we to become intimate with words, to speak them with beauty and accuracy? Fortunately, there is no mystery about the means to be employed. *Books!* There is the secret. He who would enlarge his stock of words must drink deeply of good literature.

Lincoln wrote to a young man eager to become a successful lawyer: "It is only to get the books, and read and study them carefully... Work, work, work is the main thing."

What books? Begin with Arnold Bennett's *How to Live on Twenty-Four Hours a Day*. This book is as stimulating as a cold bath. It tells you a lot about that most interesting of all subjects—yourself. It reveals how much time you are wasting each day, how to stop the wastage, and how to use what you salvage.

To learn about greatness, make Ralph Waldo Emerson your daily companion. Command him first to give you his famous essay on "Self-Reliance." Read it again and again. Dedicate yourself to Emerson's essays and you will encounter some of the highest thoughts and finest uses of words in the English language.

Finally, don't use shopworn, threadbare words and expressions. Be exact in your meaning. Avoid trite comparisons such as "cool as a cucumber" or "high as a kite." Strive for freshness. Create expressions of your own. Have the courage to be distinctive.

Chapter Eleven

# How to Get Action

If you could have the power of any talent that you now possess doubled and tripled, which one would you select? Wouldn't you likely designate your ability to influence others, to get action? That would mean additional power, additional profit, and additional pleasure.

Must this art—so essential to our success in life—remain forever a hit-and-miss affair? Must we blunder along depending upon our instinct, upon rule-of-thumb methods only? Or is there a more intelligent way to achieve it?

There is, and we shall discuss it at once—a method based on the rules of common sense, on the rules of human nature, a method that I have frequently, and successfully, used myself.

The first step in this method is to gain *interested attention*. Unless you do that people will not listen closely to what you say. We've already touched on some of the ways to do this: Talk to people about topics of vital interest—usually themselves. Be deeply in earnest about what you say. Be clear, plainspoken, and definite as to what you mean.

The second step is to gain the *confidence* of your hearers. Unless you do that, they will have no faith in what you say. And here is where many speakers fall down. Here is where many advertisements fail, where many business letters, many employees, many business enterprises go nowhere. Here is where many individuals fail to make themselves effective within the human environment.

The prime way to win confidence is to *deserve it*. I have noticed time without number that facile and witty speakers—if those are their chief qualities—

are not nearly as effective as those who are less brilliant but more sincere. There is no use trying to pretend a sympathy or sincerity that one does not feel. It won't work. It must be genuine.

The second way to gain the confidence of the audience is to speak discretely out of your own experience. This helps immensely. If you give opinions, people may question them. If you relate hearsay or repeat what you have read, it may have a second-hand flavor. But what *you yourself have lived through*, that has a genuine ring of truth and veracity. And people like it. They believe it.

Once you have won people's confidence, consider what people are looking for—from you and from the world around them. One of the strongest of human motives is *the desire for gain*. And even stronger than the money motive is the desire for *self-protection*. All health appeals are based on that. To make an appeal to someone's sense of self-protection, make it personal. Don't, for example, quote statistics to show that cancer is on the rise. No. Tie it right down to the people who are listening to you, for example: "There are thirty people in this room. If all of you live to be forty-five, three of you, according to the law of medical averages, will die of cancer."

As strong as the desire for money—and for many even stronger—is the wish to be well regarded, to be admired. In other words, pride. Ask yourself why you bought this book. Were you influenced, to some extent, by the wish to make a better impression? Did you covet the flow of inward satisfaction that comes from making a commendable talk? Won't you feel a very pardonable pride in the power, leadership, and distinction that naturally flow to the good public speaker?

There is another powerful group of motives that influence us mightily. We shall call them religious motives. I mean religious not in the sense of orthodox worship or the tenets of any particular creed or sect. I mean rather that broad group of beautiful and eternal truths that Christ taught: justice and forgiveness and mercy, serving others and loving our neighbors as ourselves.

No man likes to admit, even to himself, that he is not good and kind and magnanimous. So we love to be appealed to on these grounds. It implies a certain nobleness of soul. We take pride in that.

To summarize all we have been discussing, here are the ways that you as a speaker can get people on your side and move them to action:

### First
Get interested attention.

### Second
Win confidence by deserving it, not only by your sincerity but also by being qualified to speak on your subject, by telling us the things that experience has taught you.

### Third
State your facts clearly and educate your audience regarding the merits of your proposal or cause.

### Fourth
Appeal to the motives that make us act: the desire for gain, self-protection, pride, pleasures, sentiments, affections, and religious ideals, such as justice, mercy, forgiveness, and love.

These methods, if used wisely, will not only help the speaker in public, but also in private. They will help him in the writing of sales letters, in constructing advertisements, in managing business interviews—and in making an impact in life.

# The Richest Man in Babylon
(1926)

## by George S. Clason

*Discover the Essentials of the Legendary Guide to Wealth!*

## Contents

Introduction  *"Pay Yourself First"* by Mitch Horowitz  500
Foreword  by George S. Clason  502
Chapter One  The Man Who Desired Gold  502
Chapter Two  The Richest Man in Babylon  504
Chapter Three  Seven Cures for a Lean Purse  509
Chapter Four  Meet the Goddess of Good Luck  516
Chapter Five  The Five Laws of Gold  518
Chapter Six  The Gold Lender of Babylon  519
Chapter Seven  The Camel Trader of Babylon  520
Chapter Eight  The Clay Tablets from Babylon  524
Chapter Nine  The Luckiest Man in Babylon  529

## Introduction
# "Pay Yourself First"

"Pay yourself first." This is the key lesson of George S. Clason's guide to financial health, *The Richest Man in Babylon*, which he presented as a series of parables from the Mesopotamian empire. Clason, who is credited with coining the phrase "pay yourself first," meant that you must set aside at least ten-percent of your earnings in savings—now a standard principle in financial guides—and dedicate the remainder of your money to paying down debt, procuring a home or other investment properties, buying insurance, caring for your family, and only then allowing yourself to spend on life's pleasures.

His approach was one of thrift. "Every piece of gold you save is a slave to work for you," one of his ancient characters says. He does not endorse asceticism; indeed he wants money management approached in a spirit of joy and adventure—knowing that your prudence will pay off in comfort and security. This is the aim of his rock-ribbed lessons to personal prudence and safe investment. And he got rich himself offering them.

In the early twentieth century, Clason was a Denver-based publisher of maps and atlases. He published the first road atlas of the United States and Canada. In 1926, he hit upon an idea that later saved his own finances and preserved his name as one of the most popular self-help writers of the last century, and our own. Clason began writing a series of pamphlets on managing personal finances, which banks, insurance companies, and brokerage houses bought in bulk and distributed free to their clients. The map-maker's pamphlets proved so popular that in 1930 he grouped them together in a single volume, which he issued from his own publishing company.

Clason Publishing did not survive the Great Depression. But *The Richest Man in Babylon* did—and in the years ahead it emerged as a mainstay of popular financial literature.

Clason's outlook was ardently business-friendly. Companies that sold insurance, issued home loans, or maintained savings accounts had everything to like about it. Clason endorsed modern financial products along with a cheerful and self-sacrificing work ethic. Yet for all its institutional friendliness, Clason's book also contains solid, principled advice. There is not a fickle or unrealistic passage in it.

\* \* \*

For me, the book's most effective section is chapter seven, "The Camel Trader of Babylon," which is the about the imperative of paying down your debts, and the feelings of nobility that accrue to the individual who does so, even if incrementally. This principle reminds of a passage that I read from The Talmud as a teen: "Who is evil?" a rabbi asks his students. After rumination, the answer comes: "He who borrows and does not repay." That statement must be understood on many levels; but one cannot neglect the material level.

Keep in mind that debts mean not only monetary borrowings, but also deadlines or obligations in any area of life where you've given your word. If you've vowed to complete a task, even a seemingly small domestic chore, or to show up at a certain time, then do so. You'd be surprised how carefully people note such things, including your family. However you see yourself, you are evaluated and defined by your incremental workaday ethics. Whether you are aware, you also experience your own sense of performance and reliability internally; this can feed feelings of shame and anger, or of dignity and rightness.

It is, of course, natural to excuse yourself for those times when you feel justifiably late or in default on a commitment: aren't there exceptions for unforeseen circumstance? Yes; but you should always be very disciplined about such cases. As a friend once put it: "The only real emergency is a medical emergency." Consider this before you delay a debt, project, or commitment.

Clason helped clarify another principle for me: You should dedicate twice as much money to your debts as to your savings. Immediately save your ten percent, he wrote; but *twenty percent* should go toward debt. Debt is intrinsically a drain both in terms of interest and reputation (as well as credit score).

Because the chapters in *The Richest Man in Babylon* were first issued as individual pamphlets, there is some redundancy in the book. This is somewhat relieved by Clason's device of using a series of dramatized parables and dialogues. For this reason the book is especially ripe for condensation. This Condensed Classics edition contains all the lessons of the original, but with repetition, wordiness, or superfluous passages reduced.

You will find that Clason's lessons retain all of their original usefulness and power. Rediscovering this book has clarified important lessons for me, and put me on firmer financial footing. I hope it does the same for you, and more.

—Mitch Horowitz

### Foreword

Our prosperity as a nation depends upon the personal financial prosperity of each of us as individuals.

This book deals with the personal successes of each of us. Success means accomplishments as the result of our own efforts and abilities. Proper preparation is the key to our success. Our acts can be no wiser than our thoughts. Our thinking can be no wiser than our understanding.

This book of cures for lean purses has been termed a guide to financial understanding. That, indeed, is its purpose: to offer those who are ambitious for financial success insight that will help them acquire money, keep money, and make their surpluses earn more money.

In the pages which follow, we are taken back to Babylon, the cradle in which was nurtured the basic principles of finance now recognized and used the world over.

Babylon became the wealthiest city of the ancient world because its citizens were the richest people of their time. They appreciated the value of money. They practiced sound financial principles in acquiring money, keeping money, and making their money earn more money. They provided for themselves what we all desire: incomes for the future.

—George S. Clason

## Chapter One
# The Man Who Desired Gold

Bansir, the chariot builder of Babylon, was thoroughly discouraged. From his seat upon the low wall surrounding his property he gazed sadly at his simple home and the open workshop in which stood a partially completed chariot.

His wife frequently appeared at the open door. Her furtive glances in his direction reminded him that the meal bag was almost empty, and he should be at work finishing the chariot.

Nevertheless, his fat, muscular body sat stolidly upon the wall. His slow mind was struggling with a problem for which he could find no answer.

Bansir was shaken from his brooding by the twanging of the strings from a familiar lyre. He turned and looked into the sensitive, smiling face of his best friend—Kobbi, the musician.

"May the gods bless thee, my good friend," began Kobbi with an elaborate salute. "Pray, from thy purse which must be bulging else thou wouldst be busy in yon shop, extract but two humble shekels and lend them to me."

"If I did have two shekels," Bansir responded, "to no one could I lend them—not even to you, my best of friends; for they would be my fortune—my entire fortune."

"What!" exclaimed Kobbi. "Thou hast not one shekel in thy purse? Have the gods brought to thee troubles?"

"A torment from the gods it must be," Bansir said. "Let us talk it over together, for we ride in the same boat. We have earned much coin in the years that have passed, yet to know the joys that come from wealth, we are left to dream about them. Are we more than dumb sheep? We live in the richest city in all the world, but we have naught."

"Never in all our years of our friendship didst thou talk like this before, Bansir." Kobbi was puzzled.

"My heart is sad," the chariot maker replied. "I wish to be a man of means. What is the matter with us? Again I ask you! Why cannot we have our just share of the good things so plentiful for those who have gold?"

"Might we not find out how others acquire gold and do as they do?" Kobbi asked.

"Perhaps there is some secret we might learn if we but sought from those who knew," replied Bansir.

"This very day," said Kobbi, "I did pass our old friend, Arkad, riding in his golden chariot. So rich is he that the king himself is said to seek his aid in affairs of the treasury."

"So rich," Bansir said, "that I fear if I should meet him in the darkness of the night I should lay my hands upon his fat wallet."

"Nonsense," reproved Kobbi, "a man's wealth is not in the purse he carries. A fat purse quickly empties if there be no golden stream to refill it. Arkad has an income that constantly keeps his purse full, no matter how liberally he spends."

"Kobbi, thou bringest to me a rare thought." A new light gleamed in Bansir's eyes. "It costs nothing to ask wise advice from a good friend, and Arkad was always that. We are weary of being without gold in the midst of plenty. Come, let us go to him and ask how we, also, may acquire incomes for ourselves."

"Thou speakest with true inspiration, Bansir. Thou bringeth to my mind a new understanding. Thou makest me to realize why we have never found any measure of wealth. We never sought it. Thou hast labored patiently to build the staunchest chariots in Babylon. To that purpose was devoted your best endeavors. Therefore, at it thou didst succeed. I strove to become a skillful lyre player. And, at it I did succeed.

"In those things toward which we exerted our best endeavors we succeeded. The gods were content to let us continue thus. Now, at last, we see a new light. It biddeth us to learn more that we may prosper more. With new understanding we shall find honorable ways to accomplish our desires."

## Chapter Two

# The Richest Man in Babylon

In old Babylon there once lived a certain very rich man named Arkad. Far and wide he was famed for his great wealth. He was generous in his charities. He was generous with his family. He was liberal in his own expenses. But nevertheless each year his wealth increased more rapidly than he spent it.

Certain friends of younger days came to him and said: "You are more fortunate than we. You have become the richest man in all Babylon while we struggle for existence. Yet, once we were equal. We studied under the same master. We played in the same games. And in neither the studies nor the games did you outshine us. And in the years since, you have been no more an honorable citizen than we. Nor have you worked harder or more faithfully. Why, then, should a fickle fate single you out to enjoy all the good things of life and ignore us who are equally deserving?"

Thereupon Arkad remonstrated with them, saying, "If you have not acquired more than a bare existence in the years since we were youths, it is because you either have failed to learn the laws that govern the building of wealth, or else you do not observe them.

"In my youth," the rich man continued, "I looked about me and saw all the good things there were to bring happiness and contentment. And I realized that wealth increased the potency of all these.

"And, when I realized all this, I decided that I would claim my share of the good things of life.

"Being, as you know, the son of a humble merchant, one of a large family with no hope of an inheritance, and not being endowed, as you have so frankly said, with superior powers or wisdom, I decided that if I were to achieve what I desired, time and study would be required.

"As for time, all men have it in abundance. You, each of you, have let slip by sufficient time to have made yourselves wealthy.

"As for study, did not our wise teacher teach us that learning was of two kinds: the one kind being the things we learned and knew, and the other being the training that taught us how to find out what we did not know?

"Therefore did I decide to find out how one might accumulate wealth, and when I had found out, to make this my task.

"I found employment as a scribe in the hall of records, and long hours each day I labored upon the clay tablets. Week after week, and month after month, I labored, yet for my earnings I had naught to show.

"And one day Algamish, the moneylender, came to the house of the city master and ordered a copy of the Ninth Law, and he said to me, 'I must have this in two days.'

"I labored hard, but the law was long, and when Algamish returned the task was unfinished. He was angry, and had I been his slave, he would have beaten me. But knowing that the city master would not permit him to injure me, I was unafraid, so I said to him, 'Algamish, you are a very rich man. Tell me how I may also become rich, and all night I will carve upon the clay, and when the sun rises it shall be completed.'

"He smiled and replied, 'You are a forward knave, but we will call it a bargain.'

"All that night I carved, though my back pained and the smell of the wick made my head ache until my eyes could hardly see. But when he returned at sunup, the tablets were complete.

"'You have fulfilled your part of our bargain, my son,' he said to me. 'And I am ready to fulfill mine. Mark you well my words, for if you do not you will fail to grasp the truth that I will tell you, and you will think that your night's work has been in vain.'

"Then he looked at me shrewdly and said in a low, forceful tone: 'I found the road to wealth when I decided that a part of all I earned was mine to keep. And so will you.'

"Then he continued to look at me with a glance that I could feel pierce me but said no more. 'Is that all?' I asked.

"'That was sufficient to change the heart of a sheep herder into the heart of a moneylender,' he replied.

"But all I earn is mine to keep, is it not?" I asked.

"'Far from it,' he replied. 'Do you not pay the garment-maker? Do you not pay the sandal-maker? Do you not pay for the things you eat? Can you live in Babylon without spending? What have you to show for your earnings of the past month? What for the past year? Fool! You pay to everyone but yourself. You labor for others. As well be a slave and work for what your master gives you. If you did keep for yourself one-tenth of all you earn, how much would you have in ten years?'"

"My knowledge of the numbers did not forsake me, and I answered, 'As much as I earn in one year.'

"'You speak but half the truth' he retorted. 'Every gold piece you save is a slave to work for you. Every copper it earns is its child that also can earn for you. If you would become wealthy, then what you save must earn, and its children must earn, that all may help to give to you the abundance you crave.

"'You think I cheat you for your long night's work,' he continued, 'but I am paying you a thousand times over if you have the intelligence to grasp the truth I offer.

"'A part of all you earn is yours to keep. It should be not less than a tenth no matter how little you earn. It can be as much more as you can afford. Pay yourself first. Do not buy from the clothes-maker and the sandal-maker more than you can pay out of the rest.

"'Wealth, like a tree, grows from a tiny seed. The first copper you save is the seed from which your tree of wealth shall grow. The sooner you plant that seed the sooner shall the tree grow. And the more faithfully you nourish and water that tree with consistent savings, the sooner may you bask in contentment beneath its shade.'

"So saying, he took his tablets and went away.

"I thought much about what he had said to me, and it seemed reasonable. So I decided to try it. Each time I was paid I took one from each ten pieces of copper and hid it away. And strange as it may seem, I was no shorter of funds than before.

"A twelfth month later Algamish returned and asked me, 'Son, have you paid to yourself not less than one-tenth of all you have earned for the past year?'

"I answered proudly: 'Yes, master, I have.'

"'That is good,' he answered, 'and what have you done with it?'

"I have given it to Azmur, the brick maker, who told me he was travelling over the far seas and he would buy for me the rare jewels of the Phoenicians. When he returns we shall sell these at high prices.

"'Every fool must learn,' he said. 'Why trust the knowledge of a brick maker about jewels? Would you go to the bread maker to inquire about the stars? No, you would go to the astrologer, if you had power to think. Your savings are gone, youth; you have pulled your wealth-tree up by the roots. But plant another. Try again. And next time if you would have advice about jewels, go to the jewel merchant. Advice is one thing that is freely given away but watch that you take only what is worth having. He who takes advice about his savings from one who is inexperienced in such matters shall pay with his savings for proving the falsity of their opinions.' Saying this, he went away.

"And it was as he said. For the Phoenicians sold to Azmur worthless bits of glass. But as Algamish had bid me, I again saved each tenth copper, for I now had formed the habit and it was no longer difficult.

"Again, twelve months later, Algamish came and asked, 'What progress have you made since last I saw you?'

"'I have paid myself faithfully,' I replied, 'and my savings I have entrusted to Aggar the shield maker, to buy bronze, and each fourth month he does pay me the rental.'

"'That is good. And what do you do with the rental?'

"I have a great feast. Also I have bought me a scarlet tunic. And some day I shall buy me a young ass upon which to ride.

"To which Algamish replied, 'You eat the children of your savings. How do you expect them to work for you? And how can they have children that will also work for you? First get thee an army of golden slaves and then many a rich banquet may you enjoy without regret.' So saying he again went away.

"Nor did I again see him for two years. And he said to me, 'Arkad, hast thou yet achieved the wealth thou dreamed of?'

"And I answered, 'Not yet all that I desire, but some I have and it earns more, and its earnings earn more.'

"'And do you still take the advice of brick makers?'

"'About brick making they give good advice,' I said.

"'Arkad,' he continued, 'you have learned well. You first learned to live upon less than you could earn. Next you learned to seek advice from those who were competent through their own experience to give it. And, lastly, you have learned to make gold work for you. You have taught yourself how to acquire money, how to keep it, and how to use it. Therefore, you are competent for a responsible position. I am becoming an old man. My sons think only of spending and give no thought to earning. My interests are great and too much for me to look after. If you will go to Nippur and look after my lands there, I shall make you my partner and you shall share in my estate.'

"So I went to Nippur and took charge of his holdings, which were large. And because I was full of ambition and had mastered the three laws of handling wealth, I was enabled to increase greatly the value of his properties. So I prospered much, and when the spirit of Algamish departed, I did share in his estate as he had arranged under the law."

So spake Arkad, and when he had finished his tale, one of his friends said, "You were indeed fortunate that Algamish made of you an heir."

"Fortunate only in that I had the desire to prosper before I first met him. For four years did I not prove my definiteness of purpose by keeping one-tenth of all I earned? Opportunity is a haughty goddess who wastes no time with those who are unprepared."

"You had strong willpower to keep on after you lost your first year's savings," said another.

"Willpower!" retorted Arkad. "What nonsense. Do you think willpower gives a man the strength to lift a burden the camel cannot carry, or to draw a load the oxen cannot budge? Willpower is but the unflinching purpose to fulfill a task you set for yourself. Therefore, I am careful not to start difficult and impractical tasks, because I love leisure."

And then another friend spoke up and said, "If what you tell is true, then being so simple, if all men did it, would there be enough wealth to go around?"

"Wealth grows wherever men exert energy," Arkad replied. "No man can prophesy the limit of it. Have not the Phoenicians built great cities on barren coasts with the wealth that comes from their ships of commerce on the seas?"

"What then do you advise us to do that we also may become rich?" asked one of his friends.

"I advise that you take the wisdom of Algamish and say to yourselves, 'A part of all I earn is mine to keep.' Say it in the morning when you first arise. Say it at noon. Say it at night. Say it each hour of every day. Say it to yourself until the words stand out like letters of fire across the sky. Then take whatever portion seems wise. Let it be not less than one-tenth and lay it by. Arrange your other expenditures to do this if necessary.

"Soon you will realize what a rich feeling it is to own a treasure upon which you alone have claim. As it grows it will stimulate you. A new joy of life will thrill you. Greater efforts will come to you to earn more.

"Then learn to make your treasure work for you. Make it your slave. Make its children and its children's children work for you.

"Insure an income for thy future. Look thou at the aged and forget not that in the days to come you too will be numbered among them. Therefore invest thy treasure with greatest caution.

"Provide also that thy family may not want should the gods call thee to their realms. For such protection, it is always possible to make provision with small payments at regular intervals. Therefore the provident man delays not in expectation of a large sum becoming available for such a wise purpose.

"Counsel with wise men. Seek the advice of men whose daily work is handling money. A small return and a safe one is far more desirable than risk.

"Enjoy life while you are here. Do not overstrain or try to save too much. If one-tenth of all you earn is as much as you can comfortably keep, be content to keep this portion. Live otherwise according to your income; let not yourself get stingy and afraid to spend. Life is good and rich with things worthwhile and things to enjoy."

His friends thanked him and went away. In the following years, they frequently revisited Arkad, who received them gladly. He counseled them and gave freely of his wisdom, as men of broad experience are always glad to do. He assisted them in investing their savings to bring good interest with safety, and not be lost or entangled in investments that paid no dividends.

The turning point in these men's lives came upon the day when they realized the truth that had come to them:

### Part of All You Earn, Is Yours to Keep

## Chapter Three
# Seven Cures for a Lean Purse

The glory of Babylon endures. Down through the ages its reputation comes to us as the richest of cities. Yet it was not always so. The riches of Babylon were the results of the wisdom of its people. They first had to learn how to become wealthy.

When the good king, Sargon, returned to Babylon after defeating his enemies, he was confronted with a serious situation. The Royal Chancellor explained it to the king: "After many years of great prosperity brought to our people because your majesty built the great irrigation canals, now that these works are completed the people seem unable to support themselves. The laborers are without employment. The merchants have few customers. The farmers are unable to sell their produce. The people have not enough gold to buy food."

"But where has all the gold gone that we spent for these great improvements?" asked the king.

"It has found its way, I fear," responded the Chancellor, "into the possession of a few very rich men."

The king was thoughtful for some time. Then he asked, "Why should so few men be able to acquire all the gold?"

"Because they know how," replied the Chancellor.

The king decided that the ways of wealth must be taught to the people—and the next day he summoned to the palace Arkad, the richest man in Babylon.

"Arkad," said the king, "I desire that Babylon be the wealthiest city in the world. Therefore, it must be a city of many wealthy men. Hence, we must teach all the people how to acquire riches. Tell me, Arkad, is there any secret to acquiring wealth? Can it be taught?"

"It is practical, your majesty. That which one man knows can be taught to others. Let your chancellor arrange for me a class of one hundred men and I will teach to them the seven cures that did fatten my purse."

A fortnight later, the chosen hundred assembled in the Temple of Learning.

"As a dutiful subject of our king," Arkad began, "I stand before you in his service. Because once I was a poor youth who did greatly desire gold, and because I found knowledge that enabled me to acquire it, he asks that I impart unto you my knowledge.

"The first storehouse of my treasure was a well-worn purse. I loathed its useless emptiness. I desired that it be round and full, clinking with the sound of gold. Therefore, I sought every remedy for a lean purse. I found seven. We shall now consider each."

## The First Cure
*Start thy purse to fattening*

"Now I shall tell thee the first remedy I learned to cure a lean purse. For every ten coins thou placest within thy purse take out for use but nine. Thy purse will start to fatten at once and its increasing weight will feel good in thy hand and bring satisfaction to thy soul.

"Deride not what I say because of its simplicity. Truth is always simple. I told thee I would tell how I built my fortune. This was my beginning. I, too, carried a lean purse and cursed it because there was naught within to satisfy my desires. But when I began to take out from my purse but nine parts of ten I put in, it began to fatten. So will thine.

"Now I will tell a strange truth, the reason for which I know not. When I ceased to pay out more than nine-tenths of my earnings, I managed to get along just as well. I was not shorter than before. Also, ere long, did coins come to me more easily than before. Surely it is a law of the gods that unto him who keepeth and spendeth not a certain part of all his earnings, shall gold come more easily. Likewise, him whose purse is empty does gold avoid.

"Which desirest thou the most? Is it the gratification of thy desires of each day, a jewel, a bit of finery, better raiment, more food; things quickly gone and forgotten? Or is it substantial belongings, gold, lands, herds, merchandise, income-bringing investments? The coins thou takest from thy purse bring the first."

"The coins thou leavest within it will bring the latter. This, my students, was the first cure I did discover for my lean purse: 'For each ten coins I put in, to spend but nine.'"

## The Second Cure
*Control thy expenditures*

"Confuse not the necessary expenses with thy desires. Each of you, together with your good families, have more desires than your earnings can gratify. Therefore are thy earnings spent to gratify these desires insofar as they will go. Still thou retainest many ungratified desires.

"All men are burdened with more desires than they can gratify. Because of my wealth thinkest thou I may gratify every desire? There are limits to my time. There are limits to my strength. There are limits to the distance I may travel. There are limits to what I may eat. There are limits to the zest with which I may enjoy.

"I say to you that just as weeds grow in a field wherever the farmer leaves space for their roots, even so freely do desires grow in men whenever there is a possibility of their being gratified. Thy desires are a multitude and those that thou mayest gratify are but few.

"Study thoughtfully thy accustomed habits of living. Herein may be most often found certain accepted expenses that may wisely be reduced or eliminated. Let thy motto be one hundred percent of appreciated value demanded for each coin spent.

"Therefore, engrave upon the clay each thing for which thou desireth to spend. Select those that are necessary and possible through the expenditure of nine-tenths of thy income. Cross out the rest and consider them but a part of that great multitude of desires that must go unsatisfied and regret them not.

"Budget then thy necessary expenses. Touch not the one-tenth that is fattening thy purse. Let this be thy great desire that is being fulfilled. Remember: the purpose of a budget is to help thy purse to fatten. It is to assist thee to have thy necessities and, insofar as attainable, thy other desires. It is to enable thee to realize thy most cherished desires by defending them from thy casual wishes. Like a bright light in a dark cave thy budget shows up the leaks from thy purse and enables thee to stop them and control thy expenditures for definite and gratifying purposes."

"This, then, is the second cure for a lean purse. Budget thy expenses that thou mayest have coins to pay for thy necessities, to pay for thy enjoyments, and to gratify thy worthwhile desires without spending more than nine-tenths of thy earnings."

## The Third Cure
*Make thy gold multiply*
"I tell you, my students, a man's wealth is not in the coins he carries in his purse; it is the income he buildeth, the golden stream that continually floweth into his purse and keepeth it always bulging. That is what every man desireth. That is what thou, each one of thee, desire: an income that continues to come whether thou work or travel.

"Great income I have acquired. So great that I am called very rich. My loans to responsible traders and craftsmen were my first training in profitable investment. Gaining wisdom from this experience, I extended my loans and investments as my capital increased. From a few sources at first, from many sources later, flowed into my purse a golden stream of wealth available for such wise uses as I should decide.

"Behold, from my humble earnings I had begotten a hoard of golden slaves, so to speak, each laboring and earning more gold. As they labored for me, so their children also labored and their children's children until great was the income from their combined efforts.

"This, then, is the third cure for a lean purse: to put each coin to laboring that it may reproduce its kind as the flocks of the field and help bring to thee income, a stream of wealth that shall flow constantly into thy purse."

# THE FOURTH CURE
### GUARD THY TREASURES FROM LOSS

"Misfortune loves a shining mark. Gold in a man's purse must be guarded with firmness, else it be lost. Thus it is wise that we must first secure small amounts and learn to protect them before the gods trust us with larger.

"Every owner of gold is tempted by opportunities whereby it would seem that he could make large sums by its investment in most plausible projects. Often friends and relatives are eagerly entering such investment and urge him to follow.

"The first sound principle of investment is security for thy principal. Is it wise to be intrigued by larger earnings when thy principal may be lost? I say not. The penalty of risk is probable loss. Before parting with thy treasure, study carefully each assurance that it may be safely reclaimed. Be not misled by romantic desires to make wealth rapidly.

"Before thou loan it to any man assure thyself of his ability to repay and his reputation for doing so. Before thou entrust it as an investment in any field acquaint thyself with the dangers that may beset it."

"This, then, is the fourth cure for a lean purse, and of great importance to prevent thy purse from being emptied once it has become well filled. Guard thy treasure from loss by investing only where thy principal is safe, where it may be reclaimed if desired, and where thou will not fail to collect a fair rental. Consult with wise men. Secure the advice of those experienced in the profitable handling of gold. Let their wisdom protect thy treasure from unsafe investments."

## The Fifth Cure

*Make of thy dwelling a profitable investment*

"If a man setteth aside nine parts of his earnings upon which to live and enjoy life, and if any part of this nine parts he can turn into a profitable investment without detriment to his well-being, then so much faster will his treasures grow.

"All too many of our men of Babylon do raise their families in unseemly quarters where they pay to exacting landlords high rents. No man's family can fully enjoy life unless they do have a plot of ground wherein children can play in the clean earth and where the wife may raise not only blossoms but good rich herbs.

"I recommend that every man own the roof that sheltereth him and his.

"Nor is it beyond the ability of any well-intentioned man to own his home. Hath not our great king so widely extended the walls of Babylon that within them much land is now unused and may be purchased at reasonable sums?

"Also I say to you, that the moneylenders gladly consider the desires of men who seek homes for their families. Readily may thou borrow for such commendable purposes, if thou can show a reasonable portion of the necessary sum which thou thyself hath provided for the purpose.

"Then when the house be built, thou canst pay the moneylender with the same regularity as thou didst pay the landlord. Because each payment will reduce thy indebtedness to the moneylender, a few years will satisfy his loan.

"There come many blessings to the man who owneth his own house. And greatly will it reduce his cost of living, making available more of his earnings for pleasures and the gratification of his desires. This, then, is the fifth cure for a lean purse: Own thy own home."

## The Sixth Cure

*Insure a future income*

"The life of every man proceedeth from his childhood to his old age. This is the path of life and no man may deviate from it unless the Gods call him prematurely to the world beyond. Therefore do I say that it behooves a man to make preparation for a suitable income in the days to come, when he is no longer young, and to make preparations for his family should he be no longer with them.

"There are diverse ways by which a man may provide safety for his future. He may provide a hiding place and there bury a secret treasure. Yet, no matter with what skill it be hidden, it may nevertheless become the loot of thieves. For this reason I recommend not this plan.

"A man may buy houses or lands for this purpose. If wisely chosen as to their usefulness and value in the future, they are permanent in their value and their earnings or sale will provide well for his purpose.

"A man may loan a small sum to the moneylender and increase it at regular periods. The rental which the moneylender adds to this will largely add to its increase. When such a small payment made with regularity doth produce such profitable results, no man can afford not to insure a treasure for his old age and the protection of his family, no matter how prosperous his business and his investments may be.

"This, then, is the sixth cure for a lean purse: provide in advance for the needs of thy growing age and the protection of thy family."

## THE SEVENTH CURE
*INCREASE THY ABILITY TO EARN*

"I now speak of one of the most vital remedies for a lean purse. Yet, I will talk not of gold but of yourselves, of the men beneath the robes who do sit before me. I will talk to you of those things within the minds and lives of men which do work for or against their success.

"One of the most vital requirements to increase your earnings is a strong desire to earn more, a proper and commendable desire. Preceding accomplishment must be desire. Thy desires must be strong and definite. General desires are but weak longings. For a man to wish to be rich is of little purpose. For a man to desire five pieces of gold is a tangible desire which he can press to fulfillment. After he has backed his desire for five pieces of gold with strength of purpose to secure it, next he can find similar ways to obtain ten pieces and then twenty pieces and later a thousand pieces and, behold, he has become wealthy. In learning to secure his one definite small desire, he hath trained himself to secure a larger one. This is the process by which wealth is accumulated: first in small sums, then in larger ones as a man learns and becomes more capable.

"Desires must be simple and definite. They defeat their own purpose should they be too many, too confusing, or beyond one's training to accomplish.

"As a man perfecteth himself in his calling even so doth his ability to earn increase. In those days when I was a humble scribe carving upon the clay for a few coppers each day, I observed that other workers did more than I and were paid more. Therefore, did I determine that I would be exceeded by none. Nor did it take long for me to discover the reason for their greater success. More interest in my work, more concentration upon my task, more persistence in my effort, and, behold, few men could carve more tablets in a day than I.

"The more of wisdom we know, the more we may earn. That man who seeks to learn more of his craft shall be richly rewarded. Always do the affairs of man change and improve because keen-minded men seek greater skill that they may better serve those upon whose patronage they depend. Therefore, I urge all men to be in the front rank of progress and not to stand still.

"Many things come to make a man's life rich with gainful experiences. Such things as the following a man must do if he respects himself: He must pay his debts with all the promptness within his power, not purchasing that for which he is unable to pay. He must take care of his family that they may think and speak well of him. He must make a will of record that, in case the gods call him, proper and honorable division of his property be accomplished. He must have compassion upon those who are injured and smitten by misfortune and aid them within reasonable limits. He must do deeds of thoughtfulness to those dear to him.

"Thus the seventh and last remedy for a lean purse is to cultivate thy own powers, to study and become wiser, to become more skillful, to so act as to respect thyself."

## Chapter Four
# Meet the Goddess of Good Luck

We all hope to be favored by the whimsical Goddess of Good Luck. Is there some way we can meet her and attract, not only her favorable attention, but her generous favors? Is there a way to attract good luck?

That is just what the men of ancient Babylon wished to know.

Among the many who frequented the Temple of Learning, was a wise rich man named Arkad, the richest man in Babylon. He had his own special hall where almost any evening a large group gathered to discuss and argue interesting subjects. We now listen in to see whether they knew how to attract good luck.

"I see no reason," Arkad announced," that the good goddess of luck would take any interest in any man's bet upon a horse race or at the gaming tables. To me she is a goddess of love and dignity whose pleasure it is to aid those who are in need and to reward those who are deserving.

"In tilling the soil, in honest trading, in all of man's occupations, there is opportunity to make a profit upon his efforts and his transactions. Perhaps not all the time will he be rewarded because sometimes his judgment may be faulty, and other times the winds and the weather may defeat his efforts. Yet, if he persists, he may usually expect to realize his profit. This is so because the chances of profit are always in his favor.

"But when a man playeth the games, the situation is reversed for the chances of profit are always against him.

"We must seek good luck in such places as the goddess frequents. Now, suppose we consider our trades and businesses. Is it not natural if we conclude a profitable transaction to consider it not good luck but a just reward for our efforts? I am inclined to think we may be overlooking the gifts of the goddess. Perhaps she really does assist us when we do not appreciate her generosity.

"Who among you," Arkad asked, "have had good luck within your grasp only to see it escape?"

Many hands were raised.

"When sound opportunity stands before thee," the wise man continued, "it is offering a chance that may lead to wealth. I beg of thee, do not delay.

"Good luck waits to come to that man who accepts opportunity. To the building of an estate there must always be the beginning. That start may be a few pieces of gold or silver which a man diverts from his earnings to his first investment.

"To take his first start to building an estate is as good luck as can come to any man. With all men, that first step, which changes them from men who earn from their own labor to men who draw dividends from the earnings of their gold, is important. Some, fortunately, take it when young and thereby outstrip in financial success those who do take it later.

"Opportunity will not wait. She thinks if a man desires to be lucky he will step quick.

"There is much wisdom in making a payment immediately when we are convinced our bargain is wise. If the bargain be good, then dost thou need protection against thy own weaknesses as much as against any other man. We mortals are changeable. Alas, I must say more apt to change our minds when right than wrong. Wrong, we are stubborn indeed. Right, we are prone to vacillate and let opportunity escape. My first judgment is my best."

"The spirit of procrastination is within all men. We desire riches; yet, how often when opportunity doth appear before us, that spirit of procrastination from within doth urge various delays in our acceptance. In listening to it we do become our own worst enemies.

"The truth is this: Good luck can be enticed by accepting opportunity.

"Those eager to grasp opportunities for their betterment, do attract the interest of the good goddess. She is ever anxious to aid those who please her. Men of action please her best."

Men of Action are Favored by the Goddess of Good Luck

## Chapter Five
# The Five Laws of Gold

Gold is reserved for those who know its laws and abide by them. Hence we now reflect on the laws we have so far learned. Here are:

### The Five Laws of Gold

1. Gold cometh gladly and in increasing quantity to any man who will put by not less than one-tenth or his earnings to create an estate for his future and that of his family.
2. Gold laboreth diligently and contentedly for the wise owner who finds for it profitable employment, multiplying even as the flocks of the field.
3. Gold clingeth to the protection of the cautious owner who invests it under the advice of men wise in its handling.
4. Gold slippeth away from the man who invests it in businesses or purposes with which he is not familiar or which are not approved by those skilled in its keep.
5. Gold flees the man who would force it to impossible earnings or who followeth the alluring advice of tricksters and schemers or who trusts it to his own inexperience and romantic desires in investment.

These are the five laws of gold. I do proclaim them as of greater value than gold itself, for they demonstrate how to continually procure its safeguard.

## Chapter Six
# The Gold Lender of Babylon

The gold lender of Babylon spoke as follows:

"Gold bringeth unto its possessor responsibility and a changed position with his fellow men. It bringeth fear lest he lose it or it be tricked away from him. It bringeth a feeling of power and ability to do good. Likewise, it bringeth opportunities whereby his good intentions may bring him into difficulties.

"If you desire to help thy friend, do so in a way that will not bring thy friend's burdens upon thyself.

"The safest loans, my token box tells me, are to those whose possessions are of more value than the one they desire. They own lands, or jewels, or camels, or other things which could be sold to repay the loan. Some of the tokens given to me are jewels of more value than the loan. Others are promises that if the loan be not repaid as agreed they will deliver to me certain property settlement. On loans like those I am assured that my gold will be returned with the rental thereon, for the loan is based on property.

"In another class are those who have the capacity to earn. They labor or serve and are paid. They have income and if they are honest and suffer no misfortune, I know that they also can repay the gold I loan them and the rental to which I am entitled. Such loans are based on human effort.

"Others are those who have neither property nor assured earning capacity. Life is hard and there will always be some who cannot adjust themselves to it. Alas for the loans I make them, even though they be no larger than a pence, my token box may censure me in the years to come unless they be guaranteed by good friends of the borrower who know him honorable.

"And mind you that humans in the throes of great emotions are not safe risks for the gold lender.

"Youth is ambitious. Youth would take short cuts to wealth and the desirable things for which it stands. To secure wealth quickly youth often borrows unwisely. Youth, never having had experience, cannot realize that hopeless debt is like a deep pit into which one may descend quickly and where one may struggle vainly for many days. It is a pit of sorrow and regrets where the brightness of the sun is overcast and night is made unhappy by restless sleeping. Yet, I do not discourage borrowing gold. I encourage it. I recommend it if it be for a wise purpose. I myself made my first real success as a merchant with borrowed gold.

"But be not swayed by the fantastic plans of impractical men who think they see ways to force thy gold to make earnings unusually large. Such plans are the creations of dreamers unskilled in the safe and dependable laws of trade. Be conservative in what thou expect it to earn that thou mayest keep and enjoy thy treasure. To hire it out with a promise of usurious returns is to invite loss.

"Associate with men and enterprises whose success is established that thy treasure may earn liberally under their skillful use and be guarded safely by their wisdom.

"Ere thou goest read this which I have carved beneath the lid of my token box. It applies equally to the borrower and the lender:

### Better a Little Caution
### Than a Great Regret

## Chapter Seven
# The Camel Trader of Babylon

The hungrier one becomes, the clearer one's mind works—also the more sensitive one becomes to the odors of food.

Tarkad certainly thought so. For two whole days he had tasted no food except two figs purloined from over the wall of a garden. Never before had he realized how much food was brought to the markets of Babylon, and how good it smelled.

Lost in his thoughts, he found himself face to face with the one man he wished avoid, the tall bony figure of Dabasir, the camel trader. Of all the friends and others from whom he had borrowed small sums, Dabasir made him feel the most uncomfortable because of Tarkad's failure to repay promptly.

Upon meeting his gaze, Tarkad stuttered and his face flushed. He had naught in his empty stomach to nerve him to argue with Dabasir. "I am sorry, very sorry," he said, "but this day I have neither the copper nor the silver with which I could repay."

"Then get it," Dabasir said. "Surely thou canst get hold of a few coppers and a piece of silver to repay the generosity of an old friend of thy father who aided thee whenst thou wast in need?"

"Tis because ill fortune does pursue me that I cannot pay."

"Ill fortune! Wouldst blame the gods for thine own weakness? Ill fortune pursues every man who thinks more of borrowing than of repaying. Come with me, boy, while I eat. I am hungry and I would tell thee a tale."

Settling down in the eating house, Dabasir began. "When I was a young man I learned the trade of my father, the making of saddles. I worked with him in his shop and took to myself a wife. Being young and not greatly skilled, I could earn but little, just enough to support my excellent wife in a modest way. I craved good things which I could not afford. Soon I found that the shopkeepers would trust me to pay later even though I could not pay at the time.

"Being young and without experience I did not know that he who spends more than he earns is sowing the winds of needless self-indulgence from which he is sure to reap whirlwinds of trouble and humiliation. So I indulged my whims for fine raiment and bought luxuries for my good wife and our home, beyond our means.

"I paid as I could and for a while all went well. But in time I discovered I could not use my earnings both to live upon and to pay my debts. Creditors began to pursue me to pay for my extravagant purchases and life became miserable. I borrowed from my friends, but could not repay them either. Things went from bad to worse. My wife returned to her father and I decided to leave Babylon and seek another city where a young man might have better chances.

"For two years I had a restless and unsuccessful life working for caravan traders. From this I fell in with a set of likable robbers who scoured the desert for unarmed caravans. Such deeds were unworthy of the son of my father, but I was seeing the world through a colored stone and did not realize to what degradation I had fallen.

"One day our leaders were killed, and the rest of us were taken to Damascus where we were stripped of our clothing and sold as slaves.

In bondage I one day told my story to the wife of my new master. Rather than express pity, she replied: "'How can you call yourself a free man when your weakness has brought you to this? If a man has in himself the soul of a slave will he not become one no matter what his birth, even as water seeks its level? If a man has within him the soul of a free man, will he not become respected and honored in has own city in spite of his misfortune?

"'Have you a desire to repay the just debts you owe in Babylon?' she asked.

"Yes, I have the desire, but I see no way," I said.

"'If thou contentedly let the years slip by and make no effort to repay, then thou hast but the contemptible soul of a slave. No man is otherwise who cannot respect himself, and no man can respect himself who does not repay honest debts.'

"But what can I do who am a slave in Syria?"

"'Stay a slave in Syria, thou weakling.'

"I am not a weakling," I said.

"'Then prove it.'

"How?"

"'Does not thy great king fight his enemies in every way he can and with every force he has? Thy debts are thy enemies. They ran thee out of Babylon. You left them alone and they grew too strong for thee. Hadst fought them as a man, thou couldst have conquered them and been one honored among the townspeople. But thou had not the soul to fight them and behold thy pride hast gone down until thou are a slave in Syria.'

"Much I thought over her accusations and many defensive phrases I worded to prove myself not a slave at heart, but I was not to have the chance to use them. Three days later she came to me and said: 'Saddle the two best camels in my husband's herd. Tie on water skins and saddlebags for a long journey.'

"Deep in the desert she asked me: 'Dabasir, hast thou the soul of a free man or the soul of a slave?'

"The soul of a free man," I said.

"'Now is thy chance to prove it. 'Take these camels'—she gestured at part of the herd—'and make thy escape.'

"I needed no further urging, but thanked her and was away into the night."

"Day after day I plodded along. Food and water gave out. The heat of the sun was merciless. At the end of the ninth day, I slid from the back of my mount with the feeling that I was too weak to ever remount and I would surely die.

"I looked across into the barren distance and once again came to me the question, 'Have I the soul of a slave or the soul of a free man?' Then I realized that if I had the soul of a slave, I should give up, lie down in the desert and die.

"But if I had the soul of a free man, what then? Surely I would force my way back to Babylon, repay the people who had trusted me, bring happiness to my wife who truly loved me and bring peace and contentment to my parents.

"'Thy debts are thine enemies who have run thee out of Babylon,' the master's wife had said. Yes it was so. Why had I refused to stand my ground like a man?

"Then a strange thing happened. All the world seemed to be of a different color. At last I saw the true values in life.

"Die in the desert! Not I! With a new vision, I saw the things that I must do. First I would go back to Babylon and face every man to whom I owed an unpaid debt. I should tell them that after years of wandering and misfortune, I had come back to pay my debts as fast as the Gods would permit. Next I should make a home for my wife and become a citizen of whom my parents should be proud.

"I staggered to my feet. What mattered hunger? What mattered thirst? They were but incidents on the road to Babylon. Within me surged the soul of a free man going back to conquer his enemies and reward his friends. I thrilled with the great resolve.

"We found water. We passed into a more fertile country where were grass and fruit. We found the trail to Babylon because the soul of a free man looks at life as a series of problems to be solved and solves them, while the soul of a slave whines, 'What can I do who am but a slave?'

"How about thee, Tarkad? Dost thy empty stomach make thy head exceedingly clear? Art thou ready to take the road that leads back to self-respect? Canst thou see the world in its true color? Hast thou the desire to pay thy debts, however many they may be, and once again be a man respected in Babylon?"

Moisture came to the eyes of the youth. He rose eagerly to his knees. "Thou has shown me a vision; already I feel the soul of a free man surge within me."

"Where the determination is, the way can be found," Dabasir said, returning to his tale. "I now had the determination so I set out to find a way. First I visited every man to whom I was indebted and begged his indulgence until I could earn that with which to repay. Most of them met me gladly. Several reviled me but others offered to help me; one indeed did give me the very help I needed.

"Gradually I was able to repay every copper and every piece of silver. Then at last I could hold up my head and feel that I was an honorable man among men."

So ended the tale of Dabasir the camel trader of old Babylon. He found his own soul when he realized a great truth, a truth that had been known by wise men long before his time. It has led men of all ages out of difficulties and into success, and it will continue to do so for those who have the wisdom to understand its magic power. It is for any man to use who reads these lines:

Where the Determination Is,
the Way Can be Found

## Chapter Eight
# The Luckiest Man in Babylon

At the head of his caravan, proudly rode Sharru Nada, the merchant prince of Babylon. He liked fine cloth and wore rich and becoming robes. He liked fine animals and sat easily upon his Arabian stallion. To look at him one would hardly have guessed his secret: years earlier he had been a slave in the city that now counted him among its wealthiest citizens.

His young journeyman, Hadan Gula, broke in upon his thoughts, "Why dost thou work so hard, riding always with thy caravan upon its long journeys? If I had wealth equal to thine, I would live like a prince. Never across the hot desert would I ride. I would spend the shekels as fast as they came to my purse. That would be a life to my liking, a life worth living."

"Wouldst thou leave no time for work?" the older man asked.

"Work was made for slaves," Hadan Gula said.

"Did not thy grandfather tell thee I was once a slave?"

"He often spoke of thee but never hinted of this."

"Any man may find himself a slave. It was a gaming house and barley beer that brought me disaster."

"But tell me," Hadan Gula asked, "how didst thou regain freedom?"

Sharru Nada remembered back to his youth. "The first night I was in the slave encampment waiting to be sold the next morning, terror gripped me. I could not sleep. I crowded close to the guard rope, and when the others slept, I attracted the attention of Godoso who was doing the first guard watch.

"'Tell me, Godoso,' I whispered, 'when we get to Babylon will we be sold to the walls?' The task of building the city walls was brutal and a near-certain death sentence.

"'Why you want to know?' he asked.

"'Canst thou not understand?' I said. 'I am young. I want to live. I don't want to be worked or beaten to death on the walls. Is there any chance for me to get a good master?'

"He whispered back, 'I tell you something. Thou good fellow, give me no trouble. Most times we go first to slave market. Listen now. When the buyers come, tell 'em you a good worker, like to work hard for good master. Make 'em want to buy. You not make 'em buy, next day you carry brick. Mighty hard work.'

"After he walked away, I lay in the warm sand, looking up at the stars and thinking about work. Another slave, a wise one named Megiddo, told me that work was his best friend. It made me wonder if it would be my best friend. Certainly it would be if it helped me out of this.

"The following morning, Meggido talked to me earnestly to impress upon me how valuable work would be to me in the future: 'Some men hate it. They make it their enemy. Better to treat it like a friend, make thyself like it. Don't mind because it is hard. If thou thinkest about what a good house thou build, then who cares if the beams are heavy and it is far from the well to carry the water for the plaster. Promise me, boy, if thou get a master, work for him as hard as thou canst. If he does not appreciate all thou do, never mind. Remember, work, well done, does good to the man who does it. It makes him a better man.'

"He stopped as a burly farmer came to the enclosure and looked at us critically. Megiddo asked about his farm and crops, soon convincing him that he would be a valuable man. After violent bargaining with the slave dealer, the farmer drew a fat purse from beneath his robe, and soon Megiddo had followed his new master out of sight.

"A few other men were sold during the morning. At noon Godoso confided to me that the dealer was disgusted and would not stay over another night but would take all who remained at sundown to the king's buyer and put them to work on the walls. I was becoming desperate when a fat, good-natured man walked up to the pen and inquired if there was a baker among us.

"I approached him saying, 'Why should a good baker like thyself seek another baker of inferior ways? Would it not be easier to teach a willing man like myself thy skilled ways? Look at me, I am young, strong, and like to work. Give me a chance and I will do my best to earn gold and silver for thy purse.'

"He was impressed by my willingness and began bargaining with the dealer. At last, much to my joy, the deal was closed. I followed my new master away, thinking I was the luckiest man in Babylon.

"My new home was much to my liking. Nana-naid, my master, taught me how to grind the barley in the stone bowl that stood in the courtyard, how to build the fire in the oven, and then how to grind very fine the sesame flour for the honey cakes. I had a couch in the shed where his grain was stored. The old slave housekeeper, Swasti, fed me well and was pleased at how I helped her with the heavy tasks.

"Here was the chance I had longed for to make myself valuable to my master and, I hoped, to find a way to earn my freedom. I asked Nana-naid to show me how to knead the bread and to bake. This he did, much pleased at my willingness. Later, when I could do this well, I asked him to show me how to make the honey cakes, and soon I was doing all the baking. My master was glad to be idle, but Swasti shook her head in disapproval. 'No work to do is bad for any man,' she declared.

"I felt it was time for me to think of a way by which I might start to earn coins to buy my freedom. As the baking was finished at noon, I thought Nana-naid would approve if I found profitable employment for the afternoons and might share my earnings with me. Then the thought came to me, why not bake more of the honey cakes and peddle them to hungry men upon the streets of the city?

"When I told him of my plan to peddle our honey cakes, he was well pleased. 'Here is what we will do,' he suggested. 'Thou sellest them at two for a penny, then half of the pennies will be mine to pay for the flour and the honey and the wood to bake them. Of the rest, I shall take half and thou shalt keep half.'

"I was much pleased by his generous offer that I might keep for myself one-fourth of my sales. I worked day and night and my success at selling my honey cakes grew. My master was pleased. And as the months passed I continued to add pennies to my purse. It began to have a comforting weight upon my belt. Work was proving to be my best friend, just as Megiddo had said.

"I was happy but Swasti was worried. 'Thy master, I fear to have him spend so much time at the gaming houses,' she said.

"As I went forth with my tray of cakes every day, I soon found regular customers. One of these was none other than your grandfather, Arad Gula. He was a rug merchant and sold to the housewives, going from one end of the city to the other, accompanied by a donkey loaded high with rugs. He would buy two cakes for himself and two for his slave, always tarrying to talk with me while they ate them.

"Thy grandfather said something to me one day that I shall always remember. 'I like thy cakes, boy, but better still I like the fine enterprise with which thou offerest them. Such spirit can carry thee far on the road to success.' But how canst thou understand, Hadan Gula, what such words of encouragement could mean to a slave boy, lonesome in a great city, struggling with all he had in him to find a way out of his humiliation?

"One day in the markets Arad Gula asked me, 'Why dost thou work so hard?' Almost the same question thou asked of me today, dost thou remember? I told him what Megiddo had said about work and how it was proving to be my best friend. I showed him with pride my wallet of pennies and explained how I was saving them to buy my freedom.

"'When thou art free, what wilt thou do?' he asked.

"'I intend to become a merchant,' I said.

"At that, he confided in me. Something I had never suspected. 'Thou knowest not that I, also, am a slave. I am in partnership with my master.'

"After confiding that he was a slave," Sharru Nada continued, 'he explained how anxious he had been to earn his freedom. Now that he had enough money to buy this he was much disturbed as to what he should do. He was no longer making good sales and feared to leave the support of his master.

"I protested his indecision: 'Cling no longer to thy master. Get once again the feeling of being a free man. Act like a free man and succeed like one! Decide what thou desirest to accomplish and then work will aid thee to achieve it!' He went on his way saying he was glad I had shamed him for his cowardice.

"Back home I earned that Swasti's fears were well-founded. The master's loses had been mounting, and I discovered that he had put me up as collateral. While I was doing the baking next morning, the moneylender came with a man he called Sasi. This man looked me over and said I would do.

"The moneylender waited not for my master to return. With only the robe on my back and the purse of pennies hanging safely from my belt, I was hurried away.

"I was whirled away from my dearest hopes as the hurricane snatches the tree from the forest and casts it into the surging sea. Again a gaming house and barley beer had caused me disaster.

"Sasi was a blunt, gruff man. As he led me across the city, I told him of the good work I had been doing for Nana-naid and said I hoped to do good work for him. He offered no encouragement: he told me I was bound for the walls.

"The walls were all that I had heard. Picture a desert with not a tree, just low shrubs and a sun burning with such fury the water in our barrels became so hot we could scarcely drink it. Then picture rows of men, going down into the deep excavation and lugging heavy baskets of dirt up soft, dusty trails from daylight until dark. Picture food served in open troughs from which we helped ourselves like swine. We had no tents, no straw for beds. That was the situation in which I found myself. I buried my wallet in a marked spot, wondering if I would ever dig it up again.

"At first I worked with good will, but as the months dragged on, I felt my spirit breaking. Then the heat fever took hold of my weary body. I lost my appetite and could scarcely eat. At night I would toss in unhappy wakefulness. Yet I was just as willing to work as Megiddo; he could not have worked harder than I. Why did not my work bring me happiness and success? Was I to work the rest of my life without gaining my desires? All of these questions were jumbled in my mind and I had not an answer. Indeed, I was sorely confused.

"Several days later when it seemed that I was at the end of my endurance and with my questions still unanswered, Sasi sent for me. A messenger had come from my master to take me back to Babylon. I dug up my precious wallet, wrapped myself in the tattered remnants of my robe and was on my way.

"When we rode to the courtyard of my master's house, imagine my surprise when I saw Arad Gula awaiting me. He helped me down and hugged me like a long lost brother.

"As we went our way I would have followed him as a slave should follow his master, but he would not permit me. He put his arm about me, saying, 'I hunted everywhere for thee: When I had almost given up hope, I did meet Swasti who told me of the moneylender, who directed me to thy noble owner. A hard bargain he did drive and made me pay an outrageous price, but thou art worth it. Thy philosophy and thy enterprise have been my inspiration to this new success. We are going to Damascus and I need thee for my partner. In one moment thou will be a free man!'

"Tears of gratitude filled my eyes. 1 knew I was the luckiest man in Babylon. In the time of my greatest distress, work didst indeed prove my best friend. My willingness to work enabled me to escape being sold to slave gangs upon the walls. It also so impressed thy grandfather, he selected me for his partner.

"Life is rich with many pleasures for men to enjoy," Sharru Nada concluded to his young friend. "Each has its place. I am glad that work is not reserved for slaves. Were that the case I would be deprived of my greatest pleasure. Many things do I enjoy, but nothing takes the place of work."

## Chapter Nine
# The Clay Tablets of Babylon

Alfred H. Shrewsbury, a young archeologist at Nottingham University, was breathless with excitement at the five clay tablets that had just arrived from excavation in the ruins of Babylon.

He wrote to the excavator: "You will be as astonished at the story they relate. One expects the dim and distant past to speak of romance and adventure. When instead it discloses the problem of a person named Dabasir to pay off his debts, one realizes that conditions upon this old world have not changed as much in five thousand years as one might expect.

"It's odd, you know, but these old inscriptions rather 'rag' me. Being a college professor, I am supposed to be a thinking human being possessing a working knowledge of most subjects. Yet, here comes this old chap out of the ruins of Babylon to offer a way I had never heard of to pay off my debts and at the same time acquire gold to jingle in my wallet. Pleasant thought, I say, and interesting to prove whether it will work as well nowadays as it did in Babylon. Mrs. Shrewsbury and myself are planning to try out his plan upon our own affairs, which could be much improved."

His translations went as follows:

### TABLET ONE

Now, when the moon becometh full, I, Dabasir, who am but recently returned from slavery in Syria, with the determination to pay my many debts and become a man of means worthy of respect in my native city of Babylon, do here engrave upon the clay a permanent record of my affairs to guide and assist me in carrying through my high desires.

This plan includeth three purposes which are my hope and desire.

First, the plan doth provide for my future prosperity. Therefore one-tenth of all I earn shall be set aside as my own to keep.

Second, I shall support and clothe my good wife who hath returned to me with loyalty from the house of her father. To take good care of a faithful wife putteth self-respect into the heart of a man and addeth strength and determination to his purposes.

Therefore seven-tenths of all I earn shall be used to provide a home, clothes to wear, and food to eat, with a bit extra to spend, that our lives be not lacking in pleasure and enjoyment. But he doth further enjoin the greatest care that we spend not greater than seven-tenths of what I earn for these worthy purposes. Herein lieth the success of the plan. I must live upon this portion and never use more nor buy what I may not pay for out of this portion.

### Tablet Two

Third, the plan doth provide that out of my earnings my debts shall be paid. Therefore each time the moon is full, two-tenths of all I have earned shall be divided honorably and fairly among those who have trusted me and to whom I am indebted. Thus in due time will all my indebtedness be surely paid.

Here the professor jotted on his notepad: "Paying debt surpasses savings. One-tenth to savings; two-tenths to debt; seven-tenths to home and family."

### Tablet Three

Now that I realize how I can repay my debts in small sums of my earnings, do I realize the great extent of my folly in running away from the results of my extravagances.

Therefore have I visited my creditors and explained to them that I have no resources with which to pay except my ability to earn, and that I intend to apply two-tenths of all I earn upon my indebtedness evenly and honestly. This much can I pay but no more. Therefore if they be patient, in time my obligations will be paid in full.

Ahmar, whom I thought my best friend, reviled me bitterly and I left him in humiliation. Birejik, the farmer, pleaded that I pay him first as he didst badly need help. Alkahad, the house owner, was indeed disagreeable and insisted that he would make me trouble unless I didst soon settle in full with him.

All the rest willingly accepted my proposal. Therefore am I more determined than ever to carry through, being convinced that it is easier to pay one's debts than to avoid them.

### Tablet Four

Thus I have divided according to the plan. One-tenth have I set aside to keep as my own, seven-tenths have I divided with my good wife to pay for our living.

Two-tenths have I divided among my creditors as evenly as could be done in coppers.

I did not see Ahmar but left it with his wife. Birejik was so pleased he would kiss my hand. Old Alkahad alone was grouchy and said I must pay faster. To which I replied that if I were permitted to be well fed and not worried, that alone would enable me to pay faster. All the others thanked me and spoke well of my efforts.

Therefore, at the end of one moon, my indebtedness is reduced by almost four pieces of silver and I possess almost two pieces of silver besides, upon which no man hath claim. My heart is lighter than it hath been for a long time.

### Tablet Five

Again the moon shines full and I remember that it is long since I carved upon the clay. Twelve moons in truth have come and gone. But this day I will not neglect my record because upon this day I have paid the last of my debts. This is the day upon which my good wife and my thankful self celebrate with great feasting that our determination hath been achieved.

My wife looketh upon me with a light in her eyes that doth make a man have confidence in himself. Yet it is the plan that hath made my success. I do commend it to all who wish to get ahead. For truly if it will enable an ex-slave to pay his debts and have gold in his purse, will it not aid any man to find independence? Nor am I finished with it, for I am convinced that if I follow it further it will make me rich among men.

After completing his translation, Shrewsbury wrote again to his friend: "You will possibly remember my writing a year ago that Mrs. Shrewsbury and myself intended to try his plan for getting out of debt and at the same time having gold to jingle. You may have guessed, even though we tried to keep it from our friends, our desperate straits.

"We were frightfully humiliated for years by a lot of old debts and worried sick for fear some of the tradespeople might start a scandal that would force me out of the college. We paid and paid—every shilling we could squeeze out of income—but it was hardly enough to hold things even. Besides we were forced to do all our buying where we could get further credit regardless of higher costs.

"It developed into one of those vicious circles that grow worse instead of better. Our struggles were getting hopeless. We could not move to less costly rooms because we owed the landlord. There did not appear to be anything we could do to improve our situation.

"Then comes the old camel trader from Babylon, with a plan to do just what we wished to accomplish. He jolly well stirred us up to follow his system. We made a list of all our debts and I took it around and showed it to every one we owed. I explained how it was simply impossible for me to ever pay them the way things were going along. They could readily see this themselves from the figures. Then I explained that the only way I saw to pay in full was to set aside twenty percent of my income each month to be divided pro rata, which would pay them in full in a little over two years. Then, in the meantime, we would go on a cash basis and give them the further benefit of our cash purchases.

"They were really quite decent. Our greengrocer, a wise old chap, put it in a way that helped to bring around the rest. 'If you pay for all you buy and then pay some of what you owe, that is better than you have done.'

"Then we began scheming on how to live upon seventy percent. We were determined to keep that extra ten percent to jingle. It was like having an adventure to make the change. We enjoyed figuring this way and that to live comfortably upon that remaining seventy-percent. We started with rent and managed to secure a fair reduction. Next we put our favorite brands of tea and such under suspicion and were agreeably surprised how often we could purchase superior qualities at less cost.

"We managed and right cheerfully at that. What a relief it proved to have our affairs in such a shape we were no longer persecuted by past due accounts.

"I must not neglect, however, to tell you about that extra ten percent we were supposed to jingle. Well, we did jingle it for some time. Now don't laugh too soon. You see, that is the sporty part. It is the real fun to start accumulating money that you do not want to spend. There is more pleasure in running up such a surplus than there could be in spending it.

"After we had jingled to our hearts' content, we found a more profitable use for it. We took up an investment upon which we could pay that ten percent each month. This is proving to be the most satisfying part of our regeneration. It is the first thing we pay out of my check.

"There is a most gratifying sense of security to know our investment is growing steadily. By the time my teaching days are over it should be a snug sum, large enough so the income will take care of us from then on.

"All this out of my same old check. Difficult to believe, yet absolutely true.

"At the end of the next year, when all our old bills shall have been paid, we will have more to pay upon our investment besides some extra for travel. We are determined never again to permit our living expenses to exceed seventy percent of our income.

"The chap who carved these tablets had a timeless message, a message so important that after five thousand years it has risen out of the ruins of Babylon, just as true and just as vital as the day it was buried."

# The Secret of the Ages
(1926)

# by Robert Collier

*The Legendary Success Formula*

## Contents

Introduction  *What Is the "Secret of the Ages"?* by Mitch Horowitz  536
Chapter One  The World's Greatest Discovery  537
Chapter Two  Your Higher Self  538
Chapter Three  The Primal Cause  540
Chapter Four  This One Thing I Do  541
Chapter Five  Universal Mind  543
Chapter Six  See Yourself Doing It  544
Chapter Seven  The Formula of Success  545
Chapter Eight  The Law of Attraction  546
Chapter Nine  Your Needs Are Met  547
Chapter Ten  The Master Mind  548

## Introduction
# What Is the "Secret of the Ages"?

Robert Collier was born to a prosperous Irish immigrant household in St. Louis, Missouri, in 1885. As the nephew of publishing magnate P.F. Collier, the boy was part of a socially prominent family—but his early life was marked by tragedy. Robert's parents often lived apart and his mother died when he was eleven. He spent much of the remainder of his youth in boarding schools.

As Collier neared adulthood, however, he discovered a world of possibilities. He trained for the priesthood and, deciding it wasn't for him, tried his hand as a mining engineer, journalist, advertising man, and publisher.

Collier's prospects dimmed in the early 1920s when he suffered a chronic and debilitating case of food poisoning. For months the illness sapped his energies and resisted treatment. Searching for a cure, Collier dedicated himself to the study of Christian Science, prayer healing, autosuggestion, and New Thought, a popular metaphysical movement based on principle that *thoughts are causative*. Robust mental imaging, went the New Thought gospel, could restore health.

Using his new psycho-spiritual methods, Collier recovered. He came to wonder: Could the same mind-power metaphysics work for other needs, such as money and career success? Collier threw himself into studying the higher dimensions of the mind. The writer came to believe that as God had created man in His own image, so could man, through his powers of mental imaging, function as a creator within his earthly sphere of existence.

In 1926 Collier mapped out his program in a pamphlet series called *The Secret of the Ages*. He had actually begun publishing his series the prior year when, perhaps thinking of his miracle recovery, he called it *The Book of Life*.

Collier's "Secret of the Ages" was this: From earliest time, humanity has possessed the ability to invent, build, and advance through the creative energies of thought. Man's mental power, Collier explained, is a metaphysical *force* that lifted humankind out of caves and into the light of fire; it created the ancient civilizations of Egypt, Mesopotamia, and the Indus Valley; it built the empires of Greece and Rome; and its powers are encrypted in the ancient narratives, parabolic or otherwise, of every miracle from Aladdin's Lamp to Christ's walking on water.

Collier could be startlingly blunt about his views. "Mind is God," he wrote in 1927. "And the subconscious in us is our part of Divinity." But he was never cavalier. Collier expressed deep reverence for the teachings of Christ, which he considered a psychological blueprint to man's highest potential.

The metaphysical insights that aided Collier's recovery did not render him impervious to disease. He died of intestinal cancer in 1950, two years after revising and expanding *The Secret of the Ages*. But the facts of his and our physical limits should not engender cynicism toward Collier's work. His writing sparkles with sincerity and discovery, which is preserved in this condensation of his key principles. His ideas have contributed to the success of a wide range of readers, many of whom wrote to Collier during his lifetime, and have continued to make *The Secret of the Ages* a cornerstone of self-development literature in the decades since his passing.

—Mitch Horowitz

## Chapter One
# The World's Greatest Discovery

What, in your opinion, is the most significant discovery of our age? The finding of dinosaur eggs on the plains of Mongolia laid some 100,000,000 years ago? The unearthing of ancient tombs and cities with their specimens of bygone civilizations? The radioactive time clock by which we can estimate the age of earth at 4.5 billion years?

No—none of these. The really significant thing about this vast research from the study of bygone ages is that for the first time we are beginning to understand the existence of a "Vital Force" that—somehow, some way—was brought to earth millions of years ago.

It matters not whether you believe that mankind dates back to the primitive ape-man or sprang full-grown from the mind of the Creator. In either event, there had to be a First Cause—a source of Creation. Some Power had to bring to earth the first germ of Life.

No one can follow history down through the ages without realizing that the whole purpose of existence is GROWTH. Life is dynamic. It is ever moving forward. The one unpardonable sin of nature is to stand still, to stagnate.

Egypt and Persia, Greece and Rome, all the great empires of antiquity perished *when they ceased to grow.*

It is for men and women who refuse to stand still that this book is written. It will give you a clear understanding of your own potential, and show you how to work with and take advantage of the creative energy that surrounds you.

The evidence of this energy is everywhere. Take up some rigorous exercise—rowing, tennis, swimming, riding. In the beginning your muscles are weak, easily tired. But keep at it for a few days. The Vital Force flows into them more strongly, strengthens them, toughens them. Do rough manual labor—and what happens? The skin of your hands becomes tender, blisters, hurts. Keep it up and the Vital Force provides extra thickness, extra toughness—calluses, we call them—to meet your need.

All through daily life you will find this Life Force steadily at work. Embrace it, work with it, take it to yourself, and there is nothing you cannot do.

The fact that you have obstacles to overcome is in your favor. For when there is nothing to be done, when things run along too smoothly, this Life Force seems to sleep. It is when you need it, when you call upon it urgently, when you seem to have used up every reserve in you, that it is most on the job.

The Life Force makes no distinction between rich and poor, high and low. The greater your need, the more readily will it respond to your call. Wherever there is an unusual task, wherever there is poverty, hardship, sickness, or despair, *there* is this Servant of your Mind, ready and eager to help, asking only that you call upon it.

## Chapter Two

# Your Higher Self

The power to be what you want, to get what you desire, to accomplish whatever you are striving for, abides within you. It rests with you only to bring it forth. You must learn how to do that, of course, but the first essential is to *realize that you possess this power.*

You are not a mere clod. You are not a beast of burden relegated to spend your days in unremitting labor in return for food and housing. You are one of the Lords of the Earth, with unlimited potentialities. Within you is a power that, properly grasped and directed, can lead you out of mediocrity and place you among the elect—the lawgivers, the writers, the engineers, the great industrialists—the DOERS and the THINKERS. It rests with you to learn to use this Universal Mind that can do all things.

Carl Jung claimed that the subconscious contains not only all the knowledge that it has gathered during the life of the individual, but that it also contains all the wisdom of past ages. And that by drawing on its wisdom and power the individual may possess any good and noble thing of life.

You see, the subconscious is the connecting link between the Creator and ourselves, between Vital Force and our own bodies and affairs.

Most of us think of mind as merely the conscious part of us. But the earliest Greek religious writings taught that man is a triune being: *first*, the physical or conscious self; *second*, the subconscious, sometimes called your "Inner Mind" because it is latent within you; and *third*, the superconscious or "Higher Self."

Go back 2,000 years before Christ to the Upanishads, the earliest religious books of India, and you find a similar teaching. Study the religion of the Egyptians and you find the same belief. The great pyramids were triangular on each side, exemplifying the idea you find on many of their monuments. The Egyptians believed that the "Ka," or "Higher Self" could separate itself from the body and perform any service required of it.

You can send your Higher Self to do your will. Through it, you can protect your loved ones, you can heal, you can help in all ways.

To do so, however, you must charge the situation with your own Vital Force. You can never help another without giving something of yourself. You must consciously GIVE of your Vital Force. You must have the faith to SEE your Higher Self doing the things that you direct it to do. You must BELIEVE that it IS doing them. Given such faith, all things are possible to you.

YOU are a Creator, with the God-given power to use that Vital Force as you please. But to create *anything of good* requires four things:

1. The mental image of what you want. That is the mold.
2. Knowledge of your power, so you can consciously draw to you all the Vital Force you need—breathe it in—and then pour it into your mental mold.
3. Faith in your creative power, faith to crystalize the Vital Force into your mold, until it is manifest for all to see.
4. Doing something to convince your subconscious mind—and, through it, the superconscious—that you *believe you HAVE received*. For instance, a woman who prayed for a house got a board and nail and kept them before her, affirming that they were the beginning of the house.

As I see it, the Universal Mind is the Supreme Intelligence and Creator of the Universe, and we are partakers of the Divine Attributes. You are part of it, I am part of it, and anything we do *that is for the good of all* has the support of this Universal Mind—*provided we call upon it.*

## Chapter Three

# The Primal Cause

"Give me a base of support," said Archimedes, "and with a lever I will move the world."

Your base of support is *mind*. All started with mind. In the beginning was nothing—a fire mist. Before anything could come out of it there had to be an *idea*, a model upon which to build. *Universal Mind* supplied that idea. Therefore the primal cause is mind. Everything must start with an idea.

Matter in the ultimate is but a product of thought. Even the most materialist scientists acknowledge that matter is not as it appears. According to physics, matter, be it the human body or a log of wood, is an aggregation of distinct minute particles or atoms.

Until fairly recently, these atoms were supposed to be the ultimate makeup of matter. We ourselves—and all the material world—were supposed to consist of these infinitesimal particles, so small that they could not be seen, weighed, or touched individually—but, still, particles of matter *and indestructible.*

Now, however, these atoms have been further analyzed; and physics tells us that they are not indestructible at all—that they are mere positive and negative buttons of force or energy called protons and electrons, without hardness, without density, without solidity, without even positive actuality. In short, they are vortices in the ether—whirling bits of energy—dynamic, never static, pulsating with life.

And that, mind you, is what the solid table in front of you is made of, is what your house, your body, and the whole world is made of—*whirling bits of energy!*

Your body is about 85 percent water, 15 percent ash, phosphorus, and other elements. And they, in turn, can be dissipated into gas and vapor. Where do we go from there?

Is not the answer that, to a great degree at least, and perhaps altogether, this world is *one of our mind's own creating*?

Reduced to the ultimate—to the atom or to the electron—everything in this world is an idea of mind. All of it has been brought together through mind.

The world without is but a reflection of the world within. Your thought *creates* the conditions that the mind images. Keep before your mind's eye the image of all you want to be, and you will see it reflected in the world without.

Few of us have any idea of our mental powers. The *old idea* was that man must take this world as he found it. The basis of all democracies is that man is *not* bound by any system, that he need not accept the world as he finds it. He can remake the world to his own ideas.

As French psychologist Charles Baudouin puts it, "You will go in the direction in which you face . . ."

This new principle is responsible for all our inventions, all our progress. Man is satisfied with nothing. He is constantly remaking his world.

But there *must be an idea* before it can take form. As psychologist Terry Walter says: "The impressions that enter the subconscious form indelible pictures, which are never forgotten, and whose power can change the body, mind, manner, and morals; can, in fact, revolutionize a personality."

*Learn to control your thoughts.* Learn to image upon your mind only the things you want to see reflected there. Your thoughts supply you with limitless energy that will take whatever form your mind demands.

Begin at once, today, to use what you have learned. All growth comes from practice. All the forces of life are active—peace—joy—power.

You are "heir of God and coheir with Christ." And as such, no evil has power over you, whereas you have all power for good. And "good" means not merely holiness. Good means happiness—the happiness of everyday people.

## Chapter Four

# This One Thing I Do

It may sound paradoxical, but few people really know what they want.

Most of them struggle along in a vague sort of way, hoping for something to turn up. They are so occupied with the struggle that they have forgotten—if they ever knew—what they are struggling *for*. They are like a drowning man, using up many times the energy it would take to get somewhere, frittering it away in aimless struggles—without thought or direction.

*You must know what you want before you stand any chance of getting it.*

How did the Salvation Army get so much favorable publicity out of the First World War? They were a comparatively small part of the "services" that catered to the boys, yet they carried off the lion's share of the glory. Do you know how they did it?

By concentrating on just one thing—DOUGHNUTS!

They served doughnuts to the boys—and they did it *well*. And that is the basis of all success in business and in most parts of life: to focus on one thing and do that thing well. Better by far to do one thing preeminently well than to dabble in forty.

The greatest success rule I know in business—the one that should be printed over everyone's desk is—"This One Thing I Do."

Volumes have been written about personal efficiency. But boiled down, it all comes to six steps:

1. Know what you want.
2. Analyze the thing you must do to get it.
3. Plan your work ahead.
4. Do one thing at a time.
5. Finish that one thing and send it on its way before starting the next.
6. Once started, KEEP GOING!

In the realm of mind, the realm of all practical power, you can possess what you want at once. You have but to claim it, visualize it, and believe in it to bring it into actuality. And all you need to begin this process is an earnest, intense, well-focused DESIRE.

"But," you will say, "I have plenty of desires. I've always wanted to be rich. How do you account for difference between my wealth, position, and power and that of the rich men all around me?"

The problem is simply that you have never focused your desires into *one great dominating desire*. You have a host of mild desires. You mildly wish you were rich, you wish you had a position of responsibility and influence, you wish you could travel at will. The wishes are so many and so varied that they conflict with each other and you get nowhere in particular. You lack one *intense* desire, to which you are willing to subordinate everything else.

Take one idea, make a good distinct picture of it, and immediately your thoughts begin to group themselves, and you have the nucleus of your desire. *This one thing you do*, and ideas from the SELF within begin to collect around the one thing, and you open the way for your good to flow to you.

Watch your thoughts! Examine each thought that comes to you. It may be your calling. Open your mind, be alert to the things happening around you. Be interested in everyone you meet; you may entertain an angel unawares. He may have a vital message for you, or you for him. Watch for your special work, recognize it, be ready for it. And when it arrives equip yourself to excel in it through study, application, and arduous practice. And, above all, *focus your efforts on this one thing.*

Do you know how Napoleon so frequently won battles in the face of a numerically superior foe? By concentrating his men at the actual *point of contact!* His artillery was often greatly outnumbered, but it accomplished far more than the enemy's because instead of scattering his fire, he *concentrated it all on the point of attack!*

The time you spend aimlessly dreaming and wishing would accomplish marvels if it were concentrated upon one definite object.

If you want a thing badly enough you will have no trouble concentrating on it. Your thoughts will naturally center on it, like bees on honey.

In his ESP experiments at Duke University, Dr. J.B. Rhine demonstrated that the mind can definitely influence inanimate objects, but only when there is intense interest or desire. When the subject's interest was distracted, when he failed to concentrate his attention, he had no power over the object. It was only as he gave his entire attention to it, concentrated his every energy upon it, that he got successful results.

Dr. Rhine proved through physical experiments what most of us have always believed: that there *is* a Power over and above the merely physical powers of the mind or body; that through intense concentration we can line up with that Power; and that once we do, nothing is impossible to us.

## Chapter Five
# Universal Mind

It is not always the man who struggles hardest who wins. It is the direction as well as the energy of the struggle that counts.

To get ahead you must swim with the tide. Those who prosper and succeed work in accord with natural forces. A given amount of effort with these forces carries a man faster and farther than much more effort used *against the current*. Those who work blindly, regardless of these forces, make life difficult for themselves and rarely prosper.

It has been estimated that something like 60 percent of the factors producing success or failure lie outside of a man's conscious efforts—separate from his daily round of details. To the extent that he cooperates with the wisdom and power of Universal Mind he is successful, well, and happy. To the extent that he fails to cooperate, he is unsuccessful, sick, and miserable.

The connecting link between your conscious mind and Universal Mind is *thought*. And every thought that is in harmony with progress and good, every thought that is freighted with the right idea, can penetrate to Universal Mind. And penetrating to the Universal Mind, your thought returns with the power of Universal Mind to accomplish it. You don't need to originate the ways and means. The Universal Mind knows how to bring about any necessary results.

There is one right way to solve any problem. When your human judgment is unable to decide what that one right way is, turn to Universal Mind for guidance. You need never fear the outcome; if you heed its advice you cannot go astray.

A flash of genius does not originate in your own brain. Through intense concentration you establish a circuit through your subconscious mind with the Universal, and it is from the Higher Mind that the inspiration comes. All genius, all progress comes from this same source.

## Chapter Six
# See Yourself Doing It

What does it mean that *God created man in His own image*?

"The imagination," writes Glenn Clark in *The Soul's Sincere Desire*, "is of all the qualities in man the most Godlike—that which associates him most closely with God. The first mention we read of man in the Bible is where he is spoken of as an 'image.' 'Let us make man in our own image, after our likeness.' The only place where an image can be conceived is in the imagination."

If man was made in God's image, it stands to reason that man's imagination—like that of the Great Master—is capable of creation.

When you form a mental image of the good you wish to come to pass, make it clear, picture it vividly in every detail, BELIEVE in it, and the "Genie-of-Your-Mind" will bring it into being as an everyday reality.

The keynote of successful visualization is this: *See things as you would have them be instead of as they are.*

Close your eyes and make clear mental pictures. Make them look and act just as they would in real life. In short, daydream—but daydream with a *purpose*. Better still, get those pictures down on paper using, if you need to, pictures of similar things cut from magazines. Concentrate on one idea at a time to the exclusion of others, and continue to concentrate on that one idea until it has been accomplished.

## Chapter Seven
# The Formula of Success

What is the eternal question that stands up and looks you and every sincere person squarely in the eye each morning?

*"How can I better my condition?"* That is the real-life question that confronts you, and will haunt you every day till you solve it.

Often this question takes the form of whether you should stick to the job you have, or seek a better one. The answer depends entirely on what you are striving for. The first thing is to set your goal. What is it you want? A profession? A political career? An executive position? A business of your own?

Every position should yield you three things:
1. Reasonable pay for the present.
2. Knowledge, training, or experience that will be worth money to you in the future.
3. Prestige or acquaintances that will be of assistance in attaining your goal.

Judge every opening by these three standards. But don't overlook chances for valuable training, merely because the pay is small.

Some complain of their station in life and feel that their surroundings are discouraging. Do you feel that if you were in another's place success would be easier? Just bear in mind that your real environment is *within you*. All the factors of success or failure are in your inner world. *You* make your own inner world—and through it your outer world. You can choose the material from which to build. If you have chosen unwisely in the past, you can choose new material now. The richness of life is within you. Start right in and do all those things you feel you have it in you to do. *Ask permission of no one.*

Take the first step and your mind will mobilize all of its forces to your aid. But it is essential is that you *begin.*

Those who have made their mark on life all had one trait in common: they *believed in themselves.* "But," you may ask, "how can I believe in myself when I have never done anything worthwhile, when everything I put my hand to seems to fail?" You can't, of course. That is, you couldn't if you had to depend upon your conscious mind alone. But remember what one far greater than you said: "I can of mine own self do nothing. The Father that is within me—He doeth the works."

That same "Father" is within you. And it is by knowing that He *is* in you, and that through Him you can do anything that is right, that you can acquire the belief in yourself that is so necessary.

The starting point is *Faith.* But St. James tells us: "Faith without works is dead." So go on to the next step. Decide the one thing you want most from life. No matter what it may be. There is no limit to Mind. Visualize this thing that you want. See it, feel it, BELIEVE in it. Make your mental blueprint, and *begin to build!*

Psychologists have discovered that the best time to make suggestions to your subconscious is just before going to sleep, when the senses are quiet and the body is relaxed. So, let us take your desire and suggest it to your subconscious mind tonight. The two prerequisites are the earnest DESIRE, and an intelligent, understanding BELIEF.

Do that every night until you ACTUALLY DO BELIEVE that you have the thing you want. When you reach that point, *YOU WILL HAVE IT!*

## Chapter Eight
# The Law of Attraction

Look around you. What businesses are getting ahead? Who are the big successes? Are they the ones who grab the passing dollar, careless of what they offer in return? Or are they those who are striving always to give a little greater value, a little more work than they are paid for?

When scales are balanced evenly, a trifle of extra weight thrown on either side overbalances the other as effectively as a ton.

In the same way, a little better value, a little extra effort, makes the man of business stand out from the great mass of mediocrity, and brings results out of all proportion to the additional effort involved.

It pays—not merely altruistically, but in good, hard dollars—to give a little more value than seems necessary, to work a bit harder than you are paid for. It's that extra ounce of value that counts.

*For, the Law of Attraction is service.* We receive in proportion as we give out. In fact, we usually receive in far greater proportion.

"Whosoever shall be great among you," said Jesus, "shall be your minister, and whosoever of you will be the chiefest, shall be the servant of all." In other words, if you would be great, you must serve. And he who serves most shall be greatest of all.

If you want to make more money, instead of seeking it for yourself see how you can make more for others. In the process you will inevitably make more for yourself, too. We get as we give. *But we must give first.*

It matters not where you start—you may be a day laborer. But still you can give—give a bit more of energy, of work, of thought, than you are paid for. Try to put a little extra skill into your work. Use your mind to find some better way of doing whatever task may be set for you.

There is no kind of work or method that cannot be improved by thought. So give generously of your thought to your work. Think every minute you are at it: "Isn't there some way this could be done easier, quicker, better?" Read everything that relates to your own work, or to the job ahead of you.

Look around YOU now. How can YOU give greater value for what you get? How can you SERVE better? How can you make more money for your employers, or save more for your customers? Keep that thought ever in front of you and *you'll never need to worry about making more money for yourself.*

## Chapter Nine
# Your Needs Are Met

An old man called his children to his bedside to give them a few parting words of advice. "My children," he said, "I have had a great deal of trouble in my life—a great deal of trouble—*but most of it never happened.*"

We are all like that old man. Our troubles weigh us down, in prospect, but we usually find that when the actual need arrives, Providence has devised some way of meeting it.

In moments of great peril, in times of extremity, when the brave soul has staked its all—those are the times when miracles are wrought, if we but have faith.

That does not mean that you should rest supinely at your ease and let the Lord provide. When you have done *all that is in you to do*—when you have given your very best—don't worry or fret as to the outcome. Know that if more is needed, your need will be met. You can sit back with the confident assurance that, having done your part, you can depend upon the Genie-of-Your-Mind to do the rest.

This does not mean that you will never have difficulties. Difficulties are good for you. They are the exercise of your mind. You are the stronger for having overcome them. But look upon them as mere exercise, as "stunts" that are given you in order to better learn how to use your mind, and how to draw upon Universal Supply. Like Jacob wrestling with the Angel, don't let your difficulties go until they have blessed you—until, in other words, you have learned something from having encountered them.

## Chapter Ten
# The Master Mind

The Transcendentalist philosopher Ralph Waldo Emerson wrote: "There is one mind common to all individual men. Every man is an inlet to the same and to all of the same. He that is once admitted to the right of reason is made a freeman of the whole estate. What Plato has thought, he may think; what a saint has felt, he may feel; what at any time has befallen any man, he can understand. Who hath access to this universal mind is a party to all that is or can be done, for this is the only and sovereign agent."

The great German physicist Walther Nernst found that the longer an electric current was made to flow through a filament, the greater became the conductivity of the filament.

In the same way, the more you call upon and use your subconscious mind, the greater becomes its conductivity in passing along to you the infinite resources of Universal Mind. The wisdom of a Solomon, the skill of Michelangelo, the genius of an Edison, the daring of a Napoleon, *all* may be yours.

It rests with you only to form contact with Universal Mind in order to draw from it what you will.

Think of this power as something that you can connect with at any time. It has the answer to all of your problems. There is no reason why you should hesitate to aspire to any position, any honor, any goal, for the Mind within you is fully able to meet any need. It is no more difficult for it to handle a great problem than a small one. Mind is just as much present in your everyday affairs as in those of a big business or a great nation.

*Start something*! Use your initiative. Give your mind something to work upon. The greatest of all success secrets is *initiative*. It is the one quality, more than any other, that has put men in high places.

Conceive something. Conceive it first in your own mind. Make the pattern there and your superconscious mind will draw upon the plastic substance or energy all about you to make that model real.

The connecting link between the human and the Divine, between the formed universe and formless energy, lies in your imaging faculty. It is, of all things human, the most God-like. It is our part of Divinity. Through it we share in the creative power of Universal Mind. Through it we can turn the drabbest existence into a thing of life and beauty. It is the means by which we avail ourselves of all the good that the Universal Mind is constantly offering.

When Jesus adjured His disciples, "whatsoever ye desire, when ye pray, believe that ye RECEIVE it," He was not only telling them a great truth, but he was teaching what we moderns would call excellent psychology, as well. For this "belief" is what acts upon the subconscious mind and through it upon the superconscious. It is through this "belief" that formless energy is compressed into material form.

The Apostles were almost all poor, uneducated men, yet they did a work that is unequalled in history. Joan of Arc was a poor, illiterate peasant girl—yet she saved France. So don't allow lack of training, lack of education, to hold you back. Your mind can meet every need, and direct you to every necessary step.

The pages of history are filled with ordinary people who went on to think great thoughts, forge great nations, build and invent great things, and became religious, political, or commercial leaders. *Begin now*. Use the glorious empire of your mind to build that which you yearn to see in the world, that which would help yourself and others.

Use the infinite horizons of your mind—a part of the Universal Mind, a part of Divinity.

# The Law of Success
(1928)

## by Napoleon Hill
*The Original Classic*

## Contents

Introduction   *The Science of Success* by Mitch Horowitz   552
Foreword   The Master Mind   553
Law One   A Definite Chief Aim   554
Law Two   Self-Confidence   555
Law Three   The Habit of Saving   556
Law Four   Initiative and Leadership   557
Law Five   Imagination   557
Law Six   Enthusiasm   558
Law Seven   Self-Control   559
Law Eight   The Habit of Doing More Than Paid For   560
Law Nine   Pleasing Personality   561
Law Ten   Accurate Thought   562
Law Eleven   Concentration   564
Law Twelve   Cooperation   565
Law Thirteen   Profiting by Failure   565
Law Fourteen   Tolerance   566
Law Fifteen   The Golden Rule   567

## Introduction
# The Science of Success

You are about to experience Napoleon Hill's first comprehensive exploration of the principles of success. Hill began this project when, as a young journalist, he interviewed industrialist Andrew Carnegie in 1908. Carnegie urged the writer to make an intensive study of leaders across diverse fields to determine whether high achievers share a set of common traits.

Hill dedicated himself to this exploration for the next twenty years, and in 1928 he published his findings in a series of sixteen pamphlets called *The Law of Success*. This work became the basis for everything that followed in Hill's career, including his landmark *Think and Grow Rich* in 1937.

That later volume is primarily a digest and refinement of insights Hill first set down in *The Law of Success*. But some of Hill's most valuable ideas didn't make it into *Think and Grow Rich*. Hill's chapter here on "The Golden Rule" is one of his clearest and most poignant statements on how your thoughts directly shape your experience. Likewise, his chapters on "Self-Control," "Accurate Thought," and "Concentration" highlight some of his sharpest insights.

*The Law of Success* remains Hill's most ambitious and wide-ranging exploration of the principles upon which greatness is built. This condensed edition retains all of the core points and strategies of Hill's original work.

While technology has obviously undergone radical changes since Hill published this book, his insights into human nature and the ingredients of achievement remain strikingly relevant.

If you are pursuing any personally meaningful aim—whether launching a business, attaining distinction as an artist or professional, or repairing injustice in the world—this book may prove one of the most significant learning experiences of your life. Return to it several times; memorize its lessons; and, above all, *use it*.

—Mitch Horowitz

## Foreword
# The Master Mind

This is a course in the fundamentals of success.

Success is largely a matter of adapting to the changing circumstances of life in a spirit of harmony and poise. Harmony is based on understanding the forces around you. This course analyzes those forces and provides a blueprint to success.

To begin with, *you can never exercise power and attain success without the type of personality that influences others to willingly cooperate with you.* Each lesson teaches you how to build a winning personality through the fifteen laws of success. They are:

1. A DEFINITE CHIEF AIM
2. SELF-CONFIDENCE
3. THE HABIT OF SAVING
4. INITIATIVE AND LEADERSHIP
5. IMAGINATION
6. ENTHUSIASM
7. SELF-CONTROL
8. THE HABIT OF DOING MORE THAN PAID FOR
9. PLEASING PERSONALITY
10. ACCURATE THOUGHT
11. CONCENTRATION
12. COOPERATION
13. PROFITING BY FAILURE
14. TOLERANCE
15. THE GOLDEN RULE

The surest way to advance quickly through these principles, and into the fullness of your success, is with the aid of a Master Mind group. A Master Mind group consists of several people who coordinate their minds in pursuit of a goal.

The group may consist of any number from two or higher. Select the members of your Master Mind group carefully—the key ingredient is harmony and cooperation. You may focus on one group goal, or each member may have his own personal aims. Arrange a time to meet regularly to discuss your plans and ideas, and to exchange advice and guidance. When you're not together, hold each member's wishes and needs in your mind.

This friendly alliance, if carried out with purpose and harmony, will, in time, yield extraordinary results. For example, everyone in the group gains the ability to gather insight through the subconscious minds of all the other members. This produces a more vivid imaginative and mental state in which new ideas "flash" into your awareness.

Every high achiever I know has employed the power of the Master Mind. Do not neglect it.

## Law One
# A Definite Chief Aim

Probably ninety-five percent of all people drift aimlessly through life, without the slightest conception of the work for which they are best fitted, or even the need for a *definite* objective toward which to strive.

A person's acts are always in harmony with his dominating thoughts. Any *definite chief aim* that is deliberately fixed in the mind, with the determination to realize it, eventually saturates the subconscious until it influences all aspects of one's being.

Your *definite chief aim* should be selected with deliberate care. And after you select it you should write it out and place it where you will see it when you wake in the morning and retire at night. You must write down your aim—it is the first step towards its actualization.

You can impress your *definite chief aim* upon your subconscious through the principle called *autosuggestion*. In the simplest terms this is a suggestion that you make to yourself consistently and with deep feeling. Be certain that your *definite purpose* is constructive; that its attainment will bring hardship and misery to none; that it will bring you and your loved ones peace and prosperity; then apply the principle of self-suggestion, holding this idea constantly in your mind.

The subconscious is like a magnet, and when it has been vitalized and thoroughly saturated with any *definite purpose* it has a tendency to attract all that is necessary for the attainment of that purpose—in ideas, resources, circumstances, and people.

There is some *one thing* that you can do better than anyone else. Search until you find that particular line of endeavor, and make it your *definite chief aim*. Then direct all of your forces toward it with the belief that you are going to win. You will most likely attain the greatest success by finding what work you like best, for you generally succeed when you can thrown your whole heart and soul into something.

To be sure of success, your *definite chief aim* should be backed with a *burning desire* for its achievement. Merely desiring freedom would never release a man from prison if it were not sufficiently strong to cause him to do something to entitle himself to freedom.

You must experience your desire with a heartfelt passion. *Singleness of purpose* is essential for success.

## Law Two
# Self-Confidence

You are now at one of the most unusual chapters in this book—because it consists largely of a *personal pledge*. I want you to consider this pledge very carefully, and then write it down and sign your name to it.

Repeat this pledge at least once a day until it has become a part of your mental makeup. Keep a copy of it before you as a daily remainder. By doing so you will again be making use of *autosuggestion*—or self-suggestion—to develop the crucial trait of self-confidence.

Never mind what anyone may say about your method. Outside your Master Mind group, you don't have to talk to anyone about it. In fact, it's probably best not to. Just remember that it is your business to succeed, and this creed, if mastered and applied, will take you a long way.

> *I believe in myself. I believe in my coworkers. I believe in my employer. I believe in my friends. I believe in my family. I believe that God will lend me everything I need to succeed if I do my best to earn it through faithful and honest service. I believe in prayer and will never close my eyes in sleep without praying for divine guidance to be patient with others and tolerant of those who do not believe as I do. I believe that success is the result of intellectual effort and does not depend upon blind luck or sharp-practices or double-crossing. I believe that I will get from life what I put into it, therefore I will conduct myself toward others as I would want them to act toward me. I will not spread or listen to slander and gossip. I will not slight my work no matter what I may see others doing. I will render the best service possible because I have pledged myself to*

succeed in life, and I know that true success is the result of conscientious and efficient effort. Finally, I will forgive those who offend me because I realize that I shall sometimes offend others and I will need their forgiveness.

Remember: Write this statement out, sign it, recite it daily, and keep it where you can see it.

## Law Three
# The Habit of Saving

Saving money is a matter of habit. For this reason, we begin with a brief analysis of the *law of habit*.

The law of habit shapes your personality. Through repetition any act becomes a habit, and the mind may sometimes seem to be nothing more than a mass of motivating forces growing from our daily habits.

Here is how to develop the immensely valuable habit of saving:

### First

Through your *definite chief aim* set up in your mind an accurate and detailed description of what you want, including the amount of money you intend to earn. Your subconscious takes over this picture and uses it as a blueprint to mold your thoughts and actions into *practical plans*. Through the law of habit you keep the object of your *definite chief aim* fixed in your mind until it becomes firmly and permanently implanted there. This practice will erode the poverty consciousness and set up a prosperity consciousness. You will actually begin to DEMAND prosperity; you will begin to expect it; you will begin to prepare yourself to receive it and to use it wisely, thus paving the way for the *habit of saving*.

### Second

Having in this manner increased your earning ability you make further use of the law of habit by committing, in the written statement of your *definite chief aim*, to save a fixed percentage of all that you earn. As your earnings increase, your savings increase in proportion, and you will be on the road to financial stability.

## Law Four
# Initiative and Leadership

*Leadership* is essential for attaining success—and *initiative* is the foundation upon which *leadership* sits.

*Initiative* is that exceedingly rare quality that impels a person to do what ought to be done *without being told to*. Leadership is found only among those who have acquired the *habit of initiative*.

*Leadership* is something you must invite yourself into; it will never thrust itself upon you. If you carefully analyze all the leaders with which you are familiar, you will see that they not only exercised *initiative*, but also went about their work with a *definite purpose*. You will further see that they possessed *self-confidence*. Anyone who lacks these traits is not really a leader.

Here is the exact procedure to become a person of *initiative* and *leadership*:

### First
You must eliminate all *procrastination*. This habit gnaws at the soul. Nothing is possible until you throw it off.

### Second
You can best develop *initiative* by making it your business to interest those around you in doing the same. You learn best that which you teach.

### Third
Understand that there are two kinds of *leadership*. One is as deadly as the other is helpful. The deadly brand belongs to pseudo-leaders who *force* their will on others. The brand we are after was seen in Abraham Lincoln: his leadership brought truth, justice, and understanding. Those qualities have engraved his name upon the heart of the world. Emulate them.

## Law Five
# Imagination

You will never have a *definite purpose* in life, you will never have *self-confidence*, you will never have *initiative* and *leadership*, unless you first create these qualities in your *imagination* and see them as yours.

You may see how important *imagination* is when you stop to realize that it is the only thing in the world over which you have absolute control. Others may cheat you or deprive you of material wealth, but no one can deny you the control and use of your *imagination*.

Your imagination is the mirror of your soul, and you have every right to stand before that mirror and see yourself as you wish to be. You have *the right* to see in that mirror the mansion you intend to own, the business you plan to manage, the station in life you intend to occupy. *Your imagination belongs to you.* Use it! The more you use it the more efficiently it will serve you.

Your battle for achievement is already half won when *you know definitely what you want.*

The selection of your *definite chief aim* calls for both imagination and *decision*. The power of decision also grows with use. Prompt decision in compelling the *imagination* to create a *definite chief aim* gives you a more powerful capacity to reach decisions in other matters.

## Law Six

# Enthusiasm

Enthusiasm is a state of mind that inspires you to *action*. But it does more—it is contagious, and it arouses everyone around you.

Enthusiasm is the vital force of life. The greatest leaders know how to instill enthusiasm in their followers. Enthusiasm is the most important factor in salesmanship. It is by far the most crucial factor in public speaking.

Mix enthusiasm with your work and it will seem neither hard nor monotonous. *Enthusiasm* will so energize your body that you can get along with less than half the usual amount of sleep and perform two to three times as much work as usual, without fatigue.

*Enthusiasm* is no mere figure of speech; it is a *vital force* through which you can recharge your body and develop a dynamic personality. Some are blessed with natural enthusiasm; others must acquire it. The procedure through which it may be developed is simple. It begins by doing the work that you like best. If you cannot, for the time being, engage in such work that is all more reason to adopt a *definite chief aim*, and you will begin to move toward it.

Lack of money and many other circumstances may force you to engage in work that you do not like. But no one can stop you from determining your *definite chief aim*; nor can anyone stop you from planning ways and means for translating that aim into reality; nor can anyone stop you from mixing *enthusiasm* with your plans.

When you are enthusiastic over your goods or services, or the speech you are delivering, your mental state becomes obvious to all who hear you. The tone with which you make a statement, more than the statement itself, carries conviction or fails to convince. Words are devitalized sounds unless colored with enthusiasm.

But take note: *Never express, through words or acts, something that does not harmonize with your beliefs—or you will lose the ability to influence others.*

I do not believe that I can afford to deceive anyone about anything; but *I know that I cannot afford to deceive myself.* To do so would destroy the power of my pen. It is only when I write with the *fire of enthusiasm* that my writing impresses others. *It is only when I speak from a heart that is bursting with belief in my message* that I can move my audience to accept it.

## Law Seven
# Self-Control

*Self-control* is the force through which you direct your enthusiasm to constructive ends. Without *self-control* enthusiasm resembles unharnessed lightening—it may strike a*nywhere*, destroying life and property. The balanced person possesses both *enthusiasm* and *self-control*.

The majority of our griefs result from lack of self-control. Scripture is full of injunctions to *self-control*. It even urges us to love our enemies and to forgive those who injure us. The law of non-resistance runs like a golden cord throughout the Bible.

Where does *self-control* come from? Consider this very carefully: *Thought* is the only thing over which you have total dominion. This is of profound significance. It suggests that *thought* is your nearest approach to Divinity on this earthly plane. This fact carries another vital idea: namely, that *thought* is your most important tool; the one with which you may shape your destiny. Divine Providence did not make *thought* the sole power over which you have absolute control without associating that power with potentialities which, if understood and developed, would strain belief.

*Self-control is solely a matter of thought-control.*

You are searching for the magic key to power; and yet you have the key in your hands, and may use it the moment you learn to *control your thoughts*.

A student once asked how he could control his thoughts in a state of intense anger. I replied, *"In exactly the same way that you would change your manner and tone if you were in a heated argument with a family member and heard the doorbell ring, signaling that company was about to visit. You would control yourself because you would desire to."*

If you have ever faced a similar predicament, where you found it necessary to quickly conceal your feelings and change your facial expression, you know that it can be done *because you WANT TO!*

Back of all achievement, back of all *self-control*, back of all *thought control*, is that magic something called DESIRE! It is no exaggeration to say that you are limited only by the depth of your *desire*.

When your *desire* is strong enough you will appear to possess superhuman abilities. No one has ever explained this phenomenon of the mind, and perhaps no one ever will, but if you doubt that it exists you have only to experiment.

Don't say, "It can't be done," or that you are different from the thousands of people who have achieved noteworthy success. If you are "different" it is only because *they desired the object of their achievement with greater depth and intensity than you.*

The energy that most people dissipate through lack of self-control, or fritter away gossiping, would, if controlled and directed constructively, be sufficient to attain their *definite chief aim*, provided they have one.

## Law Eight
# The Habit of Doing More Than Paid For

Here is one of the most important laws of this philosophy: *A person is most efficient, and will more quickly and easily succeed, when engaged in work that he loves, or work that he performs for someone he loves.*

When the element of love enters any task, the quality of the work improves and the quantity increases. When engaged in work that you love it is no hardship to do more and better work than you are paid for; for this very reason you owe it to yourself to find the work you like best.

There are many reasons to do more than you are paid for, but two stand out:

## First

By establishing a reputation as someone who performs more and better work than paid for, you benefit by comparison with competitors who rarely show such commitment.

## Second

Suppose that you want to develop a strong right arm. You could develop such an arm *only by giving it the hardest use.* Out of resistance comes strength. By performing more and better service than paid for, you not only develop your skill and ability but also can *command* greater remuneration than the majority who do not perform such service.

Try this experiment: For the next six months commit to rendering useful service to at least one person every day, for which *you neither expect nor accept monetary pay.* Go at this experiment with faith that it will prove to you one of the most powerful laws of success: that you succeed best and quickest by helping others to succeed.

Law Nine
# Pleasing Personality

Your personality is the sum total of your characteristics and appearance. The clothes you wear, the lines in your face, the vitality of your body, your handshake, your tone of voice, the thoughts you think, the character you have developed by those thoughts—all are parts of your *personality.*

Whether your personality is attractive is another matter.

By far the most important part of your personality is your *character*, and is therefore the part that is not visible. The style of your clothes and their appropriateness also constitute an important part of your personality, for it is true that people derive first impressions from your outward appearance.

There is one way to express your personality that will *always attract*: *taking a heartfelt interest in others.* Study people closely enough to find something about them or their work that you *truly* admire. Talk to them about it. Show genuine interest in it. Only in this way can you develop a personality that will be irresistibly *attractive.*

Cheap flattery has the opposite effect. It repels instead of attracting. It is so shallow that even the ignorant easily detect it.

As noted, *character* is the most important factor in *personality*. How can you build *character*? Follow these steps:

## First

Identify people whose characters have the qualities you wish to emulate, and develop these qualities through *autosuggestion*.

## Second

Let the dominating thought of your mind be a picture of the person that you are *deliberately building*.

## Third

Find at least one person each day, and more if possible, in whom you see some good quality and *praise it*. But remember, this praise must be *genuine* and not insincere flattery.

I cannot over-emphasize the benefits of praising, openly and enthusiastically, the good qualities in others; for this habit will soon reward you with a feeling of self-respect and manifestation of gratitude from others, which will modify your entire personality.

## Law Ten
# Accurate Thought

You cannot succeed without *accurate thought*. *Accurate thought* involves two fundamentals. First, you must separate *facts* from mere *information*. Much "information" is not based upon facts. Second, you must divide *facts* into two classes: *important* and *unimportant*.

All facts that *aid* your pursuit of your *definite chief aim* (without violating the rights of others) are *important* and *relevant*. All that you cannot use are the opposite. If you direct your attention exclusively to the *important facts*—those that contribute to the realization of your aim—you will attain a special clarity.

You must also avoid the vulgar and self-destructive habit of spreading and listening to gossip. If you permit yourself to be swayed by all manner of information—especially rumors and gossip—you will never become an *accurate thinker*, and you will not attain your *definite chief aim*.

We will now explore a special form of *thought* that does much more than gather and organize facts. In many ways, this form of thought is the keynote of this course. We will call it *creative thought*. With a few exceptions man has not yet recognized *creative thought* as the connecting link to the power of *infinite intelligence*.

To understand how this occurs we return to the topic of *autosuggestion*. The sense impressions arising from your environment, or from the statements and actions of others, are mere ordinary suggestions; but the sense impressions that *you place in your own mind*—that you deliberately and confidently dwell upon, think of at every opportunity, and mentally picture and *feel*—are the product of self-suggestion, or *autosuggestion*.

Autosuggestion is the telegraph line over which you register in your subconscious the aim you wish to *create* in physical form.

The subconscious is the intermediary between the conscious *thinking mind* and *infinite intelligence*. You can invoke the aid of *infinite intelligence* through the *subconscious* only by giving it clear instructions as to what you want. Hence the critical need for a *definite chief aim*.

*The subconscious records the suggestions that you send it through autosuggestion, and invokes the aid of infinite intelligence in translating these suggestions into their natural physical form, through natural means which are in no way out of the ordinary.*

First, you must select the picture to be recorded (your *definite chief aim*). Then you fix your conscious mind upon this purpose with such intensity that it communicates with the subconscious through autosuggestion, and registers that picture. You then watch for and expect manifestations of the physical realization of that picture.

Bear in mind that you do not sit down and wait, nor go to sleep, with the expectation that *infinite intelligence* has granted your desire. No, you go right ahead doing your daily work *with full faith and confidence that natural ways and means for the attainment of your definite purpose will open to you at the proper time and in a suitable manner.*

*Infinite intelligence* will not build you a home and deliver it ready to enter. But *infinite intelligence* will open the way and provide the necessary means, including insights, intuitions, and ideas, which allow you to build your own house. Do not reply upon miracles for your *definite chief aim*; rely upon the power of *infinite intelligence* to guide you, through natural channels and laws, to its attainment.

## Law Eleven
# Concentration

To move safely and accurately toward a target you must *concentrate* on it. Two important laws enter into the act of *concentrating* on a given desire. One is the law of autosuggestion, which we have already reviewed; the other is the law of habit, which we will now consider in further detail.

*Habit* grows from environment and repetition—from doing and thinking the same thing over and over. Except for rare occasions when the mind rises above environment, we draw the material out of which *thought* is created from our surroundings, and *habit* crystalizes this thought into a permanent fixture.

To attain success, you must develop habits that lead toward constructive thoughts and actions in the direction of your *definite chief aim*. Follow this procedure to acquire the habits you need:

### First
At the beginning of the formation of a new habit put force and enthusiasm into your expression. *Feel what you think*. Remember that you are taking the first steps toward making a new mental path; it is much harder at first than it will be later. Make the path as clear and as deep as you can at the beginning, so that you can readily see it the next time you wish to follow it.

### Second
Keep your attention firmly *concentrated* on the new path you are building, and keep you mind far away from the old paths.

### Third
Travel over your newly made paths as often as possible. Make opportunities for doing so. The more you traverse these new paths the sooner they will become familiar and easily travelled.

### Fourth
Resist the temptation to travel over the older, easier paths that you have used in the past. Every time you resist a temptation, you grow stronger.

**Fifth**

Be sure that you have mapped out the right path as your *definite chief aim*—and then charge at it without fear or doubt.

## Law Twelve
# Cooperation

Success cannot be attained singlehandedly. It requires *cooperative effort*. Even a hermit in the wilderness is *dependent* upon forces outside himself for existence. The more he becomes a part of civilization, the more he *depends* upon *cooperative effort*.

If your philosophy is based upon cooperation instead of competition you will not only acquire the necessities and luxuries of life with less effort, but you will enjoy an additional reward in *happiness*. Fortunes acquired through cooperative effort inflict no scars upon the hearts of their owners.

Ordinary cooperative effort produces power. But cooperative effort that is based upon complete harmony of purpose develops *superpower*. Gave a person of average ability a sufficiently visualized and passionately felt motive and he will develop superpower. Men work harder for *an ideal* than they will for money. Remember this when searching for a motive to develop group cooperation.

Men generally respond to three major motivating forces:
1. The motive of self-preservation.
2. The motive of sexual contact.
3. The motive of financial and social power.

Regardless of who you are, or your *definite chief aim*, if you depend upon others—as almost all of us do—you must present them with a motive strong enough to ensure their full cooperation.

## Law Thirteen
# Profiting by Failure

What we typically call *failure* is, in reality, *temporary defeat*. Moreover, this temporary defeat often proves a blessing, for it jolts us and redirects our energies along different and more desirable paths.

Sound character is usually the outcome of reverses, setbacks, and temporary defeat.

Neither temporary defeat nor adversity spell failure to one who looks upon such things as a teacher. A great and lasting lesson appears in every reverse and defeat—and, usually, it could be learned in no other way.

Ralph Waldo Emerson explored this principle in his great essay "Compensation." If you haven't read it, do so—and reread it every three months.

I used to *hate* my enemies. But this was before I learned how well they were serving me by keeping me everlastingly on the alert, lest some weak spot in my character provide an opening through which I might be damaged. Enemies discover your defects and point them out; friends, even if they see them, say nothing.

I am convinced that failure is Nature's plan through which she hurdle-jumps men of destiny and prepares them to do their work. Failure is Nature's great crucible in which she burns the dross from the human heart and purifies the metal of a man so that it can stand the test of hard usage.

## Law Fourteen

# Tolerance

Always remember these two facts about *intolerance*.

### First

*Intolerance* makes enemies; it disintegrates the organized forces of society; it dethrones reason and substitutes mob psychology in its place. *Intolerance* is a form of ignorance that must be mastered before enduring success may be attained.

### Second

*Intolerance* is the chief disintegrating force in the organized religions of the world, where it plays havoc with the greatest power for good on earth by breaking it up into small sects, which spend as much time opposing each other as in combating evil.

Anything that impedes the progress of civilization also stands as a barrier to each individual.

I once encountered intolerance in myself, and I vowed to *unlearn much that I had previously considered the truth*. I discovered that I had acquired my views of religion, politics, economics, and many other important subjects simply by "picking up" what my family believed.

*Most of my views were unsupported by even a reasonable hypothesis, much less facts.* Imagine suddenly discovering that most of your philosophy had been built on bias and prejudice.

I urge you to learn how and where you acquired your philosophy of life in order to trace your prejudices and biases to their original source—and to discover, as I did, the degree to which you are the result of training you received before the age of fifteen.

## Law Fifteen
# The Golden Rule

For more than twenty-five years I have been observing how men behave in positions of power, and I have seen that the man who attains power in any way other than a slow, step-by-step process is in constant danger of destroying himself and all whom he influences.

For more than four thousand years humanity has preached the Golden Rule as the foundation of good conduct. But the world has accepted the letter while totally missing the spirit of this universal injunction. We acknowledge the Golden Rule merely as a sound principle—but we have failed to understand the *inner law* upon which it is based.

The Golden Rule means to do unto others as you would wish them to do unto you. But why? What is the *real* reason for this kindly consideration of others?

The reason is this: There is an eternal law by which we reap what we sow. When you select the rule of conduct by which to guide your life, you are more likely be fair and just if you *know* that you are setting into motion a *power* that will run its course in the lives of others, returning, finally, to help or hinder you, according to its nature.

It is your choice to deal unjustly with others, but if you understand the law upon which the Golden Rule is based, you must know that your unjust deals will return to you.

You cannot pervert or change the course of this law—*but you can adapt yourself to its nature and thereby use it as an irresistible power that will carry you to heights of achievement.*

This law does not stop merely by flinging back at you your *acts* of injustice and unkindness; it goes further—much further—and *returns to you the results of every thought that you release.*

Therefore, it is advisable not only to "do unto others as you wish them to do unto you." But to make full use of this great Universal Law you must "think of others as you wish them to think of you." The law upon which the Golden Rule is based begins affecting you, for good or evil, the moment you release a *thought*.

Understand this law and you understand *all* that the Bible has to reveal. The Bible presents one unbroken chain of evidence that man is the maker of his own destiny.

All your *acts* toward others, and even your *thoughts* of others, are registered in your subconscious through the principle of autosuggestion, thereby building your own character in exact duplicate. Can you see how important it is to guard those acts and thoughts?

You cannot act toward another without having first created the nature of that act in your own *thought, and you cannot release a thought without planting the sum and substance of it in your own subconscious, there to become a part of your character.*

Grasp this simple principle and you will understand why you cannot afford to hate or envy another person. You will also understand why you cannot afford to strike back at those who do you an injustice. Likewise, you will understand the injunction, "Return good for evil."

Throughout this course I have emphasized one particular principle for the purpose of revealing that your personality is the sum total of your *thoughts* and *acts*—and that you come to resemble the nature of your dominating *thoughts*.

Man, alone, has the power to transform his *thoughts* into physical reality. Use the palace of your mind methodically, carefully, and deliberately—and you will reconstruct on the outside those dreams that dwell within.

# The Magic Ladder to Success

(1930)

## by Napoleon Hill

*Your Step-by-Step Plan to Wealth and Winning from the Author of* Think and Grow Rich

## Contents

Introduction   *The Birth of a Brave Book* by Mitch Horowitz   570
Foreword   How to Read this Book for Profit   571
Lesson One   The Master Mind   573
Lesson Two   A Definite Chief Aim   578
Lesson Three   Self-Confidence   579
Lesson Four   The Habit of Saving   580
Lesson Five   Initiative and Leadership   581
Lesson Six   Imagination   582
Lesson Seven   Enthusiasm   584
Lesson Eight   Self-Control   585
Lesson Nine   Habit of Doing More Than Paid For   586
Lesson Ten   Pleasing Personality   587
Lesson Eleven   Accurate Thinking   589
Lesson Twelve   Concentration   590
Lesson Thirteen   Cooperation   590
Lesson Fourteen   Profiting by Failure   591
Lesson Fifteen   Tolerance   593
Lesson Sixteen   Practicing the Golden Rule   593
Lesson Seventeen   The Habit of Health   595
Afterword   596

## Introduction

# The Birth of a Brave Book

This book began in the mind of one of Napoleon Hill's students. After the 1928 publication of Hill's sixteen-volume *Law of Success*, the writer made a practice of holding "interviews," or what we today would call creativity sessions, with individual students.

One student proved particularly insightful. "Within fifteen minutes after her arrival at the author's office," he wrote, "she had 'stepped up' the vibrations of her mind to where she was 'tuning in' on the Master Mind principles." As a result, Hill continued, a wave of ideas began to "flash" into the student's mind. He wrote down forty of them, the first of which was: "Rewrite the Law of Success philosophy in a brief form which can be presented in one volume, at a very low cost, so it can be placed in the hands of hundreds of thousands of students who might otherwise never have the benefit of such a philosophy of success." Hill's *Magic Ladder to Success*, published in 1930, became that volume.

This Condensed Classics edition further reduces the master's original work to its essentials, so that its full range of seventeen principles are available to you in a single sitting. I have endeavored to preserve every core idea of the original, so that this work comes to you not only with brevity, but also without compromise. It is a working guide to Hill's broadest range of ideas.

One of the benefits of *The Magic Ladder to Success*—and one of the elements I have preserved in this abridgement—is that Hill writes boldly on his theory of how to use "sex energy" as a force for creativity and success. In all of his books, Hill makes the sometimes enigmatic point that the sexual urge is, in fact, the sensation of life's creative force flowing through the individual, and that if this urge, while still being respected on its physical terms, can be channeled *in the direction of achievement*, it may result in works of excellence and even genius. In brief, this technique requires *substituting* another aim or desire for the object of one's sexual urge—and then allowing your creative energies to channel in that direction. Again, Hill does not mean stifling or denying physical sexuality. Not at all. In fact, he underscores the therapeutic value of sexual contact. But rather, Hill induces the reader to become a kind of alchemist who understands redirecting intimate forces for both mental and outer ends.

Hill shrewdly notes that the motive of sexual expression is perhaps the strongest of all motives, since sexuality is the impulse of life replicating itself.

He observes that some people have arrived at great inventions, accomplishments, or business successes with the covert intention, unknown perhaps even to themselves, of wooing or pleasing a partner. This brief volume provides sufficient instruction so that you can experiment with these principles on your own.

*The Magic Ladder to Success*, in this condensation, is probably the briefest but also the most complete digest of Hill's full range of ideas. It is a wonderful entry point for newcomers and a refresher for veterans. It also provides a sense of the broadness of Hill's overall vision. May this book ignite some of your highest efforts and ideas.

—Mitch Horowitz

Foreword

# How to Read this Book for Profit

For almost a quarter century, I have been writing this book.

The task could not have been completed in less time for several reasons, not the least of which is that I had to inform myself, through years of research, what others had discovered in connection with the causes of failure and success.

Another important reason why my labors have covered nearly a quarter of a century is that I felt it necessary to prove that I could make the Law of Success philosophy work for myself before offering it to others.

I was born in the mountains of the South, in the midst of poverty and illiteracy. For three generations preceding me, my ancestors, on both sides of the house, were content to live in poverty and ignorance, and I would have followed in their footsteps had not my stepmother planted in my mind *the seed of desire* to whip poverty and illiteracy.

From her I got my first impression of the value of a *definite major aim*, and later that impression became so obviously essential as one of the factors of success that I gave it second place in the list of seventeen principles outlined in this book. Except for her influence in planting the seed of ambition in my mind, I never would have written a philosophy of success.

As you read this book, you will observe, as thousands of others have, that ideas will begin to "flash" into you mind. Capture these ideas with the aid of a notebook and pencil as they may lead you to the attainment of your coveted goal in life. Many students of this philosophy have created valuable inventions while reading the Law of Success. Clergymen have been inspired by this philosophy to write sermons that lifted them to great heights of eloquence. The Law of Success philosophy is a mind fertilizer. It will cause the mind to function as a magnet that will attract brilliant ideas.

The value of this book is not in its own pages, but in your own reaction to what you read in it. Any brain that can create new ideas in abundance is capable, also, of organizing great power! The main purpose of the Law of Success philosophy is to stimulate the *imaginative* faculties of the brain so they will readily create new and usable ideas for any emergency in life.

Read or listen to this book with pencil in hand, and as you do, note all statements that cause new ideas to "flash" into your mind. This method will serve to fix such ideas in your mind permanently. You cannot assimilate the entire subject matter of this philosophy at one reading or listening of this book. Read or listen to it many times, and each time follow the habit of marking the lines or making notes when you reach passages that inspire new ideas.

This procedure reveals one of the great mysteries of the human mind by introducing you to a source of knowledge that cannot be described adequately to any except those who have discovered this source for themselves. *In this statement lies a hint of the nature of the secret that the Law of Success philosophy has handed over to so many of its students throughout the world!* No one many ever come into possession of this secret except by the method described here.

Before we enter the experience of this book, let us first define success as:

> The power with which to acquire whatever one wants without violating the rights of others.

The factors through which power may be acquired and used in harmony with this definition number seventeen:

1. The Master Mind
2. A Definite Chief Aim
3. Self-Confidence
4. The Habit of Saving
5. Imagination
6. Initiative and Leadership
7. Enthusiasm
8. Self-Control
9. Doing More Than Paid For

10. A Pleasing Personality
11. Accurate Thinking
12. Cooperation
13. Concentration
14. Profiting by Failures
15. Tolerance
16. The Golden Rule
17. The Habit of Health

The purpose of this book is to *describe* how to apply these seventeen factors so as to acquire personal power for use in any calling and for the solution of one's economic problems. We now turn to an analysis of each factor.

## Lesson One
# The Master Mind

The Master Mind may be defined as: "a composite mind, consisting of two or more individual minds working in perfect harmony, with a definite aim in view."

Recall the definition of success, which is attainable through the application of power, and you will more quickly grasp the meaning of the term Master Mind, as it will be immediately obvious that a group of two or more minds, working in harmony and perfect coordination, will create power in abundance.

All success is achieved through the application of *power*. The staring point, however, may be described as a *burning desire* for the achievement of some specific, definite objective.

Just as the oak tree, in the embryo, sleeps within the acorn, success begins in the form of an intense *desire*. Out of strong desires grow the motivating forces that cause men to cherish hopes, build plans, develop courage, and stimulate their minds to a highly intensified degree of *action* in pursuit of some *definite* plan or purpose.

Desire, then, is the starting point of all human achievement. There is nothing back of desire except the stimuli through which *strong desire* is fanned into a hot flame of *action*. These stimuli are known and have been included as a part of the Law of Success philosophy described in this book.

It has been said, and not without reason, that one may have anything one wants, within reasonable limitations, providing *one wants it badly enough!* Anyone who is capable of stimulating the mind to an intense state of *desire* is capable also of more than average achievement in pursuit of that desire. It must be remembered that wishing for a thing is not the same as *desiring* it with such intensity that out of this desire grow impelling forces of action that drive one to build plans and put those plans to work. A wish is merely a passive form of desire. Most people never advance beyond the wishing stage.

The Basic Motivating Forces of Human Action

There are eight basic motivating forces, one or more of which is the starting point of all noteworthy human achievement. These motivating forces are:

1. The urge of self-preservation
2. The desire for sexual contact
3. The desire for financial gain
4. The desire for life after death
5. The desire for fame; to possess *power*
6. The urge of *love* (separate and distinct from the sex urge)
8. The desire for revenge (prevalent in the more undeveloped minds)
9. The desire to indulge one's egotism

Men make use of great power only when urged by one or more of these eight basic motives. The imaginative forces of the human mind become active only when spurred on by the stimulation of a well-defined *motive*! Master salesmen have discovered that all salesmanship is based upon an appeal to one or more of these eight basic motives, which impel men and women to action. Without this discovery no one could become a master salesman.

The Master Mind principle described in this lesson is the medium through which all personal power is applied. For this reason, every known mind stimulant, and every basic motive that inspires action in all human endeavor, are mentioned in this book and chapter.

A Master Mind may be created by any group of people who coordinate their minds in a spirit of perfect harmony. The group may consist of any number from two upward. Best results appear available from the blending of six or seven minds.

It has been suggested that Jesus discovered how to make use of the principle of mind chemistry, and that His seemingly miraculous performances grew out of the power He developed through the blending of the minds of his twelve disciples. It has been pointed out that when one of the disciples, Judas, broke faith, the Master Mind immediately disintegrated and Jesus met with the supreme catastrophe of His life.

When two or more people harmonize their minds and produce the effect known as a Master Mind each person in the group becomes vested with the power to connect with and gather knowledge through the subconscious minds of all the other members. This power becomes immediately noticeable, having the effect of stimulating the mind to a higher rate of vibration, and otherwise evidencing itself in the form of a more vivid imagination and the consciousness of what appears a sixth sense. It is through this sixth sense that new ideas "flash" into the mind. These ideas take on the nature and form of the subject dominating the mind of the individual.

Every public speaker has felt the influence of mind chemistry, for it is well-known that as soon as the individual minds of an audience become en rapport with the speaker (that is, attached to the rate of vibration of the mind of the speaker), there is a noticeable increase of enthusiasm in the speaker's mind, and he often rises to heights of oratory that surprise all, including himself.

It must not be presumed that a Master Mind will immediately spring, mushroom fashion, out of every group of minds that make a pretense of coordination in a spirit of *harmony*! Harmony, in the real sense of the word, is as rare among groups of people as is genuine Christianity among those who proclaim themselves Christian.

Harmony is the nucleus around which the state of mind known as the Master Mind must be developed. Without this element of harmony, there can be no Master Mind, a truth that cannot be repeated too often.

The Relationship Between Sexual Urge and Genius

The urge of sex is, by far, the most powerful of the eight basic motivating factors that stimulate the mind to *action*. Because of the importance of this subject, it has been reserved as the closing segment of the first of the seventeen factors constituting the Law of Success. It is also revisited in the lessons on enthusiasm and the habit of health.

The part that the sexual urge plays in the achievement of outstanding success was first discovered by the author in his studies of the biographies of great leaders, and in his analysis of men and women of the present age who have risen high in their fields. But to be highly sexed is not sufficient, of itself, to produce a genius. Only those who understand the nature of sexual urge, and who know how to *transmute* this powerful emotion into other channels of action than that of sexual contact, rise to the status of a genius. The urge of sex is a driving force compared to which all other motives must take second place. A mind that has been aroused through intense sexual desire becomes receptive to that impulse of ideas that "flash" into the mind from outside sources through what is ordinarily known as "inspiration."

It is the belief of this author—a belief not without considerable evidence to back it—that all so-called "revelations," of whatever nature, from religion to art, are super-induced by intense desire for sexual contact. All so-called "magnetic" people are highly sexed. People who are brilliant, charming, versatile, and accomplished are generally high sexed. Prove this for yourself by analyzing those whom you know to be highly sexed.

It is a fact well known to scientists, although not generally known to the layman, that sexual contact has a therapeutic value unknown in connection with any other human emotion. This fact may be easily verified, however, by even the most casual study of the subject, by observing the physical state of the body following sexual contact between two people who are properly mated or affinitized. What mind is so vulgar and ignorant as not to have observed that following sexual contact, between two people who are properly "balanced," or mated, the physical body becomes relaxed or calm? Relaxation, super-induced in this manner, provides the nervous system with a favorable opportunity to balance and distribute the nervous energy of the body to all of its organs.

A great, enduring love is a sufficient motive to drive even a mediocre man to unbelievable heights of achievement, a statement of fact that should be kept in mind by all spouses.

In short, *sexual urge is the most effective known agency through which the mind may be "stepped up" to where it becomes a Master Mind!*

## The Ten Major Sources of Mind Stimulation

It may be helpful here to outline the major sources of mind stimulation, in view of the fact that all great achievements result from some form of stimuli that "step up" the mind to a high rate of vibration. These stimuli are listed in the order of what the author considers their importance:

1. *Sexual contact* between two people who are motivated by a genuine feeling of love.
2. *Love* not necessarily accompanied by sexual contact.
3. *Burning desire* for fame, power, and financial gain.
4. *Music,* which acts as a mighty stimulant to a highly emotionalized person.
5. *Friendship,* between either those of the same sex or the opposite sex, accompanied by a desire to be mutually helpful in some definite undertaking.
6. *Master Mind alliance,* between two or more people who ally themselves, mentally, for the purpose of mutual help, in a spirit of unselfishness.
7. *Mutual suffering,* such as that experienced by people who are unjustly persecuted, for reasons of race, religion, or economics.
8. *Autosuggestion,* through which an individual may step up his or her own mind, through constant self-suggestion with a definite motive.
9. *Suggestion.* The influence of *outside* suggestion may lift one to great heights of achievement, or, if negatively used, dash one to the pit of failure and destruction.
10. *Narcotics and alcohol.* This source of mind stimulation is totally destructive, and leads, finally, to negation of all the other nine sources of stimulation.

Through these sources of stimulation one may commune, temporarily, with Infinite Intelligence, a procedure that constitutes all there is of genius. *The foregoing statement is definite and plain. Take it or leave it, just as you please!* The statement is made as a positive fact because this author has had the privilege of helping to raise scores of mediocre men and women out of mediocrity into states of mind that entitled them to rank as geniuses. Some have been able to remain in this exalted state, while others have relapsed to their former status, either temporarily or permanently.

Again, the desire for sexual contact is the strongest, most powerful, and most impelling of all human desires, and for this very reason it may be harnessed and transmuted into channels other than that of sexual contact in a manner that will raise one to great heights of genius. On the other hand, this powerful urge, if not controlled and so transmuted, may and often does lower man to the level of an ordinary beast.

## Lesson Two
# A Definite Chief Aim

To be successful in any sort of endeavor you must have a *definite* goal toward which to work. You must have definite plans for attaining this goal. Nothing worthwhile is ever accomplished without a definite plan that is systematically and continuously followed out day by day.

A *definite chief aim* is placed at the beginning of the Seventeen Laws of Success for the reason that without it the other Sixteen Laws would be useless, for how could one know when he had succeeded, without first having determined what he wanted to accomplish?

Careful study of more than one hundred of the leading men in practically all walks of life has disclosed that every one of these men worked with a *definite chief aim* and also a *definite plan* for its attainment.

The human mind is something like a magnet in that it will attract the counterparts of the dominating thoughts held in the mind, and especially those that constitute a *definite chief aim* or purpose. For example, if a man establishes, as his *definite chief aim*, and as his daily working purpose, the adding of, say, one hundred new customers who will regularly purchase the merchandise or service he is rendering, immediately that aim or purpose becomes a dominating influence in his mind, and this influence will drive him to do whatever is necessary to secure these additional one hundred customers.

Your first step on the road to success is to know where you are going, how you intend to travel, and when you intend to get there, which is only another way of saying that you must determine a *definite chief aim*. This aim, when decided upon, must be written out in clear language, so it can be understood by any other person. If there is anything "hazy" about your aim, it is not *definite*. A man who knew what he was saying once stated that nine-tenths of success, in any undertaking, is in knowing *what is wanted*. This is true.

The moment you write out a statement of your *chief aim*, your action plants an image of that aim firmly in your subconscious mind. Nature causes your subconscious mind to use that chief aim as a pattern or blueprint by which the major portion of your thoughts, ideas, and efforts are directed toward the attainment of the objective on which the *aim* is based.

This is a strange, abstract truth—something that cannot be weighed, meditated upon—but is a truth nevertheless!

## Lesson Three
# Self-Confidence

The third of the Seventeen Laws of Success is self-confidence. The term is self-explanatory—it means that to achieve success you must believe in yourself. However, this does not mean that you have no limitations; it means that you are to take inventory of yourself, find out what qualities you have that are strong and useful, and then organize these qualities into a *definite plan* of action with which to attain the object of your *definite chief aim*.

In all the languages of the world there is no one word that carries the same or even approximately the same meaning as *"faith."* If there are any such things as "miracles," they are performed only with the aid of super-faith. The doubting type of mind is not a creative mind. Search where and how you may, and you will not discover a single record of great achievement in any line of endeavor that was not conceived in the imagination and brought into reality through *faith*!

To succeed, you must have faith in your own ability to do whatever you make up your mind to do. Also, you must cultivate the habit of faith in those who are associated with you, whether they are in a position of authority over you, or you over them. The psychological reason for this will be covered later in the law of cooperation.

A *definite chief aim* is the starting point of all noteworthy achievement, but self-confidence is the unseen force that coaxes, drives, or leads one on and on until the object of the aim is a reality. Many people have vague sorts of aims, but they get nowhere because they lack the self-confidence to create *definite plans* for attaining these aims.

*Fear* is the main enemy of self-confidence. Every person comes into the world cursed, to some extent, with Six Basic Fears, all of which must be mastered before one may develop sufficient self-confidence to attain outstanding success.

The six basic fears are:
1. The Fear of Criticism
2. The Fear of Ill Health
3. The Fear of Poverty
4. The Fear of Old Age
5. The Fear of Loss of Love (ordinarily called jealousy)
6. The Fear of Death

Space will not permit a lengthy description of how and where these Six Fears came from. In the main, however, they were acquired through early childhood environment. Fear of Criticism is placed at the head of the list because it is, perhaps, the most common and one of the most destructive of the entire six fears.

Before you can develop self-confidence sufficient to master the obstacles that stand between you and success, you must take inventory of yourself and find out how many of these six basic fears are standing in your way. A few days of study, thought, and reflection will enable you to lay your fingers on the particular fear or fears that stand between you and self-confidence.

## Lesson Four
# The Habit of Saving

It is an embarrassing admission, but true, that a poverty-stricken person is less than the dust of the earth as far as the achievement of noteworthy success is concerned. It may be, and perhaps is true, that *money is not success*. But unless you have it or can command its use, you will not get far, no matter what may be your *definite chief aim*. As business is conducted today—as civilization stands to today—money is an absolute essential for success, and there is no known formula for financial independence except that which is connected, in one way or another, with systematic saving.

The amount saved from week to week or from month to month is not of great consequence so long as the saving is regular and systematic. This is true because the habit of saving adds something to the other qualities essential for success, which can be had in no other way.

It is doubtful if any person can develop self-confidence to the highest possible point without the protection and independence that belong to those who have saved and are saving money. There is something about the knowledge that one has some money ahead that gives faith and self-reliance such as can be had no other way.

Without money, a person is at the mercy of everyone who wishes to exploit or prey upon him. If the man who does not save and has no money offers his personal services for sale, he must accept whatever the purchaser offers; there is no alternative.

If opportunity to profit by trade, or otherwise, comes along it is of no avail to the man who has neither money nor credit, and it must be kept in mind that credit is generally based upon the money one has or its equivalent.

The amount of your income is of little importance if you do not systematically save a portion of it.

Railroad magnate James J. Hill once named a rule by which any man may test himself and determine, well in advance, whether he will succeed in life. That rule is: "He must have formed the habit of systematic saving of money."

## Lesson Five
# Initiative and Leadership

All people may be placed in one or the other of two general classes. One is known as leaders and the other as followers. The followers rarely achieve noteworthy success, and never succeed until they break away from the ranks of followers and become leaders.

There is a mistaken notion broadcast in the world to the effect that a man is paid for what he knows. This is only partly true, and like all other half-truths, it does more damage than an outright falsehood.

The truth is, a man is paid not only for what he *knows*, but more particularly for what *he does* with what he knows, or that which he *gets others to do*.

Without *initiative* no man will achieve success, no matter what he may consider success, because he will do nothing out of the ordinary run of mediocre work such as nearly all men are forced to do in order have a place to sleep, something to eat, and clothes to wear. These three necessities may be had, of a certain kind, without the aid of *initiative* and *leadership*, but the moment a man makes up his mind to acquire more than the bare necessities of life, he must either cultivate the habits of *initiative* and *leadership* or else find himself hedged in behind a stone wall.

The first step essential to the development of *initiative* and *leadership* is that of forming the habit of prompt and firm *decision*. All successful people have a certain amount of *decision*. The man who wavers between two or more half-baked and more or less vague notions of what he wants to do generally ends by doing nothing.

It is not enough to have a *definite chief aim* and a *definite plan* for its attainment, even though the plan may be perfectly practical and you may have all the necessary ability to carry it through successfully. You must have more than these. You must actually take the *initiative* and put the wheels of your plan into motion and keep them turning until your goal is reached.

Study those whom you know to be failures (you'll find them all around you) and observe that, without a single exception, they lack firmness of *decision,* even in matters of the smallest importance. Such people usually talk a great deal, but they are very short on performance. "Deeds, not words," should be the motto of anyone who intends to succeed in life, no matter what may be his calling, or what he has selected as his *definite chief aim.*

## Lesson Six
# Imagination

No man ever accomplished anything, never created anything, never built any plan or developed a *definite chief aim* without the use of his *imagination.*

Everything that any man ever created or built was first visioned, in his own mind, through *imagination.*

In the workshop of the *imagination* one may take old, well-known ideas or concepts, or parts of ideas, and combine them with still other old ideas or parts of ideas, and out of this combination create what seems to be new. This process is the major principle of all invention.

One may have a *definite chief aim* and a plan for achieving it; may possess *self-confidence*; may have a highly developed *habit of saving*; and possess both *initiative* and *leadership* in abundance—but if the element of imagination is missing, these other qualities will be useless because there will be no driving force to shape their use.

Thomas Edison developed the electric bulb by use of his *imagination* when he assembled two old and well-known principles in a combination in which they had never before been associated. A brief description of just how this was accomplished will help you to vision the manner in which *imagination* may be made to solve problems, overcome obstacles, and the lay foundation for great achievements.

Edison discovered, as others had before him, that a light could be created by applying electrical energy to a wire, thus heating the wire to a white heat. The trouble, however, came because no one had found a way to control the heat. The wire soon burned out when heated sufficiently to give a clear light.

After many years of experimentation, Edison happened to think of the old, well-known method of burning charcoal, and saw, instantly, that this principle held the secret to the needed control of heat essential in creating a light by applying electrical power to a wire.

Charcoal is made by placing a pile of wood on the ground, setting the wood on fire, and then covering it over with dirt, thereby cutting off most of the oxygen from the fire, which enables the wood to burn slowly; but it cannot blaze and the stick cannot burn up entirely. This is because there can be no combustion where there is no oxygen, and little combustion where there is little oxygen. With this knowledge in mind, Edison went into his laboratory, placed the wire with which he had been experimenting inside a vacuum tube, thus cutting off *all* the oxygen, applied the electrical power, and lo! he had a perfect incandescent light bulb. The wire inside the bulb could not burn up because there was no oxygen inside to create combustion sufficient to burn it up.

So it happened that one of the most useful modern inventions was created by combining two principles in a new way.

There is nothing absolutely new!

That which seems new is but a combination of ideas or elements of something old. This is literally true in the creation of business plans, inventions, the manufacture of metals, and everything else created by man.

To cultivate the *imagination* so it will eventually suggest ideas on its own initiative, you should make it your business to keep a record of all the useful, ingenious, and practical ideas you see in use in other lines of work outside your own, as well as in connection with your work. Start with an ordinary pocket-sized notebook, and catalogue every idea, concept, or thought that occurs to you, which is capable of practical use, and then take these ideas and work them into new plans. By and by, the time will come when the powers of your own *imagination* will go into the storehouse of your own subconscious mind, where all the knowledge that you have ever gathered is stored, assemble this knowledge into new combinations, and hand over to you the results in the shape of *new ideas*, or what appear to be new ideas.

This procedure is practical because it has been followed successfully by some of the best-known leaders, investors, and businessmen.

Let us here define the word *imagination* as: "The workshop of the mind wherein may be assembled, in new and varying combinations, all ideas, thoughts, plans, facts, theories, and principles known to man."

A single combination of ideas, which may be merely parts of old and well-known ideas, may be worth anywhere from a few cents to a few million dollars.

The dreamer who does nothing more than dream uses the imagination, but he falls short of using this great faculty efficiently because he does not add to it the impulse to put his thoughts into *action*. Here is where *initiative* enters and goes to work for him, providing he is familiar with the Laws of Success and understands that ideas, of themselves, are worthless until put into action.

The dreamer who creates practical ideas must place back of these ideas three of the laws that have preceded this one, namely:

1. The Law of a Definite Chief Aim
2. The Law of Self-Confidence
3. The Law of Initiative and Leadership

## Lesson Seven

# Enthusiasm

It seems more than coincidence that the most successful people, in all walks of life—and particularly in sales—are the enthusiastic type.

*Enthusiasm* is a driving force that not only gives greater power to the man who has it, but it is contagious and affects all whom it reaches. Enthusiasm over the work in which one is engaged takes the drudgery out of that work. Enthusiasm gives greater power to one's efforts, no matter what sort of work one is in.

The starting point of enthusiasm is "motive," or well-defined desire. Enthusiasm is simply a high rate of vibration of the mind. Elsewhere in this book may be found a complete list of the mind stimulants that will superinduce the state of mind known as enthusiasm. The urge of sexual desire is the greatest-known mind stimulant. People who do not feel a strong desire for sexual contact are seldom, if ever, capable of becoming highly enthusiastic over anything. Transmutation of the great driving force of sex desire is the basis of practically all the works of genius. By "transmutation" is meant the switching of thought from sexual contact to any other form of physical action.

It is a well-known fact that men succeed most readily when engaged in an occupation that they like best, and this for the reason that they readily become enthusiastic over that which they like best. Enthusiasm is also the basis of creative imagination. When the mind is vibrating at a high rate, it is receptive to similarly high rates of vibration, from outside sources, thus providing a favorable condition for creative imagination. It will be observed that enthusiasm plays an important part in four of the other principles constituting the Law of Success philosophy, namely, the Master Mind, Imagination, Accurate Thought, and Pleasing Personality.

Enthusiasm, to be of value, must be controlled and directed to definite ends. Uncontrolled enthusiasm may be, and generally is, destructive. The acts of so-called "bad boys" are generally nothing more than uncontrolled enthusiasm. The wasted energy of uncontrolled enthusiasm expressed through promiscuous sexual contact, and sex desire not expressed through contact, is sufficient to lift one to high achievement if this urge is harnessed and transformed into some other form of physical action.

The next chapter, on self-control, appropriately follows the subject of enthusiasm, since self-control is necessary in the mastery of enthusiasm.

## Lesson Eight
# Self-Control

Lack of self-control has brought grief to more people than any other shortcoming known to the human race. This evil shows itself, at one time or another, in everyone's life.

Every successful person must have some sort of a balance wheel for his or her emotions.

The man who lacks self-control may be easily mastered by one who has such control, and tricked into saying or doing that which may later prove embarrassing to him.

Success in life is very largely a matter of harmonious negotiation with other people, and this requires self-control in abundance.

An angry man is suffering from a degree of temporary insanity, and therefore he is hardly capable of diplomatic negotiation with others. For this reason, the angry man, or the one who has no self-control, is an easy victim of the man who has such control. No man may become powerful without first gaining control of himself.

Self-control is also a balance wheel for the person who is too optimistic and whose enthusiasm needs checking, for it is possible to become entirely too enthusiastic; so much so that one becomes a bore to all those near him.

## Lesson Nine
# Habit of Doing More Than Paid For

This law has proven a stumbling block to many promising careers. There is a general attitude among people to perform as little service as they can get by with; but if you study these people carefully, you will observe that while they may be actually "getting by" temporarily, they are not, however, getting anything else.

There are two major reasons why all successful people must practice the law of doing more than paid for:

1. Just as an arm or limb grows strong through use, so does the mind grow strong. By rendering the greatest possible amount of service, the faculties through which the service is rendered are put into use and, eventually, become strong and accurate.
2. By rendering more service than you are paid for, you will be turning the spotlight of *favorable* attention upon yourself, and it will not be long before you will be sought with fancy offers for your services, and there will be a continuous market for those services.

"Do the thing and you shall have the power," was the admonition of Emerson.

By rendering more service and better service than that for which you are paid, you also take advantage of the Law of Increasing Returns, through the operation of which you will eventually be paid, in one way or another, for far more service than you actually perform.

You will not find many people many rendering such service, which is all the better for you, because you will stand in bold contrast with practically all others who are engaged in a work similar to yours. *Contrast* is a powerful law, and you may, in this manner, profit by it.

If the author had to choose one of the seventeen laws of success as the most important, and had to discard all the others except the one chosen, he would, without a moment's hesitation, chose this Law of *Rendering More Service and Better Service than Paid for*.

Lesson Ten

# Pleasing Personality

A pleasing personality, naturally, is one that does not antagonize. Personality cannot be defined in one word, nor in half a dozen words, for it represents the sum total of all one's characteristics, good and bad.

Your personality is totally unlike any other personality. It is the sum of qualities, emotions, characteristics, appearances, etc., which distinguish you from all other people.

Your clothes form an important part of your personality; the way you wear them, the harmony of colors you select, the quality, and many other details all go to indicate much that belongs distinctly as a part of your personality. Some psychologists claim that they can accurately analyze any person, in many important respects, by turning that person loose in a clothing store where there is a great variety of clothing, with instructions to select whatever may be wanted and dress in the clothes selected.

Your facial expression, as shown by the lines of your face, or the lack of lines, forms an important part of your personality. Your voice, its pitch, tone, volume, and the language you use form important parts of your personality because they mark you instantly, once you have spoken, as a person of refinement or the opposite.

The manner in which you shake hands constitutes an important part of your personality. If, when shaking hands, you merely hold out a cold hunk of flesh and bones that is limp and lifeless, you are displaying a sign of a personality that is not mixed with *enthusiasm* or *initiative*.

A pleasing personality is usually found in one who speaks gently and kindly, selecting refined words that do not offend, in a modest tone of voice; who selects clothing of appropriate style and colors, which harmonize; who is unselfish and not only willing, but desirous, of serving others; who is a friend of all humanity, rich and the poor alike, regardless of politics, religion or occupation; who refrains from speaking unkindly of others, either with or without cause; who manages to converse without being drawn into vulgar conversations or useless arguments on such debatable topics as religion and politics; who sees both good and bad in people, but makes due allowance for the latter; who seeks neither to reform nor to reprimand others; who smiles frequently and deeply; who loves music and little children; who sympathizes with all who are in trouble and forgives acts of unkindness; who willingly grants others the right to do as they please as long as no one's rights are interfered with; who earnestly strives to be constructive in every thought and deed indulged in; who encourages others and spurs them on to greater and better achievement.

Life may be properly called a great drama in which good showmanship is of the utmost importance. Successful people, in all callings, are generally good showmen; meaning, by this, that they practice the habit of catering or playing to the crowd.

A good showman is one who understands how to cater to the masses. Success is not a matter of chance or luck. It is the result of careful planning, careful staging, and able acting of parts by the player in the game.

What is to be done about this defect by the man who is not blessed with a personality that lends itself to able showmanship? Is such a person to be doomed to failure because of Nature's oversight in not blessing him with such a personality?

Not at all. Here is where the principle of the Master Mind comes to the rescue. Those who do not have pleasing personalities may surround themselves with men and women who supply this defect. Henry Ford was not blessed, by Nature, with native ability as a good showman, and his personality was not perfect by a long way, but, knowing how to make use of the Master Mind Principle, he bridged this defect by surrounding himself with men who did have such ability.

What are the most essential characteristics of good showmanship?

First, the ability to appeal to the imagination of the public, and to keep people interested and curious concerning one's activities. Second, a keen sense of appreciation of the value of psychological appeal through advertising. Third, sufficient alertness of mind to enable one to capture and make use of the prejudices, likes, and dislikes of the public, at the psychological moment.

## Lesson Eleven
# Accurate Thinking

The art of accurate thinking is not difficult to acquire, although certain definite rules must be followed. To think accurately, one must follow at least two basic principles:
1. Accurate thinking calls for the separation of *facts* from mere *information*.
2. *Facts*, when ascertained, must be separated into two classes; one is known as *important* and the other as *unimportant*, or irrelevant.

The question naturally arises, "What is an *important fact?*" and the answer is: An *important fact* is essential for the attainment of one's *definite chief aim* or purpose, or which may be useful or necessary in connection with one's daily occupation. All other facts, while they may be useful and interesting, are comparatively unimportant as far as the individual is concerned.

No one has the right to an opinion on any subject, unless he has arrived at that opinion by a process of reasoning based upon all the available *facts* connected with the subject. Despite this, however, nearly everyone has opinions on nearly every subject, whether they are familiar with those subjects, or have any *facts* connected with them or not.

Be careful, also, that you do not indulge in wild, speculative language that is not based upon *known facts*.

It often requires considerable effort to *know facts* on any subject, which is perhaps \ why so few people take the time or go to the trouble to gather *facts* as the basis of their opinions.

You are presumably following this philosophy for the purpose of learning how you may become more successful; and if that is true then *you* must break away from the common practices of the masses who do not think and take the time to gather facts as the basis of thought. That this requires effort is freely admitted, but it must be kept in mind that *success* is not something that one may pluck from a tree, where it has grown of its own accord. Success is something that represents perseverance, self-sacrifice, determination, and strong character.

Everything has its price, and nothing may be obtained without paying the price; or, if something of value is obtained, it cannot be retained for long. The price of accurate thought is the effort required to gather and organize the *facts* on which to base the *thought*.

## Lesson Twelve
# Concentration

The jack-of-all-trades seldom accomplishes much at any trade. Life is so complex, and there are so many ways of dissipating energy unprofitably, that the habit of *concentrated effort* must be formed and adhered to by all who succeed.

Power is based upon organized effort or energy. Energy cannot be organized without the habit of *concentration* of all the faculties on one thing at a time. An ordinary reading glass may be used to so focus the rays of the sun that they will burn a hole in a board in a few minutes. Those same rays will not even heat the board until they are *concentrated* on one spot.

The human mind is something like the reading glass, because it is the medium through which all the faculties of the brain may be brought together and made to function in a coordinated fashion. It is worthy of serious consideration to remember that all the outstanding men of success, in all walks of life, concentrated the major portion of their thoughts and efforts upon one *definite purpose, objective,* or *chief aim.*

Find out what you wish to do—adopt a *definite chief aim*—then concentrate all your energies back of this purpose until it has reached a happy climax.

Observe, in analyzing the next law, on *cooperation*, the close connection between the principles outlined and those associated with the law of *concentration.*

Wherever a group of people ally themselves in an organized, cooperative spirit for the carrying out of some definite purpose, it will be observed that they are employing the law of *concentration*, and unless they do so their alliance will be without real power.

## Lesson Thirteen
# Cooperation

We are living distinctly in an age of *cooperation*. The outstanding achievements in business, industry, finance, transportation, and politics are all based upon the principle of cooperative effort.

To succeed in a big way, in any undertaking, means that one must have the cooperation of others. The winning football team is the one that is best coached in the art of *cooperation*. The spirit of teamwork must prevail in business, or the business will not get very far.

You will observe that some of the preceding laws must be practiced as a matter of habit before you can get perfect cooperation from others. For example, other people will not cooperate with you unless you have mastered and applied the law of a *pleasing personality*. You will also notice that *enthusiasm* and *self-control* and the *habit of doing more than paid for* must be practiced before you hope to gain the full cooperation from others.

These laws overlap one another, and all of them must be merged into the law of *cooperation*, which means that one, to gain cooperation from others, must form the habit of practicing the laws named.

No man is willing to cooperate with a person who has an offensive personality. No man is willing to cooperate with one who is not enthusiastic, or who lacks self-control. *Power* comes from organized, *cooperative* effort!

A dozen well-trained soldiers, working with perfectly coordinated effort, can master a mob of a thousand people who lack leadership and organization.

You may test this out, in your own way, by watching the reaction of your own mind when you are in the presence of those with whom you are friendly compared with what happens when you are in the presence of those who you do not like. Friendly association inspires one with a mysterious energy not otherwise experienced, and this great truth is the foundation stone of the law of *cooperation*.

An army that is forced to fight because the soldiers are afraid they will be shot down by their own leaders may be a very effective army, but such an army never has been a match for an army that goes into action of its own accord, with every man determined to win because he believes his side ought to win.

## Lesson Fourteen
# Profiting By Failure

Failure is one of the most beneficial parts of a human being's experience, for the reason that there are many needed lessons that must be learned before one commences to succeed, which could be learned from no teacher other than *failure*.

*Failure* is a blessing in disguise providing it teaches us some useful lesson that we could not or would not have learned without it!

However, millions of people make the mistake of accepting *failure* as final, whereas it is, like most other events in life, but transitory, and for this reason should not be accepted as final.

Successful people must learn to distinguish between failure and *temporary defeat*. Every person experiences, at one time or another, some form of temporary defeat, and out of such experiences come some of the greatest and most beneficial lessons.

In truth, most of us are so constituted that if we never experienced temporary defeat (or what some ignorantly call *failure*), we would soon become so egotistical and independent that we would imagine ourselves more important than Deity.

Headaches are beneficial, despite the fact that they are very disagreeable, because they represent Nature's language in which she calls loudly for intelligent use of the body.

It is the same regarding temporary defeat or failure—these are Nature's symbols through which she signals us that we have been headed in the wrong direction, and if we are reasonably intelligent we heed these signals, steer a different course, and come, finally to the objective of our *definite chief aim*.

One of the most starting discoveries in my research was that all outstanding successes, regardless of the field in which they were engaged, were people who met with reverses, adversity, temporary defeat, and, in some instances, actual *permanent failure* (as far as they, as individuals, were concerned). Not a single successful person was discovered whose success was attained without the experience of what, in many instances, seemed like unbearable obstacles, which had to be mastered.

It was discovered also that in exact ratio to the extent that these successful people met squarely and did not budge from defeat that they arose to the heights of success. In other words, success is measured, always, by the extent to which any individual meets and squarely deals with the obstacles that arise in the course of this procedure in pursuit of his *definite chief aim*.

Do not be afraid of temporary defeat, but make sure that you learn some lesson from every such defeat. That which we call "experience" consists, largely, of what we learn by mistakes—our own and those made by others—but we cannot ignore the knowledge that may be gained from mistakes.

## Lesson Fifteen
# Tolerance

Intolerance has caused more grief than any other of man's many forms of ignorance.

It is impossible for any man to observe the law of *accurate thought* without having first acquitted the habit of tolerance, for the reason that intolerance causes a man to slam shut the Book of Knowledge and write on its cover, "Finis, I know it all!"

Intolerance is closely related to *the six basic fears* described in the law of *self-confidence,* and it may be stated as a positive fact that intolerance is always the result of either *fear* or *ignorance.* There are no exceptions to this. The moment another person (providing he, himself, is not intolerant) discovers that you are cursed with intolerance he can easily and quickly mark you as being either the victim of *fear* and *superstition,* or, what's worse, ignorance.

Intolerance closes the doorway to opportunity in a thousand ways, and shuts out the light of intelligence.

The moment you open your mind to *facts*, and take the attitude that the last word is seldom said on any subject—that there always remains the chance that still more truth may be learned on every subject—you begin to cultivate the law of *tolerance*, and if you practice this habit for long you will soon become a thinker, with ability to solve the problems that confront you in your struggle to make a place for yourself in your chosen field.

## Lesson Sixteen
# Practicing the Golden Rule

This is, in some ways, the most important of the Seventeen Laws of Success.

Despite the fact that the great philosophers for more than five thousand years have all discovered the law of the Golden Rule, and have made comment on it, the great majority of people today look upon it as a sort of pretty text for preachers to build sermons on.

In truth, the Golden Rule is based upon a powerful law that, when understood and faithfully practiced, will enable any man to get others to *cooperate* with him.

It is a well-known truth that most men follow the practice of returning good or evil, act for act. If you slander a man, he will slander you. If you praise a man, he will praise you. If you favor a man in business, he will favor you in return.

There are exceptions to this rule, to be sure, but by and large the law works out. Like attracts like. This is in accordance with a great natural law, and it works in every particle of matter and in every form of energy in the universe. Successful men attract successful men. Failures attract failures.

The law of the Golden Rule is closely related to the law of *the habit of doing more than paid for*. The very act of rendering more service than you are paid for puts into operation this law through which like attracts like, which is the selfsame law as that which forms the basis of the Golden Rule.

This law is so fundamental, so obvious, and so simple. Yet it is one of the great mysteries of human nature that it is not more generally understood and practiced. Back of its use lie possibilities that stagger the imagination of the most visionary person. Through its use one may learn the real secret—all the secret there is—to the art of *getting others to that which we wish them to do*.

If you want a favor from someone, make it your business to seek out the person from whom you want the favor and, in an appropriate manner, render that person an equivalent of the favor you wish from him. If he does not respond at first, double the dose and render him another favor, and another, and another, and so on, until finally he will, out of shame if nothing more, come back and render you a favor.

*You get others to cooperate with you by first cooperating with them.*

The foregoing sentence is worth reading a hundred times, for it contains the gist of one of the most powerful laws available to the man who has the intention of attaining great success.

It may sometimes happen, and it will, that the particular individual to whom you render useful service will never respond and render you a similar service, but *keep this important truth in mind*—that even though one person fails to respond, someone else will observe the transaction and, out of a sportsman's desire to see justice done, or perhaps with a more selfish motive in mind, will render you the service to which you are entitled.

"Whatsoever a man soweth that shall he also reap."

This is more than mere preachment; it is a great practical truth that may be made the foundation of every successful achievement.

## Lesson Seventeen
# The Habit of Health

We come now to the last of the seventeen factors of success. In previous chapters we learned that success grows out of power; that power is organized knowledge expressed in definite action. No one can remain intensively active very long without good health. The mind will not function properly unless it has a sound body in which to function. Practically all of the other sixteen factors that enter into the building of success depend, for their successful application, upon a healthy body.

As a closing thought for this chapter, the author wishes to return to a very brief statement concerning the therapeutic value of sex energy. The foundation of fact that justifies reference to sex, as a health builder, will be laid out in the following manner:

It is a well-known fact that *thought* is the most powerful energy available to man. It is equally well known that negative thoughts of worry, envy, hatred, and fear will destroy the digestive processes and bring about illness; this is because negative thought inhibits the flow of certain glandular contents that are essential in the digestive processes.

Negative thoughts cause "short circuits" in the nerve lines that carry nervous energy (or life force) from the central distributing station, the brain, to all parts of the body, where this energy performs its natural task of nourishment and of removal of worn out cells and waste matter.

Sex energy is a highly vitalizing, positive force, when it is in a state of agitation, during the period of sexual contact, and because it is powerful it sweeps over the entire nervous system of the body and unties any "short circuits" that may exist in any of the nerve lines, thus ensuring a complete flow of nervous energy to *all* parts of the body.

Sexual emotion is the most powerful of all the human emotions, and when it is actively engaged, it reaches and vitalizes every cell in every organ of the body, thereby causing the organs to function in a normal manner. Total abstinence, sexually, was not one of Nature's plans, and those who do not understand this truth, usually pay for their ignorance out of a trust fund that Nature provided for the maintenance of health.

*Thought* controls all voluntary movements of the body. Are we in accord on this statement? Very well, if thought controls all voluntary movements of the body, may it also be made to control, or at least materially influence, all involuntary movements of the body?

Thoughts of a negative nature, such as fear, worry, and anxiety, not only inhibit the flow of the digestive juices, but they also "tie knots" in the nerve lines which carry nervous energy to the various organs of the body.

Thoughts of a *positive* nature untie these knots in the nerve lines and permit the nervous energy to pass through. *Sex emotion is the most powerful form of positive thought.* Sex energy is Nature's own "medicine," proof of which is obvious if one will observe the state of mind and the perfectly relaxed condition of the body following sexual contact.

Brief as it is, the foregoing statement should be made the starting point for some intelligent analysis of this subject by the reader of this book. No one knows the last word in connection with the subject; most of us do not even know the first word. Therefore, let us not pass judgment on a subject concerning which we know so very little until we at least have done some intelligent thinking on the subject. For all that most of us know, both poverty and ill health may be mastered through a complete understanding of the subject of sex energy, and for that reason sex energy is the most powerful mind stimulant known.

## Afterword
# The Mystery of the Power of Thought

Every man is where he is as the result of his own dominating thoughts, just as surely as night follows day. Thought is the only thing that you absolutely control, a statement of fact that we repeat because it is of great significance. You do not control, entirely, the money you possess, or the love and friendship that you enjoy; you had nothing to do with your coming into the world and you will have little to do with the time of your going; but you can make the mind *positive* or you can permit it to become *negative*, as the result of outside influences and suggestions. Divine Providence gave you supreme control of your own mind, and with this control the responsibility is now yours to make the best use of it.

The difference between success and failure is largely a matter of the difference between positive and negative thought. A negative mind will not attract a fortune. Like attracts like. Nothing attracts success as quickly as success.

Poverty begets more poverty. Become successful and the whole world will lay its treasures at your feet and want to do something to help you become more successful. Show signs of poverty and the entire world will try to take away that which you have of value. You can borrow money at the bank when you are prosperous and do not need it, but try and arrange a loan when you are poverty-stricken, or when some great emergency faces you. You are the master of your own destiny because you control the one thing that can change and redirect the course of human destinies, the power of *thought*.

Let this great truth sink into your consciousness and this book will have marked the most important turning point of your life.

# Think and Grow Rich
(1937)

## by Napoleon Hill
*The Original 1937 Classic*

## Contents

Introduction   *The Power of a Single Book* by Mitch Horowitz   600
Chapter One   Desire   The First Step to Riches   601
Chapter Two   Faith   The Second Step to Riches   603
Chapter Three   Auto Suggestion   The Third Step to Riches   605
Chapter Four   Specialized Knowledge   The Fourth Step to Riches   606
Chapter Five   Imagination   The Fifth Step to Riches   607
Chapter Six   Organized Planning   The Sixth Step to Riches   608
Chapter Seven   Decision   The Seventh Step to Riches   610
Chapter Eight   Persistence   The Eighth Step to Riches   611
Chapter Nine   The Master Mind   The Ninth Step to Riches   612
Chapter Ten   Sex Transmutation   The Tenth Step to Riches   613
Chapter Eleven   The Subconscious Mind   The Eleventh Step to Riches   614
Chapter Twelve   The Brain   The Twelfth Step to Riches   615
Chapter Thirteen   The Sixth Sense   The Thirteenth Step to Riches   616
Epilogue   A Word about Fear   616

## Introduction
# The Power of a Single Book

The book you are about to experience has probably touched more lives than any other work of modern self-help. Try a small personal experiment: Carry a copy of *Think and Grow Rich* with you through an airport, grocery store, shopping mall, or any public place—and see if more than one person doesn't stop you and say something like, "Now, *that's* a great book..."

I have met artists, business people, doctors, teachers, athletes—people from different professions and possessed of seemingly different outer goals—who have attested that *Think and Grow Rich* made a concrete difference in their lives.

This is because, whatever our individual aims and desires, all motivated people share one common trait: the drive for personal excellence. This book, better than any other I know, breaks down the steps and elements to accomplishing any worthy goal.

When journalist Napoleon Hill published *Think and Grow Rich* in 1937 he had already dedicated more than twenty years of study to discovering and documenting the common traits displayed by high achievers across varying fields. Hill observed and interviewed more than five hundred exceptional people, ranging from statesmen and generals, to inventors and industrialists.

He condensed their shared traits into thirteen principles of accomplishment—and this forms the core of *Think and Grow Rich*.

This book has sold many millions of copies around the world since its first appearance—but that is not the true measure of its success. Lots of books gain popularity for a time, but go unread and sometimes unheard of within a decade or so of their publication. But *Think and Grow Rich* has, if anything, grown in influence since Hill's death in 1970. Its ideas are at the foundation of most of today's philosophies of business motivation and personal achievement.

But there is still more to Hill's book than that—and this brings us back to the little experiment proposed at the start of this preface. *Think and Grow Rich* evokes rare and deeply felt affection among many of its readers. All over America, and in other parts of the world, it is possible to run into friendly strangers who will beckon you aside for a moment to share a brief personal connection, telling you how *Think and Grow Rich* has helped them in life.

In a sense, you are about to join an informal fraternity of strivers, from a wide range of backgrounds, who have benefited from the principles in this book. When you meet them—and you will—many will welcome you with a nod and a smile, as if to say: *We've been waiting for you.*

—Mitch Horowitz

Chapter One

# Desire

## *The First Step to Riches*

In the early twentieth century a great American salesman and businessman named Edwin C. Barnes discovered how true it is that men really do *think and grow rich.*

Barnes's discovery did not come in one sitting. It came little by little, beginning with an ALL-CONSUMING DESIRE to become a business associate of inventor Thomas Edison. One of the chief characteristics of Barnes's desire was that it was *definite.* Barnes wanted to work *with* Edison—not just *for* him.

Straight off a freight train, Barnes presented himself in 1905 at Edison's New Jersey laboratory. He announced that he had come to go into business with the inventor. In speaking of their meeting years later, Edison said: "He stood there before me, looking like an ordinary tramp, but there was something in the expression of his face which conveyed the impression that he was determined to get what he had come after."

Barnes did *not* get his partnership with Edison on his first interview. But he *did* get a chance to work in the Edison offices, at a very nominal wage, doing a job that was unimportant to Edison—but *most important* to Barnes, because it gave him an opportunity to display his abilities to his future "partner."

Months passed. Nothing happened outwardly to bring Barnes any closer to his goal. But something important *was* happening in Barnes's mind. He was constantly intensifying his CHIEF DESIRE and his PLANS to become Edison's business associate.

Barnes was DETERMINED TO REMAIN READY UNTIL HE GOT THE OPPORTUNITY HE CAME FOR.

When the "big chance" arrived, it was in a different form, and from a different direction, than Barnes had expected. *That is one of the tricks of opportunity.* It has a sly habit of slipping in by the back door, and it often comes disguised as misfortune or temporary defeat. Perhaps this is why so many fail to wait for—or recognize—opportunity when it arrives.

Edison had just perfected a new device, known then as the Edison Dictating Machine. His salesmen were not enthusiastic. But Barnes saw his opportunity hidden in a strange-looking contraption that interested no one. Barnes seized the chance to sell the dictating machine, and did it so successfully that Edison gave him a contract to distribute and market it all over the world.

When Edwin C. Barnes climbed down from that freight train in Orange, New Jersey, he possessed one CONSUMING OBSESSION: to become the business associate of the great inventor. Barnes's desire was not a *hope!* It was not a *wish!* It was a keen, pulsating DESIRE, which transcended everything else. It was DEFINITE.

*Wishing* will not bring riches or other forms of success. But *desiring* riches with a state of mind that becomes an obsession, then planning definite ways and means to acquire riches, and backing those plans with persistence *that does not recognize failure*, will bring success.

The method by which DESIRE can be transmuted into its financial equivalent, consists of six definite, practical steps.

### First
Fix in your mind the *exact* amount of money you desire. It is not sufficient merely to say, "I want plenty of money." Be definite as to the amount.

### Second
Determine exactly what you intend to give in return for the money you desire.

### Third
Establish a definite date when you intend to *possess* the money you desire.

### Fourth
Create *a definite plan* for carrying out your desire, and begin *at once*, whether or not you are ready, to put this plan into *action*.

### Fifth

Write out a clear, concise statement of the amount of money you intend to acquire, name the time limit for its acquisition, state what you intend to give in return for the money, and describe clearly the plan through which you intend to accumulate it.

### Sixth

Read your written statement aloud, twice daily, once just before retiring at night and once after arising in the morning. AS YOU READ—SEE AND FEEL AND BELIEVE YOURSELF ALREADY IN POSSESSION OF THE MONEY.

It is especially important that you observe and follow number six. You may complain that it is impossible for you to "see yourself in possession of money" before you actually have it. Here is where a BURNING DESIRE will come to your aid. If you truly DESIRE money or another goal so keenly that your desire is an obsession, you will have no difficulty in convincing yourself that you will acquire it. The object is to want it so much and become so determined that you CONVINCE yourself you will have it. In future chapters you will learn why this is so important.

## Chapter Two

# Faith

## *The Second Step to Riches*

FAITH is the head chemist of the mind. When FAITH is blended with the vibration of thought, the subconscious mind instantly picks up the vibration, translates it into its spiritual equivalent, and transmits it to Infinite Intelligence, as in the case of prayer.

ALL THOUGHTS THAT HAVE BEEN EMOTIONALIZED (given feeling) AND MIXED WITH FAITH begin immediately to translate themselves into their physical equivalent.

If you have difficulty getting a grasp of just what faith is, think of it as a special form of *persistence*—one that we feel when we *know* that we have right at our backs and that helps us persevere through setbacks and temporary failure.

To develop this quality in yourself, use this five-step formula. Promise yourself to read, repeat, and abide by these steps—and write down your promise.

### First

I know that I have the ability to achieve the object of my DEFINITE PURPOSE in life, therefore, I *demand* of myself persistent, continuous action toward its attainment, and I here and now promise to render such action.

### Second

I realize the dominating thoughts of my mind will eventually reproduce themselves in outward physical action, and gradually transform themselves into physical reality. Therefore, I will concentrate my thoughts for thirty minutes daily upon the task of thinking of the person I intend to become, thereby creating in my mind a clear mental picture of that person.

### Third

I know that through the principle of auto suggestion any desire that I persistently hold in my mind will eventually seek expression through some practical means of attaining the object back of it. Therefore, I will devote ten minutes daily to demanding of myself the development of *self-confidence*.

### Fourth

I have clearly written down a description of my DEFINITE CHIEF AIM in life, and I will never stop trying until I have developed sufficient self-confidence for its attainment.

### Fifth

I fully realize that no wealth or position can long endure unless built upon truth and justice. Therefore, I will engage in no transaction which does not benefit all whom it affects. I will succeed by attracting to myself the forces I wish to use, and the cooperation of other people. I will induce others to serve me, because of my willingness to serve others. I will eliminate hatred, envy, jealousy, selfishness, and cynicism, by developing love for all humanity, because I know that a negative attitude toward others can never bring me success. I will cause others to believe in me because I will believe in them, and in myself.

I will sign my name to this formula, commit it to memory, and repeat it aloud once a day, with full FAITH that it will gradually influence my THOUGHTS and ACTIONS, so that I will become a self-reliant and successful person.

Chapter Three

# Auto Suggestion
## *The Third Step to Riches*

AUTO SUGGESTION is a term that applies to all suggestions and self-administered stimuli that reach one's mind through the five senses. Stated another way: *auto suggestion is self suggestion.*

It is the agency of communication between the conscious and subconscious minds. But your subconscious mind recognizes and acts ONLY upon thoughts that have been well mixed with *emotion or feeling*. This is a fact of such importance as to warrant repetition.

When you begin to use—and keep using—the three-step program for auto suggestion in this chapter, be on the alert for hunches from your subconscious mind—and when they appear, put them into ACTION IMMEDIATELY.

### First

Go into some quiet spot (preferably in bed at night) where you will not be disturbed or interrupted, close your eyes, and repeat aloud (so you may hear your own words) the written statement of the amount of money you intend to accumulate, the time limit for its accumulation, and a description of the service or merchandise you intend to give in return for the money. As you carry out these instructions SEE YOURSELF ALREADY IN POSSESSION OF THE MONEY.

For example: Suppose that you intend to accumulate $50,000 by the first of January, five years hence, and that you intend to give personal services in return for the money in the capacity of a salesman. Your written statement of your purpose should be similar to the following:

"By the first day of January, I will have in my possession $50,000, which will come to me in various amounts from time to time during the interim.

"In return for this money I will give the most efficient service of which I am capable, rendering the fullest possible quantity and the best possible quality of service in the capacity of salesman of …(and describe the service or merchandise you intend to sell).

"I believe that I will have this money in my possession. My faith is so strong that I can now see this money before my eyes. I can touch it with my hands. It is now awaiting transfer to me at the time and in the proportion that I deliver the service I intend to render for it. I am awaiting a plan by which to accumulate this money, and I will follow that plan when it is received."

## Second

Repeat this program night and morning until you can see (in your imagination) the money you intend to accumulate.

## Third

Place a written copy of your statement where you can see it night and morning, and read it just before retiring and upon arising, until it has been memorized.

## Chapter Four
# Specialized Knowledge
### *The Fourth Step to Riches*

General knowledge, no matter how great in quantity or variety, is of little use in accumulating money. Knowledge is only *potential* power. It becomes power only when, and if, it is organized into *definite plans of action*, and directed toward a *definite end*.

In connection with your aim, you must decide what sort of specialized knowledge you require, and the purpose for which it is needed. To a large extent, your major purpose in life, and the goal toward which you are working, will help determine what knowledge you need. With this question settled, your next move requires that you have ACCURATE INFORMATION concerning DEPENDABLE SOURCES OF KNOWLEDGE.

Look toward many high-quality sources for the knowledge you seek: people, courses, partnerships, books—look everywhere. Some of this knowledge will be free—never undervalue what is free—and some will require purchasing. Decide what knowledge you seek—and pursue it completely. The author spent more than twenty years interviewing people and studying success methods before writing this book.

Without specialized knowledge, your ideas remain mere wishes. Once you have acquired the knowledge you need, you can use your critical faculty of *imagination* to combine your IDEAS with this SPECIALIZED KNOWLEDGE, and make ORGANIZED PLANS to carry out your aims.

This is the formula for capability: *Using imagination to combine specialized knowledge with ideas and to form organized plans.*

The connecting ingredient is imagination, which we will now learn to cultivate.

Chapter Five

# Imagination
## *The Fifth Step to Riches*

The imagination is the workshop wherein are fashioned all plans created by man. The impulse, the DESIRE, is literally given shape, form, and ACTION through the aid of the imaginative faculty of the mind.

Through the medium of creative imagination, the finite mind of man has direct communication with Infinite Intelligence. Imagination is the faculty through which "hunches" and "inspirations" are reached. It is by this faculty that all basic or new ideas are handed over to man. It is through this faculty that thought vibrations from the minds of others are received. It is through this faculty that one individual may "tune in" or communicate with the subconscious minds of others.

The creative imagination works only when the conscious mind is stimulated through the emotion of a STRONG DESIRE. This is highly significant.

What's more, the creative faculty may have become weak through inaction. Your imagination becomes more alert and more receptive in proportion to its development through *use*.

After you have completed this book, return to this section and begin at once to put your imagination to work on the building of a plan, or plans, for the transmutation of *desire* into money, or your core aim. Reduce your plan to writing. The moment you complete this, you will have *definitely* given concrete form to the intangible *desire*.

This step is extremely important. When you reduce the statement of your desire, and a plan for its realization, into writing, you have actually *taken the first* of a series of steps that will enable you to covert your *thought* into its physical counterpart.

## Chapter Six
# Organized Planning
### *The Sixth Step to Riches*

It is vital that you form a DEFINITE, practical plan, or plans, to carry out your aims. You will now learn how to build plans that are *practical*, as follows:

### First
Ally yourself with a group of as many people as you may need for the creation and carrying out of your plan or plans for the accumulation of money—making use of the "Master Mind" principle described in a later chapter. (Compliance with this instruction is essential. Do not neglect it.)

### Second
Before forming your "Master Mind" alliance, decide what advantages and benefits you may offer the individual members of your group in return for their cooperation. No one will work indefinitely without some form of compensation. No intelligent person will either request or expect another to work without adequate compensation, although this may not always be in the form of money.

### Third
Arrange to meet with the members of your "Master Mind" group at least twice a week, and more often if possible, until you have jointly perfected the necessary plan or plans for the accumulation of money.

## Fourth

Maintain *perfect harmony* between yourself and every member of your "Master Mind" group. If you fail to carry out this instruction to the letter, you may expect to meet with failure. The "Master Mind" principle *cannot* obtain where *perfect harmony* does not prevail.

Keep in mind these facts:
1. You are engaged in an undertaking of major importance to you. To be sure of success, you must have plans that are faultless.
2. You must have the advantage of the experience, education, native ability, and imagination of other minds. This is in harmony with the methods followed by every person who has accumulated a great fortune.

Now, if the first plan you devise does not work successfully, replace it with a new plan. If this new plan fails to work, replace it, in turn, with still another, and so on, until you find a plan that *does work*. Right here is the point where the majority of men meet with failure, because of their lack of *persistence* in creating new plans to take the place of those that fail.

Remember this when your plans fail: *Temporary defeat is not permanent failure.*

*No follower of this philosophy can reasonably expect to accumulate a fortune without experiencing "temporary defeat."* When defeat comes, accept it as a signal that your plans are not sound, rebuild those plans, and set sail once more toward your goal.

Finally, as you are devising your plans keep in mind these Major Attributes of Leadership—traits possessed by the greatest achievers:
1. Unwavering Courage
2. Self-Control
3. A Keen Sense of Justice
4. Definiteness of Decision
5. Definiteness of Plans
6. The Habit of Doing More Than Paid For
7. A Pleasing Personality
8. Sympathy and Understanding
9. Mastery of Detail
10. Willingness to Assume Full Responsibility
11. Cooperation With Others

## Chapter Seven
# Decision
## *The Seventh Step to Riches*

Analysis of several hundred people who had accumulated fortunes disclosed that *every one of them* had the habit of *reaching decisions promptly,* and of changing these decisions slowly, if and when they were changed. People who fail to accumulate money, *without exception,* have the habit of reaching decisions, if at all, very *slowly,* and of *changing these decisions quickly and often.*

What's more, the majority of people who fail to accumulate money sufficient for their needs tend to be easily influenced by the "opinions" of others. "Opinions" are the cheapest commodities on earth. Everyone has a flock of opinions ready to be wished upon anyone who will accept them. If you are influenced by "opinions" when you reach *decisions,* you will not succeed in any undertaking, much less in that of transmuting *your own desire* into money.

If you are influenced by the opinions of others, you will have no DESIRE of your own.

Keep your own counsel when you begin to put into practice the principles described here by *reaching your own decisions* and following them. Take no one into your confidence *except* the members of your "Master Mind" group, and be very sure in your selection of this group that you choose ONLY those who will be in COMPLETE SYMPATHY AND HARMONY WITH YOUR PURPOSE.

Close friends and relatives, while not meaning to, often handicap one through "opinions" and sometimes through ridicule, which is meant to be humorous. Thousands of men and women carry inferiority complexes with them throughout life, because some well-meaning but ignorant person destroyed their confidence through "opinions" or ridicule.

You have a mind of your own. USE IT and reach your own decisions. If you need facts or information from others to enable you to reach decisions, as you probably will in many instances, acquire these facts or secure the information you need quietly, without disclosing your purpose.

Those who reach DECISIONS promptly and definitely know what they want and generally get it. Leaders in every walk of life DECIDE quickly and firmly. That is the major reason why they are leaders. The world has a habit of making room for the man whose words and actions show that he knows where he is going.

Chapter Eight

# Persistence

*The Eighth Step to Riches*

PERSITENCE is an essential factor in transmuting DESIRE into its monetary equivalent. The basis of persistence is the POWER OF WILL.

Will power and desire, when properly combined, make an irresistible pair. Men who accumulate great fortunes are generally known as cold-blooded and sometimes ruthless. Often they are misunderstood. What they have is will power, which they mix with persistence, and place at the back of their desires to *ensure* the attainment of their objectives.

Lack of persistence is one of the major causes of failure. Experience with thousands of people has proved that lack of persistence is a weakness common to the majority of men. It is a weakness that may be overcome by effort. The ease with which lack of persistence may be conquered depends *entirely* upon the INTENSITY OF ONE'S DESIRE.

In short, THERE IS NO SUBSTITUTE FOR PERSISTENCE! It cannot be supplanted by any other quality! Remember this and it will hearten you in the beginning when the going may seem difficult and slow.

Those who have cultivated the HABIT of persistence seem to enjoy insurance against failure. No matter how many times they are defeated, they finally arrive toward the top of the ladder. Sometimes it appears that there is a hidden Guide whose duty is to test men through all sorts of discouraging experiences. Those who pick themselves up after defeat and keep on trying arrive at their destination. The hidden Guide lets no one enjoy great achievement without passing the PERSISTENCE TEST.

What we DO NOT SEE, what most of us never suspect of existing, is the silent but irresistible POWER that comes to the rescue of those who fight on in the face of discouragement. If we speak of this power at all, we call it PERSISTENCE.

There are four simple steps that lead to the habit of PERSISTENCE.
1. A definite purpose backed by burning desire for its fulfillment.
2. A definite plan, expressed in continuous action.
3. A mind closed tightly against all negative and discouraging influences, including negative suggestions of relatives, friends, and acquaintances.
4. A friendly alliance with one or more persons who will encourage you to follow through with both plan and purpose.

## Chapter Nine

# The Master Mind

## *The Ninth Step to Riches*

The "Master Mind" may be defined as: "Coordination of knowledge and effort, in a spirit of harmony, between two or more people for the attainment of a definite purpose."

No individual may hold great power without availing himself of the "Master Mind." A previous chapter supplied instructions for the creation of PLANS for the purpose of translating DESIRE into its monetary equivalent. If you carry out these instructions with PERSISTENCE and intelligence, and use discrimination in selecting your "Master Mind" group, your objective will have been halfway reached, even before you begin to recognize it.

The Master Mind brings an obvious economic advantage, by allowing you to surround yourself with the advice, counsel, and personal cooperation of a group of people who are willing to lend you wholehearted aid in a spirit of PERFECT HARMONY. But there is also a more abstract phase; it may be called the PSYCHIC PHASE.

The psychic phase of the Master Mind is more difficult to comprehend because it has reference to the spiritual forces with which the human race, as a whole, is not well acquainted. You may catch a significant suggestion from this statement: "No two minds ever come together without, thereby, creating a third invisible, intangible force which may be likened to a third mind."

The human mind is a form of energy, a part of it being spiritual in nature. When the minds of two people are coordinated in a SPIRIT OF HARMONY the spiritual units of energy of each mind form an affinity, which constitutes the "psychic" phase of the Master Mind.

Analyze the record of any man who has accumulated a great fortune, and many of those who have accumulated modest fortunes, and you will find that they have either consciously or unconsciously employed the "Master Mind."

*Great power can be accumulated through no other principle!*

Chapter Ten

# Sex Transmutation
*The Tenth Step to Riches*

The meaning of the word "transmute" is, in simple language, "the changing or transferring of one element, or form of energy, into another." The emotion of sex brings into being a unique and powerful state of mind that can be used for extraordinary intellectual and material creative purposes.

This is accomplished through *sex transmutation*, which means the switching of the mind from thoughts of physical expression to thoughts of some other nature.

Sex is the most powerful of human desires. When driven by this desire, men develop keenness of imagination, courage, will power, persistence, and creative ability unknown to them at other times. So strong and impelling is the desire for sexual contact that men freely run the risk of life and reputation to indulge it.

When harnessed and redirected along other lines, this motivating force maintains all of its attributes of keenness of imagination, courage, etc., which may be used as powerful creative forces in literature, art, or in any other profession or calling, including, of course, the accumulation of riches.

The transmutation of sex energy calls for the exercise of will power, to be sure, but the reward is worth the effort. The desire for sexual expression is inborn and natural. The desire cannot, and should not, be submerged or eliminated. But it should be given an outlet through forms of expression that enrich the body, mind, and spirit. If not given this form of outlet, through transmutation, it will seek outlets through purely physical channels.

The emotion of sex is an "irresistible force." When driven by this emotion, men become gifted with a super power for action. Understand this truth, and you will catch the significance of the statement that sex transmutation will lift one into the status of a genius. The emotion of sex contains the secret of creative ability.

When harnessed and transmuted, this driving force is capable of lifting men to that higher sphere of thought which enables them to master the sources of worry and petty annoyance that beset their pathway on the lower plane.

The major reason why the majority of men who succeed do not begin to do so until after the ages of forty to fifty (or beyond), is their tendency to DISSAPATE their energies through over indulgence in physical expression of the emotion of sex. The majority of men *never* learn that the urge of sex has other possibilities, which far transcend in importance that of mere physical expression.

But remember, sexual energy must be *transmuted* from desire for physical contact into some *other* form of desire and action, in order to lift one to the status of a genius.

## Chapter Eleven
# The Subconscious Mind
## *The Eleventh Step to Riches*

The subconscious mind is the connecting link between the finite mind of man and Infinite Intelligence. It is the intermediary through which one may draw upon the forces of Infinite Intelligence at will. It alone contains the secret process by which mental impulses are modified and changed into their spiritual equivalent. It alone is the medium through which prayer may be transmitted to the source capable of answering prayer.

I never approach the discussion of the subconscious mind without a feeling of littleness and inferiority due, perhaps, to the fact that man's entire stock of knowledge on the subject is so pitifully limited. The very fact that the subconscious mind is the medium of communication between the thinking mind of man and Infinite Intelligence is, of itself, a thought that almost paralyzes one's reason.

After you have accepted as a reality the existence of your subconscious mind, and understand its possibilities for transmuting your DESIRES into their physical or monetary equivalent, you will understand why you have been repeatedly urged to MAKE YOUR DESIRES CLEAR, AND TO REDUCE THEM TO WRITING. You will also understand the necessity of PERSISTENCE in carrying out instructions.

The thirteen principles in this book are the stimuli with which—through practice and persistence—you acquire the ability to reach and influence your subconscious mind.

## Chapter Twelve
# The Brain
### *The Twelfth Step to Riches*

More than twenty years before writing this book, the author, working with the late Dr. Alexander Graham Bell and Dr. Elmer R. Gates, observed that every human brain is both a broadcasting and receiving station for the vibration of thought.

The Creative Imagination is the "receiving set" of the brain, which receives thoughts released by the brains of others. It is the agency of communication between one's conscious, or reasoning, mind, and the outer sources from which one may receive thought stimuli.

When stimulated, or "stepped up," to a high rate of vibration, the mind becomes more receptive to the vibration of thought from outside sources. This "stepping up" occurs through the positive emotions or the negative emotions. Through the emotions the vibrations of thought may be increased. This is why it is crucial that your goal have strong emotions at the back of it.

Vibrations of an exceedingly high rate are the only vibrations picked up and carried from one brain to another. Thought is energy travelling at an exceedingly high rate of vibration. Thought that has been modified or "stepped up" by any of the major emotions vibrates at a much higher rate than ordinary thought, and it is this type of thought that passes from one mind to another, through the broadcasting machinery of the human brain.

Thus, you will see that the broadcasting principle is the factor through which you mix feeling or emotion with your thoughts and pass them on to your subconscious mind, or to the minds of others.

## Chapter Thirteen
# The Sixth Sense
## *The Thirteenth Step to Riches*

The thirteenth and final principle is known as the "sixth sense," through which Infinite Intelligence may and will communicate voluntarily, without any effort or demands by the individual.

After you have mastered the principles in this book, you will be prepared to accept as true a statement that may otherwise seem incredible, namely: Through the aid of the sixth sense you will be warned of impending dangers in time to avoid them, and notified of opportunities in time to embrace them.

With the development of the sixth sense, there comes to your aid, and to do your bidding, a kind of "guardian angel" who will open to you at all times the door to the Temple of Wisdom.

Whether this is a statement of truth, you will never know except by following the instructions described in this book, or some similar method.

The author is not a believer in, nor an advocate of, "miracles," for the reason that he has enough knowledge of Nature to understand that Nature *never deviates from her established laws.* Some of her laws are so incomprehensible that they produce what appear to be "miracles."

The sixth sense comes as near to being a miracle as anything I have ever experienced.

## Epilogue
# A Word About Fear

As you begin any new undertaking you are likely at one point or another to find yourself gripped by the emotion of fear.

Fear should never be bargained with or capitulated to. It takes the charm from one's personality, destroys the possibility of accurate thinking, diverts concentration of effort, masters persistence, turns the will power into nothingness, destroys ambition, beclouds the memory, and invites failure in every conceivable form. It kills love, assassinates the finer emotions of the heart, discourages friendship, and leads to sleeplessness, misery, and unhappiness.

So pernicious and destructive is the emotion of fear that it is, almost literally, worse than anything that can befall you.

If you suffer from a fear of poverty, reach a decision to get along with whatever wealth you can accumulate WITHOUT WORRY. If you fear the loss of love, reach a decision to get along without love, if that is necessary. If you experience a general sense of worry, reach a blanket decision that *nothing* life has to offer is *worth* the price of worry.

And remember: The greatest of all remedies for fear is a BURNING DESIRE FOR ACHIEVEMENT, backed by useful service to others.

# Alcoholics Anonymous
(1939)

## The Landmark of Recovery and Vital Living

### Contents

Introduction  *Abridging a Sacred Text* by Mitch Horowitz   620

Foreword   The Doctor's Opinion   622

Chapter One   Bill's Story   624

Chapter Two   There Is a Solution   630

Chapter Three   We Agnostics   634

Chapter Four   How It Works   638

Chapter Five   Into Action   644

## Introduction
# Abridging a Sacred Text

You are about to encounter an abridgment of probably the greatest work of modern self-help. That *Alcoholics Anonymous* has saved and revitalized countless lives since its initial publication in 1939 does not require excessive restatement here. More important is that some readers who have experienced the power of this book would understandably chaff at the notion of its abridgement. To some, *Alcoholics Anonymous* is a work of almost Scriptural significance, and condensing it can seem like an act of heresy, if not cynicism.

I can promise you that my motive is neither. As a writer, historian, and seeker, I approach this book on bended knee, and with deepest gratitude. I consider it the most effective program of spiritual self-help of the past hundred years, and perhaps beyond. My intent in condensing this work is not to replace or sidestep the complete version of the "Big Book," which I encourage you to read. My aim, rather, is to supply a resource for people who may be unready to dive into the Big Book but can be induced by this shorter and equally faithful journey. This condensed edition is also for veterans of the Big Book who wish to review or reencounter its core points. Whatever brings you to this edition, you can experience its ideas in about an hour of reading or listening. Is the length of a lunch break, or a morning commute, too much to dedicate to a philosophy of self-development that can change everything for you, or for someone you love?

*Alcoholics Anonymous* was written for alcoholics and their loved ones— but it is not for them alone. As readers and self-improvers have repeatedly discovered, the "twelve steps" of *Alcoholics Anonymous*, which are described in chapter four, are a blueprint that can be applied to virtually life-depleting habit or compulsion, such as anger, gambling, drugs, debt-spending, or chronic overeating. Although the book was written by and for those who struggle with alcohol, nearly any term or problem, like the ones I just named, can be substituted wherever the word alcohol appears.

What is an addiction? The brilliant actor Philip Seymour Hoffman, who died of a drug overdose in 2014, told a friend that "addiction is when you do the thing you really, really most don't want to be doing." Whatever repeatedly derails your life, threatens your health, and distracts you from your finest and highest tasks, represents an addiction or compulsion. The twelve-step program can direct you to fuller (and safer) existence, whatever the problem that keeps you from it.

As I consider the responsibility of abridging a work that has saved lives, reassembled broken households, and redirected people from paths leading to illness and despair, I am reminded of a recent exchange I had with a successful self-help writer. He told me that he didn't regard himself as a self-help writer at all. He considered the label gauche, and called most self-help books a sham.

In my twenty years as a writer, publisher, and user of self-help philosophies, I have heard that attitude often. It comes not infrequently from self-help writers themselves, some of whom aspire to traditional conceptions of literary recognition, and fear that the label detracts from their respectability or seriousness. I have also, and more often, heard such judgments from people who are looking for reasons to avoid books like this one, suspecting that its program will remake them into ineffectual, woo-woo automatons, unsuited to the rigors of commerce, artistry, or professionalism. Nothing could be further from the truth.

This book provides a restoration of the path toward life—and away from pettiness, compulsion, and self-destruction. Its path is, unashamedly, one of power. Not the kind of ersatz power that we seek from our self-will. If will power worked, there would be no addicts or alcoholics. Rather, this book directs you toward the power derived from having a relationship with the Highest Source of life. Do you reject or have difficulty conceiving of a Higher Power? That is no barrier to entry. The authors of *Alcoholics Anonymous* dealt with the question of belief in an intellectually serious and non-dogmatic way. They placed no ideological tollgate in front of anyone seeking help. They asked only for sincerity of intent.

In any case, my point is not to sell you on the effectiveness of this or any self-help program. Only you can make that evaluation. Rather, I wish to encourage you, as you begin this book, to understand that labels are secondary and ideas alone matter. The only measure of a practical philosophy is its efficacy. A high-sounding ethical or spiritual idea that doesn't work for the individual is worse than useless.

One word of caution: The methods and principles in this book reveal themselves only to someone who approaches them with deep seriousness. The requirements of the twelve-steps are simple but not cheap. They call for a special kind of dedication, a willingness to work with others, and a policy of zero-tolerance for cynicism, eye-rolling, or self-justification. If you can bring that kind of the commitment to the table, the twelve-steps will serve you as a life-changing resource. Of that much I am certain.

—Mitch Horowitz

### Foreword

# The Doctor's Opinion

Men and women drink essentially because they like the effect produced by alcohol. To them, their alcoholic life seems the only normal one. They are restless, irritable, and discontented, unless they can again experience the sense of ease and comfort that comes at once by taking a few drinks—drinks which they see others taking with impunity. After they have succumbed to the desire again, as so many do, and the phenomenon of craving develops, they pass through the well-known stages of a spree, emerging remorseful, with a firm resolution not to drink again. This is repeated over and over, and unless this person can experience an entire psychic change there is very little hope of his recovery.

On the other hand—and strange as this may seem to those who do not understand—once a psychic change has occurred, the very same person who seemed doomed, who had so many problems he despaired of ever solving them, suddenly finds himself easily able to control his desire for alcohol, the only effort necessary being that required to follow a few simple rules.

Men have cried out to me in sincere and despairing appeal: "Doctor, I cannot go on like this! I have everything to live for! I must stop, but I cannot! You must help me!"

Faced with this problem, if a doctor is honest with himself, he must sometimes feel his own inadequacy. Although he gives all that is in him, it often is not enough. One feels that something more than human power is needed to produce the essential psychic change. Though the aggregate of recoveries resulting from psychiatric effort is considerable, we physicians must admit we have made little impression upon the problem as a whole. Many types do not respond to the ordinary psychological approach.

I do not hold with those who believe that alcoholism is entirely a problem of mental control. I have had many men who had, for example, worked a period of months on some problem or business deal, which was to be settled on a certain date, favorably to them. They took a drink a day or so prior to the date, and then the phenomenon of craving at once became paramount to all other interests so that the important appointment was not met. These men were not drinking to escape; they were drinking to overcome a craving beyond their mental control.

There is the type of man who is unwilling to admit that he cannot take a drink. He plans various ways of drinking. He changes his brand or his environment. There is the type who always believes that after being entirely free from alcohol for a period of time he can take a drink without danger. There is the manic-depressive type, who is, perhaps, the least understood by his friends, and about whom a whole chapter could be written. Then there are types entirely normal in every respect except in the effect alcohol has upon them. They are often able, intelligent, friendly people.

All these, and many others, have one symptom in common: they cannot start drinking without developing the phenomenon of craving. This phenomenon has never been, by any treatment with which we are familiar, permanently eradicated. The only relief we have to suggest is entire abstinence.

When I need a mental uplift, I often think of a case brought in by a physician prominent in New York City. The patient had made his own diagnosis, and deciding his situation hopeless, had hidden in a deserted barn determined to die. He was rescued by a searching party, and, in desperate condition, brought to me. Following his physical rehabilitation, he had a talk with me in which he frankly stated he thought the treatment a waste of effort, unless I could assure him, which no one ever had, that in the future he would have the "will power" to resist the impulse to drink.

His alcoholic problem was so complex, and his depression so great, that we felt his only hope would be through what we then called "moral psychology," and we doubted if even that would have any effect. However, he did become "sold" on the ideas contained in this book. He has not had a drink for more than three years.

I earnestly advise every alcoholic to read this book through, and though perhaps he came to scoff, he may remain to pray.

## Chapter One
# Bill's Story

War fever ran high in the New England town to which we new, young officers were assigned, and we were flattered when the first citizens took us to their homes, making us feel heroic. I forgot the strong warnings and the prejudices of my people concerning drink. In time we sailed for "Over There." I was very lonely and again turned to alcohol.

At twenty-two, and a veteran of foreign wars, I returned home at last. My talent for leadership, I imagined, would place me at the head of vast enterprises, which I would manage with utmost assurance.

I took a night law course, and obtained employment as investigator for a surety company. The drive for success was on. I'd prove to the world I was important. My work took me about Wall Street and little by little I became interested in the market. Many people lost money—but some became very rich. Why not I? I studied economics and business as well as law. Potential alcoholic that I was, I nearly failed my law course. At one of the finals I was too drunk to think or write. Though my drinking was not yet continuous, it disturbed my wife.

By the time I had completed the course, I knew the law was not for me. Wall Street had me in its grip. Business and financial leaders were my heroes. I failed to persuade my broker friends to send me out looking over factories and managements, but my wife and I decided to go anyway. I had developed a theory that most people lost money in stocks through ignorance of markets. I discovered many more reasons later on.

We gave up our positions and off we roared on a motorcycle, the sidecar stuffed with tent, blankets, change of clothes, and three huge volumes of a financial reference service.

For the next few years fortune threw money and applause my way. My judgment and ideas were followed by many to the tune of paper millions.

Meanwhile, my drinking assumed more serious proportions, continuing all day and almost every night. The remonstrances of my friends terminated in a row and I became a lone wolf. There were many unhappy scenes in our apartment.

I began to be jittery in the morning.

Abruptly in October 1929 hell broke loose on the New York stock exchange. After one of those days of inferno, I was finished and so were many friends. The papers reported men jumping to death from the towers of High Finance. That disgusted me. I would not jump. I went back to the bar. My friends had dropped several million—so what? As I drank, the old fierce determination to win came back.

Our resources drained, we went to live with my wife's parents. I found a job; then lost it as the result of a brawl with a taxi driver. Mercifully, no one could guess that I was to have no real employment for five years, or hardly draw a sober breath. My wife began to work in a department store, coming home exhausted to find me drunk. I became an unwelcome hanger-on at brokerage places. Liquor became a necessity.

Sometimes a small deal would net a few hundred dollars, and I would pay my bills at the bars and delicatessens. This went on endlessly, and I began to waken very early in the morning shaking violently. A tumbler full of gin followed by half a dozen bottles of beer would be required if I were to eat any breakfast. Nevertheless, I still thought I could control the situation, and there were periods of sobriety which renewed my wife's hope.

Gradually things got worse. The house was taken over by the mortgage holder, my mother-in-law died, my wife and father-in-law became ill. Then I got a promising business opportunity. Stocks were at the low point of 1932, and I had somehow formed a group to buy. I was to share generously in the profits. I went on a prodigious bender, and that chance vanished.

This had to stop. I saw I could not take so much as one drink. I was through forever. Before then, I had written lots of sweet promises, but my wife happily observed that this time I meant business. And so I did. Shortly afterward I came home drunk. There had been no fight. Where had been my high resolve? I simply didn't know. It hadn't even come to mind. Someone had pushed a drink my way, and I had taken it. Was I crazy? I began to wonder, for such an appalling lack of perspective seemed near being just that.

Renewing my resolve, I tried again. Some time passed, and confidence began to be replaced by cocksureness. I could laugh at the gin mills. Now I had what it takes! One day I walked into a cafe to use the telephone. In no time I was beating on the bar asking myself how it happened. As the whiskey rose to my head I told myself I would manage better *next time*.

The remorse, horror, and hopelessness of the next morning are unforgettable. The courage to do battle was not there. My brain raced uncontrollably and there was a terrible sense of impending calamity. Should I kill myself?

No—not now. Then a mental fog settled down. Gin would fix that. So two bottles, and—oblivion.

The mind and body are marvelous mechanisms, for mine endured this agony two more years. Sometimes I stole from my wife's slender purse when the morning terror and madness were on me. Again I swayed dizzily before an open window, or the medicine cabinet where there was poison, cursing myself for a weakling. Then came the night when the physical and mental torture was so hellish I feared I would burst through my window. Somehow I managed to drag my mattress to a lower floor, lest I suddenly leap. Next day found me drinking both gin and sedative.

I could eat little or nothing when drinking, and I was forty pounds underweight.

My brother-in-law is a physician, and through his kindness and that of my mother I was placed in a nationally known hospital for the mental and physical rehabilitation of alcoholics. Under the so-called belladonna treatment my brain cleared. Hydrotherapy and mild exercise helped.

The frightful day came when I drank once more. After a time I returned to the hospital. This was the finish, the curtain, it seemed to me. My weary and despairing wife was informed that she would soon have to give me over to the undertaker or the asylum.

No words can tell of the loneliness and despair I found in that bitter morass of self-pity. Quicksand stretched around me in all directions. I had met my match. Alcohol was my master. Trembling, I stepped from the hospital a broken man. Fear sobered me for a bit. Then came the insidious insanity of that first drink, and on Armistice Day 1934, I was off again. Everyone became resigned to the certainty that I would have to be shut up somewhere, or would stumble along to a miserable end.

How dark it is before the dawn! In reality that was the beginning of my last debauch. I was soon catapulted into what I like to call the fourth dimension of existence. I was to know happiness, peace, and usefulness, in a way of life that is incredibly more wonderful as time passes.

Near the end of that bleak November, I sat drinking in my kitchen. With a certain satisfaction I reflected there was enough gin concealed about the house to carry me through that night and the next day. My musing was interrupted by the telephone. The cheery voice of an old school friend asked if he might come over. *He was sober.* It was years since I could remember his coming to New York in that condition. I was amazed. Rumor had it that he had been committed for alcoholic insanity. I wondered how he had escaped. Of course he would have dinner, and then I could drink openly with him. Unmindful of his welfare, I thought only of recapturing the spirit of other days.

The door opened and he stood there, fresh-skinned and glowing. There was something about his eyes. He was inexplicably different. What had happened? I pushed a drink across the table. He refused it. Disappointed but curious, I wondered what had got into him. "What's all this about?" I queried. He looked straight at me. Simply, but smilingly, he said, "I've got religion."

I was aghast. So that was it—last summer an alcoholic crackpot; now, I suspected, a little cracked about religion. He had that starry-eyed look. Yes, the old boy was on fire all right. But bless his heart, let him rant! Besides, my gin would last longer than his preaching. But he did no ranting. In a matter of fact way he told how two men had appeared in court, persuading the judge to suspend his commitment. They had told of a simple religious idea and a practical program of action. That was two months ago and the result was self evident. It worked!

He had come to pass his experience along to me—if I cared to have it. I was shocked, but interested. I had always believed in a power greater than myself. I had often pondered these things. I was not an atheist. My intellectual heroes, the chemists, the astronomers, even the evolutionists, suggested vast laws and forces at work. Despite contrary indications, I had little doubt that a mighty purpose and rhythm underlay all. How could there be so much of precise and immutable law, and no intelligence? I simply had to believe in a Spirit of the Universe, who knew neither time nor limitation. But that was as far as I had gone.

With ministers, and the world's religions, I parted right there. When they talked of a God personal to me, who was love, superhuman strength, and direction, I became irritated and my mind snapped shut against such a theory. To Christ I conceded the certainty of a great man. His moral teaching—most excellent. For myself, I had adopted those parts that seemed convenient and not too difficult; the rest I disregarded. The wars, the burnings, and chicanery that religious dispute had facilitated made me sick. I doubted whether, on balance, the religions of mankind had done any good. Judging from what I had seen in Europe and since, the power of God in human affairs was negligible, the Brotherhood of Man a grim jest.

But my friend sat before me, and he made the point-blank declaration that God had done for him what he could not do for himself. That he had, in effect, been raised from the dead, suddenly taken from the scrap heap to a level of life better than the best he had ever known! Had this power originated in him? Obviously it had not. There had been no more power in him than there was in me at that minute; and this was none at all.

That floored me. It began to look as though religious people were right after all. Here was something at work in a human heart that had done the impossible. My ideas about miracles were drastically revised right then. Never mind the musty past; here sat a miracle directly across the kitchen table.

I saw that my friend was much more than inwardly reorganized. He was on a different footing. Despite the living example of my friend there remained in me vestiges of my old prejudice. The word God still aroused a certain antipathy. When the thought was expressed that there might be a God personal to me this feeling was intensified. I didn't like the idea. I could go for such conceptions as Creative Intelligence, Universal Mind or Spirit of Nature, but I resisted the thought of a Czar of the Heavens however loving His sway might be. I have since talked with scores of men who felt the same.

My friend suggested what then seemed a novel idea. He said, *"Why don't you choose your own conception of God?"* That statement hit me hard.

*It was only a matter of being willing to believe in a power greater than myself. Nothing more was required of me to make my beginning.* I saw that growth could start from that point.

Thus was I convinced that God is concerned with us humans when we want Him enough. At long last I saw, I felt, I believed. Scales of pride and prejudice fell from my eyes. A new world came into view.

At the hospital I was separated from alcohol for the last time. Treatment seemed wise, for I showed signs of delirium tremors. There I humbly offered myself to God, as I then understood Him, to do with me as He would. I placed myself unreservedly under His care and direction. I admitted for the first time that of myself I was nothing. I ruthlessly faced my sins and became willing to have my newfound Friend take them away, root and branch. I have not had a drink since.

My schoolmate visited me, and I fully acquainted him with my problems and deficiencies. We made a list of people I had hurt or toward whom I felt resentment. I expressed my entire willingness to approach these individuals, admitting my wrong. Never was I to be critical of them. I was to right all such matters to the utmost of my ability.

I was to test my thinking by the new God-consciousness within. Common sense would thus become uncommon sense. I was to sit quietly when in doubt, asking only for direction and strength to meet my problems as He would have me. Never was I to pray for myself, except as my requests bore on my usefulness to others. Then only might I expect to receive. But that would be in great measure.

My friend promised when these things were done I would enter upon a new relationship with my Creator; that I would have the elements of a way of living, which answered all my problems. Belief in the power of God, plus enough willingness, honesty and humility to establish and maintain the new order of things, were the essential requirements.

Simple, but not easy; a price had to be paid. It meant destruction of self-centeredness. I must turn in all things to the Father of Lights who presides over us all.

These were revolutionary and drastic proposals, but the moment I fully accepted them, the effect was electric. There was a sense of victory, followed by such a peace and serenity as I had never known. There was utter confidence. I felt lifted up, as though the great clean wind of a mountaintop blew through and through. God comes to most men gradually, but His impact on me was sudden and profound.

Alarmed for my sanity, I called my friend the doctor. He listened in wonder as I talked. Finally he shook his head saying, "Something has happened to you that I don't understand. But you had better hang on to it. Anything is better than the way you were." The good doctor now sees many men who have such experiences. He knows they are real.

While I lay in the hospital, the thought came that there were thousands of hopeless alcoholics who might be glad to have what had been so freely given me. Perhaps I could help some of them. They, in turn, might work with others. My friend had emphasized the absolute necessity of demonstrating these principles in all my affairs. It was particularly imperative to work with others as he had worked with me. Faith without works was dead, he said. And how appallingly true for the alcoholic! For if an alcoholic failed to perfect and enlarge his spiritual life through work and self sacrifice for others, he could not survive the certain trials and low spots ahead.

My wife and I abandoned ourselves with enthusiasm to the idea of helping other alcoholics to a solution of their problems. We commenced to make many fast friends and a fellowship has grown up among us. Most of us feel we need look no further for Utopia. We have it with us right here and now. Each day my friend's simple talk in our kitchen multiplies itself in a widening circle of peace on earth and good will.

## Chapter Two
# There Is a Solution

We of Alcoholics Anonymous know countless people who were once just as hopeless as Bill. All have recovered. They have solved the drink problem.

We are average Americans. We are people who normally would not mix. But there exists among us a fellowship, a friendliness, and an understanding, which is indescribably wonderful. We are like the passengers of a great liner the moment after rescue from shipwreck when camaraderie, joyousness and democracy pervade the vessel from steerage to captain's table. Unlike the feelings of the ship's passengers, however, our joy in escape from disaster does not subside as we go our individual ways. The feeling of having shared in a common peril is one element in the powerful cement that binds us. But that in itself would never have held us together as we are now joined.

The tremendous fact for every one of us is that we have discovered a common solution. This is the great news this book carries to those who suffer from alcoholism.

An illness of this sort—and we have come to believe it an illness—involves those about us in a way no other human sickness can. If a person has cancer all are sorry for him and no one is angry or hurt. But not so with the alcoholic illness, for with it there goes annihilation of all the things worthwhile in life. It engulfs all whose lives touch the sufferer's. We hope this volume will inform and comfort those who are, or who may be affected.

Highly competent psychiatrists who have dealt with us found it sometimes impossible to persuade an alcoholic to discuss his situation without reserve. *But the ex-alcoholic who has found this solution, who is properly armed with facts about himself, can generally win the entire confidence of another alcoholic in a few hours. Until such an understanding is reached, little or nothing can be accomplished.*

How many times people have said to us: "I can take it or leave it. Why can't he?" "Why don't you try beer and wine?" "Lay off the hard stuff." "His will power must be weak." "He could stop if he wanted to." "The doctor told him that if he ever drank again it would kill him, but there he is lit up again."

These are commonplace observations on drinkers which we hear all the time. Back of them is a world of ignorance and misunderstanding. We see that these expressions refer to people whose reactions are very different from ours.

Moderate drinkers have little trouble in giving up liquor entirely if they have good reason for it. They can take it or leave it alone. Then we have a certain type of hard drinker. He may have the habit badly enough to gradually impair himself physically and mentally. It may cause him to die a few years before his time. If a sufficiently strong reason—ill health, falling in love, change of environment, or the warning of a doctor—becomes operative, this man can also stop or moderate, although he may find it difficult and troublesome, and may even need medical attention.

But what about the real alcoholic? He may start off as a moderate drinker; he may or may not become a continuous hard drinker; but at some stage of his drinking career he begins to lose all control of his liquor consumption once he starts to drink.

He may be one of the finest fellows in the world. Yet let him drink for a day, and he frequently becomes disgustingly, and even dangerously, antisocial. He has a positive genius for getting tight at exactly the wrong moment, particularly when some important decision must be made or engagement kept. He is often perfectly sensible and well balanced concerning everything except liquor, but in that respect is incredibly dishonest and selfish.

Why does he behave like this? If hundreds of experiences have shown him that one drink means another debacle with all its attendant suffering and humiliation, why is it he takes that one drink? What has become of the common sense and will power that he still sometimes displays with respect to other matters?

Opinions vary considerably as to why the alcoholic reacts differently from normal people. We are not sure why, once a certain point is reached, little can be done for him. We cannot answer the riddle.

We know that while the alcoholic keeps away from drink, as he may do for months or years, he reacts much like other men. We are equally positive that once he takes any alcohol whatever into his system, something happens, both in the bodily and mental sense, which makes it virtually impossible for him to stop.

*The fact is that most alcoholics, for reasons yet obscure, have lost the power of choice in drink. Our so-called will power becomes practically non-existent. We are unable at certain times, to bring into our consciousness with sufficient force the memory of the suffering and humiliation of even a week or a month ago. We are without defense against the first drink.*

There *is* a solution. Almost none of us liked the self-searching, the leveling of our pride, the confession of shortcomings, which the process requires for its successful consummation. But we saw that it really worked in others, and we had come to believe in the hopelessness and futility of life as we had been living it. When, therefore, we were approached by those in whom the problem had been solved, there was nothing left for us but to pick up the simple kit of spiritual tools laid at our feet. We have found much of heaven and we have been rocketed into a fourth dimension of existence, of which we had not even dreamed.

The great fact is just this, and nothing less: that we have had deep and effective spiritual experiences, which have revolutionized our whole attitude toward life, toward our fellows, and toward God's universe. The central fact of our lives today is the absolute certainty that our Creator has entered into our hearts and lives in a way that is indeed miraculous. He has commenced to accomplish those things for us that we could never do by ourselves.

If you are as seriously alcoholic as we were, we believe there is no middle-of-the-road solution. We were in a position where life was becoming impossible, and if we had passed into the region from which there is no return through human aid, we had but two alternatives: one was to go on to the bitter end, blotting out the consciousness of our intolerable situation as best we could; and the other, to accept spiritual help. This we did because we honestly wanted to, and were willing to make the effort.

A certain American businessman had ability, good sense, and high character. For years he had floundered from one sanitarium to another. He had consulted the best known American psychiatrists. Then he had gone to Europe, placing himself in the care of a celebrated physician who prescribed for him.

He wished above all things to regain self-control. He seemed quite rational and well-balanced with respect to other problems. Yet he had no control whatever over alcohol. Why was this?

He begged the doctor to tell him the whole truth, and he got it. In the doctor's judgment he was utterly hopeless; he could never regain his position in society and he would have to place himself under lock and key, or hire a bodyguard if he expected to live long.

But this man still lives, and is a free man. He does not need a bodyguard, nor is he confined. He can go anywhere on earth without disaster, provided he remains willing to maintain a certain simple attitude. Let us tell you the rest of the conversation our friend had with his doctor.

The doctor said: "You have the mind of a chronic alcoholic. I have never seen one single case recover, where that state of mind existed to the extent that it does in you." Our friend felt as though the gates of hell had closed on him.

He said to the doctor, "Is there no exception?"

"Yes," replied the doctor, "there is. Exceptions to cases such as yours have been occurring since early times. Here and there, once in a while, alcoholics have had what are called vital spiritual experiences. To me these occurrences are phenomena. They appear to be in the nature of huge emotional displacements and rearrangements. Ideas, emotions, and attitudes, which were once the guiding forces of the lives of these men, are suddenly cast to one side, and a completely new set of conceptions and motives begin to dominate them. In fact, I have been trying to produce some such emotional rearrangement within you. With many individuals the methods which I employed are successful, but I have never been successful with an alcoholic of your description."

Upon hearing this our friend was somewhat relieved, for he reflected that, after all, he was a good church member. This hope, however, was destroyed by the doctor's telling him that his religious convictions were very good, but that in his case they did not spell the necessary vital spiritual experience.

Here was the terrible dilemma in which our friend found himself when he had the extraordinary experience, which as we have already told you, made him a free man.

We, in our turn, sought the same escape, with all the desperation of drowning men. What seemed at first a flimsy reed, has proved to be the loving and powerful hand of God. A new life has been given us or, if you prefer, "a design for living" that really works.

The distinguished American psychologist, William James, in his book *Varieties of Religious Experience* indicates a multitude of ways in which men have discovered God. We have no desire to convince anyone that there is only one way by which faith can be acquired. If what we have learned, and felt, and seen, means anything at all, it means that all of us are the children of a living Creator with whom we may form a relationship upon simple and understandable terms as soon as we are willing and honest enough to try. Those having religious affiliations will find here nothing disturbing to their beliefs or ceremonies. There is no friction among us over such matters.

* * *

One more word about the outlook of the alcoholic. The idea that somehow, someday he will control and enjoy his liquor drinking is the great obsession of every abnormal drinker. It may be true that certain non-alcoholic people, though drinking foolishly and heavily at the present time, are able to stop or moderate. But the actual or potential alcoholic, with hardly an exception, will be *absolutely unable to stop drinking on the basis of self-knowledge.*

Many doctors and psychiatrists agree with our conclusions. One of them, a staff member of a world-renowned hospital, recently made this statement to some of us: "What you say about the general hopelessness of the average alcoholic's plight is, in my opinion, correct. As to two of you men, whose stories I have heard, there is no doubt in my mind that you were 100% hopeless, apart from Divine help. Had you offered yourselves as patients at this hospital, I would not have taken you, if I had been able to avoid it. People like you are too heartbreaking. Though not a religious person, I have profound respect for the spiritual approach in such cases as yours. For most cases, there is virtually no other solution."

Once more: the alcoholic at certain times has no effective mental defense against the first drink. Except in a few rare cases, neither he nor any other human being can provide such a defense. His defense must come from a Higher Power.

## Chapter Three

# We Agnostics

In the preceding chapters, you have learned something of alcoholism. We hope we have made clear the distinction between the alcoholic and the non-alcoholic.

If, when you honestly want to, you find you cannot quit entirely, or if, when drinking, you have little control over the amount you take, you are probably alcoholic. If that be the case, you may be suffering from an illness that only a spiritual experience will conquer.

To one who feels he is an atheist or agnostic such an experience seems impossible, but to continue as he is means disaster especially if he is an alcoholic of the hopeless variety. To be doomed to an alcoholic death or to live on a spiritual basis—not always easy alternatives to face.

But it isn't so difficult. About half our fellowship were of exactly that type. At first some of us tried to avoid the issue, hoping against hope we were not true alcoholics. But after a while we had to face the fact that we must find a spiritual basis of life—or else.

If a mere code of morals, or a better philosophy of life were sufficient to overcome alcoholism, many of us would have recovered long ago. But we found that such codes and philosophies did not save us, no matter how much we tried.

Our human resources, as marshaled by the will, were not sufficient; they failed utterly. Lack of power, that was our dilemma. We had to find a power by which we could live, and it had to be *A Power Greater Than Ourselves*. But where and how were we to find this Power?

Well, that's exactly what this book is about. Its main object is to enable you to find a Power greater than yourself, which will solve your problem. That means, of course, that we are going to talk about God. Here difficulty arises with agnostics. Many times we talk to a new man and watch his hope rise as we discuss his alcoholic problems and explain our fellowship. But his face falls when we speak of spiritual matters, especially when we mention God, for we have re-opened a subject that our man thought he had neatly evaded or entirely ignored.

We know how he feels. We have shared his honest doubt and prejudice. We looked upon this world of warring individuals, warring theological systems, and inexplicable calamity, with deep skepticism. We looked askance at many individuals who claimed to be godly. Yes, we of agnostic temperament have had these thoughts and experiences, and many more. Let us make haste to reassure you. We found that as soon as we were able to lay aside prejudice and express even a willingness to believe in a Power greater than ourselves, we commenced to get results, even though it was impossible for any of us to fully define or comprehend that Power, which is God.

Much to our relief, we discovered we did not need to consider another's conception of God. Our own conception, however inadequate, was sufficient to make the approach and to effect a contact with Him. As soon as we admitted the possible existence of a Creative Intelligence, a Spirit of the Universe underlying the totality of things, we began to be possessed of a new sense of power and direction, provided we took other simple steps. We found that God does not make too hard terms with those who seek Him. To us, the Realm of Spirit is broad, roomy, all inclusive; never exclusive or forbidding, to those who earnestly seek.

When, therefore, we speak to you of God, we mean your own conception of God. This applies, too, to other spiritual expressions that you find in this book. Do not let any prejudice you may have against spiritual terms deter you from honestly asking yourself what they mean to you. At the start, this is all we needed to commence spiritual growth, to effect our first conscious relation with God as we understood Him.

We needed to ask ourselves but one short question. "Do I now believe, or am I even willing to believe, that there is a Power greater than myself?" As soon as a man can say that he does believe, or is willing to believe, we emphatically assure him that he is on his way. It has been repeatedly proven among us that upon this simple cornerstone a wonderfully effective spiritual structure can be built.

Everybody nowadays believes in scores of assumptions for which there is good evidence, but no perfect visual proof. And does not science demonstrate that visual proof is the weakest proof? It is being constantly revealed, as mankind studies the material world, that outward appearances are not inward reality at all.

Instead of regarding ourselves as intelligent agents, spearheads of God's ever advancing Creation, we agnostics and atheists chose to believe that our human intelligence was the last word, the alpha and the omega, the beginning and end of all. Rather vain of us, wasn't it?

We who have traveled this dubious path beg you to lay aside prejudice, even against organized religion. We have learned that whatever the human frailties of various faiths may be, those faiths have given purpose and direction to millions.

Our world has made more material progress in the last century than in all the millennia that went before. Almost everyone knows why. Students of ancient history tell us that the intellect of men in those days was equal to the best of today. Yet in ancient times material progress was painfully slow. The spirit of modern scientific inquiry, research, and invention was almost unknown. In the realm of the material, men's minds were fettered by superstition, tradition, and all sorts of fixed ideas. The contemporaries of Columbus thought a round earth preposterous. Others like them came near putting Galileo to death for his astronomical heresies. We asked ourselves this: are not some of us just as biased and unreasonable about the realm of the spirit as were the ancients about the realm of the material?

We had to ask ourselves why we shouldn't apply to our human problems this same readiness to change the point of view. We were having trouble with personal relationships, we couldn't control our emotional natures, we were prey to misery and depression, we couldn't make a living, we had a feeling of uselessness, we were full of fear, we were unhappy, we couldn't seem to be of real help to other people.

When we saw others solve their problems by simple reliance upon the Spirit of this universe, we had to stop doubting the power of God. Our ideas did not work. But the God idea did.

Logic is great stuff. We liked it. We still like it. It is not by chance we were given the power to reason, to examine the evidence of our senses, and to draw conclusions. That is one of man's magnificent attributes. We agnostically inclined would not feel satisfied with a proposal which does not lend itself to reasonable approach and interpretation. Hence we are at pains to tell why we think our present faith is reasonable, why we think it more sane and logical to believe than not to believe, why we say our former thinking was soft and mushy when we threw up our hands in doubt and said, "We don't know."

When we became alcoholics, crushed by a self-imposed crisis we could not postpone or evade, we had to fearlessly face the proposition that either God is everything or He is nothing. God either is, or He isn't. What was our choice to be?

Arrived at this point, we were squarely confronted with the question of faith. We couldn't duck the issue. Some of us had already walked far over the Bridge of Reason toward the desired shore of faith. The outlines and the promise of the New Land had brought lustre to tired eyes and fresh courage to flagging spirits. Friendly hands had stretched out in welcome. We were grateful that Reason had brought us so far. But somehow, we couldn't quite step ashore. Perhaps we had been leaning too heavily on Reason that last mile and we did not like to lose our support.

That was natural, but let us think a little more closely. Without knowing it, had we not been brought to where we stood by a certain kind of faith? For did we not believe in our own reasoning? Did we not have confidence in our ability to think? What was that but a sort of faith? Yes, we had been faithful, abjectly faithful to the God of Reason. So, in one way or another, we discovered that faith had been involved all the time!

Hence, we saw that reason isn't everything. Neither is reason, as most of us use it, entirely dependable, though it emanate from our best minds. We finally saw that faith in some kind of God was a part of our make-up, just as much as the feeling we have for a friend. Sometimes we had to search fearlessly, but He was there. He was as much a fact as we were. We found the Great Reality deep down within us. In the last analysis it is only there that He may be found. It was so with us.

We can only clear the ground a bit. If our testimony helps sweep away prejudice, enables you to think honestly, encourages you to search diligently within yourself, then if you wish you can join us on the Broad Highway. With this attitude you cannot fail. The consciousness of your belief is sure to come to you.

## Chapter Four
# How It Works

Rarely have we seen a person fail who has thoroughly followed our path. Those who do not recover are people who cannot or will not completely give themselves to this simple program, usually men and women who are constitutionally incapable of being honest with themselves. There are such unfortunates. They are not at fault; they seem to have been born that way. They are naturally incapable of grasping and developing a manner of living which demands rigorous honesty. There are those, too, who suffer from grave emotional and mental disorders, but many of them do recover if they have the capacity to be honest.

Remember that we deal with alcohol—cunning, baffling, powerful! Without help it is too much for us. But there is One who has all power—That One is God. May you find Him now!

Half measures availed us nothing. We stood at the turning point. We asked His protection and care with complete abandon.

Here are the steps we took, which are suggested as a Program of Recovery:

1. We admitted we were powerless over alcohol—that our lives had become unmanageable.
2. Came to believe that a Power greater than ourselves could restore us to sanity.
3. Made a decision to turn our will and our lives over to the care of God *as we understood Him.*
4. Made a searching and fearless moral inventory of ourselves.
5. Admitted to God, to ourselves, and to another human being the exact nature of our wrongs.
6. Were entirely ready to have God remove all these defects of character.
7. Humbly asked Him to remove our shortcomings.
8. Made a list of all persons we had harmed, and became willing to make amends to them all.
9. Made direct amends to such people wherever possible, except when to do so would injure them or others.
10. Continued to take personal inventory and when we were wrong promptly admitted it.
11. Sought through prayer and meditation to improve our conscious contact with God *as we understood Him* praying only for knowledge of His will for us and the power to carry that out.
12. Having had a spiritual experience as the result of these steps, we tried to carry this message to alcoholics, and to practice these principles in all our affairs.

Many of us exclaimed, "What an order! I can't go through with it." Do not be discouraged. No one among us has been able to maintain anything like perfect adherence to these principles. We are not saints. The point is, that we are willing to grow along spiritual lines. The principles we have set down are guides to progress. We claim spiritual progress rather than spiritual perfection.

Our description of the alcoholic, the chapter to the agnostic, and our personal adventures before and after make clear three pertinent ideas:

(a) That we were alcoholic and could not manage our own lives.

(b) That probably no human power could have relieved our alcoholism.

(c) That God could and would if sought.

Being convinced, *we were at step three*, which is that we decided to turn our will and our life over to God as we understood Him. Just what do we mean by that, and just what do we do?

The first requirement was that we be convinced that any life run on self-will could hardly be a success. On that basis we are almost always in collision with something or somebody, even though our motives are good. Most people try to live by self-propulsion. If his arrangements would only stay put, if only people would do as he wishes, the show would be great. Everybody, including himself, would be pleased.

What usually happens? The show doesn't come off very well. He begins to think life doesn't treat him right. He decides to exert himself some more. He becomes, on the next occasion, still more demanding or gracious, as the case may be. Still the play does not suit him. Admitting he may be somewhat at fault, he is sure that other people are more to blame. He becomes angry, indignant, self-pitying. What is his basic trouble? Is he not really a self-seeker even when trying to be kind? Is he not a victim of the delusion that he can wrest satisfaction and happiness out of this world if he only manages well?

Our troubles are basically of our own making. They arise out of ourselves, and the alcoholic is an extreme example of self-will run riot, though he usually doesn't think so. Above everything, we alcoholics must be rid of this selfishness. We must, or it kills us! God makes that possible. And there often seems no way of entirely getting rid of self without Him. Many of us had moral and philosophical convictions galore, but we could not live up to them even though we would have liked to. Neither could we reduce our self-centeredness much by wishing or trying on our own power. We had to have God's help.

This is the how and why of it. First of all, we had to quit playing God. It didn't work. Next, we decided that hereafter in this drama of life, God was going to be our Director. He is the Principal, we are His agent. He is the Father, and we are His children. Most good ideas are simple and this concept was the keystone of the new and triumphant arch through which we passed to freedom.

When we sincerely took such a position, all sorts of remarkable things followed. We had a new Employer. Being all powerful, He provided what we needed, if we kept close to Him and performed His work well. Established on such a footing we became less and less interested in ourselves, our little plans and designs. More and more we became interested in seeing what we could contribute to life. As we felt new power flow in, as we enjoyed peace of mind, as we discovered we could face life successfully, as we became conscious of His presence, we began to lose our fear of today, tomorrow, or the hereafter. We were reborn.

We were now at step three. Many of us said to our Maker, *as we understood Him:* "God, I offer myself to Thee—to build with me and to do with me as Thou wilt. Relieve me of the bondage of self, that I may better do Thy will. Take away my difficulties, that victory over them may bear witness to those I would help of Thy Power, Thy Love, and Thy Way of life. May I do Thy will always!" We thought well before taking this step making sure we were ready; that we could at last abandon ourselves utterly to Him.

The wording was, of course, quite optional so long as we expressed the idea, voicing it without reservation. This was only a beginning, though if honestly and humbly made, an effect, sometimes a very great one, was felt at once.

Next we launched on a course of vigorous action, the first step of which is a personal housecleaning, which many of us had never attempted. Though our decision was a vital and crucial step, it could have little permanent effect unless at once followed by a strenuous effort to face, and to be rid of, the things in ourselves that had been blocking us.

Therefore, we started upon a personal inventory. *This was step four.* A business that takes no regular inventory usually goes broke. Taking a commercial inventory is a fact-finding and a fact-facing process. It is an effort to discover the truth about the stock-in-trade. One object is to disclose damaged or unsalable goods, to get rid of them promptly, and without regret. If the owner of the business is to be successful, he cannot fool himself about values.

We did exactly the same thing with our lives. We took stock honestly. First, we searched out the flaws in our make-up which caused our failure. Being convinced that self, manifested in various ways, was what had defeated us, we considered its common manifestations.

Resentment is the "number one" offender. In dealing with resentments, we set them on paper. We listed people, institutions or principles with whom we were angry. We asked ourselves why we were angry. In most cases it was found that our self-esteem, our pocketbooks, our ambitions, our personal relationships (including sex) were hurt or threatened.

We went back through our lives. Nothing counted but thoroughness and honesty.

It is plain that a life that includes deep resentment leads only to futility and unhappiness. To the precise extent that we permit these, do we squander the hours that might have been worthwhile. But with the alcoholic whose hope is the maintenance and growth of a spiritual experience, this business of resentment is infinitely grave. It is fatal. For when harboring such feelings we shut ourselves off from the sunlight of the Spirit. The insanity of alcohol returns and we drink again. And with us, to drink is to die. If we were to live, we had to be free of anger. The grouch and the brainstorm were not for us. They may be the dubious luxury of normal men, but for alcoholics these things are poison.

We turned back to the list. We realized that the people who wronged us were perhaps spiritually sick. Though we did not like their symptoms and the way these disturbed us, they, like ourselves were sick, too. We asked God to help us show them the same tolerance, pity, and patience that we would cheerfully grant a sick friend. When a person offended we said to ourselves "This is a sick man. How can I be helpful to him? God save me from being angry. Thy will be done."

We avoid retaliation or argument. We wouldn't treat sick people that way. If we do, we destroy our chance of being helpful. We cannot be helpful to all people, but at least God will show us how to take a kindly and tolerant view of each and every one.

Referring to our list again, where had we been selfish, dishonest, self-seeking, and frightened? Though a situation had not been entirely our fault, we tried to disregard the other person involved entirely. Where were we to blame?

We reviewed our fears thoroughly. We put them on paper, even though we had no resentment in connection with them. We asked ourselves why we had them. Wasn't it because self-reliance failed us? Self-reliance was good as far as it went, but it didn't go far enough. Some of us once had great self-confidence, but it didn't fully solve the fear problem, or any other. When it made us cocky, it was worse.

Perhaps there is a better way—we think so. For we are now on a different basis; the basis of trusting and relying upon God. We trust infinite God rather than our finite selves. We are in the world to play the role He assigns. Just to the extent that we do as we think He would have us, and humbly rely on Him, does He enable us to match calamity with serenity.

We never apologize to anyone for depending upon our Creator. We can laugh at those who think spirituality the way of weakness. Paradoxically, it is the way of strength. The verdict of the ages is that faith means courage. All men of faith have courage. They trust their God. We never apologize for God. Instead we let Him demonstrate, through us, what He can do. We ask Him to remove our fear and direct our attention to what He would have us be. At once, we commence to outgrow fear.

Now about sex. Many of us needed an overhauling there. But above all, we tried to be sensible on this question. It's so easy to get way off the track. Here we find human opinions running to extremes—absurd extremes, perhaps. One set of voices cry that sex is a lust of our lower nature, a base necessity of procreation. Then we have the voices who cry for sex and more sex; who bewail the institution of marriage; who think that most of the troubles of the race are traceable to sex causes. They think we do not have enough of it, or that it isn't the right kind. They see its significance everywhere. One school would allow man no flavor for his fare and the other would have us all on a straight pepper diet. We want to stay out of this controversy. We do not want to be the arbiter of anyone's sex conduct. We all have sex problems. We'd hardly be human if we didn't. What can we do about them?

We reviewed our own conduct over the years past. Where had we been selfish, dishonest, or inconsiderate? Whom had we hurt? Did we unjustifiably arouse jealousy, suspicion or bitterness? Where were we at fault, what should we have done instead? We got this all down on paper and looked at it.

In this way we tried to shape a sane and sound ideal for our future sex life. Whatever our ideal turns out to be, we must be willing to grow toward it. We must be willing to make amends where we have done harm, provided that we do not bring about still more harm in so doing. In other words, we treat sex as we would any other problem. In meditation, we ask God what we should do about each specific matter. The right answer will come, if we want it.

To sum up about sex: we earnestly pray for the right ideal, for guidance in each questionable situation, for sanity, and for the strength to do the right thing. If sex is very troublesome, we throw ourselves the harder into helping others. We think of their needs and work for them. This takes us out of ourselves. It quiets the imperious urge, when to yield would mean heartache.

In this book you read again and again that faith did for us what we could not do for ourselves. We hope you are convinced now that God can remove whatever self-will has blocked you off from Him. If you have already made a decision, and an inventory of your grosser handicaps, you have made a good beginning. That being so, you have swallowed and digested some big chunks of truth about yourself.

## Chapter Five

# Into Action

Having made our personal inventory, what shall we do about it? We have been trying to get a new attitude, a new relationship with our Creator, and to discover the obstacles in our path. We have admitted certain defects; we have ascertained in a rough way what the trouble is; we have put our finger on the weak items in our personal inventory. Now these are about to be cast out. This requires action on our part, which, when completed, will mean that we have admitted to God, to ourselves, and to another human being, the exact nature of our defects. This brings us to *the fifth step* in the Program of Recovery: discussing our defects with another person.

We think we have done well enough in admitting these things to ourselves. There is doubt about that. In actual practice, we usually find a solitary self-appraisal insufficient. Many of us thought it necessary to go much further. We will be more reconciled to discussing ourselves with another person when we see good reasons to do so. The best reason first: if we skip this vital step, we may not overcome drinking. Time after time newcomers have tried to keep to themselves certain facts about their lives. Trying to avoid this humbling experience, they have turned to easier methods. Almost invariably they got drunk.

They took inventory all right, but hung on to some of the worst items in stock. They only *thought* they had lost their egoism and fear; they only *thought* they had humbled themselves. But they had not learned enough of humility, fearlessness, and honesty, in the sense we find necessary, until they told someone else *all* their life story.

More than most people, the alcoholic leads a double life. He is very much the actor. To the outer world he presents his stage character. This is the one he likes his fellows to see. He wants to enjoy a certain reputation, but knows in his heart he doesn't deserve it.

We must be entirely honest with somebody if we expect to live long or happily in this world. Rightly and naturally, we think well before we choose the person or persons with whom to take this intimate and confidential step. Those of us belonging to a religious denomination that requires confession, must, and of course, will want to go to the properly appointed authority whose duty it is to receive it. Though we have no religious connection, we may still do well to talk with someone ordained by an established religion. We often find such a person quick to see and understand our problem. Of course, we sometimes encounter people who do not understand alcoholics.

If we cannot, or would rather not do this, we search our acquaintance for a close-mouthed, understanding friend. Perhaps our doctor or psychologist will be the person. It may be one of our own family, but we cannot disclose anything to our spouses or our parents that will hurt them and make them unhappy. We have no right to save our own skin at another person's expense. Such parts of our story we tell to someone who will understand, yet be unaffected. The rule is we must be hard on ourself, but always considerate of others.

When we decide who is to hear our story, we waste no time. We have a written inventory, and we are prepared for a long talk. We pocket our pride and go to it, illuminating every twist of character, every dark cranny of the past. Once we have taken this step, withholding nothing, we are delighted. We can look the world in the eye. We can be alone at perfect peace and ease.

Returning home we find a place where we can be quiet for an hour, carefully reviewing what we have done. Carefully rereading the first five proposals we ask if we have omitted anything, for we are building an arch through which we shall walk a free man at last. Is our work solid so far? Are the stones properly in place? Have we skimped on the cement put into the foundation?

If we can answer to our satisfaction, we then look at *step six*. We have emphasized willingness as being indispensable. Are we now ready to let God remove from us all the things that we have admitted are objectionable?

When ready, we say something like this: "My Creator, I am now willing that you should have all of me, good and bad. I pray that you now remove from me every single defect of character that stands in the way of my usefulness to you and my fellows. Grant me strength, as I go out from here, to do your bidding. Amen." We have then completed *step seven*.

Now we need more action without which we find that "Faith without works is dead." Let's look at *steps eight and nine*. We have a list of all persons we have harmed, and to whom we are willing to make amends. We made it when we took inventory. We subjected ourselves to a drastic self-appraisal. Now we go out to our fellows and repair the damage done in the past. If we haven't the will to do this, we ask until it comes. Remember it was agreed at the beginning *we would go to any lengths for victory over alcohol.*

As we look over the list of business acquaintances and friends we have hurt, we may feel diffident about going to some of them on a spiritual basis. Let us be reassured. To some people we need not, and probably should not emphasize the spiritual feature on our first approach. We might prejudice them. At the moment we are trying to put our lives in order. But this is not an end in itself. Our real purpose is to fit ourselves to be of maximum service to God and the people about us. It is seldom wise to approach an individual, who still smarts from our injustice to him, and announce that we have gone religious. In the prize ring, this would be called leading with the chin. Why lay ourselves open to being branded fanatics or religious bores? We may kill a future opportunity to carry a beneficial message. But our man is sure to be impressed with a sincere desire to set right the wrong. He is going to be more interested in a demonstration of good will than in our talk of spiritual discoveries.

The spiritual life is not a theory. *We have to live it.* Unless one's family expresses a desire to live upon spiritual principles we think we ought not to urge them. We should not talk incessantly to them about spiritual matters. They will change in time. Our behavior will convince them more than our words. We must remember that ten or twenty years of drunkenness would make a skeptic out of anyone.

There may be some wrongs we can never fully right. We don't worry about them if we can honestly say to ourselves that we would right them if we could. Some people cannot be seen—we send them an honest letter. And there may be a valid reason for postponement in some cases. But we don't delay if it can be avoided. We should be sensible, tactful, and considerate and humble without being servile or scraping. As God's people we stand on our feet; we don't crawl before anyone.

This thought brings us to *step ten*, which suggests we continue to take personal inventory and continue to set right any new mistakes as we go along. We vigorously commenced this way of living as we cleaned up the past. We have entered the world of Spirit. Our next function is to grow in understanding and effectiveness. This is not an overnight matter. It should continue for our lifetime. Continue to watch for selfishness, dishonesty, resentment, and fear. When these crop up, we ask God at once to remove them. We discuss them with someone immediately and make amends quickly if we have harmed anyone. Then we resolutely turn our thoughts to someone we can help. Love and tolerance of others is our code.

Every day is a day when we must carry the vision of God's will into all of our activities. "How can I best serve Thee—Thy will (not mine) be done." These are thoughts that must go with us constantly. We can exercise our will power along this line all we wish. It is the proper use of the will.

Much has already been said about receiving strength, inspiration, and direction from Him who has all knowledge and power. If we have carefully followed directions, we have begun to sense the flow of His Spirit into us. To some extent we have become God-conscious. We have begun to develop this vital sixth sense. But we must go further and that means more action.

*Step eleven* suggests prayer and meditation. We shouldn't be shy on this matter of prayer. Better men than we are using it constantly. It works, if we have the proper attitude and work at it. It would be easy to be vague about this matter. Yet, we believe we can make some definite and valuable suggestions.

When we retire at night, we constructively review our day. Were we resentful, selfish, dishonest, or afraid? Do we owe an apology? Have we kept something to ourselves which should be discussed with another person at once? Were we kind and loving toward all? What could we have done better? Were we thinking of ourselves most of the time? Or were we thinking of what we could do for others, of what we could pack into the stream of life? But we must be careful not to drift into worry, remorse, or morbid reflection, for that would diminish our usefulness to others. After making our review we ask God's forgiveness and inquire what corrective measures should be taken.

On awakening let us think about the twenty-four hours ahead. We consider our plans for the day. Before we begin, we ask God to direct our thinking, especially asking that it be divorced from self-pity, dishonest or self-seeking motives. Under these conditions we can employ our mental faculties with assurance for after all God gave us brains to use. Our thought life will be placed on a much higher plane when our thinking is cleared of wrong motives.

We ask especially for freedom from self-will, and are careful to make no request for ourselves only. We may ask for ourselves, however, if others will be helped. We are careful never to pray for our own selfish ends. Many of us have wasted a lot of time doing that, and it doesn't work. You can easily see why.

We alcoholics are undisciplined. So we let God discipline us in the simple way we have just outlined.

But this is not all. There is action and more action. "Faith without works is dead." This brings us to the vital importance of step twelve: working with others.

Practical experience shows that nothing will so much ensure immunity from drinking as intensive work with other alcoholics. It works when other activities fail. This is our *twelfth suggestion:* Carry this message to other alcoholics! You can help when no one else can. You can secure their confidence when others fail. Remember they are very ill.

Life will take on new meaning. To watch people recover, to see them help others, to watch loneliness vanish, to see a fellowship grow up about you, to have a host of friends—this is an experience you must not miss. We know you will not want to miss it. Frequent contact with newcomers and with each other is the bright spot of our lives.

To be vital, faith must be accompanied by self-sacrifice and unselfish, constructive action. Let another see that you are not there to instruct him in religion. Admit that he probably knows more about it than you do, but call to his attention the fact that however deep his faith and knowledge, he could not have applied it, or he would not drink. Perhaps your story will help him see where he fails to practice the very precepts he knows so well. We represent no particular faith or denomination. We are dealing only with general principles common to most denominations.

Helping others is the foundation stone of your recovery. A kindly act once in a while isn't enough. You have to act the Good Samaritan every day, if need be. It may mean the loss of many nights' sleep, great interference with your pleasures, interruptions to your business. It may mean sharing your money and your home, counseling frantic wives and relatives, innumerable trips to police courts, sanitariums, hospitals, jails, and asylums. Your telephone may jangle at any time of the day or night.

Your job now is to be at the place where you may be of maximum helpfulness to others, so never hesitate to go anywhere, if you can be helpful. You should not hesitate to visit the most sordid spot on earth on such an errand. Keep on the firing line of life with these motives, and God will keep you unharmed.

We are careful never to show intolerance or hatred of drinking as an institution. Experience shows that such an attitude is not helpful to anyone. Every new alcoholic looks for this spirit among us and is immensely relieved when he finds we are not witch-burners. A spirit of intolerance might repel alcoholics whose lives could have been saved, had it not been for such stupidity. We would not even do the cause of temperate drinking any good, for not one drinker in a thousand likes to be told anything about alcohol by one who hates it.

Someday we hope that Alcoholics Anonymous will help the public to a better realization of the gravity of the alcoholic problem, but we shall be of little use if our attitude is one of bitterness or hostility. Drinkers will not stand for it.

*After all, our problems were of our own making. Bottles were only a symbol. Besides, we have stopped fighting anybody or anything. We have to!*

# The Power of Faith
(1940)

# by Norman Vincent Peale

*The Founding Father of Positive Thinking
On How to Lead a Healthful Life*

## Contents

Introduction  *The Foundations of Positive Thinking* by Mitch Horowitz  650
Chapter One  The Power of Faith  651
Chapter Two  The Hidden Energies of the Mind  656
Chapter Three  Fear, Worry, and Anxiety  662
Chapter Four  Conscience and the Sense of Guilt  667
Chapter Five  Self-Criticism, Failure, and Success  670
Chapter Six  Grief and Sorrow  672
Chapter Seven  The Company of the Lonely  675
Chapter Eight  Love and Marriage  677
Chapter Nine  The Faith That Heals  679

## Introduction
# The Foundations of Positive Thinking

This short book is a condensation of Norman Vincent Peale's first collaboration with psychiatrist Smiley Blanton, originally titled *Faith Is the Answer*. Their 1940 effort presents a valuable summary of Peale's therapeutic theology and of the themes he explored to worldwide notice twelve years later in his *Power of Positive Thinking*.

But in *The Power of Faith* you will discover a different Norman Vincent Peale from the one who later authored one of the world's most popular books.

The authorial voice of *The Power of Faith* reveals the younger Peale not only as a trenchant and elegant writer, but also as a figure of considerable literary breadth. In *The Power of Faith*, Peale effortlessly weaves Scriptural analysis and little-known works of theology with the ethical insights of figures including Marcus Aurelius, William James, Henry Drummond, and Daniel Defoe, as well as the modern voices of his own congregants.

Peale wanted to be understood not only as a theologian of good tidings, but also as a true intellectual, which he was. One of the pains of Peale's life was that, despite his worldwide fame and in some ways because of it, he got rundown in lettered circles after the publication of *The Power of Positive Thinking*. Critics and academics, many of whom I doubt read or more than skimmed Peale's books, often depicted the minister a kind of philosopher for simpletons. This was a profoundly unfair judgment, which I explore in my historical treatment of Peale in *One Simple Idea: How Positive Thinking Reshaped Modern Life*.

*The Power of Faith* is less mystical in nature than many of Peale's later works. The minister had not yet fully immersed himself in the study of New Thought, Science of Mind, Christian Science, and other variants of the mind metaphysics that characterized *The Power of Positive Thinking*. Yet the telltale influence of early twentieth-century French mind theorist Emile Coué appears in *The Power of Faith*. In Peale's chapter on self-criticism he notes, "imagination is stronger than will." That was one of Coué's key insights. Coué noted that our behavioral patterns are dictated by subliminal emotion and self-image much more than by personal determination. Hence, Coué—who coined the mantra "day by day, in every way, I am getting better and better"—considered self-reconditioning essential to the pursuit of a happy and purposeful life. Peale's resonance with this principle warmed him to concepts he later discovered in New Thought, including the therapeutic uses of visualization, prayer, and affirmation. You will see that Peale also examines the Proverb "as a man thinketh," which served as the basis of the spiritual-psychology brought by early New Thought author James Allen in 1903.

Peale and psychiatrist Smiley Blanton originally wrote this book in alternating chapters. My condensation retains only the key points of Peale's own chapters. In some cases, Blanton's considerable psychological insights have been supplanted by more recent developments in neuroscience, cognitive restructuring, and psychopharmacology. But Peale's spiritual observations and Scriptural analyses remain universal, actionable, and revealing of his earliest attitudes toward the therapeutic value of faith.

I believe that in this book you will discover Norman Vincent Peale not only as a deeply appealing storyteller and communicator, but also as a man whose vision of religion as a workable, practical philosophy helped transform the spiritual landscape of the past century—and of our own. His early vision may transform your life, as well.

—Mitch Horowitz

## Chapter One
# The Power of Faith

If I were to tell you that everything troubling you, every weakness, every unhappiness can be eliminated; if I were to declare that everything about your life can be strong and effective, what would be your reaction? Probably many of you would be skeptical or at least wistful, doubtful that such marvelous results are possible. Some people have never had anything great happen to them, so they doubt that it can happen. They suffer from what a great thinker once referred to as "the vast inertia of the soul."

But it is a fact that any person's life can be so completely changed that every crippling thing known and unconscious which interferes with his well-being can be eliminated or effectively controlled. This is no academic assertion but one that can be fully documented from the experiences of many people in whom the most amazing results were obtained. These people learned the technique of faith and so tapped a curative element so potent that no malady of personality could resist its health-giving force. And like many epoch-making processes, it operates simply.

You may develop the art of having faith through two suggestions, if they are faithfully followed: (1) the practice of simple but habitual prayer and devotional meditation; (2) the surrender of your life in childlike trust to the will of God.

We shall now proceed to explain the content and operation of this workable formula.

The late Henry Drummond was one of the superior intellects and scholars of his time. Beyond this, he was a spiritual genius, one of those rare characters who gain acute insight into spiritual laws. Drummond's secret was so simple that anyone can put it into practice. He stated his formula as follows: "Ten minutes spent in Christ's society every day, aye, two minutes, will make the whole day different." Multiply one day by every day and add the cumulative effect of habit and the changed mental outlook, and you will understand how this brief period faithfully observed can change everything, even to your entire life.

We have all known men who have been like saints—strong, radiantly happy. Examination of their daily program reveals regular periods of spiritual meditation. Drummond tells us that a few minutes daily spent in thinking about Christ and in consciously and sincerely seeking to secure his power will make the whole day different. This simple practice gives control over fears, weaknesses, and those tragic ineptitudes which interfere so disastrously with success in life.

Wordsworth was another who discovered the amazing values in a daily period of spiritual meditation. Wordsworth's method was unusual but exceedingly rewarding if we may judge by the quality of his mind and character. It was his custom every day to meditate on a few of Jesus' words, reading them slowly and endeavoring to bring out their full meaning. He would stop and say, "I wonder what Jesus meant when he said that. What was the expression on his face, the tone of his voice?" This approach served to make Christ come near to Wordsworth as a vital living character and to walk with him in his own time.

The hurry and rush of our lives is often advanced as a reason why the daily period of personal prayer and meditation is impossible today. This, of course, is a specious excuse, for we have ample time for what we want to do. It is possible for every person to go apart alone for at least ten minutes every day to relax body, mind, and soul, open himself to God and allow the divine energies to flood his receptive spirit.

There is a quality of the mind through which, with practice, we can retire into ourselves, open a little door, and be in our own quiet inner temple. On a train, or bus, or rushing subway we may close our eyes, turn our minds to Christ and withdraw from the busy world into a few minutes of communion that will give us calm strength and imperturbable poise for the day.

I stress this practice, for it is a certain and workable method for developing faith. The result of this habitual daily meditation is that we come finally to believe absolutely in him and consequently develop a depth of faith that is sure and positive. Live with Christ in daily spiritual associations and your faith in God will be deep and certain. This makes God a real factor rather than a vague concept. An old blind Indian in the West, a magnificent person with inner peace and kindly spirit, revealed the source of his strength when he said, "it is easy to believe in God when you live alone with him in the dark." He knew how to have faith because spiritually he lived with God.

I could write page after page of theory about how to have faith, but I will save you much reading, and myself much labor of writing, by saying that if you will definitely set aside a few minutes, ten or even five, or, as Drummond says, two minutes, to think about God and Christ, to confess your sins, to pray for those who have done wrong against you, and to ask for strength, and if you do this consistently day after day, a true faith will before long begin to send spiritual health and power through your personality.

A Chinese gentleman, a successful broker, recently told his story in our Church Clinic. It was a spiritual narrative, full of tragedy and rising to stirring drama. He came of a wealthy family and had every opportunity that wealth and social connections afford. He ultimately lost his wife through his dissipation and his money went the same way, the bulk of it through gambling. His health failed and a nervous breakdown made him unfit for any except very limited activity. At this juncture he met some people whose joy and delight in life amazed him. It awakened the hope that there might be a way out of his sad failure. They told him the way was by faith, but the advice was futile. Faith was just the thing he did not have either in God, his fellow man, or himself. But he was one of those rare souls who, once being convinced of great possibilities, is not daunted by any obstacle however formidable.

He began a daily plan of communion with God, that being on the advice of a wise friend the sure method of gaining faith. Perseverance was difficult because of his nervous state and the dulled condition of his mind. But he kept at it desperately, feeling it was his last hope. For thirty minutes each morning he gave himself to a period of meditation and asked four questions:

What have I to thank God for during the last twenty-four hours?

What sins have I committed in the last twenty-four hours?

What does God want me to do?

Whom should I pray for?

The first two questions he limited to twenty-four hours because the memory is inclined not to be specific unless the period of analysis is short.

Our Chinese friend's story ended with his finding a restored life. He overcame his disability, his mind began to function with its old time efficiency. He is today a happy man.

Sometimes in my interviews, when deep springs of experience have been opened, I have clearly felt the presence of Christ. It was so when this gentleman asserted his positive conviction that faith in God has remade his entire life, even to his health and business acumen.

And now the second and ultimate method for having faith is simply to have faith. Many people get lost exploring abstruse procedures, unaware that the secret is to believe by an act of trust. It was for this reason that Christ, the supreme Teacher, told us we could not enter his kingdom until we had a childlike heart.

The New Testament says, "According to your faith be it unto you." We receive good in direct proportion to the amount of faith we exercise. "Lord, I believe; help thou my unbelief," is the attitude that opens the door to new life. In plain vernacular that means, "I trust you, O Lord. I believe, even though I cannot see how it can be. I believe even though shadowy questions haunt my mind." The spirit struggles to believe, triumphing over the weak doubtings of the earth-bound body. The release of power that comes with this victory of faith is the most impressive phenomenon of human experience.

I was asked to call on a patient in a tuberculosis hospital. This man said he had been helped by my radio program and wanted to talk with me. I went to see him at considerable expenditure of time, for the hospital was some distance from the city, but it proved to be very worthwhile—one of my most inspiring and enlightening experiences. I found this man lying on a mattress on a board because of the condition of his spine. His hand was off at the wrist, but he was one of the happiest men I ever met all my life long. I who had gone to comfort him was myself comforted, even thrilled by the story he told.

He was taken to the hospital in 1936 and given up to die. He had been a successful lawyer, with a wife and two sons. Everything he owned went into the battle to save his life.

At the time he became hospitalized he was having frequent hemorrhages with severe pain. He was in an apparently hopeless condition. It was at this juncture that he listened to the radio talk in which occurred this quotation from the New Testament, "I can do all things through Christ which strengthens me."

"You said," he explained, "whoever you are, wherever you are, and in whatever condition or circumstance, if you surrender your life completely to God and put your trust in him, you can obtain Divine power by which you can win over anything."

"You also spoke of the amount of faith that would help us. 'Even as a grain of mustard seed.' This seemed to me like a small investment for the return offered."

Looking straight at me, this man said, "I had heard that sort of thing all my life—that is, when I went to church, which was not too often—and it never moved me. In fact," he continued, "I guess I never really knew what it meant. I'm sure I didn't appreciate how deep it went. But this time," he declared, "it came over me as by a wave that it was true. I bowed my head," he went on, "and did just as you said. I guess I was at the end of my rope and I meant it absolutely when I put my life in God's hands. A strange thing happened. I felt a surge of peace. I came to have a conviction that regardless of the number and pain of hemorrhages nothing could ever hurt me again. I went farther, repeating my surrender every day, several times a day, and one day I came to believe that my hemorrhages would stop. That was late in 1936, and in early 1937 they did stop and I've had none to this day." (This conversation took place in 1939.)

With a happy smile, the narrator continued: "I am slowly getting better, but that is not the chief thing that has happened to me. The main thing is the strange new strength, this wonderful inner peace, this absolute sense of being attached to the very power of God himself. We, my family and I, have had to face many difficult problems. Again and again we have been caught in what seemed a blind alley with no way out, but God opened a way every time, and he always will."

I sat there looking at that heroic and inspiring man. I was listening to one of the most amazing accounts of God's grace that has ever come to my attention. We both knew that day that we were talking about no imaginary happening but were awed by the real experience of a man who in his dire need stumbled upon the greatest thing that can happen to a human being—the actual release, through faith, of the power of God into human experience. There is in religious faith and for our benefit a greater power than we realize.

## Chapter Two
# The Hidden Energies of the Mind

Men habitually use only a small part of the powers which they possess and which they might use under appropriate circumstances." The eminent psychologist William James, great genus in understanding personality, said this. Every person has it in him to be far more and accomplish far more, according to this great expert in personality.

Deep within every normal individual is a vast reservoir of untapped power waiting to be used. In most of us only a small trickle of power is seeping to the surface, and on that we live and do our work. It is little wonder that many of us are tired and unhappy, frustrated and ineffectual. A sixteen-cylinder car, if it possessed feeling and reason, would not be very happy, or in any sense satisfactory, if it went sputtering and limping along on one cylinder. That is exactly what most of us are doing. This book is intended to help people learn and practice the secret of using all their power and ability.

The first step toward being what you can be is to know what you are. That is to say, no man can have the use of all his potential power until he learns to understand himself. The trouble with so many people who fail in this life is that they go through the world thinking deep within them that they are ordinary, commonplace persons. Thus, having no fundamental belief in themselves, they dissipate their energies in undisciplined living. Such persons live aimless and erratic lives very largely because they never had a glimpse of what life really can be and what they can become. There exist possibilities for successful living in the unconscious mind. How can they be released and how can religion help?

A man has a good book in his hand when he turns the pages of the Bible. Why does the Bible retain its hold on humanity after hundreds of years? The answer, of course, is that the Bible contains more than any book ever written, the most astute insight into, and knowledge of, human beings.

In it is a story of a young man who became fed up on the orderly, decent life at the old home, and, getting a sizable sum of money from his father, went off and drank it up. We are told he went into "a far country," which is indeed an apt description. It is a far country, for some get so far into it they never get back. But this boy did get back. When his money was gone, his job lost, and he had gone the rounds of his associates getting only the cold shoulder, "He came to himself," as the Bible says with eloquent finality.

Here is an example of the remarkable insight of the Bible. Here is a man, ruining himself not because he was wicked, but because he was ignorant about himself. When he came to himself, when he came to his senses, he had the inestimable thrill of self-discovery. He saw, as in a flash, that he was on the wrong track; that he was really throwing his energies, his abilities, and his future away. "He came to himself" and saw with sharp discernment what he was and what he could become. Then, continues the Bible, he said, "I will arise." From then on life is an onward, upward movement. It becomes aggressive, victorious living.

Christianity is coming to be more widely recognized every day as possessing the surest techniques for helping people realize themselves. It has an astounding genius for touching men's ordinary lives and unlocking doors behind which their personalities have long atrophied. Many people have the mistaken notion that religion restricts and imprisons. On the contrary, sin does that, while religion swings open the door and invites men out to freer and happier lives. An old hymn sings of Christ, "He sets the prison free," and that, of course, is what many ineffectual people are—prisoners. They are prisoners of the senses, prisoners of social customs, prisoners of themselves. Christ sets them free, when, coming to themselves, they say, "I will arise and go to my Father."

One element in the adventure of self-discovery is to become aware of our innate goodness. Whether you are prepared to admit it or not, you *are* a good person basically. No man can go far in unworthy living without provoking the increasing protests of the finer self. It is impossible for any man long to escape the relentless challenge of the great personality in his soul.

Some years ago a distinguished playwright wrote a play that bore the title, *Six Characters in Search of an Author.* This was Luigi Pirandello. The play pictured a rehearsal at which several characters came bursting in, demanding to be played by the actors. That is an accurate picture of our lives. On our life's stage great characters burst out from within us demanding to identify themselves with us, to perform in us before the world.

Nathanial Hawthorne left among his papers an outline of a play, which he never wrote, but which intrigues us with its possibilities. It was to be a play in which the principal character never appears. Hawthorne with his superb genius could have made much of such an idea, but he did not have to write it for us, for you and I have lived it often enough. It is tragic to think of a man playing on the stage of life only the minor, and often unworthy, parts that are in him. He is the bigot, the coward, the defeated spirit, the sinner, the liar, or the cheat. But for a man never to play the principal character within himself—that is tragical. Never to perceive and act the hero in his life; never to see the Galahad within him, never to see the saint in him—that is deepest tragedy; that is indeed to have the principal character never appear.

In every weak person there is a strong person. In every evil person is a good person. In every defeated person is a victorious person. To become aware of this nobility and power within ourselves, is to know and to be able to practice the Art of Living.

This adventure of self-discovery is working out along another great line. Many people are discovering through their religious faith that in themselves there is a great old rugged character whom no one can discourage or defeat. Many modern people whom I happen to know had received so many blows and hard knocks that the come-back spirit, had all but gone from them. They were about ready to admit they were defeated and that they could do nothing about it except complain and grow bitter.

I have seen scores, even hundreds, of men and women turn to religious faith in earnest attempt to get power into their lives. I have seen them come, saying, "Lord, I am run down, my life is empty, circumstances are too strong for me—I can no longer do anything by my own strength." Then I have seen them do the wisest thing in the world, which is to turn the switch and contact the circuit of creative spiritual energy; that is, to put their lives, with all problems, completely into God's hands. This they have done, with wholehearted faith that God is interested in them and will turn his power into their lives like water into a reservoir long empty and dry. In the Bible we read, "But as many as received him, to them gave he power," and so He does, and modern people are finding out this great secret in increasing numbers every day.

A young businessman in his late thirties told me his experience. He was brought up in a devout home, but like many others, drifted away from the religious life in college days. Later he married and got into business and social life, and the church would see him at Easter, but that was about all. His connection with spiritual values was exceedingly tenuous. Then hard times came. Business grew difficult. His domestic situation became complicated. His and his wife's life were rooted only in material things, and such roots are insecure. To sum it up, his life crashed in on him and his courage ran out. Life had rained blow after blow upon him, and it was almost more than the spirit could bear.

Then he encountered a radiant personality who seemed to possess a depth of peace and confidence in a situation not unlike his own, a man who was not beaten. On the contrary, he was overcoming adversity by an unwavering perseverance and sustained attack. My friend saw that this man was being fed by what seemed an unfailing stream of power. He asked the secret and the answer was, Christ.

"Why, I have always believed in Christ," my friend said.

"Yes," the other man replied, "but have you ever absolutely and completely given yourself into his hands?"

My friend was forced to admit that he hadn't, but that state didn't last long. He turned to Christ in faith. Live wires now tap his personality and a spiritual transformer has stepped up his physical and mental energy. He said an interesting thing to me recently.

"All my life," he declared, "I have been more or less around religion, but it always seemed a rather dead thing to me. Strange, how different it is now." And then he concluded, "But one thing is sure, when you actually take it into your life spiritually, it does everything it says it will."

Layer upon layer of childhood influences form in the unconscious mind the basis of our moral nature. Religion attempts to govern the fundamental instincts and impulses by saturating the mind with spiritual ideals to such an extent that the automatic functioning of a man's life will be on a basis of strength and goodness. Religion teaches us to allow only good and beautiful thoughts to enter the unconscious because of the obvious fact often demonstrated that the unconscious can only send back what was first sent down. Let in bad thoughts freely and bad motivation will be sent back. Habitually send in thoughts of an elevated nature and the unconscious will inevitably return attitudes and actions of a corresponding quality.

As William James pointed out, the molecules and cells of our bodies and brains are storing up day by day every action, emotion, and thought to use either for or against us, quite automatically, in crises which ultimately arrive.

The Bible expresses the deepest insight into human nature in a well-known phrase, "As he thinketh in his heart, so is he." That is one of the profoundest truths ever set down for man's guidance. The word "heart" is used to describe the inmost part of man's thought and feeling; in all likelihood what the modern psychiatrist refers to as "the unconscious." That is to say, a man is in the last analysis what he has been predominantly sending into the controlling center of his life.

The ideas or thoughts which finally determine our actions and character are not those which we receive and examine in the conscious mind. It is not "as a man thinketh in his conscious mind" that constitutes his personality. That is only a receiving station, or perhaps it can be compared to a reception office, where thoughts, good, bad, and innocuous, are examined and passed upon. Some are rejected. If these rejected thoughts are evil, their temporary presence in the conscious mind has done little if any harm. If they are good thoughts, they have had little opportunity to have any effect. But the thought, good or bad, which is received hospitably and is ushered into the mind repeatedly with a welcome, becomes eventually the thought a man "thinketh in his heart," and presently it may be said, "So is he."

People come to us complaining of having what they describe as "bad thoughts." These are thoughts of hate, or immorality, or dishonesty, or sometimes even murder. These people are troubled by the feeling that the thought which passed through the mind has made them guilty of sin. Sometimes they have quoted the Biblical passage, "Whosoever looketh on a woman to lust after her, hath committed adultery with her already in his heart."

No sin is committed if a thought enters the mind, provided it is not made welcome. The thought first passes into an anteroom, where it stands before the mind acting as a judge. No matter how sordid or evil, it has not touched the personality with its infamy or in any way laid guilt upon the soul unless and until the mind acting as judge admits it with a welcome. If the mind decides against it and dismisses it, the personality is not only unsullied, but is, on the contrary, by this act of rejection stimulated and strengthened in moral power. You cannot prevent the birds from flying over your head but you can keep them from building nests in your hair.

A thought that enters the mind, is weighed and rejected, and is passed, condemned, from the mind, leaves no stain of guilt but instead greatly increases spiritual power.

There can be no doubt that Jesus held this point of view, for in the passage quoted above the phrase, "Looketh on a woman to lust after her" does not imply a passing and unadmitted impure thought but a definitely entertained desire. The word "lust," which is the important word in the passage, means a premeditated and active attitude implying an idea welcomed and pleasurably entertained.

In my experience as pastor I have known many people whose lives were made exceedingly unhappy by their failure to make this wholehearted distinction between the evil thought examined and rejected and an evil thought accepted and entertained.

Consideration of this problem, which affects so many people, makes it plain that a conscious mind, clear, penetrating, morally discriminating and vigorous, standing guard over the unconscious mind, is profoundly essential equipment for happy and effective living.

That which is received and accepted by the conscious mind determines ultimately the automatic reaction of the unconscious and in effect may be summed up as character. Before every deed there is a thought or more properly a succession of thoughts. Before the thief steals with his hand he steals with his mind. Before the immoral act is preformed the mind has already committed the offense. If the thought of a wrong act has never been favorably entertained by the mind, the act itself will never take place. The issue is determined, not at the moment of crisis by rational and objective thinking, but by the resistance or lack of it in the unconscious, a resistance which has been strengthened or weakened each time the conscious mind rejected or accepted the thought.

In a certain small town one family had operated the local bank for three generations. Grandfather, father, and son in succession had filled the important position of banker to the community. The family was held in the highest esteem and respect. The Great Depression came, and the son, who had become president of the bank, had been lured by the speculation mania sweeping the country and had overtaxed his ability to meet his obligations. He had to have money.

One night, alone in the bank, the thought of falsifying the books came to him, but he resolutely put it aside. It returned again and again. No one would ever know. He could make good out of his earnings before the bank examiners would discover the default. The pressure became great. In other relationships, as it later appeared, he had played fast and loose with fidelity. His inner supports had been weakened.

The unconscious could only return what he had given it, and one night the hand crept out hesitantly but surely to perform the deed which sent him to the penitentiary and broke the long and honored tradition of a fine family.

"As he thinketh in his heart, so is he." What we are will eventually appear. The mask will some day slip from the face. The truth will out.

In the unconscious are all the forces which make for our success or failure, our misery or our happiness. These forces according to their strength control the mind, determining our choices and decisions. In the unconscious lie hidden energies which can defeat us if not understood and properly used but which wisely used can endow us with great power. Religion says that when these hidden energies are brought under the influence of Christ as Master of life, the most amazing results appear in people whose lives were hitherto commonplace or defeated.

By the phrase "coming under the influence of Christ" we mean the acceptance of Christ's way of life as our own. Further than that, it requires an attitude which we like to call spiritual experience. The standard word for it is "conversion." It is a surrender of self to God by an act of faith, a wholehearted readiness to follow God's will.

This spiritual experience goes deeply into the personality laying a controlling hand upon the unconscious mind, the inner life force, holding firmly in check the destructive elements and releasing the hidden energies to produce a person of wisdom and power.

## Chapter Three
# Fear, Worry, and Anxiety

There are many businessmen in America today who are failing in business or not getting ahead. The free functioning of their intellectual and emotional capacities is inhibited by anxiety and fear. Here, for example, is a man who goes down to his office in the morning and sits down to a desk full of business.

This man needs to be able to draw upon every bit of his mental equipment in order to dispose effectively of the problems before him. But he is haunted by anxiety and fear. He is worried about the condition of the stock market, about meeting the payroll, or about holding his job. He worries about the war in Europe or the condition of this country. He worries about his family, or how to meet the payments on his home. He worries about whether he has heart trouble or high blood pressure, or fears that some sin he committed will catch up with him and put its bony and terrifying finger into his business to his undoing. His powers should be drawn to a focus as the divergent rays of the sun are caught by the glass and brought to a point of heat. But his powers are drawn off in a score of different directions by the wide sprouting of his anxieties, and the emotional and mental energy which he needs for success is lacking. Deeply buried anxiety in the unconscious mind is the cause of an astoundingly large number of inefficient and desultory careers in our time.

"What is courage?" a small boy recently asked his mother, and then added, "Is it like our cat when he arches his back and spits when he is afraid?"

His mother tried to think of a way to make the real meaning of courage clear to her son, for she believed that the first and finest lesson that parents can teach little children is courage. She took him for a long walk in the country, and they finally came to a place where a destructive forest fire had raged. In a blackened, fire-swept field they saw one little red flower.

Pointing to that little, courageous, optimistic red flower, she said, "There is courage, my son—a fragile red flower growing in a fire-swept land." It is a good symbol of courage. Soon or late, the fires of adversity will roar across the life of each one of us, and in the blackened desolation that remains it will be hard to see any hope, but in that hour we must project the flower of courage in a fire-swept land. That one flower of courage will be the forerunner of restored life.

What is the cure for anxiety and fear? How many have this kind of courage? The best answer to that question is not any comment of mine or suggestion from the experts but is a statement found in the Bible which reads, "Take no thought for your life, what ye shall eat, or what ye shall drink; nor yet for your body, what ye shall put on . . . But seek ye first the kingdom of God and his righteousness; and all these things shall be added unto you."

What does that mean? It means that we are not to worry about the necessities of life, but to strive for inner peace and mental, emotional, and spiritual harmony, developing an organized and integrated personality which will be able to meet life so effectively that these necessary things will indeed "be added unto you." This admonition from the Bible implies what is directly stated in many other Scripture references—that an habitual resting of our worries upon the goodness of God through real faith releases a power into our lives which is not of this world, the power of God, through which we accomplish what otherwise would be impossible.

One of the practical ways of putting into practice this wise advice is to develop the habit of not talking about our anxieties and our worries. The average anxious person is constantly telling everybody how worried and apprehensive he is about everything. It should be recalled that speech has greater effect on emotion than thinking has. An actor, for example, can talk himself into the desired emotions he wishes to portray. Get your anxiety out of your general conversations and it will tend to drop out of your mind. On the other hand, it is advisable to go to someone who has the insight and skill to help you become free from your worries.

Go to your minister, or your priest, or your rabbi, or to your psychiatrist and unburden yourself. Tell everything that is on your heart, including your sins, real and imaginary, the haunting sense of guilt, and every suppressed desire. This confession, this unburdening of yourself will throw sunlight into every dark corner of the mind, drive out the shadows, bring blessed relief, and open the way for complete healing of the malady of anxiety.

Religion is a practical method for solving this problem. Many people do not understand present-day religious practice; they think of it as something dull and musty, quite remote from real life. Thereby they miss the one thing that could make them happy and successful and useful. Some time ago I was in the police station—a voluntary visit—and in talking with the burly sergeant I told him I had just given a radio talk on "How Religion Can Conquer Nervousness." He was astounded and said: "I never heard of religion having anything to do with nervousness. I thought religion was just going to church and acting as decent as you can."

"Go read your Bible," I replied, "and you will find religion is a medicine for every human ill."

"I sure will," he said, "because if religion can do what you say, I'll have to try a little."

It will do everything it claims to do for the man who really tries it.

How does the fact that we turn to God in trust and faith relieve us of our fears? For one thing, when a man gets his mind on God, he gets it off himself. Fears, in reality, accompany excessive thinking about oneself. They are nurtured by the ego-centered attitude as a nest is warmed by a sitting hen. Our minds sit on the nest of our real and imaginary fears, and they grow up rapidly. We need to engage in more physical activity and less introspection if we are to eliminate fear from our lives.

Mary Ellen Chase writes in *The Good Fellowship*: "Manual labor to my father was not only good and decent for its own sake, but, as he was given to saying, it straightened out one's thoughts—a contention which I have since proved on many occasions; indeed, the best antidote I know to a confused head or to tangled emotions is to work with one's hands. To scrub a floor has alleviated many a broken heart, and to wash and iron one's clothes has brought order and clarity to many a perplexed and anxious mind."

For this reason a well-known psychologist very wisely advised a young man to run around the block every night until he was dead tired, as an effective means toward conquering his fears.

But there are other and better things to do to conquer fear than run around the block. The one sure method of eradicating fear from the mind is by surrendering one's life to God. By that I mean avoiding the mistake of attempting to pluck fear out by a process of effort and struggle or by power of will. This only serves to implant it more firmly in the consciousness. The surrender of life to God means that all fear and worry is laid before Him and the future is left in His hands in perfect trust. We are then able to avoid any worried thought for the morrow, for God knows our needs and will take care of us.

For my part, I have found it absolutely true that when I sincerely put my life in God's hands and trust him to take care of me, he does so with amazing fidelity and kindliness. This is one of the greatest secrets in the world. It gives any man peace and strength beyond calculation. Let all your fears go—give them to God. He will not let you down. Did you ever carry a tired child in your arms? You will recall the complete relaxation of the little body. The child rests in your arms perfectly free from tension. There is in him no fear that he will be dropped. Feeling this trust, you hold the little form all the closer and with the greater care, for you cannot fail such complete confidence.

If this kind of love and faith passes between grown-ups and tired, sleepy children, how much more profoundly does God take to his heart adults who are tired and worn in the dark nights of this life?

A stout heart and a courageous spirit constitute a basic necessity for this life. Samuel Johnson understood this fact when he said that courage is the primary virtue! "Unless a man have that virtue, he has no security for preserving any other."

I once spoke to the students of a New England university, and afterward went home to dinner with an old and very wise professor. As we sat by the fire that stormy day, he presented me with a little book by J.M. Barrie, saying, "You will need this often. Make a companion of it."

He was right. It was Barrie's famous essay on "Courage," and I have always kept it nearby. Its deep philosophy, written in his inimitable style, has meant much when my courage has ebbed. In it, among other things, Barrie says: "Pray for courage with your daily bread, for courage will keep you lighthearted and gay and you must keep lighthearted and gay."

How to have courage is a practical problem faced by every reader of this volume.

In a terrifying scene, Lady Macbeth—strong, masterful as well as cruel—strove to buttress her husband's ebbing courage. "But if we fail?" he asked, timorously. "Screw your courage to the sticking-place," she belligerently declared, "and we'll not fail." Granted that this illustration comes through the commission of a famous crime, it nevertheless portrays an important fact about life. There come times when courage ebbs and some more vigorous personality may admonish us to screw our courage to the sticking place. That is exactly what we must do—but how to do it?

One of the most pathetic things in the world is to see human beings struggling against great odds, trying desperately to screw their courage to the sticking place. It is pathetic, but it is also inspiring, for it reveals the magnificent heroism of the average man. The more we watch people fighting gallantly against discouragement and hardship and pain and fear, the more wonderful we feel they are. The great need of this life is to develop courage.

Many people miss the best rewards of life simply because of their inability to screw their courage to the sticking place and keep it there until the game is won. Browsing through an old library recently, I came across a book written by a very wise man of a bygone generation. The book told a story showing that ebbing courage has been a problem in every generation.

Its author had a friend who had acquired a claim in a far Western gold field. The claim was in a lonely spot in the mountains. When the friend started to dig for gold, he found evidence that much work had been done on the claim a long while before. Farthest in, in the excavation he found an old rusted pick, its handle rotted off but its point sticking firmly in the rocky soil. He threw the pick aside and went to work and to his amazement, just a few feet beyond where he had found it, he came upon a rich vein of gold. He could not escape thinking about the tragedy of the old pick, and sometime later he heard the story.

A prospector had learned of the probability of a rich strike in this locality, had staked out his claim and had gone to work. Day after day, until his back ached unbearably, he worked with his pick, but never a glimpse of gold did he see. Gradually, the acid of discouragement crept through his system, eating away his resolution. His courage slowly ebbed, and one day in desperation, and with a sense of complete futility, he drove his pick hard into the rocky earth, gathered up his belongings, and went away. The passing years rusted the pick and ate away the handle.

The tragedy of ebbing courage which failed just short of success, was not revealed until the prospector of our story many years later came and found, a few feet farther on, the vein which would have fallen to the first man had he been able to solve the problem of failing courage. The man is fortunate indeed who, no matter how desperate his condition, how unpromising his prospects, still has growing within his soul the red flower of courage.

What is the secret of this kind of courage? When courage fails the secret is to fill your mind and saturate your consciousness with simple and trusting faith in God. I emphasize this procedure, for it is the heart of the problem of fear.

There is a quotation from the Bible which every man with ebbing courage would do well to hang on his bedroom wall, where he could look at it every morning before starting out to face the day's struggle and every evening so that it might leaven his unconscious mind as he slept. That great sentence is this, "In all these things we are more than conquerors through him that loved us."

Now, I do not mean to say that every person who belongs to the church, or who believes academically in God, has the kind of faith that keeps courage from ebbing. But I do say that every individual I have ever known who truly practices the faith of the New Testament always kept a sturdy heart. I have never yet known a man who believes in and practices—and the emphasis is on "practices"—sincere faith in God to be defeated. I can produce scores of present-day people, young and old, from every walk of life who will tell you from their own experience that they have discovered that it is absolutely a fact that they have become more than conquerors "through him that loved us."

## Chapter Four
# Conscience and the Sense of Guilt

An impressive line in Axel Munthe's book, *The Story of San Michele*, says, "A man can stand a lot as long as he can stand himself. He can live without hope, without books, without friends, without music as long as he can listen to his own thoughts." Because this is so patently true, the wise thing, the absolutely necessary thing for every man is to cultivate at all costs a self with which he can live in peace and happiness. He must look to his conscience and eradicate the sense of guilt.

One thing is sure, whether you like it or not, you have to live with yourself. Goethe once said, "Beloved brother, let us not forget that a man can never get away from himself."

Lord Byron, when fleeing from England, heartbrokenly asked: "What exile from himself can flee?"

Indeed, it is a fact that a man may flee from other men and from familiar scenes and the obligations of life, and may even become a recluse in an obscure corner of the earth, he may turn his back on the social conventions and on early training and beliefs, but from himself there is no escape. I saw in a newspaper an account of a young man who was attempting to flee after having done a great wrong. He traveled the world over, but finally said this pathetic thing, "Everywhere I go I am still myself, and I myself am the penalty for the wrong I have done."

This is one of the inescapable facts of life—you have to live with what you are. For some this may be described as heaven; for others, it is literally hell. For some it is romance; for others it is intolerable boredom. In some men happiness and delight well up out of their hearts. They are alive and vibrant with the sheer joy of living. Life for them is an ever-fresh adventure. Every morning means a fresh beginning, every evening brings the deep satisfaction of a day richly lived. Such men are constantly finding within themselves unexplored riches and fresh sources of happiness. It is a joy to live with a self like that.

There are other men for whom it is not so. They have divided and conflicting personalities. In them is a contentious internecine spirit. They are at odds with themselves most of the time. They are like one of the characters in a modern novel about whom the author says, "He was not a personality, he was a civil war." Theirs is a self which desires to do right, but all too readily acquiesces in evil. Theirs is a self stung by remorse and haunted by a sense of guilt over past misdeeds. Theirs is a self which is horribly conscious of self because it is concerned only with self. To live with a self like that is hell. Nor is there any evasion, any escape. We have to live with what we are.

In the light of this grace and inescapable fact it becomes evident that the supremely important thing is to develop a self with which we can live satisfactorily. Since whether we like it or not we do have to live with ourselves, we profoundly want to become good company for ourselves. Each of us wants to be able to enjoy the self we have to live with.

The soul becomes apparent only as it develops. We are continuously building up or breaking down the self with which we were born. Through the years every thought, every emotion, every experience contributes to the quality of the self. No matter how old we are, or how set we may be, our self is in the making. We are all in the continuous process of creating the self we have to live with. Everything contributes to its greatness or littleness. You will remember Tennyson's discerning remark, "I am part of all I have met." By the same token everything we have met is part of us.

Winfred Rhodes, the helpful writer, expressed it in a great phrase, "Life's greatest achievement is the continual remaking of your self so that at last you know how to live." This constant process of self-development is expressed in such everyday remarks as: "How he has grown!" or "He is not the man he used to be."

These remarks represent a statement of the fact that we are constantly developing, whether for good or bad.

How go about developing a self we can live with happily, a self free from the domination of a wounded conscience and carrying a sense of guilt? We could indulge in much theory and speculation at this point, but a more effective method is to analyze an actual specimen in the laboratory of life. Let us take a man who had tremendous difficulty living with himself, but who solved the problem so effectively that he became one of the greatest men of all time. He is the eminent thinker, philosopher, and leader in the Christian Church, Paul, the apostle. He was a man who, by his own admission, suffered acute inner conflict and division. He once cried, "O wretched man that I am! Who shall deliver me from the body of this death?"

That is a very graphic description of inner conflict. He evidently had trouble with his good intentions too, for he complained that "The good that I would I do not: but the evil which I would not, that I do." But he won his fight with himself, and finally at the end of a life of heroic proportions, great in achievement but studded with pain, shipwreck, stonings, beatings, and prison, ending in martyrdom, he was able to say: "I have fought a good fight, I have finished my course, I have kept the faith." The man who said that was a man at peace with himself, who had developed a self with which he could live with profound inner contentment.

And what was his secret? It is expressed in these words, without which no explanation of this great life is possible: "I live; yet not I, but Christ liveth in me." That is to say, his life was now centered not in his divided and inharmonious personality, but in Christ, in whom are no divisions nor conflicts. Christ became the center around which his personality organized itself, and so the divisions in Paul's personality were healed and he became a self with whom it was pleasant for him to live.

Psychiatrists are now saying what the ministers have always said, that a clear mind, free of, or forgiven for, wrongdoing, is essential to the harmonious organization of a man's personality. Marcus Aurelius, one of the world's wisest men, knew the truth of these things. "The one thing worth living for," he declared, "is to keep one's soul pure."

The right may also be determined on the basis of results. Is wrong workable? Is it sensible? Seneca wisely declared, "If thou wouldst bring all things under subjection, subject thyself to reason." Jesus said to the man who sinned, "Thou fool, this night thy soul shall be required of thee."

Men afterward say, "I was a fool to have done that." It is not "the morning after" that is most tragic but "the years afterward."

A good skill to develop is a capacity for moral previewing, the ability to foresee the result; to project the mind ahead and see how a thing will look after it is done. A man thinking about committing a sin would do well to practice reading about it as if it had afterward become public.

The first function of religion, and I believe of psychiatry too, is to point the way to happier lives by teaching men and women how to cope with a sense of guilt which is due to their own unwisdom.

Psychiatry uses its own method of diagnosis and treatment.

Religion brings to distressed minds the knowledge of God's forgiveness and thus of the peace that passeth all understanding.

## Chapter Five
# Self-Criticism, Failure, and Success

A distinguished statesman said that in his youth he heard one sentence which, through the later years, had done him no end of good. He has, he declared, repeated it frequently all his adult life, and it has proved a marvelous source of strength. The sentence is: "You can become strongest in your weakest place."

It is a good sentence and states two important things about you and me. First, it calls attention to the obvious fact that we have weak places and a weakest place. Of course we do not like to admit that fact; we prefer to dwell on our strong points. We do not like to be honest with ourselves.

It is not easy to be absolutely honest with ourselves owing to what psychiatrists call rationalization. That is, we have a tendency not to be objective in our attitude toward ourselves. We set our minds to work, not upon dealing with the facts as they are, but upon inventing rational reasons for our courses of conduct. Our unconscious minds play tricks on us, and unless we watch our minds they will deceive us, keeping us from being entirely honest with ourselves, from realizing that we have weak places.

Second, the sentence tells us that we can be strongest in our weakest place. It does not say that we may become merely strong in the places where we are now weak, but that we may become strongest in the place which is now our weakest spot. Some of the tribes of Africa believe that when one man vanquishes another, the strength of the vanquished passes into the victor and he thereby becomes that much stronger. When you conquer a weakness, the strength that lies in that weakness, its power over you, passes into you. Each time you overcome the weakness you acquire an additional part of its strength. Its strength is diminished with each victory and your strength is correspondingly increased.

The ultimate result is the complete destruction of your weakness and your acquisition of the strength it had over you. When we vigorously set ourselves to overcome a weakness which we recognize, the direct campaign which we wage tends to bring all of our forces into play at that point. We concentrate a great measure of strength at our weakest point, making it our strongest.

Let the process known as "welding" illustrate the thought. Welding is a process in which two pieces of metal are fused at their point of contact, making a joint that is usually stronger than the parent metal itself. Intense heat is applied at the point of contact. The intense heat and resulting fusion makes the point that was weak stronger than any other.

We should keep in mind that the tendency of our personality is to palliate, to excuse and to defend our weaknesses. At times we need to be jarred out of ourselves, so as to see ourselves with such distinctness that our minds will be forced to honestly accept the fact of our woeful weakness. Holding this realization firmly in mind, attack your weakest place with determination and it will become your strongest place.

Here is an example from everyday life of the operation of the power of faith. A young man came to see me and said he had an insatiable appetite for alcohol which was fast destroying his effectiveness in business. His craving was so great that several times he had arisen in the middle of the night to get himself a drink. A psychiatrist would probably have diagnosed his case as "the will to fail,"—that is, that, basically, he wanted to fail. That is not infrequently the correct assumption in such cases. He wanted me to pray with him, comfort him, and urge him to go out and fight a fight which he confidently expected to lose, and then, having failed, come back for more prayer and more comfort. After he did just that several times, I told him there was no use trying and advised him not to try. He was amazed at this, and I explained that the gospel really does not urge us to try harder, but to believe harder. If the gospel did otherwise, it would be only for those of strong will. The only fight it urges is the fight of faith, the struggle to believe.

I assured him that however much he stirred up his will to succeed, he would probably fail because he visualized himself as failing. His will might heroically declare, "I will," but at the same time his imagination whispered, "I cannot." And because imagination is stronger than will, his will would lose. He needed to imagine himself not to be failing but winning. His faith needed to paint that picture firmly on his inner consciousness. So I asked him to believe by an act of pure faith that he would vanquish his craving—not tomorrow, or sometime in the future, but to believe that by the grace of God he was that very minute freed from its domination.

"According to your faith, be it done unto you," said Christ. He asked me if I was certain of that, and I assured him that I was. By an act of faith he accepted the idea, and whatever were the mental operations involved in the process, the fact remains that at the end of the month he told me he had not had the slightest desire for alcohol. Now, at the end of a year and a half he has had no recurrence of the desire. The moral lesion was healed by so great a curative force that no vestige of diseased tissue remains. What fruitless struggle could not do was accomplished by the tremendous power of faith in Christ. Any problem of this life can be successfully handled if by faith we merely open our minds to the power of God.

## Chapter Six

# Grief and Sorrow

Some years ago I had a friend, a great soul. He was a big man, big physically and big of heart. One stormy night his home telephone rang and at the other end was the agonized voice of an acquaintance who had just had great tragedy come to him. It was one of the most terrible tragedies that can happen to a man, the discovery of the infidelity of a beloved wife. She had gone, left his home. He was alone in the dawning knowledge that her love was a broken thing. Piteously, like a child in the dark, his heart dead within him, he called my friend over the telephone. My friend immediately got out his car, drove for a good many miles through the storm to this man's home, and found him bowed in hopeless grief. My friend walked in without a word, went up to the broken man, put his great arms about him, pulled him up close and said, "Come with me."

They gathered up a few of his belongings and got into the tight little car where the man sat with his shoulder pressed against my big bulky friend. The stricken man told me, afterward, that as they drove through the night not a word was spoken. What could be said? The unspoken attitude of human sympathy had to speak the message, and he said that as he looked upon the strong, kindly face of his friend, lighted by the dim glow of the dash light, and reflected in the windshield, there came over him a great sense of peace and protection and calm comfort. My friend had thrown his tabernacle over him. So God, who loves us with an infinite love, has spread his tabernacle over our dear departed loved ones.

Death has always been pictured as a dark angel, as a sinister figure. I wonder if the metaphor of going home to a mother, to a father, isn't a better and more accurate one. I know a man who, in the struggle in these difficult days in the heart of a great city, became overwhelmed with trouble. He is a strong, resourceful man, but life hit him many blows, and the going became exceedingly hard. He felt a deep and irresistible desire to go back to his boyhood home and have a visit with his aged mother.

He wanted, somehow, to recapture the enthusiasm and zest of life which had been drained from his spirit. Streaks of gray were beginning to show in his hair, and as Charles Lamb once said, "Our spirits grow gray before our hair," so it was with this man.

He told me afterward that he went back to the old home, and his mother, like mothers in every age and in every place, wanted to feed him, give him a good dinner such as he used to have. She put food and drink before him and talked to him about old-fashioned, intimate family matters. She was slaking his thirst, and feeding the deeper hunger of his life. As he sat at the table, as she passed by, she put her hands, soft and tender and wrinkled, on his head as if she knew the burden he carried and the pain in his heart, and was trying as only a mother can to wipe away the tears from his eyes.

He said that in the quietness of that place peace came over him and a new enthusiasm for living came stealing back into his heart. What we often find in a mother or in a loving father here on earth, our dead have found in the great mother heart, in the great father heart of God. Their eyes, closed in death, have opened in the light of an eternal home.

So I say to you who mourn, that if we are to believe the Scriptures, and I know that we can believe them, we may be sure that those whom we have "loved long since and lost awhile" are happy and peaceful and contented, for they are in the Father's house and the Father is with them.

Jesus once said, "In my Father's house are many mansions: If it were *not so*, I would have told you. I go to prepare a place for you, . . . that where I am, there ye may be also." He is there, and wherever he is cannot be other than a place of beauty and happiness and peace. Thus sorrow is lifted by our faith in the goodness of God.

But there is another and profound source of grief which we must consider. It is very common and is subtle, for the average person does not think of it as a deep grief resting upon the spirit, subtracting from life its color and enjoyment. Deep-centered grief often emanates from a loss of ideas and of faith.

Many people are trying to satisfy deep hungers and do not know how to do it. The only way that has occurred to some is loose living, compromised morality, and even dissipation. But apparently that method is proving a sad disappointment, for in ever-increasing numbers, people, and particularly younger people—for they are still honest and frank—are turning to religious experience as the only sure antidote for redundant boredom. Here is a generation in confusion, which has lost its way, not only with regard to its collective economic and social life, but also in its individual life. It may be said that multitudes have "come to grief" because their ideals have been lost.

What is the answer to this tragic condition? There is only one thinker who has the answer, the wisest man who ever lived, a man named Jesus Christ. What does he have to say? He says, and the statement shows magnificent insight, uncanny genius: "The kingdom of God is within you." What did he mean by that?

In each of us is God. If we reject him, he is still there in us just the same, for he never rejects us. But unless we give him control of our inward life he can do little for us. Weak as we are, we have the power to render the God in us ineffective. The minute a man says with sincerity to God within him, "you take control," that very minute he realizes the kingdom of God within him, and radiant life begins for him. The secret of happiness lies in exercising the spiritual power within yourself. Simply say with a whole heart: "God, you are in me—dominate me," and presently your life is at springtime, radiant and beautiful. When Jesus Christ says, "the kingdom of God is within you," he is saying what wise men have always said, namely, that in you yourself is the answer to your own happiness. This is the antidote to deep inward grief of the spirit.

## Chapter Seven
# The Company of the Lonely

In compiling a list of the world's greatest novels an eminent professor of literature gave first place to that thrilling old classic, *Robinson Crusoe* by Daniel Defoe. He justified giving the primacy to this book on the ground that not only is it the first English novel, but it is wrought, as every great novel must be, out of a fundamental fact of human experience. A great novel must deal with a profound truth about life. This *Robinson Crusoe* does with surpassing genius.

It portrays a man fallen upon a most terrible fate—that of loneliness. The highlight of the book which stirs every reader is where the cure for that loneliness is found. Every day Crusoe comes to his lookout point, where he has rigged up a cloth at the top of a pole. He stands gazing across the sea, hands shading his eyes, searching for white sails against the empty horizon.

Standing there in his tatters, skin bronzed, hair long and unkempt, the beach grass waving at his feet, utterly alone, he is a tragic figure. He longs for the touch of a human hand, the sound of a human voice, and the friendly light on a human face. His solitary vigil once again unrewarded, he turns to go but stops short, in wild surprise, for before him in the sands of his supposedly desert island is an unmistakable human footprint, not his own.

In a manner usually less dramatic but no less poignant, every man in the long voyage of the years is likely to find himself like Crusoe upon some lonely island of the spirit. Indeed, there is a fundamental loneliness which haunts all who think deeply upon human experience. Man, at birth, enters this world alone from out the vast silences. Here he comes to be closely bound to others by strong ties of love and friendship. Yet in him remains a mystic homesickness, as if he does not really belong here but is, as an old hymn says, "A pilgrim and a stranger." Literature, art, and music, man's means of expressing himself, give utterance to this cosmic loneliness.

Sculptors, painters, and writers have given us the thought that we are not detached spirits, each living his allotted three score and ten, but elements in the ceaseless flow of eternity. Sir James Jeans, the eminent scientist, touched on the same thought when he said, "It may be that each individual consciousness is a brain cell in a universal mind." We do not live, according to Jeans, as distinct entities for a limited moment of time but tarry on earth during what is called human life, passing on finally, not to extinction, as though our purpose were accomplished, but to further functioning in other capacities in the never-ending process of cosmic mind of which each of us is a constituent part. It is a noble thought and may explain that vague loneliness which the thoughtful man feels now and then as though somehow he did not really belong here but felt the pull of some mystic homeland ever drawing his restless feet toward it.

My experience as a pastor has clearly shown me that a genuine Christian is never a victim of loneliness. Mark you, I said a genuine Christian, and that, of course, does not mean everyone who goes to church and glibly recites the creeds. A genuine Christian is one who sincerely tries to live in the spirit of Christ, has a simple trust and who has mastered the workable techniques of faith. This type of Christian has a friendly and sympathetic attitude toward all men. He is kindly in his relationships, and possesses a generous spirit, which is well able to lift him above everyday frictions. Moreover, he has learned to cope with shyness and oversensitiveness, because he has conquered the ego centeredness which causes them. The Christlike spirit that actuates him makes him too big for that carping pettiness which destroys friendship, leaving us forsaken and alone.

Another thing I have noticed about the genuine Christian is that though he may be compelled by circumstances to be much alone, he is not lonely, for he has inner resources to draw upon and consequently always finds himself in good company. As a man playing solitaire whiles away the lonely hours pleasantly because he enjoys his own game, so the man with worthwhile things in his own mind can play life's game in solitary because he is interesting even to himself. The important factor is what is in a man's mind.

Many people never read anything worthwhile; some never read at all, save the newspaper headlines. The extent of this indifference to good reading is evidenced by the astonishing prevalence of picture publications. The person who stocks his mind with great thought lays up treasures and resources upon which he may live happily, finding himself interesting enough to make loneliness impossible.

Faith is the answer to the problem of loneliness. As a pastor I have seen evidence of this assertion too many times to have any doubt about it. Consider the loneliness of bereavement. A loved one has been taken by death. For a while the reaction is one of lonesomeness, the agony of separation. The bereaved one misses the object of his love withal the pain of grief. The danger is that the grief may become abnormal through the withdrawal of one's love into oneself and through a spirit of bitterness toward an unkind world. There are thousands of people today whose lives are disintegrating because they have not developed enough faith to cope with the sorrow that is breaking down their personalities.

The man of faith, although he suffers all the pain of loss, at the same time believes that "all things work together for good to them that love God." He believes that the soul is immortal and that God is a Being with absolute love in his heart. He turns to God for comfort, and God does not disappoint him. If his faith is strong enough, it makes his consciousness of the Divine compassion and protection so complete that loneliness vanishes and a sense of companionship takes its place.

An old Russian proverb says, "The hammer shatters glass, but forges steel." Some people are like glass—the hammer of circumstance breaks them in pieces. Other people are like steel—the hammer strikes and instead of breaking them, forges them into new forms of strength and beauty. Christianity puts the steel-like element in people, so that they do not break under the hammers of circumstance. That precious ingredient is given them by faith.

## Chapter Eight
# Love and Marriage

I believe any man and wife can make a success of their marriage if they enter upon it with a spiritual attitude. I advise couples to pray together the first night of their marriage and every night thereafter. I know scores of present-day young couples who say grace at meals and many more who frequently read together from the Bible. These marriages do not break. They are cemented by the greatest power in the world—faith in God.

I have seen many failing marriages saved and permanently restored when both or even one of the partners was willing to bring religion into the situation.

A young woman came to me and said she and her husband had reached the breaking point. Misunderstandings had grown to enormous proportions and frequent differences had become hateful and bitter quarreling. She was about ready for the divorce court, she said, and from what I gathered he felt the same way. But she had a sensitive conscience about divorce, and, besides, down deep, as it later appeared, she still loved her husband and, of course, wanted to save their marriage.

"Have you, as a minister, any suggestion to make?" she asked.

"Yes, I have a suggestion," I replied. "I have known it to work in other cases like yours, and, in fact, it will work in any situation if it is faithfully tried."

"What is it?" she demanded, half skeptical, half hopeful.

"Pray with your husband," I said. "Go home and get him to kneel down and pray with you."

"Oh," she answered, her face fallen with disappointment, "I couldn't do that. He would make fun of me. We used to pray together every night, when we were first married, but we gave that up long ago."

"It will work," I replied. "I want you to promise you will pray with him tonight."

She did not say she would, but the next day she was back again as radiant a young woman as I ever saw. She fairly bubbled over with excitement and joy as she told me how she had struggled all evening for courage to make the suggestion to her husband, sunk behind his paper.

Finally she went over to him and said, "Jim, we can't seem to get together any other way, and all our arguments don't get us anywhere, and, Jim, in spite of everything, I really love you. Will you do one thing for me—will you—will you pray with me like we used to?"

She said he looked at her rather strangely.

"And then what do you think he said?" she asked. "He said, 'I thought of that a couple of times myself, but I didn't have the nerve to suggest it.'"

"Why," she cried, "it was wonderful, unbelievable; we got down on our knees as we did when we were first married and we talked to God like a couple of children, and all the trouble seemed to melt away all at once."

"Keep it up," I urged her, "and you will hold that refound happiness."

Religion works when used in human relationships. If you want happiness in marriage—and, of course, you do—practice your religion, and if your husband or wife will not join you in prayer and faith, then do all the praying yourself. One person with real faith can bring to bear a spiritual force sufficient to destroy irritating differences. Faith is so potent that one partner can lift both to that higher level where understanding and unity are attained.

## Chapter Nine
# The Faith That Heals

Many miracles of prayer and faith are taking place today in the field of physical and mental health.

This was once a very important aspect of Christianity. The New Testament is full of accounts of healing by Christ and his disciples. The tendency of the Christian religion under the influence of our era's naturalistic-scientific zeal has been to ignore its healing element. But now that science is becoming more mature, and its real harmony with religion better established, it is becoming evident that even as science has set free forces in the material world, so a more scientific application of prayer and faith tends to set free once more the healing forces such as are described in the New Testament as being of usual occurrence. There is now, I feel, a happy tendency by psychiatry, and general medicine, and surgery to work together with religion, each in its own realm to be sure, but with sympathy and understanding, in the common cause of healing body, mind and soul.

One doctor put it very well: "I treated my patient and God healed her." If we will avail ourselves of the best that medical science can give us and at the same time by faith and prayer put ourselves in the hands of God, being sure to pray always that God's will be done whatever that may involve, we shall be the object of curative and restorative forces of remarkable efficacy. The head of the medical service in a great university hospital said, "One should send for his minister as he sends for his doctor when he becomes ill." That is to say that God helps the sick in two ways, through the science of medicine and surgery, and through the science of faith and prayer. This latter brings the mind and spirit of the sick into harmony with God so that his healing power may operate. The physician thereby receives a superb cooperation.

My brother, Dr. Robert C. Peale, a physician and surgeon, says: "Because of the abiding faith and trust in the Almighty of the injured or sick person, I constantly see, as a surgeon, recoveries that were thought impossible. I also see poor results because of an attempted cure by religion or science alone. I have therefore become convinced that there is a definite and fixed relationship between religion and science and that God has given us both as weapons against disease and unhappiness. Used together for the benefit of mankind, their possibilities are unlimited, separately they can only be of limited benefit."

Simple faith in God opens our lives in an amazing manner to the forces of healing and strength and growth. All serious students of mankind know that man's essential quality is not physical or material but spiritual. A man can live a purely physical and material life for a while, but he will be beaten eventually, because he has cut himself off from the source of life-giving vitality. Like a pool of water separated from the living waters of a running stream he presently becomes unhealthy. Life is unhappy and sinful because it is cut off from the flow of life-giving force. Simple faith and surrender to God correct this condition. It is remarkable what a sincere attempt to harmonize our lives with God's power will do physically, mentally, and spiritually.

If we only believe, there is no limit to the blessings God will give us. We are told that Christ came to give us an abundant life. That means something far beyond the narrow, limited, frustrated lives most of us live. The whole emphasis of the New Testament which we so tragically miss is that God wants to pour out blessings in overflowing generosity. No blessing is too great, no power too strong, no victory too complete. All is ours.

# The Secret Door to Success
## (1940)

## by Florence Scovel Shinn

*Your Guide to Miraculous Living*

## Contents

Introduction   *Last Testament of a Miracle Worker* by Mitch Horowitz   682

Chapter One   The Secret Door to Success   684

Chapter Two   Bricks Without Straw   686

Chapter Three   "And Five of Them Were Wise"   687

Chapter Four   What Do You Expect?   689

Chapter Five   The Long Arm of God   690

Chapter Six   The Fork in the Road   692

Chapter Seven   Crossing Your Red Sea   693

Chapter Eight   Look With Wonder   696

Chapter Nine   Rivers in the Desert   698

## Introduction
# Last Testament of a Miracle Worker

This book almost never saw publication. It appeared in 1940, the year that Florence Scovel Shinn died. The work of the metaphysical teacher remains a formative influence on people around the world touched by her simple message that *thoughts are destiny*.

Shinn has many times over passed the test that philosopher Ralph Waldo Emerson posed for whether someone has lived well—which is "to know that even one life has breathed easier because you have lived." I believe that Shinn, through her message of mental causation, left many thousands of people breathing easier, and living better. She may be about to do the same for you.

Shinn is best known for her 1925 classic *The Game of Life and How to Play It*. While Shinn called life a "game," her own life was not easy—and nor did she seek ease. Born Florence Scovel in Camden, New Jersey in 1871, she took a rare path as a female artist, attending the Pennsylvania Academy of Fine Arts. There she met her future husband, realist painter Everett Shinn. Married in 1898, they moved to New York's Greenwich Village, where they became part of the Ashcan School of American artists, a cohort known for depicting street scenes, tenements, and the immigrant experience. The couple divorced in 1912. While pursuing her own career as an illustrator, Shinn became a student of metaphysics, leading her to write *The Game of Life* and several other books. She also became a popular spiritual lecturer and counselor. Following an illness, she died at home in Manhattan in October of 1940.

Shinn provided a role model for many independent seekers not only by how she lived out her principles of self-creation, but also by her do-it-yourself ethic. When no publisher would accept her manuscript for *The Game of Life*, Shinn published the book herself. It became one of the most popular works of practical metaphysics of the past hundred years, and remains widely read today. She did the same with her next book, *Your Word is Your Wand*, published in 1928, and with this one. The final book that bears her name, *The Power of the Spoken Word*, appeared posthumously in 1944, four years after her death.

*The Secret Door to Success* uses the Bible as its chief point of reference. This has been a basic aspect of New Thought tradition. Shinn and her contemporaries interpreted Scripture as a psychological blueprint of individual development and personal excellence. In so doing, Shinn influenced some of the most powerful and varied voices in the positive-mind tradition, including the mystic Neville Goddard and the mega-selling Norman Vincent Peale, both of whom used Shinn's phraseology in her work. Shinn was likewise an influence on spiritual thinkers of our own generation, including writer-publisher Louise Hay and on Yolanda King, eldest daughter of Martin Luther King Jr.

Shinn's contemporary Emmet Fox eulogized her: "One secret of Shinn's success was that she was always herself . . . colloquial, informal, friendly, and humorous. She never sought to be literary, conventional, or impressive. For this reason she appealed to thousands who would not have taken the spiritual message through more conservative and dignified forms, or have been willing to read . . . at least in the beginning . . . the standard metaphysical books."

I quote from Fox's eulogy with a tinge of hesitancy. There is, I think, something of a backhanded compliment, or even a veiled putdown, in his noting that Shinn's books are for seekers who might not have taken the message through more "dignified forms." A problem with our spiritual and intellectual culture (and many of those who aspire to be a part of it) is its suspicion of simple ideas and methods.

Shinn's technique of "speaking the word"—of placing faith in God's channels and announcing the arrival of that which is needed—either works or it does not. If it works—and I say that, in great measure, it does and challenge the reader to find his or her own applications—where is the need for the more "dignified" works to which Fox alludes? We should never be embarrassed or warned off an idea because it is simple. The only true test of a religious or ethical principle is its efficacy. That may be why Shinn is far more widely read today than Fox and many of her contemporaries.

Shinn's natural, practical voice inspired a wide range of seekers and metaphysical ministers. In so doing, she gave New Thought its popular tone: one of encouragement, experiment, boldness, and boundless possibility. In this, the final book of Shinn's life, now a part of our Condensed Classics Library, the teacher left us a testament that conveys something of the woman herself.

—Mitch Horowitz

## Chapter One
# The Secret Door to Success

> "So the people shouted when the priests blew with the trumpets; and it came to pass, when the people heard the sound of the trumpet, and the people shouted with a great shout, that the wall fell down flat, so that the people went up into the city, every man straight before him, and they took the city." —JOSHUA 6:20

A successful man is always asked—"What is the secret of your success?" People never ask a man who is a failure, "What is the secret of your failure?" It is quite easy to see and they are not interested.

People all want to know how to open the secret door to success.

For each man there is success, but it seems to be behind a door or wall. In the Bible reading, we have heard the wonderful story of the falling of the walls of Jericho.

Of course all biblical stories have a metaphysical interpretation.

We will talk now about *your* wall of Jericho: the wall separating *you* from success. Nearly everyone has built a wall around his own Jericho.

This city you are not able to enter, contains great treasures; your divinely designed success, your heart's desire!

*What kind of wall have you built around your Jericho?* Often, it is a wall of resentment—resenting someone, or resenting a situation, shuts off your good.

If you are a failure and resent the success of someone else, you are keeping away your own success.

I have given the following statement to neutralize envy and resentment: *What God has done for others, He now does for me and more.*

I gave the following statement to a woman: *The walls of lack and delay now crumble away, and I enter my Promised Land, under grace.* She had a vivid picture of stepping over a fallen wall, and received the demonstration of her good, almost immediately.

It is the word of realization that brings about a change in your affairs; for words and thoughts are a form of radioactivity.

Taking an interest in your work, enjoying what you are doing opens the secret door of success.

The *Secret of Success is to make what you are doing interesting to other people.* Be interested yourself, and others will find you interesting.

A good disposition, a smile, often opens the secret door; the Chinese say, "A man without a smiling face, must not open a shop."

Living in the past, complaining of your misfortunes, builds a thick wall around your Jericho.

Talking too much about your affairs, scattering your forces, brings you up against a high wall. I knew a man of brains and ability, who was a complete failure.

He lived with his mother and aunt, and I found that every night when he went home to dinner, he told them all that had taken place during the day at the office; he discussed his hopes, his fears, and his failures.

I said to him, "You scatter your forces by talking about your affairs. Don't discuss your business with your family. Silence is golden!"

*Success is not a secret, it is a System.*

Many people are up against the wall of discouragement. Courage and endurance are part of the system. We read this in lives of all successful men and women.

Only twice is the word success mentioned in the Bible—both times in the Book of Joshua.

"Only be strong and very courageous to observe to do according to all the law which Moses, my servant, commanded thee: turn not from it to the right nor to the left, that thou mayest have good success whithersoever thou goest. This book of the law shall not depart from thy mouth, but thou shalt meditate therein day and night, that thou mayest observe to do all that is written therein, for then shalt thou make thy way prosperous and thou shalt have good success. Turn not to the right nor to the left."

The *road to success is a straight and narrow path; it is a road of loving absorption, of undivided attention.*

"You attract the things you give a great deal of thought to."

So if you give a great deal of thought to lack, you attract lack, if you give a great deal of thought to injustice, you attract more injustice.

Joshua said, "And it shall come to pass, that when they make a long blast with the ram's horn, and when ye hear the sound of the trumpet, all the people shall shout with a great shout: and the wall of the city shall fall down flat, and the people shall ascend up, every man straight before him."

The inner meaning of this story is the power of the word, your word, which dissolves obstacles and removes barriers.

When the people shouted the walls fell down.

We find in folklore and fairy stories, which come down from legends founded on Truth, the same idea—a word opens a door or cleaves a rock.

So let us now take the statement—*The walls of lack and delay now crumble away, and I enter my Promised Land, under grace.*

## Chapter Two
# Bricks Without Straw

*"There shall no straw be given you, yet ye shall make bricks without straw."*
—Exodus 5:18

In the fifth chapter of Exodus, we have a picture of every day life, when giving a metaphysical interpretation.

The Children of Israel were in bondage to Pharaoh, the cruel taskmaster, ruler of Egypt. They were kept in slavery, making bricks, and were hated and despised.

Moses had orders from the Lord to deliver his people from bondage—"Moses and Aaron went in and told Pharaoh—Thus saith the Lord God of Israel, Let my people go, that they may hold a feast unto me in the wilderness."

He not only refused to let them go, but told them he would make their tasks even more difficult: they must make bricks without straw being provided for them.

It was impossible to make bricks without straw. The Children of Israel were completely crushed by Pharaoh; they were beaten for not producing the bricks—then came the message from Jehovah.

"Go therefore now, and work; for there shall no straw be given you, yet shall ye deliver the tale (number) of bricks."

I was told the story of a woman who needed money for her rent. It was necessary to have it at once, but she knew of no channel, she exhausted every avenue.

However, she was a Truth student, and kept making her affirmations. Her dog whined and wanted to go out, she put on his leash and walked down the street, in the accustomed direction.

However, the dog pulled at his leash and wanted to go in another direction.

She followed, and in the middle of the block, opposite an open park, she looked down, and picked up a roll of bills, which exactly covered her rent.

She looked for ads, but never found the owner. There were no houses near where she found it.

The reasoning mind, the intellect, takes the throne of Pharaoh in your consciousness. It says continually, "It can't be done. What's the use!"

We must drown out these dreary suggestions with a vital affirmation!

For example take this statement: *"The unexpected happens, my seemingly impossible good now comes to pass."* This stops all argument from the army of the aliens (the reasoning mind.).

"The unexpected happens!" That is an idea it cannot cope with.

Think of the joy of really being free forever, from the Pharaoh of the oppression. To have the idea of *security, health, happiness and abundance established in the subconscious*. It would mean a life free from all limitation!

It would be the Kingdom that Jesus Christ spoke of, where all things are automatically added unto us. I say automatically added unto us, because all life is vibration; and when we vibrate to success, happiness and abundance, the things that symbolize these states of consciousness will attach themselves to us.

Feel rich and successful, and suddenly you receive a large check or a beautiful gift.

## Chapter Three
# "And Five of Them Were Wise"

"And five of them were wise, and five were foolish. They that were foolish took their lamps, and took no oil with them." —MATT. 25:2–3

My subject is the parable of the Wise and Foolish Virgins. "And five of them were wise, and five were foolish. They that were foolish took their lamps, and took no oil with them. But the wise took oil in their vessels with their lamps." The parable teaches that true prayer means preparation.

Jesus Christ said, "And all things, whatsoever ye shall ask in prayer, *believing*, ye shall receive" (Matt. 21:22). "Therefore I say unto you, what things soever ye desire, when ye pray, believe that ye receive them, and ye shall have them" (Mark 11:24). In this parable he shows that only those who have prepared for their good (thereby showing active faith) will bring the manifestation to pass.

We might paraphrase the scriptures and say: When you pray believe you have it. When you pray ACT as if you have already received.

*Armchair faith or rocking chair faith will never move mountains.* In the armchair, in the silence, or meditation, you are filled with the wonder of this Truth, and feel that your faith will never waver. You know that The Lord is your Shepherd, you shall never want.

You feel that your God of Plenty will wipe out all burdens of debt or limitations, then you leave your armchair and step out into the arena of Life. It is only what you do in the arena that counts.

I will you give you an illustration showing how the law works; for faith without action is dead.

A man, one of my students, had a great desire to go abroad. He took the statement: *I give thanks for my divinely designed trip, divinely financed, under grace, in a perfect way.* He had very little money, but knowing the law of preparation, he bought a trunk. It was a very happy trunk with a big red band around its waist. Whenever he looked at it it gave him a realization of a trip. One day he seemed to feel his room moving. He felt the motion of a ship. He went to the window to breathe the fresh air, and it smelt like the aroma of the docks. With his inner ear he heard the shriek of a seagull and the creaking of the gangplank. The trunk had commenced to work. It had put him in the vibration of his trip. Soon after that, a large sum of money came to him and he took the trip. He said afterwards that it was perfect in every detail.

In the arena of Life we must keep ourselves tuned-up to concert pitch.

Are we acting from motives of fear or faith? *Watch your motives with all diligence, for out of them are the issues of life.*

The lamp symbolizes man's consciousness. The oil is what brings Light or understanding.

"While the bridegroom tarried, they all slumbered and slept. And at midnight there was a cry made. Behold, the bridegroom cometh; go ye out to meet him. Then all those virgins arose, and trimmed their lamps. And the foolish said unto the wise, "Give us of your oil; for our lamps are gone out."

The foolish virgins were without wisdom or understanding, which is oil for the consciousness, and when they were confronted with a serious situation, they had no way of handling it.

And when they said to the wise "give us of your oil," the wise answered saying, "Not so; lest there be not enough for us and you: but go ye rather to them that sell, and buy for yourselves."

That means that the foolish virgins could *not receive more than was in their consciousness, or what they were vibrating to.*

Every day you must make a choice, will you be wise or foolish? Will you prepare for your good? Will you *take the giant swing into faith*? Or serve doubt and fear and bring no oil for your lamps?

Every day examine your consciousness and see just what you are preparing for. You are fearful of lack and hang on to every cent, thereby attracting more lack. Use what you have with wisdom and it opens the way for more to come to you.

## Chapter Four
# What Do You Expect?

"According to your faith, be it done unto you." —MATT. 9:29

Faith is expectancy—"According to your faith, be it done unto you."

We might say, according to your expectancies be it done unto you. So, what are you expecting?

We hear people say: "We expect the worst to happen," or "The worst is yet to come." They are deliberately inviting the worst to come.

We hear others say: "I expect a change for the better." They are inviting better conditions into their lives.

Change your expectancies and you change your conditions.

How can you change your expectancies, when you have formed the habit of expecting loss, lack or failure?

Begin to act as if you expected success, happiness, and abundance; *prepare for your good.*

*Do* something to show you expect it to come. Active faith alone will impress the subconscious.

If you have spoken the word for a home, prepare for it immediately, as if you hadn't a moment to lose. Collect little ornaments, tablecloths, etc., etc.!

I knew a woman who made the giant swing into faith, by buying a large armchair; a chair meant business, she bought a large and comfortable chair, for she was preparing for the right man. He came.

Someone will say, "Suppose you haven't money to buy ornaments or a chair?" Then look in shop windows and link with them in thought.

Get in their vibration: I sometimes hear people say, "I don't go into the shops because I can't afford to buy anything." That is just the reason why you should go into the shops. Begin to make friends with the things you desire or require.

I know a woman who wanted a ring. She went boldly to the ring department and tried on rings. It gave her such a realization of ownership, that not long after, a friend made her a gift of a ring. "You combine with what you notice."

The soul is the subconscious mind, and the psalmist was telling his subconscious to expect everything directly from the universal; not to depend upon doors and channels; "My expectation is from Him."

God cannot fail, for "His ways are ingenious, His methods are sure."

*You can expect any seemingly impossible Good from God; if you do not limit the channels.*

Do not say how you want it done, or how it can't be done.

"God is the Giver and the Gift *and creates His own amazing channels.*"

Now think of the blessings that seem so far off, and begin to expect them now, under grace, in an unexpected way; for God works in unexpected ways, His wonders to perform.

## Chapter Five
# The Long Arm of God

"The Eternal God is thy refuge, and underneath are the everlasting arms."
—Deut. 33:27

Have you ever felt the relief of getting out some negative thought-form? Perhaps you have built up a thought-form of resentment, until you are always boiling with anger about something. You resent people you know, people you don't know, people in the past, and people in the present, and you may be sure that the people in the future won't escape your wrath.

All the organs of the body are affected by resentment—for when you resent, you resent with every organ of the body.

I have given the following statement to many of my students: *The long arm of God reaches out over people and conditions, controlling this situation and protecting my interests.*

This brings a picture of a long arm symbolizing strength and protection. With the realization of the power of the long arm of God, you would no longer resist or resent. You would relax and let go. The enemy thoughts within you would be destroyed, therefore, *the adverse conditions would disappear.*

Spiritual development means the ability to stand still, or stand aside, and let Infinite Intelligence lift your burdens and fight your battles. When the burden of resentment is lifted, you experience a sense of relief! You have a kindly feeling for everyone, and all the organs of your body begin to function properly.

Non-resistance is an art. When acquired, The World is Yours! So many people are trying to force situations. Your lasting good will never comes through forcing personal will.

*Flee from the things which flee from thee*
*Seek nothing, fortune seeketh thee.*
*Behold his shadow on the floor!*
*Behold him standing at the door!*

I do not know the author of these lines. Lovelock, the celebrated English athlete, was asked how to attain his speed and endurance in running. He replied, "Learn to relax." Let us attain this rest in action. He was most relaxed when running the fastest.

Your big opportunity and big success usually slide in, when you least expect it. You have to let go long enough for the *great law of attraction to operate. You never saw a worried and anxious magnet.* It stands up straight and hasn't a care in the world, because it knows needles can't help jumping to it. The things we rightly desire come to pass when we have taken the clutch off.

*Do not let your heart's desire become your heart's disease. You are completely demagnetized when you desire something too intensely.* You worry, fear, and agonize. There is an occult law of indifference: "None of these things move me." Your ships come in over a don't-care sea.

So many people use their words in exaggerated and reckless statements. I find a great deal of material for my talks in the beauty parlor. A young girl wanted a magazine to read. She called to the operator, "Give me something terribly new and frightfully exciting." All she wanted was the latest moving picture magazine. You hear people say, "I wish something terribly exciting would happen." They are inviting some unhappy, but exciting, experience into their lives. Then they wonder why it happened to them.

There should be a chair of metaphysics in all colleges. *Metaphysics is the wisdom of the ages.* It is the ancient wisdom taught all through the centuries in India and Egypt and Greece. Hermes Trismegistus was a great teacher of Egypt. His teachings were closely guarded and have come down to us over ten centuries. He lived in Egypt in the days when the present race of men was in its infancy. But if you read *The Kybalion* carefully, you find that he taught just what we are teaching today. He said that all mental states were accompanied by vibrations. You combine with what you vibrate to, so let us all now vibrate to success, happiness, and abundance.

*Now is the appointed time. Today is the day of my amazing good fortune.*

## Chapter Six
# The Fork in the Road

"Choose you this day whom ye will serve." —Josh. 24:15

Every day there is a necessity of choice—a fork in the road.

"Shall I do this, or shall I do that? Shall I go, or shall I stay?" Many people do not know what to do. They rush about letting other people make decisions for them, then regret having taken their advice.

There are others who carefully reason things out. They weigh and measure the situation like dealing in groceries, and are surprised when they fail to obtain their goal.

There are still other people who follow the magic path of intuition and find themselves in their Promised Land in the twinkling of an eye.

Intuition is a spiritual faculty high above the reasoning mind, but on the path is all that you desire or require.

So choose ye this day to follow the magic path of intuition.

In my question-and-answer classes I describe how to cultivate intuition. In most people it is a faculty that has remained dormant. So we say, "Awake thou that sleepeth. Wake up to your leads and hunches. Wake up to the divinity within!"

Claude Bragdon said, "To live intuitively is to live fourth dimensionally."

Now, it is necessary for you to make a decision, you face a fork in the road. *Ask for a definite unmistakable lead*, and you will receive it.

We find many events to interpret metaphysically in the Book of Joshua. "After the death of Moses, the divine command came to Joshua, 'Now therefore, arise, go over the Jordan, thou and all thy people, unto the land which I do give to them. Every place the sole of your feet shall tread upon; to you have I given it'."

The feet are the symbol of understanding, so it means metaphysically all that we understand stands under us in consciousness, and what is rooted there can never be taken from us.

For, the Bible goes on to say: "There shall not any man be able to stand before thee all the days of thy life… I will not fail thee, nor forsake thee. Only be thou strong and very courageous, that thou mayest observe to do according to all the law, which Moses my servant commanded thee: 'turn not from it to the right hand or to the left, that thou mayest prosper whithersoever thou goest'."

So we find we have success through being strong and very courageous in following spiritual law. We are back again to the "fork in the road"—the necessity of choice.

"Choose you this day whom ye will serve," the intellect or divine guidance.

So, as we reach the fork in the road today, let us fearlessly follow the voice of intuition.

The Bible calls it "the still small voice."

"There came a voice behind me, saying, 'This is the way, walk ye in it'." On this path is the good, already prepared for you. You will find the "land for which ye did not labor, and cities which ye built not, and ye dwell in them; of the vineyards and olive yards which ye planted not, do ye eat."

Let us say: *I am divinely led, I follow the right fork in the road. God makes a way where there is no way.*

## Chapter Seven
# Crossing Your Red Sea

"Speak unto the children of Israel that they go forward."  —Ex. 14:15

One of the most dramatic stories in the Bible is the episode of the children of Israel crossing the Red Sea.

Moses was leading them out of the land of Egypt where they were kept in bondage and slavery. They were being pursued by the Egyptians.

The children of Israel, like most people, did not enjoy trusting God; they did a lot of murmuring. They said to Moses: "Is not this the word that we did tell thee in Egypt, saying, Let us alone, that we may serve the Egyptians? For it had been better for us to serve the Egyptians, than that we should die in the wilderness."

"And Moses said unto the people, Fear ye not, stand still, and see the salvation of the Lord, which he will show to you today, for the Egyptians whom ye have seen today, ye shall see them again no more forever."

"The Lord shall fight for you, and ye shall hold your peace."

We might say that Moses pounded faith into the children of Israel.

They preferred being slaves to their old doubts and fears (for Egypt stands for darkness), than to take the giant swing into faith, and pass through the wilderness to their Promised Land.

There is, indeed, a wilderness to pass through before your Promised Land is reached.

The old doubts and fears encamp round about you, but there is always someone to tell you to go forward! There is always a Moses on your pathway. Sometimes it is a friend, sometimes intuition!

"And the Lord said to Moses, Wherefore cryest thou unto me? Speak unto the children of Israel, that *they go forward!*"

Now remember, the bible is talking about the individual. It is talking about *your* wilderness, *your* Red Sea, and *your* Promised Land.

Each one of you has a Promised Land, a heart's desire, but you have been so enslaved by the Egyptians (your negative thoughts), it seems very far away, and too good to be true. You consider trusting God a very risky proposition. The wilderness might prove worse than the Egyptians. And how do you know your Promised Land really exists?

The reasoning mind will always back up the Egyptians.

But sooner or later, something says, *"Go forward!"* It is usually circumstances—you are driven to it.

I give the example of a student. She is a very marvelous pianist and had great success abroad. She came back with a book full of press clippings, and a happy heart.

A relative took an interest in her and said she would back her financially for a concert tour. They chose a manager who took charge of the expenses, and attended to her bookings.

After a concert or two, there were no more funds. The manager had taken them. My friend was left stranded, desolate, and disappointed. This was about the time that she came to me.

She hated the man, and it was making her ill. She had very little money and could afford only a cheerless room where her hands were often too cold to practice.

She was indeed, in bondage to the Egyptians—hate, resentment, lack, and limitation.

Someone brought her to one of my meetings, and she spoke to me and told her story. I said, "In the first place you must stop hating that man. When you are able to forgive him, your success will come back to you. You are taking your initiation in forgiveness."

It seemed a pretty big order, but she tried and came regularly to all my meetings.

In the meantime, the relative had started a suit to recover the money. Time went on and it never came to court.

My friend had a call to go to California. She was no longer disturbed by the situation, and had forgiven the man.

Suddenly, after about four years, she was notified that the case had come to court. She called me upon her arrival in New York, and asked me to speak the word for rightness and justice.

They went at the time appointed, and it was all settled out of court, the man restoring the money by monthly payments.

She came to me overflowing with joy, for she said, "I hadn't the least resentment toward the man. He was amazed when I greeted him cordially." Her relative said that all the money was to go to her, so she found herself with a big bank account.

Now she will soon reach her Promised Land. She came out of the house of bondage (of hate and resentment) and crossed her Red Sea. Her goodwill toward the man caused the waters to part, and she crossed over on dry land.

## Chapter Eight
# Look With Wonder

"I will remember the works of the Lord; surely I will remember thy wonders of old."

—PSALMS 77:11

The words wonder and wonderful are used many times in the Bible. In the dictionary the word wonder is defined as, "a cause for surprise, astonishment, a miracle, a marvel."

P.D. Ouspensky, in his book *Tertium Organum*, calls the 4th dimensional world, the "World of the Wondrous." He has figured out mathematically that there is a realm where all conditions are perfect. Jesus Christ called it the Kingdom.

We might say, "Seek ye first the world of the wondrous, and all things shall be added unto you."

It can only be reached through a state of consciousness.

Jesus Christ said to enter the Kingdom we must become "as a little child." Children are continually in a state of joy and wonder!

The future holds promises of mysterious good. Anything can happen overnight.

Robert Louis Stevenson in *A Child's Garden of Verses* says: "The world is so full of a number of things. I'm sure we should all be as happy as kings."

So let us look with wonder at that which is before us. That statement was given me a number of years ago, I mention it in my book, *The Game of Life and How To Play It*.

I had missed an opportunity and felt that I should have been more awake to my good. The next day, I took the statement early in the morning: "I look with wonder at that which is before me."

At noon the phone rang, and the proposition was put to me again. This time I grasped it. I did indeed look with wonder for I never expected the opportunity to come to me again.

A friend in one of my meetings said the other day that this statement had brought her wonderful results. It fills the consciousness with happy expectancy.

Children are filled with happy expectancy until grown-up people, and unhappy experiences, bring them out of the world of the wondrous!

Let us look back and remember some of the gloomy ideas that were given us: "Eat the speckled apples first." "Don't expect too much, then you won't be disappointed." "You can't have everything in this life." "Childhood is your happiest time." "No one knows what the future will bring."

These are some of the impressions I picked up in early childhood.

At the age of six I had a great sense of responsibility. Instead of looking with wonder at that which was before me, I looked with fear and suspicion. I feel much younger now than I did when I was six.

I have an early photograph taken about that time, grasping a flower, but with a careworn and hopeless expression.

I had left the world of the wondrous behind me! I was now living in the world of realities, as my elders told me, and it was far from wondrous.

It is a great privilege for children to live in this age, when they are taught Truth from their birth. Even if they are not taught actual metaphysics, the ethers are filled with joyous expectancy.

So let us become *Miracle Conscious* and prepare for miracles, expect miracles, and we are then inviting them into our lives.

Maybe you need a financial miracle! There is a supply for every demand. Through active faith, the word, and intuition, we release this invisible supply.

I will give an example: One of my students found herself almost without funds, she needed one thousand dollars, and she had had plenty of money at one time and beautiful possessions, but had nothing left but an ermine wrap. No fur dealer would give her much for it.

I spoke the word that it would be sold to the right person for the right price, or that the supply would come in some other way. It was necessary that the money manifest at once, it was no time to worry or reason.

She was on the street making her affirmations. It was a stormy day. She said to herself, "I'm going to show active faith in my invisible supply by taking a taxi cab." It was a very strong hunch. As she got out of the taxi, at her destination, a woman stood waiting to get in.

It was an old friend, a very, very kind friend. It was the first time in her life she had ever taken a taxi, but her Rolls Royce was out of commission that afternoon.

They talked and my friend told her about the ermine wrap. "Why," her friend said, "I will give you a thousand dollars for it." And that afternoon she had the check.

*God's ways are ingenious, His methods are sure.*

## Chapter Nine
# Rivers in the Desert

"Behold, I will do a new thing: now it shall spring forth; shall ye not know it? I will even make a way in the wilderness, and rivers in the desert."
—Isaiah 43:19

In this 43rd chapter of Isaiah are many wonderful statements, showing the irresistible power of Supreme Intelligence coming to man's rescue in times of trouble. *No matter how impossible the situation seems, Infinite Intelligence knows the way out.*

Working with God-Power, man becomes unconditioned and absolute. Let us get a realization of this hidden power that we can call upon at any moment.

Make your contact with Infinite Intelligence (the God within) and all appearance of evil evaporates, for it comes from man's "vain imaginings."

In my question-and-answer class I would be asked, "How do you make a conscious contact with this Invincible Power?"

I reply, "By your word." "By your word you are justified."

The Centurion said to Jesus Christ, "Speak the word, master and my servant shall be healed."

"Whosoever calleth on the name of the Lord shall be delivered." Notice the word, "call:" you are calling on the Lord or Law, when you make an affirmation of Truth.

As I always say, take a statement that "clicks," that means, gives you a feeling of security.

People are enslaved by ideas of lack: lack of love, lack of money, lack of companionship, lack of health, and so on.

They are enslaved by the ideas of interference and incompletion. They are asleep in the Adamic Dream: Adam (generic man) ate of "Maya the tree of illusion" and saw two powers, good and evil.

The Christ mission was to wake people up to the Truth of one power, God. "Awake thou that sleepeth."

*If you lack any good thing, you are still asleep to your good.*

How do you awake from the Adamic dream of opposites, after having slept soundly in the race thought for hundreds of years?

Jesus Christ said, "When two of you agree, it shall be done." It is the law of agreement.

It is almost impossible to see clearly, your good, for yourself: that is where the healer, practitioner or friend is necessary.

Most successful men say they have succeeded because their wives believed in them. I will quote from a current newspaper, giving Walter P. Chrysler's tribute to his wife, "Nothing," he once said, "has given me more satisfaction in life, than the way my wife had faith in me from the very first, through all those years." Chrysler wrote of her, "It seemed to me I could not make anyone understand that I was ambitious except Della. I could tell her and she would nod. It seems to me I even dared to tell her that I intended, some day, to be a master mechanic." She always backed his ambitions.

Talk about your affairs as little as possible, and then only to the ones who will give you encouragement and inspiration. The world is full of "wet blankets," people who will tell you "it can't be done," that "you are aiming too high."

As people sit in Truth meetings and services, often a word or an idea will open a way in the wilderness.

Of course the Bible is speaking of states of consciousness. You are in a wilderness or desert, when you are out of harmony—when you are angry, resentful, fearful or undecided. Indecision is the cause of much ill health, being unable "to make up your mind."

One day when I was on a bus a woman stopped it and asked the conductor its destination. He told her, but she was undecided. She got half way on, and then got off, then on again: the conductor turned to her and said, "Lady, make up your mind!"

So it is with so many people—"Make up your minds!"

The intuitive person is never undecided: he is given his leads and hunches, and goes boldly ahead, knowing he is on the magic path.

In Truth, we always ask for definite leads just what to do; you will always receive one if you ask for it. Sometimes it comes as intuition, sometimes from the external.

One of my students, named Ada, was walking down the street, undecided whether to go to a certain place or not. She asked for a lead. Two women were walking in front of her. One turned to the other and said, "Why don't you go Ada?"—the woman's name just happened to be Ada—my friend took it as a definite lead, and went on to her destination, and the outcome was very successful.

We really lead magic lives, guided and provided for at every step; *if we have ears to hear and eyes that see.*

Of course we have left the plane of the intellect and are drawing from the superconscious, the God within, which says, "This is the way, walk ye in it."

Whatever you should know, will be revealed to you. Whatever you lack, will be provided! "Thus saith the Lord which maketh a way in the sea and a path in the mighty waters."

"Remember ye not the former things, neither consider the things of old."

People who live in the past have severed their contact with the wonderful now. God knows only the *now*. Now is the appointed time, today is the day.

*You must live in the now and be wide awake to your opportunities.*

"Behold, I will do a new thing, now it shall spring forth; shall ye not know it? I will even make a way in the wilderness, and rivers in the desert."

This message is meant for the individual. Think of your problem and know that Infinite Intelligence knows the way of fulfillment. I say the *way*, for before you called you were answered. *The supply always precedes the demand.*

*God is the Giver and the Gift and now creates His own amazing channels.*

When you have asked for the Divine Plan of your life to manifest, you are protected from getting the things that are not in the Divine Plan.

You may think that all your happiness depends upon obtaining one particular thing in life; later on, you praise the Lord that you didn't get it.

Sometimes you are tempted to follow the reasoning mind, and argue with your intuitive leads, suddenly the Hand of Destiny pushes you into your right place, and under grace, you find yourself back on the magic path again.

You are now wide awake to your good—you have the ears that hear (your intuitive leads), and the eyes that see the open road of fulfillment.

*The genius within me is released. I now fulfill my destiny.*

# Your Faith Is Your Fortune

(1941)

## by Neville

*The Classic Guide to Harnessing Your Power Within*

## Contents

Introduction   *The Practical Mystic* by Mitch Horowitz   702
Chapter One   You Shall Decree   703
Chapter Two   The Principle of Truth   704
Chapter Three   Who Am I?   705
Chapter Four   Thy Will Be Done   706
Chapter Five   The Foundation Stone   707
Chapter Six   To Him That Hath   709
Chapter Seven   Interval of Time   710
Chapter Eight   Prayer   712
Chapter Nine   Salute No Man   713

## Introduction
# The Practical Mystic

I am writing these words on the 111th birthday of Neville Goddard in 1905. In the years that have passed since Neville's death in 1972, one might expect that this boldly experimental mystic, who independently published his books under only his first name, would have been forgotten. But, in fact, Neville's ideas are reaching more people today than during his lifetime. This condensation one of his earliest books, *Your Faith Is Your Fortune,* is a perfect entry point for those just discovering Neville, and a refresher for longtime admirers.

Neville's key principle is so radical, so audacious, so at odds with everything we've been raised to believe that many serious people immediately want to argue with it. It is this: *The human imagination is God.* This God-power within you is constantly outpicturing your thoughts into reality. Your mental and emotive states literally define your life.

Neville argued this principle in more than ten books and thousands of lectures. Part of his gift as a writer, lecturer, and thinker was his capacity to continually and elegantly restate his thesis without it once seeming stale or familiar. Whenever Neville stepped to the podium or put pen to paper, he seemed to be expressing his ideas for the first time, finding alluring illustrations and fresh methods.

Another appeal of Neville's claim is that it is completely testable. As you are about to experience, Neville challenges his audience at every step to test the principle that your thoughts and feeling states create your reality. Prove me wrong, he urged—and if you do, throw away my ideas. Given Neville's sustained popularity, it would seem that most readers who put him to the test did not walk away.

Let me set the stage for this book's appearance in 1941. Neville had previously published only one pamphlet-sized work, *At Your Command,* written two years earlier. His name was rising as a metaphysical speaker and writer. He had originally come to New York City from his native Barbados at age 17 in the early 1920s to study theater. Although the young performer won roles on Broadway and toured with a dance troupe, he abandoned his stage career to dedicate himself to mystical studies. Neville said that his metaphysical queries deepened in 1933 upon meeting a turbaned black rabbi named Abdullah, with whom he studied Scripture, Hebrew, and religious symbolism for five years.

With his tutelage to Abdullah complete, Neville branched out with his first full-length book, *Your Faith Is Your Fortune*. His ease and confidence in interpreting Scripture and various mystical traditions are evident throughout the work, as they are in his many lectures, which today are circulated online from tape recordings that he freely permitted listeners to make during his life.

You are about to experience a brief but powerful journey into a tremendously rich and challenging thought system. After more than twenty years in metaphysical publishing, I hesitate to issue the overused promise that a book can "change your life." But Neville's works are among the very few I know that can support that claim. The concepts you are about to sample are like a nourishing meal—perhaps filling a lifelong hunger. If they convince you to return for more of Neville's ideas, this brief volume will have done its job.

—Mitch Horowitz
February 19, 2016
(Neville's Birthday)

Chapter One

# You Shall Decree

*So shall my word be that goeth forth out of my mouth; it shall not return unto me void, but shall accomplish that which I please, and it shall prosper in the thing whereto I sent it.* —Isaiah 55:11

Man can decree a thing and it will come to pass.

Man has always decreed that which has appeared in his world. He is today decreeing that which is appearing in his world and he shall continue to do so as long as man is conscious of being man.

Nothing has ever appeared in man's world but what man decreed that it should. This you may deny; but try as you will you cannot disprove it for this decreeing is based on a changeless principle. Man does not command things to appear by his words, which are, more often than not, a confession of his doubts and fears. Decreeing is ever done in consciousness.

Every man automatically expresses that which he is conscious of being. Without effort or the use of words, at every moment of time, man is commanding himself to be and to possess that which he is conscious of being and possessing.

This changeless principle of expression is dramatized in all the Bibles of the world. The writers of our sacred books were illumined mystics, past masters in the art of psychology. In telling the story of the soul they personified this impersonal principle in the form of a historical document.

Today the priesthoods of the world have forgotten that the Bibles are psychological dramas representing the consciousness of man; in their blind forgetfulness they now teach their followers to worship its characters as men and women who actually lived in time and space.

When man sees the Bible as a great psychological drama with all of its characters and actors as the personified qualities and attributes of his own consciousness, then—and only then—will the Bible reveal to him the light of its symbology.

The day man does this he will know that he and his Father are one but his Father is greater than he. When man discovers his consciousness to be the impersonal power of expression, which power eternally expresses itself in his conceptions of himself, he will assume and appropriate that state of consciousness which he desires to express; in so doing he will become that state in expression.

"Ye shall decree a thing and it shall come to pass" can now be told in this manner: You shall become conscious of being or possessing a thing, and you shall express or possess that which you are conscious of being.

## Chapter Two
# The Principle of Truth

"To be absent from the body and be present with the Lord" is not given to a select few; it is a sweeping call to mankind. The body from which you are invited to escape is your present conception of yourself with all of its limitations, while the Lord with whom you are to be present is your awareness of being.

To accomplish this seemingly impossible feat you take your attention away from your problem and place it upon just being. You say silently but feelingly, "I AM." Do not condition this awareness but continue declaring quietly, "I AM—I AM." Simply feel that you are faceless and formless and continue doing so until you feel yourself floating.

"Floating" is a psychological state which completely denies the physical. Through practice in relaxation and willfully refusing to react to sensory impressions, it is possible to develop a state of consciousness of pure receptivity. It is a surprisingly easy accomplishment. In this state of complete detachment a definite singleness of purposeful thought can be indelibly engraved upon your unmodified consciousness. This state of consciousness is necessary for true meditation.

This wonderful experience of rising and floating is the signal that you are absent from the body or problem and are now present with the Lord; in this expanded state you are not conscious of being anything but I AM—I AM; you are only conscious of being.

When this expansion of consciousness is attained, within this formless deep of yourself, give form to the new conception by claiming and feeling yourself to be that which you, before you entered into this state, desired to be. You will find that within this formless deep of yourself all things appear to be divinely possible. Anything that you sincerely feel yourself to be while in this expanded state becomes, in time, your natural expression.

### Chapter Three
# Who Am I?

All men have had proof of the power of faith. The faith that moves mountains is faith in yourself. No man has faith in God who lacks confidence in himself. Your faith in God is measured by your confidence in yourself. I and my Father are one, man and his God are one, consciousness and manifestation are one.

And God said, "Let there be a firmament in the midst of the waters." In the midst of all the doubts and changing opinions of others, let there be a conviction, a firmness of belief, and you shall see the dry land; your belief will appear. The reward is to him that endureth unto the end. A conviction is not a conviction if it can be shaken. Your desire will be as clouds without rain unless you believe.

Your unconditioned awareness of I AM is the Virgin Mary who knew not a man and yet, unaided by man, conceived and bore a son. Mary, the unconditioned consciousness, desired and then became conscious of being the conditioned state which she desired to express, and in a way unknown to others became it. Go and do likewise; assume the consciousness of that which you desire to be and you, too, will give birth to your savior. When the annunciation is made, when the urge or desire is upon you, believe it to be God's spoken word seeking embodiment through you. Go, tell no man of this holy thing that you have conceived. Lock your secret within you and magnify the Lord, magnify or believe your desire to be your savior coming to be with you.

When this belief is so firmly established that you feel confident of results, your desire will embody itself. How it will be done, no man knows. I, your desire, have ways ye know not of; my ways are past finding out. Your desire can be likened to a seed, and seeds contain within themselves both the power and the plan of self-expression. Your consciousness is the soil. These seeds are successfully planted only if, after you have claimed yourself to be and to have that which you desire, you confidently await results without an anxious thought.

If I be lifted up in consciousness to the naturalness of my desire, I shall automatically draw the manifestation unto me. Consciousness is the door through which life reveals itself. Consciousness is always objectifying itself.

To be conscious of being or possessing anything is to be or have that which you are conscious of being or possessing. Therefore, lift yourself to the consciousness of your desire and you will see it automatically outpicture itself.

## Chapter Four
# Thy Will Be Done

"Not my will but thine, be done." This resignation is not one of blind realization that "I can of myself do nothing, the Father within me he doeth the work." When man wills he attempts to make something which does not now exist appear in time and space. Too often we are not aware of that which we are really doing. We unconsciously state that we do not posses the capacities to express. We predicate our desire upon the hope of acquiring the necessary capacities in future time. "I AM not, but I will be."

Man does not realize that consciousness is the Father which does the work, so he attempts to express that which he is not conscious of being. Such struggles are doomed to failure; only the present expresses itself. Unless I am conscious of being that which I seek, I will not find it. God (your awareness) is the substance and fullness of all. God's will is the recognition of that which is, not of that which will be. Instead of seeing this saying as "Thine will be done," see it as "Thy will is done." The works are finished.

When a sculptor looks at a formless piece of marble he sees, buried within its formless mass, his finished piece of art. The sculptor, instead of making his masterpiece, merely reveals it by removing that part of the marble which hides his conception. The same applies to you. In your formless awareness lies buried all that you will ever conceive yourself to be. The recognition of this truth will transform you from an unskilled laborer who tries to make it so to a great artist who recognizes it to be so.

Your claim that you are now that which you want to be will remove the veil of human darkness and reveal your claim perfectly; I AM that. Now you will see the wisdom in the words of the prophet when he states, "Let the weak say, I AM strong," Joel 3:10. Man in his blindness will not heed the prophet's advice; he continues to claim himself to be weak, poor, wretched, and all the other undesirable expressions from which he is trying to free himself by ignorantly claiming that he will be free from these characteristics in the expectancy of the future. Such thoughts thwart the one law that can ever free him.

There is only one door through which that which you seek can enter your world. "I AM the door." When you say, "I AM," you are declaring yourself to be, first person, present tense; there is no future. To know that I AM is to be conscious of being. Consciousness is the only door. Unless you are conscious of being that which you seek, you seek in vain.

## Chapter Five

# The Foundation Stone

Man moves in a world that is nothing more or less than his consciousness objectified. Not knowing this he wars against his reflections while he keeps alive the light and the images that project the reflections. "I AM the light of the world." I AM (consciousness) is the light. That which I am conscious of being (my conception of myself)—such as "I AM rich," "I AM healthy," "I AM free"—are the images. The world is the mirror magnifying all that I AM conscious of being.

Stop trying to change the world since it is only the mirror. Man's attempt to change the world by force is as fruitless as breaking a mirror in the hope of changing his face. Leave the mirror and change your conceptions of yourself. The reflection then will be satisfactory.

Freedom or imprisonment, satisfaction or frustration, can only be differentiated by the consciousness of being. Regardless of your problem, its duration or its magnitude, careful attention to these instructions will, in an amazingly short time, eliminate even the memory of the problem. Ask yourself this question: "How would I feel if I were free?" The very moment you sincerely ask this question the answer comes. No man can tell another the satisfaction of his desire fulfilled. It remains for each within himself to experience the feeling and joy of this automatic change of consciousness. The feeling or thrill that comes to one in response to his self-questioning is the Father state of consciousness or Foundation Stone upon which the conscious change is built. Just how this feeling will embody itself no one knows, but it will; the Father (consciousness) has ways that no man knows; it is the unalterable law.

All things express your nature. As you wear a feeling it becomes your nature. It might take a moment or a year—it is entirely dependent upon the degree of conviction. As doubts vanish and you can feel "I AM this," you begin to develop the fruit or the nature of the thing you are feeling yourself to be. When a person buys a new hat or pair of shoes he thinks everyone knows that they are new. He feels unnatural with his newly acquired apparel until it becomes a part of him. The same applies to the wearing of the new state of consciousness. When you ask yourself the question, "How would I feel if my desire were at this moment realized?" the automatic reply, until it is properly conditioned by time and use, is actually disturbing. The period of adjustment to realize this new potential of consciousness is comparable to the newness of the wearing apparel. Not knowing that consciousness is ever outpicturing itself in conditions round about you, like Lot's wife you continually look back upon your problem and again become hypnotized by its seeming naturalness.

Heed the words of Jesus (salvation): "Leave all and follow me." "Let the dead bury the dead." Your problem might have you so hypnotized by its seeming reality and naturalness that you find it difficult to wear the new feeling or consciousness of your savior. You must assume this garment if you would have results.

The stone (consciousness) which the builders rejected (would not wear) is the chief cornerstone, and other foundations no man can lay.

## Chapter Six
# To Him that Hath

*Take heed therefore how ye hear; for whosoever hath, to him shall be given; and whosoever hath not, from him shall be taken even that which he seemeth to have.* —LUKE 8:18

The Bible, which is the greatest psychological book ever written, warns man to be aware of what he hears; then follows this warning with the statement, "To him that hath it shall be given and to him that hath not it shall be taken away." Though many look upon this statement as one of the most cruel and unjust of the sayings attributed to Jesus, it remains a just and merciful law based upon life's changeless principle of expression.

Man's ignorance of the working of the law does not excuse him or save him from the results. Law is impersonal and therefore no respecter of persons. Man is warned to be selective in that which he hears and accepts as true. Everything that man accepts as true leaves an impression on his consciousness and must in time be defined as proof or disproof. Perceptive hearing is the perfect medium through which man registers impressions. A man must discipline himself to hear only that which he wants to hear, regardless of rumors or the evidence of his senses to the contrary. As he conditions his perceptive hearing he will react only to those impressions that he has decided upon. This law never fails. Fully conditioned, man becomes incapable of hearing other than that which contributes to his desire.

God, as you have discovered, is that unconditioned awareness which gives to you all that you are aware of being. To be aware of being or having anything is to be or have that which you are aware of being. Upon this changeless principle all things rest. It is impossible for anything to be other than that which it is aware of being. "To him that hath (that which he is aware of being) it shall be given." Good, bad or indifferent—it does not matter—man receives multiplied a hundredfold that which he is aware of being.

## Chapter Seven
# Interval of Time

*Let not your heart be troubled; ye believe in God, believe also in me. In my Father's house are many mansions; if it were not so, I would have told you. I go to prepare a place for you. And if I go and prepare a place for you, I will come again, and receive you unto myself; that where I am, there ye may be also.*

—John 14:1-3

Man is such a slave to time that, if after he has appropriated a state of consciousness which is not now seen by the world and it, the appropriated state, does not immediately embody itself, he loses faith in his unseen claim; forthwith he drops it and returns to his former static state of being. Because of this limitation of man I have found it very helpful to employ a specified interval of time in making this journey into a prepared mansion.

"Wait but a little while."

We have all catalogued the different days of the week, months of the year and seasons. By this I mean you and I have said time and again, "Why, today feels just like Sunday" or "—Monday" or "—Saturday." We have also said in the middle of Summer, "Why, this feels and looks like the Fall of the year." This is positive proof that you and I have definite feelings associated with these different days, months, and seasons of the year. Because of this association we can at any time consciously dwell in that day or season which we have selected. Do not selfishly define this interval in days and hours because you are anxious to receive it, but simply remain in the conviction that it is done—time being purely relative, should be eliminated entirely—and your desire will be fulfilled.

This ability to dwell at any point in time permits us to employ time in our travel into the desired mansion. Now I (consciousness) go to a point in time and there prepare a place. If I go to such a point in time and prepare a place, I shall return to this point in time where I have left; and I shall pick up and take you with me into that place which I have prepared, that where I AM, there ye may also be.

Let me give you an example of this travel. Suppose you had an intense desire. Like most men who are enslaved by time, you might feel that you could not possibly realize so large a desire in a limited interval. But admitting that all things are possible to God, believing God to be the ME within you or your consciousness of being, you can say, "As John I can do nothing; but since all things are possible to God and God I know to be my consciousness of being, I can realize my desire in a little while. How my desire will be realized I do not (as John) know, but by the very law of my being I do know that it shall be."

With this believe firmly established decide what would be a relative, rational interval of time in which such a desire could be realized. Again let me remind you not to shorten the interval of time because you are anxious to receive your desire; make it a natural interval. No one can give you the time interval. No one can say what the natural interval would be to you. The interval of time is relative, that is, no two individuals would give the same measurement of time for the realization of their desire.

Time is ever conditioned by man's conception of himself. Confidence in yourself as determined by conditioned consciousness always shortens the interval of time. If you were accustomed to great accomplishments, you would give yourself a much shorter interval in which to accomplish your desire than the man schooled in defeat.

If today were Wednesday and you decided that it would be quite possible for your desire to embody a new realization of yourself by Sunday, then Sunday becomes the point in time that you would visit. To make this visit you shut out Wednesday and let in Sunday. This is accomplished by simply feeling that it is Sunday. Begin to hear the church bells; begin to feel the quietness of the day and all that Sunday means to you; actually feel that it is Sunday.

When this is accomplished, feel the joy of having received that which on Wednesday was but a desire. Feel the complete thrill of having received it, and then return to Wednesday, the point in time you left behind you. In doing this you created a vacuum in consciousness by moving from Wednesday to Sunday. Nature, abhorring vacuums, rushes in to fill it, thereby fashioning a mould in the likeness of that which you potentially create, namely, the joy of having realized your defined desire.

## Chapter Eight
# Prayer

*When thou prayest, enter into thy closet, and when thou hast shut thy door, pray to thy Father which is in secret; and thy Father which seeth in secret shall reward thee openly.* —MATHEW 6:8

*What things soever ye desire, when ye pray, believe that ye receive them, and ye shall have them.* —MARK 11:24

Prayer is the most wonderful experience man can have. Unlike the daily murmurings of the vast majority of mankind in all lands who by their vain repetitions hope to gain the ear of God, prayer is the ecstasy of a spiritual wedding taking place in the deep, silent stillness of consciousness. In its true sense prayer is God's marriage ceremony. Just as a maid on her wedding day relinquishes the name of her family to assume the name of her husband, in like manner, one who prays must relinquish his present name or nature and assume the nature of that for which he prays.

The gospels have clearly instructed man as to the performance of this ceremony in the following manner: "When ye pray go within in secret and shut the door and your Father who sees in secret will reward you openly." The going within is the entering of the bridal chamber. Just as no one but the bride and groom are permitted to enter so holy a room as the bridal suite on the night of the marriage ceremony, likewise no one but the one who prays and that for which he prays are permitted to enter the holy hour of prayer. As the bride and groom on entering the bridal suite securely shut the door against the outside world, so too must the one who enters the holy hour of prayer close the door of the senses and entirely shut out the world round about him. This is accomplished by taking the attention completely away from all things other than that with which you are now in love (the thing desired).

The second phase of the spiritual ceremony is defined in these words, "When ye pray believe that ye receive, and ye shall receive." As you joyfully contemplate being and possessing that which you desire to be and to have, you have taken this second step and are therefore spiritually performing the acts of marriage and generation.

Your receptive attitude of mind while praying or contemplating can be likened to a bride or womb for it is that aspect of mind which receives the impressions. That which you contemplate being is the groom, for it is the name or nature you assume and therefore is that which leaves its impregnation; so one dies to maidenhood or present nature as one assumes the name and nature of impregnation.

Lost in contemplation and having assumed the name and nature of the thing contemplated, your whole being thrills with the joy of being it. This thrill that runs through your entire being as you appropriate the consciousness of your desire is the proof that you are both married and impregnated. As you return from this silent meditation, the door is once more opened upon the world you had left behind. But this time you return as a pregnant bride. You enter the world a changed being and, although no one but you knows of this wonderful romance, the world will in a very short while see the signs of your pregnancy, for you will begin to express that which you in your hour of silence felt yourself to be.

Millions of prayers are daily unanswered because man prays to a God who does not exist. Consciousness being God, one must seek in consciousness for the thing desired by assuming the consciousness of the quality desired. Only as one does this will his prayers be answered. To be conscious of being poor while praying for riches is to be rewarded with that which you are conscious of being, namely, poverty. Prayers to be successful must be claimed and appropriated. Assume the positive consciousness of the thing desired.

With your desire defined, quietly go within and shut the door behind you. Lose yourself in your desire; feel yourself to be one with it; remain in this fixation until you have absorbed the life and name by claiming and feeling yourself to be and to have that which you desired. When you emerge from the hour of prayer you must do so conscious of being and possessing that which you heretofore desired.

## Chapter Nine

# Salute No Man

"Salute no man by the way." This is not a command to be insolent or unfriendly but a reminder not to recognize a superior, not to see in anyone a barrier to your expression. None can stay your hand or question your ability to express that which you are conscious of being. Do not judge after the appearances of a thing, "for all are as nothing in the eyes of God."

When the disciples through their judgment of appearances saw the insane child, they thought it a more difficult problem to solve than others they had seen; and so they failed to achieve a cure. In judging after appearances they forgot that all things were possible to God. Hypnotized as they were by the reality of appearances, they could not feel the naturalness of sanity.

The only way to avoid such failures is to constantly bear in mind that your awareness is the Almighty, the all-wise presence; without help, this unknown presence within you effortlessly outpictures that which you are aware of being. Be perfectly indifferent to the evidence of the senses, so that you may feel the naturalness of your desire, and your desire will be realized. Turn from appearances and feel the naturalness of that perfect perception within yourself, a quality never to be distrusted or doubted. Its understanding will never lead you astray. Your desire is the solution of your problem. As the desire is realized the problem is dissolved.

You cannot force anything outwardly by the mightiest effort of the will. There is only one way you can command the things you want and that is by assuming the consciousness of the things desired. There is a vast difference between feeling a thing and merely knowing it intellectually. You must accept without reservation the fact that by possessing (feeling) a thing in consciousness you have commanded the reality that causes it to come into existence in concrete form. You must be absolutely convinced of an unbroken connection between the invisible reality and its visible manifestation. Your inner acceptance must become an intense, unalterable conviction that transcends both reason and intellect, renouncing entirely any belief in the reality of the externalization except as a reflection of an inner state of consciousness. When you really understand and believe these things you have built up so profound a certainty that nothing can shake you.

# The Master Key to Riches
(1945)

## by Napoleon Hill

*The Secrets to Wealth, Power, and Achievement from the Author of* Think and Grow Rich

## Contents

Introduction   *The Secrets to Power* by Mitch Horowitz   716
Foreword   Think!   717
Chapter One   The Beginning of All Riches   717
Chapter Two   The Twelve Riches of Life   719
Chapter Three   The Eight Princes   722
Chapter Four   Definiteness of Purpose   725
Chapter Five   The Habit of Going the Extra Mile   727
Chapter Six   Love, the True Emancipator of Mankind!   729
Chapter Seven   The Master Mind   730
Chapter Eight   Applied Faith   731
Chapter Nine   The Law of Cosmic Habitforce   735
Chapter Ten   Self-Discipline   741

## Introduction

# The Secrets to Power

This is probably the most unusual book Napoleon Hill ever wrote. He dramatically presents its text as a speech delivered by a "masked rich man," who decides to share his wealth secrets with the world. In using this device, Hill was borrowing a theme that has long been popular in America's alternative spiritual culture—placing lessons in the mouth of a mysterious master, who may be real, invented, or a mixture of both.

Hill's unknown speaker is basically a personification of the voice of practical wisdom that ran through all of his books. In *The Master Key to Riches*, the speaker captures the essentials of Hill's ideas and adds some additional insights that came to Hill when he published this book in 1945, toward the victorious end of World War II, with America's Great Depression finally a memory and his classic work, *Think and Grow Rich*, eight years behind him.

As with all of Hill's books, you can more or less glean the totality of his philosophy from this one, in which he states his seventeen principles of success, along with other lists and testaments that guide you through towards effectiveness, attainment, and achievement. *The Master Key to Riches* is notable in that it probably features more lists and bulleted points than ever before, and in a pleasingly compressed form so that the book serves as an introduction to the newcomer and a refresher to the veteran. In my view, a reader always benefits from a review of Hill's ideas, as each reading reveals something new or previously overlooked. That has been my personal experience.

Another important aspect of this book is that it features what I consider Hill's clearest and most sustained explanation of the power of the "applied faith." I have sometimes struggled with the idea of faith in Hill's program. Chapter eight, "Applied Faith," has proven especially helpful to me in that regard, and I direct you to pay close attention to it.

I now turn you over to the voice of Hill's "Masked Rich Man from Happy Valley," whose revelations and insights are the closest thing we have, and likely ever will, to a science of success.

—Mitch Horowitz

## Foreword
# Think!

Many centuries ago a very wealthy and wise philosopher by the name of Croesus, an adviser to Cyrus, King of the Persians, said:

> I am reminded, O King: and take this lesson to heart; that there is a Wheel on which the affairs of men revolve, and its mechanism is such that it prevents any man from being *always fortunate*.

*The Master Key to Riches* was designed for the purpose of aiding men in the mastery and control of this great Wheel, to the end that it may be made to yield them an abundance of all that they desire, including the Twelve Great Riches of Life described in the second chapter.

Remember, you who are beginning the study of this philosophy, that this same Wheel that "prevents any man from being always fortunate" may provide also that no man shall be always unfortunate, provided he will take possession of his own mind and direct it to the attain of some Definite Major Purpose in life.

## Chapter One
# The Beginning of All Riches

The largest audience ever assembled in the history of mankind sat breathlessly awaiting the message of a mysterious man who was about to reveal to the world the secret of his riches.

Slowly the curtain began to rise. The speaker walked briskly to the podium. He was dressed in a long black robe and wore a mask over his eyes. His hair was grayish, and he appeared about sixty years of age.

He stood silently for a few moments, while the cameras flashed. Then, speaking slowly, in a voice soft and pleasing, like music, be began his message:

You have come here to seek the MASTER KEY TO RICHES!

You have come because of that human urge for the better things in life, which is the common desire of all people.

You desire economic security, which money alone can provide.

Some of you desire an outlet for your talents in order that you may have the joy of creating your own riches.

Some of you are seeking the easy way to riches, with the hope that you will find it without giving anything in return; that too is a common desire. But it is a desire I shall hope to modify for your benefit, as from experience I have learned that there is no such thing as something for noting.

There is but one sure way to riches, and it may be attained only by those who have the MASTER KEY TO RICHES!

The MASTER KEY is an ingenious device with which those who possess it may unlock the door to the solution all of their problems. Its powers of magic transcend those of the famous Aladdin's Lamp.

It opens the door to sound health.

It opens the door to love and romance.

It opens the door to friendship, by revealing the traits of personality and character that make enduring friends.

It reveals the method by which every adversity, every failure, every disappointment, every mistaken error of judgment, and every past defeat may be transmuted into riches of a priceless value.

It kindles anew the dead hopes of all who possess it, and it reveals the formula by which one may "tune in" and draw upon the great reservoir of Infinite Intelligence, through that state of mind known as Faith.

It opens the doors, one by one, to the Twelve Great Riches of Life, which I shall presently describe for you in detail.

Listen carefully to what I have to say, for I shall not pass this way again. Listen not only with open ears, but also with open minds and eager hearts, remembering that no man may hear that for which he has not the preparation for hearing.

Before I describe the Twelve Great Riches let me reveal to you some of the riches you already possess; riches of which most of you may not be conscious.

First, I would have you recognize that each of you is a plural personality, although you may regard yourself as a single personality. You and every other person consist of least two distinct personalities, and many of you possess more.

One is your "other self," a positive sort of person who thinks in terms of opulence, sound health, love and friendship, personal achievement, creative vision, service to others, and who guides you unerringly to the attainment of all of these blessings. It is this self which alone is capable of recognizing and approaching the Twelve Great Riches. This is not an imaginary personality of which I speak. It is real.

When your negative personality is in control your radio station picks up only the negative thought vibrations that are being sent out by hundreds of millions of other negative personalities throughout the world. These are accepted, acted upon, and translated into their physical equivalent in terms of the circumstances of life that you do not wish.

When your positive personality is in control it picks up only the positive thought vibrations being released by millions of other positive personalities throughout the world, and translates them into their physical equivalent in terms of prosperity, sound health, love, hope, faith, peace of mind and happiness; the values of life for which you and every other normal person are searching.

I have come to reveal to you the Master Key by which you may attain these and many other riches. That mysterious key that unlocks the doors to the solution of all human problems, acquires all riches, and places every individual thought pattern under the control of one's "other self."

When I speak of "riches" I have in mind the greater riches whose possessors have made life pay off on their own terms—the terms of full and complete happiness. I call these the "Twelve Riches of Life." And I sincerely wish to share them with all of you who are prepared to receive them, in whole or in part.

You may wonder about my willingness to share, so I shall tell you that the MASTER KEY TO RICHES enables its possessors to add to their own store of riches everything of value when they share with others. This is one of the strangest facts of life, but it is a fact which each of you must recognize and respect. Now let us pass onto the description of the Twelve Riches.

## Chapter Two
# The Twelve Riches of Life

The greatest of all riches is . . .

1. **A Positive Mental Attitude.** All riches of whatever nature, begin as a state of mind; and let us remember that a state of mind is the one and only thing over which any person has complete, unchallenged right of control. It is highly significant that the Creator provided man with control over nothing except the power to shape his own thoughts and the privilege of

fitting them to any pattern of his choice. Mental attitude is important because it converts the brain into the equivalent of an electro-magnet, which attracts one's dominating thoughts, aims, and purposes. It also attracts one's fears, worries, and doubts. A positive mental attitude is the starting point of all riches, whether they are riches of a material nature or intangible wishes. It attracts the wishes of a true friendship. And the riches one finds in the hope of future achievement.

2. **Sound Physical Health.** Sound health begins with a "health consciousness" produced by a mind that thinks in terms of health and not in terms of illness, plus temperance of habits in eating and properly balancing physical activities.

3. **Harmony in Human Relationships.** Harmony with others begins with one's self, for it is true, as Shakespeare said, and there are benefits available to those who comply with his admonitions, "To thine own self be true, and it must follow, as the night the day, thou cans't not then be false to any man."

4. **Freedom from Fear.** No man who fears anything is a free man! Fear is a harbinger of evil, and wherever it appears one may find a cause that must be eliminated before he may become rich in the fuller sense. The seven basic fears that appear most often in the mind of men are: (1) fear of POVERTY, (2) fear of CRITICISM, (3) fear of ILL HEALTH, (4) fear of LOSS OF LIFE, (5) fear of LOSS OF LIBERTY, (6) fear of OLD AGE, (7) fear of DEATH.

5. **The Hope of Achievement.** The greatest of all forms of happiness comes as a result of the hope of achievement of some yet unattained desire; and poor beyond description is the person who cannot look to the future with hope that he will become the person he would like to be, or with the belief that he will attain the objective he has failed to reach in the past.

6. **The Capacity for Faith.** Faith is the connecting link between the conscious mind of the man and the great universal reservoir of Infinite Intelligence. It is the fertile soil of the garden of the human mind wherein may be produced all of the riches of life. It is the "eternal elixir" that gives creative power and action to the impulses of thought. Faith is the basis of so-called miracles, and of many mysteries that cannot be explained by the rules of logic or science. Faith is the "spiritual chemical" that, when it is mixed with prayer, gives one direct and immediate connection with Infinite Intelligence. Faith is the power that transmutes the ordinary

energies of thought into their spiritual equivalent. And it is the one power through which the Cosmic Force of Infinite Intelligence may be appropriated to the uses of man.

7. **Willingness to Share One's Blessings.** He who has not learned the blessed art of sharing has not learned the true path to happiness, for happiness comes only by sharing. And let it be forever remembered that all riches may be embellished and multiplied by the simple process of sharing them where they may serve others. And let it be also remembered that the space one occupies in the hearts of his fellowmen is determined precisely by the service he renders through some form of sharing his blessings.

8. **A Labor of Love.** There can be no richer man than he who has found a labor of love and who is busily engaged in performing it, for labor is the highest form of human expression of desire. Labor is the liaison between the demand and the supply of all human needs, the forerunner of all human progress, the medium by which the imagination of man is given the wings of action. And all labor of love is sanctified because it brings the joy of self-expression to him who performs it.

9. **An Open Mind on all Subjects.** Tolerance, which is among the higher attributes of culture, is expressed only by those who hold an open mind on all subjects at all times. And it is only the man with an open mind who becomes truly educated and who is thus prepared to avail himself of the greater riches of life.

10. **Self-discipline.** The man who is not master of himself may never become the master of anything. He who is the master of self may become the master of his own earthly destiny, the "master of fate, the Captain of his soul." And the highest form of self-discipline consists in the expression of the humility of the heart when one has attained great riches or has been overtaken by that which is commonly called "success."

11. **The Capacity to Understand People.** The man who is rich in the understanding of people always recognizes that all people are fundamentally alike in that they have evolved from the same stem; that all human activities are inspired by one or more of the nine basic motives of life: (1) the emotion of LOVE, (2) the emotion of SEX, (3) the desire for MATERIAL GAIN, (4) the desire for SELF PRESERVATION (5) the desire for FREEDOM OF BODY AND MIND, (6) the desire for SELF-EXPRESSION, (7) the desire for perpetuation of LIFE AFTER DEATH, (8) the emotion of ANGER, and (9) the emotion of

FEAR. And the man who would understand others must first understand himself.
12. **Economic Security.** The last, though not least in importance, is the tangible portion of the "Twelve Riches." Economic security is not attained by possession of money alone. It is attained by the service one renders, for useful service may be converted into all forms of human needs, with or without the use of money.

Presently I shall acquaint you with the principles by which money and all other forms of riches may be obtained, but first you must be prepared to make application of these principles. Your mind must be conditioned for the acceptance of riches just as the soil of the earth must be prepared for the planting of seeds.

*When one is ready for a thing it is sure to appear!*

This does not mean the things one may need will appear without a cause, for there is a vast difference between one's "*needs*" and one's *readiness* to receive. To miss this distinction is to miss the major benefits I shall endeavor to convey. So let me lead you into *readiness* to receive the riches that you desire.

## Chapter Three
# The Eight Princes

My riches came through the aid of others. Some of these helpers have been well known. Some have been strangers whose names you will not recognize. Among these *strangers* are eight of my friends who have done most for me in preparing my mind for the acceptance of riches. I call them the "Eight Princes." They serve me when I am awake and they serve me when I am asleep.

The Princes serve me through a technique that is simple and adaptable. Every night, as the last order of the day's activities, the Princes and I have a roundtable session, the major purpose of which is to permit me to express my gratitude for the service they have rendered me during the day. My Princes of Guidance are:

1. PRINCE OF MATERIAL PROSPERITY, I am grateful to you for having kept my mind attuned to the consciousness of opulence and plenty, and free from the fear of poverty and want.

2. PRINCE OF SOUND PHYSICAL HEALTH, I am grateful to you for having attuned my mind to the consciousness of sound health, thereby providing the means by which every cell of my body and every physical organ is being adequately supplied with an inflow of cosmic energy sufficient unto its needs, and providing a direct contact with Infinite Intelligence which is sufficient for the distribution and application of this energy where it is required.
3. PRINCE OF PEACE OF MIND, I am grateful to you for having kept my mind free from all inhibitions and self-imposed limitations, thereby providing my body and my mind with complete rest.
4. PRINCE OF HOPE, I am grateful to you for the fulfillment of today's desires, and for your promise of fulfillment of tomorrow's aims.
5. PRINCE OF FAITH, I am grateful to you for the guidance which you have given me; for your having inspired me to do that which has been helpful to me, and for turning me back from doing that which had it been done would have proven harmful to me. You have given power to my thoughts, momentum to my deeds, and the wisdom that has enabled me to understand the laws of Nature, and the judgment to enable me to adapt myself to them in a spirit of harmony.
6. PRINCE OF LOVE, I am grateful to you for having inspired me to share my riches with all whom I have contacted this day; for having shown me that only that which I give away can I retain as my own. And I am grateful too for the consciousness of love with which you have endowed me, for it has made life sweet and all my relationships pleasant.
7. PRINCE OF ROMANCE, I am grateful to you for having inspired me with the spirit of youth despite the passing of the years.
8. PRINCE OF OVERALL WISDOM, my eternal gratitude to you for having transmuted into an enduring asset of priceless value, all of my past failures, defeats, errors of judgment and of deed, all fears, mistakes, disappointments, and adversities of every nature; the asset consisting of my willingness and ability to inspire others to take possession of their own minds and to use their mind-power for the attainment of the riches of life, thus providing me with the privilege of sharing all of my blessings with those who are ready to receive to them. And thereby enriching and multiplying my own blessings by the scope of their benefit to others.

Let me now share with you the following creed, so that you may adopt it as your own.

## A Happy Man's Creed

I have found happiness by helping others to find it.

I have sound physical health because I live temperately in all things, and eat only the foods that Nature requires for body maintenance.

I am free from fear in all of its forms.

I hate no man, envy no man, but love all mankind.

I am engaged in a labor of love with which I mix play generously. Therefore I never grow tired.

I give thanks daily, not for more riches, but for wisdom with which to recognize, embrace, and properly use the great abundance of riches I now have at my command.

I speak no name save only to honor it.

I ask no favors of anyone except the privilege of sharing my riches with all who will receive them.

I am on good terms with my conscience. Therefore it guides me correctly in all that I do.

I have no enemies because I injure no man for any cause, but I benefit all with whom I come into contact by teaching the way to enduring riches.

I have more material wealth than I need because I am free from greed and covet only the material things I can use while I live.

I own the Estate of Happy Valley, which is not taxable because it exists mainly in my own mind in intangible riches, which cannot be assessed or appropriated except by those who adopt my way of life. I created this vast estate by observing Nature's laws and adapting my habits to conform therewith.

In the chapters that follow you fill find the MASTER KEY, which will unlock the door to this chamber and all others. And it will be in your hands when you have prepared yourself to accept it.

## Chapter Four
# Definiteness of Purpose

It is impressive to recognize that all of the great leaders, in all walks of life and during all periods of history, have attained their leadership by the application of their abilities to a *definite major purpose.*

It is no less impressive to observe that those who are classified as failures have no such purpose, but they go around and around, like a ship without a rudder, coming back always empty-handed, to their starting point.

Some of these "failures" begin with a definite major purpose but they desert that purpose the moment they are overtaken by temporary defeat or strenuous opposition. They give up and quit, not knowing that there is a philosophy of success which is as dependable and as definite as the rules of mathematics, and never suspecting that temporary defeat is but a test ground which may prove a blessing in disguise if it is not accepted as final.

It is one of the great tragedies of civilization that ninety-eight of out every one hundred persons go all the way through life without coming within sight of anything that even approximates definiteness of a major purpose!

We come now to the analysis of the power of definiteness of purpose, and psychological principles from which the power is derived.

### First premise:
The starting point of all individual achievement is the adoption of a definite purpose and a definite plan for its attainment.

### Second premise:
All achievement is the result of a motive or combination of motives, of which there are nine basic motives, which govern all voluntary actions. (We described these nine motives in chapter two.)

### Third premise:
Any dominating idea, plan or purpose held in the mind, through repetition of thought, and emotionalized with a burning desire for its realization, is taken over by the subconscious section of the mind and acted upon, and it is thus carried through to its logical climax by whatever means may be available.

**Fourth premise:**
Any dominating desire, plan or purpose held in the conscious mind and backed by absolute faith in its realization, is taken over and acted upon immediately by the subconscious section of the mind, *and there is no known record of this kind of a desire having ever been without fulfillment.*

**Fifth premise:**
The power of thought is the only thing over which any person has complete, unquestionable control—a fact so astounding that it connotes a close relationship between the mind of man and the Universal Mind of Infinite Intelligence, the connecting link between the two being FAITH.

**Sixth premise:**
The subconscious portion of the mind is the doorway to Infinite Intelligence, and it responds to one's demands in exactly proportion to the quality of one's FAITH! The subconscious may mind be reached through faith and given instructions as though it were a person or a complete entity unto itself.

**Seventh premise:**
A definite purpose, backed by absolute faith, is a form of wisdom, and wisdom in action produces results.

## The Major Advantages of Definiteness of Purpose

Definiteness of purpose develops self-reliance, personal initiative, imagination, enthusiasm, self-discipline, and concentration of effort, and all of these are prerequisites for the attainment of material success.

Definiteness of aim induces one to budget his time and to plan all his day-to-day endeavors so they lead toward the attainment of his MAJOR PURPOSE in life.

It makes one more alert in the recognition of opportunities related to the object of one's MAJOR PURPOSE, and it inspires the necessary courage to act upon those opportunities when they appear.

It inspires the cooperation of others.

It prepares the way for the full exercise of that state of mind known as FAITH, by *making the mind positive* and freeing it from the limitations of fear, doubt, and indecision.

It provides one with a *success consciousness*, without which no one may attain enduring success in any calling.

It destroys the destructive habit of procrastination.

Lastly, it leads directly to the development and the continuous maintenance of the first of the Twelve Riches, a *positive mental attitude*.

These are the major characteristics of DEFINITENESS OF PURPOSE, although it has many other qualities and usages, and it is directly related to each of the Twelve Riches because they are attainable only by singleness of purpose.

Definiteness of purpose can, and it should, so completely occupy the mind *that one has no time or space in the mind for thoughts of failure.*

Chapter Five

# The Habit of Going the Extra Mile

An important principle of success in all walks of life and in all occupations is a willingness to GO THE EXTRA MILE; which means the rendering of more and better service than that for which one is paid, and giving it in a *positive mental attitude.*

Search wherever you will for a single sound argument against this principle, and you will not find it; nor will you find a single instance of enduring success that was not attained in part by its application.

The principle is not the creation of man. It is a part of Nature's handiwork, for its is obvious that every living creature below the intelligence of man is forced to apply the principle in order to survive.

Man may disregard the principle if he chooses, but he cannot do so and at the same time enjoy the fruits of enduring success.

Observe how Nature applies this principle in the production of food that grows from the soil, where the farmer is forced to GO THE EXTRA MILE by clearing the land, plowing it, and planting the seed at the right time of the year, for none of which he receives any pay in advance.

But, observe that if does his work in harmony with Nature's laws, and performs the necessary amounts of labor, Nature takes over the job where the farmer's labor ends, germinates the seed he plants, and develops it into a crop of food.

And, observe thoughtfully this significant fact: For every grain of wheat or corn he plants in the soil Nature yields him perhaps a hundred grains, thus enabling him to benefit by the law of increasing returns.

Nature GOES THE EXTRA MILE by producing enough of everything for her needs, together with a surplus for emergencies and waste; for example, the fruit on the trees, the bloom from which the fruit is grown, frogs in the pond and fish in the seas.

The advantages of the habit of GONG THE EXTRA MILE are definite and understandable. Let us examine some of them and be convinced:

The habit brings the individual to the *favorable attention* of those who can and will provide opportunities for self-advancement.

It tends to make one indispensible, in many different human relationships, and it therefore enables him to command more than average compensation for personal services.

It leads to mental growth and to physical skill and perfection in many forms of endeavor, thereby adding to one's earning capacity.

It enables one to profit by the law of contrast since *the majority of people do not practice the habit.*

It leads to the development of a positive, pleasing mental attitude, which is essential for enduring success.

It tends to develop a keen, alert imagination because it is a habit that inspires one continuously to seek new and better ways of rendering service.

It develops the important quality of personal initiative.

It develops self-reliance and courage.

It serves to build the confidence of others in one's integrity.

It aids the mastery of the destructive habit of procrastination.

It develops definiteness of purpose, ensuring one against the common habit of aimlessness.

There is still another, and a greater reason, for following the habit of GOING THE EXTRA MILE. *It gives one the only logical reason for asking for increased compensation.*

The attitude of the man who follows the habit of GOING THE EXTRA MILE is this: *He recognizes the truth that he is receiving pay for schooling himself for a better position and greater pay!*

This is an asset of which no worker can be cheated, no matter how selfish or greedy his immediate employer may be.

## Chapter Six
# Love, the True Emancipator of Mankind!

Love is man's greatest experience. It brings one into communication with Infinite Intelligence.

When it is blended with the emotions of sex and romance it may lead one to the higher mountain-peaks of individual achievement through *creative vision*.

The emotions of love, sex, and romance are the three sides of the eternal triangle of achievement known as genius. Nature creates geniuses through no other media.

Love is an outward expression of the spiritual nature of man.

Sex is purely biological, but it supplies the springs of action in all creative effort, from the humblest creation that crawls to the most profound of all creations, man.

When love and sex are combined with the spirit of romance the world may well rejoice, for these are the potentials of the great leaders who are the profound thinkers of the world.

The love of which I speak must not be confused with the emotions of sex, for love in its highest and purest expression is a combination of the eternal triangle, *yet it is greater than any one of its three component parts!*

The love to which I refer is the "élan vital"—the life-giving factor—the spring of action—of all creative endeavors that have lifted mankind to its present state of refinement and culture.

It is the one factor that draws a clear line of demarcation between man and all the creatures of the earth below him. It is the one factor that determines for every man the amount of space he shall occupy in the hearts of his fellowmen.

Love is the solid foundation upon which the first of the Twelve Riches may be built, *a positive mental attitude*. Love is the warp and woof of all the remaining eleven riches. It embellishes all riches and gives them the quality of endurance.

The *habit* of GOING THE EXTRA MILE leads to the attainment of that spirit of love, for there can be no greater expression of love than love that is demonstrated through service rendered completely and unselfishly.

## Chapter Seven
# The Master Mind

*Definition: An alliance of two or more minds, blended in a spirit of perfect harmony and cooperation for the attainment of a definite purpose.*

Note well the definition of this principle, for it carries a meaning that provides the key to the attainment of a great personal power.

The Master Mind is the basis of all great achievements, the foundation stone of major importance in all human progress, whether individual or collective.

The key to its power may be found in the word "harmony"!

Without that element, collective effort may constitute cooperation, but it will lack the power that harmony provides through coordination of effort.

The tenets of major importance in connection with the Master Mind are:

1. The Master Mind principle is the medium through which one may procure the full benefit of the *experience, training, education, specialized knowledge, and native ability of others*, just as completely as if their minds were one's own.
2. An alliance of two or more minds a spirit of *perfect* harmony for the attainment of a definite purpose, stimulates each individual mind with a high degree of inspiration, and may become that state of mind known as Faith! (A slight idea of this stimulation and its power is experienced in the relationship of close friendship and in the relationship of love.)
3. Every human brain is both a broadcasting and receiving station for the expression of the vibrations of thought, and the effect of the Master Mind principles stimulates action of thought, through what is commonly known as telepathy, operating through the sixth sense.
4. The Master Mind principle, when actively applied, has the effect of connection one with the subconscious section of the mind, and the subconscious sections of the minds of his allies—a fact that may explain many of the seemingly miraculous results obtained through the Master Mind.
5. The more important human relationships in connection with which one may apply the Master Mind principle are: (a) marriage, (b) religion, and (c) in connection with one's occupation, profession, or calling.

The Master Mind principle made it possible for Thomas Edison to become a great inventor despite his lack of education and his lack of knowledge of the sciences with which he had to work—a circumstance that offers hope to all who erroneously believe themselves seriously handicapped by a lack of formal education.

There are two general types of Master Mind alliances:

1. Alliance, for purely personal reasons, with one's relatives, religious advisors and friends, where no material gain or objective is sought. *The most important of this type of alliance is that of man and wife.*
2. Alliances for business, professional, and economic advancement, consisting of individuals who have a personal motive in connection with the object of the alliance.

Never neglect forming a Master Mind alliance; great power can be attained in no other way.

## Chapter Eight
# Applied Faith

Faith is a royal visitor that enters only the mind that has been properly prepared for it; the mind that has been set in order through *self-discipline*.

In the fashion of all royalty, Faith commands the best room, nay, the finest suite, in the mental dwelling place.

It will not be shunted into servant's quarters, and it will not associate with envy, greed, superstition, hatred, revenge, vanity, doubt, worry, or fear.

Get the full significance of this truth and you will be on the way to an understanding of that mysterious power that has baffled scientists through the ages.

When the mind has been cleared of a *negative mental attitude*, the power of Faith moves in and begins to take possession!

Surely no student of this philosophy will be unfortunate enough to miss this important observation.

Let us turn now to analysis of Faith, although we must approach the subject with full recognition that Faith is a power that has defied analysis by the entire scientific world.

Faith is a state of mind that might properly be called the "mainspring of the soul" through which one's aims, desires, and purposes may be translated into their physical or financial equivalent.

Previously we observed that great power may be attained by the application of (1) the habit of GOING THE EXTRA MILE, (2) Definiteness of Purpose, and (3) the Master Mind. But that power is feeble in comparison with that which is available through the combined application of these principles with the state of mind known as Faith.

We have already observed that *capacity for faith* is one of the Twelve Riches. Let us now recognize the means by which this "capacity" may be filled with that strange power that has been the main bulwark of civilization, the chief cause of all human progress, the guiding spirit of all constructive human endeavor.

Let us remember that Faith is a state of mind that may be enjoyed only by those who have learned the art of taking *full and complete control* of their minds! This is the one and only prerogative right over which an individual has been given complete control.

Faith expresses its powers only through the mind that has been prepared for it. But the way of preparation is known, and may be attained by all who desire to find it.

The fundamentals of Faith are:

1. Definiteness of purpose supported by personal initiative or *action*.
2. The habit of GOING THE EXTRA MILE in all human relationships.
3. A Master Mind alliance with one or more people who radiate courage based on Faith, and who are suited spiritually and mentally to one's needs in carrying out a given purpose.
4. A positive mind, free from all negatives, such as fear, envy, greed, hatred, jealousy, and superstition. (A positive mental attitude is the first and the most important of the Twelve Riches.)
5. Recognition of the truth that every adversity carries with it the seed of equivalent benefit; that *temporary defeat is not failure* until it has been accepted as such.
6. The habit of affirming one's Definite Major Purpose in life in a ceremony of meditation at least once daily.
7. Recognition of the existence of Infinite Intelligence, which gives orderliness to the universe; that all individuals are minute expressions of this Intelligence; and as such the individual mind has no limitations except those that are accepted and set up by the individual in his own mind.

8. A careful inventory (in retrospect) of one's past defeats and adversities, which will reveal the truth that all such experiences carry the seed of an equivalent benefit.
9. Self-respect expressed through harmony with one's own conscience.

These are the fundamentals of major importance that prepare the mind for the expression of Faith. Their application calls for no degree of superiority, but application does call for intelligence and *a keen thirst for truth and justice.*

Remember: faith fraternizes only with the mind that is positive!

## How to Demonstrate the Power of Faith

1. Know what you want and determine what you have to give in return for it.
2. When you affirm the objects of your desires, through prayer, inspire your imagination to see yourself already in possession of them, and act precisely as if you were in the physical possession thereof. (Remember the possession of anything first takes place mentally.)
3. Keep the mind open at all times for *guidance from within,* and when you are inspired by hunches to modify your plans or to move on a new plan, move without hesitancy or doubt.
4. When overtaken by temporary defeat, as you may be overtaken many times, remember that man's Faith is tested in many ways, and your defeat may be only one of your "testing periods." Therefore, accept defeat as an inspiration to greater effort, and carry on with belief that you will succeed.
5. Any negative state of mind will destroy the capacity for Faith and result in a negative climax of any affirmation you may express. Your state of mind is everything; therefore take possession of your mind and clear it completely of all unwanted interlopers that are unfriendly to Faith, and keep it cleared, no matter what may be the cost in effort.
6. Learn to give expression to your power of Faith by writing out a clear description of your Definite Major Purpose in life and using it as the basis of your daily meditation.
7. Associate with your Definite Major Purpose as many as possible of the nine basic motives, described previously.

8. Write out a list of all the benefits and advantages you expect to derive from the attainment of the object of your Definite Major Purpose, and call these into your mind many times daily, thereby making your mind "success conscious." (This is commonly called autosuggestion.)
9. Associate yourself, as far as possible, with people who are in sympathy with your Definite Major Purpose; people who are in harmony with you, and inspire them to encourage you in every way possible.
10. Let not a single day pass without making at least one definite move toward the attainment of your Definite Major Purpose. Remember, "Faith without works is dead."
11. Choose some prosperous person of self-reliance and courage as your "pacemaker," and make up your mind not only to keep up with that person, but to excel him. Do this silently, without mentioning your plan to anyone. (Boastfulness will be fatal to your success, as Faith has nothing in common with vanity or self-love.)
12. Surround yourself with books, pictures, wall mottoes, and other suggestive reminders of self-reliance founded upon Faith as it has been demonstrated by other people, thus building around yourself an atmosphere of prosperity and achievement. This habit will be fruitful of stupendous results.
13. Adopt a policy of never evading or running away from unpleasant circumstances, but recognize such circumstances and build a counter-fire against them right where they overtake you. You will discover that recognition of such circumstances, without fear of their consequence, is nine-tenths of the battle in mastering them.
14. Recognize the truth that everything worth having has a definite price. The price of Faith, among other things, is eternal vigilance in carrying out these simple instructions. Your watchword must be PERSISTENCE!

These are the steps that lead to the development and maintenance of a *positive mental attitude*, the only one in which Faith will abide. They are steps that lead to riches of both mind and spirit as well as riches of the purse. Fill your mind with this kind of mental food.

## Chapter Nine
# The Law of Cosmic Habitforce

We now come to the analysis of the greatest of all of Nature's laws, the law of Cosmic Habitforce!

Briefly described, the law of Cosmic Habitforce is Nature's method of giving fixation to all habits so that they may carry on automatically once they have been set into motion—the habits of men the same as the habits of the universe.

Every man is where he is and what he is because of his established habits of thought and deed. The purpose of this entire philosophy is to aid the individual in the formation of the kind of habits that will transfer him from where he is to where wishes to be.

Every scientist, and many laymen, know that Nature maintains a perfect balance between all the elements of matter and energy throughout the universe; that the entire universe is operated through an inexorable system of orderliness and habits that never vary, and cannot be altered by any form of human endeavor; that the five known realities of the universe are: (1) Time, (2) Space, (3) Energy, (4) Matter, and (5) Intelligence; these shaped the other known realities into orderliness and system based upon *fixed habits.*

These are nature's building-blocks with which she creates a grain of sand or the largest stars that float through space, and every other thing known to man, or that the mind of man can conceive.

These are the known realities, but not everyone has taken the time or the interest to ascertain that Cosmic Habitforce is the particular application of Energy with which Nature maintains the relationship between the atoms of matter, the stars and the planets in their ceaseless motion onward toward some unknown destiny, the seasons of the year, night and day, sickness and health, life and death. Cosmic Habitforce is the medium through which all habits and all human relationships are maintained in varying degrees of permanence, and the medium through which thought is translated into its physical equivalent in response to the desires and purposes of the individual.

But these truths are capable of proof, and one may count that hour sacred during which he discovers the inescapable truth that man is only an instrument through which higher powers than his own are projecting themselves.

This entire philosophy is designed to lead one to this important discovery, and to enable him to make use of the knowledge it reveals, *by placing himself in harmony with the unseen forces of the universe, which may carry him inevitably into the success side of the great River of Life.*

The hour of this discovery should bring him within easy reach of the Master Key to all Riches!

Cosmic Habitforce is Nature's Comptroller through which all other natural laws are coordinated, organized, and operated through orderliness and system. Therefore it is the greatest of all natural laws.

The law of Cosmic Habitforce is Nature's own creation. It is the one universal principle through which order and system and harmony are carried out in the entire operation of the universe, from the largest star that hangs in the heavens to the smallest atoms of matter.

It is a power that is equally available to the weak and the strong, the rich and poor, the sick and well. It provides the solution to all human problems.

The major purpose of the seventeen principles of this philosophy is that of aiding the individual to adapt himself to the power of Cosmic Habitforce by self-disciple in connection with the formation of his habits of thought.

Let us turn now to a brief review of these principles, so that we may understand their relationship to Cosmic Habitforce. Let us observe how these principles are so related that they blend together and form the Master Key that unlocks the doors to the solution of all problems.

The analysis begins with the first principle of the philosophy:

1. THE HABIT OF GOING THE EXTRA MILE. This principle is given first because it aids in conditioning the mind for the rendering of useful service. And this condition prepares the way for the second principle—
2. DEFINITENESS OF PURPOSE. With the aid of this principle one may give organized direction to the principle of Going the Extra Mile, and make sure that it leads in the direction of his major purpose and becomes cumulative in its effects. These two principles alone will take anyone far up the ladder of achievement, but those who are aiming for the higher goals of life will need much help on the way, and this help is available through the application of the third principle—
3. THE MASTER MIND. Through the application of this principle one begins to experience a new and greater sense of power which is not available to the individual mind, as it bridges one's personal deficiencies and provides him, when necessary, with any portion of the combined knowl-

edge of mankind, which has accumulated throughout the ages. But this sense of power will not be complete until one acquires of art of receiving guidance through the fourth principle—

4. APPLIED FAITH. Here an individual begins to tune in to the powers of Infinite Intelligence, which is a benefit that is available only to the person who has conditioned his mind to receive it. Here the individual begins to take full possession of his own mind by mastering all fears, worries, and doubts, by recognizing his oneness with the source of all power. These four principles have been rightly called the "Big Four" because they are capable of providing more power than the average man needs to carry him to great heights of personal achievement. But these are adequate only for the very few who have other needed qualities of success, such as those provided by the fifth principle.

5. PLEASING PERSONALITY. A pleasing personality enables a man to sell himself and his ideas to others. Hence, it is an essential for all who desire to become the guiding influence in a Master Mind alliance. But observe carefully how definitely the four preceding principles tend to give one a pleasing personality. These five principles are capable of providing one with stupendous personal power, but not enough power to ensure him against defeat, for defeat is a circumstance that every man meets many times throughout his life; hence the necessity of understanding and applying the sixth principle—

6. HABIT OF LEARNING FROM DEFEAT. Notice that this principle begins with the word "habit," which means that it must be accepted and applied as a matter of habit, under all circumstances of defeat. In this principle may be found hope sufficient to inspire a man to make a fresh start when his plans go astray, as go astray they must at one time or another.

7. CREATIVE VISION. This principle enables one to look into the future and to judge it by a comparison with the past, and to build new and better plans for attaining his hopes and aims through the workshop of his imagination. And here, for the first time perhaps, a man may discover his sixth sense and begin to draw upon it for the knowledge which is not available through the organized sources of human experience and accumulated knowledge. But, in order to make sure that he puts this benefit to practical use he must embrace and apply the eighth principle—

8. PERSONAL INITIATIVE. This is the principle that starts action and keeps it moving toward definite ends. It insures one against the destructive habits of procrastination, laziness, and indifference. An approximation of the importance of this principle may be had by recognizing that it is the "habit-producer" in connection with the seven preceding principles, for it is obvious that the application of no principle may become a *habit* expect by the application of personal initiative. The importance of this principle may be further evaluated by recognition of the fact that it is the sole means by which a man may exercise full and complete control over the only thing the Creator has given him to control, *the power of his own thoughts*. But personal initiative is sometimes misdirected. Therefore it needs supplemental guidance from the ninth principle—

9. ACCURATE THINKING. Accurate thinking not only insures against the misdirection of personal initiative, but it also insures against errors of judgment, guesswork, and premature decisions. It also protects one against the influence of his own undependable emotions by modifying them through the power of reason. The individual who has mastered these nine principles will find himself in possession of tremendous power, but personal power may be, and often is, dangerous if it is not controlled and directed through application of the tenth principle—

10. SELF-DISCIPLINE. Self-discipline cannot be had for the mere asking. Nor can it be acquired quickly. It is the product of carefully established and carefully maintained habits, which in many instances can be acquired only by many years of painstaking effort. So we have come to the point at which the power of the will must be brought into action, *for self-discipline is solely a product of the will*. Numberless men have risen to great power by the application of the nine preceding principles only to meet with ultimate failure. Self-discipline must begin with the application of the eleventh principle—

11. CONCENTRATION OF ENDEAVOR. The power of concentration is also a product of the will. It is so closely related to self-discipline that the two have been called the twin brothers of this philosophy. Concentration saves one from the dissipation of his energies, and aids him in keeping his mind focused upon the object of his Definite Major Purpose until it has been taken over by the subconscious section of the mind and there made ready for translation into its physical equivalent, through the law of Cosmic Habitforce. It is the camera's eye of the imagina-

tion through which the detailed outline of one's aims and purposes are recorded in the subconscious; hence it is indispensible. But even these powers are not sufficient for every circumstance; there are times when one must have the friendly cooperation of many people, such as customers, clients, or voters, all of which may be had through the application of the twelfth principle—

12. COOPERATION. Cooperation differs from the Master Mind principle in that it is a human relationship that is needed, and may be had, without a definite alliance with others based upon a complete fusion of the minds. Without cooperation of others one cannot attain success in the higher brackets of personal achievement, for cooperation is the means of major value by which one may extend the space he occupies in the minds of others, which is sometimes called goodwill. Cooperation is attained more freely and willingly by the application of the thirteenth principle—

13. ENTHUSIASM. Enthusiasm is a contagious state of mind that not only aids one in gaining the cooperation of others, but more importantly, it inspires the individual to draw upon and use the power of his own imagination. It inspires action also in the expression of personal initiative, and it leads to the habit of concentration of endeavor. Moreover, it is one of the qualities of major importance in a pleasing personality, and it makes easy the application of the principle of Going the Extra Mile. In addition to all these benefits, enthusiasm gives force and conviction to the spoken word. Enthusiasm is the product of *motive*, but it is difficult to maintain without the aid of the fourteenth principle—

14. THE HABIT OF HEALTH. Sound physical health provides a suitable housing place for the operation of the mind; hence it is an essential for enduring success, assuming that the word "success" shall embrace all of the requirements for happiness. Here again the word "habit" comes into prominence, for sound health begins with a "health consciousness" that can be developed only by the right habits of living. Sound health provides the basis for enthusiasm, and enthusiasm encourages sound health; so the two are like the hen and the egg: no one can determine which came into existence first, but everyone knows that both are essential for the production of either. Health and enthusiasm are like that. Both are essential for human progress and happiness.

15. BUDGETING TIME AND MONEY. Nearly everyone wishes to spend time and money freely, but budget and conserve them—never! However,

independence and freedom of body and mind, the two great desires of all mankind, cannot become enduring realities without the self-discipline of a strict budgeting system. Hence, this principle is an essential part of the philosophy of individual achievement.

16. THE GOLDEN RULE *APPLIED*. Note the emphasis on the word "applied." Belief in the soundness of the Golden Rule is not enough. To be of enduring benefit, and in order that it may serve as a safe guide in the use of personal power, it must be applied as a matter of habit, in all human relationships. Quite an order, this! But the benefits that are available through the application of this profound rule of human relations are worthy of the efforts necessary to develop it into a habit. The penalties for failure to live by this rule are too numerous to describe. Now we have attained the ultimate in personal power, and we have provided ourselves with the necessary insurance against its misuse. What we need from here on out is the means by which this power may be made permanent during our entire lifetime. We shall climax this philosophy, therefore, with the only known principle by which we may attain this desired end—the seventeenth and last principle of this philosophy—

17. COSMIC HABITFORCE. *Cosmic Habitforce* is the principle by which all habits are fixed and made permanent in varying degrees. As stated, it is the comptrolling principle of the entire philosophy, into which the preceding sixteen principles blend and become a part. And it is the comptrolling principle of all natural laws of the universe. It is the principle that gives the *fixation of habit* in the application of the principles of this philosophy. Mere understanding of the sixteen preceding principles will not lead anyone to the attainment of personal power. The principles must be understood and applied as a matter of strict habit, and habit is the sole work of the law of Cosmic Habitforce. Cosmic Habitforce is synonymous with the great River of Life, for it consists of a negative and a positive potentiality, as do all forms of energy.

You now have at your command a *complete philosophy* of life that is sufficient for the solution of every individual problem. It is a philosophy of principles, some combination of which has been responsible for every individual success in every occupation or calling.

## Chapter Ten
# Self-Discipline

Self-discipline is one of the Twelve Riches, but it is much more; it is an important prerequisite for the attainment of all riches, including freedom of mind and body, power and fame, and all the material things that are called wealth.

It is the sole means by which one may focus the mind upon the objective of a Definite Major Purpose until the law of Cosmic Habitforce takes over the pattern of that purpose and begins to translate it into its material equivalent.

It is the key to the volitional *power of the will* and the *emotions of the heart*, for it is the means by which these two may be mastered and balanced, one against the other, and directed to definite ends in *accurate thinking*.

It is the directing force in the maintenance of a Definite Major Purpose.

Also it operates entirely through the functioning system of the mind. Therefore, let us examine this system so that we may understand the factors of which it consists.

## THE TEN FACTORS OF THE "MECHANISM" OF THOUGHT

The mind operates through ten factors, some of which operate automatically, while others must be directed through voluntary effort. *Self-disciple is the sole means of this direction.*

The ten factors are:

1. INFINITE INTELLIGENCE. The source of all power of thought, which operates automatically, but it may be organized and directed to definite ends through DEFINITENESS OF PURPOSE. Infinite intelligence may be likened to a great reservoir of water that overflows continuously, its branches flowing in small streams in many directions, and giving life to all vegetation and all living things. That portion of the stream that gives life to man supplies him also with the power of thought.

2. THE CONSCIOUS MIND. The individual mind functions through two departments. One is known as the conscious section of the mind; the other the subconscious. It is the opinion of psychologists that these two sections are comparable to an iceberg, the visible portion above the waterline representing the conscious section, and the invisible portion below the waterline representing the subconscious. Therefore it is obvi-

ous that the conscious section of the mind—that portion with which we consciously and voluntarily turn on the power of thought—is but a small portion of the whole, consisting of perhaps one-fifth of the available mind power. All the other essential functions are performed by the subconscious mind, which also serves as the connecting link between the conscious mind and *Infinite Intelligence*. It may be likened to the spigot of the consciousness mind, through which (by its control through self-discipline) more thought power may be turned on. Or it may be likened to a rich garden spot wherein may be planted and germinated the seed of any desired idea.

3. THE FACULTY OF WILLPOWER. The power of the will is the "boss" of all departments of the mind. It has the power to modify, change, or balance all thinking habits, and its decisions are final and irrevocable except by itself. It is the power that puts the emotions of the heart under control, and it is subject to direction only by self-discipline. In this connection, it may be likened to the Chairman of the Board of Directors whose decisions are final. It takes its orders from the conscious mind, *but recognizes no other authority*.

4. THE FACULTY OF REASON. This is the "presiding judge" of the conscious section of the mind, which may pass judgment on all its ideas, plans, and desires, and it will do so if it is directed by self-discipline. But its decisions can be set aside by the power of the will, or modified by the power of the emotions when the will does not interfere. Let us here take note that all accurate thinking requires the cooperation of the faculty of reason, *although it is a requirement which not more than one person in every ten thousand respects*. This is why there are so few accurate thinkers. Most so-called thinking is the work of the emotions without the guiding influence of self-discipline; without relationship to either the power of the will or the faculty of reason.

5. THE FACULTY OF THE EMOTIONS. This is the source of most of the actions of the mind, the seat of most of the thoughts released by the conscious section of the mind. The emotions are tricky and undependable and may be very dangerous if they are not modified by the faculty of reason under the direction of the faculty of the will. However, the faculty of the emotions is not to be condemned because of its unpredictability, for it is the source of all enthusiasm, imagination, and Creative Vision, and it may be directed by self-discipline to the development of these essentials

of individual achievement. The direction may be given by modification of the emotions through the faculties of the will and the reason. *Accurate thinking* is not possible without complete mastery of the emotions. The emotions that are most important and most dangerous are: (1) the emotion of sex, (2) the emotion of love, and (3) the emotion of fear. *These are the emotions that produce the major portion of all human activities.* The emotions of love and sex are creative. When controlled and directed they inspire one with imagination and creative vision of stupendous proportions. If they are not controlled and directed they may lead one to indulge in tremendous follies.

6. THE FACULTY OF IMAGINATION. This is the workshop wherein are shaped and fashioned all desires, ideas, plans, and purposes, together with the means of attaining them. Through organized use and self-discipline the imagination may be developed to the status of Creative Vision. But the faculty of the imagination, like the faculty of the emotions, is tricky and undependable if it is not controlled and directed by self-discipline. Without control it often dissipates the power of thought in useless, impractical, and destructive activities. *Uncontrolled imagination is the stuff that daydreams are made of!*

7. THE FACULTY OF CONSCIENCE. The conscience is the moral guide of the mind, and its major purpose is modifying the individual's aims and purposes so that they harmonize with the moral laws of nature and of mankind. The conscience is the twin-brother of the faculty of reason in that it gives discrimination and guidance to the reason when reason is in doubt. The conscience functions as a cooperative guide only so long as it is respected and followed. If it is neglected, or its mandates are rejected, it finally becomes a conspirator instead of a guide, and often volunteers to justify man's destructive habits. Thus the dual nature of the conscience makes it necessary for one to direct it through strict self-discipline.

8. THE SIXTH SENSE. This is the "broadcasting station" of the mind through which one automatically sends and receives the vibrations of thought commonly known as telepathy. It is the medium through which all thought impulses and hunches are received. And it is closely related to, or perhaps it may be a part of, the subconscious. The sixth sense is the medium through which Creative Vision operates. It is the medium through which all basically new ideas are revealed. And it is the major asset of the minds of all who are known as geniuses.

9. THE MEMORY. This is the filing cabinet of the brain, wherein is stored all thought impulses, all experiences, and all sensations that reach the brain through the five physical senses.. And it may be the filing cabinet of all impulses of thought that reach the mind through the sixth sense. The memory is tricky and undependable unless it is organized and directed by self-discipline.
10. THE FIVE PHYSICAL SENSES. These are the physical arms of the brain through which it contacts the external world and acquires information. The physical senses are not reliable, and therefore require constant self-discipline. Under any kind of intense emotional activity the senses become confused and unreliable. The five senses are easily deceived. And they are deceived daily by the common experiences of life. Under the emotion of fear the physical senses often create monstrous "ghosts" that have no existence except in the faculty of the imagination, and there is no fact of life that they will not exaggerate or distort when fear prevails. In this sense, fear is the archenemy of mankind.

Before leaving the analysis of self-discipline, which deals entirely with the mechanism of thought, let us briefly describe some of the known facts and habits of thought in order that we may acquire the art of accurate thinking.
1. All thought (whether it is positive or negative, good or bad, accurate or inaccurate) tends to clothe itself in its physical equivalent, and it does so by inspiring one with ideas, plans, and the means of attaining desired ends, through logical and natural methods.
2. Through the application of self-discipline thought can be influenced, controlled, and directed through transmutation to a desired end, by the development of voluntary habits suitable for the attainment of any given end.
3. The power of thought (through the aid of the subconscious) has control over every cell of the body and all the effects therein. These functions are carried on automatically but many may be stimulated by voluntary aid.
4. All of man's achievements begin in the form of thought, organized into plans, aims, and purposes, and expressed in terms of physical action. All action is inspired by one or more of the nine basic motives.
5. The entire power of the mind operates through the conscious and subconscious. The conscious section is under the control of the individual; the subconscious is controlled by Infinite Intelligence and is the medium of communication between Infinite Intelligence and the conscious mind.

6. Both the conscious and subconscious function in response to fixed habits, whether the habits are voluntary or involuntary.
7. The majority of one's thoughts are inaccurate because they are inspired by personal opinions that are reached without examination of the facts, or because of bias, prejudice, fear, and emotional excitement.
8. The first step in accurate thinking is that of separating facts from hearsay evidence and emotional reactions. The second step is that of separating facts, after they have been identified as such, into two classes: important and unimportant. An important fact can be used to help you attain your major purpose. All other facts are relatively unimportant.
9. Desire, based on a definite motive, is the beginning of all voluntary thought action associated with individual achievement. The presence in the mind of any intense desire tends to stimulate the faculty of the imagination with the purpose of creating ways and means of attaining the desire.

These are some of the more important of the known facts concerning the greatest of mysteries, the mystery of human thought, and they indicate clearly that accurate thinking is attainable only by the strictest habits of self-discipline.

The lights were now dimmed. The masked rich man from Happy Valley finished speaking and disappeared into the darkness as mysteriously as he had arrived, but he had given every member of that huge audience a new birth of hope, faith, and courage.

*Remember it is profoundly significant that the only thing over which you have complete control is your own mental attitude!*

If the rich man from Happy Valley has brought you nothing but this great truth he has provided you with a source to riches of incomparable value; for this is the Master Key to Riches!

# The Magic of Believing
(1948)

## by Claude M. Bristol

*The Immortal Program to Unlocking the Success-Power of Your Mind*

## Contents

Introduction   *The Metaphysics of Success* by Mitch Horowitz   748
Chapter One   How I Came to Tap the Power of Belief   749
Chapter Two   Mind-Stuff Experiments   750
Chapter Three   Suggestion Is Power   755
Chapter Four   The Art of Mental Pictures   756
Chapter Five   The Mirror Technique for Releasing the Subconscious   757
Chapter Six   How to Project Your Thoughts   760
Chapter Seven   Belief Makes Things Happen   764

## Introduction
# The Metaphysics of Success

The American metaphysical scene has produced no other figure quite like Claude M. Bristol. Born in 1891, Bristol had a background as varied as the nation itself: a veteran, a seeker, a sometime journalist, a sometime businessman, and an enthusiast of the possibilities and powers of the mind.

As a veteran, Bristol returned from World War One to witness a nation in transition. The American economy was growing but the mass of people returning from the war, many of whom came from agrarian roots and had never worked in manufacturing or large offices, were unsure of how to enter the new economy. Bristol believed that the threshold of prosperity began in the mind. He wrote his two and only books—the fullest being *The Magic of Believing*—in order to place his ideas about the powers of the mind within reach of the broadest range of people.

Within this abridgment of his immensely popular book you're going to hear about topics that are not always held in high repute these days: ESP, telepathy, and telekinesis, among them. When abridging this book, I made the decision to retain this material—and I did not do so lightly. As I've written in my own analysis of the positive-thinking movement, *One Simple Idea*, I believe that many journalists and academics today have failed to understand, or even attain basic familiarity with, the experiments to which Bristol refers, particularly those conducted by ESP researcher J.B. Rhine at Duke University beginning in the early 1930s.

I take seriously Bristol's contention that legitimate parapsychology has much to offer the motivational seeker. Speaking as a historian who has considered this field, I can vouch for the general validity of Bristol's popularizations and suggested applications of some parapsychological experiments. Indeed, Bristol was one of the few positive-mind theorists of his day who rightly highlighted the work of J.B. Rhine and his contemporaries.

I think that you will find *The Magic of Believing*, first published in 1948, a surprising and still-radical journey into the possibilities of the mind. We remain at the early stages of grappling with higher mental possibilities today, gaining a glimpse of them in a new wave of experiments in placebo studies, neuroplasticity, precognition, and quantum theorizing.

Bristol, in his way, makes very large questions about the mind seem simple—because he believed that simple, personal experiments *were* possible, and could prove the efficacy of positive-mind mechanics in daily life, including in matters of career, creativity, and relationships.

I think Bristol was right. And I invite you to approach this book with a spirit of enthusiasm, expectancy, and personal adventure.

—Mitch Horowitz

Chapter One

# How I Came to Tap the Power of Belief

Is there a something, a force, a factor, a power, a science—call it what you will—which a few people understand and use to overcome their difficulties and achieve outstanding success? I firmly believe that there is, and it is my purpose to attempt to explain it so that you may use it if you desire.

About fifteen years ago the financial editor of a great Los Angeles newspaper, after attending lectures I had given to financial men in that city, wrote: "You have caught from the ether something that has a mystical quality—a something that explains the magic of coincidence, the mystery of what makes men lucky."

I realized that I had run across something that was workable, but I didn't consider it then, neither do I now, as anything mystical, except in the sense that it is unknown to the majority of people. It is something that has always been known to a fortunate few down the centuries, but, for some unknown reason, is little understood by the average person.

When I started out years ago to teach this science, I wasn't certain that it could be or would be grasped by the ordinary individual; but now that I have seen those who have used it double and triple their incomes, build their own successful businesses, acquire homes in the country, and create sizable fortunes, I am convinced that any intelligent person who is sincere with himself can reach any heights he desires.

The science of thought is as old as man himself. The wise men of all ages have known about it and used it. The only thing the writer has done is to put the subject in modern language and bring to the reader's attention what a few of the outstanding minds of today are doing to substantiate the great truths that have come down through the centuries.

Much has been written and said about mystical powers, unknown forces, the occult, metaphysics, mental physics, psychology, black and white magic, and many kindred subjects, causing most people to believe that they are in the field of the supernatural. Perhaps they are for some, but my conclusion is that the only inexplicable thing about these powers is that it is *belief* that makes them work.

## Chapter Two
# Mind-Stuff Experiments

In order to get a clearer understanding of our subject, the reader should give thought to thought itself and to its phenomena. No one knows what thought really is, other than it is some sort of mental action; but, like the unknown element electricity, we see its manifestations everywhere. We see it in the actions and expressions of a child, in an aged person, in animals, and, in fact, to varying degrees in every living thing. The more we contemplate and study thought, the more we realize what a terrific force it is and how unlimited are its powers.

Glance around as you read this. If you are in a furnished room, your eyes tell you that you are looking at a number of inanimate objects. That is true so far as visual perception is concerned; but in reality you are actually looking at thoughts or ideas that have come into materialization through the creative work of some human being. It was a thought, first, that created the furniture, fashioned the window glass, gave form to the draperies and coverings.

The automobile, the skyscraper, the great planes that sweep the stratosphere, the sewing machine, the tiny pin, a thousand and one things—yes, millions of objects—where did they come from originally? Only one source. From that strange force— thought. As we analyze further, we realize that these achievements, and in fact all of our possessions, came as a result of creative thinking. Ralph Waldo Emerson declared that the ancestor of every action is thought; when we understand that, we begin to comprehend that our world is governed by thought and that everything without had its counterpart originally within the mind. It is just as Buddha said many centuries ago: "All that we are is the result of what we have thought."

Figuratively, thought makes giants out of pigmies, and often turns giants into pigmies. History is filled with accounts of how thought has made weak men strong and strong men weak, and we see evidence of its working around us constantly.

You do not eat, wear clothes, run for a bus, drive your automobile, go for a walk, or read a newspaper—you don't even raise your arm—without a preceding thought-impulse. While you may consider the motions you make as more or less automatic, perhaps caused by some physical reflexes, behind every single step you take in life, regardless of its direction, is that formidable and powerful force—thought.

The very way you walk, the way you carry yourself, your talk, your manner of dress, all reflect your way of thinking. A slovenly carriage is an indication of slovenly thinking, whereas an alert, upright carriage is the outward sign of inward strength and confidence. What you exhibit outwardly, you are inwardly.

You are the product of your own thought. What you believe yourself to be, you are.

Thought is the original source of all wealth, all success, all material gain, all great discoveries and inventions, and of all achievement. Without it there would be no great empires, no great fortunes, no great transcontinental rail lines, no modern conveniences; in fact, there would be no advance over life in the most primitive ages.

Your thoughts, those that predominate, determine your character, your career, indeed your everyday life. Thus it becomes easy to understand what is meant by the statement that a man's thoughts make or break him. And when we realize that there can be no action or reaction, either good or bad, without the generating force of thought initiating it, the Biblical saying, "For whatsoever a man soweth, that shall he also reap," and Shakespeare's words, "There is nothing either good or bad, but thinking makes it so," become more intelligible.

Sir Arthur Eddington, the English physicist, says that to an altogether unsuspected extent the universe in which we live is a creation of our minds; while the late Sir James Jeans, who was equally famous in the same field, suggested that the universe was merely a creation that resulted from the thought of some great universal mind underlying and coordinating all of our minds. Nothing is clearer than that the world's greatest scientists and thinkers of our age are not only voicing the ideas of the wisest men of old, but that they are confirming the fundamental principle of this book.

Almost since the beginning of the human race, the molding of men has been done by those who knew something of thought's great power. All the great religious leaders, kings, warriors, statesmen have understood this science and have known that people act as they think and also react to the thought of others, especially when it is stronger and more convincing than their own. Accordingly, men of powerful dynamic thought have ever swayed the people by appealing to their minds, sometimes to lead them into freedom and sometimes into slavery. There never was a period in history when we should study our own thoughts more, try to understand them, and learn how to use them to improve our position in life, by drawing upon the great source of power that lies within each of us.

There was a time when I would have laughed at people who talked about the magnetic force of thought, how thought correlates with its object, how it can affect people and inanimate things, even at great distances. But I no longer laugh, nor do others who know something of its power, for anyone who has any intelligence sooner or later comes to the realization that thought can change the surface of the entire globe.

The late George Russell, famous Irish editor and poet, was quoted as saying that we become what we contemplate. Undoubtedly, we become what we envisage, and he certainly demonstrated it in his own life by becoming a great writer, lecturer, painter, and poet.

However, it must be borne in mind that many of our ideas, the thoughts we think, are not ours at all, or those of our own originating. We are molded also by the thoughts of others; by what we hear in our social life, what we read in newspapers, magazines, and books; what we hear in the movies, the theater, and on the radio; even by chance remarks from the conversation of bystanders—and these thoughts bombard us constantly. Some of them that accord with our own inmost thoughts and also open the way to greater visions in our life are helpful. But often there are thoughts that are upsetting, that weaken our self-confidence, and turn us away from our high purposes. It is these outside thoughts that are the troublemakers, and later I shall point out how you can keep free of them.

One essential to success is that your desire be an all-obsessing one, your thoughts and aims be coordinated, and your energy be concentrated and applied without letup. It may be riches or fame or position or knowledge that you want, for each person has his own idea of what success means to him. But whatever you consider it to be, you can have it provided you are willing to make the objective the burning desire of your life. A big order, you say. Not at all; by using the dynamic force of believing, you can set all your inner forces in motion, and they in turn will help you to reach your goal. If you are married, you remember the stimulating and emotional experience of courting the girl you wanted for your wife. Certainly, it wasn't nerve-racking work—quite the contrary, you'll admit—but what were you using, if not this very same science, even though unconsciously. The desire to win a helpmate was uppermost in your mind from the time you got the idea until your marriage. The thought, the belief, was with you every minute of the day and perhaps it was with you in your dreams.

Now that you have a clearer idea of the part that thought and desire play in our daily lives, the first thing to determine is precisely what you want. Starting in with the general idea that you merely want to be a success, as most people do, is too indefinite. You must have a mental pattern clearly drawn in your mind. Ask yourself: Where am I headed? What is my goal? Have I visualized just what I really want? If success is to be measured in terms of wealth, can you fix the amount in figures? If in terms of achievement, can you specify it definitely?

I ask these questions, for in their answers are factors that will determine your whole life from now on. Strange as it may appear, not one out of a hundred people can answer these questions. Most people have a general idea that they would like to be a success, but beyond that everything is vague. They merely go along from day to day figuring that if they have a job today they will have it tomorrow, and that somehow they will be looked after in their old age. They are like a cork on the water floating aimlessly, drawn this way and that by various currents, and either being washed up on the shore, or becoming waterlogged and eventually sinking.

Therefore, it is vital that you know exactly what you want out of life. You must know where you are headed, and you must keep a fixed goal in view. That, of course, is the over-all picture; it makes no difference whether you want *a* job or a *better* one, a new house, a place in the country, or just a new pair of shoes. You must have a fixed idea before you'll obtain what you are after.

There is a great difference between a need and a desire. For example, you may *need* a new car for business, and you may *desire* one in order to give pleasure to your family. The one for your business you will get as a matter of necessity. The one for your family you will plan to get as soon as possible. For this car you will make an extra effort, because it is something you have never had before, something that will add to your responsibilities, and something that will compel you to seek new powers within yourself and new resources outside. It is desire for something new, something different, something that is going to change your life, that causes you to make an extra effort; and it is the *power of believing* that alone sets in motion those inner forces by which you add what I call *plus-values* to your life.

Do you know that departments of psychology in great universities have already undertaken experiments to determine whether the mind possesses the power to influence material objects, and that the experiments have already demonstrated the existence of such a power? While the experiments have not been too widely publicized, there have been stories appearing from time to time giving the general facts.

Perhaps the most outstanding work has been done at Duke University, where Dr. J. B. Rhine and his associates have demonstrated that psychokinesis, the name given to designate the power of mind by which material objects are influenced, is much more than idle theory. Dice (yes, the old army type of dice used in crap games) were thrown by a mechanical device to eliminate all possibility of personal influence and trickery. Since 1934 when experiments of this type were started, there have been many tests in which millions of throws of the dice have been made. The results were such as to cause Dr. Rhine to declare that "there is no better explanation than the subjects influenced the fall of the dice without any recognized physical contacts with them." By mentally concentrating upon the appearance of certain numbers, while at the same time they stood at a distance to avoid all physical contact with the mechanical thrower and with the dice, the experimenters were frequently able to control the dice. In a number of the experiments, the scores made under psychokinesis refuted some of the traditional mathematical odds of millions to one against the reappearance of certain combinations of numbers in repeated succession.

Meditate over this for a few minutes and then realize what it means to you. Those experiments give you some idea of what is meant by "Thought creates after its kind," "Thought correlates with its object," "Thought attracts that upon which it is directed," and similar statements that we have heard for years. Recall that it was Job who said: "For the thing which I greatly feared is come upon me." Our fear thoughts are just as creative or just as magnetic in attracting troubles to us as are the constructive and positive thoughts in attracting positive results. So no matter what the character of the thought, it does create after its kind. When this sinks into a man's consciousness, he gets some inkling of the awe-inspiring power that is his to use.

## Chapter Three
# Suggestion Is Power

After studying the various mystical religions and different teachings and systems of mind-stuff, one is impressed with the fact that they all have the same basic modus operandi, and that is through repetition—the repeating of certain mantras, words, and formulas.

One finds the same principle at work in the chants, the incantations, litanies, daily lessons (to be repeated as frequently as possible during the week), the frequent praying of the Buddhists and Moslems alike, the affirmations of the Theosophists and the followers of Unity, the Absolute Truth, New Thought, and Divine Science.

The Bible is filled with examples of the power of thought and suggestion. Read Genesis, chapter 30, verses 36 to 43, and you'll learn that even Jacob knew its power. The Bible tells how he developed spotted and speckled cattle, sheep, and goats by placing rods from trees, partially stripping them of their bark so they would appear spotted and marked, in the watering troughs where the animals came to drink. As you may have guessed, the flocks conceived before the spotted rods and brought forth cattle, "ringstraked, speckled, and spotted," and incidentally Jacob waxed exceedingly rich.

Moses, too, was a master at suggestion. For forty years he used it on the Israelites, and it took them to the promised land of milk and honey. David, following the suggestive forces operating on him, slew the mighty, heavily armed Goliath with a pebble from a slingshot.

William James, father of modern psychology in America, declared that often our faith [belief] in advance of a doubtful undertaking is the only thing that can assure its successful conclusion. Man's faith, according to James, acts on the powers above him as a claim and creates its own verification. In other words, the thought becomes literally father to the fact. For further illumination of faith and its power, I suggest that you read the General Epistle of James in the New Testament.

Recall the panic on the night of October 20, 1938, when Orson Welles and his Mercury Theater players put on the air a dramatization of H. G. Wells' novel, *The War of the Worlds*. It was a story of an invasion by some strange warriors from the planet Mars, but it caused fright among millions of people. Some rushed out-of-doors, police stations were besieged, eastern telephone exchanges were blocked, New Jersey highways were clogged. In fact, for a few hours following the broadcast, there was genuine panic among millions of listeners because they believed our earth was being attacked by invaders from Mars. Yes, indeed, belief can and does cause some strange and unusual happenings.

Let's take an example out of the war. General Douglas MacArthur declared when he left the Philippines: "I shall return." With our Pacific Fleet in ruins at Pearl Harbor, practically no airplanes or transports at the time, and with the Japanese in control of most of the South Pacific, MacArthur had no physical evidence that he would ever return. However, he must have had a mental picture of his return or he would have never made the statement. It was a statement of confidence or belief, and history relates his triumphant return. Thousands of similar cases happened during the war and are happening today.

## Chapter Four
# The Art of Mental Pictures

Emile Coué, the French hypnotherapist who threw so much light on the power of suggestion, declared that imagination was a much stronger force than willpower; when the two are in conflict, he said, the imagination always wins. In explanation, let's say you are an inveterate smoker of good cigars and decide to break yourself of the habit. You grit your teeth, shove out your chin, and solemnly declare that you are going to use your willpower to break yourself of the habit. Then suddenly comes the idea of the taste of a good cigar, its aroma and its soothing effects—the imagination goes to work and the resolution to break the habit goes out the window. The same holds true of efforts to break the drinking habit and other bad habits.

Charles Fourier, a French philosopher of more than a century ago, declared that the future of the world would grow out of the brain of man, shaped, controlled, and directed by the desires and passions by which men are moved. His prophecy is coming true, yet man through his mind has barely started shaping and controlling the world.

All of this brings us to the topic of desire and what you actually want in life. There are comparatively few people with great desires. Most are content to go along filling the tiny niches in which they find themselves. They accept their positions in life as something that fate has fixed for them, and very seldom do they make either a mental or physical effort to extract themselves from those positions. They never raise their sights or realize that it's just as easy to shoot at a bird on a limb thirty feet above the ground as it is to shoot at it on the ground the same distance away. Many engage in wishful thinking, but wishful thinking in itself is without effect simply because the power factor is missing.

But when you run across a person who is "going to town"—and there are many—you realize that the great power behind it all is projected by desire. The way seems easy for those people— and to a great degree it is—because they are putting to use the powers of their subconscious minds that, in turn, magnetize, coordinate, and then transmit to their conscious minds the electrifying vision of the object of their desire.

So let's be reminded that whatever we fix our thoughts upon or steadily focus our imaginations upon, that is what we attract. This is no mere play of words. It is a fact that anyone can prove to his own satisfaction. Whether the results come through magnetic or electrical energy is something still undetermined; while man hasn't been able to define it, manifestations of thought-attraction can be seen on every hand. It is like the electrical field itself—we do not know what electricity is, although in a material sense we know how man can generate it through various kinds of energy-producing apparatus; we see electricity manifest every time we turn on a light or snap a switch.

## Chapter Five
# The Mirror Technique for Releasing the Subconscious

I want to tell you about something called the mirror technique. It is a method of great power. Stand in front of a mirror. It need not be a full-length mirror, but it should be of sufficient size so that you may at least see your body from the waist up.

Those of you who have been in the army know what it means to come to attention—stand fully erect, bring your heels together, pull in your stomach, keep your chest out and your head up. Now breathe deeply three or four times until you feel a sense of power, strength, and determination. Next, look into the very depths of your eyes, tell yourself that you are going to get what you want—name it aloud so you can see your lips move and you can hear the words uttered. Make a regular ritual of it, practice doing it at least twice a day, mornings and evenings—and you will be surprised at the results. You can augment this by taping notes on the face of the mirror with any slogans or key words you wish, so long as they are the key to what you have previously visualized and want to see in reality. Within a few days you will have developed a sense of confidence that you never realized you could build within yourself.

If you are planning to call on an exceptionally tough prospect or are proposing to interview the boss whom you may have previously feared, use the mirror technique, and keep it up until you are convinced that you can make the proper presentation without any trepidation. If you are called upon to make a speech, by all means practice before a mirror. Gesticulate—pound your fist on the palm of your other hand to drive home the arguments—use any other gestures that come naturally to you.

As you stand before the mirror, keep telling yourself that you are going to be an outstanding success and that nothing in this world is going to stop you. Does this sound silly? Don't forget that every idea presented to the subconscious mind is going to be produced in its exact counterpart in objective life, and the quicker your subconscious gets the idea, the sooner your wish becomes a picture of power. Certainly it is not good business for you to tell anyone of the devices you employ, because you might be ridiculed by scoffers and your confidence shaken, especially if you are just beginning to learn the science.

If you are an executive or sales manager and you want to put more push into your entire organization, teach your employees the mirror technique and see that they use it, just as many organizations now do.

Much has been written about the power of the eyes. The eyes are said to be the windows of the soul; they reveal your thoughts. They express you far more than you imagine. They permit others to "get your number," as the saying goes. However, you will find that once you start this mirror practice your eyes will take on a power that you never realized you could develop (something that writers have referred to as a dynamic or fascinating power); this power will give you that penetrating gaze that causes others to think you are looking into their very souls. Sooner or later there will come an intensity that will bespeak the intensity of your thought, which people will begin to recognize. It will be recalled that Emerson wrote that every man carries in his eye the exact indication of his rank. Remember that your own gradation or position in life is marked by what you carry in your eyes. So develop eyes that bespeak confidence. The mirror will help you.

This mirror technique may be used in many different ways and with very gratifying results. If you have a poor posture, or are slovenly in your walk, you will find that practice before a full-length mirror will work wonders for you. Your mirror shows you the person others see when they look at you, and you can fashion yourself into any kind of person you would like them to see.

It is said that if you act the part you will become that part, and here again there is no better way than rehearsing your acting before the mirror. Vanity has no part in this science. Consequently, don't use the mirror in a supercilious manner, but use it to build yourself into the person you wish to be. Surely, if some of the world's most outstanding men and women use this mirror technique to build themselves and increase their influence over other people, you can use it for your own special requirements.

Much has been written about intuition, hunches, and the like. Some psychologists claim that ideas which come to us intuitively are not something "out of the blue," but come as a result of our accumulated knowledge or because of something we may have seen or heard in earlier times. That may be true to some extent with chemists, inventors, and others who work by the "trial and error" method of using their knowledge and the results of previous experiments, but it's the writer's belief that by far the greatest number of discoveries, illuminations, and inspired works come from the subconscious mind, without previous knowledge having been planted in the mind. Every custom we follow, everything we utilize was first an idea in someone's mind, and those ideas came first in the way of "hunches," intuitive flashes, or call them what you will. So it is wise to heed your intuitions and to trust them to the end.

You may have a hunch to call on or telephone a certain man. He may be the head of some concern and in a position to be of great help to you. However, because of his position you may fear to make the move and you struggle with your "hunch" on one hand and your fear on the other. The fear too often wins. The next time fear or doubt enters your mind, ask yourself this question: "What have I got to lose if I do see him or call him? What harm can I do?" Your fears and doubts can't answer that question. So obey your hunch without delay.

The writer takes it for granted that none of his readers will assume that this book is an open-sesame to riches and fame overnight. It is intended only as a key to unlock the door that opens on the roadway that will lead to the goal of your desire. Certainly it wouldn't be wise to rush into undertakings far beyond your capabilities or your development. You must have a plan of action before any program is undertaken. You wouldn't go to the corner drugstore and ask just for drugs. You would be specific and name the drugs desired. And so it is with this science. You must have a plan of action—you've got to know what you want and be specific about it.

If you have definitely determined what you want and have fixed a goal for yourself, then consider yourself extremely fortunate, for you have taken the first step that will lead to success. As long as you hold on to the mental picture of your idea and begin to develop it with action, nothing can stop you from succeeding, for the subconscious mind never fails to obey any order given to it clearly and emphatically.

## Chapter Six
# How to Project Your Thoughts

Anyone who has traveled through the great farming belts of our country and Canada can tell by a glance at the house or barn whether the farmer is alive or whether he is dying on his feet. I think of some of the great orchardists of the Pacific Northwest who twenty or thirty years ago couldn't sell a whole wagonload of pears or apples for twenty dollars; and yet men who had the idea of attractive packaging and marketing in recent years have made large fortunes. It's nothing to get people to pay two dollars or more for a dozen apples or pears carefully wrapped in tissue, waxed paper, or tinfoil; some of these alert orchardists sell their products by mail to thousands of buyers throughout the world. I happen to know personally a number of these operators and their success in each instance has been predicated upon an idea that came to them in a flash and that developed as a result of their believing.

Now consider this matter of packaging in connection with yourself. Do you have eye-appeal? Do you wear clothes to give yourself the best appearance? Do you know the effect of colors and study those which best suit your form and temperament? Does your whole appearance set you apart from many who pass unnoticed in the crowd? If not, give thoughtful attention to personal packaging, for the world accepts you as you appear to be. Take a tip from the automobile manufacturers, the Hollywood make-up artists, or any of the great show producers, who know the value of eye-appeal and package their goods accordingly. When you have a combination of proper packaging and highest quality goods within the package, you have an unbeatable combination. The *you* within can do the same thing for the *you* outside—and you, too, have the unbeatable combination.

To satisfy yourself on what the right appearance will do for you, just pass by where there is construction under way. If you are well-dressed and have an air of prosperity and importance, workmen who may be in your path will step aside as you pass. Or you might try stepping into an outer office where others may be waiting to see a certain executive. Notice that the important-looking individual with the air and voice of authority gets first attention not only from the office attendants but from the executive.

No better example of the impressiveness of a good appearance can be given than the distinction made between individuals by attendants at a police station or jail. The stylishly dressed, well-poised businessman is seldom ill treated, while the man who has the appearance of a bum lands almost immediately in a cell. As a police reporter on metropolitan newspapers for a number of years, I saw this happen times without number. The fellow who looked as though he might be "somebody" and who had been arrested for a minor law infraction, often got a chair in the captain's office until he could telephone the judge or some friend to obtain his release, while the bum was carted off to jail, to get his release when and if he could.

The head of a huge automobile distributing agency told me that he was frequently called upon to close a sale with wealthy men who always bought the most expensive cars. "Not only do I take a shower," he said, "and change all my clothes, but I go to a barbershop and get everything from a shave to a shampoo and manicure. Obviously, it has something to do with my appearance, but further than that it does something to me inside. It makes me feel like a new man who could lick his weight in wildcats."

If you are properly attired when you are starting out on some important undertaking, you will feel within yourself that sense of power, which will cause people to give way before you and will even stir others to help you on your way. The right mental attitude, keeping your eyes straight ahead and fixed on your goal, throwing around you the proper aura, which is done by an act of your imagination or an extension of your personal magnetism, will work wonders.

It is always important to remember that a negative person can raise havoc in an organization or a home. The same amount of damage can be done by a strong negative personality as good can be done by a positive personality, and when the two are pitted against one another, the negative frequently becomes the more powerful.

An extremely nervous person in a position of authority can put nearly every person associated with him into a nervous state. You can see this happen in almost any office or shop where the executive is of a nervous type. Sometimes this emotional pattern will extend throughout an entire organization. After all, as has been said, an organization is only the extended shadow of the man who heads it. Thus, to have a smoothly running organization, all its members must be attuned to the thinking of the principal executive. A strong negative personality in such an organization, who is out of tune with the ideas of the management, can extend his negative vibrations to others and do great damage.

If you would remain a positive type, avoid associating too much with anyone who has a negative or pessimistic personality. Many clergymen and personnel counselors often become victims of prolonged association with people who come to them with their troubles. The impact of the steady stream of woe and sorrow vibrations eventually reverses their positive polarity and reduces them to a negative state.

To get a better understanding of the effect of these suggestive vibrations, you need only remember your varying feelings upon entering different offices or homes. The atmosphere, which is the creation of the people habitually frequenting the office or home, can be instantly detected as being upsetting, disturbing, tranquil, or harmonious.

You can tell almost instantly whether the atmosphere is cold or warm—the arrangement of the furniture, the color scheme, the very walls themselves, all vibrate to the thinking of the persons occupying the place, and bespeak the type to which their thoughts belong. Whether the home be a mansion or a shack, the vibrations are always a key to the personality of those who occupy it.

In recent years there has been a renewed interest in telepathy or thought-transference, arising out of the experiments and investigations carried on in many colleges and universities, particularly those conducted under the direction of Dr. J. B. Rhine of Duke University. The records of both the American and British Societies for Psychical Research are filled with case reports of telepathy, clairvoyance, and similar phenomena, but many people, despite the published reports of scientific findings, are prone to scoff at the idea that telepathy exists.

It has always struck me as odd that many people who profess to believe in the Bible, in which there are countless stories of visions, clairvoyance, and telepathy, declare that today telepathy and kindred phenomena are not possible. Notwithstanding the general skepticism, some of the world's greatest scientific thinkers have declared that telepathy is not only possible but that it is a faculty that can be used by most people when they understand it. In addition to the findings of both the American and British Societies for Psychical Research, and the results made public by Dr. Rhine, there are numerous old and new books on the subject. A few of the better known ones are *Mental Radio* by Upton Sinclair; *Beyond the Senses* by Dr. Charles Francis Potter, well-known New York preacher; *Thoughts Through Space*, by Harold Sherman and Sir Hubert Wilkins, famous explorer; *Telepathy* by Eileen Garrett, editor and publisher; and *Experimental Telepathy*, by René Warcollier, Director of The Institute Metaphysique International in Paris.

When the results of Dr. Rhine's experiments at Duke University were first made public, there were many men who rushed into print to declare that the results could be laid to chance, and considerable time and money were spent in an endeavor to prove that telepathy was non-existent. Yet the experiments continue at Duke and at other leading universities. I have often wondered why many opposing so-called scientific investigators do not try to prove that the phenomena exist instead of trying to prove the contrary; but here again the writer has a theory that belief is the miracle worker, and this is partly substantiated by what Dr. Rhine himself says in his book on extrasensory perception. He declares that satisfactory results were secured when the experimenters caught the "spirit of the thing," and that the ability to transmit and receive became weakened when the original novelty wore off. In other words, while there was enthusiasm there was spontaneous interest and the belief that it could be done. But when students were called back at later dates to continue their experiments in the course of their studies, enthusiasm was lacking, and the results were not satisfactory.

I think that anyone who understands the vibratory theory of thought power can also understand why unsympathetic vibrations can be "monkey wrenches thrown into the machinery." Verification of this is found in the experiments by Dr. Rhine, who discovered in his psychokinesis tests that when a subject operated in the presence of an observer who tried to distract him and depress his scoring, the results were always below expectancy. And, contrariwise, when the same subject performed alone or in the presence of neutral or sympathetic observers, his score of successes was correspondingly high.

Despite the fact that the secretary of the London Society for Psychical Research after twenty years of investigation by its members stated that telepathy is an actuality, and the further fact that experiments at the various colleges continue to pile up amazing evidence of its existence, there are many scientific men who refuse to accept the findings. Moreover, the number of people who are carrying on investigations of their own is constantly growing, even though they are regarded in certain quarters as being eccentric and somewhat gullible. I have often wondered if those who belittle this research are really being fair, both to themselves and those interested in the phenomena, especially when the research may lead to greater discoveries than hitherto dreamed possible.

You can get the same results when visitors overstay their time in your home. When you feel it is time for them to go, simply say to yourself, "Go home now, go home now, go home now," and you will find that they glance around the room looking for the clock and say, "Guess it's about time we were leaving."

I recognize that some skeptics will say that telepathy has nothing to do with this, that your facial expressions, your bodily movements, signs of nervousness or weariness are what warn the visitor that it is time for him to leave. However, experiment for yourself; but take care that you give the visitor no outward sign, either by word or facial expression, that it is time for his departure. You will find that there are times, especially if the visitor is intent upon putting over a point or winning an argument, that this procedure will not work. But the moment there is a lull in the conversation, try it and the results will astonish you.

## Chapter Seven
# Belief Makes Things Happen

I have long held the conviction that various forms of telepathy or thought-transmission are used every day of our lives, far more than most people suspect. I believe that many great leaders, preachers, orators, executives, and so-called super-salesmen, some unconsciously and others thoroughly conscious of its workings, exercise the power to varying degrees. We meet a person, and before a word is spoken we experience a like or a dislike. What is it that causes the feeling to register but some form of thought-transmission? I believe that the only possible explanation of healing and affecting others at a distance is through the medium of this phenomenon, of which we are only now beginning to get a scientific explanation.

Some people have had the experience of walking into a darkened room and feeling the presence of someone there, even before a word was uttered. Certainly, it couldn't have been anything else but the vibrations of some unseen individual that indicated his presence to the other person. Evidence of telepathy? What do *you* think? It is maintained that if the first person in the room will, at the entry of the second person, think of something entirely foreign to himself and dismiss from his mind all thought of the possibility of his discovery, the second person will not sense his presence. There are thousands of people who have thought of someone, only to hear from them or see them shortly thereafter, and they have given no heed to the phenomena involved. These experiences are usually considered coincidences; but when we properly consider the power of thought, do we not have the real explanation? I cannot help but feel that anyone with an open mind and willing to read and experiment for himself, will sooner or later come to the conclusion that the phenomena of psychokinesis and telepathy are realities, and, as investigators have pointed out, that these powers are latent in everyone, though developed to varying degrees.

When we consider the subconscious mind of a single individual as being only an infinitesimal part of the whole and the vibrations therefrom extending to and embracing everything, we get a better understanding of the workings of psychokinesis, telepathy, and kindred phenomena.

In explaining psychokinesis, Dr. J.B. Rhine points out that there must be a mental attitude of expectancy, concentration of thought, and enthusiasm for the desired results if a person is to be successful in the experiments. Again we have the magic of believing at work. The subject must have a prior belief that he can influence the fall of the dice.

The writer knows that it is difficult for the average person who knows nothing of this subject to accept the idea that all is within; but surely the most materialistic person must realize that as far as he himself is concerned, nothing exists on the outside plane unless he has knowledge of it or unless it becomes fixed in his consciousness. It is the image created in his mind that gives reality to the world outside of him.

Happiness, sought by many and found by few, therefore is a matter entirely within ourselves; our environment and the everyday happenings of life have absolutely no effect on our happiness except as we permit mental images of the outside to enter our consciousness. Happiness is wholly independent of position, wealth, or material possessions. It is a state of mind that we ourselves have the power to control—and that control lies with our thinking.

# Think Your Way to Wealth

(1948)

## by Napoleon Hill

*The Classic on Raising Your Own Salary—Now Condensed*

## Contents

Introduction  *An Old Classic Made New* by Mitch Horowitz  768
Chapter One  Definiteness of Purpose  769
Chapter Two  The Mastermind  771
Chapter Three  Attractive Personality  774
Chapter Four  Applied Faith  781
Chapter Five  Going the Extra Mile  781
Chapter Six  Organized Individual Endeavor  783
Chapter Seven  Creative Vision  784
Chapter Eight  Self-Discipline  786
Chapter Nine  Organized Thinking  789
Chapter Ten  Learning from Defeat  792
Chapter Eleven  Inspiration  794
Chapter Twelve  Controlled Attention  795
Chapter Thirteen  The Golden Rule Applied  796
Chapter Fourteen  Cooperation  798
Chapter Fifteen  Budgeting of Time and Money  799
Chapter Sixteen  The Habit of Health  801
Chapter Seventeen  Cosmic Habit Force  801

## Introduction
# An Old Classic Made New

This book is written as a dialogue between success author Napoleon Hill and industrialist Andrew Carnegie. Hill said that he met the steel magnate for an interview in 1908, and that Carnegie pressed on him the idea of studying the principles of success and achievement found in the lives of great financiers, inventors, and high-achievers of all types. *Think Your Way to Wealth* is Hill's reproduction of that original dialogue.

The structure and language of the book are Hill's own. Written more than a decade after the appearance of his 1937 classic *Think and Grow Rich*, *Think Your Way to Wealth* gave Hill the opportunity to expand on some of the themes in his earlier book, and to call out ideas that he had omitted, such as the application of the Golden Rule and the use of what Hill called Cosmic Habit Force. Cosmic Habit Force is explored in the final and most powerful chapter of this book.

*Think Your Way to Wealth* is something of a personal milestone for me. It was the first audiobook that I narrated when I collaborated on its full-length recording in 2011. I can tell you from personal experience that you are fortunate to be encountering this abridgement. Although filled with sound and actionable ideas, Hill's original version of *Think Your Way to Wealth*, first published in 1948 (and sometimes alternately called *How to Raise Your Own Salary*), is one of his most verbose and drawn-out books. The original is uncharacteristically burdened with excess verbiage and repetition. It was probably written quickly and rushed to market. In this abridgment, I have tried to carve away the superfluous language to bring you the book's central ideas.

You will find in this abbreviated work not only a summation of Hill's best insights but a key articulation of his most important idea, which forms the foundation of his entire program: the possession of a Definite Chief Aim. If you take just one lesson from Hill's work, make it that one. You'll see why from experiencing the Hill-Carnegie dialogue in this book.

Like many lovers of Hill's work, I find that no matter how many times I experience his writings, I always find some new insight or emphasis, which refreshes my personal efforts. In this condensed edition of *Think Your Way to Wealth* I know you will discover or rediscover ideas that will lift your energies and drive you to new plans and strivings.

—Mitch Horowitz

## Chapter 1
# Definiteness of Purpose

NAPOLEON HILL: Mr. Carnegie, please go back to the beginning of your career and describe your principles of achievement.

ANDREW CARNEGIE: To begin with, there are seventeen major principles of success, and everyone who attains his objective must use some combination of these principles.

The first is the most important. You may call it the Principle of Definiteness of Purpose. Study anyone who is a permanent success, and you will find that he has a definite major goal. He has a plan for the attainment of this goal. He devotes the major portion of his thoughts and his efforts to the attainment of this one purpose.

My own major purpose is that of making and marketing steel. I conceived that purpose while working as a laborer. It became an obsession with me. I took it to bed with me at night, I took it to work with me in the morning. My Definite Purpose became more than a mere wish; it became my burning desire. That is the only sort of definite purpose that brings results.

I must emphasize the vast difference between a mere wish and a burning desire that has assumed the proportions of an obsession. Everyone wishes for the better things of life but most never go beyond the wishing stage. Men who know exactly what they want of life, however, and are determined to get it, do not stop with wishing. They intensify their wishes into a burning desire and back that desire with continuous effort based on a sound plan.

It is necessary that they induce other people to cooperate in carrying out their plan. No great achievement is possible without the aide of other minds.

HILL: How long does it require, Mr. Carnegie, for one's mental attitude to begin attracting the physical and financial requisites of one's major purpose?

CARNEGIE: That depends entirely upon the nature and extent of one's desires and the control one exercises over his mind in keeping it free from fear and doubt and self-imposed limitations. This sort of control comes through constant vigilance, wherein one keeps his mind free of all negative thoughts and leaves it open for the influx and the guidance of infinite intelligence.

HILL: Do you follow the habit of writing down your major purpose, Mr. Carnegie?

CARNEGIE: I followed that habit many years ago, while I was struggling to make the change from day labor to industrial management. Moreover, I went much farther than merely reading my written statement of my major purpose. I met with my Mastermind group nightly, and we entered into a detailed roundtable discussion for the purpose of building plans to carry out the object of my major goal. I heartily recommend this roundtable habit.*

HILL: Why do you place a Definite Chief Aim at the head of the list of the 17 Principles of Achievement?

CARNEGIE: No one may achieve success without first knowing precisely what he wants. About 98 out of every 100 people are totally without a major goal, and it is significant that approximately the same percentage of people are considered failures.

HILL: Give me your definition of the word success.

CARNEGIE: My definition of success is this: the power with which to acquire whatever one demands of life without violating the rights of others.

HILL: Well, is it not true that success is often the result of luck?

CARNEGIE: If you will analyze my definition of success, you will see that there is no element of luck about it. A man may, and sometimes men do, fall into opportunities through mere chance or luck, but they have a queer way of falling out of those opportunities the first time opposition overtakes them.

HILL: Mr. Carnegie, in your definition of success, you used the word power. You said that success is achieved through the power with which to acquire whatever one wants.

---

* You can learn more about this step in the following chapter and in *The Power of the Master Mind* by Mitch Horowitz (G&D Media).

CARNEGIE: Personal power is acquired through a combination of individual traits and habits, some of which will be explained in greater detail as we come to the remaining Principles of Achievement. Briefly, the ten qualities of personal power, which we call the 10-Point Rule of Personal Power are: 1) definiteness of purpose, 2) promptness of decision, 3) soundness of character or intentional honesty, 4) strict discipline over one's emotions, 5) obsessional desire to render useful service, 6) thorough knowledge of one's occupation, 7) tolerance on all subjects, 8) loyalty to one's personal associates and faith in a supreme being, 9) enduring thirst for knowledge, and 10) alertness of imagination.

You will observe that this 10-Point Rule embraces traits that anyone may develop. These traits lead to a form of personal power that can be used without violating the rights of others. That is the only form of personal power anyone can afford to wield.

## Chapter 2
# The Mastermind

HILL: Mr. Carnegie, we now come to the second of these principles, which you have named the Mastermind. Please define what you mean by the term.

CARNEGIE: The Mastermind is an alliance of two or more minds working together in the spirit of perfect harmony for the attainment of a definite purpose.

HILL: Do you mean to say, Mr. Carnegie, that the mere choice of a major purpose in life is not of itself enough to ensure success?

CARNEGIE: To achieve the object of one's major goal one must so relate himself to the members of his Mastermind alliance that he will procure the full benefit of their brains in a spirit of harmony. Before any alliance can constitute a Mastermind, everyone in the group must have his heart as well as his head in full sympathy with the object of the alliance, and he must be in perfect harmony with every other member of the alliance.

HILL: On previous occasions you have referred to nine major motives that unite people in the Mastermind alliance and life in general. Will you name them?

CARNEGIE: Here are the nine motives, some combination of which creates the moving spirit back of everything we do: 1) The emotion of love, the gateway to one's spiritual power. 2) The emotion of sex, which may serve as a powerful stimulant to action when transmuted. 3) Desire for financial gain. 4) Self-preservation. 5) Desire for freedom of body and mind. 6) Desire for self-expression leading to fame and recognition. 7) Desire for life after death.

The last two motives are negative but very powerful as stimulants to action. They are: 8) The emotion of anger often expressed as envy or jealousy. And, 9) The emotion of fear.

Here you have the nine major approaches to all minds. The leader of a successful Mastermind alliance must depend upon one or more of these basic motives to induce each member of his group to give the harmonious cooperation required for success.

HILL: Which emotions draw the greatest response?

CARNEGIE: The two motives to which men respond most generously in business alliances are the emotion of sex and the desire for financial gain. Most men want money more than any other thing, but they often want it mainly to please the woman of their choice. Here then, the motivating force is three-fold: love, sex, and financial gain. There is a type of man, however, who will work harder for recognition than he will for material and financial gains.

HILL: You say that all success of noteworthy proportions is the result of understanding and application of the Mastermind Principle. Are there not some exceptions to this rule, Mr. Carnegie? Couldn't a man become a great artist or a great preacher or a successful salesman without the use of the Mastermind Principle?

CARNEGIE: The answer is no. A man might become an artist or a preacher or a salesman without direct application of the Mastermind Principle, but he could not become great in these fields of endeavor without the aid of this principle. An all-wise providence has so arranged the mechanism of the mind that no single mind is complete. Richness of the mind in its fullest sense comes from the harmonious alliance of two or more minds working together toward the achievement of some definite purpose.

HILL: What is the plan for improving and maintaining romantic and household relationships, Mr. Carnegie?

CARNEGIE: The time would be well spent if married people set aside a regular hour for a confidential Mastermind meeting at least once every week during which they would come to an understanding concerning every vital factor of their relationship both in and outside of the home associations. Continuous contact between a man and his wife is an essential for harmony and cooperative effort.

HILL: Earlier you mentioned the key role of the sex emotion. Can you expand on this?

CARNEGIE: The emotion of sex is nature's own source of inspiration through which she gives both men and women the impelling desire to create, build, lead, and direct. Every great artist, every great musician, and every great dramatist gives expression to the emotion of sex transmuted into human endeavor. It is also true that men of vision, initiative, and enthusiasm who lead and excel in industry and business owe their superiority to transmuted sex emotion.

The well-informed man recognizes the possibilities available to him by combining the emotion of sex with whatever plan he adopts for the object of his Mastermind alliance with his wife. The same suggestion offers stupendous benefits to the married woman who is interested both in aiding her husband in his occupation and in holding his interest in herself. Let it be remembered, however, that the relationship of sex to be of enduring benefit as a medium of inspiration, must be kept on a high pedestal of romance.

HILL: Why do you stress the importance of romance?

CARNEGIE: Because wherever evidence of greatness in men is found, no matter in what age or calling, there one may also find evidence of this spirit of romance. The acorn yields an oak tree only in response to the stimulus of the sun's rays. The bird breaks the shell and takes to wing only in response to warmth outside itself. The seed of achievement that reposes in the brain of every man responds most quickly to the warmth of another's love and affection. Ignore the call of romance when it appeals to you from within and you hide your talents in the darkness of obscurity.

On the contrary, listen for the call of this messenger of infinite intelligence treated with civility and understanding when it arrives, and it will hand you the key to the temple of wisdom whose doors are locked within your heart and brain.

All that is great and good in man and woman comes to be there only through God's gift of love. Keep the fire of romance burning. Let it become a part, an important part, of the Mastermind ceremony, and your martial relationship will yield priceless returns in both material and spiritual measures.

HILL: From what you have said about the spirit of romance I get the impression that it is a great driving force that may be used in the pursuit of one's aim.

CARNEGIE: Precisely. The force that is born of a combination of love and sex is the elixir of life through which nature expresses all creative effort. Understand this truth, and you will know why a man's greatest use of the Mastermind Principle is that which grows out of his alliance with the mate of his choice.

The spirit of romance is born of the combination of the emotions of love and sex. Enthusiasm, driving force, keen interest, and vision are essential for success in any calling, and these states of mind can be produced at will by the person who converts the motives of sex and love, two of the strongest of the basic motives, into an obsessional interest in his occupation.

Chapter 3

# Attractive Personality

HILL: Mr. Carnegie, we now come to the third of the 17 Principles of Individual Achievement, which you have named Attractive Personality. I understand that you have separated the factors behind personality into twenty-four distinct traits, all but one of which may be developed by anyone. Please describe these characteristics of personality with special emphasis on those that you consider of greatest importance.

CARNEGIE: I will not only describe the twenty-four traits of an Attractive Personality, but I will also give you a simple formula with which all but one of these traits may be developed and maintained.

We will begin with the outline of the twenty-four factors with a description of the most important of these, which is **positive mental attitude**. One may get a fair idea of the important part mental attitude plays in the affairs of an individual's life by considering the fact that it influences the tone of voice, the expression of the face, the posture of the body, and modifies every word that is spoken as well as determining the nature of every emotion one feels.

It does more than these. It modifies every thought one releases thereby extending its influences to all within its range through the principle of telepathy.

The second is **flexibility**. By this I mean the ability to adapt quickly to changing circumstances and emergencies without losing one's sense of balance. Without this ability, an attractive personality is hardly possible, as the ever-changing conditions of life and of human relationships require individual adaptability.

The third is **sincerity of purpose**. This is one trait of character for which there is no substitute. I say it is a trait of character because it is something that reaches deeper into a human being than any mere quality of personality. Sincerity of purpose, or the lack of it, writes itself so indelibly into the words and deeds of men that even the novice at character analysis can recognize its presence or absence.

The fourth factor is **promptness of decision**. Those who dillydally around trying to make up their minds are neither popular nor successful. This is a fast-moving world, and those who do not move quickly cannot keep up. Successful men reach decisions definitely and quickly, and they become annoyed and inconvenienced by others who do not act promptly.

I call your attention also to the close relationship between promptness of decision and definiteness of purpose. The man with the vision to recognize opportunity and the promptness of decision to embrace it will get ahead. This is the way of the world. It always makes a place for the man who knows exactly what he wants and is determined to get it.

Courtesy is the fifth factor. It is an essential part of an attractive personality. And it is absolutely free. All it costs is the time required to express it in one's daily contact with others. Perhaps its very cheapness accounts for its scarcity, as it is so rare that when one comes upon it one is quick to take note of the person expressing it. Courtesy simply means respecting other people's feelings under all circumstances, going out of one's way to help any less fortunate person whenever possible, and controlling selfishness in all its forms. Courtesy is a medium with which one may project his influence to sources of opportunity he could not reach without it.

Number six is **tone of voice**. The spoken word is, by great odds, the medium through which one expresses his personality most often, therefore, the tone of one's voice should be so thoroughly under control that it can be colored and modified so as to make it carry a meaning quite in addition to the mere words expressed, for it does carry a separate meaning, whether one is conscious of this or not. The idea, therefore, is to so cultivate the voice that it can be used to convey the particular meaning desired.

Factor seven is the **habit of smiling**. Now, don't make the mistake of feeling that this simple habit of smiling is not important, and don't forget that it is a habit that is directly associated with mental attitude. If you aren't sure about this, just try smiling when you are angry. I suggest that one should stand before a mirror when practicing voice control because there are certain expressions of speech that cannot be dramatized properly unless they are accompanied by a smile.

The eighth factor is **facial expression**. You can tell a great deal of what is going on in one's mind by the expression on his face. Master salesmen can tell by careful observation of a prospective buyer's facial expression much about what his real thoughts are. If they cannot do this, they are not master salesmen. Moreover, the cleverest salesman also learns to judge what is going on in the other fellow's mind by the tone of his voice. Thus, the smile, the tone of voice, the expression of the face constitute an open window through which all who will may see and feel what takes place in the minds of people. This naturally suggests to the smart person the use of caution in connection with this open window. The smart person will know when to keep the window closed. He will also know when to open it.

We are up to number nine, which is **tactfulness**. There is always a right and a wrong time for everything. Tactfulness consists of the habit of doing and saying the right thing at the right time, and I'm going to enumerate for you a list of the more common ways in which people show their lack of tactfulness: 1) Carelessness in tone, often speaking in gruff, antagonistic tones. 2) Speaking out of turn when silence would be more appropriate. 3) Interrupting others. 4) Constantly referring to yourself. 5) Asking impertinent questions. 6) Injecting intimately personal subjects into conversation where such action is embarrassing to others. 7) Going where one has not been invited. 8) Boastfulness. 9) Flouting the rules of society in matters of personal adornment. 10) Making personal calls at inconvenient hours. 11) Holding people on the telephone with needless conversation. 12) Writing people whom one has no reasonable excuse for addressing. 13) Volunteering opinions when not asked. 14) Openly questioning the soundness of others' opinions. 15) Declining requests in an arrogant manner. 16) Disparaging people in front of their friends. 17) Rebuking those who disagree with you. 18) Speaking of people's physical afflictions in their presence. 19) Correcting subordinates and associates in the presence of others. 20) Complaining when requests for favors are refused. 21) Presuming upon friendship in asking favors. 22) Using profane or offensive language. 23) Expressing dislikes too freely. 24) Speaking of ills and misfortunes. 25) Criticizing some other person's religion. 26) Overfamiliarity on all occasions.

Tenth place goes to **tolerance**. Let us define tolerance simply as open-mindedness. The tolerant person is one who holds his mind open for new facts, knowledge, and viewpoints on all subjects. Observe, too, how closely related are tolerance and tactfulness.

The eleventh trait of Attractive Personality is **frankness of manner and speech**. Everyone mistrusts the man who resorts to subterfuge instead of dealing frankly with his daily associates. I have known men who were so slippery that you could not pin them down to a direct, clear-cut statement on any subject. I have never yet seen a man of this type who could be depended upon. This sort of man doesn't come right out and lie, but he does what amounts to exactly the same thing by deliberately withholding important facts. Men of sound character always have the courage to speak and deal directly with people, and they follow this habit even though it may, at times, be to their personal disadvantage. Men who resort to subterfuge to deceive others seldom have very much confidence in themselves.

Number twelve is **a keen sense of humor**. A well-developed sense of humor aids a man in becoming flexible and adjustable to the varying circumstances of life. It keeps a man from taking himself and life too seriously, a tendency toward which altogether too many people are inclined. A sense of humor even serves to give one a better physical appearance, as it helps to keep the lines of the face softened. It also leads to the habit of smiling, which is one of the important traits of Attractive Personality, and there is a definite relationship between a sense of humor and mental attitude. A keen sense of humor encourages a positive mental attitude.

Now we come to the most profound and far-reaching of all the elements comprising an Attractive Personality: **Faith in Infinite Intelligence**. Faith is woven into every principle of the Philosophy of Achievement since the intangible power of faith is the essence of every great achievement, no matter what may be its nature or purpose. In short, the power that operates the exquisitely finely tuned machine called the brain is a form of energy which comes from the outside, and faith is the master gate through which an individual may give his brain full and free access to the great universal power which operates it.

The hand that opens the gate and permits the free entry of the power that operates the brain is desire or motive. No one has ever discovered any other method of opening the gate. There are various degrees to which it can be opened, all depending upon motive and desire. Only those desires which take on the proportion of an obsession, burning desires, serve to open wide the valve.

A burning desire in the sense that I am using this term is one that is accompanied by a deep, emotional feeling. Mere head desires growing out of pure reason do not open the gate to the brain as widely as heart desires that are mixed with emotion. I wish to make this point very clear and to emphasize it in every way possible *for it is the very warp and woof of the subject of faith.*

The next trait is a **keen sense of justice**. It seems trite to remind people that an individual cannot hope to become popular and attractive unless he deals justly with others. Justice, as I use the term means intentional honesty. Many people are honest for the sake of expediency, but their brand of honesty is so flexible that they can stretch it to fit any circumstance. We are talking about deliberate honesty that is so rigidly adhered to that the individual is motivated by it under circumstances that may not be to his immediate benefit, the same as to those that promise the greatest possible reward. In addition to its many benefits, this establishes a basis of confidence, without which no one can have an attractive personality. It builds a fundamentally sincere and sound character which of itself is one of the greatest of all attracting forces. It not only attracts people, but it offers opportunities for personal gain in one's occupation. It gives one a feeling of self-reliance and self-respect.

Number fifteen is **appropriateness of words**. Among cultured people, there is perhaps no greater source of annoyance than the careless use of words. Colloquialisms and slang may be passable at times, but the less these are used, the better. Proper use of language is an indelible mark of culture and persuasiveness.

The sixteenth trait of an attractive personality is **emotional control**. Most of us are directed less by reason than by emotion. We do things, or we refrain from doing them because of *how we feel*. Emotion, therefore, may be defined with one word: feeling. This is a mighty important word since it defines the motivating force that controls most of our actions throughout life. We certainly owe it to ourselves to learn as much as possible about the force that lifts us to great achievement or hurls us downward to defeat.

The seventeenth trait may be called **alertness of interest in persons, places, and things**. Without the ability to fix one's interest at will on any subject or person and hold it there for whatever time the occasion requires, no one will have an attractive personality. You can pay another person no greater compliment, generally speaking, than that of concentrating your attention upon him when he desires your attention.

The eighteenth trait of an attractive personality is **effective speech**. The person who cannot stand on his feet and speak with force and conviction on any subject within his range of knowledge is under a great handicap. The same applies to the man who cannot express himself forcefully in ordinary conversation and in small-group gatherings such as business conferences. The ability to dramatize words and express them forcefully at all times, under all conditions, is among the greatest of human achievements. In fact, some people place this power at the head of the list of all personal achievements.

The ability to dramatize speech comes through habit. Therefore, one should begin this habit by speaking forcefully in ordinary conversation. There is where great speakers learn the art of effective speech. They practice on every person with whom they converse. They never utter a word without placing back of it the necessary feeling to make it penetrate the mind of the listener. This simple procedure will make an effective speaker of anyone who follows it as a matter of daily habit.

The nineteenth trait of a pleasing personality is **versatility**. It is hardly necessary to mention the obvious fact that people who lack a general understanding of their world, including at least a surface knowledge of human nature, are seldom interesting or attractive. A general interest in things and people is one of the essentials of flexibility of personality.

The twentieth trait is a **genuine fondness for people**. People recognize individuals who like people, and they resent those who have a natural distain.

The Law of Retribution always operates so that people are judged and dealt with, not alone by their deeds, but by their dominating mental attitudes. It is inevitable, therefore, that the person who dislikes people will be disliked.

The twenty-first trait is **humility of the heart**. Arrogance, greed, vanity, and egotism are never found in the man who has a pleasing personality.

Number twenty-two is **good showmanship**. Showmanship is the ability to combine facial expression, tone of voice, personal adornment, choice of words, control of the emotions, courtesy, effective speech, versatility, mental attitude, sense of humor, emphasis, and tactfulness in such a manner as to dramatize any circumstance or occasion so as to attract favorable attention.

The twenty-third trait is **clean sportsmanship**. The man who can win without boasting and lose without squealing generally has the admiration of other people.

The twenty-fourth and final trait is **personal magnetism**. Let us be frank at the outset and say that personal magnetism is a polite way of describing sex energy, for that is precisely what it means. Now, we need not evade the admission that sex energy is something with which an individual is born, and it therefore cannot be developed by personal effort. Sex energy is nature's own device with which she creates and perpetuates every living thing from God's smallest creature to his greatest handiwork, man. I see no reason, therefore, for subterfuge in connection with the analysis of sex emotion as one of the most important traits of personality, but I do see a reason for making it plain that this universal power adds attractive qualities to the personality only when it is controlled and used properly.

I am referring to transmutation, which means diverting sex emotion from physical expression into whatever constructive purpose one wishes to carry out. It is a well-known fact that when a man who is highly sexed organizes this irresistible, creative force and places it at the back of his occupational endeavors, he has but little difficulty in persuading people to cooperate with him.

The emotion of sex must be considered as one of the most important factors of an attractive personality. Therefore, I have given here a clue from which anyone smart enough to recognize it may add greatly to his ability to influence people through his personality.

## Chapter 4
# Applied Faith

HILL: Mr. Carnegie, how may one develop faith?

CARNEGIE: Clearing the mind of its enemies may develop faith. Clear the mind of negative thoughts, fears, and self-imposed limitations, and faith fills the place without effort. There is no great mystery about the state of mind known as faith. Give it a place to dwell, and it will move in without ceremony or invitation.

HILL: From what you have said, Mr. Carnegie, the best way to start developing faith is by choosing an objective and beginning at once to attain it through whatever media available.

CARNEGIE: Exactly. The development of faith is largely a matter of understanding the astounding power of the mind. The only real mystery about faith is man's failure to make use of it. I speak from personal experience when I say that faith is a state of mind that can be acquired and used as effectively and easily as any other state of mind. It is all a matter of understanding and application. Truly, faith without works is dead.

My early days of youth were cursed by poverty and limitation of opportunity, a fact with which all who know me are acquainted. I am no longer cursed by poverty because I took possession of my mind, and that mind has yielded to me every material thing I want and much more than I need. Faith is no patented right of mind. It is a universal power as available to the humblest person as it is to the greatest.

## Chapter 5
# Going The Extra Mile

HILL: Mr. Carnegie, I have heard some men say that success is often the result of luck. Do you attribute any portion of your success to luck or favorable breaks?

CARNEGIE: Your question gives me a starting point for describing the fifth of the 17 Principles of Achievement, which is called the Habit of Going the Extra Mile. This means rendering more service and better service than one is paid for.

First, I will answer your question by saying yes, indeed, there is a wheel of life that controls human destinies, and I am happy to be able to tell you that this wheel can be definitely *influenced* to operate in one's favor. If this were not true, there would be no object in organizing the rules of personal achievement.

First of all, to control the wheel of fortune, one must understand and apply the 17 Principles of Achievement. Now, the habit of doing more than one is paid for is one that an individual may practice without asking the permission of others. Therefore, it is under one's own control. Many other beneficial habits can be practiced only through the consent and cooperation of other people.

Until a man begins to render more service than that for which he is paid, he is not entitled to more pay than he receives for that service since, obviously, he is already receiving full pay for what he does.

I think I can make the point clear by calling attention to the simple illustration of the farmer. Before he collects pay for his services, he carefully and intelligently prepares the soil, plows and harrows it, fertilizes it if need be, then plants it with seed. Up to this point, he has gained nothing whatsoever for his labor, but understanding the Law of Growth as he does, he rests after his labor while nature germinates the seed and yields him a crop.

Here, the element of time enters into the farmer's labor. In due time, nature gives him back the seed he planted in the ground together with an abundant over-plus to compensate him for his labor and his knowledge. If he sows a bushel of wheat in properly prepared soil, he gets back the bushel of seed together with, perhaps, as many as ten additional bushels as his compensation.

Here, the Law of Increasing Returns has stepped in and compensated the farmer for his effort and his intelligence. If there were no such law, man could not exist on this earth since obviously there would be no object in planting a bushel of wheat in the ground if nature yielded back only a bushel of grain.

It is this over-plus which nature yields through the Law of Increasing Returns that makes it possible for man to produce from the ground, but little imagination is needed to see that the man who renders more service and better service than that for which he is paid thereby places himself in a position to benefit by this same law.

Often, I have heard working men say, "I'm not paid to do that," or, "This is not my responsibility." You've heard statements like that. Everyone has. Well, when you hear a man talking like this, you may mark him down as one who will never get more than a bare living from his work. Moreover, that sort of mental attitude makes one disliked by his associates, and it therefore discourages favorable opportunities for self-promotion.

Successful men are not looking for short hours and easy jobs, for if they are truly successful, they know that no such circumstance exists. Successful men are always looking for ways to lengthen instead of shorten the working days.

Emerson said, "Do the thing, and you shall have the power." He never expressed a more truthful thought. It applies to every calling and to every human relationship. Men who gain and hold power do so by making themselves useful to others.

## Chapter 6
# Organized Individual Endeavor

HILL: You have stated, Mr. Carnegie, that Organized Individual Endeavor is the sixth of the 17 Principles of Individual Achievement. Will you analyze this principle in its relationship to personal achievement?

CARNEGIE: Personal initiative may be likened to the steam in the boiler in this respect. It is the power through which one's plans, aims, and purposes are put into action. It is the antithesis of one of the worst of all human traits, procrastination. Successful men are known always as men of action. There can be no action without the exercise of one's initiative. There are two forms of action: 1) that in which one indulges from force of necessity; and 2) that which one exercises out of choice of his own free will. Leadership grows from the latter. It comes as the result of action in which one engages in response to his own motives and desires.

HILL: When, and under what circumstances, should one begin to exercise personal initiative?

CARNEGIE: The time to begin using personal initiative is immediately following one's definite decision as to what one wishes to accomplish. The time to begin is right then. If the plan chosen turns out to be weak, it can be changed for a better one, but any sort of plan is better than procrastination. The universal evil of the world is procrastination, the terrible habit people have of waiting for the time to begin something to be just right. It causes more failures than all the weak plans of the world.

HILL: But, shouldn't one consult others and get their opinions before beginning important plans?

CARNEGIE: Opinions are like the sands of the desert, and most of them are about as slippery. Everyone has an opinion about practically everything, but most of them are unworthy of trust. The man who hesitates because he wants the opinion of others before he begins to exercise his personal initiative usually winds up by doing nothing.

Of course, there are exceptions to this rule. There are times when the counsel and advice of others are absolutely essential for success, but if you refer to idle opinions of bystanders, let them alone. Avoid them as you would an epidemic of disease for that is exactly what idle opinions are, a disease. Everyone has a flock of them, and most people hand them out freely without being asked. When you need information for your endeavor, seek expertise—never opinion.

## Chapter 7
# Creative Vision

HILL: Mr. Carnegie, you have said that Creative Vision is the seventh Principle of Individual Achievement. Will you analyze this principle and describe how to use it?

CARNEGIE: First of all, let us have a clear understanding of the meaning of the term Creative Vision as we are using it by explaining that this is but another name for imagination. There are two types of imagination. One is known as *synthetic imagination* and the other as *creative imagination*.

*Synthetic imagination* consists of the act of combining recognized ideas, concepts, plans, facts, and principles in new arrangements. The old axiom that there is nothing new under the sun grew out of the fact that the majority of things that seemed to be new are nothing but a rearrangement of that which is old. Practically all the patents recorded in the patent office are nothing more than old ideas that have been arranged in a new order or given a new use.

*Creative imagination* has its source, as far as science has been able to determine, in the subconscious mind wherein exists through some power unknown to science, the ability to perceive and interpret basically new ideas. It is believed by some that the faculty of a creative imagination truly is the workshop of the soul through which man may contact and be guided by infinite intelligence. Of this, however, there is no conclusive evidence save only that which is circumstantial.

Let us, therefore, be content to accept the reality of creative imagination and make the best possible use of it without endeavoring to define its source. Of one fact we can be sure, and that is the undeniable reality of the existence of a faculty of the mind through which some men perceive and interpret new ideas never before known to man.

HILL: Which of the two types of imagination is used more often in business?

CARNEGIE: Synthetic imagination is more commonly used. Creative imagination, as the name implies, is used only by those who, generally speaking, have attained to some form of leadership or unusual skill. Inventors and artists rely on creative imagination. To tap into this power you must intensify your desires until they become obsessional. A deep, burning desire is picked up by the subconscious and acted upon much more definitely and quickly than an ordinary desire. A mere wish appears to make no impression on the subconscious. Many people become confused as to the difference between a wish and a burning desire that has been stimulated into obsessional proportions by the repetition of thought in connection with the desire.

HILL: Then, anyone may make use of creative imagination by the simple process of charging his subconscious mind with definite desires?

CARNEGIE: Yes, there is nothing to hinder anyone from using this principle, but you must remember that practical results are obtained only by those who have gained discipline over their thought habits through the process of concentration of interest in desire. Fleeting thoughts, which come and go intermittently and mere wishes, which are about the extent of the average person's thinking, make no impression whatsoever on the subconscious mind.

HILL: Why is it that so few people appear to have a well-developed imagination?

CARNEGIE: The faculty of imagination, like all other faculties of the mind, can be developed through use. The reason so many people seem not to have a keen imagination is obvious. Most people allow the faculty of imagination to atrophy through neglect. But in those with a strong enough desire it builds.

## Chapter 8

# Self-Discipline

HILL: Mr. Carnegie, you have designated Self-Discipline as the eighth Principle of Individual Achievement. Please describe the part that self-discipline plays in personal achievement and how to cultivate it.

CARNEGIE: Self-discipline begins with the mastery of one's thoughts. Without control over thoughts, there can be no control over deeds. Let us say, therefore, that self-discipline inspires one to think first and to act afterward. The usual procedure is just the reverse. Most people act first and think afterward, if and when they think at all. Thinking is power.

HILL: I judge from what you have said previously that personal power is something that must be used with discretion, or it may turn out to be a curse instead of a blessing.

CARNEGIE: I've always made it a part of my business philosophy to caution my associates against the dangers of indiscreet use of personal power and especially those who, through promotions, have but recently come into the possession of increased power. Newly acquired power is something like newly acquired riches. It needs watching closely lest a man become the victim of his own power.

Here is where self-discipline gives a good account of itself. If a man has his own mind under complete control, he makes it serve him in a manner that does not antagonize other people.

HILL: I deduce that self-discipline is largely a matter of the adoption of constructive habits.

CARNEGIE: That is precisely the idea. That which a man is, that which he accomplishes, both his failures and his successes are the results of his habits. Fortunately, habits are self-formed. They are under the control of the individual. The most important of these are the habits of thought. A man finally comes to resemble in his deeds the nature of his thought habits. When he gains control over his thought habits, he has gone a long way toward the attainment of self-discipline.

Definite motives are the beginning of thought habits. It is not difficult for a man to keep his mind on the thing that serves as his greatest motive, especially if the motive becomes obsessional. Self-discipline without definiteness of motive is impossible. Moreover, it would be without value.

HILL: In terms of discipline, should a man attempt to control his life with his reasoning faculty and leave the emotions out of his decisions and plans?

CARNEGIE: That would be very unwise, even if it were possible. Emotions provide the driving power, the action force that enables a man to put his head decisions into operation. The aim is control and discipline of the emotions, not elimination. The emotions of man are something like a river in that their power can be damned up and released in whatever proportions and whatever directions one desires, but they cannot be eliminated. Through self-discipline, a man can organize all his emotions and release them in a highly concentrated form as a means of attaining the object of his plans and purpose.

The two most powerful emotions are love and sex. These emotions are inborn, the handiwork of nature, the instruments through which the Creator provided for both the perpetuation of the human race and for social integration by which civilization evolves from a lower to a higher order of human relationship. One would hardly wish to destroy so great a gift as the emotions, even if this were possible for the reason that they represent man's greatest power.

If you destroy hope and faith, what would you have left that would be of use to man? If you remove enthusiasm, loyalty, and the desire for achievement, you would still have left the faculty of reason, the head power, but what good would it be? There would be nothing left for the head to direct.

Now, let me call your attention to an astounding truth. The emotions of hope, faith, enthusiasm, loyalty, and desire are nothing but specialized applications of the inborn emotions of love and sex diverted or transmuted into different purposes. As a matter of fact, every human emotion outside of love and sex has its roots in these two natural inborn traits of man. If these two natural emotions were destroyed in a man, he would become as docile as a domesticated animal.

HILL: Self-discipline, then, is the tool with which a man may harness and direct his inborn emotions in whatever direction he chooses?

CARNEGIE: That is correct. Now, I wish to call your attention to another astounding truth. Creative Vision is the result of self-discipline through which the emotions of love and sex are transmuted into some specialized plan or purpose. There has never yet been born a great leader in any form of human endeavor who did not attain his leadership by mastery and direction of these two great inborn emotions.

The great artists, musicians, writers, speakers, lawyers, doctors, architects, inventors, scientists, industrialists, salesmen, and the outstanding men and women in all walks of life attain their leadership by harnessing and directing their natural emotions of love and sex as a driving force behind their endeavors. In most instances, the diversion of these emotions into specialized endeavor is done unconsciously as the result of a burning desire for achievement. In some instances, the transmutation is deliberate.

HILL: Then, it is no disgrace for one to be born with great capacity for the emotions of love and sex.

CARNEGIE: No. The disgrace comes from the abuse of these natural gifts. The abuse is the result of ignorance, the lack of training as to the nature and potentialities of these great emotions.

HILL: I get the impression that the most important application of self-discipline is that through which one takes possession of his sex emotion and transforms it into whatever form of endeavor he desires. Is that true?

CARNEGIE: Yes, and I may add that when a man once acquires discipline over his sex emotion, he will find it easy to discipline himself in all other directions, and the reason for this is that the emotion of sex reflects itself either consciously or unconsciously in practically everything a man does. Failure to gain control over the emotions of love and sex generally means failure to gain control over other traits.

Chapter 9

# Organized Thinking

HILL: You have explained that the ninth Principle of Individual Achievement is Organized Thought. You have also stated that no one may be sure of success without the ability to organize his thinking habits. I have a general idea what it means, but I would like to have a detailed statement of its meaning.

CARNEGIE: Before discussing the organization of thought, let us examine thought itself. What is thought? With what do we think? Is thought subject to individual control? Thought is a form of energy that is distributed through the brain, but it has one peculiar quality unknown in connection with all other forms of energy.

It has intelligence. Thought can be controlled and directed toward the attainment of anything man may desire. In fact, thought is the only thing over which any person has complete, unchallenged control. The system of control is so complete that no one may penetrate the mind of another without his consent although this system of protection often is so loosely guarded that one's mind may be entered at will by any person skilled in the art of thought interpretation.

Many people not only leave their minds wide open for others to enter and interpret their thoughts, but they voluntarily disclose the nature of their thoughts by unguarded expressions of speech and their personal conduct, their facial expression, and the like.

HILL: Is it safe for one to leave his mind open to free entry by others?

CARNEGIE: Just about as safe as leaving the door to one's house unlocked with all of one's valuables left inside the house, except that the loss of purely material things is as nothing compared with the loss one may suffer by leaving his mind open to entry by any stray who may wish to go in and take possession.

The habit of leaving one's mind open and unguarded not only permits other people to enter and become familiar with one's most private thoughts, but this habit permits all sorts of errant thoughts released from the minds of others to enter one's mind.

HILL: You believe, then, that thoughts do pass from one mind to another through the principle of telepathy?

CARNEGIE: That fact has apparently been established by men of science, but I have evidence of its existence from my own personal experience. Yes, one's mind is being constantly bombarded with the impulses of thought released from the minds of others, especially those with whom we come into close contact daily. That is one of the major reasons why I have emphasized the importance of harmony. The chemistry of the brain is such that the mind power of a group of men can be organized so it functions as one unit of power only when there is perfect rapport between the minds of the individuals.

HILL: One of the important steps in Organized Thought seems to be that of the Mastermind alliance through which men pool their mind power, their experience, education, and knowledge and move in response to a common motive. Is this the right idea, Mr. Carnegie?

CARNEGIE: You have stated the matter perfectly. You might have said that the Mastermind alliance is the most important step one may take in connection with Organized Thought, for that is true, but Organized Thought begins with the organization of the individual's thinking habits. To become an effective member of a Mastermind alliance, an individual must first form definite, controlled habits of thought. A group of men working together under the Mastermind principle, each of whom has so disciplined himself that he controls his thought habits, represents Organized Thought of the highest order.

As a matter of fact, there can never be full assurance of harmony in a Mastermind group unless each member of the group is so self-disciplined that he can control his own thoughts.

HILL: Do I understand you to say that an individual may actually discipline himself so that he controls the nature of his thoughts?

CARNEGIE: That is true, but remember that one gains control over his thoughts by forming definite thought habits. You know, of course, that when habits are once formed, they function automatically without any voluntary effort on the individual's part.

HILL: But, isn't it very difficult for one to force his mind to function through definite habits? How may one go about this sort of self-discipline?

CARNEGIE: No. There is nothing difficult about the formation of habits. As a matter of fact, the mind is constantly forming thought habits without the conscious knowledge of the individual responding, as the mind does, to every influence that reaches it from one's daily environment.

Through self-discipline, one may switch the action of his mind from the response to the casual influences around him to subjects of his own choice. This is accomplished by setting up in the mind a definite motive based on a definite purpose and intensifying that purpose until it becomes an obsession.

HILL: Then, Organized Thought begins with Definiteness of Purpose?

CARNEGIE: Everything man achieves begins with Definiteness of Purpose. Name a single instance, if you can, where a man has achieved any form of success without a definite motive based on a definite purpose carried out through a definite plan, but you must remember that there is one more factor that must be considered in connection with Definiteness of Purpose. The purpose must be expressed in terms of intense action.

Here is where the power of the emotions gives an account of itself. The emotional feeling of desire for the attainment of a definite purpose is the power that gives life and action to that purpose and influences one to move on his own initiative.

To ensure satisfactory results, one's definite purpose should be given obsessional proportions. It should be backed by a burning desire for its attainment. Desires of this sort take full possession of one's mind and keep it so fully occupied that it has no inclination or opportunity to entertain stray thoughts released by the minds of others.

HILL: I believe I see what you mean. For example, a young man who is in love has no difficulty in keeping his mind on the object of his love, and not infrequently, his mind works out ways and means of inducing response to his affections from the woman of his choice. In this sort of circumstance, one has no difficulty in forming controlled thought habits.

CARNEGIE: A good illustration. Now, switch it over to some other sort of purpose such, for example, as the development of a business or a profession or the attainment of a definite position or the accumulation of money, and you will have an idea of how these ends are attained, through obsessional desire for their attainment.

## Chapter 10
# Learning from Defeat

HILL: Mr. Carnegie, you have stated that defeat can be converted into a priceless asset if one takes the right attitude toward it. Will you explain that right attitude?

CARNEGIE: The right attitude toward defeat is that which refuses to accept it as anything more than temporary, and this is an attitude that one can best maintain by so developing his willpower that he looks upon defeat as a challenge to test his mettle. That challenge should be accepted as a signal that has been deliberately hoisted to inform him that his plans need mending.

Defeat should be looked upon in precisely the same manner that one accepts the unpleasant experience of physical pain, for it is obvious that physical pain is nature's way of informing one that something needs attention and correction. Pain, therefore, may be a blessing and not a curse.

The same is true of the mental anguish one experiences when overtaken by defeat. While the feeling is unpleasant, it may be nevertheless beneficial because it serves as a signal by which one may be stopped from going in the wrong direction.

HILL: I see your logic, but defeat sometimes is so definite and severe that it has the effect of destroying one's initiative and self-reliance. What is to be done in such a circumstance?

CARNEGIE: Here is where the Principle of Self-Discipline comes to one's rescue. The well-disciplined person allows nothing to destroy his belief in himself and permits nothing to stop him from rearranging his plans and moving ahead when he is defeated. You see, he changes his plans if they need change but not his purpose. If one has mastered the Principle of Organized Thought, one knows that the power of will is equal to all the circumstances of life. He allows nothing to destroy his will to win.

HILL: You mean, I assume, that defeat should be accepted as a sort of mental tonic that can be made to serve as a means of stimulating one's willpower.

CARNEGIE: You've stated it correctly. As I told you previously, *every negative emotion can be transmuted into a constructive power and used for the attainment of desirable ends.* Self-discipline enables one to change unpleasant emotions into a driving power, and every time this is done, it helps to develop one's power of will.

You must remember also that the subconscious mind accepts and acts upon one's mental attitude. If defeat is accepted as permanent instead of being regarded as a mere stimulant to greater action, the subconscious mind acts accordingly and makes it permanent. You see, therefore, how important it is that one form the habit of searching for the good there is to be found in every form of defeat. This procedure becomes the finest sort of training of the willpower and serves, at the same time, to bring the subconscious mind into action in one's behalf.

## Chapter 11

# Inspiration

HILL: Mr. Carnegie, your eleventh Principle of Individual Achievement is Inspiration. You also call this Applied Enthusiasm. How may one develop this?

CARNEGIE: Inspiration is the result of desire expressed in terms of action and based upon motive. Inspiration is a form of animation that creates enthusiasm. No normal person ever goes into a heat of enthusiasm without a motive. It is obvious, therefore, that the beginning of all enthusiasm is desire based on motive. Enthusiasm, which is an expression of one or more of the emotions, stimulates the vibration of thought and makes it more intense, thus starting the faculty of the imagination to work in connection with the motive which inspired the enthusiasm. Enthusiasm gives tone quality to one's voice and makes it pleasing and impressive. A salesman or public speaker would be ineffective without the ability to turn on his enthusiasm at will. The same is true of one who engages in ordinary conversation. Even the most prosaic subjects can be made interesting if they are expressed with enthusiasm. Without it, the most interesting subjects can become tiresome.

Enthusiasm inspires initiative both in thought and in physical action. It is very difficult for one to do well at that for which he has no feeling of enthusiasm. Enthusiasm dispels physical fatigue and overcomes laziness. It has been said that there are no lazy men. What appears to be a lazy man is one who is moved by no motive over which he becomes enthusiastic.

Enthusiasm stimulates the entire nervous system and causes it to perform its duties more efficiently including, in particular, the function of digestion of food. For this reason, the meal hour should be the pleasantest hour of the day, and it should never become the occasion for settling personal or family differences of opinion, nor should it become the time for the correction of the faults of the children.

Enthusiasm stimulates the subconscious section of the brain and puts it to work in connection with the motive, which inspires enthusiasm. In fact, there is no known method of stimulating the subconscious mind voluntarily except that of inspired feeling.

Here, let us emphasize the fact that the subconscious mind acts upon all feeling, whether it is negative or positive. It will act on the emotion of fear as quickly as it will act on the emotion of love, or it will go to work on the worry over poverty as quickly as it will act on the feeling of opulence. It is important, therefore, to recognize that enthusiasm is the positive expression of feeling.

HILL: Is it not possible for one to display too much enthusiasm for his own good?

CARNEGIE: Yes. Uncontrolled enthusiasm often is as detrimental as no enthusiasm. For example, the man who is so enthusiastic over himself and his own ideas that he monopolizes the conversation when conversing with others is sure to be unpopular.

Then there is the man who becomes too enthusiastic over the roulette wheel or the horses and the man who becomes more enthusiastic over ways and means of getting something for nothing than he does over rendering useful service. This sort of uncontrolled enthusiasm may be very detrimental.

But enthusiasm directed toward constructive ends, and properly controlled by Organized Thinking, can heighten the vibrations of thought in such a way as to elevate a man into the category known as genius.

## Chapter 12
# Controlled Attention

HILL: Mr. Carnegie, you have named the twelfth principle of the Philosophy of Individual Achievement, Controlled Attention. Please describe how this principle can be applied in the practical affairs of life.

CARNEGIE: Controlled Attention is the act of combining all the faculties of the mind and concentrating them upon the attainment of a definite purpose. The time involved in the act of concentration of thought on a given subject depends upon the nature of the subject and upon that which one expects in connection with it.

Take my own case, for example. The dominating forces of my mind are, and have been for many years, concentrated upon the making and marketing of steel. I have others allied with me who likewise concentrate their dominating thoughts upon the same objective. Thus, we have the benefit of Controlled Attention in collective form consisting as it does of the individual mind power of a great number of people, all working toward the same end, in a spirit of harmony.

It is important to note that splitting one's attention has the effect of dividing one's powers. The best plan for anyone to follow is to devote all his energies to some specific field. This concentration enables one to specialize in that field. Specialization through concentration of effort gives one greater power. It saves lost motion in both thought and physical action. It harmonizes with the Principle of Definiteness of Purpose, the starting point of all achievement.

## Chapter 13

# The Golden Rule Applied

CARNEGIE: We now come to the 13th Principle of Individual Achievement, The Golden Rule Applied, the principle which nearly everyone professes to believe, but few people practice, due I suspect, to the fact that so few people understand the deep underlying psychology of this principle.

The real benefits of the Golden Rule Applied do not come from those in whose favor it is applied, but they accrue to the one applying the rule in the form of a strengthened conscience, peace of mind, and the other attributes of sound character, the factors which attract the more desirable things of life, including enduring friendships and fortune.

To get the most from the Golden Rule, it must be combined with the Principle of Going the Extra Mile, wherein consists the applied portion of the Golden Rule. The Golden Rule supplies the right mental attitude while Going the Extra Mile supplies the action feature of this great rule. A combination of the two gives one the power of attraction which induces friendly cooperation from others as well as opportunities for personal accumulation.

Passive belief in this rule will accomplish nothing. It is the application of the rule that brings benefits, and they are so numerous and varied that they touch life through almost every human relationship. These are some of the more important benefits.

A, the Golden Rule Applied opens the mind for the guidance of Infinite Intelligence through faith.

B, develops self-reliance through a better relationship with one's conscience.

C, builds sound character sufficient to sustain one in times of emergency; develops a more attractive personality.

D, attracts the friendly cooperation of others in all human relationships.

E, discourages unfriendly opposition from others.

F, gives one peace of mind and freedom from self-established limitations.

G, gives one immunity against the more damaging forms of fear since the man with a clear conscience seldom fears anything or anyone.

H, enables one to go to prayer with clean hands and a clear heart.

I, attracts favorable opportunities for self-promotion in one's occupation, business, or profession.

J, eliminates the desire for something for nothing.

K, makes the rendering of useful service a joy that can be had in no other way.

L, provides one with an influential reputation for honesty and fair dealing, which is the basis of all confidence.

M, serves as a discouragement to the slanderer and a reprimand to the thief.

N, makes one a power for good, by example, whenever he comes into contact with others.

O, discourages all the baser instincts of greed and envy and revenge, and gives wings to the higher instincts of love and fellowship.

P, brings one within easy communicating distance of the Creator through the medium of an undisturbed mind.

Q, enables one to recognize the joys of accepting the truth that every man is, and by right should be, his brother's keeper.

R, establishes a deeper personal spirituality.

These are no mere opinions of mine. They are self-evident truths, the soundness of which is known to every person who lives by the Golden Rule as a matter of daily habit.

## Chapter 14

# Cooperation

HILL: In terms of the fourteenth Principle of the Philosophy of Achievement, do you mean that friendly cooperation is necessary for success?

CARNEGIE: Personal power is acquired through friendly coordination of effort and in no other way. In this country, we have an economic system based upon this sort of cooperation. That is why ours is the richest and most powerful nation in the world. We have found a practical way of coordinating the efforts of groups of individuals in all walks of life, and this coordination has given us great power.

If you are a close observer, you will have noticed that the individuals who have attained the highest degree of cooperation in their relationships with others are those who have achieved the greatest success in their chosen callings.

HILL: You believe then that government regulation of industry is for the common good of all. Why?

CARNEGIE: Because regulation within the bounds of reason discourages the greedy and the selfish individuals from seeking monopolies and protects the public against unfair practices in business.

Just as there must be unbiased umpires who see that the rules of the game are observed for the benefit of all the players, there must also be an unbiased governmental umpire who will see that the sound rules of industry are carried out for the benefit of all.

Every well-managed business has executives who see to it that all individuals work together in a spirit of teamwork. These executives serve as the umpires who coordinate all factors essential for the successful operation of the business. Their sense of fairness and their wisdom determine the degree of success the business enjoys.

HILL: And, you believe that a business cannot be successful without the aid of unbiased coordinators known as management?

CARNEGIE: That is the idea. Small, one-man businesses may operate successfully without a coordinator, but the moment any business requires more than one man for its operation, some individual must assume the responsibility of coordinating the factors that affect the business, or it will not succeed.

HILL: Summed up in a few words, what you were saying is that the coordination of individual efforts is essential for success in any business, and the majority of men lack the ability or the inclination to cooperate with others in an efficient, friendly manner?

CARNEGIE: That is precisely what I've been saying, and it is supported by the experience of all able business leaders. The best evidence of its soundness may be found in the well-known fact that while ordinary manual labor is always plentiful, managerial ability always is scarce. This is because men with the temperament, education, experience, and personal inclination to coordinate the efforts of others are scarce. This scarcity accounts for the fact that able managerial ability always commands its own price because here, as elsewhere in the field of economics, the Law of Supply and Demand obtains.

## Chapter 15
# Budgeting of Time and Money

HILL: Mr. Carnegie, you have named the Budgeting of Time as one of the essentials for individual achievement. What methods should one adopt to make the best use of his time?

CARNEGIE: Every successful person plans his life as carefully as a successful businessman plans his business. He begins by adopting a Definite Major Purpose, and he follows through by devoting a definite proportion of his time to attaining the object of that purpose.

Of course, sound health demands balanced physical and mental habits, but successful people have learned how to arrange their work time and their free time so that the free time provides recreation along lines that contribute to and harmonize with the duties they perform during their work time.

HILL: I see the logic of your argument, Mr. Carnegie, but is it not true that a well-rounded life calls for play and recreation? That old saying that all work and no play makes Jack a dull boy seems to be sound.

CARNEGIE: That may be a sound saying, but there are many misconceptions. Speaking for myself, and from my observations of the successful people I have known, I can say that there is no better form of play than that which is associated with the planning and attaining of one's major purpose. It would be a mistake to say that I work hard, for the truth is that I look upon my work as the finest sort of play. So does every other man who is succeeding in the true sense of that term.

A man's work can be a recreation if he does it in a spirit of intense enthusiasm and likes what he is doing. Enthusiasm recreates. An interest in one's work may therefore be recreation.

HILL: But, Mr. Carnegie, wouldn't some people consider it selfish for one to cultivate relationships only with those whom he desired to use?

CARNEGIE: No matter how one may view this habit, it is an essential for personal achievement. Personally, I see nothing selfish about it provided one so relates himself to others that he gives as well as receives, and I have made it clear that I have always followed this practice.

HILL: And what about budgeting your money?

CARNEGIE: The successful man, the one who attains economic success, budgets the use of his money and material assets as carefully as he budgets his time. He sets aside a definite amount of his income, usually determined on a definite percentage of the total for 1) food, clothing, and household expense; 2) life insurance; 3) savings which he puts to work in some form of investments; and 4) charity and recreation.

All four of these items are controlled by a strict budget from which no deviation is made except in cases of emergency. This ensures the saving of a definite percentage of one's income and leads to economic security.

What difference would it make whether a man's income were $100 a month or $1,000 a month if he allowed it all to go for living expenses or spent it for recreation or for any other purpose that did not yield a material return of some sort? I must tell you, however, that the majority of the American people make this very mistake. No matter how much they earn, it all goes out in one way or another because they have no established budget system for saving and properly using a percentage of it. I have known men to receive salary increases only to spend every cent of it on living expenses.

## Chapter 16
# The Habit of Health

HILL: To maintain a health consciousness requires not only healthy physical habits involving exercise and diet, but one must also think in terms of sound health, not in terms of illness and disease. For whatever the mind dwells upon, the mind brings into existence, whether it be financial success or physical health.

Émile Coué, the great French psychologist, gave the world in one sentence a very simple but practical formula for the maintenance of a health consciousness. "Day by day, in every way, I'm getting better and better." He recommended that this sentence be repeated thousands of times daily until the subconscious section of the mind picked it up, accepted it, and began to carry it out to its logical conclusion in the form of sound health.

The wise ones smiled, not too tolerantly, when they heard of the Coué formula. The not-so-wise accepted it in good faith, put it to work in earnest, and discovered that it produced marvelous results, for it started them on the road toward the development of a health consciousness, and here is the reason why a positive mental attitude is essential for the maintenance of sound health.

## Chapter 17
# Cosmic Habit Force

HILL: Cosmic Habit Force is the particular application of energy with which nature maintains the existing relationship between the atoms of matter, the stars and planets, the seasons of the year, night and day, sickness and health, life and death, and more important to us right now, it is the medium through which all habits and all human relationships are maintained, the medium through which thought is translated into its physical equivalent.

You, of course, know that nature maintains a perfect balance between all the elements of matter and energy throughout the universe. You can see the stars and planets move with perfect precision, each keeping its own place in time and space, year-in and year-out. You can see the seasons of the year come and go with perfect regularity. You can see that night and day follow each other in unending regularity.

You can see that an oak tree grows from an acorn, and a pine grows from the seed of its ancestor. An acorn never produces a pine, nor does a pinecone ever produce an oak, and nothing is ever produced that does not have its antecedents in something else which preceded it.

These are simple facts that anyone can see, but what most people cannot see or understand is the universal law through which nature maintains perfect balance between all matter and energy throughout the universe forcing every living thing to reproduce itself.

We caught a fragmentary glimpse of this great law of nature, which holds our little Earth in its proper position and causes all material objects to be attracted toward the center of the earth when Newton discovered what he called the Law of Gravitation.

And if Newton had gone a few steps beyond where he stopped, perhaps he would have discovered that the same law which holds our little Earth in space and relates it to all the other planets in both time and space, relates human beings to one another in exact conformity with the nature of their own thoughts, he would have discovered that the same force which draws all material things toward the center of this Earth also builds man's thought habits in varying degrees of permanency.

He would have discovered that negative thought habits of whatever nature attract to their creator physical manifestations corresponding to their nature as perfectly as nature germinates the seed of the acorn and develops it into an oak tree.

Also, he would have discovered that positive thoughts reach out through the self-same law and attract physical counterparts of their nature. We are here concerned only with the method by which nature takes a hold on the mind through the operation of the law.

Before we go any further, let us briefly describe an important function of Cosmic Habit Force through which it controls all human relationships and determines whether an individual will be a success or a failure in his chosen occupation. This description can best be made by the statement that nature uses this law as a medium by which every living thing is forced to take on and become a part of the environment in which it lives and moves daily.

We are ruled by habits, all of us. Our habits are fastened upon us by repetition of thought and experience, therefore, we can control our earthly destinies just to the extent that we control our thoughts. It is a profoundly significant fact that over the power of thought a person may have complete control. Everything else is subject to forces outside of one's control. Nature has given man the privilege of controlling his thoughts, but she has also subjected him to the power of Cosmic Habit Force through which his thoughts are made to clothe themselves in their physical likeness and equivalent.

If a man's dominating thoughts are of poverty, the law translates those thoughts into physical terms of misery and want. If a man's dominating thoughts are of opulence, the law transforms them into their physical counterpart. Man builds the pattern through his thoughts, but Cosmic Habit Force works that pattern into its physical likeness and builds it into permanency.

"But, how can a law of nature make something out of nothing," some will ask? It is but natural that any practical person would want to know the exact manner in which, for example, Cosmic Habit Force could transmute thoughts of opulence into material riches or thoughts of poverty into material evidence of poverty. We are happy to raise the question and to answer it.

To begin with, let us recognize the fact that Cosmic Habit Force is silent, unseen, and unfelt and works in complete harmony with all of nature's other forces such as gravitation, electricity, evolution, etc., but it differs from all other natural forces in that it is the sole source of their power and serves as nature's controller through which every form of power and every law of nature must work. It is the master key to the universe, so great in power that it controls every living thing and every atom of matter, the control being carried out through established habit force.

The method by which Cosmic Habit Force converts a positive impulse or mental desire into its physical equivalent is simple. It merely intensifies the desire into a state of mind known as faith, which inspires one to create definite plans for the attainment of whatever is desired, the plans being carried out through whatever natural methods the resourcefulness of the individual can command. Cosmic Habit Force does not undertake to transmute the desires for money directly into bank balances but it does set into motion the mechanism of imagination through which the most easily available means of converting the desire into money is provided in the form of a definite idea, plan, or method of procedure.

This force works no miracles, makes no attempt to create something out of nothing, but it does help an individual, nay it forces him to proceed naturally and logically to convert his thoughts into their physical equivalent by using all the natural media available to him which may serve his purpose. The force works so quietly that the individual, unless he is of a philosophical trend of mind, does not recognize his relationship to what is happening to him.

On one occasion, an idea will present itself to his mind in a form that he calls a hunch, and it will inspire him with such definite faith that he will begin at once to act upon it. His entire being has been changed from a negative to a positive state of mind with the result that related ideas flow into his mind more freely. The plans he creates are more definite, and his words have more influence with other people.

Because he does not understand the source from which his hunch came, he may dismiss the matter and imagine the newly discovered idea or plan with which he achieves success was the creation of his own brain. The hunch is simply a desire that has been given the intensity to enable Cosmic Habit Force to take it over and give it the necessary momentum to convert it into a definite idea or plan of action.

From that point on, the individual must move on his own by using such opportunities, human relationships, and physical conveniences as may be available to him for carrying out his desire. At times, one is inspired with awe by the coincidental combination of favorable circumstances with which he is favored in carrying out his plans such as voluntary cooperation from unexpected sources, some fortunate transaction in business that provides unexpected money, etc., but always these strange and unexplained things happen through perfectly natural procedure similar to daily experiences.

What the individual cannot see or understand is the method by which Cosmic Habit Force gives to one's thoughts that peculiar quality, which gives them the power to surmount all difficulties, overcome all resistances, and achieve seemingly unattainable ends through simple but natural procedure.

That is one secret of nature that is not yet revealed, but neither has she revealed the secret by which she causes a seed of wheat to germinate, grow, and reproduce itself bringing back with it 100 additional grains for good measure.

Cosmic Habit Force guided me through an awe-inspiring maze of experiences before revealing itself to me. All through those years of struggle, there was one definite purpose uppermost in my mind, the burning desire to organize a philosophy with which the average man can become self-determining.

Nature had no alternative but that of yielding to me the working principle of Cosmic Habit Force because I unwittingly complied with the law, by persistently seeking the way to its discovery. If I'd known of the existence of the law and of its working principle at the beginning of my research, I could have organized the Philosophy of American Achievement in a much shorter period of time.

It is profoundly significant that the Law of Cosmic Habit Force was revealed after a daily contact of minds through the Mastermind Principle covering a period of almost two years. A major portion of this time was devoted to the analysis of problems which had nothing to do with the voluntary search for the law, but the important thing I wish here to emphasize is the fact that our habit of bringing our minds into rapport for a definite purpose daily actually had the effect of giving us the benefit of Cosmic Habit Force before we knew of the existence of the law.

If your life is not what you wish it to be, you can truthfully say that you drifted into your present, unhappy condition through the irresistible force of Cosmic Habit Force, but you cannot stop there because you shall know presently that time and Definiteness of Purpose backed by Cosmic Habit Force, can give you rebirth no matter who you are or what may be your circumstances.

You may be in prison without friends or money with a life sentence hanging over you, but you can walk through the front gate and back to the outside world of free men if you adapt yourself to this force in the proper manner. How do I know this can be done? Because it has been done before, because your common sense will tell you that it can be done once you understand the working principle and catch the full significance of its relationship to time and Definiteness of Purpose.

You may be suffering with ill health, which prevents you from using your mind. In that event, unless your illness is of a nature that can be cured, you may not be able to order your life just as you would have it, but you can make changes that will give you ample compensation for your trouble in living.

You're going to make another outstanding discovery in connection with this force. You're going to learn that every failure brings with it the seed of an equivalent advantage. You're going to discover beyond any room for doubt that every experience, every circumstance of your life is a potential stepping-stone or stumbling block due entirely to the manner in which you react to the circumstance in your own mind.

You are going to discover that your only limitations are those that you set up in your own mind, but more important still, you're going to know that your mind can remove all limitations it establishes. You're going to know that you may be the master of your fate, the captain of your soul because you can control your own thoughts.

You are going to learn that failure is one of nature's methods by which he breaks up the grip of Cosmic Habit Force and releases the mind for a new start. You are going to understand that nature breaks the grip of Cosmic Habit Force on human beings through illness that forces them to rest the organs of the body and the brain. You are going to understand, too, that nature breaks the grip of the law on the people of an entire nation through wars and economic collapses known as depressions, thereby breaking up the monopolies and opportunity and reducing all men to substantially the same level.

I have given you a working knowledge of the relationship between Cosmic Habit Force, drifting, time, and Definiteness of Purpose. I have shown you through illustrations based on actual experience exactly how and why 98 out of every 100 people are failures.

I want you to know that the failures of life become such because they fall into the habit of drifting on all matters affecting their economic life, that Cosmic Habit Force carries them swiftly along in this drifting path until time fastens the habit permanently, after which there can be no escape except through some circumstance of catastrophe which breaks up their established habits and gives them an opportunity to move with Definiteness of Purpose.

I wish you to see that you are where you are and what you are today because of the influences which have reached your mind through your daily environment plus the state of mind in which you have reacted to these influences. I wish you to see and to understand that you can move with purpose and make your environment to order, or you can drift with circumstances and allow your environment to control you.

In both cases, Cosmic Habit Force is an irresistible force. It carries you swiftly toward a definite goal if you have one, and if you are definitely determined to reach that goal, or if you have no goal, it forces you to drift with time and circumstances until you become the victim of every stray wind of chance that crosses your path.

Everything in life worth having has a definite price upon it. There is no such reality as something for nothing. Having had the full advantage of studying Emerson's conclusions on this subject, plus the advantage of analyzing men and women representing the great successes and the outstanding failures, I am prepared to describe why every desirable thing in life has a price that must be paid, but I cannot pass this information onto the person who is not willing to face facts and admit to his own shortcomings. A willingness to look at oneself through unbiased eyes is a part of the price one must pay for the formula that leads to self-determination spiritually, economically, and physically.

Every person who succeeds must make use of some combination of the principles of this philosophy. The power that gives life and action to these principles is Cosmic Habit Force. Whenever any combination of the principles has been used successfully, as far as I have been able to determine by my research and personal experience, the law was unconsciously applied. I mean by this that those who have made successful application of the law have done so by mere chance without recognizing the real source of the power back of their achievements.

Observe the importance of the element of time as an essential factor with which the Principles of Achievement and Cosmic Habit Force becomes related. Cosmic Habit Force is so inexorable that it automatically takes over habits and makes them permanent.

If Cosmic Habit Force crystalizes an impulsive thought of illness and pain into a habit, think how much more quickly it will translate into permanency the pleasant, positive sensations of life. When nature has a message to convey to mankind, she does not release it to those who are indulging in dissipation, nor does she hand it over to those who have been pampered and protected from struggle, but she picks as her torch bearers those who have been seasoned by defeat until they have become self-determining.

This is your destiny. Embark on it.

# Atom-Smashing Power of Mind

(1949)

## by Charles Fillmore

*The Life-Changing Classic on Your Power Within*

## Contents

Introduction  *Charles Fillmore: The Man Who Never Stood Still* by Mitch Horowitz  810
Chapter One   The Atomic Age   811
Chapter Two   The Restorative Power of Spirit   814
Chapter Three   Spiritual Obedience   816
Chapter Four   I AM or Superconsciousness   818
Chapter Five   Day of Judgment   820
Chapter Six   Thou Shalt Decree a Thing   821
Chapter Seven   Thinking in the Fourth Dimension   822
Chapter Eight   Is This God's World?   824
Chapter Nine   Truth Radiates Light   826
Chapter Ten   The Only Mind   828
Chapter Eleven   The Body   830
Chapter Twelve   Faith Precipitations   832
Chapter Thirteen   The End of the Age   833

## Introduction
# Charles Fillmore: The Man Who Never Stood Still

Spiritual experimenters through the ages, from ancient astrologers and alchemists to contemporary chaos magicians and mind-power mystics, have always availed themselves of the latest technologies of their eras. The New Thought pioneer Charles Fillmore, who founded the vibrant and ongoing Unity movement, was a great example of this.

Born in 1854 on an Indian reservation near St. Cloud, Minnesota, Fillmore and his wife and intellectual partner Myrtle, organized their Kansas City-based Unity ministry into one of the nation's first mass-media ministries. As early as 1907, the Fillmores staffed phone banks with round-the-clock volunteers ready to assist callers with distance prayers. The Unity ministry made early use of radio, targeted mailings, correspondence courses, pamphlets, and well-produced magazines aimed at the large demographic range of Unity's congregants. This included the children's monthly *Wee Wisdom*, which launched the literary career of bestselling novelist Sidney Sheldon when it published the ten-year-old's first poem in 1927.

Up to the eve of his death in 1948, Charles Fillmore remained well versed in the science and technology of the newly dawned atomic era. Fillmore sought to unite the insights of science and practical mysticism in the collection of writings that make up *Atom-Smashing Power of the Mind*, which appeared the year after his death.

This 1949 book is one of Fillmore's finest literary efforts. It serves as a powerful and stirring summation of his theology of mind-power metaphysics. At the same time, Fillmore relates the higher abilities of thought to the revolutions in atomic energy that entered public awareness in the years immediately preceding his death. Of this, Fillmore makes a creditable effort, foreseeing future developments in wireless, microwave, and cellular technology. When I consider my failings to stay fully versed in the digital technology of our own era, I am all the more admiring of a frontier boy who grew up not only to establish a major religious denomination but who never stopped learning about the radically changing world around him. Within those changes, Fillmore discovered confirmation of his own universal ideals.

This condensation of *Atom-Smashing Power of Mind* captures the verve, spirit, and soaring language of his original, while retaining his key points and practical insights. I consider Fillmore's book one of the finest mid-century statements of New Thought philosophy. It is the kind of work that should inspire those of us today who believe that all knowledge—scientific, technological, psychological, medical, and spiritual—ultimately converge. Of this, Charles Fillmore was absolutely certain.

—Mitch Horowitz

## Chapter One

# The Atomic Age

The majority of people have crude or distorted ideas about the character and the location of Spirit. They think that Spirit plays no part in mundane affairs and can be known by a person only after his death.

But Jesus said, "God is Spirit;" He also said, "The kingdom of God is within you." Science tells us that there is a universal life that animates and sustains all the forms and shapes of the universe. Science has broken into the atom and revealed it to be charged with tremendous energy that may be released and be made to give the inhabitants of the earth powers beyond expression when its law of expression is discovered.

Jesus evidently knew about this hidden energy in matter and used His knowledge to perform so-called miracles.

Our modern scientists say that a single drop of water contains enough latent energy to blow up a ten-story building. This energy, existence of which has been discovered by modern scientists, is the same kind of spiritual energy that was known to Elijah, Elisha, and Jesus, and used by them to perform miracles.

By the power of his thought Elijah penetrated the atoms and precipitated an abundance of rain. By the same law he increased the widow's oil and meal. This was not a miracle—that is, it was not a divine intervention supplanting natural law—but the exploitation of a law not ordinarily understood. Jesus used the same dynamic power of thought to break the bonds of the atoms composing the few loaves and fishes of a little lad's lunch—and five thousand people were fed.

Science is discovering the miracle-working dynamics of religion, but science has not yet comprehended the dynamic directive power of man's thought. All so-called miracle workers claim that they do not of themselves produce the marvelous results; that they are only the instruments of a superior entity. It is written in I Kings, "The jar of meal wasted not, neither did the cruse of oil fail, according to the word of Jehovah, which he spake by Elijah." Jesus called Jehovah Father. He said, "The works that I do in my Father's name, these bear witness of me."

Jesus did not claim to have the exclusive supernatural power that is usually credited to Him. He had explored the ether energy, which He called the "kingdom of the heavens;" His understanding was beyond that of the average man, but He knew that other men could do what He did if they would only try. He encouraged His followers to take Him as a center of faith and use the power of thought and word. "He that believeth on me, the works that I do shall he do also; and greater works than these shall he do."

Have faith in the power of your mind to penetrate and release the energy that is pent up in the atoms of your body, and you will be astounded at the response. Paralyzed functions anywhere in the body can be restored to action by one's speaking to the spiritual intelligence and life within them. Jesus raised His dead bodies in this way, and Paul says that we can raise our body in the same manner if we have the same spiritual contact.

What have thought concentration and discovery of the dynamic character of the atom to do with prayer? They have everything to do with prayer, because prayer is the opening of communication between the mind of man and the mind of God. Prayer is the exercise of faith in the presence and power of the unseen God. Supplication, faith, meditation, silence, concentration, are mental attitudes that enter into and form part of prayer. When one understands the spiritual character of God and adjusts himself mentally to the omnipresent God-Mind, he has begun to pray rightly.

Audible prayers are often answered but the most potent are silently uttered in the secret recesses of the soul. Jesus warned against wordy prayers—prayer uttered to be heard of men. He told His disciples not to be like those who pray on the housetop. "When thou prayest, enter into thine inner chamber, and having shut thy door, pray to thy Father who is in secret, and thy Father who seeth in secret shall recompense thee."

The times are ripe for great changes in our estimate of the abiding place and the character of God. The six-day creation of the universe (including man) described in Genesis is a symbolic story of the work of the higher realms of mind under divine law. It is the privilege of everyone to use his mind abilities in the superrealms, and thereby carry out the prayer formula of Jesus:

"Seek ye first his kingdom, and his righteousness; and all these things shall be added unto you."

Of all the comments on or discussions of the indescribable power of the invisible force released by the atomic bomb none that we have seen mentions its spiritual or mental character. All commentators have written about it as a force external to man to be controlled by mechanical means, with no hint that it is the primal life that animates and interrelates man's mind and body.

The next great achievement of science will be the understanding of the mental and spiritual abilities latent in man through which to develop and release these tremendous electrons, protons, and neutrons secreted in the trillions of cells in the physical organism.

Here is involved the secret, as Paul says, "hid for ages and generations... which is Christ [superman] in you, the hope of glory." It is through release of these hidden life forces in his organism that man is to achieve immortal life, and in no other way. When we finally understand the facts of life and rid our minds of the delusion that we shall find immortal life after we die, then we shall seek more diligently to awaken the spiritual man within us and strengthen and build up the spiritual domain of our being until, like Jesus, we shall be able to control the atomic energy in our bodies and perform so-called miracles.

The fact is that all life is based upon the interaction between the various electrical units of the universe. Science tells us about these activities in terms of matter and no one understands them, because they are spiritual entities and their realities can only be understood and used wisely by the spiritually developed man. Electricians do not know what electricity is, although they use it constantly. The Christian uses faith and gets marvelous results, the electrician uses electricity and also gets marvelous results, and neither of them knows the real nature of the agent he uses so freely.

The man who called electricity faith doubtless thought that he was making a striking comparison when in fact he was telling a truth, that faith is of the mind and it is the match that starts the fire in the electrons and protons of innate Spirit forces. Faith has its degrees of voltage; the faith of the child and the faith of the most powerful spiritual adept are far apart in their intensity and results. When the trillions of cells in one's body are roused to expectancy by spiritual faith, a positive spiritual contact results and marvelous transformations take place.

Sir James Jeans, the eminent British scientist, gives a prophecy of this in one of his books. He says in substance that it may be that the gods determining our fate are our own minds working on our brain cells and through them on the world about us.

This will eventually be found to be true, and the discovery of the law of release of the electronic vitality wrapped up in matter will be the greatest revelation of all time.

When we awake to the fact that every breath we draw is releasing this all-potent electronic energy and it is shaping our lives for good or ill, according to our faith, then we shall begin to search for the law that will guide us aright in the use of power.

## Chapter Two

# The Restorative Power of the Spirit

Not only our Bible but the scriptures of all the nations of the world testify to the existence of an invisible force moving men and nature in their various activities. Not all agree as to the character of this omnipresent force, universal Spirit, but it serves the purpose of being their god under whatever name it may appear. Different nations ostensibly believe in the same scriptures, but they have various concepts of the universal Spirit; some conceive it to be nature and others God. Robert Browning says, "What I call God ... fools call Nature."

Our Bible plainly teaches that God implanted in man His perfect image and likeness, with executive ability to carry out all the creative plans of the Great Architect. When man arrives at a certain point in spiritual understanding it is his office to cooperate with the God principle in creation.

As the animating life of all things God is a unit, but as the mind that drives this life He is diverse. Every man is king in his own mental domain, and his subjects are his thoughts.

People in this atomic-age civilization ask why God does not reveal Himself now as He did in Bible days. The fact is that God is talking to people everywhere, but they do not understand the message and brush it aside as an idle dream. We need to divest ourselves of the thought that Daniel and Joseph, in fact all the unusually wise men of the Bible, were especially inspired by God, that they were divinely appointed by the Lord to do His work. Everything points to their spiritual insight as the result of work on their part to that end.

The body is the instrument of the mind, and the mind looks to the Spirit for its inspiration. Not only the Scriptures that we look to for authority in our daily living but also the experience of ourselves and our neighbors proves that those who cultivate communion with the Father within become conscious of a guiding light, call it what you will.

Those who scoff at this and say that it is all the work of the imagination are deluding themselves and ignoring a source of instruction and progress that they need above all things. If this sense world were the only world we shall ever know, the attainment of its ambitions might be sufficient for a man of meager outlook and small capacity, but the majority of us see ourselves and the world about us in a process of transformation that will culminate in conditions here on the earth far superior to those we have imagined for heaven.

Jesus was very advanced, and His radiant body was developed in larger degree than that of anyone in our race, but we all have this body, and its development is in proportion to our spiritual culture. In Jesus this body of light glowed "as he was praying." Jesus' body did not go down to corruption, but He, by the intensity of His spiritual devotion, restored every cell to its innate state of atomic light and power. When John was in the state of spiritual devotion Jesus appeared to him, "and his eyes were as a flame of fire; and his feet like unto burnished brass." Jesus lives today in that body of glorified electricity in a kingdom that interpenetrates the earth and its environment. He called it the kingdom of the heavens.

We do not have to look to the many experiences recorded in the Bible of the spiritually illumined to prove the existence of the spiritual supersubstance. People everywhere are discovering it, as they always have in every age and clime.

The metaphysical literature of our day is very rich with the experiences of those who have found through various channels the existence of the radiant body. This prompts me to tell of my development of the radiant body, during half a century's experience. It began when I was mentally affirming statements of Truth. Just between my eyes, but above, I felt a "thrill" that lasted a few moments, then passed away. I found I could repeat this experience with affirmations. As time went on I could set up this "thrill" at other points in my body and finally it became a continuous current throughout my nervous system. I called it "the Spirit" and found that it was connected with a universal life force whose source was the Christ. As taught in the Bible, we have through wrong thinking and living lost contact with the parent life. Jesus

Christ incarnated in the flesh and thereby introduced us by His Word into the original Father life. He said, "If a man keep my word, he shall never taste of death." I have believed that and affirmed His words until they have become organized in my body. Sometimes when I make this claim of Christ life in the body I am asked if I expect to live always in this flesh. My answer is that I realize that the flesh is being broken down every day and its cells transformed into energy and life, and a new body is being formed of a very superior quality. That new body in Christ will be my future habitation.

I have found that the kingdom of God is within man and that we are wasting our time and defeating the work of the Spirit if we look for it anywhere else.

## Chapter Three
# Spiritual Obedience

Zeal is the great universal force that impels man to spring forward in a field of endeavor and accomplish the seemingly miraculous. It is the inward fire that urges man onward, regardless of the intellectual mind of caution and conversation.

Zeal should be tempered with wisdom. It is possible to be so zealously active on the intellectual plane that one's vitality is consumed and there is nothing left for spiritual growth. "Take time to be holy." Never neglect your soul. To grow spiritually you should exercise your zeal in spiritual ways.

Above all other Bible writers Paul emphasizes the importance of the mind in the transformation of character and body. In this respect he struck a note in religion that had been mute up to this time; that is, that spirit and mind are akin and that man is related to God through his thought. Paul sounds again and again in various forms this silent but very essential chord in the unity of God and man and man and his body.

When the scientific world investigates the so-called miracles of religion and discovers that they are being duplicated continually, the power of mind over matter will be heralded as of great importance to both religion and science.

Prayer gives spiritual poise to the ego, and it brings forth eternal life when spiritually linked with the Christ. "If a man keep my word, he shall never see death."

To one who gains even a meager quickening of the Spirit, Christianity ceases to be a theory; it becomes a demonstrable science of the mind.

We must not anticipate better social and economic conditions until we have better men and women to institute and sustain those conditions.

Jesus said that He was the bread and substance that came down from heaven. When will our civilization begin to realize and appropriate this mighty ocean of substance and life?

A finer civilization than now exists has been conceived by many from Plato in his "Republic" to Edward Bellamy in "Looking Backward." But a new and higher civilization will be developed only through the efforts of higher and finer types of men and women. Philosophers and seers have looked forward to a time when this earth would produce superior men and women, but save Jesus none has had the spiritual insight to declare, "Verily I say unto you, This generation shall not pass away, until all these things be accomplished."

"Behold, the man!" Jesus Christ is the type of a new race now forming in the earth. Those who incorporate into consciousness the Christ principles are its members.

The dominion that God gave to man in the beginning, as recorded in Genesis, is a dominion over spiritual ideas, which are represented in the allegory by material symbols.

Hence to exercise his dominion man must understand the metaphysical side of everything in existence.

Divine Mind is the one and only reality. When we incorporate the ideas that form Divine Mind into our mind and persevere in those ideas, a mighty strength wells up within us. Then we have a foundation for the spiritual body, the body not made with hands, eternal in the heavens. When the spiritual body is established in consciousness, its strength and power is transmitted to the visible body and to all the things that we touch in the world about us.

In the economy of the future man will not be a slave to money. Humanity's daily needs will be met in ways not now thought practical.

In the new economy we shall serve for the joy of serving, and prosperity will flow to us and through us in rippling streams of plenty. The supply and support that love and zeal set in motion are not yet largely used by man, but those who have tested this method are loud in their praise of its efficiency.

## Chapter Four
# I AM or Superconciousness

Superconciousness is the goal toward which humanity is working. Regardless of appearances there is an upward trend continually active throughout all creation. The superconsciousness is the realm of divine ideas. Its character is impersonal. It therefore has no personal ambitions; knows no condemnation; but is always pure, innocent, loving, and obedient to the call of God.

The superconsciousness has been perceived by the spiritually wise in every age, but they have not known how to externalize it and make it an abiding state of consciousness. Jesus accomplished this, and His method is worthy of our adoption, because as far as we know, it is the only method that has been successful. It is set forth in the New Testament, and whoever adopts the life of purity and love and power there exemplified in the experiences of Jesus of Nazareth will in due course attain the place that He attained.

Jesus acknowledged Himself to be the Son of God. Living in the superconsciousness calls for nothing less on our part than a definite recognition of ourselves as sons of God right here and now, regardless of appearances to the contrary. We know that we are sons of God; then why not acknowledge it and proceed to take possession of our God heirdom? That is what Jesus did in the face of the most adverse conditions. Conditions today are not so inertly material as they were in Jesus' time. People now know more about themselves and their relation to God. They are familiar with thought processes and how an idea held in mind will manifest itself in the body and in affairs; hence they take up this problem of spiritual realization under vastly more favorable conditions. An idea must work out just as surely as a mathematical problem, because it is under immutable law. The factors are all in our possession, and the method was demonstrated in one striking instance and is before us. By following the method of Jesus and doing day-by-day work that comes to us, we shall surely put on Christ as fully and completely as did Jesus of Nazareth.

The method by which Jesus evolved from sense consciousness to God consciousness was, first, the recognition of the spiritual selfhood and a constant affirmation of its supremacy and power. Jesus loved to make the highest statements: "I and the Father are one." "All authority hath been given unto me in heaven and on earth." He made these statements, so we know that at the time He was fully aware of their reality. Secondly, by the power of His word He penetrated deeper into omnipresence and tapped the deepest resources of

His mind, whereby He released the light, life, and substance of Spirit, which enabled Him to get the realization that wholly united His consciousness with the Father Mind.

In the light of modern science the miracles of the Bible can be rationally explained as Mind acting in an omnipresent spiritual field, which is open to all men who develop spiritually. "Ye who have followed me, in the regeneration when the Son of man shall sit on the throne of his glory, ye also shall sit upon twelve thrones, judging the twelve tribes of Israel."

"He that overcometh, I will give to him to sit down with me in my throne."

Overcoming is a change of mind from error to Truth. The way of overcoming is first to place one's self by faith in the realization of Sonship, and second, to demonstrate it in every thought and act.

The Word is man's I AM. The Holy Spirit is the "outpouring" or activity of the living Word. The work of the Holy Spirit is the executive power of Father (mind) and Son (idea), carrying out the creative plan. It is through the help of the Holy Spirit that man overcomes. The Holy Spirit reveals, helps, and directs in this overcoming. "The Spirit searcheth all things, yea, the deep things of God." It finally leads man into the light.

Science rightly understood is of inestimable value to religion, and Christianity in order to become the world power that its founder envisioned, must stress the unfoldment of the spiritual mind in man in order that he may do the mighty works promised by Jesus.

When Jesus went up into the mount to pray He was transfigured before His apostles

Peter, James, and John. True prayer brings about an exalted radiation of energy, and when it is accompanied by faith, judgment, and love, the word of Truth bursts forth in a stream of light that, when held in mind, illumines, uplifts, and glorifies.

Jesus recognized Mind in everything and called it "Father." He knew that there is a faith center in each atom of so-called matter and that faith in man can move upon the faith center in so-called matter and can remove mountains.

Jesus taught that the realities of God are capable of expression here in this world and that man within himself has God capacity and power. Jesus was crucified because He claimed to be the Son of God. Yet the Scriptures, which the Pharisees worshiped, had this bold proclamation, which Jesus quoted to them from Psalms 82:

> "I said, Ye are gods,
> And all of you sons of the Most High."

The reports by His followers of what He taught clearly point to two subjects that He loved to discourse upon. The first was the Son of God: He was the Son of God. Secondly: We might all become as He was and demonstrate our dominion by following Him in the regeneration.

In order to follow Jesus in the regeneration we must become better acquainted with the various phases of mind and how they function in and through the body.

In spiritual understanding we know that all the forces in the body are directed by thought and that they work in a constructive or a destructive way, according to the character of the thought. Medicine, massage, and all the material means accomplish but incomplete, unsatisfactory, temporary results, because they work only from the outside and do not touch the inner springs that control the forces. The springs can only be touched by thought. There must be a unity between the mind of man and Divine Mind so that ideas and thoughts that work constructively unto eternal life may be quickened in the mind and organism of man.

We are told in John that the world could not contain the books that would be written if all the things that Jesus did were put into writing. But enough is given in the story of His life and in the writings of the apostles concerning Him to bear witness to that which is daily being revealed in this day of fulfillment. Those who are consecrated to Truth and fully resolved to follow Jesus all the way are spiritualizing the whole man, including the body, which is being redeemed from corruption. Those who are living as Jesus lived are becoming like Him. "God is not the God of the dead, but of the living." Resurrection takes place in people who are alive.

Chapter Five

# The Day of Judgment

It is said we are to be judged after death according to deeds done in the body, which are kept on record like books that are balanced; and if the balance is found to be in our favor we go up, and if against us we go down. But if we are spiritual now—divine—this spiritual part has dominion, and we begin to exercise this dominion. The moment we catch sight of this we begin to judge. We begin to put the thoughts that are good on the right and the others on the left. All our ideas of the attributes of our divine self we put on the right hand of power, while the thoughts of disease, death, limitation and lack we put on the left—denied, cut off.

This is not to occur after death. It is to begin right now!

Now is the time to plant the seed thought of the conditions we desire by saying, "Come my good thoughts, let us inherit our kingdom."

We do not fear anything, for we have separated our sheep from our goats; we have set our true thoughts on the right and have denied our error thoughts any power whatever.

Come into the kingdom of mind. Here everything that is in Principle is yours.

Everything, all good, is to be gathered up, and everything is good at its center. The essence of your body is good and of true substance. When you sift your consciousness of all but the real and true, the body becomes full of light.

The diamond owes its brilliance to the perfect arrangement of the innumerable little prisms within it, each of which refracts the light of the other. Man's body is made up of centers of consciousness—of light—and if arranged so they radiate the light within you, you will shine like the diamond. All things are in the consciousness and you have to learn to separate the erroneous from the true, darkness from light. The I AM must separate the sheep from the goats. This sifting begins right now and goes on until the perfect child of God is manifest and you are fully rounded out in all your Godlike attributes

## Chapter Six

# Thou Shalt Decree a Thing

To decree with assurance is to establish and fix an ideal in substance. The force behind the decree is invisible, like a promise to be fulfilled at a future time; but it binds with its invisible chains the one who makes it. We have only a slight conception of the strength of the intangible. We compare and measure strength by some strong element in nature. We say "strong as steel." But a very little thought will convince us that mental affirmations are far stronger than the strongest visible thing in the world. The reason for this is that visible things lack livingness. They are not linked with energy and intelligence as are words. Words charged with power and intelligence increase with use, while material things decrease.

It is not necessary to call the attention of metaphysicians to the fact that all visible things had their origin in the invisible. The visible is what remains of an idea that has gradually lost its energy. Scientists say that this so-called solid earth under our feet was once radiant substance. Nothing is really "solid" but the atomic energy latent in everything. They tell us that it takes some six billion years for uranium to disintegrate and become lead, and this rate of disintegration has helped scientists determine the age of the earth as about two billion years.

Since nothing is lost in the many transformations that occur in nature, what becomes of the energy that is being released in the disintegration that is going on in our earth? The answer is that a new earth is being formed in which matter will be replaced by atomic energy. This process of refining matter into radiant substance is taking place not only in the natural world but in our bodies also. In fact the speed with which the transformation takes place depends on the character of the thoughts that we project into our brains and through them into our bodies and the world about us. This is why we should spiritualize our thoughts and refine the food we eat to correspond.

At the present writing there is a housing shortage everywhere and the lack of materials and competent labor indicate that several years will elapse before the need is met. This is counted a calamity; but is it? The inventive genius of man is planning houses of glass and other materials that will be much less expensive—more durable and in every respect superior to the present homes. When man gets his ingenious mind into action he always meets every emergency with something better. Every adverse situation can be used as a spur to urge one to greater exertion and the ultimate attainment of some ideal that has lain dormant in the subconsciousness.

## Chapter Seven
# Thinking in the Fourth Dimension

Scientists tell us that the discoveries that their efforts are revealing convince them that they are just on the verge of stupendous truths. Christianity spiritually interpreted shows that Jesus understood the deeper things of God's universe. He understood exactly what the conditions were on the invisible side of life, which is termed in His teaching the "kingdom of God" or the "kingdom of the heavens." We are trying to connect His teaching with modern science in order to show the parallel; but as He said in Mark 4:23, "if any man hath ears to hear, let him hear." This means that we must develop a capacity for understanding in terms of the atomic structure of the universe.

Unless we have this spiritual capacity we do not understand. We think we have ears, but they are attuned to materiality. They do not get the radiations from the supermind, the Christ Mind. Physiology working with psychology is demonstrating that hearing and seeing can be developed in every cell in the body, independent of ears and eyes. We hear and see with our minds working through our bodies. This being true, the capacity to hear may extend beyond the physical ear into the spiritual ethers, and we should be able to hear the voice of God. This extension of hearing is what Jesus taught. "If any man hath ears to hear, let him hear."

Then we are told that we must "take heed" what we hear. Many of us have found that as we develop this inner, spiritual hearing, we hear voices sometimes that do not tell the truth. These deceptive voices can be hushed by affirming the presence and power of the Lord Jesus Christ.

As you unfold your spiritual nature, you will find that it has the same capacity for receiving vibrations of sound as your outer, physical ear has. You do not give attention to all that you hear in the external; you discriminate as you listen. So in the development of this inner, spiritual ear take heed what you hear: discriminate.

Jesus said, "For he that hath, to him shall be given: and he that hath not, from him shall be taken away even that which he hath." How can what a man has not be taken away? We believe in our mortal consciousness that we have attained a great deal, but if we have not this inner, spiritual consciousness of reality our possessions are impermanent. Then we must be careful what we accumulate in our consciousness, because "he that hath, to him shall be given." The more spiritual Truth you pile up in your mind, the more you have of reality, and the larger is your capacity for the unlimited; but if you have nothing of a spiritual character, what little you have of intellectual attainment will eventually be taken away from you.

The mysteries of the supermind have always been considered the property of certain schools of occultists and mystics who were cautious about giving their truths to the masses for fear that in their ignorance these might misuse them. But now the doors are thrown wide open, and whosoever will may enter in.

Our attention in this day is being largely called to the revolution that is taking place in the economic world, but a revolution of even greater worth is taking place in the mental and spiritual worlds. A large and growing school of metaphysicians has made its advent in this generation, and it is radically changing the public mind toward religion. In other words, we are developing spiritual understanding, and this means that religion and its sources in tradition and in man are being inquired into and its principles applied in the development of a new cosmic mind for the whole human family.

## Chapter Eight
# Is This God's World?

"Why doesn't God do something about it?" This oft-repeated query, uttered by the skeptical and unbelieving, is heard day in and day out. Imitating the skeptics, Christian believers everywhere are looking to God for all kinds of reforms in every department of manifest life and also are charging Him with death and destruction the world over.

One who thinks logically and according to sound reason wonders at the contradictions set up by these various queries and desires.

Is God responsible for all that occurs on this earth, and if not all, how much of it?

The Bible states that God created the earth and all its creatures, and last of all man, to whom He gave dominion over everything. Observation and experience prove that man is gaining dominion over nature wherever he applies himself to that end. But so much remains to be gained, and he is so small physically that man counts himself a pygmy instead of the mental giant that he is.

All the real mastery that man attains in the world has its roots in his mind, and when he opens up the mental realm in his being there are no unattainables. If the conquests of the air achieved in the last quarter century had been prophesied, the prophets would have been pronounced crazy. The fact is that no one thinking in the old mind realm can have any conception of the transformation of sound waves into electromagnetic waves and back again into words and messages of intelligence. Edison admitted that his discovery of the phonograph was an accident and that he never fully understood how mechanical vibrations could be recorded and be reproduced in all forms of intelligent communication.

Now that man has broken away from his limited visualizations and mentally grasped the unhampered ideas of the supermind, he is growing grandly bold and his technical pioneers are telling him that the achievements of yesterday are as nothing compared to those of tomorrow. For example, an article by Harland Manchester condensed in the *Reader's Digest* from *Scientific American* tells of the "microwaves" that are slated for a more spectacular career in the realm of the unbelievable than anything that has preceded them. This article describes in detail some of the marvels that will evolve out of the utilization of microwaves, among which may be mentioned "private phone calls by the hundreds of thousands sent simultaneously over the same wave band without wires, poles or cables. Towns where each citizen has his own radio frequency, over which he can get voice, music, and television, and call any phone in the country by dialing. Complete abolition of static and interference from electrical devices and from other stations. A hundred times as much 'space on the air' as we now have in the commercial radio band. A high-definition and color television network to cover the country. And, perhaps most important of all, a nationwide radar network, geared to television, to regulate all air traffic and furnish instantaneous visual weather reports to airfields throughout the land."

Add to this the marvels promised by the appliers of atomic energy and you have an array of miracles unequaled in all the bibles of all the nations of the world.

It is admitted by those who are most familiar with the dynamic power of these newly discovered forces that we do not yet know how to protect our body cells from the destructiveness of their vibrations. Very thick concrete walls are required to protect those who experiment with atomic forces. One scientist says that the forces released from the bombs that were used on the Japanese cities in 1945 may affect those who were subjected to them and their descendants for a thousand years. Experimentation proves that we have tapped a kingdom that we do not know how to handle safely.

## Chapter Nine
# Truth Radiates Light

Spiritual light transcends in glory all the laws of matter and intellect. Even Moses could not enter the Tabernacle when it was aglow with this transcendent light.

It is written that the Israelites did not go forward on days when the cloud remained over the Tabernacle, but when the cloud was taken up they went forward. This means that there is no soul progress for man when his body is under the shadow of a "clouded" mind, but when the cloud is removed there is an upward and forward movement of the whole consciousness (all the people).

We are warned of the effect of thoughts that are against or opposed to the commandments of Jehovah. When we murmur and complain we cloud our minds, and Divine Mind cannot reach us or help us. Then we usually loaf until something turns up that causes us to think on happier things, when we go forward again.

Instead of giving up to circumstances and outer events we should remember that we are all very close to a kingdom of mind that would make us always happy and successful if we would cultivate it and make it and its laws a vital part of our life. "The joy of Jehovah is your strength."

You ask, "How can I feel the joy of Jehovah when I am poor, or sick, or unhappy?"

Jesus said, "Come unto me, all ye that labor and are heavy laden, and I will give you rest."

Here is the first step in getting out of the mental cloud that obscures the light of Spirit. Take the promises of Jesus as literally and spiritually true. Right in the midst of the most desperate situation one can proclaim the presence and power of Christ, and that is the first mental move in dissolving the darkness. You cannot think of Jesus without a feeling of freedom and light. Jesus taught freedom from mortality and proclaimed His glory so persistently that He energized our thought atmosphere into light.

The Scriptures state that when Moses came down from Mount Sinai with the Ten Commandments his face shone so brilliantly that the Children of Israel and even Aaron, his own brother, were afraid to come near him until he put a veil over his face. The original Hebrew says his face sent forth beams or horns of light.

The Vulgate says that Moses had "a horned face;" which Michelangelo took literally, in his statue of Moses representing him with a pair of horns projecting from the head. Thus we see the ludicrous effect of reading the Bible according to the letter.

Our men of science have experimented with the brain in action, and they tell us that it is true that we radiate beams when we think. The force of these beams has been measured.

Here we have further confirmation of the many statements in the Bible that have been taken as ridiculous and unbelievable or as miracles.

Persons who spend much time in prayer and meditate a great deal on spiritual things develop the same type of face that Moses is said to have had. We say of them that their faces fairly shine when they talk about God and His love. John saw Jesus on the island of Patmos, and he says, "His countenance was as the sun shineth in his strength."

I have witnessed this radiance in the faces of Truth teachers hundreds of times. I well remember one class lesson during which the teacher became so eloquent that beams of light shot forth from her head and tongues of fire flashed through the room, very like those which were witnessed when the followers of Jesus were gathered in Jerusalem.

We now know that fervent words expressed in prayer and song and eloquent proclamations of spiritual Truth release the millions of electrons in our brain cells and through them blend like chords of mental music with the Mind universal.

This tendency on our part to analyze and scientifically dissect the many supposed miracles recorded in the Bible is often regarded as sacrilegious, or at least as making commonplaces of some of the very spectacular incidents recorded in Scripture.

In every age preceding this the priesthood has labored under the delusion that the common people could not understand the real meaning of life and that they should therefore be kept in ignorance of its inner sources; also that the masses could not be trusted with sacred truths, that imparting such truths to them was like casting pearls before swine.

But now science is delving into hidden things, and it is found that they all arise in and are sustained by universal principles that are open to all men who seek to know and apply them.

Anyone who will search for the science in religion and the religion in science will find that they harmonize and prove each other. The point of unity is the Spirit-mind common to both. So long as religion assumes that the Spirit that creates and sustains man and the universe can be cajoled and by prayer or some other appeal can be induced to change its laws, it cannot hope to be recognized by those who know that unchangeable law rules everywhere and in everything.

Again, so long as science ignores the principle of intelligence in the evolutionary and directive forces of man and the universe, just so long will it fail to understand religion and the power of thought in the changes that are constantly taking place in the world, visible and invisible.

## Chapter Ten

# The Only Mind

say, "An idea comes to me." Where did it come from? It must have had a source of like character with its own. Ideas are not visible to the eye, they are not heard by the ear, nor felt, nor tasted, yet we talk about them as having existence. We recognize that they live, move, and have being in the realm that we term mind.

This realm of mind is accepted by everybody as in some way connected with the things that appear, but because it is not describable in terms of length, breadth, and thickness, it is usually passed over as something too vague for consideration.

But those who take up the study of this thing called mind find that it can be analyzed and its laws and modes of operation understood.

To be ignorant of mind and its laws is to be a child playing with fire, or a man manipulating powerful chemicals without knowing their relation to one another. This is universally true; and all who are not learning about mind are in like danger, because all are dealing with the great cause from which spring forth all the conditions that appear in the lives of all men and women. Mind is the one reservoir from which we draw all that we make up into our world, and it is through the laws of mind that we form our lives. Hence nothing is as important as a knowledge of mind, its inherencies, and the mode of their expression.

The belief that mind cannot be understood is fallacious. Man is the expression of mind, dwells in mind, and can know more clearly and definitely about the mind than the things that appear in the phenomenal world.

Mind is the great storehouse of good from which man draws all his supplies. If you manifest life, you are confident that it had a source. If you show forth intelligence you know that somewhere in the economy of Being there is a fount of intelligence. So you may go over the elements that go to make up your being and you will find that they draw their sustenance from an invisible and, to your limited understanding, incomprehensible source.

This source we term Mind, because it is as such that our comprehension is best related to it. Names are arbitrary, and we should not stop to note differences that are merely technical. We want to get at the substance which they represent.

So if we call this invisible source Mind it is because it is of like character with the thing within our consciousness that we call our mind. Mind is manyfold in its manifestations. It produces all that appears. Not that the character of all that appears is to be laid to the volition of Mind; no, but some of its factors enter into everything that appears. This is why it is so important to know about Mind, and how its potentialities are made manifest.

And this is where we have set up a study that makes of every atom in the universe a living center of wisdom as well as life and substance.

We claim that on its plane of comprehension man may ask the atom or the mountain the secret that it holds and it will be revealed to him. This is the communication of mind with Mind; hence we call Mind the universal underlying cause of existence and study it from that basis.

God is Mind, and man made in the image and likeness of God is Mind, because there is but one Mind, and that is the Mind of God. The person in sense consciousness thinks he has a mind of his own and that he creates thought from its own inherent substance. This is a suppositional mind that passes away when the one and only real Mind is revealed. This one and only Mind of God that we study is the only creator. It is that which originates all that is permanent; hence it is the source of all reality. Its creations are of a character hard for the sense man to comprehend, because his consciousness is cast in a mold of space and time. These are changeable and transient, while the creations of the one Mind are substantial and lasting. But it is man's privilege to understand the creations of the one Mind, for it is through them that he makes his world. The creations of the one Mind are ideas. The ideas of God are potential forces waiting to be set in motion through proper formative vehicles. The thinking faculty in man is such a vehicle, and it is through this that the visible universe has existence. Man does not "create" anything if by this term is meant the producing of something from nothing; but he does make the formless up into form; or rather it is through his conscious cooperation that the one Mind forms its universe.

Mind is the storehouse of ideas. Man draws all his ideas from this omnipresent storehouse. The ideas of God, heaven, hell, devils, angels, and all things have their clue in Mind. But their form in the consciousness depends entirely upon the plane from which man draws his mental images. If he gets a "clue" to the character of God and then proceeds to clothe this clue idea with images from without, he makes God a mortal. If he looks within for the clothing of his clue idea he knows God to be the omnipresent Spirit of existence.

So it is of the utmost importance that we know how we have produced this state of existence which we call life; and we should be swift to conform to the only method calculated to bring harmony and success into our life, namely to think in harmony with the understanding derived from communion with the God-Mind.

## Chapter Eleven

# The Body

You see at once that man is not body, but that the body is the declaration of man, the substantial expression of his mind. We see so many different types of men that we are bound to admit that the body is merely the individual's specific interpretation of himself, whatever it may be. Man is an unknown quantity; we see merely the various ideas of man expressed in terms of body, but not man himself. The identification of man is determined by the individual himself, and he expresses his conception of man in his body.

Some persons have tall bodies; some have short ones. Some have fat bodies; some have slim ones. Some have distorted bodies, some have symmetrical ones. Now, if the body is the man, as claimed by sense consciousness, which of these many bodies is man?

The Bible declares that man is made in the "image" and after the "likeness" of God. Which of the various bodies just enumerated is the image and likeness of God?

Let us repeat that the body of man is the visible record of his thoughts. It is the individual's interpretation of his identity, and each individual shows in his body just what his views of man are. The body is the corporeal record of the mind of its owner, and there is no limit to its infinite differentiation. The individual may become any type of being that he elects to be. Man selects the mental model and the body images it. So the body is the image and likeness of the individual's idea of man. We may embody any conception of life or being that we can conceive. The body is the exact reproduction of the thoughts of its occupant. As a man thinks in his mind so is his body.

You can be an Adam if you choose, or you can be a Christ or any other type of being that you see fit to ideate. The choice lies with you. The body merely executes the mandates of the mind. The mind dictates the model according to which the body shall be manifested. Therefore as man "thinketh within himself [in his vital nature], so is he." Each individual is just what he believes he is.

It is safe to say that nine hundred and ninety-nine persons out of every thousand believe that the resurrection of the body has something specifically to do with the getting of a new body after death; so we find more than ninety-nine per cent of the world's population waiting for death to get something new in the way of a body. This belief is not based on the principles of Truth, for there is no ready-made-body factory in the universe, and thus none will get the body that he expects. Waiting for death in order to get a new body is the folly of ignorance. The thing to do is to improve the bodies that we now have; it can be done, and those who would follow Jesus in the regeneration must do it.

The "resurrection" of the body has nothing whatever to do with death, except that we may resurrect ourselves from every dead condition into which sense ignorance has plunged us. To be resurrected means to get out of the place that you are in and to get into another place. Resurrection is a rising into new vigor, new prosperity; a restoration to some higher state. It is absurd to suppose that it applies only to the resuscitation of a dead body.

It is the privilege of the individual to express any type of body that he sees fit to ideate. Man may become a Christ in mind and in body by incorporating into his every thought the ideas given to the world by Jesus.

Divine mind has placed in the mind of everyone an image of the perfect-man body. The imaging process in the mind may well be illustrated by the picture that is made by light on the photographic plate, which must be "developed" before it becomes visible. Or man's invisible body may be compared to the blueprint of a building that the architect delivers to the builder. Man is a builder of flesh and blood. Jesus was a carpenter. Also He was indeed the master mason. He restored the Lord's body ("the temple of Jehovah") in His mind and heart (in Jerusalem).

The resurrection of the body is not dependent for its demonstration on time, evolution, or any of the man-made means of growth. It is the result of the elevation of the spiritually emancipated mind of the individual.

Step by step, thought added to thought, spiritual emotion added to spiritual emotion—eventually the transformation is complete. It does not come in a day, but every high impulse, every pure thought, every upward desire adds to the exaltation and gradual personification of the divine in man and to the transformation of the human. The "old man" is constantly brought into subjection, and his deeds forever put off, as the "new man" appears arrayed in the vestments of divine consciousness.

How to accomplish the resurrection of the body has been the great stumbling block of man. The resurrection has been a mere hope, and we have endeavored to reconcile a dying body with a living God, but have not succeeded. No amount of Christian submission or stoical philosophy will take away the sting of death. But over him who is risen in Christ "death no more hath dominion."

## Chapter Twelve
# Faith Precipitations

When asked what electricity is, a scientist replied that he had often thought of it as an adjunct to faith, judging from the way it acts.

This linking of faith and electricity seems at first glance fantastic, but when we observe what takes place when certain substances in solution and an electric current are brought in conjunction, there seems to be a confirmation of the Scripture passage: "Now faith is assurance of things hoped for."

Just as the electric current precipitates certain metals in solution in acid, so faith stirs into action the electrons of man's brain; and acting concurrently with the spiritual ethers, these electrons hasten nature and produce quickly what ordinarily requires months of seedtime and harvest.

Speedy answers to prayer have always been experienced and always will be when the right relations are established between the mind of the one who prays and the spiritual realm, which is like an electrical field. The power to perform what seems to be miracles has been relegated to some God-selected one; but now we are inquiring into the law, since God is no respecter of persons, and we find that the fulfillment of the law rests with man or a group of men, when they quicken by faith the spiritual forces latent within them.

The reason why some prayers are not answered is lack of proper adjustment of the mind of the one who prays to the omnipresent creative spiritual life.

Jesus was the most successful demonstrator of prayer of whom we have any record, and He urged persistence in prayer. If at first you don't succeed, try, try again. Like Lincoln, Jesus loved to tell stories to illustrate His point, and He emphasized the value of persistence in prayer. He told of a woman who demanded justice of a certain judge and importuned him until in sheer desperation he granted her request.

Every Christian healer has had experiences where persistent prayer saved his patient. If he had merely said one prayer, as if giving a prescription for the Lord to fill, he would have fallen far short of demonstrating the law. Elijah prayed persistently until the little cloud appeared or, as we should say, he had a "realization;" then the manifestation followed.

## Chapter Thirteen
# The End of the Age

In all ages and among all people, there have been legends of prophets and saviors and predictions of their coming.

The fact that all who believe in the principle of divine incarnation have long strained their eyes across the shining sands in an effort to catch sight of the coming of one clothed with the power of heaven, should make us pause and consider the cause of such universality of opinion among peoples widely separated. To dismiss the subject as a religious superstition is not in harmony with unprejudiced reason. To regard these prophecies merely as religious superstitions rules out traditions that are as tenable and as reliable as the facts of history. There is a cause for every effect, and the cause underlying this almost unanimous expectation of a messiah must have some of the omnipresence of a universal law.

In considering a subject like this, which demonstrates itself largely on metaphysical lines, it is necessary to look beyond the material plane to the realm of causes.

The material universe is but the shadow of the spiritual universe. The pulsations of the spiritual forces impinge upon and sway men, nations, and planets, according to laws whose sweep in space and time is so stupendous as to be beyond the ken or comprehension of astronomy. But the fact should not be overlooked that higher astronomy had its votaries in the past. The Magi and the illumined sages of Chaldea and Egypt had astronomical knowledge of universal scope. It was so broad, so gigantic, so far removed from the comprehension of the common mind of their day that it always remained the property of the few. It was communicated in symbols, because of the poverty of language to express its supermundane truths. In the sacred literature of the Hindus are evidences of astronomical erudition covering such vast periods of time that modern philosophers cannot or do not give them credence, and they are relegated to the domain of speculation rather than of science. However the astronomers of the present age have forged along on material lines until now they are beginning to impinge upon the hidden wisdom of the mighty savants of the past.

There is evidence that proves that the ages of the distant past knew a higher astronomy than do we of this age, and that they predicted the future of this planet through cycles and aeons—its nights of mental darkness and the dawn of its spiritual day—with the same accuracy that our astronomers do its present-day planetary revolutions.

Jesus evidently understood the aeons or ages through which earth passes. For example, in Matthew 13:39, our English Bible reads: "The enemy that sowed them is the devil: and the harvest is the end of the world; and the reapers are angels." In the Diaglott version, which gives the original Greek and a word-for-word translation, this reads: "THAT ENEMY who SOWED them is the ADVERSARY; the HARVEST is the End of the Age; and the REAPERS are Messengers." In this as in many other passages where Jesus used the word "age," it has been translated "world," leading the reader to believe that Jesus taught that this planet was to be destroyed.

So we see that the almost universally accepted teaching of the end of the world is not properly founded on the Bible. The translators wanted to give the wicked a great scare, so they put "the end of the world" into Jesus' mouth in several instances where He plainly said "the end of the age."

The Bible is a textbook of absolute Truth; but its teachings are veiled in symbol and understood only by the illumined.

In accordance with the prophecies of the ancients, our planetary system has just completed a journey of 2,169 years, in which there has been wonderful material progress without its spiritual counterpart. But old conditions have passed away and a new era has dawned. A great change is taking place in the mentality of the race, and this change is evidenced in literature, science, and religion. There is a breaking away from old creeds and old doctrines, and there is a tendency to form centers along lines of scientific spiritual thought. The literature of the first half of the twentieth century is so saturated with occultism as to be an object of censure by conservatives, who denounce it as a "lapse into the superstition of the past." Notwithstanding the protests of the conservatives, on every hand are evidences of spiritual freedom; it crops out in so many ways that an enumeration would cover the whole field of life.

It is evident that Jesus and His predecessors had knowledge of coming events on lines of such absolute accuracy as to place it in the realm of truth ascertained, that is, exact science.

Do you belong to the old, or are you building anew from within and keeping time with the progress of the age? The "harvest" or "consummation of the age" pointed out by Jesus is not far off. This is no theological scare; it is a statement based on a law that is now being tested and proved.

Listen to your inner voice; cultivate the good, the pure, the God within you. Do not let your false beliefs keep you in the darkness of error until you go out like a dying ember. The divine spark is within you. Fan it into flame by right thinking, right living, and right doing, and you will find the "new Jerusalem."

# How to Attract Good Luck

(1952)

## by A.H.Z. Carr

*The Unparalleled Classic On Lucky Living*

## Contents

Introduction  *Good Luck Is No Accident* by Mitch Horowitz  838
Chapter One  Chance Versus Luck  839
Chapter Two  How Zest Exposes Us to Luck  840
Chapter Three  How Generosity Invites Luck  841
Chapter Four  Turning Points  842
Chapter Five  Our Desires and Our Luck  843
Chapter Six  Our Abilities and Our Luck  844
Chapter Seven  Judgment as an Element In Luck  845
Chapter Eight  Safeguarding Luck with Self-Respect  846
Chapter Nine  The Intuitive Approach to Luck  847
Chapter Ten  The Power of Response  848
Chapter Eleven  How Increased Energy Produces Luck  848
Chapter Twelve  Imagination and Luck  849
Chapter Thirteen  The Luckiness of Faith  850
Chapter Fourteen  The Will to Be Lucky  852
Chapter Fifteen  Lucky Habits: Takeaway Points  853

## Introduction
# Good Luck Is No Accident

Do you want good luck? Of course you do. We all depend, to one degree or another, on fortuitous opportunities to put our skills to use, to meet people who provide vital openings for us, and to discover information that makes a crucial difference in our lives.

You are about to experience a condensation of one of the most intriguing and little-known books in the self-help tradition: *How to Attract Good Luck*. The book offers a straightforward and ethical recipe for cultivating your ability to identify and prepare for those crucial moments where life's currents lift you, or at least help you along. The title *How to Attract Good Luck* may sound like it belongs to a gambling guide. But this book is the furthest thing from it.

Economist, journalist, and diplomat A.H.Z. Carr wrote *How to Attract Good Luck* in 1952. Carr had served as an economic adviser in the presidential administrations of Franklin Roosevelt and Harry Truman, and spent time on economic and diplomatic missions in Europe and the Far East. He amassed a great deal of experience observing how most personal misfortune arises from impetuous, shortsighted, or unethical behavior. By "luck" Carr was referring not to blind chance but rather to how we can bend circumstances to our favor through specific patterns of behavior.

In an entertaining and incisive fashion, his book catalogues the insights he gleaned on how *virtue pays*. In a certain sense, Carr's book is really a guide to honorable living, which, in his estimation, pays dividends in success, stability, and peace of mind. Carr's work is an exegesis of a statement attributed to scientist Louis Pasteur: "Chance favors the prepared mind." Preparation, in Carr's view, is based not only in rigor and study, but also in a kind of personal comportment that makes one ready to take authority or act decisively when the need arises.

In an age where people gobble up copies of blatantly amoral success guides like *The 48 Laws to Power*, I find something distinctly appealing and rock-solid in Carr's work. This is a self-help book that can be used by someone who tries to live by the Beatitudes or the Boy Scouts Code of Honor. And why *wouldn't* we want to live by enduring guides to decency and ethic solidity? Carr tells us, in effect, that we can both achieve in the world and remain appealing as people. In fact, he maintains, very persuasively, that sound behavior and achievement are intimately united. Do you doubt that? Put his ideas to the test.

Without sardonicism or irony, I wish you a heartfelt *good luck*.

—Mitch Horowitz

Chapter One

# Chance Versus Luck

People have always sought ways to improve their luck. Their efforts have generally centered around portents, omens, and black magic. The Roman augur, interpreting the flights of birds, has been succeeded in modern times by numerologists and clairvoyants. But these practices have degraded the subject of luck. At the very mention of the word, many intelligent people understandably lift a skeptical eyebrow.

But our understanding of luck can be lifted from a black-cat level to an infinitely higher and broader plane. Psychology has opened the gate to a new and rational approach to luck. Armed with modern insights, those who seek can discover the true nature of luckiness. Luck is not a mere matter of poker winnings and the like but rather a *specific condition of mind*. This book shows how the lucky condition of mind can be attained.

At the outset, we must clarify the difference between "chance" and "luck." Chance comprises the infinite number of unpredictable happenings, both great and trivial, that are constantly at work in the world, whether a volcanic eruption or a sparrow's flight. Most of the chances we perceive in life seem remote and meaningless. But now and then a chance will touch the interests of an individual—and then it becomes very personal and significant indeed. *For as soon as human emotions are affected by a chance, it has been transformed into luck*. Luck, then, is the effect of chance on our lives.

But—and this is of vital importance—chance is not the only element in luck. Another factor is involved—ourselves. For it is our *response* to chance that provides the counterpoint in the harmony of events that we call luck. Whether and how a chance affects us is largely determined by our own attitude and behavior. Chance and response, between them, provide the warp and woof of existence, and the pattern of every life.

The central theme of this book is: *We can improve our luck by making ourselves readier for the chances of life as they come to us.* Shakespeare put it this way: "If it be not now, yet it will come. The readiness is all." These words have profound meaning. For the vigor of effort that we make to be ready for luck may well be the deciding factor between a lucky and unlucky life.

It lies within our power to influence, not chance, but our relation to chance. And in that sense none of us can escape a measure of responsibility for his own luck.

## Chapter Two
# How Zest Exposes Us to Luck

Good luck usually strikes into the world of men with the suddenness of lightening. How can we attract this beneficent lightening in our lives?

Over many years hundreds of people have told me their stories of good luck. More than half of them had one thing in common: the lucky episode began for the person concerned at a time when he was exposed to others—*when someone else unexpectedly said something important to him.* Most of our good luck—the beneficial effect of chance upon our lives—comes to us through other people. To expose ourselves to luck, then, means in essence to come into healthy human relationships with more people. The more luck-lines a person throws out, the more luck he is likely to find.

A high proportion of lucky chances comes to us through strangers, or people we know only slightly. This is not really surprising. Most of our well-worn contacts rarely offer us a new perspective, or a new piece of important information. But displaying "unexpected friendlessness" toward people we do not know is the secret of much of the luck of life. Ancient myths and parables repeatedly tell of rewards heaped upon someone who is kind to a travelling stranger—only to discover that the seeming stranger is a god or angel.

Of course, not every stranger merits our trust. We must guard against the aggressive bore, the gossip, or the ruthless peddler. But do not allow fear or indifference to block you off to the potential luck of The Stranger.

In enabling us to throw out luck-lines to strangers and old acquaintances alike, one quality has almost magical power—the quality of zest. Philosopher Bertrand Russell has called zest "the most universal and distinctive mark of happy men." Zest is also the mark of most lucky men—a quality which, in the struggle of life, often overshadows and outweighs serious character flaws and limitations of mind.

Never confuse zest with greed or gluttony. Zest means to take an explorer's interest in the world. The zestful person upon meeting others is curious not what they may think of him, how much money they make, or what they can do for him. Rather, he wants to discover their personalities and ways of life. He is capable of sincere enthusiasm, praise, and appreciation. The zestful person may feel angered or disquieted by events, but he loves life in all its follies. We need zest to counteract feelings of anxiety, which lay waste to human relationships.

Experimentation of almost any kind leads to zest. So does the discovery of a meaningful avocation or hobby—any well-defined core activity that stimulates thought and beckons new skill.

Frequently the things we read with zest are coupled directly with strokes of luck. Even a sentence or two, found by chance, can set off a train of lucky events. This is why books have a special place in luck development. The effort of attention needed to read a book, and especially a book with serious content, impresses it strongly on the memory, so that its ideas can be readily evoked by passing chance and brought into lucky use.

Chapter Three

# How Generosity Invites Luck

Some people put out luck-lines that get them nowhere. Things may start out all right but they find that instead of good luck they have been tempting misfortune. Sometimes we reach out to people—but our *unchecked* ego gets in our way.

Probably no human frailty is more likely to bring bad luck than an exaggerated need for appreciation. This unhappy state of mind, which usually grows out of a rooted feeling of insecurity, drives its victim to advertise his importance and demand that the busy world pay attention to him. The egotist tends to be inattentive when others are talking, he causes acquaintances to take a passive position in conversation and to therefore withhold valuable information and ideas. Even more serious, such a person tends to brag and boast, if sometimes in subtle and indirect ways.

The chronic egotist is always a candidate for bad luck. But the strong characteristic opposite to egotism, generosity of spirit, consistently acts as a magnet for favorable chances.

Note that we're speaking of *uncalculated generosity*. A distinction should also be drawn between genuine generosity and the compulsive and almost frantic displays of giving which some neurotic people make.

The luck that comes to us as a result of true generosity seldom takes the form of spectacular, immediate blessings out the blue. The real reward of the generous is invisible and secret. It lies partly in their own psychological health and partly in the hearts of others—in the reservoir of good will they build up. The generous person creates an unsuspected potential of good luck that needs only a touch from chance to burst all at once into happy reality.

In luck-development we need to keep in mind this seemingly obvious yet easily neglected fact: *In order to have real friends, a man must be capable of being one.* We can, for example, try a little hard to understand the problems of a friend, and give him such assistance as we're able without seeking return. When a friend is suffering, we can suppress remarks that would only add to his pain. Likewise, when a friend is fortunate, we can fight down our envy and try to enter his gladness.

The key point is that *every act of true friendship and generosity is proof of a rising luck-potential within us.*

## Chapter Four
# Turning Points

It is actually possible to anticipate favorable chances. Chance, which produces the effects in our lives that we call luck, has its own way of behaving. We need to become aware of two marked tendencies in the fall of chance: *rhythm* and *interconnection.*

Chance follows the same rhythm of nature. It is not an even, unbroken rhythm. We can learn to expect the alternation of runs of chance; moreover we can learn to expect it more at certain times than others. *The runs of chance in life are normally short.* After similar chances have appeared in succession several times, we have every reason to expect a change. This calls for expectancy and alertness.

As the rhythm of chance often points to the turning points of life, so does the characteristic that I have called *interconnection*. From time to time, two or more interlocking chances in close succession touch almost every life. And it is at these points where luck reveals its power most dramatically. At such times, by alertness, we can often "pyramid" our luck, using the luck of the first chance as a steppingstone to the greater luck of the others.

It is a fact of many, and perhaps most lives, that large fulfillments come not at a steady pace but by sudden leaps. After a single lucky chance we are wise to keep all of our senses alert for other chances that may interlock with the first, and provide a major turning point of life. The conscious effort to be alert to chance seems especially productive of turning points in periods of pronounced social change, when the old order is upturned.

Enthusiasm for the spectacular and impatience with the commonplace chances of life are likely to result in peaks of good luck alternating with deep valleys of misfortune. The reservoir of luck in each of us is far more often tapped by chance in frequent little jets than in big bursts.

We must also keep alert in the face of *crucial chances*. To do so we need to maintain our physical energy at a high level. A sound regimen of diet, sleep, and exercise, helps assure the ability of our alertness and mental acuity. Beyond this, we can generate alertness through *imaginative anticipation*. Obviously we cannot anticipate all eventualities, but we can often decide in advance what we shall do if certain common chances befall us.

Finally, when the occurrence of a chance seems fairly probable, a single preparatory action can go far to maintain the essential alertness until the event takes place.

## Chapter Five

# Our Desires and Our Luck

There is no reason to believe that opportunity knocks only once; but whether it knocks once, twice, or ten times, only the self-knowing mind, the mind that knows what it wants and what it will risk, is likely to recognize the real nature of the chance and act accordingly. Often the claims of competing desires are so strong as to make a decision difficult. No matter how complex the problem presented by chance, a firm set of values for our various desires helps us to find the lucky answer.

By testing chances against our personal values we sometimes perceive luck where others would see none. By knowing what you really want in life, you may detect opportunities that others may not understand or value.

Here is a core principle of life: *The person who knows the relative importance, for himself, of conflicting desires is best prepared to recognize the favorable chance as it passes, and to transform it into luck.* It is not easy to prioritize your desires, but it is absolutely vital if you want to bring more luck into your life. Fortunately, modern psychology has greatly clarified this problem. It tells us that a person's desires are not fixed and rigid; rather, they are malleable, ever-changing, and evolving in us from cradle to grave.

As adults we have ten basic, universal desires:
1. Love, both romantic and the affections of friends and family.
2. Procreation, with the urge to sex, marriage, and children.
3. Group status, or a firm place in the community or group.
4. Prestige, or recognition by others of our talents and distinctions.
5. Economic security and a satisfying standard of living.
6. Self-respect, or a sense of living up to meritorious standards of behavior.
7. Self-expression, or the use of one's abilities and talents.
8. Faith, or belief in a universal purpose or goal outside ourselves.
9. Long life, specifically the prospect of long-term physical and mental vigor.
10. Good health and freedom from illness.

The evaluation of desires is a highly personal matter. Everyone has, in effect, a private blend of desires. Some want more love than others, some more prestige, some more economic security, and so on. This difference profoundly affects our ideas of what is lucky. We must also distinguish honestly between basic desires versus compulsions or obsessions. Unchecked desires can balloon into obsessions or addictions, which destroy our luck.

## Chapter Six
# Our Abilities and Our Luck

One of the major elements in appraising the luck-content of a chance can be expressed in the question: *Does it accord with my abilities?* Unless our estimate of our abilities is realistic, we can be tempted by chance into foolhardy and disastrous ventures.

Part of the basic formula for a lucky life is: *Make the most of what you are, and do not try to be more than you can be.* The man who tries to live beyond his capacities, physically, psychologically, or economically, invites misfortune.

The more that you know about the requirements and hazards of a given chance, the more likely you are to find good luck in it, and avoid bad luck—*if you have a realistic understanding of your own abilities and limitations.* Nothing is more promising of good luck than the chance that accords with desire and ability; nothing is more dangerous than chance that appeals to desire but is not backed up by requisite ability.

So long as your judgment is mature and sound, there is a role for *inner conviction* in assessing one's abilities. When internal conviction asserts itself with sufficient power, it can often bring luck in spite of the most adverse judgments.

In sum, only when a given chance conforms both to basic desire and to demonstrated or indicated ability does it give genuine promise of good luck.

## Chapter Seven
# Judgment as an Element in Luck

Judgment has been called the eye of the mind. When people demonstrate bad judgment it is usually due less to defects in thinking than to emotional factors that have clouded the mind's outlook.

An appalling amount of bad luck can be attributed to three emotional states: boredom, anxiety, and overconfidence. Use these principles to your benefit: 1) Beware of boredom. 2) Allow for anxiety. 3) Overcome overconfidence. These rules are important markers on the road to better luck.

When a person is bored he hungers for an event that will lead to a better life. He looks with favor upon anything that seems to promise a thrill. This makes him highly vulnerable to bad luck because he does not assess the risks of the chances that he takes. Boredom has pushed many people into tragic misfortune.

Similarly in forming our judgment of chances, we must allow for inevitable and natural anxiety. Anxiety can cause us to reject favorable chances, even when they come straight at us, by making us think that we that we see peril and risk where there is none. In order to be lucky, we are not required to give up anxiety (some of which is healthy); but we must make allowances for the appearance of anxiety, and bring our fears to the surface for appropriate judgment.

In some ways, the more important rule for protecting our judgment from unstable emotions is the need to "overcome overconfidence." A dangerous sense of overconfidence can result from: 1) a run of luck, 2) a lack of experience, and 3) a misunderstanding of motive.

We sometimes believe that we understand people's motives when we actually do not. Too many of us accept, at face value, the motives put forward by people with whom we must deal in chance situations. Not that we need to be cynical about the motives of other people. Cynicism is, in truth, only an inverted form of naiveté, twisting one's view of reality. At the same time, when we have no sound reason to believe in the other person's purity of motive, we do well to pause for reflection.

## Chapter Eight
# Safeguarding Luck with Self-Respect

It is always unlucky to forfeit self-respect. The test of self-respect is especially important when chance demands an instantaneous decision and allows no time for judgment to probe and consider.

It is not always easy to tell which course of action in a complex situation will best maintain self-respect. And, curiously enough, some people even shrug at the term self-respect, failing to realize the decisive role it plays in good luck. They think that enjoying life is the only measure of success. The stifling of conscience, however, means that *the psychic trouble within us seeks other outlets*, such as the warping of the personality through neurotic fear or vicious criticism.

At the same time, there can be no doubt that self-respecting behavior frequently results in strong new luck-lines, over which material benefits flow. For example, the courage displayed by an act of selfless honesty, such as owning up to a serious mistake and not letting others take the fall for it, often marks someone as accountable and deserving of trust with serious responsibilities.

It is never too late to reaffirm self-respect. Fortunately for us, the occasional violence we do to our self-respect *is* only occasional. A single self-respecting action, taken when the personality was in danger of becoming permanently enfeebled, can perform a miracle of regeneration.

At this point a warning should be posted. It is easy to confuse self-respect with pride—and pride is a positively unlucky trait. In contrast to self-respect, pride—whether over origin, beauty, position, achievement, or anything else—is fundamentally an expression of insecurity, with its roots in illusion. It is a sign that someone is trying to cover up a feeling of spiritual weakness by pointing to a superficial advantage or external superiority.

When we sharply separate self-respect from pride and vanity, it serves us best in the selection and rejection of chances.

## Chapter Nine
# The Intuitive Approach to Luck

Below the threshold of consciousness is a kind of secret reference library of unspoken knowledge and forgotten impressions. The unconscious mind at certain times will pull out the evidence that bears on a risk before you, delivering its verdict in the mysterious form of *intuition*.

Our intuitive judgments of others may sometimes arise from unconscious impressions of previous experiences with people of similar characteristics. The wife of a friend once cautioned her husband to avoid Jim, a new acquaintance at work. The friend later told me: "Jim was a good fellow, but I felt highly competitive toward him. He brought out the worst in me." The wife had demonstrated sound intuition. No one can afford to forget that while he is influencing other people, they are also influencing him, for better or worse. Getting involved with competitive people often brings bad luck.

Little mishaps in the home or office have many times been preludes to larger misfortunes. This is certainly not to say that we should seek for omens. But there is nothing superstitious about recognizing the implications of our unconscious actions. Sigmund Freud stressed this point, noting: "The Roman who . . . withdrew from an undertaking because he had stumbled on his threshold . . . was a better psychologist than we . . . For his stumbling could demonstrate to him the existence of a doubt . . . the force of which could weaken the power of his intention at the moment of its execution. For only by concentrating all psychic forces on the desired aim can one be assured of its success."

Never confuse intuition with a mere *wish* for something. Apparent intuitions that coincide with feverish wishes, and which involve high risks—such as the desire to romantically win over an uninterested or deeply flawed lover—should always be regarded with suspicion.

## Chapter Ten
# The Power of the Response

Some acts of chance, like a fatal accident, leave no room for response. The vast realm of luck, however, is ruled not by chance alone but jointly, by chance and by ourselves.

Even seeming disasters can be converted or redirected by a sound response, which makes us more educated, more resilient, and more knowledgeable. Sometimes the response may aid us in some other area that seems distant from the event itself.

Underlying the sound responses of lucky people to chance are three predominant character traits: *high energy, vigorous imagination, and strong faith.*

These are the "big three" that can transform raw chance into good fortune. If you are lacking in one or two of these and are willing to try to do something about it, that willingness alone is the gateway to better luck. A vigorous effort to develop ourselves in any lucky direction can itself bring us into closer harmony with chance.

We will now review the importance of each trait, and how to strengthen it.

## Chapter Eleven
# How Increased Energy Produces Luck

Here is a statement so obvious that one may easily lose sight of its significance: *Much of our greatest luck comes to us when our energy is high.*

Heightened energy manifests itself to us in a number of specifically luck ways—sometimes in a display of muscular power to meet a sudden chance, but more frequently in a state of mind. Notably, three psychology attitudes are closely linked to luck: *presence of mind, confidence, and determination.*

**Presence of mind** is a kind of alertness. As soon as we have identified the chance, the alert condition undergoes a profound change. We no longer watch concentratedly for something to happen. It has happened. Our problem now is how to respond. Instead of keeping attention focused entirely on the chance event, we survey our surroundings—we "get the picture"—we see what things or circumstances near us can be of use in responding to the chance. The more "present" our mind is, the more likely we are to respond luckily to the chance.

**Confidence** is vital to our luck development. Preparation induces confidence. Especially in those instances that involve other people, like your subject if you are a journalist, or your partners if you are an investor. *Preparatory study of the facts makes for luck.* Of course, no one is confident all the time, or in the face of all chances. Our need is to *use periods of high energy to prepare for the chances of life that seem most probable.*

Like confidence and presence of mind, the quality of **determination** is also associated with high energy. Some people are more determined than others because they are able to *renew their energy* in relation to an activity. Often a person has high energy at the outset of a project, but it dissipates. *Determination grows out of the repeated tapping of your energy reserves in the pursuit of a single purpose.* This usually occurs: 1) When you are focused on a definite purpose, and you keep your aim constantly in sight, stimulating hope and renewing incentive. 2) When you prevent yourself from growing stale through an occasional change of activity, which makes possible a zestful return to the attack.

High energy is in large degree the expression of an attitude toward life. "A single successful effort of moral volition," wrote William James, "such as saying 'no' to some habitual temptation, or performing some courageous act, will launch a man on a higher level of energy for days or weeks, will give him a new range of power."

It must also be said that anyone who fails to make an effort to eat and drink wisely, to get enough exercise and rest, and to shake off his worries, greatly weakens his power to respond successfully to life's chances. Any effort we make to raise the level of our energy by improvement in these essential aspects of living automatically tends to improve our luck potential.

## Chapter Twelve
# Imagination and Luck

Wherever luck is most impressive, it is usually because energy has been directed by imagination, which reveals the potentialities of a chance.

Not every imagination, as we all know, makes for good luck. Notably, the egocentric imagination, which evokes images concerned primarily with selfish gratifications, invites unluckiness. One of its distinguishing products is the *daydream*—the fantasy that is always concerned with the future of the dream and which leads to the fictional fulfillment of some desire. Heedlessly indulged, the daydream can be a menace to good luck. It weakens one's hold on reality and reduces the energy available for the real tasks of life.

Another unlucky way the egocentric imagination expresses itself is morbidity. The morbid imagination tends to focus on the unpleasant perceptions that fit into its dark and distorted picture of life, and to ignore constructive or encouraging elements. Where this condition exists, a trivial chance can easily produce a major increase of unhappiness.

*The unmistakable characteristic of the healthy and lucky imagination is that it readily turns outward, away from the self.* It does not confuse the world of external reality with the images conjured up by desire or anxiety. The healthy imagination also has a high capacity for empathy, which enables you to share in the feelings of others in given situations. A great part of human luck depends on other people. When we share in their states of mind, we are more likely to respond to chances in ways that link them to us emotionally, making for a greater probability of luck for all concerned.

Just as a strong empathic imagination can bring good luck out of unfavorable circumstances, such as forming a bond with a gifted person who has experienced a temporary setback, a counter weakness area can lead to disastrous failures. This is *irrational prejudice*. Irrational prejudice includes snobbishness, religious or racial bigotry, and class discrimination. The creeping vine of intolerance chokes off the empathic imagination. What's more, prejudice dwells in insecure minds, which are natural targets for trouble.

## Chapter Thirteen
# The Luckiness of Faith

The word "faith" is used here, not in the sense of conventional lip service to a religious creed, but to signify the state of mind of those who are either wholly at one with their religion, or who profoundly hold a philosophic belief from which flows an affirmation of life and a moral principle.

Sometimes men and women who have neither religion nor philosophy try to fill this void in their lives by pinning their faith on their children or their work. Love of one's children and respect for one's work can be strengthening influences. They cannot, however, take the psychological place of a profound identification between the self and some large religious or philosophic conviction of good, which provides a moral basis for behavior.

When we lack the steadying power of faith, the insecurity feelings latent in all of us tend to run away with our behavior. A psychologist recently made an informal study among his university students of three negative traits: bragging, snobbishness, and secretiveness, all of which express insecurity. When he correlated the results with what he knew of the students' backgrounds and beliefs, there seemed to be an unmistakable link between the presence of these unlucky flaws and the absence of religious or philosophic faith.

We can cite very specific reasons why luck is most likely to be found in the faith-directed way of life. Faith tends to develop in the individual certain attributes that go far to ensure successful responses to chance. Courage is one of these attributes. But no less important are two traits that are in good part the psychological offspring of faith: *integrity* and *sense of proportion*.

It is through integrity that faith chiefly affects our responses to chance. Not that we find integrity in every person who professes a religion or a philosophy. But whenever we do find a person of genuine integrity, there, almost by definition, we find a core of faith. The exaltation of moral principle manifests a belief in universal law.

Together with courage and integrity, a third lucky characteristic flows from faith—the wide-horizoned attitude of mind that we think of as a *sense of proportion*. This attitude expresses itself in the personality through humility and through humor. The man who sees his actual position in the universe, and who can endure the revelation of his personal unimportance, gains enormous inner strength. Throughout life the sense of proportion links with chance to produce good luck and to mitigate misfortune.

The same quality, the sense of proportion derived from religion or philosophy, has a further bearing on our fortunes through its power in combatting envy, among the unluckiest of human characteristics. Competitive beings that we are, we all experience envy. But if envy is quickly controlled by a sense of proportion, it does little harm. In fact, a feeling of envy may be transformed to admiration and spur you to make more of your abilities. The great polar explorer Amundsen said that when he heard that Commodore Peary had reached the North Pole, his first thought was, "Then I shall visit both Poles." And he did. The danger to luck arises when envy in unchecked and becomes a permanent state of mind, which engenders bitterness, scheming, and cynicism.

The envy-resisting sense of proportion, rooted integrity, and sustained courage—those are stars of luck's constellation; and faith is their parent-quality. The need of effort to develop these attributes is too plain to need much discussion. What must be stressed is the point that any such effort, if it is to succeed, must follow the spiritual and intellectual route toward faith.

## Chapter Fourteen
# The Will to Be Lucky

The conscious steering of our actions, which is the peculiar privilege of man, is a skill that must be learned. The successful steersman in life, the lucky man, requires a degree of mastery of difficult arts of behavior and self-expression. Certain specific qualities of character and personality must be developed in us before we can find a lucky way through life.

When men have a keen sense of responsibility for their own fortunes, they can influence their luck far more than they dream. The chances of life, from which luck flows, are a kind of cosmic committee, constantly testing our readiness for membership in the lodge of the lucky. The *will to be lucky* is the crux of our internal development.

To modify destructive habits, which often have strong roots, *we must feel active resentment of the insecurity feelings that push us into inferior patterns of behavior*—and that make us unlucky in life. That gives us the requisite strength of feeling to challenge and change depleting habits of behavior.

*Any effort we make, however slight, to prevent the dictation of our behavior by insecurity feelings is a step toward luckiness.* A single modest improvement at a time is often enough to produce far-reaching consequences in one's fortunes. We have examined the importance to our luck of a number of characteristics which have a close relationship to the workings of chance: zest and generosity, with the power to attract luck into our lives; alertness, self-knowledge, judgment, self-respect, and intuition—all of high value in the recognition of favorable chances; and qualities of special significance in our responses to chance—energy, with its bearing on the presence of mind, confidence, and determination—imagination—and courage, sense of proportion, and integrity, which grow out of faith.

By doing a few relatively simple things over a period of a few months, you can often develop the lucky side of your personality to an extent that can seem miraculous. Vast and ungovernable is the power of chance; and yet, as we have seen, its influence on our luck is profoundly shaped by our own actions. The presence of this book is itself a chance, and your response to it may go far to affect your fortune to come.

## Chapter Fifteen
# Lucky Habits: Takeaway Points

In order to retain the material we've covered in this book, here are gleanings to consider:

- Demonstrate "unexpected friendliness" to colleagues, strangers, or casual acquaintances. In the history of religion and myth, displays of unwarranted hospitality or friendliness often prove the turning point that results in rewards being showered on someone who unknowingly aids an angel, the gods, or a disguised royal.
- Pursue topics or lines of work for which you feel zest. This is a recipe for fortuitous connections and relationships.
- Boredom is a harbinger of bad luck. Boredom leads you to rash or frivolous actions in pursuit of relief and excitement. Stay busy and engaged.
- Generosity is almost always rewarded one way or another.
- Watch for "small chances" to accomplish your aims. A small step either in conjunction with other small steps or by itself can produce unexpected results.
- Stay alert for larger "critical chances"—be watchful.
- It is lucky to know what we want. Focus brings us right action.
- Never imagine yourself more formidable or skilled than you really are. Be realistic about your current level of abilities and where they must grow.
- Healthful self-respect keeps you out of trouble.
- Avoid hyper-competitive colleagues and acquaintances. Those who make us feel competitive easily can tempt us into unlucky displays of egotism.
- Always look for how to turn chance events into good use.
- William James wrote: "A single successful effort of moral volition, such as saying 'no' to some habitual temptation, or performing some

courageous act, will launch a man on a higher level of energy for days or weeks, will give him a new range of power."
- Prejudice brings bad luck.
- Ethical courage, not impulsiveness or truculence, imbues you with nobility. Defending a loved one is almost always a lucky act.
- Acting without integrity invites misfortune.
- Envy moves you to foolish actions and pettiness. It is the bug zapper of good luck.
- Any effort we make, however slight, to prevent the dictation of our behavior by insecurity feelings is a step toward luckiness.

# The Power of Awareness
(1952)

## by Neville

*The Extraordinary Guide to Your Limitless Potential—Now in a Special Condensation*

## Contents

Introduction  *Doer of the Word* by Mitch Horowitz  856
1. Consciousness  857
2. Power of Assumption  859
3. Desire  860
4. The Truth That Sets You Free  861
5. Attention  862
6. Renunciation  863
7. Preparing Your Place  863
8. Creation  864
9. Subjective Control  865
10. Acceptance  865
11. Effortless Way  866
12. Essentials  867
13. Free Will  868
14. Failure  869
15. Destiny  871

## Introduction
# Doer of the Word

*The Power of Awareness* is, in many respects, the perfect Neville book. The mystic wrote it in full bloom of his abilities as an author and speaker. The book sums up Neville's philosophy of creative imagination with exquisite clarity—indeed *The Power of Awareness* makes me think that of all the writers to emerge from the American metaphysical scene in the last century, Neville was the most elegant as a literary figure and communicator. (In this regard, he's closely rivaled by Alan Watts.)

The book's essential point is that you are a composite of exactly *what you believe to be true about yourself*. Your persistently held assumptions and mental pictures *are* your destiny, more than any past event or present circumstance. This is a message of extraordinary self-liberation.

It is also a deeply challenging message, especially for those experiencing health difficulties or physical maladies. Are such things really malleable to a change of mentality? And, in the face of chronic pain or other tactilely felt conditions, is a change in psyche even possible?

These are areas for the reader to experiment with. It is possible that in order to experience the full sway of our mental powers we must begin with conditions that we feel we can more readily effect, and watch for changes to arrive through already established channels, before moving on to more ambitious aims. It is also possible, as I explore in *The Miracle Club*, that we may be unable to experience, from within our present mentality, the ultimate role of awareness as the shaper of reality. But this should not serve as a deterrent to our personal experiments. Extraordinary events *do* occur, large and small, and Neville urges us to probe such occurrences for correlation between sustained mental picture and outer activity.

Every one of us lives by assumptions, whether or not we acknowledge them. We all harbor untested, psychologically conditioned, and second-hand notions about life, which we seldom scrutinize. Acknowledging that this is so gives us remarkable freedom to select and road-test new personal philosophies and approaches. That is the spirit in which I hope you will approach this book. You have everything to gain by embracing your freedom to experiment with a new inner creed. That is what Neville offers.

One of Neville's traits that I most love is his continual challenge to the reader or listener to simply *try*. To test his ideas, this very minute, and see if they do not bring results. If not, he urges, forget all about me; but if so then dig deeper.

I want to add on a personal note that you will not be alone in these experiments. I and many others who love Neville's work are laboring with you. I hold a deep conviction that not only was Neville the most beautiful writer and speaker to emerge from the American metaphysical scene in the last century, but that he also conveyed ideas of remarkable and mysterious truth. These ideas will not simply disclose themselves on the page or through a speaker's voice, however. They require application and perseverance. You will likely encounter tantalizing successes and, at times, dispiriting failures, a topic that Neville addresses forthrightly in one of the last chapters in this book.

My hope is that this condensation *The Power of Awareness* will provide you with a springboard to action, and with a lesson plan that can be absorbed in a single sitting. And after you take it in, become, as Neville and Scripture urges, a "doer of the Word." See what transpires.

> This book is to reveal your infinite power, against which no earthly force is of the slightest significance.
> It is to show you who you are,
> your purpose and your destiny.

—Mitch Horowitz

# 1. Consciousness

It is only by a change of consciousness, by actually changing your concept of yourself that you can "build more stately mansions"—the manifestations of higher and higher concepts. (By manifesting is meant experiencing the results of these concepts in your world). It is of vital importance to understand clearly just what consciousness is.

The reason lies in the fact that *consciousness is the one and only reality, it is the first and only cause-substance of the phenomena of life*. Nothing has existence for man save through the consciousness he has of it. Therefore, it is to consciousness you must turn, for it is the only foundation on which the phenomena of life can be explained.

If we accept the idea of a first cause, it would follow that the evolution of that cause could never result in anything foreign to itself. That is, if the first cause-substance is light, all its evolutions, fruits and manifestations would remain light. The first cause-substance being consciousness, all its evolutions, fruits and phenomena must remain consciousness. All that could be observed would be a higher or lower form or variation of the same thing. In other words, if your consciousness is the only reality, it must also be the *only* substance. Consequently, what appears to you as circumstances, conditions and even material objects are really only the products of your own consciousness. Nature, then, as a thing or a complex of things external to your mind, must be rejected. You and your environment cannot be regarded as existing separately. You and your world are *one*.

Therefore, you must turn from the objective appearance of things to the *subjective center* of things, your consciousness, if you truly desire to know the cause of the phenomena of life, and how to use this knowledge to realize your fondest dreams. In the midst of the apparent contradictions, antagonisms and contrasts of your life, *there is only one principle at work*, only your consciousness operating. Difference does not consist in variety of substance, but in variety of arrangement of the same cause-substance, your consciousness.

The world moves with motiveless necessity. By this is meant that it has no motive of its own, but is under the necessity of manifesting your concept, the arrangement of your mind, and *your mind is always arranged in the image of all you believe and consent to as true*. The rich man, poor man, beggar man or thief are not different minds, but different arrangements of the same mind, in the same sense that a piece of steel when magnetized differs not in substance from its demagnetized state but in the arrangement and order of its molecules. A single electron revolving in a specified orbit constitutes the unit of magnetism. When a piece of steel or anything else is demagnetized, the revolving electrons have not stopped. Therefore, the magnetism has not gone out of existence. There is only a rearrangement of the particles, so that they produce no outside or perceptible effect. When particles are arranged at random, mixed up in all directions, the substance is said to be demagnetized; but when particles are marshalled in ranks so that a number of them face in one direction, the substance is a magnet. Magnetism is not generated; it is displayed. *Health, wealth, beauty and genius are not created; they are only manifested* by the arrangement of your mind—that is, by your concept of yourself. The importance of this in your daily life should be immediately apparent.

The basic nature of the primal cause is consciousness. Therefore, the ultimate substance of all things is *consciousness*.

## 2. Power of Assumption

Man's chief delusion is his conviction that there are *causes other than his own state of consciousness*. All that befalls a man—all that comes from him—happens as a result of his state of consciousness. A man's consciousness is all that he thinks and desires and loves, all that he believes is true and consents to. That is why a change of consciousness is necessary before you can change your outer world.

"Be ye transformed by the renewing of your mind."

To be transformed, the whole basis of your thoughts must change. But your thoughts cannot change unless you have *new ideas*, for you think from your ideas. All transformation begins with an intense, burning desire to be transformed. The first step in the 'renewing of the mind' is *desire*. You must want to be different before you can begin to change yourself. Then you must *make your future dream a present fact*. You do this by *assuming the feeling of your wish fulfilled*. By desiring to be other than what you are, you can create an ideal of the person you want to be and *assume that you are already that person*. If this assumption is persisted in until it becomes your dominant feeling, the attainment of your ideal is inevitable. The ideal you hope to achieve is always ready for an incarnation, but unless you yourself offer it human parentage it is incapable of birth. Therefore, your attitude should be one in which—having desired to express a higher state—you alone accept the task of incarnating this new and greater value of yourself.

In giving birth to your ideal you must bear in mind that the methods of mental and spiritual knowledge are entirely different. This is a point that is truly understood by probably not more than one person in a million. You know a thing mentally by looking at it from the outside, by comparing it with other things, by analyzing it and defining it; whereas you can know a thing spiritually only by becoming it. You must be the thing itself and not merely talk about it or look at it.

Just as the moth in his desire to know the flame was willing to destroy himself, so must you in becoming a new person be willing to die to your present self.

You must be conscious of *being* healthy if you are to know what health is. You must be conscious of *being* secure if you are to know what security is. Therefore, to incarnate a new and greater value of yourself, you must assume that you already are what you want to be and then live by faith in this assumption—which is not yet incarnate in the body of your life—in confidence that this new value or state of consciousness will become incarnated through your absolute fidelity to the assumption that you are that which you desire to be. This is what wholeness means, what integrity means. They mean submission of the whole self to the feeling of the wish fulfilled in certainty that that new state of consciousness is the renewing of mind which transforms.

Imagination is the only redemptive power in the universe. However, your nature is such that it is optional to you whether you remain in your present concept of yourself (a hungry being longing for freedom, health and security) or choose to become the instrument of your own redemption, imagining yourself as that which you want to be, and thereby satisfying your hunger and redeeming yourself.

## 3. Desire

The changes which take place in your life *as a result of your changed concept of yourself* always appear to the unenlightened to be the result, not of a change of your consciousness, but of chance, outer cause or coincidence. However, the only fate governing your life is the fate determined by your own concepts, your own assumptions; for an assumption, *though false*, if persisted in will harden into fact. The ideal you seek and hope to attain will not manifest itself, will not be realized by you, until you have imagined that you are already that ideal. There is no escape for you except by a radical psychological transformation of yourself, except by your assumption of the feeling of your wish fulfilled. Therefore, make results or accomplishments the crucial test of your ability to use your imagination.

Everything depends on your attitude towards yourself. *That which you will not affirm as true of yourself can never be realized by you* for that attitude alone is the necessary condition by which you realize your goal.

*You must imagine that you are already experiencing what you desire.* That is, you must assume the feeling of the fulfillment of your desire until you are possessed by it and this feeling crowds all other ideas out of your consciousness.

If you do not believe that you are He (the person you want to be) then you remain as you are. Through the faithful systematic cultivation of the feeling of the wish fulfilled, *desire becomes the promise of its own fulfillment.* The assumption of the feeling of the wish fulfilled makes the future dream a present fact.

# 4. The Truth That Sets You Free

The drama of life is a psychological one in which all the conditions, circumstances and events of your life are brought to pass by your assumptions.

Since your life is determined by your assumptions you are forced to recognize the fact that you are either a slave to your assumptions or their master. To become the master of your assumptions is the key to undreamed of freedom and happiness. You can attain this mastery by deliberate conscious control of your imagination. You determine your assumptions in this way: Form a mental image, a picture of the state desired, of the person you want to be. Concentrate your attention upon the feeling that you are already that person. First, visualize the picture in your consciousness. Then *feel* yourself to be in that state as though it actually formed your surrounding world. By your imagination that which was a mere mental image is changed into a seemingly solid reality.

The great secret is a controlled imagination and a well sustained attention firmly and repeatedly focused on the object to be accomplished. It cannot be emphasized too much that, by creating an ideal within your mental sphere, by assuming that you are already that ideal, *you identify yourself with it and thereby transform yourself into its image.* This was called by the ancient teachers, "Subjection to the will of God" or "Resting in the Lord", and the only true test of "Resting in the Lord" is that all who *do* rest are inevitably transformed into the image of that in which they rest. You become according to your resigned will, and your resigned will is your concept of yourself and all that you consent to and accept as true. You, assuming the feeling of your wish fulfilled and continuing therein, take upon yourself the results of that state; not assuming the feeling of your wish fulfilled, you are ever free of the results.

## 5. Attention

Attention is forceful in proportion to the narrowness of its focus, that is, when it is obsessed with a single idea or sensation. It is steadied and powerfully focused only by such an adjustment of the mind as permits you to see one thing only, for you steady the attention and increase its power by confining it. *The desire which realizes itself is always a desire upon which attention is exclusively concentrated*, for an idea is endowed with power only in proportion to the degree of attention fixed on it. Concentrated observation is the attentive attitude directed towards some specific end. The attentive attitude involves selection, for when you pay attention it signifies that you have decided to focus your attention on one object or state rather than on another.

Therefore, when you know what you want you must deliberately focus your attention on the feeling of your wish fulfilled until that feeling fills the mind and crowds all other ideas out of consciousness.

The power of attention is the measure of your inner force. Concentrated observation of one thing shuts out other things and causes them to disappear. *The great secret of success is to focus the attention on the feeling of the wish fulfilled without permitting any distraction*. All progress depends upon an *increase* of attention.

To aid in mastering the control of your attention practice this exercise. Night after night, just before you drift off to sleep, strive to hold your attention on the activities of the day *in reverse order*. Focus your attention on the last thing you did, that is, getting *in* to bed and then move it backward in time over the events until you reach the first event of the day, getting *out* of bed. This is no easy exercise, but just as specific exercises greatly help in developing specific muscles, this will greatly help in developing the "muscle" of your attention. Your attention must be developed, controlled and concentrated in order to change your concept of yourself successfully and thereby change your future. Imagination is able to do anything *but only according to the internal direction of your attention*.

When you attain control of the internal direction of your attention, you will no longer stand in shallow water but will launch out into the deep of life. You will walk in the assumption of the wish fulfilled as on a foundation more solid even than earth.

# 6. Renunciation

There is a great difference between *resisting evil and renouncing it.*

When you resist evil, you give it your attention, you continue to make it real. When you renounce evil you take your attention from it and give your attention to what you want. Now is the time to control your imagination and

> "Give beauty for ashes, joy for mourning, praise for the spirit of heaviness, that they might be called trees of righteousness, the planting of the Lord that He might be glorified."

You give beauty for ashes when you concentrate your attention on things as you would like them to be rather than on things as they are. You give joy for mourning when you maintain a joyous attitude regardless of unfavorable circumstances. You give praise for the spirit of heaviness when you maintain a confident attitude instead of succumbing to despondency. In this quotation the Bible uses the word tree as a synonym for man. You become a tree of righteousness when the above mental states are a permanent part of your consciousness.

# 7. Preparing Your Place

All is yours. Do not go seeking for that which you are. Appropriate it, claim it, assume it. *Everything* depends upon your concept of yourself. That which you do not claim as true of yourself, cannot be realized by you. The promise is

> "Whosoever hath, to him it shall be given, and he shall have more abundance; but whosoever hath not, from him shall be taken away even that which he seemeth to have."

Hold fast, in your imagination, to all that is lovely and of good report for the lovely and the good are essential in your life if it is to be worthwhile. Assume it. You do this by imagining that you *already are* what you want to be—and *already have* what you want to have.

> "As a man thinketh in his heart so is he."

Be still and know that you are that which you desire to be, and you will never have to search for it.

In spite of your appearance of freedom of action, you obey, as everything else does, the law of assumption. Whatever you may think of the question of free will, the truth is *your experiences throughout your life are determined by your assumptions*—whether conscious or unconscious. An assumption *builds a bridge of incidents that lead inevitably to the fulfillment of itself.*

Man believes the future to be the natural development of the past. But the law of assumption clearly shows that this is not the case. Your assumption places you psychologically where you are not *physically*; then your senses pull you back from where you were psychologically to where you are physically. *It is these psychological forward motions that produce your physical forward motions in time.* Pre-cognition permeates all the scriptures of the world.

## 8. Creation

Creation is finished. Creativeness is only a deeper receptiveness, for the entire contents of all time and all space while experienced in a time sequence actually co-exist in an infinite and eternal now. In other words, all that you ever have been or ever will be—in fact, all that mankind ever was or ever will be, exists *now*. This is what is meant by creation and the statement that creation is finished means that nothing is ever to be created, it is only to be manifested. *What is called creativeness is only becoming aware of what already is.*

*The whole of creation exists in you and it is your destiny to become increasingly aware of its infinite wonders and to experience ever greater and grander portions of it.*

If creation is finished, and all events are taking place now, the question that springs naturally to the mind is "what determines your time track?" That is, what determines the events which you encounter? And the answer is *your concept of yourself.* Concepts determine the route that attention follows. Here is a good test to prove this fact. Assume the feeling of your wish fulfilled and observe the route that your attention follows. You will observe that as long as you remain faithful to your assumption, so long will your attention be confronted with images clearly related to that assumption. For example; if you assume that you have a wonderful business, you will notice how *in your imagination* your attention is focused on incident after incident relating to that assumption. Friends congratulate you, tell you how lucky you are. Others are envious and critical. From there your attention goes to larger offices, bigger bank balances and many other similarly related events. Persistence in this assumption will result in *actually experiencing in fact that which you assumed.*

The same is true regarding any concept. If your concept of yourself is that you are a failure you would encounter in your imagination a whole series of incidents in conformance to that concept.

## 9. Subjective Control

Your imagination is able to do all that you ask *in proportion to the degree of your attention.* All progress, all fulfillment of desire, depend upon the control and concentration of your attention.

Your attention is directed from within when you deliberately choose what you will be preoccupied with mentally. It is obvious that in the objective world your attention is not only attracted by but is constantly *directed* to external impressions. But, your control in the *subjective state* is almost non-existent, for in this state attention is usually the servant and not the master—the passenger and not the navigator—of your world. There is an enormous difference between attention directed objectively and attention directed subjectively, and the *capacity to change your future depends on the latter.* When you are able to control the movements of your attention in the subjective world you can modify or alter your life as you please. But this control cannot be achieved if you allow your attention to be attracted constantly from without. Each day, set yourself the task of deliberately withdrawing your attention from the objective world and of focusing it *subjectively.* In other words, concentrate on those thoughts or moods which you deliberately determine.

You will no longer accept the dominance of outside conditions or circumstances. You will not accept life on the basis of the world without. Having achieved control of the movements of your attention, and having discovered the mystery hid from the ages, that *Christ in you is your imagination,* you will assert the supremacy of *imagination* and put all things in subjection to it.

## 10. Acceptance

However much you seem to be living in a material world, *you are actually living in a world of imagination.*

Whenever you become completely absorbed in an emotional state you are at that moment assuming the feeling of the state fulfilled. If persisted in, whatsoever you are intensely emotional about you will experience in your world. These periods of absorption, of concentrated attention, are the beginnings of the things you harvest.

This shock reverses your time sense. By this is meant that *instead of your experience resulting from your past, it now becomes the result of being in imagination where you have not yet been physically*. In effect, this moves you across a bridge of incident to the physical realization of your imagined state. The man who at will can assume whatever state he pleases has found the keys to the Kingdom of Heaven. The keys are *desire, imagination and a steadily focused attention on the feeling of the wish fulfilled*.

Assume the spirit, the feeling of the wish fulfilled, and you will have opened the windows to receive the blessing. To assume a state is to get into the spirit of it. Your triumphs will be a surprise only to those who did not know your hidden passage from the state of longing to the assumption of the wish fulfilled.

The Lord of hosts will not respond to your wish until you have assumed the feeling of already being what you want to be, for *acceptance is the channel of His action*. Acceptance is the Lord of hosts in action.

## 11. The Effortless Way

The principle of 'Least Action' governs everything in physics from the path of a planet to the path of a pulse of light. Least Action is the minimum of energy, multiplied by the minimum of time. Therefore, in moving from your present state to the state desired, you must use the minimum of energy and take the shortest possible time. Your journey from one state of consciousness to another, is a psychological one, so, to make the journey you must employ the psychological equivalent of 'Least Action' and the psychological equivalent is mere assumption.

The day you fully realize the power of assumption, you discover that it works in complete conformity with this principle. It works by means of attention, minus effort. Thus, with least action through an assumption you hurry without haste and reach your goal without effort.

Because creation is finished, *what you desire already exists*. It is excluded from view because you can see only the contents of your own consciousness. It is the function of an assumption to call back the excluded view and restore full vision. *It is not the world but your assumptions that change.* An assumption brings the invisible into sight. It is nothing more nor less than seeing with the eye of God, i.e., imagination.

## 12. Essentials

The essential points in the successful use of the law of assumption are these: First, and above all, *yearning, longing, intense burning desire*. With all your heart you must want to be different from what you are. Intense, burning desire *is* the mainspring of action, the beginning of all successful ventures. In every great passion desire is concentrated.

"As the hart panteth after the water brooks, so panteth my soul after Thee, O God."

"Blessed are they that hunger and thirst after righteousness for they shall be filled."

Here the soul is interpreted as the sum total of all you believe, think, feel and accept as true; in other words, your present level of awareness. God means I AM, the source and fulfillment of all desire. This quotation describes how your present level of awareness longs to transcend itself. *Righteousness is the consciousness of already being what you want to be.*

Second, *cultivate physical immobility*, a physical incapacity not unlike the state described by Keats in his 'Ode to a Nightingale'.

"A drowsy numbness pains my senses, as though of hemlock I had drunk."

It is a state akin to sleep, but one in which you are still in control of the direction of attention. You must learn to induce this state at will, but experience has taught that it is more easily induced after a substantial meal, or when you wake in the morning feeling very loath to arise. Then you are naturally disposed to enter this state. The value of physical immobility shows itself in the accumulation of mental force which absolute stillness brings with it. It increases your power of concentration.

"Be still and know that I am God."

In fact, the greater energies of the mind seldom break forth save when the body is stilled and the door of the senses closed to the objective world.

The third and last thing to do is to *experience in your imagination what you would experience in reality had you achieved your goal*. Imagine that you possess a quality or something you desire which hitherto has not been yours. Surrender yourself completely to this feeling until your whole being is possessed by it. This state differs from reverie in this respect: it is the result of a *controlled imagination and a steadied concentrated attention*, whereas reverie is the result of an uncontrolled imagination—usually just a daydream. In the controlled state, a minimum of effort suffices to keep your consciousness filled with the feeling of the wish fulfilled. The physical and mental immobility of this state is a powerful aid to voluntary attention and a major factor of minimum effort.

Apply these three points:
- Desire
- Physical immobility
- The assumption of the wish already fulfilled

This is the way to at-one-ment or *union with your objective*.

## 13. Free Will

The question is often asked, "what should be done between the assumption of the wish fulfilled and its realization?" *Nothing*. It is a delusion that, other than assuming the feeling of the wish fulfilled you can do anything to aid the realization of your desire. You think that you can do something, you want to do something; but, actually you can do nothing. *The illusion of the free will to do is but ignorance of the law of assumption* upon which all action is based. Everything happens automatically. All that befalls you, all that is done by you—*happens*. Your assumptions, *conscious or unconscious*, direct all thought and action to their fulfillment. To understand the law of assumption, to be convinced of its truth, means getting rid of all the illusions about free will to act. Free will actually means *freedom to select any idea you desire*. By assuming the idea *already* to be a fact, it is converted into reality. Beyond that, *free will ends* and everything happens in harmony with the concept assumed.

It is impossible to *do* anything. You must *be* in order to do.

If you had a different concept of yourself, everything would be different. You are *what you are*, so everything *is as it is*. The events which you observe are determined by the concept you have of yourself. If you change your concept of yourself, the events ahead of you in time are altered, but, thus altered, they *form again a deterministic sequence* starting from the moment of this changed concept. You are a being with powers of intervention, which enable you, by a change of consciousness, to alter the course of observed events—in fact, to *change your future.*

Deny the evidence of the senses, and assume the feeling of the wish fulfilled. Inasmuch as your assumption is *creative* and forms an atmosphere, your assumption, if it be a noble one, increases your assurance and helps you to reach a higher level of being. If, on the other hand, your assumption be an unlovely one, it hinders you and makes your downward way swifter. Just as the lovely assumptions create a harmonious atmosphere, so the hard and bitter feelings create a hard and bitter atmosphere.

Make your assumptions the highest, noblest, happiest concepts. There is no better time to start than *now*. The present moment is always the most opportune in which to eliminate all unlovely assumptions and to concentrate only on the good.

If you would change your life, you must begin at the very source *with your own basic concept of self.* Outer change, becoming part of organizations, political bodies, religious bodies, is not enough. The cause goes deeper. The essential change must take place *in yourself,* in your own concept of self. You must assume that you are what you want to be and continue therein, for the *reality of your assumption has its being in complete independence of objective fact,* and will clothe itself in flesh if you persist in the feeling of the wish fulfilled. When you know that assumptions, if persisted in, harden into facts, then events which seem to the uninitiated mere accidents will be understood by you to be the logical and inevitable *effects* of your assumption.

The important thing to bear in mind is that you have *infinite free will in choosing your assumptions,* but no power to determine conditions and events. You can create nothing, but your assumption determines what portion of creation you will experience.

# 14. Failure

This book would not be complete without some discussion of *failure* in the attempted use of the law of assumption. It is entirely possible that you either have had or will have a number of failures in this respect—many of them in really important matters. If, having read this book, having a thorough knowledge of the application and working of the law of assumption, you faithfully apply it in an effort to attain some intense desire and fail, what is the reason? If to the question, did you persist enough?, you can answer yes—and still the attainment of your desire was not realized, what is the reason for failure?

The answer to this is the most important factor in the successful use of the law of assumption. *The time it takes your assumption to become fact, your desire to be fulfilled, is directly proportionate to the naturalness of your feeling of already being what you want to be—of already having what you desire.*

The fact that it does not feel *natural* to you to be what you imagine yourself to be is *the secret of your failure*. Regardless of your desire, regardless of how faithfully and intelligently you follow the law if you do not feel *natural* about what you want to be *you will not be it*. If it does not feel natural to you to get a better job you will not get a better job. The whole principle is vividly expressed by the Bible phrase "you die in your sins"—you do not transcend from your present level to the state desired.

How can this feeling of naturalness be achieved? The secret lies in one word *imagination*. For example, this is a very simple illustration. Assume that you are securely chained to a large heavy iron bench. You could not possibly run, in fact you could not even walk. In these circumstances it would not be natural for you to run. You could not even *feel* that it was natural for you to run. But you could easily *imagine* yourself running. In that instant, while your consciousness is filled with your *imagined* running, you have forgotten that you are bound. In *imagination* your running was completely natural.

The essential feeling of naturalness can be achieved by *persistently filling your consciousness with imagination*—imagining yourself being what you want to be or having what you desire.

Progress can spring only from your imagination, from your desire to transcend your present level. What you truly and literally *must* feel is that *with your imagination, all things are possible*. You must realize that changes are not caused by caprice, but by a change of consciousness. You may fail to achieve or sustain the particular state of consciousness necessary to produce the effect you desire. But, once you know that consciousness is the only reality and is the sole creator of your particular world and have burnt this truth into your whole being, then you know that success or failure is entirely in your own hands. Whether or not you are disciplined enough to sustain the required state of consciousness in specific instances has no bearing on the truth of the law itself—that an assumption, if persisted in, will harden into fact. The certainty of the truth of this law must remain despite great disappointment and tragedy—even when you "see the light of life go out and all the world go on as though it were still day." You must not believe that because your assumption failed to materialize, the truth that assumptions do materialize is a lie. If your assumptions are not fulfilled it is because of some error or weakness in your consciousness. However, these errors and weaknesses *can be overcome*. Therefore, press on to the attainment of ever-higher levels by feeling that you *already are* the person you want to be. And remember that the time it takes your assumption to become reality is *proportionate to the naturalness of being it*.

## 15. Destiny

Your destiny is that which you must inevitably experience. Really it is an infinite number of individual destinies, each of which when attained is the starting place for a new destiny.

Since life is *infinite* the concept of an ultimate destiny is inconceivable. When we understand that consciousness is the only reality, we know that it is the only creator. This means that your consciousness is the creator of your destiny. The fact is, you are creating your destiny every moment, *whether you know it or not*. Much that is good and even wonderful has come into your life without you having any inkling that you were the creator of it.

However, the understanding of the causes of your experience, and the *knowledge that you are the sole creator of the contents of your life, both good and bad, not only make you a much keener observer of all phenomena but through the awareness of the power of your own consciousness, intensifies your appreciation of the richness and grandeur of life.*

Regardless of occasional experiences to the contrary it is *your destiny to rise to higher and higher states of consciousness, and to bring into manifestation more and more of creation's infinite wonders*. Actually you are destined to reach the point where you realize that through your own desire you can consciously create your successive destinies.

The study of this book, with its detailed exposition of consciousness and the operation of the law of assumption, is the master key to the conscious attainment of your highest destiny.

This very day start your new life. Approach every experience in a new frame of mind—with a new state of consciousness. Assume the noblest and the best for yourself in every respect and continue therein.

Make believe—great wonders are possible.

# Magic of Faith
(1954)

## by Joseph Murphy

*The Groundbreaking Classic on the Creative Power of Thought by the author of* The Power of Your Subconscious Mind

## Contents

Introduction   *The Bible as Blueprint* by Mitch Horowitz   874
Chapter I   The Song of Triumph   875
Chapter II   The Practice of the Presence of God   880
Chapter III   Realizing Your Desire   886
Chapter IV   The Magic of Faith   890
Chapter V   Steps to Happiness   893
Chapter VI   Harmonious Human Relations   897
Chapter VII   How to Control Your Emotions   901
Chapter VIII   Changing the Feeling of "I"   906

## Introduction
# The Bible as Blueprint

For Joseph Murphy the Bible was a metaphysical blueprint to the individual's self-development. In this regard, Murphy was similar to his contemporary and friend, the great mystic Neville Goddard. Late in life, Murphy told an interviewer that the two men, coming of age as writers and seekers in New York City in the 1930s—Murphy a recent transplant from Ireland and Neville from the West Indies—had the same teacher, a black-Jewish spiritual master named Abdullah.

In this vein, I am particularly struck by chapter three of this book, "Realizing Your Desire," in which Murphy sounds very much in harmony with Neville. Like his fellow seeker, Murphy taught that desire is God's voice speaking to you. "Desire pushes man," Murphy wrote, "it is the goad of action. It is behind all progress. Desire is really the cosmic urge in all of us, impelling us to go forward, onward, upward, and Godward."

Passages like this one helped me clarify my personal search. Mine is a path of aspiration. This divided me for many years. I wasn't sure how to truly practice the teaching, "Thy will be done." Murphy makes it clear that there is no "I" and "Thy"—all is One. The voice of higher forces reaches you through your wishes and desires, which are the impetus toward progress, achievement, and self-actualization. Murphy teaches you to trust your desires.

In a striking and daring passage, Murphy writes: "*Jesus* means your desire which, if realized, would be your savior. Jesus comes into your mind as an idea, desire, plan, purpose, vision, or some new undertaking."

In *Magic of Faith*, which Murphy wrote in 1954, nine years before his classic *The Power of Your Subconscious Mind*, Murphy, like Neville, highlighted the uses of Scripture as a symbolical and practical guidebook to understanding the creative potentials of your mind. Murphy also used case studies to drive home his points of application. The sum total of what he wrote can give you a larger, more epic sense of yourself and your possibilities.

Neville taught that the imagination is God. Murphy saw God functioning in us through the imagination. But the difference is minor. Both men believed that you, the individual, have far too small a sense of who you really are: a branch of the Divine clothed in flesh. Murphy wrote this book, distilled here to its essentials, to introduce you to that greater life. It is not outside of you. It is your very birthright.

—Mitch Horowitz

## Chapter I

# The Song Of Triumph

You sing the Song of God, or the mood of triumph, when you subjectively feel that you are that which your five senses tell you you are not; you are then God-intoxicated and seized with a Divine frenzy—a sort of mad joy.

Haven't you at times seen a person bubbling over with enthusiasm and intoxicated with joy? That person is singing the Song of God at that moment. "In thy presence *is* fulness of joy; at thy right hand *there are* pleasures for evermore."

The real You is a spiritual, eternal, perfect being. You are a living expression of God now. "I have said, Ye *are* Gods; and all of you are children of the most High."

When you pray, it is a romance with God or your Good. Your desire, when realized, brings you joy and peace. In order to realize the desire of your heart, which is depicted in *The Song of Solomon* as your beloved, you must woo it; let that desire of yours captivate, hold, and thrill you. Let it fire your imagination. You will always move in the direction of the desire that dominates your mind.

If you are saying to yourself, "I can't. It is too late now. I am too old, and I don't know the right people"—in other words if you are mentally feeding on all the reasons why you cannot do something, or be what you want to be, you are not making "thy flock to rest at noon."

*At noon* the sun casts no shadow; likewise, when you pray, you are not to permit any shadow of fear or doubt to cross your path, or deflect you from your goal or aim in life. The world of confusion shall be rejected, and you shall mentally eat of or meditate on the reality of your desire.

Once I talked to an alcoholic who said, "Don't say anything about this God-stuff to me. I don't want God. I want a healing." This man was deeply resentful toward a former wife who had remarried; moreover, he was full of grudges against several people. He needed the *doves' eyes,* which means he needed to see the truth that would give him peace of mind.

I asked him, "Will you pray with me now? All I ask is that you be sincere; if you are, you will experience an inner peace which passeth all human understanding."

He relaxed his body, and I said to him, "Imagine you are talking to the Invisible Presence within you—the Almighty Power which created the Cosmos. It can do all things. Say, 'Thank you, thank you, for this inner peace.' Say it over and over again."

After ten minutes in silent meditation, he was blinded by an interior, Inner Light. It seemed to come from the floor where he was. The whole room was flooded with Light!

He exclaimed, "All I see is Light! What's wrong?" Then he relaxed into sleep in my office, and his face did truly shine as the sun. He awakened in about fifteen minutes, and was completely at peace saying, "God truly is! God is!" This man had found his Beloved; It had *doves' eyes*.

As you fall asleep at night, tell your desire how fair it is, and how wonderful you would feel in realizing it. Begin to fall in love with your ideal. Praise it; exalt it. "Arise my Love!" Feel that you are what you want to be. Go to sleep in the consciousness of being or doing what you long to do.

I told a man in one of the islands one time "to sleep" on the idea of success. He was selling magazine subscriptions. He became a great success by following this procedure: I suggested that he think of success prior to sleep; i.e., what success meant to him; what he would do if he were successful. I told him to use his imagination; then as he was about to go to sleep, fall in love with the idea of success this way: Repeat the one word, "Success," over and over again. He should get into the mood of success; then fall off to sleep in the arms of his Everlasting Lover. Your Lover—your Divine Presence—will bring to pass whatever you accept as true. The conditions, experiences, and events of your life are called children of your mind.

You know when there is no longer any argument or doubt in your conscious or subconscious mind, your prayer is answered, because the two have agreed as touching upon it, and it is so.

I had a long talk with a man in England who had trouble with his leg. He had been confined to his home for nine months, and was unable to lean on his leg or walk. The first thing I did was to ask him what he would do if he were healed? He said, "I would again play polo, swim, golf, and climb the Alps which I used to do every year." That was the answer I was seeking.

I told him in the simplest way how to achieve the perfect use of his legs again. The first thing was to imagine he was doing the things he would do. I painted an imaginary picture for him. For fifteen or twenty minutes three times a day he sat in his study and imagined he was playing polo; he assumed the mental mood of actually performing the role of a polo player. He became the actor; an actor participates in the role.

Note carefully that he did not see himself playing polo; that would be an illusion. He *felt* himself playing polo. He actualized it by living the drama in his mind or *banquet house.*

At noon he would quiet the mind; still the body, and feel his Alpine clothes on him. He would feel and imagine he was climbing the Alps; he would feel the cold air on his face, and hear the voice of his old associates. He lived the drama and felt the naturalness and the tangibility of the rocks.

At night prior to sleep, before going into the Arms of his Beloved—His Deeper Self—he would play a game of golf. He would hold the club; touch the ball with his hand; put it in place, and tee off. He would swing his clubs, and delight in watching where the ball went.

Within two months this man's leg was healed. He did all the things he imagined he would do. The *idea* of climbing the Alps, plus the *desire* to play polo again, said to this man, "Arise, my love, my fair one, and come away," from your belief in a physical handicap; that is what he did.

The law of the subconscious is one of compulsion. When you subjectively feel you are swimming—for example, when you feel the chill of the water, and the naturalness of your various swimming strokes—you will sooner or later be compelled to swim. Whatever the handicap, whether fear or a physical condition, you will do what you subjectively felt you were doing.

Your desire, dream, ambition, goal, or aim is your savior! It is walking down the corridor of your mind, saying to you, "Arise, my love, and come away," and enjoy the good and glorious things of life.

No matter what the problem is, or its magnitude, you have really nothing to do but convince yourself of the truth that you are affirming. As quickly as you succeed in convincing yourself of the reality of your desire, results will automatically follow. Your subconscious mind will faithfully reproduce what you impregnated within it.

The Bible says, "Choose you this day whom ye will serve." You have the freedom to choose the tone, feeling, or mood you enter into. The manifestation of your feeling or conviction is the secret of your lover or subconscious mind. Your external actions are, therefore, determined by your subconscious beliefs and impressions.

Your thought and feeling determine your destiny. The knowledge of the truth is saying to you now, "The winter is past, the rain is over *and* gone." *The winter* represents that cold state when the seeds are frozen in the bosom of the earth and nothing is growing. The winter and all the seasons are in your mind.

Do everything from the standpoint of the One God and His Love. For instance, when you shop, pray before purchasing. Say, "God guides me in all my purchases." Say quietly to the saleslady or salesman, "God is prospering him."

Whatever you do, do it with love and good will. Pour out love, peace, and good will to all. Claim frequently that God's Love and Transcendent Beauty flow through all my thoughts, words, and actions. Make a habit of this. Fill your mind with the eternal verities; then you will see that "The flowers appear on the earth; the time of the singing of *birds* is come!" You will begin to *flower;* yes, you will begin to blossom forth.

When you go into a home, and you see confusion, quarrelling, and strife, you will realize within yourself, that the peace of God reigns supreme in the minds and hearts of all those in this house; you will see the flower of peace made manifest and expressed.

Where you see financial lack and limitation, you will realize the infinite abundance and wealth of God forever flowing, filling up all the empty vessels, and leaving a Divine surplus. As you do this, you will live in the garden of God where only orchids and all beautiful flowers grow; for only God's ideas circulate in you.

Tennyson said, "Speak to Him, thou, for He hears, and Spirit with Spirit can meet—closer is He than breathing, and nearer than hands and feet."

One time as a boy I was lost in the woods. I sat down under a tree, and remembered a prayer that starts with, "Our Father, He will show us the way; let us be quiet, and He will lead us." I quietly repeated, "Father, lead us."

A wave of peace came over me, which I can still recall. *The voice of the turtle dove* became real. *The turtle dove* is intuition which means being taught from within. An overpowering feeling came over me to go in a certain direction as if I were being pushed ahead. Two of the boys came with me; the others did not. We were led out of that thick jungle, as if by an Unseen Hand.

Great musicians have listened and heard the music within; they wrote down what they heard inwardly. In meditation Lincoln listened to the principle of liberty; Beethoven heard the principle of harmony.

If you are intensely interested in the principle of mathematics, you are loving it; as you love it, it will reveal all its secrets to you.

Jesus heard *the voice of the turtle dove* when he said, "Peace, I leave with you; my peace I give unto you; not as the world giveth, give I unto you. Let not your heart be troubled; neither let it be afraid." How wonderful you will feel as you drink in these words and fill your mind with their therapeutic potency.

Job heard *the voice of the turtle* when he said, "Acquaint now thyself with Him, and be at peace." "Thou wilt keep *him* in perfect peace, *whose* mind is stayed *on thee:* because he trusteth in thee." "For God is not *the author* of confusion, but of peace."

If you want guidance, claim Infinite Intelligence is guiding you now; It will differentiate Itself as right action for you. You will know you have received the answer, for *the dove of peace* will whisper in your ear, "Peace be still." You will know the Divine answer, for you will be at peace, and your decision will be right.

A girl recently was wondering whether to accept a position in New York for considerably more money or remain in Los Angeles in her present position. At night as she went to sleep, she asked herself this question, "What would be my reaction if I had made the right decision now?" The answer came to her, "I would feel wonderful. I would feel happy having made the right decision." Then she said, "I will act as though I had made the right decision," and she began to say, "Isn't it wonderful! Isn't it wonderful!" over and over again, as a lullaby, and lulled herself to sleep in the feeling, "It is wonderful."

She had a dream that night, and the voice in the dream said, "Stand still! Stand still!" She awakened immediately, and knew of course that was *the voice of the turtle dove*—the voice of intuition.

The fourth dimensional-self within her can see ahead; it knows all and sees all; it can read the minds of the owners of the business in the east. She remained in her present position. Subsequent events proved the truth of her Inner Voice; the Eastern concern went into bankruptcy. "I the Lord will make myself known unto him in a vision, *and* will speak unto him in a dream."

By realizing and knowing these qualities and attributes of God are being expressed through you, and that you are a channel for the Divine, every atom of your being begins to dance to the rhythm of the Eternal God. Beauty, order, harmony, and peace appear in your mind, body, and business world as you feed among the lilies; you feel your oneness with God, Life, and God's Infinite Riches. You are married to your Beloved, for you are now married to God; you are a bride of the Lord (I AM). From this moment forward you will bring forth children of your Beloved; they will bear the image and likeness of their Father and Mother.

The *father* is God's idea; the *mother* is the emotionalizing of the idea, and its subjective embodiment. From that union of idea and feeling come forth your health, abundance, happiness, and inner peace.

When you go to sleep tonight, forgive everyone, and imagine and feel your desire is fulfilled. Become absolutely and completely indifferent to all thought of failure, because you now know the law. As you accept the end, you have, as Thomas Troward so beautifully stated, willed the means to the realization of the end. As you are about to enter sleep, galvanize yourself into the feeling of being or having your desire. Your mental acceptance or your feeling as you go to sleep is the request you make of your Beloved; then She looks at your request (conviction in the subconscious mind), and being the Absolute Lover, she must give you what you asked.

When you pray, accept as true what your reason and five senses deny and reject. Remain faithful to your idea by being full of faith every step of the way. When your consciousness is fully qualified with the acceptance of your desire, all the fear will go away. Trust in the reality of your ideal or desire until you are filled full of the feeling of being it; then *the day will break and all shadows will flee away.* Yes, the answer to your prayer will come, and light up the heavens of your mind bringing you peace.

No matter what the problem is, how acute, dark, or hopeless things seem to be, turn now to God, and say, "How is it in God and Heaven?" The answer will softly steal over your mind like the dew from heaven: "All is peace, joy, bliss, perfection, wholeness, harmony, and beauty"; then reject the evidence of your senses, and *feed among the lilies of God and Heaven,* such as peace, harmony, joy, and perfection. Realize what is true of God must be true of you and your surroundings. Continue in this abiding trust and faith in God "until the day breaks and the shadows flee away."

## Chapter II

# The Practice of the Presence of God

*"Whither shall I go from thy Spirit? or whither shall I flee from thy presence? If I ascend up into heaven, thou ART THERE, If I take the wings of the morning, AND dwell in the uttermost parts of the sea; Even there shall thy hand lead me, and thy right hand shall hold me."*

This one hundred and thirty ninth Psalm is one of the most beautiful Psalms in the Bible. It is a matchless, priceless gem of truth. The language of this Psalm is unsurpassed for beauty and elegance. David's marvelous conception of the Omnipresence of God was found in this passage.

The religion outlined in the Bible is the practice of the Presence of God. To understand and to intelligently practice this truth, you will find is the way to health, harmony, peace, and spiritual progress. The practice of the Presence is powerful beyond imagination. Let us not overlook it, because of its utter simplicity.

The first step is to realize that God is the Only Power. The next thing to become aware of is that all things—no matter what they are—represent God in manifestation. The whole world is God in infinite differentiation, as God never repeats Himself; this is the whole story, and the greatest of all truths. It is really the all-inclusive, all-encompassing truth.

I know many students who sit down for five or ten minutes every day, and meditate on the fact that God is the Only Presence and the Only Power. They let their thoughts dwell on this profound truth; they look at it from all angles; then they begin to think that every person they meet is an expression of God; that in fact everything they see is God made manifest; it is God dramatizing Himself for the joy of expressing Himself. As they do this, they find their whole world changing; they experience better health; outer conditions improve, and they are possessed of a new vitality and energy.

Your whole world will change as you really begin to see God in everything and in everyone. "For thou shalt be in league with the stones of the field: and the beasts of the field shall be at peace with thee. And thou shalt know that thy tabernacle *shall* be in peace." This means that the man who begins to see God everywhere, and who follows and practices the good, will not be afraid of anything. As a matter of fact the whole world will be his friend, and everything will extend the offer of help whether animate, or what the world calls inanimate.

The only way to magnify the Presence of God in the eyes of others is to radiate at all times the sunlight of God's Love. Love God or Truth, and you will be under a Divine compulsion for good. You cannot go wrong. You will find that you will never make any real mistake or a wrong choice. Love of all things good, or of the truth, is really the touch of Midas.

In a building the superstructure depends upon the foundation. Let *your* foundation be God and Him alone. You are always practicing the Presence of God when you activate your mind with true ideas, which heal and strengthen you. Your mind needs constant cleansing, disciplining, and direction. By practicing the Presence of God, you are constantly cleansing your mind; this is prayer.

Think all day long from the standpoint of the One God about every person and every situation you meet. Pray at work by realizing God is your partner, and God is in action through all your associates.

Pray driving your car, by realizing the vehicle is God's idea moving from point to point freely, joyously, and lovingly.

Pray when you go into a store by realizing God directs your purchases, that God is prospering the clerk who waits on you, and that the store is being governed and directed by God's Wisdom.

Let prayer be the orderly, right way of doing everything. Practice the Golden Rule in all your transactions; then you are writing God's Law in your heart.

It is essential for you to get the right concept and understanding of God. Have you meditated? or have you asked yourself what God is? Your concept of God molds, fashions, and shapes your whole future. Your real belief about God is of supreme importance. It is done unto you as you believe. If you say and believe God is the only Presence, the only Power, Infinitely Good, Perfect, Boundless Love, and Limitless Life, your whole life will be transformed.

If you say, "Oh, I do not know what I think of God; my thoughts are confused and muddled," confusion will reign in your life. It does not really matter whether you call God: Reality, Infinite Intelligence, Being, Life, Allah, or Brahma; the real Name of God, in so far as you are concerned, is your concept or your belief about God.

A man said to me one time, "I believe in God, and that is all that matters." I asked him, "But tell me, what sort of God do you really believe in?" He said, "I believe in the laws of nature." That was his idea of God, and he cannot transcend this belief. He is subject to that belief, thereby limiting his Inner Powers. He had no idea that God was his own Life, that he could contact this Presence with his thought, that he could be guided, and that he could heal his body by prayer. He was bound by his limited belief about God. Many have said to me that God is some kind of a man in the skies—a sort of a glorified man. Others say and believe there are three persons in God. You will always manifest the result of your belief. If you believe that God is some sort of a tyrannical, inscrutable being living in the skies, ready to judge and punish you for your mistakes and violations of man-made laws and religious taboos, you are bound by that belief, and you cause pain, misery, guilt complexes, and so forth. This is why Phineas Quimby said, "Man is belief expressed."

Your concept of God enters into all departments of your life; it is bound to have its effect upon you. God is Life, and Life seeks to express Itself as Love, Light, Truth, and Beauty. Life cannot wish death, sickness, or disease. To say that Life wishes death would be a violation of its own nature. Life cannot have a tendency toward limitation of any kind. Life is a Oneness, a Wholeness, a Unity, and It seeks to express that Unity in the formed universe.

In order to practice the Presence, you must do the will of God. What does this mean? *The will of God* must always be the nature of God. You can rest assured the will of God must always be something wonderful and glorious. "His name shall be called Wonderful, Counsellor, The Mighty God, The Everlasting Father, The Prince of Peace."

If your desire, idea, or intention is constructive, if it will bless others, and if it is in keeping with the universal principle of harmony, your will or desire is God's will. Your desire for wealth, true place, abundance, security, and better living conditions conforms to the will or tendency of Life or God.

Life is forever seeking to express Itself through you along higher levels. Enthrone in your mind the concept that God is the Only Presence, the Only Power, and that God is Infinitely Good and Perfect. Think of some of God's qualities and attributes, such as Boundless Love, Infinite Intelligence, Indescribable Beauty, Omnipotence, Omniscience, and Omnipresence. Believe these truths about God, and your whole life will change. You will begin to express more and more God-like qualities every day. Believe that God is All Life, All Love, All Truth, and All Beauty; accept It in the same way as you accept the sun in the heavens each morning; then you will find a great sense of peace and goodwill stealing over your mind and heart.

Do you believe in a vengeful, capricious, anthropomorphic Deity who sends sickness, trials, and tribulation to you? Watch the effect of such a belief. If you do, you will be like the man who said to me one time, "God sent this arthritis to me for a good purpose, and I suppose I must just bear it." This is superstition; such an attitude of mind has no foundation. He had arthritis for fifteen years, and he could not overcome it.

When this man with arthritis got a new concept of God, and he learned to forgive those whom he deeply resented, by realizing the Love of God was dissolving in his mind and body everything unlike Itself, he was healed, even though it took some months. This man's concept of God worked out, and made Itself manifest in his body according to his belief.

It is not your theoretical belief about God that manifests itself, but it is your real, deep, subconscious belief.

There are people who forget to practice the Presence when a lawsuit or verdict goes against them. Even though the judge rendered a verdict which seems unjust to you, continue to believe that it is God in action, and that there is a Divine, harmonious solution for all concerned; the matter will come right in due season. You cannot lose; you can only win by practicing the Presence.

God is Pure Spirit, Infinite Mind, and Infinite Intelligence. The Bible calls the Name of God, "I AM," meaning Pure, Unconditioned Being. No one can, of course, define God, for God is Infinite, but there are certain Truths which the illumined of all ages have perceived as true of God, and that is why the Bible says, "I AM THAT I AM." What is "I AM?" It is your True Being—your Real Self; nobody can say, "I AM," for you. That is the Presence of God in you, and your Real Identity. Whatever you affix to "I AM," and believe, you become. Always claim, "I am strong, powerful, radiant, happy, joyous, illumined, and inspired;" then you are truly practicing the Presence, for all these qualities are true of God.

When you say, "I am weak," "I am inferior," "I am no good," you are denying God in the midst of you, and lying about Him.

Brother Lawrence of the 17th century was a monk. He was a saintly man, and wholly devoted to God. The book entitled *The Practice of the Presence of God* reveals a great humility, simplicity, and a mystic touch with God. "To do the will of God was," as he said, "his whole business." Brother Lawrence practiced the Presence when washing the dishes or scrubbing the floor. His attitude was that it was all God's work. His consciousness and awareness of the Divine Presence was no less when employed in the kitchen, than when he was before the altar. The way to God was to Brother Lawrence through the heart and through Love. His superiors marveled at the man who, though only educated to the point of reading and writing, could express himself with such beauty and profound wisdom. It was the Voice of God within him that prompted all his sayings.

This is how he daily practiced God's Holy Presence: He said in effect, "I have put myself in Your Keeping; it is Your Business I am about, and so everything will be all right." How beautiful! How simple, yet how soul-stirring is this prayer! He said the only sorrow he could experience would be the loss of the sense of God's Presence, but he never feared that, being wholly aware of God's Love and Absolute Goodness.

In his early life he feared he would be damned; this torture of his mind persisted for four years; then he saw the whole cause of this negativity was lack of faith in God; seeing that, he was freed and entered into a life of continual joy.

Begin now to practice the Presence by keeping your eyes on God, or all things Good, by seeing God in everyone you meet, and by constantly affirming, "It is God in action in all departments of my life." Calmly trust God's Holy Presence to lead you to green pastures and still waters. Love the Truth with a love that leaves no room for care or doubt. No matter what your work may be, as you go to your business say, "God walks and talks in me. I rely on God's guidance and wisdom completely." Give thanks for the perfect day. Do as Brother Lawrence suggests, whenever your attention wanders away on fear or doubt, bring it back to the contemplation of His Holy Presence.

To secure and know the life of peace and joy, school yourself daily to have an intimate, loving, familiar, humble conversation with God all day long. In this way you will draw upon God's grace abundantly. You shall become illumined by an Inner Light, and you will behold the inner vision of God, your Beloved.

# Case Histories

### CASE HISTORY NUMBER ONE

This interesting case from my files may bless many of you. This man invested a large sum of money in a certain organization. He had a very high regard for the two men who were active partners in this business. They appropriated the money that he gave them for themselves, and a little later they went into bankruptcy. He was very bitter and resentful, because he had practically put his life's savings into this venture. He was also ill, due to the hatred in his heart.

I explained to this man that resentment is never justified, and that many people make investments in land, stocks, bonds, etc., and have lost their money, but that it is absurd to blame the broker or the real estate man, because we erred in judgment. In a great measure this man's resentment was caused by a feeling of guilt for his own mistake, which he refused to admit. He was blaming the other men by an active resentment for his own shortcoming and failure. He prayed his way through it by the practice of His Presence in this way: "I now radiate love and goodwill to these two men. I humbly, sincerely, and honestly wish for them God's guidance, inner peace, and Divine Love. I wish for each one of them: prosperity, success, and a richness of life. It is God in action in all departments of their life. I mean this; I am sincere. My mind is now clear, clean, poised, serene, and expectant of happiness. God is guiding me in all ways. Nobody can take happiness, peace, or wealth away from me. I am one with God, and my business is God's Business. I am now minding my own business. The money I gave these men comes back to me in peace and harmony." He prayed like this night and morning, and during the day when hateful thoughts would come, he would say, "God is with me now."

In two weeks he was at peace with the world. All the resentful thoughts were burned up in his deeper mind; they were withered away by realizing God in action in his own life, and the life of those whom he said wronged him. A relative died in the interim, and a most interesting thing happened: He was bequeathed the exact amount he lost in that business venture. "For as the heavens are higher than the earth, so are my ways higher than your ways."

## Chapter III
# Realizing Your Desire

Desire is the power behind all action. We could not lift our hand or walk unless we had the desire or urge to move. Desire is the gift of God. As Browning said, "Tis thou, God, who giveth, 'tis I who receive."

It is man who receives—not a few of the gifts of life, but all of them! "Son thou art ever with me, and all that I hath is thine." All things whatsoever the Father hath are mine. *Our Father* holds within Himself all things we require, such as peace, harmony, abundance, guidance, joy, and infinite expression. We must grow unceasingly. We can never exhaust the Infinite Storehouse.

Let us realize a few simple truths: It is due to desire that we jump out of the way of an oncoming bus. The reason we do this is because we have a basic desire to preserve our life. Self-preservation is the first law of nature.

By example, the farmer plants seed due to his desire to attain food for himself and his family. Man builds airplanes due to his desire to collapse time and space. Similar illustrations are found throughout our whole course of life.

Desire pushes man; it is the goad of action. It is behind all progress. Desire is really the cosmic urge in all of us, impelling us to go forward, onward, upward, and Godward.

Desire is the angel of God—the messenger of the Divine—saying to each one of us, "Come on up higher."

Desire is behind all progress. It is the push of life. We find that we follow the desire that captivates and holds our attention. All of us find ourselves moving in the direction of the idea that dominates our mind for the time being.

Desire is an angel of God, telling us of something which, if accepted by us, will make our life fuller and happier. *The greater the expected benefit from the desire, the stronger is our desire.* Where there is no expected benefit, gain, or advancement accruing, there is no desire; consequently no action is found.

"I am alpha and omega, the beginning and the end, saith the Lord." Our ideal murmuring in our hearts is the alpha; in order that it become the omega, we must enter into the feeling that it is ours *now,* and walk the earth knowing that it is so.

Failure to realize our desire over a long period of time results in frustration and unhappiness. I have talked to many men in different parts of the country; their frequent complaint is that for years they have tried in vain to attain a certain ideal or position in life, and that they have failed miserably. They did not know that the desire to be, to do, and to have was the Still Small Voice speaking to them, and all that was necessary was for them to say, "Yes, Father, I accept and believe it"; then walk the earth knowing that, "It is done."

It is foolish to blame or accuse others, as we must realize that others are witnesses telling us who we are—"As within, so without." If there is discord within, there will be discord without. If we dwell in a mood of lack and limitation, others must come and testify to our lack.

I knew a woman in London one time, and on three occasions her purse was snatched from her by a thief in the tube of London; she was a wealthy woman. The explanation for this is that she was living in the fear of having her purse stolen; this was really an expectancy. "What I fear most has come upon me."

The mood, feeling, or conviction in which we walk determines the movements and actions of others towards us. In the eleventh chapter of Mark it says, "All things whatsoever ye shall ask in prayer, believe that ye receive them, and ye shall receive them."

The word *whatsoever* in the above quotation means anything you wish; it is all inclusive. There are no specific conditions set forth; you do not have to be a church-goer, or belong to a certain creed, or make any sacrifices. "I rejoice not in the sacrifices of man, not by power, not by might, but by the spirit saith the Lord." "For what purposes is the multitude of thy sacrifices. I am full of the blood of rams and the fat of beast, I rejoice not in the blood of rams or he goats." The only requisite is to believe that you have it now, or that you are the being you long to be.

*Believe* means to live in the state of being it; this means a complete mental acceptance where there is no longer any doubt or question in your mind. This is the state of consciousness called "a conviction." All other procedures as cited by Isaiah are foolishness and superstition. The only prerequisite is to believe that you have received; then comes the manifestation of your ideal.

We grow through desire. It is desire that pushes us forward, for it is the cosmic urge.

Let us realize that we are all channels of the Divine—individualizations of God-consciousness. The desire that lingers in your heart, that murmurs quietly—perhaps it has been there for months making itself known to you—is the Voice of God speaking to you, telling you to come on up higher— to arise and shine. Maybe you have looked around you and said to yourself, "What chance have I?" "Mary can, but I can't." "Perhaps, someday!" "It is just wishful thinking, etc." Have many such expressions come to your mind? Remember it is your five senses and worldly reason arguing with your Higher Self. We must remember that in prayer we always shut out the evidence of our senses and reason, plus everything that contradicts or denies what we truly want; then, as Jesus commands, we go within; shut the door, and pray to our Father in secret; the Father who seeth in secret will reward thee openly. Let us now proceed to enter into this Secret Place, and perform the spiritual, creative act in our own mind.

Sit down in an armchair, relax, and let go. Practice the Nancy School technique by getting into a drowsy, meditative state, a state of effortless effort, wherein effort is reduced to a minimum.

By example if you want to be a singer on the radio, imagine you are before a microphone; the microphone is now in front of you, and you see the imaginary audience; you are the actor. ("Act as though I am, and I will be.") You *feel* yourself into the situation; you are singing now (in your imagination); enter into the joy of it; feel the thrill of accomplishment! Continue to do this in your imagination until it begins to feel natural for you; then go off to sleep. If you have succeeded in planting your desire in your subconscious mind, you will feel a great sense of peace and satisfaction when you awaken. An interesting thing will have happened: You will have no further desire to pray about it, because it is fixed in consciousness. The reason for this is that the creative act has been finished, and you are at rest.

After true prayer when you have reached an inner conviction, there steals over you a sense of inner peace, calm, and certitude which tells you, "All is well." This is called *the sabbath* in the Bible, or period of stillness, or rest; it is the interval that elapses between the subjective realization of your desire and its manifestation. The manner of manifestation is not known to you; that is the secret of the subjective. "My ways are past finding out."

The answer or manifestation comes as a thief in the night. You know a thief comes when you least expect him; there is always an element of surprise; perhaps when you are sound asleep, the thief will come. If you sit up watching and waiting for the intruder, he will not come. Likewise we must go about our daily business, and the moment we think not, the answer will come. You are now at peace, made whole so to speak. You do not have to assist this Infinite Intelligence; It is All Powerful. It would be foolish to try to add power to Power.

The trouble with many people is this: When they pray, they are tense, anxious, and impatient. They say, "I wonder when it will come?" Others say, "Why has it not happened yet?"

If I say, "Why?" it means I am anxious and lack faith. If I *know* a thing is true, I do not question my prayer. Let us remember, therefore, anytime we ask, "Why?" to ourself or another, it means we have not reached a conviction within ourselves.

When we possess something in consciousness, we do not seek it; we have it! Another point I want to stress here is: When the student questions, "How will it come?" he shows lack of faith and conviction.

# Case Histories

### CASE HISTORY NUMBER TWO

Several years ago the author was lecturing in the Park Central Hotel in New York City. A man spoke to me at the end of the meeting saying, "I desire desperately to go to Pittsburgh, and I have no money."

I said to him, "Did you hear the lecture?" He said, "Yes, but—." I told him to ignore the doubts in his mind. We made a simple statement of truth together in that lovely lecture room. The statement was, "I am now at home in Pittsburgh with my people. All is peace and harmony." He was at home with them during those few minutes of silence in his imagination and feeling.

He phoned me later saying, "I went to the restaurant, and a man who sat next to me said, "You know I am driving to Pittsburgh. I would love to have someone share in the driving; I would pay him also. Do you know anyone? You look like a mechanic." This was the way Infinite Intelligence answered this man's prayer.

## Chapter IV
# The Magic of Faith

The purpose of this chapter is to teach you the spiritual truth of your dominion and freedom. "In all thy ways acknowledge him, and he shall direct thy paths." (Prov. 3:6). "I will lift up mine eyes unto the hills, from whence cometh my help." (Psm. 121:1).

In the above verse from Proverbs you are told to acknowledge the Infinite Intelligence within you, and that It shall direct you in all ways. The answer to your problem will come when you turn in faith and recognition to the Divine Principle within.

It was Shakespeare who said, "Our doubts are traitors, making us lose the good we oft might win, by fearing to attempt." Fear holds us back. *Fear* is a lack of faith in God or the Good.

A man told me one time that he was a member of a sales force for a large chemical organization which had two hundred men in the field. The sales manager died, and the vice president offered him the position; however he turned it down. He realized later that the only reason he rejected the offer was due to fear. He was afraid to attempt the responsibility. This man lacked faith in himself and his Inner Power. He hesitated, and the wonderful opportunity passed him by.

This salesman came to me for consultation, and I learned he was condemning himself, which was like a destructive, mental poison. In place of condemnation, he began to realize that there were other opportunities. I explained to him that faith is a way of thinking, a positive mental attitude, or a feeling of confidence that what you are praying for will come to pass.

For example, you have faith that the sun will rise tomorrow. You have faith that the seed you deposited in the ground will grow. The electrician has faith that electricity will respond to his proper use of it. A scientist has an idea for an ediphone; he proceeds to bring it to pass by having faith in the execution of the invisible idea.

Opportunity is always knocking at your door. The desire for health, harmony, peace, and prosperity is knocking at your door now. Perhaps you are offered a promotion; are you going to act like Peter of old who walked on the waters? ("And when Peter was come down out of the ship, he walked on the water, to go to Jesus. But when he saw the wind boisterous, he was afraid; and beginning to sink, he cried, Lord, save me.")

Besides being historical, this drama of Peter and Jesus takes place in your own mind. *Peter* means faith, perseverance, and determination. *Jesus* means your desire, which, if realized, would be your savior. Jesus comes into your mind as an idea, desire, plan, purpose, vision, or some new undertaking. The realization of your dreams, plans, or purpose would bring you and others great satisfaction and inner joy; this would be your Jesus. You must now call Peter, which is faith in the God-Power to bring all things to pass. Look at Peter and Jesus as dramatizations of the power of truth within you.

Oftentimes as you attempt something new—for example, a new position—doubt comes into your mind; this is *Peter* in you looking at the *boisterous wind and sinking*. This represents the impingement in your mind of the belief in failure, lack, and limitation.

You must cremate, burn up, and destroy that negative thought immediately. Doubt and fear hold men in bondage of sickness and failure. These false concepts cause you to vacillate, waver, equivocate, and hesitate to go ahead. The way to overcome is to increase your faith and awareness of your deep, spiritual potencies. Be like Peter; he succeeded, because he went forward; he had faith and confidence, knowing he would succeed.

A general in the field cannot afford to vacillate and waver on the battlefield. He has to come to a decision. Failure to come to a decision, plus a constant wavering in the mind, leads to a nervous breakdown and mental confusion. When you find yourself being pulled two ways that is a sign of doubt and fear.

Your good comes to you in the form of your desire. If you are sick, you wish health. If you are poor, you desire wealth. If you are full of fear, you desire faith and confidence. Jesus comes as your desire walking down the streets of your mind.

Ideas are our lords and masters. Ideas govern and rule us. The dominant idea that you now entertain is your lord; it generates its own emotion. Emotions compel you to express them. The dominant idea of success enthroned in the mind generates its own mood or feeling. This feeling compels you to right action, so that whatever you do under the mood of faith and confidence will be successful. The desire or idea of yours now is your lord. Mentally appropriate your desire, kiss it, love it, let it captivate your mind; feel the reality of it.

Is your desire lofty, inspiring, and wonderful enough to lead you forward? This ideal of yours is real, just the same as the idea of a radio was real in the mind of the inventor; or the idea of an automobile was real in the mind of Ford; or the idea of a house is real in the mind of an architect. It is not idle fancy or a daydream.

Peter is within you; i.e., *Peter* is faith, perseverance, stick-to-it-iveness, and an abiding trust in an Almighty Power that responds to man's thought and belief. This Formless Awareness within you takes the form of your belief and conviction. It is really all things to all men. It is strength to you, if you need strength. It is guidance, if you need guidance. It is food and health also.

All great scientists, mystics, artists, poets, and inventors are gifted or possessed by an abiding faith and trust in the Invisible Powers within.

As you read this, turn your desire or request over to the subjective mind within you, acknowledging in your heart it has the answer and the "know how" of accomplishment, and that its ways are past finding out. When you are relaxed and peaceful, you will know you have succeeded in impregnating your deeper mind. Signs follow; the wave of peace is the sign; this is inner conviction. You now walk above all the waters of confusion, chaos, and false beliefs, because in a little while what you felt as true will be experienced.

# Case Histories

### CASE HISTORY NUMBER THREE

I visited a man in prison a few months ago. The first thought in his mind was freedom; this is symbolized in the Bible as Jesus walking on the waters of your mind. This prisoner was very bitter and cynical. I explained to him that he had placed himself in prison by his actions, which were contrary to the golden rule. He was living in a psychological prison of hatred and envy. He changed his mental attitude by calling forth Peter, which was his faith in an Almighty Power to bring to pass the cherished desire of his heart.

I gave detailed instruction to this prisoner. He began to pray for those he hated by saying frequently, "God's love flows through them, and I release them." He began to do this many times a day. At night prior to sleep, he imagined himself home with his family. He would feel his little daughter in his arms and hear her voice saying, "Welcome, daddy." All this was done in his imagination. After awhile he made this so real, natural, and vivid, that it became a part of him. He had impregnated the subconscious with the belief in freedom.

Another interesting thing happened; he had no further desire to pray for his freedom; this was a sure psychological sign to him that he had embodied the desire for freedom subjectively. He was at peace, and though he was behind bars, he knew subjectively that he was free. It was an inner knowing. You no longer seek that which you have. Having realized his desire subjectively, he had no further desire to pray about it.

A few weeks passed and this young man was liberated from prison. Friends came to his rescue, and through the proper channels, the door was opened to him for a new life.

## Chapter V
# Steps to Happiness

Happiness is a state of consciousness. Faith and fear are moods of the soul. Your faith is a joyous expectancy of the best. Fear comes to challenge your faith in God or the Good. You must look upon fear as man's ignorance or his false beliefs which try to overcome his conviction in the good.

Never entertain or accept the suggestions of sickness, weakness, or failure. If you listen to negative suggestions and become fearful, begin to affirm the Truths of God, such as Love, Peace, Joy, etc. Know that thought and feeling are the causes of conditions and experiences.

Fear is based on the false beliefs that there are other powers, and that external things and conditions can hurt you. Fear must leave you, because it has nothing to sustain it; there is no reality behind it; its claims are false. Come back to the simple truth: "Only your thought has power over you, and the One Almighty Power now moves on your behalf, because your thoughts are in tune with the Infinite One."

I met a farmer one time on the west coast of Ireland. I lived in his house for a few days. He seemed to be always happy and joyful. I asked him to tell me his secret of happiness. His answer was, "It is a habit of mine to be happy." This is the whole story! Prayer is a habit; happiness is likewise a habit.

There is a phase in the Bible: "Choose ye this day whom ye will serve." You have the freedom *to choose* happiness; this may seem extraordinarily simple—and it is. Perhaps this is why people stumble over the way to happiness; they do not see the simplicity of the key to happiness.

Perhaps you say to yourself, "Business is bad. It is going to get worse." Furthermore, you may say to yourself, "The worst is yet to come!" If you have this attitude of mind the first thing in the morning, you will attract all these experiences to you, and you will be very unhappy.

On the other hand you can choose happiness. This is how you do it: When you open your eyes in the morning, say to yourself, "All things work together for good to them that love God." Remember that in all languages God and Good are synonymous.

Love is an emotional attachment. Continue to become attached to the good in the morning in this way: Look out the window, and say, "This is God's day for me. I am Divinely guided all day long. Whatever I do will prosper. I cast the spell of God around me. I walk in His Light. Whenever my attention wanders away from God or the Good, I will immediately bring it back to the contemplation of God and His Holy Presence. I am a spiritual magnet attracting to myself all things that bless and prosper me. I am going to be a wonderful success in all my undertakings today. I am definitely going to be happy all day long."

Start each day in this manner; then you are choosing happiness, and you will be a radiant, joyous person.

You can experience nothing outside your own mentality. Your dominant, mental mood is the way you think and feel inside about yourself, others, and the world in general. What is your present mental attitude? How do you feel inside? Are you worried, confused, angry, or concerned about other people's actions? If you are, you are not happy, because you are dwelling mentally on limitation.

Begin to anchor your mind on thoughts of peace, success, and happiness; this is really prayer. Do this frequently; then you will be like the Irish farmer who said, "It is a habit of mine to be happy." Your dominant mental attitude rules and governs all your experiences; therefore nothing can come into your world but the out-picturing of your mental attitude. Love all things good, and even your so-called "enemies" will be constrained to do you good.

Oftentimes you read in psychological and metaphysical literature that the world you behold is the world you are; this means you can control your relationship with the world. The world you really live in is a mental world of thoughts, feelings, sensations, and beliefs. As a matter of fact every person, circumstance, and experience you meet becomes a thought in your mind. How you mentally feel and react to life and conditions depend on what you believe about life and things in general. If your knowledge about life and the world is false, you can be very unhappy. If you have true knowledge and the right ideas, you can control your emotional reactions to life and have inner peace.

I knew a woman in England who had rheumatism for twenty years. She would pat herself on the knee, and say, "My rheumatism is bad today. I can't go out; my rheumatism keeps me miserable." This dear, elderly lady got a lot of attention from her son, daughter, and the neighbors. She really wanted her rheumatism; she enjoyed her "misery," as she called it. This person did not really want to be happy.

I suggested a curative procedure given in the Bible. I wrote down some biblical verses, and said if she gave her attention to these truths, she would be healed, but she was not interested. There seems to be a peculiar, mental streak in many people, whereby they seem to enjoy being miserable and sad.

Jesus said, "If you know these things, happy are ye if ye do them." "We should become as little children." The reason for this is that a child is happy, because it is close to God. The child knows intuitively where to find happiness. You do not have to become old, dull, crotchety, petulant, and cantankerous; neither do you have to become jaded and depressed in spirit. The simple truths of life, and not the opinions of man, produce and generate happiness within us. There are a great number of people trying to buy happiness through the purchase of radios, television sets, automobiles, and a home in the country, but happiness cannot be purchased or procured that way.

The Kingdom of God is within you, and the kingdom of happiness is in your thought and feeling. Too many people have the idea that it takes something artificial to produce happiness. Some people say, "If I had a million dollars, I would be happy." Others say, "If I was elected mayor, or the president of the organization, I would be happy." The answer is, "We must *choose* happiness." We must make it a habit to be happy. It is a mental and spiritual state. Happiness comes through your daily visits with God and in silent communion with His Holy Presence.

Begin now to eat the bread of the silence; you do this by meditating on the fact that, "In Him there is fullness of joy." As you dwell on these words, imagine the joy and the love of God are flowing through your mind and heart as a living current or stream; then you are stirring up the gift of God within you.

Within you is the Power to overcome any situation. You were born to win, to succeed, and to conquer. There is a great thrill in mastering a difficult assignment; the joy is in overcoming. Stand up against the problem now. Take up that shining sword of truth, and say, "I go forth conquering and to conquer!" The Power of the Almighty is within you; It will reveal to you the perfect solution. It will show you the way you should go. Conquer and overcome every negative emotion within you. Love casts out fear. The peace of God casts out pain. Good will casts out envy. In the midst of all kinds of adversity, look for that which is good, and that which is right; in other words look for the Divine answer.

# Case Histories

### CASE HISTORY NUMBER FOUR

I knew an alcoholic in London who had sunk to the depths of degradation. When I met him, he was begging pennies on the street for drink. At one time he was a highly respected lawyer. I spent some time with him in Hyde Park, London, telling him a few simple truths. I wrote these words for him to repeat: "I surrender myself completely to God and His Boundless Love and Goodness. My mind and heart are now open to the Spirit of Almighty God, which flows through me now. God fills my mind and heart with His Joy and His Love. I do not see the wind, but I feel the breeze upon my face; likewise I feel God's Presence stirring in my heart. God's river of Love flows through me, and I am clean and made whole."

I told him to relax, and slowly articulate the above meditation fifteen minutes, three times a day. All that was necessary was sincerity and humility on his part; then he was assured he would be free from the habit and blessed beyond his wildest dreams. This man became childlike in his simplicity. He fulfilled his promise. In less than a week he was engaged in a romance with God. Truly he touched the hem of His garment. As he meditated aloud, he imagined that the words were seeds sinking down into his soul. On the sixth day his whole being, and his room were flooded with an Interior Light which seemed to blind him temporarily. He was completely healed.

## Chapter VI
# Harmonious Human Relations

*"All things whatsover ye would that men should do unto you, do ye even so to them."*

The first thing you learn is that there is no one to change but yourself. The above truth has outer and inner meanings: As you would that men should *think* about you, think you about them in like manner. As you would that men should *feel* about you, feel you also about them in like manner. As you would want men to *act* toward you, act you toward them in like manner. This Biblical passage is the key to happy, human relationships in all walks of life.

Do you observe your "inner talking"? For example, you may be polite and courteous to someone in your office, but when his back is turned, you are very critical and resentful toward him in your mind. Such negative thoughts are highly destructive to you; it is like taking poison; you are actually taking a mental poison that robs you of vitality, enthusiasm, strength, guidance, and good will.

The suggestion you give to the other, you give to yourself. Ask yourself now, "How am I behaving internally toward this other fellow?" This interior attitude is what counts. Begin now to observe yourself; observe your reactions to people, conditions, and circumstances. How do you respond to the events and news of the day? It makes no difference if all the other people were wrong, and you alone were right, if the news disturbs you, it is your evil, because your bad mood affected and robbed you of peace and harmony. You do not have to react negatively to the news or the comments of the broadcaster. You can remain unmoved, undisturbed, and poised, realizing he has a right to his expression and beliefs. It is never what a person says or does that affects us; it is our reaction to what is said or done that matters.

Mentally divide yourself into two people: Your present mental state and that which you desire to be. Look at the thoughts of envy, jealousy, and hatred, which may have enslaved and imprisoned you. You have divided yourself into two people for the purpose of disciplining yourself: One is the race mind working in you, the other is the Infinite or the God-Self seeking expression through you. Be honest with yourself and determine which mood shall prevail.

For example, if someone gossips about you or criticizes you, what is your reaction? Are you going to engage in the typical way by getting excited, resentful, and angry? If you do you are letting the world-mind work in you. You must positively refuse to react in this mechanical, stereotyped, machine-like way. Say positively and definitely to yourself: "The Infinite One thinks, speaks, and acts through me now; this is my Real Self. I now radiate love, peace, and good will to this person who criticized me. I salute the Divinity in him. God speaks through me as peace, harmony, and love. It is wonderful." You are now a real student of truth. Instead of reacting like the herd that returns hate for hate, you have returned love for hatred, peace for hurt, good will for ill will. You have come into truth to think and react in a new way. When you come into truth, you make a new set of reactions to supplant the old. If you find yourself always reacting in the same way to people and conditions, you are not growing. Instead you are standing still, deeply immersed in the conditioned mind.

You know that you do not have to accept negative thoughts. You can become what you want to be by refusing to be a slave to old thought patterns.

Become the real observer, and practice observing your reactions to the events of the day. Whenever you discover that you are about to react negatively, say firmly, "This is not the Infinite One speaking or acting"; this will cause you to stop your negative thinking; then the Divine Love, Light, and Truth will flow through you at that moment. Instead of identifying yourself with anger, resentment, bitterness, and hatefulness, identify immediately with peace, harmony, poise, and balance; with this attitude you are really practicing the art of separation. You are separating yourself from the old (your present, mental state), and you are identifying yourself with the new (that which you desire to be).

Remember this great truth: You do not have to go along with, believe in, nor consent to negative thoughts or reactions. Begin to positively refuse to react mechanically as you formerly did. React and think in a new way. You want to be peaceful, happy, radiant, healthy, prosperous, and inspired; therefore, from this moment forward you must refuse to identify with negative thoughts, which tend to drag you down.

You are the cause of your own anger. If someone called you a fool, why should you get angry? You know you are not a fool. The other person is undoubtedly very disturbed mentally; maybe his child died during the night, or perhaps he is very ill psychologically. You should have compassion on him, but not condemn him. Realize God's peace fills his mind, and that His Love flows through him; then you would be practicing the Golden Rule. You would be identifying not with anger or hatred but with the law of goodness, truth, and beauty.

Would you condemn a person who had tuberculosis? No, you would not. In all probability if he told you, you would realize the Presence of God, harmony, and perfection where the trouble was; that would be compassion. *Compassion* is the Wisdom of God functioning through the mind of man, shown when you forgive all men, and see the God in them.

A person who is hateful, spiteful, envious, and jealous, and who says nasty, mean, scandalous things is very ill psychologically; he is just as sick as the man who has tuberculosis. How are you going to react to such a man? Where is your truth? Where is your wisdom and understanding? Are you going to say, "I am one of the herd; I react in kind; I return spite for spite, hate for hate, and anger for anger?" No, you would stop, and say, "This is not the Infinite One acting through me. God sees only perfection, beauty, and harmony. I see, therefore, as God sees." "Thou art of purer eyes than to behold evil, and canst not look on iniquity." I am going to see all men and women as God sees them. When your eyes are identified with beauty, you will not behold the distorted picture.

You are not living with people, you are living with your concept about them. How are you now responding to John Jones who is next to you on the bench? The fellow who works next to him likes him; his wife loves him; his children think he is wonderful. Perhaps members of his club believe he is generous, kind, and cooperative. Are you thinking of him as mean and petty? Are you resenting him? Who is this fellow? Is he *your* concept, or are all the others wrong? Would it not be wise to look within yourself and determine what it is in you that is causing him to be ugly or a stumbling block to you? I am sure you will find it within yourself.

Maybe you are saying to your son or father when you go home, "That fellow Jones annoys the life out of me. He irritates me beyond words." You are so upset, you cannot digest your dinner properly. According to your description he is impossible.

Where was Jones during the time you were saying all these things? Perhaps he was at the opera with his family; perchance he was out fishing in the stream having a wonderful, glorious time. As a matter of fact if someone said to you, "Where is Jones now?" You would answer, "I do not know." Be honest with yourself now, and admit he is in your own mind as a thought, a concept, or a mental image. You are revealing yourself and your own perturbed state of mind.

Quimby used to say that the suggestion we give to the other, we give to ourselves. You can now see how true that is. As a matter of fact, that is the basis of the Golden Rule. Never suggest to another, or think anything about another, that you would not wish the other to think, suggest, or feel about you.

Watch your hidden conversation to yourself. How do you meet people in your mind when they are thousands of miles away? You may be nice to their face, but the way you think about them is what counts. If you are negative, you are poisoning yourself. There are mental, corrosive poisons, just the same as there are physical, corrosive poisons; they are just as destructive also. If you are now disturbed, agitated, and angry over the way someone has acted toward you, it means you have a very negative thought-pattern in your consciousness, which you should heal instantly.

Be sure that you are not one of those people who will give all the reasons why they should be angry. Stop giving alibis; cease all self-justification. How could you be justified in hating or resenting someone? Do you have a special license? If you do, who gave you this authority? If you are agitated toward another, you are responsible for your unhappiness.

Now you can decree how your thoughts and emotions shall be directed. You are now a king over your own household (mind). Your thoughts, ideas, and feelings are your servants. You issue the command; their mission is to obey. You are here to control, and not to be controlled by angry, wild emotions.

Now when you say to yourself, "Who is the thinker in me?" you must answer, "I am!"

## Chapter VII
# How to Control Your Emotions

The ancient Greeks said, "Man, know thyself." As you study yourself, you seem to be made up of four parts: Your physical body, emotional nature, intellect, and the Spiritual Essence, which is called the Presence of God. The I AM within you, the Divine Presence, is your Real Identity, which is Eternal.

You are here to discipline yourself, so that your intellectual, emotional, and physical nature are completely spiritualized. These four phases of your nature are called the four beasts of *The Book of Revelation.* (*The Revelation of St. John* means God revealing himself as man.)

The real way for you to discipline and bridle your intellectual and emotional nature is by the Practice of the Presence of God all day long.

You have a body; it is a shadow or reflection of the mind. It has no power of itself, no initiative, or volition. It has no intelligence of itself; it is completely subject to your commands or decrees. Look upon your body as a great disc upon which you play your emotions and beliefs. Being a disc, it will faithfully record all your emotionalized concepts and never deviate from them; therefore, you can register a melody of love and beauty, or one of grief and sorrow upon it. Resentment, jealousy, hatred, anger, and melancholia are all expressed in the body as various diseases. As you learn to control your mental and emotional nature, you will become a channel for the Divine, and release the imprisoned splendor that is within you.

Think over this for a moment: You cannot buy a healthy body with all the money in the world, but you can have health through riches of the mind, such as thoughts of peace, harmony, and perfect health.

Let us dwell now on the emotional nature of man. It is absolutely essential for you to control your emotions if you want to grow spiritually. You are considered grown up or emotionally mature when you control your feelings. If you cannot discipline or bridle your emotions, you are a child even though you are fifty years old.

You must remember that the greatest tyrant is a false idea, which controls a man's mind holding him in bondage. The idea you hold about yourself or others induces definite emotions in you. Psychologically speaking, emotions compel you for good or evil. If you are full of resentment toward someone or possessed by a grudge, this emotion will have an evil influence over you, and govern your actions in a manner which has nothing to do with what you say is the original cause. When you want to be friendly and cordial, you will be ugly, cynical, and sour. When you want to be healthy, successful, and prosperous in life, you will find everything going wrong. Those of you reading this book are aware of your capacity to choose a concept of peace and good will. Accept the idea of peace in your mind, and let it govern, control, and guide you.

Quimby pointed out that ideas are our masters, and that we are slaves to the ideas we entertain. The concept of peace with which you now live will induce the feeling of peace and harmony. Your feeling is the Spirit of God operating at the human level; this feeling of peace and goodwill compel you to right action. You are now governed by Divine Ideas, which are mothered by the Holy Spirit.

Uncontrolled or undisciplined emotion is destructive. For example, if you have a powerful automobile, it will take you through the roughest country, or to the top of a high hill; however, you must control the automobile. If you do not know how to drive, you may hit a telegraph pole or another car. Should you step on the gas instead of the brake, the car may be destroyed.

It is wonderful to posses a strong, emotional nature provided you are the master. Your emotions are controlling you if you permit yourself to get angry over trifles or agitated over practically nothing. If you get upset over what you read in the newspapers, you are not controlling your emotions. You must learn to blend your intellect and emotions together harmoniously. The intellect of man is all right in its place, but it should be anointed or illumined with the Wisdom of God.

There are many people who are always trying to intellectualize God. You cannot define the Infinite. Spinoza said that to define God is to deny him. You have met the highly intellectual man who says that man cannot survive death, because he does not take his brain with him. Somehow he is so clever he really believes the brain thinks by itself. Such a man is looking at everything from a three-dimensional standpoint; that is where the intellect ceases.

The intellect, as I said previously, is all right in its place—for example, in our everyday work, and in all kinds of science, art, and industry. However as we approach the Living Spirit Almighty within, we are compelled to leave the world of the intellect, and go beyond into the realm of spiritual values, which are perfection, and where dimension is infinity.

When man's intellect is blended with the emotions of love, peace, and goodwill, he will not use explosives and knowledge of chemistry for the destruction of mankind. The reason man uses the atomic bomb, submarine, and other implements of warfare to destroy his fellow creature is because his spiritual awareness and knowledge lag so far behind his intellectual achievements.

Let us see how emotions are generated. Suppose you observe a cripple; perhaps you are moved to pity. On the other hand you may look at your young, beautiful child, and you feel an emotion of love welling up within you. You know that you cannot imagine an emotion, but if you imagine an unpleasant episode or event of the past, you induce the corresponding emotion. Remember it is essential to entertain the thought first before you induce an emotion.

An emotion is always the working out of an idea in the mind. Have you noticed the effect of fear upon the face, eyes, heart, and other organs? You know the effect of bad news or grief on the digestive tract. Observe the change that takes place when it is found the fear is groundless.

All negative emotions are destructive and depress the vital forces of the body. A chronic worrier usually has trouble with digestion. If something very pleasant occurs in his experience, the digestion becomes normal, because normal circulation is restored, and the necessary gastric secretions are no longer interfered with.

The way to overcome and discipline the emotions is not through repression or suppression. When you repress an emotion, the energy accumulates in the subconscious and remains snarled there. In the same manner as the pressure increases in the boiler, if all the valves are closed, and you increase the heat of the fire, finally there will be an explosion.

Today in the field of psychosomatics we are discovering that many cases of ill health, as arthritis, asthma, cardiac troubles, and failure in life, etc., may be due to suppressed or repressed emotions, perhaps occurring during early life or childhood.

These repressed or suppressed emotions rise like ghosts to haunt you later on. There is a spiritual and psychological way to banish these ghosts, which walk in the gloomy gallery of your mind. The ideal way is the law of substitution. Through the law of mental substitution, you substitute a positive, constructive thought for the negative. When negative thoughts enter your mind, do not fight them; just think of God and His Love; you will find the negative thoughts disappear. "I say unto you, That ye resist not evil." (Math. 5:39) If a person is fearful, the positive emotion of faith and confidence will completely destroy it.

If you sincerely wish to govern your emotions, you must maintain control over your thoughts. By taking charge of your thoughts, you can substitute love for fear. The instant you receive the stimulus of a negative emotion supplant it with the mood of love and good will. Instead of giving way to fear, say, "One with God is a majority." Fill your mind with concepts of peace, love, and faith in God; then the negative thoughts cannot enter.

It is far easier to cremate, burn up, and destroy negative thoughts at the moment they enter the mind, rather than try and dislodge them when they have taken possession of your mind. Refuse to be a victim of negative emotions through controlling your thought and thinking of God and His Attributes. You can be master of all your emotions and conditions. "He that *is* slow to anger is better than the mighty; and he that ruleth his spirit than he that taketh a city."

*The Book of Revelation* deals with the control of the intellectual and emotional life of man. It says in Chapter 4, verses 6, 7, and 8: "And before the throne *there was* a sea of glass like unto crystal: and in the midst of the throne, and round about the throne, *were* four beasts full of eyes before and behind.

"And the first beasts *was* like a lion, and the second beasts like a calf, and the third beast had a face as a man, and the fourth beast *was* like a flying eagle.

"And the four beasts had each of them six wings about *him;* and *they were* full of eyes within: and they rest not day and night, saying, Holy, holy, holy, Lord God Almighty, which was, and is, and is to come."

*The sea of glass before the throne* means the inner peace of God, for God is peace. Deep in the centre of your being, the Infinite One lies stretched in smiling repose. It is the Living Presence of God within you. You stand before this throne. *The throne* is a symbol of authority. Your emotional conviction of a deep, abiding faith in the God-Power is your authority in consciousness. To say it simply: Your inner conviction is your throne in heaven, because therein lies your power. "According to your faith it is done unto you." *Faith* is a positive, emotional attitude knowing that the good I seek is mine now.

*The four beasts forever before the throne* are the four phases of your being: spiritual, mental, emotional, and physical. In order to get your emotional nature on a spiritual basis, it is necessary to understand these four beasts; in doing so you learn the gentle art of scientific prayer which in the final analysis is the answer to all problems. Study these four potencies of consciousness.

*The lion* is the king of the jungle; it means God, your I AMNESS.

*Taurus* means the bull or beast of burden. *Your burden* is your desire. You labor in your imagination to make your desire a part of your consciousness.

*Aquarius* means the water bearer; it means meditation. The word *meditation* means to eat of God or your good, to feast upon your ideal. You pour water on your ideal, meaning you dwell upon and pour love on it, which is the water of life. Something happens as you mentally feast upon your ideal; you generate an emotion; the latter is the spirit of God moving on your behalf. Your emotion is the Holy Spirit moving at human levels. God is a reactive, reciprocal Power within you. Your emotion responds according to the nature of the idea. As you emotionalize your idea, it sinks into the subconscious mind as an impression; this is called the *Eagle* or *Scorpio*, meaning the Divine impregnation. These are the four stages of the unfoldment or manifestation of an ideal or desire. Whatever is impressed is expressed.

The four beasts had each of them six wings. *The six wings* refer to the mental, creative act. When idea and feeling blend together in harmony and faith, there has taken place a wedding ceremony in the mind. Knowledge of this mental, creative act gives you wings; enables you to soar aloft above the storms and struggles of the world, and find peace and strength in your own mind.

# Case Histories

### CASE HISTORY NUMBER FIVE
A soldier who has returned from Korea told me that when he was seized with fear, he would say to himself over and over again, "God's Love surrounds me, and goes before me." This affirmation impressed his mind with the feeling of love and faith. This mood of love supplanted his fear. "Perfect Love casteth out fear." This procedure is the answer to the process of freedom from fear.

### CASE HISTORY NUMBER SIX
A mother, whose only child died, was grief stricken. The grief was affecting her vision, and she suffered from migraine headaches. She was in a deep state of depression. I suggested to her that she go to a hospital, and offer her services in the children's ward. She was a former nurse. In offering her time at a local hospital, she began to pour out love on the children; she coddled them; cared for them, and fed them. The love was no longer bottled up within her; she became a channel for the Divine, and began to release the sunshine of God's Love. She practiced sublimation, which was a redirection of the energy

lodged within her subconscious mind. In this manner she drained off the poison pockets of her subconscious mind.

## CASE HISTORY NUMBER SEVEN

A woman who comes to our meeting told me that she was accustomed to fits of temper and anger periodically by the action of neighbors. Instead of letting the anger and hatred affect her mentally and physically by pushing it back into the subconscious, she transmuted it into muscular energy by getting a gallon of water and washing the windows or the floor. Sometimes she would begin to dig in the garden, saying to herself aloud, "I am digging in the garden of God, and planting God's ideas." She would do this for fifteen minutes at a time. When washing the windows, she would say aloud, "I am cleansing my mind with the waters of love and life." The above illustrations are simple methods of working off negative emotions in a physical way.

## Chapter VIII
# Changing the Feeling of "I"

If you say, "I," to everything you think, feel, say, or imagine, you cannot transform your emotional life. Remember all kinds of thoughts can enter your mind; all kinds of emotions may enter your heart. If you say, "I," to all negative thoughts, you are identifying yourself with them, and you cannot separate internally from them. You can refuse to attach "I" to negative emotions and thoughts. You make it a practice to avoid muddy places as you walk along the road; likewise you must avoid walking down the muddy roads of your mind where fear, resentment, hostility, and ill-will lurk and move. Refuse to listen to negative remarks. Do not touch the negative moods, or let them touch you. Practice inner separation by getting a new feeling about yourself, and about what you really are. Begin to realize that the real "I" in you is the Infinite Spirit, the Infinite One.

Begin to identify yourself with the Qualities and Attributes of this Infinite One; then your whole life will be transformed. The whole secret in transforming your negative, emotional nature is to practice self-observation. To observe and *to observe* oneself are two different things. When you say, "You observe..." you mean you give your attention to external things. In self-observation the attention is directed inwards. A man may spend his whole lifetime studying the atom, stars, body, and the phenomenalistic world—namely, knowledge of the external world; this knowledge cannot bring about an interior change. Self-observation is the means of interior change—the change of the heart. You must learn to differentiate, to discern, to separate the chaff from the wheat.

You practice the art of self-observation when you begin to ask yourself, "Is this idea true? Will it bless, heal, and inspire me? Will it give me peace of mind, and contribute to the well-being of humanity?" You are living in two worlds: the external and the internal; yet they are both one. One is visible and the other invisible (subjective and objective). Your external world enters through your five senses, and is shared by everyone. Your internal world of thought, feelings, sensations, beliefs, and reaction is invisible and belongs to you. Ask yourself, "In which world do I live? Do I live in the world revealed by my five senses, or in this inner world?" It is in this inner world you live all the time; this is where you feel and suffer. Suppose you are invited to a banquet. All you see, hear, taste, smell, and touch belong to the external world. All that you think, feel, like, and dislike belong to the inner world. You attend two banquets recorded differently: namely, one the outer, and one the inner. It is in your inner world of thought, feeling, and emotion in which you rise and fall and sway to and fro.

In order to transform yourself, you must begin to change the inner world through the purification of the emotions, and the correct ordering of the mind through right thinking. If you want to grow spiritually, you must transform yourself. *Transformation* means the changing of one thing into another.

In order truly to observe yourself, you must see that regardless of what happens, your thought and feeling are fixed on this great truth: "How is it in God and Heaven?" This will lift you up, and transform all your negative thoughts and emotions. You may be inclined to say that other people are to blame, because of the way they talk or act, but if what they say or do makes you negative, you are inwardly disturbed; this negative state is where you now live, move, and have your being.

P.D. Ouspensky used to point out that people became upset easily, because their feeling of "I" was derived from negative states of consciousness. The feeling of "I" was one of his favorite expressions, and some of his ideas are incorporated in this chapter.

When you say, "I think this..." "I think that..." "I resent this..." or "I dislike this..." which "I" is speaking? Is it not a different "I" speaking every moment? Each "I" is completely different. One "I" in you criticizes one moment; a few minutes later another "I" speaks tenderly. Look at and learn about your different "I's," and know deep within yourself that certain "I's" will never dominate, control, or direct your thinking.

Take a good look at the "I's" you are consorting with. With what kind of people do you associate? I am referring to the people that inhabit your mind. Remember your mind is a city; thoughts, ideas, opinions, feelings, sensations, and beliefs dwell there. Some of the places in your mind are slums and dangerous streets; however Jesus (your savior) is always walking down the streets of your mind in the form of your ideal, desire, and aim in life.

One of the meanings of Jesus is your desire; for your desire, when realized, is your savior. Your aims and objectives in life are now beckoning to you; move toward them. Give your desire your attention; in other words take a lively interest in it. Go down the streets of love, peace, joy, and good will in your mind; you will meet wonderful people on the way. You will find beautifully lighted streets and wonderful citizens on the better streets of your mind.

Never permit your house, which is your mind, to be full of servants that you do not have under control. When you were young, you were taught not to go with what your mother called, "bad company." Now when you begin to awaken to your inner powers, you must make it a special point that you do not go with wrong "I's" (thoughts) within you.

I had an interesting chat with a young man who studied mental discipline in France. His procedure was to take, as he said, "mental photographs of himself from time to time." He would sit down, and think about his emotions, moods, thoughts, sensations, reactions, and his tones of voice; then he would say, "These are not of God; they are false. I will go back to God and think from that Standard or Rock of Truth." He practiced the art of inner separation. He would stop when he got angry, and say, "This is not the Infinite One, the real 'I' speaking, thinking, or acting; it is the false 'I' in me."

Return to God like this young man. Every time you are prone to get angry, critical, depressed, or irritable, think of God and Heaven, and ask yourself, "How is it in God and Heaven?" *There* is the answer to becoming the new man; this is how you become spiritually reborn or experience what is called the second birth. (*The second birth* is internal discipline and spiritual understanding.)

The saint and the sinner are in all of us; so are the murderer and the holy man; likewise are God and the world mind. Every man basically and fundamentally wants to be good, to express good, and to do good. This is "the positive" in you. If you have committed destructive acts, as for example, if you have robbed, cheated, and defrauded others, and they condemn you, and they hold you in a bad light, you can rise out of the slum of your mind to that place in your own consciousness where you cease to condemn yourself; then all your accusers must still their tongues. When you cease to accuse yourself, the world will no longer accuse you; this is the power of your own consciousness; It is the God in you.

*The other self* represents the many "I's" in you, for instance the many negative ideas and beliefs that there are powers outside your own consciousness; the belief that others can hurt you; the elements are unfriendly, plus the fears, superstitions, and ignorance of all kinds. Finally prejudices, fears, and hates drive and goad you to do that which you would not otherwise do. The ideal way to change the feeling of "I" is to affix to the real "I" within you everything that is noble, wonderful, and God-like.

Begin to affirm, "I am strong. I am radiant. I am happy. I am inspired. I am illumined. I am loving. I am kind. I am harmonious." Feel these states of mind; affirm them, and believe them; then you will begin to truly live in the Garden of God. Whatever you affix to the "I AM" and believe, you become. The "I AM" in you is God, and there is none other. "I AM" or Life, Awareness, Pure Being, Existence, or the Real Self of you is God. It is the Only Cause. It is the Only Power making anything in the world. Honor It.

# How to Attract Money
(1955)

# by Joseph Murphy

*The Original Classic of Abundance—
from the Author of*
The Power of Your Subconscious Mind

## Contents

Introduction   *The Book You've Been Waiting For* by Mitch Horowitz   912

Chapter One   Your Right to be Rich   914

Chapter Two   The Road to Riches   931

## Introduction
# The Book You've Been Waiting For

I am often asked: If I were to select one New Thought book to recommend to someone approaching the philosophy of mental causation for the first time, or maybe someone who is willing to sample one and just one book, which would it be?

The answer has eluded me. I have been uncertain whether to recommend a "mainstream" work like Earl Nightingale's wonderful lecture *The Strangest Secret*, which lays out New Thought in a precise, businesslike manner, omitting most mystical themes. For someone from a strictly nonreligious background, I might recommend surgeon Maxwell Maltz's *Psycho-Cybernetics*, which is a secular, psychological exploration of the mind's formative abilities. Or, finally, if I see that someone has a key goal in mind, and is open to both spiritual and psychological language, I would recommend Napoleon Hill's evergreen *Think and Grow Rich*.

But in writing these words, I realize that the book I should be recommending—and that I plan to from now on—is one that I've been reading for years, but never fully appreciated: Joseph Murphy's slender 1955 masterpiece, *How to Attract Money*.

I think that I have previously resisted recommending *How to Attract Money* because I felt slightly embarrassed by its acquisitive-sounding title. Thoughtful people are taught to believe that overt expressions of money-getting are vulgar or "unspiritual." Reading this book with fresh eyes, however, I am disabused of that notion. First of all, money—in whatever form it takes, whether bills, goods, or commodities—is part of the natural human exchange, and is indelibly tied to all phases of our lives. More importantly, Murphy, in his genius as a communicator, uses the topic of money, something that we all need, as a metaphor for the point he's really making: which is that we are generative, causative beings who channel the power of higher creativity through the medium of our thoughts, which take form in the overt circumstances of our lives.

Not everyone approaching New Thought, or this book, must be spiritual in outlook. One could venture psychological explanations for the link between thoughts and events, something that Maltz does compellingly in *Psycho-Cybernetics*, where he compares the mind to a homing device, like a heat-seeking missile, which is programed by our subconscious beliefs. And that is valid. But New Thought, at its heart, is spiritual, by which I mean it posits a non-material, extra-physical basis for life. In this short volume, Joseph Murphy explains this perspective, and provides precise techniques for using your thoughts, prayers, mental images, and affirmations in a manner that exerts and channels the creative intelligence of cosmos, or what we call God.

When Murphy writes about using the powers of your mind while in a drowsy, pre-sleep state, and when he asserts that the Bible is a symbolical book of inner development, his ideas converge with those of his contemporary seeker, spiritual teacher Neville Goddard. Murphy recalled studying with Neville (who wrote under his first name) when the two men—Murphy a recent immigrant from Ireland and Neville from the West Indies—were coming up as metaphysical teachers on the New York scene in the 1930s. In interviews toward the end of his life in 1981, Murphy said that he and Neville shared the same teacher: a mysterious, turbaned black rabbi named Abdullah.

If all that is a little too mystical for you, don't worry. Murphy's philosophy doesn't require credulity; it requires experimentation. And the experiments in this book are exquisitely private—they are yours alone. They require no membership or label. And, most especially, there is no need to disclose what you're doing to anyone else. In fact, it's better not to. These ideas don't need another's approval or approbation—only your engagement.

This short book, written eight years before the 1963 publication of Murphy's worldwide bestseller *The Power of Your Subconscious Mind*, captured his philosophy in its totality. Murphy's communicative powers, always considerable, are at their peak. His words here are effective, truthful, and, I think, demonstrably good and beneficent.

I have been reading New Thought literature for about twenty years, and yet *something*—I cannot quite say what—awakened in me when I recently reread this little book in the early morning hours, while my home in New York City remained covered in predawn darkness and the activity of the streets was briefly stilled. I wish a similar experience for you. And if you, like me, come to feel that you want to share this book with friends and curious people, you will be spreading seeds of mental creativity, which may grow in your life and in the lives of others in ways that surprise you. That, too, I wish for all who approach this volume.

—Mitch Horowitz
New York City, 2017

## Chapter One
# Your Right to be Rich

It is your right to be rich. You are here to lead the abundant life, and be happy, radiant, and free. You should, therefore, have all the money you need to lead a full, happy, prosperous life.

There is no virtue in poverty; the latter is a mental disease, and it should be abolished from the face of the earth. You are here to grow, expand, and unfold, spiritually, mentally, and materially. You have the inalienable right to fully develop and express yourself along all lines. You should surround yourself with beauty and luxury.

Why be satisfied with just enough to go around when you can enjoy the riches of the Infinite? In this book you will learn to make friends with money, and you will always have a surplus. Your desire to be rich is a desire for a fuller, happier, more wonderful life. It is a cosmic urge. It is good and very good.

Begin to see money in its true significance—as a symbol of exchange. It means to you freedom from want, and beauty, luxury, abundance, and refinement.

As you read this chapter, you are probably saying, "I want more money." "I am worthy of a higher salary than I am receiving."

I believe most people are inadequately compensated. One of the causes many people do not have more money is that they are silently or openly condemning it. They refer to money as "filthy lucre," or "Love of money is the root of all evil," etc. Another reason they do not prosper is that they have a sneaky, subconscious feeling there is some virtue in poverty; this subconscious pattern may be due to early childhood training, superstition, or it could be based on a false interpretation of the Scriptures.

There is no virtue in poverty; it is a disease like any other mental disease. If you were physically ill, you would think there was something wrong with you; you would seek help, or do something about the condition at once. Likewise if you do not have money constantly circulating in your life, there is something radically wrong with you.

Money is only a symbol; it has taken many forms as a medium of exchange down through the centuries, such as salt, beads, and trinkets of various kinds. In early times man's wealth was determined by the number of sheep or oxen he had. It is much more convenient to write a check than to carry some sheep around with you to pay your bills.

God does not want you to live in a hovel or go hungry. God wants you to be happy, prosperous, and successful. God is always successful in all His undertakings, whether He makes a star or a cosmos!

You may wish to make a trip around the world, study art in foreign countries, go to college, or send your children to a superior school. You certainly wish to bring your children up in lovely surroundings, so that they might learn to appreciate beauty, order, symmetry, and proportion.

You were born to succeed, to win, to conquer all difficulties, and have all your faculties fully developed. If there is financial lack in your life, do something about it.

Get away immediately from all superstitious beliefs about money. Do not ever regard money as evil or filthy. If you do, you cause it to take wings and fly away from you. Remember that you lose what you condemn.

Suppose, for example, you found gold, silver, lead, copper, or iron in the ground. Would you pronounce these things evil? God pronounced all things good. The evil comes from man's darkened understanding, from his unillumined mind, from his false interpretation of life, and his misuse of Divine Power. Uranium, lead, or some other metal could have been used as a medium of exchange. We use paper bills, checks, etc.; surely the piece of paper is not evil; neither is the check. Physicists and scientists know today that the only difference between one metal and another is the number and rate of motion of the electrons revolving around a central nucleus. They are now changing one metal into another through a bombardment of the atoms in the powerful cyclotron. Gold under certain conditions becomes mercury. It will only be a little while until gold, silver, and other metals will be made synthetically in the chemical laboratory. I cannot imagine seeing anything evil in electrons, neutrons, protons, and isotopes.

The piece of paper in your pocket is composed of electrons and protons arranged differently; their number and rate of motion is different; that is the only way the paper differs from the silver in your pocket.

Some people will say, "Oh, people kill for money. They steal for money!" It has been associated with countless crimes, but that does not make it evil.

A man may give another $50 to kill someone; he has misused money in using it for a destructive purpose. You can use electricity to kill someone or light the house. You can use water to quench the baby's thirst, or use it to drown the child. You can use fire to warm the child, or burn it to death.

Another illustration would be if you brought some earth from your garden, put it in your coffee cup for breakfast, that would be your evil; yet the earth is not evil; neither is the coffee. The earth is displaced; it belongs in your garden.

Similarly if a needle were stuck in your thumb, it would be your evil; the needle or pin belongs in the pin cushion, not in your thumb.

We know the forces or the elements of nature are not evil; it depends on our use of them whether they bless or hurt us.

A man said to me one time, "I am broke. I do not like money; it is the root of all evil."

Love of money to the exclusion of everything else will cause you to become lopsided and unbalanced. You are here to use your power or authority wisely. Some men crave power; others crave money. If you set your heart on money, and say, "That is all I want. I am going to give all my attention to amassing money; nothing else matters," you can get money and attain a fortune, but you have forgotten that you are here to lead a balanced life. "Man does not live by bread alone."

For example, if you belong to some cult or religious group, and become fanatical about it, excluding yourself from your friends, society, and social activities, you will become unbalanced, inhibited, and frustrated. Nature insists on a balance. If all your time is devoted to external things and possessions, you will find yourself hungry for peace of mind, harmony, love, joy, or perfect health. You will find you cannot buy anything that is real. You can amass a fortune, or have millions of dollars; this is not evil or bad. Love of money to the exclusion of everything else results in frustration, disappointment, and disillusionment; in that sense it is the root of your evil.

By making money your sole aim, you simply made a wrong choice. You thought that was all you wanted, but you found after all your efforts that it was not only the money you needed. What you really desired was true place, peace of mind, and abundance. You could have the million or many millions, if you wanted them, and still have peace of mind, harmony, perfect health, and Divine Expression.

Everyone wants enough money, and not just enough to go around. He wants abundance and to spare; he should have it. The urges, desires, and impulses we have for food, clothing, homes, better means of transportation, expression, procreation, and abundance are all God- given, Divine, and good, but we may misdirect these impulses, desires, and urges resulting in evil or negative experiences in our lives.

Man does not have an evil nature; there is no evil nature in you; it is God, the Universal Wisdom, or Life seeking expression through you.

For example, a boy wants to go to college, but he does not have enough money. He sees other boys in the neighborhood going off to college and the university; his desire increases. He says to himself, "I want an education, too." Such a youth may steal and embezzle money for the purpose of going to college. The desire to go to college was basically and fundamentally good; he misdirected that desire or urge by violating the laws of society, the cosmic law of harmony, or the golden rule; then he finds himself in trouble.

However if this boy knew the laws of mind, and his unqualified capacity through the use of the Spiritual Power to go to college, he would be free and not in jail. Who put him in jail? He placed himself there. The policeman who locked him up in prison was an instrument of the man-made laws which he violated. He first imprisoned himself in his mind by stealing and hurting others. Fear and a guilt consciousness followed; this is the prison of the mind followed by the prison walls made of bricks and stones.

Money is a symbol of God's opulence, beauty, refinement, and abundance, and it should be used wisely, judiciously, and constructively to bless humanity in countless ways. It is merely a symbol of the economic health of the nation. When your blood is circulating freely, you are healthy. When money is circulating freely in your life, you are economically healthy. When people begin to hoard money, to put it away in tin boxes, and become charged with fear, there is economic illness.

The crash of 1929 was a psychological panic; it was fear seizing the minds of people everywhere. It was a sort of negative, hypnotic spell.

You are living in a subjective and objective world. You must not neglect the spiritual food, such as peace of mind, love, beauty, harmony, joy, and laughter.

Knowledge of the spiritual power is the means to the Royal Road to Riches of all kinds, whether your desire is spiritual, mental, or material. The student of the laws of mind, or the student of the spiritual principle, believes and knows absolutely that regardless of the economic situation, stock market fluctuation, depression, strikes, war, other conditions, or circumstances, he will always be amply supplied regardless of what form money may take. The reason for this is he abides in the consciousness of wealth. The student has convinced himself in his mind that wealth is forever flowing freely in his life, and that there is always a Divine surplus. Should there be a war tomorrow, and all the student's present holdings become valueless, as the German marks did after the First World War, he would still attract wealth, and be cared for regardless of the form the new currency took.

Wealth is a state of consciousness; it is a mind conditioned to Divine supply forever flowing. The scientific thinker looks at money or wealth like the tide; i.e., it goes out, but it always comes back. The tides never fail; neither will man's supply when he trusts a tireless, changeless, immortal Presence which is Omnipresent, and flows ceaselessly. The man who knows the workings of the subconscious mind is never, therefore, worried about the economic situation, stock market panics, devaluation, or inflation of currency, since he abides in the consciousness of God's eternal supply. Such a man is always supplied and watched over by an overshadowing Presence. *Behold the fowls of the air: for they sow not, neither do they reap, nor gather into barns; yet your heavenly Father feedeth them. Are ye not much better than they?* MATTHEW 6:26

As you consciously commune with the Divine-Presence claiming and knowing that It leads and guides you in all your ways, that It is a Lamp unto your feet, and a Light on your path, you will be Divinely prospered and sustained beyond your wildest dreams.

Here is a simple way for you to impress your subconscious mind with the idea of constant supply or wealth: Quiet the wheels of your mind. Relax! Let go! Immobilize the attention. Get into a sleepy, drowsy, meditative state of mind; this reduces effort to the minimum; then in a quiet, relaxed, passive way reflect on the following simple truths: Ask yourself where do ideas come from? Where does wealth come from? Where did you come from? Where did your brain and your mind come from? You will be led back to the One Source.

You find yourself on a spiritual, working basis now. It will no longer insult your intelligence to realize that wealth is a state of mind. Take this little phrase; repeat it slowly four or five minutes three or four times a day quietly to yourself, particularly before you go to sleep: "Money is forever circulating freely in my life, and there is always a Divine surplus." As you do this regularly and systematically, the idea of wealth will be conveyed to your deeper mind, and you will develop a wealth consciousness. Idle, mechanical repetition will not succeed in building the consciousness of wealth. Begin to feel the truth of what you affirm. You know what you are doing, and why you are doing it. You know your deeper self is responsive to what you consciously accept as true.

In the beginning people who are in financial difficulties do not get results with such affirmations as, "I am wealthy," "I am prosperous," "I am successful"; such statements may cause their conditions to get worse. The reason is the subconscious mind will only accept the dominant of two ideas, or the dominant mood or feeling. When they say, "I am prosperous," their feeling of lack is greater, and something within them says, "No, you are not prosperous, you are broke." The feeling of lack is dominant so that each affirmation calls forth the mood of lack, and more lack becomes theirs. The way to overcome this for beginners is to affirm what the conscious and subconscious mind will agree on; then there will be no contradiction. Our subconscious mind accepts our beliefs, feelings, convictions, and what we consciously accept as true.

A man could engage the cooperation of his subconscious mind by saying, "I am prospering every day." "I am growing in wealth and in wisdom every day." "Every day my wealth is multiplying." "I am advancing, growing, and moving forward financially." These and similar statements would not create any conflict in the mind.

For instance if a salesman has only ten cents in his pocket, he could easily agree that he would have more tomorrow. If he sold a pair of shoes tomorrow, there is nothing within him which says his sales could not increase. He could use statements, such as, "My sales are increasing every day." "I am advancing and moving forward." He would find these would be sound psychologically, acceptable to his mind, and produce desirable fruit.

The spiritually advanced student who quietly, knowingly, and feelingly says, "I am prosperous," "I am successful," "I am wealthy," gets wonderful results also. Why would this be true? When they think, feel, or say, "I am prosperous," they mean God is All Supply or Infinite Riches, and what is true of God is true of them. When they say, "I am wealthy," they know God is Infinite Supply, the Inexhaustible, Treasure- House, and what is true of God is, therefore, true of them, for God is within them.

Many men get wonderful results by dwelling on three abstract ideas, such as health, wealth, and success. *Health* is a Divine Reality or quality of God. *Wealth* is of God; it is eternal and endless. *Success* is of God; God is always successful in all His undertakings.

The way they produce remarkable results is to stand before a mirror as they shave, and repeat for five or ten minutes: "Health, wealth, and success." They do not say, "I am healthy," or "I am successful"; they create no opposition in their minds. They are quiet and relaxed; thus the mind is receptive and passive; then they repeat these words. Amazing results follow. All they are doing is identifying with truths that are eternal, changeless, and timeless.

You can develop a wealth consciousness. Put the principles enunciated and elaborated on in this book to practice, and your desert will rejoice and blossom as the rose.

I worked with a young boy in Australia many years ago who wanted to become a physician and surgeon, but he had no money; nor had he graduated from high school. For expenses he used to clean out doctors' offices, wash windows, and do odd repair jobs. He told me that every night as he went to sleep, he used to see a diploma on a wall with his name in big, bold letters. He used to clean and shine the diplomas in the medical building where he worked; it was not hard for him to engrave the diploma in his mind and develop it there. I do not know how long he continued this imaging, but it must have been for some months.

Results followed as he persisted. One of the doctors took a great liking to this young boy, and after training him in the art of sterilizing instruments, giving hypodermic injections, and other miscellaneous first aid work, he became a technical assistant in his office. The doctor sent him to high school and also to college at his expense.

Today this man is a prominent doctor in Montreal, Canada. He had a dream! A clear image in his mind! *His wealth was in his mind.*

*Wealth* is your idea, desire, talent, urge for service, capacity to give to mankind, your ability for usefulness to society, and your love for humanity in general.

This young boy operated a great law unconsciously. Troward says, "Having seen the end, you have willed the means to the realization of the end." The end in this boy's case was to be a physician. To imagine, see, and feel the reality of being a doctor now, to live with that idea, sustain it, nourish it, and to love it until through his imagination it penetrated the layers of the subconscious, becoming a conviction, paved the way to the fulfillment of his dreams.

He could have said, "I have no education." "I do not know the right people." "I am too old to go to school now." "I have no money; it would take years, and I am not intelligent." He would then be beaten before he started. His wealth was in his use of the Spiritual Power within him which responded to his thought.

The means or the way in which our prayer is answered is always hidden from us except that occasionally we may intuitively perceive a part of the process. *My ways are past finding out.* The *ways* are not known. The only thing man has to do is to imagine and accept the end in his mind, and leave its unfoldment to the subjective wisdom within.

Oftentimes the question is asked, "What should I do after meditating on the end and accepting my desire in consciousness?" The answer is simple: You will be compelled to do whatever is necessary for the unfoldment of your ideal. The law of the subconscious is compulsion. The law of life is action and reaction. What we do is the automatic response to our inner movements of the mind, inner feeling, and conviction.

A few months ago as I went to sleep, I imagined I was reading one of my most popular books, *Magic of Faith* in French. I began to realize and imagine this book going into all French-speaking nations. For several weeks I did this every night, falling asleep with the imaginary French edition of *Magic of Faith* in my hands.

Just before Christmas in 1954, I received a letter from a leading publisher in Paris, France, enclosing a contract drawn up, asking me to sign it, giving him permission to publish and promote abroad to all French-speaking countries the French edition of *Magic of Faith*.

You might ask me what did I do about the publishing of this book after prayer? I would have to say, "Nothing!" The subjective wisdom took over, and brought it to pass in its own way, which was a far better way than any method I could consciously desire.

All of our external movements, motions, and actions follow the inner movements of the mind. Inner action precedes all outer action. Whatever steps you take physically, or what you seem to do objectively, will all be a part of a pattern which you were compelled to fulfill.

Accepting the end wills the means to the realization of the end. Believe that you have it now, and you shall receive it.

We must cease denying our good. Realize that the only thing that keeps us from the riches that lie all around us is our mental attitude, or the way we look at God, life, and the world in general. Know, believe, and act on the positive assumption that there is no reason why you cannot have, be, and do whatever you wish to accomplish through the great laws of God.

Your knowledge of how your mind works is your saviour and redeemer. Thought and feeling are your destiny. You possess everything by right of consciousness. The consciousness of health produces health; the consciousness of wealth produces wealth. The world seems to deny or oppose what you pray for; your senses sometimes mock and laugh at you.

If you say to your friend, you are opening up a new business for yourself, he may proceed to give you all the reasons why you are bound to fail. If you are susceptible to his hypnotic spell, he may instill fear of failure in your mind. As you become aware of the spiritual power which is one and indivisible, and responds to your thought, you will reject the darkness and ignorance of the world, and know that you possess all the equipment, power, and knowledge to succeed.

To walk on the Royal Road to Riches, you must not place obstacles and impediments on the pathway of others; neither must you be jealous or envious of others. Actually when you entertain these negative states of mind, you are hurting and injuring yourself, because you are thinking and feeling it. "The suggestion," as Quimby said, "you give to another, you are giving to yourself." This is the reason that the law of the golden rule is a cosmic, divine law.

I am sure you have heard men say, "That fellow has a racket." "He is a racketeer." "He is getting money dishonestly." "He is a faker." "I knew him when he had nothing." "He is crooked, a thief, and a swindler." If you analyze the man who talks like that, he is usually in want or suffering from some financial or physical illness. Perhaps his former, college friends went up the ladder of success and excelled him; now he is bitter and envious of their progress. In many instances this is the cause of his downfall. Thinking negatively of these classmates, and condemning their wealth, causes the wealth and prosperity he is praying for to vanish and flee away. He is condemning the things he is praying for. He is praying two ways. On the one hand he is saying, "God is prospering me," and in the next breath, silently or audibly, he is saying, "I resent that fellow's wealth." Always make it a special point to bless the other person, and rejoice in his prosperity and success; when you do, you bless and prosper yourself.

If you go into the bank, and you see your competitor across the street deposit twenty times more than you do, or you see him deposit ten thousand dollars, rejoice and be exceedingly glad to see God's abundance being manifested through one of his sons. You are then blessing and exalting what you are praying for. What you bless, you multiply. What you condemn, you lose.

If you are working in a large organization, and you are silently thinking and resenting the fact you are underpaid, that you are not appreciated, and that you deserve more money and greater recognition, you are subconsciously severing your ties with that organization. You are setting a law in motion; then the superintendent or manager says to you, "We have to let you go." You dismissed yourself. The manager was simply the instrument through which your own negative, mental state was confirmed. In other words he was a messenger telling you what you conceived as true about yourself. It was an example of the law of action and reaction. The action was the internal movement of your mind; the reaction was the response of the outer world to conform to your inner thinking.

Perhaps as you read this, you are thinking of someone who has prospered financially by taking advantage of others, by defrauding them, in selling them unsound investments in property, etc. The answer to this is obvious, because if we rob, cheat, or defraud another, we do the same to ourselves. In reality in this case we are actually hurting or robbing from ourselves. We are in a mood of lack in the first place, which is bound to attract loss to us. The loss may come in many ways; it may come in loss of health, prestige, peace of mind, social status, sickness in the home, or in business. It may not necessarily come in loss of money. We must not be shortsighted and think that the loss has to come just in dollars and cents.

Isn't it a wonderful feeling to place your head on the pillow at night, and feel you are at peace with the whole world, and that your heart is full of goodwill toward all? There are some people who have accumulated money the wrong way, as by tramping on others, trickery, deceit, and chicanery. What is the price? Sometimes it is mental and physical disease, guilt complexes, insomnia, or hidden fears. As one man said to me, "Yes, I rode roughshod over others. I got what I wanted, but I got cancer doing it." He realized he had attained his wealth in the wrong way.

You can be wealthy and prosperous without hurting anyone. Many men are constantly robbing themselves; they steal from themselves: peace of mind, health, joy, inspiration, happiness, and the laughter of God. They may say that they have never stolen, but is it true? Every time we resent another, or are jealous, or envious of another's wealth or success, we are stealing from ourselves. These are the thieves and robbers which Jesus cast out of the temple; likewise you must cast them out incisively and decisively. Do not let them live in your mind. Cut their heads off with the fire of right thought and feeling.

I remember in the early days of the war reading about a woman in Brooklyn, New York, who went around from store to store buying up all the coffee she could. She knew it was going to be rationed; she was full of fear that there would not be enough for her. She bought as much as she could, and stored it in the cellar. That evening she went to church services. When she came home, burglars had broken down the door, stolen not only the coffee, but silverware, money, jewelry, and other things.

This good woman said what they all say: "Why did this happen to me when I was at church? I never stole from anyone."

Is this true? Was she not in the consciousness of lack and fear when she began to hoard supplies of coffee? Her mood and fear of lack was sufficient to bring about loss in her home and possessions. She did not have to put her hand on the cash register or rob a bank; her fear of lack produced lack. This is the reason that many people who are what society calls "good citizens" suffer loss. They are good in the worldly sense; i.e., they pay their taxes; they obey the laws, vote regularly, and are generous to charities, but they are resentful of others' possessions, their wealth, or social position. If they would like to take money when no one was looking, such an attitude is definitely and positively a state of lack, and may cause the person who indulges in such a mental state to attract charlatans or knaves who may swindle or cheat them in some business transaction.

Before the outer thief robs us, we have first robbed ourselves. There must be an inner thief, before the outer one appears.

A man can have a guilt complex, and be accusing himself constantly. I knew such a man; he was very honest as a teller in a bank. He never stole any money, but he had an illicit romance; he was supporting another woman, and denying his family. He lived in fear that he would be discovered; a deep sense of guilt resulted. Fear follows guilt. Fear causes a contraction of the muscles and mucous membranes; acute sinusitis developed. Medication only gave him temporary relief.

I explained to this client the cause of his trouble, and told him the cure was to give up his outside affair. He said he couldn't; she was his soul mate, and that he had tried. He was always condemning and accusing himself.

One day he was accused by one of the officials of the bank of having embezzled some money; it looked serious for him, as the evidence was circumstantial. He became panic stricken, and realized that the only reason he was wrongfully accused was that he had been accusing and condemning himself.

He saw how mind operates. Inasmuch as he was always accusing himself on the inner plane, he would be accused on the outer.

He broke off the relationship immediately with the other woman due to the shock of being accused of embezzling, and began to pray for Divine harmony and understanding between himself and the bank official. He began to claim, "There is nothing hidden that is not revealed. The peace of God reigns supreme in the minds and hearts of all concerned."

Truth prevailed. The whole matter was dissolved in the light of truth. Another young man was discovered as the culprit. The bank teller knew that only through prayer was he saved from a jail sentence.

The great law is, "As you would that men should think about you, think you about them in the same manner. As you would that men should feel about you, feel you also about them in like manner."

Say from your heart, "I wish for every man who walks the earth, what I wish for myself. The sincere wish of my heart is, therefore, peace, love, joy, abundance, and God's blessings to all men everywhere." Rejoice and be glad in the progression, advancement, and prosperity of all men. Whatever you claim as true for yourself, claim it for all men everywhere. If you pray for happiness and peace of mind, let your claim be peace and happiness for all. Do not ever try and deprive another of any joy. If you do, you deprive yourself. When the ship comes in for your friend, it comes in for you also.

If someone is promoted in your organization, be glad and happy. Congratulate him, rejoice in his advancement and recognition. If you are angry or resentful, you are demoting yourself. Do not try and withhold from another his God-given birthright to happiness, success, achievement, abundance, and all good things.

Jesus said, "Sow up for yourselves treasures in heaven, where the moth and the rust doth not consume, and where thieves cannot break through and steal." Hatred and resentment rot and corrode the heart causing us to become full of scars, impurities, toxins, and poisons.

*The treasures of heaven* are the truths of God which we possess in our soul. Fill your minds with peace, harmony, faith, joy, honesty, integrity, loving kindness, and gentleness; then you will be sowing for yourself treasures in the heavens of your own mind.

If you are seeking wisdom regarding investments, or if you are worried about your stocks or bonds, quietly claim, "Infinite Intelligence governs and watches over all my financial transactions, and whatsoever I do shall prosper." Do this frequently and you will find that your investments will be wise; moreover you will be protected from loss, as you will be prompted to sell your securities or holdings before any loss accrues to you.

Let the following prayer be used daily by you regarding your home, business, and possessions: "The overshadowing Presence which guides the planets on their course and causes the sun to shine, watches over all my possessions, home, business, and all things that are mine. God is my fortress and vault. All my possessions are secure in God. It is wonderful." By reminding yourself daily of this great truth, and by observing the laws of Love, you will always be guided, watched over, and prospered in all your ways. You will never suffer from loss; for you have chosen the Most High as your Counsellor and Guide. The envelope of God's Love surrounds, enfolds, and encompasses you at all times. You rest in the Everlasting Arms of God.

All of us should seek an inner guidance for our problems. If you have a financial problem, repeat this before you retire at night: "Now I shall sleep in peace. I have turned this matter over to the God-Wisdom within. It knows only the answer. As the sun rises in the morning, so will my answer be resurrected. I know the sunrise never fails." Then go off to sleep.

Do not fret, fuss, and fume over a problem. Night brings counsel. Sleep on it. Your intellect cannot solve all your problems. Pray for the Light that is to come. Remember the dawn always comes; then the shadows flee away. Let your sleep every night be a contented bliss.

You are not a victim of circumstances, except you believe you are. You can rise and overcome any circumstance or condition. You will have different experiences as you stand on the rock of spiritual Truth, steadfast, and faithful to your deeper purposes and desires.

In large stores, the management employs store detectives to prevent people from stealing; they catch a number every day trying to get something for nothing. All such people are living in the consciousness of lack and limitation, and are stealing from themselves, attracting at the same time all manner of loss. These people lack faith in God, and the understanding of how their minds work. If they would pray for true peace, Divine expression, and supply, they would find work; then by honesty, integrity, and perseverance they would become a credit to themselves and society at large.

Jesus said, "For ye have the poor always with you; but me ye have not always." The *poor states* of consciousness are always with us in this sense, that no matter how much wealth you now have, there is something you want with all your heart. It may be a problem of health; perhaps a son or daughter needs guidance, or harmony is lacking in the home. At that moment you are poor.

We could not know what abundance was, except we were conscious of lack. "I have chosen twelve, and one of you is a devil."

Whether it be the king of England or the boy in the slums, we are all born into limitation and into the race belief. It is through these limitations we grow. We could never discover the Inner Power, except through problems and difficulties; these are our *poor states* which prod us in seeking the solution. We could not know what joy was, except we could shed a tear of sorrow. We must be aware of poverty, to seek liberation and freedom, and ascend into God's opulence.

The *poor states*, such as fear, ignorance, worry, lack, and pain are not bad when they cause you to seek the opposite. When you get into trouble, and get kicked around from pillar to post; when you ask negative, heart-rending questions, such as "Why are all these things happening to me?" "Why does there seem to be a jinx following me?" light will come into your mind. Through your suffering, pain, or misery, you will discover the truth which sets you free. "Sweet are the uses of adversity, like a toad ugly and venomous, yet wears a precious jewel on its head."

Through dissatisfaction we are led to satisfaction. All those studying the laws of life have been dissatisfied with something. They have had some problem or difficulty which they could not solve; or they were not satisfied with the man-made answers to life's riddles. They have found their answer in the God-Presence within themselves—the pearl of great price—the precious jewel. The Bible says, "I sought the Lord, and I found him, and He delivered me from all my fears."

When you realize your ambition or desire, you will be satisfied for only a period of brief time; then the urge to expand will come again. This is Life seeking to express Itself at higher levels through you. When one desire is satisfied, another comes, etc. to infinity. You are here to grow. Life is progression; it is not static. You are here to go from glory to glory; there is no end; for there is no end to God's glory.

We are all poor in the sense we are forever seeking more light, wisdom, happiness, and greater joy out of life. God is Infinite, and never in Eternity could you exhaust the glory, beauty, and wisdom which is within; this is how wonderful you are.

In the absolute state all things are finished, but in the relative world we must awaken to that glory which was ours before the world was. No matter how wise you are, you are seeking more wisdom; so you are still poor. No matter how intelligent you are in the field of mathematics, physics, or astronomy, you are only scratching the surface. You are still poor. The journey is ever onward, upward, and Godward. It is really an awakening process, whereby you realize creation is finished. When you know God does not have to learn, grow, expand, or unfold, you begin to gradually awaken from the dream of limitation, and become alive in God. As the scales of fear, ignorance, race belief, and mass hypnosis fall from your eyes, you begin to see as God sees. The blind spots are removed; then you begin to see the world as God made it; for we begin to see it through God's eyes. Now you say, "Behold, the Kingdom of Heaven is at hand!"

Feed the "poor" within you; clothe the naked ideas, and give them form by believing in the reality of the idea, trusting the great Fabricator within to clothe it in form and objectify it. Now your word (idea) shall become flesh (take form). When you are hungry (poor states), you seek food. When worried, you seek peace. When you are sick, you seek health; when you are weak, you seek strength. Your desire for prosperity is the voice of God in you telling you that abundance is yours; therefore, through your poor state, you find the urge to grow, to expand, to unfold, to achieve, and to accomplish your desires.

A pain in your shoulder is a blessing in disguise; it tells you to do something about it at once. If there were no pain and no indication of trouble, your arm might fall off on the street. Your pain is God's alarm system telling you to seek His Peace and His Healing Power, and move from darkness to Light. When cold, you build a fire. When you are hungry, you eat. When you are in lack, enter into the mood of opulence and plenty. Imagine the end; rejoice in it. Having imagined the end, and felt it as true, you have willed the means to the realization of the end.

When you are fearful and worried, feed your mind with the great truths of God that have stood the test of time and will last forever. You can receive comfort by meditating on the great psalms. For example: "The Lord is my shepherd; I shall not want." "God is my refuge, my salvation, whom shall I fear?" "God is an ever-present help in time of trouble." "My God in Him will I trust." "He shall cover me with His feathers, and under His wings shall I rest." "One with God is a majority." "If God be for me, who can be against me?" "I do all things through Christ which strengtheneth me." Let the healing vibrations of these truths flood your mind and heart; then you will crowd out of your mind all your fears, doubts, and worries through this meditative process.

Imbibe another great spiritual truth: "A merry heart maketh a cheerful countenance." "A merry heart hath a continual feast." "A merry heart doeth good like a medicine; a broken spirit drieth the bones." "Therefore I put thee in remembrance that thou stir up the gift of God within thee." Begin now to stir up the gift of God by completely rejecting the evidence of senses, the tyranny and despotism of the race mind, and give complete recognition to the spiritual Power within you as the only Cause, the only Power, and the only Presence. Know that it is a responsive and beneficent Power. "Draw nigh unto it, and it will draw nigh unto you." Turn to It devotedly with assurance, trust, and love; it will respond to you as love, peace, guidance, and prosperity.

It will be your Comforter, Guide, Counsellor, and your heavenly Father. You will then say, "God is Love. I have found Him, and He truly has delivered me from all my fears." Furthermore, you will find yourself in green pastures, where abundance and all of God's riches flow freely through you.

Say to yourself freely and joyously during the day, "I walk in the consciousness of the Presence of God all day long." "His fullness flows through me at all times filling up all the empty vessels in my life."

When you are filled full of the feeling of being what you long to be, your prayer is answered. Are all the vessels full in your life? Look under health, wealth, love, and expression. Are you fully satisfied on all levels? Is there something lacking in one of these four? All that you seek, no matter what it is, comes under one of these classifications.

If you say, "All I want is truth or wisdom," you are expressing the desire of all men everywhere. That is what everyone wants, even though he or she may word it differently. Truth or wisdom is the overall desire of every man; this comes under the classification of expression. You wish to express more and more of God here and now.

Through your lack, limitation, and problems, you grow in God's Light, and you discover yourself. There is no other way whereby you could discover yourself.

If you could not use your powers two ways, you would never discover yourself; neither would you ever deduce a law governing you. If you were compelled to be good, or compelled to love, that would not be love. You would then be an automaton. You have freedom to love, because you can give it, or retain it. If compelled to love, there is no love. Aren't you flattered when some woman tells you she loves you and wants you? She has chosen you from all the men in the world. She does not have to love you. If she were forced to love you, you would not be flattered or happy about it.

You have freedom to be a murderer or a Holy man. This is the reason that we praise such men as Lincoln and others. They decided to choose the good; we praise them for their choice. If we believe that circumstances, conditions, events, age, race, religious training, or early environment can preclude the possibility of our attaining a happy, prosperous life, we are thieves and robbers. All that is necessary to express happiness and prosperity is to feel happy and prosperous. The feeling of wealth produces wealth. States of consciousness manifest themselves. This is why it is said, "All that ever came before me (feeling) are thieves and robbers." Feeling is the law, and the law is the feeling.

Your desire for prosperity is really the promise of God saying that His riches are yours; accept this promise without any mental reservation.

Quimby likened prayer to that of a lawyer pleading the case before the judge. This teacher of the laws of mind said he could prove the defendant was not guilty as charged, but that the person was a victim of lies and false beliefs. You are the judge; you render your own verdict; then you are set free. The negative thoughts of lack, poverty, and failure are all false; they are all lies; there is nothing to back them up.

You know there is only one spiritual Power, one primal cause, and you, therefore, cease giving power to conditions, circumstances, and opinions of men. Give all Power to the Spiritual Power within you, knowing that It will respond to your thought of abundance and prosperity. Recognizing the supremacy of the Spirit within, and the Power of your own thought or mental image is the way to opulence, freedom, and constant supply. Accept the abundant life in your own mind. Your mental acceptance and expectancy of wealth has its own mathematics and mechanics of expression. As you enter into the mood of opulence, all things necessary for the abundant life will come to pass. You are now the judge arriving at a decision in the courthouse of your mind. You have, like Quimby, produced indisputable evidence showing how the laws of your mind work, and you are now free from fear. You have executed and chopped the heads off all the fear and superstitious thoughts in your mind. Fear is the signal for action; it is not really bad; it tells you to move to the opposite which is faith in God and all positive values.

Let this be your daily prayer; write it in your heart: "God is the source of my supply. That supply is my supply now. His riches flow to me freely, copiously, and abundantly. I am forever conscious of my true worth. I give of my talents freely, and I am wonderfully, divinely compensated. Thank you, Father!"

## Chapter Two
# The Road to Riches

Riches are of the mind. Let us suppose for a moment that a physician's diploma was stolen together with his office equipment. I am sure you would agree that his wealth was in his mind. He could still carry on, diagnose disease, prescribe, operate, and lecture on materia medica. Only his symbols were stolen; he could always get additional supplies. His riches were in his mental capacity, knowledge to help others, and his ability to contribute to humanity in general.

You will always be wealthy when you have an intense desire to contribute to the good of mankind.

Your urge for service—i.e., to give of your talents to the world—will always find a response in the heart of the universe.

I knew a man in New York during the financial crisis of 1929, who lost everything he had including his home and all his life's savings. I met him after a lecture which I had given at one of the hotels in the city. This was what he said: "I lost everything. I made a million dollars in four years. I will make it again. All I have lost is a symbol. I can again attract the symbol of wealth in the same way as honey attracts flies."

I followed the career of this man for several years to discover the key to his success. The key may seem strange to you; yet it is a very old one. The name he gave the key was, "Change water into wine!" He read this passage in the Bible, and he knew it was the answer to perfect health, happiness, peace of mind, and prosperity.

*Wine* in the Bible always means the realization of your desires, urges, plans, dreams, propositions, etc.; in other words, it is the things you wish to accomplish, achieve, and bring forth.

*Water* in the Bible usually refers to your mind or consciousness. Water takes the shape of any vessel into which it is poured; likewise whatever you feel and believe as true will become manifest in your world; thus you are always changing water into wine.

The Bible was written by illumined men; it teaches practical, everyday psychology and a way of life. One of the cardinal tenets of the Bible is that you determine, mold, fashion, and shape your own destiny through right thought, feeling, and beliefs. It teaches you that you can solve any problem, overcome any situation, and that you are born to succeed, to win, and to triumph. In order to discover the Royal Road to Riches, and receive the strength and security necessary to advance in life, you must cease viewing the Bible in the traditional way.

The above man who was in a financial crisis used to say to himself frequently during the days when he was without funds, "I can change water into wine!" These words meant to him, "I can exchange the poverty ideas in my mind for the realization of my present desires or needs which are wealth and financial supply."

His mental attitude (water) was, "Once I made a fortune honestly. I will make it again (wine)." His regular affirmation consisted of, "I attracted the symbol (money) once, I am attracting it again. I know this, and feel it is true (wine)." This man went to work as a salesman for a chemical organization. Ideas for the better promotion of their products came to him; he passed them on to his organization. It was not long until he became vice president. Within four years the company made him president. His constant mental attitude was, "I can change water into wine!"

Look upon the story in John of changing water into wine in a figurative way, and say to yourself as the above-mentioned chemical salesman did: "I can make the invisible ideas, urges, dreams, and desires of mine visible, because I have discovered a simple, universal law of mind."

The law he demonstrated is the law of action and reaction. It means your external world, body, circumstances, environment, and financial status are always a perfect reflection of your inner thinking, beliefs, feelings, and convictions. This being true, you can now change your inner pattern of thought by dwelling on the idea of success, wealth, and peace of mind. As you busy your mind with these latter concepts, these ideas will gradually seep into your mentality like seeds planted in the ground. As all seeds (thoughts and ideas) grow after their kind, so will your habitual thinking and feeling manifest in prosperity, success, and peace of mind. Wise thought (action) is followed by right action (reaction).

You can acquire riches when you become aware of the fact that prayer is a marriage feast. The *feast* is a psychological one; you meditate (mentally eat of) on your good or your desire until you become *one* with it.

I will now cite a case history from my files relating how a young girl performed her first miracle in transforming "water into wine." She operated a very beautiful hair salon. Her mother became ill, and she had to devote considerable time at home neglecting her business. During her absence two of her assistants embezzled funds. She was forced into bankruptcy, losing her home and finding herself deeply in debt. She was unable to pay hospital bills for her mother, and she was now unemployed.

I explained to this woman the magic formula of changing water into wine. Again we made it clear to her that wine means answered prayer or the objectification of her ideal.

She was quarreling with the outside world. She said, "Look at the facts: I have lost everything; it is a cruel world. I cannot pay my bills. I do not pray; for I have lost hope." She was so absorbed and engrossed in the material world, that she was completely oblivious to the internal cause of her situation. As we talked, she began to understand that she had to resolve the quarrel in her mind.

No matter what your desire or ideal is as you read this book, you will also find some thought or idea in your mind opposed to it. For example your desire may be for health; perhaps there are several thoughts such as these in your mind simultaneously: "I can't be healed. I have tried, but it is no use; it's getting worse." "I don't know enough about spiritual mind healing."

As you study yourself, don't you have a tug of war in your mind? Like this girl, you find environment and external affairs challenging your desire of expression, wealth, and peace of mind.

True prayer is a mental marriage feast, and it teaches us all how to resolve the mental conflict. In prayer you "write" what you *believe* in your own mind. Emerson said, "A man is what he thinks about all day long." By your habitual thinking you make your own mental laws of belief. By repeating a certain train of thought you establish definite opinions and beliefs in the deeper mind called the subconscious; then such mental acceptances, beliefs, and opinions direct and control all the outer actions. To understand this and begin to apply it is the first step in changing "water into wine," or changing lack and limitation into abundance and opulence. The man who is unaware of his own inner, spiritual powers is, therefore, subject to race beliefs, lack, and limitation.

Open your Bible now, and perform your first miracle, as this beauty operator did. You can do it. If you merely read the Bible as a historical event, you will miss the spiritual, mental, scientific view of the laws of mind with which we are concerned in this book.

Let us take this passage: "And the third day there was a marriage in Cana of Galilea; and the mother of Jesus was there." *Galilee* means your mind or consciousness. *Cana* means your desire. The *marriage* is purely mental or the subjective embodiment of your desire. This whole, beautiful drama of prayer is a psychological one in which all the characters are mental states, feelings, and ideas within you.

One of the meanings of *Jesus* is illumined reason. The *mother of Jesus* means the feeling, moods, or emotions which possess us.

"And both Jesus was called, and his disciples, to the marriage." *Your disciples* are your inner powers and faculties enabling you to realize your desires.

"And when they wanted wine, the mother of Jesus saith unto him, They have no wine." *Wine*, as we have stated, represents the answered prayer or the manifestation of your desire and ideals in life. You can now see this is an everyday drama taking place in your own life.

When you wish to accomplish something as this girl did, namely, finding work, supply, and a way out of your problem, suggestions of lack come to you; such as, "There is no hope. All is lost, I can't accomplish it; it is hopeless." This is the voice from the outside world saying to you, "They have no wine," or "Look at the facts." This is your feeling of lack, limitation, or bondage speaking.

How do you meet the challenge of circumstances and conditions? By now you are getting acquainted with the laws of mind which are as follows: "As I think and feel inside, so is my outside world; i.e., my body, finances, environment, social position, and all phases of my external relationship to the world and man." Your internal, mental movements and imagery govern, control, and direct the external plane in your life.

The Bible says, "As he thinketh in his heart, so *is* he." The *heart* is a Chaldean word meaning the subconscious mind. In other words your thought must reach subjective levels by engaging the power of your subliminal self.

Thought and feeling are your destiny. Thought charged with feeling and interest is always subjectified, and becomes manifest in your world. *Prayer* is a marriage of thought and feeling, or your idea and emotion; this is what the marriage feast relates.

Any idea or desire of the mind felt as true comes to pass, whether it is good, bad, or indifferent. Knowing the law now that what you imagine and feel in your mind, you will express, manifest, or experience in the outside, enables you to begin to discipline your mind.

When the suggestion of lack, fear, doubt, or despair (they have no wine) come to your mind, immediately reject it mentally by focusing your attention at once on the answered prayer, or the fulfillment of your desire.

The statement given in the Bible from John 2, "Mine hour is not yet come," and "Woman, what have I to do with thee," are figurative, idiomatic, oriental expressions.

As we paraphrase this quotation, *woman* means the negative feeling that you indulge in. These negative suggestions have no power or reality, because there is nothing to back them up.

A suggestion of lack has no power; the power is resident in your own thought and feeling.

What does God mean to you? *God* is the Name given to the One Spiritual Power. *God* is the One Invisible Source from Which all things flow.

When your thoughts are constructive and harmonious, the spiritual power being responsive to your thought flows as harmony, health, and abundance. Practice the wonderful discipline of completely rejecting every thought of lack by immediately recognizing the availability of the spiritual power, and its response to your constructive thoughts and imagery; then you will be practicing the truth found in these words, "Woman what have I to do with thee?"

We read, "Mine hour is not yet come." This means that while you have not yet reached a conviction or positive state of mind, you know you are on the way mentally, because you are engaging your mind on the positive ideals, goals, and objectives in life. Whatever the mind dwells upon, it multiplies, magnifies, and causes it to grow until finally the mind becomes qualified with the new state of consciousness. You are then conditioned positively, whereas before you were conditioned negatively.

The spiritual man in prayer moves from the mood of lack to the mood of confidence, peace, and trust in the spiritual power within himself. Since his trust and faith are in the Spiritual Power, his mother (moods and feeling) registers a feeling of triumph or victory; this will bring about the solution or the answer to your prayer.

*The waterpots* in the story from the Bible refer to the mental cycles that man goes through in order to bring about the subjective realization of his desire. The length of time may be a moment, hour, week, or month depending on the faith and state of consciousness of the student.

In prayer we must cleanse our mind of false beliefs, fear, doubt, and anxiety by becoming completely detached from the evidence of senses and the external world. In the peacefulness and quietude of your mind, wherein you have stilled the wheels of your mind, meditate on the joy of the answered prayer until that inner certitude comes, whereby *you know that you know.* When you have succeeded in being one with your desire, you have succeeded in the mental marriage—or the union of your feeling with your idea.

I am sure you wish to be married (one with) to health, harmony, success, and achievement in your mind at this moment. Every time you pray you are trying to perform the *marriage feast of Cana* (realization of your desire or ideas). You want to be mentally identified with the concept of peace, success, wellbeing, and perfect health.

"They filled them up to the brim." *The six waterpots* represent your own mind in the spiritual and mental creative act. You must fill your mind *to the brim*, meaning you must become filled full of the feeling of being what you long to be. When you succeed in filling your mind with the ideal you wish to accomplish or express, you are full to the brim; then you cease praying about it; for you feel its reality in your mind. You *know*! It is a finished state of consciousness. You are at peace about it.

"And he saith unto them Draw out now, and bear unto the governor of the feast." Whatever is impregnated in our subconscious mind is always objectified on the screen of space; consequently when we enter a state of conviction that our prayer is answered, we have given the command, "Bear unto the governor of the feast."

You are always governing your mental feast. During the day thousands of thoughts, suggestions, opinions, sights, and sounds reach your eyes and ears. You can reject them as unfit for mental consumption or entertain them as you choose. Your conscious, reasoning, intellectual mind is the governor of the feast. When you consciously choose to entertain, meditate, feast upon, and imagine your heart's desire as true, it becomes a living embodiment, and a part of your mentality, so that your deeper self gives birth or expression to it. In other words what is impressed subjectively is expressed objectively. Your senses or conscious mind sees the objectification of your good. When the conscious mind becomes aware of "water made into wine," it becomes aware of the answered prayer. *Water* might be called, also, the invisible, formless, spiritual power, unconditioned consciousness. *Wine* is conditioned consciousness, or the mind giving birth to its beliefs and convictions.

*The servants* which draw the water for you represent the mood of peace, confidence, and faith. According to your faith or feeling, your good is attracted or drawn to you.

Imbibe, cherish, fall in love with these spiritual principles which are discussed in this book. In the first recorded miracle of Jesus, you are told that prayer is a marriage feast, or the mind uniting with its desire.

Love is the fulfilling of the law. Love is really an emotional attachment, a sense of oneness with your good. You must be true to that which you love. You must be loyal to your purpose or to your ideal. We are not being true to the one we love, when we are flirting or mentally entertaining other marriages with fear, doubt, worry, anxiety, or false beliefs. Love is a state of oneness, a state of fulfillment. (Refer to the book by the author, *Love is Freedom*.)

When this simple drama was explained to the beauty operator mentioned about, she became rich mentally. She understood this drama, and she put it into practice in her life. This is how she prayed: She knew that the water (her own mind) would flow, and fill up all the *empty vessels* in response to her new way of thinking and feeling.

At night this client became very quiet and still, relaxed her body, and began to use constructive imagery. The steps she used are as follows:

First step: She began to imagine the local bank manager was congratulating her on her wonderful deposits in the bank. She kept imagining that for about five minutes.

The second step: In her imagination she heard her mother saying to her, "I am so happy about your wonderful, new position." She continued to hear her say this in a happy, joyous way for about three to five minutes.

The third step: Vividly she imagined the writer was in front of her performing her marriage ceremony. This woman heard me saying as the officiating minister, "I now pronounce you man and wife." Completing this routine, she went off to sleep feeling filled full, i.e., sensing and feeling within herself the joy of the answered prayer.

Nothing happened for three weeks; in fact things got much worse, but she persevered, refusing to take "No" for her answer. She knew that in order to grow spiritually, she too, had to perform her first miracle by changing her fear to faith, her mood of lack to a mood of opulence and prosperity, by changing consciousness (water) into the conditions, circumstances, and experiences she wished to express.

Consciousness, Awareness, Beingness, Principle, Spirit, or whatever Name you give It is the cause of all; it is the only Presence and Power. The Spiritual Power of Spirit within us is the cause and substance of all things. All things—birds, trees, stars, sun, moon, earth, gold, silver, and platinum—are its manifestations. It is the cause and substance of all things. "There is none else."

Understanding this she knew that *water* (consciousness) could become supply in the form of money, true place, or true expression for herself, health for her mother, as well as companionship and fullness of life. She saw this simple—yet profound—truth in the twinkling of an eye, and said to me, "I *accept* my good."

She knew that nothing is hidden from us; all of God is within us, waiting for our discovery and inquiry.

In less than a month this young girl got married. The writer performed the ceremony. I pronounced the words she heard me say over and over again in her meditative, relaxed state, "I now pronounce you man and wife!"

Her husband gave her a check for $24,000 as a wedding present, as well as a trip around the world. Her new expression as a beauty operator was to beautify her home and garden, and make the desert of her mind rejoice and blossom as the rose.

She changed "water into wine." *Water* or her consciousness became charged or conditioned by her constant, true, happy imagery. These images, when sustained regularly, systematically, and with faith in the developing powers of the deeper mind, will come out of the darkness (subconscious mind) into light (objectified on the screen of space).

There is one important rule: Do not expose this newly developed film to the shattering light of fear, doubt, despondency, and worry. Whenever worry or fear knocks at your door, immediately turn to the picture you developed in your mind, and say to yourself, "A beautiful picture is being developed now in the dark house of my mind." Mentally pour on that picture your feeling of joy, faith, and understanding. You know you have operated a psychological, spiritual law; for what is impressed shall be expressed. It is wonderful!

The following is a sure, certain way for developing and manifesting all the material riches and supply you need all the days of your life. If you apply this formula sincerely and honestly, you should be amply rewarded on the external plane. I will illustrate this by telling you of a man who came to see me in London in desperate financial straits. He was a member of the Church of England, and had studied the working of the subconscious mind to some extent.

I told him to say frequently during the day, "God is the source of my supply, and all my needs are met at every moment of time and point of space." Think also of all the animal life in this world, and in all the galaxies of space which are now being taken care of by an Infinite Intelligence. Notice how nature is lavish, extravagant, and bountiful. Think of the fish of the sea which are all being sustained, as well as the birds of the air!"

He began to realize that since he was born, he had been taken care of; fed by his mother; clothed by his father, and watched over by tender, loving parents. This man got a job and was paid in a wonderful way. He reasoned that it was illogical to assume that the Principle of Life which gave him life, and always took care of him would suddenly cease to respond to him.

He realized that he had cut off his own supply by resenting his employer, self-condemnation, criticism of himself, and by his own sense of unworthiness. He had psychologically severed the cord which joined him to the Infinite Source of all things—the Indwelling Spirit or Life Principle, called by some "Consciousness or Awareness."

Man is not fed like the birds; he must consciously commune with the Indwelling Power and Presence, and receive guidance, strength, vitality, and all things necessary for the fulfillment of his needs.

This is the formula which he used to change water into the wine of abundance and financial success. He realized God or the Spiritual Power within him was the cause of all; furthermore he realized that if he could sell himself the idea that wealth was his by Divine right, he would manifest abundance of supply.

The affirmation he used was, "God is the source of my supply. All my financial and other needs are met at every moment of time and point of space; there is always a divine surplus." This simple statement repeated frequently, knowingly, and intelligently conditioned his mind to a prosperity consciousness.

All he had to do was to sell himself this positive idea, in the same way a good salesman has to sell himself on the merits of his product. Such a person is convinced of the integrity of his company, the high quality of the product, the good service which it will give the customer, and the fact that the price is right, etc.

I told him whenever negative thoughts came to his mind, which would happen, not to fight them, quarrel with them in any way, but simply go back to the spiritual, mental formula, and repeat it quietly and lovingly to himself. Negative thoughts came to him in avalanches at times in the form of a flood of negativity. Each time he met them with the positive, firm, loyal conviction: "God supplies all my needs; there is a Divine surplus in my life."

He said as he drove his car, and went through his day's routine, that a host of sundry, miscellaneous, negative concepts crowded his mind from time to time; such as, "There is no hope." "You are broke." Each time such negative thoughts came, he refused their mental admission by turning to the Eternal Source of wealth, health, and all things which he knew to be his own spiritual awareness. Definitely and positively he claimed, "God is the source of my supply, and that supply is mine now!" Or, "There is a Divine solution. God's wealth is my wealth," and other affirmative, positive statements which charged his mind with hope, faith, expectancy, and ultimately a conviction in an ever-flowing fountain of riches supplying all his needs copiously, joyously, and endlessly.

The negative flood of thoughts came to him as often as fifty times in an hour; each time he refused to open the door of his mind to these gangsters, assassins, and thieves which he knew would only rob him of peace, wealth, success, and all good things. Instead he opened the door of his mind to the idea of God's Eternal Life Principle of supply flowing through him as wealth, health, energy, power, and all things necessary to lead a full and happy life here.

As he continued to do this, the second day not so many thieves knocked at his door; the third day, the flow of negative visitors was less; the fourth day, they came intermittently, hoping for admission, but receiving the same mental response: "No entrance! I accept only thoughts and concepts which activate, heal, bless, and inspire my mind!"

He reconditioned his consciousness or mind to a wealth consciousness. "The prince of this world cometh, and hath nothing in me"—This conveys to your mind: The negative thoughts, such as, fear, lack, worry, anxiety came, but they received no response from his mind. He was now immune; God intoxicated, and seized by a divine faith in an ever-expanding consciousness of abundance and financial supply. This man did not lose everything; neither did he go into bankruptcy; he was given extended credit; his business improved; new doors opened up, and he prospered.

Remember always in the prayer-process, you must be loyal to your ideal, purpose, and objective. Many people fail to realize wealth and financial success, because they pray two ways. They affirm God is their supply, and that they are divinely prospered, but a few minutes later they deny their good by saying, "I can't pay this bill." "I can't afford this, that, or the other things." Or they say to themselves, "A jinx is following me." "I can't ever make ends meet." "I never have enough to go around." All such statements are highly destructive, and neutralize your positive prayers. This is what is called, "praying two ways."

You must be faithful to your plan or your goal. You must be true to your knowledge of the spiritual power. Cease making negative marriages, i.e., uniting with negative thoughts, fears, and worries.

Prayer is like a captain directing the course of his ship. You must have a destination. You must know where you are going. The captain of the ship, knowing the laws of navigation, regulates his course accordingly. If the ship is turned from its course by storms or unruly waves, he calmly redirects it along its true course.

*You* are the captain on the bridge, and you are giving the orders in the way of thoughts, feelings, opinions, beliefs, moods, and mental tones. Keep your eye on the beam. *You go where your vision is!* Cease, therefore, looking at all the obstacles, delays, and impediments that would cause you to go off your course. Be definite and positive. Decide where you are going. Know that your mental attitude is the ship which will take you from the mood of lack and limitation, to the mood and feeling of opulence, and to the belief in the inevitable law of God working for you.

Quimby, who was a doctor, a wonderful student, and teacher of the mental and spiritual laws of mind, said, "Man acts as he is acted upon." What moves you now? What is it that determines your response to life? The answer is as follows: Your ideas, beliefs, and opinions activate your mind and condition you to the point that you become, as Quimby stated, "An expression of your beliefs." This illustrates the truth of Quimby's statement: "Man is belief expressed."

Another popular statement of Quimby's was, "Our minds mingle like atmospheres, and each person has his identity in that atmosphere." When you were a child, you were subject to the moods, feelings, beliefs, and the general mental atmosphere of the home. The fears, anxieties, superstitions, as well as the religious faith and convictions of the parents were impressed on your mind.

Let us say the child had been brought up in a poverty-stricken home, in which there was never enough to go around, financially speaking; he heard constantly the complaint of lack and limitation.

You could say, like Salter in his conditioned reflex therapy, that the child was conditioned to poverty. The young man may have a poverty complex based on his early experiences, training, and beliefs, but he can rise above any situation, and become free; this is done through the power of prayer.

I knew a young boy aged 17, who was born in a place called Hell's Kitchen, in New York. He listened to some lectures I was giving in Steinway Hall, New York, at the time. This boy realized that he had been the victim of negative, destructive thinking, and that if he did not redirect his mind along constructive channels, the world-mind with its fears, failures, hates, and jealousies would move in and control him. "Man acts as he is acted upon."

It stands to reason, as Quimby knew, that if man will not take charge of his own house (mind), the propaganda, false beliefs, fears, and worries of the phenomenalistic world will act as a hypnotic spell over him.

We are immersed in the race mind which believes in sickness, death, misfortune, accident, failures, disease, and diverse disasters. Follow the Biblical injunction: "Come out from among them, and be separate." Identify yourself mentally and emotionally with the Eternal Verities which have stood the test of time.

This young man decided to think and plan for himself. He decided to take the Royal Road to Riches by accepting God's abundance here and now, and to fill his mind with spiritual concepts and perceptions. He knew, as he did this, he would automatically crowd out of his mind all negative patterns.

He adopted a simple process called, "scientific imagination." He had a wonderful voice, but it was not cultivated or developed. I told him the image he gave attention to in his mind would be developed in his deeper mind and come to pass. He understood this to be a law of mind—a law of action and reaction—i.e., the response of the deeper mind to the mental picture held in the conscious mind.

This young man would sit down quietly in his room at home; relax his whole body, and vividly imagine himself singing before a microphone. He would actually reach out for the "feel" of the instrument. He would hear me congratulate him on his wonderful contract, and tell him how magnificent his voice was. By giving his attention and devotion to this mental image regularly and systematically, a deep impression was made on his subconscious mind.

A short time elapsed, and an Italian voice instructor in New York gave him free lessons several times a week, because he saw his possibilities. He got a contract which sent him abroad to sing in the salons of Europe, Asia, South Africa, and other places. His financial worries were over; for he also received a wonderful salary. His hidden talents and ability to release them were his real riches. These talents and powers within all of us are God-given; let us release them.

Did you ever say to yourself, "How can I be more useful to my fellow creature?" "How can I contribute more to humanity?"

A minister-friend of mine told me that in his early days he and his church suffered financially. His technique or process was this simple prayer which worked wonders for him, "God reveals to me better ways to present the truths of God to my fellow creature." Money poured in; the mortgage was paid in a few years, and he has never worried about money since.

As you read this chapter, you have now learned that the inner feelings, moods, and beliefs of man always control and govern his external world. The inner movements of the mind control the outer movements. To change the outside, you must change the inside. "As in Heaven, so on earth;" or as in my mind or consciousness, so is it in my body, circumstances, and environment.

The Bible says, "There is nothing hidden that shall not be revealed." For example if you are sick, you are revealing a mental and emotional pattern which is the cause. If you are upset, or if you receive tragic news, notice how you reveal it in your face, eyes, gestures, tonal qualities, also in your gait and posture. As a matter of fact your whole body reveals your inner distress. You could, of course, through mental discipline and prayer, remain absolutely poised, serene, and calm, refusing to betray your hidden feelings or mental states. You could order the muscles of your body to relax, be quiet, and be still; they would have to obey you. Your eyes, face, and lips would not betray any sign of grief, anger, or despondency. On the other hand with a little discipline, through prayer and meditation, you could reverse the entire picture. Even though you had received disturbing news, regardless of its grave nature, you could show and exhibit joy, peace, relaxation, and a vibrant, buoyant nature. No one would ever know that you were the recipient of so-called bad news.

Regardless of what kind of news you received today, you could go to the mirror, look at your face, lips, eyes, and your gestures, as you tell yourself, and imagine you have heard the news of having received a vast fortune. Dramatize it, feel it, thrill to it, and notice how your whole body responds to the inner thrill.

You can reverse any situation through prayer. Busy your mind with the concepts of peace, success, wealth, and happiness. Identify yourself with these ideas mentally, emotionally, and pictorially.

Get a picture of yourself as you want to be; retain that image; sustain it with joy, faith, and expectancy; finally you will succeed in experiencing its manifestation.

I say to people who consult me regarding financial lack to "marry wealth." Some see the point, others do not. As all Bible students know, your wife is what you are mentally joined to, united with, or at one with.

In other words what you conceive and believe, you give it conception. If you believe the world is cold, cruel, and harsh, that it is a "dog eat dog" way of life, that is your concept; you are married to it, and you will have children or issue by that marriage. The children from such a mental marriage or belief will be your experiences, conditions, and circumstances together with all other events in your life. All your experiences and reactions to life will be the image and likeness of the ideas which fathered them.

Look at the many wives the average man is living with, such as fear, doubt, anxiety, criticism, jealousy, and anger; these play havoc with his mind. Marry wealth by claiming, feeling, and believing: "God supplies all my needs according to his riches in glory." Or take the following statement, and repeat it over and over again knowingly until your consciousness is conditioned by it, or it becomes a part of your meditation: "I am divinely expressed, and I have a wonderful income." Do not say this in a parrot-like fashion, but know that your train of thought is being engraved in your deeper mind, and it becomes a conditioned state of consciousness. Let the phrase become meaningful to you. Pour life, love, and feeling on it, making it alive.

One of my class-students recently opened a restaurant. He phoned me saying that he got married to a restaurant; he meant that he had made up his mind to be very successful, diligent, and persevering, and to see that his business prospered. This man's *wife* (mental) was his belief in the accomplishment of his desire or wish.

Identify yourself with your aim in life, and cease mental marriages with criticism, self-condemnation, anger, fear, and worry. Give attention to your chosen ideal, being full of faith and confidence in the inevitable law of prosperity and success. You will accomplish nothing by loving your ideal one minute, and denying it the next minute; this is like mixing acid and an alkali; for you will get an inert substance. In going along the Royal Road to Riches, you must be faithful to your chosen ideal (your wife).

We find illustrations in the Bible relating to these same truths. For instance, "Eve came out of Adam's rib." *Your rib* is your concept, desire, idea, plan, goal, or aim in life.

*Eve* means the emotion, feeling nature, or the inner tone. In other words you must mother the idea. The idea must be mothered, loved, and felt as true, in order to manifest your aim in life.

The *idea* is the father; the *emotion* is the mother; this is the marriage feast which is always taking place in your mind.

Ouspensky spoke of the third element which entered in or was formed following the union of your desire and feeling. He called it the neutral element. We may call it "peace"; for God is Peace.

The Bible says, "And the government shall be on his shoulders." In other words let Divine Wisdom be your guide. Let the subjective Wisdom within you lead, guide, and govern you in all your ways. Turn over your request to this Indwelling Presence knowing in your heart and soul that it will dissipate the anxiety, heal the wound, and restore your soul to equanimity and tranquility. Open your mind and heart, and say, "God is my pilot. He leads me. He prospers me. He is my counsellor." Let your prayer be night and morning, "I am a channel through which God's riches flow ceaselessly, copiously, and freely." Write that prayer in your heart, inscribe it in your mind. Keep on the beam of God's glory!

The man who does not know the inner workings of his own mind is full of burdens, anxieties, and worries; for he has not learned how to cast his burden on the Indwelling Presence, and go free.

The Zen monk was asked by his disciple, "What is Truth?" He replied in a symbolic way by taking the bag off his back, and placing it on the ground.

The disciple then asked him, "Master, how does it work?"

The Zen monk still silent, placed the bag on his back, and walked on down the road singing to himself. The bag is your burden, or your problem. You cast it on the subjective Wisdom which knows all, and has the "know-how" of accomplishment. It knows only the answer.

*Placing the bag again on his back* means though I still have the problem, I now have mental rest and relief from the burden, because I have invoked the Divine Wisdom on my behalf; therefore I sing the song of triumph, knowing that the answer to my prayer is on the way, and I sing for the joy that is set before me. It is wonderful.

"Every man at the beginning doth set forth good wine; and when men have well drunk, then that which is worse; but thou hast kept the good wine until now." This is true of every man when he first enters a knowledge of the laws of mind. He sets out with high spirits and ambitions. He is the new broom which sweeps clean, and he is full of good intentions; oftentimes he forgets the Source of power. He does not remain faithful to the Principle within him, which is scientific and effectual, that would lift him out of his negative experiences, and set him on the high road to freedom and peace of mind. He begins to indulge mentally and emotionally with ideas and thoughts extraneous to his announced aim and goal. In other words he is not faithful to his ideal or wife.

Know that the subjective or deeper self within you will accept your request, and being the great fabricator, it will bring it to pass in its own way. All you do is release your request with faith and confidence, in the same way you would cast a seed on the ground, or mail a letter to a friend, knowing the answer would come.

Did you ever go between two great rocks and listen to the echo of your voice? This is the way the Life Principle within you answers. You will hear the echo of your own voice. Your voice is your inner, mental movement of the mind—your inner, psychological journey where you feasted mentally on an idea until you were full; then you rested.

Knowing this law and how to use it, be sure you never become drunk with power, arrogance, pride, or conceit. Use the law to bless, heal, inspire, and lift up others, as well as yourself.

Man misuses the law by selfishly taking advantage of his fellow man; if you do, you hurt and attract loss to yourself. Power, security, and riches are not to be obtained externally. They come from the treasure-house of eternity within. We should realize that the *good wine* is always present, for God is the Eternal Now. Regardless of present circumstances, you can prove your good is ever-present by detaching yourself mentally from the problem, going on the High Watch, and go about your Father's business.

*To go on the High Watch* is to envision your good, to dwell on the new concept of yourself, to become married to it, and sustain the happy mood by remaining faithful—full of faith every step of the way—knowing that the wine of joy, the answered prayer, is on the way. "Now is the day of salvation." "The kingdom of heaven is at hand." "Thou hast kept the good wine until now."

You can—this moment—travel psychologically in your mind, and enter mentally through divine imagination into any desired state. The wealth, health, or invention you wish to introduce are all invisible first. Everything comes out of the Invisible. You must subjectively possess riches, before you can objectively possess wealth. The feeling of wealth produces wealth; for wealth is a state of consciousness. *A state of consciousness* is how you think, feel, believe, and what you mentally give consent to.

A teacher in California receiving over five or six thousand dollars a year looked in a window at a beautiful ermine coat that was priced at $8,000. She said, "It would take me years to save that amount of money. I could never afford it. Oh, how I want it!" She listened to our lectures on Sunday mornings. By ceasing to marry these negative concepts, she learned that she could have a coat, car, or anything she wished without hurting anybody on the face of the earth. I told her to imagine she had the coat on, to feel its beautiful fur, and to get the feel of it on her. She began to use the power of her imagination prior to sleep at night. She put the imaginary coat on her, fondled it, caressed it, like a child does with her doll. She continued to do this, and finally felt the thrill of it all.

She went to sleep every night wearing this imaginary coat, and being so happy in possessing it. Three months went by, and nothing happened. She was about to waver, but she reminded herself that it is the sustained mood which demonstrates. "He who perseveres to the end shall be saved." The solution will come to the person who does not waver, but always goes about with the perfume of His Presence with him. The answer comes to the man who walks in the light that "It is done!" You are always using the *perfume of His Presence* when you sustain the happy, joyous mood of expectancy knowing your good is on the way. You saw it on the unseen, and you *know* you will see it in the seen.

The sequel to the teacher's drama of the mind is interesting. One Sunday morning after our lecture, a man accidently stepped on her toe, apologized profusely, asked her where she lived, and offered to drive her home. She accepted gladly. Shortly after he proposed marriage; gave her a beautiful diamond ring, and said to her, "I saw the most wonderful coat; you would simply look radiant wearing it!" It was the coat she admired three months previously. (The salesman said over one hundred wealthy women looked at the coat, admired it immensely, but for some reason always selected another garment.)

Through your capacity to choose, imagine the reality of what you have selected, and through faith and perseverance, you can realize your goal in life.

All the riches of heaven are here now within you waiting to be released. Peace, joy, love, guidance, inspiration, goodwill, and abundance all exist now. All that is necessary in order to express God's riches is for you to leave the present now (your limitation), enter into the mental vision or picture, and in a happy, joyous mood become one with your ideal. Having seen and felt your good in moments of high exaltation, you know that in a little while you shall see your ideal objectively as you walk through time and space. As within, so without. As above, so below. As in heaven so on earth. In other words you will see your beliefs expressed. Man *is* belief expressed!

# The Power of Your Subconscious Mind

(1963)

## by Joseph Murphy

*The Original Classic*

## Contents

Introduction   *The Power of Thought* by Mitch Horowitz   950
Chapter One   The Treasure House Within You   951
Chapter Two   How Your Mind Works   952
Chapter Three   The Miracle-Working Power of Your Subconscious Mind   953
Chapter Four   Prayer and Your Subconscious Mind   954
Chapter Five   How to Get the Results You Want   955
Chapter Six   How to Use Your Subconscious Mind for Wealth   955
Chapter Seven   Your Subconscious Mind as a Partner in Career Success   957
Chapter Eight   The Inventiveness of Your Subconscious Mind   958
Chapter Nine   Your Subconscious Mind and Marital Problems   959
Chapter Ten   Your Subconscious Mind and Happiness   960
Chapter Eleven   Your Subconscious Mind and Harmonious Relationships   961
Chapter Twelve   How Your Subconscious Mind Removes Mental Blocks   962
Chapter Thirteen   How to Stay Young in Spirit Forever   964

## Introduction
# The Power of Thought

This may be one of the most personally important books you ever encounter. I say that not because I agree with every one of its premises or ideas. But, rather, because author and New Thought minister Joseph Murphy identifies and expands upon one immensely important and undervalued principle: *What you think dramatically affects your quality of life.*

This idea has been restated from antiquity to the present. John Milton put it this way in *Paradise Lost*: "The mind is its own place, and in it self can make a Heav'n of Hell, a Hell of Heav'n."

Murphy presents this principle as an absolute. He argues that thought governs health, finances, relationships, and all facets of life. I am personally unconvinced that *every* element of existence yields to thought alone. But within the folds of this idea—that mind is the master builder—can be found great truths. They are yours to discover, test, and benefit from. All that is required is to change how you think.

Murphy's philosophy is profoundly simple—but it is not for the weak or myopic. If you take seriously what you find in this book—and I urge you to—you will discover that redirecting your thoughts toward resiliency and constructiveness requires a lifetime of effort. But it is a task worthy of every motivated, mature person.

You will also learn that your emotions must be brought into play for any real self-change to occur. Emotion is more powerful than thought—never confuse or conflate the two. The mind says, "be satisfied with your portion"—emotion shouts, "I want more!" The mind says, "be calm"—emotion wants to run away. The mind says, "I'm happy for my neighbor"—emotion feels envy. Murphy supplies exercises to help align your emotions and thoughts in pursuit of a personal goal.

Murphy's message that *new thought means new life* has touched countless people since this book first appeared in 1963. This is not because Murphy's outlook is cloying or wishful; but because it is essentially true. We *all* feel that we should be practicing more dignified, generous, and self-respecting patterns of thought, tones of speech, and person-to-person relations. We harbor the conviction that we are *not* leading the lives we should be—that our abilities are underdeveloped, our decisions too hesitant and timorous, and our attitudes too selfish. Almost all of us sense the potential of a larger existence within us. This is a near-universal instinct.

*The Power of Your Subconscious Mind* is an instruction manual toward seeking that greater scale of life. Pay close attention to the book's principles, methods, and exercises. And, above all, *use them*.

It may be the most important step you ever take.

—Mitch Horowitz

## Chapter One
# The Treasure House Within You

What, in your opinion, is the master secret of the ages? Atomic power? Thermonuclear energy? Interplanetary travel? No—not any of these. What, then, is the master secret? Where can one find it, and how can it be contacted and brought into action? The answer is extraordinarily simple. The secret is the marvelous, miracle-working power of your own subconscious mind.

You can bring into your life more ability, more health, more wealth, and more happiness by learning to contact and release the hidden forces of your subconscious.

As you follow the simple techniques in this book, you can gain the necessary knowledge and understanding to unlock your subconscious depths. Within them are infinite wisdom, infinite power, and infinite supply. Begin now to recognize these potentialities of your deeper mind, and they will take form in the world without.

The infinite intelligence within your subconscious can reveal to you everything you need to know at every moment, provided you are open-minded and receptive. You can receive new thoughts and ideas enabling you to bring forth new inventions, make new discoveries, or write plays and books. You can attract the ideal companion. You can acquire resources and wealth. You can move forward in abundance, security, joy, and dominion.

It is your *right* to discover this inner world of thought. Its miracle-working powers and eternal laws of life existed before you were born, before any religion or church appeared, and before the world itself came into being. It is with these thoughts that I urge you in the following chapters to lay hold of this wonderful, magical, transforming power that is your subconscious mind.

Chapter Two

# How Your Mind Works

There are two levels of mind, conscious and subconscious. You think with your rational, conscious mind—and whatever you habitually think seeps down into your subconscious mind, which creates according to the nature of your thoughts.

Once the subconscious mind accepts an idea, it begins to execute it. Your subconscious does not engage in *proving* whether your thoughts are good or bad, but responds according to the *nature* of your thoughts or suggestions. If you consciously assume something is true, even though it may be false, your subconscious will accept it and proceed to bring about results that must necessarily follow.

Your conscious mind is the "watchman at the gate." Its chief function is to protect your subconscious from false impressions. You now know one of the basic laws of mind: Your subconscious is amenable to *suggestion*.

From infancy on, many of us have been given negative suggestions. Not knowing how to thwart them, we unconsciously accepted them. Here are some of the negative suggestions: "You can't." "You'll never amount to anything." "You'll fail." "You haven't got a chance." "It's no use." "It's not what you know, but who you know." "You're too old now." And so on.

If you look back, you can easily recall how parents, friends, relatives, teachers, and associates contributed to a campaign of negative suggestions. Study the things said to you, and you will discover that much of it was said to control you or instill fear in you. Check regularly on the negative suggestions that people make to you today. You do not have to be influenced by destructive suggestion.

Never say: "I can't." Overcome fear of failure by substituting the following statement: *I can do all things through the power of my subconscious mind.*

Never allow others to think for you. Choose your own thoughts, and make your own decisions. Always remember that *you have the capacity to choose*. Choose life! Choose love! Choose health! Choose happiness! Whatever your conscious mind assumes and believes, your subconscious mind accepts and brings to pass.

Chapter Three

# The Miracle-Working Power of Your Subconscious Mind

The power of your subconscious mind is enormous. It inspires you, guides you, and reveals to you names, facts, and scenes from the storehouse of memory.

Your subconscious mind never sleeps or rests. You can discover its miracle-working power by plainly stating to your subconscious prior to sleep that you wish to accomplish a certain thing. You will be delighted to find that forces within you will be released, leading to the desired answer or result.

William James, the father of American psychology, said that the power to move the world resides within your subconscious mind. Your subconscious is at one with infinite intelligence and boundless wisdom. It is fed by hidden springs. The law of life operates through it. Whatever you impress upon your subconscious, it will move heaven and earth to bring it to pass. You must, therefore, impress it with right ideas and constructive thoughts.

What is your idea or feeling about yourself right now? Every part of your being expresses that idea. Your body, vitality, finances, friends, and social status are a perfect reflection of the idea you have of yourself. What is impressed in your subconscious mind is expressed in all phases of your life.

Worry, anxiety, and fear can interfere with the normal rhythm of your heart, lungs, and other organs. Feed your subconscious mind with thoughts of harmony, health, and peace, and all the functions of your body will become normal again.

Feel the thrill of accomplishment, imagine the happy ending or solution to your problem, and what you imagine and feel will be accepted by your subconscious mind and brought to pass. The life principle will flow through you rhythmically and harmoniously as you consciously affirm: *I believe that the subconscious power that gave me this desire is now fulfilling it through me.*

Your subconscious mind can and will accomplish as much as you allow it to.

## Chapter Four

# Prayer and Your Subconscious Mind

In building the Golden Gate Bridge, the chief engineer understood mathematical principles, stresses, and strains. Secondly, he had a picture of the ideal bridge across the bay. The third step was his application of tried and proven methods, which were implemented until the bridge took form. Likewise, there exist techniques and methods by which your prayers are actualized.

Prayer is the formulation of an idea concerning something you wish to accomplish. Your desire *is* your prayer. It comes out of your deepest needs and it reveals what you want in life. *Blessed are they that hunger and thirst after righteousness: for they shall be filled.* That is really prayer: life's hunger and thirst for peace, harmony, health, joy, and other blessings.

We will now explore the "passing over" technique for impregnating the subconscious mind with your desire. This involves inducing the subconscious to *take over* your prayer request as handed it by the conscious mind. This *passing over* is best accomplished in a reverie-like state. Know that within your deeper mind exist infinite intelligence and infinite power. Just calmly think over what you want; and see it coming into fuller fruition from this moment forward.

Your prayer—*your mental act*—must be accepted as an image in your mind before the power of your subconscious will play upon it and make it operative. You must reach a point of *acceptance* in your mind, an unqualified and undisputed state of agreement.

This contemplation should be accompanied by a feeling of joy and restfulness in foreseeing the accomplishment of your desire. The basis for the art and science of true prayer is your knowledge and complete confidence that the movement of your conscious mind will gain a definite response from your subconscious mind.

The easiest and most obvious way to formulate an idea is to visualize it, to see it in your mind's eye as vividly as if it were alive. You can see with the naked eye only what already exists in the external world; in a similar way, that which you can visualize in your mind's eye *already exists* in the infinite realms of thought. Any picture that you have in your mind is *the substance of things hoped for and the evidence of things not seen.* What you form in your imagination is as real as any part of your body.

Your ideas and thoughts are *real*—and will one day appear in the objective world if you remain faithful to your mental image.

## Chapter Five
# How to Get the Results You Want

The principle reasons for failure when trying to tap your subconscious are: 1) lack of confidence, and 2) too much effort.

Many people block answers to their prayers by failing to fully comprehend the nature of their subconscious. When you know how your mind functions, you gain a measure of *confidence*. You must remember that whenever your subconscious accepts an idea, it immediately begins to execute it. It uses all its mighty resources to that end, and mobilizes all the mental and spiritual faculties of your deeper mind. This law is true for good ideas or bad. Consequently, if you use it negatively, it brings trouble, failure, and confusion. When you use it constructively, it brings guidance, freedom, and peace.

The right answer is inevitable when your thoughts are constructive and loving. The only thing you have to do to overcome failure is to get your subconscious to accept your idea or request by *feeling its reality now*, and the law of your mind will do the rest. Turn over the request with faith and confidence, and your subconscious will take over and see it through.

You will always fail to get results by trying to use *mental coercion*—your subconscious does not respond to coercion; it responds to your faith or conscious-mind acceptance. Relaxation is the key. *Easy does it*. Do not be concerned with details and means, but rest in the assured end.

*Feeling* is the touchstone of all subconscious demonstration. Your new idea must be *felt subjectively*, not in the future but in a finished state, as coming about now. Get the *feel* of the happy solution to your problem. Remember how you felt in the past when you solved a major problem or recovered from a serious illness. Live in this feeling, and your subconscious depths will bring it to pass.

## Chapter Six
# How to Use Your Subconscious Mind for Wealth

Wealth is a subconscious conviction on the part of the individual. You will not become a millionaire by saying, "I am a millionaire, I am a millionaire." Rather, you will *grow into a wealth consciousness* by building into your mentality the idea of wealth and abundance.

Perhaps you are saying to yourself now, "I need wealth and success." Follow these steps: Repeat for about five minutes to yourself three or four times a day, "Wealth—Success." These words have tremendous power. They represent the inner power of the subconscious. Anchor your mind on this substantial power within you; then corresponding conditions and circumstances will be manifested in your life.

Again, you are not merely saying, "I am wealthy." You are dwelling on real powers within you. There is no conflict in the mind when you say, "Wealth." Furthermore, the *feeling* of wealth will well up within you as you dwell on the idea of wealth.

I have talked to many people during the past thirty-five years whose usual complaint is: "I have said for weeks and months, 'I am wealthy, I am prosperous,' and nothing has happened." I discovered that when they said, "I am prosperous, I am wealthy," they felt within that they were lying to themselves. One man told me, "I have affirmed that I am prosperous until I am tired. Things are now worse. I knew when I made that statement that it was obviously not true." His statements were rejected by the conscious mind, and the very opposite of what he outwardly affirmed was made manifest.

Your affirmation succeeds best when it is specific and when it does not produce a mental conflict or argument; hence, the statements made by this man made matters worse because they suggested his lack. Your subconscious mind accepts what you really feel to be true, not just idle words or statements.

Here is the ideal way to overcome this conflict. Make this statement frequently, particularly prior to sleep: *By day and by night I am being prospered in all of my interests.* This affirmation will not arouse any argument because it does not contradict your subconscious mind's impression of financial lack.

Many people tell themselves, "I deserve a higher salary." I believe that most people are, in fact, underpaid. One reason why many people do not have more money is that they are silently or openly condemning it. They call money "filthy lucre" or say "love of money is the root of all evil." Another reason they do not prosper is that they have a sneaky subconscious feeling that there is some virtue in poverty. This subconscious pattern may be due to early childhood training, superstition, or a mistaken interpretation of Scripture

Cleanse your mind of all conflicting beliefs about money. Do not regard money as evil or filthy. If you do, you cause it to take wings and fly away from you. You lose what you condemn.

At the same time, do not make a god of money. It is only a symbol. Remember that the real riches are in your mind. You are here to lead a balanced life—and that includes acquiring all the money you need.

There is one emotion that causes lack of wealth in the lives of many. Most people learn this the hard way. It is envy. To entertain envious thoughts is devastating; it places you in a negative position in which wealth flows *from* you rather than *to* you. If you are ever annoyed or irritated by the prosperity of another, claim immediately that you truly wish him greater wealth in every possible way. This will neutralize your negative thoughts, and cause an ever-greater measure of wealth to flow to you.

## Chapter Seven
# Your Subconscious Mind as a Partner in Career Success

Let us discuss three steps to success. The first step is to discover the thing you love to do, and then do it. Success is in loving your work.

Some may say, "How can I put the first step into operation? I do not know what I should do." In such a case, pray for guidance as follows: *The infinite intelligence of my subconscious mind reveals to me my true place in life.* Repeat this prayer quietly, positively, and lovingly to your deeper mind. As you persist with faith and confidence, the answer will come to you as a feeling, a hunch, or a tendency in a certain direction. It will come to you clearly and in peace, as an inner awareness.

The second step to success is to specialize in some particular branch of work, and to know more about it than anyone else. For example, if a young man chooses chemistry as his profession, he should concentrate on one of the many branches in that field. He should give all of his time and attention to his chosen specialty. He should become sufficiently enthusiastic to know all there is about it; if possible, he should know more than anyone else.

The third step is the most important. You must be certain that the thing you want to do does not build your success only. *Your desire must not be selfish; it must benefit humanity.* The path of a complete circuit must be formed. In other words, your idea must go forth with the purpose of blessing or serving the world. It will then come back to you pressed down, shaken together, and running over. If it is to benefit you alone, the circle or circuit is not formed.

A successful person loves his work and expresses himself fully. True success is contingent upon a higher ideal than mere accumulation of riches. The person of success is one who possesses great psychological and spiritual understanding, and whose work benefits others.

## Chapter Eight
# The Inventiveness of Your Subconscious Mind

Nikola Tesla was a brilliant electrical scientist who brought forth amazing inventions in the late-nineteenth and early twentieth centuries. When an idea for a new invention entered Tesla's mind, he would build it up in his imagination, knowing that his subconscious would construct and reveal to his conscious mind all the parts needed for its manufacture. Through quietly contemplating every possible improvement, he spent no time in correcting defects, and was able to give technicians perfect plans for the product.

"Invariably," he said, "my device works as I imagined it should. In twenty years there has not been a single exception."

When you have what you term "a difficult decision" to make, or when you fail to see the solution to a problem, begin at once to think constructively about it. If you are fearful and worried, you are not really thinking. True thinking is free from fear.

Here is a simple technique to receive inner guidance on any subject: Quiet the mind and still the body. Go to a quiet place where you won't be disturbed—preferably lying on a bed, sofa, or in a recliner. Mobilize your attention; focus your thoughts on the solution to the problem. Try to solve it with your conscious mind. Think how happy you would be with the perfect solution. Sense the feeling you would have if the right answer were yours now. Let your mind play with this mood in a relaxed way; then drop off to sleep. When you awaken, and do not have the answer, get busy about something else. When you are preoccupied with something else, the answer will probably come into your mind like toast pops from out of a toaster.

The secret of guidance or right action is to mentally devote yourself to the right answer, until you find its response in you. The response is a feeling, an inner awareness, and an overpowering hunch whereby *you know that you know*. In such cases, you have used the infinite power of your subconscious to the point where *it begins to use you*. You cannot fail or make a false step while operating under the subconscious wisdom within you.

## Chapter Nine
# Your Subconscious Mind and Marital Problems

Recently a young couple, married for only a few months, was seeking a divorce. I discovered that the young man had a constant fear that his wife would leave him. He expected rejection, and he believed that she would be unfaithful. These thoughts haunted him and became an obsession. His mental attitude was one of separation and suspicion. His own feeling of loss and separation operated through the relationship. This brought about a condition in accordance with the mental pattern behind it.

His wife left home and asked for a divorce, which is what he feared and believed would happen.

Divorce occurs first in the mind; the legal proceedings follow. These two young people were full of resentment, fear, suspicion, and anger. These attitudes weaken and debilitate the whole being. The couple began to realize what they had been doing with their minds. These two people returned together at my suggestion and experimented with *prayer therapy*, a method we will learn.

Each one practiced radiating to the other love, peace, harmony, health, and good will. They alternated in reading the Psalms every night. Their marriage began growing more beautiful every day.

Now, divorce is an individual problem. It cannot be generalized. In some cases, no marriage should have occurred to begin with. In other cases, divorce is not the solution. Divorce may be right for one person and wrong for another. A divorced woman may be far more sincere and noble than many of her married sisters, who are perhaps living a lie.

For couples that wish to *stay together* the solution is to *pray together*. Here is a three-step program in prayer therapy.

## First

Never carry over from one day to another accumulated irritations arising from little disappointments. Forgive each other for any sharpness before you retire at night. The moment you awaken, claim infinite intelligence is guiding you in all ways. Send out thoughts of peace, harmony, and love to your partner, to all family members, and to the entire world.

## Second

Say grace at breakfast. Give thanks for the wonderful food, for your abundance, and for all your blessings. Make sure that no problems, worries, or arguments enter into the table conversation; the same applies at dinnertime. Say to your partner, "I appreciate all you are doing, and I radiate love and good will to you all day long."

## Third

Spouses should alternate in praying each night. Do not take your marriage partner for granted. Show your appreciation and love. Think appreciation and good will, rather than condemnation, criticism, and nagging. Before going to sleep read the 23rd, 27th, and 91st Psalms; the 11th chapter of Hebrews; the 13th chapter of I Corinthians; and other great texts of the Bible.

As you practice these steps, your marriage will grow more blessed through the years.

## Chapter Ten
# Your Subconscious Mind and Happiness

There is a phrase in the Bible: *Choose ye this day whom ye will serve.*

You have the freedom to *choose happiness*. This may seem extraordinarily simple—and it is. Perhaps this is why so many people stumble over the way to happiness; they do not see the simplicity of the key to happiness. The great things of life are simple, dynamic, and creative.

St. Paul reveals how you can think your way into a life of dynamic power and happiness in these words: *Finally, brethren, whatsoever things are true, whatsoever things are honest, whatsoever things are just, whatsoever things are pure, whatsoever things are lovely, whatsoever things are of good report; if there be any virtue, and if there be any praise, think on these things.* (Philippians 4:8)

There is one very important point about being happy. You must sincerely *desire* to be happy. Some people have been depressed, dejected, and unhappy for so long that when they are suddenly made happy by some joyous news they actually feel uncomfortable. They have become so accustomed to the old mental patterns that they do not feel at home being happy. They long for the familiar depressed state.

Begin now to choose happiness. Here is how: When you open your eyes in the morning, say to yourself: *Divine order takes charge of my life today and every day. All things work together for good for me today. This is a new and wonderful day for me. There will never be another day like this one. I am divinely guided all day long, and whatever I do will prosper. Divine love surrounds me, enfolds me, and enwraps me, and I go forth in peace. Whenever my attention wanders away from what is good and constructive, I will immediately bring it back to the contemplation of that which is lovely and of good report. I am a spiritual and mental magnet attracting to myself all things that bless and prosper me. I am going to be a wonderful success in all my undertakings today. I am definitely going to be happy all day long.*

Start each day in this manner; you will then be choosing happiness.

## Chapter Eleven
# Your Subconscious Mind and Harmonious Relationships

Matthew 7:12 says, *All things whatsoever ye would that men should do unto you, do ye even so to them.*

This passage has outer and inner meanings. We are interested in its inner meaning, which is: As you would that men should *think* about you, think about them. As you would that men should *feel* about you, feel about them. As you would want men to *act* toward you, act toward them.

For example, you may be polite and courteous to someone in your office, but inside you are critical and resentful. Such negative thoughts are highly destructive to you. You are actually taking mental poisons, which rob you of enthusiasm, strength, guidance, and good will. These negative thoughts and emotions sink into your subconscious, and cause you all kinds of difficulties and maladies.

Matthew 7:1-2 says, *Judge not, that ye not be judged. For with what judgment ye judge, ye shall be judged; and with what measure ye shall mete, it shall be measured to you again.*

The study and application of these verses, and their inner truth, provides the key to harmonious relations. To judge is to think, to reach a mental verdict or conclusion in your mind. Your thoughts are creative, therefore, you actually create in your own experience what you think and feel about another person. It is also true that the suggestion you give to another, you give to yourself.

Now, there *are* difficult people in the world who are twisted and distorted mentally. They are malconditioned. Many are mental delinquents, argumentative, uncooperative, cantankerous, and cynical. They are sick psychologically. Many people have deformed and distorted minds, probably warped during childhood. Many have congenital deformities. You would not condemn a person who had tuberculosis, nor should you condemn someone who is mentally ill. You should have compassion and understanding. *To understand all is to forgive all.*

At the same time, do not permit people to take advantage of you and gain their point by temper tantrums, crying jags, or so-called heart attacks. These people are dictators who try to enslave you and make you do their bidding. Be firm but kind, and refuse to yield. *Appeasement never wins.* You are here to fulfill your ideal and to remain true to the eternal verities and spiritual values of life.

Give no one the power to deflect you from your goal, your aim in life, which is to express your hidden talents to the world, to serve humanity, and to reveal more and more of God's wisdom, truth, and beauty. Know definitely that whatever contributes to your peace, happiness, and fulfillment must, of necessity, bless all who walk the earth. The harmony of the part is the harmony of the whole, for the whole is in the part, and the part in the whole.

## Chapter Twelve
# How Your Subconscious Mind Removes Mental Blocks

A young man asked Socrates how he could get wisdom. Socrates replied, "Come with me." He took the lad to a river, pushed the boy's head under the water, held it there until the boy was gasping for air, then relaxed and released his head. When the boy regained his composure, the teacher asked, "What did you desire most when you were under water?"

"I wanted air," said the boy.

Socrates told him, "When you want wisdom as much as you wanted air, you will receive it."

Likewise, when you possess an intense desire to overcome any block or addiction, and you reach a clear-cut decision that there is a way out, and that is the course you wish to follow, then victory and triumph are assured.

If you are an alcoholic or drug addict, begin by admitting it. Do not dodge the issue. Many people remain alcoholics because they refuse to admit it. If you have a burning desire to free yourself from any destructive habit, you are fifty-one percent healed. When you have a greater desire to give up a habit than to continue it, you will gain complete freedom.

Whatever thought you anchor the mind upon, the mind magnifies. If you engage the mind on the concept of freedom from habit and peace of mind, you generate feelings that gradually emotionalize the concept of freedom and peace. Whatever idea you emotionalize is accepted by your subconscious and brought to pass.

Use these steps to help cope with addiction:

### First

Get still; quiet the wheels of the mind. Enter into a sleepy, drowsy state. In this relaxed, peaceful, receptive state you are preparing for the second step.

### Second

Take a brief phrase, which can readily be graven on the memory, and repeat it over and over as a lullaby. Use the phrase: *Sobriety and peace of mind are mine now, and I give thanks.* To prevent the mind from wandering, repeat the phrase aloud or sketch its pronunciation with your lips and tongue as you say it mentally. This helps its entry into your subconscious. Do this for five minutes or more. You will find a deep emotional response.

### Third

Just before going to sleep, imagine a friend or loved one in front of you. Your eyes closed, you are relaxed and at peace. The loved one or friend is subjectively present, and is saying to you, "Congratulations!" You see the smile; you hear the voice. You mentally touch the hand; it is all vivid and real. The word "congratulations" implies *complete freedom*. Hear it over and over until you get the subconscious reaction that satisfies.

## Chapter Thirteen
# How to Stay Young in Spirit Forever

Your subconscious never grows old. It is part of the universal mind of God, which was never born and will never die.

Patience, kindness, veracity, humility, good will, harmony, and brotherly love are eternal attributes, which never age. If you continue to generate these qualities, you will remain young in spirit.

During my many years of public life, I have studied the careers of famous people who have continued their productivity well beyond the normal span of life. Some achieved their greatness in old age. I have also met and known countless individuals of no prominence who, in their lesser sphere, belong to those hardy mortals who have proven that old age of itself does not destroy the creative powers of the mind and body.

My father learned French at sixty-five, and became an authority on it at seventy. He made a study of Gaelic when he was over sixty, and became a well-regarded teacher of the subject. He assisted my sister in a school of higher learning and continued to do so until he passed away at ninety-nine. His mind was as clear at ninety-nine as it was at twenty. Moreover, his handwriting and reasoning powers improved with age.

A Hollywood screenwriter told me that he had to write scripts that would cater to the twelve-year-old mind. This is a tragic state of affairs if the great masses of people are expected to be emotionally and spiritually mature. It means the emphasis is placed on youth in spite of how youth stands for inexperience, lack of discernment, and hasty judgment.

Old age really means the contemplation of the truths of God from the highest standpoint. Realize that you are on an endless journey, a series of important steps in the ceaseless, tireless, endless ocean of life. Then, with the Psalmist, you will say, *They shall still bring forth fruit in old age; they shall be fat and flourishing.* (Psalm 92:14)

You are a child of Infinite Life, which knows no end, a child of Eternity.

# The Million Dollar Secret Hidden in Your Mind

(1963)

## by Anthony Norvell

*The Lost Classic on How to Control Your Thoughts for Wealth, Power, and Mastery*

### Contents

Introduction   *A Better Path to Power* by Mitch Horowitz   966
Chapter One   Dynamic Thinkers Rule the World   967
Chapter Two   The Undiscovered Genius Within Your Mind   968
Chapter Three   You Are Greater Than You Think   970
Chapter Four   Tap the Hidden Treasures Within Your Mind   971
Chapter Five   Magnetism, the Law of Universal Attraction   973
Chapter Six   The Magic Genie Within Your Subconscious Mind   974
Chapter Seven   Duplicate the Power of the Great Men of History   977
Chapter Eight   The Million-Dollar Personality That Wins   978
Chapter Nine   Ten Steps That Can Make You a Mental Giant   979
Chapter Ten   Become a Receiving Station for Great Ideas   983
Chapter Eleven   How to Seek and Win the Aid of Important People   985
Chapter Twelve   Take These Seven Steps Up the Ladder of Success   988

## Introduction
# A Better Path to Power

You may have noticed a lot of books on attaining power making the rounds lately. Many of them, in my view, are unappealing. They encourage the pursuit of success without nobility, proffering methods like taking credit for other people's efforts or ideas, intimidating acquaintances, withholding information, and being a general sneak.

There is a better way. And it appears in the condensation you are about to experience of an overlooked and underestimated work from 1963: *The Million Dollar Secret Hidden in Your Mind*. Its author, Anthony Norvell, was a jack-of-all-trades success guru who reached his highest watermark with this practical, shrewd, and principled book. In it, Norvell makes memorable and substantive points about the non-exploitative pursuit of worldly success.

Norvell wrote with more edge than a Dale Carnegie, but always with an eye on legitimate personal growth. For example, Norvell pushes you to cultivate influence through the "law of proximity," which means seeking the company of people who encourage your finest traits, provide good examples to emulate or imitate, do not indulge your lowest habits, and challenge you to match them in mental acumen, not in money. Norvell observed how the most retrograde influences in your life are likely to come from "old neighborhood" friends and acquaintances, who forever see you as you were in childhood, and who nudge you toward past, and often dysfunctional, patterns of behavior.

Here are some of my favorite Norvell aphorisms. They may seem elementary but their meaning is deeper than may first appear.

- "Most people have a tendency to minimize themselves and their abilities."
- "To be great, you must dwell in the company of great thoughts and high ideals."
- "Do not be afraid to ask important people to help you."
- "Your subconscious mind will give you valuable ideas, but if you do not write them down, they leave suddenly, and it is difficult to recall them again."
- "Your mind likes *definiteness*. Give yourself a five-year plan for study, growth, and evolvement."
- "You must create a need in your life for the things you want."
- "Determine that you will never use your money for any destructive or degrading act."

- *"Know what you want of life."*
- "You build your sense of self-importance by studying constantly."

Yes, there are more sophisticated works of mental therapeutics than Anthony Norvell's. You can read the essays of Ralph Waldo Emerson and William James (and you should); you can approach the complex metaphysics of Mary Baker Eddy and Thomas Troward; or you can immerse yourself in the luminous spiritual visions of Neville Goddard and Ernest Holmes. But there exists in Norvell's work a sapling of all those figures. What's more, Norvell writes with a delightful, infectious simplicity.

I often think of how to reply when asked to recommend a single book on mind power. This could be such a book. It is easily digestible and surprisingly broad in scope. You'll enjoy its ideas—but, above all, you must use them. Proof of their depth is in application.

—Mitch Horowitz

## Chapter One
# Dynamic Thinkers Rule the World

A legend is told of the time when the Gods created man and the universe. They held a conference and one of them said, "Let us give man the same creative power that we ourselves possess. Where shall we hide this priceless gift?"

Another answered, "Let us hide it where man will never think to look for it; within his own mind."

And this is where the Million Dollar Secret resides; within your own mind, your own consciousness. Here it is that you can find all the creative power you will ever need to make a fortune or to give yourself a million dollars worth of health, happiness, friendship, love, and enjoyment in life.

The great philosopher Descartes had a philosophy that can be summarized in one dynamic sentence: "I think, therefore I am."

Dynamic thinking can set into motion a series of reactions that are cataclysmic in their effects.

Ask yourself: "What do I think?" Then answer candidly.

Do you think of yourself as a failure in life?

Do you think you are inferior and inadequate?
Do you think you are doomed to poverty all your life?
Do you think your personality is unattractive?

If you are thinking these negative thoughts, you are short-circuiting the dynamic power of your brain and creating the image of these negative conditions in the outer circumstances of your life. Thoughts are a psychological reality. We each live in a world colored and dominated by our own private thought atmosphere.

Change the picture of your thoughts from negative to positive. Dynamic thinking will cause you to **be** that which you **think**.

Think you are successful.

Think that you are adequate, that you are equal to others.

Think that you can achieve the riches that others have.

Think that your personality may become magnetic and attractive.

You are using the magical power of dynamic thinking in the moment that you think in a positive manner. "I think, therefore I am." Write that down on a card, which you can consult several times daily, and on that card also write, "I think and talk success, health, happiness, and achievement. I think great thoughts, therefore I am great."

## Chapter Two
# The Undiscovered Genius Within Your Mind

There is a popular expression:

> Sow a thought, reap a habit;
> Sow a habit, reap a character;
> Sow a character, reap a destiny.

Actually you build your future destiny thought by thought, and as these thoughts become more dynamic and perfect, they begin to shape your character and destiny in paths of greatness.

Now you are embarked upon the thrilling voyage of discovery that will lead you to the finding of new worlds, but there are shoals and pitfalls which I must warn you about.

Most of the pitfalls are your own relatives and friends. They have lived with you for many years and have been used to the shrinking violet you may have become under the regime of weak, negative thinking of the past. These friends and relatives feel comfortable in the presence of the small ego that fits their concept of your totality of power. When the slumbering mental giant that is within your mind begins to stir restlessly and tries to shake off the chains that bind it to mediocrity, failure, poverty, and ignorance, these people are apt to set up a clamor that will shock the giant back into his somnolent state of immobility and inertia.

Just remember that every genius of history has had to go through discouragement, often from people close to him, before breaking the bonds of negativity and frustration. A prophet is without honor in his own country, Scripture tells us. Those closest to you are sometimes the very last ones to recognize the genius within you or to give you recognition for having great talent.

Use these three steps to release the undiscovered genius within your mind:

1. Each day try to originate some new and daring concept of thought in relation to your life. Write these down in a notebook and begin to apply them to your activities.
2. Live in your imagination at least one half hour a day. See yourself as the person you wish to be. Visualize yourself as the manager of the department where you work See yourself owning your own business. Imagine yourself taking trips to foreign countries. Build the new concept of your great powers by seeing how many refinements you can make on inventions and technologies. Write down ideas for great stories, novels, movies. You may not intend to be a writer but this mental exercise will extend your thinking to the realm of creative ideas and cause the subconscious mind to release more power to your everyday activities.
3. Pick some outstanding genius of history each day and emulate his philosophy, his thinking, his inspiration. Study the lives of great geniuses of history, searching for great thoughts which you may make a part of your own mental equipment. For instance, Pasteur. Concentrate on his persistence and patience. Edison. Borrow his vision and curiosity, and apply those qualities to your own life, seeing how many things you can mentally create, and how many useful facts you can discover.

## Chapter Three
# You Are Greater Than You Think

Most people have a tendency to minimize themselves and their abilities. Such people depreciate their own talents, their personalities, and tend to put others on a pedestal.

You cannot achieve a great destiny or a big fortune if you constantly believe yourself inferior and unworthy. Some people have subconscious feelings of guilt, put into their minds by their parents when they were children, and these guilt feelings hound them throughout life, making them unhappy, and dooming them to live lives that are inferior and inadequate. You may have been told that it is wrong and sinful to want to be successful, famous, and rich, and that only the "Meek shall inherit the earth." You must break such negativity at once, and believe *that you are greater than you think*.

The natural intelligence is greater in you than it is in all of nature's other creatures, for you represent the highest form of creation in the universe. When you discover the unlimited realm of the mind you can use it to shape the world you desire. This inner intuitive power that is in every animal, insect, bird and beast, is awaiting your recognition and bidding. When you once discover this power and learn through this study how to channel it correctly, you will be able to achieve seeming miracles in your own life.

Begin today to realize that you live in an unlimited universe, with unlimited resources. There are billions of worlds in outer space and science is now beginning to realize that more worlds are being born every day. The secret power back of all creation is intelligence.

To be great you must dwell in the company of great thoughts and high ideals. Your mind becomes stronger and more intelligent when you pass through it great thoughts, when you desire great things in your life, when you strive for high achievements. To expand your thinking into an area of importance and success, there must be a corresponding degree of inspiration and energy-drive in your thinking. If the idea held in consciousness is big enough, all the actions that follow will be of a like quality and degree.

It takes no more energy mentally to think of a big job, with good pay, than it does to think of an inferior position with small pay. People will set the value on you and your talents that you set on yourself.

All great men who have ever achieved anything worthwhile or enduring, have been infused with this higher purpose in living. There must be a change in your mental concept first; the idea that you want to express, the work you want to do, the home you want to live in; when you once **know for sure** what it is you want, and you hold tenaciously to that idea, your circumstances of life will gradually begin to change. Do not worry about how this higher mind within you is going to produce the change. You cannot tell this infinite intelligence, which rules the world, how to create an oak tree; this is God's secret. But you can plant the tiny acorn in the soil and then, under the universal laws of growth and capillary attraction, that acorn will attract to itself all the nourishment it needs from the soil and rain, to make a giant oak tree a hundred feet tall.

Do these things to become greater:

1. Build your sum of knowledge. You grow in mental power as your fund of knowledge grows.
2. Learn to crawl before you walk, but try to run as quickly as you gain strength and confidence in your power to walk. In other words, do not remain in a position that is inferior.
3. Make decisions quickly. Do not vacillate after making a decision, but act on your decision promptly.
4. Write to important people presenting your great ideas. Some people have won promotion and success through this process of calling attention to themselves.
5. Do not be afraid to ask important people to help you. They are human and are often flattered to think that you believe they are important enough to give you assistance.

Chapter Four

# Tap the Hidden Treasures Within Your Mind

You may not think your ideas are valuable because they came from your brain. Change your attitude about the value of your thoughts. Some of the greatest things in the world were accomplished by men and women like you, who had just one good idea and made it pay dividends.

When I was lecturing in Honolulu, I met a man at my lectures who had invented the silent mercury switch for electric lights. He had been awakened so many times by the noise of the electric switch when his wife would turn it on at night that his mind began to think of some way to make the turning on of a light switch silent.

Your own ideas may be worth a fortune. You must sit quietly in your own room for at least half-an-hour daily and probe the goldmine of your mind. You should then write down all new ideas that come to you for improving your life, perfecting some product, marketing some merchandise you have created.

Start with whatever field you are in now, and do not wait for some better time or more improved conditions. Look around you, see what could be changed or improved, and then set about doing it. Start this process now and continue it the rest of your life, and you will see amazing results.

Epictetus said, "No great thing is created suddenly, any more than a bunch of grapes or a fig. If you tell me that you desire a fig, I answer you that there must be time. Let it first blossom, then bear fruit, then ripen."

Use this daily regimen for tapping the hidden treasures of your mind:

1. Begin each day, when you waken in the morning, by passing through your mind a series of big ideas relating to your life, your work, your environment. Ask yourself: "What can I do today to improve my situation in life? How can I improve my business? What ideas can I incorporate in my work that will pay me rich dividends in the future?"

2. Check your mind and see if you are using all the power that you possess or if you are wasting it on petty, unimportant things. Could you use more daring, courage, patience, persistence, thrift, sociability, optimism, humor in your relations with others? Are you using the gifts and talents you possess as steppingstones to greatness? Are you using the knowledge you possess fully? Do you seek the aid of important people you've met to help you achieve your goals?

3. Keep a daily diary in which you jot down each night the outstanding ideas you had during that day. Let your imagination soar without restraint, and carefully note the ideas and suggestions that flash into your mind. Then write them down for future use. Many times your subconscious mind will give you valuable ideas, but if you do not write them down they leave suddenly and it is difficult to recall them again. Edison kept a notebook by his bedside, and his biggest ideas for his many inventions came to him while he slept. He wrote them down at once, and the next day acted on these inspirational ideas.

4. Stir your mind to action by holding in your mind each day a desire to achieve something important and worthwhile. An artist cannot paint his picture until he first has the visual image in his mind. The desire to create that particular picture stirs him into action and he projects his mental

picture onto the canvas before him. You must do the same thing: hold in your mind daily the pictures of the things you wish to achieve. Do not worry how you will attain them. The law of cause and effect takes over the moment you have a strong idea in mind.

Chapter Five

# Magnetism, the Law of Universal Attraction

You can magnetize what you want in life. You must image it mentally; clearly and emotionally, feeling it is already yours. You must write it down. You must visualize the persons, conditions, money, success—whatever it is you want clearly and as often as possible. The process known as daydreaming is helpful in fixing the image clearly in your mind. Daydream yourself in the situations in life you desire, such as singing, speaking or acting. Do the entire performance as if you were actually before that audience. Picture yourself in the job you desire, seeing yourself as an executive, giving orders, having other employees under you. Follow this process based on whatever desires you hold.

Energy and matter are interchangeable. The energy of the mind can be converted into material substance. For instance, the idea to build a bridge is only mental energy, but it can become externalized in the building of the actual bridge. The idea for a painting, a literary work, an invention, or a business is just as real and has a dimension that is as solid and actual as matter. The *idea for a thing* has inherent in it the ability to magnetize the thing itself and bring it into being. This is the way that your mental energy has in itself the equivalent of the thing you are holding in your mind. Be sure then that you magnetize *only* positive things.

The Bible speaks of it as, "As ye sow, so shall ye reap." This is the great mental law of attraction at work in nature.

Take these six steps for greater magnetic power:

1. Picture clearly the things that you want to magnetize and attract. Sit quietly in your room and run these pictures through your mind like film through a movie projector. Review these pictures daily, as often as possible, especially at night just before going to sleep. See them clearly; do *not* keep changing them, but have the pictures the same each time. Have as many things as you want to magnetize, taking them up one at a time, and giving about ten minutes to picturing each thought.

2. Write down the things you wish to magnetize. Write them clearly and briefly. This serves to imprint them on your subconscious more forcibly.
3. Engage in constructive daydreaming when possible. The moments you spend waiting for a car or bus, the time you take out for coffee or a break at work—use these precious moments to daydream. In these daydreams, see yourself as your ideal.
4. *Do not tell anyone* of the secret power you are using. They will tend to laugh at you, discourage you, and they may short-circuit your magnetic attraction with their negative ideas. The acorn grows in the secret, hidden womb of the earth, safe from all interference, and becomes an oak tree because of this secrecy. What if someone tore it up by the roots every few days to see if it was growing? It would die. So, too, your dreams die if they are shattered by others.
5. Have faith in the invisible intelligence that resides in nature to produce the things you are trying to magnetize. The secret power that can make a baby in nine months knows how to release the energy to bring your idea or dream to fruition. But you must have faith in this invisible power that creates all life.
6. Share your good with the world. There is magnetism in giving to others.

### Chapter Six
# The Magic Genie Within Your Subconscious Mind

In Aladdin's Lamp resided a Magic Genie, who would carry out any wish Aladdin had. All he had to do was rub the magic lamp and the Genie would appear ready to carry out his bidding.

Your subconscious mind might be likened to this Genie. It is ready to carry out any command that you give it. And like the Magic Genie, your subconscious mind is a powerful aid, a dynamic force that can be harnessed for great achievement.

When you see a great pianist like Vladimir Horowitz sit at the piano and play a difficult concerto with such ease and fluency, it is because he has spent years in building the habit patterns of perfection in his mind. The subconscious stores these memoires and releases them under automatic control, so the pianist need not consciously think of how he going to play the difficult score.

All your habit patterns can be built in your subconscious mind so they become automatic responses of your body functions. You can learn how to become a great speaker, writer, composer, musician, inventor, or business success. You may consciously choose the things you want your subconscious to do for you automatically, and then by constant repetition of the act or thought, you will imprint it on your subconscious mind, making it a part of the automatic reflex action of your subconscious.

Modern psychosomatic medicine has shown that one's mental attitude also has much to do with sickness or health. When you constantly repeat positive statements such as, "I am healthy. I am happy. I am young. I have vitality and energy," you actually help raise the energy levels of your body and release the stored sugar in your liver, giving you greater vitality.

The subconscious accepts as truth whatever you tell it often enough. When you repeat an idea over and over again, your subconscious mind automatically accepts it as gospel, and sets to work making it a reality in your life. In psychology, this is known as the Law of Predominant Mental Impression. It simply means that you must keep repeating an idea, saying it over so often that it becomes a law for your subconscious mind.

For instance, if you keep telling yourself, "I can't do that, I'm afraid I'll fail, I'm inferior and inadequate, I'm tired and weak, I'm afraid I'll catch cold," you will make these negative statements the laws of your subconscious mind. As this mind automatically carries out everything you think or say many times, the sympathetic nervous system will set these negative forces into motion. You will become more and more fearful. You will do things that make you fail. You will become inferior. You will be constantly tired and weak. You set the mental stage for the action you imprint upon the subconscious mind.

One of the best ways to reach your subconscious mind and imprint upon it the things you want it to do, is to begin to act the part you wish to play in life. If you want to be rich and successful, act as though you already are. If you want to be happy, begin to act as though you are already happy: smile, be optimistic, talk about the good things of life instead of the sad and evil things. Your subconscious reacts according to the emotional pattern that you set for yourself. If you act happy and successful, your subconscious will send positive pulsations to your glands and the entire rhythm of your body will change to a positive one.

When Napoleon decided he would become Emperor of France, he called in François-Joseph Talma, one of the nation's leading tragedians, to show him how to walk, talk, and look like an emperor. Napoleon had a real problem, for he was scarcely five feet tall. The actor made him strut back and forth, giving commands as an emperor would; he showed him how to stand, how to talk, how to think like an emperor. Finally, when Napoleon was ready to declare himself Emperor Napoleon the First, he carried such conviction that the crowed heads of Europe bowed before him.

If you act a part long enough, your subconscious mind will be impressed by it, and make it living reality. You can begin to achieve a strong, more dynamic personality by this art of impersonation. Stand before a mirror and speak to yourself. Tell yourself that you are strong, dynamic, good looking: really believe the things you are going to become. Then go around *being* the person you wish to be. Soon, it will become second nature. You will be guided to doing the things you have long acted out. People will begin to see you as the person you have mentally thought yourself to be.

Elsewhere we are told of the importance of writing down your desires and ambitions. Now it is time for you to know how this simple act works to imprint upon your subconscious mind the suggestions you write down. Your subconscious mind believes everything that is repeated to it often enough—things that are said or written down. The kinetic action of *doing* something with your hands more forcibly impresses the subconscious than if you just *think* a thing.

Another great secret for releasing subconscious power is to read or talk aloud. There is something magical about the hypnotic power of the human mind. When you give yourself autosuggestions, and believe what you are telling yourself, you are deeply imprinting the subconscious mind with what you say.

Review these facts for great subconscious power:

1. Turn over the automatic function of your body completely to your subconscious mind. Stop worrying about the way your body works and trust your subconscious to take care of it.
2. Use the system of autosuggestion devised by French mind theorist Emile Coué, and every night just before you drift off to sleep whisper to yourself at least twenty times, "Every day in every way, I am getting better and better." Do the same immediately upon waking in the morning.
3. Memorize other autosuggestions which you repeat every day when you have a few minutes of time, such as, "I can do this job perfectly. I will win a promotion and a raise in salary. I like other people, and they like me. I

can be a big success. I am bigger than I think." You can make up your own suggestions to fit your needs.
4. Write down your main dream or goal at least once a week, and keep where you can see it every day. Keep reviewing it in your mind until it becomes second nature.
5. Sit quietly for ten minutes a day and pass through your imagination mental pictures of yourself doing things you really want to do, such as singing, acting, being in your own business, living in a new house, buying a car, taking a long trip. The important thing is to keep reviewing the picture in detail, until it is such a big part of your consciousness that your subconscious will take it up and act on it.

## Chapter Seven
# Duplicate the Power of the Great Men of History

When Thomas Edison failed time after time in perfecting his electric light bulb he never stopped trying to find some substance that would last more than a few seconds in the filaments of his lamps. He was so resourceful that he tried thousands of different substances, and each time he failed. But still he did not give up. One day his assistant become so discouraged that he said, "Mr. Edison you've tried ten thousand times and failed, why don't you give up?"

Edison replied, "No, I can't give up. Now we know ten thousand things that won't work." And soon he found something that *did work*.

If you wish to be great and make your fortune, learn how to duplicate the power of the greatest men and women in history. These figures discovered The Million Dollar Secret, some by accident, others through inspiration or sheer dint of hard work and persistent effort.

There are three things that will make you outstanding in any business field, and these three things were present in the works of all geniuses:
1. Ability to know your own talents and possibilities.
2. Daring to attempt the seeming impossible.
3. Courage to persist in the face of obstacles.

The step of determining what you want, and letting your desires guide you to the path you wish to take, is the most important in applying the Million Dollar Secret to your own life and success.

Follow this step-by-step formula to greatness:

1. Pick the field you wish to specialize in; learn all you can about it, study the lives of its outstanding successes, then strive to emulate their pattern of thinking.
2. Each day strive to put into action one or more of the qualities or traits that you have learned from the lives of great men. Imitate these thoughts, if need be, at first, then you will gradually begin to originate great thoughts and actions of your own.
3. Get specialized training to perfect your gifts and talents. Assemble facts about the work you choose; see the good and bad sides, then, if you remain interested, let no one divert you from your goal.
4. Let what I call Divine Discontent motivate you in your desire to achieve perfection. Never be satisfied with your present accomplishments or progress. When you are satisfied, you cease to grow. Everything in nature is in constant flux, from an imperfect to a more perfect state. Constantly desire change and evolvement.
5. Aim for the stars, even though you may not achieve them; at least such an ambition will assure you of reaching some kind of high goal. Browning said, "Ah, but a man's reach should exceed his grasp, / Or what's a heaven for?"
6. Create a vortex of mental activity about yourself. Break the inertia that may be holding you back by doing *something*, almost anything is preferable to sitting back and refusing to make an effort.
7. Never be satisfied with the limitations that life seems to have placed on you and your expression of your talents. There are means and possibilities all about you—search them out and use them. Part of our Million Dollar Secret is the building of mental power, so you may better express your God-given gifts and talents.

## Chapter Eight
# The Million-Dollar Personality That Wins

Some people seem to be born lucky. They grow up in circumstances that seem favorable for their maturing into well-balanced, integrated personalities. They seem to possess charm and attractiveness; everyone seems to like them, and want to help them.

Others are less fortunate. They are born in environments that may be negative and shabby, surrounded by people who are negative, fearful, financially pinched, and constantly worried. These people acquire mental habits that are difficult to break in adult life.

Epictetus said of habit: "Every habit and faculty is preserved and increased by correspondent actions, as the habit of walking, by walking, or running, by running."

The more you practice thinking or doing a thing, the easier it becomes, until finally, by building positive mental habits you are able to perform consistently at a high level of action in the expression of your personality.

It is possible for you now to choose the type of persona you want to be, just as you choose the suit or dress you want to wear. Psychologists tell us that we are conditioned by our own minds through suggestions and opinions we hold, or tell ourselves. If you constantly tell yourself you are inferior, you will gradually begin to take on the hangdog appearance of an inferior person. You will shrink from contact with people. They will sense your reactions and shy away from you.

If you make it a point to reinforce your ego by telling yourself you are worthy of the best life has to offer, and that you are likeable, pleasant, happy, and loving towards others, people will instantly feel your power and gravitate toward you.

Building a magnetic personality is easy when you once know how. It is a matter of satisfaction to be able to win friends and hold them, but it has intrinsic value also that can be counted in actual dollars and cents. Tests given by psychologists proved that men and women who had studied their personalities and worked to perfect and polish them actually got more jobs as executives than those who had inferior personalities but great ability. If it comes to a choice between a pleasant, cheerful, happy-appearing person for a job, and one who is morose and sullen all the time, ability being equal, the pleasant person will be selected every time.

## Chapter Nine
# Ten Steps That Can Make You a Mental Giant

Before you begin your study of this part of the Million Dollar Secret, I ask that you rid your mind of all doubts and uncertainties, and do *really believe you can do the things I am going to tell you about.* Remove the shadows of fear and doubt and limitation that may fill your mind, and then become imbued with only one thought: *you can do anything you desire!*

Make these ten steps part of your life:

1. **Listen to the Master Mind within.** There is a vast intelligence in all of nature that regulates and operates the entire universe. This Master Mind also works through your own mind; if you learn how tap its power you will have increased your mental capacity at least fifty percent. See how this Master Mind works in nature. The maple tree produces seed that the Master Mind has given wings, like a parachute. Why wings? Because this Intelligence *knows* that if maple seeds fall in the shade of the mother tree they will have little chance to survive, so they have wings that the wind can catch and blow to a sunny patch of ground. This Intelligence leaves nothing to chance to assure the success and perpetuity of her creation; she gives the maple tree literally thousands of winged seed, to be sure that some of them will survive the caprices of Fate. Learn to listen to the Master Mind within. Be in tune with it; it wants your success and happiness *more than you do!*

2. **Expand your thinking to encompass broader fields of experience and action.** Most people limit themselves to habit-patterns of thought that include their small, everyday happenings. They never allow themselves to soar into the unlimited world of creative thought where they envision wonderful experiences, better jobs, bigger income, the accumulation of a fortune. The habit patterns of thought become chains that bind them to lives of inactivity, poverty, and limitation. Learn to *think big!* Your brain cells are aching for exercise in big thinking. Consider the limitations of thought in those people you know. Most of them are in positions where they make a limited income and they are doing nothing to change their mode of thought or life. Samuel Johnson said: "The true, strong, and sound mind is the mind that can embrace equally great things and small."

3. **Gather as much knowledge as you can consciously—then let your subconscious take over.** Most people make too much effort to do the really big things of life. They seem to feel, somehow, that they have to do the actual work. Stop and ask yourself what power it is within you that does your breathing, that digests your food, that works your mind. You

will then realize that the really big things are done for you by your subconscious. To let your subconscious work better for you, gather as much knowledge as you can consciously about the subjects you wish to become expert in, then turn over this mass of material to your subconscious and let it do the work of sorting out, storing, filing, and using the knowledge you have accumulated.

4. **Give yourself a five-year plan for mental growth.** Your mind likes *definiteness*. Give yourself a five-year plan for study, growth, and evolvement. In that time promise yourself a completely new mental viewpoint, new environment, new work, new friends, a higher income, and better standards of living. Your mind likes such a challenge as this. It will rise to the occasion and give you the mental power you may need to achieve your five-year goal. Do not stop, however, with a five-year plan; keep expanding and changing this plan as the years go on, so that you always have an unfinished symphony of life which you are working to complete. This gives added purposefulness to living. Pick the books you want to study in that five-year plan, the courses you wish to take, the steps you wish to use to set up a new social life, the friends you wish to cultivate. *Do more than just think about these things*; write them down, make a comprehensive list of your plans and aspirations, so you can consult your list frequently and see that you are on the right path.

5. **Create a need in your life for something you want.** Do not vaguely say, "I want more money," "I'd like to visit Europe next year," or "I'd like to get married." These kinds of statements are weak and inconclusive. Everyone thinks such thoughts once in a while. You must create a need in your life for the things you want. If you want more money, *find a need for more money*. What do you want more money for? Be specific and tell yourself what you will do with it. Why do you want to go to Europe? For fun? For cultural improvement? To meet a rich marriage partner? For relaxation and rest? Have a real need, and keep reaffirming that need, until it crystallizes in your mind as a dynamic demand on the universal life intelligence.

6. **Make your mind do some creative act each day.** Nothing builds latent mental powers so much as each day making your mind do some creative act. You may not see any immediate results in these small creative efforts but you can take my word for it, they will gradually build giant mental

power. Victor Herbert wrote music for more than forty years *without winning recognition*, but every day he sat down and courted the creative muse within, writing a little, patiently waiting and perfecting his talents. Forty years later he won his great success with *Babes in Toyland*, and established himself for all time in the light opera and musical comedy field.

7. **When you experience defeats come back and try again.** A muscle grows by repeated exercise; a brain cell grows *only* when you keep trying, thinking, studying to develop your mind. You need persistent and daily mental exercise if you wish to build your mental power to its fullest capacity. Increase your mental capacity by repeating your efforts over and over, even in the face of seeming defeats. When someone asked the mighty Babe Ruth what he thought about when he stood on the diamond waiting for the pitcher to throw the ball, the great Babe replied, "I think of only one thing; of hitting the ball!" Your mind must have this persistent and determined feeling about the goal you are trying to achieve.

8. **Accept no limitation on your mental powers.** This priceless ingredient of our Million Dollar Secret is vitally important. Many times it is not the knowledge, the talent, the greatness that a person possesses that brings him success, fame, and fortune. A little talent will go a long way if a person refuses to accept limitations on his abilities.

9. **Organize your thinking by organizing your life.** Order and harmony are God's first laws for creation. If you live in a constant state of confusion and disorder, you cannot have an orderly mind. You can begin today to organize your thinking. You start by first organizing your life. Have a daily schedule and organized surroundings. This will help you acquire the habit of neat and orderly thinking, and your mind will soon release power to do these things in an easier manner than if left to haphazard chance.

10. **Be inspired by noble emotions and high ideals.** No person has ever achieved great heights who was not first inspired by noble emotions and high ideals. Absorb great works of art, writing, and music—read inspiring biographies and emulate their examples. Create beauty and greatness.

## Chapter Ten
# Become a Receiving Station for Great Ideas

There is a saying in philosophy, "As above, so below." This means that the microcosm, man, reflects all the processes and creative principles that exist in the macrocosm, or the larger universe. Microcosm relates to an organism, regarded as a world in miniature. Man is actually a world in miniature, and he reflects in all his mental and physical processes, all the universal processes of growth, attraction, reproduction, and refinement. The seedling of reality is in man's own mind; his mind is where he creates the world in which he lives.

Once you understand this principle, you will know that part of the Million Dollar Secret lies hidden in your mind as the creative power that every person has locked within his own human consciousness.

There is a picture or pattern within your mind, which has its counterpart in Universal Intelligence—the same intelligence that creates the rose and the oak tree. There is only one major difference between use of this Creative Power within your mind and that in nature: You, being a creature of volition and choice, *may choose the pictures you wish to create in the outer world*, whereas animals, birds, insects, and growing organisms in nature are *forced to create according to a set pattern*.

What one man has thought, experienced, or done may be the common property of all creative minds. You can reflect the knowledge of all the great minds since the beginning of time. Just as all chicks within the hen's egg know how to peck their way out of the shell, so too, your Creative Intelligence knows how to work out all your problems, knows how to give you the ideas and inspiration to make your dreams come true.

You can become a receiving station for great ideas, just as the famous men of history did. You can unlock the creative power of this higher mind within you, just as Napoleon did, as Michelangelo did in his creative masterpieces of marble and canvas. The power that was used by Lincoln, Columbus, Newton, Edison, Washington, and Benjamin Franklin is a part of your own higher consciousness. You may tap the creative mind within and receive from it all the inspiration you need to build your future destiny in the pattern of greatness and genius.

Here is how to use this method to become a receiving station for great ideas:

1. Each night before going to bed spend a few moments picturing in your mind's eye the things you want to achieve, the things you wish to attract, the qualities and talents you want for your own, and even the people you want in your life. Feel that these things are already in existence awaiting your joyous discovery.

2. Ask the "Father Within" to point the way to right work, to the finding or making of the money you need to pay your debts; to the knowledge you need to get a better salary; to the finding of lost or hidden objects. The great ESP researcher Dr. J.B. Rhine tells in his book *Extra-Sensory Perception* of how a girl, whose father had died, needed money desperately. She dreamed one night that her father came to her and told her to look in the secret compartment of an antique dresser. She found it, and stuffed in there were many big bills. How was this knowledge conveyed? Telepathy? Spiritualism? Vibration? Science does not yet know, but there is something at work in another dimension of the universe, which seems to represent a higher mind. Put your problems to this higher mind within, ask for a solution, and then quietly go to sleep confident that the answer will come to you, either in a dream or when you awaken.

3. If you wish to pick up thoughts of greatness, such as those that inspired the geniuses of the past, sit quietly in your room alone, and meditate on the great person whose imagination you wish to contact. If it is Beethoven, hold his name in your mind; acquire as much knowledge as you can of his life; be conversant with his great music; then sit and wait for the highest inspiration to come through to you. Do the same with any great figure: a scientist, inventor, or business success.

4. You can convey messages to others through this process of speaking to the higher mind within you. Tell the higher mind what you want to convey; hold the name and face of the person in mind; then talk to them as you would if they were there in person. You can also receive mental messages from others through this same process of concentration and visualization. Hold in mind the face of the person you wish to receive messages from; concentrate your mind on that person for a while, and then sit perfectly still and wait and see what thoughts come into your mind.

## Chapter Eleven
# How to Seek and Win the Aid of Important People

You've heard the saying, "Nothing succeeds like success." Also, "Money seeks out money." It is true, if you wish to win fame and fortune, you can seldom do it on your own. You must seek out the aid of wealthy and important people.

The Quaker father advised his daughter, "Marry thee not for money, but go thee where money is."

The working of the law of proximity is influential in the lives of many people who have achieved success in their chosen profession. It isn't so much *what* they know as *whom* they know. This has become a cliché in American business, but is nevertheless true. Few of the great geniuses in history could have possibly succeeded without the aid of others.

Edison was a great inventor, but his inventions would have been worthless to the world if they *had not been marketed*. Ford had a great idea in building his horseless carriage, but he needed capital and backing before he could mass-produce his motorcar. Raphael and Michelangelo created great masterpieces in art but they needed their reigning princes of state and church, and the aid of influential, wealthy men and women to give them the means to achieve their great works of art.

It is said, "A man is known through the company he keeps." Most people achieve greatness through reflection. It is just as easy in life to choose the company of friends who are important, politically powerful, creatively active, and wealthy, as to associate with people who are shabby, disorderly in their thinking, lazy, disreputable, shiftless, and negative.

It is important, in building your future career, to choose friends who are striving for the same goals as you; or people who *have already achieved these goals*. It is just as easy to form friendships with people who are going places as to select those who are doomed by their negative habits to failure.

"Hitch your wagon to a star" is a saying that applies to the forming of friendships. Everyone you admit into your life on a close, personal basis should measure up to certain standards. Ask yourself:

- Will our friendship by mutually good?
- What have I to offer this person, and what has he to give?
- Does he have habits that are negative and that might impede my course in life?

- Are his standards high?
- Have I anything to learn from my association with this friend?

It is not selfish for you to be concerned about these new associations, for if you see a person more than three times, he has the power to change your life. You want to be sure that, given such tremendous power, these new friends will change your life for the better.

So many people plan every detail of their lives carefully, and yet completely ignore their social lives. More business is done over cocktails and on golf courses than in offices. It is true that very often, important, busy executives snatch these opportunities of relaxation and conviviality to discuss business matters and make important decisions. Take advantage of this psychological fact. It is easier after a businessman has had a few drinks and eaten a good meal to get his attention than it is to go to his office and get through a retinue of assistants and secretaries.

I recall two meetings with noted authors that came about in such relaxed surroundings in my own career. One was the great humorist, Irvin Cobb, who was a guest of honor at a luncheon I attended. The other was Rupert Hughes, a great American writer, who I met at a party. Because he was slightly deaf and wore a hearing aid, many people found it difficult to talk to the noted author. I made it a special point to speak distinctly and loudly when addressing him, keeping my face turned towards him so he could read my lips. I spent an instructive and pleasant hour in his company, and when the evening was over, he invited me to lunch, and at another time to play golf with him at the Lakeside Country Club near Hollywood. At the club that day alone, Mr. Hughes introduced me to some of the biggest directors, producers, and stars who later helped my career immeasurably. I was then in my early twenties, and *such contacts would have been impossible without the aid of a well-known and important person.*

Use these secrets for winning the aid of important people:

1. Offer your services and aid to civic betterment groups in your community. Here you will meet people who are in key positions and who can help you immeasurably in achieving your goal.
2. Become affiliated with your local political groups, for they have prestige and power. Many a man has started as a lowly assistant in a political ward, and risen to a position of power and prominence. You can meet lawyers, judges, and those who are big in politics, and through their aid and influence you can be selected to big-paying jobs.

3. Join a veteran's group, or the American Legion, if you qualify, or any other group that is active in your community. Not only does this pave the way to social activity, but it can lead to an expansion of your business contacts and a position of prestige.
4. Get in the habit of writing to important people, suggesting ideas for the betterment of the community, or offering your help in some charitable work being undertaken. Occasionally write a letter praising the official, and he will definitely take note of you. I have known people who got in to see the heads of some of the biggest businesses in the country through this practice.
5. Use your vacation time profitably. Plan your vacation so that you come in contact with people who might prove valuable to your career.
6. Do not be afraid to present your ideas to important business executives or wealthy people. They are constantly searching for new ideas, new talent, new markets. If you bring them an idea that changes their business for the better, you may work yourself right into an important position. I know one young man who sent a suggestion to the Canadian Pacific Railroad president for ways of increasing tourist riders, and the president instantly arranged an interview that led the young man to lucrative post.
7. In making contacts with important people, show interest in them and their work. Have respect for their advice and opinions. They have risen in their profession because of specialized skills; respect their judgment.
8. Build the other person's ego, for if he *is* important he will appreciate recognition of that fact. Even great people have their low moments.
9. When you meet people who are important and who might prove helpful, find a common ground of interest, which you can use as a basis for a friendship. This might be work you have in common, school friends you both know, a sport that you can share, and so on.
10. Try to discuss things that are pleasant and noncontroversial. Avoid politics and religion. You are judged by the things you talk about.
11. Package your personality so it shows your best side. This means you should have a pleasant, affable, and relaxed personality, one that is easy to get along with. Practice smiling, and learn how to have a good, hearty laugh, for a good laugh is infectious and often helps win friends. Everyone wants to laugh; no one really wants to share your sad experiences and cry.
12. Give freely of yourself, if you wish to attract and hold the interest of important people. If you have nothing else of value to give the world, give

yourself, your interest, your enthusiasm, your charm, your attention, your consideration, and, *most important of all*, your sincere friendship.

## Chapter Twelve
# Take These Seven Steps Up the Ladder of Success

There is a formula for success that is as definite as the laws that govern mathematics. Success consists of several different component parts, and these are as absolute as the law of gravity.

### Step 1. The Desire to Achieve
We have spoken elsewhere of desire, but in connection with achieving success, it is vitally important that you use this Emotion of Desire correctly. Everyone wants to succeed. Everyone wants fame and fortune. What you must do is *define exactly the type of success you desire*. The concrete image must exist in your mind first. It is the pattern by which Universal Intelligence can cut the cloth to make the suit you have chosen.

### Step 2. Your Dream or Inner Vision
All outward forms of creation in the world began with a dream or inner vision. Everyone has some kind of dream of the world in which he wishes to live. This dream resides in the mind, and is instilled by our early childhood thoughts and experiences. You played house, and expressed the idea of love and marriage and having your own family some day. You played doctor and had the dream of someday being one in real life. Dreams crystalize into reality when you apply this formula correctly. It has been said that an idea, when it comes with the force of revelation, will lead to a revolution in your life. The overpowering *idea you hold in your mind* about the life you wish to lead is *the dream or inner vision* that will shape your entire future. You must have this dream firmly fixed and never stray from it.

### Step 3. Release Creative Imagination
Literally, imagination means the act or power of forming mental images of what is not present. It is also the act or power of creating new ideas by combining previous experiences. Creative Intelligence carries you a step further, however, than just forming mental images; it means to cause to come into

existence, to make or originate, to cause, to produce, to bring about. When you creatively imagine something you are actually causing it to come into being, for you are *forming it first in your own mind.*

## Step 4. The Power of Concentration

A lightening bolt can split a giant oak tree because of its concentrated power. The power of concentration is terrific when released in your mind. Most people scatter their mental energy and force by spending ninety percent of their time in thinking over past defeats and disappointments. Their minds spend hours dwelling on the negative aspects of their lives: the failures, the tragedies, the sicknesses, the lost investments. This tendency to concentrate on the negative aspects of life only helps to inscribe these things deeper into the workings of the brain. In using the positive power of concentration, learn to reverse your failures, not to rehearse them, which only tends to make them more real in your mind.

## Step 5. The Power of Intuition

The humming bird needs no instructor in the art of constructing his thistle-down-lined, swinging nest. Something within him *knows how to construct it perfectly!* The ant requires no one to tell him how to organize his nest and build an anthill. This is an intuitive function within his mind. Emerson spoke of this Intuitive Mind Within in these brilliant words:

> A man should learn to detect and watch that gleam of light which flashes across his mind from within, more than the lustre of the firmament of bards and sages. Yet, he dismisses without notice his thought, because it is his. In every work of genius we recognize our own rejected thoughts; they come back to us with a certain alienated majesty. Trust thyself; every heart vibrates to that iron string.

## Step 6. Habit Patterns of Success

Study the following questions carefully, for each is a key to the building of new habit patterns of success:
- Are you efficient?
- Are you punctual?
- Are you honest?

- Do you give full value?
- Are you positive?
- Are you confident?
- Are you thrifty?
- Do you know how to handle money?
- Are you able to organize people?
- Are you outgoing in your personality?
- Are you orderly, clean, neat?
- Do you recognize big ideas?
- Do you persist in the face of obstacles?
- Do you believe in yourself?
- Do you think and talk only success?

## Step 7. Faith in Your Destiny

Faith in yourself and faith in your destiny—this is an essential step in your climb up the ladder of success. Many talented people never make it because they do not possess this essential ingredient of the Million Dollar Secret.

The twentieth-century novelist Howard Fast wrote a book some years ago. He sent it out to several publishers. They all turned it down. No one had faith in it. Fast had such faith in the ultimate success of the book that he raised $1,000 and published it himself. Only a few hundred copies existed, and undoubtedly, for a time, for a very small sum, anyone could have bought the movie rights.

Then one day a producer read the book, and offered Fast a large sum for the movie rights. *Spartacus* was the name of the book that Howard Fast had faith in. It became one of the great motion pictures of its time, and also smashed the infamous Hollywood blacklist.

Faith in yourself is the "open sesame" to riches and fame. It matters not that others lack faith in you or your works; if you really believe in yourself and your talents, you will build inspiration and power to persist until you have achieved your life goal.

"All things are possible to him that believeth."

# About the Authors

## James Allen
JAMES ALLEN was born in Leicester, in central England's industrial heartland, on November 28, 1864. He took his first job at age 15 to support his family after his father was murdered while looking for work in America in 1879. Allen worked as a factory knitter and later as a private secretary with various manufacturing companies. In 1901, he published his first book, *From Poverty to Power*. The following year, he left secretarial work to devote himself fulltime to writing, and in 1903 published his third and best-known work, *As a Man Thinketh*. At this time, Allen moved with his wife, Lily, and daughter, Nora, to Ilfracombe, England, where he continued to write books and articles, and, with Lily, to publish his spiritual journal, *The Light of Reason*, later retitled *The Epoch*. He died at age 47 on January 24, 1912, most likely of tuberculosis. Allen completed nineteen books during his career, several of which were published posthumously. *As a Man Thinketh* is considered one of the formative classics of modern inspirational thought.

## Claude M. Bristol
Born in 1891 in Portland, Oregon, CLAUDE M. BRISTOL worked for nearly forty years as a newspaper reporter and editor, during which time he also studied law, became an investment banker, and traveled extensively. After serving in World War One, Bristol became an advocate for the rights of veterans, whom he believed could attain success in civilian life by harnessing the powers of the mind. Bristol spent most of his adult life researching and tracking discoveries in psychical abilities and ESP, which he believed held the key to greater human potential. He died in 1951, three years the publication of his classic guide *The Magic of Believing*.

## Andrew Carnegie
Born in Scotland in 1835, ANDREW CARNEGIE migrated with his parents to the United States in 1848 at age twelve. The family settled in Allegheny, Pennsylvania, where Andrew took his first job at age 13 at the local cotton mill. After

a series of jobs and ventures, Carnegie became a steel manufacturer in Pittsburgh where he grew wealthy through supplying steel during the nation's industrial boom. By 1901, he sold Carnegie Steel to JP Morgan making Carnegie arguably the richest man in the world. The industrialist spent the remaining two decades of life writing and organizing his fortune into philanthropic trusts. He died in Lennox, Massachusetts, in 1919.

## Dale Carnegie

Born in northwestern Missouri in 1888, DALE CARNEGIE was one of the pioneers of motivational and self-help philosophy. World famous for his 1936 classic, *How to Win Friends and Influence People,* Carnegie began his career as a writer and teacher in 1912 when he offered courses on public speaking at a YMCA in New York City. Carnegie was one of the first business minds of the twentieth century to grasp the importance of being able to communicate ideas and concepts clearly to colleagues, coworkers, clients, and customers. His pioneering book, *Public Speaking: A Practical Course for Business Men*, from which this volume is abridged, first appeared in 1926. It is regarded as the seminal work on how to speak with power and skill. Carnegie died in New York City in 1955.

## A.H.Z. Carr

Born in Chicago in 1902, A.H.Z. CARR was an economic adviser to the presidential administrations of Franklin Roosevelt and Harry Truman, and participated in economic and diplomatic missions in Western Europe and East Asia. He also served as a consulting economist to several large corporations. Carr wrote for magazines including *Harper's, Reader's Digest,* and *The Saturday Evening Post.* He died in 1971.

## George S. Clason

Born in Missouri in 1874, GEORGE S. CLASON attended the University of Nebraska and served in the U.S. Army during the Spanish-American War. Soon after the war he founded the Clason Map Company of Denver, Colorado, where he published the first road atlas of the U.S. and Canada. In 1926, Clason began issuing a series of pamphlets on personal financial management using fictionalized parables set in ancient Babylon. His pamphlets were first distributed free to clients by banks and insurance companies, and in 1930 Clason collected and published them in book form, where they became famous as *The Richest Man in Babylon.* Clason died in Napa, California, in 1957.

## Robert Collier

Born in St. Louis, Missouri, in 1885, ROBERT COLLIER trained for the priesthood before entering a career in business. He achieved success in the fields of advertising, publishing, and engineering. After struggling with a severe and chronic case of food poisoning, Collier recovered using methods of Christian Science, New Thought, prayer therapy, and autosuggestion. He made an intensive study of the new metaphysics and distilled what he learned into a popular and influential pamphlet series first called *The Book of Life* in 1925 and renamed *The Secret of the Ages* in 1926. Collier assembled *The Secret of the Ages* into a single volume, which he revised and expanded in 1948. The author of many books on the mystical dimensions of the mind, Collier died in 1950.

## Russell H. Conwell

Born in western Massachusetts in 1843, RUSSELL H. CONWELL trained as lawyer, served as an officer in the Union army, and worked as an international journalist. He was ordained and worked as a Baptist minister before founding Temple University in Philadelphia in 1884. Conwell founded the school to educate poor and working-class students, and funded it largely through speaking fees earned from his famous motivational and character-building lecture *Acres of Diamonds*, which he began delivering in the 1870s. Conwell gave the talk more than 6,152 times throughout the nation before his death in 1925. He served as Temple University's first president, and his Conwell School of Theology became the Gordon-Conwell Theological Seminary, one of the largest interdenominational seminaries in the United States.

## Theron Q. Dumont

"Theron Q. Dumont" was one of several pseudonyms used by WILLIAM WALKER ATKINSON, a popular and innovative New Thought writer and publisher in the early twentieth century. Born in Baltimore, Maryland, in 1862, Atkinson became a successful attorney in 1894. Following a series of illnesses, he immersed himself in New Thought literature. He soon became an important figure in the early days of the movement, publishing magazines such as *Suggestion, New Thought,* and *Advanced Thought*. Under the aegis of his own publishing company, Yogi Publication Society, Atkinson wrote many self-bylined works, and many titles under the pseudonyms Yogi Ramacharaka, Magus Incognito, Theron Q. Dumont, and Three Initiates. Under the last of these, Atkinson wrote his most popular and enduring work, *The Kybalion*. Published in 1908 by Atkinson's Chicago-based press, *The Kybalion* is perhaps the most widely read occult book of the twentieth century. Atkinson died in California in 1932.

## Ralph Waldo Emerson

Born in 1803 in Boston, Massachusetts, RALPH WALDO EMERSON was one of America's preeminent men of letters. The inspiration for the school of philosophy called Transcendentalism, Emerson, in his essays, journals, lectures, and letters, traced out a view of life that located man as an extension and reflection of the Divine, owing his existence and allegiance to none but the highest insights of his own nature. An inspiration on figures ranging from his contemporary Henry David Thoreau to William James, Emerson formulated what can be called the American spiritual vision: non-dogmatic, nonsectarian, and based in the integrity and primacy of the individual spiritual search. In that sense, Emerson is also the founding figure of much of the modern spiritual culture in the West. After many years as a writer, publisher, lecturer, and seeker, he died in 1882 in Concord, Massachusetts, where his house still stands today.

## Charles Fillmore

One of the pioneering leaders of the New Thought movement, CHARLES FILLMORE (1884–1948), with his wife Myrtle, founded the worldwide Unity ministry. An early visionary in using mass media to spread religious and inspirational messages, Fillmore was widely known for his metaphysical interpretations of the Bible, and for his books including *Prosperity; Christian Healing; Talks on Truth; Atom-Smashing Power of Mind;* and *The Twelve Powers.*

## Khalil Gibran

Born in Lebanon in 1883, KHALIL GIBRAN migrated with his family to Boston in 1895. As a youth and into adulthood, Gibran excelled in painting, poetry, and philosophy. He is best known for his 1923 work *The Prophet*, which has been translated into more than twenty languages and is one of the most widely read works of verse in history, ranking in readership and influence with Shakespeare, Lao Tzu, and Rumi. Gibran died in New York City in 1931.

## Neville Goddard

NEVILLE GODDARD was one of the most remarkable mystical thinkers of the past century. In more than ten books and thousands of lectures, Neville, the solitary public name that he used, expanded on one radical principle: *the human imagination is God.* As such, he taught, everything that you experience results from your thoughts and feeling states. Born to an Anglican family in Barbados in 1905, Neville traveled to New York City at age seventeen in the early 1920s to study theater. Although he won roles on Broadway and toured internationally with a dance troupe, Neville abandoned the stage in the early 1930s to dedicate himself to metaphysical studies and chart a new career as a writer and lecturer. He was a compelling presence at metaphysical churches, spiritual centers, and auditoriums until his death in West Hollywood, California, in 1972. Neville was not widely known during his lifetime, but today his books and lectures, which he permitted to be freely recorded and are now circulated online, have attained bounding popularity. Neville's principles about the creative properties of the mind prefigured some of today's most radical quantum theorizing, and have influenced several major spiritual writers, including Carlos Castaneda and Joseph Murphy. Many of Neville's books are available in Gildan audio editions.

## Napoleon Hill

NAPOLEON HILL was born in 1883 in Wise County, Virginia. He was employed as a secretary, a reporter for a local newspaper, the manager of a coalmine and a lumberyard, and attended law school, before he began working as a journalist for *Bob Taylor's Magazine,* an inspirational and general-interest journal. In 1908 the job led to his interviewing steel magnate Andrew Carnegie. The encounter changed the course of Hill's life. Carnegie believed success could be distilled into definite principles that anyone could follow. He urged Hill to interview the greatest industrialists, financiers, and inventors of the era to discover these principles. Hill pursued the challenge for twenty years, resulting in his landmark volume *The Law of Success* in 1928. The sixteen-volume work formed the basis for Hill's worldwide sensation *Think and Grow Rich* in 1937. Hill dedicated the rest of his life to documenting and refining the principles of success. The motivational pioneer died in 1970 in South Carolina.

## Mitch Horowitz

MITCH HOROWITZ is a historian of alternative spirituality and one of today's most literate voices of esoterica, mysticism, and the occult. Mitch is the PEN Award-winning author of books including *Occult America, One Simple Idea, The Miracle Club, Daydream Believer, Uncertain Places, Modern Occultism,* and *Happy Warriors. The Washington Post* says Mitch "treats esoteric ideas and movements with an even-handed intellectual studiousness that is too often lost in today's raised-voice discussions." *Filmmaker Magazine* calls him "a genius at distilling down esoteric concepts." Mitch hosts Discovery/HBO Max's *Alien Encounters: Fact or Fiction,* SpectreVision's podcast, *Extraordinary Evidence: ESP Is Real,* and plays himself in Shudder's *V/H/S/BEYOND,* a Critics Choice Award nominee. A former vice president at Penguin Random House, Mitch has written on alternative spirituality for *The New York Times, The Wall Street Journal, The Washington Post, Time, Politico,* and appeared widely in national media. Mitch's writing has called attention to the worldwide problem of violence against accused witches, helping draw notice to the human-rights element of the issue. Mitch's work has been translated into French, German, Arabic, Hebrew, Chinese, Italian, Spanish, Korean, Japanese, and Portuguese. He is censored in China.

## Elbert Hubbard

Journalist ELBERT HUBBARD was born in Bloomington, Illinois, in 1856. A founder of the Arts and Crafts movement community Roycroft, in East Aurora, New York, Hubbard acted as publisher and editor of two popular cultural magazines, *The Philistine* and *The Fra*. Hubbard and his second wife Alice died aboard the British steamer the Lusitania in 1915, after it was torpedoed and sunk by a German submarine. He was en route to Europe, on a trip to encourage the end of World War One. Famous for his motivational writing and social-reform journalism, Hubbard's *A Message to Garcia* is one of the most widely read works in history.

## Niccolò Machiavelli

Born in Florence in 1469, NICCOLÒ MACHIAVELLI was a widely traveled and deeply read diplomatic envoy for Italy's royal court. Also a politician, historian, philosopher, humanist, writer, playwright, and poet, he has been called the founder of modern political science for his efforts to arrive at a cause-and-effect formula for how to attain and hold power and conduct statecraft. Machiavelli's classic *The Prince* was posthumously published in 1532. It was made up of earlier papers and letters that he had prepared for his royal patrons. A short work of considerable innovation, *The Prince* is one of the most enduring and widely read pieces of Renaissance literature. Although the term "Machiavellian" came to refer to actions or people characterized by cunning ruthlessness, contemporary critics and scholars are taking fuller note of Machiavelli's ethics and reformist sympathies. The writer died in 1527 in Florence at age fifty-eight.

## Joseph Murphy

JOSEPH MURPHY was born in 1898 on the southern coast of Ireland. Raised in a devout Catholic family, Murphy had planned on joining the priesthood. As a young man he instead relocated to America to make his career as a chemist and druggist. After running a pharmacy counter at New York's Algonquin Hotel, Murphy began studying mystical and metaphysical ideas. In the 1940s he became a popular New Thought minister and writer. Murphy wrote prolifically on the autosuggestive and mystical faculties of the human mind. He became widely known for his metaphysical classic, *The Power of Your Subconscious Mind*, which has sold millions of copies since it first appeared in 1963. Considered one of the pioneering voices of New Thought and affirmative-thinking philosophy, Murphy died in Laguna Hills, California, in 1981.

## Anthony Norvell

Born in 1908 in Upstate New York, ANTHONY NORVELL was a popular writer on occult and esoteric topics, particularly the uses of visualization and mind metaphysics. He lectured widely on both coasts, including weekly talks at New York's Carnegie Hall. *The Million Dollar Secret Hidden in Your Mind*, originally published in 1963, is his most popular and enduring book. He died in 1990.

## Norman Vincent Peale

NORMAN VINCENT PEALE (1898–1993) was among the most influential and prolific ministers of the twentieth century. His worldwide classic *The Power of Positive Thinking*, published in 1952, revolutionized the field of self-help and practical spirituality, and it popularized mystical themes of mind-power metaphysics throughout the world.

## Florence Scovel Shinn

FLORENCE SCOVEL SHINN was born in Camden, New Jersey, in 1871. She attended the Pennsylvania Academy of Fine Arts, where she met her husband, the realist painter Everett Shinn. She worked for many years as an artist and illustrator of children's literature in New York City before writing her New Thought landmark, *The Game of Life and How to Play It*. Unable to interest New York presses, Shinn published the book herself in 1925. She went on to write three more books: *Your Word is Your Wand,* published in 1928; *The Secret Door to Success*, published in 1940; and *The Power of the Spoken* Word, published posthumously in 1944. Shinn was also a sought-after spiritual lecturer and counselor. She died in New York City in 1940.

## Henry David Thoreau

Born in 1817 in Concord, Massachusetts, HENRY DAVID THOREAU was one of America's preeminent naturalists, essayists, critics, memoirists, poets, and philosophers. His 1854 book *Walden* is a classic the world over. By turns considered an anarchist, tax-resister, and mystic, Thoreau was one of the founding voices of Transcendentalism and is also seen as the father of the simple-living movement. He died in 1862 at age 44.

## Three Initiates

"Three Initiates" is one of several pseudonyms used by WILLIAM WALKER ATKINSON, a popular and innovative New Thought writer and publisher in the early twentieth century. Born in Baltimore, Maryland, in 1862, Atkinson became a successful attorney in 1894. Following a series of illnesses, he immersed himself in New Thought literature. He soon became an important figure in the early days of the movement, publishing magazines such as *Suggestion, New Thought*, and *Advanced Thought*. Under the aegis of his own publishing company, Yogi Publication Society, Atkinson authored many bylined works and many titles written under the pseudonyms Yogi Ramacharaka, Magus Incognito, and Theron Q. Dumont. *The Kybalion* is the most popular and enduring work published by Atkinson's Chicago-based publishing house, and is perhaps the most widely read occult work of the twentieth century. Atkinson died in California in 1932.

## Ralph Waldo Trine

A pioneering figure in the New Thought movement and one of the most popular voices in American metaphysics, RALPH WALDO TRINE was born in 1866 in Mount Morris, Illinois. The author of more than a dozen books, Trine began working as a journalist before writing his classic *In Tune With the Infinite* in 1897, which went on to sell more than two million copies and inspired a generation of spiritual and motivational writers. He died in Claremont, California, in 1958.

## Sun Tzu

Little is known about SUN TZU, who is estimated to have been born in 544 BC in the latter-era of China's Zhou dynasty, and died in 496 BC. Historians generally agree that Sun Tzu—an honorific title meaning "Master Sun"—was a commander in the dynastic army. His ancient treatise on strategy is one of the most widely read works of antiquity.

LIONEL GILES, whose groundbreaking 1910 translation of Sun Tzu is used in this abridgment, was a British sinologist and curator who also translated the works of Confucius and Lao Tzu. Born in 1875, he died in 1958.

## Frederick van Rensselaer Dey

FREDERICK VAN RENSSELAER DEY (February 10, 1861–April 25, 1922) was an American dime novelist and pulp fiction writer. He was born on February 10, 1861 in Watkins Glen, New York. He was educated at the Havana (N.Y.) Academy, and later graduated from the Law School of Columbia University. He practiced law and was a junior partner of William J. Gaynor (afterwards Mayor of New York and quite famous for having been photographed while being shot in the head).

Dey took up story writing for amusement while convalescing from a serious illness, and later made it his life work. His first full-length story was written for Beadle and Adams in 1881.

In 1891, Street & Smith hired him to continue a series of novelettes, begun by John R. Coryell, relating the adventures of a detective named Nick Carter. Most of his Nick Carter stories appeared under the pseudonyms "A Celebrated Author" and "The Author of 'Nick Carter.'" It is said that Dey wrote between one thousand and eleven hundred Nick Carter stories, comprising over forty million words, all written longhand. Besides these he wrote more serious books and serials. Two of his earlier books, before his dime-novel days, "The Magic Word" and "The Magic Story," written in 1899, were extremely popular and passed through some twenty editions.

He also wrote stories, of various kinds, under pseudonyms, and it is highly unlikely that his bibliography will ever be fully established, so that his importance for the nineteenth-century American literature of the fantastic is more a matter of assertion than sure knowledge. Writing as "Varick Vanardy," he created "The Night Wind," who appeared in stories from 1913 to the early 1920s.

Dey also worked in the newspaper industry as a police reporter, general reporter, special correspondent, and at various editorial desks. He was married twice.

## Wallace D. Wattles

A progressive social reformer and New Thought pioneer, WALLACE D. WATTLES was born in 1860 in the United States. He popularized creative-thought principles in his groundbreaking classics *The Science of Getting Rich*, *The Science of Being Great*, and *The Science of Being Well*. A great influence on future generations of success writers, he died in 1911.

## Bill Wilson

AA cofounder BILL WILSON (1895–1971), was the chief voice and writer behind *Alcoholics Anonymous*—often called "The Big Book"—on which he collaborated with many figures, including his wife and intellectual partner LOIS WILSON (1891–1988), his AA cofounder BOB SMITH (1879–1950), pioneering AA member HENRY PARKHURST (1895–1954), and a wide range of early AAs who contributed stories and strategies.

www.ingramcontent.com/pod-product-compliance
Lightning Source LLC
Chambersburg PA
CBHW072139070526
44585CB00015B/973